The Barbour

BIBLE STUDY

Companion

Easy-to-Understand Study Notes
for Genesis–Revelation

CHRISTOPHER D. HUDSON
General Editor

BARBOUR BOOKS
An Imprint of Barbour Publishing, Inc.

© 2013 by Barbour Publishing, Inc.

Previously published as *The Layman's Concise Bible Commentary*

Produced with the assistance of Christopher D. Hudson & Associates. Project contributors include Christopher D. Hudson, Tremper Longman, Mark Strauss, Carol Smith, Peter Barnes, Stan Campbell, Ralph Davis, Bob Deffinbaugh, Ian Fair, Joe Guglielmo, David Guzik, John Hanneman, W. Hall Harris III, David Hatcher, J. Hampton Keathley III, Stephen Leston, Stephen C. Magee, Doug McIntosh, Eugene H. Merrill, Jeff Miller, Richard D. Patterson, Robert Rayburn, and Derek W. H. Thomas.

Print ISBN 978-1-68322-293-4

All scripture quotations are taken from the King James Version.

Published by Barbour Books, an imprint of Barbour Publishing, Inc., P.O. Box 719, Uhrichsville, Ohio 44683, www.barbourbooks.com

Our mission is to publish and distribute inspirational products offering exceptional value and biblical encouragement to the masses.

Member of the
Evangelical Christian
Publishers Association

Printed in China.

Contents

Introduction

A book as important as the Bible deserves a commentary as user-friendly as this one.

Many commentaries are big and bulky, too academic, and difficult to understand. Some readers are discouraged when the commentary they looked to for help confuses them even more. To overcome these challenges, we created *The Barbour Bible Study Companion.*

Though pastors and scholars can benefit from this volume, we really wrote it for "average" readers who want to better grasp God's Word during their own Bible study and devotional time. *The Barbour Bible Study Companion* will enhance the understanding of anyone who finds scripture occasionally daunting or confusing.

The Bible is a life-changing book. We wanted to provide tools to help you understand God's Word and apply it to your own life. You'll find that this commentary contains clear explanations for passages from Genesis 1:1 through Revelation 22:21. On every page, in plain, everyday English, you'll find

- historical perspectives
- definitions of important terms
- explanation of confusing cultural references
- clarification of translation, with reference to the original languages
- cross references to other passages, with chapter and verse direction
- personal, practical applications

The Barbour Bible Study Companion also includes brief introductions to all sixty-six Bible books, giving you additional context on the purpose, author, and occasion of each. And a map section at the end provides additional help for understanding the geographical context of the passages you study.

We pray this book serves as the key to unlocking God's truth in your copy of His Word.

THE EDITORS

THE FIRST BOOK OF MOSES, CALLED

GENESIS

INTRODUCTION TO GENESIS ■ The first eleven chapters of Genesis trace events such as creation, the fall, the flood, and the establishing of the nations. The accounts of four great people complete the book in chapters 12–50: Abraham, Isaac, Jacob, and Joseph. Genesis comes from the Greek word *geneseos*, meaning "origin, source, generation, or beginning."

AUTHOR ■ Although Genesis does not directly name its author, Jesus and the writers of scripture clearly believed that Moses was the author of the Pentateuch (the first five books of the Bible, often referred to in the New Testament as "the law"; see Mark 10:3–5; Luke 24:44).

OCCASION ■ Genesis spans more time than any other book in the Bible. In fact, it covers more years than all of the remaining sixty-five books of the Bible put together (approximately 2,400 years). The total duration is from the time of creation to the time when the Israelites arrive in Egypt and grow into a nation (about 1800 BC). The date of Genesis is sometime after the Exodus, during the fifteenth century BC.

1:1–2:25 The initial recipients of this story are the Israelites of Moses' day. Because it is written to the people of God, Genesis is much more of a declaration than a defense. These chapters are not intended to give an account of the creation that would answer all of the scientific problems and phenomena. Rather, an air of mystery permeates these two chapters, and within that mystery is the fact that God created this world and it exists within His control.

1:1 The word *God*, a rendering from the Hebrew word *Elohim*, is a plural noun. This implies that God is plural, even as God is singular.

1:16 The moon is called the "lesser light" and the sun is called the "greater light" for a reason. Among Israel's pagan contemporaries, the sun and moon were designations for deities. Even today in astrology people use stars and planets for guidance, but here they are simply referred to as lights. They were appointed to regulate the fundamental rhythms of human life by defining day and night and the seasons of the year.

1:26 The idea that humanity is created in God's image has far-reaching implications: A relationship can exist between God and humanity, and men and women can reflect God's nature. As part of that reflection, people rule over nature. The idea of ruling carries with it the connotation of responsible management rather than dictatorial control or exploitation.

1:27 This verse is in the form of poetry. While some translations use the word *man*, this is a reference to all of humanity, not simply to Adam. God created humanity, both male and female.

1:28 God's blessing is a central theme in Genesis. *Blessed* denotes all that fosters human fertility and assists in achieving dominion. Interpreters have generally recognized "Be fruitful, and multiply" as commands to Adam and Eve (and later to Noah; see 9:1) as the heads of the human race, not simply as individuals. That is, God has not charged every human being with begetting children.

1:31 God evaluates only this day's work as "very good."

2:4–25 This begins a descriptive account, with humanity as the central theme. This section is not meant to be chronological. Genesis 2:7 is simply an elaboration of 1:27. The two accounts look at a similar series of events from two distinct points of view. The first chapter emphasizes man as one created with authority; Genesis 2 emphasizes man as one under authority.

2:7 The word *formed* describes the activity of a potter, forming vessels out of clay—ground and water. The fact that God forms man out of dust reflects man's lowly origin (see also 3:19). The Hebrew word for *man* (Adam) sounds like, and may be related to, the Hebrew word for *ground*.

2:18–25 These verses are considered the apex of the first two chapters. Everything up until this point is called "good," but now the Lord says it is "not good."

2:20 The word translated *help meet* does not mean a servant. It signifies the woman's essential contribution, not inadequacy.

3:1–5:32 This passage reveals how sin enters the world and how sin can be overcome. At the end of Genesis 2, life seems ideal—paradise. Then the events described in this section forever change the world. Fear and shame enter and judgment begins. But the seeds of redemption can be found as well.

3:4–5 The first thing Satan does is deny God's judgment and cast doubt on God's command. To make this direct contradiction of God's word seem reasonable, Satan invents a false motive for God. Thus, the serpent stands in direct conflict with God as He has revealed Himself.

3:9–10 God's question carries the implied question of why Adam and Eve are there. It is a demand that Adam take personal responsibility for his actions. Adam's response does not express personal responsibility, but it does acknowledge something important: Life has changed. Shame, fear, and guilt have entered paradise. (Verse 10 is the first time fear is mentioned in the Bible.)

3:15 This is one of the foundational verses of the Bible. Many see this as the first glimpse of the gospel of Jesus.

3:16–19 The woman will experience suffering in having children and in her desire for her husband. Adam will suffer in his attempts to control his domain. The very dust he came from will force him to struggle to survive. Man's natural or original relationship to the ground—to rule over it—is reversed; instead of submitting to him, it now resists and eventually swallows him.

3:22–24 This passage contains a certain amount of irony, in that the human race, which has been created in God's image (1:26), seeks to be like God by eating the fruit (3:5–7) but afterward finds itself no longer in union with God.

4:3–5 There may be clues in the description of the offerings themselves as to what was the problem with Cain's offering. Abel offers the first of his flock (see Exodus 34:19; Deuteronomy 12:6; 14:23) and the fattest (see Numbers 18:17). Abel gives what cost him most—the firstborn and the choicest selections. On the other hand, Cain's offering is not described as his first or his best, merely as the fruit. This difference in quality and attitude may be the key to God's differing reactions to the offerings.

4:9 God's question to Cain mirrors His question to Adam in 3:9. And like his father, Cain responds with a lie and defensiveness.

4:10–16 God's judgment is that Cain would be an outcast wanderer. This is the first instance in scripture where a human is cursed. When God pronounced judgment on Adam, it was the ground that actually was cursed. While in modern culture, the death penalty is considered the ultimate punishment, in this ancient world, disenfranchisement was possibly worse than death. It was a loss of roots and a loss of all that defined someone.

4:17–19 These verses begin a history of Cain's descendants. Verse 19 introduces Lamech as a man with two wives. Bigamy was common in the ancient Near East. It is not unheard of even among the fathers of the faith.

5:1 Here begins a second genealogy (the first is Genesis 4:17–26). This fifth chapter is a list of the ten descendants of Adam to Noah. The technique of mixing narrative and genealogy is found throughout the book of Genesis. A primary purpose seems to be to show the development of the human race from Adam to Noah and to bridge the gap in time between the two.

5:22–24 The phrase "walked with God" is only used of two men: Enoch and Noah (5:22; 6:9). *Walk* is a biblical figure for fellowship and obedience that results in divine blessing. It describes the closest communion with God—as if walking at His side.

6:1–2 Many view these two groups ("the sons of God" and "the daughters of men") as a way of describing the descendants of Cain and the descendants of Seth (4:1–26). The assumption, then, is that the descendants of Seth are God-following people, while the descendants of Cain are not. If this is the case, then the events described

here represent a mingling of the godly with the ungodly. Other interpretations of this passage include the idea that these are marriages between angels and humans, or between aristocrats and commoners.

6:3 "An hundred and twenty years" likely refers to the time remaining between this announcement of judgment and the coming of the flood.

6:5 Humanity's evil is far more than a surface foolishness.

6:11–12 The earth is described as *corrupt.* The Hebrew word translated here is rich in meaning. It was used to describe a shirt that was stained too badly to be used or a clay pot that was marred in the production process, making it unusable.

6:14–16 Noah receives detailed instructions that he is to follow in building the ark. The ingredients are gopher wood and pitch. While the Bible doesn't give enough detail to know exactly what the ark looked like, it probably was shaped like a shallow rectangular box topped with a roof, with an 18-inch space under the roof, interrupted only by roof supports, so that light could get into the vessel from every side. This design would use space efficiently and would have been stable in the water.

6:17–18 This is the first use of the word *covenant*, which refers to a binding promise. It will mean safety for Noah and his family, even in the midst of tragic judgment.

7:2 God does not reveal the basis for His distinction between clean and unclean animals here. Noah predated Moses, who wrote down the dietary laws regarding which animals were ceremonially clean to eat, but the understanding of clean and unclean animals was already common. Even Israel's pagan neighbors observed distinctions between clean and unclean animals.

8:1 The word *remembered* is a high point of this story. God remembers His people and the promises He made to them.

8:4 During the eleventh to twelfth centuries AD, Mount Ararat became the site traditionally associated with Noah's landing. The Bible does not indicate a specific peak and refers generally to its location as the "mountains of Ararat."

8:20 This is the first time an altar is mentioned in the Bible.

9:1 Chapter 9 opens with a renewal of God's first blessing and commission to Adam (1:28). Like Adam, Noah and his sons are blessed and are commanded to reproduce and fill the earth. The word *bless* is key in Genesis. It means "to confer benefit."

9:4–5 What is the purpose of God's restriction that Noah and his sons drain the blood of the animals they use for food? One reason is probably respect for life and the giver of life. In the centuries to come, as the Jewish laws were developed and documented, God's people were again forbidden to consume the blood, which was considered the life of the creature.

9:6 This verse upholds the sanctity of human life and human responsibility before God to protect that life. It is the acknowledgment of God's image borne by every person.

9:8–17 God promises not to flood the earth again. He clearly makes this an eternal promise and marks it with the sign of the rainbow.

9:21–23 The word translated *uncovered*, the description of Noah in his tent, means "to be disgracefully exposed." Ham gloats over his father's shame and does nothing to preserve his father's dignity. In contrast to Ham, Shem and Japheth walk in backward and cover Noah. They honor their father and win the approval and blessing of God (9:26).

10:1–11:32 The genealogy in Genesis 10 includes reference to the separation of nations (10:5, 20, 31) that occurs at the Tower of Babel, which is described in chapter 11. This is a modified genealogy, and it uses the words *son* and *father* even more flexibly than do the other genealogies. *Son* in Genesis 10 may mean "descendant," "successor," or "nation." *Father* may mean "ancestor," "predecessor," or "founder."

10:1–5 Japheth's descendants settled in India and Europe.

10:6–20 Ham's descendants, the Canaanites, are significant because of the part they play in the future history of Israel, particularly the events at Babel (Babylon), Mizraim (Egypt), and Canaan.

10:21–31 The descendants of Shem are the Semitic peoples who inhabit the eastern lands: modern-day Iraq, Iran, and eastern Saudi Arabia.

11:3–4 The motivation for building a city is to make a name for themselves and to keep from scattering across the land. This is not an act of worship, but rather an act of pride.

11:5–7 God's response to the people's efforts is anthropomorphic; it describes God in human terms. It simply means that God wants a good look at what people are doing on earth. God, of course, doesn't need to leave heaven to see what is happening on earth. God spoke of Himself in this same plural form early in Genesis (1:26).

11:27 This verse marks a new division in the book of Genesis. This book covers more than 2,000 years and more than 20 generations; yet it spends almost a third of its text on the life of this one man: Abraham, the forefather of the Israelite nation (11:27–25:18).

11:28 It is generally held that Ur is located in southern Mesopotamia, near the Persian Gulf. Some, however, contend that Ur is located to the north and east of Haran.

11:30 Sarai's childlessness is a major factor in the upcoming account. Childlessness in the ancient Near East involved shame and social ridicule and implied that the woman, or the couple, was not in the favor of the gods.

12:6–7 Sichem becomes sacred to the Israelites because, while this is God's second revelation of Himself to Abram, it is the first revelation in the promised land. Sichem is near the geographic center of Canaan (Joshua 20:7).

12:10–20 Though Abram is held up as a model of faith, this passage gives us a peek into his humanity. Out

of fear, Abram asks Sarai to pretend to be his sister rather than his wife. While Sarai is indeed Abram's half sister, this is a ruse intended to deceive, and he is trusting in his deception to protect him instead of trusting in the Lord. While he has proven himself to be a man of faith, in this case he is more afraid of the Egyptians than of God.

13:1–16:16 Everything that Abram receives in Egypt later causes him trouble. Because of the great wealth he acquires from Pharaoh, Abram and Lot choose to separate. Hagar, the Egyptian maidservant whom Pharaoh gives to Abram, brings division and sorrow with far-reaching consequences.

13:14–17 God's revelation contains three specifics: (1) God will give the land to Abram and his descendants forever. (2) Abram's heir will be his own child. (3) Abram's descendants will be innumerable.

14:1–12 These verses describe the first war ever recorded in scripture—a war between four eastern kings and five southern kings. Shinar (Babylon, modern-day Iraq) initiates this war (14:1–2). (It is in Shinar where the first families after the flood settle and then attempt to build a tower at Babel.)

14:17 Abram's victory also benefits the cities of Sodom and Gomorrah. A special welcoming committee had evidently been appointed, headed by the king himself, to confer upon Abram the usual reward for a conquering hero.

14:18 *Melchizedek* is probably a title rather than a proper name. It means "King of Righteousness." Salem, of which Melchizedek is king, may be the shortened name for Jerusalem (Psalm 76:2), which at that time was occupied by the Canaanites. Melchizedek was a Canaanite, but he is called a priest of the *Most High God*. The biblical record does not mention Melchizedek's parents, his ancestry, his birth, or his death. In that sense he is different from any other individual found in this narrative.

15:2–3 Abram's response to God is recorded for the first time. Inherent in his response is the pain of having wealth and success but no heir to pass it on to. It was a common practice in the ancient Near East for a childless couple to adopt a son, who would care for them in their old age and inherit their possessions and property. Abram suggests that he adopt his chief servant, Eliezer.

15:6 Some consider Genesis 15:6 to be the most important verse in the Old Testament: God declares Abram righteous (clean, morally right) on the basis of Abram's faith. The idea is that God is crediting Abram's faith as righteousness. While this connection between faith and righteousness is most often considered a New Testament concept, this verse confirms that God has always desired faith from His people.

15:7–21 In Abram's day, legal agreements were formalized by means of a very graphic covenant ceremony: The dividing of an animal sealed the covenant. The animal was cut in half, and the two parties would pass between the halves while repeating the terms of the covenant. By doing so, the two parties were stating, "If

I fail to fulfill my commitments to this covenant, may I suffer the same fate as this animal."

16:1–6 Ancient documents reveal that when a woman could not provide her husband with a child, she could give her female slave as a wife and claim the child of this union as her own. While Hagar is not on equal standing with Sarai, her status does change when she becomes a slave wife. If she produces the heir, she could be the primary wife in the eyes of society. According to verses 4–5, in Hagar's opinion Sarai had been demoted. The Hebrew word translated *despised* means "to be treated lightly or with contempt."

16:12 This prophecy about Ishmael is not an insult. The wild donkey lives a solitary existence in the desert away from society. Ishmael would be free-roaming and strong. His free-roaming lifestyle would put him in conflict with those who followed social conventions. This is not a prophecy of open warfare, only of friction because of his antagonism to others' ways of life.

16:13 This is the only place in the Bible where a person names God. Hagar names God *El Roi*—"the God who sees."

17:5 It is at this time that God changes Abram's name. Abram means "exalted father," a name that probably refers to God's nature more than Abram's. Here God changes Abram's name to Abraham, which means "father of a multitude."

17:6–8 God makes five "I will" statements in verses 6–8.

17:7–14 Circumcision is an outward sign of an inward commitment. It is to an Israelite what a wedding ring is to a bridegroom. It is important to note that circumcision is not a condition of the covenant, but a sign of Abraham's participation in it.

17:15–16 Sarai's name is changed to Sarah. The names are two different forms of a word meaning "princess."

18:2–8 Abraham's reaction to the three visitors is typical of ancient Middle Eastern hospitality. He hurries to serve them and bows before them. He also makes his best food available. In the ancient world, a person's hospitality was often determined by the ability to provide an extravagant welcome. Also, though Abraham has servants available to him, he is personally involved in the care of these guests.

18:11–12 Verse 11 offers background information that reveals that what the guest proposes—Sarah's pregnancy—is a natural impossibility. Sarah certainly believed it to be impossible, and her laughter is not simply from being caught off guard by the idea; it reveals her unbelief.

18:17 The Lord chose to disclose His intentions toward Sodom and Gomorrah because He had chosen Abraham to be a channel of blessing to all the nations of the earth and because of Abraham's relationship with God. The Bible certainly doesn't represent Abraham as a perfect man, yet his faith in God put him in relationship with God; Isaiah 41:8 even refers to Abraham as His friend. Therefore, God trusted him with this information about Sodom and Gomorrah.

18:20–21 Here we find God's basic plan for Sodom and Gomorrah. The word translated *cry* in verse 20 is used to describe cries of the oppressed and brutalized. In this case, the term may have two meanings: It may mean (1) the outcry against Sodom caused by its injustice and violence, or (2) the cry of its rebellion against God (19:13).

18:22–33 Abraham's conversation with the Lord is a prayer-negotiation for the righteous people of Sodom and Gomorrah. This is the first time in the scriptures so far that a man has initiated a conversation with God. Keep in mind that these wicked cities are where Abraham's nephew Lot has settled.

19:1 After Abraham's negotiation, two angels approach Lot at the gate of Sodom. The city gate is where the civic leaders met to finalize legal and business transactions. It is a place of prominence and influence. The implication is that Lot had achieved a fair amount of success within the city.

19:4–9 This is a chilling testament to the wickedness of both the Sodomites and even Lot himself, as the Sodomites demand to be given access to the guests and Lot offers his daughters instead. Though there is some debate on this account, the verb traditionally translated *know* in verse 5 is most often translated as sexual intercourse. This idea seems to be confirmed by Lot's offer of his virgin daughters to the men. Lot's offering of his daughters is unfathomable to a modern society. We understand it a little more when we consider the low place of women in the pre-Christian world and the high standing of any guest in terms of Middle Eastern hospitality.

19:18–22 Even as the angels are rescuing Lot from the cities, he is fighting for his own self-preservation. Rather than trusting these messengers, he fights to stay within his comfort level.

19:24–29 Archaeologists believe that today these cities are buried under the Dead Sea. As for Lot's wife, the Hebrew verb translated *looked back* signifies an intense gaze, not a passing glance, even though their rescuers had warned them to keep moving ahead (19:17, 26).

19:30–38 This follow-up account is remarkably similar to the story of the last days of Noah after his rescue from the flood (9:20–27). In Noah's case, he became drunk with wine and uncovered himself in the presence of his children. In both narratives, the act has grave consequences. Thus, at the close of the two great narratives of divine judgment—the flood and the destruction of Sodom—those who are saved from God's wrath subsequently fall into a form of sin reminiscent of those who died in the judgment. This is a common theme in the prophetic literature (Isaiah 56–66; Malachi 1). The mention of the Ammonites and Moabites is significant since these neighboring nations are mentioned in the nation of Israel's later journey to occupy the promised land.

20:1–18 This account is quite similar to another account, described in Genesis 12:10–20, where Abram and Sarai devise a scheme to avoid potential problems with the pharaoh in Egypt.

21:1–4 *Isaac* means "He laughs," or "May [God] smile." Abraham also obeys God by circumcising his son on the eighth day (21:4). This was God's command to Abraham and His covenant with him.

21:6–10 The scene shifts to Sarah, alluding to her laughter of unbelief when the Lord announced that she would give birth (18:10–15). In verses 9–10, the Egyptian Hagar again has a role in the narrative. Fourteen years earlier, Hagar had given birth to Ishmael, and for most of the intervening period, Abraham had treated Ishmael as the heir. By this point Ishmael is a teenager.

21:11–13 At Sarah's demand that Abraham banish Ishmael, Abraham receives a direct word from God for the sixth time since coming to the land of Canaan.

21:15–16 Single mothers without the support of family or friends faced a dire plight. While Hagar does cry out to God, it is the boy's cries that God hears. This offers special meaning to the fact that Ishmael means "God hears" (16:11; 21:17).

21:17–21 Even though Hagar suffers, her need for support is met. God does not forget His promise to greatly multiply her descendants (16:10). God has compassion on Hagar's plight and becomes like a father to Ishmael.

21:22 Abimelech reenters the account, arriving with his enforcer, Phichol, to sign a treaty with Abraham. The term *Phichol* may be a title rather than a proper name. The same name is used in Genesis 26:26 of Abraham's military commander.

21:25–26 In contrast to Abraham's previous fear of Abimelech, he now boldly stands up to this powerful king. Abraham brings up the matter of the well that Abimelech's servants had seized from him. Wells were of extreme importance to semi-nomadic people like Abraham. The Hebrew verb translated *reproved* implies that Abraham had to complain several times.

21:30–32 The passage concludes with the men naming the well *Beer-sheba*. By granting Abraham rights to a well, Abimelech has made it possible for Abraham to live there permanently and acknowledged his legal right, at least to water. Abraham now owns a small part of the land God promised him.

21:33 By planting a grove, Abraham indicates his determination to stay in that region. The grove is meant to be a lasting landmark to God's provision and a focal point of Abraham's worship. It serves as an appropriate symbol of the enduring grace of the faithful God.

22:1–14 God tested Abraham. There is a vast difference between God's purpose in testing a person and Satan's purpose in testing a person. God tests to confirm and strengthen; Satan tests to corrupt and weaken (see Job 1). The repetition of the words *son* and *only son* reiterates the severe nature of this test. This terminology can refer to an infant (Exodus 2:6) or a young man (1 Chronicles 12:28). Abraham obeys God's commands immediately and unquestioningly (Genesis 22:3–4).

22:5–8 Abraham's obedience is based on faith. He believes God will provide the sacrifice. The word *worship* in verse 5 means "to bow oneself close to the ground."

22:11–12 These verses don't imply that God is just now learning that Abraham fears Him. God is omniscient. The angel of the Lord is saying to Abraham, "By your faithful actions I experientially know that you fear God." The language is accommodated to the human understanding, uttered, as it were, from a human point of view.

22:13–24 Abraham's obedience is rewarded in three ways. First, God provides the very thing He demands from Abraham (22:13–14). Fittingly, Abraham names this place "The Lord will provide." Second, God provides assurances of His promises (22:15–19). It is unusual for God to speak with an oath. Abraham's supreme act of obedience draws forth God's supreme assurance of blessing. Finally, God provides for future needs (22:20–24).

22:15 This verse contains the final recorded instance of God speaking to Abraham. God spoke directly to Abraham eight times (12:1, 7; 13:14; 15:1; 17:1; 21:12; 22:1, 15).

23:2 Abraham mourns and weeps, indicating that he goes through the traditional mourning customs of his day: tearing his clothes, cutting his beard, spreading dust on his head, and fasting. This is all done in the presence of the dead body. The Israelites had a very elaborate process that they went through when someone died. This is the first record of a man's tears in the Bible.

23:19 The ancient Israelites placed great importance on the location of their own and family members' burial sites. It was normally important to be buried in one's homeland. Remember that Abraham and Sarah's family roots were in Ur (11:31). Despite the importance of burial location, family roots, and Abraham's current alien status, he insists on burying Sarah in Canaan, even though doing so is costly. Why? Because Abraham is not looking backward to where he came from, nor is he looking at his present situation—living in a tent because he does not possess even one acre of the promised land. Abraham is looking forward.

24:1–67 This chapter contains a great love story. The Lord, who never speaks in this chapter, is nevertheless the main character. He is mentioned seventeen times. The agreement that Abraham makes with his servant seems a little bizarre, as does the servant's placing his hand under Abraham's thigh. Yet this is customary in Abraham's day (see also 47:29).

24:10 The description of the servant's travels actually encompasses hundreds of miles and several months, as the servant assembles a caravan and makes his way to Mesopotamia. The city of Nahor could refer to a city by that name, or it could simply mean that Abraham's brother Nahor lives there. The servant's arrival at the proper place is all a part of the divine blessing. God's hand is in the events of this story.

24:15–21 This passage records Rebekah's appearance and her family connections; it also records that she does exactly what the servant had prayed, exhibiting a servant's heart by going beyond his request and watering his camels. It should be noted that a typical ancient well was a large, deep hole in the earth with steps leading down to the springwater. Each drawing of water required substantial effort. Camels can consume up to twenty-five gallons of water in ten minutes, and the servant had ten camels with him. One more fact: A typical water jar held about three gallons of water. All of this together means Rebekah made many descents into the well. Her labors could have taken well over an hour.

24:34–49 The servant seeks to obtain the approval of Rebekah's family. Genesis 24, as a whole, is an excellent example of the ancient storyteller's art. In those days people enjoyed repetition—in fact, they preferred it—as they listened to tales or read them. The servant's repetition of the details that led up to his search is probably deliberately employed as an effective literary device.

24:50–54 The tension is resolved by the family's approval. Again, the servant responds appropriately by bowing to the ground in worship and gratitude. The gifts the servant offers may have been the bride price, which would finalize the agreement. Abraham's servant does not want to delay his leaving, which presents a difficult choice for Rebekah. She would leave her family and everything familiar and go to a new land with a man she had just met in order to marry another man she had never seen (24:55–61). Rebekah's courageous willingness seems to be another testimony to God's leadership in this situation.

24:67 Ultimately, this entire story is about God's faithfulness. He protects and guides the servant on his journey, and He brings Rebekah, along with just the right servant-spirit, to the well at just the right time. From our historical perspective centuries later, we can see how God used the remarkable obedience of a few family members to accomplish His purposes.

25:1–6 Before he dies, Abraham passes on his legacy: the promises he received from God. According to verses 2–4, the six sons Abraham had with Keturah become the ancestors of several Far East tribes. Abraham wills everything he owns to Isaac, because he is the legal firstborn. But while he is alive, he honors his other sons with gifts.

25:9–10 Abraham is buried in the field that he purchased from Ephron the Hittite (Genesis 23:1–20), once again affirming that he believed God would grant the land to Abraham's descendants.

25:12–18 In between the major sections of Genesis dealing with Abraham (11:27–25:11), Jacob (25:19–35:29), and Joseph (37:2–50:26), there are smaller sections dealing with Ishmael (25:12–18) and Esau (36:1–37:1). Genesis 25:12–18 looks briefly at Ishmael before continuing the story. In this small passage, there is reference to God's promise that twelve princes will be born to Ishmael (17:20). God had pronounced that Ishmael would live in hostility toward his brothers (16:12). The description in verse 18 of Ishmael's descendants seems to confirm that pattern.

25:17 Like his father, Abraham, Ishmael is also "gathered unto his people," indicating that he is a believer in God and shares in the spiritual blessings of all who die in the faith.

25:23 This idea of the younger serving the elder appears in several places in Genesis: (1) The offering of Cain, the older brother, is rejected, whereas the offering of the younger brother, Abel, is accepted (4:1–5). (2) The line of Seth, the younger brother of Cain, is the chosen line (4:26–5:8). (3) Isaac is chosen over his older brother, Ishmael (17:18–19). (4) Rachel is chosen over her older sister, Leah (29:18). (5) Joseph, the younger brother, is chosen over all the rest of Jacob's sons (37:3). The intention behind each of these reversals is the recurring theme of God's sovereign plan of grace.

25:25–28 Esau's name means "hairy one"; Jacob's name means "God will protect." The Hebrew word for *Jacob* is similar to *heel*, reminiscent of Jacob grasping Esau's heel during birth. From this comes the nickname "heel holder," which has a connotation of a wrestling term but also indicates a scoundrel.

25:29–34 These verses recount the well-known story of Esau's trading his birthright for some stew. In the original Hebrew, a bit more texture is revealed in this account than in modern English. Esau's so-called request is actually a forceful demand. Not only does Esau demand food, but he demands to devour it. The word translated *eat*, or better yet, *gulp down*, is a word that normally describes the feeding of cattle. Jacob's counterdemand, on the other hand, suggests that he has long premeditated his act and is exploiting his brother's weakness.

26:1–35 Genesis 26 is the only chapter of Genesis devoted exclusively to Isaac. While he is mentioned in other chapters, he is not the focus of attention. Here Isaac's life is summed up in the events described, all of which have a striking parallel in the life of his father, Abraham.

26:7–22 These verses continue the parallel between Isaac's and Abraham's lives: Isaac lies about Rebekah's identity out of a fear for his own survival. The Abimelech mentioned in verse 8 is probably the son, or even the grandson, of the Abimelech who ruled over Gerar in Abraham's time (20:2). The parallel between Isaac's life and that of his father is again evident in this account of the disputes over the wells (26:12–22).

26:23–25 God appears to Isaac in Beer-sheba (His second revelation), calming Isaac's fears and reviewing the promises He had given previously (26:2–5). Isaac's response is to build an altar, worship the Lord, and settle down there. These verses seem to confirm the fact that Isaac's decision to move out of Philistine territory pleased God.

26:34–35 This passage is best read as an introduction to Genesis 27. Esau marries at age forty, just as his father, Isaac, did (25:20). Esau, however, marries two Hittite women from the land of Canaan (36:2). Abraham had warned his servant not to take a wife for Isaac from among the wicked Canaanites, who would not give up their gods for their husbands (24:3). Thus, the servant finds Rebekah from the country and family of Abraham (chapter 24). Note that Isaac seems to have had no hand in Esau's wife-taking, though Esau is, at one point, his favorite son, according to Genesis 25:28. Compare this with Isaac's own experience with his father, Abraham, who sent a servant five hundred miles to get a suitable wife for Isaac (24:2–4).

27:1–4 In the willfulness of his old age, Isaac is determined to pass on the blessing to Esau, despite what the Lord has said (25:23) and what the boys have shown with their lives. The fact that he attempts to make this transaction—which should have been a family event—without the knowledge of his wife, Rebekah, and his son Jacob, compounds his sin. Isaac's insistence on a good meal before the blessing recalls Esau's own trading of the birthright for a pot of stew, and thus casts Isaac in a similar role to that of Esau (25:27–34).

27:18–29 In this scenario, who is deceiving whom? On one hand, Jacob is definitely deceiving his father, Isaac. However, Isaac—because he thinks Jacob is really Esau—thinks he is deceiving Jacob by giving the blessing to Esau. Both intend to deceive the other, yet only Jacob succeeds. Even through this act of deception, God's will is done, and the family blessing continues through Jacob.

27:30–45 When Esau discovers the ruse, he is enraged. Once the blessing was given, it had the force of a legal contract and could not be revoked. The two losses that Rebekah feared may have been Isaac's death and then Jacob's death at the hand of Esau, or Jacob's death at the hand of Esau and then Esau's necessary departure.

27:46–28:9 When Rebekah fears for Jacob's life, she manipulates Isaac into sending Jacob away. In effect, she gives Isaac a cover story. Her real goal is to protect him, not to find him a wife. Isaac agrees, calling Jacob to his side, repeating the Abrahamic blessing, and sending him off to Haran to find a wife. In one sense, the plot to receive the blessing from Isaac is a great success. However, in another sense, it is a terrible failure. Jacob receives the blessing, but he has to leave the inheritance with Esau.

28:10 Jacob's journey retraces the steps of his grandfather Abraham, who came from Haran to the promised land many years before. It is natural that Jacob's mother, Rebekah, would think of Haran when she cast about for a safe haven for her wayward younger son. The trek from Beer-sheba to Haran was far enough that Esau wouldn't follow Jacob there. Yet there was family at Haran, so Jacob wouldn't be alone.

28:16–17 Jacob wakes up amazed by his experience, sure that the God of his fathers is the source of it. Jacob acknowledges God. Pouring oil on the pillar constitutes an act of consecration. The pillar becomes a monument marking the place and the event. The name given to the place means "house of God."

28:20–22 Jacob's vow is understood by some to be another form of his scheming nature. Others suggest that he is simply making a commitment, acknowledging the need for God's help in order to keep that commitment.

29:11 When Jacob meets Rachel, he kisses her. Most likely, he kisses her on both cheeks, a traditional greeting.

29:16–17 These verses introduce Laban's other daughter, Leah. In Hebrew, Leah means "cow," and Rachel means "ewe lamb." There is some mystery regarding Leah's eyes. A few English translations understand Leah's eyes to be her best quality, so they translate the Hebrew word as *tender* or something similar. However, most scholars suggest that Leah's eyes are a detriment in some way. The point seems to be that she does not measure up to her beautiful sister.

29:18–25 How could Jacob marry the wrong woman? According to contemporary Western customs, no man could be fooled in this way. The most likely explanation is that when Laban brings his daughter Leah to Jacob, it is dark, and she is veiled from head to toe. It seems that the wedding feast hosted by Laban is an intentional ploy to dull Jacob's senses with wine (29:22).

29:26 Laban's explanation that he must see his firstborn daughter marry first seems ironically appropriate in this story. Jacob had dishonored the principle of the firstborn by cheating his brother out of the birthright and the blessing. Now God forces him to honor the principle he had violated by marrying Leah first. The deceiver is deceived. God trains Jacob by allowing him to meet his own sins in someone else.

29:27–30 Jacob receives Rachel seven days after he consummated his marriage to Leah. Jacob marries two women in eight days.

29:31 When Leah is referred to as *hated*, this does not mean that Jacob truly hates her, but rather that he loves her less than Rachel. Leah's becoming a mother ensures that her importance will increase in Jacob's estimation, as well as in the estimation of her family and society in general.

30:1–2 Although her husband loves her, Rachel does not consider her life worth living without children. Jacob responds in anger. In fact, the word translated *anger* here is quite graphic. It means "to breathe hard, be enraged, flare the nostrils." Jacob's anger is heated as he, in essence, says Rachel's childlessness is not his fault.

30:4 Rachel's solution is an ancient custom that allows an infertile woman to offer her female servant as a wife, then claim the child of this union as her own. This was culturally acceptable and completely legal, and in fact, it was a solution that had been employed by Abraham and Sarah, Jacob's grandparents (16:1–3).

30:14–21 Mandrakes are plants that bear bluish flowers in winter and yellowish, plum-size fruit in summer. In ancient times, mandrakes were reputed as being aphrodisiacs (Song of Solomon 7:13) and aiding in conception. The fruit was even called "love apples." In this story, both women want what the other has. Leah feels that having sons for Jacob will somehow earn his love, while Rachel is as desperate for children.

30:22–24 After fourteen years, Rachel conceives a son named Joseph. The theme of the entire narrative is the movement from barrenness (29:31) to birth (30:22). For all the maneuverings of the sisters, it is still God who opens the womb.

30:25 After the birth of Joseph, Jacob asks to be released from Laban's authority. Unlike today, Jacob could not simply pack his bags and leave. The authority structure in this Eastern extended family is far more complex and restrictive—as it is still today in some Eastern cultures. There is a shared ownership of Jacob's wives and children. To leave without his father-in-law's permission and blessing could lead to outright war within the family clan.

30:37–43 It was generally believed that by placing visuals before the animals as they were mating, it was possible to influence the appearance of their offspring.

31:1–5 Both Laban and his sons are unhappy about Jacob's growing herds. Essentially, Laban's sons are accusing Jacob of stealing their inheritance. From their perspective, it is disappearing right before their eyes. As a result, they become envious and bitter toward Jacob. Laban also treats Jacob differently.

31:3 The last recorded revelation that Jacob received from God was twenty years earlier, while he was still in the land of promise (28:10–22). God had promised to bring Jacob back to the land (28:15); now, at last, God gives Jacob the divine directive to return to the promised land.

31:14–16 Rachel and Leah agree with Jacob's assessment. After all, their father, Laban, had stolen their inheritance, treated them like foreigners, sold them, and used up the money from their dowry.

31:17–18 It was nearly three hundred miles from Haran to the mountains of Gilead. Jacob travels with the knowledge that Laban might be pursuing him from behind in order to kill him, and Esau, his brother, might be waiting ahead, also wanting to kill him.

31:19–21 Rachel steals her father's household idols while he is busy at work shearing his sheep. These idols are small figurines (probably 2 to 3 inches long) used in divination and to bring good luck. Why does she steal them? No exact reason is given, but it may have been simply for protection and good fortune, which would have revealed some attachment to the religion of her father.

31:29 Laban catches up to Jacob, a journey that takes seven days since Jacob had a three-day head start. It is interesting that God reveals Himself to Laban, a man who, thus far in this account, has not expressed the kind of faith we associate with messages from God.

31:36–55 After an uneventful search in which Rachel sits on the idols to hide them, Jacob unleashes twenty years of pent-up frustration. In his rebuke to Laban, Jacob shows himself to be a man of faith (31:31–42). This part of the story concludes in 31:43–55. Jacob takes a stone and sets it up as a pillar (31:45). This may have been in the form of a heap of stones that functioned both as a table for the meal and as a memorial of the event. Standing stones sometimes marked supposed dwelling places of the gods (compare 28:17–18) or graves (2 Samuel 18:17). In this case, it seals a treaty.

32:1–3 Jacob leaves Laban and goes on to Canaan. He does this in obedience to God's command (31:3). The angels who meet him join Jacob's company of travelers for his protection. This is the reason for the name *Mahanaim* ("double host" or "double camp"). These angels were apparently intended to reassure Jacob of God's protective presence.

32:2–21 These verses describe Jacob's preparations for meeting Esau. At the news that Esau has four hundred men with him, Jacob becomes afraid (32:6–7). Esau may have had a large army because he'd had to subjugate the Horite (Hurrian) population of Seir. His soldiers probably consisted of his own servants, plus the Canaanite and Ishmaelite relations of his wives.

32:7–18 Why does Jacob send such an impressive gift to Esau? As a bribe or payoff for his sin of deception and theft? Possibly, but it could have been an act of restitution and reconciliation. It also could have been for the practical reason that he wants Esau to know he is wealthy (verses 14–15 list more than 550 animals given as gifts) and is not returning for the inheritance.

32:22–23 Hebrew narrative style often includes a summary statement of the whole passage, followed by a more detailed report of the event. In this case, verse 22 provides a summary statement while verse 23 begins the detailed account. It is when Jacob is alone, having done everything he could to secure his own safety, that God comes to him. God has arranged the circumstances so that He could get Jacob alone at a moment when he felt completely helpless.

32:25 Why does the man touch Jacob's thigh? Because the thigh is the largest and strongest muscle connection of the body. He is deliberately crippling Jacob at the point of his greatest strength (32:24–30).

32:28–30 The new name Jacob receives, *Israel*, means either "God strives," or "he who strives with God." If the latter interpretation is the one intended by the wrestler who blesses Jacob, then the name fits well with Jacob's character as one who, throughout his life, struggles with God. The name given to this place, Peniel, means "the face of God."

33:1–3 Jacob has every reason to believe that twenty years has not diminished Esau's anger, as he sees Esau marching toward him with four hundred men. By going ahead of his family to meet Esau, Jacob shows that he has overcome the fear that had formerly dominated the old Jacob. He also shows valor in protecting his family. Bowing to the ground before Esau demonstrates humility. This is ancient court protocol for approaching a lord or king (33:3, 6–7).

33:4–5 In Esau's culture, men walked; they didn't run. By running to Jacob, Esau is breaking the cultural norms and humbling himself. His kiss seems to be an indication of forgiveness.

33:9 The fact that Esau refuses Jacob's herds as gifts is significant. Esau is not the taker that Jacob has been.

33:10 Jacob's comparison of seeing Esau to seeing God's face may seem like flattery or overstatement.

It could also have been recognition on Jacob's part of God's character in the life of his brother.

33:12–17 Jacob claims to be going to Seir, but he goes to Succoth instead. Succoth is to the north and west; in other words, it is in the exact opposite direction from Esau. Perhaps Jacob did not want to face his father, or perhaps reconciling with Esau was a different matter than living side by side. It also could have been a practical concern regarding pastures for the herds. As a result of Jacob's choice to settle away from his brother, he never saw his father again.

33:18 Jacob settles near the city of Shechem, even though God had commanded him to settle in Bethel (28:19–21; 31:3, 13). This may have been fear-based. In spite of Esau's warm greeting, Jacob probably didn't trust him. Nevertheless, he builds his first altar, as Abraham had also done at Shechem when he first entered Canaan (12:6–7). This is the first instance in which an altar is named (33:20; see also 35:7; Exodus 17:15; Judges 6:24).

33:20 *El-elohe-Israel* means "The mighty God is the God of Israel." Jacob uses his own new name, Israel (Genesis 32:28). Here he acknowledges God as the God of Israel, his own God.

34:1–31 This horrific account serves to warn us of the high price of compromise. The tragedies that take place in this chapter are the result of Jacob's failure to be obedient to God's command to return to Bethel.

34:5–7 Jacob seems far less affected by the news of Dinah's assault than her brothers.

34:7 The name *Israel* is used here for the first time as a reference to God's chosen people. The family of Jacob had a special relationship to God by divine calling, reflected in the name Israel ("prince with God").

34:13 As was customary in their culture, Jacob's sons take an active part in approving their sister's marriage (see 24:50). They were correct in opposing the end in view: the mixing of the chosen seed with the seed of the Canaanites. Yet they were wrong in adopting the means they selected to achieve their end (34:13–17). The sons are following in their deceitful father's footsteps.

34:13–24 Regarding the proposal made by Jacob's sons, the men of the city become convinced on financial grounds. While Shechem has fallen in love with Dinah, to these men circumcision seems a small price to pay if it results in a huge financial windfall from the alliance.

34:25–29 The slaughter outrages Jacob on an unexpected level. He seems to think only of his lowered standing among the local inhabitants. His selfish response (34:30) reflects his focus on himself.

35:1 Chapter 35 opens with God's renewed command to Jacob to go to Bethel. It is at Bethel that Jacob has his first real encounter with God and is told about God's plan to bless him. It is also at Bethel that Jacob first builds an altar of worship to the Lord.

35:5 The inclusion of the phrase "the sons of Jacob" suggests that the other cities fear Jacob's boys because of what they had done to the people of Shechem. Yet it also seems evident that as Jacob obeys the Lord, the Lord protects Jacob and his family by causing a fear to fall on the surrounding cities (Deuteronomy 11:25).

35:7–15 Jacob faithfully fulfills his vow to God at Luz, which he renames Bethel, or "house of God."

35:16–20 Rachel's death is recorded. Rachel, who had so longed for a child, dies bearing her second son. She gives him the name *Ben-oni*, which can mean "son of my sorrow"; but the name that Jacob gives is *Benjamin*, which means "the son of the right hand."

35:22 A concubine, as Bilhah is described, was sometimes a slave with whom her owner had sexual relations. She enjoyed some of the privileges of a wife, and people sometimes called her a wife in patriarchal times, but she was not a wife in the full sense of the term. Reuben's relations with Bilhah are a power move as much as anything else. In that culture, a man who wanted to assert his superiority over another man might do so by having sexual relations with that man's wife or concubine. Reuben's actions may also have been an effort to elevate his own mother's (Leah's) standing in the home. With the death of Rachel, who had been Jacob's favorite, Bilhah, Rachel's servant, may have been able to move into a favored role. Reuben's actions make Bilhah detestable to Jacob; thus Leah has a better standing in the household.

36:2 Esau, in open defiance, takes wives from the idolatrous Hittites and brings them to his tents within the camp, where they make life miserable for Esau's parents, Isaac and Rebekah (see 26:35). Verse 3 indicates that he also added a third wife from the descendants of Ishmael.

36:6–8 The dividing of territory between Esau and Jacob described here is reminiscent of the episode between Abraham and Lot in 13:1–13. There are two reasons for Esau's move: (1) There isn't sufficient water and pasture for both flocks and herds, and (2) Esau has finally come to accept that the promised land of Canaan is to be passed on to Jacob.

36:8–43 Esau and his descendants are men of great political power. They are called dukes (36:15) and kings (36:31). These men reign as kings in Edom before any king reigns in Israel. While Esau's sons and grandsons become rulers, Jacob's sons remain lowly shepherds for generations (47:3).

37:1–50:26 While the last fourteen chapters of Genesis include Jacob, the story line focuses on Jacob's sons. And of his twelve sons, special interest is given to Joseph, who is mentioned twice as much as Jacob. This means a quarter of the book of Genesis is devoted to Joseph.

37:2 Elsewhere, the word *report* is used in the negative sense of an untrue report (the same word is translated "slander" in Proverbs 10:18). This may imply some exaggeration or inaccuracies on Joseph's part, which would have added fire to the rivalry between him and his brothers.

37:3 Jacob's favoritism, signified by the colorful tunic he gives his favorite son, is no help. While it's not clear exactly what the tunic looked like, the idea that it is a coat of many colors comes from the Greek translation of the Old Testament. The tunic sets Joseph apart as the favored one. Favoritism and rivalry have a long history in Jacob's family. Jacob's father, Isaac, preferred Esau. His mother, Rebekah, claimed Jacob as a favorite. In Jacob's own family, his preference for Rachel set up resentment between not only Rachel and her sister (also Jacob's wife), Leah, but probably between their children as well.

37:5–11 Joseph probably reveals part faith and part foolishness in sharing these dreams with his already contentious family.

37:12–17 Joseph is sent to check on his brothers. It is not uncommon for shepherds to lead their flocks many miles from home in search of pasture. Shechem was about fifty miles north of Hebron. When he doesn't find his brothers at Shechem, Joseph goes to Dothan, a location fifteen miles north of Shechem.

37:18–22 When Joseph finds his brothers, there is a shift in perspective. Suddenly the story is told from his brothers' point of view. Reuben, who advocates for Joseph's life, is the firstborn and the decision-maker in the family (37:21–24). He is apparently not part of the family group that was plotting to kill Joseph. That group consisted probably of Dan, Naphtali, Gad, and Asher—the four sons against whom Joseph brought a bad report (37:2).

37:23–28 These verses record how the brothers capture Joseph and subsequently sell him to the Midianite merchants for twenty pieces of silver. Slave-trading was common in Egypt. The price agreed on for Joseph was the same price that was later specified for a slave between the ages of five and twenty years under the Mosaic economy (Leviticus 27:5).

37:29–32 When Reuben returns to find Joseph gone, he knows that as the oldest, he will have to answer to his father for whatever has happened. Thus evolves the brothers' scheme. Though the brothers never actually say Joseph is dead, they successfully deceive their father.

37:36 Joseph ends up in Egypt, in the home of one of the most responsible officers of Pharaoh's administration.

38:1–11 Judah leaves home and moves to Canaan, where he lives among people whom his family considered unclean. When Judah's oldest son, Er, dies, Er's wife, Tamar, becomes a childless widow. Since carrying on the bloodline is of the highest value in this culture, the custom of the day is for Er's brother to marry Tamar and supply Er with an heir. This custom, called *levirate marriage*, is described in Deuteronomy 25:5–10. A son born from this new marriage is considered the heir to the deceased man and does not increase the wealth of the younger brother at all. This is why Onan does not cooperate in providing Er with an heir. After Onan dies, Tamar expects that the third son of Judah will provide her an heir when he is old enough, but that is never Judah's intent.

38:12–19 When Tamar realizes that Judah lied to her, she plans a ruse to make him take responsibility for the situation. Tamar tricks Judah into sleeping with her.

38:24 When Judah finally hears the stories of pregnant Tamar, he calls for her judgment by burning.

38:25 Going to execute judgment on Tamar, Judah faces the woman who has his personal belongings and is pregnant with his twin sons. There is evidence that among ancient Assyrian and Hittite peoples, part of the levirate responsibility could pass to the father of the widow's husband, if there were no brothers to fulfill it. Thus Tamar was, in one sense, claiming what was due her. She had tricked Judah into fulfilling the levirate responsibility and now would bear his children. (See study note at 38:1–11.)

38:27–30 Tamar and Judah have two sons: Pharez and Zarah. *Pharez* means "a breach" or "one who breaks through." Pharez becomes the ancestor of David (Ruth 4:18–22), who in turn becomes the ancestor of Jesus Christ (Matthew 1:3). *Zarah* means "a dawning or brightness." The struggle between the twins at birth is reminiscent of the struggle of Jacob and Esau, Judah's father and uncle.

39:3 After Joseph's brothers sell him into slavery, the Midianites take him down to Egypt and sell him to Potiphar (37:36). Potiphar is the chief executioner or chief of police. Even in these less-than-ideal circumstances, Potiphar notices God's hand on Joseph.

39:6 This verse describes Joseph's outward appearance. The Bible rarely offers this kind of description. The only other men who are referred to in this way are David (1 Samuel 16:12) and Absalom (2 Samuel 14:25).

39:7–20 Genesis describes Joseph's life in Potiphar's house, and particularly his interaction with Potiphar's wife. According to verse 7, she carefully scrutinizes Joseph and then eventually propositions him. When he refuses, she manipulates the situation to make it appear that Joseph has acted inappropriately, and so he is thrown in jail. In this time and place, attempted rape was a capital offense. The milder punishment Joseph receives suggests that Potiphar does not believe his wife. Furthermore, the king's prison was a place for political prisoners and would hardly have been expected to accommodate foreign slaves guilty of crimes against their masters. Another very telling observation is that the prison was in the basement of Potiphar's house (40:3, 7). Joseph was thus demoted.

39:21–23 Joseph maintains persistent good character. He is not enslaved by his circumstances.

40:1 While Joseph is in Potiphar's jail, God brings some influential and unexpected guests: Pharaoh's butler (or cupbearer) and baker. The butler and baker are not guilty of some minor indiscretion or inadvertent offense against Pharaoh; they had greatly offended him (40:1–3).

40:4–11 Joseph's role is to act as a servant to these men, and in the course of serving them, he also interprets some dreams for them. He recognizes that their dreams are revelations from God and invites the two prisoners to relate their dreams to him. He is careful, however, to give God the glory for his interpretative gift (40:8; 41:16, 25, 28, 39).

40:12–19 Here we read of Joseph's interpretations—one having a positive outcome and the other having a harrowing outcome. In some translations, Joseph is credited with saying that the baker's head would be lifted up, but that is actually a reference to a hanging. The baker would not simply suffer execution, but his corpse would be impaled and publicly exposed.

40:20–23 Joseph's predictions come true just as God had said. One of the men is reinstated by Pharaoh, and the other is executed. Between the end of chapter 40 and the beginning of chapter 41, however, two years pass without the butler fulfilling his promise to remember Joseph and his interpretive gifts.

41:1–7 Two years after the butler's return to court, Pharaoh has two dreams symbolic enough to require interpretation. In the first dream, seven fat cows are eaten by seven gaunt cows. In the second dream, seven plump ears of grain are eaten by seven thin ears.

41:8 The magicians Pharaoh sends for shouldn't be confused with contemporary magicians, who perform simple tricks. These were the wise, educated men of Pharaoh's kingdom. They were schooled in the sacred arts and sciences of the Egyptians. Yet they are unable to help Pharaoh.

41:9–14 Though it was two years earlier that the butler had promised to remember Joseph, it is these troubling dreams that finally make it happen. He summons Joseph for Pharaoh. Notice that part of Joseph's preparations for meeting Pharaoh is to shave. The Egyptians preferred to shave all the hair off their bodies and wear wigs.

41:15–16 Once in Pharaoh's presence, Joseph makes it clear that he can interpret the dreams only in God's power. In essence, Joseph tells Pharaoh (who is considered a god in his own country) that his God is superior to and sovereign over Pharaoh and the gods of Egypt. This is quite a stand to take.

41:17–36 Pharaoh explains his dreams to Joseph, and Joseph interprets the dreams and discusses a plan of action with the great king of Egypt. Three times in this section, Joseph attributes the outcome of Pharaoh's dreams to God (41:25, 28, 32).

41:37–45 Because of these events, Joseph becomes an advisor to and an officer of the Egyptian government. To naturalize Joseph, Pharaoh gives him an Egyptian name (41:45; compare Daniel 1:7) and an Egyptian wife from an appropriate level of society. Joseph's name, *Zaphnath-paaneah*, is probably Egyptian for "God speaks; He lives."

41:45 Joseph's marriage to an Egyptian seems out of place. The patriarchs generally avoided marriage to Canaanites, but this was a marriage to a non-Canaanite Gentile, which was less serious. Under the circumstances, it doesn't seem that Joseph is given much choice. Perhaps more important, it's clear from the names given to their two sons that Joseph doesn't allow his wife's pagan background to influence him away from God. It is this falling away that is the issue with mixed religious marriages in the Old Testament.

41:50–52 God blesses Joseph with two sons. Joseph names his firstborn *Manasseh*, which means "making to

forget." He names the second *Ephraim*, meaning "God has made me fruitful in the land of my affliction." If the name of Joseph's first son (Manasseh) focuses on a God who preserves, the name of Joseph's second son (Ephraim) focuses on a God who blesses. Joseph gives his boys Hebrew names that are testaments to God's faithfulness.

42:1 The seven years of famine that Joseph predicted are now in full force. The famine has spread to Joseph's family in Canaan.

42:2 What would have kept Jacob's sons from going to Egypt until their father instructed them? For one thing, the trip was long (250 to 300 miles) and dangerous, and a round trip could consume six weeks' time. Even after arriving in Egypt, the brothers couldn't be certain of a friendly reception. As foreigners from Canaan, they would be vulnerable and could even be arrested and enslaved.

42:6 When the brothers arrive in Egypt and are ushered into Joseph's presence, the predictions of Joseph's dreams from long ago (37:5–7) are fulfilled as his brothers bow before him.

42:7 His brothers did not recognize him. The last time the brothers had seen Joseph, he was a seventeen-year-old boy who was in a position of weakness, being carried off into slavery by the Midianites (37:28). At this point in the story, though, Joseph is nearly forty, the governor of Egypt, wearing the royal clothing of a king; and to top it off, he is powerful and confident in his role.

42:9 The Bible is clear that Joseph never indulges in any resentment against others who had injured him (45:5; 50:18–21). Joseph's purpose in speaking harshly and accusing his brothers of spying is not motivated by bitterness but by a desire to covertly discover information regarding the health and well-being of his father, Jacob, and his younger brother, Benjamin. He also is testing their character—have they changed in how they care for each other?

42:18 Joseph gives his brothers a glimmer of hope when he tells them he fears God. The name he uses for God is the name of the Hebrews' God (*Elohim*). The brothers would not have expected this from the seemingly harsh Egyptian prime minister. But there is enough hope of fair treatment in those words to keep them from despairing.

42:24 Joseph's pent-up emotions simply have to come out, so he leaves the room and weeps privately. This is the first of six such experiences. Joseph also weeps when he sees his brother Benjamin (43:29–30), when he reveals himself to his brothers (45:2), when he meets his father in Egypt (46:29), when his father dies (50:1), and when he assures his brothers that they are truly forgiven (50:17). The scripture does not say why Joseph chooses to imprison Simeon rather than any of the other brothers. Perhaps the reason is in the brothers' discussion of their guilt in having sold Joseph into slavery. In that discussion, Joseph learns for the first time that Reuben, the oldest son of the family, had kept the other brothers from killing Joseph. If Joseph had intended to imprison the oldest brother, he may have had a change of heart. Simeon, being the second oldest, would have been the one responsible for their collective wickedness.

42:25–28 Before his brothers leave, Joseph hides their payment for the grain in their grain sacks. Perhaps this is to test his brothers to see if they could still be bought with money. Joseph wanted to know if they would do to Simeon what they did to him. The brothers panic because they could be accused of stealing this money.

42:29–36 When they return home, Jacob's sons share with their father what happened. Unfortunately, Jacob's response only serves to prolong their return, Simeon's imprisonment, and his reunion with his long-lost son.

42:37–38 Reuben's offer may have made sense to Reuben, but basically he is only offering to increase his father's sense of bereavement by causing him to lose two grandsons in addition to his youngest son.

43:3–10 Judah steps up and offers to be the collateral for Benjamin. This is the first evidence of real character we find in Judah so far in Genesis. Up until now, he has been like his father, self-centered and self-absorbed. When Jacob finally allows the brothers to make the trip with Benjamin, he employs his gift-giving strategy of diplomacy. It is the same strategy he employed when he was preparing to meet his brother, Esau (33:10–11). Jacob's gift-giving isn't motivated by love or friendship; it is intended to soften the heart of the Egyptian leader.

43:15–25 When the brothers are reunited with Simeon, they go from agony to ecstasy in a matter of moments. Then Joseph hosts a meal for the brothers, who years before had callously sat down to eat while he languished in a pit (37:24–25). We aren't told whether Joseph even acknowledges the gifts that Jacob sent.

43:33 The brothers are seated in order by age by a host who presumably is entirely ignorant of their birth order. The chances of that happening are approximately one in forty million. It must have seemed like magic.

43:34 Joseph shows respect to Benjamin as his distinguished guest by giving him larger and better servings of food than his brothers receive. Special honorees frequently received double portions, but a fivefold portion was the sign of highest privilege. With this favor, Joseph not only is honoring Benjamin but may have been testing his other brothers' feelings toward Benjamin. He may have wanted to see if they would hate him as they had hated his father's former favorite.

44:2 Joseph continues his effort to discover the truth—to find out whether his brothers are still the selfish, godless, wicked men who sold him into slavery twenty years earlier. A silver cup like the one he had placed in Benjamin's sack is, of course, valuable.

44:4–14 When the accusation of theft is made, the brothers are no doubt indignant because they are confident in their righteousness. But when the silver cup is discovered in Benjamin's sack, they are broken and show evidence that they had become a family (44:3–9).

44:18–34 Fourteen times in this speech, Judah mentions his father, Jacob. Jacob would eventually

crown Judah with kingship (49:10), because he demonstrates that he has become fit to rule according to God's ideal of kingship—that the king serves the people, not vice versa. Judah is transformed from one who sold his brother as a slave to one who is willing to be the slave for his brother.

45:1–15 Joseph reveals his identity. The response of the brothers to Joseph's revelation of his identity is a term translated *dismayed* or *dumbfounded*. This is a term used for paralyzing fear as felt by those involved in war (Exodus 15:15; Judges 20:41; 1 Samuel 28:21; Psalm 48:5). But after a threefold expression of Joseph's goodwill toward his siblings (weeping, explaining, and embracing), his brothers are finally able to talk to him.

45:5, 7–9 Throughout the course of Joseph's life, he has discerned God's providential control of events. Four times he states that God, not his brothers, is behind what has happened.

45:24 Upon parting, Joseph's admonition to his brothers not to quarrel on their journey is a bit unclear. Probably he means just that—not to become involved in arguing and recriminations over the past. The brothers had already quarreled over their sin against Joseph (42:21–22). Joseph may have known that as soon as these men left his presence, they would be tempted to assign blame to one another.

45:26 Jacob is stunned to receive news that his favorite son, Joseph, is alive. At the age of 130, he prepares the family to leave Canaan and head out to join Joseph in Egypt.

46:1 Why sacrifices at Beer-sheba? Beer-sheba was at the southernmost boundary of Israel. In essence, it was the point of no return. Furthermore, Beer-sheba was a significant place to Jacob's family. This is where Abraham had dug a well, planted a grove, and called on the name of the Lord (21:30–33). Abraham even lived in Beer-sheba after offering Isaac on Mount Moriah (22:19). Isaac also lived in Beer-sheba (26:23, 32–33) and built an altar there (26:23–25). It is perhaps at this altar where Jacob presents his sacrifices.

46:2–4 God appears once more to Jacob, as He had to Jacob's grandfather Abraham (22:11). God identifies Himself in virtually the same way as when He spoke to Jacob during his vision of the stairway up into heaven (28:13). He also offers the fourth and final "fear not" consolation recorded in Genesis (see 15:1; 21:17; 26:24). After hearing directly from the Lord, Jacob and his family leave Beer-sheba and travel to Egypt (46:5–7).

46:8–27 This is a list of every tribe (and every major family group within that tribe) that later formed the nation of Israel. Every Hebrew knew his family ancestry. The division of labor, the organization of the army, and the parceling of the land all were done according to tribe. This list of names reminds original readers of their identity as God's people in fulfilling His purposes.

46:28 The fact that Jacob chooses Judah to be the guide indicates that he trusts his son, which suggests that the men had told their father everything and were in his good graces again. Now Jacob can see the hand of God in all that has happened. In spite of his past failures, Judah now proves he is faithful, and his descendants are eventually named the royal tribe (49:8–12).

46:29 The reunion between Jacob and Joseph recalls Jacob's former meeting with Esau (33:4). In both situations, after a long period of separation, Jacob sends a party ahead to meet the relative. Previously, Jacob had said that the loss of his sons would bring him to his grave in mourning (37:35; 42:38). But finding Joseph alive enables his father to find a measure of peace.

46:34 Goshen had some of the best pastureland in all of Egypt. It would be a place to keep the Hebrews isolated and insulated from the culture and religion of Egypt, since the Egyptians considered sheep unclean and Hebrews detestable (43:32). One of the greatest dangers to the covenant promises of God was intermarriage between the Hebrews and the Egyptians, because intermarriage would inevitably lead to spiritual compromise and the worship of the false gods of the Egyptians.

47:1–6 Joseph explains to Pharaoh the needs of his family. He even introduces five of his brothers to Pharaoh. After the brothers answer Pharaoh's questions, they ask his permission to live in Goshen. Pharaoh agrees to their request and even offers any capable brothers a job—to be put in charge of Pharaoh's livestock.

47:7 Jacob's blessing of Pharaoh is unusual in that it implies Jacob is superior, even though Pharaoh is a man of immense worldly power and influence. The precise meaning of the Hebrew verb translated *blessed* is difficult in this passage, because the content of Jacob's blessing is not given. The expression could simply mean that he greets Pharaoh, but that seems insufficient. Jacob probably praises Pharaoh, for the verb is used this way for praising God. It is also possible that he pronounces a formal prayer of blessing, asking God to reward Pharaoh for his kindness.

47:13–27 This passage demonstrates the fulfillment of Jacob's blessing on Pharaoh (46:31–47:10). Joseph is able to save Egypt and its neighbors from a severe famine and alleviate the desperate plight of the Egyptians. God blesses Pharaoh because he has blessed the Israelites with the best of Egypt.

47:22 Joseph gives preferential treatment to the Egyptian priests. More than a sign of religious support, this concession is probably due to the powerful lobby that the priests have with Pharaoh.

47:24 The tax described is not out of line with what was common in that day in the ancient Near East. It was lower than the average 33.3 percent.

47:28 The account of Jacob begins to draw to a close. Jacob enjoys the blessings of God for seventeen more years—ironically, the same number of years he enjoyed Joseph until Joseph was sold into slavery to Egypt by his older brothers (37:2).

47:29–31 Why does Jacob insist on being buried in Canaan? This would remind his descendants that Egypt was not home, but only a place to sojourn until God brought them back to their true home, Canaan, the land of promise (Hebrews 11:22).

48:1–49:33 Jacob is coming to the end of his life. He has not always honored God but is an example of a man who finishes well. Before he dies, Jacob passes the torch on to those who follow. It is likely that in the seventeen years Jacob lived with Joseph in Egypt, he invested in Joseph's sons Manasseh and Ephraim. These sons were born during the seven years of abundance, before the first year of the famine (41:50). Jacob went down to Egypt somewhere around the end of the second year of the famine (45:6) and lived seventeen years after he arrived (47:28). Since Jacob is near death, the sons of Joseph must have been about twenty years old.

48:5–6 Jacob effectively adopts his grandsons. Ephraim and Manasseh go from being Jacob's grandsons to his number one and two sons. This action displaces Reuben and Simeon as the two oldest sons. Thus, in future lists of the twelve tribes of Israel, Ephraim and Manasseh are normally included in the place of Joseph. Both Reuben and Simeon had disqualified themselves from positions of status and leadership in Israel's family because of their sin: Reuben due to his sin of lying with Bilhah, Jacob's concubine (35:22; 49:4; 1 Chronicles 5:1–2), and Simeon due to his violent murder of the men of Shechem (Genesis 34:25). In essence, Jacob is giving Joseph the double blessing that is generally reserved for the firstborn (Reuben). In the future, Joseph's other children will be incorporated into the tribes of Ephraim and Manasseh.

48:13–20 This is the first of many scriptural instances of the laying on of hands. By this symbolic act, a person transfers a spiritual power or gift to another. In this case, Jacob symbolically transfers a blessing from himself to Joseph's sons. Ephraim and Manasseh do become great tribes. At one time, Ephraim was used as a synonym for the kingdom of Israel. Jacob's blessing of Ephraim and Manasseh also carries prophetic significance and force (48:19–20). This is the fourth consecutive generation of Abraham's descendants in which the normal pattern of the firstborn assuming prominence over the secondborn is reversed: Isaac over Ishmael, Jacob over Esau, Joseph over Reuben, and Ephraim over Manasseh.

49:3–4 Jacob's three oldest sons are disinherited for their unfaithfulness. The firstborn son normally has two rights. First, he becomes the leader of the family, the new patriarch. Second, he is entitled to a double share of the inheritance. But Reuben is not to receive this blessing because he is reckless and destructive. The picture painted with these descriptive words is of water that floods its banks and goes wildly out of control. The result is an evaluation of Reuben that points to wildness and weakness, an undisciplined life. This is a reference to Reuben's misconduct in Genesis 35. True to Jacob's prophecy, the Reubenites never produce a leader of any kind for Israel. They never enter the promised land (Numbers 32). They build unauthorized places of worship (Joshua 22:10–34). The tribe produces no significant man, no judge, no king, and no prophet.

49:5–7 When Jacob says that Simeon and Levi are brothers, it is not a statement simply about their family relationship as brothers as much as a statement about their similarity in character—they are two of a kind. Interestingly, Jacob still characterizes his sons as angry men. He doesn't say their anger was fierce; instead, he says it is fierce. These men have remained angry. Jacob's prophecy that these tribes will be scattered is fulfilled, as the tribe of Simeon later inherits land scattered throughout Judah's territory (Joshua 19:1–9; see also 1 Chronicles 4:28–33, 39, 42). The tribe of Levi becomes priests with no inheritance but scattered throughout the rest of the tribal lands. Even though these first three tribes suffer loss for their sins, Jacob's prophecies about them are still a blessing. They retain a place in the chosen family and enjoy the benefits of God's promises as Jacob's heirs. Yet they are disqualified from the reward that could have been theirs because of their failure to repent of their sin (see Numbers 32:23–24; Ezekiel 18:30).

49:8–27 Jacob gives the seven acceptable sons responsibilities, and the two most faithful sons receive greater responsibility. True to the poetic qualities of the text, the images of the destinies of the remaining sons are, in most cases, based on wordplays of the sons' names. Most notably, Judah will be preeminent among his brothers, and they will praise him. Judah's hand will be on the neck of his enemies, and his brothers will bow down to him. But leadership of his descendants will not be fully realized until the days of King David, some 640 years later (49:8).

49:22–26 Joseph's blessing is especially abundant. Judah receives the leadership of the tribes, but Joseph obtains the double portion of the birthright (1 Chronicles 5:2). The two tribes bearing his sons' names will see the fulfillment of the blessing, even though during his lifetime Joseph faced much opposition.

50:1–8 Joseph was a man of faith and a man of sensitivity. The only tears recorded in Joseph's life are not for himself but for the plight of his brothers and the loss of his father. The Egyptians show great honor to Jacob and to Joseph in their seventy days of mourning after Jacob's death. This length of time is only two days short of the length of mourning for a pharaoh. When Joseph goes to bury his father, all of Pharaoh's servants and elders, and all of the elders of Egypt, accompany him.

50:14 God's promises are all connected to Canaan, but Joseph does not choose to stay there. He knows his calling concerns Egypt. He takes one look at the land of promise, which he has not seen since he was seventeen years old, and then goes back to the place where God had called him.

50:15–18 Joseph's brothers exhibit some negative and positive responses when their father dies. Initially, they respond negatively due to guilt, fear, and paranoia. They assume that Joseph has been simply biding his time out of respect for his father, Jacob. But now that Jacob is gone, they are gripped with the terrifying expectation of punishment for their sins. So they falsely claim that Jacob has issued a charge for Joseph to forgive his brothers. However, Jacob never did this, because he recognized that Joseph had completely forgiven his brothers. Positively, though, the brothers own their sin against Joseph. They beg for forgiveness, bow down before Joseph, and offer themselves up as slaves.

50:19–21 Joseph recognizes God as the only One who is able to judge. While not diminishing the manner in which his brothers wronged him, he recognizes God's greater purpose. Joseph's claim that God meant for good what his brothers meant for evil is the theme of the entire Joseph narrative.

50:22–26 Joseph was a man who experienced God's blessing. More than fifty years elapse between verses 21 and 22. During this period, God abundantly blesses Joseph with a long life, the privilege of seeing his great-great grandchildren, and a remarkable faith. It is only fitting that the book of Genesis ends on a note of blessing, since it has been a consistent theme throughout the book.

50:25–26 Although God's people would spend four hundred years in Egyptian bondage, Joseph already saw the day when God would bring them back to the promised land. In light of this faith, Joseph makes known his wish to be buried in the promised land. This is an expression of faith and confidence that God's covenant promises will come to pass. Joseph dies and is placed in a coffin in Egypt. Unlike his father, Jacob, Joseph's body isn't buried immediately. Instead, his coffin lay above ground for more than four hundred years, until the people of Israel take it back to Canaan as they leave Egypt under Moses' leadership. So there it sat in Egypt, for four hundred years, as a silent witness to Joseph's confidence that Israel was going back to the promised land, just as God had said (Exodus 13:19). Joseph's faith in God's promises to his forefathers provides a fitting climax for the book of Genesis.

EXODUS

INTRODUCTION TO EXODUS ■ Exodus tells the story of the birth of the nation of Israel through its deliverance from bondage in Egypt and the receiving of God's instructions, based on His covenant, for building the nation to honor Him.

AUTHOR ■ Though there is debate among scholars about the authorship of Exodus, Moses is considered the author by most evangelical scholars.

OCCASION ■ The main purpose of the book of Exodus is to describe God's rescue of His enslaved people and His making them a nation. This book chronicles God's faithfulness to His people—in spite of their sin. The book of Genesis closes with the family of Israel making a home in Egypt under the leadership of Joseph. Exodus picks up centuries later in Egypt after the family of Israel has grown into the nation of Israel. While Joseph had saved the Egyptians from starvation, his family's descendants had become slaves. Exodus follows the story of God's people from the birth of Moses, the leader of Israel during this period in their history, through their deliverance from bondage, the giving of the law, and the construction of the tabernacle in the desert.

1:1 The beginning of Exodus links the events of Genesis to those recorded in Exodus—two books intended to be understood in relationship to each other. Genesis provides an excellent backdrop for Exodus, reminding Israel of its roots and of the basis for God's blessings, which were soon to be experienced.

1:1–6 These verses sum up the history of Israel as a clan, as described more thoroughly in Genesis 12–50. They remind us that all that is going to take place in this book is directly related to what has gone before. Most importantly, this portion of the introduction to the book of Exodus links the existence and rapid growth of Israel as a nation to the covenant that God made with Abraham (Genesis 12:1–3; 15:12) and reiterated to the patriarchs (Genesis 26:2–5, 24; 28:13–15). The sons of Israel and their families are seventy in number when they arrive in Egypt. But when the sons of Israel leave Egypt, they do so as a great nation (Exodus 1:7, 12, 20; 12:37).

1:7 This verse fills in a nearly four-hundred-year gap, covering the period from the death of Joseph to the time of the Exodus. Periods of silence similar to the gap in the history of Israel exist throughout scripture. During these periods, God is at work behind the scenes and in ways that at the time are not immediately apparent. Verses 8–22 demonstrate that during periods of apparent silence, God is at work providentially, bringing His purposes to pass and preparing history for another of His dramatic interventions into the affairs of people.

1:8–14 There is considerable disagreement among scholars as to the identity of this new king who does not know about Joseph. It is most likely that the king referred to here is new in a very significant sense. He represents not only a new person but also a new dynasty. The fears of Pharaoh are of interest. He fears the numerical strength of the Israelites and seeks to diminish them. He fears that they will become allies with the enemy, overcome the Egyptians, and leave Egypt. Pharaoh's plan is to enslave the Israelites and tighten control over them. A substantial part of this plan seems to be that of intimidation and oppression, so demoralizing and frightening the Israelites that they will not dare to resist their masters. Yet just as the Israelites had greatly multiplied during the time of Joseph (Genesis 47:27) and after his death, so they continue to multiply under the cruel hand of their taskmasters. The Egyptians came to dread the Israelites and worked them ruthlessly.

1:15–22 Pharaoh's demands of the midwives are quite abominable. Not only does he propose acts of violence on the innocent, but he also passes on all responsibility for the death of these Hebrew infants. He wants the midwives to solve this national dilemma of the Hebrew birthrate. But the midwives fear God more than Pharaoh, so they refuse to put the infant boys to death. Pharaoh's plan backfires. God rewards the midwives for fearing Him by enabling them to be fruitful themselves (some scholars suggest that barren women were often made midwives). God also records the names of two of these God-fearing Hebrew midwives as an example to believers throughout the centuries.

2:1–25 Few stories in the Bible are more familiar than that of Moses set afloat in the waters of the Nile and his rescue by the daughter of Pharaoh. Exodus 2 shows how God's hand is at work in the history of Israel, preserving the life of one child who will become Israel's deliverer.

2:2 Moses is exceedingly well formed and beautiful, and his parents perceive that God has a special purpose for their child. But Moses is not suggesting that God moved his parents to hide him because they were convinced that he was particularly special in appearance or in purpose, but rather that they saw something special about him as a child of God. This verse could simply be rendered, "She saw that he was good." The Hebrew word meaning "goodly" (or "good") is frequently used by Moses in the five books of the Law, and in most it has the sense of goodness that is the result of being made (or given) by God and of being declared good by Him. The frequent expression in Genesis 1 and 2, "It was good," employs the same term.

2:6 Pharaoh's daughter comes face-to-face with the implications of her father's policy of genocide. What Pharaoh had commanded was not only unthinkable; it was undoable. She names the boy *Moses*, a name rooted in the event of her finding him as a baby at which time she drew him out of the Nile.

2:11 This verse passes over nearly forty years (see Acts 7:23), taking up the story of Moses as an adult. Moses makes the critical decision to identify with his people before he goes out to observe the affliction of his brethren (as described in Hebrews 11:24–26), which informs us that the reason Moses visits his brethren is due to his decision to identify with them and even suffer with them.

2:12 Moses' premeditated murder cannot be defended. Yet while Moses' method of dealing with this problem is wrong, we see that his motivation is commendable. Moses sought to defend the oppressed. When he seeks to rebuke his Hebrew brother for wrongly mistreating another Hebrew (2:13), Moses reveals, once again, the disposition of a deliverer.

2:15–17 Rather than taking his place as a deliverer of his people, at this point Moses flees to find himself delivering the oppressed elsewhere. At the well, Moses does not like how the women are being pushed in line by the shepherds. Moses once again delivers the oppressed. Moses cannot look the other way, even when advantage is being taken of strangers.

2:21–22 With great economy of words, Moses briefly records that this chance encounter leads to a lengthy stay in Midian, his marriage to Zipporah, and the birth of a son, Gershom. Moses names the child *Gershom* because he felt like an alien in a foreign land. In Midian, a land closer to Canaan than Egypt, Moses thought of himself as an alien and a sojourner. He still thought of Egypt, not Canaan, as his homeland. One can hardly think of this time as one of great faith or purpose in Moses' life. The faith and commitment to the people of God with which verse 11 began have somehow eroded into something far less.

2:23–25 In spite of appearances, God is at work. Humanly speaking, it looks as though everything is working against Israel, yet this passage reiterates that God is very much informed, involved, and intent upon fulfilling His purposes and promises. This section ties together the agony of God's people in Egypt (described in chapter 1, but overshadowed by the personal account of Moses in chapter 2) with the deliverance about to take place in the following chapters.

3:2–3 The burning bush not only made a profound impact on Moses and the nation of Israel, but also continued to serve as a key event in history. This passage of scripture is one that must have been well known to the Jews of Jesus' day. The account of the burning bush is so central to the thinking of the Gospel writers Mark and Luke that they (perhaps like most men in their day) came to call this section of scripture "the bush" portion (Mark 12:26; Luke 20:37). The bush is apparently a typical common desert bush, but the fire is far from ordinary. The closer Moses gets to the bush, the more incredible the scene becomes. Moses surely had to wonder about this phenomenon. Scholars have offered numerous "natural" explanations for the burning bush over the years, not wanting to acknowledge a full-fledged miracle. Yet we know from the biblical account that this is truly a unique intervention of God in time and space.

3:8 This entire chapter introduces a significant change in the drama of the deliverance of God's people from Egypt. From God's providential dealings in the life of the nation of Israel, we move to God's direct intervention through Moses and the miracles He performs. We move from the silence of God over the past four hundred years to God's speaking directly to Moses from the bush, and later on, from the same mountain.

3:14 Scholars have spent a great deal of effort to determine the exact meaning of the expression "I AM THAT I AM." As the "I AM," God is not the God who was anything, in the sense that He changes. Whatever He was, He continues to be, and He will be forever. God exists independently and unchangeably. Therefore, whatever God has begun to do He will bring to completion, because there are no changes that necessitate any alterations in His original plans and purposes.

3:16–22 Now that God has revealed Himself, He reveals His plan for Moses and for Israel. Moses is to repeat the words that God has spoken to him from the burning bush, request a three-day "leave" for the Israelites to worship God in the desert, and finally, collect the wages that are owed to the people of God for their hard work in Egypt. These commands are all based on the promise and the prophecy God had previously given Abraham in Genesis 15:12–20. The real struggle now is between Moses and God, and whether he will do what God commands. As the next section reveals, Moses will learn that God's commands are not to be refused.

4:1 In the past, Moses doubted his calling; now he is doubting the word of God, for the Lord has just told him the leaders of Israel will accept him (3:18). From the words that follow this assurance, we know that Moses is told not only that the leaders of Israel will accept his leadership, but that it will all work out, just as God has said. Moses is guilty of unbelief.

4:2–9 God still graciously deals with the weakness of Moses by granting him the ability to perform three signs. For the Israelites, these signs are visible evidence that God did appear to Moses in the burning bush. Not only do these signs emphatically prove the existence of the God of the Hebrews, but they give evidence of His superior power.

4:10 Rather than acting on the basis of who God is, Moses retreats on the pretext that he is not a gifted communicator.

4:11 God reminds Moses that, as his Creator, He fashioned him precisely as He intended, and he is therefore fully able to carry out his commission. The problem of what to say is one that the Lord will handle in due time. While Moses is worrying about what he will say when he gets to Egypt, God is spurring him to get going. Moses is looking too far down the path.

4:13 This verse reveals the truth: Moses does not want to go. It is not that he lacks the assurance or the authority; he simply lacks the courage to act.

4:14–17 God is longsuffering and patient, but now He is angry. God's anger is not only reflected in a visible way; it is evident in His answer to Moses. Aaron could speak fluently, so why not let him speak for Moses? As later events indicate, the presence of Aaron is a burden for Moses and at times a stumbling block for others (32:1–5; Numbers 12:1–12).

4:22–23 Here, for the first time, the nation of Israel is referred to as the firstborn son of God. Because Pharaoh would not release Israel, God's firstborn son, to worship Him in the desert, God would have Moses tell Pharaoh that He will kill his firstborn. The mention of Israel as Yahweh's firstborn is significant in this larger context. The firstborn son was to the Egyptians not only special, but in many respects sacred. It is therefore most interesting that the people of God are regarded as firstborn in this passage.

4:24–26 To the Israelites, the covenant God made with Abraham and reiterated to the patriarchs and Moses was their "gospel." Circumcision was the sign of the covenant—evidence of the parents' faith in the promise of God to Abraham that through his seed blessings would come to Israel and to the whole world (see Genesis 12:1–3). As a testimony of the parents' faith in God's covenant promise, every male in Israel was to be circumcised. Moses was about to go to Egypt and tell the Israelites that God was about to fulfill His promises, based upon His covenant. And yet Moses had not yet circumcised his son. And if this son is his firstborn, he has had many years in which to do so.

5:1–21 In this passage, Moses first uses God's powerful (and now popularized) phrase: "Let my people go." God desires to be alone with *His* people, but Pharaoh is annoyed by the arrogance of the request. He even says he suspects Moses is lying about receiving divine revelation. Even though Pharaoh is warned there will be consequences, he remains arrogant himself—without any fear or reverence for the God of the Israelites. His heart is already hardened to the plight of the Hebrews. In response to the Israelites' request, he further complicates their situation by demanding bricks without providing straw for them to be made.

5:22–6:13 God reiterates to Moses His commitment to deliver the Israelites from bondage in Egypt—these are the promises of the Abrahamic Covenant. Yet even the promise of deliverance does little to raise the hopes of the beleaguered people. The Hebrew word for *redeem* (verse 6) is the same word used in the story of Ruth, when she is redeemed by the house of Boaz. It refers to the right of family members to acquire persons or

property belonging to other family members who are at risk—just as God redeems His people during their time of need in Egypt and ultimately purposes to save their souls through the work of Jesus Christ.

6:14–27 Evidently the genealogy of Moses and Aaron is partially truncated since only four generations are recorded for the four-hundred-year period during which the Israelites wander in the desert. This record introduces the team that God has chosen to lead His people, His children, out of slavery. The genealogy testifies to how intimately connected the Israelites would always be with Egypt, because scholars note that it includes Egyptian names—like Phinehas and Putiel.

6:28–7:7 God likens the relationship between Moses and his brother, Aaron, to the one between God and His prophet. Aaron will speak for Moses. Later on in this story, when the Israelites commit idolatry under Aaron's watch (chapter 32), Moses will discover what a frustrating and disappointing relationship this can often be! Aaron is Moses' mouthpiece in part because of Moses' own lack of faith in himself. Another significant description here is the hardening of Pharaoh's heart. Throughout the story of Israel's deliverance, both God and Pharaoh play a role in this process, which will ultimately bring great sorrow and destruction to the Egyptians through the plagues and defeat in the Red sea.

7:8–13 The miracle of turning the rod into a snake is a demonstration of Moses and Aaron's God-given powers. Though the Egyptian sorcerers were able to imitate the miracle to a point—changing their rods to serpents— their power was inferior to the power God gave Aaron and Moses. The point of this supernatural ability on the part of Moses and Aaron is also to demonstrate to Pharaoh, who was considered a god himself, that Moses has been divinely appointed and anointed and is an opponent to be reckoned with. The demand increases from the request for an opportunity for communion with God to a demand for release of the Israelites from slavery.

7:14–25 These verses record the first plague: the River (or the Nile) turns into blood. The Nile is virtually the lifeblood of Egypt. Without the silt it provides during its times of overflow and the water it provides to sustain life, Egypt would be almost uninhabitable. The meaning of the miracle of turning the Nile to blood can best be understood in light of God's later prophecy, recorded in Ezekiel 29:2–6, where He concludes that by this miracle all of Egypt will know that He is the Lord. This plague also serves as an attack on one of the Egyptian gods. The Egyptians believed that Hapi, a god of fertility, was also the god of the Nile.

8:1–15 The beginning of chapter 8 tells of the second plague: the frogs. Frogs were common in Egypt, especially around the Nile River, but there had never been this many. From this account, one can visualize frogs hopping and croaking all over Egypt, and even overrunning the palace of the pharaoh. The frogs got into the food, into the kneading troughs, and into the ovens. When Egypt is finally rid of the frogs, thanks to Moses, huge heaps of dead frogs are piled all over the country, creating a stench that is a plague in and of itself. God is making the Israelites' presence a real nuisance to the Egyptians. Soon it is their groaning, not the Hebrews', that will accomplish God's purpose.

8:16–19 Here we read of the third plague: lice. It is not altogether certain what is meant by the Hebrew term translated *lice*. Some have suggested that it was a plague of gnats or mosquitoes. It does not really matter exactly what is meant. The insects plagued both humans and animals. The significance of this plague is that the magicians of Egypt are unable to produce these insects themselves, which leads them to tell Pharaoh that it is the work of God (8:19).

8:20–32 With Pharaoh's heart hardened, God brings a fourth plague: flies. With this plague, the second sequence of three plagues is commenced. Here, discrimination is made between the Egyptians and the Israelites. While the exact species of flies that plagues Egypt is not certain, one can assume that they are bigger and more difficult than the lice previously set loose on the Egyptians. Because the flies are so bothersome, Pharaoh is willing to negotiate with Moses. Pharaoh's request, "Intreat for me" (8:28), indicates his self-centered interests. Moses leaves, but with the warning that there must be no more deceit on Pharaoh's part regarding his promise to let Israel go. But when the flies are gone, so is Pharaoh's motivation to release Israel.

9:1–7 God sends a fifth plague: the death of the livestock. The fifth plague is directed against the livestock of the Egyptians, but not the cattle of the Israelites. There is only speculation as to the cause of death. By whatever means, God virtually wipes out the cattle of the Egyptians. Since wealth was measured largely in terms of cattle, this was an economic disaster. The gods of Egypt were once again proven to be lifeless and useless.

9:8–12 A sixth plague strikes: blains (or boils). There is a subtly humorous note here. The magicians are not only unable to rid the land of Egypt of the boils; they are also so afflicted themselves that they cannot even show up to stand before Moses.

9:13–35 God uses the weather to bring a seventh plague: the storm. God often uses weather to humble people and to demonstrate His power. Describing this as the plague of hail is only partly true. In reality, the plague is the worst thunderstorm in Egypt's history, and the death and destruction that occur are the result of both hailstones and lightning.

10:1–20 An eighth plague strikes the Egyptians: locusts. The previous plague of the thunderstorm had destroyed the flax and barley crops, but the wheat and spelt crops were not destroyed since they matured later (9:31–32). The locusts, however, would wipe out the remaining crops. This plague brings Pharaoh to a point of humility before Moses and God, but still no deal is made between them.

10:21–22 Consider how striking the frightening plague of darkness must have been. The three days of darkness had a tremendous emotional and psychological impact on the nation as a whole. The plague of darkness struck hard at one of the chief Egyptian deities, the sun god Re, of whom Pharaoh was a representation. Re was responsible for providing sunlight, warmth, and productivity. Other gods, including Horus, were also associated with the sun. Nut, the goddess of the sky, would have been humiliated by this plague. It was God's way of demonstrating that He alone has power over any other being in His creation. The plagues were an indictment and judgment of the gods of Egypt and demonstrated God's existence and power.

10:24–29 Pharaoh offers to allow the Israelites to leave Egypt to worship God but insists that the cattle must remain behind. When this offer is rejected, Pharaoh hotly warns Moses that he must leave his presence, and to return will be to his death.

11:1–10 Moses' purpose is not merely a chronological review of historical events but to explain theologically the significance of what happens to Egypt and Israel as a result of the plague of the firstborn and the first passover. Thus, he sacrifices chronological smoothness in deference to theological explanation. Verses 4–8 are Moses' final retort to Pharaoh, made immediately after his demand that Moses leave. Verses 1–3 are cited before the announcement of Moses to Pharaoh that the firstborn of Egypt will be slain. This explains how Moses knew that this was the final plague, and why Pharaoh will nonetheless reject the warning. Verses 9–10 are also a parenthetical explanation of why Pharaoh stubbornly refuses to heed the warning of the plagues.

12:1–36 Like the feast of unleavened bread and the redemption of the firstborn, the passover was to become a permanent part of Israel's religious liturgy. There were several purposes for the passover celebration, some of which were to be understood at a later time. The passover is a memorial of the deliverance of Israel, accomplished by the mighty power of God (3:20; 13:9, 14). The passover and its related celebrations, the feast of unleavened bread and the redemption of the firstborn, were intended to serve as occasions for instruction for the future generations of Israel (12:26–27; 13:8, 14–16).

For the Israelites, the passover and the tenth plague serve as a judgment on the gods of Egypt, whom the Israelites had worshipped (Joshua 24:14), and as evidence of the grace of God in the lives of His people. The plagues point out the sin of the Egyptians and their need to repent and believe in the God of Israel.

The firstborn of Israel are not spared because they are more worthy or more righteous than the Egyptians, but because of the grace of God alone. God made provision for non-Israelites to partake of the passover if they were circumcised (acknowledging their faith in the Abrahamic Covenant; see Genesis 17:9–14; Exodus 12:48–49). Since there were many non-Israelites who left Egypt with Israel (12:38), it is likely that a number were converted and physically spared from death through the process of the plagues and the provision of the passover.

12:31–42 These verses give a historical overview of the Exodus, from the command to leave issued by Pharaoh to an account of the departure, showing that God's promises have been carried out in accord with His schedule—to the very day.

12:43–51 This chapter concludes with further instructions for the Israelites regarding the celebration of the passover in the future, especially focusing on the participation of foreigners. God would have the Israelites (and the readers of New Testament times as well) know that the institution of the passover was done in accordance with direct divine revelation—designed and prescribed by God. The passover is proof of God's possession of Israel. The firstborn of Israel belonged to God as a result of the passover, and all of Israel was God's possession as a result of the Exodus. All of the commandments and requirements that God placed on the Israelites were predicated on the fact that they were a people who belonged to Him.

13:17–18 Israel's passing through the Red Sea is one of the most dramatic events recorded in the Old Testament. It rid the Israelites, once and for all, of Pharaoh's dominion and released them from their obligation to return to Egypt after traveling a three-day journey into the wilderness to worship God (as had been described by Moses to Pharaoh). This was, in fact, the birth of the nation of Israel. It may seem strange that God wants to avoid a military confrontation, when verse 18 (see also 6:26; 12:41) reads that the Israelites are armed for battle. These verses seem to refer to the orderly way in which the Israelites (nearly two million people, counting women and children; see 12:37) departed Egypt.

13:21–22 These verses describe a cloud and fire in which God is present (14:24; 40:38; Numbers 9:15–23; 14:14; Deuteronomy 1:33; Nehemiah 9:12, 19; Psalms 78:14; 105:39; 1 Corinthians 10:1). These provide the Israelites with a visible manifestation of His presence, protection, and guidance.

14:1–9 Moses' leadership was to bring about a change of course for the Israelites, one that would perplex the people. The Israelites are instructed to turn back and camp near Pi-hahiroth, between Migdol and the sea. God's instructions explain that this change of course, while it puts the people in a seemingly vulnerable position, is intended to encourage Pharaoh's pursuit. God knew Pharaoh would think that recovering them would be easy. Pharaoh's attack would result in his defeat, to the glory of God.

14:10–14 The Israelites are terrified by the sight of the rapidly approaching Egyptians. They begin to reason that God has failed them. Moses, confident that God will deliver them from the Egyptians, tries to reassure the people. Even Moses begins crying out to God, not unlike the Israelites before him, anxious for deliverance.

14:15–20 Why does God rebuke Moses? Because Moses knows that God has guided the Israelites to this place—between the Red Sea and the Egyptians. The pillar has led them there (13:21–22; 14:19), and God

has explained His plan to Moses—so that He could gain glory through Pharaoh and his army (14:1–4). Moses knew that God had promised to bring the Israelites into the land of Canaan, which was across and beyond the Red Sea (Genesis 15:13–21; Exodus 3:7–8, 16–17; 6:4; 12:25; 13:5). Moses also knew that God had given him power through the use of his rod. God's gentle rebuke of Moses implies that Moses should have understood these things. In spite of Moses' lack of faith, God graciously responds to his cry for help. He instructs Moses to raise his rod and stretch out his hand over the sea, making it possible for the Israelites to pass through on dry ground.

14:21–23 Stretching forth his hand over the sea, Moses brings about a strong wind, turning the seabed to dry ground. Even more amazing than the courage of the Israelites to enter the seabed is the fact that the Egyptians follow them there. The Egyptians are blind to the incredible dangers of doing so by the hardness of their hearts.

14:24 God brings confusion to the Egyptian troops. The poetic description of Psalm 77:16–19 makes it seem that a thunderstorm causes the confusion. The Egyptians try to retreat but instead plunge headlong into the waters.

15:1–12 Moses apparently wrote the song and led the Israelites as they sang it. In psalm-like fashion, the acts of God are viewed as evidence of His nature and character. With dramatic poetic strokes, the song tells how God's sovereignty is evidenced by His control over the forces of nature (wind) and His ability as the Creator to cause nature to act unnaturally (the piling up of the water). In spite of the Egyptians' power and confidence, God simply blew them away, causing them to sink in the sea. The greatest army on the face of the earth is no match for the God of Israel. The greatness and the goodness of God are recognized by the Israelites as they reflect on God's victory over their enemies.

15:13–21 The second half of the song focuses on Israel's deliverance that is yet to come and the defeat of the enemies who will resist Israel in Canaan. This song provides the Israelites with a mechanism for recalling God's great act of deliverance at the Red Sea, and it directs their attention to the character of God, producing hope and confidence in His future protection and blessing.

15:22–27 The Israelites travel into the wilderness of Shur, and for three days they find no water. When they realize the water at Marah is bitter, they quickly turn to anger at Moses for leading them to such a place. This reveals their lack of faith and hardness of heart. The transformation of the waters of *Marah*, which means "bitter" (Ruth 1:20), is a miracle. No known wood could produce the result described here. The casting of the wood into the water was a symbolic act, like Moses' raising his rod over the waters of the Red Sea.

16:1–3 In this passage, there is a definite relationship between the Israelites' growling stomachs and their grumbling lips. They greatly exaggerate the benefits of Egypt and the direness of their current predicament, and they fail to perceive the hand of a sovereign God in their sufferings. They are struggling with submitting to the wisdom of their leaders, and they are complaining because they feel like they have no control over their situation.

16:4–36 God reveals His glory to the Israelites by manifesting Himself in the cloud and satisfies their physical needs by providing quail and manna. God's daily provision of manna in the wilderness teaches the Israelites to look daily to God for their sustenance. The regulations for collecting the manna—gathering only the needs of the day—taught them self-control that kept their hope for deliverance in God and not in the manna. The greatest danger Israel faced was not starvation in the midst of a wilderness but the wrath of God.

17:1–7 Moses names the place where he draws water from the rock *Massah* ("test") and *Meribah* ("quarrel"). This incident is typical of Israel's stubbornness and rebellion against God (Deuteronomy 9:6–8, 24; Hebrews 3:10). The grumbling of the Israelites in the wilderness is a persistent problem. Furthermore, the sin of this first generation of Israelites is almost identically reproduced by the second generation of Israelites some years later (Numbers 20:1–13). The problem of grumbling is common to every generation, in every age. Thus, we find the events of Massah and Meribah frequently referred to throughout scripture (Numbers 20:1–13; Deuteronomy 6:16–17; 8:15; Psalm 95:7–9; 1 Corinthians 10:1–13; Hebrews 3; 4). Israel's lack of water is by divine design, for God is testing them by their response to adversity (Deuteronomy 8:2, 16; Psalm 81:7). It reveals the sinful condition of their hearts and is a reminder that God is always blessing them on the basis of His grace, not their works.

17:8–16 Scripture often reveals one dramatic event immediately after another. The attack of the Amalekites right after the Israelites' testing of God is an opportunity for them to demonstrate their confidence in God's desire for their good. The image of Moses holding up his rod to call on the power of God to defeat the Amalekites is a powerful one. What a simple but powerful picture of the interplay between our limited strength and God's all-powerful might. The image of *Jehovah-nissi* (the Lord is His people's Banner) is used elsewhere in the Bible.

18:1 Moses' father-in-law, Jethro, having heard of God's protection and deliverance of the Israelites, comes to visit in order to reunite Moses with his wife and children. The first half of chapter 18 reveals several symptoms of a serious problem in Moses' life, which prompts not only Jethro's arrival but also his advice about achieving balance.

18:2–6 The arrival of Jethro, accompanied by Zipporah, Gershom, and Eliezer, is apparently a pleasant surprise for Moses. We are not told precisely when or why Moses and his family are separated, but the last mention of them is in chapter 4. One might conjecture that Moses sent his family back to Jethro at a time when he feared for their safety. Perhaps, too, he felt that the pressures of confronting Pharaoh and of leading Israel were too

great to have the additional responsibilities of a husband and father. Jethro acts out of wisdom, compassion, and concern for Moses' best interest.

18:9–10 Jethro rejoices with Moses, praising God for His grace manifested toward Israel, as evidenced by Moses' report. Also, Jethro seems to acknowledge, for the first time, the superiority of God over all other gods—unique in that Midianites were generally idolaters (Numbers 25:17–18; 31:16).

18:12 Jethro demonstrates his faith by offering sacrifices to God and sharing the sacrificial meal.

18:13–16 Jethro is baffled by the inefficiency he has witnessed. It is apparent from his questioning that he does not agree with the way Moses is handling things. Moses' response reveals his distorted perception and several misconceptions regarding his role as a leader.

18:17–20 While Moses deals with the Israelites individually, Jethro advocates dealing with them collectively. Moses is unable to manage because he fails to see that he needs a strong team to support him. He is dealing with nearly two million people, and he is trying to do so by himself. He is, according to Jethro, wearing himself out. Moses has allowed his sense of public duty to overshadow his sense of personal responsibility. Jethro's advice is that Moses rearrange his time so that priority is given to teaching the people God's principles and precepts, and prescribe guidelines for solving problems when they arise.

19:1–4 God uses an image of the eagle's care for its offspring. In the book of Deuteronomy, Moses explains the image more fully (Deuteronomy 32:11). While there are times when God seems (to the Israelites) to have abandoned His people, in reality God is simply stirring up the nest, forcing the Israelites to try their wings.

19:1–25 Chapter 19 serves as a preamble to the commandments given by God to Israel. It reveals the purpose of the commandments, as well as the perspective we should have toward them.

19:5–6 God's declaration also describes how Israel's deliverance was for the purpose of being brought to God so that the nation could be His prized possession. In the Abrahamic Covenant, God promises Abraham that Israel will become a great nation and the special object of His blessing. The blessing of Israel is also meant to be a source of blessing to all nations (Genesis 12:2). While this would ultimately be fulfilled by the coming of the Messiah, there is also a more immediate application. God purposed to bless the nations by establishing Israel, His servant, as a mediatory people, sharing with the nations the way of entering into fellowship with God.

19:7–15 To this point, God has only indicated that the people must keep their covenant by obeying the laws that He is about to set down. The Israelites anticipated the law with eagerness, demonstrating their implicit trust in the character of God. Verses 10–15 outline the steps the Israelites must take in order to purify and prepare themselves for the appearance of God on the third day. These are important because irreverence is the by-product of an inadequate sense of the holiness of God.

19:16–25 This text describes the splendor and the majesty of God as He manifests Himself to Israel on the mountain. Exodus 19 prepares us for the glorious giving of the law by God to His people—an occasion marked by God's purity, power, and holiness.

20:1–17 In Exodus 20, God expresses the essence of the Old Testament law in ten principal statements. In chapter 19, we learn that the giving of the law is directly related to Israel's calling to be a kingdom of priests and a holy nation (19:6). If Israel is to represent God, they must be like God. The law defines how God's holiness is to be manifested in the lives of men and women. The Ten Commandments are both a corporate constitution for Israel and an intensely personal revelation from God to His children. The *thou (you)* in the commandments is not plural, but singular. Each individual is therefore urged to enter into the joy of service by adopting this covenant and by obeying the laws contained therein. The Decalogue is not only a constitution; it is God's standard for Israel's culture.

20:18–21 These verses contain the account of the Israelites' reaction to the giving of the law. They also offer God's reason for giving it as He did—to keep the people from sinning. While God evidently spoke the Ten Commandments in the hearing of all the Israelites (19:9; 20:19, 22) the people were so struck by the revelation that they asked Moses to act as a go-between for them from then on, which he did. Verse 20 mentions two kinds of fear. First, the people are told not to fear, but then they are told the fear of God will be with them. The first fear is a tormenting fear (which enslaves). The second is a respectful fear (which demonstrates trust with acknowledgment of power). The latter is the fear that will keep the people from sinning.

20:22–26 These verses include specific instructions regarding worship. Idolatry is clearly prohibited, but also there seems to be a prohibition against making images to represent God. An altar, on the other hand, was an acceptable form of worship. The Israelites built altars both at a central location once they settled and along the way when God revealed Himself (Genesis 35:7; Joshua 8:30). The specific instruction regarding hewn (uncut) stones was probably to distinguish the Israelite altars from the Canaanite altars. Another distinction between the two was the prohibition of steps leading up to the altar. This seems to be simply to keep the priest from exposing himself as he went to the altar to make a sacrifice. The simple construction of the altar—made of earth or stone—could serve to keep the emphasis on the worship on God rather than human efforts.

21:1–22:15 The Ten Commandments set out in broad strokes God's law for His people—outlining how we are to relate to Him and honor His image in others. The Mosaic Law continues for two more chapters in Exodus (chapters 21 and 22), outlining God's design for protecting servants, persons, and property, and further explaining the roles of social responsibility, mercy, and justice in the nation of Israel. The laws in chapter 21 relate to the commandments in which God prohibits killing and stealing. Though they differ from contemporary times and customs, they do explain the moral law and the rules of natural justice. God's people are to have a unique approach to everything, including their servants and property. God commands the Israelites to respect their servants as human beings—even preserving their family bonds and allowing their families to go free with them in what became known as the year of jubile (Jubilee). In being made free, servants become a picture of God's mercy and a living example of the eventual freedom that is possible in Christ, through His own sacrifice and grace.

22:16–31 The people of God answer to God, not only for what they do maliciously but for what they do without intent. In this portion of the law, God calls His people to always be ready to show mildness and mercy, according to the spirit of these laws. When one does harm to a neighbor, he or she should make it right, even when not compelled by law. God calls upon the Israelites to honor those around them and God Himself by being generous and living justly.

23:1–9 The Law of Moses includes many straight-forward, practical requirements. Every element of the law enables the Israelites to act as God's people and to worship Him with their conduct, thus separating themselves from the pagan world. The Israelites are called to remain fair and honest, allowing nothing to compromise God's justice by lessening faults, aggravating small ones, excusing offenders, accusing the innocent, or misrepresenting the truth in any way.

23:10–19 The sabbath laws require that both the seventh day of each week and each seventh year are treated as sacred opportunities for rest and rejoicing in God's provision and power. They teach not only the importance of mercy but the need for dependence on God by forcing people to trust that God will bless their faithfulness with plenty. The Israelites have a weakness for idolatry, and therefore God requires them to be rigorous in honoring Him during three annual festivals. They are required to come together before the Lord, rejoicing in and honoring His faithfulness. They are not to arrive empty-handed but with sacrifices that demonstrate their loyalty and love for God.

23:20–33 In the closing verses of Exodus 23, God promises to prepare the way for the nation of Israel, drive out their enemies, and bring them into the promised land. He commands the Israelites to be sensitive and attentive to the angel He is sending ahead of them and to worship Him alone. He promises to provide for them and make them prosper in their new home.

24:1–11 The ratification of the Mosaic Covenant is the key to the remainder of the book of Exodus. God is the initiator of this covenant with His people Israel. A distinction is drawn between the Israelites and God, but there is also a distinction made between Israelites. These same distinctions are paralleled in the tabernacle, where the priests have greater access to God than the people, and the high priest alone can enter the most holy place, once a year. Such distinctions are abolished in the new covenant. Moses understood that the covenant God was making with Israel needed to be ratified by the nation. Once the Israelites have verbally ratified this covenant, Moses carries out the ratification process by the use of symbols and representatives. Moses offers covenant sacrifices (these are not sin offerings), making an altar with twelve pillars for the twelve tribes of Israel. The blood sprinkled upon the altar and upon the people links the people with the covenant sacrifices.

24:1–18 Centuries before the scenes described in this text, God promised Abraham a seed (a son, who would become a great nation), a land (the land of Canaan), and the promise that this nation would be blessed and be a blessing to all nations (Genesis 12:1–3). The promises God made were ratified as a covenant between Himself and Abraham in Genesis 15. Now the Mosaic Covenant, which has been spelled out in the Ten Commandments, is formally imposed upon Israel by the God who has delivered them out of Egypt.

24:11 The covenant meal, eaten by the seventy-five leaders of Israel in the presence of God, is the final act of ratification. The leaders (seventy elders, plus Nadab and Abihu, Aaron, Moses, and his servant Joshua) are representatives who act on behalf of the entire nation, teaching and interpreting the law. The ratification of the Mosaic Covenant had great meaning for the Israelites of that day. It clearly defined Israel's relationship with God and what was expected of each Israelite. The covenant also spelled out the consequences, both of obedience and of disobedience. The Israelites could always know where they stood with God.

24:12–18 The second call of Moses to the top of mount Sinai is for the purpose of giving him the commandments written on stone by the finger of God. It is also for the purpose of revealing the blueprints for the tabernacle. From chapter 25 to the end of Exodus, the tabernacle is the principal subject. The tabernacle was designed to institutionalize God's presence among His people on an ongoing basis, as the mountain had served on a onetime basis.

25:1–9 The gifts for the tabernacle are given voluntarily, as an act of gratitude. God also required compulsory giving and sacrificing by the Israelites; however, in this instance, there is no need to compel the people to get excited about building God's dwelling place among them. And as we see later, their giving actually exceeds what could be used. Exodus refers to the structure that was to be built as a *sanctuary* ("place of holiness") and a *tabernacle* ("dwelling place"). These words stress the fact that God is worthy of worship and that He is choosing to live with His people.

25:10–22 The ark of the covenant functioned as God's throne. The solid gold lid of the box was called the mercy seat. This is where the high priest made his yearly offering on the day of atonement (Leviticus 16).

25:23–30 The table for the shewbread was replenished weekly. This was a constant thank offering placed before God. Some think it was also a reminder of the testimony that Israel was to be to the world around them.

25:31–40 The candlestick, the *menorah*, is often seen today as a symbol of Israel. Some see the place of this candlestick in the original tabernacle as a symbol of God's Word that lights the darkness. Others see it as a symbol of Jesus, light of the world.

26:1–35 The curtains and the vail (veil) were carefully constructed. The curtains outlined the tabernacle while the vail provided a boundary for the innermost holy chamber.

26:35 God is very specific in His description of the other elements of the tabernacle; nearly everything is not only functional but also symbolic and instructive in its form.

27:1–8 The altar of burnt offerings stood just inside the entrance to the court. Some see this as an apt picture of this sacrifice being the first step to fellowship with God.

27:9–19 The curtain around the courtyard was an added boundary, though a shorter one, to protect the innermost holy place of the tabernacle. It was in the courtyard that the priests did their work and the people offered their sacrifices.

27:20–21 These instructions regarding the oil that was in the lamps form a transition from this information about the tabernacle furnishings to the following information about the priests' ministry.

28:4 The ephod was an apron-like piece of clothing that fit over the robe. Verses 6–14 describe the ephod in detail.

28:15–30 Here we find instructions for creating the breastplate. While we often think of metal military breastplates, this one was made from the same material as the ephod.

28:29–30 These verses outline the decision-making function of the breastplate. There is much we do not know about the Urim and Thummim. We know they helped with decisions, probably yes-or-no kinds of decisions, and were kept in the pockets of this breastplate. They are usually compared to casting lots or throwing dice, but we don't have enough details to understand the exact process by which the priest used them.

29:1–46 In the consecration of the priests—Aaron and his sons—God demands solemnity and ceremony. Ultimately, the model for the priesthood is Jesus, called by God to intercede for His people and anointed by His Spirit, clothed with glory and beauty (Hebrews 3:1–2). The book of Hebrews indicates that in the new covenant all believers are priests, offering spiritual sacrifices and relating directly to God. For the Israelites, the priesthood established here would be their intercessors and their representatives before God for generations to come.

30:1–38 The priests are instructed to burn incense every morning and evening, at the same time the daily burnt offerings are made. The incense is to be left burning continually throughout the day and night as a pleasing aroma to the Lord. It is made of an equal part of four precious spices (stacte, onycha, galbanum, and frankincense) and is considered holy. The offering of incense foreshadows the gifts brought to the infant Jesus by the wise men.

31:1–18 This passage reveals how God gifts His servants. God chose Bezaleel and Aholiab and anointed them with His Spirit. Indeed, God equipped these two skilled artists so that they could construct the temple exactly according to His commandments. The example of these two artists commissioned and gifted by God Himself reminds us that whatever our life's work or calling, we can use it to honor God.

32:1–6 There is a cause-and-effect relationship between the absence of leadership and the practice of idolatry. While Moses is gone for forty days and nights (24:18), receiving instructions about building the tabernacle, the Israelites use his absence as a pretext for taking immoral action, seizing the opportunity for creating an image of God.

32:1–35 In the story of the molten (or golden) calf, the Israelites are guilty of being impatient for God's manifestation in the tabernacle, but it is their idolatry that condemns them.

32:7–14 The Mosaic Covenant, ratified approximately one month before Israel's idolatry, defines the relationship Israel has with God. In Moses' appeal for his people on mount Sinai, he does not refer to the Mosaic Covenant, because the law can only condemn; it cannot save. When Moses appeals to God, he appeals to the Abrahamic Covenant, made centuries before. The law is God's provisional covenant, given to humanity because of its depravity, but it is not the cure. If the promises of the Abrahamic Covenant are to be fulfilled, it would have to be by some other covenant than the Mosaic Covenant. The Mosaic Covenant could not change human hearts— the root problem of sin. Striving to keep the law in order to be saved or sanctified is true folly, because we all suffer from the same ailment—sin. Idolatry seeks to replace what cannot be seen with something that can be seen—it is physically oriented. Thus the underlying issue of idolatry is faith, since faith focuses on what is not seen (Hebrews 11:1).

32:15–35 The irony of the dialogue between Moses and God earlier in Exodus (chapters 3–4), in which God provides Aaron as Moses' spokesman, is shown here. Moses is empowered by his fear of God, whereas Aaron is fumbling because of his failure. God reveals His righteousness in response to the sins of the Israelites; Aaron reveals his unrighteousness. It is not enough for us merely to recognize the depravity of humanity; we must resist it.

33:3 The grace of God is seen even in God's threat to remove Himself from Israel's midst. God states that the purpose for keeping a distance between Himself and the Israelites as they travel on toward the promised land is that their sinfulness would require Him to destroy them. The threatened consequence for Israel's idolatry is losing God's intimate presence among them. God's grace is evident as well in the provision of Moses as the mediator for the people.

33:4 Because of Israel's sin, God deals with His people from a distance as they travel through the wilderness. Although this is a fulfillment of Israel's first inclination and request (20:18–21), when it actually happens the nation mourns.

33:6 Israel's removal of ornaments and jewelry is an appropriate act of repentance, because these ornaments

are similar to those that had been contributed to make the molten (or golden) calf (32:2–4) and were associated in the ancient Near East with pagan gods. In the midst of Israel's sin and the threat of God withholding His presence, God provides a tent where not only Moses but all the people can go to seek God. This provides the people a means of worshipping God and offers them a hope for a future fellowship with God.

33:12–13 Now more than ever, Moses is aware of the rebelliousness and waywardness of the Israelites. And Aaron has so far proven to be a liability. Also, the Mosaic Covenant, which gave such hope initially, is now known to pronounce only a curse and not to promise blessing, due to the sinfulness of the people. No wonder Moses is concerned about setting out for Canaan. Moses wants to know not only the people God is sending with him but also the plan God has for the people. He is also seeking to know God more intimately, to know God's character in order to better understand how to please Him.

33:14 God promises Moses He will be with him and provide the means to get the Israelites to Canaan. Furthermore, He promises Moses that the Israelites will ultimately live safely in Canaan. This is indicated by the term *rest*, used here and elsewhere in the Old Testament. This word conveys the end of an evil, an enemy, hostility, or adversity. When God promises Moses rest, He assures him that the things Moses fears most will be overcome, and that the task God has given him will be completed.

33:15–17 Moses is not willing to enjoy God's favor alone while Israel's destiny hangs in the balance. So in his second request, he petitions that God's presence be not only with him but with everyone. Notice how Moses twice links himself with Israel in order to associate God's favor for them with His favor for Moses. God assures Moses that He will be present with Israel as well as with him.

33:18–23 The glory of God is almost always some visible manifestation of God's presence and splendor. For Moses, and ultimately for the entire nation, the sight of God's glory would serve as an assurance of God's presence. The Bible consistently teaches that no person is able to see God face-to-face and live. God speaks of Moses as being able to see His back, but not His face. In the context of the passage, this means that Moses will be able to see all of God's goodness, but not some of His other attributes. Let us not fail to appreciate the wonder and the honor of this revelation of God to Moses. While it is only the back of God, it is all Moses can survive—and it is more than any person had yet been privileged to see.

34:10–11 The covenant made here is virtually a renewal of the former covenant; however, there are some differences. The first covenant was based on the miracles God had done in delivering the Israelites from Egyptian bondage, while this covenant looks forward to the miracles that are instrumental in Israel's possession of the land of Canaan. Ironically, the miracles God formerly accomplished in Egypt resulted in the Egyptians driving the Israelites out of their land; now, the miracles God promises to accomplish will drive the Canaanites out of Israel's land.

34:29–35 Predictably, the people are at first frightened by the brightness of Moses' countenance, but then they are eventually able to draw near enough to hear Moses speak and to accept his words as from God Himself. Moses begins to employ a vail (veil) that he will remove when he speaks with God and leave off until he has conveyed God's words to the people. Then the vail (veil) will be put on until the next time he speaks with God. The text indicates that Moses does this on a number of occasions, with some degree of regularity.

35:1–36:7 The excitement and enthusiasm of the Israelites are evidenced by the abundance of their gifts. In fact, the text informs us that the gifts exceed the need, so much that Moses is asked to command the people to stop giving. The Israelites' giving includes both material goods and technical services—both of the highest quality. Because giving is done willingly, joyfully, and unanimously, it is not mandatory—the motivation of the Israelites is extremely high. The tabernacle is the means of God personally dwelling among His people (25:8), and the people are eager to have this promise fulfilled. This is a onetime need, and the people have been amply enabled to contribute to it. With such motivation, God could easily allow the nation to provide the skills and materials for the tabernacle voluntarily. There were other ongoing needs in Israel, however, that were not so glamorous, and of a much longer duration. To ensure these needs are met, God makes giving a compulsory matter. There is an ongoing need for the support of the priests and Levites, who devote themselves to the service of God in the tabernacle.

36:8–39:43 The description of the tabernacle provides the first biblical revelation as to how God dwells among His people and what this suggests for the church today. When the people left Sinai for Canaan, they needed some portable place for God's presence to be manifested. The tabernacle serves as a meeting place between God and humans, and it becomes known as the tent of meeting. Since the tabernacle is a tent, the problem of portability is solved. The tabernacle also solves the problem of having a holy God dwell in the midst of sinful people. The tent curtains, and especially the thick vail (veil), serve as a dividing barrier between God and the people. Beyond this, the tabernacle is sanctified and set apart as a holy place. Also, the tabernacle is a place of sacrifice so that the sins of the Israelites can be atoned for. While the solution is not permanent, it does facilitate communion between God and His people. The tabernacle displays wealth and beauty in a reflection of God's glory within. According to this calculation, there would be some 1,900 pounds of gold, 6,437 pounds of silver, and 4,522 pounds of bronze. The excellence of the tabernacle, in both its materials and its workmanship, is a reflection of the excellence of God. The tabernacle is also a holy place, because abiding in it is a holy God (30:37–38). While the tabernacle is composed of varied elements, it is its unity—in design, function, and purpose—that is celebrated and emphasized in the text. It is God's masterwork amid His people, proclaiming His presence and hinting at His glory.

40:1–16 There is a distinct change in the personal pronoun employed in chapter 40 from *they* (39:43) to *thou* (40:2). The shift is from the construction of the tabernacle, in which all the people were involved, to the setting up of the tabernacle and the anointing of it, which were the responsibility of Moses. There is a descending order of holiness of the items referred to in the chapter. We begin in the most holy place (known also as the holy of holies) in the tabernacle and end in the courtyard, the least holy place.

40:1–38 This is the climax of the story of Exodus: The tabernacle is completed, and the glory of God descends upon it. It is also an introduction to Leviticus. God commands the anointing of the priesthood, who will dominate the next story in the history of the Israelites and receive God's instructions regarding the use of the carefully constructed tabernacle.

40:17–33 There is a mood of excitement and anticipation among the Israelites, who have spent months carefully following God's specific instructions. Amazingly, the tabernacle is constructed on Israel's first anniversary as a free nation (12:2), and just about nine months from the time of the people's arrival at mount Sinai. It also appears that the tent is erected on this one day, since the materials are all made and ready before this time (39:32–43). God's precise timing emphasizes how far the Israelites have come since they escaped Egypt. Moses' role finally seems to have evolved into something more provisional (almost priestly), which continues until Aaron and his sons are anointed and installed as the official priesthood of Israel. Moses offers incense and burnt and meal (or grain) offerings, and also washes himself, like Aaron and his sons.

40:34–38 Since the cloud has been present with the Israelites from the time they left Egypt and never departed from them, there is a sense in which nothing new occurs here. What was once distant (either before or behind the nation, or far away, atop mount Sinai) is now in the very midst of the camp. The appearance of the glory of God in the tabernacle takes place after Israel's great sin (the golden calf), which is reported in chapter 32. Finally, the glory of God settles on the tabernacle to abide there, not just as a momentary manifestation of God. The glory of God descending upon the tabernacle is the realization of Israel's highest hopes, of Moses' noblest and most impassioned petition. The glory of God in the tabernacle is so awesome that even Moses cannot enter it. Remember that Moses had seen more of God's glory than any other human being alive—in the burning bush (chapter 3), in the plagues and exodus of Israel, and from inside the cloud atop mount Sinai (chapters 19, 24). At his request, he had seen even more of God's glory when he was privileged to view the back of God (33:17–34:9). But the glory of God in the tabernacle is greater than that which Moses (or any other Israelite for that matter) can behold.

THE THIRD BOOK OF MOSES, CALLED
LEVITICUS

INTRODUCTION TO LEVITICUS ■ Though many see Leviticus as a book addressing the priests of Israel, the information here was actually written for the people, yet includes specific instructions for the priests. The laws relate to the entire nation of Israel, but it was the priests who were to teach others how to live as God's holy people and to regulate worship in the tabernacle (also called sanctuary, or tent of meeting), where God's holy presence dwelled.

AUTHOR ■ Moses is generally ascribed as the author of the first five books of the Old Testament, or the Pentateuch (which means "five books" or "five scrolls").

OCCASION ■ The book served as a handbook for the priests God put in place after the institution of the Mosaic Covenant at mount Sinai. The laws on both ceremonial holiness and personal holiness were supposed to teach the Israelites about their holy God and how to live set apart as His people. Not only does God tell the Israelites how to worship, but He gives them practical ways to live out holiness in everyday life.

1:1–2 The Israelites were camped at the base of mount Sinai when Moses received their instructions. The burnt offering is a voluntary and personal offering, and instructions are given for individuals. The sacrifice is not for specific sins but rather for the general state of sinfulness. The purpose of the burnt offering is to make atonement for the sin of the offerer and to gain God's acceptance.

1:3–9 The sacrificial animal had to be the best quality (without defect) and male. Bullocks (bulls) were valuable livestock, and the male would be able to produce additional offspring. It would be a true sacrifice for an Israelite to offer a young, productive animal.

Both offerer and priest participate in the sacrifice. The offerer is responsible for the slaughter, and the priest handles the sprinkling of blood and burning of the offering on the altar of sacrifice. By laying his hands on the animal, the offerer identifies his sins with the offering. The animal becomes a substitute for the individual. While many sacrifices benefit both the offerer and the priest, because both are allowed to eat from the sacrificed animal, the burnt offering is completely consumed by fire.

When an Israelite wanted to find acceptance with God in order to worship, he had to come with a burnt offering. This is to acknowledge and make provision for his sinfulness. The sacrifice allowed the Israelites to come into the presence of a holy God in the tabernacle.

1:10–13 Sheep and goats were livestock of considerable value, and the best male of the flock was required as the offering. One of the unique contributions of the burnt offering is that it illustrates sacrifice in its purest form. A valuable animal is given up wholly to God without expectation of anything in return, other than the benefit of finding acceptance with God.

1:14–17 God gives some options for animal sacrifices. This is because the poor could not afford a bull, sheep, or goat. God did not keep people from coming into His presence because they could not afford to sacrifice (14:21–22, 30–32). A turtledove or young pigeon was a true sacrifice for those who were poor, just as a bull or goat was a sacrifice for those who owned livestock, making it pleasing to God.

2:1 The King James Version of the Bible translates grain offerings as "meat offerings." The word *meat*, as it was used by the translators of this Bible, did not have the same meaning as the term today. This was a term that simply referred to food, and in a general way could refer to grain (in either its raw or cooked form). The Israelites are instructed to make the meat (or grain) offering after the burnt offering (Numbers 28; Joshua 22:23, 29; Judges 13:19, 23). Since no blood is shed in this offering, it does not atone for sin. A person's contribution to the meat (or grain) offering is allowed because his or her sinfulness has already been atoned for in the burnt offering.

2:1–3 The grain had to be fine, meaning finely ground flour. To make fine flour entailed a great deal of extra effort. The meat (or grain) offering was also sacrificed by fire and produced a pleasing aroma to the Lord. At this time, the Israelites were camped in the desert, where they could not grow grain, so this offering (most likely wheat or barley) was a great sacrifice. To sacrifice this seed to God was an act of faith because they would have to depend on God to provide more.

2:4–10 The oil used in this offering probably would have been olive oil, also a sacrifice since it was not readily available in the desert. All the sacrificial materials were difficult to obtain in the days of Moses, though of course, these laws would continue on into the settlement of the land. Only a handful of the meat (or grain) offering was burned on the altar; the rest was given to the priests, Aaron and his sons. The greater portion of the offering served as the livelihood of the priests, just as the tithe was God's means for supporting the Levites (Numbers 18:21–24).

2:11–13 Through the meat (or grain) offering, the Israelites acknowledge God's provision for their needs. Since the purpose of the meat (or grain) offering is worship, not atonement, the offerer could contribute. However, only certain additions were allowed. Salt was allowed, but leaven and honey were forbidden. The Hebrew word translated *honey* indicates fruit (not bee) honey. When fruit honey is burned, it ferments—a form of decay that is associated with death and thus is to be avoided (the same is true of yeast). The meat (or grain) offering was associated with the burnt offering, and the blood sacrifice could not be associated with leaven, which was known to corrupt. Known to preserve and purify, salt was added to the meat (or grain) offering. Salt may have reminded Israel of the enduring covenant with God, since salt does not burn or turn into a gas but basically stays the same through fire.

2:14–16 The meat (or grain) offering of firstfruits was that which was first harvested from a crop (Exodus 23:19). The offering was accompanied by incense as a sensory symbol of the pleasure the offering would bring God. Again, the expense was a reminder that sacrifice is costly, but pleasing God is the highest good.

3:1–5 In the day of Moses, an Israelite would begin to make a peace offering by selecting an animal without any defect (male or female) from his herd or flock. He would then take this animal to the doorway of the tabernacle, where he would lay his hand on its head, identifying his sin with the animal and himself with its death, and slaughter it. Inside the tabernacle, the priests would collect the shed blood and sprinkle it around the altar. After skinning the animal and cutting it into pieces, the priests would then burn the fat, kidneys, and part of the liver on the altar. The process is much like that for the burnt offering, except in the peace offering the entire animal is not consumed. The blood, fat, and organs are burned, but the rest is given to the priests and the offerer (7:30–34; 10:14–15).

3:6–17 The process for a sacrifice from the flock is the same as one from the herd. At the end of the chapter, though, the Israelites are instructed never to eat the fat or blood of an animal (3:16–17; 17:10–13).

4:1–35 Offerings in Leviticus 1–3 are organized by sacrificial animal. The sin offering in chapter 4 is organized by categories of people: high priest (4:3–12); congregation of Israel (4:13–21); ruler (4:22–26); and individual Israelite (4:27–35). The sin offering is for a specific sin, as opposed to a state of sinfulness addressed by the burnt offering. Also, while chapters 1–3 are concerned with the process of sacrifice, chapters 4–6 emphasize the result of the process: forgiveness. (The sin offering is further explained in 5:1–13 and 6:24–30.)

4:1–2 The sins addressed through the sin offering are those that, for some reason, are not immediately apparent but are eventually known. Later, this chapter notes that the sin offering is to be made immediately after the knowledge of sin is present.

4:3–12 If the high priest sinned, he would bring guilt on the entire congregation of Israelites, so this offering was necessary to atone for the sin for everyone. The priest himself would bring a bullock (bull) to the tabernacle, lay his hand on it, and slaughter it. He would then sprinkle some of the blood on the tabernacle vail (veil) and some on the altar of incense. The remaining blood was poured at the base of the altar of burnt offering. The fat of the offered bull was burned as with the peace offering, but its body was burned completely outside the camp. The offerer received none of the meat.

4:13–21 When the entire community sins, there is a sin offering to atone for the collective sin. The process is the same as that for the sin offering of the priest.

4:22–26 Even unintentional sin makes a person guilty. When a ruler is aware of his sin, he is to sacrifice a male goat as a sin offering. The process is similar to that for the priest's offering, with two exceptions: Blood is not sprinkled at the vail (veil), and the animal's body is not burned. (The meat of these sacrificial animals could be eaten in a holy place by the male priests [6:24–30].)

4:27–35 An individual Israelite could offer a female goat or a female lamb as a sin offering. The process would have been the same as that for the ruler sin offering. In chapter 4 we see a repeated sequence: There is sin, resulting in guilt; there is a blood sacrifice, resulting in atonement and forgiveness. This explains why only the blood and fat of the sin offering are used and the rest is thrown away. God is demonstrating in a dramatic way that only blood can atone for Israel's sin.

5:1–6 Chapter 5 addresses specific sins such as ignoring a call to testify, touching something or someone ceremonially unclean, or speaking without thinking. The guilty person would confess his or her sin and give a female lamb or goat as a sin offering.

5:7, 11 These verses show God's grace in providing an exception for those who are poor. They could offer a less expensive blood sacrifice (turtledoves or pigeons), or even fine flour. So while not everyone could afford a peace offering, everyone was afforded the opportunity to experience forgiveness.

5:14–19 The trespass offering is similar to the sin offering. The trespass offering seems to have been used for a breach of God's commandments, even if unintentional or for a sin where restitution could be made. Just as with the sin offering, atonement could be found through a trespass offering. Unlike the sin offering, restitution was also necessary to make up for what a person did or did not do by giving part of the value of the sacrificial ram to the priest.

6:1–7 A trespass offering was necessary in the case of disobedience against God's laws, specifically those relating to other people. If, for example, an Israelite cheated his neighbor, he would need to make a trespass offering. The same goes for a number of sins that affected others. A sin against one person was seen as a sin against the entire community, and ultimately

God. The penalties teach that restitution is necessary before forgiveness.

6:8–13 Priests would sacrifice burnt offerings every morning and evening for the congregation of Israel. These verses focus heavily on how to make sure sacrifices are completely consumed by not allowing the fire to go out, and how to handle disposing of ashes.

6:8–7:38 This section of Leviticus addresses Aaron and his sons, the priesthood, directly. It forms a kind of handbook of priestly procedures. The priests were keepers and protectors of the law, so these specific and serious words would have been written, not handed down through oral tradition.

6:14–23 These details show priests how to burn the memorial portion of the meat (or grain) offering and what to do with the leftovers. The priests could eat what remained, but only in a consecrated area since it was still a holy offering. The seemingly tedious details ensure that priests are obedient to God rather than following their own way.

6:24–30 These additional rules relate to holiness. The tabernacle is a holy place because the presence of God dwells there, and the sin offering is a serious, sacred ritual that the priests are not to take lightly.

7:1–10 The first verses of chapter 7 give additional regulations concerning the trespass offering. The focus is on keeping it holy; it is not something to be taken lightly. Because of the offering's holy nature, only the priests (or males in their family) could partake in eating the meat of a sacrificed animal after the kidneys and the fat around them were burned on the altar to God. Likewise, the cooked meat (or grain) offering belonged to the priests. Even then, they could be eaten only in a holy place.

7:11–38 Along with the fat of a sacrificial animal that is offered to God, an appropriate meat (or grain) offering is also necessary. If the peace offering is out of thanksgiving, both leavened and unleavened cakes are to be offered. Part is burned on the altar, and the rest goes to the priests. Since the fat and blood of the animal are offered to God, and the breast and the right shoulder go to the priest, the rest of the sacrificial animal is left for the offerer. So after the ceremonial sacrifice, the Israelite would eat a festive meal with what remained. This is perhaps the most striking feature of the peace offering.

7:15–18 Throughout scripture, the meal has a deeply religious significance. The festive meal that was part of the peace offering added to this significance. Here, the meal is a symbol of the peace the Israelite has with God and with others through the sacrifice. The leftovers from the peace offering (see also 19:5–8) had to be eaten on the day of the sacrifice in the case of thanksgiving, or by the next day in the case of a vow or voluntary offering. Anyone who was unclean or had touched something unclean could not eat of the meal.

7:20, 25 For an Israelite to be cut off from his people was the ultimate punishment. The Israelites were a communal people, so to be cut off signified loss of identity and covenant relationship. The phrase *cut off* indicates the offender was taken outside the camp and put to death or possibly banished forever.

7:22–27 Here we find another reminder that the Israelites are absolutely not to eat any of the fat or blood of sacrificed animals (or any other animals, for that matter). Eating fat means the possibility of an Israelite being cut off from his people, and eating blood means he will certainly be cut off.

7:28–35 The fat of the sacrificial animal, along with its breast meat and right shoulder, are offered to the Lord, but the priests keep the meat after burning the fat. This is one of the ways that God provides for the physical care of the priests.

8:1–4 God announces Aaron's ordination through Moses. Aaron was made high priest and his sons were made priests because God had chosen them, not because of any merit they possessed on their own. The Aaronic priesthood is just being formally established in chapter 8, but the concept of priesthood is not new to the Pentateuch, the first five books of the Bible. In a curious incident in the life of Abraham, a priest-king by the name of Melchizedek is introduced (Genesis 14:18). Also, Joseph's wife is the daughter of an Egyptian priest (Genesis 41:45, 50; 46:20), and Jethro, Moses' father-in-law, is known as "the priest of Midian" (Exodus 2:16; 3:1). At mount Sinai, God proclaimed that He had delivered Israel from bondage and set the nation apart to be a "kingdom of priests" (Exodus 19:6). Instead of the nation introducing the concept of priests, Leviticus 8 is the first mention of Israelite priests.

8:5–13 Worship of God is a serious matter, shown in part through the detailed preparation in these verses. While other Israelites are often purified through washing their hands, the priests are symbolically purified through full-body baths. The elaborate ceremonial garments would have set apart the priests in appearance and in service to God. The oil represents a divine anointing.

8:14–36 Before the priests could be accepted into God's holy presence, they would have to make sacrificial offerings. Moses had been serving in the high priest function before Aaron's ordination, so he performs the sacrificial rites of the sin offering and burnt offering (see chapters 1, 4). In a special ordination ritual, a second ram is used to symbolize how the priest should hear God's voice, do righteous deeds with his hands, and walk in the ways of God. Additional offerings are made, and the portions that are not burned are given to Aaron and his sons for a ceremonial meal. The ordination is complete seven days later, only after the priests show their obedience to God.

8:35 God took the sin of His priests very seriously. Being in close proximity to God brought with it correspondingly high standards of conduct. This is indicated in several ways in Leviticus. God frequently indicates that disobedience to His commands could bring death (10:6–7, 9; see also Exodus 28:35, 43; 30:20–21). Chapter 10 shows this played out with two priests and demonstrates the implications it has for the entire priesthood.

9:1–14 After the ordination of Aaron and his sons is complete, Moses calls them and the leaders of Israel. He tells Aaron to make a sin offering and burnt offering for his own atonement, and then he tells him to educate the Israelites about their responsibilities. The Israelites obey and draw near to God. Aaron and his priestly sons perform their first ritual duties. Aaron makes a sin offering and burnt offering for himself and his family. They would have to be pure before God before they could offer sacrifices on behalf of the people.

9:15–24 As God's representative of the nation of Israel, Aaron makes a sin offering, burnt offering, meat (or grain) offering, and peace offering for the people (see chapters 1–4). The purpose of these offerings is to make preparations for the revelation of God's glory to the people. The Israelites' response to God's presence is joyful worship.

9:24 At the sight of God's glory, the people fell facedown. This was a typical symbol of submission in the Near Eastern cultures.

10:1–5 The exact sin committed by Nadab and Abihu, the two oldest sons of Aaron, is not clear; the text says they were offering "strange fire" before God. What is clear is that their actions were in direct disobedience to God's commands. The death of Nadab and Abihu dramatically conveys that priests were allowed to approach God, but that privilege demanded corresponding honor toward Him and His laws.

10:6–7 After taking Aaron's oldest sons outside the camp, Moses gives additional rules so Aaron and his other sons do not become unclean as a result of improper mourning.

10:8–11 God speaks directly to Aaron. His words indicate that Nadab and Abihu may have sinned as a result of drinking while on duty, and He makes a clear distinction between what is holy and what is common. He also emphasizes the priests' role of teaching the Israelites God's law.

10:12–20 Here are instructions to the Aaronic priests conveyed through Moses. They provide a backdrop for understanding Moses' anger when he suspects the sin offering is not properly carried out. Typically, when a goat is given for a sin offering, the breast meat is eaten by the priests. When Moses does not see the meat, he thinks Aaron's other sons have disobeyed God's instructions, but the situation is handled successfully by Aaron. Because of the recent tragedy, Aaron thinks eating of the offering is inappropriate, so it is burned.

11:1–8 Chapter 11 explains clean/unclean food regulations in particular. (There is no clear reason why certain creatures were considered clean and others were not.) Three animal categories are listed: land, water, and flying creatures. These same distinctions are found in Genesis 1, where God creates all life that is in the heavens, on earth, and under the waters.

11:4–8 Two basic stipulations must be met before a land animal can be considered clean and, therefore, something

an Israelite could eat: The creature must have a divided split hoof and chew its cud. Of course, some animals fit one category but not the other, but the rules are clear that both are necessary.

11:9–12 To be considered clean, animals that live in the sea have to meet two qualifications as well: They must have fins and scales. The Israelites are not only to avoid unclean creatures but to detest them.

11:13–23 Instead of qualifications for birds, God provides a list of unclean birds to avoid. The list includes birds that eat other animals or feed off dead carcasses. Flying insects are also mentioned. Essentially, all flying insects are unclean, unless they have jointed jumper legs.

11:29–31 An additional category of unclean animals includes ones that creep or swarm, such as mice and lizards. Touching an unclean creature that is dead would make an Israelite categorically unclean. Even eating a clean animal without going through the proper sacrificial procedure would do the same thing (11:39).

11:32–35 The offenses in chapter 11 are relatively minor, so a person or object could be made clean with water, and the state of uncleanness lasted only until evening. The exception is an earthen vessel (clay pot) or oven; it had to be destroyed. "Clean" and "unclean" are categories more than conditions. There is a direct relationship between what is clean and what is holy in scripture. Only what is clean can become holy. God emphasizes the Israelites' identification as His people by reminding them that He is the God who brought them out of Egypt and they should be holy.

11:39–40 Essentially, the death of even a clean creature made it unclean, which would, of course, make it difficult to eat since generally all animals are killed before they can be eaten. So all meals that include meat would become an act of worship, since the only way an animal could be killed and stay clean is if it were offered as a sacrifice to God in front of the door of the tabernacle (see Leviticus 17).

12:1–5 These verses describe the categorical uncleanness a woman experiences after childbirth. The act of having a child itself is not considered sinful, but the flow of blood and other discharges associated with birth cause uncleanness. It may be that reproductive blood and semen are seen as holy fluids. When one comes into contact with something holy, it renders one temporarily unclean. After the birth of a boy, a woman is isolated at home for seven days. After the child's circumcision on the eight day, she is required to wait another thirty-three days before worshipping at the tabernacle. After the birth of a girl, a mother's period of uncleanness doubles, with fourteen days at home and sixty-six days before she is allowed to go to the tabernacle. The reason for this discrepancy is unclear, though some think that *life* is the issue here, and the longer one is unclean, the longer one is in contact with principles of life—so, since a baby girl has a womb, the period of uncleanness is twice as long.

12:6–8 An unclean mother has to sacrifice both a burnt offering (lamb) and a sin offering (pigeon or turtledove) to be considered clean again. Provisions are made for mothers without much money by allowing them to substitute two birds for a lamb.

13:1–2 The term *leprosy*, used in chapter 13, is most likely not used to describe the disease we know as leprosy. It is more likely a generic term referring to a number of skin disorders rather than a specific disease. If an Israelite had any kind of symptom of a skin disease, he was taken to a priest to be examined through clinical-type instructions.

13:3–44 A deep sore or raw skin would indicate decay and therefore cause a person to be unclean. Infection also indicated decay and made a person unclean. If a priest was unsure, the affected Israelite was quarantined, followed by additional examination. A condition that did not spread was purified through water, but a spreading rash or other disorder pointed to infection. A chronic disease was also considered infection and made a person unclean for the duration of the disease. If a disease was cured or shown not to be infectious, the person was considered clean. While the practices described in this section certainly have potential for health benefits, it appears that, at the most fundamental level, the issue is "wholeness." Notice in verses 12–13 that if a person is covered from head to toe, he is considered clean.

13:24–44 The same rules apply for suspicious spots or burns. A man who experiences normal balding is clean, but a disorder on the skin of his head is examined the same way other disorders are examined by a priest.

13:45–46 Any person found to have an infectious skin disease was to be put outside the camp to live. He was forced to announce his unclean state to anyone he encountered and to take on the posture of a mourner. He would also be cut off from fellowship with other Israelites and could not approach God in worship.

13:47–59 The Israelites are instructed to deal with garments that are plagued (i.e., mildewed clothing) in a similar way to diseased skin. Just as infectious diseases could spread, so could mildew. Priests examined and isolated contaminated clothing. Clothes with spreading mildew, or mildew that would not wash out, were burned.

14:1–8 Those with symptoms of skin disease were sent outside the camp in a kind of quarantine, presumably so others would not catch the disease. This would have been significant, as it separated an individual from both his community and the sanctuary of God. If the priest finds the condition to be healed after a week, there is then a cleansing ceremony including hyssop and two clean birds. Additional bathing and washing then took place, along with shaving all hair to allow the person back into the camp.

14:9–32 After the ceremonial cleansing, the affected person has seven days of additional examination that includes additional shaving. That is followed by the sacrifice of three lambs for trespass, sin, and burnt offerings, along with a meat (or grain) offering. The

ceremonial smearing of blood is similar to the priestly consecration ritual (see 8:24). The oil ritual accompanies the atonement that makes the unclean person clean. Three sacrificial lambs would have been expensive, so special exceptions were made for the poor, as with the other offerings.

14:33–57 Rules relating to a plague in the house (a general term for anything from mildew or mold to dry rot), which was something that would cause decay in the home, are similar to those relating to human skin disease. These instructions deal with the homes the Israelites would build once in Canaan. Verse 34 likely indicates that God is the Creator of all living things, not that He is sending mildew as some kind of test or punishment.

14:37–53 The examination periods are similar to those for skin disease in chapter 13. In the same way an unclean person is sent out of the camp, contaminated building stones are put outside the city. The cleansing ritual for a home is the same as for the person who is unclean.

15:1–18 These verses refer to a man with an issue (discharge) from his body as unclean. The word translated *flesh* could mean a person's body, but it is also used as a euphemism for a man's sexual organ. The nature of this particular discharge is not clear, but it is likely some kind of infection. Because infections often contain dead matter, the man would be considered unclean. And since some infections can spread, anything or anyone the man touched would also be unclean.

15:13–15 These verses address a male's purification process. Those who touch the unclean man could become clean simply by washing their clothes and bathing. The man himself has a period of isolation and then can renew relationships with God and fellow Israelites after sacrificing birds as a sin offering and burnt offering.

15:16–18 Here we find instructions on semen discharge, a normal male function. The answer to the day-long unclean condition is to bathe and wash any affected clothing. Even intercourse between a married couple resulted in both the man and woman being unclean until evening and having to bathe.

15:19–24 A woman's regular menstruation would make her unclean for seven days (until the period is completely over). Anything she sat on was considered unclean, and anyone who touched her or anything she had touched would be unclean for a day, requiring bathing and washing. If the woman's husband had sex with her, then he would also be unclean for seven days. Purification came through water.

15:25–30 These verses address an unusually long period or other associated discharge, which is considered to make a woman unclean. The same rules apply as with normal menstruation, but the woman has to go through the same sacrificial ceremony as the man with the abnormal discharge.

15:31 The final verse of this chapter emphasizes the reason for the clean/unclean laws. Since the tabernacle housed the presence of a holy God, those who were declared categorically unclean could not enter into that presence. In addition, the laws reminded the Israelites that they were a people who had been set apart by God. As Christians today, our holiness is not judged by these kinds of laws, but it is good to remember that when we approach God through prayer or worship, we are approaching a holy God.

16:1–5 Even the high priest could not enter into the holy place whenever he wanted, so the opening instructions are to prepare Aaron to enter into that sacred place (Exodus 28, 39). Before he could enter into the Lord's presence, Aaron would have to make a sin offering for himself and his family, as well as a burnt offering. He would also go through an elaborate bathing and dressing process to illustrate the contrast between God's purity and human sinfulness.

16:6–19 The two goats Aaron brings on behalf of the people serve a special purpose. One will become the sacrificial sin offering for the people; the other will provide atonement by symbolically taking on the people's sin and then being sent away. The bullock (bull) sacrifice is a sin offering for Aaron and his family, and the subsequent goat sacrifice is a sin offering for the people. God's dwelling place (the tabernacle) is emphasized with the cloud of incense to veil the glory of God so that Aaron can enter into His presence. Atonement is made for the holy place, including the altar, since the sin of the people defiles the tabernacle.

16:20–34 After taking care of the holy place, Aaron symbolically lays the sins of the entire nation on the head of the second goat and sends it away in the wilderness (desert) so it cannot return. Atonement is made complete with burnt offerings for Aaron and the people and completion of the sin offerings. The people participate in the day through solemn rest and intentional humility. Unlike the other Jewish holidays, the day of atonement was not a festive event. It was a day of national mourning and repentance. The Israelites were told to humble themselves, which most likely included fasting. No work was done since it was on the sabbath. This would thus be the only appointed holy day characterized by mourning, fasting, and repentance. The day of atonement was a time for dealing with unknown sins that had gone unaddressed in the past year. Even unknown sins hinder our fellowship with God and others. This kind of reflection and repentance should be a regular part of the Christian life.

17:1–9 These verses presuppose that an Israelite will be tempted to slaughter one of his animals for its meat. The slaughtering of any animal is to take place as an offering at the tabernacle (see chapters 1–7, 16); otherwise it is considered bloodshed. An Israelite has to make a peace offering in order to voluntarily slaughter and eat an animal.

17:10–16 The regulation of verses 10–13 prohibits anyone living in Israel to eat the blood of any animal. Blood is equated with life and God's atonement of the

Israelites, so anyone who eats it will be "cut off" from his people, an expression that, at best, means expulsion from the nation and, at worst, execution. Hunters are instructed to cover the blood of game they kill. An animal killed by another animal may be eaten, but the one who does so will become unclean (11:39–40).

18:1–5 These verses address the Israelites' motivation for obeying the laws that God is going to lay down in the following chapters. God reminds the Israelites of their relationship to Him. Knowing they have a tendency to mimic the cultures around them, He also gives specifics for how they should live as the people of God by following His ways and statutes.

18:6–18 These verses begin with the closest relationship (mother and child) and progress from there to a man and his sister-in-law. In ancient Israel, familial relationships were the social cornerstone of the community, so keeping them pure would have been extremely important.

18:19–23 Here we find a law reiterated from chapter 15, and verse 20 is a reminder of the seventh commandment. Verses 21–23 remind the Israelites not to imitate the pagan people around them.

18:24–30 For the Israelites, the land of Canaan represents God's blessings. The last part of this chapter stresses the fact that the sins of the Canaanites defiled the land and would lead to their expulsion. It also warns the Israelites that if they fail to live according to God's laws when in Canaan, they will lose the blessing of the land. At the conclusion of Leviticus, God spells out in greater detail the blessings of obeying Him (chapter 26).

19:1–8 God had Moses assemble all the Israelites to offer His command to be holy. The law is God's standard of holiness, instructions on how to imitate His character. What follows is a refresher course on the Ten Commandments and a repeat of ceremonial law surrounding the peace offering.

19:9–17 After the reminders, God inserts new instructions that lead to God's second overarching command: Love your neighbor as yourself. Holiness would be practiced as the Israelites loved their neighbors. This includes the vulnerable (19:9–11, 14–15), fellow Israelites, strangers, and even enemies.

19:18 After God led the Israelites out of captivity in Egypt, He made a covenant with His people, known as the Mosaic Covenant because it was communicated through Moses. God introduced the Ten Commandments, part of the covenant, with the words "I am the LORD" (Exodus 20:2). When the covenant was reiterated to the next generation, the same phrase was used (Deuteronomy 5:6). In Leviticus 18, it shows up again. The words, used more than forty times in chapters 18–26, are a reminder to the Israelites of their identity as people of God.

19:19–37 The rest of the chapter lists miscellaneous laws. They are reminders to be a set-apart people who do not mix with other cultures. The people are reminded to create God-honoring relationships, to maintain fairness, and to practice compassion rather than oppression.

20:1–6 These verses show a co-participation between God and His people in condemning those who are guilty of capital crimes. In fact, those who close their eyes to sin also become guilty. The child sacrificed here is a reflection of the surrounding pagan cultures.

20:7–21 The relational sins listed in chapter 18 are repeated here, this time with a penalty for each.

20:22–27 When God made certain sins crimes as well, the Israelites were strongly motivated to obey God's laws and to avoid sin. In these verses, God gives a general exhortation to follow His laws. The result of disobedience will be loss of their promised land in Canaan. God had promised the Israelites a land flowing with milk and honey, a symbol for blessing, but He requires obedience and sanctified (set apart) lives that imitate His own character. As an example, He lists another crime that is influenced by pagan culture and deserving of the death penalty.

21:1–9 Priests had to remain ceremonially clean so that they could approach God and make offerings on behalf of the people. This meant they could not bury the dead, except in the case of close blood relatives. All Israelites (especially priests) were forbidden to shave their heads or the edges of their beards or to cut their skin as a sign of mourning (19:27; Deuteronomy 14:1). An ordinary Israelite had greater freedom in choosing a wife; priests could marry a widow but not a divorcée. Even a priest's daughter was held to higher standards.

21:10–15 If there is a high standard for the priests, there is an even higher standard for the high priest. The high priest could not participate in standard mourning traditions or even leave the tabernacle to take part in burying near relatives. And the high priest could marry only a virgin of his own people.

21:16–24 The Aaronic priesthood began with Aaron and his sons and would continue through his line of descendants. Those who had physical defects would not be able to participate in sacrificial offerings. The sacrificial animal had to be without defects, and so did the priest doing the offering. The priest with the defect could eat the food the priests were allowed, but he could not approach the altar. Aaron's position as high priest did not make him holier than others, though it did hold him to a higher standard. God chose Aaron and his descendants just as God chose the Israelites. A look at Aaron's life reveals that neither he (Exodus 32) nor his sons (Leviticus 10) were holy by their own merit. Even though a priest was ceremonially pure, he still could approach God only by means of sacrifice and atoning blood.

22:1–9 Priests were tasked with approaching God's holy presence in the tabernacle and offering blood sacrifices that would atone for sin. This means they had to remain clean. Attempting priestly duties while unclean would cause defilement, and that person would be cut off from God. The priests were to respect the rules for cleanness and uncleanness (see chapters 11–15). The nature of defilement is not that of specific sin but of

external ceremonial defilement. Leviticus begins by defining defilement in very concrete terms, but as the Old Testament revelation unfolds, the prophets emphatically teach that God is not nearly as interested in the external ceremonial acts of people as He is in the attitudes of their hearts and the resulting righteousness.

22:10–16 These verses add a few details regarding how priests are to handle the food left over after sacrificial offerings (see chapters 2–7).

22:17–33 Here are additional regulations for sacrificial offerings (see chapters 1–7). Because the blood is atoning or purifying in nature, a sacrificial animal has to be without defect. Those who had defects, some simply in their appearance, were not to be offered. The priests followed laws related to holiness in order to teach the Israelites that God is holy.

23:1–3 *Sabbath* means "rest." The sabbath celebration has its roots in the creation of the world (Genesis 2:1–3). God blessed the seventh day and sanctified it, separating it from the others in kind and character. The sabbath becomes a day of rest in a week otherwise filled with toil and work.

23:4–8 The Israelites celebrate passover and the feast of unleavened bread together. The first month in the sacred Jewish calendar is marked by passover, a day celebrating Israel's deliverance from captivity and birth as a nation. It is the most important festival. The feast of unleavened bread is an extension of passover. This is a time for the Israelites to remember their identity as God's people.

23:9–14 The festival of firstfruits is a time for the Israelites who were camped in the desert to be reminded of the hope of future blessings in Canaan. On this day, the first sheaf of barley is harvested, but nothing can be eaten until the sheaf is waved before God as an act of thanksgiving for His provision. The priest would also make a burnt offering together with a meat (or grain) offering and a drink offering of wine.

23:15–22 The festival of pentecost, or the feast of weeks, gets its name from the counting of fifty days from the sabbath following passover. It coincides with and celebrates God's giving of His law at mount Sinai. The feast also includes several offerings to God, and the Israelites are instructed to leave the edges of their crops unharvested for the poor and the foreigner as well.

23:23–44 The festival of trumpets is known today as Rosh Hashanah. It is a day marked by assembling together and doing no regular work, and it is commemorated by blowing trumpets with fanfare. It is a reminder that the day of atonement is approaching and a time for the Israelites to reflect on the year and their relationship to God. Following the somber reflection of the day of atonement, the feast of tabernacles is the joyous holiday of the manifest presence of God. As a reminder to younger generations of God's deliverance of the Israelites from Egypt, they are all to live in booths (temporary shelters made of tree branches and palm leaves) for seven days.

24:1–4 The golden candlestick has already appeared in the Pentateuch several times (Exodus 25:31–40; 27:20–21; 37:17–24; 40:25–26). It is housed in the holy place to provide light in the darkness of the tabernacle. Even in the daytime, the many layered coverings of the tent would keep out sunlight, so the light of this candlestick is required. The emphasis of these verses is that the light must be kept burning at all times. The key word is *continually*. Virtually the entire nation plays a role in this task of keeping the golden candlestick burning.

24:5–9 There are two reasons the continual changing of the cakes is important. First, they are a part of the sacrificial offerings. To fail to provide fresh cakes each week would hinder the sacrificial process, which is symbolic of an everlasting covenant. Second, these cakes (or, more accurately, what remains of them) are a part of the food that sustains and nourishes the priests. To fail to provide for the priesthood would be to hinder the priestly process, so the cakes are always to be on hand.

24:10–23 The next group of verses addresses the case of a man who had blasphemed God's name. The Israelites were not sure how to interpret God's law, so they asked for a ruling. In clarifying the law as it applies to this man's offense, Israel is taught how the law applies to them personally. In addition, God's people are taught some important principles that apply to a much wider range of offenses. The one who defames God's character is to be taken outside the camp. All the witnesses lay their hands on his head as an act of recognizing their part in the crime, and then the entire congregation of Israelites would stone the offender as a way to identify with God and His holiness. God then gives general rules for how to deal with blasphemy. God's holiness is emphasized by the severe punishment prescribed for someone who blasphemes.

25:1–7 During the sabbath year, the land is given its rest. Following these commands would require great faith, since letting fields lie fallow for a year would mean trusting God to provide as He promises (25:18–22). The land regulations are also a provision for the poor, since anyone is allowed to eat from the crops but no one could harvest them for sale. This provided them with food in times of need and the possibility of a new beginning.

25:8–34 The year of jubile (commonly called *Jubilee*) was like a super sabbath. Every fifty years, God proclaimed a year of freedom and liberation from bondage following the day of atonement. In the sabbath year, all debts are canceled (Deuteronomy 15:1–2), but in the year of Jubilee, the Israelite who has sold himself to another is released, and the land that has been leased to another is restored to its original owner. The year of Jubilee is a reminder that God owns the land. Loans were to be made without any consideration of how many years were left to repay the loan (Deuteronomy 15:7–11), but leases were made by calculating the number of years remaining until the Jubilee. One is an act of generosity, considered more a gift than a loan, and the other is a business arrangement that is regulated to ensure a fair deal.

25:35–46 The first type of poverty addressed is temporary. God's solution is a no-interest loan. God instructs the Israelites how to help a fellow Israelite who is so poor he has to sell himself. That person is to be treated not as a slave but with dignity as a hired worker who could leave his employment if treated unfairly (see Deuteronomy 15:16–17; 24:15). In the year of jubile (or Jubilee), the servant has to be released so he can return to the property of his forefathers. While an Israelite could not be a slave because he was ultimately God's servant, not another person's, non-Israelites could be bought as slaves. However, they were also to be treated well.

25:47–55 A poor Israelite could sell himself to a wealthy foreigner, but he kept the right to redemption at any time by a relative or himself (because he ultimately belonged to God). If that did not happen, though, the nation of Israel was responsible to make sure he was not mistreated and that he was released in the year of jubile (or Jubilee).

26:1–13 God reminds the Israelites that they are His people and then promises blessings if they will act as His people. In their broadest definition, God's blessings are conditioned by Israel's keeping of the Mosaic Covenant. At the heart of that covenant is worshipping God alone and observing the sabbath. The blessings God promises Israel are directly related to their possession of the land of Canaan: peace, prosperity, and the presence of God. Those promises end with a reminder of past blessings and of God's faithfulness.

26:14–39 The curses are virtually a reversal of the promised blessings. Instead of prosperity, disobedience will bring poverty. Instead of peace and security, disobedience will bring insecurity, peril, and fear. Instead of God's presence, disobedience will bring separation.

26:40–46 God deals with Israel's sin and with repentance at their roots, at the level of motivation. Israel's disobedience is the result of their hatred of God's laws (26:15). But God's motivation in discipline is to have Israel turn back to Him. God assures Israel of an ultimate hope by reaffirming His love for them. In the end, God assures Israel that He will restore them not based on obedience to the Mosaic Covenant but because of His own faithfulness.

27:1–8 People could be devoted to God (Judges 11:30–31; 1 Samuel 1:11) to serve in ministry or to serve the priests in non-ceremonial roles. The monetary values set for these different categories of people (based on age and gender) serve to discourage vows that are not well thought out, as the money would have to be presented if the offered person was not presented to fulfill what had been promised.

27:9–13 In these verses, regulations are given regarding the gift of clean and unclean animals that could be offered to God and used or sold. The vowed animals had to meet sacrificial standards and could not be replaced with a less valuable offering. If a man wanted to renege on a vow, he had to buy back the animal and pay a penalty.

27:14–21 The house in verses 14–15 is not attached to family land but is a piece of property that would not revert to the owner in the year of jubile (or Jubilee). The value of the house would be established by the priest, and if the offerer wanted to redeem the house, he had to pay that value plus a penalty. A portion of inherited family land could be dedicated to God, but it would revert to the owner or his heirs in the year of Jubilee. To redeem the field, the donor would be required to pay fifty shekels of silver for every certain amount of seed required for planting. The number of years remaining until Jubilee would determine the value of the gift. If the man who dedicated this field attempted to negate his vow by selling this property to another, then it would become property of the priests in the Jubilee year.

27:22–25 Someone could purchase another person's fields and devote them to God. In that case, the priest determines the property value and expects payment the same day, but the land would revert to the original owner at jubile (or Jubilee).

27:26–34 Unacceptable gifts include things that already belong to God, such as tithes.

NUMBERS

INTRODUCTION TO NUMBERS ■ The book of Numbers derives its name from the two censuses taken of the nation of Israel at the beginning and the end of this book. Before being referred to as Numbers, this writing had also been known as In the Desert (or Wilderness), referring to the fact that the Israelites spent forty years in the desert.

AUTHOR ■ Many evangelical scholars consider Moses the author of Numbers. Additional support for Moses as the author is found in the fact that Jesus calls the first five books of the Bible "the law of Moses" (Luke 24:27, 44).

OCCASION ■ This book covers a history of thirty-nine years in the travels of the Israelites from mount Sinai to the border of the promised land. Throughout this book, Israel is sometimes seen as a complaining and rebellious nation, often needing God to intervene with discipline. In the midst of His discipline, however, God will still keep His covenant and will continue to provide for the needs of His people. Thus, Numbers does not end with failure but with a generation ready to enter the promised land because of God's mercy and grace.

1:1 The first verse of Numbers gives us a telling reference point. This census takes place in the second month of the second year after the Israelites have left Egypt. The passover described in Numbers 9 was to have happened in the *first* month of the second year. So, while the facts and figures are included at the beginning of the book of Numbers, the census actually happens after the first passover feast is commemorated.

1:1–16 The Lord commands Moses to take a census of all the Israelites, with an exclusive emphasis on those who will be able to function as soldiers. This census is taken by tribe, with a tribal leader listed. Each tribe is identified by the son of Jacob from whom they descended. Jacob was the grandson of Abraham. His name was later changed to *Israel*; thus the people as a whole are referred to as *Israelites*.

1:17–46 Moses provides the results of the census, with the numbers rounded off to the nearest hundred. The total is 603,550 men.

1:32–54 Notice that Ephraim and Manasseh are both sons of Joseph. This means actually only eleven of Jacob's sons are represented. The missing son (and tribe) is Levi. God has a special purpose for the descendants of Levi. The Levites are not to be included as soldiers but are to care for the tabernacle and all that belongs to it. They are to camp around it, protect it, and be responsible for dismantling it and setting it back up as the camp moves. This assignment elevates the role of the Levites and puts a priority on the role of worship among the people.

2:1–34 In order for the Israelites to live their nomadic lifestyle without falling into complete chaos, there would have to be some structure. In this case, the tabernacle becomes the hub around which the tribes are organized. The campsites are described in relation to the tabernacle—north, east, south, or west. This order held significance not only for camping and breaking camp but also for traveling. The ark of the covenant always leads the way, carried by the priests; and the tribes to the east and south march ahead of the tabernacle, while those to the west and north march behind it.

2:2 Each tribe has a "standard" (or banner) that displays the tribe's symbol.

3:1–4 The opening verses of chapter 3 include the names of the sons of Aaron: the first high priest, Nadab (the firstborn), and Abihu, Eleazar, and Ithamar. We don't know the exact nature of the error that causes Nadab and Abihu to be killed in the line of duty, but we know it was an improper worship connected to the censers (or "strange fire" found in Numbers 26:61).

3:1–37 The priests are given the care of the tabernacle. Once the people enter Canaan, the Levites will have no specific piece of land. Instead, they will be scattered throughout the land and will live off a portion of the offerings brought by the people. The remainder of chapter 3 and chapter 4 offers a double census of the descendants of Levi and a description of their responsibilities. The organization of the Levites through the rest of Numbers is according to the three sons of Levi. The priests, however, are a subset of the descendants of Kohath, those who would descend specifically from Aaron's family line. Descendants of Gershon were responsible for the curtains and coverings. Descendants of Kohath were responsible for the furniture and utensils. Descendants of Merari were responsible for the boards and bars.

3:40–51 These verses discuss the substitution of the Levites for the firstborn sons and cattle of each of the other tribes. Traditionally, the firstborn belonged to the Lord, so they could be expected to be offered to the tabernacle for service (the sons) and sacrifice (the livestock). In this case, though, the Levites stand in the place of these firstborn, offering their service to the tabernacle instead. When a family came to offer their firstborn to the tabernacle, or later, the temple, they had the opportunity to give money to redeem their son back into family life. The same thing happens here with the 273 firstborn who outnumber the Levites. A price is paid for their redemption—1,365 shekels, which is given to Aaron and his sons. This practice of redeeming provides a kind of foreshadowing picture of the ransom that Christ paid in being the only begotten Son of God, who took our place and became the sacrifice.

4:1–20 While chapter 3 lists the duties of each family of Levi's descendants, chapter 4 delves deeper into their ministries. The Kohathites between thirty and fifty years of age numbered those who could care for the holy objects of the tabernacle after the priests had prepared them for removal. Rather than loading these objects onto wagons or animals, the Kohathites carried them. The items had to be covered before the Kohathites dealt with them so they wouldn't be killed by touching them or looking at them. This is not an affirmation of the worth of these items so much as a testament to the purity of God.

4:21–28 The census of the Gershonites between thirty and fifty years of age numbered those who would carry the curtains of the tabernacle under the direction of Aaron and his sons, especially Ithamar.

4:29–33 The census of the Merarites between thirty and fifty years of age numbered those who would carry the poles and tent pegs of the tabernacle, also under the direction of Ithamar. These items would have been quite burdensome.

4:34–39 These verses summarize the census, which numbers the Levites for service at 8,580.

5:1–31 As the Israelites prepare to go on the move, they must purify themselves. This pursuit of purity is meant to impact all their social interactions. In this chapter, God focuses the attention of the nation on dealing with three specific issues: physical impurities, moral impurities, and marital impurities.

5:1–4 Moses is to identify the ceremonially unclean people: any man or woman who has a skin disease. Though the King James Version describes the people who suffer from this kind of disease as "lepers," these people are not necessarily afflicted with literal *leprosy*. Someone who had this kind of skin disease, a discharge (whether natural or related to infection), or contact with a dead body—either human or animal—is unclean. While the purpose here is associated with purity rather than health, the actions probably benefited the whole community.

5:5–10 These verses deal with moral impurities. The Lord orders anyone who has wronged another to make full restitution to the one who was wronged. This restitution involves not just returning the offended person to the point before the loss, but also adding 20 percent. If the restitution can't be made directly to the person, then it is made to the family. If not the family, then to the priest. Under these guidelines, there is no excuse for not making wrongs right again. This is more than a matter of community; it is a matter of cleansing oneself before God, who sees all.

5:11–31 These verses, which deal with marital impurity, outline a test by which a man can ferret out suspected infidelity on the part of his wife. The test requires an offering and a drink of holy water with tabernacle dust (some consider this to imply a bitter herb) mixed in. The result of the test depends on how the woman's body responds to the liquid. While this test seems foreign to contemporary minds, the first purpose it serves is to put

the man and his wife in the midst of spiritual leadership—the tabernacle priest. An important point of this procedure is that it places the woman before God for Him to determine if she is guilty or innocent. The husband isn't free to act on his suspicions any way that he chooses.

6:1–20 These verses outline the vow of the Nazarite. This is typically a temporary vow of spiritual dedication. There are three marks of this vow, called a separation to God: abstaining from wine and grape products, not touching dead bodies, and not cutting one's hair. The first two conditions are similar to the rules for priests during their terms of service. Wine would hinder the priests' vigilance (Leviticus 10:6–11), and the high priest could not even enter the place where a relative's corpse lay, although the ordinary priests could attend to a close relative (Leviticus 21:1–4, 11). Uncut hair, however, is peculiar to the Nazarite and symbolizes his commitment. The word translated *Nazarite* is related to a Hebrew term that carries the idea of both a vow and a crown. This may contain a deliberate suggestion that the long hair functions as a crown—evidence of the vow.

6:9–12 If the Nazarite vow is broken—for instance, if someone can't escape touching a dead body—the Nazarite must pay a penalty and start fresh.

6:13–21 When the period of dedication ends, the Nazarite has to shave his head and burn the hair in the peace offering.

6:22–27 These verses contain the blessing God gives the Israelites. It is a frequently quoted spiritual blessing. God's "face," described in this blessing as shining on His people, is a symbol of His presence. His favor is implied by the picture of Him turning His face toward the Israelites. Thus this blessing is a prayer for God's presence and favor.

7:1 Chapters 7–9 describe the dedication of the tabernacle. The events of chapters 7–9 actually precede the events described in chapters 1–6. Numbers 7 is the second longest chapter in the Bible. It describes the twelve-day festival in which the people bring gifts to be used in the tabernacle. Each day different tribes send a representative to offer the gifts. There is much repetition, but to the original readers of Numbers, this repetition is understood as emphasis.

7:2–11 The leaders of the tribes offer six covered wagons (one for every two leaders) and twelve oxen (one for every leader). Moses daily accepts the wagons and oxen for twelve days. He gives two wagons and four oxen to the sons of Gershon, to carry the curtains and coverings of the tabernacle (3:21–26). He gives four wagons and eight oxen to the sons of Merari, to carry the heavy boards and bars of the tabernacle (3:33–37). None are offered to the sons of Kohath, though. They are required to carry the holy objects on their shoulders (3:27–32).

7:12–83 Even though the tribes offer the same gifts, Moses lists them separately, honoring each one.

8:1–4 God gives instructions regarding the lamps. They are to be mounted so their light falls forward, resembling a tree. This symbolizes the fact that God is the giver of life to humankind. It also may symbolize the fact that

Israel is to be a light to the world. The light from this candlestick also shines brightly upon the shewbread, which symbolizes the daily provision of God.

8:5–26 These verses prescribe how the whole Levite workforce (in place of the firstborn Israelites; 3:40–51) is dedicated and purified for its work, and how those who retire at age fifty may continue to help the younger Levites as guards in the tabernacle. The male members of the Levites are to be set apart by being cleansed by water and shaving their hair; washing their clothes; and offering burnt and sin offerings. Without being made clean through an offering and a spiritual washing, the Levites could not serve God.

8:26 In Numbers 8, God is establishing what it means to be set apart for His service. Though we worship differently today, this issue of seeing ourselves as God's servants is still important. First Peter 2:9 tells us that all believers are a "royal priesthood." We are set apart unto God for His purposes and glory. When Jesus Christ came, He did not do away with the priesthood; instead, He widened it so that all those who come to God through faith in Him become a holy priesthood, set apart for the work of God.

9:1 On the first month of the second year after the people had come out of Egypt, God commands them to commemorate the passover. Comparing Numbers 9:1 with Numbers 1:1 makes it obvious that this celebration must have preceded the census described at the opening of Numbers.

9:2–3 The passover is the celebration that remembers God's faithfulness in protecting the Israelites from the angel of death. The passover also shows the grace of God. God not only spared the firstborn but also rescued the people and brought them out of slavery to the promised land. The Israelites are to celebrate the passover annually, as a way of remembering the grace and the mercy of God. These two great themes come to their fullest expression on the cross of Jesus, where Jesus stood as the passover Lamb for humankind.

9:13 There are provisions made for those who are unable to celebrate the passover at the appointed time, but the death penalty awaits those who do not celebrate at the appointed time if they are able. This underscores the priority on worship that runs throughout Numbers.

9:15–16 The means of guidance for the sons of Israel is the movement of the cloud over the tabernacle and the sounding of two silver trumpets (10:1–10). Despite the failings of the nation, the cloud is always present. In fact, the presence of the Lord is seen at all times: as a cloud by day and a pillar of fire by night. The Israelite people are not only reminded of the past; they also have the daily reminder of the present: God is with them. He is their God and they are His people.

9:18–23 When the cloud moves, the Israelites are to move. God directs the people to go where He wants them to go, when He wants them to go. The people, then, must respond by obeying His direction. This passage contains eight references to God's orders and the Israelites'

obedience. This underscores a subtheme of Numbers: It is a dangerous thing to know what God demands and not do it.

10:1–10 God commands Moses to make two hammered trumpets of silver. They are to be blown for several reasons: to gather the people, to sound an alarm for the camps to begin to move, and to mark solemn days. According to verse 9, these trumpets also act as a kind of prayer that God will hear His children and rescue them from their enemies.

10:11–36 On the twentieth day of the second month of the second year, Israel sets out in military array for the first time. The cloud leads them from the wilderness of Sinai to the wilderness of Paran.

10:29–30 Moses talks his brother-in-law, Hobab, into continuing on in the journey. Hobab understands where to camp and how to function in the desert, so his presence has some advantages. Moses even promises Hobab that if he comes along, he will share in the blessings promised to the Israelites. (Though Hobab initially resists, he apparently changes his mind because his descendants are listed with the Israelites in Judges 1:16 and 4:11.) Though Hobab's expertise is certainly useful to the Israelites, God does the leading.

10:35–36 This pair of verses includes two short hymns that celebrate God's direction. The first is a prayer for protection as the group moves. The other is a prayer for fellowship as the group settles.

11:1–3 Only three days into their journey from Sinai, the people begin to complain about their difficulties—and God responds. "Fire of the Lord" may imply lightning, but the text is not that specific. When the people cry for help, Moses intercedes for them. The place is called *Taberah*, which means "burning." Yet, in the following verses, the complaining continues.

11:4 The "mixt multitude," sometimes interpreted *rabble* or *riffraff*, that seems to instigate this round of grumbling is not clearly defined here, though it likely refers to the non-Israelites who traveled with the group out of Egypt (Exodus 12:38).

11:5–7 The Israelites still don't return their attention to God and instead keep their focus on the next problem in their lives. In this case, they complain about the food God has provided: manna. It seems that they have forgotten the sweat, labor, pain, and enslavement that had been a part of their lives in Egypt and remember only the food.

11:8–9 The manna God provides is like a seed of grain and looks like small, clear drops. The name is commonly thought to be derived from an expression of surprise: "What is it?" More likely it derives from a word that means "to allot," denoting an allotment or a gift. Generally, manna has been associated with a by-product of the tamarisk tree found in northern Arabia.

11:16–17 Moses is instructed to appoint seventy elders among the Israelites. Seventy of these men, a number suggestive of a full complement of persons, are to be endowed with the Spirit of God for assisting Moses in bearing the burdens of the people as spiritual leaders.

This spiritual dimension differentiates this group from those appointed for administrative and judicial tasks in Exodus 18:25–26.

11:18 *Sanctify* is a term used here to describe the process of purification through bathing. The purpose, which is what makes it a spiritual process, is to be prepared to receive the presence of the Lord. Ritual purity was necessary before offering sacrifices and as preparation for celebrating festivals such as passover. Here, it is to prepare for God's blessing.

11:18–23 God provides directions for the larger populace to consecrate themselves prior to receiving the blessing from the Lord. In this case, though, the so-called blessing described in verses 19–20 is one that will wear out its welcome. Notice the emphatic nature of the description in verse 19—not one, two, five, ten, or even twenty days, but for an entire month they will receive meat.

11:25–26 The promise God gives in verse 17 is fulfilled here, but according to the text, it seems to be a onetime event that proved God's presence. Two of the men—Eldad and Medad—who had been registered among the seventy elders remained in the camp and prophesied there.

11:28–30 Moses' response to Joshua contrasts considerably with his earlier expressions of complaint and despair. Instead of feeling threatened, Moses commends the event. An undercurrent in Moses' response may be his own desire for further relief from the heavy responsibility of leadership, but it also reveals a heart open to God's leadership.

11:31–32 These verses describe the wind that brought the quail to the camp. The magnitude of the quail is measured in three ways: (1) the breadth of distribution: a day's journey in each direction, or twelve to fifteen miles; (2) the depth of the piles: about three feet high (though some interpret this as the level at which the quail flew); (3) the amount individually collected: at least ten homers over a two-day period, a volume estimated at between thirty-eight and sixty-five bushels. The *homer* is the largest dry volume measure in the Hebrew vocabulary.

11:33 Some of the birds are eaten right away, while most of them are spread out around the camp, presumably for drying the meat after cleaning and salting it. While the people are processing and eating the quail, the Lord's anger burns against many of those who had gathered too much, and they are struck down and die, possibly from food poisoning.

11:35 The journey continues toward Hazeroth. The precise location is conjecture.

12:1 The Hebrew grammar of the opening verses of chapter 12 suggests that Miriam is the one leading the attack against Moses, but she is backed by her brother Aaron. This conflict is bigger than a family squabble. Miriam and Aaron have national religious positions of leadership, and they are challenging the leadership of Moses as sole mediator between God and Israel. Though

the question seems to be about Moses' wife's ethnicity, it is really Moses' right to lead that is at the heart of the issue.

12:2–3 The gravity of Miriam and Aaron's objections is amplified in the last words of verse 2: "The Lord heard it." Verse 3 interjects a kind of character witness on behalf of Moses.

12:4–8 All three siblings are summoned to come out to the tabernacle, a central locale that offers a reminder of the presence of the Lord. The Lord affirms Moses' unique commission as a prophet of God, a man who stands above the others among the Israelites, such as the recently endowed seventy elders, as well as above Miriam and Aaron. He is also the mediator of the covenant, hearing from God directly. Since this is the case, how could Miriam and Aaron dare to speak against him? To speak against God's servant is tantamount to speaking against God Himself.

12:9–10 The immediate response of the Lord to Miriam is one of anger, followed by withdrawal. The charges against Moses are dismissed and judgment meted out. When the cloud of God's presence withdraws, Moses and Aaron witness their sister's leprosy (or skin disease) that requires her separation from the tabernacle and from the community itself. That Miriam rather than Aaron is plagued by the disease reinforces the idea that Miriam is the chief instigator of the dispute. The term *leprosy* can have many meanings. Whatever the skin disease Miriam contracted, she would become an outcast from society, forced to live outside the holy camp. The laws regarding various skin diseases required the afflicted to live on the outskirts of the camp or town so as not to defile the purity of the community (Leviticus 13:45–46).

12:11–13 Aaron immediately apologizes to Moses, addressing him as "lord" and submissively confessing his sin of rebellion. This may have been an attempt to lighten the potential judgment against himself in the face of Miriam's judgment. But out of concern for his sister, he begs Moses for her healing, and Moses begs God for the same.

12:15 Israel will not disembark on the next stage of the journey until the Lord leads them by the cloud. The rebellion of Miriam has consequences for the entire community as they wait for her purification. The camp waits until Miriam is ready.

12:16 This verse marks the departure from Hazeroth toward the wilderness of Paran in the modern southern Negev, or northeast Sinai region. The Paran wilderness is the goal of the first phase of the journey (10:11), and from that area the spies are to be sent to explore Canaan (13:3).

13:1–16 This chapter records one of the biggest mistakes made by the nation of Israel. At the heart is the question of whether circumstances can outpower God's plan. In Exodus 3:8, Moses had been told by God that Canaan would be spacious and have an abundance of food. Here in Numbers, Moses chooses twelve leaders from the tribes of Israel to explore Canaan. While these leaders were chosen from the tribes, they weren't the tribal leaders.

13:17–25 These spies were to evaluate the people, the land, and the cities. The twelve spies travel from the south (wilderness of Zin) to the north (Rehob) and return after forty days with their report.

13:26–33 Except for Caleb, the spies report that although the land is rich, it also is inhabited by mighty people who could outpower them. Ten of the spies report that in relation to these giants, the people of Israel look like grasshoppers. The spies who make the majority report only saw the giants, whereas Joshua and Caleb saw victory. The descendants of Anak, the giants, are noted for their great size and strength.

14:1–5 The people responded to the spies' report with despair, prompting Moses and Aaron to prostrate themselves in the presence of God. The people's despair is a rejection of faith. When God is rejected, people become disillusioned and turn toward their past bondage.

14:6–9 To Caleb and Joshua, God is bigger than their enemies. These two see the land through the eyes of faith. To the other ten spies, the problems seem bigger than God. They minimize the greatest resource they have—the fact that God has already promised them the land. When a person acknowledges the power of God, he or she will not minimize the divine resources available.

14:10 After Joshua and Caleb stand against the majority, the people want to stone them. Then God appears. The Israelites' actions are actually a rebellion against God Himself more than a rejection of the two men.

14:11–19 When God speaks of destroying the people, Moses intercedes on the basis of God's character. He reasons that the nations will hear about this destruction and it would impugn God's character. Moses declares God's glory and seeks to protect it.

14:20–35 The people are pardoned, but because of their sin, the generation from age twenty and older (except for Caleb and Joshua) would wander for forty years (one year for every day of the spies' investigation) and die in the wilderness. These people had treated God with contempt. Although He provided them with proof over and over again that He was their deliverer, they still refused to believe Him.

14:36–38 After the plague that attacks the spies, only Joshua and Caleb remain of the group that had investigated Canaan.

14:39–45 Taking matters from bad to worse, the people continue to demonstrate their rebellion by entering the land against all instruction from Moses. This is an attempt to reverse their consequences, but of course they are soundly defeated by the Amalekites and Canaanites.

15:1–13 This chapter also marks the first set of instructions for the people who now know they will wander in this wilderness until their deaths. Notice that this section begins with the reaffirmation of worship. The first thing God does after the pronouncement of the

consequences of Israel's sin is reestablish the worship He wants from His people.

15:14–16 Just as the foreigners living among the Israelites are able to take part in the passover, they are also included in worship. While the Israelites are considered the people of God, their God accepts worship from anyone who is willing to be in right relationship with Him.

15:17–21 When the Israelites enter Canaan, they are to offer from the food of the land the first of their dough throughout their generations. This is an expression of gratitude for the harvest of grain.

15:22–29 These instructions deal with unintentional sins—sins of omission rather than commission. When the nation or an individual (native or alien) inadvertently sins against the commands of God, they are to make a sin offering.

15:32–36 If one sins defiantly, it is considered blasphemy, a capital crime. These verses give an example of a man who is found gathering wood on the sabbath. He is brought before Moses and Aaron and then stoned by the congregation outside of the camp as God commands. While this is an extreme and uncomfortable example for the contemporary mind, it is the full knowledge with which the man committed the sin, rather than the details, that prompted his judgment.

15:37–41 God commands Moses to tell the Israelites to put fringes (or tassels) on the corners of their garments with a ribband (cord) of blue through each. These fringes are to be constant reminders, not of one particular law, but of the relationship they solidified with God by their obedience. The color blue is related to both heaven and royalty in the minds of the Israelites.

16:1–3 This chapter marks another complaint of the Israelites in the desert, this time against the authority of Aaron and his priestly line. The chief rebel is Korah, who descended from Levi through his son Kohath. As a Kohathite, he has high duties at the tabernacle—but he isn't a priest. Just as Korah wants more power, so do Dathan, Abiram, and On (who is not mentioned again). The rebels rise up against Moses and Aaron with 250 leaders of the community. The heart of their accusation is Moses' arrogance in claiming a special relationship with God. These rebels want the same privilege.

16:4–7 When the leaders accuse Moses and Aaron of exalting themselves, Moses does not try to convince the rebels of his calling. Although it's clear that he's angry, he will let God defend him, if God so chooses.

16:8–11 Moses also rebukes the Levites under Korah and his company, making it clear that their rebellion is against God, because they want to exalt themselves rather than wait for Him to exalt them.

16:12–15 Moses summons Dathan and Abiram to come to him, but they refuse.

16:16–24 The glory of God appears with the intention to destroy the entire congregation, except for Moses and Aaron. Moses quickly asks God to spare those who did not follow the sin of Korah, Dathan, and Abiram.

16:25–39 Moses announces the severity of what will happen—the Lord opens the ground and swallows up the households of the rebels, and the 250 men who were offering incense also perish. This event leaves no question as to God's stance on the rebellion, nor do His orders to Eleazar to use the censers of the rebels to plate the altar—an ongoing reminder.

16:41 Perhaps not surprisingly, the next day the people complain again, accusing Moses and Aaron of causing the death of Korah and his men. The truth, however, is that Moses and Aaron had asked for the survival of the same people who are continuing to complain against them.

16:43–50 A plague that kills 14,700 follows the complaining of the people. The deaths only stop because of Aaron's intercession. We aren't given a lot of details about the nature of this plague or what Moses' actions may have been in the midst of it, but the account serves to set up a transition to the next passage regarding Aaron's leadership.

17:1–10 The rods (or staffs) of the twelve tribal leaders are to be brought inside the innermost holy chamber and placed before the throne of God. This placement demonstrates the gravity of the occasion. The staff that sprouts leaves, then, will represent the leader whom God has appointed to stand before Him. Only God can impart life to that which is dead, and this test will show the combined tribes of Israel that God has conferred a special blessing upon the tribe whom He chooses. The following morning, Moses enters the inner tabernacle of witness and finds that not only has Aaron's staff sprouted but God has caused it to bud, blossom, and produce almonds. The almond is one of the earliest trees to bud and blossom in the spring, and the fruit ripens in early to mid summer. But for a dead limb to sprout, bud, blossom, and produce ripe almonds overnight is a remarkable wonder, a natural process made supernatural. The almond branch in Israelite art and literature was a symbol of the life that derived from their Maker. The bud and flower were shaped so elegantly that the three golden bowls on each side of the tabernacle candlestick were patterned after them (Exodus 25:31–40).

17:11–13 The priority of the Aaronic priesthood is vindicated. The unanswered question closing Numbers 17—Are we all going to die?—will be resolved in the following two chapters, which contain the instructions from God concerning a proper approach to a holy and just God.

18:1–7 These verses reiterate (and build upon) certain aspects of the priestly roles outlined in Numbers 3–4 (also Leviticus 8–10). The most basic responsibility is to be accountable for any potential sacrilege against the innermost holy place (the tabernacle of witness) in the tabernacle. The priests must monitor their own purity as well.

18:8–11 The priests are allowed to keep some of the offerings given by the people. This priestly tribute is divided into two levels of sanctity, the *most* holy offerings

and the generally "hallowed" (or "holy") offerings. The holiest of the offerings, which are to be consumed by the priests, are meat (or grain) offerings, sin (purification) offerings, and trespass (reparation) offerings. The meat (or grain) offering, as described in 2:1–13 and 6:14–23, is an unleavened mixture of fine flour, oil, and incense. A memorial portion is burned on the altar as a sweet savour to God, and the remainder is eaten by the priests.

18:12–18 The second level of tribute (the first level is the most holy offerings) consists of the variety of firstfruits and firstborn gifts. The first fruit from the trees and offspring from the womb (people and livestock) are treated as special gifts from God that are to be returned to Him.

18:15 God has much to say about firstborn gifts. The firstborn is the first male from the womb of the mother, whether human or animal. Animals defined by Levitical law as clean—such as cattle, sheep, and goats—are to be offered as sacrifices. Since humans cannot be sacrificed (nor unclean animals), a redemption price is established to be given instead of the firstborn. The process of human and animal redemption has a teaching purpose, too. It reminds the Israelites of their redemption from Egypt.

18:19 The offerings from Israel are a gift from God for the members of the priestly families, both male and female. God calls this an everlasting "covenant of salt." Though the origin of this covenant is unknown, the function of salt in ancient Near Eastern society included the concepts of preservation and permanence.

18:20–24 Though the Levites receive no land, God is their inheritance. This is not to say that the priests and Levites somehow owned God. Instead, what physically accrued to God from the territorial inheritance of the Israelites would belong to them. These gifts become the Levites' birthright instead of territorial grant.

18:24 The tithe, or *tenth*, is the required percentage of the productivity of Israelite labors that is to be rendered to God at the tabernacle (18:21). The statutes on tithing and the relationship between the Levites and the other Israelites are expanded in Deuteronomy 12:17–19 and 14:22–29. During the wilderness journey, the Levites camp immediately around the tabernacle, serving as a barrier between the tabernacle and the community at large. This responsibility was a perpetual one. The contributions of the Israelites to God are, in turn, His gifts to these Levites for their dedicated service.

18:25–32 The previous verses contain rules and regulations found elsewhere in the Pentateuch. Starting in verse 25, however, a new law emerges. The Levites are responsible to tithe to God, and thus to the priesthood, out of the tithes they receive. Furthermore, they are to contribute, in this tithe of the tithe, the very best of what is bestowed upon them. The original tithe, designated as the Levite inheritance in exchange for their service in the tabernacle, is treated like income. Like the other Israelites, the Levites are to tithe on this income.

19:1 This chapter offers the cleansing process for those who have been in contact with a dead body. This is an important ceremony for the Israelites, because the nation will encounter many deaths on a daily basis for several decades. Thus they must know how to remain ceremonially clean after dealing with a dead body.

19:2 This chapter outlines a ritual involving an unblemished "red heifer." The cow is to be brought to Eleazar, the priest, and slaughtered outside of the camp. The animal designated for sacrifice is a young cow. The color red may symbolize blood, but that is uncertain. The exact age of the animal is not made clear by the Hebrew, but the fact that it is not to be allowed to pull the plow or do any other type of work suggests it may have just reached maturity.

19:3 Eleazar is the one who is to receive the animal. He is the second, or deputy, high priest, and he is selected for this duty because the job causes the participant to incur temporary defilement, which the high priest cannot.

19:4–10 Eleazar is to sprinkle some of the cow's blood toward the front of the tabernacle before the cow is completely burned. After burning, its ashes are to be mixed with cedar wood, hyssop, and scarlet material; then it is to be used to clean those who have touched a corpse. Some details that set this ritual apart from the sacrifices at the tabernacle are that the animal is led out of the camp rather than being slaughtered at the altar. Also, every part of the cow is consumed by fire except the blood used in sprinkling. The ingredients mixed with the ashes are the same as those employed in the sprinkling of lepers (Leviticus 14:4–7). Numbers 19:14–22 explains the use for this mixture. Anyone who even enters the tent of a dead person needs to be sprinkled with this mixture of water and ashes from the red cow on the third and seventh days (after the contact with the dead body) in order to be cleansed. In addition, the one who performs the sprinkling, as well as all the things that the unclean person touches, will be considered unclean until evening. These rituals for dealing with the dead, though mysterious, helped preserve the sanitary conditions of the camp.

20:1 When the Israelites come in the first month to the desert of Zin and stay at Kadesh, Miriam dies and is buried there. Miriam is the leading female character in the story of the Exodus. This account of her death sets the somber mood for the rest of the chapter.

20:2–11 At Kadesh, the people resume their murmuring about lack of water and rebel against Moses and Aaron because of it. They again lose sight of the plan of God and are caught in the misery of the moment. God commands Moses to take the rod, gather the community, and speak to the rock; then it will bring forth water. For unknown reasons, Moses instead takes the rod, gathers the community, speaks to them with a hasty and passionate voice, and then strikes the rock twice.

20:12 There are two things that Moses and Aaron get wrong: the first is their unbelief, and the second is their lack of obedience. Believing is not just mentally agreeing with God; it is actually doing what God says. The consequence of their actions is severe—they will be prevented from bringing the people into Canaan.

20:13 The waters are called *Meribah* because the meaning of this name reflects the fact that Israel contended with God, but God proved Himself holy among them. Such naming of locations was meant to teach future generations about the history of Israel and about all that God did in that region.

20:14–21 Following the two great blows already described in chapter 20—Miriam's death and the conflict at Meribah—Moses has to deal with the Edomites, who will not allow them to pass to Canaan. Moses makes a diplomatic request to go through the land of Edom, but the Edomites declare they will attack Israel before letting them pass through. Moses counters: What if they only pass via the main roads? And if any of the livestock drink any of their water, they will pay for it. Edom still refuses, and the Israelites find another way. The Edomites are descendants of Esau, who was the twin brother of Jacob, forefather of the Israelites. The story of these brothers, told in Genesis 25–27, is filled with conflict. Understanding the distant family history, generations past, adds to the conflict described here in Numbers 20.

20:22–29 Chapter 20 opens with the death of Miriam and closes with the death of Aaron. When the Israelites come to mount Hor, near the border of Edom, Moses, in obedience to God, takes Aaron and his son Eleazar up the mountain. (Scholars are not certain where mount Hor is located, despite an early tradition identifying it with Jebel Nebi Harun near Petra.) There he gives Aaron's garments to Eleazar, and Aaron dies. When Moses places Aaron's vestments on Eleazar's shoulders, he is also transferring his responsibilities as Israel's high priest, the supreme mediator between God and Israel. The people mourn for Aaron for thirty days. This point in the lives of the Israelites seems to be the lowest so far. Yet God is allowing the next generation to take over, to carry on the work. God is still working and preparing the next generation to live in Canaan.

21:1–3 After Aaron's death, Moses alone leads the Israelites closer to Canaan. As they move northward, the king of Arad attacks them and takes captives. This is an important first battle because it establishes a pattern. God will do the winning. The Israelites acknowledge that unless God gives their foes into their hands, they will not have any success. The Israelites vow that if God will give the Canaanites into their hands, they will obey Him by completely destroying the cities. After this battle, the location is called *Hormah*, which means "destruction." Hormah became an ancient town on the southernmost borders of Palestine, not far from Kadesh. Tel Arad marks the spot today.

21:4 When the people are traveling from mount Hor to the Red Sea, they begin to grumble again about their circumstances and food. Remember that they are on this longer road to the promised land because the king of Edom refused to allow them to travel through his land (20:14–21). Perhaps because this journey is long, morale sinks.

21:5–7 When one complains, he or she is essentially saying that God has not provided the way He should have. It is an attack. This is why God responds by sending "fiery serpents." The desert near the head of the gulf of Akaba is known for being infested with venomous reptiles. In fact, there are lizards that raise themselves in the air and swing themselves from branches, and scorpions, which are particularly dangerous because they lie hidden in the grass. The people now face a threat, and in humility, they admit their misstep and ask for help from Moses.

21:8–9 According to God's instructions, Moses fashions the brass serpent and elevates it in plain sight of everyone in the camp. Every bitten Israelite who looks to it will be healed. Why this method? It is not that the brass snake or the pole is magical; it is the people's opportunity to choose faith and obey. Thus salvation is brought to the nation for their sin. This is the last recorded occasion on which Israel grumbles about the food and yearns for Egypt.

21:10–21 Israel moves to the eastern frontier of the Edomites, in the valley of Zared. Then they pitch their tents on the other side of Arnon (now called El-Mojib). This is a deep, broad, and rapid stream, dividing the land of the Moabites and Amorites. In both places, God provides camp space and water.

21:14 In addition to the Bible, other written sources from this era record the history of Israel. Two sources were "*the book of Jashar* (see Joshua 10:13; 2 Samuel 1:18) and "*the book of the wars of the Lord*," mentioned in this verse. Based upon these three short mentions, these two books were collections of victory songs and stories of the powerful acts of God working through His leaders during the early formation of Israel. Unfortunately, neither book survived, but their mention shows some of the alternate ways that God worked in spreading the word of His mighty power in calling, forming, growing, and protecting the nation of Israel.

21:21–32 In the account of Sihon, king of the Amorites, Israelite messengers request permission to march through their land, promising not to take anything and to leave the city and its supplies alone. In addition, they will stay on the king's high way, the ancient trade route used by many merchants. This request is rejected, and Sihon sends troops to fight Israel. Unlike the similar situation with the Edomites (20:14–21), Israel has no alternate route, so they must stand and fight. In this case, they are victorious. Earlier, in Genesis 15:16, God promised that the Israelites would be brought back to the land of the Amorites, and as a form of judgment, they would defeat the Amorites and take their land, just as it happens here.

21:33–35 The Israelites make their way through various villages, clearing out many of the Amorites. God then directs them to turn and go up by the way of Bashan, a hilly region east of the Jordan, lying between the mountains of Hermon on the north and those of Gilead on the south. There lies an intimidating foe, Og, who is a giant (see Deuteronomy 3:11). This likely describes the size of the inhabitants who scared the spies in Numbers 13. The Lord tells Moses not to fear this man and gives

Og over to the Israelites. God clearly shows the Israelites that they need Him at every turn on this journey.

22:1 The deceptively simple but profound story of Balaam and his donkey begins a period in which the Israelites—poised on the border of the promised land—encamp for an apparently lengthy time at the foot of the mountains of Moab, not unlike their encampment four decades prior at Sinai. These accounts are humorous as well as somber. Some characters are stupid and stubborn, and there is more spiritual awareness in the donkey than in the humans. Structurally, watch for threes: the donkey avoids the angel three times, Balaam arranges for three sets of sacrifices, he has three encounters with God, and so on. The narrative itself extends over six days, through Numbers 24.

22:2 As this account begins, Israel is about four months away from the end of the forty years' desert exile. When the sons of Israel camp in the plains of Moab, Balak, son of the king, becomes afraid. He has heard about Israel's victory over the Amorites.

22:4–7 Balak comes up with a plan. He seeks to defeat Israel by having Balaam, a Mesopotamian prophet, proclaim a curse upon Israel. An ancient text, the *Tell Deir 'Alla*, suggests that Balaam is a soothsayer of great renown in this region. The local text of that region suggests that he sees visions and dreams. Thus, he is an obvious choice for Balak to turn to for spiritual help. Balak sends a message requesting help and a fee.

22:8–20 When Balaam seeks direction from God, it is clear that the children of Israel are a blessed people and that it would be wrong to put a curse upon them. Yet Balak sends another, more impressive delegation with a promise of more money in payment for the curses. In the end Balaam goes, but with the determination to speak only God's words.

22:21–35 These verses tell the story of Balaam's journey. As he begins to leave with the leaders of Balak, he is stopped by his donkey. An angel of the Lord is in the road with a sword in his hand. This signifies that if Balaam tries to go to Balak, he will be killed. Balaam's donkey saves his life by not walking, despite being beaten. Three times the donkey tries to avoid the angel. Then the donkey is given the ability to speak and converses with Balaam. Finally, Balaam sees the angel, who reveals that the donkey saved his life and that Balaam must speak only God's words. This is not to say that God tells Balaam to go and then gets mad at him for going. The account probably implies that Balaam was not planning to carry out what God had requested.

22:36–41 Balak comes to meet Balaam, a gesture of some import, because the son of the king could have waited until Balaam came to him. Balak is upset with Balaam for not coming when first invited. Balak holds a banquet for Balaam and takes him to the high place of Baal to see a portion of Israel, perhaps hoping that this will make Balaam's curses stronger. Each of Balaam's blessings that follow in the subsequent chapters reiterates and confirms the promises of the Abrahamic

Covenant. What is about to take place in the life of Israel is a part of the fulfillment of what was spoken to Abraham in Genesis 12.

23:1 Some scholars portray Balaam as a saintly seer; others as a money-hungry heathen sham. In the beginning of the story, he appears positive, intent on listening to God. Other Bible passages aren't so flattering, for instance, Deuteronomy 23:4–5; 2 Peter 2:15; Jude 11; and Revelation 2:14.

23:7–10 The message of the first parable is that Israel will be multiplied like the dust of the earth.

23:18–24 The second parable proclaims that with God as their strength, the Israelites are indestructible and mighty. God cannot change His promise.

24:3–9 The third parable describes Israel as inheriting the land, and nothing will stop this from happening. The fact that Agag, the Amalekite king, is mentioned confirms specifically that Canaan is in mind here. This blessing also states that Israel will devour hostile nations. This fulfills the promise that they will possess their enemies' cities. The last words of this blessing bring home a key point of the Abrahamic Covenant: May those who bless you be blessed, and those who curse you be cursed!

24:15–19 The fourth parable promises a king in the distant future who will defeat Israel's enemies and crush the corners of Moab. This passage seems to anticipate King David's victories and the promise of his throne: the promise of the Messiah whom the Gentiles will obey. By this point, Balaam knows that the curse is not coming to Israel but to Balak. This fourth parable is actually a series development of the third one (see 24:3–9), explicitly describing the distant future.

24:20–24 Finally, Balaam describes the future destruction of those leaders who are present: Amalek, Asshur, Eber, and the Kenites.

25:1 After Balaam goes home, a new and subtler assault on Israel spreads through the immense population. And, as we find out later (31:8, 16), Balaam is tied to it. This strategy uses Moabite women—possible temple prostitutes—to seduce the men of Israel and lead the whole nation to ruin through idolatry. God hates sexual immorality, especially when it is tied to idol worship. Therefore, if Moab could not take down Israel through a curse from Balaam, it hoped to use the lust of the flesh.

25:1–3 While the Israelites are at Shittim, the region across the Jordan from Jericho, they are drawn into the worship of Moab's god, Baal-peor, through Moabite women. Baal is a fertility god whose worship often involves sexual immorality. Israel would be drawn into sin with Baal more than once in its history.

25:4–5 The Lord commands Moses to slay all of the leaders of Israel so that He might turn His anger away from the entire people. Moses orders the judges to slay the men who have coupled themselves with Baal-peor.

25:6–7 When one of the leaders of Israel blatantly brings a Midianitish (or Midianite) woman into the camp to have sexual relations with her, Phinehas, the grandson of Aaron through Eleazar, spears them both

with one stroke. This stops the plague of apostasy and sexual immorality, which leads to the death of 24,000 Israelites—a number even larger than the 14,700 who died in Korah's rebellion (chapter 16).

25:10–13 God affirms Phinehas, offering him a perpetual priesthood. Phinehas shows that he shares in God's jealousy for uprightness among the people. Therefore, the Lord proclaims that Phinehas has His covenant of peace. This means that he possesses a perpetual priesthood, having made atonement for the sons of Israel.

25:14–18 The Israelite who committed the sexual sin was Zimri, a leader of the Simeonites. The Midianitish (or Midianite) woman who participated was Cozbi, a daughter of Zur, who was a leader in Midian. Because this woman was a Midianite, the Lord commands Moses to be in perpetual war with the Midianites, who are closely associated with the Moabites. Moses is to attack them because they had been a part of the plot at Peor to lead the Israelites away from God into idolatry and sexual immorality.

26:1–2 Preparations are now beginning for the Israelites to take the land. The first thing that must take place is a census, in which men age twenty and older within each tribe are counted. The counting of the people provides several things for the Israelites: (1) It confirms the reality of God's promise of the land in Genesis 12:7. God makes good on His promises. (2) It focuses the people on the step before them. They are going to get land that will be big enough for their clan, but they are going to have to fight for it. Thus, numbering the men for war makes that point abundantly clear. (3) It reaffirms God's faithfulness to Israel. Even though people from every tribe rebelled against God, He did not wipe out every tribe. Therefore, this walk down memory lane reminds the people that God is trustworthy, just, kind, and reliable.

26:3–51 Here are the results of the census. On the plains of Moab by the Jordan, across from Jericho, Moses and Eleazar carry out the command. The census is to be of men twenty years and older who are able to go to war. It is important that a breakdown of the nation, its family distribution, and its military size be established. The total amount numbers the men at 601,730 and the Levites at 23,000. Now that the census has been taken, the land can be distributed, and the leadership knows the size of the army.

26:52–56 The Lord commands Moses to divide the land by lot. The larger inheritance is to go to the larger families; the smaller inheritance is to go to the smaller families. Because God is in charge of the outcome of the lots, there will be no fighting over who gets what land. Many understand these lots to resemble a specially made set of dice. The people could not control the way these dice fell, so it seemed to the people that God had room to lead. Some consider these lots to be the Urim and Thummim (Exodus 28:30). When decisions were made in this way, no one could argue that the decision was the result of politics, nepotism, or favoritism.

26:57–62 In the first census, the Levites are numbered separately because they are not to serve in the army. For the census described here, the Levites are omitted from the main census because they are not going to serve in the army nor receive any land. Thus we see a post-census count of the Levites. The Levites numbered 23,000 from a month old and upward.

26:63–65 With the exception of Moses, Joshua, and Caleb, there is no one left from the first census. The punishment on the people for their disbelief when they first faced the border was not entering the land (chapters 13–14). That original generation has died in the journey through the wilderness.

27:1–4 There is an issue of inheritance among the daughters of Zelophehad. These five women approach the tabernacle to implore Moses for help, an unprecedented act of courage and conviction. Zelophehad had died without sons. Therefore, when the land distribution plan was set, his daughters would be left without land. Facing Moses, they want to know if it is fair for them to not have any land because they have no brothers. They also are concerned about the preservation of their father's name. Zelophehad apparently was one of the followers of the skeptical spies; therefore he died in the wilderness (14:10–12).

27:5–11 Moses seeks the Lord, who commands him to allow the daughters to receive their father's inheritance. Then God prescribes a set of rules for the succession of the inheritance when other difficult cases arise: If a man dies without any sons, his inheritance is to be transferred to his daughter. If he has no daughter, then the inheritance goes to his brothers. If he has no brothers, the inheritance goes to his father's brothers. If his father has no brothers, the inheritance goes to his nearest relative in his own family to posses it. This ensures that everyone will get the land that was promised to Abraham.

27:12–23 The Lord commands Moses to go up to the mountain of Abarim to see the land He is giving to the nation of Israel. After Moses views his final destination, he will die. God appoints Joshua as Moses' successor. Before all the people, Moses brings Joshua before Eleazar, the high priest, and transfers some of his authority to Joshua.

28:1–2 The Lord prescribes specific daily and yearly observances for the sons of Israel to keep when they enter into the land. The entire calendar for the nation is to be governed by worship. The Lord commands Moses to be careful to present the various offerings at their appointed times, not as rote actions, but as prayers of dependence.

28:1–8 Two spotless male lambs are to be offered each day as burnt offerings to the Lord. One is to be offered in the morning and the other at twilight, with a meat (or grain) offering and a drink offering.

28:9–10 In addition to the daily offering, two one-year-old male lambs without defect are to be offered to the Lord on the sabbath. They are to be accompanied with a meat (or grain) offering and a drink offering.

28:11–15 In addition to the daily offering, the nation is to offer two bullocks (or bulls), one ram, seven one-year-old male lambs without defect, and a male goat. These are for a sin offering, along with appropriate meat (or grain) offerings and a drink offering at the beginning of each month.

28:16–25 The passover is to be celebrated on the fourteenth day of the first month. This is in association with the feast of unleavened bread (Leviticus 23:4–8), which begins the next day and runs for the next seven days. On passover, Israel is to rest and to present an offering of two bulls, one ram, and seven one-year-old male lambs without defect along with their meat (or grain) offering, and a male goat for a sin offering to make atonement for them in addition to the offerings above.

28:26–31 Fifty days after the feast of unleavened bread, on the day of firstfruits, the sons of Israel are to rest. In addition, they are to offer two young bullocks (bulls), one ram, and seven one-year-old male lambs with their meat (or grain) offerings and drink offerings, as well as one male goat to make atonement. This is to be done in addition to the offerings mentioned above.

29:1–6 On the first day of the seventh month the Israelites are to rest as well as offer one bullock (bull), one ram, seven one-year-old male lambs without defect, the appropriate meat (or grain) offerings, and one male goat as atonement for them. These are to be offered in addition to the other offerings and drink offerings.

29:7–11 The day of atonement is on the tenth day of the seventh month. The Israelites are to rest and offer one bullock (bull), one ram, seven one-year-old male lambs without defect, appropriate meat (or grain) offerings, and a male goat for atonement, in addition to the other offerings and drink offerings.

29:12–38 The feast in these verses became known as the feast of tabernacles. This feast runs the fifteenth to the twenty-first of the seventh month. On the first day, the Israelites are to rest and offer thirteen bullocks (bulls), two rams, fourteen one-year-old male lambs without defect, the appropriate meat (or grain) offerings, and a male goat as atonement. These sacrifices are to be repeated on the second through seventh days, minus one bull each day.

29:35–38 On the eighth day of the feast of tabernacles, the children of Israel are to rest and offer one bull, one ram, seven one-year-old male lambs without defect, the appropriate meat (or grain) offerings, and one male goat for a sin offering in addition to the regular offerings.

29:39 There is not a season, month, or week that goes by that does not have a time of worship associated with it. These offerings of worship are to be seen as prayers—prayers of dependence, repentance, salvation, and sanctification.

30:1–2 Vows are commitments made to God that are over and above what is required by the law. Moses introduces the topic by reminding the leaders of Israel that vows obligate the vow makers to follow through.

30:3–5 If a young woman makes a vow to the Lord while she is still at home under her father's authority, her father can undo the vow and release the girl from all responsibility. Girls only are mentioned, but many theologians believe that all minors who reside under the parental roof are included.

30:9–12 We learn that if a widow or divorced woman makes a vow to the Lord, she is bound by it. The only way she can get out of it is if she had taken it in her husband's house, and he had forbidden it on the day that he learned of it.

30:13–15 A husband may confirm or annul an oath of his wife. If he does not annul the oath upon hearing it, the vow remains binding. If he does annul the vow sometime after he has heard of it, he will be held responsible. In other words, he must not wait to annul it or he will be guilty before the Lord for breaking the vow.

30:16 The seriousness with which an oath is to be taken should motivate us to take a serious look at all our speech. The intent of this law is to teach us to watch what we say as unto the Lord. Whenever one considers oaths, pledges, and vows, he or she should not forget the words of Jesus on this issue, found in Matthew 5:33–37.

31:1–2 This chapter is a call to war. The Israelites are to go to war with the Midianites. The Midianites were the principal instigators of the wicked scheme of seduction in Numbers 25, in which they planned to entrap the Israelites into the double crime of idolatry and licentiousness. The Lord tells Moses that he is to treat the Midianites as enemies and to kill them. Now is the time for their destruction.

31:3–16 The Lord tells Moses exactly what to do. Moses speaks the command of God to the people and says to prepare for war. They gather twelve thousand men (one thousand from each tribe), as well as Phinehas, the son of Eleazar, the priest with the holy vessels and trumpets, to fight against the Midianites. This war is to be fought in the manner that God prescribes because the offense was not against Israel but against God.

31:7–12 When the sons of Israel go to war against the Midianites, they gain an incredible victory. They kill every Midianite male; kill the five kings of Midian; kill Balaam, the son of Beor (from chapter 25); capture the women and children; plunder Midianite livestock; burn Midianite cities; and take all the spoil, which they present to Moses, Eleazar, and the entire Israelite camp at the plains of Moab.

31:13–24 Moses is angry that the army has returned with Midianite women. Earlier, the Midianite women had brought a plague upon Israel by leading the people into idolatry. Moses commands that all of the male children be killed, that only the virgin girls be allowed to live, and that the army purify itself (for contact with the dead) and wait seven days before they reenter the camp. The judgment of God is very thorough. He does not take sin lightly, and the sin that drives the heart of this people brings certain death to their city.

31:25–47 The Lord commands Moses, Eleazar, and the leaders of the tribes to divide the booty between the warriors and the congregation. Moses also must issue a tax—one out of every five hundred captured persons and animals goes to the Lord. Half of the booty from the warriors goes to Eleazar, the high priest, and one out of fifty from the congregation goes to the Levites. The priests and the Levites are not to go to war, and the only way they will ever get any spoils is from taxation.

31:48–54 Not one of the sons of Israel is found to be missing in action. As a result, the warriors provide a memorial offering of thanksgiving (6,700 ounces of gold) to the Lord. They want to celebrate God's goodness, as well as make atonement for all that they did in going to war.

32:1–5 As the entire nation looks across the river to the promised land, there are two tribes, Reuben and Gad, who see that the land of Gilead will be suitable for their numerous livestock. They request that they be allowed to settle in this region rather than going across the Jordan.

32:6–15 Moses severely rejects Reuben and Gad's proposal. He perceives it to be a sin like that of their fathers, who did not want to enter the promised land (chapters 13–14).

32:16–19 The leaders of Gad and Reuben modify their request. Even though they would like for their inheritance to be in the land of Gilead, they will go and fight with the rest of the Israelites to help them acquire their inheritance. All they want is to be able to live in this spot after the land has been taken.

32:20–27 Moses agrees to let these two tribes settle in the land of Gilead if they will keep their word and go to war. If they do not fight, then they will be sinning against the Lord.

32:28–30 Moses tells Eleazar, Joshua, and the heads of the tribes that the sons of Gad and Reuben say they will fight with the sons of Israel in the promised land if they can be given the land of Gilead. Moses says that if they do not fight, they will be apportioned a possession in Canaan and will have to accept what they are given. Moses puts in place a contingency for their disobedience, just in case they get too comfortable where they are.

32:31–38 The sons of Gad and Reuben agree to the plan. Moses gives to the sons of Gad, Reuben, *and* the half tribe of Manasseh the kingdoms of Sihon, king of the Amorites, and Og, the king of Bashan, with all of its cities and territories. The first land is distributed to these families.

32:39–42 The sons of Machir, the son of Manasseh, take Gilead from the Amorites, and Moses gives the land to them. More land is being taken, and these tribes are getting settled in their new home. The problem has been averted, obedience to God's plan is still going to be carried out, and the nation is about to experience what God promised to Abraham many years ago.

33:1–4 This new generation of followers needs to be reminded that God delivered them from Egypt and will deliver them from the enemies in the promised land. Their God is dependable.

33:5–15 The beginning of the journey following their deliverance from Egypt was a time of intense testing for Israel.

33:16–36 As they travel from the desert of Sinai to Kadesh, the people are reminded of their grumbling against Moses and his leadership. It is here where the discontent of the people's hearts is put on display—and as a result they reject God's will for entering the land and suffer a great consequence for their rebellion. The children entering the land need to be reminded of this colossal failure so that they will not make the same mistake as their parents.

33:37–49 Then, in the journey from Kadesh to Moab, even the leaders of Israel sin and suffer for their sin. Miriam, Aaron, and Moses all sin and face grave consequences. None of them are allowed to enter into the promised land. Here we see that no one is exempt from following God in the manner and fashion that God determines.

33:50–56 The Lord instructs Moses to tell the people to take the land. As they take the land, they must drive the inhabitants out of the land and destroy all their false worship. If they do not do this, the current inhabitants will be a snare to the Israelites. In other words, the people who are in the land will draw them away from God.

34:2 Throughout Numbers, God has reiterated in multiple ways His promise that the people would reach Canaan (see 13:2; 14:8, 16, 23, 30; 15:2, 18; 27:12; 32:7, 9, 11). Now, the children of Israel are about to hear what portions of the land will be assigned to each tribe. This continues to affirm the certainty of this promise. God will distribute the land before they take it, because it is a sure thing that they will have the land.

34:3–12 The Israelites never occupy the entire land—they do not drive out all the inhabitants. One of the main enemies that emerges after Israel takes the land is the Philistines. They have strongholds in the western frontiers. This keeps the nation from enjoying all that God has provided for them.

34:13–29 The two and a half tribes of Gad, Reuben, and Manasseh would not be included in the apportionment of the land, since they already have their portion in the land of Gilead (also known as the Transjordan). Eleazar the priest, Joshua the son of Nun, and a chosen leader from each of the remaining nine and a half tribes divide the land for the remaining tribes.

35:1–8 The Levites are to be given a portion of each tribe's inheritance. This is because the Levites are to devote their lives to the worship of God. The Levites are not to be given just one specific area of land; instead, they are allocated forty-eight towns with pastureland around them. The surrounding land extends around the city 500 yards (1,000 cubits) and extends 1,000 yards (2,000 cubits) around the city walls.

35:9–34 Six of the Levites' forty-eight towns are to be set apart as cities of refuge, to which a person who has killed someone may go for safety. The Lord is fully aware that there will be conflict between people. Thus, if someone kills another accidentally, he may flee to this place of refuge for protection until he can stand trial for his action.

35:16–21 To ensure that everyone understands what these cities of refuge are for, God explains in these verses. A person who commits deliberate murder—if he strikes someone with an iron object, a stone, a wooden object, or his hand, by lying in wait or in enmity—is not allowed a place of refuge, but instead, the blood avenger is to put the murderer to death. If a person commits involuntary manslaughter, if he pushes his victim suddenly without enmity, throws something at him without lying in wait, or strikes him with any deadly object without being his enemy or seeking his injury, then that person is allowed to have protection until a trial can be given. Here is the way it works: If someone commits involuntary manslaughter, the congregation sends him to the city of refuge, where he is to stay until the death of the high priest. The victim's family is not allowed to hurt the person. If he leaves the city of refuge before the death of the high priest, the blood avenger is allowed to take the life of the one who committed the act.

36:2–3 In Numbers 27:1–11, there is land that is to be distributed to the daughters of Zelophehad, who had died without sons. The daughters want to know if they will get land since there are no men left in their family. God says they will. Now the question arises, what happens if these girls marry? Do they lose their land? This brought up a question about marriage and land being inherited by other families. Could one family begin to marry women in another family, and thus begin to amass a giant amount of land? It would be very natural for individuals to become self-centered and try to acquire wealth and take from others, to their own detriment.

36:5–11 God speaks to the issue of marriage within tribes to ensure that there will be fairness. People must marry within their own tribe so that the land will remain distributed in the same fashion as it was first given. No inheritance is to pass from tribe to tribe. Land ownership is something that is very important to the nation. God does not want one family member to lose out on the inheritance, and He protects each family to ensure that each generation will have what their forefathers originally received.

36:12–13 It is important to note how Numbers ends. The daughters of Zelophehad do marry within their tribe: They obey the word of the Lord. One of the great themes of the book of Numbers is the importance of obedience. God must be taken seriously, and obedience to Him must be more than a goal; it must be a lifestyle.

THE FIFTH BOOK OF MOSES, CALLED

DEUTERONOMY

INTRODUCTION TO DEUTERONOMY ■ Deuteronomy might be called the Romans of the Old Testament. It is chock-full of the great themes of scripture. It is a wonderfully down-to-earth book that provides counsel about both the large and small issues and questions of life. It addresses itself both to private matters such as the inner conflicts of the believing soul, the way of faith under trial, marriage and family, and to such public and corporate issues such as worship and the proper stewardship of the environment.

AUTHOR ■ Moses is clearly identified as the author of Deuteronomy in verse 1. Moses' authorship is claimed throughout Deuteronomy (1:5, 9; 5:1; 27:8; 29:2; 31:1, 30) as well as in other Old Testament books (1 Kings 2:3; 8:53; 2 Kings 14:6; 18:6, 12). Jesus also identified Moses as the author of Deuteronomy (Matthew 19:7–8; Mark 10:3–5; John 5:46–47), as did Peter (Acts 3:22), Stephen (Acts 7:37–38), and Paul (Romans 10:19; 1 Corinthians 9:9). The final chapter, recording Moses' death and burial (34:1–12), was most likely added by another writer after Moses' death.

OCCASION ■ The book of Deuteronomy records Moses' last words to the people of Israel as they are poised to enter the promised land after forty years of wandering in the wilderness. Moses reminds the people of all that the Lord has done for them to this point and calls them to a life of faithful obedience in the land they are about to receive.

1:1 Archaeological discoveries of international treaties have shed new light on the literary structure of the book of Deuteronomy. Ancient Middle Eastern treaties had a standard form: (1) opening preamble (paralleled in 1:1–5); (2) historical introduction (1:6–4:49); (3) particular stipulations of the treaty (chapters 5–26); (4) blessings and curses that would result from keeping or breaking the treaty (chapters 27–28; 32–33); (5) some form of oath (chapters 29–30); (6) provisions for the perpetuation of the covenant after the death of the particular kings who signed it (chapter 31). Most ancient Middle Eastern treaties were "suzerainty treaties," or treaties of sovereignty of a stronger king over a weaker one. The Lord had given Moses this covenantal revelation in the form drawn from the custom of ancient Middle Eastern diplomacy. It provides a wonderful example of God's condescension, of His employing a literary form that would have been easily appreciated and understood in Moses' day. He wanted to be understood and wanted His covenant to be kept.

1:1–5 Deuteronomy appears to be an almost perfect example of the ancient Middle Eastern treaty form. It begins, as did the treaties of that time, with a preamble, giving the geographical and historical setting.

1:9–12 The Lord had promised Abraham that his descendants would be as numerous as the stars in the sky (Genesis 15:5; 22:17; 26:4). Moses observes that this promise has come true and with it the conclusion that leading the people is more work than one man can do.

1:13–18 Moses reminds the people that they approved the appointment of leaders and agreed to be subject to their authority. Chapters 16–18 will further refine the system of leadership in Israel.

1:19–21 The account of Israel's cowardly refusal to enter the land that God had promised is an instructive beginning to the book of Deuteronomy, because it shows

that God's fundamental requirement is not obedience to the law, but faith. The event that Moses recounts had happened thirty-eight years earlier at Kadesh-barnea.

1:22–28 As Moses continues to recollect, the Lord has already given them the land, as it were, and all they have to do is walk in and take possession. But they are unnerved by the spies' reports of fortified cities and warlike people.

1:29–33 The Lord has already proved His might and His faithfulness to His people by bringing them out of Egypt and providing their food and water in the wilderness. Now they stand poised to enter the promised land, but they do not do so.

1:34–46 When the people realize that as a result of their lack of faith they will never be permitted to enter Canaan, they see the error of their ways and march across the border. The Lord does not go with them, and they are soundly thrashed by Canaanite armies and chased back into the wilderness. They gather in the camp and weep before the Lord, but He will not relent.

2:1 Moses, at the end of the forty years of desert wanderings, is recalling for the people their history. Chapter 1 ends with the Lord's decree that the generation who left Egypt will not enter the promised land of Canaan. Chapter 2 begins the saga of Israel's forty-year sojourn in the wilderness. Poised on the brink of the promised land, the Israelites now have to turn around and retrace their steps toward the Red Sea. Hidden in this narrative of Israel's travels through the wilderness from Kadesh-barnea to the river of Arnon is a lovely and profoundly important truth: The Lord shows kindness to the large part of humanity that lies beyond the boundaries of the church and His kingdom.

2:1–8 God has concern for the people living in Seir. He gives careful instructions to Israel that they are not to engage them in battle, for God has no intention of letting

Israel take the land from them. What is more, all the food and water they consume while passing through is to be paid for in cash, which they can easily afford because God has provided; they lack nothing.

2:10–12, 20–23 Historical asides about the previous inhabitants of the land remind the readers that in these cases, as in the case of Israel's conquest of Canaan, it is the Lord who drives out the nations and who gives ownership of the land.

2:24–29 Verse 24 signals a change in the way God commands Israel to deal with other nations. They *will* engage in battle, but according to God's plan. The Lord is telling them what will occur. Peace can still be genuinely offered.

2:30–37 These verses not only recount the first victory recorded in the book but also introduce some hard sayings. Verse 30 states that God hardens Sihon's heart so that he will not allow Israel to pass through his territory peacefully, because God had determined to give Sihon and his kingdom into Israel's hand. This is the only explanation given of this statement.

2:34 The word translated *destroyed* is the Hebrew term that means "to dedicate or devote something to God." Sometimes it has a positive sense—such as when objects are devoted for use in the temple and its worship—but more often it refers to the compulsory devotion of something that impedes or hinders God's work. In that case, the object is devoted to utter destruction. God had already given the nations ample time to repent.

3:1 This chapter continues the historical prologue that precedes the covenant laws and decrees that make up the bulk of Deuteronomy. The Israelites' desert wanderings have come to an end, and they are engaged in the business of conquering and claiming the land.

3:2 It is essential for a true estimation and appreciation of this history to realize that the destruction of Bashan (3:1–11) is, in fact, God's judgment and God's doing. Israel is His instrument. This point is made here, where it is clear that, in the campaign against Og, Moses and Israel are acting on orders given them by God. It isn't Moses' idea to destroy the women and children; it is a direct order from the Lord Himself. In respect to both the specific instructions Moses is given and the general instructions God gave Israel for waging wars, Israel does precisely as they are told by the Lord God when they exterminate the population of Bashan.

3:6 The word rendered *destroyed* is in fact a technical term and means, more precisely, "devoted"—separated for a holy use. It is true that these people were devoted to destruction, but they were destroyed precisely to further the interests of the kingdom of God. They are destroyed because they stand in the way of God's good purpose. That is the sense of the word *destroyed*, which is also used in much more positive ways to refer to things that are consecrated to the service of God.

3:12–17 The accounts of Israel's history that precede the law-giving conclude with a summary of the allotment of land Israel had conquered up to this point. All the land

that had been taken was east of the Jordan; Israel had not yet crossed into Canaan proper. Only the tribes of Reuben and Gad and the half tribe of Manasseh receive land east of the Jordan—perhaps because they had a lot of livestock (3:19) and needed a large range for them.

3:18–23 These verses detail the responsibilities of the tribes that live east of the Jordan to the rest of Israel. They are to accompany the other tribes across the Jordan and fight alongside them. Only after all the tribes have received their territories may any man settle down in his new home.

3:24–29 We have in these verses one of the most striking and important examples of God saying no to the prayer of one of His children. Moses' prayer recorded here, asking God to relent and allow him to set foot in the promised land, is apparently not his first. During the months, perhaps years, that had passed from Moses' striking the rock (see Numbers 20:1–13) to this point, with Israel poised on the east side of the Jordan, ready at last to enter Canaan, Moses apparently had pled often with the Lord. That is the suggestion of Deuteronomy 3:26.

4:1–8 The first three chapters of Deuteronomy recall God's faithfulness and power. Now Moses begins to lay out the commandments that God calls Israel to obey in response to what He has already done. Before setting out any specific laws, Moses speaks more generally about the importance of obedience. The obedience that Israel is here summoned to give to God is not for the purpose of making them God's children; it is not for earning salvation. This obedience they owe to God *because* God has saved them and because they are already His children. Throughout the chapter, beginning with verse 2, the law is referred to as "the commandments of the Lord your God." The Israelites are already God's people.

4:5–8 Living by the commandments of God will make this people wise and understanding, so wise as to be the envy of their neighbors. The law is God's good gift and blessing to His people, demonstrating His nearness and involvement in their lives.

4:9 Just as the Lord is the God of Israel's forefathers, He is the God of the generations yet to come as well. This generation is to teach God's law to their children.

4:10–13 There is a significant difference between obeying commandments to earn God's approval and acceptance and obeying commandments because one has already been graciously given God's approval and acceptance. The latter is the case here, very clearly. Israel does not receive the law of God at mount Sinai until after they are delivered from their bondage in Egypt. Salvation comes first, then obedience; grace first, then the believer's grateful response to God's goodness.

4:14 God's law is not some set of unreasonable and onerous requirements that God imposes simply to test His people's loyalty or fortitude. God's law is His wisdom, His instructions for how human life should be lived if it is to be lived right. It is God's fatherly counsel to His children so that they might live happily, fruitfully, and safely in the land He is giving them.

4:15–23 There is no particular reason why Israel should be so captivated by graven images (idols), but Moses here clearly regards this as the standing danger of the people's religious life. God has never appeared to His people in a form that they could pattern an idol after. They had never seen God—a point Moses reminds them of. They are not to make or worship an image of any shape—not images of humans, birds, animals, or fish. Nor are they to worship any object of God's making, such as the sun, moon, and stars. As Moses points out, having delivered them from bondage in Egypt as He did, God has every right to demand that He be worshipped by His people in the way that He deems right and proper.

4:19 The peoples of the ancient Middle Eastern world made and worshipped graven images (idols) of every kind. Gods and goddesses were represented as animals—fish, bulls, calves, and the like—or as human beings in figurine form, or as poles and pillars. What is more, they not only worshipped gods through images that represented them, but also actually considered heavenly bodies as gods themselves. Idolatry was a universal institution and a part of the fabric of life for all of these people, save one: Israel.

4:24–28 Moses warns Israel not to forget what kind of God the living and true God is: invisible, immortal, transcendent in glory, infinite in power and might. All idolatry thus becomes both dangerous and utterly foolish. It will bring God's punishments instead of His blessings—for Israel it means that they will lose the promised land—and it will turn the idolaters into fools who spend their lives chasing after the ridiculous. That is the dripping irony of verse 28.

4:29–31 The warning of verses 24–28 is not without hope. Those who look for the true God will find Him.

4:32–40 Here we have the climactic conclusion of the historical prologue and some of the most beautiful prose in the book of Deuteronomy. The elevated style is the result of the subject matter: the glorious works of Almighty God.

4:36 The instruction mentioned here is that of a father instructing his child. (This is made explicit in 8:5.) God has established a parent-child relationship between Himself and His people.

4:37–40 Moses here speaks to the people as if they were personally present at the Exodus and mount Sinai, even though many of them clearly had not been. The oldest among those to whom Moses is speaking had been children during those days of the deliverance from Egypt and the two years at Sinai, but many more would have been born in the years since Israel left Sinai and began their wanderings in the wilderness. Moses has a very practical purpose in speaking this way to his contemporaries. Reminding them of their history, he expects them (and us) to live according to it. He wants them to consider the past, take it seriously, and draw from it courage to face the challenges of life in the promised land. He desires his listeners to fear God and develop a solemn determination to keep His

commandments, to be ever thankful and hopeful, and to possess a sense of great obligation to pass this history on to future generations.

4:41–43 At the conclusion of this historical prologue, Moses tends to some logistical details for the tribes receiving territories east of the Jordan. He establishes cities of refuge, one for each tribe.

5:1 The book of Deuteronomy follows the pattern of ancient Middle Eastern treaties. The preamble in 1:1–5 gives the historical and geographical setting. The historical prologue in 1:6–4:49 comprises a lengthy review of God's dealings with Israel and serves to provide a rationale for obedience. In chapter 5, we begin the particular stipulations of the covenant: the commandments that occupy the largest part of the book.

5:1–5 Moses addresses the people as if the Ten Commandments have been given directly to them, rather than to the generation before ("The LORD our God made a covenant with us in Horeb"; He "talked with you face to face in the mount." And "*ye* were afraid by reason of the fire.") In the statement recorded in verse 3, Moses seems to draw special attention to this foreshortening of history by saying that God made His covenant at Sinai not with the people who were present there at the time, but with those who would come after them.

5:6–21 The Ten Commandments are a summary of the entire law of God. All the rest of the commandments in God's Word are applications or elaborations of these fundamental duties. Their character as a general summary is further indicated by the fact that both in the Old and the New Testaments these ten can be further summarized by only two commandments: to love God with all your heart and soul and to love your neighbor as yourself (see, for example, Deuteronomy 6:5; Luke 10:27).

5:28–29 Some of this fear is clearly the result of the people's faithlessness. They did not have a true and living trust in God; they feared God for His justice and His wrath and His power. But that is not the whole explanation. God does not dispute the request the people make of Moses. Indeed, He commends it, and then He goes on to say that His people will always fear Him as they feared at Sinai. It is only through this fear that they will be blessed and things will go well with them and their children forever. The fear of God spoken of here could be defined as an apprehension of the true majesty and glory of God. It is the awe one should have in the presence of God's greatness and wonder; it is high reverence, which is appropriate to creatures before their Creator, finite persons before the infinite and almighty God.

5:30–33 If God's people truly fear Him as they should, that fear will bring them blessing and prosperity. Nothing leads to obedience more certainly than a true reverence for God, than some sense of His majesty, His immensity. Before such a God, a God who sits enthroned in the heavens, any and all disobedience seems absurd, irrational, and unquestionably wicked. Sin is not likely to find much welcome in a soul often overwhelmed with God's sublime splendor.

6:1 Deuteronomy 5 looked to the previous generation and emphasized how essential it was for the current generation to embrace as their own the covenant made with their parents and grandparents. Deuteronomy 6 takes a forward view to the next generation. In it we read of God's exhortations for parents to nurture their children in the faith of the covenant God.

6:1–3 After exhorting the people to fear the Lord as had the generation at Sinai (5:29), Moses extends that charge—and the promised blessings—to their children and the children after them.

6:4–7 Two essentials form the core of what each generation must know: the truth about who God is and how the people are to relate to Him. This covenant succession from parents to children is too important to be left to chance. Parents must be intentional and passionate about passing on the faith.

6:7–10 The Word of God is never to be far from their lips and should often be popping into the conversation that fathers and mothers have with their children. What are the commandments that parents are to impress upon the hearts of their children? They are the commandments we read in verse 5, which are summed up in this: that they are to love God with absolutely everything they have.

6:10–19 Children cannot follow where their parents do not lead. So parents are called upon to maintain their own close walk with God. In prosperity, they must not let materialism crowd out God. In a secular culture, they must not follow the crowd. In times of deprivation, they must not succumb to ingratitude. At all times, they are to do what is right and trust the Lord with the consequences.

7:1 God drives out the nations so that Israel may possess the land. Here we find a strong statement of the principle of sovereign and electing grace. Out of all the peoples of the world, God chose Israel to be His own people. He chose them, not because they deserved His favor—they most certainly did not—but entirely and mysteriously because He loved them. As the apostle Paul would later put it: "So then it is not of him that willeth, nor of him that runneth, but of God that sheweth mercy" (Romans 9:16).

7:1–10 Election is given a double aspect here in Deuteronomy 7. If it is true that God has chosen Israel, it is also true that He has not chosen the other nations. God makes this distinction between sinful and unworthy people, to call some to Him and to leave others unsummoned. The election of Israel as a people was the first step in that process by which God set apart to Himself those who would be saved. It is His gracious choice in each case, not human action or merit, that is the final explanation for anyone's salvation.

7:11 Moses' point is not merely that God has chosen His people but that they should be deeply grateful for the salvation they do not deserve but have been given as a gift, and that in their gratitude they ought to seek the Lord's pleasure by keeping His commands.

7:12–15 Here we read the remarkable promise of blessing that the Lord makes to His people if they walk faithfully and obediently before Him. If they are faithful to

His covenant, He will make their lives rich and happy in every way. They will enjoy good health. Their farms will prosper and they will become very successful, while all their enemies will suffer ruin. It is a dramatic passage in its extravagance and in the absence of all qualification or limitation.

7:16–26 Here we read the flip side of the promises in verses 12–15: Not only will God's faithful people prosper, but the wicked nations around them will suffer defeat at their hands. This defeat is also a part of Israel's faithfulness: God's people are to destroy the graven images (idols) in Canaan so that they will not be tempted into idolatry. Those who are not faithful in rejecting these rival "gods" will not receive the promises of the faithful, but rather destruction.

8:1 In this chapter of Deuteronomy, Moses warns the people of God of the ease with which they can forget the Lord and His great kindnesses to them. He urges them to be careful not to do so, but to remember the Lord and all that He has done.

8:2–5 This generation has much to remember. They have just finished long years in the wilderness, which were necessary, after all, only because their parents had rebelled against the Lord and faithlessly refused to trust His promise to bring them into Canaan in triumph, even though He had brought them so miraculously and triumphantly out of bondage in Egypt. They should also remember how often they had tested the Lord and complained against Him and how, nevertheless, He patiently and generously met their needs with manna, clothing, and fatherly discipline.

8:6–14 The appropriate response to what God has done, Moses points out, is to obey Him, walk with Him, and give reverence to Him. And God's blessings are not simply part of Israel's history; at that moment God was in the process of bringing Israel into a good land of their own. The blessings of prosperity, it seems, come with their own temptations: to become proud and forget God.

8:15–18 To emphasize his point, Moses again reiterates what God has done and that which Israel is to remember. How true all of God's promises had proven themselves to be; how safely Israel had lived according to the Word of God. It was not by their own skill or effort or endurance that they had managed those long years in the desert, but by the goodness and provision of God. All of this was fresh in their minds as they sat poised on the eastern bank of the Jordan, ready to cross and possess the promised land.

8:19–20 If you are going to live a faithful life, Moses tells the Israelites, then make a determined and heartfelt effort to keep God's commandments, for love's sake. The kind of remembering Moses is speaking of here is that which stirs the heart, breaks pride and willfulness, and awakens faith, hope, and love.

9:1–3 Moses again assures the people that they will be successful in conquering the land—successful even against the fearsome Anakims. And he reminds them yet again that their success will be a result not of their own strength but of the Lord's power and faithfulness.

9:4–6 Moses clearly states, not once, but twice, that God's driving out of the nations is not because of Israel's righteousness, but because of the nations' wickedness and because of God's faithfulness to His covenant promises. This ought to be a cause of humility for the Israelites, but Moses recognizes that Israel may turn it into a source of pride. The fact is, they, too, are guilty of the sins of their parents. Their parents were unworthy of the promised land, but the current generation is as well. They, too, are stubborn people, always saying and doing things that offend the Lord. And here the Lord is reminding them, in the most emphatic way, that the land He is about to give them they do not deserve.

9:7–21 In chapter 8, we read the charge to remember what God has done. Now the charge is to remember what Israel has done. It is not a list to be proud of. At the very moment that God is carving His covenant with Israel into stone, Israel is making a golden statue and calling it the God who had led them out of Egypt. The full account of the golden calf is in Exodus 32.

9:22 Moses lists three other places where the people had angered the Lord: Taberah, Massah, and Kibroth-hattaavah. In each of these places, the people doubted God's provision and complained about what He did provide. At Taberah, the people's complaints angered the Lord so much that He sent fire to burn the outskirts of the camp (Numbers 11:1–3). Massah is the place where the people claimed that Moses (and, by implication, God) had led them into the desert to die of thirst (Exodus 17). Kibroth-hattaavah was the place where the people complained that they were sick of manna and whined that the food had been better in Egypt (Numbers 11:4–35).

9:23–29 Moses reminds the people of the sin that led to forty years of desert wandering: the refusal to enter the promised land because their fear of the Canaanites was greater than their trust in the Lord. They escaped destruction, Moses explains, only because God was faithful to His promises to Abraham, Isaac, and Jacob. Again, the message is that the gift of the promised land is because God is faithful, not because Israel is deserving.

9:28–29 Interestingly, all of the examples Moses uses in this chapter, demonstrating how unworthy the Israelites are of the gift they are about to receive, are from the life of the previous generation, not this generation about to cross into the promised land. Those who aroused the Lord's anger at mount Sinai, who cavorted before the golden calf, and who later rebelled at Kadesh-barnea—they all lie dead and buried back in the wilderness. They had forfeited the promised land by their faithlessness. But, with that sense of family solidarity that is so common to the Bible, the present generation is addressed as if they, too, had been at Horeb, they, too, had worshipped the golden calf, they, too, had participated in the cowardly refusal to enter the promised land at Kadesh-barnea.

10:1–5 These verses continue the account of what happened immediately after Israel's blatant unfaithfulness when they made the golden calf. Israel had broken covenant with God when they made that calf, and any

other treaty-maker would have considered that covenant over. But God does not turn away; instead, He rewrites the very same words of the covenant treaty that He had written on the stone tablets that Moses had broken. God gives the people another chance—exactly the same opportunity He had given them before they turned to idolatry, just as if they had never betrayed Him.

10:6–9 Here is a parenthetical summary not only of the people's travels but of the development of the priesthood. Aaron, the original priest, dies, and the Lord sets apart the tribe of Levi to serve as priests. The Levites would inherit no land. Their needs were provided for in the stipulations about offerings (see Leviticus 6:18; 7:28–36).

10:16 Circumcision was the original sign of God's covenant with Abraham and Abraham's descendants (Genesis 17). It was an outward, physical sign, but the command in Deuteronomy to circumcise one's heart indicates that circumcision was always intended to reflect an internal reality, not merely external obedience. Moses seems to be saying that it is the heart that matters, and there will never be true loyalty to God and faithfulness to His covenant unless they come from the heart.

11:1 It is imperative that the Israelites understand that the key to staying in the land is to obey God. All obedience to God starts with love. A person who does not love God cannot obey God. For this reason, Moses reiterates the call to love. Everything that happened in the history of Israel had been for the purpose of motivating the people to love God with their whole hearts. For this reason, they are called to love God.

11:2–7 Moses urges the people to remember all that God has done for them. He rescued them, provided for them, and disciplined them so that they would grow in their obedience to Him. The call to love is grounded in the love that God had given to them.

11:10–12 Mentioning the contrasts between the promised land and Egypt was no doubt prompted by those who wanted to return there, as Dathan and Abiram had (11:6). The land of Canaan had far more potential than Egypt ever had. What God provided clearly exceeded what Egypt offered. The people in Egypt had to depend on irrigation; God's people would have rain from heaven. Unlike human irrigation, rain is in the complete control of God. Thus, God is again showing the people that He will care for them and give them what they need to survive.

11:16 Because of the importance of obedience and the seduction of false religion, Moses again warns Israel against worshipping other gods. Many of the gods worshipped in Canaan were fertility gods (gods of grain, oil, rain, etc.).

11:17 If the people transfer their trust for the prosperity of their land to one or more of these false gods, the Lord will withdraw His gifts of rain and produce.

11:25 God will put terror and fear in their enemies so that they are not able to fight successfully against Israel. God will deliver this nation and provide for the people in extraordinary ways.

11:26–32 The Lord clearly set before the people the simple reality for obedience: If you obey, you will be blessed; if you disobey, you will be cursed. Longevity, prosperity, and security are based not on following pagan practice but on loving God and following Him all the days of their lives. A formal proclamation of blessings and curses will reemphasize this truth once the people enter the land. (The blessings and curses proclaimed from mount Ebel are recorded in 27:9–26.)

12:1 This chapter opens the next major section of Deuteronomy. The first four chapters are a historical introduction, or prologue, an account of the previous relationship between the Lord and His people Israel. Chapters 5–11 set out the general commandments or stipulations of the covenant with repeated exhortations to Israel to keep the covenant that God had made with them. Chapter 12 begins the third and longest section of the book, stretching from 12:1 to 26:15. These chapters contain the specific stipulations, or legislation, covering matters as diverse as worship and the management of criminal cases in court.

12:2–4 Pluralism and religious tolerance are not to be a part of Israel's experience. The people are not only to avoid pagan forms of worship; they are to destroy both the places of worship and the instruments used in that worship. This introductory section concludes with the summary prohibition in verse 4.

12:3 The pillars referred to are stone monuments used in Canaanite worship, probably engraved to represent Canaanite gods. Groves were wooden poles set up to honor Asherah, the Canaanite goddess of love and war.

12:5–28 This passage contains regulations governing the right worship of God. Worship must be offered according to the directions and the specifications of God's law. The Holy Spirit, through Moses, insists that worship be joyful, but He is still more insistent that Israel's worship of God be offered according to the many laws and regulations that have been laid down. They may not worship in various places as the pagans do, but only where God says. They must worship the Lord in the specific ways they have been taught, with certain kinds of offerings and gifts to be given in a certain way. More regulations follow regarding sacrificial meals and the proper way they are to be taken.

12:32 These warnings are all brought to a conclusion, where the Lord says again that Israel is to worship Him only as He has taught them.

13:1 This chapter continues the warnings about worshiping other gods. Here, however, the source of temptation is not the Canaanites, as in chapter 12, but rather people among the Israelites themselves.

13:1–5 The Israelites are warned that their own prophets may undermine the truth and that Israel must stand ready to oppose even those with authority and reputation if they contradict the Word of God. The remarkable warning in verse 2, that false teachers may be able to work miraculous signs, reminds us that Moses is writing in an age of miracles—even Egyptian magicians

had performed at least one miracle. It is a further demonstration of the general fact that falsehood will always have its powerful inducements and arguments.

13:12–18 Moses warns that in the towns especially there may be a general revolt that takes place against the Word and law of God as fashions and tastes change from time to time. One commentator speaks of "urban revolutionaries," but he is probably referring to people with modern ideas who appear in every generation, arguing that in one way or another the Word of God is out of date and needs revision. If the Israelites catch even a whiff of the scent of such infidelity, they are to take immediate action to find out whether the rumors and reports have substance. They are not to wait to see if heresy comes to full flower; they are to make every effort to locate it and nip it in the bud.

14:1–20 There is much that remains obscure in these particular laws distinguishing between clean and unclean animals recorded here. In fact, the identity of some of the animals named in the verses is not certain. But, more important, the principle of why one animal is clean and another unclean is also by no means certain.

14:21 These laws bring the demands of divine holiness into every aspect of a faithful Israelite's life. At every turn, he or she is faced with the demand that God's people be holy because God is holy and in their midst. God's holiness is to prevail also at their tables and at the taking of meals; they are the people of God, and in their eating and drinking, as in every other part of their lives, they are to be holy as their God is holy. The family could not sit down to a meal without the requirements of their heavenly Father's holiness impinging upon them. In this way, Israel is constantly impressed with the need to be fit for God's service, fit to approach Him, fit to worship Him, and fit to reflect something of His glory in the world.

14:22–26 The Israelites are required by the law of God to tithe. As verse 23 makes clear, they are to tithe not only from their harvested crops, but also from their livestock. One-tenth had to be given as an actual gift to the Lord (Leviticus 27:13). The tithe also provides for worship for the entire household. The sanctuary meal would have been one of the great occasions of the year for an Israelite family, and their tithe is put against the cost of the meal. Moses spells out the lesson of the tithe in verse 23. God's people are to tithe in order to learn to fear Him.

14:29 Regular tithing is God's appointed way to drive home to His people that their prosperity does not depend, as appearances might suggest, on the bounty of the land or their own skill as farmers and herdsmen, but upon the blessing and the provision of their heavenly Father. The people, with their produce and income, give back a portion to the One who has given it all to them in the first place; year after year they must reckon with the fact that everything they have is a gift from God.

15:1–2 God weaves mercy into the fabric of Israel's life by commanding that debts be canceled every seven years. Opinions vary as to whether the entire debt was to be permanently terminated, or whether payments were only suspended for the seventh year. The latter is more probable, and this provision has to do with the fact that, according to the Law of Moses, in that same seventh year the land was to lie fallow. Many poor people, without the income of the land, would be unable to make payments on their debt and would therefore experience even greater hardship, such as being forced into servanthood, which is discussed in verses 12–18.

15:12–18 The servanthood referred to here could as easily be called slavery. Unlike slavery as we think of it today, this form of slavery provided a solution to the person who could no longer support himself. He could sell himself with the assurance that his servitude was only temporary and that he would not go away empty-handed when his time of service ended. Lest the wealthy think this freeing of servants is too much to ask, God reminds them that they were slaves in Egypt and were given their freedom by God. God's lavish love for them has become the pattern of their lives; loving God and wanting to honor Him, they seek to imitate Him in the extravagance of love.

15:16 A servant can choose to forgo emancipation and remain in service to his master. David later describes the custom of piercing a servant's earlobe to show his willingness to serve God (Psalm 40:6), and the writer of Hebrews quotes David when describing Jesus' willingness to become a servant (Hebrews 10:5–10).

15:19–23 These verses briefly touch on setting aside the firstborn animals for the Lord. Like the tithed animals (14:22–29), these animals belong to the Lord and may be eaten only by those who offer them. This section, along with the section on tithing in chapter 14, frames the instructions on debts and servants, putting concern for the impoverished in the context of what is owed to God.

16:1 The chapter gives only a summary statement on the three great yearly feasts of the Israelite calendar. More complete legislation is found in Exodus 12; 23:14–17; Leviticus 23; and Numbers 28:16–31.

16:1–4 The month of Abib is later called *Nisan*. On today's Jewish calendar, it marks the beginning of the religious year. The festival of passover celebrates the Lord's passing over the homes of believing Israelites in Egypt.

16:5–8 While only the adult males are required to attend the passover ritual at the central tabernacle, and later the temple in Jerusalem, all Israelite families participate in their homes, starting in the evening as on the first passover. The tents to which the men are to return are their temporary lodgings at the sanctuary where they stay for the six days of the festival.

16:9–12 The feast of weeks is so called because it begins seven weeks after the offering of a sheaf of new grain. The date is given more precisely in Leviticus 23:15–16 as fifty days after the beginning of passover, which is the reason the festival is also called Pentecost (*pente* means "fifty"). In Exodus and Numbers, it is also called harvest and firstfruits, because the freewill offering comes from the first produce of the harvest. The celebration includes a trip to Jerusalem and the temple,

wonderful food, grand ceremonies, and no normal labor, allowing free time for sightseeing and recreation—and all of it is made more special because of the sacred and holy connotations of the festival itself.

16:13–17 The feast of tabernacles is celebrated at the autumn harvest of produce (grapes, olives, dates, figs). In Exodus it is also called the feast of harvest. Part of the festival involves camping out for the week, living in booths as a reminder of their camping in the wilderness following the Exodus from Egypt. Every Israelite man is required to celebrate these three feasts every year (16:16). Giving to God (via the tabernacle or temple offerings) is an essential part of all three festivals.

16:18–20 Each town has its own legal system, though there is also a central, or national, system. The officers referred to here likely hold a role similar to that of police officers (their appointment was described in Deuteronomy 1:9–18). Judges and officers must rule according to the will of God. They are to enact justice—which means to enforce the laws and commandments of God and those only. If by the faithful exercise of their office the judges ensure that God's people are living according to God's Word, the people of God will live and prosper in the land.

17:8–11 It isn't at all hard to imagine what the difficulties in judgment might be, for they were the same as we face today. Difficulties arise when courts are faced with a set of complex circumstances that the law doesn't precisely address. Such cases are to be submitted to priests for judgment. The priest's comprehensive knowledge of the scripture helps ensure that the judgment rendered is in keeping with God's Word. No doubt, after a time, a body of precedents will be compiled to aid judges in adjudicating cases, just as in modern times.

17:12 The point is made again that priests and judges are ministers of the Lord. A minister is one who does not act for himself or in his own name but carries the authority of another and speaks and acts in His name and with His authority.

17:14–18 This is a highly interesting passage of scripture for the way in which it places together the three great offices of the Old Testament religious structure. God communicates His presence directly to the hearts of His people by His Spirit, and He also uses people as instruments of His presence. He speaks to His people through prophets, He grants forgiveness of sins and maintains fellowship with them through priests, and He rules over them through kings.

17:14–20 The instructions here assume that in the future Israel will want a king. In these guidelines, God is not *recommending* that Israel have a king but rather *allowing* them to have one.

18:1 Every man in the tribe of Levi is part of the priesthood. Rather than working the land, they are to offer sacrifices on behalf of the people.

18:2–8 Since their work does not produce a livelihood, the Levites are to be supported by the rest of the people. Like the judges, courts, and king, priests exercise their office for the Lord's sake and in His name.

18:9 Between sections devoted to Israel's priesthood and prophecy, several verses forbid them to recognize or make any use of the priestly and prophetic practices of Canaan.

18:10–14 God forbids sacrifices offered to false gods, and here He specifically forbids human sacrifice as well. Divination, interpreting omens, and consulting the dead are ways of trying to predict the future or discover things through human intervention rather than through God's divine intervention through His prophet. The Israelites are to separate themselves from these practices.

18:15–22 Moses promises that God will raise up a Prophet like him. A prophet's job is to deliver God's messages to God's people. Moses reminds Israel that he fulfilled this prophetic role at Horeb. Prophecy that is proven wrong or that conflicts with God's Word is evidence of a false prophet. Peter (in Acts 3:22–23) quotes this verse about the Prophet to come. He says Jesus is a prophet like Moses but greater than Moses.

19:1 The apparent subject of the chapter is the laws governing murder and its punishment. But really the subject of the chapter is the purpose of all of these laws, which is stated in Deuteronomy 19:10—that innocent blood not be shed in the land. This is the purpose of all that we read in this chapter.

19:1–7 In addition to the three cities already set aside east of the Jordan mentioned in Deuteronomy 4:41–43, the people are to establish three cities on the west of the Jordan. This is an expansion of the law of Exodus 21:12–14, according to which the altar is a sanctuary, or asylum, for someone who has accidentally killed another. There he cannot be molested by anyone bent on vengeance. But when Israel enters the land, the altar is too far away, and a person fleeing to it might not reach it before being overtaken by the avenger of blood. Hence three centrally located cities.

19:10 The purpose of these cities of refuge is that no innocent blood is shed. Executing an innocent man is equivalent to murder, making the community as a whole guilty of bloodshed.

19:11–13 Another way that innocent blood might be shed is to let a murderer go unpunished. If executing an innocent man is a crime to be avoided at all costs, so is the failure to punish a murderer by execution. Failure in that case also renders the community guilty of bloodshed.

19:14 A "landmark" marks the edge of a person's property. To move it is essentially to rob a person of that portion of land.

19:15 Trials are to be conducted in every case. One witness, even an eyewitness, is not sufficient to prove the guilt of an accused murderer. There must be two or three, which is a cryptic way of saying that the evidence must be incontestable. The scripture clearly entertains the possibility that guilty men might go free for want of adequate evidence.

19:16–19 Witnesses are sworn to the truth upon the most serious penalty should they be found to have perjured themselves. If a witness's lie results in the condemning of an innocent man to death, the witness is executed.

19:21 The principle of justice by equity is stated here. Punishments are to be, as far as possible, the exact equivalent of the crime. An eye for an eye, a hand for a hand, and a life for a life means that justice requires that a murderer forfeit his own life. Anything less or more is not retribution in proportion to the crime. Other ancient Near Eastern law codes (famously, the Code of Hammurabi) sometimes insisted on excessive punishments, so the guidelines here function to guard against that excess.

20:1 Here begins a section of the book of Deuteronomy devoted to particular laws addressing many different issues. In certain cases, they reiterate points that have already been made in previous chapters. This chapter, for example, recapitulates some of what was already stated in chapter 7: laws governing the conduct of war.

20:2–4 Israel's strength lay not in the size or equipment of their army, but in their God, and this is a matter not only of faith but of their own experience. Egypt has a far greater army than the ill-equipped and untrained Israelite people, but it is the vaunted army of Egypt that is destroyed in the Red Sea. Before the battle, the priest is to remind the soldiers of the fact that God is worth many armies.

20:5–8 The officers mentioned in verse 5 probably refer to officials of the tribes of Israel, not to army officers, as is confirmed in verse 9. These men, knowing their tribe, would know which ones qualify to be exempted from service. God thinks it important to ensure that no man dying in battle should be deprived of the pleasure of seeing his new vineyard begin to bear fruit, and that no young man miss the joy of marrying his bride. God doesn't require the same thing of the fainthearted that He does of the brave.

20:9 It is clear that Israel, at least at this early stage, does not maintain a standing army or has very little of one. For each war, the army has to be recruited separately.

20:10–15 It is often overlooked that outside of the promised land, God commands that the Israelites offer peace before attacking cities. Only if the rulers of the city reject the offer of peace are the Israelites to attack. Even then, the women and children are to be spared. Deuteronomy 15 outlines rights of the captives and provisions for incorporating them into the Israelite community.

20:16–18 The rules for attacking the neighboring cities are given here. The laws laid out in Deuteronomy 7:1–6 are summarized here, along with the reason for them: to keep Israel from being led astray.

20:19–20 Ancient military powers often destroyed everything they found on the land they conquered. But God's covenant with Noah extends to the earth as well; the trees are not to be destroyed. This provision allows the land to remain productive.

21:1 The point of mentioning a field in the land from God is that a person murdered in the promised land is killed on sacred soil. For this reason, the sin is elevated—it isn't just a sin against this person who dies and his family but also a sin against God because it desecrates His land.

21:5 The priests, chosen by the Lord not only to offer sacrifices and pronounce blessings but also to function in judicial capacities (see 17:9; 19:17), assume a role in the proceedings. Since the murderer is unknown, it is the guilt or innocence of the community at large that is at stake. The entire point of this ritual is to make the community clean.

21:6–9 The town elders, on behalf of all the people, are to symbolize the innocence of the community by washing their hands over the carcass of the heifer, state their collective innocence of the deed, plead with the Lord to accept their act of exculpation, and absolve them of any blame for the death of the victim.

21:10–14 A bride taken as a captive is to shave her head, trim her nails, discard her native clothing, and fulfill a month of mourning for her parents before becoming a wife of an Israelite. All these procedures represent cutting off all ties to the former life. It is important that the bride enter into her new life fully and unreservedly.

21:15–16 A husband's attitude toward his wife is not to affect his legal responsibilities to her and her children. If he has two wives and the one he does not love gives him the firstborn male, he cannot favor the firstborn son of the wife he does love. The matter of law that is pertinent here is the proper bestowal of inheritance rights.

21:17 On the basis of what appears to be a long-standing custom, the eldest son is to receive a double portion of his father's estate. This is a stipulation first recorded here in biblical law. The motive for this regulation is clearly articulated: The firstborn is the first sign of his father's strength. What this means is that a man first gives indication of his virility and capacity to sire succeeding generations when his first son is born (see Genesis 49:3; Psalm 105:36). It is only fitting that the son who gives the father such recognition be recognized himself for what he symbolizes. Therefore, the rights of the firstborn are based not on feelings or relationships but on what the firstborn son represents.

21:18–20 Specifically, the charge is that a child who is stubborn-minded against his father and mother is disobeying the fifth commandment ("to honour thy father and thy mother," Deuteronomy 5:16). This rebellious son is to be brought to the gate, that is, the broad plaza just outside the gate where matters of public interest are conducted. The court before which the case is presented consists of elders, not those of a district or the whole nation but the rulers of the local village.

21:21 Once the case is heard and the elders judge the child to be guilty as charged, the townsmen execute the felon by stoning. Only by this drastic means can the evil be purged from the community. Since this child proves to be nothing more than a plague on the society, he has to be removed. This is the last step in dealing with a child's rebellion—not the first step.

22:1–4 The brother referred to in verse 1 is related not by blood but by membership in the same spiritual

community. There is to be no "finders, keepers" among brothers; possession is not nine-tenths of the law.

22:5 The command about clothing is not a statement about fashion so much as it is about real confusion of genders, specifically transvestism. Some suggest this command is related to pagan practices in the nations around Israel at that time.

22:6–7 The instruction to leave a dam (mother bird) on the nest is a law of conservation. The potential for future supply is not to be destroyed for the sake of immediate gain. Only if the Israelites take care of the resources around them will it be well with them.

22:8 Roofs were flat and used for sleeping in the summer, for certain chores, and for entertaining, so it is not inconceivable that someone could fall off an unfenced roof. Protecting people from this danger is the homeowner's responsibility.

22:13–22 If a man slanderously accuses his wife of not being a virgin when they married, her parents can bring proof of her virginity to the city elders, who will require the husband to pay a fine to the girl's father and deny the right to divorce. Should the charge be true, however, the woman will be stoned. Note that the men of the village, not just the husband, carry out the execution, indicating that the sin affects the entire community.

22:23–27 The laws about sex between single, unmarried people take into account a number of factors. First, the offense is more serious if the woman is engaged to another man. If the liaison took place in the city, both the offending man and the woman are considered equally deserving of execution, on the assumption that the sex was consensual (if the woman had cried for help in a city, someone would have heard and rescued her). She could not get away with falsely accusing her lover of rape. In the field (or country), however, the woman is given the benefit of the doubt; she may have resisted without anyone being close enough to hear her. In this case, only the rapist receives the death penalty.

22:28 A man who raped a woman who was not engaged did not receive the death penalty, but he was responsible both to marry the woman and to pay a bride-price to her father (Exodus 22:16–17; Deuteronomy 21:29).

23:2 This verse can be translated to exclude either those born of a forbidden marriage or those of illegitimate birth. In either case, it refers to a child of an incestuous relationship, a child born out of pagan worship, or a child born outside of marriage. Such a child comes from that which is an affront to God's laws and is thus not allowed at the ceremonies.

23:3–6 The Ammonites and Moabites are not allowed to join the worship of Israel because they refused to provide bread and water to the Israelites as they were moving toward the promised land.

23:7–8 Edomites are considered the Israelites' brothers because they descended from Esau, the brother of Jacob.

23:9–14 God wants the army to remember that He is the One who fought for them, and He is in their presence. With this in mind, they must not be trite about the way they handle their human waste. If a man has nocturnal emissions, out of respect for God, he is required to stay outside the camp until he has bathed himself. This way the camp of the Lord remains clean—both for health reasons and also so that the people will remember that God must always be treated with respect and dignity.

23:15 The servants referred to in this verse are not Israelites. In most Middle Eastern treaties there is a provision that servants (or slaves) seeking refuge are to be returned to their owners. But Israel is not to have allegiances to other nations.

23:17–18 Another way that Israel is to be different is in the way that they reject the practice of temple prostitution. This practice was common in the Near East. God rejects this type of religious practice because it degrades sex and it degrades holy worship. In addition to temple prostitution, the nation is not to practice prostitution at all. The money that is gained from this practice is degraded money, and therefore a vow is not to be paid with money obtained in this manner.

23:19–20 The context of this law is of a brother who has become poor or is in severe need (see Exodus 22:25; Leviticus 25:35–37); he is not borrowing money to engage in a capitalistic endeavor. The point is that to charge a poor brother usury (interest) will only worsen his condition. Mercy, kindness, and grace are all virtues that must mark this nation.

23:21–23 In this law, God wants the Israelites to make sure that when they speak, they speak with honesty and integrity. The vow is a commitment that is not forced upon anyone—it is made out of the volition of the person. Yet once it is made, it is to be kept without question.

24:1–4 The Old Testament always regards divorce as a tragedy (see Malachi 2:16). The commands here, then, are given to regulate an already existing practice rather than introducing a new idea. The precise meaning of the word *uncleanness* is not known.

24:6 Millstones were used daily in homes to grind grain in preparing meals. To take both or one of these as collateral for a debt would deprive a man of his daily bread and therefore contradict the spirit of generosity. Thus, when a loan is made, collateral should never be something that will hurt someone.

24:7 The crime of kidnapping was common in the ancient Middle East. The law codes of both Mesopotamia and the Hittite Empire mention this issue. In fact, it is still an issue today in this area. Since the kidnapper is depriving his victim of his freedom, the kidnapper is to be punished by death—as though he has taken the victim's life.

24:8 Leprous diseases refer to a broad range of skin diseases, not exclusively leprosy. Instead of repeating the legislation concerning these diseases, Moses refers the people to his original instruction in Leviticus 13–14. Motivation to obey this ceremonial legislation is furnished by Miriam, who opposed Moses and was struck with leprosy (see Numbers 12).

24:12–13 If the borrower is so poor that all he can offer as a pledge is his raiment (a cloak, which serves as a

blanket at night), then the lender is to return it before nightfall. By acting in this manner, the lender shows love, kindness, and mercy, which must govern all civil relationships in Israel.

24:16 The edict that fathers should not be executed for their children's crimes must be held in tension with other teachings and laws. This refers primarily to legal responsibility, but even then, there are exceptions (such as Achan's family in Joshua 7).

24:18 Lest they forget, Moses reminds the people that they were all once powerless slaves in Egypt. Just as the Lord looked out for them, they are to look out for others.

24:19–21 Another way of looking out for the needy is by making it possible for them to provide for themselves honestly. Women, in particular, have few vocational options other than prostitution. The practice of leaving part of every harvest—whether it be in the field, the orchard, or the vineyard—allows those who do not own land to work honestly for their food.

25:1–3 Vigilante justice has no place in Israel. They are to allow a judge to handle disputes and determine the appropriate punishment. The guilty party is not to be flogged more than forty times, so as to provide a consequence without permanently hurting the person.

25:4 The command not to muzzle an ox while it is treading corn stresses kindness and fairness to the animals that help the people survive. Mercy and kindness should extend to animals.

25:5–6 The marriage described is also called *levirate*, from the Latin word that means "brother-in-law." This marriage happens when the deceased relative has died without a male heir. The point of the levirate marriage is to provide a male heir who, in turn, can care for the parents in their old age and keep the property in the family. God is so concerned about people not losing their family line that the first son born from the levirate marriage is given the deceased brother's name. This shows that God cares about family legacy.

25:7–10 If a widow's brother-in-law refuses to fulfill his duty, she is to tell the elders of his town about it. She could then remove one of his shoes and spit in his face. This would mark him, for the entire town to see, as a man who does not care for others. The levirate law and a variation of the ritual with the shoe are played out in the life story of Ruth (Ruth 4:1–8).

25:11–12 This law is the only time when physical mutilation serves as punishment. This command intends to protect both womanly modesty and the capacity of a man to produce heirs. This also shows God's seriousness in regard to the next generation, which is probably why this law follows the one on levirate marriages.

25:17–19 The Israelites are to wipe out the Amalekites when they enter the land. The reason is clear: Since the Amalekites have shown no mercy to Israel, they are to receive none. Israel is to blot out the memory of Amalek from under heaven.

26:1 The book of Deuteronomy is a reiteration of the law for the children of those who were brought out of Egypt and allowed to enter into the promised land. As such, it is stated in its simplest form. Chapter 26 describes some of the rituals that are to be followed as soon as they enter the land.

26:3, 5, 13 Tithing and giving firstfruits were not unfamiliar requirements for the Israelites. Legislation regarding firstfruits and the tithe had already been given in Deuteronomy (14:28–29; 18:3–5). What is unique in this passage, however, is the declaration ritual for each offering. It seems that these declarations were meant to be practiced only once: for the firstfruits after Israel's first harvest and for the tithe after being in the land three years. They were given in order to celebrate Israel's transition from a nomadic existence to a settled community through the power of the Lord.

26:12–14 After the third year in the land, the people are to pay a tithe to the Lord. This tithe is to be given to those in need (Levite, strangers, orphans, widows) so that there will be food for them to eat in their towns. It is a sacred offering, intended to show the same mercy and kindness that they themselves have received. Because of its sacredness, the offering may be given only by someone who is ritually clean, as described in the declaration accompanying this offering.

26:15 The prayer for blessing emphasizes Israel's dependence on the Lord and on His grace. He is so transcendent that He dwells in heaven, but at the same time He is so near to His people that He hears their prayers on earth. God is good and provides for His people.

26:16–19 These verses are the conclusion to the entire section that began in 5:1, where Moses begins to reiterate the law. Two things are mentioned here: the responsibility of Israel and the responsibility of God.

27:1 This chapter begins a new section in the ancient Near Eastern treaty form that structures the book. Following the opening preamble (1:1–5), historical introduction (1:6–4:49), and particular stipulations of the treaty (chapters 5–26), chapter 27 opens the section of blessings and curses that will result from keeping or breaking the treaty.

27:3, 8 The reference to "the law" probably refers to the entire book of Deuteronomy rather than just parts of it.

27:4–6 The stones are to be set up on mount Ebal, at the base of which lies the city of Shechem. The altar will commemorate God's faithfulness in giving them the land.

27:7 The covenant is to be renewed not only by the writing of the law but also with sacrificial offerings. The burnt offerings express the people's total dependence on the Lord. The peace offerings express their thankfulness to Him and their joy in His provision.

27:8–10 The final reminder to write the law very clearly emphasizes the supreme importance of the role of God's law in the promised land. It is important that God's law be central to all that happens. This section, then, ends with a second call to obey God.

27:12–13 After the altar is set up on mount Ebal, six tribes are to assemble on mount Gerizim to bless the people, and six are to assemble on mount Ebal to

pronounce curses. The six tribes on mount Gerizim are from Jacob's wives, Rachel and Leah. Four of the six tribes on mount Ebal are descended from Jacob's concubines, Bilhah and Zilpah. The other two are Reuben, Jacob's firstborn who forfeited his birthright through incest (Genesis 35:22; 49:3–4), and Zebulun, Leah's youngest son.

27:15 God hates idolatry, both public and private. If a person tries to keep his or her idolatry secret, the Lord will see it and the idolater will be cursed.

27:16 Anyone showing dishonor to parents is cursed. This again shows that God is a God who believes that authority should be respected. God takes the family lineage seriously.

27:18 A blind man cannot care for himself. If someone comes along pretending to care for a blind man but really seeks to take advantage of him, this person is cursed.

27:20–23 These four curses are directed to one who engages in one of four forbidden sexual relationships. The marriage bed is to be held in high honor, and sexual relations are not to be perverted by taking them out of a proper marriage context. Some of these perversions show that when sexual relations are taken outside of God's context, they turn into horrible and degrading practices.

28:1 In this chapter, Moses sets before Israel the blessings and curses of the covenant they are renewing. The curses section is about four times longer than the blessings section. This underscores the importance of obedience. God is making the point that if you fail to obey, there is no such thing as success; every area of life will be impacted in a great way. This commitment is intended to make a strong point—they should obey God.

28:3–6 If Israel obeys the Lord, then every aspect of life will be blessed greatly by God. Both the merchant and the farmer will be blessed. Israel can expect fertility in both humanity and animals. There will always be food in their homes for daily meals, the land will never experience a famine, and in all their daily work, the Israelites will enjoy God's blessings.

28:7–13 Three areas of blessing are singled out. The first one deals with Israel's relationship to the nations around them. Israel will have supernatural military success and financial prosperity that will cause them to be above other nations. The fruit of this is that they will never borrow from other nations, and they will always lead and never follow. The second deals with agricultural endeavors. Israel will experience abundant prosperity in farming and family. The third deals with Israel's reputation. By being God's obedient and holy people, the Israelites will enjoy such a close relationship with God that they will be a testimony to all the peoples on earth who witness it.

28:15 What if they do not obey God? Just as obedience will bring blessings, so disobedience will bring curses. No middle ground exists.

28:16–19 The four curses in these verses are the exact opposite of the four blessings cited in verses 3–6. The point here is that all the great blessings will be undone with disobedience to God. Disobedience is ultimately rejection of God and His ways. If you reject God, there are grave consequences.

28:20–68 In addition to the reversal of the blessings mentioned in 28:1–14, several more major judgments will come upon Israel for disobeying: destruction, disease, drought, defeat in battle, diseases of Egypt, oppression and robbery, exile, crop failure and economic destruction, siege by the enemy, and disease that brings death and exile. Each of these judgments essentially has one goal: to turn Israel from disobedience. God's heart is to turn the nation back to Him through these punishments. The point here is that the process that leads to this level of pain and destruction is disobedience. Israel must know that they have to obey God. If they fail in this area, then all the blessings will be taken away, and pain and destruction will follow. They should take this warning seriously.

29:2–8 This review is unique for one reason—it makes the point that Israel has not really understood the significance of what God has done for them. They do not understand the real significance of the deliverance from Egypt or the hand of God in their life. Because their minds do not fully grasp what God is ultimately doing, it is easy for them to rebel against God. To miss the heart of God is to miss the motivation to obey.

29:9 Moses brings the nation back to the most fundamental of all issues, one that is a running theme in Deuteronomy—obedience. The people must obey God in order to prosper. Moses is focusing on the present. He wants the people at that moment in time to realize they need to commit themselves to God, and God is going to commit Himself to them. This moment is a part of God's plan to make good on His promise to Abraham.

29:15 Yet there is more than just the moment focused on in this text. The scope of this covenant renewal also includes future generations. Therefore, the obedience of the present generation has a great effect on those not yet born. They are to pass on to the next generation the importance of obedience to God. With this great call to multigenerational obedience, Moses will again focus on the curses that befall disobedience.

29:16–17 Moses reminds the Israelites that they are not naive concerning abominations (idolatry). They witnessed them in Egypt and had fallen into idolatry on the way to Canaan (Exodus 32; Numbers 25). These people understood how one act of idolatry was a bitter poison. For this reason, they are told to be diligent against this sin when they enter the land of Canaan. Once they enter this land, they will face new temptations to idolatry over and over again.

29:18 *Wormwood* is often associated with poison in scripture (Jeremiah 9:15; 23:15; Amos 5:7; 6:12).

29:19–21 These words are reminders that if the people are not vigilant, then an idolatrous foothold can take place through a single person who might think he or she is safe from judgment because the Lord has said Israel is His people.

29:22–28 The devastation will be so intense that the nations will ask why Israel's God allowed it to happen. The judgment will be so severe that it will seem almost unlikely that God would bring such a harsh punishment upon His own people. The point is that God hates all rebellion, no matter who does it.

29:29 The "secret things" probably refer to future details that God has not revealed to the nation. There are many things that God has not yet revealed to Israel— things according to His will that no one knows. God is bigger and is working with a view of history that no one can see or understand.

30:1 In chapter 29, the language seems to assume the reality that the people of Israel will fall into exile because of their tendency toward idolatry. Chapter 30, then, is the good news—they will eventually be brought out of exile. God will not abandon His people, even in the midst of the worst punishment—that of losing the land they believe God had promised them.

30:1–3, 8–10 While chapter 30 sheds some light on the end of the journey the Israelites have set out upon, their repentance of idolatry will be insufficient to reverse all the effects. For this reason, God Himself will intervene and with tender compassion gather the nation and bring the people back to their land. This restoration will be a time of spiritual prosperity greater than the nation has ever known. During this time, God will work a miracle that will change the fortunes of the people forever.

30:6 God is going to deal with His people's hearts—the very source of the problem. God promises to circumcise their hearts. Circumcision is the requirement God put on Abraham. It was one of the ways the Hebrews were set apart from the nations around them. Here, the idea of circumcision is used as an image of God claiming the people's hearts for Himself, marking them irrevocably. He will give them a new will to obey. With this new heart they will experience the abundant blessing that comes from obedience. In fact, the ultimate goal of God's covenant with the Israelites is to bring about this new heart. God is at work in the life of this nation, not just to give them a land, but to give them a heart that will obey Him (Jeremiah 31:31; Ezekiel 36:24–32).

30:7 When this restoration happens, all the enemies of Israel will receive all the curses mentioned in this book.

30:11, 14 God's commands are not beyond the Israelites' ability to understand. Though the law has a heavenly origin, God clearly reveals it to Israel directly. Israel did not need a special interpreter before they could obey the law.

30:15–26 The point of this passage is not the salvation of the souls of the nation. Instead, it is about the fellowship of these people with God. Genesis 15:6 makes it clear that a person is made righteous by faith. The verses here explain how a believing people can then have fellowship with God. For the Israelites, their full enjoyment of life depends on their obedience to God's Word.

30:17–19 Anyone who disregards the law can easily be drawn back into idolatry (see also 29:18), which would bring catastrophic judgment into that person's life. In this way, the law serves the purpose of keeping the nation (as well as the individuals) in check and providing a barrier to unfettered sin. So the life of the Israelites as they live in the land is to consist of obeying the Lord. This obedience can be passed down from one generation to another.

31:1 Here, at the end of their journey through the wilderness and at the doorstep of the conquest, Moses prepares to step out of the way. He is now going to transfer leadership from himself to Joshua. Moses' priority is ensuring that the next generation places a priority on their relationship with God.

31:2–6 Moses has been forbidden to enter Canaan because of an earlier act of unbelief (Numbers 20:1–13), but God's plan does not depend on any one human leader. Instead, God's plan depends only on God's power to fulfill His own promises to His people. Therefore, in light of God's past faithfulness, Moses charges the nation to be obedient and fearless. There is nothing that they should be afraid of—God will make good on His promises.

31:7 After his strong charge to the people, Moses commissions Joshua with the same charge: "Be strong and of good courage." God will bring victory to this nation. Joshua is not the one responsible to take the land; he is the one responsible to lead the nation to be faithful to the God who will take the land for them.

31:9–11 Moses records God's law and then commissions the priests to ensure that it is read every seven years to the entire nation. The priests are to read the law during the feast of tabernacles. Entire families are required to attend this holiday, which means the most people possible will hear the reading. As a nation, they will be reminded of what God requires for them to remain an acceptable nation before Him.

31:14–18 The commissioning of Joshua begins rather ominously. After Joshua is called to the tabernacle, God addresses both him and Moses. He tells Moses that the people are going to rebel after they enter the land. Their idolatry will bring on God's judgment. In hearing God's revelation to Moses, Joshua is prepared for what will come. As a leader, he will understand the full spiritual context of what is about to take place.

31:19–22 God commissions Moses to write a song to outline the rebellion of the people. This way, when the people rebel and run from God, the song will serve as a reminder and a point of accountability. Moses' song includes both the path of repentance and a warning of the judgment to come when the people fall away from their faith. God is fully aware of the tendency of the human heart to stray from Him and the extent to which these people will stray. Yet rather than rejecting the nation outright, He will use them and provide hope that they can have a changed heart.

31:23–30 In spite of this knowledge that the people will fall, the Lord formally commissions Joshua, giving him a charge to be strong and courageous and assuring him of success—God will be true to His plan. The book of the law is to be placed beside the ark, rather than inside of it. Only the Ten Commandments are placed inside (Exodus

25:16). This placement of the law is a witness that the people are not going to follow this law. Though this is a harsh reality, it is also an expression of God's grace.

32:1 There are seven themes in Moses' song. These seven themes take us on a journey from the great goodness of God to the horrible sin of humanity to the grace and kindness of the Lord.

32:3 At the opening of the song, we are told that it is for everyone in the entire world to hear and learn from. In other words, these historical events reveal eternal and binding truth for all humanity. These words are to water the earth and give meaning for all creation, for the God of all creation is going to be declared to the entire world.

32:4–10 God is described as a rock and as perfect and just. This description is presented in contrast to humanity in verse 5. The faith of His people had become so skewed that they bore no family resemblance to their Father. Even with the deliverance God has already provided in a variety of ways, the people still rebel, highlighting how extremely foolish and faithless humanity really is.

32:11 As this nation is growing and developing in some rather difficult circumstances, God is there. The metaphor of the eagle speaks of God's wise and loving parental care. Like an eagle, the Lord remains ready to catch them when necessary.

32:13 The idea of getting honey and oil from the rock suggests that even the most barren places will become fertile. In the goodness of God, the people will be blessed in miraculous ways.

32:15 Throughout the centuries, many lives have revealed that prosperity is often more dangerous for the faithful than adversity. In adversity, a person calls out to God as a way of life, while in prosperity it is easy to give lip service to faith but not make it a true priority. Israel (in verse 15, ironically referred to as *Jeshurun*, "the upright one") abandoned the Lord, their only hope for salvation, when they became prosperous. The mention of *kicked* builds on the metaphor of an animal kicking at its owner. It suggests the mindless nature and complete foolishness of Israel's rebellion against God.

32:16–18 The downfall of Israel took shape in idol worship. They actually made sacrifices to something that God created rather than to God Himself. Put in its proper perspective, this is devil (demon) worship—pure evil. Moses compares God to both a father and a mother. Yet in spite of His provision, the people scorn Him and His great love.

32:21 In His righteous indignation, God will withdraw His presence and judge Israel with a foreign nation. This means that while God may have provided protection to Israel from the attacks of surrounding enemies, because of Israel's lack of faithfulness, God would remove His protection.

32:30–33 The evidence of God's supernatural judgment through other nations will be clear. Those coming against Israel will have such strength and power that only God could be behind them. This judgment could not be attributed to the gods of Israel's enemies. In fact, the enemies who will execute God's judgment on Israel are as evil as Sodom and Gomorrah. God allows the worst of the worst to come against Israel so that the people can see how far they have fallen.

32:35 Though the Lord will use Israel's enemies to execute His judgment, He will still hold those enemies accountable for their wickedness and repay them for their evil. God will use their evil to chastise Israel, but He does not condone that evil.

32:36 In bringing judgment on Israel, God will have compassion on them. God's judgment here is interpreted by some to mean that He will judge *for* them, or vindicate them. Yet Israel will not experience God's compassion until they abandon all trust in their own efforts and in the false gods to which they have turned.

32:37–38 Moses calls on Israel to turn for help to the false gods so that they can plainly understand that these gods cannot help them. God's goal in judging Israel is not to extinguish the nation. Instead, it is to bring the people to understand that there is no god besides the Lord.

32:39–43 God wants Israel to understand that He alone has power over death and life. He is the only hope for humanity, the only power for salvation, and the only God to trust in for help and deliverance. When Israel comes to this realization, then God will take vengeance on the nation's adversaries. The turning point will be the nation's true repentance.

32:46 After reciting all the words of the song, Moses tells the people to consider them seriously. If the people will meditate on the certainty and severity of the judgment that the Lord will bring, this song could serve as a powerful deterrent for their rebellion. If they will repent of the sin that is in their hearts right then, God will forgive them. The threat of the Lord's discipline is a warning for them to turn from their wicked ways. This fear of the judgment set forth in the song would also enable them to teach their children the need to obey the words of this law.

32:49–52 Moses goes up to view the land that he had earlier in his life hoped to enter with his people. Because of his break with faith (Numbers 20:8–12), the view from mount Nebo is as close as he will get to Canaan.

33:1 The blessing of Moses given here, just before his death, is very important and common for that day. It was typical for a father to impart a blessing just before his death. Moses, leader of the Exodus and mediator of the covenant, served in a fatherly capacity for the nation.

33:2 Moses begins this blessing with praise for the greatness of God, including a description of the Lord's appearance at Sinai when He gave the Ten Commandments (Exodus 19–20). This verse is written in poetic language that describes the light of God shining on Sinai in the south, and then on Seir in the northeast, and then on Paran in the north. The idea is that God's law engulfed the land.

33:5 The proclamation of the Lord's kingship over *Jeshurun* (a name for Israel; 32:15; 33:26) is a reference back to the nation's deliverance from Egypt and the giving of the law (when the leaders and the tribes assembled to receive God's commands). When God brought the law to the people, they gathered under His rule, and He became their official king. The giving of the law was then the event that ratified His kingship over the nation.

33:8–11 The tribe of Levi was set apart to care for the tabernacle and to provide priests to serve there. The *Thummim* and *Urim* are used by priests to cast lots, a method of receiving direction from God (some compare their use to throwing dice in order to leave the outcome out of human hands). Thus the tribe of Levi was entrusted with the great work of mediating between God and humanity. At first, the faithfulness of Levi is praised because they are faithful at Massah, also called Meribah (Exodus 17:1–7). Then the tribe is praised collectively for their faithfulness to execute God's judgment in the matter of the golden calf (Exodus 32:25–29). Moses' blessing here is a prayer for supernatural ability so that the Levites will use their skills in God's work.

33:26–28 *Jeshurun* ("the upright one") is a name for Israel. Verse 26 honors the God of Israel as incomparable in power. He rides on the heavens and the sky. Because God is eternal and a refuge for His people, His everlasting arms will protect Israel in times of trouble. God will destroy their enemies. Having such a wonderful and powerful God, the nation can walk in the full assurance that God will provide for them the promised land. They also can have the confidence that, once in the land, they will live in both safety and prosperity.

34:1–3 At the close of the book of Deuteronomy, Moses ascends to the mountain of Nebo as the Lord told him to do. Though Moses is not to lead the people into the land, God allows Moses to see the land. Moses sees from the mountain starting in the north and following to the south in a counterclockwise direction. Though one could not normally view the utmost sea (the Mediterranean) from the mountain of Nebo, God may have allowed Moses to supernaturally do so in order to see the great promise that was made years before.

34:4 God's mention of the oath reminds Moses that He will still be faithful to His promise to the great ancestors of the Israelites—Abraham, Isaac, and Jacob (Deuteronomy 1:8; 6:10; 9:5, 27; 29:13; 30:20)—and bring Israel into their new land.

34:6 God bestows an honor on Moses by being the One who buries him. Moses' last moments on earth were evidently spent in fellowship with God. The place of his grave is unknown today. In Jude 9 we learn that there might have been a supernatural struggle over the body of Moses. Moses' death, at the age of 120, was an ending of an era for Israel. It was time for a new beginning.

34:9 After Moses' death, Joshua is empowered with the wisdom necessary to take Israel to the next step in experiencing the fulfillment of God's promise. Since this job is truly a spiritual job, Joshua will need supernatural insight and power to carry out the will of God. The Israelites accept Joshua's leadership, and in a sense, even this is an honor to Moses' leadership.

THE BOOK OF
JOSHUA

INTRODUCTION TO JOSHUA ■ For centuries, the descendants of Abraham had anticipated possessing the land God had promised to the patriarch in the Abrahamic Covenant (Genesis 12:1–3; 15:5–8) and then reiterated to Isaac and Jacob. Joshua is the compelling history of the fulfillment of that promise.

AUTHOR ■ There is some tradition that claims Joshua as the author of this book. But the author is unknown, as is the date of writing.

OCCASION ■ This is an account written to reveal God's faithfulness and how, by faith in God's promises, God's people can overcome and experience His life-changing deliverance.

1:1 In Joshua, we are introduced to the leadership of Moses' successor. Joshua is first mentioned in Exodus as a military leader fighting the Amalekites (Exodus 17:9–13). The book of Numbers reveals that he served as Moses' servant (Numbers 11:28). Joshua's name means "Yahweh is salvation." As the Hebrew equivalent of the name *Jesus*, Joshua typifies the saving work that would later come for all people through Jesus, whose saving life provides believers with redemption and the power to enter into the possession of our inheritance in Christ.

1:5 Joshua is given the promise, "There shall not any man be able to stand before thee," but this promise is also a warning. While the land is theirs for the taking, it would not be taken without conflict or battle. This is a wake-up call, a reality that must be faced: Life is full of battles and conflicts, even for God's people.

1:6 The issue before Joshua and the people is God's call to be strong and courageous. God is calling Joshua to a special yet difficult ministry, one with tremendous challenges and obstacles far beyond his own skill or abilities.

1:7–8 Joshua's courage is the direct result of knowing God's will (Ephesians 5:9–10). Also, Joshua is reminded that he has already been prepared for this as the servant of Moses (Joshua 1:1). Regardless of the obstacles, Joshua is commanded to act on God's will by faith in the Lord's person, promises, and provision. Now Joshua begins to survey the land, size up the enemy, and prepare the people for battle.

1:10–15 Note Joshua's immediate and obedient response, regardless of the obstacles that lay before them. There is a note of urgency, certainty, expectancy, and faith in Joshua's commands to the people. As God commanded, the new leader is taking charge and following the Lord's orders with confidence.

2:1 Jericho lay just five miles on the other side of the Jordan and was one of the most formidable fortresses in the land. Very likely, Rahab's house is the only place where the men can stay with any hope of remaining undetected; plus they will be able to gather information. Rahab's house also offered an easy way of escape since it was located on the city wall.

2:3 The king may have assumed that the spies were staying with Rahab, but he would have had reason to expect that she would do her patriotic duty and turn the spies in. The ancient Code of Hammurabi contains a provision for putting to death prostitutes who harbor felons. And yet Rahab had faith in God's ability to deliver her against all odds.

2:4 Was Rahab's lying justified? Most commentaries approve of her faith but disapprove of her lie. In essence, they approve of her hiding the spies but not telling the lies. In 6:17 Joshua explains that Rahab is to be spared because she hid the spies, and she did this as an ally. The question of whether her lie was justified by God because it was a matter of warfare is debated by theologians. Obviously, her faith was recognized as sincere regardless of whether her lie was excused by the circumstances.

2:10–13 Rahab's faith, which gives her strong convictions about God, causes her to act to the point of putting her life on the line. She knew Israel would eventually attack the city and destroy it, and she wanted to be delivered and to be on God's side. Rahab is confident in the Lord's power. Somehow she knew what had occurred at the Red Sea and that it was the product of the sovereign power of Israel's God. Rahab is concerned not only about herself but also her family. This attitude of concern demonstrates God's plan for evangelism—sharing the hope we have in the Lord with those closest to us.

2:11 Rahab is saved because she believes in the God of Israel (see 6:17; Hebrews 11:31; James 2:25). Hiding the messengers is an outworking of her faith. She has come to believe that the God of Israel is indeed the God of the heavens.

2:23 Joshua and the men of Israel see the words and actions of Rahab as clear evidence of the sovereign providence and blessing of the Lord. This passage demonstrates God's concern and work to deliver each person who calls on Him (2 Peter 3:9). The story also demonstrates that the only thing that can hinder us in doing the will of God and fulfilling our calling is our own unbelief. Our faith should lead to action and ministry to and for others. Rahab reaches out both to the spies and to her household (John 1:35–51; 4:28–29, 39).

2:24 The inhabitants of the land are terror stricken. Mentally and emotionally, they are defeated. God had already given the people of Jericho into the Israelites' hands. Note the irony: Jericho's inhabitants are looking at Israel's God and shaking in their sandals. The Israelites, who have seen the mighty works of God over and over again, often looked at their problems instead of focusing on God.

3:3 Aside from the miraculous way the river is crossed, the most important feature of this chapter is the ark of the covenant. Its prominence is stressed in the number of times it is mentioned in chapters 3 and 4 and by the nature of the commands and statements given in its regard.

3:7–10 To be effective, leaders need the right credentials—solid biblical training under people of God who truly know His Word. So it is time that God establishes Joshua as His representative to guide the nation. It is significant that it is God who does the exalting (4:14). The natural tendency is to exalt ourselves, but Joshua, in reporting God's communication to him, says nothing about this promise of being exalted. Instead, he focuses their attention on the fact that it is the living God who is among them, and it is He and He alone who will dispossess the enemies of the land.

3:13 Since the priests carry the ark of the covenant, and since the ark represents God's person and power, they alone are to take it to the edge of the water and stand still. What do we gather from this? It reminds us of our part in the plan of God. We must learn to step out in faith and obedience to the principles and promises of scripture.

3:16 These chapters reinforce the concept of grace. They show that crossing the Jordan and dispossessing the enemies (like all aspects of our salvation and sanctification) are the works of God. The things we do in consecration are not works of righteousness that merit God's favor or overcome our enemies. Rather, the acts of consecration (like confession) remove the barriers to God's power and to fellowship, and so prepare our hearts to receive God's grace; they build our faith so we will put our feet in the water, cross over, and go up against the enemy.

3:17 Many insist that this is no miracle since the event can be explained as a natural phenomenon. Earthquakes on record have caused the high banks of the Jordan to collapse and dam up the river for extended periods of time, but never during flood season. Admittedly, God could have employed natural causes such as an earthquake and a landslide, and the timing still would have made it a miraculous intervention. But considering all the factors involved, it seems best to view this occurrence as a special act of God brought about in a way unknown to humans.

4:19–20 The name *Gilgal* means "a circle of stones." Every time Israel returns to Gilgal, they will see the circle of stones and remember what God has done to roll away

the waters of the Jordan. The very sight of the stones was to be an encouragement, but also a reminder of the sovereign power of the Lord over nations and creation so they might fear the Lord forever and remain faithful to their purpose in the plan of God.

4:24 The stones (see verse 20) are a testimony to other nations. Here, God is again reminding Israel of their purpose as a nation of priests (Exodus 19:4–6; 1 Peter 2:5, 9–11).

5:1 This chapter bridges the crossing of the Jordan and the beginning of the military campaigns. Israel needed a preparation of heart and willingness to submit to God's directions that they might experience His power and overcome the enemy. The Canaanites are, in essence, already defeated. They are fearful of the nation of Israel because of the mighty works of God. God's people need to recognize and understand that the Lord is mightier than all their enemies (John 16:33; 2 Corinthians 2:14).

5:2–8 This is the second time a group circumcision is observed among the Israelites as a nation, the first being while the older generation was still in Egypt. Circumcision was not unique to the Israelites. For instance, it was an Egyptian practice with religious connotations reserved for the priests and upper-class citizens. In associating it with God's covenant, however, the Israelites gave a significance to circumcision that other nations did not.

5:9 The renewal of the rite of circumcision is necessary because none of the men born after the Israelites came out of Egypt had been circumcised—that generation of men had died. Circumcision symbolized their faith that God would enable them to posses the land.

5:10 This instance is only the third passover God's people have kept. The first was in Egypt (Exodus 12:1–28), and the second was at mount Sinai (Numbers 9:1–5). By partaking of the passover, they reexperience their deliverance and redemption out of Egypt and look forward to other victories—to the defeat of the Canaanites and also to the victory to come in Christ's work on Calvary.

5:12 For more on manna, see the study note at Numbers 11:8–9.

5:14 The Lord reminds Joshua of God's personal presence and His powerful provision. Joshua responds how each of us should respond when confronted with God's power—in worship and submission.

6:2 The words *have given* describe a future event or action as having already been accomplished. Future victory was already assured by the promise of an omnipotent, faithful, and immutable God. God's plan for victory will serve to teach Israel and God's people for all ages.

6:7 Joshua does not unfold the entire plan at first, but day by day he gives the people instructions. Each day they go out and march silently around the city. Though nothing seems to happen, they do not murmur or complain or question Joshua's instructions. They simply obey, day after day, until the seventh day when they give the great shout and the walls come tumbling down by their faith in the mighty hand of God (Hebrews 11:30).

6:17 Rahab is mentioned eight times in scripture (Joshua 2:1, 3; 6:17, 23, 25; Matthew 1:5; Hebrews 11:31; James 2:25), and in six of these occurrences, her name is found with a specific descriptive noun—*harlot.*

6:20 In spite of the taunts that were perhaps hurled down at them from the walls as they marched silently around Jericho, the Israelites were willing to look foolish for the Lord. He was their source of strength.

6:22 The promises to Rahab are kept—she and her family are delivered. While it is not stated, evidently that part of the wall on which Rahab's house was built did not collapse.

6:26 The prophecy against any who would seek to rebuild Jericho demonstrates God's severity and the surety of His Word. This prophecy came to be fulfilled in the days of Ahab (1 Kings 16:34), in keeping with God's faithfulness to keep His promises. Jericho was occupied sporadically after its destruction, but never to the previous degree.

7:1 This chapter reminds us of the reality of the ever-present threats and contrasts of life—victory is always followed by the threat of defeat. Never is the child of God in greater danger of a fall than after a victory (1 Corinthians 10:12). The problem facing the Israelites as a nation is not their enemies as much as their own unfaithfulness. The Lord holds the whole camp of Israel accountable for the act of one man.

7:2 The distance between a great victory and a terrible defeat is one step—and often a short one at that. Ai is the next objective in the path of conquest because of its strategic location.

7:5 There is an irony in the defeat of Ai. The name itself means "ruin," so it is being contrasted with the powerful city of Jericho. Jericho falls easily because God fights for obedient Israel, whereas Ai, the dump, defeats them because of Achan's sin.

The defeat at Ai demoralizes God's people. It creates misgivings and a lack of hope in the Lord. Rather than examine their own lives as the source of their defeat, they begin to doubt the Lord.

7:6 Joshua's dismay shows us his humanity and encourages us in our own failures to know that God will still accept us if we turn to Him for forgiveness. God can greatly use us if we will trust Him. Failure is not the end—often it is a test. Defeat and failure often enable people to grow in faith.

7:11 Nothing escapes the omniscience of God, especially sin (Numbers 32:23). God sees the sin in our lives and desires for us to deal with it, not hide it. Even though the Lord died for our sins and stands at God's right hand as our advocate and intercessor, God does not and cannot treat sin in our lives lightly (James 4:5–6).

7:19 The consequences of unconfessed sin are weakness and an inability to serve and live for the Lord. We each have the capacity to live victoriously for the Lord, but the ability to do so always depends on

fellowship with the Savior in the power of the Spirit; we must walk in the light (1 John 1:5–9).

7:26 God calls for a restoration to fellowship and faith in the power of God. Joshua is to call the people's attention to the sin of someone taking things that are under the ban, which is also the cause of their failure in the battle against Ai. As the Lord had emphasized to Joshua, he is to call the people's attention to both the cause and the consequences of the sin.

8:1 Often God engineers defeat before He engineers victory. Sometimes success comes through the back door of failure. In this chapter, we again see the grace of God and the truth of restoration. Defeat never has to be the end.

8:2 God's new revelation to Joshua is meant to both encourage him and give him directions for victory. God encourages His people. His words remind us that God is a God of comfort and that He wants to encourage us through His Word. With the battle at Ai, we are reminded that we should not expect God to work the same way always. We need to be open and sensitive to the various ways God may lead. As the sovereign God of the universe, He is never limited to one particular method to accomplish His purposes.

8:3–9 The strategy for the capture of Ai is ingenious. The plan works perfectly (8:14–22). Thus Israel, out of their failure, comes not only to a second chance but to a great victory along with some much-needed lessons. Though we should never seek to fail, failure can be the back door to success; for God is willing to forgive and restore us if we will deal with our sin appropriately and sincerely.

8:7 Just like at Jericho, victory at Ai will come by the power of God. The irony of God's blessing is that the spoils of Ai and its livestock can now be taken by Israel. As the firstfruits of the land, Jericho has been placed under the ban, but this is not the case with Ai. Achan's dissatisfaction actually caused him to miss precisely what he longed for and much more.

8:30–31 The altar here is for those who acknowledge their sin and come not as righteous but as sinners to the place of sacrifice. The altar, constructed of whole (uncut) stones without human workmanship, is a negation of humanism and salvation by works. It shows that human beings can add nothing to the work of God for salvation or for spirituality. We are saved by God's work.

8:33–35 Instead of further pursuing the military campaign following the victory at Ai, Joshua leads the Israelites on a spiritual pilgrimage for a special time of worship. Moses had commanded it (Deuteronomy 27:1–8) because of what this event would stand for in the lives of the Israelites. Joshua leads the entire nation—men, women, children, and cattle—to the place specified by Moses, the mountains of Ebal and Gerizim. These mountains are located in the geographic center of the land.

9:1 Powerful alliances begin immediately to form in both the north and the south of Canaan. Where tribal warfare had gone on for years, suddenly deadly enemies come together in alliances as they unite against the invasion of God's people into the land.

9:2 It appears that all the city-states in mountainous regions join forces against Israel as a means of keeping Joshua and his army from attacking one city at a time, as had been done with Jericho and Ai. In resisting Israel, however, these kings are resisting God. Their stubborn rebellion against God is an eloquent testimony that the sin of the Amorites had reached its full measure.

9:3–7 Not all are willing to go openly against Israel in view of Israel's victories. The Gibeonites, including a league of cities (9:17), concoct a clever ruse designed to deceive the Israelites and hide their true identity. They evidently somehow know that God had commanded the Israelites to totally destroy all the inhabitants of the land.

9:8–13 The Gibeonites play on the Israelites' sympathies by appearing as weary travelers who have been on a long journey. They also play on their egos and their sense of pride. They insist they came from a great distance to show their respect for the power of the God of the Israelites and want to be allowed to live as the servants of Israel.

9:14 The primary mistake here is a failure to seek counsel from the Lord. The Israelites should have sought direction from the Lord through the Urim and Thummim. Here we see the peril of presumption through prayerlessness.

9:18 The text tells us that once the ruse is discovered, the people grumble against their leaders because they judged them to be responsible. Though the Israelites erred by leaning on their own understanding rather than consulting the Lord, they honor their agreement with the Gibeonites. To break the covenant would dishonor God's name and bring down His wrath.

9:22–23 While Israel could not go back on their pledge, the Gibeonites had deceived them, so a punishment fitting their sin must be prescribed. First, Joshua rebukes them for their dishonesty and then sentences them to perpetual slavery. In the ruse of the Gibeonites, they had offered to be the subjects of the Israelites (9:8, 11). By this they are merely offering to become Israel's vassals. In return, they expect Israel, the stronger of the two, to protect them from their enemies (10:6). Their plan backfires and they become "hewers of wood and drawers of water" (woodcutters and water-bearers) for the Israelites, especially in relation to the tabernacle service. In God's grace, this turns out to be a great blessing.

9:27 The very thing the Gibeonites hoped to retain—their freedom—was lost. But the curse eventually becomes a blessing. It is on behalf of the Gibeonites that God later works a great miracle (10:10–14). Later, the tabernacle of the Lord will be pitched at Gibeon, and the Gibeonites (who may have been later known as Nethinims) will replace the Levites in temple service (Ezra 8:20). That is the amazing way the grace of God works. God not only forgives, but in many cases He actually overrules our mistakes and brings blessing out of sin.

10:1–5 The defection of the Gibeonites is cause for great alarm for three reasons: (1) It is discouraging to see such a large city surrender to the enemy, (2) without Gibeon the southern coalition is severely weakened, and (3) they constitute a fifth column to fight with Israel in time of war. Though it has no king, Gibeon is like a royal city; it is just as strong and influential as any city-state (11:12).

10:6–7 Faced with the armies of the coalition and certain destruction, the Gibeonites send a messenger to Joshua asking for help based on their treaty with Israel. Humanly speaking, this is the perfect opportunity for Joshua to get rid of the Gibeonites. Yet Joshua is a man of integrity who honors his word and does not consider that an option. The Israelites had given their word and are duty bound to honor it. Plus, the situation now provides a unique military opportunity to defeat and destroy several armies at once.

10:11 The Canaanites worshipped gods in the images of natural forces. What a shock when it seems that their gods, in which they have placed their faith, are helpless against the God of Israel, who sends a hailstorm to defeat them.

10:12 This battle includes the greatest of four miracles found in the book of Joshua, often called "Joshua's long day" or "the day the sun stood still." It is noon, and the hot sun is directly overhead when Joshua utters his prayer. The petition is quickly answered by the Lord. Joshua prays in faith, and a great miracle results.

10:13 While the details of how the sun stood still are not described in scripture, what is made clear is that God did something completely amazing to give the Israelite armies a complete and decisive victory.

10:15–19 The five kings and their armies have left the safety of their fortified cities to fight Joshua and his army out in the open, which gives Joshua a great advantage. He is determined to keep them from escaping to the safety of their walls, which will prolong the campaign against that portion of the land.

11:1–4 King Jabin believes the only hope for the kingdoms in north Canaan is to unite into one powerful army to fight off the coming Israelites. This strategy provides yet another opportunity for God to demonstrate that it is His power and His plan that will prevail. Strategically, it allows Joshua and the Israelites to fight a collective army rather than having to go through the work of taking each city one at a time.

11:5 The threat of annihilation forces the kings of the north into an unlikely partnership. Prior to Israel's imminent threat, the kings of the north were hostile to one another and had no alliances. This new united force makes an impressive army—militarily speaking, they have a distinct upper hand. Josephus, a Jewish historian of the first century AD, estimated that this northern alliance included 300,000 infantry soldiers, 10,000 cavalry troops, and 20,000 chariots. With such a huge army, it would appear from outside observation that Joshua and his army had good reason for fear.

11:6 As the remaining Canaanite forces gather and take position, Joshua is moving, too. The Israelites are not staying in one place waiting for the battle to come to them. They are marching directly toward Merom, a five-day trek from their home base. It is during this journey that God speaks to Joshua and reminds him again that He will deliver provision and victory. The promise God gives Joshua echoes the promises of victory He has been giving to Joshua from the very beginning.

11:9 Not only is Israel going to see this army delivered over to them, but God even tells Joshua specifically to cripple their horses and burn their chariots. These acts may seem brutal, but they send a strong message to the Canaanite kings. Not only have the Israelites defeated their spectacular force, but they have destroyed their hope and resources for future attacks. Destroying these weapons holds a lesson for Israel as well: They are to depend not on superior weaponry but on the Lord.

11:10–11 Hazor alone among the northern cities is both seized and burned. This city was by far the largest and most prominent city of ancient Palestine (200 acres in size, compared with Megiddo at 14 and Jericho at 8). Hazor was also ruled by King Jabin—the instigator of the alliance among the northern cities. It was strategically positioned at the center of several branches of an ancient highway that led from Egypt to Syria, Assyria, and Babylon. Because it was the hub of a trade route, Hazor was a very wealthy city. If Hazor could not escape the power of God, the remaining cities would be forced to acknowledge their own vulnerability to the Israelites.

11:16–17 The battles fought by Joshua and his troops ranged over lands that stretched from border to border, from south to north, and from east to west. The entire land was covered in Israel's amazing conquest. Chapter 12 includes a description of the conquered geographic areas and a list of the defeated kings. This information is recorded to make sure everyone knows and understands the great work that God has done. Reviewing God's provision builds faith and serves as a reminder of God's blessings.

11:22 Forty-five years before, the Israelites failed to enter the land for fear of giants—the Anakims (Numbers 13:33). Under Joshua, those fearful enemies were almost completely destroyed. Only a few remained in Gaza, Gath, and Ashdod.

12:1–24 The list in this chapter is the only complete list of the kings Israel conquered. This list is a testimony to the power of God to accomplish His purposes, overcome earthly powers, and provide for His people in a magnificent manner.

12:2–6 Sihon was the king over a piece of land about ninety miles south to north from the Arnon river at about the midpoint of the salt sea (or sea of Arabah, today called the Dead Sea) up to the sea of Chinnereth (Sea of Galilee). Og ruled over a piece of land extending north from Sihon's northern boundary for about sixty

miles (Numbers 21:21–35; Deuteronomy 2:24–3:17). This territory was given to the tribes of Reuben and Gad and the half tribe of Manasseh (Numbers 32; Joshua 13:8–13).

12:9–24 The sixteen kings of southern Canaan whom the Israelites defeated under Joshua's leadership are listed first. This is followed by the list of the fifteen kings of northern Canaan. Not only is this list impressive because of the number of kings, but it serves to highlight the power of God to carry out His promises.

12:24 Consider the number of kings who reigned in the small region that would be Israel: thirty-one kings in a land approximately 150 miles from north to south and 50 miles from east to west. This may seem strange considering the nation-states we are familiar with today. However, these kings reigned over city-states and were more like governors or mayors over cities than kings of a nation.

13:1 Joshua is now growing old and becomes more of an administrator for the nation of Israel rather than a military leader. The land has to be assigned to the various tribes, and Joshua is instructed to oversee these important transactions.

13:1–33 This chapter deals with an exciting time for the Israelites—the distribution of the land. After four hundred years in bondage in Egypt, forty years of wandering in the desert, and years of long, hard fighting, they now are able to enjoy and possess the promised land.

13:2–3 To many people, this section of the book of Joshua, with its detailed lists of boundaries and cities, seems boring to read. Keep in mind that this is not just some boring list of boundaries; instead, it is the complete and literal fulfillment of the promise of God. When God gives a promise, He fulfills it perfectly and literally. As you read this section, do not forget that God is a promise-keeping God.

13:5–6 The land that remains to be taken is described from south to north and includes Philistia and Lebanon. All this land is now to be allotted to the nine and a half tribes because God promised to drive out all the enemies.

13:8–13 Joshua confirms the provision and land division that had already been done by Moses on the east side of the Jordan. The tribes of Reuben and Gad and the half tribe of Manasseh, possessing large herds of cattle, had been anxious to settle in the rich grazing lands of the valley east of Jordan. They are given this privilege only after their men agree to fight alongside their brothers to win Canaan proper (Numbers 32).

13:9–12 The text provides a survey of the area east of the Jordan. It is interesting to note that Geshur and Maacah (already mentioned in 12:5) are not defeated by the Israelites. The reason for this is not stated, but it is something that was a present reality for the original readers of the book. These countries were located east and northeast of the sea of Chinnereth (the Sea of Galilee).

13:14 We are told that the tribe of Levi receives no specific territory of land (see 13:33; 14:3–4; 18:7). Instead, the Levites receive forty-eight towns with pastureland for their flocks and herds (14:4; 21:41) as Moses had specified (Numbers 35:1–5). God wanted to make sure that the Levites were set aside as His servants and, therefore, freed from the cares of the land. They are given cities in which to raise their animals and provide housing for their families.

13:15–23 Reuben receives the territory previously occupied by Moab, east of the salt sea (Dead Sea).

13:24–28 The tribe of Gad inherits the portion in the center of the region, in the original land of Gilead.

13:29–31 The half tribe of Manasseh receives the rich tableland of Bashan, east of the sea of Chinnereth (Sea of Galilee).

14:1–5 The beginning of this chapter introduces how Joshua is going to the divide the remainder of the promised land. The explanation is repeated regarding the dealings with the Reubenites, the Gadites and the half tribe of Manasseh, as well as the arrangements for the tribe of Levi (13:14, 33; 18:7). The method by which the land is to be distributed is by lot (18:8; 19:51).

14:6 This chapter describes the process by which the land is distributed to the rest of the nine and a half tribes. The first inheritance is given to Caleb. This is fitting because Caleb, along with Joshua, is one of the only two left from those who had been freed from Egypt, and they were the only two who believed all along that God was powerful enough to give the land to Israel. Here, Caleb gets his reward.

14:7 Caleb's remarks provide important information to help us determine the length of the conquest of Canaan by the Israelites. Caleb states that he was forty years old when he went to spy the land. Then he adds that the years Israel spent wandering in the wilderness lasted thirty-eight years. Finally, at the time of the conquest, Caleb was eighty-five years old. That tells us that the conquest lasted seven years. This is confirmed by Caleb's reference (14:10) to God's sustaining grace for forty-five years since Kadesh-barnea (thirty-eight years of the wanderings plus seven years of the conquest).

14:12 In order to take possession of this particular portion of land, Caleb still has some battles to win. Yet even at eighty-five, he feels as strong and confident in the Lord as he did years before. Thus Caleb is ready to fight the Anakims at Hebron and take that city for his own inheritance. His faith is steadfast and sincere, and he wants to see God deliver that land to Israel.

14:15 A historical note explains that the previous name of Hebron was *Kirjath-arba*. Arba was a giant among the Anakims, a nation of giants. Yet, although these giants scared most of Israel, they were taken down by God through Caleb, and thus Hebron was renamed. The giants proved no match for God or the faith of His servant Caleb.

15:1 Judah receives the largest portion because it is the largest tribe. In the distribution of the land to Judah,

some words spoken by Jacob have a remarkable bearing on this tribe. The great patriarch Jacob had prophesied several specifics concerning his sons. In regard to Judah, Jacob had predicted that his tribe would grow to be strong and fierce because they would be surrounded by their enemies (Genesis 49:8–9). With the land they are given, Judah's tribe is surrounded by the Moabites to the east, Edomites to the south, Amalekites to the southwest, and Philistines to the west.

15:13–14 Included in Judah's portion of land is the city of Hebron (Kirjath-arba; 14:15). This city has been granted to Caleb. Caleb has to drive out the Anakims in order to take possession of his land, specifically their three leaders: Sheshai, Ahiman, and Talmai. These three kings are mentioned earlier (Numbers 13:22) as having been at Hebron when Caleb and the other spies were sent by Moses to scope out the land forty-five years earlier. A very redemptive victory indeed.

15:15–17 After his victory over Hebron, Caleb turns his attention to the nearby city of Debir (10:38–39; 11:21). Caleb puts an offer out to his men—whoever helps him take this city will be given his daughter Achsah's hand in marriage. Othniel captures the city and receives Achsah as his wife. Othniel is part of the Kenizzite clan, and he is also Caleb's nephew, which keeps the land in the family. Othniel is later one of the twelve judges whom God uses (Judges 3:9–11).

15:18–19 According to the text, Achsah urges someone to seek a piece of land from Caleb. It is not entirely clear whom she is asking, but it seems that she is asking her husband, Othniel, to acquire a piece of land for them. This is the second time someone has specifically requested a portion of the land—ironically, the first had been Caleb. This account is set apart from the rest of the text, forming an aside to the main story. The text moves abruptly to a conversation between Achsah and Caleb. The father asks his daughter what she wants, and she adds two more things to the land: a blessing and some springs. Natural springs would give her and her new husband the resources to prosper. The Negev (the southern region) has little water. The blessing that she seeks is the special favor of God upon her so that she will truly prosper in the land. Her father, Caleb, complies.

15:21–32 God is clearly providing for each tribe as He promised. But there is one thing in the list that seems to be a contradiction; the number of towns in the Negev is said to be twenty-nine, but thirty-six are listed. The reason for the difference is that seven of these towns were separated out later and given to Simeon's tribe (19:1–7).

15:63 The distribution for the tribe of Judah ends on a dark note: Judah could not remove the Jebusites, who were living in Jerusalem. Was this lack of victory because they simply weren't strong enough, or was it because they failed to trust God? Joshua does not say. Unfortunately, the Jebusites will prove to be a snare to Israel later.

16:1–5 The boundary line for the sons of Joseph began in the east, near Jericho, which was north of Judah's boundary. Ephraim's territory does not butt up against Judah, because sandwiched in between Ephraim and Judah is Benjamin. The territory given to Ephraim in Canaan is in many respects the most beautiful and fertile.

16:6–9 The specific allotment for the tribe of Ephraim is located immediately north of the territory to be assigned to Dan and Benjamin. The allotment of Ephraim stretches from the Jordan to the Mediterranean and includes the sites of some of Joshua's battles as well as Shiloh. This location is the sacred place where the tabernacle will remain for close to three hundred years. To foster unity between the two tribes, some of Ephraim's towns are located in the territory of Manasseh.

16:10 Just like the men of Judah, the men of Ephraim do not completely drive out the Canaanites from their region. In fact, they greedily keep the Canaanites around as forced laborers. This provides a labor force for free and fosters economic growth—for a season. In the time of the judges, the Canaanites rise up and enslave the Israelites.

17:1–10 Half of the tribe of Manasseh had settled in the region east of the Jordan (13:29), while the other half settled in Canaan proper. Machir is Manasseh's firstborn (Genesis 50:23; Numbers 26:29). His descendants represent the half tribe of Manasseh that had already received a separate portion east of the Jordan, in Gilead and Bashan (Joshua 13:29–31). The rest of Manasseh's allotment is west of the Jordan. The remaining heirs settle in Canaan proper and are given the territory north of Ephraim, extending from the Jordan to the Mediterranean Sea.

17:3 One descendant, Zelophehad, a great-great grandson of Manasseh, had already died with no male heirs. In fact, Zelophehad had five daughters but no sons. Hebrew culture demands that the inheritance go to the son, not to the daughter. This is because women entered into a new family when they were married and were not able to own land or receive an inheritance. The Lord declared that because their father died without any sons, the daughters could receive his inheritance (Numbers 27:1–11). The only requirement is that they not marry outside the tribe so that the land would not switch out to another tribe.

17:12–13 Several cities located in the tribes of Issachar and Asher are given to Manasseh. Apparently it is considered necessary for military purposes that these cities be held by a strong tribe. The sons of Manasseh, like the Ephraimites, however, choose tribute over triumph: Rather than driving out the Canaanites, they enslave them.

17:14 In this passage, the sons of Joseph speak as one. These two tribes are discontented with their allotted territory, challenging Joshua for more land. The episode unfolds through two verbal exchanges between Joshua and the tribes. This is the fourth narrative of people wanting to talk about land.

17:15 Joshua handles the complaint with skill. He challenges them to clear the trees and settle in the forested hill country.

17:18 Joshua suggests that the sons of Joseph combine their energies to drive out the Canaanites. Joshua's advice is wise—if they need more land, then they should clear out land from the forests where the Perizzites and giants (or Rephaites) live. In short, there is more land; they just need to possess it.

18:1 Prior to this point, Israel's central encampment in the land appears to have been at Gilgal, near Jericho. It is at this camp where the nation observes several ceremonies (4:19–20; 5:2–12) worth commemorating. Now the people are moved about fifteen miles northwest of Jericho to Shiloh. This place will remain an important Israelite religious center for several hundred years.

18:4–8 To begin the process of dividing the rest of the land, Joshua instructs that three men from each of the seven remaining tribes be appointed as surveyors. The role of these surveyors will be to travel throughout the land and record its description. They are to write down their findings. This is highlighted three times; God is making sure that all generations will know the land division. The previous allotments are reviewed to remind the remaining people how God has provided for all the people of Israel. The Lord was with the nation, not only in the tabernacle, but also in the casting of lots for the remaining allotments. The Levites' special inheritance is important, so Joshua mentions it again. He will make sure that those set apart for God's service are cared for and given everything they need.

18:11–28 Of the remaining tribes, Benjamin's allotment is given in the most detail (eighteen verses). This is probably because Benjamin's geographical location is between Judah on the south and Joseph (Ephraim) on the north.

19:1–9 The tribe of Simeon's inheritance is unique because they are not given an independent allotment but rather receive land scattered within Judah's allotment. Judah's portion was more than they needed. Simeon's tribe was small relative to Judah's (1 Chronicles 4:27). Jacob's prophecy describes why Simeon does not inherit any land. Simeon and Levi were brothers with a bent toward violence. Both men committed acts of violence against the inhabitants of Shechem when they annihilated every man in the city while the men were recuperating from circumcision (Genesis 34:24–30). Simeon's cities fall into two groups: thirteen cities in the southern portion, the Negev, and four additional cities—two in the Negev and two in the western foothills, the Shephelah. One additional city in the far south is mentioned for a total of eighteen.

19:15 The city named *Bethlehem* mentioned here is not the same as the one in Judah—famous for being the birthplace of the Messiah (Judges 17:7; Ruth 1:1; 1 Samuel 16:1; Micah 5:2; Matthew 2:1). Rather, it is in Zebulun, the site where Ibzan, the judge, is buried (Judges 12:8–10). Three cities within Zebulun's boundaries later became Levitical cities: Jokneam (Joshua 19:11; 21:34), Nahallal (19:15; 21:35), and Daberath (19:12; 21:28).

19:22–23 Issachar is the second small tribe in the north, in the region of Galilee. Its boundary description consists of only three cities, and its city list contains thirteen cities. Issachar's general location is clear: It is north of western Manasseh, east and south of Zebulun, west of the Jordan, and south of Naphtali.

19:24–31 The tribe of Asher's territory lay in a long, narrow strip in the far northwest. The land is bordered on the west by the Mediterranean Sea and the tribe of Zebulun, and on the east by Manasseh's western boundary. This territory, by virtue of its position, serves as a major land of protection from northern coastal enemies (including, for example, the Phoenicians). By the time David is king, this tribe had lost much of its significance. One notable fact connects this tribe to the Messiah: Anna, the prophetess who blesses Jesus, is from this tribe (Luke 2:36–38).

19:27 The text provides very few details about the inheritance of these five smaller tribes beyond standard boundary and city lists for each. Zebulun was a small tribe whose territory was nestled between Issachar, western Manasseh, Asher, and Naphtali. According to Jacob's prophecy (19:10–16), Zebulun would live by the seashore and become a haven for ships. In this text we see that Zebulun is assigned land in lower Galilee. This land extends to the Mediterranean Sea, forming an enclave in Issachar's territory.

19:32–39 Naphtali receives the rich, forested land in the heart of the Galilee region. Asher is to the west, Zebulun to the south, and the Jordan River and eastern Manasseh to the east. This region does not play a highly significant role in the Old Testament period. Yet in the New Testament, this is the region where Jesus centers His Galilean ministry. It is in this region where Jesus fulfills the prophecy of Isaiah (Isaiah 9:1). Naphtali's allotment includes a list of fortified cities. Because of these well-protected cities, the tribe of Naphtali enjoys periods of prosperity, especially when Israel's kings are strong.

19:40–48 The final lot is cast for the tribe of Dan. This territorial allotment is in the south, abutting Judah and other tribes. Yet Dan is listed in this chapter with the northern tribes in Galilee. They are unable to take their own land, so they move north and attack the city of Leshem, which is opposite the northern part of Naphtali, and settle there (Genesis 49:17; Judges 1:34; 18). Thus they are included among these smaller tribes with allotments in Galilee, because this is where they eventually settled.

19:49–51 Caleb's inheritance is settled first (14:6–15); Joshua's is last. Joshua evidently wanted to make sure that his work had been accomplished before he would take what belonged to him. He allows all of the land to be distributed and takes from what is left over. In no way does he exercise his position for selfish gain; his choice of land demonstrates his humility.

20:1–9 The instructions governing the cities of refuge are based on legislation established by Moses. In the Pentateuch, the Israelites were instructed that six cities should be established within their nation as cities of refuge, where a man could flee if he accidentally killed someone (Exodus 21:12–14). The all-knowing God of the Israelites recognizes that people are often victims of the fallen world in which they live. These cities were establishments of grace and mercy in a nation where murderers were normally condemned to death. No place in the land was more than a day's journey from one of these cities of refuge. All six of these cities are mentioned again in the next chapter, since they also were Levitical cities. Despite their importance here and in the Pentateuch, however, they do not appear again in the Old Testament. The six designated cities were located on both sides of the Jordan River. On the west side were Kedesh in Galilee, Shechem in Ephraim, and Hebron in Judah. The cities on the east side were Bezer in the south, Ramoth in the region of Gilead in the tribe of Gad, and Golan in the northern territory of Bashan in Manasseh's tribe.

21:1–45 The last act of distribution is now taking place. Because the Levites are not given an allotment of their own territory, they are scattered (like Simeon's tribe; see 19:1–9). The Levites' inheritance is the honor that they have been set apart to serve God. The call to service is a gift greater than wealth or territory, and the Levites are reminded here to treasure what God has already blessed them with so abundantly.

21:4 The distribution for the Levites takes place according to the three main branches of the tribe of Levi. These three main branches correspond to Levi's three sons: Kohath, Gershon, and Merari. This detail is included to show the reader that not one aspect of God's promise is missed.

21:8–19 Thirteen towns for the Kohathites are listed first. Nine are in the territory belonging to the tribes of Judah and Simeon. Hebron is listed as a city of refuge because the Levites are responsible for these cities.

21:20–26 Ten more cities, including Shechem (another city of refuge), are listed. These cities are assigned to the other branches of the Kohathites in Ephraim, Dan, and western Manasseh. The priestly cities fall primarily within the southern kingdom of Judah. It is in the southern region where the temple will be built in Jerusalem, so it makes sense for the Levites to be nearby.

21:41 To have the Levites dispersed within the land is a great blessing for the nation. The Levites are to instruct Israel in the law of the Lord, to maintain the knowledge of His Word among the people. The blessing of this inheritance allows the nation to have the constant reminder and the continual discipleship of the way of God. God is, in essence, sending His ministers all throughout the land to build up, protect, and equip all generations in the way of the Lord. No one in Israel lives more than ten miles from one of the forty-eight Levite cities. This means that every Israelite has access to one of God's men who can shepherd the people. Keep in mind that for the nation to stay in the land, they must obey God (Leviticus 26). God provides the shepherds and leadership that the people need to obey the Lord.

22:1–4 The eastern tribes of Reuben and Gad and the half tribe of Manasseh have served the rest of the nation and fought alongside their brothers. Now it is time for them to return to their land. Joshua praises them for their efforts and for their commitment to their promise—to fight with the rest of the nation before they take their land (Numbers 32; Joshua 1:16–18; 4:12–14). They had been faithfully fighting for seven years, and during this time they had been away from their families and their homes. These men are being honored for their service.

22:5 The returning soldiers are given six commands by Joshua before they leave: First, be very careful to keep the commandment and the law. Second, love the Lord your God. Third, walk in all His ways. Fourth, keep His commands. Fifth, cling to Him. And finally, serve Him with all your heart and all your soul.

22:8 Leaving for home, the men from the eastern tribes take with them much of the spoils from the enemy. They are instructed to share the spoils with those who remained at home to care for and protect the land. The rule that is being established here surfaces again in the history of the Israelites (1 Samuel 30:24). The principle is that those who serve in support of war but who do not actually do the fighting are able to share in the full spoils of war. Support roles are of equal importance.

22:11–12 The act of building this altar is interpreted as an act of apostasy. The rest of the tribes of the western side of the border meet at Shiloh. This is significant because this is where the one true altar is located. It is here that they decide to go to war against the armies of the eastern tribes. They conclude that this new altar is rebellion against God. From their perspective, they believe that the others have set up a second altar of sacrifice contrary to the Mosaic Law (Leviticus 17:8–9). The western tribes believe that if their brethren are going to mock God and set up an alternate place of worship, then they will go to war to defend the integrity of worship. As difficult as this must have been, the rest of the tribes are prepared to go to war against their own brothers. Eleazar's son, Phinehas, is passionate for the Lord (Numbers 25:6–18). He heads a force to confront the eastern tribes.

22:22 The eastern tribes do not fight back or act in a defensive manner. Rather, the eastern tribes respond with humility to the charge that the altar they erected is in rebellion against God. They present their hearts before God as a witness and they swear twice by His names—*El, Elohim, Yahweh* (the Mighty One, God, the Lord)—strongly stating that if their act was in rebellion against God and His commands, then they deserve His judgment. Despite their initial misunderstanding, we see in this account that both tribes handle this situation correctly—with humility and a willingness to listen.

22:29 The eastern tribes make it clear that they are fully aware of God's laws governing worship. The point of this altar is not to replace the place for burnt offerings, but to show all generations that the eastern tribes have the right to worship God with the western tribes; in short, they are a part of the community.

22:32 The explanation of the eastern tribes is fully accepted by Phinehas and his delegation. Indeed, this response causes the western tribes to rejoice and praise God. Phinehas expresses joy and thankfulness that no sin has been committed and that the wrath of God is not going to be called down upon their eastern brothers.

23:1–2 Some years after the end of the conquest and distribution of the land, Joshua summons Israel's leaders, probably to Shiloh where the tabernacle is located. This gathering serves a very serious and solemn purpose—to warn the leaders of the dangers of not taking God and His commands seriously.

23:3–16 Joshua has one theme that he repeats three times: God has been faithful to Israel, so Israel must serve and obey Him all the days of their lives. There is no more important message for followers of God in any age. God must be taken seriously, obedience must be a way of life, and sin must be treated as an abomination to the Lord.

23:10 Joshua reminds the people that their enemies have been defeated solely because the Lord has fought for them. The battles that they fought were the Lord's, and God provided the victories. Scripture tells us that every good and perfect thing we have is from God (James 1:17).

23:13 Joshua reminds the leaders that the Lord will push the Canaanites, who are still scattered throughout the country, out of the land entirely if they rely on God. God remains committed to creating their nation if they rely on His strength, and He has promised to enable them to carry out the task of taking full possession of the land.

24:1 Shechem is the place where Abraham first received the promise that God would give his seed the land of Canaan. Abraham responds by building an altar to demonstrate his faith in the one true God (Genesis 12:6–7). Jacob, too, stops at Shechem on his return from Padan-aram and buries the idols his family had brought with them (Genesis 35:4). After the Israelites complete the first phase of the conquest of Canaan, they journey to Shechem, where Joshua builds an altar to Yahweh, inscribes the law of God on stone pillars, and reviews these laws for all the people (Joshua 8:30–35).

24:2 Joshua is reminding the people what God Himself has said. In other words, this is God speaking to the people, reviewing with them what He has done and reminding them what lies at the heart of their covenant. First He brought them out of Ur of the Chaldees (24:2–4; see Genesis 11:31). Then they were delivered out of bondage to Gentile worship and brought to the land of blessing. Next they were brought out of Egypt (24:5–7) and into Canaan (24:8–13). Again they were delivered from the bondage and slavery of the Egyptians and brought to the freedom of the promised land.

24:3–13 God uses "I" seventeen times to underscore that these good things, these amazing deliverances and victories, were performed by Him and not the Israelites. God is the One who pulled them out of every mess, out of every conflict, and out of every problem. God is the One who delivered them from all of their trials and the One who brought them into the land flowing with milk and honey.

24:15 Israel must fear the Lord and serve Him. Joshua personalizes this command, saying that whatever the leaders' choice is in regard to serving God, his own mind was made up.

24:16 The initial response of the people is good. They are still so close to the time of the conquest that they despise the very thought of forsaking God. They had the firsthand experience of being delivered by God.

24:19 Joshua is not at all satisfied with the people's verbal commitment. He knows the human heart and how people can easily be led astray, and he knows how deceptive sin can be. He is quite aware that an emotional commitment made at a moment in time does not mean as much as it might appear. Joshua bluntly declares to the Israelite leadership that they are not able to serve the Lord. He is a holy God and a jealous God. He will not forgive their rebellion and their sins.

24:20 Joshua does not mean that God is not a God of forgiveness. He means that God is not to be worshipped or served lightly. To forsake Him deliberately and to serve idols will be willful sin against God, and to sin in this manner under their circumstances will be unforgivable under the law (Numbers 15:30). This type of sin will result in disaster. Again the people respond to Joshua's probing words, earnestly reaffirming their purpose to serve the Lord.

24:22–24 Joshua calls Israel to serve as witnesses against themselves if they do turn aside from God. The

people immediately reply "yes." Joshua then speaks again, reminding them of the point he had mentioned at the beginning—that they must get rid of their idols. They have already begun the slow and steady slide to disobedience. Joshua challenges them to prove their sincerity by their works and get rid of the idols. It is interesting to note that without the slightest hesitation, the people shout their dedication to God.

24:26–27 Joshua makes a covenant with the people this day. He writes down their agreement in the book of the law of God, which is probably placed beside the ark of the covenant (Deuteronomy 31:24–27). As a final reminder, Joshua also inscribes the statutes of the covenant on a large stone slab, which is set up beneath the oak at this sacred location. Joshua says that the stone is a witness to this covenant. It bears the words of the covenant for all generations to see.

24:29 Three burials—each of them in Ephraim—mark the close of the book of Joshua. First it is recorded that Joshua dies at the age of 110 years. He is buried in his own town (19:50). No greater tribute can be paid to him than the fact that he is called "the servant of the LORD." Such should be the highest goal of everyone.

24:32 The burial of Joseph's bones is recorded. Joseph's dying request was that he be buried in the promised land (Genesis 50:25). Moses, knowing of this request, took Joseph's bones with him in the Exodus (Exodus 13:19). Finally, Joseph's remains, which had been embalmed in Egypt more than four hundred years earlier, are laid to rest in Shechem (Genesis 33:18–20; 50:26).

24:33 The third burial mentioned in these last verses of Joshua is that of the high priest Eleazar, son and successor of Aaron. Joshua, Joseph, and Eleazar once lived in a foreign nation where they received God's promise to take His people back to Canaan. Now all three are laid to rest within the promised land. God kept His word to these men, just as He had kept His promise to the Israelites. These burials testify to the faithfulness of God.

THE BOOK OF

JUDGES

INTRODUCTION TO JUDGES ■ The book of Judges gets its name from its main characters: the people God graciously selected to save ancient Israel from itself. It tells the stories of colorful and imperfect individuals with charismatic qualities God uses to break the yoke of oppression that Israel experienced, time after time, as a result of its own sinfulness. Through these types of saviors, God calls His children back to Himself.

AUTHOR ■ Although Samuel was traditionally thought to be the author of Judges, no one knows who put it together. Experts say it could have been a single author, because the material is well shaped into a coherent whole; or there may have been more than one compiler.

OCCASION ■ Judges is a compilation of selected independent stories, mostly centered on one individual. But there is one overall message: Israel's repetitive cycle of sin, and God's consistent and merciful response.

1:3 The tribe of Simeon would have lived in close proximity to the tribe of Judah. Simeon was given territory within the boundaries of the southern kingdom, taking land out of Judah's territory (Joshua 19:1–9). This connectedness to Judah, while it may have had advantages, also meant that the tribe of Simeon lost some of its distinct identity. Many trace this loss back to the curse that Jacob put on his son Simeon, the ancestor of this tribe, in Genesis 49.

1:4–7 We're told of the destruction of ten thousand men. This count of ten thousand is more of a representative number than an actual head count. The destruction includes Adoni-bezek (lord of Bezek). While Judah's treatment of Adoni-bezek seems extreme, it also carries a sense of justice. He is receiving the same kind of treatment that he often dished out—for instance, rendering his victims unable to run or bear weapons. Adoni-bezek dies in Jerusalem.

1:8 Jerusalem is set on fire, but the Israelites do not occupy the city at this time. Eventually, of course, Jerusalem will become the capital city of the Israelite territory of Judah. The day will come when King David, a descendant of Judah, will rule from there.

1:11–16 Othniel, to win his bride, destroys a great city of wickedness. Caleb, the father figure, gives the bride to his nephew and grants them a land of peace. The bride seeks a blessing, an outpouring of water, from her father. Moses had persuaded some of his father-in-law's (Jethro's) family to come with him to the land of promise. Those who believed and followed Moses came through his line of Levi and found a place to flourish in the land of Judah.

1:12 Caleb is one of the twelve spies who, forty years earlier, entered Canaan on reconnaissance to report back to Israel before they entered the land. Of the twelve spies, only Joshua and Caleb believed that God could and would give them the land He had promised. As a result of their faith, these two men were the only spies who actually entered Canaan.

1:17 *Hormah* means "placed under the ban, totally destroyed." If this utter destruction is done according

to God's decree (see Deuteronomy 20:16–18), then it is considered a whole burnt offering to the Lord. Simeon may be mentioned, because this time (as opposed to his actions in Genesis 34) he is faithfully bringing God's wrath to bear.

1:19–21 Judah takes several Philistine cities and the hill country, but he cannot take the valley due to the strength of the Canaanites' iron chariots. Judah initially takes Jerusalem (also called Jebus), which is in the land given to Benjamin, but Benjamin is not able to drive out the Jebusites living there. In the end, they allowed these pagans to dwell with them. In both of these cases, only a partial victory is obtained. This is significant in that it represents only a partial obedience to what God told the tribes to do. The land was supposed to be claimed for God entirely. Any non-Israelites who remained there should have been incorporated into the worship of the Israelite God Yahweh rather than taken on as simply co-inhabitants.

1:22–26 Spies are sent to Luz (Bethel), and they find help from within. But this time (unlike the story of Rahab in Joshua 2:1–13; 6:17) when the city is taken, the saved family does not repent and join Israel but flees and sets up another pagan city.

1:27–30 Manasseh does not drive out the Canaanites but puts them under tribute, clearly against the Lord's commands (see Exodus 23:32). Ephraim and Zebulun act similarly. In this way, these tribes have not only ignored God's commands but put themselves at risk spiritually by allowing the current religions to still be practiced.

1:31–33 Asher and Naphtali allow the previous inhabitants to dwell among them. What this means is that the Canaanites are predominate in these lands. Rather than Asher and Naphtali allowing the Canaanites to live there under each Israelite tribe's dominion, this situation is closer to the other way around. This is a great evidence of weakness for these tribes.

1:34 The tribe of Dan is forced to live in the mountains. Their wickedness is revealed in much more detail in chapters 17–18.

2:1 The angel of the Lord is specifically charged to bring judgment upon sinful Israel (see Exodus 23:20–23). The charges in this passage suggest that this angel visitor is the Lord Himself, probably a preincarnate visitation of Jesus. There are several events in the Old Testament in which an angelic visitor seems more like an appearance of Jesus than simply an angel. See, for example, the accounts of Hagar (Genesis 16:7–12) and Abraham (Genesis 22:15–16).

2:4–5 In rejecting the Lord's commands, what the Israelites may have thought would be pleasures in their new lives in Canaan would become deep thorns in their sides.

2:9 Joshua is buried in a region that became known as the "Portion of the Sun." This may be reminiscent of one of God's great works during Joshua's conquest of Canaan when He made the sun stand still during the great battle at Gilgal (Joshua 10).

2:13 The gods Baal and Ashtaroth were the male and female counterparts of the representation of the power of nature. These two powers interacted (had intercourse), thus the sexual rituals included in Baal worship), and the fruit of their union was considered creation. Adherents to the worship of these deities believed religious orgies in the temples would motivate Baal and Ashtaroth to once again bring forth better crops in the land.

2:16–19 These verses describe a terrible cycle. God's children do not listen to judges God raises up for them. Instead, they spiritually prostitute themselves to other religions such as Baal worship. Then they *groan*, a word used before only in Exodus 2 and 6, under oppression. Each time, the Lord raises up a man to judge and deliver them again, but once he dies, the people quickly fall back into spiritual adultery. And unfortunately, each generation of Israelites falls more deeply into this cycle than the one before.

2:20–23 Many times when God's judgments come into play, the very act of compromise becomes the means God uses to chastise His children. This is not merely the impassioned rage of God but probably an ordained means of revealing humanity's sin in terms that are easily accessible.

3:8 In this case, since the people do not want to follow God, He is sending them back, giving them over to their sin. Interestingly, this is also the place where one day, further down the line in Israel's story, Assyria and Babylon will come and take the people into exile, one that will be far worse than their famous bondage in Egypt. Through these eight years of subjection to a foreign power, the Israelites have an opportunity to experience life without God, since they seem to be choosing that life, after all.

3:10 As expected, the children of Israel cry out to God, who raises up a deliverer: Othniel. Othniel's victory is due to the work of the Spirit. The result of this victory is a full generation of rest (which most likely indicates a rest from war): forty years, until Othniel dies.

3:12–13 After Othniel dies, Israel falls away from the God of their salvation once again and faces some

ironic twists of circumstances that should draw their attention back. Through God's hand, Eglon, king of Moab, overpowers Israel. He takes the city of palm trees (believed to be Jericho) and forces Israel to pay tributes to him. These tributes may very well have been the firstfruit sacrifices, first harvests of crops and herds, which should have been rendered to the Lord.

3:13 Joining Eglon are the people of Ammon and the Amalekites. After they conquer the Israelites, the people suffer eighteen long years of oppression before meeting their next deliverer. The Amalekites, who also partnered with Eglon, were sworn enemies of God and Israel. Exodus 17:8 describes a time when Israel defeated Amalek, but here in Judges 3 the roles are reversed.

3:15 Ehud, a Benjamite, is a "lefthanded" warrior. He is also trusted by Eglon to present the required tribute. Ehud makes a dagger and straps it to his right thigh.

3:19–26 This shrewd deliverer takes advantage of his situation to bring about the salvation of his people from the tyranny of Eglon. This is not the act of an individual in a domestic dispute. Ehud is at war, and Eglon is an unlawful king in Israel's homeland.

3:30 The day began with a tribute to an enemy king and ended with that kingdom routed and ashamed. God's people are free.

3:31 In what can seem like a strange and out-of-place addendum, this story ends with a single verse about another judge, Shamgar. Although we know little of his story now, he was apparently well known in the days of Deborah, the one female judge mentioned in this book (chapters 4–5). Shamgar's name reveals that he was most likely not an Israelite but a convert to the Lord.

4:2–3 When the Israelites continue their cycle of spiritual downfall—again—God lets them fall into the hand of a wicked king called Jabin. This may have been a title instead of a personal name, much as the Egyptians called their kings Pharaoh. Jabin's commander, Sisera, cruelly oppresses the Israelites in Harosheth of the Gentiles. This area, in the north, is the land of Zebulun and Naphtali, north and west of the sea of Chinnereth (or Sea of Galilee). Sisera commands nine hundred iron chariots, the same tools of battle that Judah had feared generations before according to 1:19.

4:4 During Jabin's twenty-year rule, Deborah, a prophetess whose name means "bee," acts as a judge in Israel. Deborah stands out because of her gender. It is unusual (though not unheard of) in this era in the history of Israel to find a woman filling the role of prophet or judge.

4:5 Deborah held court under a tree. The image of trees is a significant one in the Bible. Trees were a source of comfort and shade. They provided not only shelter but sometimes food as well. They are often included in important biblical events and images. Humanity was first judged at a tree, and that judgment is paid by a Savior who hangs on a tree. The tabernacle is pitched under a great tree where the book of the law of God was kept (Joshua 24:26). It was a place that represented a gate to heaven, a place of righteousness and justice, and (later) a place of healing and food (Revelation 22:2).

4:9 Deborah's response to Barak's struggle to believe is a rebuke, but a gentle one. Barak does believe, raises up an army of ten thousand, and leads them to victory (more details are revealed in chapter 5). He is included in a list of faithful ancestors in Hebrews 11 as an example to follow.

4:17–22 Jael's husband, Heber the Kenite, has moved away from his fellow Kenites' alliance with Israel and made peace with Sisera. Apparently Jael, whose name means "goat," does not approve. When she recognizes the fleeing Sisera, she courageously deceives this enemy of the Lord into coming into her tent, where she offers him milk (perhaps goat's milk) and then slays him. Then she faces up to Barak and shows him her handiwork—an honor Barak was told would not be his.

5:1 Deborah and Barak praise God for His victorious strength. They exalt those who keep their word and serve the Lord in battle, and they chastise those who fall back in their comfortable religion. They contrast the true and living God with Baal, the false god, and mince no words in describing the violent victory of the righteous and the violent debauchery of the fallen.

5:7 The song recalls threatening scenes of normal life before the arrival of Deborah, a mother of Israel. And following this maternal motif, Deborah does bring new life to the nation of Israel.

5:10–15 These verses are somewhat obscure but appear to be summoning all of the people—the rich and the poor, men in arms and the common people at the watering places. All are to recount the righteous acts of God and thus stir one another up to serve God by coming down to the gates of the city. Though Deborah's song celebrates those who came to fight, it is clear that the Lord does not need help to win a battle.

5:16–17, 23 Deborah praises those who respond in faith and join the battle, and she mocks those who are too comfortable, too busy, or too frightened to fight.

5:20–21 Baal is impotent compared to the true Lord of the stars and clouds. This mention of stars and clouds may be a dig at the Canaanite astrologers. We have no record of the village of Meroz, cursed in verse 23.

5:24–31 These verses celebrate the story of Jael, the Kenite woman who assassinated Sisera. In contrast to Meroz, Jael shows more zeal, courage, and faith. Jael refuses to compromise with her husband, and when the Lord grants her the opportunity, she serves Him honorably. Conversely, Deborah's words toward Sisera's mother are a form of mockery toward the woman for sitting and wondering why her son has not returned home.

6:1–6 "Did evil" is a phrase used in the book of Judges to refer to idolatry. Israel strays again, which brings the typical consequences—the nation weakens, and the people have to leave their homes and hide in caves as foreign invaders come in and wipe out their crops and livestock. When Israel lives according to God's laws,

they live under God's blessing—the Israelites get to reap what others sow (Joshua 24:13). On the other hand, when the Israelites live in disobedience, others reap what Israel has sown (Deuteronomy 28:29, 31). And true to form, we are told that Israel finally cries out to God again for deliverance.

6:8 Before He sends Israel a deliverer, God sends them a prophet. This unnamed prophet, in essence, prepares the way for the deliverer. This prophet does not bring new prophecies; he declares what has been forgotten.

6:10 We are reminded that the main problem is not oppression but false worship, false gods, and disobedience to the Lord.

6:11 The angel of the Lord appears at the foot of an oak tree. Gideon is threshing in a winepress, trying to hide what little wheat his father has from the marauding band. All of this symbolism points to a lack of communion with God.

6:12 The angel declares that the Lord is with Gideon. Because God is with him, Gideon will be a valiant warrior. Gideon's response is one of faith, for he acknowledges that the oppression is from the hand of God.

6:14 The source of Gideon's might is that God is sending him. Gideon is dumbfounded at this idea. He is of the weakest clan in a half tribe of Israel, he is the least in his father's house, and he is down in an empty winepress threshing wheat like an ox. In the history of Israel, however, there have been other situations in which a younger (and thus weaker in position) son was chosen: Abel over Cain, Isaac over Ishmael, Jacob over Esau, Joseph over his ten older brothers. Strength comes from God's appointment of a person rather than his or her human rank or glory.

6:16–17 The Lord rewards Gideon's humility with a promise. Because God is with him, Gideon's victory will be total. Moses was considered the meekest man in the old covenant; and like Moses, Gideon now asks for a sign.

6:19–21 Gideon prepares an offering (a modified peace offering), and the fire that consumes it leaves no room for doubt—Gideon has been with God.

6:25 Gideon's first task is to tear down an altar to Baal, which apparently is on his father's property. This task by itself reveals that Gideon grew up in an idolatrous home.

6:28–32 The morning after Gideon's sacrifice, everyone knows what has happened. Baal's altar is wrecked, the nearby grove (perhaps an Ashtaroth pole) is now destroyed, and Joash's prize bull has been sacrificed as a sign of the Lord's favor. The men of the town demand that Joash turn over his son, but Joash, in biting sarcasm, reveals that his household is now following Gideon and the Lord. Then Gideon's father renames him *Jerubbaal*, the Baal-fighter.

6:33 The Midianites were descended from Abraham and his second wife, Keturah. God is now using the Midianites as a judgment upon Israel.

6:34 The idea is that the Spirit encompasses Gideon like clothing. Here we see also a pattern—a sacrifice for sin and the gift of repentance, followed by the equipping of God's people by His Spirit to finish the work that was already definitively accomplished by God in the sacrifice. Gideon is now clothed as a new man, re-created after the image of God. He calls the people of God to battle. The Midianites have come again, but this time God has sent messengers who gather the people back to Himself, back to the battle at hand.

6:37–40 The dew and fleece may represent Gideon being anointed and then, through him, all of Israel being blessed. As to miracles, the God of scripture is eternally active in His provision of all things.

7:2 Gideon's messengers gather a fighting force of some 32,000 men. That may seem like a lot, but the Midianites have more than 135,000. Nevertheless, the Lord wants to make clear that He alone is delivering Israel, and He alone is to receive the glory.

7:3–4 Gideon first reduces the troops to ten thousand. This is in line with God's commands in Deuteronomy 20:8. Holy war cannot be fought except by men of faith who have confidence in the Lord and no fear.

7:5–7 God further reduces the number. The second reduction comes through choosing men who drink water in a unique way. This leaves Gideon with the three hundred men God wants. The ratio is now 450:1. God's providence has made His people recognize their utter dependence on Him for their salvation.

7:10–15 When Gideon accepts God's offer of assurance, God kindly strengthens his faith. God's message of encouragement comes through a Midianite private, who correctly interprets his friend's dream. Note that Gideon's reputation is known among his enemies. This soldier recognizes that the barley cake—the bread of the poor—flattening the Midianite tent means doom. Overhearing this, Gideon bows in worship before the Lord.

7:25 Two commanders of the Midianite army are captured and killed by Ephraim. The places where they are killed become landmarks of God's sense of irony. The Israelites used to hide in rocks (6:2), but now Oreb is killed, possibly trying to hide in a rock himself. Gideon once hid in a winepress (6:11), but now Zeeb is killed at a winepress.

8:1–3 Ephraim's concern is for personal glory. But Gideon decides to turn away their anger with a soft answer (Proverbs 15:1). Ephraim can be commended for what they have done right, even if it is wrapped in a quest for personal gain (see Philippians 1:15–18). Gideon does mildly rebuke them, noting that God delivered these princes into their hands.

8:5–7 Succoth refuses to risk their immediate safety by openly trusting God's promise of deliverance in the light of risky circumstances. They will not side with the Lord in His blessing, and so they come to know the Lord in His discipline (8:16).

8:8–11 The city of Penuel is not afraid of the enemy, but their trust is not in the Lord. Their trust is in their big tower. Gideon's judgment upon them is not only to

destroy their tower but to kill the men of the city as well. God is a jealous God, and He will not share His glory with any other.

8:12–20 Gideon, as Jerubbaal, the servant of the Lord for the people of Israel, has the right and obligation to put to death these kings of Midian. But in this short discourse, we see the beginnings of something dark taking place. Gideon does not correct Zebah and Zalmunna when they imply he is a king. Perhaps misusing his power for vengeance, he seeks to disgrace them by having his young son slay them (and, like his father was earlier, Jether is afraid).

8:22–23 The people now seek to establish a dynasty in Gideon. But he only judges as one appointed by God, and it was the Lord who delivered them. The people's trust is moving away from the Lord again, toward an earthly throne. Unfortunately, the story doesn't end after Gideon's faithful answer.

8:27 Gideon probably justifies making a new ephod out of the Midianite plunder because God had instructed him to sacrifice and had spoken to him specifically. The original ephod, in the distant tabernacle, was a golden tunic worn by the priests. It bore the Urim and Thummim, used by the high priest to determine the word and will of God. With this new object, located in Gideon's hometown of Ophrah, the Israelites begin to follow Gideon as a pseudo king and priest.

8:28–29, 32 These verses emphasize the fact that Gideon's life was blessed by God and that overall, his service to the Lord was faithful. Nevertheless, notice the name change from *Jerubbaal* to *Gideon* between verses 29 and 32. This suggests that Gideon does not end up acting as a Baal-fighter but as a pagan king, influenced by Baal-like gods.

8:31 Abimelech, Gideon's son of a concubine, is named "my father is king." Most of us know the struggle of making our practice as holy as our theology. Gideon has denied the throne, but in his dreams and in some of his actions, he has been letting this temptation simmer, slowly and quietly permeating the aroma of his life.

8:33 Gideon's time as a judge is a mixed bag. But he must have restrained the worship of Baal effectively, because it isn't until after his death that the Israelites begin engaging in Baalism again. *Baal-berith* is literally "lord of the covenant." This vague, inclusive title could appeal to God-fearing Israelites and Baal-worshipping Canaanites alike (similar to a phrase like "God bless America"). But this mushy theology leads to a terrible curse and judgment on the true Lord of the covenant.

9:1–3 Gideon's half-Canaanite son Abimelech confronts Shechem's leaders, his uncles on his mother's side. He calls for loyalty to Baal-berith and not to the Baal-fighter and his God. Implied is Abimelech's argument that for Shechem to make a clean break, all of Jerubbaal's sons must be killed, for surely their intent is to rule over them.

9:7–20 Gideon's youngest son, Jotham, proclaims a parable from the mount of blessing, Gerizim. It is a curse and a call to repentance. The people have obviously been seduced to believe that what they have done is right and just, and that they have acted in truth and sincerity. Jotham warns them that if they do not turn from their loyalty to Abimelech, they will be burned by this same tyrant. Once again, rebellious sin becomes the very instrument of judgment upon the people.

9:23–25 Evil is self-destructive; evil people will be at one another's throats soon enough. But in His graciousness to His own people, God sends an evil spirit to speed things along. The people of Shechem turn against Abimelech, who has ruled them for three years, and begin to rob travelers passing by.

9:26–29 Gaal, in the midst of a great harvest festival (Baal is a god of the harvest), calls for pure devotion to the god and people of Shechem. In the drunkenness of the feast, he calls on Abimelech to come out and fight.

9:30–38 Zebul, a city leader, hears about Gaal and warns Abimelech, who then plans a preemptive strike. Gaal spots movement, but Zebul convinces him he sees shadows until it's too late. Zebul gets the last laugh before the battle. Gaal and his Canaanite followers are chased from town. But like a brush fire, Abimelech's wrath has just begun.

9:45 The people of Shechem figure that the crisis is over and head back out to the harvest. But Abimelech, fresh from one victory, comes down upon the field and the city, destroys, kills, and curses the land with salt (see Deuteronomy 29:23). We begin to see the hand of the Lord bringing His judgment on the land using the instrument of Abimelech, who is himself an enemy of the Lord.

9:46 The leaders of the tower flee to the inner chamber of the house of the god Berith (which means "God of the covenant"). Just as Gideon had burned the altar of Baal, so Abimelech now brings bramble-fire judgment upon Baal's house.

9:50–53 Abimelech's lust for power presses him farther, to what appears to be an easier target: Thebez. God's irony is everywhere. Another tower, another woman, another stone—but this time, his own head is crushed. Although we clearly see the chastisement of God upon Gideon's family, still these verses declare that God is at work avenging the family of Gideon, the Baal-fighter.

10:1–3 These verses provide a quick description of two judges of Israel. Tola served as judge for twenty-three years, yet no children are listed. Jair's description includes thirty sons.

10:4 What we can see in this opening description, as with the account of Gideon, is the struggle to establish a dynasty. Keep in mind that there was not a prohibition against having many wives in the Old Testament, and having many children was a sign of blessing. This is why the count of children is significant here.

10:6 Often the book of Judges records that the Lord grants rest after the work of the first judges (3:11, 30; 5:31; 8:28). With these regimes following Abimelech,

though, there is no mention of rest for the people. Life goes on, but it is as if the people are constantly falling away from their faith. Instead of rest, there is only more human activity. The fact that God keeps raising up judges to rescue and protect and lead His people is a sign of His grace. This verse and 13:1 both point to the fact that after these judges rule, Israel falls back into idolatry. This seems to tell us that, during their administrations, they kept the people from idolatry.

10:15–16 God has given fair warning that He will respond in kind (Deuteronomy 32:37–38). These frightening words, however, are used by God as a means to lead Israel to true repentance. They once again put away their false gods and serve the Lord. Notice that the text does not say God is impressed or moved by the repentance of the people. In fact, it says that God's soul cannot endure their misery. This is a reminder that hope in the mercy of God does not rest in the sincerity of a person's repentance but in the intensity of God's compassion. Repentance, like faith, is never the ground of our salvation or pardon. Instead, that ground is the mercy of God.

11:1–6 Jephthah is rejected, much as God is rejected in chapter 10 (10:6). Then Gilead comes to Jephthah, much as Israel made an attempt to return to the Lord (10:10).

11:7–11 Jephthah at first rejects the cry of his family members, who call out to him because they need his help. When Gilead appeals, Jephthah does return to his family—in some fashion like the second cries of Israel and the answer of the Lord (10:15–16). The parallel here is more flawed, for Jephthah is imperfect in his motives.

11:12 In sending messengers to Ammon, Jephthah is revealed to be a man of peace.

11:13 The Ammonites claim that Israel has taken their land. Jephthah responds with a series of diplomatic arguments.

11:14–18 First argument: As Israel passed through the eastern side of the Jordan, they always attempted to remain at peace with the nations of Edom, Moab, and Ammon, respecting their borders.

11:19–22 Second argument: The disputed land that Israel took was the territory of the Amorites under King Sihon, not the Ammonites.

11:23 Third argument: The Lord gave this land to Israel.

11:24 Fourth argument: Jephthah charges them to live with what their god, Chemosh, has given them. One God is greater than another, and Jephthah makes that case clear.

11:25 Fifth argument: Jephthah attempts to avoid war with threats. Balak couldn't contend with Israel, so what makes Ammon think they can?

11:26 Sixth argument: Israel has occupied the land for three hundred years.

11:27 Seventh argument: Jephthah's true faith is seen here. His final appeal is to the Lord, who is the true Judge of Israel.

11:28 Even faced with these arguments, however, Ammon rejects Jephthah's diplomacy. When Ammon rejects the proposal for peace, the nation brings judgment upon itself. In this case, rejecting Jephthah's words is, in effect, rejecting the word of God, because Ammon refuses to surrender to God's will as defined by the Israelite judge.

11:30–31 Jephthah is given a great victory over Ammon, but we are given very little information on the battle. Rather, the focus of the story is on the vow that Jephthah makes and the results of that vow.

11:34–40 These verses constitute one of the most debated passages in the Old Testament. Did Jephthah actually take his daughter to the tabernacle, where the Levites would kill, skin, and section her, offering her up as a burnt offering? Some would argue that this is the only interpretation this scripture allows. Others disagree. Another perspective is that the word translated "burnt offering" (11:31) is not a Hebrew word that necessarily implies the *burning* of the offering (other offerings not referred to as burnt offerings were indeed burnt). Instead, an offering that is burnt up can carry with it the idea that the entire offering ascends to God. No portion is reserved back, even for the priests. Another insight that seems relevant is that Leviticus 27:1–7 describes the redemption contract for those who have been consecrated by a vow to the Lord. There are those who are irrevocably devoted to God and cannot be redeemed, however, as in this case. In a holy war ban, also, those who had been irrevocably devoted to God would be killed. (These deaths were not considered human sacrifices.) However one interprets Jephthah's vow, it is a vow of dedication to the Lord for victory, and it includes the promise to devote the firstfruits of peace coming from his home to the Lord.

12:1–4 This is the second time in the book of Judges that Ephraim claims they have been left out of the action and the resulting glory (8:1–3). Here, they actually threaten God's appointed judge—something the law condemns (Deuteronomy 17:12).

12:5–6 These verses reveal how Jephthah's men capture the passages (or fords) of the Jordan where the Ephraimites had to cross to return to their home (after they had made an offensive attack on Gilead). Because of the ingenuity of Jephthah's men, 42,000 Ephraimites fall under God's judgment.

12:8–15 As with the opening of chapter 10, chapter 12 closes with a brief history of three judges: Ibzan, Elon, and Abdon. The last in this list of minor judges, Abdon, has seventy sons (or grandsons), yet Elon has no children listed. Ibzan, like Jair in the opening of chapter 10, has thirty sons listed. Also, as with the list at the opening of chapter 10, these short histories give facts regarding not only the number of children but also the places of burial. While these judges rule for a time, theirs is not an ongoing dynasty.

13:2–4 The Danites lived in great compromise (1:34–36; see also 15:11 and chapters 17–18). This time, there is no narrative of the people crying out for deliverance. Instead, they are a people seemingly so used to bondage that they do not even call out for relief.

13:5 In these verses, and also in Numbers 6:1–8, we learn that *nazar* generally means "to be separated, consecrated," and it can be used as a crown of sorts, signifying the one set apart for something special. Nazarites are like priests, set apart for a particular service for the Lord, either for a particular time or, as we see in some cases, for their entire lives. By his life and by his death, Samson will begin a process of deliverance. But it will take Samuel and, finally, David before the Philistines will be completely crushed.

13:12–13 Manoah wants to know about this boy, what they will do for him, and what his work will be. The angel of the Lord returns and answers, coming first to the woman and answering Manoah's questions about the boy by speaking about the requirements for his mother. God is not going to give Manoah any more details for now.

13:16 Communion, the peace-meal with God, could not occur because, in Manoah's day, the people had not cried out to the Lord; there was no peace with God and humankind (13:1). First an *olah*—a whole burnt offering, an ascension offering—must be made. The writer parenthetically tells us that Manoah is not confused regarding the order of offerings (as we might be). Rather, it is only because he does not yet know that this is the angel of the Lord that he wrongly offers to sit and eat in peace with this man.

13:17–22 Manoah has another question: "What is thy name?" The God whose name is *Wonderful* (Isaiah 9:6) did wondrous things in the sight of Manoah and his wife. The angel of the Lord (who is the Lord Himself) ascends in the flame of the offering. Then Manoah knows that he has seen the Lord.

13:24 While so much attention is given to the events surrounding the birth of Samson, after his birth we learn very little about him until his adult ministry is initiated. We are told that from this point, God's Spirit began to move in him. God's wonders will be displayed not only on behalf of this deliverer but actually through him.

14:1–4 Instead of getting ready for war, Samson is in the mood for a wedding. Against his parents' desires, he finds a woman among the Philistines. We find ourselves easily siding with the parents on this one. But that would be siding against the Lord, who is intending to do something about the dominion of the Philistines over Israel even with as unwitting an accomplice as Samson seems to be.

14:5–9 The Nazarite finds himself in the vineyards of Timnath, where the fruit of the vine is to be enjoyed in this glorious land given to Israel by the Lord. But it has been taken from them. A lion (an unclean beast) attacks Samson, but the Spirit of the Lord comes mightily upon him, and he tears the lion apart with his bare hands.

Later, Samson comes back and finds honey in the carcasses, scrapes some out and eats it, and then gives some to his parents. But he keeps these strange events to himself. As a Nazarite, Samson is not supposed to touch the unclean carcasses. Yet he enjoys and shares a token of what is promised by his deliverance in that the land would again be a land of milk and honey for God's people.

14:10–18 Samson's father provides a wedding for his son, and a seven-day feast ensues. During this time, the occasion comes to move against the Philistines, but with a riddle. Samson really wins because the Philistines have to coerce his wife through fear to squeeze the information out of Samson. The point is not Samson's weakness but his wife's unfaithfulness. The bride is supposed to forget her own people (Psalm 45:10), come out, and be made one with her husband.

14:19–20 Like the lion, the Philistines have attacked Samson in the contest of the riddle, and the Spirit of the Lord comes mightily upon Samson again. This isn't a fit of rage—this is the Lord's administration of justice upon the Philistines. Afterward, Samson's anger is roused toward his wife and he leaves her, going back up to his father's house.

15:1–5 We are not told why Samson returns to his father's home without his wife. The story picks up as Samson returns to have relations with her. It is important to note this because it bears upon the eye-for-an-eye justice he will bring. The problem lies with the Philistines of Timnath. They have robbed him of his wife and fertility, and so he responds by attacking their fertility. The choice of foxes (wild animals—possibly jackals), three hundred of them, sent in pairs, leads to questions that are hard to answer. It is clear that this is not a fit of rage on Samson's part when we hear his words in verse 3.

15:6–8 Samson's wife has been afraid of being burned by her own people, and so she betrays her husband (14:15). She ends up receiving the very judgment she sought to escape. But she is Samson's wife, and so he brings vengeance with a great slaughter. Those who do not turn in repentance after receiving a slighter judgment will find that God has been patient in withholding His full wrath.

15:9–13 Like Samson's wife, the men of Judah fear the Philistines more than God. In fact, they are quite bothered by the ruckus that Samson has raised. They may have been enslaved by the Philistine culture, but at least they are at peace. Judah is the tribe that originally had faithfully gone into battle (1:1–20); they have now become cowards. But something else is being pictured here. God's own people are betraying their messiah, and this messiah is going along with it, with a greater plan of judgment and deliverance.

15:14–17 Once again, the Spirit of the Lord comes upon Samson, frees him, and sets him on a holy war. Picking up the fresh jawbone of a donkey (another unclean animal), Samson kills a thousand Philistines, one by one. Then the Nazarite throws the jawbone away, separating himself from that which is unclean.

15:18–20 If we do not have water, we die in a matter of days. God, in a clear reference to the forty-year wilderness wanderings, humbles this deliverer to show him that God alone must provide for all his needs.

16:1–3 Judges 15 concludes as each story of deliverance in the book of Judges concludes: with judgment on Israel for many years. The first verse of Judges 16 begins with the same pattern established back in 2:16–17. Samson is being led by his lusts just as Israel has been led by theirs. Samson goes deep into Philistine territory, where he sleeps with a harlot. When he finds out that he is going to be attacked, he thwarts the attackers' plans with a preemptive strike. He picks up the gates of the city and puts them where Hebron can see that Gaza is ripe for the picking.

16:4–5 Samson continues to forsake his calling and his vows. Delilah will be the one who betrays him this time. She turns him over for silver.

16:6–14 Samson has fun ridiculing the Philistines' belief in magic. But we also see Samson playing around with his vow. He mentions the number seven and later mentions his hair. Samson does not need to fear magic, but he does need to fear compromise, and Delilah playfully pouts and seduces her way to the truth.

16:15–21 Samson's focus is primarily upon his lusts, and he has lulled himself into thinking he is invincible. Giving in to Delilah's vexing, Samson tells her that if his hair is shaved, he will lose his strength. Like Israel, Samson chases after other lovers, taking God's grace as license for any sin that pleases him. And like Israel, Samson is sent into exile.

16:22 This verse mentions that Samson's hair is growing back. This is a sign of the stupidity of the Philistines, and also a sign of Samson's strength returning.

16:23–25 The Philistines call for a great party, and their victory is their theme. But Dagon has nothing to do with their victory; it is not Dagon's power but the Lord's absence. They bring out Israel's great deliverer and publicly mock him, and we should see the foreshadowing of another Deliverer, betrayed for silver, blinded and mocked by the Roman guards (Luke 22:64).

16:28–31 The servant of the Lord will be avenged, for the Lord's name will be avenged. The Lord answers the prayer of His suffering servant—Samson's death does not picture a suicide but a victorious self-sacrifice.

17:1–3 In Judges 16, Samson has been betrayed with 1,100 pieces of silver (16:1–5), and in the opening of Judges 17, we see 1,100 pieces of silver again surrounding a betrayal. Micah steals the silver from his mother but returns it because he fears her curses. While Micah returns what he has taken, he makes no restitution as required by laws, such as those in Leviticus 6:1–7, nor is any trespass offering made.

17:4–5 Micah's mother, unnamed in this passage, dedicates the silver to the Lord but then uses it to make a carved image and a molded image, openly breaking the second commandment. Micah has a shrine (a false tabernacle), an ephod (a false garment for fortune-telling), and household idols. These idols are *teraphim*—little messengers to gods—as opposed to the seraphim who serve God. Micah also sets up his son as the priest of his own worship house.

17:7–13 From Micah's perspective, things seem to get better. A Levite from Bethlehem (which means "the house of bread") comes looking for work. This maverick priest is hired to serve in Micah's false tabernacle before false idols in false worship. This priest will even get a suit of clothes (contrasted with the first high priest's garments of glory and beauty). As presented in the Old Testament, priests are also to be like fathers, leading and protecting and teaching their flock. But Micah's priest becomes like a son, manipulated by Micah rather than rebuking him (Malachi 2:7–9). Micah manipulates the gods he owns rather than submitting to the true Lord. Once he determines that he has this perverted form of religion under control, he believes that the Lord will bless him for sure.

18:1–2 In the days when there was no king in Israel, and long before the mighty Samson, the Danites were unable to conquer the portion of the land that had been given to them when the Israelites returned to the land. When they didn't establish their promised inheritance, they made an attempt to establish their own, sending spies to explore possible sites.

18:3–6 These verses describe these spies' interaction with Micah's personal priest. Even though the priest readily admits that he is Micah's priest (rather than God's), the spies ask him to predict their future. Rather than go to Shiloh, the place where the Israelites worshipped, these men go to this priest, who tells them just what they want to hear.

18:7–12 The spies return with news that the land is good and an attack could be successful. In contrast to the first spies during the Exodus, who were afraid to trust the Lord and go into the land, these spies are not afraid. Unfortunately, what looks like trust in the Lord is really a justification to disobey. This becomes obvious when they arrive at Micah's house.

18:13–21 The spies recruit Micah's Levite. The law requires that they burn Micah and his shrine to the ground. But what do they do? Their perspective seems to be that since they are going to take land, they will need a priest and an altar. In some twisted way, they construe this Levite as God's provision. There is even a great promotion for their good friend the priest. The priest was happy in his place among the Danites (contrast this with Numbers 2:17).

18:22–26 Micah was a thief and an idolater. In the end, he could not stop his gods from being stolen. The thief is robbed, and the idolater's gods are in the control of men.

18:27–29 As with Jericho, the Danites come in and burn the first city of their conquest to the ground. The Lord calls for holy war, and in certain cases, whole cities are to be utterly destroyed. The people are to represent the Lord's holy fire of judgment.

18:30–31 These verses describe a final tribute to Dan that includes an element of irony given the mention of the house of God in Shiloh along with the idols Micah had made. The graven images that the Danites set up are idols clearly prohibited by the Law of Moses. Yet the people remained successful even though they openly worshipped these idols. This is a good example of the fact that the consequences of breaking God's law are not always immediate. Eventually, at the hand of the Philistines, the Danites' "luck" ran out.

19:1–3 Here we have the account of a concubine. In this era and culture, in places where polygamy was practiced, a concubine was like a second-class citizen, a second wife. The male head of the household was still considered her husband, but she wasn't always referred to as his wife. In this case, the Levite's concubine is unfaithful and finally deserts her husband to return to her father's household. After he waits for her return for four months, he seeks to win her back to himself by traveling to the father's house.

19:4–9 The Levite's father-in-law repeatedly delays the departure. There is nothing wrong with this display of hospitality in itself. But the way the story is told, we sense the Levite's anxiousness to be on his way, and so the repeated delay seems awkward. The Levite needs to return, but we do not know why.

19:10 Jerusalem is referred to as Jebus in verse 10. This was the name of the city before the Israelites settled there. The traveling family should have been able to stay in Jebus, but the fact that it had not yet become an Israelite city is troublesome for the Levite.

19:14–15 They travel on to Gibeah, an Israelite city, but find it empty, dark, and ominous. Their choice to wait in the city square is not unusual in this day. Hospitality, even to strangers, was expected. They would have expected to be invited to someone's home for the night.

19:16–21 When they finally do receive a single offer, it is not from a citizen of Gibeah but from an old man transplanted from Ephraim.

19:22–24 In the Genesis account of Lot in Sodom, the wicked men who attack the household are struck blind, and the attack ends. Here in Judges, there is no such rescue. The woman is victimized and killed. Once the Levite and those traveling with him settle into the old man's home, wicked men of Gibeah pound the doors requesting that the Levite have sex with them. The response from within is awful. First the old man offers his daughter and the Levite's wife. Then the Levite forces his wife out to be victimized by the men. The fate of the virgin daughter and especially of the concubine is so horrible that it is remembered throughout Israel (Hosea 9:9; 10:9).

19:25–30 In Judges 17–18 we see the consequences of a Levite living for himself. Here in verses 25–28, we see the consequences of a Levite failing to protect his wife, even if she is a concubine. And in verses 29–30, he makes the corpse of his bride some kind of message to Israel. What is the point of the Levite's actions here?

He creates a kind of picture of Israel. She is dead, torn apart, in her sin and treachery. Idolatry has given birth to immorality, and that has resulted in captivity and death.

20:1–11 At the opening of Judges 20, the tribes gather to hear the Levite's story and to decide how to respond. All of Israel, from Dan in the north to the southernmost city of Beer-sheba, gather as one in full fighting force to respond to the evil the Levite and his concubine endured.

20:12–17 While all the rest of Israel has gathered together in Mizpeh, a city in Benjamin, the tribe of Benjamin remains absent. An offer of peace is made to them if they will turn over the men who are guilty of raping and killing the woman, following the laws of war in Deuteronomy 20:10–11. But Benjamin refuses and instead prepares for battle. This reveals the hearts of the people of Benjamin, that they would fight for those who had victimized the powerless.

20:18–25 The campaign against Benjamin begins just as the battles against the Canaanites began in Judges 1. Judah is selected to go first. Two battles and two terrible losses later, we are reminded of the battle of Ai in Joshua.

20:26–28 The Lord purifies His people. This time there is weeping and fasting. Also, this time there is a burnt offering and a peace offering. The fasting portrays their need for God over anything else. Their burnt offering is the atonement granted by a substitute, wholly offered to God. Their peace offering is the communion meal, when fellowship is restored. The Lord purifies and nourishes His people. The covenant with Yahweh is renewed. Now they are ready for battle.

20:27–28 The ark of the covenant was Israel's holiest shrine, a box made to God's specifications that held artifacts like the first high priest's rod and a sampling of the manna that provided food for the Israelites in the desert. The ark was usually kept in the national place of worship and was naturally where the people would go to seek God's will. It was considered God's presence, and there were even times when the armies would carry the ark into battle with them in the hopes that it would imbue them with God's power (1 Samuel 4:2–3).

20:29–36 The battle of Benjamin described here is reminiscent of a previous battle at Ai, at least in terms of strategy (Joshua 8:1–26). This battle, however, is not only a battle against the Benjamites but a victory for Israel over the spirit of the Canaanites. Verse 35 offers a theological summary of the battle when it states that it is God who won the battle. The strategy of the battle is an ambush.

20:37–48 Drawing the Benjamites out of the city, Gibeah is burned to the ground. There is a relentless pursuit of the fleeing Benjamites. It is a brutal and awful scene. Just as the concubine's life was cut down, Gibeah is cut down. A small remnant finds refuge in the battle at the rock of Rimmon and stays there four months. Besides them, the destruction is total—men, women, animals, and cities fall under the wrath of the Lord.

21:1–3 Six hundred men of Benjamin are left at the rock of Rimmon (20:47), but they have no wives. Why? Israel had sworn an oath, a curse upon themselves if they gave any daughters to Benjamin (21:1, 18). In light of the wicked heart of Benjamin, this was an honorable vow (Deuteronomy 7:3–4). But the excommunication of the tribe of Benjamin brings no joy to Israel; it is not a moment of triumph. Instead, it is heartbreaking for even one tribe to fail. Their question—*Why?*—is in essence a prayer for restoration.

21:4 Israel had already offered sacrifices for their sins, but in this verse they do so again for all of Israel, including Benjamin, as they cry out to the Lord for Benjamin's restoration. While the motivation had some national interest unique to this situation, it still stands as an example of the kind of covenant connection that would serve the church well when a member has fallen away from the faith (1 Corinthians 5:6; Ephesians 4:4–6).

21:5–9 The sacrifices described in verses 2–4 provide a basis for the tribe of Benjamin's forgiveness and restoration, but they don't provide one practical need—wives so that the remnant of the tribe can repopulate. Therefore, Israel is still mourning. But the nation had taken another vow as well. Jabesh-gilead became the loophole that could solve the problem. This tribe had refused to come to Israel's assistance when every other city had sent men to battle the Benjamites. By doing nothing, Jabesh-gilead had stood against the efforts of Israel—and thus the perceived efforts of the Lord.

21:10–14 This story is reminiscent of the one that occurred in 1:17. In the days of Phinehas, twelve thousand men are gathered together and all are killed, leaving only the virgin women. This is a repeat of yet another slaughter against the Midianites described in Numbers 31. After the destruction, there were four hundred women to give as wives to the six hundred Benjamites.

21:16–18 The Benjamites are brought to Shiloh, the place of rest (peace), to receive the first four hundred wives and to provide them with this episode of peace and reconciliation with God and with His people. These verses reveal that the remainder of Israel wants to see the full restoration of Benjamin in spite of the curse placed upon these men.

21:18–24 This dance of virgins at the festival in Shiloh must have declared the desire of these women to be married or their father's declaration to give them in marriage, maybe in a way similar to when we see a group of women scrambling to catch the bouquet at a wedding. The fathers had declared that they would never give their daughters to Benjamin, but the fact that the men took the women during the festival provided an end run around that declaration. In an unexpected way, the tribe of Benjamin is reborn.

RUTH

INTRODUCTION TO RUTH ■ Ruth is a small book, only four chapters, that reveals God's work of providence in the details of people's lives.

AUTHOR ■ Even though there has been speculation about possible authors, no one knows who wrote the book of Ruth. We do believe, however, that the book was written during the time of King David. This seems reasonable because of the genealogy included at the end of the book, a genealogy that includes David's ancestors.

OCCASION ■ One purpose of this book is to reveal how a Moabite—a non-Jew—can become a faithful follower of Yahweh, Israel's God. Another purpose is that it is meant to be a contribution to the genealogy of David, an ancestor to Jesus. The book of Ruth illustrates how simple, obedient people can be saved by God's providence and become part of His larger plan.

1:1 This chapter has a poignant lesson: God's providence is certain and He makes no mistakes. As He unfolds the intricacies of His divine purpose in our lives, He does so with a goal in mind. We also see how the saving purposes of God often begin in the sometimes dark periods in someone's life.

1:3–5 Elimelech's family leaves Judah, the only land to which God has given specific promises of blessing, for the neighboring country of Moab. Soon Elimelech dies, leaving Naomi with her two sons, Mahlon and Chilion, and their Moabite wives, Orpah and Ruth. After about ten years, Naomi's sons die, leaving her alone with her daughters-in-law. Naomi is away from the land of her God, her immediate family, and any extended family. Naturally she would long for her home and for the company of people with similar faith.

1:6–11 Naomi hears that the Lord has returned blessing to Bethlehem but sees a problem with her daughters-in-law returning there. They cannot be guaranteed marriage partners. According to Jewish customs, the women would be married to their nearest relative in order to continue the family inheritance of their deceased husbands. But as Naomi points out, she has no other sons and is too old to have more.

1:8 As widows, all three would be poverty-stricken beggars, scraping out an existence. As foreign Moabites, the daughters-in-law would struggle even more than Naomi herself.

1:9–13 At first, both daughters-in-law refuse to leave Naomi despite her recommendation that they stay in Moab, but Naomi explains that their best chance for remarriage is to stay. Naomi, even in difficult circumstances, believes in the faithfulness of God's providence.

1:19–21 As Naomi returns home, her look has changed; pain and sorrow have etched their way into her very visage. She had gone away full, but she has come back empty, even requesting she be called by the name *Mara*, which means "bitter," rather than *Naomi*, which means "pleasant."

2:1–3 When Ruth offers to go glean in the field of Boaz, a man related to Elimelech, Naomi encourages her. The national religious laws of Israel state that after a field is harvested, a certain amount must be left on the side of the field and in the corners of the field for the poor and for those who cannot provide for themselves (Leviticus 19:9–10; Deuteronomy 24:19–22). Often women and widows used this provision to find sufficient grain to make food for one, two, or even three days, but no more than that. To survive only from the grain gleaned from a harvested field was a menial and difficult existence.

2:4–7 Boaz is a businessman, yet his first words to his workers are of God. The writer presents Boaz as a man of character. His inquiry about Ruth alludes to an attraction toward her. His workers explain that she has asked to be allowed to glean and is currently resting.

2:8–9 Boaz finds Ruth and advises her to stay in this particular field and to follow his maids. He tells her he has ordered his servants not to touch her, an indication that such fields can be dangerous, but he is providing for her safety. He also allows her to drink from his servants' water jars. Boaz is providing for Ruth beyond what is required by Levitical law.

2:12 Boaz asks God's blessing on Ruth's work, noting that Ruth has come to Israel to seek God's shelter. He uses the metaphor of being under God's wings, a protective gesture of mother hens for their baby chicks. And as the narrative unfolds, similar language is used about Boaz's relationship to Ruth; Boaz takes a surrogate role of protector and becomes responsible for Ruth. He takes her under his wing, just as he prays God will do for her.

2:15–17 Boaz is going well beyond the requirements of the law. Because of his generosity, Ruth is able to work in the field all day, with access to water and a full meal, and leave the field that evening with about thirty pounds of barley.

2:18–20 The text tells us that Ruth takes her thirty pounds of barley back to Naomi and shares it with her. Naomi must have known that the volume of the harvest is more than expected, because she asks God's blessing on the generous person. When Ruth tells her it is Boaz's field, Naomi repeats her blessing and explains that he is one of their closest relatives.

2:20 In addition to the law of gleaning, the Hebrew people also operated under the law of the kinsman redeemer: If a woman was left as a widow and childless, the nearest relative would take her as his wife, yet any children she bore would be considered the heirs of her previous husband (Deuteronomy 25:5–6). In this way, the kinsman redeemer was helping continue that family line rather than his own. Naomi may have been already hoping that this kinsman's kind treatment of Ruth would lead to a marriage.

3:1–3 Naomi presents a plan to Ruth that would ensure Ruth's future. As a widow and a nonnative of Israel, her future most likely consists of gleaning for survival. Naomi reminds Ruth of the kinsman relationship to Boaz and the promising relationship between Ruth and his maids. On a night when Naomi knows that Boaz will be at the threshing floor, she instructs Ruth to wash, anoint herself, put on her best clothes, and go to him. Knowing the dangers of harvesttime, her suggestion that Ruth go to the threshing floor both after dark and after the men have been eating and drinking carries some risk.

3:9 In response to Boaz's question about her identity, Ruth's answer is pointed. She identifies herself as one of his maids and uses a phrase that asks him to take her under his wing, a word picture he has already used with her. In this case, Ruth's request is a pledge of marriage. She even uses the language that will remind him that he is a close relative with a right and possibly a responsibility in this situation.

3:12–13 Boaz's response to Ruth's presence indicates his intention to treat her with honor. However, he explains that while he is, indeed, a close relative, there is someone even more closely related to Ruth who, according to the law of kinship, has first claim to her. Boaz will defer to this relative. In other words, while Boaz's heart has been won over by Ruth, he will do what is right according to God's law.

3:14 When morning arrives, Boaz makes sure no one knows Ruth came to the threshing floor. The message here is that Boaz wants Ruth's reputation to remain unblemished. Boaz, however, also wants his commitment to Ruth and Naomi to be clear.

3:15-18 Boaz sends Ruth home with another significant load of barley. Hearing Ruth's summary of the night, and seeing this message from Boaz, Naomi assures Ruth that Boaz will move to marry her.

4:1–3 Boaz waits at the town gate, the place of business in the ancient world, and finds the man who is related to Naomi's deceased husband, Elimelech—her closest relative. Boaz also finds ten men to witness the transaction. In ancient times, the city gate was the place where justice was administered. If you had a case that needed to be resolved in some way, you would go to the city gate and call upon the elders to make a judgment.

4:4 Boaz explains his interest in Naomi's land but defers this option to the nearest kinsman, who agrees to purchase it from Naomi, until he realizes that the land comes with the widow Ruth.

4:6–7 Because this man would jeopardize his own family's future by taking on another wife, he hands over the right of redemption to Boaz. In this culture, the passing on of this responsibility is symbolized by handing over a shoe.

4:9–10 For the record, Boaz announces to all the witnesses the result of the transaction: He has acquired everything that belongs to Naomi, and Ruth will be his wife in order to continue Elimelech's line.

4:11–12 When the people ask that the Lord make Ruth like Rachel and Leah (wives of Jacob), they are stating their hopes for a large family. Rachel and Leah bore Jacob twelve sons. The reference to Pharez here is because he is the ancestor of Boaz, revealing the family connection. This section reveals the answer to Naomi's prayer in Ruth 1:8 for her daughter-in-law.

4:13–17 Boaz and Ruth marry and have a son. The narrator's phrasing emphasizes the belief that children are a gift from God. The women of Bethlehem respond to Naomi, and her situation is significantly more hopeful than when she returned from Moab. They ask God's blessing on Naomi's grandson and describe Ruth as someone who is better to Naomi than seven sons, a powerful indication of Ruth's standing in the eyes of the community. Naomi becomes the nurse to her grandson, Obed, whose name means "servant," and who will become grandfather to King David.

4:16–22 The genealogy here traces the line of Judah. These names hold significance; they show that God's plan of sending the Messiah through the house of David will be fulfilled and that God can work through all kinds of circumstances to ensure His plan of salvation.

THE FIRST BOOK OF
SAMUEL
OTHERWISE CALLED
THE FIRST BOOK OF THE KINGS

INTRODUCTION TO 1 SAMUEL ■ The book of 1 Samuel is best understood after a thorough review of the book of Judges. This was a dark era of history for the nation of Israel. God had delivered the Israelites from slavery in Egypt to the promised land in Canaan. The transition had not been a smooth one, yet under the leadership of Joshua the people had done reasonably well. However, after the death of Joshua, Israel went through repeated cycles of blessing and discipline—the result of their obedience or rebellion. Judges ends with the bleak statement: "In those days there was no king in Israel: every man did that which was right in his own eyes" (Judges 21:25). That is the situation as 1 Samuel begins.

AUTHOR ■ What we know as 1 Samuel and 2 Samuel were originally a single book (along with 1 and 2 Kings in its final form), and Jewish tradition credits Samuel as the author. But since Samuel's death is included halfway through the (combined) book, other sources clearly were involved.

OCCASION ■ The books of 1 and 2 Samuel were recorded to provide historical accounts of a crucial period of Israel's past. The book of 1 Samuel spans Samuel's life from birth to death, chronicles Saul's entire reign as the first king of Israel, and reveals the lengthy transition David underwent from shepherd boy to heir to the throne.

1:2 The book of 1 Samuel is known for its grand accounts of Samuel (the great prophet, priest, and judge), Saul (Israel's first king), and the rise of the great King David. But it begins with the story of a humble and burdened young woman. Hannah's story is a model of the value of ongoing faithfulness and prayer, even when life's circumstances seem overwhelming.

1:3–8 Hannah is one of two wives of a man named Elkanah, the other being a woman named Peninnah. Elkanah is a godly descendant of Levi, designated as an Ephraimite because of his place of residence. Peninnah had borne a number of children to Elkanah, but Hannah was barren. Each year the family traveled some twenty miles or so north of Jerusalem to Shiloh, where the tabernacle was stationed. Three annual feasts (with required attendance for Jewish males) attracted many visitors. The event referred to in this passage may have been the feast of tabernacles (Leviticus 23:33–36), a time to rejoice and recall the exodus from Egypt.

1:6 It is unlikely that Hannah and Peninnah would have had much contact on a daily basis. They probably lived and ate in separate tents, well distanced from each other. But on journeys they would be thrown together, and Hannah would be forced to endure Peninnah's provocations.

1:9–19 Hannah's inability to conceive a child is bad enough, but traveling with Elkanah's taunting wife makes things worse. On arrival at Shiloh, Hannah hurries off to the temple, where she pours out her heart to God. Eli, the priest, sees her distressed body language but hears no verbal prayer, and he jumps to the conclusion that she is drunk. He has no idea she is making a

solemn vow to God as she pleads for a son. After a short conversation, however, Eli sends her away in peace with his endorsement of whatever she has been praying for.

1:20–28 The year after Samuel's birth, Hannah doesn't go on the annual trip to Shiloh. Her child is still weaning, and she is not yet able to honor her promise to God. But after Samuel is weaned, and still quite young, she takes him to Shiloh and presents him to God, leaving him in the care of Eli.

2:1–10 Despite knowing that she will give up her long-desired firstborn son, Hannah takes great joy in Samuel's birth. Her prayer in response to his birth has a number of features worth noting. It employs parallelism and symbolism, indicative of the format of a psalm. Like other biblical psalms, Hannah's prayer is addressed to God and reflects her praise and thanksgiving. What began as her personal expression of gratitude has become part of scripture for all to read and repeat as edification of the soul. Her words of praise seem to reflect Israel's past experiences, particularly the Exodus. (Note her use of "rock" in 2:2 [Deuteronomy 32:30–31] and "horn" in 2:1 [Deuteronomy 33:17].) Hannah's psalm does not concentrate on her sorrow, her suffering, or even her blessings. Rather, it focuses on her God, who is holy, faithful, omniscient, gracious, all-powerful, and a sovereign reverser of circumstances. Hannah's is a magnificent expression of faith at a time when she is giving up her (at the time) only child.

2:10 Hannah speaks of God giving strength to His king, although Israel had never had a human king at this time. In this sense, her song is prophetic. Her son, Samuel, will eventually anoint the first two kings of Israel.

2:12–26 Hophni and Phinehas should have known better than to abuse their sacred positions. The sons of the first high priest, Aaron, had acted improperly and had been judged and killed as a result (Leviticus 10:1–3; Numbers 3:4; 26:60–61). The maturity of Samuel—physically and spiritually—is seen in stark contrast to Eli's sons. Their offenses go beyond the liturgical abuse of the priesthood into moral corruptions. Their disregard for God's law is blatant.

2:19 It is worth noting that each year, Hannah makes not just clothes to take to Samuel, but priestly garments. It might be presumed that she and Elkanah continue to have a positive influence on their son, even as he is growing up in the shadows of Hophni and Phinehas.

2:22–26 Samuel's first assignment as a prophet will be to tell Eli something that isn't pleasant to hear (3:17–18). Yet it seems that his mentor, Eli, cannot do the same with his own sons. If he attempts to rebuke them, he lacks force and authority. Eli learns of everything they are doing yet allows the problem to continue. Samuel is a direct contrast.

2:27–36 The situation with the priesthood is, of course, evident to God. He makes known His displeasure and intent by sending a prophet to Eli—a rare event (3:1). The prophet addresses the priesthood in a proper historical and theological perspective. He first recalls the Exodus, when the Aaronic and Levitical priesthood had been established and respected. Then he looks to the future, when God will build a new house of priests. As for the present, judgment is in store for Eli and his sons—they will all die on the same day, after which God will establish a faithful priest. (The accusation that the priests are fattening themselves on the offerings [2:29] may have hit home with Eli; he is later described as a heavy old man [4:18].)

3:1 In this passage, Samuel is called a "child"—a term flexible enough to refer to a newborn or a young man. Most likely, several years have passed between chapter 2 and chapter 3, and Samuel is probably entering his teen years.

3:4 During this period in Israel's history, the people have stopped listening to God, so God does not communicate with them very often. Therefore, when God speaks to Samuel, the youngster assumes the voice is that of his mentor, Eli. It takes three times before the more experienced priest suspects what is happening and instructs Samuel to reply directly to God.

3:10 When Samuel finally acknowledges God's voice, God gives him a solemn message concerning Eli. God is about to bring judgment on Eli and his house because Eli has done nothing to hinder the offensive behavior of his sons. Judgment is now imminent. No longer will sacrifice or atonement set the record straight (3:14).

3:13 Eli did not restrain his sons. The result is that Eli and his sons have passed the point of no return.

3:15–17 Not surprisingly, the young Samuel is reticent to approach Eli with the message he has received from God. He doesn't bring it up until Eli confronts him. (Eli,

of course, has already heard a similar message from a different prophet [2:27–36].) When pressed by Eli, Samuel reluctantly tells him the entire message.

3:21 God continues to speak to Samuel, and Samuel speaks for God. The people soon notice his evident call as a true prophet (Deuteronomy 13:1–5; 18:14–22; 1 Samuel 3:19). As Samuel continues to listen and respond, the young prophet will soon become a righteous priest and judge as well.

4:1–3 At this point the Philistines have dominated the Israelites for some time (4:9). In a previous battle, Israel lost four thousand soldiers, after which they questioned why God would allow such a thing to happen. But rather than consulting God and praying and fasting, they decide to carry the ark of the covenant into the next battle, assuming it will guarantee God's presence with them.

4:5–8 When the ark first arrives at the Israelite camp, a great shout goes out. The soldiers are confident and assured of victory. In fact, the cheering is so loud that it is heard in the Philistine camp. After the Philistines discover the ark has been summoned, they presume that they will be doing battle against Israel's gods as well as their soldiers. (They are well aware of Israel's past victories in which the ark was prominent.)

4:9 Rather than causing the Philistines to cower, the news of the presence of the Israelites' ark of the covenant (4:6–8) motivates them to fight harder and die like men, if it comes to that. As fighting ensues, the tragedies accumulate for Israel: They lose the battle, thirty thousand men die (including both of Eli's sons), and the ark is captured and carried away by the Philistines.

4:13–15 Eli has stationed himself by the road, anxiously awaiting word. A Benjamite who had escaped eventually comes by. His clothes are torn and he has dust on his head—signs of mourning and defeat. Eli's vision is poor and he may not have detected the visible signs, but he could certainly hear the commotion (3:11).

4:18 When the messenger confirms the worst, the news is more than Eli's ninety-eight-year-old body can handle. He collapses and breaks his neck. As had been foretold (2:34), he and his sons die on the same day.

4:19–22 Tragedy also strikes Eli's pregnant daughter-in-law (the wife of Phinehas). The deaths of Eli and her husband, Israel's defeat, and the loss of the ark all hasten her labor. She refuses comfort or help from others and dies during the delivery. But before she does, she names her son I-chabod ("no glory"). She comments that the glory of God departed with the capture of the ark.

5:8 Prior to the battle, the Philistines had been fearful of Israel's God because they knew He had inflicted the Egyptians with all kinds of plagues (4:8). After the incident in Dagon's temple, a plague begins to spread throughout Ashdod. The local citizens quickly reason that the only way to be rid of the plague is to get rid of the ark, so they send it on to another of their cities, Gath.

5:9 The exact nature of the plague is unknown ("emerods in their secret parts"). Some people have suggested the outbreak of tumors was a widespread bout of severe hemorrhoids, although the number of deaths might indicate something more serious. Since the tumors and deaths appear to be associated with rodents (6:4), another possibility is that the epidemic might have been a manifestation of the bubonic plague or something similar.

5:10 The citizens of Gath immediately experience the same plague faced by the Ashdodites, and they attempt to forward the ark on to the city of Ekron. By then the Philistines have determined that the plagues seem to be directly associated with the presence of the ark. They strongly suspect that their trouble is the result of God's judgment on them and their god, Dagon.

5:11 The Philistines make no effort to renounce Dagon, cease their idolatry, or worship the God of Israel. Instead, they simply want to distance themselves from Israel's God.

6:1–3 After seven months of plagues, the Philistine priests are more than ready to discuss the best way to return the ark to Israel. In their eagerness to be rid of the ark, they still want to exercise caution.

6:4 The Philistines fashion a trespass offering of five gold emerods (or tumors) and five gold mice to send back with the ark.

6:7–12 The Philistines transport the ark on a cart pulled by two milch kine (milk cows), whose nursing calves have just been separated from them. The mother cows should not be willing to leave their calves under any circumstances, so when they pull the cart straight toward Israel without turning aside, it is a clear sign that the plagues are no coincidence. The Philistines follow at a distance and see the cart and its cargo come to a halt in Israel.

6:13–14 If the Philistines are glad to be rid of the ark, the Israelites of Beth-shemesh are ecstatic when they realize it has returned. The people reaping in the fields use the wood from the cart as fuel and the kine (cows) as an offering.

6:19 The festive occasion quickly comes to an end when some of the people look into the ark—a serious violation of the law. As a result, a plague breaks out and a significant number of people are struck dead.

6:21 The ark is transferred to Kirjath-jearim, where it remains for twenty years. David eventually arranges for its transport to Jerusalem.

7:1–4 Samuel is strangely absent from the accounts in chapters 4–6. But while the ark is set aside for two decades, Samuel is an essential part of Israel's spiritual revival. With the absence of the ark as a "security blanket" (as Israel had attempted to use it during the battle), the people have to look elsewhere for security.

7:5–10 Israel gathers with Samuel at Mizpeh, where Samuel promises to pray to the Lord on their behalf as the people fast. While they are there, the Philistines prepare to attack. Samuel offers a burnt offering to God and asks for His deliverance. In response, God sends thunder that creates great confusion among the Philistines and enables the Israelites to overcome them.

7:12 After the Israelites chase the fleeing Philistines,

Samuel erects a stone between Mizpeh and Shen. He calls it *Eben-ezer* ("stone, rock of my help"). It served as a lasting commemoration that the battle had been won with God's help.

7:13–17 After the battle, the Philistine domination over Israel ends for a while. Peace is also established between the Israelites and Amorites, all largely because of the influence of Samuel. From his home in Ramah, he will travel throughout Israel as a kind of circuit rider, fulfilling the roles of priest, prophet, and judge.

8:1–4 Considerable time has passed as 1 Samuel 8 begins. Samuel has adult sons and is old enough that the people are already beginning to discuss who will replace him. He has gained the respect of the Israelites, but his sons are corrupt. Perhaps Samuel deals with his dishonest offspring, because the problem is never mentioned again, yet the Israelites are unwilling to support them as leaders of the nation.

8:5 Since all the other nations around them have kings, the Israelites want one, too. They don't just make a request to Samuel—they demand a king. The people's desire for a king is not only equivalent to firing Samuel as a judge; they are also firing God as their King.

8:6–7 Samuel is disappointed in the people, not because of the personal affront, but because their request is wrong and sinful. But rather than spout off a quick retort to the elders of Israel, he affirms his godly character by turning to God in prayer. God's response confirms Samuel's assessment of the situation.

8:10–18 In response to the people's demand for a king, Samuel is explicit about the demands a king will place on the people.

8:19–22 Clearly, a king will require a costly and demanding government. Everyone will feel the effects. But the Israelites will not be dissuaded.

9:1–2 Saul comes into contact with Samuel in a manner that makes the prophet certain that Saul is God's choice for Israel's king. Saul's father, Kish, is a Benjamite of some reputation. A "mighty man of power" can refer to courage, military skill, success, or even wealth. Saul is physically impressive, but many other qualities are yet to be determined.

9:3–21 Saul is sent off with a servant to find some lost livestock. After covering a lot of ground on an unsuccessful three-day search, the servant realizes they are near the home of a man of God. Neither of them appears to have known Samuel by name, but the servant, at least, is aware of his reputation as a prophet. They ask for directions, and some young women tell them they have arrived at an opportune moment. From the women's point of view, Saul and his servant are lucky, but the biblical account makes it clear that Saul was expected at Samuel's—even after three days of aimless wandering.

9:22–23 Samuel has been told to anticipate the person God will choose as Israel's first king, but Saul has no such knowledge. As Saul sits down to eat, Samuel even sends for a choice piece of meat that has already been set aside for the guest of honor.

10:1–4 The next morning, Samuel assures Saul that his father's donkeys have been found. He then has Saul send the servant ahead, and he anoints Saul as ruler over Israel. He also gives specific instructions and tells Saul exactly what to expect on his way home, including where he will find provisions for the journey.

10:9 Samuel's words and actions must have been affirming to Saul. Moreover, as soon as Saul leaves Samuel to return home, God changes him.

10:11–12 Upon meeting a group of prophets along the way, Saul joins them in prophesying, giving rise to a new proverb. The significance of Saul's prophesying with the prophets is to publicly demonstrate that God has empowered him to judge the nation. When Moses had appointed seventy judges to share his workload (Exodus 18), all of them prophesied before the eyes of the nation, demonstrating that the Spirit of God was upon them (Numbers 11:16–17, 24–25). Saul's similar experience is the first public indication that he is to be Israel's king.

10:14–16 When Saul arrives home, people naturally want to hear about his journey. His uncle seems especially interested to learn that Saul had an encounter with Samuel. Saul provides only sketchy details about the trip, focusing on the search for the donkeys rather than his being anointed. Saul's silence is telling. It will be Samuel who publicly introduces Saul as Israel's king.

10:17–19 Samuel summons all of Israel to Mizpeh— the location where they had repented and turned to God at the beginning of his ministry (chapter 7). His audience is enthusiastic and optimistic, eager to hear the coming announcement. But first Samuel reminds them once more that their demand for a king is a manifestation of unbelief and disobedience. No human king will deliver them from their difficulties. Their source of deliverance has always been God, and always will be.

10:19–23 Although Samuel has already anointed Saul, God's designation of Saul is confirmed through the casting of lots. But when Saul's name is chosen, he is nowhere to be found. They find him hiding among the "stuff" (or baggage). He is then brought forward to the acclaim of (most of) the nation. From a merely physical perspective, Saul is an impressive king.

10:24–27 Samuel presents Saul to the nation, clarifies all the ordinances that pertain to kingly rule, and then sends the people home. One group of valiant men accompanies Saul, not unlike a secret service unit. Another group, however, voices disdain for Saul and refuses to offer gifts. Saul chooses to remain silent and do nothing for the moment.

11:1–5 What the Israelites really want is a king who will deliver them from their enemies. The immediate threat is from Nahash, the king of the Ammonites (12:12), who had besieged the Israelite town of Jabesh-gilead. He had told the city's men that they could avoid all-out conflict only by agreeing to lose their right eyes (both humiliating them and rendering them unable to fight effectively).

11:6–13 When Saul is informed of the situation in Jabesh-gilead, he takes immediate (and attention-getting) action to recruit an army. He soon has 330,000 soldiers, whom he leads to deliver a crushing defeat of the Ammonites. Saul becomes an instant hero. His qualifications of being among the prophets and chosen by lot have certainly been impressive proofs of his designation as king. But his ability to rally the nation and defeat an imposing enemy really gets everyone's attention. In fact, the majority want to execute the group of naysayers who have refused to support Saul from the beginning. But Saul earns even more credibility and respect by giving God credit for the victory and granting amnesty to those who opposed him.

12:2–5 The Israelites' accusations against Samuel's sons were true (8:1–5), but Samuel could not be accused of such behavior. In addition, it appears that Samuel may have attended to the problem with his sons. Unlike his predecessor, Eli, Samuel seems to be without fault in the discipline of his children.

12:6–7 Israel's history as a kingdom began at the Exodus. Samuel points out that their present demand to have a king like the rest of the nations is just one more instance of their rebellion against God. He emphasizes that Moses and Aaron were not the ones who had delivered Israel from Egyptian bondage—it was God. God works through human leaders, but He is the One who delivers His people.

12:8–13 Samuel summons the Israelites to take their stand before God. In a sense, they are on trial and he is their prosecutor. History is a witness to the fact that the blessings they have received are not the result of their own righteousness. Rather, history shows that the nation's deliverance has been achieved thanks to God's righteous deeds, performed on Israel's behalf, and always in the context of their sin. Repeatedly, God has graciously delivered the people from their enemies, but the people persistently forget the Lord and turn to other gods. Samuel briefly scans Israel's history, citing illustrations from the major periods (the Exodus, the wilderness wanderings, the possession of the land under Joshua, and the periods of the judges) to demonstrate a consistent pattern. Then he links Israel's past with their current situation. Like the Israelites of old, they are once again oppressed by a neighboring nation. Yet while previous generations had realized that outside oppression was a result of sin and had repented before crying out to God for deliverance, this time they have not acknowledged their sin or repented. Instead, they have blamed their circumstances on bad leadership and demanded a king so they will be like all the other nations.

12:17–18 Samuel underscores the importance of what he is saying with a sign of divine intervention. It is not the rainy season. The people have no reason to expect showers, much less storms. Yet in response to Samuel's prayer, a great thunderstorm immediately blows in—right at harvest season. This would have frightened the people because it would have threatened to destroy the crops. The unexpected rain reminds Israel that both calamity and blessing come from the Lord (Isaiah 45:5–7).

12:19–25 Samuel's message—punctuated by the sudden storm—results in great fear among the people. They are beginning to comprehend the severity of their sin in general and their demand for a king in particular. They want no further discipline, and they plead with Samuel to pray for them. Suddenly they are looking not to a king for deliverance but to Samuel.

13:1–2 The Israelites remain under Philistine control. In fact, it appears that the Philistines have no intention of wiping out the Israelites, who are positioned as a buffer between the Philistines and other more aggressive nations. So even though Saul has a standing army of three thousand soldiers, Israel remains in subjection to the much larger Philistine force.

13:3–5 The delicate détente between the two nations ends when Saul's son, Jonathan, attacks a Philistine garrison without his father's permission. Jonathan's reasoning is not provided, though it is logical to assume from other passages that he is acting on faith, believing that God still wants His people to drive out the nations inhabiting the land He has given Israel. Regardless of Jonathan's motivation, the Philistine response is predictable.

13:8–9 Saul has specific instructions from Samuel: Go to Gilgal and wait seven days for the prophet to arrive. When he arrives there, Samuel will offer sacrifices to God and provide further instructions (10:8). But as the seven days go by, Saul agonizes while he watches his army shrink. Saul manages to make it through six days and most of the seventh. But when Samuel still hasn't shown up, Saul calls for the burnt and peace offerings. It appears that he makes the offerings himself.

13:10 Just as Saul makes the offering, Samuel arrives—in plenty of time to have made the offerings himself. Rather than Saul being able to rebuke Samuel for being late, Samuel demands an explanation from Saul. Saul's excuse falls flat.

13:11–14 Samuel's response is direct and stern. Saul's actions are foolish and willfully disobedient to Samuel's instructions. If Saul had obeyed the command of God, his kingdom would have endured forever. But his disobedience costs him a dynasty.

13:15–18 Samuel departs without giving Saul any guidance for how to handle the Philistine threat (10:8). Saul takes a count of his troops and discovers he has only six hundred men ready for battle. In addition, of all the Israelites, only Saul and Jonathan have a spear or sword. And if the difficulty with the main Philistine army isn't enough of a challenge, the Philistines are sending raiding parties in various directions throughout the land. Those destructive raiders appear to be a special force of troops whose task is to destroy human life, cattle, buildings, and crops.

14:1–5 Jonathan has a definite sense of God's will that prompts him to take action. He is troubled by the influence the Philistines hold over Israel, and he is eager to do something about it. He recruits his armorbearer to go out on a mission with him. He neither asks permission from nor informs his father. While Saul doesn't want to cause trouble with the Philistines, Jonathan wants to be troubled by them no longer.

14:6 Jonathan appears to know much about the will of God from Israel's history and from the nature of God Himself. His words to his armorbearer are filled with a sense of faith and duty. The question in Jonathan's mind is not whether God can deliver the Philistines into the hands of the Israelites, but whether it is God's intent to do so at the time. So he determines another way to discern the will of God.

14:12–14 After Jonathan approaches with only his armorbearer, the Philistines do indeed tell the two of them to come on up. Imagine the soldiers' surprise when Jonathan begins wielding his sword as soon as he has climbed to the top. Before long twenty Philistines are dead, and the Michmash pass is opened, allowing the Israelites to pursue the fleeing enemy.

14:15–16 A close reading of 1 Samuel 13–14 reveals an interesting wordplay. In 13:7 we read that the Israelites are trembling because of the Philistines. But here the ground is trembling beneath the Philistines as God sends an earthquake. Their smug sense of security on top of the Michmash pass must have quickly disappeared when that former position of safety became the most dangerous place in the area.

14:18–19 At long last, Saul decides to consult God. Apparently the method involves the ark of God and the outstretched hand of Ahiah the priest, and it seems as though the process is time-consuming. However, Saul is not a patient person. The commotion in the Philistine camp convinces Saul to act right away, so he instructs the priest to withdraw his hand.

14:19–23 The Israelite army goes in pursuit of the panic-smitten Philistines, with Jonathan and his armorbearer leading the charge. The ranks of Israel's army swell that day as the six hundred soldiers are joined by the deserters who had been hiding and the Israelites who had previously gone over to the Philistines.

14:31–32 The other Israelites comply with Saul's senseless order not to eat until evening (14:24), but fewer Philistines are killed as a result. Additionally, the Israelites are famished. When they come upon the Philistine cattle that evening, they kill them and eat the meat while it is still dripping with blood, in clear defiance of the Mosaic Law (Leviticus 17:10; 19:26). It is unfortunate that they fear disobeying Saul's commands more than breaking God's law.

14:33 When the Israelites' grievous behavior is brought to Saul's attention, he self-righteously points an accusing finger at his famished men. Saul's foolish demand has initiated the damage, and now he attempts damage control. He builds an altar of stone where the soldiers can sacrifice their offerings. Yet this can hardly be considered sincere worship. It is merely an attempt to satisfy the appetites of the soldiers so they do not sin further.

14:35 Ironically, this is the first altar Saul builds. Did it take a crisis for him to seek to worship his God? This is not exactly a holy moment in Israel's history. In addition is the irony that Saul had forbidden eating in the attempt to save time. Yet to correct the situation, Saul takes the time to build an altar and then ensure that each person's sacrifice is properly slain and prepared.

14:36–39 At long last the meal is over, and Israel is again ready to fight. But when the priest tries to get direction from God, the Lord provides no answer. Saul immediately jumps to a number of conclusions: that someone has sinned, that the sin is the violation of his (foolish) order rather than God's law, and that the sin is worthy of death. Perhaps it is no coincidence that he singles out Jonathan. It seems he feels that in the area of war, Jonathan is a nuisance at best and a liability for sure. It also appears that Saul *expects* Jonathan to be selected by lot, and perhaps he even feels the situation is perfectly suited to do away with his son.

14:41–43 After Jonathan is identified by the casting of lots, he confesses that he has indeed eaten a bit of honey. Although Jonathan had no knowledge of his father's command and had not affected the army in any negative way, Saul supposes that he is the reason for Israel's failure to finish the battle. He feels it is better to kill his son than to admit his own sin and foolishness. Jonathan makes no excuses for himself or any indictments against his father.

14:44–52 Saul pontificates about the certainty of Jonathan's death. But the other soldiers recognize the foolishness of Saul's actions and are unwilling to let him put Jonathan to death. It is Jonathan, not Saul, whom they credit with their deliverance.

15:1–2 Saul had done battle against the Ammonites, Philistines, Moabites, Edomites, and others (14:47). This time God instructs him to attack the Amalekites, a group dwelling in the southern part of Canaan. Saul is to render God's judgment.

15:3 God's instructions to Saul appear harsh to modern sensibilities. But Saul, and anyone familiar with the history of Israel, would have had a different perspective. The law provided the reasoning behind the intentional deaths of entire nations, and even their cattle (Leviticus 27:28–29). Joshua had the same instructions as Saul after the walls of Jericho fell.

15:4–9 Saul has specific instructions to attack and destroy the Amalekites without sparing anyone or anything. He doesn't fully comply with the order. Saul slaughters everyone there except their king and some of their best sheep and cattle. His disobedience to God's command, therefore, appears to be self-serving rather than mercy-based. He would have gained a measure of popularity among the Israelites—they could use Amalekite animals for their sacrifices (without killing their own), and they could feast on the meat. Meanwhile, the Amalekite king Agag would have been a living trophy

of Saul's prowess and power. Saul will defend his partial obedience to Samuel, attempting to justify his actions as doing what God had instructed. Samuel (and God), however, will interpret Saul's partial obedience as disobedience.

15:10–13 God speaks to Samuel before dealing with Saul, expressing disappointment in Saul's performance as king. From God's perspective, Saul has turned away from Him and has not followed clear instructions. Samuel is so troubled that he cries out to God all night. He gets up early the next morning to deal with Saul, who can't be found at first because he is busy setting up a monument in his own honor. When Samuel finally catches up with him, Saul speaks first, proudly affirming that he has carried out God's instructions.

15:14 It is hard for Saul to claim that he has killed all the flocks and herds of the Amalekites when the best of the bunch are standing there making noise.

15:21–23 After Saul discovers his level of obedience is unacceptable to God, he first tries to blame the soldiers of Israel. But Samuel is hearing no excuses. God prefers obedience to sacrifice. Saul's lack of obedience is tantamount to arrogance and rebellion. It is severe enough for God to reject Saul as king of Israel.

15:27–28 When Samuel turns to leave, Saul grabs the skirt (hem) of the prophet's robe, and it tears. Samuel uses the incident as an illustration of how God has torn the kingdom away from Saul. It will soon be given to another.

15:32–33 Rather than attempting to mollify Saul, Samuel turns his attention to finishing what Saul started by calling for Agag. The Amalekite king is confident that since he has not been executed by now, the danger is over. But if God's command had been to annihilate the Amalekites, how could the one who had led them in their wickedness be spared? Samuel kills him on the spot. The text doesn't say, but it is likely that Samuel saw that all remaining Amalekite cattle were also put to death.

16:1–3 It isn't long after God has rejected Saul as king that He sends Samuel to anoint the next ruler of Israel. The Lord has narrowed His choice down to a certain family—the sons of Jesse of Bethlehem—but does not designate a specific individual. However, Samuel isn't particularly eager to take on this assignment. He fears that Saul will kill him. After all, Saul has just annihilated (nearly) all the Amalekites and previously had been willing to put his own son to death.

16:4 When Samuel arrives, it is the townspeople who are frightened. When a prophet shows up unannounced, he doesn't always have good news. The elders are trembling, and they want to know if Samuel has come in peace. He assures them that everything is fine and has them prepare for the sacrifice.

16:5–13 When he had been instructed to anoint Saul, Samuel knew exactly what to expect (9:15–17). This time, however, he has no idea which of Jesse's sons God will choose. The oldest, Eliab, appears to be an ideal candidate, but he is not chosen. Neither are the next six sons who stand before Samuel. It is the youngest—the one out doing the childish, mundane chore of shepherding—who is chosen. It is David. God's Spirit falls powerfully upon him.

16:14–16 In terms of logistics, how does a young unknown shepherd even begin to replace an established and paranoid king? It will be a lengthy and difficult transition, but this section explains how God providentially begins to bring about the change. With Samuel no longer available to the king, Saul is at a loss for spiritual guidance. And it is at this point when an evil spirit begins to terrorize Saul.

16:18 One of Saul's attendants knows of David's musical ability and arranges to have him come to the royal court on a regular basis. In addition to being a gifted musician, David is already a courageous warrior (against bears and lions [17:34–35]) and a person of godly wisdom. The same characteristics that enable David to serve the king are traits that qualify him to serve *as* king.

16:19–22 Ironically, David's initial contact with Saul is made in response to Saul's personal request. Before long, he is one of Saul's armorbearers—someone with a close and trusted relationship with the king.

17:3–10 The Philistines are still the primary threat to Israel, and one particular Philistine is especially threatening. Twice a day for forty days, a towering individual named Goliath has challenged Israel to send someone out to fight. The winner of the one-to-one combat will determine which nation will serve the other.

17:12 Note what a contrast is made when David is introduced to the story. Goliath is described in physical terms: appearance, weaponry, aggressiveness, and so forth. But nothing is said of David's stature, strength, or weapons. Rather, he is introduced in the context of his family. One reason has already been mentioned: David was chosen because of his *heart*, not his outer physical qualities (1 Samuel 13:14; 16:7). Another reason is that the Messiah will come from the tribe of Judah and from Bethlehem (Genesis 49:8–12; Micah 5:2). Jesus will eventually trace His human ancestry back to David.

17:13–19 Jesse's three oldest sons join the Israelite army, and occasionally David delivers things from home for them.

17:16 Forty days seems like a lengthy standoff. Saul and his army don't really want to fight, and they seem content with the stalemate. But the Philistines aren't in an ideal position for battle either. Their chariots work well on level ground, but not on mountain slopes. Both sides apparently want to avoid a full-scale battle.

17:20–28 David witnesses Israel's army shouting a war cry while running toward the Philistines, but then running away as soon as they get close to Goliath. He keeps asking why someone doesn't do something about Goliath. He learns that Saul has issued a call for a volunteer to fight the Philistine and has offered a number of substantial rewards for any takers. David's oldest brother overhears David talking to the soldiers and rebukes him with a series of false accusations. No

doubt Eliab still feels the sting of rejection from seeing his youngest brother anointed in front of him (16:13).

17:24 The Israelites are growing more and more intimidated by Goliath. He stands between nine and ten feet tall, and his armor seems impenetrable. It gets to the point where, when the Israelites see him, they run in fear. Their lack of faith is reminiscent of former generations who had sent spies into the promised land and had been fearful of the giants there (Numbers 13:27–33).

17:40–50 The next section contains one of the best-known stories in the Bible—the confrontation between David and Goliath. Goliath first tries to intimidate David verbally, but his empty boasts do not faze David. The young shepherd understands it will not be his own strength that will win the contest but God's strength. His faith is rewarded. Although Goliath is armored from head to foot, protected by shield and armorbearer, he still needs an opening around his eyes so he can see. David's accuracy with a sling sends the first stone into Goliath's exposed forehead, and the giant falls. David, who had no sword, uses Goliath's own weapon to cut off his head.

17:55, 58 Saul immediately wants to find out more about David's family. He should have known David, who was one of his armorbearers and musicians (16:21, 23). But perhaps Saul is interested in knowing exactly where David acquired the wherewithal to face off against Goliath as he had done. One might raise the question, however, of why Saul (the king) and Abner (the commander of the army) are standing around discussing genealogy while the rest of the soldiers are in pursuit of fleeing Philistines. This is a big day for Israel and the first introduction to David for most of them. But David's instant popularity will soon create problems for him.

18:1–3 Previous passages have shown that Jonathan has an outstanding faith and eagerness to serve God (13:2–3; 14:1–14), so it should come as no surprise that he is impressed with David's stand against Goliath. He overhears David's conversation with Saul, and an immediate bond forms. David and Jonathan become kindred spirits from this point onward.

18:5 Jonathan isn't the only one intrigued by David. From that day onward, Saul does not let David return home. David will have other things to do besides tend sheep and make deliveries. In fact, David excels at whatever assignment Saul gives him, which impresses both the army officers and the people of Israel.

18:6–9 David's heroism is soon depicted in song. Women come out to greet the returning army singing, dancing, and playing instruments. But the lyrics are irksome to Saul. Most likely the singers have no intent to compare Saul with David. They are simply elated that David and Saul have rid the nation of so many of their enemies. Yet Saul's envy grows quickly.

18:10–14 When God once again sends a spirit that troubles Saul, David returns to playing the harp with the intent of soothing the king as before (16:23). But this time, Saul attempts to kill David with his spear. David twice escapes. Then Saul's strategizing becomes subtler. He gives David a big promotion, placing him over one thousand soldiers. The battlefield is a dangerous place where Saul hopes David will meet his death and be forgotten. But God is with David and gives him great success.

18:17–19 Saul offers David one of his daughters in marriage, on the condition that David continues to fight. Whether or not this is intended as part of the reward for fighting Goliath (17:25) is uncertain. But Saul is not prepared for David's response. David rejects Saul's offer, not because he is reluctant to endanger himself in battle, but because he is a truly humble man who considers his station in life unworthy of such a gift. After David declines the offer, Saul allows that daughter to marry another man.

18:20–30 Another of Saul's daughters, Michal, loves David. Saul takes the opportunity to offer David another deal. If David feels he lacks the wealth or social status to be the king's son-in-law, Saul will consider another dowry altogether: one hundred Philistine foreskins. Saul sends word of this offer to David, who responds with enthusiasm. Saul's stated intent is to take revenge on his enemies, but his real desire is to have David killed by the Philistines. Saul's hopes are dashed again as David returns with twice the dowry Saul had demanded.

19:1–7 When Saul's subtle attempts to kill David continue to fail, the king tries to recruit help from others. He instructs his attendants to kill David, but he also tells Jonathan, who immediately warns David. Rather than openly defy his father, Jonathan wisely sets out to convince Saul to rescind the order. He has David lie low while he tries to reason with his father. Jonathan's plan works (this time), and Saul again welcomes David. But Saul's tolerance doesn't last long.

19:8–9 Scripture provides no indication that Saul is going out to do battle against the Philistines. Yet when David goes out to fight and comes back a hero, Saul is overcome with jealousy and anger. Perhaps Saul's powerful negative emotions are somehow connected with the evil spirit that came upon him.

19:10 As David is attempting to minister to Saul by playing the harp, Saul again tries to kill him with a spear, and again misses.

19:11–12 Saul orders a stakeout of David's home. Soldiers are ordered to kill David when he comes out in the morning. But Michal knows her father well and emphatically urges David to escape during the night. After David leaves, she uses a household idol and some goat hair to make it appear that David is sick in bed. By the time Saul's soldiers question her, hear her cover story, report to Saul, and return to find they have been deceived, David has had plenty of time to escape.

19:18 David goes to Ramah, where he finds Samuel and informs him of his experiences with Saul. The two of them then go to nearby Naioth, where apparently a number of prophets gathered.

19:20 The king soon learns of David's whereabouts and sends three successive groups of soldiers to retrieve him. But each time, as soon as the group of soldiers approaches the group of prophets, the Spirit of God causes the soldiers to begin to prophesy.

19:23–24 After three failed attempts, Saul decides to go in person to get David. But as he approaches, he too begins to prophesy, lying naked half the day and through the night. What had originally been a sign of God's endorsement of Saul as king of Israel (10:9–13) has become God's method of protecting His new choice of king.

20:1–4 David leaves Naioth and goes to see Jonathan. After a short initial conversation, the two friends discover that Saul is not being completely honest with either of them. To David's credit, he assumes potential blame for the problem with Saul. Jonathan can hardly believe his father was so intent on doing harm to David, but he is convinced by David's urgent persuasion.

20:5–16 David has a plan to confirm that what he is telling Jonathan is true. On the next day is a special festival (Numbers 10:10; 28:11–15) that David will be expected to attend with the members of Saul's family. He plans to be absent. If Saul asks why he isn't there, Jonathan will say that David's family in Bethlehem is making a special annual sacrifice and that David asked to be excused to be with them. If the king becomes angry, it is likely because he has malicious intent. Twice already David has dodged Saul's spear. He has also escaped from Saul's soldiers, both in his own home and in Ramah with Samuel. It is only natural to be suspicious that perhaps Saul is looking for yet another opportunity to kill David.

20:11, 18–23 The gravity of the situation seems to register with Jonathan at this point. Before even answering David, he waits until the two of them have gone to a nearby field, out of range of curious eyes and finely tuned ears. In the field, Jonathan can also point to landmarks as he explains what he intends to do. After speaking to Saul, Jonathan will shoot three arrows. If he yells to his assistant that the arrows are short of the mark, then all will be well and David will be safe. But if he remarks that they are beyond the mark, David needs to leave for his own safety.

20:35–39 The next morning Jonathan goes out with a young boy to the place where he knows David is hiding and watching. He shoots an arrow and gives the verbal signal that lets David know Saul indeed wants him dead.

21:1–2 David travels a few miles north and east of Jerusalem to Nob, the city of the priests. Ahimelech, the high priest, is no fool. He does not know about the schism that has formed between David and Saul, but he does know David is supposed to have a number of troops. When he sees David coming alone, he is troubled. David has a story prepared. Aware of Saul's influence and potential for violence, David does not disclose all the details of his sudden appearance, perhaps hoping to avoid involving the priests in his feud with Saul. Instead, he tells Ahimelech he is on a secret mission for Saul, and that his men are hidden nearby. If Ahimelech doubts David's cover story, he has the tact not to say anything.

21:3–7 David comes to the reason for his visit. First, he needs some provisions. The only food available is the shewbread (Exodus 25:30)—sacred bread normally eaten only by the priests. Ahimelech is willing to share the bread with anyone who is ceremonially clean. The gift is witnessed by the chief of Saul's shepherds, an Edomite named Doeg.

21:8–9 David asks Ahimelech for a weapon, which again may have raised the priest's eyebrows. What kind of soldier on a special mission would be without a sword or spear? At the time, few weapons could be found in the entire kingdom—much less in the city of the priests. In fact, the only sword on the entire premises is the sword of Goliath, a trophy/memorial of the victory God gave Israel through David. It belongs to David anyway, so Ahimelech willingly gives it to him. David takes the sword and bread and promptly leaves.

21:10–12 David's next move is a bold one. He leaves Israel and goes into Philistine territory. In fact, the city of Gath is Goliath's hometown, and David boldly enters carrying Goliath's sword. The fact that David is willing to take such a risk illustrates how strongly Saul desires to kill David.

21:13–15 While Achish begins to rethink his offer of sanctuary, David feigns madness, slobbering and scribbling on the gates. The Philistine leader Achish is presented as gullible and less than astute.

22:1–2 David leaves Philistine territory and goes into Judah. The exact site of the cave of Adullam is unknown but appears to have been a safe, secluded hideout not too close to King Saul. Word begins to spread that David is there. He soon has a band of about four hundred people.

22:3 David's next stop is the territory of Moab, where he arranges for his elderly parents to stay. The move appears to put David's parents out of harm's way during the years he is fleeing from Saul.

22:6–8 Word of David's movements are bound to reach Saul eventually. He blames his officials for everything. He had found out too late about Jonathan's covenant with David. Even worse, he accuses them of conspiring against him.

22:9–10 Saul's chief shepherd, Doeg, speaks up with some information that Saul might find useful. He had seen David in Nob, receiving help from Ahimelech and the priests. Doeg tells Saul that he had seen Ahimelech equip David with provisions and Goliath's sword. But what Doeg *doesn't* say (and perhaps he does not know) is that David never informed the priests that he was fleeing from Saul. Neither David nor the priests had ever said or done anything to conspire against the king. But Saul's blinding jealousy and devotion to protecting his throne took precedence over getting the facts straight.

22:12–14 It should have been the responsibility of the priests to enlighten Saul and others in Israel about the judgments of God. But here it is Saul who presumes to pass judgment on the entire priesthood.

22:16–19 Saul is not listening to reason. His mind is apparently already made up. He commands his guards to kill Ahimelech and all the other priests. But no one moves. As much as these men fear Saul, they are not willing to act on his heinous command. Saul then turns to Doeg, a non-Israelite, who doesn't appear to have the same qualms about killing God's priests. But he and Saul don't stop with that terrible crime. Doeg then travels to Nob, where he also kills the priests' families and cattle. Eighty-five priests die that day. And how ironic it is that while Saul had defied God's order to annihilate the people and property of the Amalekites (15:1–3, 7–9), he readily wipes out his own spiritual leaders.

22:20–21 Only one priest escapes Saul's wrath: one of Ahimelech's sons named Abiathar. He runs to David and tells him what Saul has done. David assumes full responsibility. He had seen Doeg at Nob, but who could have predicted how far Saul would go in his hatred of David? David could do nothing more for those who had been killed, but he does offer sanctuary to Abiathar.

23:7–9 Saul learns of David's whereabouts and is pleased to discover that David is in a city with gates and bars. Those protections won't keep Saul out for long, but they will keep David trapped. When David gets word of Saul's intent, he again has Abiathar bring the ephod to consult God. One would think that the citizens of Keilah would be grateful to David and offer him some protection. But God lets him know that Saul is indeed on his way and that the people of Keilah will turn him over to Saul when the king arrives. So before that can happen, David leaves.

23:9–13 When David seeks direction from the Lord, the answers he receives are hypothetical. For example, God tells him that he will be turned over to Saul, but that is conditional on his staying in the city. He can take action to avoid that ominous result. After David leaves with his men, Saul doesn't bother making the trip.

23:14–15 David takes his troops to the desert where they can hide in various strongholds and hilly areas. Saul keeps looking for him, but God is watching over him, and Saul is never able to find him.

23:16–18 Jonathan does all he can to affirm David. It is more than a pep talk; he helps David renew his strength in God. Jonathan encourages David not to be afraid. Yes, Saul is doing everything in his power to find and kill David. But Jonathan—and even Saul—realizes that God is protecting David because David is certain to be the next king of Israel. Jonathan reaffirms that he is secondary to David—his most loyal servant and supporter. Then Jonathan returns home while David goes back into hiding.

23:19–20 At this time some of the locals (the Ziphites) report David's location to King Saul. Perhaps they want to curry his favor, or maybe they simply want to avoid his anger. But their willingness to betray David is particularly grievous because they, too, are from the tribe of Judah.

23:21 Upon receiving the report from the Ziphites, Saul responds with pious-sounding language. Yet his holy-sounding words are only a front for the wickedness of his intended actions.

23:22–25 This time Saul doesn't go rushing out with his army. David has escaped his efforts several times already, and it won't look good to come back empty-handed. Instead, he instructs the Ziphites to watch David closely, making note of his habits and hiding places. When he feels the time is right, Saul makes the journey himself.

24:1–3 As soon as Saul deals with the Philistines, he returns to his pursuit of David. He takes three thousand trained soldiers to fight David's six hundred men. But before Saul has even found David, he stops at a cave to have some privacy to relieve himself. Little does Saul know that he has chosen the very cave where David and his men are hiding.

24:4–7 Saul has probably thrown his robe aside for the moment, and David uses the cover of darkness to slip over and cut off a piece of cloth. David's soldiers want to do much more, of course. They are surely weary of being on the run and in perpetual danger, and they interpret the remarkable coincidence of Saul's appearance—alone and defenseless—as God's way of delivering David's enemy into his hands.

24:8–11 David shows reverence and submission to Saul. He appeals to Saul to set aside any rumors he might have heard and to judge David's guilt or innocence for himself, based on David's actions.

24:13–14 David assures Saul he has no evil intent, and he likens himself to a dead dog or a single flea—no threat at all to Saul and his kingdom. Then David rests his case, looking to God for justice and protection, and waits for Saul's response.

24:16–20 Saul begins to weep, responding to David's affectionate address ("my father") by calling him his son. And for the first time, Saul acknowledges the truth. He had heard from Samuel that his kingdom will not endure (13:14) and that God has rejected him as Israel's king (15:26). He had seen that David's popularity could easily allow David to possess his kingdom (18:8–9). He had privately admitted that as long as David was alive, Jonathan would never become king (20:31). Yet he had resisted all those truths, treating David as a traitor to the nation and pursuing him with the intent of killing him. Here, however, Saul publicly admits that God is taking his kingdom away from him and that David's ascent to the throne is a certainty.

24:21 Saul wants David to swear that he will not kill off all of Saul's descendants. It is common practice of the time for new kings to kill off every other possible heir to the throne—especially descendants of the preceding king.

25:1 The death of Samuel is succinctly summarized at this point—without much fanfare, considering his significance to the nation. Samuel's death must have been particularly hard on David, who had just said good-bye to Jonathan for the last time (23:18) and had left his parents in care of the king of Moab (22:3).

25:4–11 David sends ten of his group to Nabal to report that they have been treating Nabal's shepherds with great respect and to ask for any provisions Nabal could spare. However, Nabal refuses to acknowledge that David's men have helped protect his shepherds and their flocks. He doesn't even send a token gift. Instead, he insults David.

25:12–13, 22 When David is told what transpired with Nabal, he becomes irate. David has acted honorably. His men could easily have taken whatever they needed from Nabal's flocks but had not done so. David expected a positive response in return for his positive actions. When he determines that Nabal is being unjust, David determines to achieve justice himself. He orders his men to arm themselves, and he sets out to kill Nabal and every male in his household.

25:14–19 Nabal would have suffered dire consequences had it not been for his wise wife, Abigail. One of Nabal's servants had gone to her with an account of what had happened, including a warning that David was likely to retaliate. She wastes no time gathering generous portions of food, packing everything on donkeys, and sending it ahead to David. One might wonder how she could gather so much food so quickly. The timing is convenient because Nabal had planned a fit-for-a-king banquet (25:36). He probably never missed what Abigail sent to David.

25:20 Abigail works her way down the mountain, out of sight of David and his men. David likewise comes from higher ground, still grumbling about Nabal's insults and rehearsing what he will do when he finds the ungrateful despot. Without either party realizing what is happening, David and Abigail converge and suddenly find themselves face-to-face with each other.

25:24–25 Abigail is everything Nabal is not: polite, well spoken, submissive, honest, and ready to take responsibility and blame. She repeatedly refers to herself as David's "handmaid" and calls David her "lord." She doesn't try to cover for her husband; she calls him a fool, and in doing so she may have saved his life. David knows from experience there is no honor or status in killing fools. Abigail isn't attempting to exaggerate her husband's faults through name-calling: *Nabal* literally means "fool," and there is little doubt that he lives up to the name.

25:26–35 Next Abigail tactfully points out how taking vengeance will be detrimental to David. God had prevented him from shedding blood for personal revenge. Abigail acknowledges the hand of God on David, and she exhorts him to avoid wrongdoing. She pleads with David to accept the gift she has brought and asks him to forgive *her* transgression. Abigail's words stop David in his tracks. He knows she is right, and he praises her in front of his men. She has literally been a godsend, used by God to prevent David from taking vengeance on Nabal and shedding other innocent blood. Had she not acted so quickly, David would have carried out his plan. He thankfully accepts her gift and sends her home in peace. David leaves vengeance in God's hands, and it comes rather quickly.

25:36–37 Nabal is drunk when Abigail gets home, so she waits until the next morning to tell him about her encounter with David. Upon hearing the news, his heart fails, and he dies ten days later.

25:39 David rejoices in the news, not so much that Nabal is dead, but that thanks to Abigail, David hadn't acted hastily and done something he would always regret. And David wastes no time asking Abigail to marry him. Her action had been selfless, and it is quickly rewarded.

25:44 During this time, Saul has a change of heart and is about to take up the pursuit of David once more. He even gives his daughter Michal (David's wife) to another man while David is gone.

26:7 David's first close encounter with Saul had been in a cave where David was hiding. This time David seeks out Saul's position and finds him out in the open, asleep and surrounded by his entire army. Saul and Abner, the commander of his army, are in the center of a large circle. David doesn't realize that the entire army is in a divinely induced slumber, yet he is willing to approach the king anyway. He and a volunteer, Abishai, walk through the sleeping soldiers, right up to Saul. The king's spear is stuck in the ground nearby, and his water jug is near his head.

26:8–12 Abishai is a stouthearted soldier (2 Samuel 23:18–19). Every instinct tells him to take the spear and do away with Saul with one good thrust. After the cave incident, perhaps Abishai thinks David might be squeamish about killing Saul, and he is more than willing to do the job himself. But David had spared Saul not out of fear but out of respect for the king's position and reverence for God's right to remove the king whenever He deemed that the time was right. In addition, David's recent encounter with Abigail may have strengthened his resolve not to be hasty in bloodshed. He tells Abishai to take Saul's spear and water jug, and they go to a neighboring hillside, within earshot of the Israelite army.

26:14 David shouts over, but to Abner, not Saul. As commander of the army, Abner is primarily responsible for Saul's protection. David points out the absence of the spear and water jug, and he makes it clear that if his intent had been to destroy the king, Saul would be dead by now. Indeed, David prevented Saul's murder by Abishai, making him a more reliable defender of Saul than anyone else in Israel.

26:17–20 Still groggy, Saul finally recognizes the voice as David's and calls over to him. David then begins to address Saul, giving a personal defense much as he had done previously (1 Samuel 24:8–15). In essence, David accuses the king of listening to other people who endeavored to make David serve other gods. (As soon as someone left Israelite soil, he or she was quickly exposed to the various gods of the various peoples of the area, and David was being kept away from his community of worship.)

26:21 Saul again is quick to confess and repent. He invites David to return. David arranges for someone to come over and retrieve Saul's property. Then the king goes home as David again goes on his way, no doubt anticipating another encounter.

27:1–2 David has just gotten a reprieve from Saul's persistent pursuit (26:21), but he knows it will only be a matter of time before Saul renews the manhunt. Until this point, David has been sounding confident and faithful (24:15; 26:23–24), and Abigail confirmed those qualities (25:28–29). David's change of heart is not explained.

27:3–4 If David primarily wants to stop worrying about Saul, he succeeds. After he arranges with King Achish to live in Philistine territory, David has no more trouble from Saul. However, the move will soon create other problems.

27:6 David had hidden out among the Philistines before (21:10–15). He survived, but left the city perceived as a scribbling, slobbering lunatic. This time he is not alone; he has his six hundred men, their wives and families, and his own two wives. At first their accommodations seem ideal. Achish gives David the city of Ziklag, where his group resides. Ziklag is about twenty-five miles from Gath, so Achish won't be privy to David's every activity.

27:8–11 David and his men regularly fight enemies of Israel, killing all the people (to eliminate any witnesses) and accumulating livestock and clothing. Anytime Achish asks about their raids, David tells him they have been fighting the Israelites. It also appears David may have given Achish a portion of the spoils.

27:12 In time, Achish comes to trust David. He assumes that David can never go home again, and it seems that Achish will always benefit from having David as an ally.

28:1–2 King Achish decides to join a larger Philistine coalition marching against Israel, and he enlists David's help. Though taken by surprise, David tells Achish what he wants to hear, and the king responds by bestowing on David an honored position. How amazing that David has gone from being armorbearer for King Saul (16:21) to being bodyguard for a Philistine king. Of course, now David has the dilemma of how to keep from actually fighting against Israel without Achish discovering his true loyalties.

28:3–9 Saul's uneasiness progresses from fear to terror to sheer panic. Even though he has been responsible for removing everyone involved in occult practices, he decides to find a medium and seek some direction. His prior action had been in compliance with God's law (Leviticus 19:31; 20:6, 27; Deuteronomy 18:10–14), so this decision reflects clear disregard for God's will. Getting to the medium requires an eight-mile trek from Gilboa to Endor (at risk of encountering the Philistines).

28:12–13 After arriving, Saul's secret identity doesn't last long. Saul asks the woman to contact Samuel, but when she does, she grows alarmed. Her response suggests that this is no ordinary conjuring. She immediately discerns Saul's identity.

28:14–19 Saul falls on the ground before Samuel, and the two have a short conversation. Saul wants to know what to do. Samuel has frequently spoken to

Saul for God, and his messages have been consistent: Because of Saul's disobedience, he is going to lose his kingdom (13:13–14; 15:27–29). If Saul is hoping for a different message this time, he is sorely disappointed. In fact, Samuel says that the next day the Philistines will soundly defeat the Israelites, and Saul and his sons will be with him.

29:1–2 At this point, the flow of 1 Samuel returns to David's dilemma. Not only are David and his men marching out with the Philistine king Achish to do battle against Israel, but they are honored with the crucial position of rear guard, where the bravest and most highly skilled warriors are placed. Apparently each of the five key Philistine cities had its own king and troops. But this time the Philistines are combining forces to march against Israel.

29:3–5 When the other leaders discover that King Achish has included David among his troops, they are incensed. They feel that Achish is being deceived (which he is) and that David will be a real threat if the Philistines go into battle and he starts fighting for Israel. They even remind Achish of the song that has been written about David concerning how many people he has killed, and they insist that David return to Ziklag.

29:6–8 In an almost comical scene, the Philistine king gives David the disappointing news that he will not be allowed to fight against Israel. Achish even invokes the name of David's God (Yahweh) in praise of David. With the matter already settled by the Philistines, David even protests their decision. In reality, it is the best thing that could have happened to extract him from a delicate situation.

30:1–6 David and his men find Ziklag burned. Missing are all their family members and livestock, and many of their possessions. Their initial emotion, naturally, is grief. They all weep until they have no more strength. But the next emotion is bitterness, and they begin to blame David for all that has gone wrong. They even talk of stoning him.

30:7–8 This event seems to turn David back to God. He calls for the priest and the ephod to determine whether God will have them pursue the raiders. God assures him of success in rescuing everything.

30:10 The trouble is that David's group had been physically challenged during the almost sixty-mile march from Aphek back to Ziklag. Then the emotional toll of finding their city in ruins and their families absent makes things worse. Not everyone is up to marching off with David right away. They all start, but a third of them are too exhausted to continue. The other two-thirds leave some of their gear with the two hundred staying behind in order to move faster.

30:11–15 The trail is indeed cold. David doesn't even know whom he is chasing. But then his men find an Egyptian slave who hasn't had food or water for three days. They feed him and discover it had been the

Amalekites who had raided Ziklag. After being promised protection, the Egyptian even agrees to lead David to the Amalekite camp.

30:16–20 The timing couldn't have been better. When David's men arrive, the much larger group of Amalekites is celebrating their easy conquest—drinking and disorganized. David and his men attack, resulting in a slaughter that lasts many hours. Four hundred young men escape on camels, but every other Amalekite soldier is killed. The next day David recovers everything that had been taken from Ziklag—wives, families, animals, and possessions—not to mention plunder from the Amalekites.

30:22 When David's fighting men return, there are those among them who don't want to share the plunder they have accumulated with the two hundred men who remained behind.

30:26–31 David steps in and sees that his soldiers all get equal shares. In addition, David sends some of their new wealth to friends and elders at various places throughout Judah. His decision will have far-reaching effects. Many of the recipients are men of considerable influence who will soon be among the first to embrace David as king.

31:1–3 As has already been shown several times in 1 Samuel, when life is going well for David, it is taking a downturn for Saul. The book concludes with one final, graphic example. At about the time that David is in pursuit of the Amalekite raiders, Saul and the Israelite army are fighting the Philistines. David returns with only good news, but the Israelites are soundly defeated. Among the casualties are Saul and his sons.

31:4–5 Saul is critically wounded and asks his armorbearer to kill him so he will avoid any torment by his enemies. His armorbearer is afraid and refuses, so Saul falls on his own sword. The armorbearer follows suit. A passing Amalekite later takes credit for delivering the death blow to Saul (2 Samuel 1:8–10), though he might have been lying in hopes of receiving a reward from David.

31:8–11 When the Philistines discover Saul's body, they cut off his head, place his armor in the temple of Ashtaroth, and hang his body on the wall of one of their cities. But the inhabitants of Jabesh-gilead remember how Saul had previously kept them from humiliation at the hands of the Ammonites (1 Samuel 11:1–11). When they hear what has happened to Saul, many of their brave men march through the night, retrieve the bodies of Saul and his sons, and return them to Israel for a proper burial. Saul's boldness toward the Ammonites at Jabesh had been his finest hour, and it was not forgotten by those whom he had saved.

31:13 The book of 1 Samuel appears to end rather abruptly at this point, because 1 Samuel and 2 Samuel were originally a single book. So the story will continue as 2 Samuel begins.

THE SECOND BOOK OF

SAMUEL

OTHERWISE CALLED

THE SECOND BOOK OF THE KINGS

INTRODUCTION TO 2 SAMUEL ■ This book tells the story of how David sets out to establish his throne with God's blessing following King Saul's death. David is a man after God's own heart, but he is still simply a man with real shortcomings, and his sin with Bath-sheba has a myriad of truly tragic consequences. The text recounts the events of the second half of King David's life during which his reign unites Israel and testifies to God's faithfulness to His servant David and to all His children.

AUTHOR ■ There is no mention of the author in the books of Samuel, though Jewish tradition states that Samuel wrote the first twenty-four chapters of what was originally one book of Samuel. In fact, 1 and 2 Samuel and 1 and 2 Kings are thought to be a single historical work edited by the same theological circle during the exile.

OCCASION ■ The book of 1 Samuel ends tragically, with King Saul a virtual madman. He turns against David, his loyal servant and friend, and seeks to kill David as though he is a traitor. He fails to obey God's Word and so brings about his own downfall and demise. Saul even goes so far as to consult with a medium. The closing chapter of 1 Samuel is the account of his death at the hand of the Philistines and his own hand as well. As sad as it is, we breathe a sigh of relief, for now David's days of fleeing from Saul as a fugitive are over. Second Samuel starts immediately afterward to tell how David will reign in Saul's place.

1:1–2 From the time he parted ways with the Philistines, David has been greatly concerned for Saul and his beloved friend Jonathan, not to mention the rest of his countrymen. During his pursuit of the Amalekite raiding party and the ensuing battle, David had little time to think about how things were going back in Israel. Now for three days David and his men have been back in Ziklag, wondering how the war is going or, perhaps, how it concluded.

1:3–4 The Amalekite messenger who brings David the news ran some one hundred miles to reach him at Ziklag. His clothing is torn, and dust is upon his head. It is a sign of mourning. Reaching David, this young man falls on the ground before him, prostrating himself as though approaching royalty. He brings David news of the death of many Israelites, including Saul and Jonathan.

1:5–10 David is unwilling to accept this man's report without some verification and immediately begins to question him. The young man explains how he came upon Saul, mortally wounded, on mount Gilboa. There he obliged the king's request to slay him. The messenger seems to think that David will be ready to reward him, even for his role in Saul's death. The young man sees Saul as David's enemy, an obstacle to David's rise to the throne. He sees Saul's death as good news to David and killing Saul as putting him out of his misery. But David sees it much more simply: This man killed the Lord's anointed.

1:11–16 David's response is quite different from what the young Amalekite expects it to be. He is grief-stricken over the defeat of Israel and the death of Saul. He is devastated by the death of his closest friend, Jonathan. Any thought of personal gain at the expense of others is cast aside. David sets the pace in the mourning, and his men promptly follow his lead.

1:17–27 This eulogy, or dirge, is a special labor of David's love. It is a psalm that mourns the deaths of Saul and Jonathan. It says nothing negative about Saul but instead honors both Saul and Jonathan as fallen heroes. David not only restrains himself from speaking ill of the dead, but honors Saul and Jonathan as war heroes, as men worthy of respect and honor. David's psalm begins by focusing on Saul and ends with the focus on Jonathan.

2:1–4 David seeks divine guidance and is divinely directed to go up to the city of Hebron. After David, his wives, and the rest of his followers arrive at Hebron with their families, the men of Judah anoint David as king.

2:5–7 David's graciousness toward the men of Jabesh-gilead gives the people of Israel an excellent opportunity to make David their king as well.

2:8–11 Abner poses a problem for David. This cousin of Saul opposes David's reign in Saul's place and orchestrates events so that Ish-bosheth, a surviving son of Saul, becomes king over the rest of Israel. This delays David's reign for several years.

2:12–17 The rivalry between the Benjamites and the house of David continues to grow. Their military leaders are Abner (Benjamites/Israelites) and Joab (Judah).

2:18–25 In the midst of the fighting, Asahel, brother of Abishai and Joab, is hot on the heels of Abner. Abner does not wish to kill Asahel, but the young man is not willing to give up the chase. Finally, after failing to talk Asahel out of his pursuit, Abner kills him. It is almost an act of self-defense, but Joab will never accept the death of his brother at the hand of Abner. He is intent upon revenge.

2:26–3:1 Both Abner and Joab pave the way for a future division. This text describes the origin of one of many cracks in the foundation of the united nation of Israel, and this crack will develop over time into a gaping chasm, one that seems almost impossible to bridge.

3:1–5 God brings blessing on the house of David, and it grows stronger and larger even in the midst of trial and waiting for David to become king of a united Israel. This family register of births also fleshes out what we know of David's household, mentioning (in addition to the two wives he brought with him) four more wives. Also notable is the introduction of Amnon and Absalom, who later play a prominent role in the tumultuous period of David's kingship following his sin with Bath-sheba.

3:6–16 Abner approaches David with the offer to make him king. He claims that the land is his and that he is in charge. If David will but make a covenant with Abner, Abner will handle the rest. He promises to bring all Israel over to David. David initially accepts Abner's offer of the kingdom with one condition: that he be given back his wife Michal. David has loyalty to his wife (1 Samuel 25:44) and regards her return as an important reunion for his household, especially because she is from the house of Saul. Ish-bosheth grants this request to David.

3:17–21 Before his death, Abner meets with the leaders of both sides. There is an agreement in principle. It seems that if he had lived, he would have done as he promised.

3:22–27 Joab returns from a raid and discovers that David has formed an alliance with Abner, with whom he is still angry over the death of his brother Asahel. He does not kill Abner in the context of war—which would be viewed not as a murder but as a necessary part of war (see 3:28–34; 1 Kings 2:30–33). Instead, Joab clearly believes his own position is threatened and calls Abner back. In a private conversation of which David is unaware, Joab murders Abner to avenge the blood of his brother.

3:28–29 When David learns of Joab's murder of Abner, he publicly renounces the actions of Joab as reprehensible. There is no excuse for what he has done. David condemns the murder and calls down divine judgment on Joab and his family.

3:31–39 David mourns the death of Abner, seeing to it that his burial is honorable, even if his death is not. David not only walks behind the bier, weeping loudly and chanting a lament for Abner, but also refuses to eat all day long. It is obvious to all that David had no part in the death of Abner. David's standing with the people continues to increase.

4:1 Although the Lord had anointed David as the next king, Abner had installed Ish-bosheth as Saul's replacement. With the death of Abner at the hand of

Joab, Ish-bosheth loses all his courage. He could hardly stand up to Abner, let alone even think about standing up against David. Now Ish-bosheth is on his own, knowing that Abner had already set up David to rule in his place.

4:2–8 Two men think they can provide a solution to remove the rivalry. These men are fellow members of the tribe of Benjamin and commanders of divisions of Israelite soldiers. They take matters into their own hands and proceed to brutally kill Ish-bosheth in his own home while he is lying in bed. They do not understand David's love for Saul or his commitment to protect the lives of his offspring and the honor of his name (1 Samuel 24:16–22).

5:4–5 David waits fifteen years from the time he is first anointed by Samuel to the time he becomes king over Judah. Even after David is anointed as king of Judah, he must wait a full seven years to be anointed king of all Israel. This means David waited more than twenty years of his life to be made king.

5:6–10 David finally obtains a place of his own. The place has been known as Jebus up to this point in time, and its inhabitants are called the "Jebusites." But from this text onward, Jebus becomes Jerusalem, and Zion is called the City of David. God continues to bless and increase David's power and his household. In the next chapter, Jerusalem will become the dwelling place of God as the ark of the covenant is brought to the city where Solomon will later build the temple and where Israel's coming king, Jesus Christ, will eventually ride in triumphantly on a donkey one week before His crucifixion.

5:9 The possession of Jerusalem as David's new capital will unite Israel. The city is virtually on the border of Judah and Benjamin. It is a city that neither the sons of Judah nor the sons of Benjamin have been able to capture. Thus, taking this city as David's capital will not seem to favor either of these two tribes. In addition to all of this, its natural setting makes it difficult to defeat (which is why the Israelites had not taken and held it before). It is in the hill country, on the top of more than one mountain, and is surrounded by valleys. With a little work, it becomes a fortress.

5:17–22 The Philistines, unlike the Israelites, will not submit to David as God's king. They attack David, seeking to kill him and to remove the threat that he and a united Israel pose. Not once, but twice, these Philistines come against David and the army of Israel. And twice God gives David the victory over his enemies. Those who receive David as God's king are blessed; those who reject David as God's king are crushed.

5:23–25 It is interesting to note that once David is established as king of Israel, the first enemy he meets is the Philistines. This battle parallels the first battle that David ever finds himself in after he is anointed by Samuel as the future king—his battle with Goliath, the giant Philistine who had frightened all of Israel's forces (1 Samuel 17). The picture here is of God going ahead of David into the battle—as indicated by the sound of marching in the treetops—and delivering the victory to His servant.

6:1–8 The ark is holy. It is not to be touched. By using poles, men could transport the ark without touching the ark itself. And these men, walking in step with one another, give the ark stability. Putting the ark on the ox cart made it susceptible to the movements of the cart and less stable, and thus more likely to fall off the cart. Uzzah is a reminder to us that God's holiness is such that sinful people cannot draw near to Him unless He provides the means to do so.

6:9–12 David is struck with fear of the Lord and decides to let the ark remain outside the city in the house of Obed-edom the Gittite. God's blessing on the house of Obed-edom, where the ark rests for three months, assures David that the nearness of the ark is a blessing but that it must be brought to Jerusalem in accordance with God's directions. David resumes bringing the ark into the city—this time being careful to observe God's instructions.

6:13–15 The ark is carried six steps, and then a sacrifice is offered. Those first six steps are no doubt the tensest steps of the entire journey. As the journey continues, the men's courage and joy increase. Soon there is great celebration as they make their way to the holy city. Along the way, David and his entourage dance and worship God and offer sacrifices as signs of humility before God.

6:16–23 It seems there is only one person in all of Israel who does not and will not enter into the spirit of rejoicing and celebration, and that person is Michal, David's wife. Michal has no intention of being a part of the celebration, and she proceeds to distract from David's praise and blessing. She is not angry with David for doing something wrong and standing out from the rest of the people. She is angry with David for behaving like the common people and not acting like a king as he worships God.

7:1–5 David is referred to as the "king," but when God refers to David, He calls him His "servant." The question God asks David sets the tone for what is to follow: Are you the one who should build My house?

7:6–7 God gave Israel the tabernacle; the temple is David's idea. God explains that as the Creator of all things, He neither requires nor can be confined by a dwelling made by human hands. In short, God does not need a temple, and He does not ask for one. God reminds David who is taking care of whom. God gently rebukes David for this heady plan. David has taken the wrong posture of helping out God, rather than being the one who has constantly been helped *by* God.

7:8–15 After pointing out all that He has done for David and Israel in the past, God goes on to tell David that he hasn't seen the best of it yet. God promises to appoint a place for His people where they will be planted. They will have a place of their own (as David intended to give God a place of His own), and they will dwell in peace there because the wicked will no longer afflict them. God

has been behind all of David's successes, and now He is promising even greater glory. God announces to David that He is going to build a house for him by blessing his descendants and ultimately bringing the Messiah through his bloodline.

7:16–17 David will have sons who will rule over Israel. But there will be one very special Son, and through Him all of the promises God has made here and elsewhere (pertaining to the kingdom of God) will be fulfilled, either in His first coming or in His return to the earth. It is in this Son that all of David's hopes, all of Israel's hopes, and all of humanity's hopes are fulfilled—this is the essence of what is often called the Davidic Covenant.

7:18–24 David now stands in awe of the fact that God takes him, a man of no status or standing, and makes him king of Israel. This, too, is what God has reminded David through Nathan (7:8–9). David sees his standing and status as Israel's king as the result of God's sovereign grace and not as the recognition of his potential greatness.

8:1 The Philistines, located to Israel's west, are troublesome to Israel (Genesis 26:1, 8, 14–15, 18), especially from the time of the judges onward (Judges 3:3, 31; 10:6–7). Once David becomes king, the Philistines think it's best to attack quickly in an attempt to nullify the threat he will pose to them. They fail, and now David will subdue them, ending their tyranny for some time.

8:2 The killing of the Moabites seems amazingly harsh and barbaric. But standard warfare rules during this era usually dictated killing all of one's enemies. So the fact that David spares one-third of the Moabites demonstrates his mercy. As king of Israel, David is God's representative. These Moabites are enemies of Israel, and therefore they are enemies of God. As such, they all deserve to die. The wonder is not that two-thirds of the Moabites are killed but that one-third is left to live. And in the killing of the two-thirds, any thought of resisting David or rebelling against him is laid to rest.

8:3–14 This is a period for David in which Israel celebrates many victories. The outcome of all of David's activities is that he defeats his enemies. Israelite garrisons are found among the neighboring nations, whereas foreign garrisons had once been in Israel (1 Samuel 10:5; 13:3–4). This means they will no longer be able to resist, harass, or oppress Israel for some time. There will be peace in the land, just as God promised.

9:1–2 David is a man who makes promises and keeps them. Before he became Israel's king, he made promises to both Jonathan and Saul. To Jonathan, he promised to protect his life and to show loving-kindness to his house forever (1 Samuel 20:12–17). To Saul, he vowed not to cut off his descendants after him (1 Samuel 24:21–22). Now Saul and Jonathan are dead, and David is king.

9:3 David not only remembers his commitment to Saul but goes far beyond it. It seems as though all of Saul's descendants are dead. No descendant of Saul approaches David, seeking his favor. David is now in a position to carry out his promise to Jonathan—all he needs is one of his descendants. David inquires as to whether there is a descendant of Saul to whom he may show kindness for Jonathan's sake (9:1). David speaks of this act of kindness as the kindness of God.

9:4–13 Only one of Jonathan's sons is still living—Mephibosheth, who is crippled in both feet. Ziba doubts David will want him to be the one to whom he shows favor. Yet David summons him and promises to restore to Mephibosheth all the land that had belonged to his father, and that he had evidently lost sometime after the death of Saul and his father. Not only will David restore all that to which Mephibosheth is heir, but he will make him his regular guest at the palace.

10:1–4 Hanun is the son of Nahash, who as king of the Ammonites has been on good terms with David. When David hears of Nahash's death, he sends a delegation to Ammon to convey his respect for Nahash and to mourn his death. The advisors of this newly installed king give him some bad counsel. They assure Hanun that David's intentions cannot be honorable. He is only sending these men as spies to obtain intelligence so that he can attack them, as he has so many other nations. This explanation of events gives Hanun the excuse he is looking for—a reason to break the alliance his father made with David and Israel.

10:5 David receives word that his delegation has been abused and humiliated. Their beards are, for the Hebrews, a mark of dignity. Hanun has half of the beard of each man shaved off. In addition, he has their garments cut off to embarrass them. David takes pity on the dishonored delegation.

10:6–7 We are not told that David summoned his troops, intending to go to war. We are told that the sons of Ammon recognize that they have angered David. Rather than apologize or attempt to reconcile with David, the sons of Ammon seek to make an alliance that will strengthen them in their conflict with Israel. Syrians from several regions are hired as mercenaries. Only after David learns of this military buildup does he call his army into active duty.

10:8–11 David and his forces draw up to battle with the Ammonites and their Syrian mercenaries. This coalition army divides into two groups, intending to attack the Israelites from the front and the rear. When Joab sees this, he divides the army of Israel into two forces. He leads one division, and his brother Abishai leads the other. Joab sets himself against the Syrians, and Abishai is to fight the Ammonites. If either of the two becomes hard-pressed by his opponent, the other is to come to his aid.

10:13–19 The political and military intrigue in 2 Samuel 8 and 10 is used providentially by God to give Israel the land and the victory God had long before promised His people (Genesis 12:1–3). The tribute that David obtains from his subjected enemies seems to provide the raw materials that will be required for the building of the temple. These events fulfill not only the promise of God made to David in 2 Samuel 7 but also the promises God made long before to Abraham and the patriarchs and to Moses.

11:1–4 A relaxed and aimless King David, shirking his duties in battle, spies a beautiful woman bathing one evening while strolling on his rooftop. He learns that she is married to a Hittite named Uriah, who is a soldier in his army. Bath-sheba is perhaps the most famous object of desire in the whole Bible because David, a man after God's own heart, is brought down from a place of glory because of his adultery with her and the resulting cover-up.

11:5–27 One of the tragic aspects of this story is that the sequence of sin in David's life does not end with his adulterous union with Bath-sheba. It instead leads to a deceptive plot to make her husband, Uriah, appear to be the father of David's child with Bath-sheba and culminates in David's murder of Uriah and his marriage to Bath-sheba.

11:6 It seems likely that David and Uriah are not total strangers but that they know each other to some degree. Uriah is listed among the mighty warriors of David (2 Samuel 23:39; 1 Chronicles 11:41). Some of these mighty men came to David early, while he was in the cave of Adullam (1 Samuel 22:1–2), and likely among them were brothers Joab, Abishai, and Asahel (2 Samuel 23:18, 24; 1 Chronicles 11:26). Others joined David at Ziklag (1 Chronicles 12), and still other great warriors joined with David at Hebron (1 Chronicles 12:38–40).

11:14–26 When the deception of making the child appear to be Uriah's fails, David, instead of repenting, escalates the sin by ordering to have Uriah sent to the front lines of the battle—a virtual death sentence for an innocent man. Certain biblical figures may cause us to question whether they really ever came to faith in God, such as Balaam, Samson, and Saul. But we have no such questions regarding David. He is not only a believer; he is a model believer—a man after God's heart. Nevertheless, David, in spite of his trust in God, in spite of his marvelous times of worship and his beautiful psalms, falls deeply into sin. If David can fall, anyone can. And that is precisely what Paul warns believers about in 1 Corinthians 10:11–12.

12:1–4 Nathan is a prophet and a friend to David. Even one of David's sons is named Nathan (5:14). David informs Nathan of his desire to build a temple in 2 Samuel 7. Nathan will name Bath-sheba and David's second son (12:25). He will remain loyal to the king and to Solomon when Adonijah seeks to usurp the throne (1 Kings 2). Nathan does not come to David only as God's spokesman; he comes to David as his friend.

12:5–6 Nathan confronts David about his sin by telling him a story about sheep—one greedy shepherd has taken everything from a lowly farmer who had only one sheep. The story, of course, parallels the actions of David with Bath-sheba and Uriah. David does not see what is coming. The story Nathan tells makes David furious. David is furious because a rich man stole and slaughtered a poor man's pet. He does not yet see the connection to his lack of compassion over stealing a poor man's beloved companion, his wife. The slaughtering of Uriah is most certainly an act that lacks compassion. The crowning touch in David's display of righteous indignation is found in the religious flavoring he gives it by the words "as the LORD liveth."

12:7–8 David has just sprung the trap on himself, and Nathan is about to let him know about it. The first thing Nathan does is dramatically indict David as the culprit. In stunned silence, David now listens to the charges against him.

12:9–10 David is thinking only in terms of the evils the rich man committed against his neighbor, stealing a man's sheep and depriving him of his companion (12:1–6). Put another way, David thinks only in terms of crime and socially unacceptable behavior, not in terms of sin. God wants David to understand that David's evil actions violate God's revealed Word.

12:11–12 Nathan draws David's attention to his sin against God and the consequences God has pronounced for his sin. First and foremost, David's sin is against God.

12:13 David's repentance is the culmination of a painful process, climaxing in Nathan's confrontation of David. David had broken at least three laws. He coveted his neighbor's wife, he committed adultery, and he committed murder (Exodus 20:13–14, 17). David's confession follows shortly after the account of his sin. But the text itself indicates that David's sin took place over a considerable period of time, slightly more than nine months by estimation. David knew what he did was wrong, but he chose to persist for a time. He does not confess his sin, and the result is torturous (Psalm 32). While sin has its momentary pleasures (Hebrews 11:25), it grieves the Spirit who indwells us, and thus the believer's spirit can no longer take pleasure in that sin.

12:16–18 In spite of David's sorrow, sincerity, and persistence in petitioning God to spare the child's life, his request is denied. The child indeed dies.

12:19–23 David has a remarkable peace about the death of his first child by Bath-sheba, a peace that causes those who witness it to marvel and to question David about it. And, as we can see from David's response to the questions posed by his servants, he is able to praise and worship God at a time of loss and sorrow for his child.

13:1–22 The characters in this story have much to teach the modern reader. Amnon warns about the pursuit of fleshly lusts (compare 1 Corinthians 10). Jonadab warns about the danger of using the sins of others to further our own interests, making them a part of our own agenda, rather than paying the price for rebuke and correction. David instructs us concerning passivity toward sin. This story of betrayal, lust, rape, and murder demonstrates the divisive power of sin—breaking bonds between individuals and families and, most seriously, with God. Sin is the root of disunity and division. Amnon has confused his "love" for his sister Tamar with lust. Love is not synonymous with sex. Amnon's brand of love is not at all concerned about respecting the other person or doing what is right, both of which characterize the love that God encourages and prescribes (see 1 Corinthians 13).

13:15–20 Tamar is one of the strongest women in the Bible—and yet she suffers terribly as a result of her brother's sin. She begs him to spare her, and still he rapes her and then sends her away to fend for herself. Her brother Absalom takes her in, but because of the sexual crime against her, she remains desolate.

13:23–36 David is furious about the crime committed against his daughter, yet it seems that he does nothing about it. His tangled web of loyalty paralyzes him. David's inaction facilitates the sin of others (13:21–22). Absalom is not willing to deal with Amnon appropriately; he wants to get his revenge in his own way. This he does, and in doing so becomes a murderer and a fugitive who will famously challenge his father's throne. From Absalom, we learn the danger of resentment and bitterness even in the midst of righteous anger.

13:37–39 After Absalom murders Amnon, he chooses political asylum in Geshur with his grandfather. David is not wrong to still love this son and yearn to see him. But it would not have been right for David to pardon him so he could return. It would not even have been right to visit him in Geshur. God uses Absalom to continue to draw David closer to Him.

14:1–20 Using trickery and deception, Joab pursues his own self-serving agenda in seeking to manipulate David into bringing Absalom back to Israel. Presumably using Joab's words, a woman from Tekoah is able to get David to commit himself to the safety of her son. Finally, David rules with a divine oath that this son is not to be harmed. Now the woman can appeal to the precedent David has just set (which it seems cannot be changed) and press David to deal similarly with his own son (whose guilt is much clearer).

14:21–24 David gives in, reluctantly, to Joab's prodding. He tells Joab that he can bring Absalom back to Israel. The assumption is that he will not allow anyone (any avenger) to take Absalom's life. But somewhere along the line, David considers what he has done and makes a change in plans. Absalom is not to be brought back to Israel as though an innocent man, free to come and go as he pleases. Absalom is to be under house arrest, confined to Jerusalem and his own house.

14:24 There is a kind of poetic justice in this confinement, as it is Absalom who had confined his sister Tamar to quarters (13:20). By confining Tamar to his house, Absalom kept her quiet. He also kept her desolate. All of this enabled him to carry out his evil plan to murder Amnon. Now, David confines Absalom to the same quarters in which he confined his sister.

14:25–33 Absalom has a great deal going for him. He is a good-looking man, without a single flaw. His hair is his crowning glory, and everybody knows it. He has three sons and a beautiful daughter, who also add to his standing. He is a celebrity of that day. He requests to see the king's face, accepting that the consequence may be death. Even though he is a murderer, his actions prove that he believes he is on the side of justice and that his heart is not repentant.

15:1–6 Absalom is very charming and wins the hearts of the Israelites by promises of justice and displays of affection. Absalom uses his freedom to undermine David's reputation and standing with the people. Absalom's betrayal is the ultimate tragedy—much like Saul's attempts to kill David or Judas's kiss that betrays Christ. Soon, Absalom is in full rebellion, which leads to the division of Israel.

15:7–12 As the old saying goes, Absalom is a man who "bites the hand that feeds him." He lacks any sense of debt to his father, and there is no evidence of gratitude on his part. But more than this, there is absolutely no true submission to his father-king. Absalom sees himself as next in line for the throne. He uses his position and power to undermine his father's authority and to disrupt his kingdom. Behind his father's back, he speaks ill of his father, making him look bad in the eyes of others. And he does all of this to get ahead.

15:14 Instead of giving the order to prepare for battle, David gives the order to prepare to flee from Jerusalem. There are a number of reasons David makes the decision to flee. David knows that God will bring about troubles in his kingdom from within his own family (12:10–12). If the rebellion of Absalom is a part of the divine discipline he has brought upon himself, David is not sure whether he should resist it. Additionally, David does not want to precipitate a fight with his son.

15:16 In fleeing from Jerusalem, David has not indicated his intention to abdicate the throne. This is why he leaves ten concubines behind to keep his house. He is leaving town, but he is not leaving his throne.

15:23–29 David demonstrates that he has learned something valuable by commanding Zadok to return the ark of the covenant to Jerusalem. He knows that if God is truly with him, then He will bring David back to Jerusalem, back to the place where God has chosen to dwell. If God is not with him, David knows the ark will do him no good.

15:30–31 David ascends mount Olivet, weeping as he makes his way toward the top. His head is covered and his feet are bare, as is the case with all those accompanying him. The report reaches David that Ahithophel has joined Absalom in his revolt. This is a devastating blow because Ahithophel's counsel is so reliable (16:23). While the loss of Ahithophel is a devastating loss for David's administration, it should not come as a great surprise because of his relationship to David—Ahithophel is Bath-sheba's grandfather (11:3; 23:34). Ahithophel very likely feels toward David as Absalom feels toward Amnon, so it is little wonder that he decides to side with Absalom at this point.

15:32 Hushai's coat is torn and he has cast dust on his head, both signs of mourning. This is indeed a most terrible thing that has happened. Hushai is ready to accompany David wherever he is going. David changes Hushai's plans.

15:33–34 The king informs Hushai that if he does accompany him into hiding, he will only be an added burden. Hushai can perform a much more valuable

service to David by returning to Jerusalem and pretending to become one of Ahithophel's loyal supporters. This way, Hushai will be in a position to counter the counsel of Ahithophel.

15:36 David informs Hushai that Zadok and Abiathar are also loyal supporters. When Zadok and Abiathar hear something from the palace, they can send a message to David by their sons: Ahimaaz, Zadok's son, and Jonathan, Abiathar's son.

16:1 David and his followers have just passed the summit of mount Olivet. There he is met by Ziba, the servant of Mephibosheth. Ziba was a servant of King Saul. In order for David to fulfill his covenant with Jonathan, he needed to find an heir of Saul to whom he could show favor for Jonathan's sake. He was told of Ziba, who was formerly Saul's servant. Ziba was summoned and informed David about Mephibosheth. When David brought Mephibosheth into his home, to eat at his table, he also restored to Mephibosheth all that was his as the heir of Saul and Jonathan. David also appointed Ziba and his family to serve Mephibosheth as his servants, as they had done before Saul's death.

16:2–4 Ziba meets David with provisions for the journey ahead. David asks Ziba why he is bringing these supplies, and Ziba tells him they are for the king and those with him, since the journey will prove difficult. David then asks Ziba where his master, Mephibosheth, is. Ziba tells David that Mephibosheth has gone to Jerusalem, hoping that his father, Saul's, kingdom will be restored to him. On the basis of Ziba's account, David gives to Ziba and his sons all that had been given to Mephibosheth.

16:15–21 David's flight from Jerusalem certainly prompts Absalom's bold advance to the city and his possession of it. Once in the city, Absalom turns to Ahithophel for counsel as to what he should do next. Ahithophel counsels Absalom to symbolically declare himself king in a way that will make a statement to David and to all Israel. Ahithophel recommends that Absalom take the ten concubines and publicly sleep with them, as a symbol of his possession of the throne (along with the harem). The taking of a king's harem certainly symbolizes the taking of his place.

16:20–17:4 Ahithophel's counsel is exceedingly shrewd in several ways. It offers an appealing course of action to Absalom. He, not unlike his father, David, can stay home from the battle with his wives while Ahithophel and his army are at war with David. Absalom can quickly enter into his possession of the throne, yet without the dangers or discomforts of going into battle. As an added incentive, he can indulge himself with David's wives in a way that gets back at David and hurts and humiliates his father. Only David, Absalom's real enemy, will be killed (according to Ahithophel's plan).

17:5–20 Ahithophel proposes a quick, easy victory for Absalom. It is almost too good to be true, but Absalom (like his father) believes that Ahithophel speaks wisely. The fact is that plan might have worked, but God has other plans for David and for Absalom. These plans are brought to pass through David's friends: Hushai, Zadok, and Abiathar, their sons Ahimaaz and Jonathan, a farmer's wife in Bahurim, and a number of other faithful friends and supporters of David. Hushai challenges the assumptions on which Ahithophel's plans are based. He proposes a very different plan. Hushai insists that Ahithophel has dangerously underestimated David and his ability to defend himself and his kingdom. Hushai reminds Absalom and the elders of Israel about the kind of man David is. He is no mental weakling, but a tough and seasoned warrior. Absalom's rebellion will not break David's spirit; it will antagonize him. David will be fighting mad and fighting ready.

17:11–14 Hushai's plan brings about a bigger battle, so that not only will many of Absalom's supporters die, but Absalom himself will be killed, thus ending the revolution. In reality, Hushai's plan gives David the time he needs to plan his battle. It allows David to fight on his turf. Hushai's plan makes Ahithophel's counsel seem foolish, which is exactly what David had prayed for (15:31). It brings about the deliverance of David and the defeat of his enemies.

17:23 Ahithophel remains in Jerusalem only long enough to be convinced that his counsel is not going to be heeded by Absalom. Once it is clear that Hushai's counsel has prevailed, Ahithophel knows he is finished. He has gambled everything on the assumption that Absalom will prevail over David. Now he knows that Absalom is destined to be defeated. He makes his way to his own home, sets his business in order, and kills himself.

17:24 As Absalom prepares to cross the Jordan in hot pursuit of David, David and his men flee to the gates of Mahanaim. This is indeed a city with history. It was Jacob who gave this city its name. Is David fearful about meeting up with his son Absalom? We know from later events that he wishes to avoid a confrontation that will end in death. He should have remembered that God always protects His people, His promises, and His purposes, even by the use of angels if needed.

17:27–29 The supporter who comes to David's aid at Mahanaim is Machir, the son of Ammiel from Lo-debar. This is the man who takes in Mephibosheth after the deaths of King Saul and Jonathan (9:4–5). Finally, Barzillai the Gileadite, an elderly man of great wealth, brings supplies for David and those with him. We learn even more about this man in 19:31–40. What an encouragement these men and their assistance must be to David.

18:1–5 David is wisely advised—because of his status as the priority target—to stay behind while his men go to battle. As David's men head off to fight Absalom's men, David charges them to deal gently with Absalom. Everyone hears these words. How different from the advice of Ahithophel (17:2), who intends to kill David alone and let the rest of the people live. David allows his men to kill any other Israelite, but not his son, the leader of the revolution. He commands those who are risking their lives for him to fight, but not to fight to win.

18:6–8 Absalom's forces suffer a great defeat, not only at the hand of David's men, but even from the forest itself.

Absalom's men are not cut out for this kind of warfare. A total of twenty thousand men die in this slaughter. It is a great victory for David, and a devastating defeat for Absalom.

18:9–11 We do not know whether Absalom is running for his life or not, but he does seem to be alone at the time his mule runs under the branches of a great oak tree and Absalom's head is wedged in the branches. None of Absalom's men seem to be around to rescue him. (They may have been fleeing for their lives.) One of Joab's men comes upon Absalom and mentions it to his commander. Joab is incensed that this young man did not kill Absalom on the spot.

18:14 It is ironic that it is Joab who kills Absalom, since it was Joab who had orchestrated amnesty for Absalom and brought him back to Jerusalem. And yet, for all Joab had done for Absalom, this man set out to take the throne away from his father and to set another as commander over Israel's forces (16:9–18). Joab, who would kill a righteous man at David's request (Uriah), kills David's own son in direct violation of his orders. David, who abused his almost absolute authority to take Uriah's wife and have him killed at Joab's command, is powerless to save his own son from death at the hand of Joab.

18:19–29 Joab knows his king well. He knows that David will not take the news of Absalom's death lightly. That is why he is reluctant to send Ahimaaz to David with the news. This is also why Ahimaaz hedges his answer to David's specific question about Absalom's well-being. David has been waiting for news of the outcome of the battle.

18:28–33 There is more space devoted to the messengers who report to David than there is about the war between the two opposing armies, including the account of the death of Absalom. Besides the space devoted to the relaying of the message, the text emphasizes the good news. The good news that Ahimaaz proclaims to David is that God has given him the victory by the death of his son. But this news is not good for David.

19:1–4 The scene of this victorious army returning to Mahanaim must have been jubilant. There would be shouting and celebration. What a great day of victory. But King David is not with his army. Instead, the triumphant soldiers learn that David is grieving over the death of his son. Now, instead of feeling proud of what they have done, David's men feel ashamed. David's warriors, who risked their necks to save their king, now hang their heads in shame. A day of victory is suddenly transformed into a day of mourning. The soldiers begin to sneak into the city, as though they have done something wrong.

19:5–7 Joab rightly rebukes David for putting everyone who has come with him from Jerusalem to shame, not just his soldiers, but his wives, children, and concubines as well. He has shown total disregard for those who are willing to give their all for their king. Joab puts it as bluntly: David would rather have heard that his entire army was slaughtered and that his son Absalom was alive than to learn that his army had prevailed but that Absalom was dead.

19:9–15 The people who had supported Absalom as king and remained in Israel need to be handled carefully so they will be convinced to accept David as their king again. Word of their reluctance to accept him reaches David while he is still residing in Mahanaim. He acts in a way that makes it easier for the Israelites to welcome him back. David sends word to Zadok and Abiathar (the priests who were in Jerusalem and had remained loyal to him), instructing them to speak to the elders of Judah. This is David's tribe, the tribe that first anointed David as their king when he was in Hebron. These are David's closest kinsmen. It is logical that they should take the lead in bringing David back to Jerusalem.

19:16–23 Shimei is no stranger to David. He is the descendant of Saul who harassed David and those with him when they fled from Jerusalem (16:5–14). He hurled rocks, dirt, accusations, and insults at David. Abishai had wanted to shut this man's mouth permanently then, but David refused, assuming God was, in some way, rebuking him through Shimei. Now, on his return, David must pass through Bahurim, Shimei's hometown. Shimei knows he is in serious trouble. David is once again the king of Israel, and he may reasonably view Shimei as a traitor who needs to be removed.

19:24–30 Ziba, his sons and servants, and Mephibosheth are there to greet David and help him on his journey through the Jordan and on to Jerusalem. Contrary to the report in chapter 16, Ziba is the one who appears to have forsaken David, while Mephibosheth seems to be in good standing. Rather than trying to reconcile conflicting reports, David divides the land he had given to Mephibosheth. David declares that Mephibosheth's land (which David had given him earlier and then given to Ziba) will be divided evenly between him and his servant Ziba. David will give both men the benefit of the doubt and make a judgment that might facilitate their reconciliation.

19:31–39 David wishes to show his gratitude to the elderly Barzillai and invites him to accompany him to Jerusalem, where the king promises to provide abundantly for him. Barzillai graciously declines David's offer. He is too old, he admits, to appreciate the gifts. David's delicacies would be wasted on him; and besides, he does not have all that much time left. He prefers to stay in his own home, near the place where his parents are buried and where he, before long, will be buried as well. Barzillai does not wish to personally benefit from the generous offer David makes him, but he does propose an alternative. Barzillai commends a young man, Chimham, to the king, asking David if he will confer his blessings on this lad, as if upon him.

19:40–20:2 As David and his men return to Jerusalem, the quarrelling continues between the men of Judah and the other ten tribes of Israel. Petty jealousy and strife prevail, so much so that the ten tribes become angry and embittered toward the men of Judah. Tensions are at an all-time high. David has not even reached Jerusalem, and his kingdom is already a divided one.

20:3 The first thing David does after arriving in Jerusalem is deal with the ten wives (or concubines) he left behind to keep the house. Absalom has slept with these women in public; there is no way David can go back to the way things were. He will never sleep with any of these women again. He appoints a place for them to stay and provides generously for them, but they have been defiled by Absalom.

20:4–13 David turns his attention to the rebellion that is under way, led by Sheba. He orders Amasa to assemble the armed forces, but his new general does not do so. Instead, David calls for Abishai, the brother of Joab. David would not ask Joab to do the job, for it would appear to be an admission that he has erred in replacing him with Amasa. But when Abishai goes out from Jerusalem, leading David's select warriors in pursuit of Sheba, he is accompanied by Joab. When Joab and Amasa meet, Joab promptly kills him. Joab assumes command again.

20:14–26 Joab and his forces finally track down Sheba at Abel of Beth-maachah. When they hear that Sheba has sought refuge in this fortified city, they put the city under siege. A wise woman sizes up the situation and takes the initiative. She goes to the wall, calls down, and asks to speak to Joab. He comes near, and she recounts to him how this city has been highly esteemed as a source of wisdom and counsel. It is a place known for ending disputes. Why then would Joab want to destroy such a place? She goes on to tell Joab that she is among those in the city who are peaceable and faithful in Israel. They have done nothing to deserve this assault. The woman assures Joab that Sheba's head will be thrown over the wall to him. The woman then convinces the people of the city to execute Sheba, and his head is thrown down to Joab and his army. With this, Joab blows the trumpet, indicating the cessation of hostilities.

21:1–14 These Gibeonites were among those living in Canaan whom God had commanded Israel to annihilate (Exodus 33:2; 34:11; Deuteronomy 7:1–2). This would have been the case except for a strange turn of events, which is described in the book of Joshua (chapter 9). God is angry with Israel because Saul and his house commenced a program of genocide against the Gibeonites. The Gibeonites must bless Israel, the people of God, in order for God to once again bless Israel. It seems to be almost an exact reversal of the Abrahamic Covenant, where God promises to bless those who bless the Israelites. Here the Israelites have violated the Gibeonites, however, which deeply angers God. Being God's chosen people does not give them a license to sin. God hears the cries of the oppressed and judges sin, even when that sin is committed by His chosen people. This passage also emphasizes the importance of covenants. Throughout Old Testament history, God deals with people through covenants (Genesis 9:1–17; 12:1–3; 17:1–22; Exodus 19–20; 31:12–17; Deuteronomy 5; 2 Samuel 7:12–17). Then, in the New Testament, He ushers in the new covenant by the Lord Jesus Christ through the shedding of His blood (Jeremiah 31:31–34; Luke 22:20; 1 Corinthians 11:25; 2 Corinthians 3:6;

Hebrews 9:11–22). David's dealing with the Gibeonites, at its roots, is a matter of keeping covenant. Israel had made a covenant with the Gibeonites. Even though this covenant is four hundred years old, it is still to be honored. No matter how good Saul's intentions might have been, the covenant must be kept. The breaking of that covenant had serious consequences.

21:15–22 It is not yet the end of David's reign as king of Israel, but it is the end of his military career. David will no longer go out to fight with his men. David's military career began with a contest with Goliath and a victory over the Philistines (1 Samuel 17). The ending of David's military career is a final battle with one of Goliath's offspring and the defeat of the Philistines.

22:1–3 David wrote this psalm after God delivered him from the hand of his enemies and from the hand of Saul. It would seem then that the psalm was written shortly after Saul's death and at the outset of David's reign as king. David now occupies the throne, and from this vantage point, he reflects on God's gracious dealings in his life to fulfill His promise that David would be Israel's king. God is David's fortress and his stronghold. He is David's shield and the horn of his salvation.

22:4–20 David called to God for deliverance, and God responded in a way that signaled His sovereignty over all creation. When God heard David's cry, He responded, as evidenced by all of His creation. God is angered by the enemies who have endangered His anointed king, and all of creation reflects God's anger. This is a description of a God who is not just eager to save His king, but intent on destroying the enemies who threaten His king. God reaches down and plucks His servant from the waters, delivering him from his strong enemy and setting him down in a broad place on solid ground. Though David's enemies are stronger, God delivers him from their hand. He is David's support when they confront him.

22:21–30 In the Law of Moses, God made it clear to His people that He would bless them as they trusted in Him and kept His law (Deuteronomy 7:12–16). On the other hand, it was also clear that their righteousness attained by their works was not the basis for God's grace. David understood that God saves the righteous and condemns the wicked. It is for this reason that God hears David's cry for help and comes to his rescue from his wicked enemies. Not only does God save the righteous, but He saves the afflicted while He condemns the proud. Very often God will have us play a role in His deliverance. In such cases, it is God who gives us the strength and ability to prevail over our enemies. David stood up to Goliath and prevailed, but it was God who gave the victory. David describes the strength God supplies in terms of waging warfare. God's strength enables him to leap over a wall and to overrun a troop of men. Military strength begins in the mind. David had the moral courage to stand up to Goliath as well as the God-given skill to strike him down with his sling.

22:31–50 The basis for strength of courage (faith) is God's Word. God's Word (both direct and indirect

revelation) guides David's actions. God not only sets David on the high places (the place of military advantage), but He gives David the sure-footedness that enables him to fight from this position. God is the one who trains David's hands for battle, who gives him the strength to break the difficult steel bow. He gives him the shield of His salvation, and then gives him firm footing with which to stand and fight. Reflecting on God's deliverance and enabling strength, David's conclusion is one full of hope and anticipation. David is God's anointed king, but his reign is soon to end. God has proven to be David's Deliverer, and will continue to bless him.

22:51 Because of the covenant God made with David, he will have an eternal throne. David's psalm reminds us that if God is our refuge, there is no need to fear.

23:1–5 David confidently speaks of a reign of righteousness for his house. This is not due to David's merits or self-righteousness, but rather to the grace of God, assured through His covenant with David (7:14). Based on God's covenant with him, David is assured of an eternal reign of righteousness, signed, sealed, and delivered in the covenant of God as fulfilled (ultimately and permanently) in the person of Jesus Christ. This is David's ultimate salvation and desire, brought about by God, the author and finisher of all salvation. David's song of salvation is centered in God. The message of the Bible is not the promise of salvation and eternal life for all people; it is the offer of salvation to all people. David celebrates God's offer of universal salvation in this passage.

24:1–25 Divinely incited, David decides to number the fighting men of Israel and Judah. Numbering is not necessarily wrong. Moses numbered the fighting men of Israel in preparation for battle (Numbers 1:1–4). Moses also numbered the Kohathites (Numbers 4:2) and the Gershonites (Numbers 4:22) for priestly service. Saul numbered the Israelites to defend the people of Jabesh-gilead by fighting the Ammonites (1 Samuel 11:8). David numbered those loyal to him in preparation for defending himself against an attack by his son Absalom (2 Samuel 18:1). In none of these cases is numbering wrong. Numbering the men of Israel seems to produce the knowledge that David is forbidden to have, a knowledge of his greatness and military strength (compare Deuteronomy 17:14–20). He wants to see his strength and power, and, even though forbidden, it is what his heart desires. The Lord is angry with Israel, and the pestilence that came to His people was justly deserved—not only because of David's sin but because of Israel's sin. How ironic that David seeks to learn how many Israelite warriors are at his disposal, and as a result of his finding out, the numbers are changed by seventy thousand men. David's faith in God for judgment is well founded. God had poured out His wrath on His people, but now He takes compassion on them. The destroying angel of the Lord is standing by the threshing floor of Araunah the Jebusite when he is ordered to halt (24:16).

THE FIRST

BOOK OF THE KINGS

OTHERWISE CALLED
THE THIRD BOOK OF THE KINGS

INTRODUCTION TO 1 KINGS ▪ First Kings was originally joined with 2 Kings in one book. The narrative covers almost five hundred years, tracing the history of Israel and Judah from the last days of the monarchy under David to the disintegration and capture of the divided kingdoms.

AUTHOR ▪ The author of this book is unknown. While there is a Jewish tradition that points to the prophet Jeremiah as the author, there is more evidence that the book evolved over a long period of time.

OCCASION ▪ The purpose of 1 Kings is not explicitly stated. However, the fact that Kings doesn't mention the return of the exiles to Jerusalem suggests that the book is written in order to answer the question, "Why are we in exile?" This book serves as a kind of warning about the consequences of falling away from faith and the practice of that faith. In the same way, it serves as an encouragement toward consistent obedience. Many scholars believe that the exilic author(s) of Kings is looking at the history of Israel and Judah through the prism of Deuteronomy. He is evaluating how well they have observed the law, and of course the answer is not well at all.

1:1 David is now so old that he can't even keep himself warm, much less rule the nation. All this is happening with the question of his successor hanging in the air.

1:2 The selection of a beautiful virgin to warm David up may sound strange or even immoral, but it was a recognized treatment in the ancient world. When Josephus describes this practice in his *Antiquities of the Jews*, he says it was a medical treatment, and he calls the servants mentioned in this verse "physicians."

1:3 David almost certainly makes this young woman, Abishag the Shunammite, his concubine, which is not at this time illegal or prohibited by God. Later, in chapter 2, Adonijah will condemn himself to death for asking for Abishag as a wife. His request would only be so outrageous if Abishag had belonged to David as a concubine. A concubine in ancient culture was not simply a mistress; she was a wife of secondary rank. Some have associated Abishag with the Shulamite addressed in the Song of Solomon (Song of Solomon 6:13), concluding that she became romantically involved with David's son Solomon. This is conjecture.

1:6 The writer of 1 Kings observes that David doesn't challenge Adonijah on his behavior. This reveals a flaw in the way David raised his sons. Second Samuel 3:2–5 describes the sons of David and lists Adonijah as the fourth son.

1:7 Adonijah gains the key support of Joab (David's chief general) and Abiathar (the high priest of Israel), both once trusted associates of David. Joab's participation may have been an attempt at revenge for David's choice of Amasa over him (2 Samuel 19:13). Joab is one of the more complex characters of the Old Testament. He was David's nephew (1 Chronicles 2:16), and while fiercely loyal to David, he was not strongly obedient. He disobeyed David when he thought it was in David's best interest, and he was cunning and ruthless in furthering his own position.

1:9–10 The idea behind Adonijah's exclusive feast is that he will burn the fat of these animals as a sacrifice to the Lord and use the meat to hold a dinner honoring and blessing only his supporters.

1:11 Nathan, David's old friend and prophet, knows that if Adonijah does become king, he could very well kill every potential rival to his throne—including Bath-sheba and Solomon. The last mention of the prophet Nathan was in 2 Samuel 12, where he rebuked his friend David over the scandal with Bath-sheba and murder of Uriah. Bath-sheba and Nathan plan to address David.

1:13–14 The specific promise Nathan and Bath-sheba refer to is not recorded in 1 Kings, but we know from 1 Chronicles 22:5–9 that David does in fact intend for Solomon to succeed him as king.

1:23 Now, at the end of his days, David receives Nathan, and it seems he remains a trusted friend. David did not treat Nathan as an enemy when he confronted him with the painful truth, and he responds again when Nathan informs him of Adonijah's rebellion.

1:28–32 When David confirms Solomon, Bath-sheba's response is a customary expression of thanks and honor, though it is ironic since David's death is near. The three leaders he calls do not support Adonijah but remain loyal to David.

1:32–35 This is a rare glimpse of all three offices in cooperation—prophet, priest, and king. David's plan will leave no doubt that Solomon is his successor.

1:36–37 Benaiah reacts with an exuberant "Amen!" This underscores an important principle: Unless the Lord God blesses the selection of Solomon, he will not stand. Benaiah senses that this is the Lord's will and offers the prayer that God would in fact declare it. His wish that Solomon's reign would be greater than David's is, on a human level, fulfilled. But on a spiritual level, it is not.

1:38 Gihon is outside Jerusalem and is its major source of water, making it a popular place for the people to gather. The mule in ancient Israel was rare and expensive. It had to be imported and was ridden only by royalty. (Everyone else rode donkeys.) No one could use anything owned by royalty without permission. Thus Solomon riding on David's mule was a sign that David had appointed him as his successor.

1:42–49 Hearing King David's words of praise to God confirms for Adonijah that even his father, David, is completely behind Solomon. Thus, there is no hope for his future as king.

1:50 The altar in Jerusalem is a traditional place of refuge. This reveals that Adonijah fears for his life and is asking for mercy.

2:1 See 1 Chronicles 28 and 29 for an expanded account of David's last speech, which emphasizes Solomon's duty to build the temple.

2:2 David's advice to be strong was a typical exhortation for new leaders, not just in Israelite literature but more broadly in ancient Near Eastern literature. See Joshua in Joshua 1.

2:4 David alludes to the covenantal promise from God that as long as David's sons walked in obedience, they would keep the throne of Israel (see 2 Samuel 7:12–16). God's promise to David is an amazing one. No matter what the Assyrians or the Egyptians or the Babylonians did, as long as David's sons were obedient and followed God, He would establish their kingdom. He would take care of the rest. (Unfortunately, they didn't hold up their end of the bargain.)

2:7 Barzillai the Gileadite supported David when he was fleeing Absalom (see 2 Samuel 19:31–39). In saying that Barzillai's sons should be allowed to eat at the king's table, David is providing them the equivalent of a pension, food and clothing, and a house and land to support them.

2:8–9 Shimei, the son of Gera, was an angry follower of Saul whom David had vowed not to kill (see 2 Samuel 16:5–13).

2:12 This connects the establishment of Solomon's kingdom with the fulfillment of the promise made to David in 2 Samuel 7:12–16. That promise is ultimately fulfilled in Jesus, the Son of David; but it also has a definite and partial fruition in Solomon and all of David's heirs down to Zedekiah.

2:16–17 Adonijah's audacious request to take the concubine widow, Abishag from Shunem, as his wife is more than it seems. In 2 Samuel 16:20–23, Absalom—the brother of Adonijah—asserts his rebellious claim to David's throne by taking David's concubines. Adonijah wants to build a claim to Solomon's throne by taking David's concubine as his wife, as revealed by Solomon's request in verse 22. Why would Adonijah, knowing the warning Solomon made in 1:52, make the outrageous request for King David's concubine? Perhaps he felt that Solomon was too young, too inexperienced, or too timid to do the right thing. He soon found out that Solomon was a decisive leader.

2:18 By agreeing to make the request to Solomon, Bath-sheba is also agreeing to inform Solomon of Adonijah's intent.

2:22–25 Solomon understands that this is Adonijah's attempt to declare his claim to the throne of Israel. He acts according to the parole terms granted to Adonijah in 1:52. Adonijah made a wicked, treasonous request and is executed because of it.

2:26 Abiathar, the priest who supports Adonijah as the next king in defiance of both the will of God and the will of King David (1:7), deserves death. This is treason against both God and the king of Israel. Solomon lets Abiathar know that he still can be executed.

2:28 When Joab hears of Adonijah's execution and Abiathar's banishment, he knows he's next. Now he imitates Adonijah's attempt to find refuge by taking hold of the horns of the altar (1 Kings 1:50–53).

2:29–34 Although it was almost a universal custom in the ancient world to find sanctuary at a holy altar, Solomon knows that this tradition is not used in Israel to protect a guilty man (see Exodus 21:14). Since Joab refuses to leave, Solomon has his rival, Benaiah, execute him right at the altar.

2:36–38 When it comes to the rebellious Shimei, who is associated with the household of the former King Saul and shows himself as a threat to the house of David (2 Samuel 16:5–8), Solomon again shows mercy. David had instructed Solomon not to allow Shimei to die in peace (1 Kings 2:8–9). Solomon places him under house arrest. Shimei knows this is mercy on Solomon's part.

2:39–46 When Shimei violates his house arrest to retrieve runaway servants, it seems to have been due mainly to forgetfulness, but it is criminal to neglect a royal covenant. Thus Shimei pays with his life.

3:1 Marriage to fellow royalty was a common political strategy in the ancient world and continues in the modern age. It was not only because royalty wanted to marry other royalty, but also because conflicts between nations were avoided for the sake of family ties. This is not Solomon's first marriage. First Kings 14:21 tells us that his son Rehoboam came to the throne when he was forty-one years old, and 11:42 tells us that Solomon reigned forty years. This means that Rehoboam was born to his mother—a wife of Solomon named Naamah the Ammonitess—before Solomon came to the throne and before he married this daughter of Pharaoh.

3:4 The huge size of Solomon's sacrifice demonstrates both his great wealth and his heart to use it to glorify God. This is an important event marking the beginning of Solomon's reign. According to 2 Chronicles 1:2–3, the entire leadership of the nation goes with Solomon to Gibeon. What set Gibeon apart was that the tabernacle was there, even though the ark of the covenant was in Jerusalem. How did that come to be? Saul moved the tabernacle to Gibeon (see 1 Chronicles 16:39–40), but David brought the ark to Jerusalem and built a temporary tent for it (see 2 Samuel 6:17; 2 Chronicles 1:4). Why didn't David bring the tabernacle from Gibeon to Jerusalem? There are a few possibilities: (1) He may have believed that if the tabernacle was in Jerusalem, the people would be satisfied with that and lose the passion for the temple God wanted built; (2) it may be that the tabernacle was only moved when it was absolutely necessary, as when disaster came upon it at Shiloh or Nob; or (3) David simply focused on building the temple, not continuing the tabernacle.

3:5 Solomon's dream is one of the more significant dreams in the Bible. God's response, beginning in verse 11, reflects that Solomon's heart truly is surrendered to Him.

3:9 Solomon asks for more than knowledge; he wants understanding. The ancient Hebrew word translated *understanding* means "hearing." Solomon wants a hearing heart, one that will listen to God.

3:11–14 God is pleased by Solomon's request and by the fact that he did not ask for riches, fame, or power. God answers Solomon beyond all expectations. Solomon experiences God's ability to do far beyond all that we ask or imagine (see Ephesians 3:20).

3:15 Solomon awakes and realizes it is a dream, but at the same time he knows it is a message from God. God does answer Solomon's prayer and makes him wise, powerful, rich, and influential. His reign is glorious for Israel, yet Solomon tragically wastes the gifts God gave him. Though he accomplished much, he could have done much more—and his heart was led away from God in the end (see 11:4–11).

3:16–28 Solomon's solution to this problem (a sword) at first seems foolish, even dangerous. The wisdom of his creative approach is only understood when the matter is settled. In the same way, the works and the judgments of God often first seem strange, dangerous, or even foolish. Time shows them to be perfect wisdom.

4:2–6 The government is structured much like that in modern nations. There are chief officials who serve as ministers, or secretaries, over their specific areas of responsibility. Jehoshaphat had also served under David (see 2 Samuel 8:16; 20:24). His role of recorder is more than a historian. Scholars say he was like a chief of protocol, or even a secretary of state.

4:7–19 Solomon's twelve district governors were responsible for taxation in their individual districts. The districts were strictly separated by tribal borders, as had been done in the past, but often according to mountains, land, and region. Each governor made provision for one month of the year. These taxes were paid in grain and livestock, which were used to support the royal court and the central government.

4:20 Solomon's reign is a golden age for Israel. The population has grown robustly, and it is a season of great prosperity, allowing plenty of leisure time and pursuit of good pleasures.

4:21 Solomon's reign encompasses all kingdoms from the river Euphrates to the border of Egypt. Solomon is not a warrior—he reaps the blessings of peace achieved by King David.

4:22 Thirty measures equaled 220 liters or about 55 gallons. We can accurately picture thirty 55-gallon drums full of fine flour being delivered for every day.

4:23 The daily provision was not for Solomon only. It was for his entire household, his royal court, and their families. Some estimate that this much food every day could feed 15,000 to 36,000 people.

4:26 Solomon's famous stables show what a vast cavalry he has assembled for Israel. Second Chronicles 9:25 is a parallel passage and has 4,000 chariots instead of 40,000: The smaller number seems correct, and the larger number is probably due to copyist error. Even with the smaller number, however, Solomon's actions seem to go against the teaching in Deuteronomy 17:16 that a king must avoid having too many horses.

4:29–34 Solomon becomes a prominent and famous man, even among kings. In a strong sense, this is the fulfillment of the great promises to an obedient Israel described in Deuteronomy 28:1, 10.

4:31 Ethan the Ezrahite is the author of Psalm 89, and Heman is the author of Psalm 88. The other names are mentioned only in this passage in the Bible. Only some of Solomon's three thousand proverbs are preserved in the book of Proverbs. He composes songs, but few psalms.

5:1–2 Solomon benefits from the alliances and friendships with neighboring nations that David wisely built during his own reign. This is evident when Hiram reaches out to Solomon.

5:3–6 Solomon's words refer to Hiram's knowledge of David's wish to build a temple. This means that David had told Hiram spiritual things.

5:3–4 David couldn't build the temple until he had vanquished his enemies and no natural disasters threatened. Now Solomon enjoys that peace and intends to take advantage of it.

5:5 Solomon proposes to build a house to honor God. He wants to show reverence by setting the plan apart from pagan practices, in which builders would construct actual residences for their gods (see 2 Chronicles 2:5–6).

5:6 The cedar trees of Lebanon were legendary for their excellent timber. This means Solomon wants to build the temple out of the best materials possible. Though Solomon begins to obtain the materials needed for the temple, he doesn't start from scratch. David had already gathered some supplies.

5:7 The king of Tyre is pleased by Solomon's message and request. We don't know if Hiram is a believer, but he seems to have respect for the God of Israel—perhaps due to David's godly influence.

5:10–12 The two leaders enjoy peace and a good business arrangement leading to a treaty.

5:13–14 Solomon's wisdom is evident in the way he employs this great workforce. First, he wisely delegates responsibility to men like Adoniram. Second, instead of making the Israelites work constantly away from home, he works them in shifts.

5:15–18 These verses seem to suggest that those who carry burdens and quarry stone are Canaanite slave laborers.

5:16 The chiefs of Solomon's officers form the middle management team, administrating the work of building the temple.

6:2–3 The temple's length is 60 cubits, its width 20 cubits, and its height 30 cubits. Assuming that the ancient cubit was approximately 18 inches (perhaps one-half meter), this means that the temple proper was approximately 90 feet (30 meters) long, 30 feet (10 meters) wide, and 45 feet (15 meters) high. Allowing for the outside storage rooms, the vestibule, and the estimated thickness of the walls, the total size of the structure was perhaps 75 cubits long (110 feet, 37 meters) and 50 cubits wide (75 feet, 25 meters). This was not especially large as ancient temples go, but the glory of Israel's temple was not in its size.

6:7 During the temple's construction, no hammer or chisel or any iron tool was heard at the site itself. The stones used to build the temple were all cut and prepared at another site. The stones were only assembled at the building site of the temple. This speaks to the way God wants His work done. The temple had to be built with human labor. Yet Solomon did not want the sound of anyone's work to dominate the site of the temple. He wanted to communicate, as much as possible, that the temple is of God and not of man.

6:10 The dimensions of the temple tell us that it was built on the same basic design as the tabernacle, but it was twice as large. This means that Solomon meant for the temple to be a continuation of the tabernacle. The difference, however, is that the temple was a permanent structure. The last of the internal enemies of Israel had been conquered, and the people were permanently established in the land.

6:13 God promises an obedient Solomon that he will reign and be blessed, fulfilling the promises God made to David about his reign (2 Samuel 7:5–16). He does not say He will live *in* the temple, the way pagans believe their gods live in temples. He will dwell *among* the children of Israel. The temple is a special place for people to meet with God.

6:14–15 Solomon installs beautiful finishing touches. For example, he panels the temple with beams and boards of cedar; these are some of the finest building materials available. The impression is of a magnificent building.

6:20–22 There is gold everywhere in the temple. The gold chains hung across the vail (veil) separating the holy place from the most holy place accentuate the idea that the most holy place is inaccessible. In further verses the walls are covered with it, the floor is covered with it (6:30), and gold is hammered into the carvings on the doors (6:32).

6:23–29 The walls all around the temple, both the inner and outer sanctuaries, are carved with figures of cherubim, palm trees, and flowers. This is modeled after the pattern of the tabernacle, which had woven designs of cherubim on the inner covering. The curtain was a deep blue with cherubim. The idea was that the person who saw it would know he was in heaven on earth.

6:36 Under the old covenant, the temple was not for the people of Israel; it was only for the priests to meet with God on behalf of the people. The inner court is the court of the priests, where the altar and laver are set and sacrifices conducted. Outside is the great court, where the people gathered and worshipped.

6:38 It takes Solomon and his thousands of workers seven years to finish the temple. It is a spectacular building. It is easy for Israel to focus on the temple of God instead of the God of the temple. Yet without the people's continued faithfulness to God, the temple's glory quickly fades. This glorious temple will be plundered just five years after the death of Solomon (see 14:25–27).

7:1 Solomon may have taken seven years to build the temple, but he puts almost twice that (thirteen years) into building his palace. First Kings 10:16–17 says that three hundred gold shields hang in the house of the forest of Lebanon (Solomon's palace). Isaiah specifically calls this building an armory in Isaiah 22:8.

7:2–12 Noteworthy is the prevalence of cedar wood from Lebanon—so much so that the structure comes to be known as the palace of the forest of Lebanon. Walking in the richly paneled halls of the palace is like walking in a forest. The roof is cedar also (7:3).

7:13–14 Solomon hires the best brass craftsman in the business: Hiram from Tyre, who is half Israelite and half Gentile. Hiram makes the needed furnishings for the temple after the pattern of the tabernacle furnishings.

7:15 The two pillars of brass were structures so impressive that they were given names: *Jachin*, meaning "He shall establish," and *Boaz*, meaning "in strength" (7:21). Some take this to mean they are a reminder that kings rule by God's appointment and with God's strength. They're also mentioned in 2 Chronicles 3:17. Others believe that the pillars are meant to remind Israel of the twin pillars from the Exodus: The pillar of fire by night and the pillar of cloud by day were constant reminders of the presence of God in the wilderness.

7:23–38 Hiram makes the sea—a laver—of cast brass, 10 cubits from one brim to the other. The huge laver is more than 15 feet (5 meters) across and is to be used for the ceremonial washings connected with the temple. In addition, Hiram makes ten identical lavers of brass, with each laver containing forty baths. It is significant that the sea was a symbol of chaos, and here God has tamed chaos.

7:48 On the golden table sits the bread. Second Chronicles 4:8 says there are ten individual tables of shewbread, though here they are referred to as one.

7:51 God told David that he could not build the temple, but David was still able to collect furnishings and treasures for the temple that his son would build (see 1 Chronicles 29).

8:1 In what must have been a celebration on the scale of our modern installation of a new pope, Solomon assembles the elders of Israel, the heads of the tribes, and the chiefs of the families for the dedication of the temple.

8:2 Solomon chooses the seventh month for the dedication, eleven months after the temple is finished (6:38). This may have been because it was the time for the feast of tabernacles.

8:3 By making it clear that the priests are the ones who carry the ark, the author of 1 Kings shows how Solomon is carefully obeying what God commanded about transporting the ark of the covenant. He will not repeat the error of his father, David, in 2 Samuel 6:1–8.

8:5 The description of sacrificing so many sheep and cattle seems to imply Solomon goes overboard in his effort to honor God.

8:9 The reminder of the deliverance from Egypt is significant, because there is a sense in which what is happening during Solomon's reign—some five hundred years after the Exodus—is the culmination of the deliverance from Egypt. Out of Egypt and into the wilderness, Israel, out of necessity, lived in tents—and the dwelling of God was a tent. Now, since Solomon built the temple, the dwelling of God among Israel is a *building*, a place of permanence and security.

8:9 The ark holds nothing but the two tablets of stone that Moses put there at Horeb. Yet earlier in Israel's history, the ark held the golden pot that contained manna (Exodus 16:33) and Aaron's rod that had budded (Numbers 17:6–11), as well as the tablets of the covenant (Exodus 25:16). We don't know what happened to the golden pot of manna and Aaron's rod, but they are not in the ark when Solomon sets it in the most holy place.

8:10 After the ark is in place, the temple fills with the cloud of glory. This glory remains at the temple until Israel utterly rejects God in the days of the divided monarchy. The prophet Ezekiel sees the glory depart the temple (Ezekiel 10:18).

8:11 The cloud of God's glory that filled the temple in the most holy place—later called the Shekinah glory—is hard to define. We might call it the radiant outshining of His character and presence. It's so intense that the priests have to stop performing their service.

8:16 Solomon presses the remembrance of the Exodus. Though it happened five hundred years before, it is as significant for Israel as the day it happened.

8:22 Solomon does not dedicate the temple from *within* the temple. It would be inappropriate for him to do so, because he is not a priest. As he prays, he spreads out his hands toward heaven. This is the most common posture of prayer in the Old Testament.

8:27 Solomon recognizes God as transcendent and asks God to dwell in this place and honor those who seek Him here. From statements in verses 12–13, we might think Solomon had a superstitious idea that God actually lived *in* the temple. That makes his comments here even more important. God cannot be restricted to

a structure built by human hands—even heaven itself is not big enough for Him.

8:28–30 Solomon asks God to incline His ear toward the king and his people when they pray from the temple. For this reason, many observant Jews still pray facing the direction of the site of the temple in Jerusalem.

8:31–32 The temple grounds were used as a place to verify and authorize oaths. When a dispute came down to one word against another, Solomon asked that the temple would be a place to properly swear by.

8:41–43 Solomon doesn't forget the people outside Israel who seek God. When God mercifully answers the prayers of foreigners, it draws those from other nations to the God of all nations. While the temple was in Israel, it was always intended to be a house of prayer for all nations (Isaiah 56:7). The first-century temple included a court of the Gentiles where the nations could come and pray. The violation of this principle makes Jesus angry in Matthew 21, when He comes to the temple and finds the outer courts—the only place where the Gentile nations could come to pray—more like a swap meet than a house of prayer. He drives out the moneychangers and the merchants.

8:46 What Solomon states here is a theme Paul reiterates in Romans 3:23: All human beings sin and fall short of God's glory.

8:63–65 The sacrifice of 22,000 oxen and 120,000 sheep is enough to feed a vast multitude for two weeks. It appears that the celebrations are followed by the regular observance of the feast of tabernacles.

8:66 The dedication of the temple ends where the story of the temple begins: with David, not Solomon, and with the people glad in heart for what the Lord had done for His servant David and His people Israel. The writer remembers that it was David's heart and vision that started the work of the temple (2 Samuel 7:1–3).

9:1 Approximately twenty-four years after Solomon came to the throne, he has finished his greatest accomplishments: the temple and the palace in Jerusalem. Some experts comment that the verb here conveys a desire like that of a bridegroom toward his bride, and this obsession may have been the start of Solomon's fall.

9:4–5 God's answer to Solomon's prayer has a great condition. If Solomon walks before God in obedience and faithfulness, he can expect blessing on his reign and the reign of his descendants, and the dynasty of David will endure forever. God does not demand perfect obedience from Solomon. David certainly did not walk perfectly before the Lord, and God tells Solomon to walk before Him as his father, David, walked.

9:6–9 If Solomon or his descendants turn from following Him, God promises to correct a disobedient Israel. God's answer to Solomon's prayer in chapter 8 was not an unqualified promise to bless the temple in any circumstance. Under the old covenant, God promised to use Israel to exalt Himself among the nations one way or another. If Israel obeyed, He would bless them so much that others couldn't help but recognize the hand of God upon Israel. If Israel disobeyed, He would chastise them so severely that the nations would know that the Lord had brought calamity on them.

9:10–11 Solomon makes a new agreement with King Hiram of Tyre, who had supplied him with cedar and pine and gold for the temple and palace. Tyre, the prominent city of the land just north of Israel, in what is now modern Lebanon, was noted for its fine wood.

9:11–14 The twenty settlements Solomon mortgages to Hiram do not please the king. Hiram nicknames the cities *Cabul*, which means "good for nothing." It's not clear why, but they appear to be fairly insignificant towns. Solomon, apparently a shrewd dealer, receives a large amount of gold in return, an estimated four tons.

9:20–23 This forced labor, bondservice, came from remnant Canaanite peoples. Solomon gathered the workforce to complete massive building projects. Archaeology is a witness to the ambitious and successful building projects of Solomon. Unfortunately, this is another apparent compromise by Solomon. God strictly commanded that the remnants of these tribes be driven out of the land, not used as slave laborers in Israel. Solomon doesn't make Israelites forced laborers, but he uses them to oversee the remnants of the Canaanite tribes.

9:28 No one knows where Ophir was located. Suggestions have included southern Arabia, the eastern coast of Africa, and India.

10:1 Sheba, also known as Sabea, was where modern-day Yemen is today in southern Arabia. We know from geography that this was a wealthy kingdom, with much gold, spices, and precious woods. History also tells us that Sheba was known to have queens as well as kings. The trip to Israel was long, about 1,500 miles, or 2,400 kilometers. The queen probably came as part of a trade delegation, as implied in 10:2–5, but there is no doubt that she was highly motivated to see Solomon and his kingdom.

10:2 The queen of Sheba visits Solomon and Israel at their material zenith. She travels in the manner of queens—with a large royal procession, heavily laden with gifts and goods for trade.

10:4–8 The queen obviously is familiar with the world of royal splendor and luxury. Yet she says Solomon's court is twice as magnificent as she expected. Not only that, but she notices that his staff and servants are happy.

10:9 The queen draws the connection to Solomon's God. Taken in context, her beautifully phrased language may only be a diplomatic response to the astonishing blessing evident in Solomon's Jerusalem, rather than a statement of faith. She acknowledges how Solomon was chosen by God. This statement is especially meaningful because Solomon is not necessarily the most logical successor of his father, David. There were several sons of David born before Solomon.

10:10 The queen of Sheba's reaction to God's blessing on Solomon and Israel is an example of what God wanted to do for Israel under the promises of the old covenant. God promised Israel that if they obeyed under the old covenant, He would bless them so tremendously that the world would notice and give glory to the Lord of Israel (Deuteronomy 28:1, 10).

10:14–15 Solomon is an extremely wealthy ruler. The 660 talents of gold itself is a vast amount of gold even by today's standards. Implicit here is a warning. In the instruction for future kings in Deuteronomy 17:14–20 (specifically verse 17), God tells rulers not to multiply silver and gold for themselves.

10:16–27 These are examples of Solomon's wealth and prosperity. He is so rich that silver holds no value. In fact, verses 24–25 imply he is the richest man on earth, and the whole earth wants an audience (and is willing to bring gifts to get one).

10:17 These golden shields are beautifully displayed in Solomon's palace, but they are of no use in battle. Gold is too heavy and too soft to be used as a metal for effective shields. This shows Solomon in the image of a warrior king, but without the substance.

10:28–29 Solomon's horses are imported from Egypt, in direct disobedience to Deuteronomy 17:16. Yet perhaps the importation of horses from Egypt began as trading as an agent on behalf of other kings. From this, Solomon could say, "I'm importing horses from Egypt, but I am not doing it for myself. I'm not breaking God's command." Many examples of gross disobedience begin as clever rationalizations.

11:1–2 Solomon not only loves foreign women who worship other gods—from nations God specifically told Israel not to intermarry with—but he also loves many women, rejecting God's plan from the beginning for one man and one woman to become one flesh in marriage (see Genesis 2:23–24; Matthew 19:4–6). Solomon eventually collects a thousand foreign wives and concubines, which makes him more than just a bad example. His lust ruins his spiritual life.

11:3 Seven hundred wives and three hundred concubines is an almost unbelievable number of marriage partners. Solomon had so many marriage partners because he followed the bad example of his father, David, who had many wives and concubines himself (2 Samuel 5:13–16). In those days, a large harem was a status symbol.

11:4–10 God has twice warned Solomon explicitly, and still Solomon seeks after other gods. Solomon's sin shows ingratitude and a waste of great spiritual privilege. God promised the entire kingdom of Israel to the descendants of David forever *if* they remained obedient. David reminded Solomon of this promise shortly before his death (2:4). Yet Israel could not remain faithful even one generation.

11:13 Many passages in the Old Testament (such as 2 Chronicles 11:12) tell us that the southern kingdom was made up of two tribes, Judah and Benjamin. Several times in this chapter, the southern kingdom is referred to as one tribe. This is because either Benjamin is swallowed up in Judah, or the idea is one tribe in addition to Judah.

11:14–25 Solomon's reign has been glorious, but not without problems. Such problems included adversaries like Hadad (who returned from Egypt) and Rezon (out of Aram in the north country). We are not told specifically how the two warriors attacked Solomon, only that they troubled his reign.

11:26–28 Jeroboam is a fellow Israelite, which sets him apart from the previously mentioned adversaries (11:23–25). Solomon himself had chosen Jeroboam to oversee the projects listed in 11:27. It is not immediately apparent why these construction projects cause Jeroboam to rebel against Solomon. But it is obvious from the comments in 12:4 that the oppression of these projects was a reality.

11:29–33 Jeroboam receives a prophecy from Ahijah, perhaps a newly appointed prophet. Ahijah's object lesson is the message that Jeroboam will lead ten tribes of a divided Israel after the death of Solomon.

11:34–36 This divided kingdom became Israel's history for hundreds of years after the death of Solomon. From this description, it might seem that the ten tribes under Jeroboam would be larger, greater, and more enduring than the one tribe left unto the house of David. As it works out, just the opposite happens, because the ten tribes forsake the Lord, while the one tribe is more obedient.

11:37–38 God promises to make a lasting dynasty for Jeroboam *if* he will do what is right in the sight of the Lord. An obedient Jeroboam has the opportunity to establish a parallel dynasty to the house of David. Both Jeroboam and David are appointed by God to follow after disobedient kings. David waited upon the Lord to make the throne clear, and God blessed his reign. Jeroboam does not wait on God and makes his own way to the throne, and God does not bless his reign.

11:40 The fact that Solomon seeks to kill Jeroboam is more startling evidence of his decline. God specifically says the breakup of the kingdom will happen *after* the death of Solomon and *in judgment* of Solomon's disobedience. Solomon thinks he can defeat God's will in this, but he is unsuccessful.

11:41–43 Many commentators believe that Solomon became king when he was about twenty years old and died around 932 BC, after forty years (a generation) of reign. This means that Solomon did not live a particularly long life.

12:1 Shechem is a city with a rich history. Abraham worshipped there (Genesis 12:6). Jacob built an altar and purchased land there (Genesis 33:18–20). Joseph was buried there (Joshua 24:32). It was also the geographical center of the northern tribes. Having to meet the ten northern tribes on their territory instead of demanding that representatives come to Jerusalem is a weak start for Rehoboam.

12:2–3 When Jeroboam hears of the gathering in Shechem, he returns. He had been in Egypt hiding after

Solomon sought to kill him (11:40). He joins the elders who address Rehoboam.

12:4 Solomon was a great king, but he took a lot from the people. Israel seeks relief from the heavy taxation and forced service of Solomon's reign, and they offer allegiance to Rehoboam if he agrees to this.

12:6–7 The elders of Israel make no spiritual demand or request of Rehoboam. Seemingly, Solomon's idolatry doesn't bother them enough to cause them to seek a change.

12:10–15 The younger advisors' response suggests a harsh approach, which sets up destruction. God did not *make* Rehoboam take this unwise and sinful action. God simply allowed him to make the critical errors his sinful heart wanted to make. Rehoboam's foolishness makes Israel reject him and the entire dynasty of David. They reject the descendants of Israel's greatest king.

12:17 From this point on in the history of Israel, the name *Israel* refers to the ten northern tribes, and the name *Judah* refers to the southern tribes of Benjamin and Judah. There was a long-standing tension between the ten northern tribes and the combined group of Judah and Benjamin. An earlier rebellion occurred along this line of potential division in the days after Absalom's rebellion (2 Samuel 19:40–43) that developed into the rebellion of Sheba (2 Samuel 20:1–2).

12:18–19 Adoram was the wrong man for Rehoboam to send. He was famous for his harsh policy of forced labor (4:6; 5:14). Rehoboam probably sent him because he wanted to make good on his promise to punish those who opposed him.

12:20 At the time the prophecy of Ahijah (11:29–39) was made, it seemed unlikely that Jeroboam would prevail; but here we see God's Word fulfilled. King Jeroboam is sometimes called Jeroboam I to distinguish him from a later king of Israel also named Jeroboam, usually known as Jeroboam II (see 2 Kings 14:23–29).

12:25 In his first acts as leader of the northern kingdom, Jeroboam makes Shechem his capital, because Jerusalem is in the territory of Judah and Benjamin, the southern kingdom. He builds the strategic defensive town of Penuel across the river Jordan.

12:26–27 Instead of following Ahijah's prophecy, in which God promises him an enduring house if he follows God's ways, Jeroboam promotes false religion to serve his purposes. The fact that the kingdom is divided does not mean that the northern tribes are exempt from their covenant obligations; they are still under the Law of Moses as much as the southern tribes. Jeroboam fears the *political* implications of yearly trips down to the capital city of the southern kingdom of Judah. So he appeals to a natural desire for convenience when he sets up idols in Bethel and Dan (12:29).

12:28–33 Jeroboam repeats the same claim as Aaron did about five hundred years before when he presented the golden calf to the Israelites as their god (Exodus 32:4). He continues to make more places of worship than the main centers at Bethel and Dan. He then goes so far as to establish a priesthood of his own liking, rejecting the commandments of God regarding the priesthood of Israel. He even serves as a priest himself.

13:1–2 This man of God says a child named Josiah will be born to the house of David. Addressing the altar, he says Josiah will sacrifice false priests on it. The man of God's prophecy is more than a pronouncement of judgment against the altar; it also announces that the judgment will come through a ruler of Judah (the house of David). This is a special rebuke and source of concern to Jeroboam, who has always been aware of the threat from his neighbor to the south (see 12:27). This remarkable prophecy will be precisely fulfilled 340 years later (2 Kings 23:15).

13:3 The altar splitting and its ashes pouring out will be a direct rebuke of the idolatrous worship at that altar.

13:4 Jeroboam seeks to silence the messenger rather than respond to the message. When Jeroboam's hand dries up, God judges him at the precise point of his most glaring sin: ordering, with illegitimate authority, action against a man of God.

13:5 The altar splits, as prophesied in verse 3, and Jeroboam turns not to his golden calf but to the Lord. As the subsequent chapters will show, Jeroboam doesn't really repent here; or if he does, it is only for a moment. Wanting to receive something from God is not the same as repentance.

13:6 To his credit, the man of God shows great grace to Jeroboam. He quickly moves from being under arrest to being an intercessor for his persecutor. This mercy reflects the great mercy of God, who answers his prayer.

13:7–10 Jeroboam quickly—and naturally, given the circumstances—embraces the man of God as a friend. He wants to refresh and reward him, without any repentance for the sin the man of God denounced. But the man of God refuses the invitation, based on a prior warning from God. To accept Jeroboam's invitation would demonstrate fellowship with his idolatry.

13:11–17 The old prophet asks the man to come home with him and eat, an invitation he refuses under the same reason he refused Jeroboam—that Jeroboam had specifically told him to return to Judah without accepting hospitality, and to return a different way.

13:18–19 No matter how natural and enticing this gesture of hospitality was, it is the duty of the man of God to resist it. He had a word from God to guide his actions and should receive no other word except through dramatic and direct confirmation by God's Spirit. In this way, this man lives much like Israel, being drawn to the prophets who say what they want to hear, rather than the truth, however harsh.

13:20–22 The old prophet of Bethel will be used for one more prophecy now. At his table, God uses him to foretell the man's doom. God judges the man of God far more strictly than He seems to judge Jeroboam or the prophet from Bethel. They are guilty of worse sins (leading national idolatry and delivering a false prophecy), yet the man of God receives the most severe verdict—an unburied body

is a curse, and it was a disgrace to be buried among strangers, away from family.

13:23–25 The results are swift. The details of the incident (for instance, the man being killed but the donkey remaining unharmed) demonstrate that this is no mere accident, but something unique from God. Not only does the lion not attack the donkey, but it doesn't eat the carcase (carcass) or attack the men who pass by.

13:26 The old prophet hears of the incident and guesses rightly who the victim is. He is sympathetic to the man of God from Judah, even in his disobedience and resulting judgment. The old prophet himself appears not to be a particularly righteous man or good prophet, having used a deceptive prophecy to lead the man of God into sin and judgment. He recognizes the common weakness of this fellow servant of God.

13:27–32 The prophet retrieves the body, buries it in his own tomb, and confirms that the judgment is of the Lord. It is not the tomb of the fathers of the man of God, in fulfillment of the previous prophecy. But although he lied to him, led him into sin, and prophesied judgment against him, perhaps the old man from Bethel still respected the man of God, recognizing he had the courage to speak against Jeroboam that he himself did not have.

13:33–34 Jeroboam has great opportunity, especially in light of the promise of God through Ahijah, recorded in 11:38. But he does not obey God and honor His commandments, and he never fulfills his potential or promise. Instead he keeps consecrating anyone who wants to be a priest, leading to the destruction of his name from the face of the earth.

14:1–4 Jeroboam sends his wife to the prophet Ahijah to ask him the fate of their son Abijah. Even kings have troubles common to all people, and consulting prophets was a common practice (see 2 Kings 1:2; 4:22; 5:3). This is a familiar pattern for Jeroboam. In his time of need, he turns to the true God and men of God. He knows that idols cannot help him in any true crisis. Perhaps it is because he knows that he had rejected God and His prophets that he tells his wife to wear a disguise. Notice that he does not tell his wife to pray for the boy or to ask Ahijah to pray. He wants to use Ahijah the prophet as a fortune-teller more than to seek him as a man of God.

14:4–6 The woman's disguise and Ahijah's blindness don't matter, because God has told Ahijah what is going on. When Ahijah greets the woman, he informs her that though she was sent to Ahijah by her husband, in truth Ahijah was sent by God with a message to her and Jeroboam. She also learns right away that the news will be bad.

14:7–11 Jeroboam could have had a lasting dynasty, but he wasted the promise of God with his unbelief, idolatry, and outright rejection of God. Jeroboam is worse than all who have ruled before him. Saul was a bad man and a bad king. Solomon was a good king but a bad man. Jeroboam is far worse. He has thrust God behind his back, a powerful description of contempt (see Ezekiel 23:35).

14:12–16 Jeroboam's wife hears an immediate judgment and a distant one. First, their son will die, but such great judgment is coming upon the house of Jeroboam that all will see that, by comparison, this son was blessed in his death. Second, God will uproot Israel from the land He gave them and scatter them, a judgment that will be fulfilled some three hundred years later. God knew that the root of Jeroboam's apostasy would eventually result in national exile.

14:17–20 The immediate judgment of Jeroboam is fulfilled in the death of his child (14:12), demonstrating the truth of the future prophecy of the judgment of Israel (14:15). The rest of Jeroboam's reign is recorded elsewhere. According to 2 Chronicles 13:20, the Lord strikes him down, and after twenty-two years of rule, he dies.

14:25–28 Shishak takes the treasures of the house of the Lord and the treasures of the king's house. Solomon left great wealth to his son Rehoboam, both in the temple and in the palace. After only five years, that wealth is largely gone. Rehoboam's replacement brasen (or bronze) shields paint a perfect picture of the decline under the days of Rehoboam. He places them in the hands of the commanders of the palace guard, hidden away in a protected guardroom until they are specifically needed for state occasions. This is the enacting of a farce.

15:1–2 The son of Rehoboam, Abijam, rules Judah for three years. The brevity of his reign indicates God did not bless him. There are more details about his reign in 2 Chronicles 13, where he is referred to as Abijah. There we learn that there is war between Jeroboam of Israel and Abijam of Judah and that Abijam challenges Jeroboam on the basis of righteousness and faithfulness to God. When victory seems certain for Israel over Judah, Abijam cries out to the Lord, and God wins a victory for Judah that day.

15:3–5 By comparing the 1 Kings 14 account with 2 Chronicles 13, we can tell that Abijam knows something of the Lord and even knows how to preach, but he does not uproot the idolatry and sexual immorality that were introduced by his father, Rehoboam. His heart is not devoted to God, as was David's. This is his real problem. David sinned during his reign, but his heart stayed loyal to his God. God allows Abijam's rule, not because of the character of David's descendants, but to preserve David's dynasty.

15:9–15 Abijam's son Asa succeeds him and reigns forty-one years. Unlike his father, Asa does right as measured against David and begins a series of reforms. He banishes the state-sanctioned temple prostitutes who were introduced into Judah during the reign of Rehoboam. He deposes his own grandmother, Maachah, because she keeps a repulsive idol associated with the fertility cult of Asherah. This demonstrates the thoroughness of Asa's reforms. He is able to act righteously even against his own family.

15:16–19 During Asa's reign, the struggle for dominance with the northern kingdom of Israel continues. The current king of Israel, Baasha, gains the upper hand in the days of Asa because he effectively blocks a main route into Judah at the city of Ramah. Asa counters by gathering the silver and gold from the palace treasuries to buy the favor of Ben-hadad of Syria so that he will withdraw support from Israel. Apparently, Baasha of Israel could not stand against Judah by himself; he needs the backing of Syria.

15:20 Because of the league Asa forged with Ben-hadad, Syria moves against Israel, forcing Baasha to withdraw from Ramah. We learn from 2 Chronicles 16:7–10 that God is not pleased by Asa's deal with Ben-hadad. He sends the prophet Hanani to tell Asa this and to prophesy that because of his foolishness, Asa will face wars from this point on. Asa becomes a portrait of a man who rules well and seeks God for many years, yet he fails in a significant challenge of his faith and then refuses to hear God's correction. (See 2 Chronicles 14–16 for additional details about Asa's reign.)

15:23–24 The last years of Asa's life are marked by unbelief, hardness against God, oppression against his people, and disease.

15:25–32 In the northern kingdom, the short reign of Nadab, king of Israel, does not go well. This son of Jeroboam does as his father did, continuing in his idolatry and hardness toward God. His assassination by Baasha, and the murder of all his family, effectively fulfills God's prophecy that the house of Jeroboam would be destroyed.

15:33–34 Baasha, the son of Ahijah, becomes king over all Israel and ushers in a dreadful period for the nation, both spiritually and politically. He does evil in the sight of the Lord and walks in the way of Jeroboam. Though Baasha is not a genetic descendant of Jeroboam (having murdered his family), he is certainly a spiritual descendant of Jeroboam.

16:1 Apparently Jehu had a long career as a prophet. Second Chronicles 19:2 mentions another work of Jehu the son of Hanani. Some fifty years after this word to Baasha, Jehu speaks to Jehoshaphat, the king of Judah. Jehu also wrote specific books of history regarding kings of Israel (2 Chronicles 20:34). His father, Hanani, is also mentioned in 2 Chronicles 16:7–10, which describes how he suffered imprisonment because he was a faithful prophet in speaking to King Asa.

16:2 In lifting Baasha out of the dust to rule over Israel, God uses Baasha to bring judgment upon the house of Jeroboam; yet God does not cause Baasha to do this. He rightly judges Baasha even though He used Baasha's wicked choices to bring judgment upon Jeroboam.

16:3–4 Because Baasha is a wicked king after the pattern of Jeroboam, he will face the same judgment as Jeroboam and his house. This judgment has special relevance to Baasha because he was the instrument of judgment God used to bring justice to the house of Jeroboam. It is considered a particular disgrace to have your dead corpse desecrated and kept from proper burial.

16:8–10 Zimri, an officer in the army of Israel, assassinates Elah.

16:11–12 The killing of a king's household was a common practice in the ancient world (and was exactly what Baasha did to the house of Jeroboam in 15:29). David's treatment of the house of Saul was a glorious exception to this common practice.

16:16 Omri's rise to power shows that the democratic influence in Israel is greater than many realize. The people—especially the army—simply do not want Zimri to reign as king over them. They therefore reject his authority and appoint Omri in his place.

16:18 Zimri commits one of the few suicides recorded in the Old Testament, along with Samson (Judges 16:30), Saul (1 Samuel 31:4), and Ahithophel (2 Samuel 17:23).

16:21–22 Civil war breaks out as soon as Zimri dies, with half of Israel supporting Omri and the other half supporting Tibni, son of Ginath. Scholars say the conflict continues for five years, until Omri's forces defeat those loyal to Tibni. Tibni dies, presumably killed by Omri, whose rise to full power is the beginning of another dynasty in Israel.

16:25–28 In the records of secular history, Omri is one of the more successful and famous kings of ancient Israel. But it's clear that Omri follows Jeroboam's evil ways. Omri is a political and economic success for Israel but a spiritual failure. He dies and is buried in Samaria, the city he founded. Ahab picks up where his father left off.

16:29–30 While Asa is ruling for forty-one years in Judah, there are seven different kings in Israel. Omri's son Ahab distinguishes himself by being worse than Jeroboam.

16:31–33 Ahab takes as his wife Jezebel, the daughter of the Zidonian king Ethbaal, whose name means "with Baal." Jezebel is famous for her hostility and cruelty. Their marriage is also politically expedient, as the alliance with the Zidonians, or Phoenicia, gives Ahab a powerful ally. Ahab introduces the worship of completely new pagan gods. In his disobedience Jeroboam said, "I will worship the Lord but do it my way." Ahab said, "I want to forget about the Lord completely and worship Baal." In his later years, King Solomon worshipped pagan gods, yet Ahab was far worse in that he commanded the worship of idols (see Micah 6:16).

16:34 After Jericho's previous destruction, Joshua had prophesied that anyone rebuilding the city would cause peril to his firstborn and his youngest (Joshua 6:26). Here the language is much the same with Hiel laying the foundation at the cost of Abiram, his firstborn, and setting up the gates at the cost of his youngest son, Segub.

17:6 The food that comes to Elijah is from the beak of an unclean animal. He has to put away his traditional ideas of clean and unclean or he will die of starvation. Through this incident, God teaches Elijah to emphasize the spirit of the law before the letter of the law.

17:7 Elijah stays by the brook until it dries up, the start of the drought he had predicted. He does not pray for rain to come again, even for his own survival. He keeps the purpose of God first, even when it adversely affects him.

17:8–9 Zarephath, a Gentile city, is in the general region of the wicked Queen Jezebel. Elijah is entering enemy territory.

17:10 Widows were known for their poverty in the ancient world. When He is rejected by His own people, Jesus uses this example of Elijah's coming to the widow of Zarephath as an illustration of God's right to choose a people to Himself (see Luke 4:24–26). Once in Zarephath, Elijah sees a woman gathering sticks, a sign she is poor.

17:15–16 The widow obeys in faith and is immediately rewarded with food every day for both Elijah and her family. God uses her as a channel of supply, and her needs are met as a result.

17:17–18 The death of the son is a double blow to this widow. Not only does she suffer as any mother who loses a child, but she also suffers as one who has lost her only hope for the future. The expectation was that her son would grow and provide for her in her old age. Now that expectation is shattered. She indirectly blames Elijah and more directly blames herself and her unnamed sin. Whatever her sin is, the guilty memory of it is always close to her.

17:19–21 Elijah prays with great heart and intimacy with God. He brings the seemingly unexplainable and irredeemable situation to God in prayer. Since he knows God led him to this widow, Elijah asks Him to remedy the situation.

18:1 Earlier God told Elijah to *hide* himself (17:3). Now it is time to *present* himself. There is a time to hide and be alone with God, and there is also a time to make ourselves active in the world.

18:7–15 Reverence turns to fear when Elijah asks Obadiah to announce to Ahab that he wants an audience. Obadiah fears that if he announces that he met Elijah and the prophet disappears again, Ahab will kill Obadiah for letting Elijah get away. Kindly and wisely, Elijah responds to Obadiah's legitimate fears and assures him that he will meet with Ahab. He will not make Obadiah a martyr for Elijah's deeds.

18:17–18 According to King Ahab's theology, Elijah is to blame for the drought. The king believes in Baal so much that his government promotes and supports Baal worship and persecutes the worshippers of Yahweh. Ahab believes that Elijah has angered Baal, and therefore Baal has withheld rain. Ahab may have thought that Baal would hold back the rain until Elijah was caught and executed.

18:21 The appeal of Elijah makes it clear that there is a difference between the service of Baal and the service of Yahweh. The people of Israel want to give some devotion to *both* Yahweh and Baal. But the God of Israel is not interested in such divided devotion. Yet Elijah knows it can never be this way; you either serve Baal or serve Yahweh. Confronting and eliminating these prophets of Baal before God sends rain to the land of Israel is crucial so that everyone understands that the rain comes from Yahweh, not from Baal. The people do not answer Elijah's appeal. They lack the courage either to defend their position or to change it.

18:25–29 The prophets of Baal take up the challenge and pray for fire from their god. They pray long and with great passion. Yet because they do not pray to a *real* God, their prayer means nothing. Elijah mocks the prophets of Baal for their foolish faith, and the prophets work even harder. They cry louder and cut themselves, a common practice to arouse the deity's pity.

18:30–35 Elijah repairs a broken altar with twelve stones—one for each tribe of the twelve tribes of Israel. In this way, Elijah is reviving something that once was. Then he prepares the altar so that there can be no question of trickery. Elijah requires more of Yahweh than he does of Baal. Elijah does not even suggest to the prophets of Baal that they wet down their sacrifice once or twice, much less three times. He believes it is no harder for God to ignite a wet sacrifice than it is for Him to set a dry one ablaze.

18:38 Within what appears to be minutes, God answers. When the fire falls, its work is beyond expectation. It would have been enough if only the cut-up pieces of the bull on the altar were ignited, but God wanted more than simple vindication—He wanted to glorify Himself among the people.

18:39 The people fall on their faces. At this moment, the people are persuaded. Asked to choose between Baal and Yahweh, they have no choice to make. Obviously the Lord is the one true God. Tragically, this is only a momentary persuasion. The people are decidedly persuaded but not lastingly changed.

18:45–46 The amazing day ends with dark clouds and heavy rains and a supernaturally empowered fourteen-mile, cross-country run. We don't know exactly why it is important to God for Elijah to reach Jezreel first.

19:3–4 Once at the distant city of Beer-sheba, Elijah goes from the high point of having won a contest with the prophets of Baal to this low point of post-traumatic depression. Elijah secludes himself, lies down, and prays to die. But Elijah's prayer is not answered. (In fact, Elijah is one of the two men in the Bible to never die.) This mighty man of prayer—mighty enough to make the rain and the dew stop for three and a half years, and then mighty enough to make it start again at his prayer—has given up. His work is stressful and exhausting and seems to accomplish nothing. The great work on mount Carmel did not result in a lasting national revival or return to the Lord.

19:5–8 God rejects Elijah's request to die and ministers to his physical needs before doing anything else. The angel God sends twice orders Elijah to eat and drink and then sends him on his 200-mile journey to mount Horeb, also known as mount Sinai. Elijah takes forty days, four times as long as needed for a straight trip. God does not demand an immediate recovery from Elijah. He allows the prophet time to recover from his spiritual depression.

19:9–10 Once Elijah reaches Horeb, God allows him to vent his frustrations. Elijah goes into a cave, perhaps like the cave or cleft of the rock in which Moses hid when God appeared to him (Exodus 33:22). God asks him what he is doing there. God knows the answer, of course, but it is good for Elijah to speak to the Lord freely and to unburden his heart. So Elijah vents about the bad situation he's in. His claim to be the only prophet left is not accurate, but it reflects how Elijah feels. Discouraging times make God's servants feel more isolated and alone than they truly are.

19:15 Immediately after ministering to Elijah, God gives him work to do. The prophet needs a task to focus on. He needs to stop looking at himself and his own (admittedly difficult) circumstances. He needs to get on with what God wants him to do.

19:18 The final encouragement to Elijah is God's promise that He has reserved seven thousand in Israel, all whose knees have not bowed to Baal. Elijah repeatedly bemoans that he is alone among the true followers of God (see 19:10, 14). This promise assures him that he is not alone and that his work as a prophet has indeed been fruitful. His quiet ministry through the years actually bears more fruit than the spectacular ministry at mount Carmel.

19:19–21 Elijah finds Elisha at work and commissions him to ministry. The mantle is the symbol of Elijah's prophetic authority. This act signifies that Elijah is calling Elisha as his successor. Elisha begs to say good-bye to his parents. It appears that Elijah begrudgingly gives permission. Elisha sacrifices his twelve oxen (having that many indicates his relative wealth), burns his equipment as fuel to cook the meat, and shares it with the community. This demonstrates Elisha's complete commitment to following Elijah. He destroys the tools of his trade in a going-away party for his family and friends.

20:5–6 Ben-hadad makes demands. Officials will come and search Ahab's house and those of his servants, to take away anything valuable. This is a greater demand than what Ben-hadad made in verses 2–4.

20:7–8 It would have been wiser for Ahab to seek the counsel of the elders *before* he surrendered to the Syrians. Now, in the brief time between the message of surrender and the actual abduction of his women and the plundering of his goods, he seeks counsel. The elders of Israel see clearly that surrender to Ben-hadad and the Syrians is the first step to a total loss of sovereignty for Israel. If they want to remain a kingdom at all, they have to resist this threat.

20:13 As the two sides prepare for war, a prophet approaches Ahab. This nameless prophet does not seem to be either Elijah or Elisha. He must be one of the seven thousand God had told Elisha that He has reserved in Israel who are quietly faithful to Yahweh (19:18). Through this prophet, God promises victory, a generous gesture to an idolatrous ruler. Israel's hardened rejection of God deserves divine abandonment. Yet God is rich in mercy, and He shows His mercy to Ahab and Israel.

20:14 Ahab asks God who will make the promised victory happen. He is looking around at his army and military leaders and wondering how God can bring a victory against a mighty enemy. Ahab also asks who will lead the battle, and God answers that Ahab himself will. God wants to win this victory by working through the unlikely people Ahab already has on his side.

20:16–21 Israel goes out to fight Ben-hadad, who at the start of the conflict is seen getting drunk at the command post. (In part, he is defeated by his own weak character.) Despite great odds, Israel wins the battle.

20:22 The same nameless prophet advises preparation again. The victory over Ben-hadad does not end the conflict between Israel and Syria. Ahab will need to prepare for a Syrian attack in the coming spring. God works through the careful preparation of His people.

20:23–25 The Syrians strategize to meet the Israelites on the plains, where they think Israel's God is weakest. The idea of the *localized deity* was prominent in the ancient world. The ancients felt that particular gods had authority over particular areas. Because the recent victory was won on hilly terrain, the servants of the king of Syria believe that the God of Israel is a localized deity with power over the hills, not the plains. The action they recommend is logical, given their theology. Their theological belief directs their strategy and action.

20:26–29 The armies muster, and Israel routs Ben-hadad in an even more spectacular victory. A casualty count of one hundred thousand Syrian foot soldiers in one day is clearly a miracle, yet it is a miracle working through the existing Israelite army, not by another outside agency. God wants to show that as unlikely as it seems, God *can* work through this outwardly weak and ineffective instrument.

20:34 Previously, the king of Syria promised to return certain cities to Israel in exchange for leniency after defeat in battle. Apparently there was a city (possibly Ramoth-gilead; see 22:3–4) that Ben-hadad never returned to Israel, and it is in a strategically important location.

20:43 Ahab has the sorrow of being a sinner and knowing the consequences of sin, without having sorrow for the sin itself.

21:1–3 The account of Naboth and his land began as a simple real estate transaction. Ahab wanted the vineyard, but Naboth's response was an emphatic *no*. His rejection of the otherwise reasonable offer is rooted in the ancient Israelite idea of the land. The land was seen as an inheritance from God, parceled out to individual tribes and families according to His will. Therefore land was never really sold, only leased—and only under the direst circumstances.

21:4–6 Ahab pouts before Jezebel for being refused this small portion of land. This seems entirely characteristic of Ahab, a man who reacts this way when he meets any kind of adversity or disappointment.

21:7–8 Jezebel's manner of speech reveals her authority in the palace of Israel. She begins to plot

Naboth's murder with Ahab's collusion, since he allows letters in his name to be sealed with his seal.

21:13–14 Two scoundrels accuse Naboth of blasphemy, and the punishment is stoning. Naboth is completely innocent of such accusations and is murdered without cause. The stoning of Naboth over a piece of land shows the brutal and immoral character of Jezebel and Ahab.

21:15–16 Ahab takes possession of Naboth's land, which adds evil to evil. Even with Naboth dead, the land does not belong to Ahab or the royal house of Israel. It belongs to the family of Naboth. Ahab probably claimed the land as a royal right because the crown seized the land of any executed criminal.

21:17–24 God sends Elijah to confront Ahab as he is enjoying his new possession. Elijah does what few other men have the courage to do: confront this wicked, brutal, and immoral king and queen of Israel. He pointedly charges them with the two crimes: murder and theft of Naboth's land. Notice that Elijah confronts Ahab over the sin of Jezebel and her wicked associates. God clearly holds Ahab responsible for this sin as husband, as king, and as beneficiary of this crime. He predicts that dogs will lick Ahab's blood on the same field on which Naboth died. Elijah's is a severe judgment against anyone, but in particular against a king. A king's legacy is in his posterity succeeding him on the throne, and here God announces an end to the dynasty of Omri (Ahab's father). His dynasty would come to a dead end just like the dynasties of Jeroboam and Baasha. The judgment on Jezebel—that she would be eaten by dogs—was not only horrible by any standard but also held an element of disgrace.

21:25–26 The writer of 1 Kings here summarizes Ahab's great wickedness, likening his sin to the sin of the Amorites. Thus God prepares the ground for the future eviction of Israel from the promised land.

21:27–29 For all his wickedness, Ahab responds to this prophecy of judgment exactly as he should. He understands that the prophecy is in fact an invitation to repent, humble one's self, and seek God for mercy. However, it's clear that his repentance is outward and superficial, arising from fear and not from sincere belief. God nevertheless honors Ahab's actions. This shows the power of both prayer and humble repentance. If Ahab did not humble himself in this way, then the judgment would have come in his own day. This shows that God gave the prophecy of judgment as an invitation to repentance, and God opened the door of mercy when Ahab properly responded to that invitation. There is no record of Jezebel's humility or repentance. Therefore we can expect that God's judgment will come upon her exactly as He first announced.

22:1–4 During a visit from Judah's king Jehoshaphat, Ahab sets his eyes upon Ramoth-gilead in the north and asks Jehoshaphat to help him. Ramoth-gilead is only forty miles from Jerusalem, but there is probably another reason for Ahab's request. It seems clear that Jehoshaphat is in a treaty relationship with Ahab, and Jehoshaphat is the subordinate partner in the alliance.

22:7–9 Jehoshaphat still wants to hear from a prophet of Yahweh. Ahab knows of one more, Micaiah, whom he hates because he never says anything good. Yet he is willing to call him when the king of Judah responds that Ahab should listen to Micaiah.

22:10–12 It was an ancient custom to hold court and make decisions at the gates of the city. There were even thrones for high officials to sit on at the gates of the city of Samaria. Ahab and Jehoshaphat are there, surrounded by the unfaithful prophets (such as Zedekiah) who are prophesying in the name of the Lord, but not truthfully. Perhaps these were true followers of Yahweh who were seduced by Ahab's sincere but shallow repentance three years before (21:27–29). After that, they began to align with Ahab uncritically. Three years later they are willing to prophesy lies to Ahab if that is what he wants to hear.

22:11–12 The prophet Zedekiah uses a familiar tool of ancient prophets, an object lesson, to convey his prophecy. He uses horns of iron to illustrate the thrust of two powerful forces, armies that would rout the Syrians. Zedekiah has the agreement of four hundred other prophets (all the prophets prophesied so).

22:13–14 Into this dramatic scene comes Micaiah, the faithful prophet, in rags and chains straight out of prison (see 22:26). The messenger who retrieved him has already told him what's happening and advised him to go along with the basic message. Micaiah assures him that he will simply repeat what God says to him.

22:15–17 Micaiah first mimics the false prophets. King Ahab recognizes the mocking tone of Micaiah's prophecy and demands the truth. Micaiah now changes his tone from mocking to serious. He says that not only will Israel be defeated but also that their leader (the shepherd) will perish.

22:19–23 King Ahab and others at the court may have found it hard to explain how one prophet could be right and four hundred wrong. Micaiah goes on to reveal the inspiration behind the four hundred prophets. He describes the throne of God, with God asking who will entice Ahab to attack Ramoth-gilead and die. Apparently one of the fallen angels volunteers for this task. Since Ahab wants to be deceived, God will give him what he wants, using a willing fallen angel who works through willing unfaithful prophets.

22:32–33 Finding himself as the only identifiable king in the battle, Jehoshaphat realizes he is in mortal danger. He cries out to God and is saved when his attackers see

that he is not the king of Israel. Second Chronicles 18:31 makes it clear that the Lord hears Jehoshaphat's cry and rescues him.

22:34–37 A bowman at random strikes Ahab, as if the arrow is a sin-seeking missile. God orchestrates unintended actions to result in an exercise of His judgment. Ahab orders his body propped up in his chariot, facing his enemies, to inspire his troops. All day long he lingers, but by evening he dies, and the battle is over. The word through the prophet Micaiah proves true. King Ahab never returns to Samaria or Israel in peace.

22:38–39 When the soldiers go to wash Ahab's chariot, the dogs lick his blood. This is almost the fulfillment of God's word through Elijah in 1 Kings 21:19, where Elijah prophesies that dogs will lick the blood of Ahab. This proves true, but not in the place Elijah said it would happen. God relents from His original judgment against Ahab, but because of Ahab's false repentance and continued sin, a very similar judgment comes upon him. Another prophecy is also fulfilled in the death of Ahab—the word from the anonymous prophet of 20:42, that Ahab spares Ben-hadad's life at the expense of his own. By materialistic standards, the reign of Ahab was a success. He was generally militarily successful and enjoyed a generally prosperous economy. Yet spiritually his reign was a disaster, one of the worst ever for Israel.

22:41–43 Jehoshaphat, son of the good king Asa, is described here as following in Asa's footsteps and doing what is right in the eyes of the Lord. The one accusation, however, that he does not take away all the high places, the places where idols are worshipped is a serious shortcoming.

22:48–49 Jehoshaphat builds ships at Ezion-geber, a territory of the Edomites, who are without a king at the time. After a disastrous shipping venture, Jehoshaphat is tempted to make an alliance with Ahaziah of Israel, Ahab's successor, but Jehoshaphat will not. This is to his credit. He learned the lesson of not entering a partnership with the ungodly.

22:51–53 The book of 1 Kings ends with mention of the son of Ahab, Ahaziah, who reigns for two years, walking in the same evil ways as his father and his grandfather, Jeroboam. This is a low note in the history of the nation. The book began with the twilight of Israel's greatest king, David. It ends with the sad reign of one of the most wicked kings in the history of God's people.

THE SECOND

BOOK OF THE KINGS
OTHERWISE CALLED
THE FOURTH BOOK OF THE KINGS

INTRODUCTION TO 2 KINGS ■ The books of 1 and 2 Kings were originally joined in one book. The narrative covers almost five hundred years, tracing the history of Israel and Judah from the last days of the monarchy under David to the disintegration and capture of the divided kingdoms.

AUTHOR ■ The author of this book is unknown. While there is a Jewish tradition that points to the prophet Jeremiah as the author, there is more evidence that the book evolved over a long period of time.

OCCASION ■ First and Second Kings were written to the people of the southern kingdom of Judah to explain that the fall of the northern kingdom of Israel was God's judgment on their idolatry, to call the southern kingdom to repentance for following Israel's example, and to remind them of the hope promised through the royal—and ultimately messianic—line of David.

1:1 The book of 1 Kings ends with King Ahab's death and his son Ahaziah's ascension to the throne. The reign of Ahab had been a spiritual disaster for Israel, the northern kingdom, but it was also a time of political security and economic prosperity. Moab, the land just south of Israel and west of the Dead Sea, had been under Israelite domination since the days of David (see 2 Samuel 8:2, 11–12). After Ahab's death, the land of Moab rebels against Israel. This rebellion of Moab in the days of Ahaziah signifies the decline of Israel's power and the judgment of God.

1:3 There is little doubt that King Ahaziah believes that Yahweh lives, but Elijah's question points out that Ahaziah lives as if there is no God in Israel. He is a practical atheist, and the way he seeks Baal-zebub instead of the Lord demonstrates this.

1:5–6 Although Ahaziah had sent the messengers to seek a word from the pagan priests of Baal-zebub, the word from Elijah persuades them so much that they do not follow through on their original mission.

1:7–8 Ahaziah clearly suspects it was the prophet Elijah who spoke the word that deterred his messengers' word. His suspicion is confirmed when the man is described as being hairy and wearing a leather belt around his waist. The Hebrew words translated *hairy man* mean "possessor of hair." Most likely this description refers to clothing made of hairy animal skins. Identifying Elijah by his clothes also connects him to the ministry of John the Baptist, who dresses in hairy skins from animals (Matthew 3:4). When the priests and Levites see him, they ask, "Art thou Elias?" (John 1:19–21).

1:9 This should have been plenty of men to capture one prophet. Clearly Ahaziah sends more men than are normally required. There are many reasons Ahaziah wants to arrest Elijah, even though he has already heard Elijah's prophecy. Perhaps he wants Elijah to reverse his word of doom and is willing to use force to compel him to do it. Perhaps he just wants to show his rage against this prophet who has troubled him and his father, Ahab,

for so long. Perhaps he wants to dramatically silence Elijah to discourage future prophets from speaking boldly against the king of Israel.

1:11–12 The second captain repeats the same error as the first captain, but with even more guilt because he knew what happened to the first captain. The judgment upon the first group should have warned this second captain and his fifty men, but the specific request of the second captain ("Come down quickly") shows that he makes his request even more bolder and more demanding. Elijah leaves the matter in God's hands, and God again responds in dramatic judgment.

1:13–15 The third captain approaches his mission in a completely different manner, recognizing that Elijah really is a man of God. Perhaps the fate of the first two captains convinced him. When the request is made wisely and humbly, Elijah goes, but he has God's assurance that there is nothing to fear.

1:16–17 Elijah gives the same answer to the king that he gave to the messengers sent by the king. The message from God does not change just because Ahaziah doesn't want to hear it the first time. The proof of Elijah's credibility is in the result—his prophecy is fulfilled just as spoken. Ahaziah does not recover from his fall through the lattice.

2:1 Chapter 2 picks up the story at the end of Elijah's ministry and tells the account of his miraculous departure in a whirlwind and of Elisha's succession as prophet. The Lord is about to take Elijah into heaven by a whirlwind.

2:2 Elijah knows that God has a dramatic plan for the end of his earthly life, yet he is perfectly willing to allow it all to take place privately, without anyone else knowing. He seems to test the devotion of Elisha by telling him to stay behind.

2:3 Apparently Elijah's departure is somewhat common knowledge. Elijah, Elisha, and the sons of the prophets all knew, but we are not told specifically how they knew.

2:7-8 The water dividing is a strange and unique miracle, though it was reminiscent of the crossing of the Red Sea during the Exodus and the stopping of the waters of the Jordan when the Israelites entered Canaan. Elijah walks in the steps of Moses and Joshua as one whom God uses to miraculously part waters.

2:13 Elisha takes up the mantle of Elijah that had fallen from him. Since the mantle is the special mark of a prophet, this is a demonstration of the truth that Elisha has inherited the ministry of Elijah.

2:14 When Elisha strikes the water, it is divided. This shows that Elisha immediately has the same power in ministry that Elijah had. He goes back over a divided Jordan the same way that he and Elijah came over the river. Elisha's question reveals that he knows that the power in prophetic ministry does not rest in mantles or fiery chariots. It rests in the presence and work of the living God. If the God of Elijah is also with Elisha, then he will inherit the same power and direction of ministry.

2:15 The succession of Elisha to the power and office of Elijah is apparent to others. Elisha doesn't need to persuade or convince them of this with words. God's blessing on his actions is enough to prove it.

2:16-17 The sons of the prophets wonder if the chariot of fire had not merely taken Elijah to another place in Israel.

2:23 The ancient Hebrew word translated *little children* refers to young men in a very broad sense. This term applied to Joseph when he was thirty-nine (Genesis 41:12), to Absalom as an adult (2 Samuel 14:21; 18:5), and to Solomon when he was twenty (1 Kings 3:7). These youths are from Bethel, and their mocking shows the continuing opposition to a true prophet in Bethel, the chief center of pagan calf-worship. The young men mock Elisha both because of his apparent baldness and because of his connection with the prophet Elijah. The idea behind the words *go up* is that Elisha should go up to heaven like Elijah did. It mocks Elisha, his mentor, Elijah, and the God they serve.

2:24-25 Elisha leaves any correction of these young men up to God but pronounces a curse on them in the name of the Lord. In response to the curse of Elisha, God sends two female bears and they maul (cut up, not kill) the young men. Forty-two in all are mauled. The bear attack has the effect of breaking up the gang, while Elisha continues on his way unharmed.

3:2-3, 13 Jehoram is the ninth consecutive bad king over the northern kingdom, which never had a godly king. Though he is better than his father and mother, he is still a wicked man. The sins of Jeroboam that Jehoram perpetuates include setting up golden calves for the people to worship in Bethel and Dan (1 Kings 12:25-32). Possibly Jehoram tears down the image of Baal out of bad motives—either because he is frightened of the repercussions or because he wants to impress Jehoshaphat so the Judean king will agree to an alliance. Something must have been amiss, because Elisha isn't impressed with Jehoram's actions against the false god.

3:9-10 Because the combined armies of Judah, Israel, and Edom have to travel a considerable distance to attack Moab from the south, they find themselves in the wilderness with no water. Jehoram's guilty conscience convinces him that this calamity can be attributed to the hand of God. His own sin makes him think that everything that has happened against him is the judgment of God.

3:11 Both Jehoram and Jehoshaphat believe there is a divine element to their current crisis. Jehoram believes that God is to be avoided because of the crisis, while Jehoshaphat believes that God should be sought because of the crisis. The description of Elisha pouring water on the hands of Elijah has the connotation of personal assistant. This is a wonderful title for any servant of God. Elisha is the humble and practical servant of Elijah. This is spiritual service that prepares him for further spiritual service.

3:12 The decision to go to Elisha is a reflection of some kind of humility on the part of these three kings. Normally kings demand that others come see them. These three are willing to go to the prophet.

3:16-17 Water will be provided, but not through just any rain or storm. The people must dig ditches in order to catch what God will provide. The injunction to dig, however, is in keeping with the principle that God wants us to prepare for the blessing He wants to bring. Listening to Him, we are to anticipate His working and get ready for it. Digging ditches was something the people of God could do. God didn't ask them to do more than they were able to do. When God wants us to prepare for the blessing He will bring, He gives us tasks that we can really do.

3:26-27 That the king of Moab is willing to sacrifice his own son and heir shows how desperate he is. He does this to honor his pagan gods and to show his own people his determination to prevent defeat. The radical determination of the king of Moab convinces the kings of Israel, Judah, and Edom that they cannot completely defeat Moab. They leave content with their near-complete victory.

4:1 We are not told precisely when the events recorded in chapter 4 occurred. In contrast to the faithlessness of King Ahaziah and King Jehoram described in chapters 1-3, here we read of simple people with profound faith. The widowed wife of one of the sons of the prophets has debts, and the only way she can pay them is to give her sons as indentured servants to her creditor.

4:2-7 Elisha instructs this woman to borrow vessels (pots, jars, bowls, etc.), and she obeys. Each vessel has to be gathered, assembled, emptied, and put in the right position and filled. As she fills these vessels, the oil miraculously continues to pour until all the borrowed vessels are filled—enough oil to pay her debt and provide for her future. It is significant that Elisha pushes her to do this, rather than doing it for her. The miracle is given according to the measure of the widow's faith in borrowing vessels; when the vessels are full, the oil ceases. The principle of this miracle is the same as the principle of the ditches in chapter 3. The amount of one's work determines the amount of blessing and provision actually received. God's powerful provision invites our hard work and never excuses laziness.

4:8–13 The remarkable relationship between Elisha and the Shunammite woman begins when the woman seeks to do something for the prophet and offers him a meal. Elisha doesn't seek anything from this woman; she simply offers her hospitality. The Shunammite woman then seeks to do more for the prophet, offering a room for Elisha to stay in on his frequent travels through the area. She asks for nothing in return.

4:14–17 It is Gehazi, Elisha's servant, who identifies what the woman needs: a son to care for her in her old age. To this barren woman, this promise seems too good to be true. The stigma associated with barrenness was harsh in the ancient world, and this promised son would answer the longing of her heart and remove that stigma of barrenness. The woman, who so generously provides material things for the prophet of God, is now blessed by the God of the prophet, blessed beyond material things.

4:18–24 When the woman's son dies, she shows her faith by fetching Elisha. She prepares for the resurrection of the boy, not his burial. Perhaps she heard that Elijah had raised the widow of Zarephath's son to life (1 Kings 17).

4:25–27 The Shunammite woman doesn't want Elisha to learn of her grief through his assistant, Gehazi. Elisha seems mystified that this woman (whom he presumably often prays for) is in a crisis that he is not aware of. In this circumstance, Elisha is more surprised that God didn't speak to him than if God had spoken to him.

4:29 Elisha's sending Gehazi ahead with his staff seems to follow the previous pattern in Elisha's ministry: He does not do things for people directly but gives them the opportunity to work with God and to trust Him for themselves. Earlier he had told the widow to gather vessels and pour the oil herself (4:1–7).

4:30–37 It may be that the Shunammite woman fails under this test, because she thinks that the power to heal is connected with Elisha himself, and she refuses to leave his presence. The child is not healed by the laying on of the staff, but God does heal the boy in response to Elisha's prayer. He prays after the pattern shown to him by his mentor, Elijah (1 Kings 17:20–23). Elisha prays with great faith because he knows God worked in this way in the life of Elijah. He also prays with great faith because he senses that God wants to raise this boy from the dead.

5:1 The disease called leprosy begins as small red spots on the skin. Before long the spots get bigger and start to turn white, with a shiny or scaly appearance. Pretty soon the spots spread over the whole body and hair begins to fall out—first from the head, then even from the eyebrows. As things get worse, fingernails and toenails become loose, start to rot, and eventually fall off. Then the joints of fingers and toes begin to rot and fall off piece by piece. Gums begin to shrink until they can't hold teeth anymore, so each tooth is lost. Leprosy

eats away at the face until literally the nose, the palate, and even the eyes rot—and the victim wastes away until death.

5:2–3 The girl who serves as a maid to Naaman's wife is an unwilling missionary, taken captive from Israel and now in Syria. She may have been taken from her family at a young age, but she still becomes an outstanding example of a faithful witness in her current circumstance. She cares enough to speak up, and she has faith enough to believe that Elisha can heal Naaman of his leprosy. God allows the tragedy of her captivity to accomplish a greater good, illustrating the mysterious ways God works.

5:4–6 It seems that 2 Kings is not necessarily arranged chronologically, so this event probably occurred during a time of lowered tension between Israel and Syria. Unless this were so, considering the record of wars between Israel and Syria described in the previous chapters, it would be odd for the king of Syria to send a letter of recommendation with his general Naaman along with over one million dollars' worth of gold, silver, and merchandise. All this together shows how desperate Naaman's condition is and how badly the king of Syria wants to help him.

5:7 When the king of Israel (Jehoram) reads the letter, he is understandably upset. First, it is obviously out of his power to heal Naaman's leprosy. Second, he has no relationship with the prophet of the God who does have the power to heal. This lends some credence to his assumption that the king of Syria seeks a quarrel.

5:9–12 Naaman is accustomed to being honored, so when Elisha doesn't even meet with him in person but sends a messenger instead, the experience is humbling. Even more humbling are the simple instructions. In his great need, Naaman has anticipated a way in which God will work, and he is offended when God doesn't work the way he expects. Because his expectation is crushed, Naaman wants nothing to do with Elisha. If the answer is washing in a river, Naaman knows there are better rivers in his own land.

5:14–16 Naaman's response of faith, when he finally becomes willing, is generously rewarded—with complete and miraculous healing. Elisha's absence makes it clear that the miracle is from God, not from Elisha. The healing, connected with the word of the prophet, is convincing evidence to Naaman that the God Elisha represents is the true God in all the earth. Naaman's desire to give a gift to Elisha is a fine display of gratitude. There is no evidence in the text that Naaman has any ulterior motive in this gesture, yet Elisha steadfastly insists that he will take nothing from Naaman.

5:17–19 Naaman reveals some superstition even in his faith. He holds the common opinion in the ancient world that particular deities have power over particular places. He thinks that if he takes a piece of Israel back with him to Syria, he can better worship the God of Israel. As an official in the government of Syria, Naaman is expected to participate in the worship of the Syrian gods. He asks Elisha for allowance to direct his heart to Yahweh even when he is in the temple of Rimmon. Some commentators believe that Naaman asks forgiveness for his previous idolatry in the temple of Rimmon, instead of asking permission for future occasions. Apparently the Hebrew will allow for this translation, though it is not the most natural way to understand the text. By generally approving, but not giving a specific answer, Elisha seems to leave the matter up to Naaman and God. Perhaps he trusted that the Lord would personally convict Naaman of his idolatry and give him the integrity and strength to avoid it.

5:20–25 Gehazi may have thought that God was blessing his venture when he ran after the gifts from Naaman that Elisha had refused. After all, Naaman is happy to give him more than he asked for. However, the fact that Gehazi deliberately hides the silver from Elisha suggests that he knows he has done wrong.

6:4–6 Losing the iron axe head in the water is a significant loss. At this time, iron was not common enough to be cheap. The man who loses the axe head is rightly sensitive to the fact that he lost something that belongs to someone else, making the loss more acute. There is no trickery in the way Elisha puts the stick in the water; it is simply the expression of his faith that God honors.

6:8–13 The king of Syria is naturally mystified by the way the king of Israel knows all of Syria's plans beforehand. He is convinced there is a traitor among them, until one servant reveals that Elisha, the prophet in Israel, knows and reveals these things.

6:15–16 When Elisha's servant sees the horses and chariots and the great Syrian army that has come to seize Elisha, he is naturally afraid. He knows that there is little chance of escaping or surviving an attack from so many. When Elisha says he and the servant have more men, this is not empty hope or wishful thinking; it is a real reason for confidence, even if the servant cannot see it.

6:17 Elisha does not pray that God will change anything in the situation, nor does he try to persuade the servant of the reality of those who are with them. His only request is that his servant can actually see the reality of the situation. When a person is blind to spiritual reality, only God can open his or her eyes. The previous lack of perception on the part of Elisha's servant does not make the reality of the spiritual army any less real. The invisible army of God has more firepower than the horses and chariots of the Syrians. The spiritual army has chariots of fire all around Elisha.

6:21–23 Elisha commands the king of Israel to treat the soldiers with kindness and generosity. This practice of answering evil with good successfully changes the policy of freelance raiders from Syria, and the bands of Syrian raiders no longer invade the land of Israel.

6:25–29 The famine is such that a donkey's head or dove droppings become so expensive that only the rich can afford them. The price of five shekels of silver is more than a month's wages for a laborer. Mothers are so hungry that they even eat their own children. Deuteronomy 28 contains an extended section where God warns Israel about the curses that will come upon them if they reject the covenant He made with them. Part of that chapter describes the horrors fulfilled in this chapter.

6:30–33 The king is deeply grieved and angry—but not with himself, with Israel, or with their sin. The king is angry against the prophet of God—and with God Himself.

7:1 Though the king of Israel blames God for the calamity that came upon Israel and Samaria, God still has a word for the king and the nation—and it is a good word. God's promise through Elisha is that in twenty-four hours the economic situation in Samaria will be completely reversed. Instead of scarcity, there will be such abundance that food prices will radically drop in the city. By the standards of that time, the prices listed are not cheap, but they were nothing compared to the famine conditions associated with the siege.

7:2 The king's officer doubts the prophecy, and his doubt is based on several faulty premises. First, he doubts the power of God, that if God wills it, He can drop food from the sky. Then he doubts God's creativity, that He can bring provision in a completely unexpected way. Finally, he doubts the messenger of God who has an established track record of reliability. Through Elisha, God pronounces a harsh judgment upon the king's doubting officer. He will see the word fulfilled, but he will not benefit from its fulfillment.

7:3–4 The four stay at the entrance of the gate because they are not welcome in the city. Their leprous condition makes them outcasts and untouchables. Their logic is perfect. They will soon die from the famine if they stay in the city. If any food becomes available, they will certainly be the last to receive it. So they decide that their chances are better if they surrender to the Syrians.

7:6–7 Israel is powerless against this besieging army, but God isn't powerless. He attacks the Syrian army simply by causing them to hear noises of an army. Perhaps God does this by putting the noise into the air; perhaps He simply creates the perception of the noise in the minds of the Syrian soldiers. The same God who struck one Syrian army so they could not see what was there (6:18) now strikes another Syrian army so they hear things that are not there. As a result, the siege for Samaria is over—even though no one in the city knows it or enjoys it.

7:10–15 The lepers call to the porters (or gatekeepers) of the city. Since the lepers are not welcome in the city, they can only communicate with the porters. The good news from the lepers is communicated in the simplest way possible. It goes from one person to another, until the news reaches the king himself, whose officers go to check the accuracy of the report. This is the sensible reaction to the good news that started with the report of the lepers. The report might be true or it might not be; it only makes sense to test it and see.

7:16–18 When the good news is found to be true, there is no stopping the people. Because they know their need, they are happy to receive God's provision to meet that need. Through Elisha, God had announced the exact prices in the Samaritan markets, and the prophecy is proven to be precisely true.

8:1–3 Second Kings 4 describes Elisha's previous dealings with this woman—and her husband—godly, generous people who help the prophet. Through Elisha's prayer they were blessed with a son, who was also brought miraculously back to life. At the advice of the prophet, the woman and her family leave Israel because of a coming famine. In the land of the Philistines, they are spared the worst of the famine, but upon leaving Israel and going to the land of the Philistines, the woman forfeits her claim to her ancestral lands. To regain them requires intervention from the king.

8:4 The king is talking with Gehazi, the same servant of Elisha who was cursed with leprosy (5:20–27). It seems strange that a severely afflicted leper would be a counselor to a king, so it seems that either Gehazi is granted healing from his leprosy or this actually takes place before the events of chapter 5. Of course, it is still possible that the king has this conversation with Gehazi when he is a leper and the king simply keeps his distance.

8:7–9 The leaders of Syria had at one time tried to capture or kill Elisha. But since God has miraculously delivered the prophet so many times, he is now respected and welcome in the courts of the Syrian king. He is especially welcome on account of the king's illness. Wanting to know the outcome of his present illness, the king of Syria asks the prophet what will happen—and with his extravagant gift attempts to prompt a favorable message.

8:13–15 Perhaps Hazael had planned this assassination and simply pretends to be ignorant at Elisha's announcement. Perhaps he has not yet planned it and does not know the evil capabilities in his own heart. Either way, he should have taken this warning as an opportunity to confront himself and to do right, instead of turning an accusation back upon Elisha.

8:16, 21–24 It is easy to confuse the variation between Jehoram and Joram; but in this case, they are two variants of the same name. On the other hand, it's also easy to confuse Jehoram of Judah with King Jehoram of Israel, mentioned in chapter 3. That Jehoram is called Joram in verse 16.

8:19 God will not destroy Judah, for David's sake. The implication is that Jehoram's evil is great enough to justify such judgment, but God withholds it because of David's faithfulness.

8:20–22 The Edomite revolt against Judah is evidence of the weakness of the kingdom of Jehoram. He thinks that the marriage alliance with Ahab and the kingdom of Israel will make Judah stronger, but this act of disobedience only makes them weaker.

8:24 According to 2 Chronicles 21:12–15, Elijah writes Jehoram a letter condemning him for his sins and predicting that not only will judgment come upon him but also disaster will come upon the nation. At the age of forty, Jehoram is struck with a fatal intestinal disease, and he dies in terrible pain (2 Chronicles 21:19). The short life and reign of Jehoram (he reigns only eight years and dies at age forty) should have warned his son Ahaziah.

8:25–29 Ahaziah's brief reign (one year) shows he was even less blessed than his father. His close association with the wicked house of Ahab develops into a war alliance with Israel against Syria. His connection with his mother's family (she is a daughter of Ahab and Jezebel, 8:18) is so strong and sympathetic that he pays a visit to the injured and sick King Joram of Israel.

9:2–3 Though Israel has abandoned God, God has not abandoned Israel. He still has the right to interfere among them as described here. He will appoint and allow kings as He chooses, either to bless an obedient Israel or to curse a disobedient nation, according to the terms of His covenant with them at mount Sinai.

9:7–10 The young prophet's message about the destruction of Ahab's family is more than Elisha told him to say in 9:1–3. Either Elisha told him to say this and it was not recorded previously, or he came under the inspiration of the Spirit when he did what Elisha told him to do and spoke these words in spontaneous prophecy to Jehu. Clearly God intends to use Jehu as a tool of judgment against the royal house of Ahab.

9:14–18 Upon seeing the company of Jehu approaching, King Joram wants to know if this mysterious group comes in peace. As he waits to recover full strength in Jezreel, Joram is fundamentally insecure in his hold on the throne and easily suspects threats. Jehu's reply means that the soldier should not regard this as a time of peace but a time of conflict—a time to violently overthrow the throne of Joram and the dynasty he comes from.

9:19–20 When two messengers do not return but instead join the company of Jehu, it shows that he enjoys popular support among the troops of Israel, and King Joram does not. Jehu is such an intense man that his personality can be easily seen in the way he drives a chariot.

9:22–26 Jehu's condemnation of Jezebel shows that he takes his previous anointing by Elijah (1 Kings 19:16–17) and his more recent anointing by one from the school of the prophets seriously. Jehu's words as he has Joram's body dumped on Nabal's property confirm that Jehu sees himself as a fulfiller of God's will in bringing judgment on the house of Ahab. Jehu's mind is not filled with thoughts of political gain and royal glory. Rather, he acts as a conscious executor of divine judgment against the house of Ahab.

9:28 When Ahaziah is killed in battle, he receives a dignified burial—not for his own sake, but because his ancestor Jehoshaphat was a godly man (2 Chronicles 22:9).

9:30–31 Jezebel compares Jehu to Zimri, who assassinated King Baasha of Israel (1 Kings 16:9–12) when Zimri was a commander in Baasha's army. It is her way of calling Jehu a despicable rebel. It is also an implied threat, because the brief reign of Zimri was ended by Omri, the father of Ahab and the father-in-law of this same Jezebel. By implication, Jezebel is saying that the dynasty of Omri will defeat Jehu just like it defeated Zimri.

10:1–3 Ahab's seventy sons are a significant danger to the anointed King Jehu. First, they are the descendants of Ahab and have a great interest in battling to keep the throne of Israel among the dynasty of Omri. Second, they are in Samaria, the capital city of Israel—meaning they are away from Jehu, who killed King Joram in Jezreel. In light of all this, Jehu challenges any partisans of the house of Omri to declare themselves and prepare to fight for their master's house.

10:4–5 Having sent a challenge to those who might contest the throne, Jehu receives a message back from Ahab's sons promising not to put any of the princes on the throne as king.

10:6–8 Jehu's letter—and his previous bold action against Joram and Ahaziah—persuades the leaders of Israel to execute the sons of Ahab on behalf of Jehu. The nobles are so afraid of Jehu that they send grim evidence of their obedience: the princes' heads in a basket. Jehu doesn't ask for the severed heads on a whim. It is the custom in this era to display the heads of rebels at the city gate as a public warning against further rebellion.

10:12–14 Since Jehu is committed to execute all those connected with the house of Ahab, these men are also targets of judgment. Ahaziah is a descendant of King Ahab through his mother (who is the daughter of Ahab and Jezebel). Therefore, their mention of the queen mother does not help them. None of them escape. This is characteristic of Jehu—wholehearted and energetic obedience to his mission.

10:15 Jehonadab, the son of Rechab, was the mysterious founder of the Rechabites, a reform movement among the people of God protesting the immoral and impure lives of many in Israel and Judah. In Jeremiah 35, God uses the Rechabites and the memory of Jehonadab as an example of faithfulness and obedience to rebuke His unfaithful and disobedient people. Jehonadab is optimistic about Jehu as an energetic reformer, and Jehu is hungry for the approval of Jehonadab as a popular religious leader and reformer. As politics go, it would be reasonable to think that Jehu wants to use Jehonadab's influence to add legitimacy to his reign as king.

10:18–28 Jehu feigns devotion to Baal to lure the priests and worshippers of Baal into the temple, which is being used as a trap. Ahab had built this temple for his wife, Jezebel (1 Kings 16:32); Jehu tears it down. He works to completely eliminate the worship of Baal from Israel, making him a unique king among the other rulers of the northern kingdom.

10:29 Even though Jehu stood against the worshippers of Baal, he still promotes a false kind of worship of the true God. God had commanded His people not to make

any image to worship (Exodus 20:4). Here, however, after the pattern of Jeroboam, Jehu sets up the golden calves that had been at Bethel and Dan (1 Kings 12:28–32).

10:31–36 Though incomplete in his own goodness, Jehu is the best of a bad group, and his goodness is rewarded with a twenty-eight-year reign. This is a long reign, but it is notable only at its beginning. Jehu has the energy and influence to truly turn the nation back to God, but his half-commitment to God leaves that potential unfulfilled.

11:1 Athaliah is the daughter of Ahab and Jezebel and is given to Jehoram, king of Judah, as a bride. She is a bad influence on both her husband and her son (King Ahaziah of Judah). Here, she uses the occasion of her son's death to take power for herself. She is from the family of Ahab, and Jehu has completely destroyed all of Ahab's descendants in Israel. After Jehu's coup in chapter 10, Athaliah works to save something for Ahab's family by trying to eliminate the house of David in Judah.

11:2 Jehosheba, a little-known woman, had an important place in God's plan. Through her courage and ingenuity, she preserves one member of the royal line of David, the bloodline through which the Messiah will come. Evil people like Athaliah will begin their work, but God can always raise up a Jehosheba.

11:4 Jehoiada is a godly man who is concerned with restoring the throne of David to the line of David and taking it away from this daughter of Ahab and Jezebel. From the place—the temple—where Jehoiada charges the guards with an oath of loyalty, and from the context of the oath, we learn that the worship of the true God is not dead in Judah. These captains and bodyguards and escorts respond to their responsibility before the Lord.

11:5–12 It is a dramatic moment when Jehoiada brings out the young prince, Joash, secret heir to David's throne. Jehoiada chooses the sabbath for the day of the coup, because that is the day when the guards change their shifts, and they can assemble two groups of guards at the temple without attracting attention. It is fitting for these soldiers to use weapons that had belonged to King David himself.

11:13–14 For the usurper queen mother, the coronation of Joash was a horrifying sight. For six years, she believed there were no legitimate claimants to the throne of David. Now she sees that one son of Ahaziah—Joash, her own grandson—escaped her murderous intent.

11:15–16 The execution of Athaliah is both righteous and prudent. It is a just sentence against this woman who had murdered so many, and prudent precautions are taken so she cannot mount a resistance. As a priest, Jehoiada has a great concern for the sanctity and reputation of the temple, so Athaliah is not executed there but in the place where horses enter the palace grounds.

11:20 One reason the people resent the worship of Baal in Jerusalem is because, according to 2 Chronicles 24:7, Athaliah had directed that sacred objects from the temple of the Lord be relocated into the temple of Baal.

12:1–3 Jehoash, previously referred to as Joash (11:2), has a long and mostly blessed reign. He falls short of full commitment and complete godliness, but he does advance the cause of God in the kingdom of Judah.

12:4–5 There is regular income coming into the temple from several different sources—census, assessments or taxes, and voluntary gifts. King Jehoash wants to put that money toward a particular purpose: repairing the temple. The temple needed restoration because it had been vandalized by Athaliah and her sons (2 Chronicles 24:7). It would be natural for Jehoash to have a high regard for the condition of the temple, because it was his home as a young boy (see 11:3).

12:6–9 King Jehoash has to wait a very long time until the damages of the temple are repaired. The work is going far too slowly; the priests and the Levites have taken the money for their own use. Under the direction of King Jehoash, the priests give the people the opportunity to give.

12:10–16 King Jehoash gets to the heart of the problem—poor administration and financial misman-agement. Through Jehoiada the priest, he implements a system where the money will be set aside, saved, and then wisely spent for the repair and refurbishing of the temple. Through good administration of the project, they are able to find men who can be trusted to use the money wisely and honestly. In the end, the project succeeds without taking anything away from the priests. They still receive money from the trespass offerings and sin offerings.

12:17–19 The kingdom of Syria attacks Judah. Instead of trusting God, Jehoash trades prior blessing—the sacred treasures of the temple—to protect his capital and kingdom against the attacking Syrians. There is no record of repentance on Jehoash's part.

12:20–21 The officers' conspiracy against Jehoash is startling, and it shows that the blessing of God had long before vanished from the compromised king who began so well but failed to finish well.

13:1–3 Jehoahaz follows in the footsteps of both Jeroboam and his father, Jehu—two wicked kings. So the Lord delivers the kingdom of Israel into the hand of Hazael, king of Syria. Israel retains its own name and king, but it is a tributary and subservient nation to Syria. In the general history of this time, the Assyrian Empire kept the Syrians weak and unable to expand their domain into Israel. But there was a period when internal problems made the Assyrians bring back their troops from the frontiers of their empire, and the Syrians took advantage of this time of Assyrian distraction.

13:4–5 Jehoahaz is an ungodly man, and his prayer does not mark a lasting or real revival in his life. Yet God listens to his prayer because of His great mercy and because of His care for Israel. The identity of the deliverer in verse 5 is unknown.

13:6–7 Though God answers their prayer and sends a deliverer, Israel continues in their false worship of the true God. Israel's repentance is only halfhearted; they repent because they suffer rather than because they regret their sin.

13:10–11 Jehoash is the grandson of King Jehu, founder of this dynasty. He continues in the same sins as his father.

13:14 King Jehoash's response to Elisha's illness might seem strange since he does not have a reputation as a godly king. Keep in mind, however, that Jehoash is not a worshipper of false gods; he is a false worshipper of the true God. He has some respect for the true God and therefore some regard and honor for Elisha.

13:15–17 Jehoash is concerned that the true strength of Israel is about to depart from this earth. Therefore, Elisha uses this illustration of the arrow shot through the window to show him that the arrow of the Lord's deliverance is still present, and all Jehoash has to do is shoot the arrow in faith. Elisha makes it clear that there is a connection between the shooting of the arrows toward the east and a strike against the Syrians that will bring deliverance to Israel.

13:18–19 The phrase *smite upon* the ground can be used for arrows hitting the ground. Elisha asks Jehoash to shoot the arrows through the window at no particular target, not to pound them on the floor. Jehoash timidly receives this invitation. He shoots three arrows and stops, not sensing what he should—that the arrows represent victories in battle over the Syrians. Because King Jehoash does not seize the strategic moment, Israel will enjoy only three victories over the Syrian army instead of the many more they could have enjoyed.

13:21 There is little explanation for the resurrection of the corpse that touches the bones of Elisha. The silence of the record suggests that there is not inherent power in the bones of Elisha to resuscitate others. This seems to be a onetime miracle bringing honor to the memory of this great prophet.

13:24–25 Elisha had promised Jehoash these three victories over the Syrians (13:15–19). We can suppose that, especially after the third victory, King Jehoash wished he had shot more arrows through the window at the invitation of Elisha, since for every arrow he shot he would have won a victory.

14:5 Amaziah's execution of the servants who had murdered his father eliminates those who would find the assassination of the king a reasonable way to change the kingdom. It is the standard practice of the ancient world to execute not only the guilty party in such a murder but also their family. Amaziah goes against the conventional practice of his day and obeys the word of God instead (see Genesis 9:5–7; Deuteronomy 24:16).

14:7 Amaziah's victory over the Edomites shows the military might of Amaziah and that he successfully subdues the weaker nations surrounding Judah. Second Chronicles 25:5–16 gives more background to the battle against the Edomites. Amaziah gathers a huge army in Judah to go against Edom (three hundred thousand). He also hires one hundred thousand mercenary soldiers from Israel. But a prophet comes and warns him not to use the soldiers from Israel, because God is not with that rebellious and idolatrous kingdom. Amaziah is convinced to trust God, send the mercenaries from Israel away, and accept the loss of the money used to hire them. God blesses this step of faith and gives them a convincing victory over the Edomites.

14:8 Proud from his success against Edom, Amaziah decides to make war against the northern kingdom of Israel. He has reason to believe he will be successful. He had recently assembled an army of three hundred thousand men that killed twenty thousand Edomites in a victory over Edom (2 Chronicles 25:5, 11–12).

14:9–18 The reply of Jehoash, king of Israel, is both wise and diplomatic. He counsels Amaziah to glory in his previous victory over Edom but then to stay at home. Instead, Amaziah provokes a fight he should have avoided and does not consider the effect his defeat will have on the whole kingdom.

14:19–20 The embarrassing loss against Israel undermines Amaziah's support among Judah's leaders. He flees to Lachish, but he meets a similar end to that of his father—assassination (12:20–21).

14:23–25 King Jeroboam II of Israel is a wicked king who continues the politically motivated idolatry of his namesake, Jeroboam the son of Nebat. During his reign, the prophets Jonah and Amos spoke for God. This is almost certainly the same Jonah who is famous for his missionary trip to Nineveh.

14:26–28 The reign of Jeroboam II is a time of prosperity for Israel because of God's mercy. Around the year 800 BC, the mighty Assyrian Empire defeated Syria and neutralized this power that hindered Israel's expansion and prosperity. With Syria in check, Israel can prosper.

14:29 Zachariah, Jeroboam's son, succeeds to the throne after his father's death. It was prophesied that the dynasty of Jehu would continue for four generations—Zachariah is the fourth generation (10:30).

15:1–4 Azariah is also called Uzziah in 15:13 and many other places in 2 Kings, 2 Chronicles, and Isaiah. His reign is largely characterized by the good he does. His godliness is rewarded with a long reign of fifty-two years. As with Jehoash (12:3) and Amaziah (14:4), however, the reforms of Azariah do not reach so far as to remove the traditional places of sacrifice. Second Chronicles tells us much more about the successful reign of Azariah (2 Chronicles 26:5–15).

15:5–7 Azariah comes into the temple as an arrogant king, and he leaves—indeed, he hurries to get out, because the Lord has struck him (2 Chronicles 26:16–21)—as a humbled leper. And so he is to the day he dies.

15:8–10 The reign of Zachariah is both short and wicked. He continues in the state-sponsored idolatry begun by Jeroboam. Zachariah is so despised by his own people that Shallum assassinates him in public. This is the end of the dynasty of Jehu, which began with such potential but ends (as God has foretold) in great darkness.

15:13–15 Shallum's reign is even briefer than Zachariah's—four weeks. The violence that marks Shallum's rise to and fall from power shows that he does not reign with the blessing of God.

15:16–21 When Menahem's enemies fail to surrender, his soldiers rip open the pregnant women. This brutal act is commanded by Menahem himself—the next king of Israel. Menahem's reign is evil and a continuation of the state-sponsored idolatry of Jeroboam. He puts the kingdom of Israel under tribute to the Assyrian Empire, purchasing the backing of the Assyrian king with money raised from the wealthy people in his kingdom. Therefore he rules with the strength of Assyria supporting him.

15:22–26 The two kings of Israel who ruled before Menahem do not establish any kind of dynasty to pass to a son. Menahem rules well enough to pass the kingdom to Pekahiah. The blessing of God is obviously not on Pekahiah, whose reign ends with assassination after only two years.

15:32–34 King Jotham of Judah does what is right in the sight of the Lord. This stands in strong contrast to the evil done by the kings mentioned in the previous chapters of 2 Kings.

15:35 Though the high places still exist, work is accomplished on the temple. Throughout Israel's history, when kings and leaders are concerned about the house of the Lord, it reflects some measure of spiritual revival. Jotham's father, Azariah (Uzziah), had misunderstood the link between the royal house and the house of God, demanding to hold the authority not simply of a king but of a priest (2 Chronicles 26:16–21). Many kings before him wanted no link between the royal house and the house of God. Jotham understands that he is a king and not a priest, yet he wants a good, open link between the palace and the temple. The building of this link is one of the chief ways that he prepares his way before God.

15:36–38 Judah begins to be chastened for their partial obedience. It is the hand of the Lord that sends foreign rulers.

16:5 King Pekah of Israel joins forces with King Rezin of Syria against Judah. This is part of Pekah's anti-Assyria policy. He thinks that with Judah defeated, Syria and Israel together can more effectively resist the resurgent power of the Assyrian Empire. The combined armies of Syria and Israel are strong enough to capture many cities of Judah but not strong enough to defeat Jerusalem and overthrow the government of Ahaz. Judah suffers terrible losses from this attack. King Ahaz loses 120,000 Judean soldiers and 200,000 civilian hostages in these battles with Israel and Syria (2 Chronicles 28:5–8). It is a dark time for Judah, and it looks as if the dynasty of David will soon be extinguished, as so many dynasties in the northern kingdom of Israel had ended.

16:6 According to the 2 Chronicles account of this event, these captives were taken to Samaria (the capital city of the northern kingdom of Israel) and kept there until a prophet named Oded calls on the army to return them to Judah. The leaders in Israel respond, realizing that they have already offended the Lord and risk offending Him even further. So they clothe and feed the captives (who had before this been treated terribly) and return them to Judah (2 Chronicles 28:8–15).

16:7–9 Ahaz sends messengers to Tiglath-pileser, king of Assyria, asking for help. In this way, he surrenders to one enemy in order to defeat another. He refuses to trust in the God of Israel and instead submits himself and his kingdom to an enemy of Israel.

16:10–13 Ahaz serves as a priest at the altar of his own design, showing a direct disregard for God's commands regarding priests (see Numbers 18:7). Urijah not only allows Ahaz to do this, but he participates. Ahaz's grandfather Azariah (also known as Uzziah) dared to enter the temple and serve God as a priest (2 Chronicles 26). Yet at least Azariah falsely worshipped the true God (by using idols). In this case, Ahaz falsely worships a false god of his own creation.

16:14–18 Ahaz cannot bring in his pagan, corrupt innovations without also removing what had stood before at the temple—this is an ungodly exchange, taking away the good and putting in the bad—including the king's outer entrance built in the days of his father, King Jotham. Collectively, all these things serve to discourage the worship of the true God. All this takes place at the temple Solomon built for the Lord, but the location does not make it true worship.

17:1–2 We last saw Hoshea, in 15:30, as the man who led a conspiracy against Pekah, the king of Israel. After the successful assassination, Hoshea takes the throne and starts his own brief dynasty. Though he is an evil man, he is by no means the worst of the kings of Israel. It is during his reign, however, that the kingdom of Israel is effectively destroyed. This reminds us that judgment may not come at the height of sin. The actual events of judgment may come after the worst is over.

17:3–4 In the pattern of King Menahem before him (15:17–22), Hoshea accepts the status of vassal or servant unto the king of Assyria. As is typical of the politics of the day, if he pays his tribute money and does as king of Assyria pleases, he will be allowed to continue on the throne of Israel. King Hoshea hopes to find help among the Egyptians, who are in a constant power struggle with the Assyrian Empire. Because of this conspiracy against his oppressor, and the failure to pay the yearly tribute money, Hoshea is imprisoned by the king of Assyria.

17:5–6 The king of Assyria embarks on a long, dedicated campaign to crush the rebellious kingdom of Israel that had defied the power of the Assyrian Empire. Though it takes three years, it is worth it to the Assyrians. When Samaria finally falls and the northern kingdom is conquered, the Assyrians implement their typical policy toward conquered nations: They deport all but the very lowest classes back to the key cities of their own empire to utilize the talented or to enslave the able. When the Assyrians depopulate and exile a conquered community, they lead the captives away on journeys of hundreds of miles, with the captives naked and attached to one another with a system of strings and fishhooks pierced

through their lower lips (see Amos 4:2–3).

17:7 The fundamental reason for the conquering and captivity of the northern kingdom, at the root, is a problem with sin rather than geopolitical changes or social causes. First, they had feared other gods. In the central act of redemption in Old Testament history, God brought Israel up out of the land of Egypt. Remembrance of this act alone should prompt Israel to uphold a single-hearted commitment to the Lord. Yet they do not remember this and instead fear other gods, breaking the covenant God made with His people.

17:8–15 Included in a list of accusations against Israel is the charge that they conformed themselves to the godless nations around them. Before Israel occupied Canaan in the days of Joshua, the promised land was populated by degenerate, pagan peoples who practiced the worst kinds of idolatry and human sacrifice. One of the fundamental sins of Israel was that they followed in these ancient Canaanite ways. God cast out the Canaanite nations in the days of Joshua because of these sins. Now He has cast out the northern kingdom of Israel for the same sins. God's judgment is not against the ancient Canaanites because of race or ethnicity; it is because of their conduct.

17:16–17 The two calves mentioned here refer to the infamous sin of Jeroboam (1 Kings 12:26–29). This state-sponsored idolatry does not immediately ruin the kingdom—the northern kingdom of Israel lasts as an independent nation for another two hundred years following the time of Jeroboam. Yet it certainly was the beginning of the end.

17:18–23 When the kingdom finally falls, the people are dispersed by the Assyrians. Some assimilate into other cultures, but others keep their Jewish identity as exiles in other lands. The ten northern tribes are lost in terms of their existence as a separate entity. According to 2 Chronicles 11:13–16, however, when the nation started to fall away from God in the days of Jeroboam, the legitimate priests and Levites who lived in the northern ten tribes moved from the northern kingdom of Israel to the southern kingdom of Judah so that they could keep their faith pure. In the end, then, the southern kingdom of Judah contained Israelites from all of the tribes.

17:24–27 The typical policy of the Assyrian Empire is to remove rebellious, resistant people and to resettle the lands of those people with Assyrian citizens from other parts of the empire. In this case, God defends the land against these newcomers with lions. God demands to be feared among the people of the land, even if they come from other nations. Though Assyria responds, any faith in God among these resettled people is founded in simple fear of the lions.

17:28–34 This nameless, corrupt priest teaches the new inhabitants of the land a corrupt religion. The new residents of Israel give a measure of respect to the God of Israel, yet they also serve their own gods and pick and choose among religious and spiritual beliefs as they please (as was typical of this historical era). This mixed religion first promoted by the Assyrians continues for many centuries in Samaria, existing even until New Testament times.

17:35–41 The basis of God's covenant with His people is a purity of worship. Had the kingdom adhered to its part of the covenant, it would still stand. Theirs was an act of self-destruction.

18:1 Hezekiah comes to the throne of Judah as the kingdom of Israel is ending. Three years after the start of his reign, the Assyrian armies lay siege to Samaria, and three years after that the northern kingdom is conquered. The sad fate of the northern kingdom is a valuable lesson to Hezekiah. He sees firsthand what happens when the people of God reject their God.

18:3–8 Hezekiah's unique passion and energy are even more remarkable in light of the fact that his father, Ahaz, was one of the worst kings to have reigned in Judah (16:10–20).

18:14–16 Hezekiah's tribute to Assyria reveals a clear lack of faith on his part. He feels it is wiser to pay off the Assyrian king and become his subject than it is to trust God to defend Judah against this mighty king. Hezekiah hopes that this policy of appeasement will make Judah safe. He is wrong, and his policy only impoverishes Judah and the temple and makes the king of Assyria bolder than ever against Judah.

18:17–18 *Rab-shakeh* is not a name but a title. It describes the field commander of the Assyrian army, who represents the Assyrian king Sennacherib and is translated "chief of staff" by some. The Rab-shakeh seems to be in complete command of the situation. He is able to walk right into the city of Jerusalem and stand at the crucial water supply—which is Jerusalem's lifeline in a siege attack.

18:19–21 Instead of trusting the Lord, Hezekiah has put his hope in an alliance with Egypt, and the Rab-shakeh wants him to lose confidence in that alliance. In this way, he makes an attempt at demoralizing Judah and driving them to despair. The Rab-shakeh can see the truth of Egypt's weakness better than many of the leaders of Judah can.

18:23–24 The Rab-shakeh's whole strategy is to make Judah give up. He had the superior army—he could have just attacked Jerusalem without this speech. But the Rab-shakeh prefers Judah to surrender out of fear, discouragement, or despair. His basic message is, "We could beat you with one hand tied behind our backs!"

18:25 The Rab-shakeh's lowest blow is a spiritual one, claiming Hezekiah's God is on Assyria's side. Since at this time God's favor was often measured by an army's success, it might have been easy for Hezekiah and his men to believe this. After all, hadn't the Assyrians been wildly successful, and didn't they have the most powerful army?

18:26–27 Since he is speaking in Hebrew, everyone can understand what the Rab-shakeh is saying. The request for him to speak in Aramaic goes against his

mission. The more fear, discouragement, and despair he can spread, the better.

18:28–34 This speech is intended to glorify the enemy facing God's people, to make God's people doubt their leaders, to build fear and unbelief in God's people, and to make surrender an attractive option. He refers to the policies of ethnic cleansing and forced resettlement practiced by the Assyrians. When they conquer a people, they forcibly resettle them in faraway places, to keep their spirits broken and their power weak. The Rab-shakeh's speech is intended to make this terrible fate seem attractive.

18:35 The final point of the speech is intended to destroy the people's trust in God. His message is simple: "The gods of other nations have not been able to protect them against us. Your God can't protect you either." Anyone in Judah who had the spiritual understanding to see it could have started planning the victory party right then. It is one thing to speak against Judah, its people, and its leaders; it is another thing altogether to mock the God of Israel this way and count Him as just another god. With this statement, the Rab-shakeh simply oversteps his bounds.

19:1–2 The tearing of clothes and the wearing of sackcloth (a rough, burlap-type material) are expressions of deep mourning, usually for the death of a loved one. Hezekiah takes this report regarding the Rab-shakeh seriously, knowing how dedicated this enemy is to completely conquering Jerusalem. Understanding this, he turns to the Lord through the temple and the prophet.

19:3 Hezekiah's image is one of disaster—a woman so exhausted by labor that she cannot complete the birth.

19:5–7 Isaiah's prophecy will be entirely provable. Either it will happen or it will not happen. Isaiah will be known as either a true prophet or a false prophet. Significantly, in this initial word from the prophet Isaiah, there is no mention of Jerusalem's deliverance or the defeat of the Assyrian army. God focuses this word against the Rab-shakeh personally.

19:10–13 In his letter, the Rab-shakeh repeats his earlier mistake. In counting the true God of Israel among the gods of the nations, the Rab-shakeh again blasphemes the Lord and invites judgment.

19:14–15 As recorded in Isaiah 37:16, Hezekiah also uses another title when he addresses God: "Lord of hosts." This title for God essentially means "Lord of armies." Hezekiah is in a crisis that is primarily military in nature, so it makes sense for him to address God first according to the aspect of God's nature that is most needful for him. In recognizing God as Creator, Hezekiah sees that God has all power and all rights over every created thing—including Assyria and the Rab-shakeh.

19:17–19 In his prayer, King Hezekiah draws the contrast between the living God and the false gods of the nations the Assyrians had already conquered. Those false gods are not gods but the work of human hands, so they are not able to save them from the Assyrians. But Hezekiah prays confidently that the living God will save them, that all the kingdoms of the earth may know that He alone is God.

19:27–28 This is an especially dramatic statement, because the kind of treatment described here is exactly how the Assyrians cruelly march those whom they force to relocate out of their conquered lands. They line up the captives and drive a large fishhook through the lip or the nose of each captive, stringing them all together. God will do the same to the Assyrians.

19:29 The invasion has interfered with planting crops, but the Lord promises that enough will grow on its own to provide for the people until they can plant again.

19:30–34 In ancient times, when a city was under siege, it was surrounded by a hostile army and trapped into a slow, suffering starvation. King Hezekiah and the people of Jerusalem lived under the shadow of this threat, but God's promise through Isaiah assures them that Sennacherib and the Assyrian army not only will fail to capture the city but won't even begin a siege.

19:37 Between this verse and the previous one, twenty years pass. Perhaps Sennacherib thought he had escaped the judgment of God, but he hadn't. He meets death at the end of swords held by his own sons.

20:1 We are not told how Hezekiah becomes sick. We do know from comparing 18:2 with 20:6 that Hezekiah is thirty-nine years old when he learns he will soon die.

20:2–3 Hezekiah lived under the old covenant, and at that time there was no confident assurance of the glory in the life beyond. Also, under the old covenant, Hezekiah would have regarded his fatal illness as evidence that God was displeased with him.

20:6 God gives two gifts to Hezekiah: the gift of an extended life and the gift of knowing he only has fifteen years left. The latter gift gives King Hezekiah the motivation to walk rightly with God and to set his house in order. The fact that God answers Hezekiah's prayer is a reminder that when God announces judgment, it is almost always an invitation to repent and to receive mercy.

20:9–11 God shows even more mercy to Hezekiah with this promise to make the shadow on the sundial move backward instead of forward. This is a wonderfully appropriate sign for Hezekiah. By bringing the shadow of the sundial backward, God gives more time in the day—just as God gave Hezekiah more time to live.

20:14–15 Isaiah probably already knows the answers to the questions he asks Hezekiah. This is Hezekiah's opportunity to answer honestly (which he does) and to see his error himself (which he apparently does not). It seems that Hezekiah is proud to tell Isaiah all this, missing the point of the conversation.

20:16–18 Hezekiah thinks that this display of wealth (20:13) will impress the Babylonians, but it simply shows the Babylonians what can be stolen from Judah. Worse than taking the material riches of the kings of Judah, the king of Babylon will take the sons of the king of Judah. This prophecy is fulfilled under the Babylonian king Nebuchadnezzar (24:10–13; 25:11–17). It is at this time that Daniel and his companions are taken into captivity (Daniel 1:1–4). Because of the promise in verse 18, many think that Daniel and his companions are made eunuchs when they are taken to serve in the palace.

20:20 Hezekiah builds an aqueduct to ensure fresh water inside the city walls even during sieges. The tunnel bringing water into the city is an amazing engineering feat. It is more than 650 yards long through solid rock, begun on each end and meeting in the middle. It can still be seen today, and it empties into the pool of Siloam.

20:21 There is no doubt that Hezekiah starts out as a godly king, and overall his reign is one of outstanding godliness (18:3–7). Yet his beginning is much better than his end; Hezekiah does not finish well. God gave Hezekiah the gift of fifteen more years of life, but the added years do not make him a better or godlier man.

21:1–3 Manasseh is twelve years old when he becomes king. This means that he is born in the last fifteen years of Hezekiah's life, the additional fifteen years that Hezekiah prayed for. Those additional fifteen years bring Judah one of its worst kings. Manasseh's reign is both remarkably long and remarkably evil.

21:4–6 Manasseh doesn't only allow idol worship in Judah; he also corrupts the worship of the true God at the temple and makes it a place of idol altars, including those dedicated to his astrological worship. He sacrifices his own son to the Canaanite god Molech, who is worshipped with the burning of children, and he invites direct satanic influence by his approval and introduction of occult arts.

21:11 The Amorites were among the Canaanite tribes who populated the promised land before Israel captured it, and they were infamous for their violent, immoral, and depraved culture. The accusation that Manasseh acts more wickedly than these people is a severe one.

21:16 Manasseh persecutes the people of God. This puts Manasseh, king of Judah, in the same spiritual family as Ahab, king of Israel. Under both of these kings—among others—the people of God are persecuted by the religion of state-sponsored idolatry. The extent of it is so great that it can be metaphorically said that Manasseh filled Jerusalem from one end to another with the blood of his victims.

21:17–18 Second Chronicles 33:11–19 describes a remarkable repentance on the part of Manasseh. Because he and his people will not listen to the warnings of God, the Lord allows the Babylonians to bind King Manasseh and take him as a captive to Babylon. There he humbles himself before God, and God answers his prayer and restores him to the throne. Manasseh then proves that his repentance is genuine by taking away the idols and the foreign gods from Jerusalem. This is a wonderful example of Proverbs 22:6. Manasseh was raised by a godly father, yet he lived in defiance of his father's faith for most of his life. Nevertheless, at the end of his days, he truly repents and serves God. In this way, we can say that it is true that Manasseh rests with his fathers.

21:19–26 Amon's unusually short reign is an indication that the blessing of God is not upon it. Amon sins as Manasseh had sinned, but without repentance. This story of conspiracy and assassination seems more like something that would happen among the kings of Israel, not Judah. Yet when the kings and people of Judah begin to imitate the sins of their conquered northern neighbors, they slip into the same chaos and anarchy that mark the last period of the northern kingdom's history.

22:1–7 The young King Josiah comes to the throne at eight years of age because of the assassination of his father, Amon. Josiah understood that the work of repairing and rebuilding the temple needed organization and funding. He paid attention to both of these needs when he commanded Hilkiah to begin the work on the temple.

22:8 The fact that Hilkiah has to find the book of the law makes it clear that it has been lost. According to Deuteronomy 31:24–27, there was to be a copy of the book of the law beside the ark of the covenant, beginning in the days of Moses. The Word of God was with Israel, but it was greatly neglected in those days. This neglect could only happen because Judah was in prolonged disobedience to God.

22:12–13 King Josiah knows that the kingdom of Judah deserves judgment from God. He cannot hear the Word of God and respond to the Spirit of God without seriously confronting the sin of his kingdom.

22:14 We know little of Huldah the prophetess other than this mention here (and the similar account recorded in 2 Chronicles 34:22). With the apparent approval of King Josiah, Hilkiah the priest consults this woman for spiritual guidance. She is not sought out because of her own wisdom and spirituality, but she is recognized as a prophetess and can reveal the heart and mind of God.

22:15–17 Judah and its leaders have walked against God for too long and will not genuinely repent so as to avoid eventual judgment. God's Word is true, even in its promises of judgment. God's faithfulness is demonstrated as much by His judgment upon the wicked as it is by His mercy upon the repentant.

23:1 Josiah hears the promise of both eventual judgment (22:16) and the immediate delay of judgment (22:20). He does not respond with indifference or simple contentment that he will not see the judgment in his day. He wants to get the kingdom right with God, and he knows that he can't do it by himself—he needs all the elders of Judah to join in broken repentance with him.

23:2–3 Josiah is so concerned that the nation hear the Word of God that he reads it to them himself. We do not read of any command for the people to stand to the covenant; it is clearly the work of God among the people, but God works through the example and leadership of King Josiah.

23:4–6 There are idols dedicated to Baal, to Asherah, and to all the host of heaven in the very temple itself. Throwing the ashes of the idols on the graves outside the city is not intended to defile the graves. Any contact with

death was believed to be an act of defilement, so scattering the dust on the graves serves to defile the idols.

23:5–9 From this account, it seems that Josiah begins the cleansing reforms at the center and works outward. Josiah's reforms remove not only sinful things but also the sinful people who promote and permit these sinful things. The idols that fill the temple do not get there or stay there on their own—idolatrous priests are responsible for these sinful practices.

23:10–15 The official idolatry in Judah is widespread, elaborate, and heavily invested in. Previous kings of Judah had spent a lot of time and money to honor these pagan idols. King Josiah even takes down altars located in the former kingdom of Israel. He removes the pagan altar at Bethel that Jeroboam set up hundreds of years earlier.

23:16–20 This is the remarkable fulfillment of a prophecy made hundreds of years earlier, recorded in 1 Kings 13:1–2. Josiah is careful to honor the gravestone of this anonymous prophet, but he executes the pagan priests.

23:21–23 The celebration of the passover had become so neglected that this was a remarkable observance. Passover remembers the central act of redemption in the Old Testament: God's deliverance of Israel from Egypt in the days of Moses. The neglect of passover proves that this nation had neglected to remember God's work of redemption for them. It would be like a group of modern Christians completely forgetting the celebration of the Lord's Supper, which remembers Jesus' work of redemption for us.

23:29 The alliance between Egypt and Assyria is part of the geopolitical struggle between the declining Assyrian Empire and the emerging Babylonian Empire. The Assyrians make an alliance with the Egyptians to protect against the growing power of the Babylonians.

23:31–37 The reforms of King Josiah are not long lasting. After the defeat of King Josiah in battle, the Egyptian pharaoh is able to dominate Judah and make it effectively a vassal kingdom and a buffer between Egypt and the growing Babylonian Empire. He imposes on the land a tribute, imprisons King Jehoahaz, and puts on the throne of Judah a puppet king, Eliakim (renamed Jehoiakim), a brother of Jehoahaz.

24:1 Nebuchadnezzar, king of the Babylonian Empire, is concerned with Judah because of its strategic position in relation to the empires of Egypt and Assyria. Therefore it is important to him to conquer Judah and make it a subject kingdom (his vassal), securely loyal to Babylon. This happens in 605 BC, and it is the first (but not the last) encounter between Nebuchadnezzar and Jehoiakim. There will be two later invasions (597 and 587 BC). This specific attack is documented by the Babylonian Chronicles, a collection of tablets discovered as early as 1887 and held in the British Museum. Excavations also document the victory of Nebuchadnezzar over the Egyptians at Carchemish. Archaeologists found evidences of battle, vast quantities of arrowheads, layers of ash, and a shield of a Greek mercenary fighting for the Egyptians. The campaign is interrupted suddenly when Nebuchadnezzar hears of his father's death and races back to Babylon to secure his succession to the throne. He travels about five hundred miles in two weeks—remarkable speed in that day. Nebuchadnezzar only has the time to take a few choice captives (such as Daniel), a few treasures, and a promise of submission from Jehoiakim—which doesn't last.

24:2–6 It might seem that God will honor the Judean independence movement of Jehoiakim, but He does not bless it. Jehoiakim is a patriot of the kingdom of Judah but not a man submitted to God. The various peoples mentioned in verse 2 are probably allies who are willing to join the fight.

24:7 In the geopolitical struggle between Egypt and Babylon, Nebuchadnezzar of Babylon defeats the army of Egypt and then becomes the dominant power in that part of the world.

24:8–9 Jehoiachin succeeds his father, Jehoiakim. He carries on in the tradition of the wicked kings of Judah.

24:10–12 The previous king of Judah, Jehoiakim, had led a rebellion against Nebuchadnezzar. Jehoiachin hopes to appease Nebuchadnezzar by submitting himself, his family, and his leaders to the Babylonian king. But God allows Jehoiachin to be taken as a bound captive back to Babylon.

24:13 Some ancient traditions tell us that Jeremiah hides the ark of the covenant before the temple is looted, so that it is not among the things that are cut up and carried back to Babylon.

24:14–16 Nebuchadnezzar takes captive anyone with any skills or abilities. Among these captives is the prophet Ezekiel, who compiles his book of prophecies while in captivity in Babylon.

24:17 Nebuchadnezzar thinks Mattaniah will submit to Babylon, so he chooses him as leader and changes his name to Zedekiah, which means "the Lord is righteous." Zedekiah is an uncle of Jehoiachin and a brother to Jehoiakim.

24:18–19 Second Chronicles 36:11–20 tells us more of the evil of Zedekiah, specifically that he does not listen to Jeremiah or other messengers of God. Instead, he mocks and disregards the message.

25:1–3 When Nebuchadnezzar attacks Jerusalem, he uses the common method of attack in those days of securely walled cities. A siege, as described here, was intended to surround a city, prevent all business and trade from entering or leaving, and eventually starve the population into surrender. After a year and a half, Nebuchadnezzar and the Babylonians are at the point of victory over Jerusalem.

25:4–5 King Zedekiah makes a last-chance effort to escape the grip of the nearly successful siege—a secret break through the city walls and the siege lines of the Babylonians. He gets a considerable distance from Jerusalem before the enemy army overtakes him in the plains of Jericho.

25:6–7 The Babylonians are not known to be as cruel as the Assyrians, who conquered the northern kingdom of Israel some 150 years earlier, yet they make certain that the last sight King Zedekiah sees is the murder of his own sons. Zedekiah's capture fulfills the mysterious promise God makes through Ezekiel regarding Zedekiah shortly before the fall of Jerusalem (Ezekiel 12:13).

25:8–10 The captain of Nebuchadnezzar's guard returns to Jerusalem and sets fire to the temple. It will stay a ruin for many years, until it is humbly rebuilt by the returning exiles in the days of Ezra. He also destroys the walls of Jerusalem—the physical security of the city. Jerusalem is no longer a place of safety and security. The walls will remain a ruin until they are rebuilt in the days of Nehemiah.

25:11–17 This is the third major wave of captivity, taking all the remaining people, except for the poor of the land, as well as the remaining valuables from the temple. Jerusalem is completely plundered.

25:18–21 The last leaders of Jerusalem and Judah are captured and put to death. The tribes of Israel had possessed this land for some 860 years; they took it by faith and obedience, but they lose it through idolatry and sin.

25:22–24 The king of Babylon has made Gedaliah governor in what remains of Judah. Gedaliah is a friend of the prophet Jeremiah (see Jeremiah 26:24; 39:14). He advises the people to live peacefully and serve the king of Babylon. It seems unpatriotic and perhaps ungodly to do this, but it is the best they can do in this situation of deserved and unstoppable judgment. The Babylonians are doing the work of God in bringing this judgment upon the deserving kingdom of Judah. Here to resist the Babylonians is to resist God. The situation greatly bothers the prophet Habakkuk. Even though Judah is wicked and deserves judgment, how can God use an even more wicked kingdom like Babylon to bring judgment? Habakkuk deals with these difficult questions in Habakkuk 1:5–2:8.

25:24 The Chaldees are representative of the Babylonians as a whole, since the territory of Chaldea is the largest of the Babylonian territories.

25:25–26 Because Gedaliah submits to the Babylonians (here referred to as the Chaldees), he is seen as a traitor to the resistance movement and is thus assassinated.

25:27–30 Jehoiachin had previously been taken away to Babylon in bronze fetters (24:10–12). These last events of the book of 2 Kings occur after Jehoiachin has been a captive for many years. The book of 2 Kings ends with the smallest hopeful note—simply that King Jehoiachin begins to receive better treatment in Babylon. For the writer of this book, this small thing is evidence that God is not done blessing and restoring His people, foreshadowing even greater blessing and restoration to come.

THE FIRST BOOK OF THE

CHRONICLES

INTRODUCTION TO 1 CHRONICLES ■ In the Hebrew, 1 and 2 Chronicles are one single book. The title means "the events of the times." The book of 1 Chronicles covers the same time period and many of the same events as portions of 1 and 2 Samuel and the first chapters of 1 Kings, but it has a unique perspective. While the books of Samuel and Kings focus more on the political history of Israel and Judah, the Chronicles dwell more on the religious history and stay focused primarily on Judah. The information included in the Chronicles helps the people of Judah understand their history so they can live well in the present.

AUTHOR ■ Many scholars believe that Ezra wrote 1 and 2 Chronicles, which is quite possible. The book of 2 Chronicles flows smoothly into the book of Ezra, and the time frame (450 to 430 BC) is reasonable. However, the author's identity cannot be proven beyond reasonable doubt, so it has become traditional to refer to him as "the Chronicler."

OCCASION ■ The Israelites are captives of a powerful foreign empire, but some of the citizens are being allowed to return home. Their current status seems uncertain, so the Chronicler goes back to Adam (1:1) and reviews their history up to the current time (2 Chronicles 26:23). In doing so, he supports his outlook with various citations from the books of law, the Psalms, the prophetic books, and other sources. His repeated emphasis is on the covenants, the temple, and other reminders of how God has always provided for and delivered His people. As they look to return home and rebuild the temple that the Babylonians left in ruins, the Chronicler wants to assure them that God will continue to be with them.

1:1–9:44 The first nine chapters of 1 Chronicles cover a number of genealogies going all the way back to Adam. While such lists of family histories are sometimes perceived to be insignificant (or even boring) to modern readers, the Hebrew mind-set was quite different. Such lists helped define who the Hebrews were as a people and were a reminder of the blessings of their past. In particular for this group of exiles returning home, the genealogies grounded them in their history.

1:1–27 When approaching any section of biblical genealogy, many people automatically assume it will be dry and essentially meaningless. However, God does not place anything in His Word that is unimportant. With a little effort, the significance of many of these names will become both apparent and relevant to our modern faith. It has been said that some of the greatest treasure is found in the driest places. The primary focus of the genealogies in 1 Chronicles is the line of the Messiah. Other genealogies are included but usually run through a few names and are then dropped. Those that connect Adam to David to the ancestors of Jesus, however, are much more prominent.

1:1–4 The sequence from Adam to Noah is brief but afterward becomes more detailed because it is the sons of Noah who are assigned to repopulate the earth after the flood. Noah has three sons.

1:5–7 Japheth and his descendants live in the area of the north—what is now Europe and some of the former Soviet states.

1:8–16 Ham's descendants settle on the continent of Africa and in the area known as Canaan. Perhaps the most prominent name in his progeny is Nimrod, a

mighty hunter and warrior whose name is connected with both Babylon and Nineveh (Genesis 10:8–12). The Jewish Targum, a paraphrase of the Old Testament, attributes no small measure of wickedness to Nimrod, crediting him with creating the false religious system at the tower of Babel.

1:17–27 The messianic line goes through Noah's remaining son, Shem (from whom we get the word *Semites*). His descendants take up residence in the Middle East.

1:19 The mention of the dividing of the earth during the days of Peleg has created varying schools of thought. Some believe the reference is to the dividing of Earth's land masses into continents, but how could this be? They would have had no knowledge of this in antiquity. Others feel it means that during the time of the tower of Babel, God divided languages, and thus people, into separate groups.

1:27–31 The final entry in Shem's list of descendants is Abram, or Abraham, and the genealogy picks up there with his families. Ishmael, the son Abraham had with Hagar, has a number of sons.

1:32–33 Abraham himself has a number of additional children with a woman he married after Sarah died. However, the son whose line the Chronicler will follow is Isaac, the only son of Sarah.

1:34–43 Isaac has two sons: the twins Jacob and Esau. However, Jacob's name isn't used in this section of 1 Chronicles. Instead, he is identified as Israel, the name he receives from God and by which the entire nation eventually comes to be known. (*Jacob* means "heel catcher"; *Israel* means something like "wrestling or struggling God.") Esau has several sons and many grandchildren. His line eventually comes to be called the Edomites. But it will be the children of Jacob—the Israelites—who will get the most attention in this genealogical list.

2:1 Israel has twelve sons. Judah is fourth in birth order but rises to prominence after Jacob's older sons commit harsh actions that prevent them from receiving their father's blessing (Genesis 34:25–30; 35:22; 49:1–12). Still, Judah is hardly a perfect son or citizen.

2:3–5 Judah's first two sons, Er and Onan, are killed by the Lord for their wickedness (Genesis 38:6–10). Judah is reluctant to let his third son marry the same woman, Tamar, which was the tradition of the time. Tamar is therefore unable to remarry or have children. Seeing a unique opportunity, she poses as a prostitute and is approached by Judah himself, who unknowingly impregnates her without ever discovering her identity. Months later, when she is discovered to be pregnant, Judah wants to have her killed, but she produces some of his possessions she had taken as collateral. Only then does he realize he is the father of her child, which turns out to be children—twins (Genesis 38:13–30). One of the offspring is named Pharez, and as it turns out, he is in the messianic line.

2:7 Another notorious member of Judah's family is Achar, known in Joshua as Achan. He plunders Jericho after Israel's victory, in defiance of God's and Joshua's explicit instructions (Joshua 7). His life is summed up in one phrase: "troubler of Israel."

2:12 Other memorable names of a more honorable reputation are Boaz, the kinsman-redeemer and husband of Ruth, and his grandson Jesse, who was the father of David.

2:13–15 The account of Samuel anointing David as king in 1 Samuel 16:6–13 provides the names of David's three oldest brothers, but 1 Chronicles provides the names of those three and three more. David has seven older brothers, but only six are listed in 1 Chronicles. Perhaps the difference is to promote David to seventh position, since seven is a significant number throughout scripture.

2:16–17 David's nephews are decent warriors, yet they create a lot of unnecessary stress during David's conflict with Saul. Saul's commander, Abner, kills Asahel. Later, even though David has established a peace treaty with Abner, Joab kills Abner out of revenge. David tries to remove Joab as general, but Joab holds on to his job, although he is not a man to be trusted. It is Joab who later kills David's son Absalom in direct disobedience to David's orders (2 Samuel 18:14–15).

2:18–54 Backing up a bit, the Chronicler records the family of Caleb. Caleb had represented the tribe of Judah when Moses selected one person from each tribe to spy out the promised land before entering it (Numbers 13:3–16). Of the twelve spies, only Caleb and Joshua return with the recommendation to move ahead in faith. Sadly, they are outvoted. The other spies are terrified

of the inhabitants of the land, and their fear spreads to the entire nation. As a result, all the tribes are forced to wander in the wilderness for forty years because of their unbelief. Caleb, however, has a strong and consistent faith throughout his lifetime (Judges 1:8–20).

3:1–9 Historically, perhaps the most famous Old Testament character who comes through the line of Judah, whose descendants are listed in this section. After the opening genealogies of chapters 1–9, most of the rest of this book reviews David's life.

3:5 Two of David's children born to Bath-sheba (*Bathshua* in Hebrew), Nathan and Solomon, continue David's lineage in the messianic line. Nathan's descendants continue to the family of Mary, the mother of Jesus (see Luke 3). Solomon's descendants go to Joseph, the adopted father of Jesus (see Matthew 1), which links Jesus to the royal line of David but avoids the blood curse that had been placed on Jehoiachin and his descendants (Jeremiah 22:28–30).

3:5–9 Even a brief mention of David's sons and daughters tends to trigger recollections of tragic stories. David's daughter Tamar is raped by David's son Amnon (2 Samuel 13:1–22). In response, Tamar's full brother, Absalom, bides his time for two years before assassinating Amnon (2 Samuel 13:23–39). Absalom later leads a revolt against David in an effort to take the throne but is killed in the process (2 Samuel 18:1–18). Still later, another son named Adonijah attempts a coup and is also put to death (1 Kings 1; 2:13–25). All these events follow the declaration of the prophet Nathan that "the sword shall never depart from [David's] house" (2 Samuel 12:10) a prophecy that was delivered immediately after David's adultery with Bath-sheba and his murder of her husband, Uriah (2 Samuel 11). Yet the Chronicler's list of David's sons also includes Solomon, which serves as a reminder of God's grace and forgiveness. Even after David's sins, his son would sit on the throne of Israel during the most peaceful and prosperous era in their history.

3:10–16 After the kingdom is divided, the northern tribes will have eight different families/dynasties on the throne. The southern kingdom of Judah, however, has only one dynasty: David's. And it is from David's lineage that the Messiah will eventually come. These verses list the kings of Judah who follow David. All the kings of Judah are descendants of David, up to Zedekiah, the last king before the majority of the people are taken away captive to Babylon. A curse is placed on Jehoiachin because of his great wickedness, ensuring that he will never have a descendant on the throne (Jeremiah 22:28–30). Zedekiah, who follows Jehoiachin, is a son of Josiah (Jeremiah 37:1), but Jehoiachin outlives Zedekiah to become the last surviving king in the line of David—until the arrival of Jesus.

4:1 Hezron is the father of Caleb, who had been an exemplary soldier and follower of God. Yet he is not included in the messianic line. The line runs through Pharez instead. (The listing of Judah's descendants is not a group of siblings but rather a sequential series of families.)

4:9–10 The account of Jabez is short but fascinating. He is a man in pain who seeks the Lord, and his prayers are answered. God honors his request and blesses him.

4:24–8:32 After spending much time detailing the family of Judah, the son of Israel through whose line the Messiah will eventually come, the Chronicler moves on to the other sons of Israel and their family lines. These non-messianic lines are considerably more abbreviated. The Chronicler's extensive coverage of the family of Judah is due to both David's involvement and the anticipation of the Messiah to come from that line. Reuben is actually the oldest son of Jacob (Israel), but he loses the privileges that were usually bestowed on the firstborn. He not only misses out on the birthright that would connect him with the Messiah but also forfeits the double portion of the inheritance that traditionally would have been his. That honor goes to Joseph. (This is why there is no tribe of Joseph. Instead, there are two tribes named for Joseph's sons, Ephraim and Manasseh [see 5:1–2].)

4:24–43 Simeon, along with his brother Levi, had offended their father in an incident involving their sister, Dinah (Genesis 34). However, in this example provided by the Chronicler, the Simeonites are good models of faith and action. Their families have grown, along with their flocks and herds. They feel restricted and need more room, so they seek to destroy their enemies and enlarge their borders. Too frequently the problem with the Israelites (as well as with believers of all ages) was that they became complacent during good times. After they entered the promised land, they settled and stopped struggling as soon as they had acquired a little personal comfort—before they had dealt with the problems around them. Consequently, they remained vulnerable to the attacks of their enemies. The Simeonites are an admirable exception in this instance.

5:1–26 The tribes of Reuben and Gad and the half tribe of Manasseh have the common bond of settling on the east side of the river Jordan.

5:18–24 In one account recalled by the Chronicler, these tribes go into battle and are victorious—not because of their own strength but because they cry out to God. God gives them victory because they express confidence and trust in Him. In addition to their victory, they receive the spoils of battle, including land and numerous animals.

5:25–26 In time, however, this cluster of tribes becomes unfaithful to God. When the Assyrian army invades, led by Tilgath-pilneser (or Pul), they are easily defeated and taken into exile. They had not crossed the river Jordan, a line of defense, to settle in Canaan, so they were easily the first to be taken away captive.

6:1–81 The Levites are placed in charge of the tabernacle and matters of worship, with each of the sons of Levi given a specific duty. Gershon and his descendants are responsible for the fabrics of the tabernacle, the coverings, tents, clothes, curtains, cords,

and so forth. Kohath and his descendants (including Aaron) are to care for the ark, the table of shewbread, the oil-burning lamp, the altars of burnt offering and incense, the sacred vessels, the veil, and related furnishings. The Merarites (descendants of Merari) take care of the boards, sockets, walls, floors, and such.

6:31–48 The Gershonites, Kohathites, and Merarites are still going strong as David becomes king. David is a man of worship who is determined to provide qualified people to worship. Imagine being able to walk by the temple day or night and hear the worship of God being sung out.

6:49–53 The descendants of Aaron become the priestly line in Israel.

6:54–81 The Levites do not inherit any land because the Lord is to be their inheritance. (It is important to note as well that Jacob cursed Levi's tribe in Genesis 49.) Instead, forty-eight cities are designated throughout Israel in which the Levites live and minister. Under this arrangement, no one in the other tribes is more than a day's journey from one of the Levitical cities.

7:13 Biblical genealogies aren't altogether unlike the average family tree: Some members are going to be more prominent than others. In this section of Israel's family tree, there are fewer familiar names. And while some of the tribes have lengthy sections with name after name and generation after generation, the tribe of Naphtali gets but a single verse with four names.

7:15 More of the story of Zelophehad, who had only daughters, is provided in Numbers 27:1–11, where the daughters go to Moses and the other leaders of Israel upon the death of their father, pointing out that the law made no provision for inheritances of families without sons. Moses takes their case to the Lord, who determines that the daughters certainly do have a right to inherit their father's land.

7:21–27 Interesting tidbits are recorded for some of the biblical families, just as every modern family has its favorite stories that are told and retold. For example, two men in the line of Ephraim are killed in an altercation over livestock. The father grieves for them many days but then has other children and goes on with life.

7:27 One noteworthy name in Ephraim's family is Jehoshuah—also known as Joshua, the assistant to Moses, spy of the promised land, and leader of the nation when the Israelites conquer Jericho and march triumphantly into the land.

8:1–40 When Samuel first approaches Saul about being the first king of Israel, Saul's initial response is skepticism. He is well aware that he is not only from Israel's smallest tribe but also from the least significant clan within the tribe (1 Samuel 9:21). Since that time, however, it appears that being the source of the first king of Israel had helped the tribe of Benjamin increase in status. The Chronicler has already included a short genealogy of the tribe, and here he inserts another, more detailed, family line. This list begins with a background of the Benjamites in general.

8:28 The note that these Benjamites all lived in Jerusalem indicates the author's awareness that David had eventually conquered the city and established it as Israel's capital. That act had not yet taken place during the lifetime of Saul.

8:29–40 The names included here are the Benjamites to whom Saul is specifically related. Similar lists of names are found elsewhere in scripture and do not always coincide exactly. Sometimes the term *son* might actually refer to a grandson or perhaps even a more distant relative. And depending on the writer's intent, he might be selective in how many names he provides. This particular section is more comprehensive than others of a similar nature (see Genesis 46:21; Numbers 26:38–40).

9:1 After Israel divides into a northern and southern kingdom, the northern kingdom is first to fall, but to the Assyrian Empire. More than a century later, the Babylonian Empire begins making incursions into the southern kingdom, each time carrying away segments of the more trained and useful people. The first invasion is in 605 BC, the second in 597 BC. By 586 BC, the Babylonians level the city of Jerusalem, destroying the temple in the process. The invaders also take the majority of the leaders back to Babylon, leaving only the poor to take care of the land. In 539 BC, the Persian Empire conquers Babylon. The Persians allow the Israelites to go back to their homeland. However, by then not many of them want to return because they have become very comfortable in Babylon. The religious leaders are the first to return.

9:2–16 The priests would normally attend to and minister in the temple, but the temple is no longer standing. They are assisted by the Levites.

9:17–32 The porters are a specified group of Levites in charge of opening and closing the gates of the temple. They ensure that only those who are permitted to be in the temple area are allowed in, and they keep out those who do not belong there. Some of the people in this group have no responsibilities other than being in the temple and singing worship songs to the Lord. Music and worship could be heard day and night. The Chronicler will have more to say about the priests, singers, porters, and other groups in chapters 23–26.

9:35–44 This passage parallels 8:29–38. It is reviewed here as a portion of Saul's genealogy that functions as a prologue to the account of his death in chapter 10. A much more extensive account of Saul's life is found in 1 Samuel 9–31.

10:8–12 One of Saul's first acts as king had been to rescue the men of the Israelite city of Jabesh-gilead from hostile Ammonites (1 Samuel 11:1–11). When the citizens of that city hear of the Philistines' despicable treatment of the bodies of Saul and his sons, they conduct a night raid, heroically retrieve the bodies, and carry them back to Jabesh for a decent burial (1 Samuel 31:11–13).

10:13–14 When Israel demands a king, God gives them Saul and promises to bless the new king if he will be obedient (1 Samuel 12:13–15). Saul, however, does not obey God. Consequently, his dynasty lasts only some forty years. He is replaced by David, a leader divinely ordained by God, whose dynasty lasts more than ten times as long—from 1011 BC until 586 BC.

11:1 By the time Saul dies, David is more than ready to be the next king. He had already been anointed years before, yet he was insistent on leaving the timing of the transition in God's hands. He had had two ideal opportunities to kill King Saul but refused each time (1 Samuel 24; 26). In the meantime, he continues to serve God and his nation. His victory over Goliath and subsequent battles against the Philistines garner him national attention. Not only is it evident that he is a great military figure, but the people also recognize the hand of God in David's life. Even when David was a shepherd, God had been training him to be king.

11:3 After Saul dies, the people in Judah immediately turn to David as their next leader, and he establishes a headquarters in Hebron (2 Samuel 2:1–4). The rest of the nation, however, recognizes Saul's son Ish-bosheth (2 Samuel 2:8–10). (They had wanted a king in order to be like the other nations, and the other nations tended to pass down their royal status through family lines.) For a long while, war rages between the supporters of David and the supporters of Saul (2 Samuel 3:1). As time passes, David's influence expands as the house of Saul gets weaker. It takes seven and a half years, but finally the entire nation gathers to endorse David's leadership as king.

11:4–7 David's next step displays good political sense, insightful wisdom, and military courage. Rather than choose an established city in Israel as a capital (which would likely upset some of those in Judah) or a city from the south (which could reignite the still-delicate feelings of Saul's supporters), David chooses the city Jebus, located between Judah and the northern tribes. But unfortunately the city is inhabited by Israel's enemies. The citizens of Jebus had withstood all former assaults for hundreds of years and were not worried about David's desire to conquer them. David conquers Jebus, and from that point forward it is known better as the city of Jerusalem and will always be known as the city of David.

11:6 Jebusites had inhabited the city of Jebus since before the Israelites had entered the promised land. If God's people had done as He instructed (Joshua 23:6–13) and driven out all their enemies before settling comfortably in the land, they could have avoided a lot of problems—including the one of a fortified city established on a hill that was thought to be impenetrable. But David accomplishes what all the Israelites before him failed to do.

11:6 David's victory at Jebus also allows someone else an opportunity to prove himself. As David steps into the role of king, his army is left without a commander in chief, so he promises the position to whoever leads the attack on the Jebusites. The challenge is accepted by one of David's nephews—a man named Joab. He is seen in scripture as a tough, though at times unethical, warrior. Exactly how Joab is able to breach the defenses of Jebus when others could not is not fully explained. One possible scenario is that David knew of a 45-foot shaft from which the Jebusites brought water into the city, and Joab is able to climb up the shaft and open the doors for Israel's soldiers (see 2 Samuel 5:8).

11:10–47 David had a reputation as a great warrior, and he seemed to attract others who were also noteworthy in battle. He collects a small army of about six hundred men while on the run from King Saul (1 Samuel 27:2). Several of their names are recorded. A sampling of their exploits is also provided, although few details are given. Slight variations in names and details occur between this Chronicles account and the parallel account in 2 Samuel 23, but the list is overall quite consistent.

12:1 Ziklag is a Philistine city that had been given to David when he took shelter under the care of the Philistine king Achish. When David and his men return to Ziklag, they discover the Amalekites have burned it and taken all their wives and possessions. At this point, David's men are ready to stone him. David seeks the Lord, who assures him that they will defeat the Amalekites and retrieve everything that has been taken, which is exactly what happens (1 Samuel 30). The author of Samuel provides much information about David's experiences in Ziklag (1 Samuel 27:6–7; 29:1–30:19). The author of Chronicles adds that it is during all these events that various groups of warriors come to Ziklag to join David.

12:1–15 David's men are from three of the twelve tribes of Israel: Benjamin (thus related to Saul), Gad, and Manasseh. When David is sent back to Ziklag, these men go with him.

12:16–18 As each group comes to David, he goes out to receive them. He welcomes all who come in peace to support him, but he warns against any attempt to betray him. It is only natural for him to be a bit suspicious since Saul is looking for David in order to destroy him.

12:23–40 David soon has a great army. By the time Saul dies and David moves on to Hebron, men are joining his ranks by the thousands, from all the tribes. After all that David has been through—dodging Saul, negotiating with the Philistines, and leading all those who have come to him—this is a relaxing and joyous time. Volunteers have provided plentiful supplies of food, and David and his group spend three days eating and drinking. It is a well-deserved break for the new king of Israel.

12:38 Once anointed the next king of Israel, David had to wait a decade or so until God determined King Saul's reign should come to an end. Saul tried persistently to capture and kill David, but it was Saul who died on the battlefield after drifting away from God. David is initially the king of only the territory of Judah, but he eventually wins over all the Israelites and receives their endorsement as king. This section describes some of his early acts in his official leadership role.

13:1–3 The original location for the ark of the covenant was in the tabernacle, the portable center of worship used by the Israelites as they traveled. At times, however, Moses had taken the ark into battles because it reminded the people of God's presence and power. After settling in Canaan, the ark was eventually captured by the Philistines during battle (1 Samuel 4:1–11). Upon its return, the Israelites stored the ark in a personal residence, and there it remained for twenty years (1 Samuel 6:21–7:1).

13:5–10 The ark had been designed with rings on the sides. Poles could be slipped through the rings, and then the priests, rather than touching the ark itself, could lift it with the poles. The poles were not to be detached (Exodus 25:10–16). The Philistines, in returning the ark to Israel, had transported it on a cart—the method adopted by those in David's processional. Had the Israelites used the intended mode of transportation, instability would not have been an issue and Uzza wouldn't have had to reach out and touch the ark.

14:1 Before continuing the story of the ark, the Chronicler inserts a few interesting facts about David's early experiences as king. One of David's tasks is to build his living quarters. To help with the construction of the palace, David enlists the assistance of Hiram, king of Tyre. This is the beginning of an alliance that will carry on through the reign of Solomon and an attempt to hire the most qualified people to do the best possible work so God will be honored.

14:8–12 Not long before this, David and his followers were living in a Philistine city and even going out to march (or pretending to) against Israel (1 Samuel 27:1–6; 29). Some had suspected his true convictions, while others had considered him a genuine ally. David knew the Philistine tactics as well as anyone, but still he stops to consult God before deciding to fight.

14:13–17 The Philistines regroup and attack again. David doesn't take anything for granted or make the assumption that he will again defeat them. He once more inquires of God and receives a different battle plan than before. As a result of David's victory, his reputation spreads throughout the land—not just as a mighty warrior but also as a spiritual man.

15:1 Prior to its capture by the Philistines, the ark had been located in Shiloh, tended to by Eli the priest and his family (1 Samuel 4:4). But now that Jerusalem has been established as Israel's capital, David sets up a temporary tent there to house the ark. The tabernacle that Moses had used in the wilderness is also still in use, located in Gibeon (1 Chronicles 16:39–40), a town in Benjamin, northeast of Jerusalem.

15:2–11 David had apparently used the interval of time since his first attempt to move the ark to determine what he had done wrong. This time he allows no one but the Levites to handle the transportation of the ark, using God's guidelines rather than his own. He isn't going to make the same mistake twice. He recruits Levites from various families to participate.

15:12–15 David's anger toward and fear of God from the first time he tried to move the ark and failed had abated by now. He makes no excuses for his previous failure. He appears ready to right his mistake and move forward.

15:16–24 Worship is an integral element planned for moving the ark toward Jerusalem. Singers are appointed to sing joyful songs with musical accompaniment. And this is no ad hoc group; everyone has specific assignments, and the leader is skilled at what he does. In addition to the worship music is the aspect of sacrifice. As the priests methodically progress toward Jerusalem with the ark, every six steps they stop and two animals are offered to God (2 Samuel 6:13).

15:29 David isn't just watching the processional; he is actively participating. The account in 2 Samuel says that David dances before the Lord with all his strength (2 Samuel 6:14). Michal, his wife, is appalled. Michal was the daughter of King Saul, and David's first wife. When David was forced to flee Saul and leave Michal behind, Saul gave her to a man named Phalti as his wife. When David eventually gained the throne after Saul's death, he sent for Michal. After Michal's scolding of David for dancing, she remains childless for the rest of her life (2 Samuel 6:20–23).

16:1–3 When the ark arrives and is positioned in the tent that David has provided, more offerings are made. David realizes that he has been blessed by God, and he wants to share those blessings with the people around him.

16:4–6 Levites were appointed for regular petition, thanksgiving, and praise of God. In essence, their job was to remember and commemorate what God had done. Music would continue to be an essential element of worship.

16:8 When the word Lord is written with small capital letters, it signifies the *name* of God (Yahweh). When it is written *Lord*, it refers to God's *title* as lord or master. God's name indicates action: *Yahweh* means "the becoming one."

16:23–36 When David tells the people to give God glory and strength, he is speaking of serving Him with all their ability.

16:37–42 With the ark in its new location in Jerusalem, and the tabernacle still in operation in Gibeon, there are now two primary centers of worship. David ensures that both places are staffed with competent and attentive spiritual leaders. Consequently, this is a unique period in which two high priests are designated: Zadok is the priest in charge of the tabernacle, and David appoints Abiathar to attend to the ark in Jerusalem (15:11).

16:43 This has been a big day for Israel. The ark is not only back in their land, but it has finally been reestablished in a place of prominence. Their new king is showing spiritual strength that the former king lacked. David will continue to inspire his people throughout the early years of his reign.

17:1–2 David has become king, united the nation, moved the ark to Jerusalem, and built his palace. He is becoming a popular leader, respected by the people,

but he feels he needs to do more to honor God. He mentions his idea to Nathan the prophet, who thinks it is admirable. In fact, it seems that Nathan automatically assumes God will endorse the idea, and he tells David to go ahead before he even consults the Lord.

17:3–5 God speaks to Nathan, telling him that David isn't the right person to build a temple to house the ark. Later, as David recalls the story, he explains that God had declared that the one who builds His house should not be someone who has shed as much blood as David has (28:2–3). As a warrior, David had killed hundreds, if not thousands, of people (see 1 Samuel 18:27). Rather than having a temple constructed by those hands of violence, God reserves that right for a person of peace: David's son Solomon, whose name means "peace."

17:5–6 God's words here show little concern for having a house of cedar in which to live. The phrase "from tent to tent" does not imply that God moved from one tent of worship to another, or from one tabernacle to another. Rather, in the five hundred or more years that the tabernacle had been in existence, surely portions of it had worn out and had been replaced. But the Lord's presence with the Israelites had remained consistent.

17:5 In the first century, when John writes that "the Word was made flesh, and dwelt among us" (John 1:14), his use of the word *dwelt* suggests a tabernacle or tent. So the presence of God has included, but has not been limited to, a tent in the wilderness, the temple that would replace the tabernacle, and the person of Jesus Christ. Today the residence of God is not in a building but in believers (1 Corinthians 3:16).

17:7–14 Rather than expecting David to build Him a house, God said He would set David over a house. God had been with David all along, from shepherd to king. Under David's leadership, all of God's people are being blessed. And David's house will continue.

17:14 Like so many other prophetic passages, this promise of God has two intended fulfillments: one in the near future and a second that is more long-range. David's house will continue first through his son Solomon, who will become the next king. In fact, the long series of kings of Judah will be from the Davidic line—an ongoing continuation of his "house." But beyond that, of course, is the anticipation of the Messiah who is to come from the lineage of David and who will sit on the throne and rule forever.

17:15–19 After Nathan delivers God's message, David is humbled. He realizes he has failed at times, and he feels unworthy to receive such abundant blessings from God. Yet David rightly acknowledges that the Lord is a God of grace who gives His people gifts, not because of their goodness, but because of *His* goodness.

17:23–27 If taken out of context, David's final response might sound excessively bold. But David is only agreeing to the things that God has already promised him; he is affirming what God has said. It is because of his knowledge of God's will for his life that David can pray with such boldness.

18:1 David's skill as a warrior is evident throughout his career. As king, he is a natural leader against Israel's enemies. One major accomplishment is his subjugation of the Philistines, who had been a recurring problem ever since Israel had entered the promised land.

18:2 The Moabites were descendants of Lot, originating from an incestuous relationship between Lot and his older daughter shortly after their narrow escape from the destruction of the city of Sodom (Genesis 19:36–37). David has strong ties to Moab: His great-grandmother is Ruth, who accompanied Naomi back from Moab. But since the Moabites continue to oppose Israel, David defeats them, and they offer tribute to him as his subjects.

18:3–6 David is victorious over all these persistent foes of Israel because God is with him (18:13). After conquering large numbers of enemy soldiers, David takes steps to minimize future conflict with the same groups. Establishing garrisons and demanding tribute kept such nations in line. He also hamstrings enemy horses—a practice that essentially eliminates their effectiveness in war yet allows them to live and serve a peaceful purpose.

18:7–11 David begins to accumulate many valuable items from spoils of war, tributes received, and gifts from those who want to ally with him. He dedicates those assets to the Lord. Although David has not been allowed to build a temple for God, he is preparing for it. Solomon will later use the materials David is acquiring.

19:1–2 David doesn't see the need to fight when diplomacy will work just as well. He had formed an alliance with Nahash, the king of the Ammonites. When David hears of the death of Nahash, he sends a delegation of his men to express condolences to Nahash's son Hanun.

19:4–5 Hanun's advisors feel that the visit of David's men is only a ruse to allow Israel to spy on Ammon. Because of this, the Ammonites treat David's men with the utmost disdain, utterly humiliating them by shaving off half of each man's beard and cutting off the bottoms of their garments so that the men's buttocks are exposed (2 Samuel 10:4). A beard was a sign of masculinity at the time, which made the Ammonite insult intentional, shameful, and personal. David's delegation doesn't even want to return to Jerusalem out of shame, thus David's instructions to remain in Jericho until their beards have grown back.

19:10–13 The Israelites divide into two forces: one led by Joab (the regular army commander) and a second commanded by his brother Abishai. While Joab deals with the outer circle of Syrians, Abishai confronts the Ammonites. Each brother agrees to back up the other if the need arises.

19:14–19 As soon as the fighting starts, the Syrians quickly begin to flee, leaving the Ammonites on their own. The Ammonites immediately retreat into the safety of Rabbah (20:1), their capital city, while the Syrians recruit more of their countrymen to stand against the Israelites. The combined forces of the Syrians face off against David's army, and this time the entire Syrian army is defeated, becoming David's subjects, effectively ending the Ammonite/Syrian alliance. Meanwhile, the Ammonites remain within the protection of their city. They have weather on their side (for now) because fighting was usually suspended during the winter (rainy) season. Chariots, a primary mode of transportation, and the horses that pulled them couldn't navigate well in muddy terrain.

20:1–2 While David remains in Jerusalem, Joab neutralizes the threat of the Ammonite army. But when the city is ready to fall, Joab summons David to come lead the final charge and receive credit for the victory. The Ammonite king has a magnificent (though hardly functional) crown made of gold and precious stones that weighs seventy-five pounds. The crown is removed from the Ammonite king and placed on David's head. David acquires much other plunder as well, and he puts the conquered people to work doing common labor, thus adding the Ammonites to the list of peoples ruled by Israel.

20:5–7 Goliath's brother is one of the Philistines mentioned by name. The shaft of Lahmi's spear is likened to a weaver's beam, which is the same description given for Goliath's spear (1 Samuel 17:7). In what seems like a parallel event, another huge man taunts the Israelites, and David's nephew kills him. When Goliath first challenged the Israelites, it had taken six weeks or so before he could convince even a single Israelite soldier to confront him (1 Samuel 17:16).

20:4–8 After David killed Goliath, David's faith and courage became legendary. But more than that, his action was also inspirational and motivational. The soldiers are no longer sitting around waiting for David to act on their behalf. In this passage, at least three others become legendary giant-killers in their own right.

21:5–8 David's problem seems to be a matter of pride, of placing confidence in his military instead of in the Lord. Whatever David's inner motivation, it is clear that he later recognizes and acknowledges his sin. The author of Samuel says that because God is angry with Israel (the reason is not provided), He tells David to take a census (2 Samuel 24:1). The Chronicler, however, writes that it is Satan who incites David's action. This is not actually a contradiction. God does not tempt anyone, but He can withdraw His control of a situation, allowing Satan to step in. In this case, David succumbs to some kind of temptation. As a result, God is then able to deal with David's pride as well as chasten the nation of Israel.

21:9–12 Even though David is sorry, sin has consequences. In this case, God allows David to *choose* which of three consequences he prefers. God presents these options to David through the prophet Gad, someone who has advised David well in times past (1 Samuel 22:3–5).

21:13–16 As soon as the plague falls on Israel, seventy thousand people die. The angel of the Lord then stands between heaven and earth, with a sword drawn to destroy Jerusalem. It is at this point that David's insight into God's character proves valuable. God deems that enough suffering has taken place, and He relents. In this instance, God does not complete the entire three days of plagues that He said would happen.

21:17 When David sees the angel about to destroy Jerusalem, he pleads with God to punish him rather than the people. David, it seems, still has the heart of a shepherd. In this case, the shepherd is attempting to protect the people under his leadership.

21:18–20 The trouble is that David doesn't own the land. The angel had been halted while standing on the threshing floor of a man named Ornan. In fact, Ornan and his four sons are in the process of threshing wheat when they see the angel, and the sons immediately run to hide.

21:21–25 The amount that David pays is a point on which there seems to be a discrepancy between the account in 2 Samuel (fifty shekels of silver) and the one here (six hundred shekels of gold). But it is reasonable to assume that, as specified in 2 Samuel 24:24, the lower amount only applies to the threshing floor and oxen. The greater total specified in verse 25 is for the site, which likely includes the surrounding land.

22:1 David's isn't the first altar to be constructed in this location. As it happens, the threshing floor of Ornan is on the same spot where Abraham had traveled centuries earlier, intending to offer his son Isaac to God. It is the site where Solomon will soon build the temple. And roughly one thousand years later, Christ will be crucified approximately three blocks away at the location of Golgotha, in history's ultimate sacrifice.

22:2–5 David had been denied permission to build the temple for God, so David decides to do what he *can* do. He begins to gather the supplies he knows will be needed to construct the temple. David's preparations are extensive. While the Chronicler continues to follow the life and exploits of David, from this point onward Solomon becomes a prominent figure as well. The building will come to be known as Solomon's Temple, but its construction is a team effort.

22:6–13 David is apparently able and willing to open up to others about his unfulfilled personal desires. His account to his son Solomon is one such example. David is both supportive and encouraging as he charges Solomon to begin his task. He makes clear that as long as Solomon is careful to follow God's laws, he will find success in all he does.

22:13 David's charge to Solomon will not be the last challenge Solomon receives to be obedient. God Himself reminds Solomon of the importance of obedience on different occasions (see 1 Kings 3:14; 9:4–9; 2 Chronicles 7:17–22). But, ultimately, Solomon will reject this wise advice, resulting in the deterioration of the kingdom that David worked so hard to establish and unite.

22:14–16 The quantities of precious metals that David gathers are overwhelming, translating roughly as 3,750 tons of gold and 37,500 tons of silver. Other metals are so abundant they are not even measured.

22:17–19 David doesn't just give Solomon the assignment of building the temple; he also enlists the support of all the people for his son's work. By this point in David's life, he is preparing to turn the kingdom over to Solomon. In this section, David turns his attention to the personnel who will work in the temple. While much of the content of 1 Chronicles has a corresponding version in Samuel or Kings, most of the content of this section is not found elsewhere.

23:23 It may seem a bit strange to see David once again counting the people, because that same action caused problems previously (21:1–8). This time, however, his motive is entirely different. Rather than lining up his fighting men to determine his military strength, now he is seeing how many people will qualify to serve in the temple. The Levites are one of the two tribes that weren't included in the previous census (21:6), so they are counted at this time—apparently late in David's life.

23:3–5 Traditionally, a priest or Levite had to be thirty years old before he was allowed to minister before the Lord, and he retired from service at age fifty (Numbers 4:1–3). David's count finds thirty-eight thousand Levites in that category. David assigns twenty-four thousand of them to supervise temple work. Six thousand others will serve as officials and judges; four thousand will be porters; and the final four thousand will be musicians. David even provides the instruments that are needed.

23:6–23 The Levites are subdivided into three smaller groups: the Gershonites, the Kohathites, and the Merarites (descendants of the three sons of Levi: Gershon, Kohath, and Merari). The Chronicler has already provided a similar breakdown in 6:16–30 and will do so again in 24:20–30. Each subgroup has specific duties to perform. The official priests, however, all come from the Kohathites—specifically, the line of Aaron. The other Levites assist the priests (23:28, 32).

23:24–32 A previous list of Levite duties included guarding the facilities, opening the temple each morning, keeping up with the inventory, baking, mixing spices, playing music, and so forth (9:22–33). Here the Chronicler adds their ongoing responsibilities of caring for the temple's courtyards and side rooms, purifying the sacred objects, and offering praise to God every morning and evening and during sabbaths and festivals. The extent of the work is so demanding that David enlists additional help by lowering the age requirement from thirty to twenty.

24:1–3 When the Chronicler begins to enumerate the line of people in the priesthood, beginning with Aaron, he briefly notes that Aaron's older sons, Nadab and Abihu, died before their father. Their deaths were a tragic story from Israel's history, recounted numerous times in scripture. Nadab and Abihu had ministered in an inappropriate manner, and they were consumed by fire from the Lord (Leviticus 10:1–5). They had not yet had children of their own. Replacing Nadab and Abihu were two of Aaron's other sons, Eleazar and Ithamar (Leviticus 10:12). Zadok, the priest who attended to the tabernacle, was a descendant of Eleazar. Ahimelech (son of David's other high priest, Abiathar) descended from Ithamar.

24:4–19 Eleazar has twice as many descendants as Ithamar, so lots are drawn to provide a fair and random assignment. A total of twenty-four families are available to serve (sixteen from Eleazar and eight from Ithamar). As the lots are cast, the assignments are duly recorded by Shemaiah, the scribe. The priests' work is assigned in two-week shifts, so one full rotation lasts just about a year with each family serving once. (Later on, a shift is made to one-week commitments, with each family serving twice during the year.) The Chronicler provides no details as to the importance of the priesthood or the specific functions the priests perform, although his readers would have been familiar with such information since this text was written later recounting history.

24:20–30 This list of the other descendants of Levi is quite similar to the list in 23:6–23. For some reason, the author again lists the Kohathites and Merarites, but not the Gershonites, and he adds one extra generation.

24:31 Just as they had done for the assignments of the priests, David and his two high priests oversee the casting of lots to determine the responsibilities of the Levites. Since the casting of lots is a random decision-making system, somewhat like throwing dice, every family receives equal treatment with no favoritism.

25:1 It's hard to miss the fact that music is an integral part of Israelite worship. The Psalms (the Israelites' hymnbook) are an extensive portion of scripture, centrally located in most Old Testaments. This portion of 1 Chronicles shows that such an emphasis on music is quite intentional. Much thought and planning went into the musical elements of Israel's worship life. The people weren't merely encouraged to sing; the music was modeled for them on a regular basis by gifted and well-trained Levites.

25:1 It might seem strange for David to work with the commanders of the army while assigning singing ministries. However, a different usage of the Hebrew language would allow for a translation of "leaders of the Levites" rather than "captains of the host"—a usage some scholars find more likely because of the focus on the Levites in the preceding chapter. Three key families are devoted to the music ministry: Asaph, Heman, and Jeduthun. The ministry of the singers/instrumentalists is clearly a musical one, yet their work is called *prophesying*, probably because they are telling forth the mighty works of God through their music.

25:5 Though a musician, Heman is referred to as the king's *seer*, another word for *prophet*. In other portions of scripture, the same title is also applied to Asaph (2 Chronicles 29:30) and Jeduthun (2 Chronicles 35:15). Of the three main families designated to serve as musicians, Heman appears to be the most prominent. Not only is he the one of the three identified as a seer here; he has more than twice as many sons as the other two. Yet after the exile of Israel, references are found to

the descendants of Asaph and Jeduthun, but there is no further mention of the descendants of Heman.

25:3–31 In light of the twenty-four divisions among the priestly families (24:7–18), it is interesting to note these three musical men have a total of twenty-four sons: Asaph with four, Jeduthun with six, and Heman with fourteen. Each of the twenty-four musical divisions is comprised of a twelve-person contingent, resulting in a total of 288 people. It appears likely that one group of musicians/singers is paired with one division of priests on each assignment at the temple.

26:1 It is difficult to think of a contemporary job that compares to that of the temple porters. In one sense, they acted simply as ticket takers, but some of their tasks resemble those of security guards. Entering the temple was a serious matter. There were sections where unauthorized people were prohibited from going, and the penalty for entering the forbidden areas was death.

26:1–4 Names that look odd to us may have been quite common in Old Testament times. Consequently, when we see a strange name that is used in different places, we may wrongly tend to presume that it is the same person, when instead it might be someone else with the same name. For example, the Asaph identified as one of the leaders of the singers in the previous chapter *may* be the one mentioned here. Or the latter reference may be to a man named Ebiasaph, but using an abbreviation of his name. Similarly, some contend that one man named Obed-edom tended to the ark of the covenant (13:14), served as a musician (15:21), and was a part-time porter (15:18), while another man with the same name was a full-time porter (16:38).

26:13–17 Casting lots (a form of random selection) is the method of determining which porters will be assigned to each gate. The east gate is the primary entrance to the temple. It has two additional posts and requires more guards than the other sides. The Shallecheth gate is not mentioned anywhere else in scripture.

26:17–18 Only twenty-two jobs for porters are listed. However, these are probably the positions of the chief men (26:12). With four thousand porters available for service (23:5), each of the leaders had people who served *with* him.

26:20 Unlike the unfamiliar function of porter, the job of treasurer is more understandable today. The Chronicler writes of two different areas requiring treasurers—the house of God and the dedicated things. The "treasures of the house of God" refers to the storehouse of wealth for the temple.

26:26–28 The treasuries for the dedicated things are a collection of spoils of war that have been set aside for God. In the days of Joshua, God had given specific instructions that everything from the defeat of Jericho should be devoted to Him (Joshua 6:17–19, 24). Others of God's military leaders had apparently continued this practice on a voluntary basis. However, none of the specific examples in verse 28 are referred to elsewhere in scripture, with the possible exception of Saul (1 Samuel 15:21).

27:1–15 The Lord had blessed David with a strong army that had made possible the current peace and prosperity in Israel. The army had played its part, but it couldn't take credit for all the victories—that credit went to God. Many of the people David names to head divisions of the army are previously listed among the mighty men who had fought alongside him: Jashobeam, Dodai, Benaiah, and others. Asahel and Joab had been close to David from the beginning. Twelve divisions established, one to be on duty each month.

27:15 Twelve divisions of twenty-four thousand men each yields an army of 288,000 soldiers. That total may have been a potential maximum number, however, rather than the actual count. Based on the original language, it is appropriate, and perhaps preferable, to understand that each army division had twenty-four *units*, with each unit comprised of *up to* one thousand soldiers.

27:16–22 Leaders of tribes were referred to as rulers, and the exact job description that goes with the title is unknown. These people may have been appointees of David, initiating a transition between the former system of individual tribes to a more unified and centralized system of government. Most of those on the list are not mentioned elsewhere in scripture.

27:20–21 These tribal divisions are not traditional. Asher and Gad are omitted for some reason. The total remains at twelve; however, Manasseh is designated twice: once for the half tribe on the western side of the river Jordan and again for the tribe on the east.

27:24 Numerous historic journals are mentioned in scripture that have been lost to us today (or have not yet been discovered). For example, 1 and 2 Kings refer to the chronicles of the kings of Israel and the chronicles of the kings of Judah. Here the Chronicler mentions the chronicles of King David, which would have preceded those other books.

27:25–34 Last on David's series of lists are overseers of various aspects of the king's business: storehouses, field hands, vineyards, herds and flocks, olive and fig crops, and so forth. One of the last names on the list, Ahithophel is a leader who didn't last. Even though he was David's top advisor, he later sided with Absalom when Absalom tried to take the kingdom away from David. But after Absalom decided not to take Ahithophel's advice on a crucial matter, Ahithophel realized it would only be a matter of time until David regained control, so he went home and hanged himself (2 Samuel 17:1–14, 23).

28:1–3 After David makes all the appointments recorded in chapters 23–27, he gathers all the designated leaders for a series of speeches. He is the greatest of Israel's kings, yet even at the close of his reign he considers the Israelites not his subjects but rather his brothers. David has done much to prepare for the soon-to-be-constructed temple of the Lord, but he takes no credit for it. He makes it clear that God directed him all along the way. He wisely realizes that God is never confined to a building. The temple in Jerusalem will not be like other temples of the time, perceived as a residence for the god to which it is dedicated. Instead, it is built to honor God's name. God's throne and residence are in heaven, but the temple will be His footstool.

28:3–6 David reiterates his personal desire to build the temple and God's veto of his plans due to all the blood David had shed. Yet David feels honored and humbled to be a part of God's plan. Judah had not been the oldest son of Israel, David had not been the oldest son of Jesse, and Solomon is not the oldest son of David. But in each case, God chose the person for the task He had in mind. Solomon is God's choice to be the next king and the builder of His temple. After Solomon, no subsequent king of Israel or Judah will be referred to as *chosen*. The Chronicler had previously recorded a similar speech by David (22:5–19). In both cases, David addresses both Solomon and the leaders of Israel. In the prior instance, however, more of the emphasis was on Solomon. Here David spends more time attempting to prepare the Israelites to support their new king and new temple.

28:7–9 David's speech repeatedly highlights obedience as a crucial element of the ongoing success of the kingdom. God will perpetuate Solomon's kingdom as long as the young king remains faithful. Yet the imperative of obedience extends to the entire nation. As long as the people maintain their strong relationship with the Lord, He will bless their lives in the land He has given them, and the land will be an inheritance to their descendants.

28:11–13 The plans David had prepared for the temple are not vague. Just as God had given Moses detailed instructions for how to construct the tabernacle in the wilderness, the Spirit of God had worked through David to provide specifics for the temple to be built. The temple is far more than a one-room sanctuary. The plans include porches, storerooms, inner rooms, altars, treasury storehouses, and more.

28:14–19 The temple plans are so complete that David specifies the designated weights of various implements: gold and silver candlesticks, tables, forks, bowls, pitchers, dishes, and such. Especially important is the design of the golden cherubim with outspread wings that are to sit atop the ark of the covenant to shelter it. And lest there be any confusion about what David says should be done, he assures Solomon that everything is written down for him.

28:20–21 The construction of the temple is an enormous project, and Solomon is a young and inexperienced king, so David repeats his challenge to be strong and to get the work done. This time, however, he adds much assurance and encouragement. Far from being alone in this project, Solomon has the entire nation aligned behind him—every willing person skilled in any craft. Much more important, however, is the confidence that God will be overseeing the project and will neither fail nor forsake Solomon until the work is complete.

29:1 David again appeals to the entire assembled group, imploring them to support their new, young, inexperienced king. No one in Israel had faced the magnitude of the task ahead of Solomon. This is no ordinary structure, no stately palace for a regal human occupant. Rather this will be the temple of their unseen, all-powerful, loving, and merciful God.

29:6–9 David encourages the people to contribute, and their response reflects their enthusiasm. Inspired by the example of their leaders, they give freely and sincerely, resulting in a one-day commitment of 5,360 tons of valuable materials needed for the temple. This is in addition to the staggering 41,250 tons of gold and silver (and brass and iron too abundant to measure) that David had previously provided (22:14). The people's willing and generous giving is another parallel between the temple and the Old Testament tabernacle. After Moses made known the needs for the construction of the tabernacle, the people had come day after day with contributions until Moses had to issue an order for them to stop bringing their gifts (Exodus 36:2–7). Similarly, the Israelites pour out abundant financial support for the temple.

29:7 A *dram* was a gold coin of Persia, first used around the reign of Darius I (522–486 BC).

29:10–19 David is overjoyed to see the response from the people. He responds to all the giving with a prayer. Despite all David has done, and as important a project as the building of the temple is, neither David nor the temple is prominent in the prayer. Indeed, David acknowledges his own insignificance as he maintains a focus on the attributes of God. Certainly, without God's provision for His people, none of their gifts would have been possible.

29:22–24 David's high priest, Zadok, is again anointed to acknowledge his continued role under Solomon. We know from 1 Kings 1–2 that the transition from David to Solomon is not as smooth as they may have wished, but the Chronicler chooses to focus on the support that Solomon receives, not the opposition.

29:26–28 It is not known how long David continues to live after Solomon's coronation, but it probably isn't very long. His life is briefly summarized as 1 Chronicles concludes. He ruled a total of forty years, at first just as Judah's leader, but soon as the king of the united nation of Israel. David had received three often-mentioned blessings of God: long life, wealth, and honor. And he lived to see Solomon begin to rule in his own right.

29:29–30 The sources cited by the Chronicler ("the book of Samuel the seer," "the book of Nathan the prophet," and "the book of Gad the seer") most likely include the parallel accounts of 1 Samuel and possibly Kings. Samuel, Nathan, and Gad were all involved at various critical stages of David's life and rule as king. The reign of Solomon will be impressive, but in the long line of kings until the fall of Jerusalem, no other leader will surpass David's lifelong reputation as a faithful king to his people and a devoted man of God. David was a man who, during his lifetime, was guilty of sexual indiscretions, coped with intense family turmoil, and had his share of spiritual questions and dilemmas. Yet at the end of his life, those who had observed him had nothing but good to say about him.

CHRONICLES

INTRODUCTION TO 2 CHRONICLES ■ The books of 1 and 2 Chronicles were originally written not as two books but as one continuous history. The majority of 2 Chronicles describes the history of Israel after Solomon's reign as the kingdom divided into northern Israel and southern Judah. This is not a history written as it was happening, however. Instead, it is a history written long after the fact to remind the people of Judah of the journey of their ancestors.

AUTHOR ■ The author of the books of 1 and 2 Chronicles is not explicitly stated in the text. Many scholars ascribe the work to Ezra, citing a unified authorship of the Chronicles and the books of Ezra and Nehemiah. However, there are parts of the book that are obvious additions and expansions on the original work, and it is difficult to date the entire book within Ezra's lifetime. The author was a wise and God-fearing person, writing with tremendous knowledge and insight into the significance of the community of God's people during this period.

OCCASION ■ While the accounts recorded in 2 Chronicles describe Israel's history during Solomon's reign and the fall of Israel afterward, the occasion of the writing is much later. It was written after the Jews had been exiled away from their homeland and had been given permission to return again. Therefore, it begins with Solomon, but it ends with Cyrus's decree that allowed the people passage back to Jerusalem.

1:1–6 The tabernacle, the portable worship structure Moses had built some five hundred years earlier during their wilderness wanderings, was located in Gibeon. With the tabernacle, besides the other temple articles, is the brasen (bronze) altar in which the sacrifices are offered. Thus Solomon needs to go to Gibeon and offer his sacrifices to the Lord (see Leviticus 17:11).

1:4 This event is recorded in 2 Samuel 6:2–17.

1:6 The burnt offering was given totally to the Lord, completely burned up, symbolizing the offerer's consecration to Him. On the other hand, the peace offering, described in Leviticus 3, was partly given to the Lord and partly eaten by those making the offering. It symbolized communion with the Lord. Historically, in this part of the world, when a person ate with someone, they formed an intimate relationship in a sense. Thus the connection between the names—peace and fellowship.

1:7–10 Solomon is only fourteen years old at this time (David reminds him of his youth in 1 Chronicles 29:1). Solomon's prayers echo those of his father, David, who asked that God would give him wisdom and understanding to lead his people, for he rightly recognized he could not do it on his own.

1:13–17 As Solomon takes power in Jerusalem, he begins to amass wealth—and the seeds of destruction for the nation of Israel are being sown. Solomon is gathering chariots, horses, and riches. He becomes an arms merchant as he traffics in chariots, even going to Egypt to obtain them, and he also takes multiple wives. This is precisely what God had warned the Israelites against when He brought them into the promised land (Deuteronomy 17:14–17). God knew that these harbingers of military and economic power would distract His people from worshipping Him.

2:1–5 Solomon gathers together a tremendous group of forced labor gangs—mostly foreigners and prisoners

of war—to build his own palace and the temple of God, according to David's plans. Solomon requests manpower and materials from a nearby neighbor, Huram of Tyre. His letter of request begins by emphasizing how magnificent and great the house of the Lord will be.

2:6 The temple that Solomon is building is indeed a place for worship, but Solomon realizes that the presence of God fills the universe.

2:7–10 Solomon needs fine wood and skilled craftsmen to build the temple. The amounts he lists here for payment for the work he is commissioning on the temple equal 160,000 bushels of wheat and barley and 150,000 gallons each of wine and oil.

2:11–13 The skilled craftsman the king will send is the son of an Israelite mother (from the tribe of Dan) and a Gentile father. While Solomon has sought to enlist the world's most skilled people, God ultimately provides an Israelite to do the job. The fact that this craftsman is from the tribe of Dan creates a parallel with Moses' preparation of the tabernacle in which God appointed a Danite to oversee the work (Exodus 31:6–11).

2:13–18 For the transport of the lumber, the logs are tied together and they float down the Mediterranean Sea, some seventy miles, to the only seaport in the area, Joppa. From Joppa they are carried across land some twenty or thirty miles to the city of Jerusalem, where they will be used in the construction of the temple. Solomon takes stock of the foreign labor force at his disposal and puts them to work according to the construction needs. Similar notes about aliens as laborers are made elsewhere in the Old Testament (1 Chronicles 22:2; Isaiah 60:10–12).

3:1–2 Solomon began this construction project around 966 BC, about 480 years after the Exodus (according to 1 Kings 6:1, which many use to date the Exodus around 1446 BC). The temple is being built on the threshing floor of Ornan, which is located on mount Moriah, the place where Abraham went to offer his son Isaac a thousand years earlier (Genesis 22:2–14).

3:3–8 The temple is ninety feet long by thirty feet wide, roughly twice the size of the tabernacle, which was forty-five feet long by thirty feet wide and fifteen feet high. The most holy house, or holy of holies, is thirty feet long by thirty feet wide. This is where the ark of God resides. The holy place is sixty feet long by thirty feet wide. But the whole temple area is much bigger— some fifty acres in all. Thus this area has to be built up and secured with various structures to help support it. Today the temple area still exists, with some additions that Herod made, and is an area that is claimed as a holy site by Jews, Muslims, and Christians.

3:9–14 Inside the holy of holies (the most holy house), standing above the ark of the covenant and the mercy seat, are two giant cherubim with a wingspan of fifteen feet each. One of their wings touches the wing of the other, and their other wing touches the wall, thus filling the whole place.

3:15–17 Two freestanding pillars flank the entrance of the temple. The names of the pillars reminded anyone who came to the temple, before he or she entered, that God had established this nation, and it is only by His strength that it will stand. It is unclear from the information here whether the pillars are load-bearing elements of the construction or simply a part of the aesthetics. Some have imagined them as freestanding pillars with bowls at the top that could be filled with oil and thus used for lighting (much like large oil lamps).

4:1 The brass altar of sacrifice is thirty feet long by thirty feet wide and about seventeen feet high. It stands in the courtyard directly in front of the temple.

4:2–5 The sea of cast brass, or the laver, is Solomon's version of the laver of brass in Moses' tabernacle (Exodus 30:18). It is fifteen feet across, forty-five feet in circumference, and seven and a half feet deep. It can hold between twelve and fifteen thousand gallons of water. It is used by the priests for ceremonial cleansing and is located to the south side of the temple, or on the left as you walk in. The twelve oxen mentioned are probably symbolic of the twelve tribes of Israel but also demonstrate how Solomon had adopted the Phoenician symbol of fertility (the bull), representative of God's life-giving rain.

4:6–8 The ten portable lavers are used for washing. Each laver is able to hold some 230 gallons of water, and they are placed on carts for mobility. These are located on the sides of the temple, five on each side. The tabernacle only had one menorah and one table of shewbread, while Solomon makes ten of each, placing five on each side of the temple.

4:9 The court of the priests and the great court are both mentioned in 1 Kings 6:36 and 7:12. The larger court is intended for the laity.

4:18 Note that they have so much brass for use in the temple that they do not bother to weigh it. The temple is a seven-year building project.

5:2 The city of David, also called Zion, was actually the easternmost hill in what we now know as Jerusalem. It was there that David had placed the ark in a tent. During the time of David, Zion was only about half of a city block wide and about two city blocks long, built upon the lower ridge of mount Moriah. The account given here in 2 Chronicles follows almost verbatim the account given in 1 Kings 8:1–13.

5:4–5 The transportation of the ark was to be done by the Levites, specifically the Levites who descended from Kohath. When it was time for the children of Israel to move, the tabernacle was to be dismantled, and the Kohathites had the responsibility of caring for the ark and the other temple implements. They would walk into the holy of holies backward, carrying a covering for the ark. Next they would place the covering over the ark and then lift the ark by two poles that were inserted through four rings located on the sides of the ark. The poles were then placed upon the shoulders of the priests (Exodus 25:10–16; Numbers 4:15).

5:7–8 The temple proper consists of two main rooms: The holy place is sixty feet long by thirty feet wide, and the most holy place is thirty feet long by thirty feet wide. It is in the most holy place, or the holy of holies, that the ark is to be placed. The wings of two cherubim form a canopy for the ark within the holy of holies. Each cherub has a wingspan of fifteen feet.

5:11 David had divided the priests into twenty-four divisions, each serving two weeks at a time. After their work is done, they return to their city until the time of their next service. The priests have forty-eight Levitical cities spread throughout the land of Israel in which to live. Here, for the dedication of the temple, all who were present during this time of celebration assisted in the sacrifices.

5:12–14 The words of praise recorded in verse 13 are used at other times in the accounts of 2 Chronicles (7:3; 20:21). After this time of worship and praise, the Shekinah glory, the presence of God, fills the temple. God inhabits the praises of His people.

6:1–2 Solomon explains that the Lord has said He will dwell in the dark cloud (Leviticus 16:2; Psalm 97:2). Throughout the scriptures, the full glory of the Lord is shrouded from the people, because it would consume those unworthy (Exodus 33:20). The Bible says that God allows His children to see His presence through a veil, as if through dark glasses, but one day we will see Him face-to-face, in all His glory, as we go to be with Him (1 Corinthians 13:12).

6:3–6 When God chose David to be the first king of the Israelites, He also declared that Jerusalem would be the place for the temple. Solomon honors God by building the temple according to His instructions and choice.

6:7–9 God does not allow David to build the temple because he has been too busy with war. Yet God, and Solomon in this speech, honors David for desiring to build a place centered on the purpose of worship.

6:26–31 Solomon considers how God often uses disasters—such as a drought or famine to get His children's attention. Disasters such as these force people to awaken out of spiritual slumber and turn to God. God is warning His people, through Solomon, that these things will come to pass if they fail to repent of their sins and cling to Him.

6:32–36 God opens the door for all to come to Him, not just the Israelites—an invitation not typically found in the Old Testament. Solomon asks the Lord to forgive all who come in repentance, even the foreigners. He prays that no matter where the people may be, God will hear their prayer and sustain them. Solomon's prayer is for mercy, because there is no one who does not sin.

7:1–3 In chapter 7 the glory of God fills the temple for a second time. The first time it is in response to worship, and this time it is in response to prayer. When God consumes the sacrifices, it is a sign of acceptance of those offerings. There are other examples in the Old Testament where this occurs. For instance, the same thing happened when the priests began their work in the tabernacle (Leviticus 9:23–24). Also, after David's unauthorized census, he offered sacrifices that were miraculously consumed (1 Chronicles 21:26).

7:6 The influence of David is clear in this passage. He invested heavily in the worship life of ancient Israel. He organized the worship leaders and the worship times, both day and night. He made the instruments used in worship and even wrote songs and psalms of praise to the Lord.

7:7 The brasen altar is the altar of sacrifice, which stands fifteen feet high by thirty feet long by thirty feet wide. Even so, it isn't big enough for all the sacrifices that are being offered. So Solomon sanctifies the entire outer court in order to offer all the sacrifices. The priests are in attendance for all the sacrifices and the work that needs to be done.

7:12–14 Solomon's prayer is answered with a tremendous promise: God will hear His children's cry for repentance, forgive the people's sins, and heal their land. This promise is especially powerful considering that the original audience for whom the Chronicler was writing was the remnant of Jews who had returned home from their Babylonian exile. A promise of restoration would have given them great hope.

7:19–20 Why had these people, the original audience of the Chronicles, been exiled? Basically because of the very warning recorded here from Solomon—they had forsaken the God of their fathers and worshipped idols. In light of that, the city of Jerusalem and their temple, the very temple whose dedication this section describes, had been destroyed. The Israelites as a nation and a culture had become a byword to many of their neighbors. The journey of this ragtag group to reassemble as a nation is filled with hardships. In some cases, however, it is only because of these trials that God's people will turn to Him. When they do, He will protect and heal them.

7:21–22 The reason for the captivity is simple: The Israelites turned away from the Lord. Solomon is warned against precisely that kind of rebellion, and yet he and future kings do not heed this warning.

8:1 Solomon spends seven years building the temple and thirteen years building his own house and administrative buildings. There is nothing wrong with building projects unless they become the focus of one's life, as with Solomon. Remember that when Solomon became king, he was just fourteen years old and dependent upon the Lord to guide him and give him wisdom to lead his people. Now twenty years have passed, and Solomon has become more self-reliant. He has placed his faith in himself instead of the Lord.

8:2–8 The cities Solomon builds up are located on the trade routes. Hamath-zobah is located 300 miles north of Jerusalem. Tadmor is a desert oasis located on the main highway from Mesopotamia, about 150 miles northeast of Damascus. Beth-horon is located about ten miles northwest of Jerusalem, on the border between Judah and the northern tribes. Baalath is located in the territory of Dan. These cities serve as places of prosperity and protection for the growing kingdom of Israel under Solomon's reign. Unfortunately, in many instances, the natives of the conquered cities remained and established a foothold within Israel. God had warned His people against not driving out the enemy—they pose a threat to Israel's religious faithfulness.

8:9–10 Solomon only uses foreigners—and not his own brethren—as a forced labor force, or slaves. The children of Israel are placed in higher positions, overseeing the work. Later, however, when the Israelites look back on Solomon's reign, they describe him as a harsh master (10:4).

8:11–15 Although Solomon is moving away from God's instruction in so many areas—for example, by marrying a foreign wife with her foreign gods—he continues to follow many customs taught him by his father (see also 1 Samuel 15:22–23).

8:17–18 The Israelites aren't a seafaring people, even though they sail and fish on the sea of Galilee. So Solomon again hires Huram, king of Tyre, to assist him in obtaining riches from other nations by his ships. The Phoenicians are a seafaring people. Their ships returned every three years full of riches and possessions from various nations. Solomon acquires 450 talents of gold from Ophir, which is a small amount compared to the 3,000 talents of gold David acquired from Ophir during the same amount of time.

9:1–4 The queen of Sheba travels some twelve hundred miles from Arabia to test Solomon's wisdom. Tradition tells us that Solomon is tested with riddles. Tradition also suggests that one of the riddles that the queen of Sheba gives to Solomon has to do with two bouquets of flowers. One is real and the other fake. As she stands at a distance that makes it impossible to tell with the naked eye which is which, Solomon has bees released and they fly into the real flowers. Solomon thus solves the riddle.

9:10–11 When algum wood, or juniper wood, is cut, it releases a sweet fragrance that does not decrease in its intensity. Also, this wood does not rot like other kinds of wood do. It is a marvelous gift to bring.

9:13–14 Solomon places a heavy tax burden on the people, but he does not need it any longer. The temple and the buildings are all completed, and he could have offered some relief to his people. His son Rehoboam is going to be asked to bring tax reform to the nation, but he refuses, and as a result, the nation is divided.

9:16–22 The house of the forest of Lebanon is one of Solomon's homes. This structure is 150 feet long by 75 feet wide and 45 feet tall. It is surrounded by forty-five cedar pillars, so as you look at the building, it looks like a forest. Solomon has his throne made of ivory, and then he covers the ivory with gold. The people are hurting from the heavy burden of taxes, but even so Solomon is living a life of luxury.

9:23–24 Solomon is charging people to share in this gift God has given to him. God gave him this wisdom, and now he is making a profit from it. He is doing everything that God told him not to do (Deuteronomy 17).

9:30–31 Solomon's death marks a transition. Now his son Rehoboam is on the throne, and instead of following the spiritual influence of King David, Rehoboam continues riding the materialistic wave that began with Solomon. The downward spiral that this creates in Israel will continue until the people's captivity.

10:1 Note that Rehoboam travels to Shechem to be approved as king, rather than Jerusalem where his father, Solomon, was anointed. Shechem was a significant place to several Jewish fathers. It was a strategic battle site as well as a religious site. Abraham and Jacob built altars there (Genesis 12:6–7; 33:18–20). After the final conquest of Canaan, Joshua's covenant renewal happened there (Joshua 24). Rehoboam reigns for seventeen years. In that amount of time, Israel deteriorates into a second-class nation. At one time, people from near and far came to see the glory of this kingdom, but that is going to change very quickly.

10:2 Jeroboam is a young and industrious man of whom Solomon had taken notice. Solomon placed him in charge of the labor force over the house. We know from 1 Kings 11:28–40 that Ahijah the Shilonite, a prophet of God, meets with Jeroboam in a field. Ahijah takes the garment of Jeroboam, tears it into twelve pieces, and tells him to take ten of those pieces. Solomon heard about this situation and tried to stop it by attempting to kill Jeroboam, who then fled to Egypt for safety. Now that Solomon is dead, Jeroboam returns from Egypt to Jerusalem.

10:3–4 The people's request reveals something about Solomon's reign. The people are tired and feel they have been overburdened by Solomon. Now that Rehoboam is king, they want him to ease up on their burden of taxation.

10:8–11 Although the text refers to these advisors as young men, they are no teenagers. Rehoboam has grown up with these men, and he is over forty years old himself. Nevertheless, due to inexperience, if not youth, their counsel is foolish.

10:16–17 The nation divides—the ten northern tribes separate from Judah and Benjamin in the south. Up to this point, both the northern and southern tribes are referred to as Israel. Here the conflicting groups are identified as the house of David and the house of Israel. Eventually, however, the northern tribes come to be known as Israel and the southern tribes come to be known as Judah.

10:17–19 When the northern tribes kill the messenger, Hadoram, Rehoboam recognizes the trouble Israel is in and flees from Shechem, traveling about twenty-five miles south to Jerusalem.

10:19 The term *Israel* refers to the northern tribes. The term *rebellion* is more than a description of the civil conflict. Here the northern tribes have rebelled against the covenant God had made with David, that his house would rule all of Israel.

11:1–4 The division of Israel grieves God, and yet He allows it. The northern kingdom of Israel begins and ends in idolatry. They have no king who leads them in the ways of the Lord. The southern kingdom of Judah has its problems as well but at least has its share of godly kings who bring reform to the land. Thus this division is healthy, in a sense, for the southern kingdom of Judah. The references to Judah and Benjamin in verses 1 and 3 refer to tribes as well as locations.

11:5–12 Rehoboam is fortifying Judah's cities with military strength because he has legitimate concerns about his kingdom being overthrown by surrounding nations.

11:13–17 There is a religious fallout to the civil rebellion. The priests—relieved of their duties by Jeroboam—head to Jerusalem to continue the work they are called to do. Not only do the priests begin to leave, but some of the people do as well, in light of the idolatry that Jeroboam is bringing into the land.

11:15 The calf idols are reminiscent of the earlier act of rebellion in which the Israelites created and worshipped a golden calf after they left Egypt but as they were still on the way to Canaan (Exodus 32:1–10; Deuteronomy 9:16).

11:22–23 The king is concerned that his sons might be murdered, so he spreads them out throughout the land to prevent them from being wiped out. Whereas Solomon's rule represented a time of great peace, King Rehoboam fears rebellion from within and attack from outside. Israel has very little promise of stability.

12:1–4 Rehoboam starts his regime looking to the Lord for help, but this attitude deteriorates over time because of pride and self-reliance. Shishak is God's judgment upon Rehoboam and the southern kingdom of Judah because they turned away from Him.

12:1 The reference to "all" of Israel is a reference to the southern kingdom. At this point, many of the faithful from the northern kingdom have migrated southward. So this is a reference to all those of Israel who remain in the southern kingdom of Judah. Keep in mind that the writer of Chronicles is describing these events many years after they happened. He recounts the beginnings of the fall of the nation and thus reminds the people of the price of disobedience.

12:5–8 God's prophet Shemaiah helps the king and his leaders recognize their failure and see the righteousness of God. God is waiting with His forgiveness, and as soon as they humble themselves before Him and repent of their sin, He forgives them. God is not going to allow Egypt to wipe Judah out, but He is going to allow them to oppress Judah. The contrast that is placed before Judah is clear: Serving a holy and merciful God is far more rewarding than serving a wicked and cruel earthly king.

12:9–11 When Shishak takes the gold shields, which may have been more a tribute paid by Rehoboam to Shishak than an actual theft, Rehoboam makes brass shields to replace them. Brass is worthless, but it can be polished so that from a distance it gives the appearance of gold. The king goes through all the motions, making it look like nothing has happened.

12:14–16 Rehoboam's heart is not fixed on the Lord, and thus the fruit of his life is evil. This account of Rehoboam's reign is much longer than the parallel account in 1 Kings. The extrabiblical documents listed in verse 15 may have supplied additional information. The mention of these documents reminds us that these writers were real-life people with records to keep and an interest in historical documentation.

13:1–3 Civil war breaks out between the northern and southern kingdoms of Israel. Abijah, king of the southern kingdom of Judah, is outnumbered two to one.

13:4–8 Abijah tries to talk his way out of this battle, explaining that David and his descendants have the right to the throne and Jeroboam doesn't. The covenant of salt speaks of preservation—the dynasty of David is not to end.

13:9–10 To become a priest under Jeroboam, all one needs is a young bull and seven rams—Jeroboam's priesthood functions like an auction. Yet serving God is not an item for sale; it is a calling. Abijah declares that Judah has not forsaken God; their priests are of the Levite lineage, and they are doing what God has told them to do.

13:12 Abijah declares that God is on his side; thus to fight against Abijah's kingdom is to fight against God's purposes. This highlights the importance of the covenant God made with David, that his house would rule forever. This covenant is Abijah's claim and his judgment against Jeroboam.

13:18 Here is the key to Judah's victory—they trusted the God of their ancestors. They were not relying on their own strength. This statement would serve as a reminder to the original hearers of this document to return to the faith of their ancestors if they would have any hope of reestablishing themselves as a nation.

14:1 In many ways, this period of turmoil and war with the north strengthens Judah, and when Abijah dies, his son Asa will reign during some of the most peaceful years in this era of Israel's history.

14:2–5 Asa is one of the few godly kings to rule the southern kingdom of Judah. Not only is he going through the motions of serving the Lord, but his heart is in the right place as well. Asa brings spiritual reform to the southern kingdom of Judah, destroys the worship of foreign gods, and follows after the Lord. But, like many spiritual revivals, it does not go far enough.

14:9–11 Zerah the Ethiopian (or Cushite) brings an army of a million men. This army far outnumbers Judah's forces, so Asa cries out to God for help—the key turn of events in this situation. God does not need a whole army to win. Asa is at peace, because he trusts God. Asa's prayer stands as a model still for us today. He acknowledges God's power, acknowledges his own helplessness and need, and then requests God's help, not on behalf of the convenience of the people but on behalf of God's glory and reputation.

14:12–15 After Asa's victory over the Ethiopians, Judah has no more battles with Egypt until Josiah meets Pharaoh Neco in 609 BC.

15:1–3 The prophet Azariah comes to Asa after this great victory and reminds him to continue walking with the Lord—warning that if he forgets to rely on the Lord for strength, God will forsake him. Azariah recounts Israel's history: Before there were priests, before there was the law, God was the One who was still faithful even though His people were not.

15:4–5 The trouble mentioned here is not identified as a specific era or event in the history of Israel. Throughout Israel's history, however, there were cycles of a falling away from the faith, the consequences that falling away incurred, and then God's deliverance of His people from the destruction faced in light of those consequences.

15:8–12 As word spreads to the northern kingdom about the spiritual reform in the southern kingdom of Judah, and how God is blessing Asa, many come down to Judah to reap some of those blessings. The nation comes together, though just for a time, and they make a covenant to seek the Lord wholeheartedly.

15:13–15 The Israelites have good intentions, but they go too far when they put to death those who refuse to turn to God. You can't force love for God. The people come before the Lord in prayer and worship, not because they have to, but because they have the desire to; it flows from their lives.

15:16 Asa removes Maachah, who is either his mother or his grandmother, from office because of her idolatry. His first loyalty is to the Lord; no one is given special treatment. The grove was an indicator of the Canaanite fertility god named Asherah. Moses clearly forbade the Israelites to set up any worship centers for this goddess (Deuteronomy 16:21).

16:1 Baasha, king of the northern kingdom of Israel, builds up Ramah, which is located about five miles north of Jerusalem on the border between the two kingdoms and on an important trade route linking Egypt and Mesopotamia. He does this to stop the migration of his people to Judah. In the process, Baasha brings his men and supplies to prepare for war against Judah.

16:2 Asa is in trouble again, but instead of turning to God, as he did in chapter 14, he turns to a human. Asa takes the treasuries of God and gives them to Ben-hadad, king of Syria, to get help with his problems.

16:3–6 Ben-hadad has a treaty with Baasha, but he is bought out by Asa's and so comes to Judah's aid. Baasha is down in Ramah, in the southern part of his kingdom, so Ben-hadad strikes Israel at its northern borders. The plan works. Asa is free of Baasha, but this success does not mean God is pleased.

16:7–8 God rebukes Asa through the prophet Hanani, a seer about whom we know nothing more than what is recorded here (except for a mention of his son, Jehu, in 19:2). Hanani reminds Asa that when the Ethiopians came upon him, he turned to the Lord for help and not simply to another human.

16:9 Asa's life parallels his great-grandfather Solomon's. Solomon started out young and inexperienced and asked God for wisdom to lead his people. He looked to the Lord for strength until he grew strong and wealthy. He then took his focus off the Lord as he grew confident in his own strength. Asa also takes his eyes off the Lord and places his confidence in his own strength toward the end of his life.

16:11–14 God illustrates how trusting in the Lord as a last resort has become a pattern in Asa's life. Asa's walk with the Lord has been hampered. He no longer has an intimate relationship with the Lord, and his spiritual walk is hindered by his disease. Asa's life, like Solomon's, looks promising, and yet it has very low points of disappointment. At significant times he trusts more in humankind than he trusts in the Lord, particularly in the latter part of his life. Still, 2 Chronicles 15:17 describes Asa as a person whose heart was fully committed to God. Perhaps his legacy cannot be determined by any one downfall or disappointment (as is described in chapter 16). At his best moments, his hope was in God's strength, not his own.

17:3 Jehoshaphat does not seek Baalim (the nature gods) to make the land fertile, but instead he seeks the Lord. The Lord had told His people not to make graven images or idols for themselves (Leviticus 19:4). God is the only true God.

17:4–6 At this time, the northern kingdom of Israel is ruled by wicked King Ahab and his wife, Jezebel. Ahab and Jezebel introduce Baal worship to the Israelites and even set up altars to worship this false god. Meanwhile, Jehoshaphat and the southern kingdom of Judah follow the Lord.

17:7–11 Jehoshaphat does not simply condemn people for being wrong; he leads them in the ways they should go. This good king enjoys times of peace and prosperity as a result of his faithfulness to God. Even the Philistines, who are a constant thorn in the side of Israel, are subdued during this time.

17:12–19 Jehoshaphat, like his father, brings spiritual reform to the southern kingdom of Judah. This brings the fear of the Lord to the kingdoms around Judah so that they do not seek war against Judah.

18:1 Perhaps Jehoshaphat joins this alliance with Ahab in order to heal the wounds between the two kingdoms, but just as oil and water don't mix, neither do good and evil. An alliance between the two kingdoms, and between Jehoshaphat and Ahab, would be strange and unworkable at best.

18:5–7 The false prophets are not the prophets of Baal, destroyed by Elijah at mount Carmel prior to this time (1 Kings 18). These prophets are likely the false prophets of the calf worship that Jeroboam had established. So they claim to be worshipping Yahweh, but they worship Him by worshipping an idol, a direct violation of the second of the Ten Commandments. Ahab's prophets speak to please the king and use the name of God even though it is meaningless to them. Jehoshaphat recognizes that something is not right, for God has given him discernment as he looks for a true prophet of God. Ahab is not interested in the truth.

18:8–10 As both of these kings sit before the four hundred prophets, the prophet Zedekiah uses horns to illustrate that Ahab and his men are going to push back and defeat the Syrians, but these are not the words of God.

18:11–13 These false prophets know of Yahweh, but they do not follow after His commands. Micaiah speaks the truth, but no one is interested if the truth isn't a positive message.

18:14–17 The prophet says what the king wants to hear, but the king is not convinced. Perhaps he picks up on the prophet's sarcasm. When Micaiah does reveal the bad news, it is clear that Ahab doesn't want to hear it. He shuns the words of the prophet, claiming Micaiah was predisposed to prophesy a negative outcome.

18:18–22 This can be a difficult passage—questioning how a holy and righteous God can send forth a lying spirit. In the end, however, God does give all of us a choice: If we reject the truth, then we open ourselves up to receive a lie, just as Ahab does. Ahab hears the truth, but he rejects it, and because of this he opens himself up to be deceived by the enemy.

18:28–29 After hearing these words of Micaiah, Jehoshaphat follows after Ahab anyway, even though God tells him not to go. In this way, Jehoshaphat actually fulfills Micaiah's prophecy that he will be lured into destruction (18:20–22). Ahab, concerned that the prophecy of his death may come true, disguises himself as a regular soldier so he will not draw fire as someone dressed like an officer or a king would.

18:30–32 As is common in military strategy, the king of Syria tells his men to focus on the king and destroy him. This confirms Ahab's decision to disguise himself. Unfortunately, Jehoshaphat has worked so hard to be agreeable with Ahab that he has put himself in a precarious position by wearing Ahab's robes.

18:33–34 As the archer releases his arrow, not trying for any particular target, it strikes Ahab between his armor with a mortal wound. In Ahab's story is the lesson that you simply cannot escape the judgment of God no matter how hard you try. You cannot hide from God.

19:1–3 Jehu is the son of Hanani who rebuked King Asa of Judah when he entered into an alliance with a foreign king (1 Kings 16:1–9). In this case, Jehoshaphat was fellowshipping with Ahab, and it put him in a position to be led astray. Jehu rebukes Jehoshaphat for his actions. But Jehu also mentions the good that Jehoshaphat has done and the fact that he seeks after God, which tends to be a theme in Chronicles.

19:5–11 As opposed to being merely representatives of the king, these judges represent God and His justice in the social order of Israel. In this way, Jehoshaphat seeks to restore godliness to the system in Israel since it is supposed to be a nation guided by God. Note that he appoints two "attorney generals" of sorts: Amariah for religious matters and Zebadiah for civil matters.

20:1 Three people groups come to make war. The Moabites and Ammonites are blood relatives of Israel. Both people groups descended from the daughters of Lot, Abraham's nephew. Their ancestors were the children of an incestuous relationship between Lot and his two daughters after the destruction of Sodom and Gomorrah (Genesis 19). The third group, "other beside the Ammonites," is a people associated with the Edomites in this passage, but it is sometimes translated Menuites. While the Menuite territory was associated with Mount Seir, a mountain range in Edom, they are a separate nation.

20:2 This verse gives a description that implies the Edomites: "beyond the sea on this side Syria." Edom is related to Israel (as are the Moabites and Ammonites). Esau, the son of Isaac and the brother of Jacob (from whom the nation of Israel descended), is the ancestor of the Edomites (Genesis 36).

20:3–4 As often is the case, fear causes Jehoshaphat to refocus on the Lord and look to Him for strength. He calls the national fast as a way for the people to purify themselves and hopefully add more power to their prayers.

20:9 When Solomon dedicated the temple, he prayed that God would answer the cry of His people when they were in trouble (1 Kings 8:22–30). Jehoshaphat is echoing the prayer of Solomon here. When the Israelites had come out of Egypt, Ammon, Moab, and Edom had refused Israel passage through their land, and God had forbidden Israel from destroying them (Edom, Numbers 20:18–20; Ammon, Deuteronomy 23:3–4; Moab, Judges 11:17–18). Now these people groups are joining forces to destroy Judah.

20:10–13 Jehoshaphat recognizes that he cannot win on his own, and so his eyes are upon the Lord. It is when we lose the consciousness of God in our lives that things get out of focus and we become anxious and terrified. Just like the Israelites, we often find ourselves surrounded by the enemy.

20:14–21 Jahaziel reminds Israel that it's God's battle. The battle plan is simple: Go into battle with praise and worship, and see the salvation that the Lord will bring. It seems like a foolish military plan, but God uses it to bring about a great victory. Tekoa is located

approximately twelve miles south of Jerusalem and about six miles southeast of Bethlehem. It is located on high ground between two watersheds. The area around it is referred to as the wilderness of Tekoa.

20:22–26 When Jehoshaphat's army enters singing God's praises, the enemy, confused by the people's spirit of praise in the midst of difficulty, ends up killing one another. What was once the valley of the shadow of death God has now made the valley of Berachah, or the valley of blessing.

20:27–30 When the other nations see what the Lord has done, how He fought for Judah, the fear of the Lord comes upon them. In this way, God gives the southern kingdom of Judah some rest from its enemies.

20:31–35 Though Jehoshaphat is a godly king, he continues to make alliances with the ungodly kings of the northern kingdom in a misguided effort to bring unity between the two nations. Here he makes an alliance with Ahaziah, the son of Ahab. Treaties, however, are not going to smooth over the real differences that exist between the split nation that is now Israel and Judah.

20:33 The continuing problem with the nation of Israel is that they are still not wholehearted in their faith. Even after seeing God's provision, they had not set their hearts on God, clearing away the debris of idolatry around them (1 Kings 22:43).

20:36–37 God is not going to bless an endeavor of those who are rebelling against His law. Here Jehoshaphat makes an alliance with Ahaziah to gather some merchant ships, but before it even gets off the ground, God puts an end to it, refusing to bless the venture.

21:1–6 Though Jehoram was preceded by a father and grandfather who led Judah to faith and prosperity, he instead begins his reign with the murder of all his brothers (to remove competition for the throne) and leads the people of Judah into idolatry. The people and things you surround yourself with always affect your own walk of faith. Such was the case with Jehoram. The wickedness that flows from Ahab and Jezebel, rulers of Israel, not only affects their daughter Athaliah, who becomes Jehoram's wife, but also the king of Judah himself.

21:7–11 God could choose to destroy Jehoram, and thus the reign of a descendant of David, because of Jehoram's wickedness. Instead, He honors His promise to David to establish his throne forever (2 Samuel 7:13; 1 Kings 15:4–5; 2 Kings 8:19; 1 Chronicles 17:4–14). Nevertheless, judgment does come upon the nation by various nations rising up against them.

21:12–15 Some have called into question the authorship of the letter attributed to Elijah, since Elijah's death had been recorded in 2 Kings during Jehoshaphat's reign. Others point out, however, that Jehoram and Jehoshaphat ruled together for a time. Elijah would have been elderly but could have been alive long enough to be aware of Jehoram. The text does not say what affliction Jehoram is struck with, but it is serious enough to cause him a slow death.

21:18–19 Just as Jehoram experienced God's judgment in the form of a physical ailment, so did Asa, the king of Judah who suffered from a foot disease but refused to ask for God's help (1 Kings 15:23), and Uzziah, the king of Judah who was cursed with a skin rash (2 Chronicles 26:18–20).

22:1–2 In 2 Kings 8:26 we are told that Ahaziah is twenty-two years old when he becomes king (not forty-two years old, as is stated here in 2 Chronicles). Scholars agree that it seems likely the copyediting error is here in 2 Chronicles. This minor discrepancy is often cited as evidence that the Bible, especially the Old Testament, is unreliable. The earliest manuscripts of the Old Testament still in existence today are from the Dead Sea Scrolls, which date around 125 BC. In comparing those scrolls with a scroll of Isaiah from 900 AD, scholars find only 5 percent variation, consisting chiefly of spelling differences. No significant change in meaning is found. The scriptures have been one of the most highly analyzed books of antiquity and are found to be one of the most reliably and carefully transmitted works available today.

22:3–4 Families can be forces for good and supportive environments, or they can be sources of great strife, bad influences, and true tragedy. Athaliah greatly influences her son to rule wickedly. Ahaziah saturates himself with evil counselors, including his mother, and evil is what flows from his life.

22:6–9 At this point in history, the relationships in the intermarriages between the rulers of Israel in the north and the rulers of Judah in the south are becoming increasingly messy. Jehu's killing spree—King Joram of Israel, forty-two of Ahaziah's brothers, and Ahaziah—places Jehu on the throne in the northern kingdom of Israel, while in the southern kingdom of Judah the throne is vacant. Athaliah's response—killing all the royal heirs—is her own power play and a direct attack on God's promise to David that his descendants will remain on the throne. Note that with the other rulers, the Chronicler bookends their accounts with a kind of summary report. In Athaliah's case, however, no such summary appears, which reveals a lack of credibility for her reign.

22:10–12 By God's grace, Athaliah has not been entirely successful in her campaign to wipe out the heirs to the throne, and the Davidic dynasty barely survives. This time the only surviving heir is one-year-old Joash, hidden by his aunt for six years in one of the chambers that surrounds the temple.

23:1–8 Jehoiada resists Athaliah even as he is raising the hidden heir to the throne. Given the political power plays in the kingdom—including murder—it is risky to make the attempt to restore the throne to someone from the line of David. That is why extreme measures are being taken to protect the young heir, who is the final link to the Messiah whom God had promised.

23:13–15 Joash is only seven years old at the time he takes the throne from Athaliah. Note the irony as Athaliah cries treason—she who usurped the throne and

committed murder to attempt to ensure her power. While Jehoiada is credited with Joash's rise to the throne, it seems clear that the coup had both religious and political roots.

23:19–21 The porters, or doorkeepers, are needed not only to prevent anything that is unclean from entering and defiling the temple but also to allow those who belong in the temple to freely enter. Now that the proper king, Joash, a descendant of David, is in place, peace returns to the land for a brief period.

24:1–3 At this point, high priest Jehoiada is the power behind the throne. He is a good role model for Joash, and the people of Judah are blessed by his actions.

24:4–7 Joash wants to rebuild and repair the temple of God that was plundered by Athaliah and her sons. He sets the Levites in charge of this project, but they don't do it quickly and are dragging their feet. They have no heart to restore the worship of God.

24:7 Since we have a record of Athaliah murdering any possible rivals to the throne, the term *sons* here may refer to political followers rather than biological sons.

24:8–14 A half-shekel is already given each year, by every male over twenty years old, for the upkeep of the tabernacle and later the temple (Exodus 30:14–16). With Joash's offering chest, the people have a way to give more than the minimum requirement if they desire, and the people respond with a willing spirit by rejoicing in the opportunity to participate in the Lord's work.

24:15–16 The description of Jehoiada's old age signifies honor and respect. He was a positive influence in the life of Joash, and the nation was blessed by God as a result. His burial is in sharp contrast to that of Jehoram (21:19–20). Jehoiada is buried with the kings because the people loved him for bringing spiritual reform to the nation and for putting God back on the throne.

24:17–19 Joash is like a spiritual chameleon, changing his behavior to fit those who are around him. As the story unfolds, we see that he never really has a heart for the Lord himself, but is more influenced by others. God's desire is not to bring judgment and destroy Joash but to see him turn from his evil ways and live; thus He sends warnings through prophets.

24:18 Asherah is a fertility goddess of the Canaanite religions and mythologies. Often associated with Baal, her shrines took the form of upright wooden pole; thus her worship sites were often referred to as groves. The tree was a symbol associated with Ashtaroth worship (worship of Asherah).

24:20–22 Zechariah must have been like a brother to Joash, because they grew up together. Joash has a choice to heed the warnings from this close confidant, but instead he orders the death of Zechariah to be carried out at the very place he was anointed king by Jehoiada. It is a terrible sign of how quickly he has fallen from the truth.

24:23–24 Chronicles equates the military defeat of Judah—at the hands of the Syrians—with the judgment of God against Joash's sin. This is meant to both remind and warn the remnant of Israel, the audience for this book. Just as with the other evil kings, no fanfare surrounds Joash's death, which transpired at the hands of his own servants. He is not even buried with the other kings—a stark contrast to how his mentor was celebrated in his death in verses 15–16.

25:1–5 Amaziah is not wholeheartedly devoted to the Lord, although he responds to the prophetic warning in Deuteronomy.

24:16 Jesus is speaking to Amaziah's kind of commitment when He speaks of those who honor God with their lips while their hearts are far from Him (Matthew 15:8).

25:6–9 Amaziah hires one hundred thousand mercenaries from Israel, the northern kingdom that is famous for wickedness, to assist him in battle. The prophet warns him against this because wicked Israel would not have God on its side; thus they would not have God's help in the battle.

25:13 Mercenaries are typically paid to fight, but they can add to their fee by taking spoils from the battle. The Israelite soldiers received their fighting fee but did not get to add to it. On their way home to Israel, the mercenaries attack some of the cities and villages in Judah, getting back some of the spoil they would have gained if they had been able to fight against the Edomites.

25:14–17 In response to Judah's God-granted victory, Amaziah immediately strays, gathers the gods of the people he has just defeated, and worships them. This looting of the temple idols is not uncommon. At the time, these were considered war trophies. First Samuel, in fact, describes a time when the Israelite's ark of the covenant was captured and held on display by the Philistines (1 Samuel 5:1–2). Amaziah's worship of these gods, however, clearly disregards God's commands and sets him on a path of destruction. When God's prophet warns the king, Amaziah's sharp rebuff reveals the hardness of his heart.

25:18–24 The king of the northern kingdom of Israel is a different Joash than Amaziah's predecessor. The king of Israel cautions Amaziah against attacking them, reminding him that his victory against the Edomites was God's doing. Verse 20 seems to offer the idea that Amaziah's hardness of heart is somehow from God. As a result, Judah is defeated because of the people's sin. Not only is the house of God plundered, but so, too, is the king's house, and many are taken away captive as slaves.

25:25–28 The suffering of Judah is a reminder of the consequences of sin—it affects our worship of God, destroys and robs us of our witness, and eventually enslaves us completely. Amaziah has led the people astray, and their anger burns into a murderous rage. His sin has pushed them over the edge and bred their own sinfulness.

26:1 After only six years of Amaziah's reign, his son Uzziah co-reigns with him for twenty-three years. After his father's death, Uzziah is the sole king in the kingdom of Judah, reigning for another twenty-nine years. Uzziah is a good king and a strong leader, which is the reason the people place him on the throne at the age of sixteen.

26:2–10 After the death of his father, Uzziah begins to recapture cities that were lost to the enemy and restore them or build them up. The nation enjoys a time of prosperity, not because Uzziah is doing good works but because he places God before everything else in his life. God has begun to once again bless the southern kingdom of Judah with victory over its enemies. The cycle is clear: When the Israelites seek God, they become mighty. Under Uzziah's leadership, the people begin to honor God and also return to cultivating the land. As a result, it blossoms once again.

26:11–15 Uzziah is able to achieve success in three areas: winning victory in war, overseeing massive building projects, and making the land fruitful again. The strength of his army and his ability to develop weapons of war also help to put down the enemy.

26:16–23 Uzziah becomes too self-important for his own good. He is a king, not a priest, and thus not allowed in the temple to offer incense to the Lord. But because of his pride, he approaches God without humility. As a result, God strikes him with leprosy, and he is banished from the city, forced to co-reign with his son Jotham.

27:1–2 In contrast to the mixed records of his predecessors, Jotham is a good king. His only flaw is that he avoids the temple, most likely because he witnessed what happened to his father, Uzziah, in that temple (26:19–21).

27:3–6 Ophel is where the old city of David was located, farther down the slope of mount Moriah. Jotham looks to the Lord for guidance, but he never really has a true heart of worship. Still, his victory over the Ammonites highlights God's approval of him.

27:7–9 When Ahaz, Jotham's son, takes the throne, whatever strides had been made toward following the Lord are pushed back by the new king. The kingdom of Judah will never fully recover from the influences of King Ahaz.

28:1–2 When God associates a king with the kings of Israel, it is a rebuke. The kings of Israel were wicked. In this case, Ahaz of Judah is just as wicked as the northern kings were. He is not at all like David, the standard by which all kings are to be judged.

28:3–4 Ahaz even sacrifices his own children by fire, a pagan ritual mentioned elsewhere in scripture (Leviticus 18:21; Deuteronomy 12:31; 2 Kings 16:3). The place where they offer these children to the god Molech, by passing them through the fire, is located in the valley of Hinnom, which is just south and west of Jerusalem. In the New Testament, this area is used as a garbage dump, which continued to burn day and night. Jesus uses the valley of Hinnom as an illustration of hell, Gehenna (Matthew 10:28).

28:5–13 God uses the Arameans, or Syrians, and the northern kingdom of Israel to carry out His judgment on Judah. But Israel goes overboard and takes back home with them many slaves, which God forbids. Though the kingdom had divided, the people of Judah and Israel were one people. The Israelites were enslaving their own.

The prophet Oded rebukes the Israelites for thinking that they are better than Judah, and for once, the Samarians take the prophet's words to heart. The people in Samaria actually obey the prophet's warning. They recognize that they are not perfect, that the nation has many problems, and by continuing to disobey God's commands, they are fearful that they will add to their sin and judgment.

28:14–15 It was a common practice to humiliate captives, and many times they were taken away completely unclothed. Thus, because the Israelites are mending their ways, these captives are given clothes and food, and the weak are given donkeys to ride home. The Israelites do the right thing in releasing their captives.

28:22–23 Ahaz hardens his heart even more and refuses to look to God. His was a typical perspective for his era. If a king won a battle, then it was assumed that he had his god's approval and that his god was stronger than the god of the army he had defeated. If Damascus defeated Judah, then to Ahaz, Damascus's gods were more powerful than Ahaz's.

28:24–27 After Ahaz's death, Hezekiah reigns in Judah. Although he is a great king, he will not be able to overcome the spiritual darkness that was brought on by his father, King Ahaz. The kingdom of Judah is only about 110 years away from the Babylonian invasion. Even one bad leader can affect the course of a nation for generations to come.

29:1 Judah never fully recovers from Ahaz's negative influence, and judgment in the form of the Babylonian captivity is looming a mere 110 years down the road. Even a good king like Hezekiah could not reverse the wicked influence of the previous generations.

29:2 Hezekiah is probably the best king since the time of David. He brings spiritual reform to the nation, and he is also able to remove the idols that had crept into the people's practice of worship, including the bronze serpent that Moses had used to challenge the people to stop grumbling in the desert following their deliverance from captivity in Egypt (Numbers 21:4–8). It's been about eight hundred years since their ancestors wandered in the wilderness, and the people are now worshiping this bronze serpent on a pole (2 Kings 18:4).

29:3–5 Hezekiah is sandwiched between his father, Ahaz, and his son Manasseh, who both led wicked regimes. Yet clearly God is the focus of Hezekiah's life. Isaiah the prophet influences Hezekiah's life in a positive manner (Isaiah 36–39). Hezekiah wastes no time in bringing spiritual reform to the nation, beginning with the reopening of the temple. He begins immediately to cleanse, repair, and restore it to usher in an era of spiritual revival. Under his father, the temple had become a place to store junk—an appropriate metaphor for the clutter in the hearts of the people. Hezekiah is ready to de-clutter.

29:6–11 Hezekiah asserts that Judah is under judgment for its neglect of the temple—including the rituals that God had given the people to remember His faithfulness, such as lighting the menorah. Hezekiah is going to gather the religious leaders to see that they get right with God and consecrate their hearts before the Lord.

29:17–19 It takes sixteen days to clean the temple proper and to restore the house of God to a place of worship. Imagine the amount of garbage that needed to be hauled out. This is a major project of restoration.

29:20–36 The ceremony of restoring the temple consists of three crucial elements: atonement sacrifices brought by the leaders, arrangement of music, and sacrifices of thanksgiving from the people. The process takes less than three weeks.

29:27 From here on in the Chronicles, the term *Israel* is used to refer to Judah together with the refugees from the northern tribes.

30:1–9 The northern kingdom of Israel has been carried away captive by the Assyrians for its idolatry. Only a few people remain in the land, and Hezekiah reaches out to them and urges them to get right with God. Hezekiah began his reign the first month of the ecclesiastical (or religious) year, which was the month of Nisan, or March/April. The passover was also celebrated in the month of Nisan. The problem was that the temple was not cleaned until the sixteenth of the month, and passover began on the fourteenth of the month, followed by the feast of unleavened bread. God made a provision to the people, through Moses, that if they could not celebrate passover in the first month, they could celebrate it on the fourteenth day of the second month, so this is precisely what Hezekiah begins to institute (Numbers 9:9–11). The king also invites those who have escaped from the hands of the Assyrians in the northern kingdom not only to join in the passover celebration but to return to the Lord and restore unity to the kingdom.

30:10–12 Even after many have been carried away captive, some Israelites in the north still refuse to repent of their sin. They laugh in the face of God. Some do respond and go to Jerusalem to celebrate the passover. In Judah, they experience unity in the Lord, which unites them as one nation.

30:13–20 According to Deuteronomy 16:16–17, during the feast of passover, a worshipper would take his own lamb, without spot or blemish, and sacrifice it himself. In this case, the Levites sacrificed the lambs for those worshippers who were unclean. These people were seeking God, and thus they came as they were without knowledge of what they would do to be ceremonially clean. This shows flexibility and insight on the part of Hezekiah, who understood that it is not the religious ritual that makes one acceptable to God; it is a matter of the heart.

30:21–24 When true revival breaks out, studying the Word of God also becomes a focus again. The energy is so amazing that they extend their celebration, and Hezekiah gives out of his own possessions unto the Lord.

31:1–4 The spiritual revival is leading now to social changes, as the false worship places are destroyed—as well as the sexual perversion and carnality that accompany them. This is not only affecting the southern kingdom of Judah but has also spread northward, into Israel. Hezekiah is following the example that David laid out regarding temple service for the priests. In David's kingdom, each division served for two weeks out of the year in the temple, and the rest of the time they ministered to those in their hometown. Remember that during the time of David, the priests were spread out throughout the land of Israel in forty-eight Levitical cities so that no one was more than a day's journey from a priest.

31:5–15 When people's hearts are touched by God, one of the evidences is the way they give. Included here is a record of abundant giving. For four months the people bring gifts to help support the priests and their families, so much so that the offerings are in heaps. The priests and Levites are blessed beyond measure—they have more than they need.

31:16–19 Hezekiah makes sure everyone gets what is rightfully his or hers. Throughout the land, anyone who works in the temple receives a portion for every family member over three years old. (Children younger than three were still nursing, but once they were weaned from breast milk, they received their portion.)

31:20–21 Hezekiah and the nation prosper, because his heart is set on doing what is right before the Lord. His eyes are properly focused on God, and his priorities are right. He puts God first in his life.

32:1–4 King Ahaz, Hezekiah's father, had made a treaty with Tiglath-pileser, king of Assyria, for protection (2 Kings 16:7). Now that Hezekiah is on the throne, he breaks any treaties that his father had made (2 Kings 18:7), and there are sure to be repercussions. Jerusalem has two main sources of water, the watercourse of Gihon in the Kidron Valley and the spring of En-Rogel, which was two miles to the south. Hezekiah has two groups of workers—one group working from the watercourse of Gihon, digging a tunnel through solid rock toward the city, and another group digging from the pool of Siloah out of the city. His goal is to bring the water supply into the city so that even if the city is under attack, the people can still survive. This tunnel, which is some 1,777 feet long, is a constant source of fresh water. This tunnel Hezekiah builds exists in Israel to this day.

32:5–8 Hezekiah fortifies the city, rebuilds what was broken, builds towers on the walls, and prepares weapons for war. He does all that he can do, and then he commits the rest to God. Hezekiah strengthens not only himself but his people as well—by sharing with them the Word of God.

32:9–15 Lachish is about thirty miles southwest of Jerusalem. It's from this nearby location that Sennacherib, the king of Assyria, sends his representatives to Jerusalem to give the Israelites an ultimatum to surrender or die fighting. Intimidation plays a big role in the Assyrian tactics. Rab-shakeh, the field commander—thinking that Hezekiah had removed the places of all worship rather than simply false worship—tells them that their God is not going to spare them when their own king has destroyed all

the worship sites. This only reveals his ignorance of the God of Israel. As Rab-shakeh speaks his threats in their native tongue, Hebrew (2 Kings 18:26), he is trying to intimidate the crowd.

32:20–22 Hezekiah and Isaiah are prayer partners, lifting their concerns up to the Lord, the only One who can help them and give them peace in the middle of this storm. One angel wipes out 185,000 Assyrians in one night, so that when Israel wakes that morning, they see all the dead bodies of their enemy. Sennacherib, king of Assyria, heads home in retreat and goes into his temple to worship his god, and while he is there his two sons kill him.

32:23–33 With the southern kingdom of Judah victorious, Hezekiah is exalted, and this may be the spark that sends him on a downward trend. This account of Hezekiah's pride is fleshed out in more detail in 2 Kings 20 and Isaiah 38. First his pride begins to build, but Hezekiah recognizes it and repents of it. Because of that, God says judgment will not come in his days but in future generations. Again Hezekiah greatly prospers, which again leads to pride in his life. As ambassadors from Babylon come, he opens all the storehouses and shows off his wealth. Isaiah tells him he acts foolishly and warns of the coming captivity (Isaiah 39:6–7). Hezekiah is a great king and comparable to King David in his actions. However, even his godly reforms are not enough to rescue the future of a rebellious people.

33:1–9 Manasseh was arguably the most wicked king in Judah's troubled history. He destroys the reforms of his father with remarkable speed. He even goes so far as setting up an idol in the holy of holies, sacrificing his children to the god Molech, and going after all the abominations practiced by the nations that were driven from the land. The parallel account of Manasseh in 2 Kings 21:1–18 is even harsher than this one in Chronicles.

33:10–20 Manasseh should have been wiped out, and yet God is calling to him, trying to get him to listen and gain the attention of the nation, but he refuses. Tradition tells us that during Manasseh's reign, he takes Isaiah the prophet captive, places him in a hollowed-out log, and saws him in two pieces. He does not want to hear what the prophets have to say, for they go against what he is doing. Since he refuses to listen to the prophets, God tries to get his attention through the Assyrians, who humiliate him and carry him away. Manasseh's conversion is very similar to that of Nebuchadnezzar, king of Babylon. Nebuchadnezzar's pride brings him to a state of madness until he finally looks up to the true and living God.

33:21–25 Amon does not repent of his sin but remains lost, moving in the opposite direction of God. The die is cast, and the nation sinks lower and lower, drowning in its wickedness. Amon is king for only two years before his own men assassinate him. With Amon's death, Josiah becomes king and brings about the last revival before the southern kingdom of Judah is taken into captivity by the Babylonians.

34:1–2 It is thirty-four years before Babylon's first invasion of Judah. Israel has already been in Assyrian captivity for eighty years. God brings judgment upon the northern kingdom of Israel via military defeat and enslavement, and Judah still does not repent. Since the split, Judah has had five good kings who try to steer the nation back toward God—Asa, Jehoshaphat, Joash, Hezekiah, and here Josiah.

34:3–7 Josiah is the fulfillment of a prophecy from three hundred years earlier (1 Kings 13:1–2), when God calls Josiah by name. He takes the throne in Judah when he is only eight years old. Then when he turns sixteen, he begins to seek the Lord with all his heart. By the time he is twenty years old, he is purging the land of all the false worship that his grandfather Manasseh had started. Jeremiah's ministry begins in Josiah's thirteenth year as king, when Josiah is twenty-one years old, and continues some forty-one years—into the Babylonian captivity.

34:8–15 The massive temple restoration project begins. As they purge the temple of garbage, Hilkiah finds a copy of the books of Moses. According to Deuteronomy 31:24–27, there is to be a copy of the book of the law beside the ark of the covenant, beginning in the days of Moses. The Word of God was with Israel, but it was greatly neglected in those days.

34:16–19 Josiah tears his clothes because the Word of God pierces his heart. He understands why judgment has come upon God's people. Josiah rightly recognizes that not only does he stand guilty before God but so does the entire nation.

34:20–22 Josiah wants Hilkiah and his men to go to Huldah the prophetess to inquire of God as to what they should do next. Their sin is exposed and they need wisdom. Huldah tells them God will spare Josiah; however, judgment is still coming for the nation—God is not convinced that their hearts are sincere. Jeremiah describes Judah's reform as pretense rather than wholehearted repentance (Jeremiah 3:10). God rebukes Judah for their false loyalty (Jeremiah 7:8).

34:29–33 The temple and the rituals of faith have become a false mask for the people's true convictions (34:23–28). Instead of giving up in the face of coming judgment, Josiah leads the people by giving them the Word of God and being an example to them. Just as his great-grandfather Hezekiah had done, Josiah reinstitutes the passover celebration. Josiah also follows in his forefather's footsteps by properly organizing the priests (1 Chronicles 24; 2 Chronicles 8:14).

35:1–9 Josiah reinstitutes the passover, a feast that remembers the central act of redemption in the Old Testament: God's deliverance of Israel from Egypt in the days of Moses. The neglect of passover proves that this nation had neglected to remember God's work of redemption for them.

35:10–19 The people celebrate the passover with urgency, just as they did in Egypt during the first passover (Exodus 12:11). This passover celebration is even bigger than Hezekiah's.

35:20–27 It is 610 BC, and the Assyrian Empire is on the decline. Nineveh has fallen to the Babylonians in 612 BC, forcing the Assyrians to concentrate their forces around Haran and Charchemish, in the area of the upper river Euphrates. Egypt also is weak and ineffective. So Pharaoh Neco is coming to Charchemish to make an alliance with Assyria to fight off the Babylonians. Pharaoh Neco warns Josiah not to get involved in this battle, but Josiah does not listen. It costs him his life.

36:1–13 The Chronicler quickly traces the reigns and disobedience of Josiah's three sons (Jehoahaz, Johoiakim, and Zedekiah) and his grandson (Jehoiachin). The account is expanded in 2 Kings 23:31–24:20, but here it underscores how the Israelites are tumbling ever nearer to the inevitable exile from the promised land.

36:6–14 The southern kingdom of Judah was in captivity for seventy years because of their idolatry and failure to follow God. God had lead them into the promised land and commanded them to work there for six years, allowing the land rest every seventh year—a year of sabbatical that was meant to purge and restore, and during which time all debts were forgiven. But the Israelites neglected to obey God's command for 490 years. Scholars note that God gave the land its seventy years of rest and taught His people about trusting in Him during their time in captivity.

36:15–21 The events of this chapter coincide with Jeremiah's prophecy. Often nicknamed "the wailing prophet," Jeremiah is crying out that it is all over and warning not to fight against the Babylonians, for this is of God (Jeremiah 21:3–10). The nation is sinking deeper and deeper into idolatry, becoming more and more wicked, even after the judgment of God has begun. God tries to warn them over and over again by sending them prophets, but they refuse to listen and mock the messengers of God. God's long-suffering has come to an end, and the people and the nation have come to the point of no return (Jeremiah 32:1–5). The time is now 586 BC, and the Babylonians make their final invasion into Jerusalem, destroying the city and the temple and taking with them the rest of the people, killing many. Zedekiah and his sons are captured. Then the Babylonians put out the eyes of Zedekiah—the last thing he sees before being led away captive to Babylon is the death of his sons, who are executed before his eyes.

EZRA

INTRODUCTION TO EZRA ■ The book of Ezra is a chronicle of hope and restoration. Originally, Ezra and Nehemiah were together as one book, recording the stories about a remnant of God's chosen people who had been taken captive by the Babylonians after the destruction of Jerusalem and who were returning to the promised land to rebuild their nation. The dramatic narrative starts in 538 BC.

AUTHOR ■ Bible experts have long suggested that the author of Ezra also wrote 1 and 2 Chronicles and Nehemiah, referring to the writer as "the Chronicler." But recent scholars question this assumption and conclude that Ezra and Nehemiah were not written by the Chronicler. As to who wrote Ezra and Nehemiah, there is support for the Jewish tradition that teaches that Ezra was the writer of both books. It's interesting to note that the narration switches from third person to first person after Ezra appears in the story (chapter 7). The book was likely written between 460 and 440 BC, but there are competing views regarding the date.

OCCASION ■ Ezra, with Nehemiah, tells the story of God's faithfulness to His promises regarding His chosen people, restoring them to their land after seventy years of captivity.

1:1 The Jews' freedom came through Cyrus, the Persian conqueror. Note the prophecies about him in Isaiah 44:24–28 and 45:1–6, especially verse 4. It is the Lord who stirs the spirit of Cyrus, king of Persia, thus Cyrus's edict in verses 2–4. Cyrus's permission for the Jews to return home and to rebuild Yahweh's house is consistent with his practices in Babylon toward conquered people. They are reflected in the famous Cyrus Cylinder, the cuneiform-covered clay cylinder that recounts his rule after the conquest of Babylon.

1:2–4 Under Cyrus's edict, quoted in Ezra, the Jews are allowed to return to Judah and rebuild the temple. But behind this event is the word that Yahweh had spoken years previously to Jeremiah (see Jeremiah 25:12; 29:10–11). Jeremiah had said there were seventy years for Babylon. The numeral is approximate. It was seventy-three years from the fall of Nineveh (612 BC) to the fall of Babylon (539 BC). From the accession of Nebuchadnezzar and the taking of the first crop of Judean exiles (605 BC) to the fall of Babylon, it was sixty-six years.

1:5–8 Seeking God in public worship is the heart of the Jews' existence and usually a factor that reveals their spiritual fitness. Here, they have to be stirred up by God to tend to the task. Nebuchadnezzar originally takes the vessels mentioned in these passages to Babylon in 605 BC and places them in the "house of his gods." Since Yahweh's furniture is pilfered, Yahweh is considered "weaker" than Babylon's gods.

1:9–11 This seemingly mundane inventory of items returned to the temple actually constitutes, item by item, signs that Yahweh is restoring His people and His worship.

2:1 These people represent the remnant of God's chosen ones, descendants of Nebuchadnezzar's captives who had not forgotten the promised land or God's promises—and who had not been forgotten by God. They returned in 538 BC, the first group led by Zerubbabel years before Ezra comes on the scene. There's a parallel passage in Nehemiah 7.

2:2 Zerubbabel is the grandson of King Jehoiachin of Judah. There are ten others, eleven if Nahamani, listed in Nehemiah 7:7, is included.

2:3–35 The laypeople are listed either by a recognized family or clan or by hometown. The totals do not exactly match Nehemiah 7, probably a result of copying errors as ancient manuscripts were copied by hand through the years. These small discrepancies do not diminish the significance of this return to the land.

2:36–39 These are the tallies of four clans of priests. The total of the priests constitutes approximately 10 percent of the total found in 2:64, which means one in ten of the returnees is a priest. Why so many? Because they long to serve at the altar in a restored temple and participate in public worship of God, serving where they are meant to serve.

2:40–42 Those mentioned here are Levites, 341 in all. Some scholars think that only the seventy-four mentioned in verse 40 directly assisted the priests. That's one Levite to every fifty-eight priests. This is precious few to do the chores and the tasks connected with temple worship—a lot of work and little recognition.

2:43–58 This passage contains two sections of names: the temple servants and the sons of Solomon's servants, totaling 392 people. According to 8:20, David had given these temple servants to the Levites to assist them. Their work, therefore, consists of the most menial tasks around the temple complex. Three-quarters of the temple servants' names and more than a third of Solomon's servants' names are foreign. The speculation is that these people are descendants of prisoners of war (during David's time) or of the pagans whom Solomon pressed into slavery (see 1 Kings 9:20–21). If so, now the descendants of these pagan ancestors are listed among the covenant people of God as they are restored to their land.

2:59–63 Three lay families and three priestly families are unable to prove their ancestry. This is not to say they are not Israelites or priests, but they cannot *prove* it. However, it does not keep them from coming up from Babylon, joining the pilgrim people, and returning to Jerusalem. They remain among the people of God even though this uncertainty hangs over them.

2:64–69 The gift of the heads of households consists of 61,000 drams (about 1,133 pounds) of gold and 5,000 pounds of silver. The numbers in the Nehemiah 7 account differ somewhat. Note the number of servants in light of the overall number—about one servant to every six freemen. This means that some of the returnees must have substantial wealth, and though there is reason to hold it back in view of the uncertain times, they instead give generously.

3:1 A less-than-enthusiastic attitude toward life typifies the Jewish remnant around 538 BC. Life is hard and times are tough. The focus in the following verses is not on the temple but on the altar. Observe how the text describes Israel and, by implication, all God's people.

3:3 The exiles set up the altar. The people they are fearful of are apparently not only the Samarians but also those of the surrounding territories. You can be fearful and faithful at the same time.

3:4–6 Joshua and company join Zerubbabel and the others in building the altar to offer burnt offerings. Then they celebrate the feast of tabernacles. They are establishing a program of regular, ongoing worship. Note the reference in verse 4 to observing the feast of tabernacles, also known as the feast of booths (see Leviticus 23:39–40, 42–43; Numbers 29:12–38). The feast of tabernacles is meant to remind Israel of their wilderness experience post-Egypt. During this week, they live in huts (booths), which conjure up their precarious existence during the wilderness years.

3:8–11 Israel looks beyond restoring the altar. The exiles start to plan to rebuild the temple. Much preparation is involved, including gathering of materials, organization, and celebration.

3:10–11 These verses bring to mind the promise of Jeremiah 33:7, 10–11. Against all human likelihood, God's people see God's goodness again.

3:12–13 The memory of the first temple clouds the day for some. The older individuals can still recall the magnificence of the original temple (see 1 Kings 5–7), and this projected temple will have none of the style of Solomon's. There is no problem here with the candor of their weeping, but there is a danger in the negativity of these people.

4:1–3 Here is hatred under the guise of friendship. The people who approach Zerubbabel seem trustworthy because they say they seek God, though they are actually enemies. This reference to the Assyrian king reveals these people to be, to a large degree, pagan imports who probably have a religion that combines various deities (see 2 Kings 17:24–41, especially verses 33, 41). The discoveries of fourth-century papyri at Wadi Daliyeh

(located some distance north of Jericho) seem to support this. A great number of skeletons were also found here, the remains of families of Samaria who had fled the advance of Alexander the Great in 331 BC. Their names include references to such false deities as the Canaanite Baal and the Babylonian Nebo.

4:4–5 The enemies launch a withering campaign of hostility against the people of Judah. The Hebrew text stresses the ongoing, wearing effect of this opposition—not merely that they did these intimidating things but that they continue doing them.

4:6–8 Scholars point out that when the emperor Darius dies at the end of 486 BC, Egypt rebels. His successor, Ahasuerus, has to march west to suppress the revolt. The Persians gain control by the end of 483 BC. If the accusation in verse 6 has to do with an innuendo alleging revolt by Judah during this time, one can imagine the Persians would be concerned, with Egypt already on their hands. The accusation included in verse 7 is leveled during the reign of Artaxerxes. Then verse 8 indicates a third accusation, also under Artaxerxes, of which we have a copy preserved in 4:11–16.

4:6–23 These verses constitute brackets of information, like a parenthesis, breaking up the chronology of the chapter. It feels as though the writer, who is relating the earlier days after the return from exile, begins telling about the opposition Judah has experienced from the beginning and then decides that he will simply go on and pile up all the opposition that Judah has experienced through the years. By verse 23, though, it is as if he is ready to return to the time period chapter 4 really concerns: 520 BC, early in Darius's reign, when the work on the temple stopped because Judah seemed under so much duress.

4:24 Here we return to the story begun in verses 1–5.

5:1 Note how verse 1 speaks of Haggai and Zechariah prophesying in the name of their God. Ultimately, neither the king of Persia nor any other ruler is master. Only the God of Israel rules over the people.

5:3–5 No sooner do Judah's leaders obey God's Word than they run into renewed opposition. Tatnai, the governor, and Shethar-boznai, his assistant, ask Judah for authorization for this project, but apparently theirs is not the blatant opposition related in Ezra 4.

5:5 The Aramaic verb *betel* is used, meaning "stop." This is an example of negative providence: something God does not allow to happen (compare Psalms 124 and 129). Judah may be under investigation, and another potential frustration is pending, but Judah is allowed to keep building in the meantime.

5:6 The letter beginning here and ending in verse 16 is written to King Darius by Tatnai and Shethar-boznai. In it they lay out the background to their inquiry and ask Darius to verify the people of Judah's claims. The letter was probably delivered using the Persian Royal Road, a kingdomwide communication network. Every fifteen miles or so sat a postal station where couriers could replace exhausted horses with fresh mounts. Scholars estimate that a courier could average 240 miles a day, in contrast with a caravan, which would average 19 miles. If Darius's road system was fully operational early in his reign, the correspondence noted in Ezra 5–6 could have been completed in a month or two at most.

5:11–16 Tatnai and Shethar-boznai quote the response that the exiles gave when challenged about their authority for rebuilding. In one sense, these words are a response of praise. And yet they are also words of confession, as verse 12 makes clear. Judah admits that they are a people who have been under Yahweh's wrath, and He had taken the temple and land from them.

6:1–4 Darius finds a copy of Cyrus's original decree in the archives, confirming what the people of Judah had said. Not only is Judah granted freedom from interference from Tatnai and company, but the elders of Judah also receive provision for the maintenance of the temple worship. Darius will underwrite the functioning of the temple with state funds and punish anyone who stands in his way. Verse 3 shows that the dimensions of the temple in Ezra are sixty cubits high and broad, possibly indicating the limits of what the Persians would underwrite. This occasion in chapter 6 reveals the same kind of providence that is evident in Exodus 2:1–10, where Moses' mother not only gets her baby back but raises him under state protection, and with a salary to boot. Here also the Jews receive far more than mere permission to build. After Tatnai and Shethar-boznai carry out Darius's decree, the elders of the Jews finish building according to God's decree.

6:15 Adar, the last Babylonian month, is the time frame of February–March. The temple is finished on March 12, 515 BC, a little over seventy years from the destruction of the first temple. Renewed work had begun on September 21, 520 BC (see Haggai 1:4–15), so a sustained effort continued for over four years to complete it.

6:22 The king is Darius, king of Persia. Why is he called the king of Assyria here? There is evidence from the ancient Near East that new rulers or foreign rulers were incorporated into the lists of kings of a particular country. Because Darius was also the sovereign of Assyria, he could easily have been called the king of Assyria.

7:1 This chapter introduces the scribe Ezra himself into the narrative. It's now 458 BC, decades after the first group of returnees returned from Babylonian captivity under Zerubbabel. Ezra 7 summarizes that King Artaxerxes authorizes Ezra to lead another, smaller group to Judea, and Ezra 8 gives the details. A thematic element that binds these chapters together is the repeated reference to the hand of God.

7:1 The phrase *after these things* is a clue that time has passed since the last event mentioned. Though it can seem immediate, it is not. Ezra 7 is set almost sixty years after the events narrated in Ezra 6. The writer is very selective as to what is included in the section. Not every detail is given, only what is significant for the people of God. At this point, the book is placing focus on different concerns: not only on restored worship

(chapters 1–6) but also on reformed life according to the law and the Word of God (chapters 7–10).

7:7–9 The date described here might be anywhere between 428 BC and 398 BC. Keep in mind, however, that the significance of the events is the same no matter the exact date.

7:10 God prospers the venture because of Ezra's purpose. Ezra has set his heart to study the law, practice it, and teach it.

7:12–26 This decree of Artaxerxes gives more people permission to return to Judah, but there are several other concerns and purposes. It is, in part, a fact-finding mission. It also includes specific instructions regarding the temple, even the utensils to be used there.

7:20–22 Needs were to be met from the royal treasury, up to 3.75 tons of silver, 650 bushels of wheat, 600 gallons of wine, and 600 gallons of oil.

7:24 This is a cautionary note to Artaxerxes' regional IRS agents. The clergy (priests, Levites, singers, porters, and servants) are to be kept tax-free.

7:26 Ezra's mission is to teach the people of God afresh the law and to discipline them to live according to it. Hence, the focus of Ezra 1–6 is God's temple, while that of Ezra 7–10 is God's law.

7:27 King Artaxerxes may make the decree and grant the permission, but it is God who turns the king's heart whichever way He desires (Proverbs 21:1). Yet Yahweh's sovereignty is not always blatant—frequently it is hidden and subtle. Yahweh chooses to carry out His decrees through the decrees and decisions of the lesser kings and rulers of the earth.

7:28 Note the juxtaposition of the power heads of the Persian Empire (the king, his counselors, all the king's mighty princes) and Ezra's position. There is something astounding in how this one Judean could command such favor from the bureaucracy of Persia! Ezra revels in the thought. Clearly God placed Ezra in a position of authority in Babylon for His purposes, but Ezra doesn't neglect to give credit to the hand of God, who is the anchor of his story.

8:1–14 Those who come back with Ezra tend to have had other family members return in 538 BC. Compare this list to that in Ezra 2. The list of households in this section may provide a flicker of hope for the nation of Israel. In it is a descendant of the royal line of David, Hattush. If you scrutinize the listing of Davidic descendants in 1 Chronicles 3:17–24, it seems that the main thread of the list goes from Jeconiah, Pedaiah, Zerubbabel, Hananiah, Shechaniah, Shemaiah, to Hattush. Hattush is then the fourth generation after Zerubbabel. If Zerubbabel was born around 560 BC, and if one allots approximately twenty-five years per generation, then Hattush appears here about 458 BC, which fits the traditional date of Ezra's arrival in Jerusalem.

8:15–20 It's unclear where or what Casiphia is, but apparently it is a site near Babylon, perhaps a Judean study center. The appeal to Casiphia nets a total of 38 Levites and 220 temple servants.

8:21-23 Ezra calls for fasting and a time of prayer for the people to humble themselves before God (see Leviticus 16:29, 31). This pleading and confession is an expression of their faith. The exiles are undertaking a 900-mile journey, exchanging the familiar for home. If the Levites are to go with Ezra back to Judea, they will leave a life where they may have a good bit of autonomy from the strict routines of the temple. In Judea, life would be perhaps more about hardship and obedience.

8:24-26 The twelve leading priests Ezra entrusts with oversight of this wealth are called holy, as are the utensils they guard. In the latter case, *holy* means, in part, "off-limits."

8:26-27 The details of this inventory will come out a bit differently depending on the commentator. But the amounts on any scheme are substantial: 650 talents of silver equals 49,000 pounds, or about 25 tons. One hundred gold talents equals 7,500 pounds, or 3.75 tons.

9:1 Ezra and his group of exiles have been in Jerusalem about four and a half months when the problem of intermarrying, and therefore rejection of the law and its demand for spiritual purity, is brought to his attention. The old problem of intermarriage with pagans, in violation of the Torah (Exodus 34:11-16; Deuteronomy 7:1-5), is a problem of sanctification. The people would be hard-pressed to stay true to their religious faith if they are mingling that faith with the idolatry of the cultures around them. Since the spiritual leaders such as the priests and the Levites are implicated as well, this is an extensive and serious issue.

9:3-4 Ezra visibly reacts by tearing his clothes, hair, and beard and sitting down appalled (desolated, devastated). He seems simply beside himself in helpless frustration. Others share Ezra's essential reaction, even if theirs does not duplicate his exactly.

9:6-7 Note how Ezra switches to the plural pronoun *our* in verse 6, in identification with the sins of his people. The immensity of the guilt involves quantity: Ezra tries to express the huge mass of guilt in these pictures. It also involves history: It goes back to their fathers, is long-standing, and has been experienced in judgments, the effects of which continue to the present time.

9:8 The *nail* could refer to a tent peg, driven into the ground as anchorage for a tent; or it could refer to, as in Isaiah 22:23, a peg or nail securely fastened in a wall so that items can be hung on it. Some theologians have taken the peg to refer to the rebuilt temple. Either way, the idea is that Israel has been given some degree of security in their otherwise tenuous postexilic experience.

9:10-12 Ezra highlights the folly of unfaithfulness and acknowledges that God's people have confronted the problem before. Hence, they are without excuse. There is both suspense here, in that there is no definite, particular plea that Ezra makes, and frustration. Ezra can only throw Israel upon the mercy of Yahweh.

10:1 Ezra may have been a highly respected leader, but he is willing to throw sophistication to the wind in his grief. The effect is to motivate his people to repent. Not just men, but women and children gather to weep and lament.

10:2-4 Here is a minor character with a major role in the story. Shechaniah puts Israel's corporate unfaithfulness into words. The hope he refers to is based on a call to covenant with God, in which there is fruit that shows repentance. It is a repentance that takes the hard road: to send away the foreign women and children.

10:3-4 Shechaniah calls Ezra and the other leaders to courageous action and offers him the support of the people.

10:5-6 Johanan's chamber is apparently in the temple. We are not told who he is. Ezra's fasting has been called a reflection of Moses' fasting (see Exodus 34:28; Deuteronomy 9:18) after the golden calf episode of Exodus 32. It would not be unreasonable to see Ezra as a kind of "second Moses."

10:7-11 The leaders call the assembly. The people generally live within fifty miles of Jerusalem. Non-participation means excommunication. The date given in verse 9 (ninth month, twentieth day) is December 19, 458 BC. It is the rainy season, in which temperatures are in the forties.

10:11-16 What we see in Ezra 9-10 is Deuteronomy 7:1-5 applied in a new postexile situation.

10:13-14 The leaders recognize that it will be logistically impossible to have the entire assembly make confession out in the open because it's cold and it will take more than a few days. So they make a proposal that offenders appear to representatives by appointment. They should be accompanied by the elders and judges of their towns—an important element, supporting a fair investigation.

10:15 The few who resist likely oppose the whole process, perhaps thinking it too harsh or wanting to protect relatives. The *Meshullam* of verse 15 may be the same person named as a son of Bani in verse 29, who himself had married a foreign wife.

10:16-17 The hearings last from the first day of the tenth month until the first day of the first month. That's three months of work, finishing on March 27, 457 BC.

10:18-43 Offenders, in terms of the intermarriage, included people of all levels: priests, Levites, and laity. According to the lists, the offenders included seventeen priests, six Levites, one singer, three gatekeepers, and eighty-four laity. This indicates careful work. Assuming they take the sabbath off, it takes about seventy-five days to complete the investigations of all the cases. If the names recorded in Ezra 10 represent the total number of men who had taken a foreign wife, it's a very small percentage of the entire community. Estimates of its size at this point total 30,000 or maybe 50,000.

THE
BOOK OF NEHEMIAH

INTRODUCTION TO NEHEMIAH ■ The book of Nehemiah is one of the Old Testament's historical books. Until the fifteenth century AD, Ezra and Nehemiah were considered to be one book, and we see evidence of this with Ezra's abrupt ending. The events of Nehemiah pick up naturally where Ezra leaves off, with the continual rebuilding of Jerusalem and the return of the final group of exiles from Babylon in 445 BC.

AUTHOR ■ Nehemiah is believed by some scholars to have written the majority of the text—much of the book of Nehemiah is written in the first person, and 1:1 identifies the speaker as Nehemiah, son of Hacaliah, an exiled Jew who served as the cupbearer to the Persian king Artaxerxes I. Yet Jewish tradition holds that Ezra authored the books of Ezra and Nehemiah. Because Ezra and Nehemiah were one book, Nehemiah may have been edited by Ezra, or the two may have been combined by a historical chronicler. No one knows for certain.

OCCASION ■ The events recorded in the book of Nehemiah are dated from circa 445 to 431–432 BC. The book begins with Nehemiah returning to Jerusalem in the twentieth year of King Artaxerxes I of Persia (1:1), approximately thirteen years after Ezra returned with the second group of exiled Jews. Nehemiah leaves Jerusalem for a brief period of time in the thirty-second year of the reign of Artaxerxes I and returns shortly thereafter (13:6–7), dating the events at the end of the book around 432 BC.

1:1 The reference to the twentieth year is to the year of Artaxerxes I, or 445 BC. Comparing Ezra 7:7, we note that this is thirteen years after Ezra's coming. The month of Chisleu is November–December. Shushan (or Susa) was in what is now southwest Iran, in the alluvial plain 150 miles north of the Persian Gulf. It serves as a winter palace for the Persian kings.

1:2–4 Although Nehemiah lived most of his life in Babylon, his home is Jerusalem, and he still has concern and affection for his homeland and its people. Nehemiah's grief and distress over Jerusalem in ruins have been ongoing for some time.

1:5–6 The remainder of this chapter is made up of Nehemiah's prayer of grief over the fact that Jerusalem is in ruins, the city wall destroyed. The fact that the broken walls remained untouched reflected the oppression that crippled the Jewish people. Jerusalem was the holy city of the Jews, and a wall in ruins was a visible reminder of the city's prior destruction, the Jewish exile, and an overall loss of national identity and pride.

1:5 Nehemiah begins his prayer by identifying God as both awe-inspiring and faithful. Note how these two aspects of God's character complement one another: God is both frightening and dependable. Nehemiah goes on to state that God is approachable as well.

1:7 Nehemiah doesn't point an accusing finger at others but instead identifies with his people. The offenses have been committed in violation of the revelation of God's law received through Moses.

1:8–9 These verses correspond with Deuteronomy 30:1–10. The language of verse 9 links up with the promise of help and restoration from judgment in Deuteronomy 30:3–5.

1:10 When Nehemiah uses the verb *redeemed*, he is likely referring to redemption from Egypt and the resulting covenant, not to redemption from Babylon after the exile. It's as if Nehemiah says, "Look at what you have done for them. Do you mean all of that to go for nothing?"

1:11 Nehemiah's prayer is in reference to the grave crisis of the people of Judah as well as to the suspense over what the king's reaction might be. Nehemiah refers not merely to his own prayer but to the prayers of others. Nehemiah does not stand alone in prayer; there is a fellowship of intercession.

1:11 Because Nehemiah was the king's cupbearer, he had access the throne. The position of cupbearer was one of great responsibility and influence. Kings wanted a cupbearer they could trust. When Nehemiah makes his cupbearer remark, he is recognizing that Yahweh's providence has been at work long before this moment. He was high up in the civil service with access to the king and, therefore, in a favorable position to seek good for the people of Judah.

2:1 Nehemiah doesn't act hastily on his desire to return to Jerusalem and lead in the rebuilding of the walls. Following his prayer in chapter 1, he waits four months before taking the first step toward returning—asking King Artaxerxes' permission to leave.

2:2 Nehemiah cannot keep his depression about the state of his homeland from showing—and this may have been a breach of royal court etiquette. Nehemiah's fear likely arises in light of the accurate diagnosis and the knowledge that this king has nullified precisely what Nehemiah seeks to do (see Ezra 4:7–23). At this point, Nehemiah does not explicitly mention Jerusalem.

2:4–6 Here is the moment of opportunity—and of uncertainty—hence Nehemiah's resort to impromptu prayer. This is a reflection of Nehemiah's piety, and also his balance between dependence and boldness. Royal permission is his reward.

2:7–8 The care, planning, and thought Nehemiah has given to this matter are reflected in his request for official letters and to obtain materials. The explanation of Nehemiah's success comes not merely as information but also as praise. The king gives provision, but it is by Yahweh's hand that he does so.

2:9 Whereas Ezra rejected an armed escort as a matter of faith in Ezra 8:21–23, here we have Nehemiah's acceptance of an escort as a matter of wisdom. It will add authority and support to his position and work.

2:12–13, 15–16 There is also a sense of divine calling on Nehemiah's part. This is not just Nehemiah's desire but one spurred by God-given motivation. Nehemiah conducts a nighttime survey of the conditions of the wall. By inspecting the wall himself, he obtains direct knowledge of the condition of the wall. If there are any objections, he will know on what basis to answer.

2:18–20 Nehemiah identifies with the people of Judah. His appeal is based on their current shame—they should rebuild so they will no longer be a mockery. He also intends for them to be moved by seeing how God has been at work as had been shown in the king's authorization of the project. In response to Nehemiah's motivation, the people agree to his plan to rebuild, and they begin the work. But the dissenters—Sanballat, Tobiah, and Geshem—make their voices heard; the enmity is expressed by both ridicule and innuendo. Nehemiah's response is to the point.

3:1 The priests lead by example. The high priest and other priests are the first people named as helpers in the rebuilding effort. They apparently do not think such work is beneath them. Rather, those with sacred office take the lead in the restoring work. Many names are mentioned in this chapter as those who helped rebuild, evidencing that this was a task that demanded all hands on deck.

3:3 Because it is such a large city, Jerusalem is a necessary stop on many trade routes. Its size also requires many gates by which to enter the city. The fish gate is the entrance for one of the main roads, and it likely received its name because of the fish market that was just outside the gate (2 Chronicles 33:14).

3:5 It seems that there are some from the town of Tekoa, the nobles, who refuse to assist in the work. Perhaps they think it is beneath them. By contrast, however, this chapter is full of others with social and political clout who avidly contribute their share to the work (3:9, 12, 15, 19). The men from Tekoa who do help evidently work on more than one section of the wall (see also 3:27). Meremoth, the son of Urijah, is mentioned in verses 4 and 21. This taking on more than one's share speaks well for these workers.

3:6–8 The old gate, also called the Jeshanah Gate, is repaired by a group of Jebusites, whose descendants were the original owners of the land on which the temple was built. The stretch of wall from the old gate to the broad wall includes a wide range of people.

3:11 From the broad wall (3:8), the building continues around to the tower of the furnaces, which is located on the western wall of the city.

3:12 There are some who seem marked by special zeal for the work. Shallum's zeal leads to making the rebuilding a family affair—even his daughters help in his section of repair.

3:13–15 The valley gate is likely located near the southwest corner of the city. The dung gate, which received its name because it was the gate that led to Jerusalem's landfill, is next along the wall's repair route. The fountain gate and the pool of Siloah mark the southernmost point of Jerusalem. From there the wall route Nehemiah is tracing turns northeasterly along the valley of the brook Kidron.

3:17–32 This list catalogues those who worked on the eastern portion of the wall between the fountain gate and the horse gate. The horse gate is at the easternmost part of the wall. The Miphkad, or inspection gate, is the last gate before returning back to the sheep gate, where Nehemiah begins his record. It marks the northern part of the eastern wall. The names here constitute a roll of honor of Yahweh's workers, recorded for lasting remembrance.

4:2 The army of Samaria is present, which indicates Sanballat has armed help at hand. And yet he can hardly benefit from it because Nehemiah has official permission from the king, which surely frustrates Sanballat.

4:3 Not being able to use military force against God's people, Sanballat turns to mockery. Tobiah's fox remark is said in reference to walls that are undoubtedly thick and capable of withstanding strong military force.

4:4–5 Note that Nehemiah does not send a retort to the mockers but instead turns to God. Nehemiah's prayer is a prayer for justice against sin. As such, it is a prayer for God to act. Nehemiah is not presuming to take vengeance into his own hands; he commits that to God. These are not personal enemies but enemies of God's kingdom. There is no indication that Sanballat, Tobiah, or their men seek repentance.

4:7–9 In all four directions the builders are surrounded, with Samaria to the north, Arabs to the south, Ammon to the east, and Ashdod to the west. Sanballat has been angry, but now he and his cohorts are furious, so much so that there is a possibility of an armed assault.

4:10–12 The discouragement of the builders is evident, perhaps because of the threat described in verses 7–9. It also sounds as though the Jews living in neighboring villages pick up the threats and propaganda from the enemies and repeat them to the workers. Perhaps the enemies leak word of the plans that are being made, and then those Jews come to Jerusalem and repeat the rumors among the workers. It is all intended to demoralize.

4:16–19 In the revised building scheme there seem to be several groups of workers. Some are permanent guards. Some serve as load haulers, who carry both loads and their weapons at the same time. Then there are the builders, each with his sword strapped on his side. Finally, there is an alarm system in place.

4:20–23 Nehemiah's claim that God would fight for him and his people reveals the confidence that undergirds their toil. And with that reminder, the wall continues to go up. Commuting is done away with, and the people are constantly on guard. The unusually perilous circumstances call for uncommon measures for the immediate future.

5:1–5 While the threat of external assault has been the fear, internal dissension begins to take place in this chapter. There are three groups raising dissension. The first group consists of families who may have owned no land for food, and thus taking time to work on the wall diminishes their ability to earn wages. The second group consists of those who are mortgaging their land, farms, and homes in order to get food, and these people will lose this security completely if they cannot pay their debts from the annual harvest. The third group consists of those having to borrow, with fields and vineyards as collateral, in order to pay the king's taxes. Some of their family members are in debt-slavery because of this hardship.

5:8–10 These profiteers in chapter 5 are fellow Jews (5:1, 7). The problem is probably not interest/usury but debt-slavery, with loan sharks possessing the pledge or the collateral. Apparently some Jews had been sold to surrounding peoples and redeemed, meaning that some of the loan sharks must have sold their fellow Jews obtained by debt default to surrounding peoples. Nehemiah admits that he and his associates have also made loans of money and grain for collateral, but there is no reason to suppose that Nehemiah had pressed the claims and profiteered from the loans he'd made. In fact, he says that all claims are not to be pressed; they are to be abandoned.

5:11–13 Nehemiah's order is for the profiteers to restore collateral they have taken as well as surcharges they have demanded. The moneylenders give their consent to Nehemiah's directive. However, Nehemiah presses for even more clout and calls the priests to administer an oath, after which Nehemiah dictates the curse that will overtake those who renege on their obligation.

5:14–19 These verses are an extract out of Nehemiah's diary that interrupts the chronological flow of the narrative in progress, but they are likely placed here to set forth a positive sample of Nehemiah's walking in the fear of God over against the heartlessness of the profiteering Jews in verses 1–13. Nehemiah has certain rights by virtue of his position as appointed governor—a food allowance, or a stipend—but he voluntarily relinquishes them. He also doesn't allow his staff to lord their stipends over the people as the underlings of past governors had. Apparently Nehemiah pays for his stock and food supply.

6:1–19 The schemes recorded here are directed toward Nehemiah, either to eliminate him or at least to discredit him. Undoubtedly his enemies want to bring trouble to his exemplary leadership. Note the emphasis on fear throughout the chapter (6:9, 13–14, 19).

6:2–7 At this point there has been substantial progress on the wall. Now Sanballat and those influenced by him want a consultation with Nehemiah. Nehemiah's perception is likely an accurate one: They intend to harm or do evil to him, so he resists. Their persistence shows their helplessness or weakness, since they can't think of any other approach except to repeat the last ploy. The fifth time Sanballat sends an open letter.

6:9 The second half of this verse is an interjected prayer.

6:10–11 Shemaiah's being behind closed doors could be a prophetic action reinforcing his warning to Nehemiah to hole up in the temple. Here Shemaiah is referring to the temple itself, not merely its courtyards. A layman cannot go into the temple; thus Nehemiah would be transgressing by doing so. This is a privilege and right that is off-limits to laymen (see Numbers 18:7; 2 Chronicles 26:16–20).

6:12–14 Shemaiah's intent is to get Nehemiah to commit a ritual transgression and thereby be discredited. But Nehemiah discerns that God has not sent Shemaiah but that Tobiah and Sanballat have paid him off. It is all a plot to lead Nehemiah into sin. And Shemaiah is only a *part* of the problem; the prophetess Noadiah and other prophets are conspiring together, seeking to magnify Nehemiah's danger and send him into paranoia.

6:14 This is a prayer for vengeance, a plea for God to remember and deal with the deeds and designs of the likes of Shemaiah. There is nothing wrong with such a prayer. What can be more wicked than placing one's office as bearer of God's Word up for hire, using the Lord's Word as a tool to manipulate people and gain power over them? This sort of ploy is so tricky because it involves a revelation claim—an alleged word from the Lord—and not just from one person but a plurality of people.

6:19 There are two elements to notice here: intimidating letters from Tobiah and a constant stream of gossip, part of which is propaganda about the good deeds of Tobiah. This propaganda is continuous. There is no doubt that Tobiah is powerful, and his power combined with his desire to see Nehemiah's plans fail make for an intimidating combination. Whether Nehemiah is intimidated or not, Tobiah's threats don't stop him, and the wall is still completed in an extraordinarily short amount of time.

7:2–4 Nehemiah makes a series of necessary arrangements after the completion of the wall. First, he appoints guards to the city's gates in order to ensure the city's safety. Second, he establishes new security regulations that include opening the gates to the city only during the busiest parts of the day, and having various people throughout the town stand guard over their neighborhoods. Third, Nehemiah notices the town's vacancy and the need for people to fill it. A city the size of Jerusalem is safer with more inhabitants.

7:5–73 This list reproduces the record found in Ezra 2. The figure of 42,360 appears as the total in both Ezra

2:64 and Nehemiah 7:66, yet the individual items add up to three different totals. There is general agreement that the divergences are copying errors, arising from the special difficulty of understanding or reproducing numerical lists. More than anything, the list shows God's faithfulness in preserving His chosen people. Genealogies are also important because Jews used them to prove their bloodline as descendants of Abraham. Two of the three synoptic Gospels include genealogies that trace Jesus back to David and Abraham as well.

8:1 The covenant renewal of Nehemiah 8–10 can be seen on a plane with the temple restoration of Ezra 3. Ezra 3 stresses the people and temple, while Nehemiah 8 stresses the people and law. One depicts worship restored and the other depicts the Word restored.

8:1 Although Ezra had been in Jerusalem since before Nehemiah (Ezra 7:6–9), this is the first mention of him in the book of Nehemiah. In addition to being the scribe, Ezra also serves as a priest. Nehemiah governs the people, but Ezra is in charge of their spiritual well-being. The book of the law mentioned here is probably the Jewish Torah, or Genesis–Deuteronomy.

8:2–6 This audience consists of men, women, and all who can listen with understanding. This hearing of the Word is marked by patience, attention, reverence, and worship. The Levites circulate among the people, perhaps doing exposition of the Word in small groups.

8:8 Many scholars have discussed the participle *mephorash*, which qualifies the verb *read*. Some hold that it means "translating." Others hold that it means "making distinct," or as an adverb, "clearly." Still others take it as "paragraph by paragraph," breaking it down into manageable chunks. Probably the second or third option is preferable: breaking it down and explaining the meaning. The intent, in any case, is to make the Word of God clear, to highlight the insight it holds, and to make its applications obvious.

8:9–12 The assembly takes place on the first day of the seventh month, which is the feast of trumpets (Leviticus 23:23–25; Numbers 29:1–6). The weeping of the people may be over sin exposed through the reading of the Torah. They have to be ordered by Nehemiah and company—three times—to be joyful. Note that this is a social joy, not a selfish joy. The last line of verse 10 contains the primary argument against sadness—God is the people's strength. Perhaps there is the suggestion that ongoing sorrow and grief, while proper at times, can leave the people of God vulnerable. The text implies that joy and delight in Yahweh fulfill a protective function in believers' lives, keeping them, perhaps, from being swallowed up in despair.

8:13–18 The heads of households meet for ongoing study of God's Word. They find written in the Torah the regulations about the feast of tabernacles (see Leviticus 23:33–43; Deuteronomy 16:13–15). The celebration of tabernacles (booths) was an appropriate activity for postexilic Judah, as it should be for the Lord's people in all ages. The booths (or huts) were meant to force Israel

to recall their tenuous post-Egyptian existence during the wilderness journey. In the midst of Israel's settled life in the promised land, they need to remember their former hand-to-mouth existence. In the midst of what is also a harvest festival, they remember that life can be a wilderness, and their only sustainer is Yahweh. They must never forget their humiliation in the wilderness (Deuteronomy 8) or the God who sustained them through it.

9:1–2 The reading of the Word of God is a catalyst for the Israelites' reformation. It reminds them that a change on their part is necessary. They must get back to the business that had them so upset in Nehemiah 8:9.

9:3 First comes the reading of the Torah and then confession and worship. The worship is built upon the Word. The Levites begin with a call to worship.

9:6 Observe the historical moments covered by the prayer that makes up the remainder of this chapter: creation (9:6); Abraham (9:7–8); the exodus (9:9–12); Sinai (9:13–14); the wilderness (9:15–21); conquest (9:22–25); the judges and following (9:26–37). The majority of the first section focuses on Yahweh as redeemer. However, this verse expresses homage to Yahweh as creator. It lauds Yahweh not only as creator of all things (heaven, earth, seas, and their contents) but as life-giver and sustainer as well. And for all this He receives worship from those conscious, invisible beings, the heavenly hosts.

9:7–8 This part of the prayer highlights redemption and covenant. The root of covenant is election, as seen in the idea that God chose Abram. The concern of the covenant is place (the land) and people (Abram's descendants). The anchor of the covenant is fidelity.

9:9–14 Though the note of compassion is not lacking, there is a stress on the judgment aspect of Yahweh's deliverance. Yahweh does not grant redemption while withholding direction. Sinai is the assurance that Yahweh does not redeem a people from bondage only to abandon them to ambiguity.

9:15 This part of the prayer reflects on the provision aspect of God's redemption. Episodes like those of Exodus 16–17 are in view here, where provision in extremity (hunger, thirst) is delivered in unpredictable ways: from heaven and from a rock.

9:16–17 The strong language here reflects no momentary lapse on Israel's part but instead a deliberate, open-eyed resistance to God's will. Rebellion is absurd in light of all the preceding acts of grace. This is the phenomenal character of Yahweh: In all this, God never turned away. This passage tells us that our hope is not in denying or explaining away our rebellion but simply in the character of God.

9:26–31 These verses describe the behavior of Israel when settled in the promised land during the period of the judges. Israel again commits great sin, and for this Yahweh brings them into distress, but the wonder is that there is deliverance. But nothing changes. Israel is in a cycle of repeated infidelity.

9:36 Even though the people are back in the promised land, they recognize that this is not a state of blessing, because they are ruled over and taxed by others. There is no directive, no particular petition here. There is, however, an implied petition in light of the whole prayer. They are asking, "You will not now forsake us, will You?"

10:1–27 The names here include both the leadership and the laity. Nehemiah and Zidkijah (Zedekiah) seem to be by themselves; then the priests, listed mostly according to family names (10:2–8); followed by the Levites, listed as individuals rather than families (10:9–13); and then the leaders (10:14–27; verses 14–19 follow Ezra 2; these are mostly lay families).

10:28–29 The people are entering under a curse, calling down judgment on themselves if they do not keep their oath (see Jeremiah 34). Covenant renewal cannot thrive on generalities and vague resolutions. The promises included here are precise.

10:30 The covenantal promise to not intermarry with foreigners does not imply that God looks negatively on those who are not Israelites simply because of their nationality. Rather, this ensures that the Israelites maintain households that honor and serve Yahweh. The nations around the Israelites were pagan nations with a variety of deities and religious practices. It was this religious intermingling that was the concern. The Old Testament accounts of intermarrying with pagan nations never produce positive results (see 1 Kings 11:1–11).

10:31 This verse prohibits trade in Jerusalem on the sabbath, maintaining that Yahweh, and not money, is the God of the Israelites. The promise that every seventh year individuals will stop working the land and cancel all debts is a reiteration of the sabbath law as recorded in Exodus 23:10–11 and Deuteronomy 15:1–2.

10:32–34 The people make a promise that they will participate in the giving of funds for worship maintenance. Because the temple is now rebuilt, the people promise that temple taxes and offerings will also be restored. The law is even so specific as to include the provision of firewood to ensure the sacrifices can be burned on the altar. The people's covenant includes a lots system (random selection, so not given to partiality) for calendaring when families are in charge of providing the wood.

10:35–39 The people also assume responsibility for bringing a number of offerings to the temple each year. These provisions deal with the maintenance of the temple worship itself, particularly the temple staff—the Levites who receive the tithe. Provisions include the firstfruits of their crops, firstborn sons, the firstborn of all their animals, and a tithe of their crops. The people promise that they will keep worship a priority in their lives.

11:1–2 The present situation in Jerusalem is a far cry from what is described in Isaiah 2, a place that welcomes all nations. Nehemiah proposes that with the casting of lots, one out of ten families living in the territory of Judah should relocate and reside in Jerusalem. In this way, they cannot bear a grudge against Nehemiah; they have been drafted by the Lord. The move into the city for those whose lots were chosen is a sacrifice. They do not prefer to live in Jerusalem or they already would have settled there. So they face the trouble of uprooting themselves from homes and means of livelihood, leaving everything for the city.

11:3–24 The listing for Jerusalem is part of a list of the population of the whole province of Judah in the times of Ezra and Nehemiah, both the newcomers and all others who were already in Jerusalem. If the tallies are followed (11:6, 8, 12–14, 18–19), there are 3,044, so after including wives and children, one could estimate a population of 10,000 to 12,000 people.

11:25–36 As citizens of one empire, these people are free to settle where they want if they keep the peace. There is a hint of the fidelity of God in the geography of Judah here.

12:1–26 The list of names continues with the names of the priests and Levites who return from exile. These are the priestly families and Levites at the time of Zerubbabel and Jeshua in 536 BC (see 1 Chronicles 24:7–19; Ezra 2:40–42). Verses 10–11 list the high priests from Jeshua's line. Continuing in verses 12–21 is a list of the heads of twenty-one priestly families during Joiakim's time, the second generation. The notes and records from the book of the chronicles, mentioned in verses 22–23, include the list of Levites that follows.

12:27 We are not sure how long after the completion of the wall this dedication occurred. One gets the impression that the dedication takes place after the events of chapters 7–11, but there may have been other, more pressing concerns at the time when the wall was finished.

12:30–43 After purification, the celebration begins with two large choirs circumnavigating the top of the wall, in opposite directions, singing songs of praise and thanksgiving. The choirs are accompanied by the Levites named here. The first choir, which covers the wall from the valley gate counterclockwise, is led by Ezra, while the second group, covering the wall from the valley gate clockwise, is led by Nehemiah. The two groups meet at the temple, where they continue to worship and offer sacrifices as they are joined by the women and children.

12:45 The dedication of the wall in Jerusalem marks a fully restored city—the religious community is fully restored to the holy city. Once again the temple functions as it once had, as the center of worship for a spiritually strong people. The Israelites have not had such a sense of security since before the exile, so to the very last detail they ensure worship will resume as it once had been carried out. Among these details is the appointing of a staff to keep up with the tithes that are received. This will be a large accumulation; therefore this staff will be required to collect the offerings and redistribute them to the temple workers who receive portions of the tithe.

12:46–47 The repeated mention of David in Nehemiah's account of the temple organization leads one to perceive

Nehemiah as doing for the postexilic temple what David did for the original one. Because music had been such an important part of David's design for worshipping the Lord, Nehemiah guarantees provisions will be made for the singers and musicians.

12:47 See Numbers 18:21–32 for the portions referred to here.

13:1–3 The reference to the book of Moses is to Deuteronomy 23:3–6. How do they interpret that passage? Do they infer from the mention of Ammonites and Moabites that the text intends the exclusion of all foreigners? Observe how in 13:2 they recall not merely the threat of humankind but the protection of God.

13:4 This is the same Tobiah who made himself an enemy of Nehemiah by opposing the rebuilding of the wall. Not only that, but he is also an Ammonite and, as such, is prohibited to enter the temple. There is a note of defiance in Eliashib's action. The ease of compromise is clear: Eliashib is close to Tobiah. This may mean he is closely associated with him, or it could mean he is related to him. There may have been a marriage tie (see 6:17–19), and if so, his behavior simply shows that blood is thicker than covenant. Eliashib believes pleasing people matters more than showing fidelity to God.

13:6–9 The compromise of Eliashib is in clear opposition to the Word of God (13:1–3), and therefore it has to be dealt with harshly instead of gently.

13:11 The Levites are to live on tithes that are given (Numbers 18:21), but they have not received them—the procedures of Nehemiah 12:44–47 having gone into eclipse. So the Levites flee to the towns and to their fields to gather what living they can. Hence, the house of God is forsaken.

13:15–16 The issue of work on the sabbath arises. The offense is twofold: The people of Judah are working on the sabbath, bringing loads of food into Jerusalem and (apparently) selling them. And the foreign Tyrians do their fish selling on the sabbath as well.

13:17–18 Nehemiah's rebuke is a theological one: These sabbath-breakers are placing Israel under the anger of Yahweh again. See this same argument pressed by the prophet Jeremiah in the preexilic period (Jeremiah 17:19–27).

13:19–22 To prevent further offense, Nehemiah both closes and guards the gates, placing his own men there to prevent traders from entering. Then he makes threats against the people trying to hang around outside the walls hoping to draw citizens outside the city to buy. He institutes a more lasting provision to ensure compliance.

13:23–25 The issue of intermarriage resurfaces, with the cultural ties of the children landing closer to the mother's roots. Eventually this will prove true for religious ties as well. Nehemiah's cursing of the people means that they reap the negative consequences of the covenant they established with God. Nehemiah calls God's judgment into effect.

13:26 The oath Nehemiah requires is what the people have already sworn to do in 10:28–30. Nehemiah presses an argument upon them—a biblical, theological, and historical argument, based on Solomon's drift toward paganism. He enjoyed vast privileges but came to ruin because of this very offense.

13:28 Marriages to pagans had occurred even among the priestly circles of the community. A grandson of the high priest became son-in-law to Sanballat. A priest should have been an exemplar of piety and covenant fidelity (see Numbers 25:13).

THE
BOOK OF
ESTHER

INTRODUCTION TO ESTHER ■ The book of Esther is a good complement to the books of Ezra and Nehemiah. While those books describe the trials and challenges of the Jewish exiles who were finally allowed to return to their homeland, Esther shows the plight of the Jewish people in Persia during the same period of time. Some people uphold Esther and Mordecai as heroic figures, yet others question whether they were actually godly individuals. God is not once mentioned by name in this book, yet it is a testament to divine providence.

AUTHOR ■ The author is unknown yet certainly appears to be a Jewish individual who had remained in Persia after other Jews had departed.

OCCASION ■ The account of Esther is a magnificent work purely on the grounds of literature: character, plot, conflict, and so on. But it was probably written to provide the background and setting for the creation of the Jewish holiday of Purim.

1:1 Due to their disobedience and pursuit of idols and other gods, the people of Israel and Judah have been carried into captivity by Assyria and Babylon. The Babylonians, in turn, are conquered by the Medes and Persians, so the group of Jews who originally went to Babylon is now under Persian rule. It is a trying time, but the story of Esther demonstrates how God's people obtain not only a voice but also an advocate in the king of Persia himself.

1:2 The king in this passage is Xerxes. The Hebrew form of his name is *Ahasuerus*. He has been in power for three years after conflicts with Babylon and Egypt. His residence is in Shushan (Susa), the capital of ancient Elam, which his father, Darius I, had rebuilt as a winter capital.

1:3 What had begun as an alliance between the Medes and the Persians (Daniel 5:28; 6:8, 12, 15) has by this time become the kingdom of Persia and Media (Esther 1:3, 14, 18–19), showing that Persia has become the dominant nation. Indeed, Ahasuerus is the great king of the Persians whom Daniel had prophesied would rise to power (Daniel 11:2).

1:4 The text does not provide the reason for Ahasuerus's elaborate six-month banquet, but history tells us that the following year he will (unwisely) wage war against the Greeks. This celebration may well have been an occasion for gathering support, rallying his group, and planning the military campaign. If so, Ahasuerus would have wanted everyone to see that he was richer and more powerful than anyone else.

1:5–9 After six months, the king's extravagance continues with a local weeklong banquet. Fine art is on display for the people of Shushan (Susa)—rich and poor—as they recline on expensive furniture, eat gourmet food, and drink fine wine. While the king entertains the men, the women have their own celebration, with Queen Vashti as his hostess.

1:10–12 Much speculation is made about this section of the book of Esther. We know that at the end of the

banquet, King Ahasuerus summons his wife, Vashti, to come wearing her crown to let everyone see how beautiful she is. But Vashti refuses to make an appearance. Is the king (who has been enjoying wine) unreasonable in asking his wife to appear before a crowd of drunken men, exposing her to potential embarrassment and shame? Or does Vashti coldly refuse a reasonable request to appear for the grand finale of the party? Opinions vary. But the result is clear: The king becomes furious.

1:13–21 To his credit, Ahasuerus calls his counselors and asks them how he should handle the situation. Consequently, out of fear that Vashti's actions will negatively influence the women of the kingdom, they recommend that she be banned from ever again appearing with the king. Not only that, but they suggest she be replaced by a woman more fit to be queen. Ahasuerus acts on their advice with an irreversible decree.

2:1–4 After a number of years pass (1:3; 2:16), King Ahasuerus is again ready for a queen. If he hadn't passed an official ban against Vashti, perhaps he would have relented and taken her back. But instead, his advisors recommend a national search for young virgins from whom the king can select his next queen. Not surprisingly, Ahasuerus gladly agrees with their suggestion.

2:5–8 Mordecai was one of the Jews living in Shushan (Susa). He is raising his cousin Esther (*Hadassah* in Hebrew) as a daughter because her parents have died. She is very beautiful, and she is chosen to be among those contending for queen.

2:6 The actions and direction of God are evident throughout the story of Esther, even though the name of God is never mentioned in the book. However, some hold the perspective that the book of Esther even more so reflects the struggles of Jewish exiles who became too attached to the land of their captivity and thus dishonored God by not returning to their homeland when they were able to. From this perspective, God's providential care for the Jews in Persia was accomplished not because of their faithfulness but in spite of their unfaithfulness.

2:5–7 Esther was born as a captive in a foreign land where she had neither social status nor power. Yet she will become queen over one of the greatest empires in the world. If nothing else, her story seems to demonstrate how God places the right person in the right place at the right time. Those who willingly allow Him to use them—where they are—may be surprised at what can be accomplished.

2:8–14 The Persian king had little regular interaction with his harem as a group. To ensure propriety, the women who associated with the king were attended to by eunuchs—men who had been castrated. One eunuch, Hegai, is designated to prepare the contestants for their interview with the king. The young women will spend an entire year getting ready, and then each will spend one night with King Ahasuerus. Afterward, they are placed in his harem of concubines under the supervision of another eunuch, Shaashgaz. Unless the king requests one of them by name, these women will never meet with him again.

2:15–18 Everyone who sees Esther is impressed by her, and the king chooses her over all the other young women in the kingdom to become his new queen. He throws another great banquet to celebrate, but throughout the year-long process, Esther keeps her Jewish identity secret (2:10, 20).

2:19 The second group of virgins may have been a regrouping of the first group (2:8) or yet another selection of beauties. Either way, the king would most likely have been preoccupied with them, and it would not have been the best time for Esther to approach him.

2:21–23 Mordecai's position in the city gate suggests he had a respectable degree of status, which he uses here to pass information to the king through Esther. Persian justice is swift; the two conspirators are immediately executed, and the details of their arrest and judgment are recorded. The record of the event will be important later in the story. Also essential to the account is the fact that Esther never got around to telling her new husband that she had been among the Jewish people exiled to Persia.

3:1–2 One of the few things we are told about Haman is that he is the son of an Agagite, from the family of the Amalekite king Agag. In contrast, Mordecai is a Benjamite (2:5)—the same tribe King Saul is from. By Persian times, the term *Agagite* might have been a reference to a geographic area rather than a specific bloodline, yet Israelites and Amalekites had long been bitter enemies, which might help explain Haman's widespread resentment toward the Jewish people. Before the Israelites had even crossed from Egypt to Canaan, they contended with the Amalekites, and God promised Moses their eventual destruction (Exodus 17:8–16; Deuteronomy 25:17–19). Later, King Saul had been instructed to kill King Agag of the Amalekites (1 Samuel 15). Understanding this history sheds light on Mordecai's attitude.

3:8–11 Haman's appeal to the king is calculated and intentionally vague in that it never mentions the Jews specifically, and he mixes truths with half-truths and lies. For example, as a captive people, the Jews had been instructed to cooperate with their host nations (Jeremiah 29:7). Haman's charge that they disobey the king's laws is unfounded. Haman gives Ahasuerus two incentives to grant his request: (1) a promised reduction of rebellion in the kingdom and (2) a generous contribution to the national treasury. Although Ahasuerus appears to decline the monetary offer, his initial disinterest may be a customary oriental bargaining exercise. Perhaps the king expected to benefit both from Haman's initial payment and from later portions of the spoils that would be confiscated.

4:1–8 The Persian king and his malevolent second-in-command have celebratory drinks after agreeing to the extinction of an entire people group, but the Jews across the Persian nation are soon fasting, weeping, and tearing their clothes. Although letters have gone out to all sections of the empire, the news still hasn't reached Esther. She finds out because she hears that Mordecai is just outside the city gate, mourning loudly and publicly. She then sends a messenger to see exactly why Mordecai is so distraught. Mordecai supplies all the details and sends the messenger back with a plea for Esther to intercede with the king.

4:16 Many people don't realize that Esther can be seen as a reluctant heroine. Readers often presume that the fasting of her people also includes prayer and repentance, yet that is not necessarily the case. Isaiah 58:3–5 points to a kind of fasting whose function is merely to get an answer from God, rather than to set oneself apart in order to hear God better. Even Esther's words, considered by some to be a statement of faith ("If I perish, I perish"), are actually a declaration of fatalism.

5:1 After observing a three-day fast along with the other Jews in Shushan (Susa; 4:16), Esther approaches King Ahasuerus. Little is said about her state of mind, but she has numerous reasons to be fearful. To begin with, if she interrupts or interferes with the king at the wrong time, she might be put to death. And even if he welcomes her visit, she is going to have to confess to him that she is Jewish, convince him to reverse a law he has just instated (1:19; 3:10–11), and reveal that his closest companion (Haman) is a terrible villain. Most likely the king will feel deceived by Esther and/or Haman, and not many royal leaders like to admit to such poor judgment. Still, Esther goes ahead with her plan.

5:2–7 Dressed in her royal robes, Esther is graciously received by Ahasuerus. The reasons for her delay—two banquets prepared for the king and Haman—are not explained, although during the interval God prepares the king to respond as He desires.

5:9–14 The invitations by the queen put Haman in a good mood, but it doesn't last long because of Mordecai. Haman's solution—build a gallows and have Mordecai hanged—seems easy since Haman is so close to the king. He can get an edict to have Mordecai hanged right away.

5:14 In Persian culture, hanging was not the same as people today usually envision it. The execution was performed not with a rope around the neck but by impaling the convicted person on a sharpened pole. The "hanging" is in reference to the impaled body displayed to public view.

6:1–3 Ironically, while Haman plots against Mordecai, the king is thinking about how to reward Mordecai.

6:4–13 Haman arrives, rehearsing his request for Ahasuerus to grant him the right to kill Mordecai. But before he can even ask, the king asks how to reward a man. Haman, of course, assumes the king is referring to him, and answers in that context. What a bitter and shaming experience it must have been after Ahasuerus told him to go out and do all those things for Mordecai. Haman rushes home in grief but receives no sympathy from his friends and family. They interpret it as a sign of bad things to come.

7:7–8 After a big meal and plentiful wine, the enraged king goes into the palace garden. (Perhaps to get some fresh air or control his anger? To think of how to punish Haman? To give some thought to Esther's dilemma?) Haman approaches Esther but falls onto the couch. This put them in an awkward position since Esther was reclining. It was Persian tradition to recline while eating. The Greeks and Romans would do the same, and at some point the Jews adopted the habit. After the king assumes the worst, he accuses Haman of molesting the queen and orders him to be led away.

7:9–10 One of the king's servants is aware of the newly constructed gallows beside Haman's house. In a final irony, the king commands that Haman be executed on the gallows he had created to murder Mordecai.

8:1–2 After Haman's death, King Ahasuerus's actions—giving everything Haman had owned to Esther and rewarding Mordecai with the position that Haman had held—were made official by the gift of the king's signet ring. The ring's seal would also provide authenticity for any missive sent out from the capital, Shushan (Susa).

8:3–6 Even though Haman has died, his order to kill all the Jews is still in effect. Addressing that threat is Esther and Mordecai's next priority. After Esther pleads with Ahasuerus to rescind the order that Haman sent out, the king sends for his scribes. Rather than a request based on the Word of God, the Abrahamic covenant, or some other spiritual basis, Esther's appeal to the king is solely on the basis of his affection for her and on what the destruction of the Jews would do to her.

8:7–10 Mordecai dictates a new letter that is recorded and translated in the king's name and sealed with the king's ring. And lest anyone doubt where the king stands on this issue, the couriers ride the king's own horses. The previous order as written by Haman was supposed to be irreversible, but Ahasuerus makes it known that he now supports the Jews.

8:11 The king's order doesn't just provide *protection* for the Jewish people and give them permission to defend themselves; it authorizes them to *avenge* themselves.

8:15–17 Mordecai clearly has the king's favor. He leaves the palace attired in royal clothes, a distinctive purple robe, and a golden crown. The Jews in Shushan (Susa) are celebrating and feasting, as are those throughout the kingdom. And along with the sudden shift of power, many non-Jewish people are converting, perhaps more from fear of the Jews than genuine faith.

9:1–10 Nearly nine months pass, but the mood among the Jews remains jubilant. The new law enacted by Mordecai gives them the right to fight back when attacked by their enemies on the thirteenth day of the twelfth month. They are ready. Mordecai has become a powerful man in the king's administration, and the people are terrified of him and his people. The Jews have no trouble killing and destroying their enemies. In a single day they kill five hundred opponents in Shushan (Susa) alone, including the ten sons of Haman.

9:10 Interestingly, although the Jews have been authorized to acquire the plunder of those they defeat (8:11), they choose not to do so (see also 9:15–16). So the only Jewish person to profit from the exposure of Haman is Esther (8:1).

9:12–17 The king is still willing to accommodate a request by Esther, so she requests a one-day extension for the Jews in Shushan (Susa) to continue eliminating their enemies. She wants Haman's sons to be hanged, their bodies publicly displayed. So while the Jews in other territories have a day of celebration and rejoicing, those in Shushan (Susa) kill another three hundred men and do their celebrating the following day.

9:18–27 The celebration becomes an annual event among the Jews that continues today. The name *Purim* is taken from the plural of *pur*, the die that Haman cast to determine what day the Jews would be annihilated. Purim is different from most other Old Testament feasts and celebrations. It was not established by God but by people. It is a celebration of human achievement rather than God's deliverance. Rather than centering on worship as most other feasts do, Purim involves generosity and gift-giving that can border on self-indulgence. There is no element of sacrifice—just celebration.

9:20–22, 29–32 Letters go out one more time to all the Jews in Persia. But this time they aren't forewarnings of death to come or a call to take up arms and fight their enemies. This time the news is to celebrate their victory over their enemies.

10:1–3 The book of Esther concludes with two tributes. King Ahasuerus (Xerxes) is king of one of the greatest empires of all time, yet all that is said of him is that he taxed his kingdom. Mordecai, on the other hand, is given lavish praise. Ahasuerus will soon be assassinated, which presumably ends Mordecai's influence as well. About 150 years later, the glory of Persia will come to an end at the hands of Alexander the Great.

THE BOOK OF

JOB

INTRODUCTION TO JOB ■ Many people who read the book of Job miss the God-centered message because they are focused on the man-centered problems. Why the righteous suffer is never really answered in this book. As God shows Job, knowing the answers to life's problems is not as important as knowing and understanding the awesomeness of God and how wise He is.

AUTHOR ■ The author of the book of Job is unknown. Most likely he was an Israelite, because he uses the Israelite covenant name for God (Yahweh, or the LORD).

OCCASION ■ We do not know when Job was written, though the account describes history around the time of Abraham—that is, around 2000 BC. The first eleven chapters of Genesis predate the story of Job, but they were not written down in a book form until the time of Moses, around 1500 BC.

1:1 In describing Job as upright, God is giving insight into the character of Job so that, as we read this story, we won't misinterpret what is going to happen to this man. Job is a morally upright person—a good man who loves God. He fears God—meaning that he has a correct perspective of God as holy and righteous. Because he has this perspective, he shuns evil—meaning he turns away from it.

1:2–3 Job is a wealthy man who is blessed with ten children. His number of animals indicates his wealth. Money is not a part of his culture. The sheep are used for clothing and food, the donkeys and camels for transportation (while donkeys are for short distances, camels—the workhorses of the desert—are used for cross-country). The oxen are for food, plowing, and milk.

1:4–5 It seems that Job's children like to party. With the wine flowing at these parties and clouding their judgment, Job fears that his children may have taken the name of the Lord a little too lightly. By their actions they could be dishonoring God. Thus Job intercedes for his children, getting up early and offering ten sacrifices, one for each child.

1:7 Notice the restlessness of the accuser, going to and fro over the earth. Why? To see who he can destroy and what lives he can ruin. As 1 Peter 5:8 says, "Be sober, be vigilant; because your adversary the devil, as a roaring lion, walketh about, seeking whom he may devour." It's important to remember that Satan could have access to the throne of God, the very presence of God, but he is *not* God, nor is he equal to God. Satan is not omnipotent, omnipresent, or omniscient, as God is.

1:8 God points out to Satan this man Job and his goodness. The word *considered* is a military term that is used of a general who is studying a city before he attacks it so that he can develop a strategy to destroy it. So God is asking Satan if he has found any weakness in Job by which Satan might gain control or cause him to stumble. God's implication is that Satan can find nothing to cause Job to stumble.

1:12 Key to our understanding of Satan is that here he can do nothing unless God allows it.

1:13–19 Tragedies begin to fall upon Job's household. Verse 16 is noteworthy because the servant says that the fire of God fell from heaven. Yes, God allows it, but Satan is behind it.

1:20–21 After hearing his bad news, Job mourns, then worships. Job realizes that all his material possessions, his wealth, and even his children are on loan to him from God. Job does not understand why this happens to him, but he knows his God and thus he does not bring a foolish charge against God for what transpires. Those who feel they are entitled will be angry and bitter toward God when their things are taken away. Nothing is ours to keep; we are God's stewards, watching over that which He has entrusted to us.

1:22 Job passes the first test. Satan is wrong; it is not the material blessings that cause Job to worship God. But Satan is not going to give up easily.

2:1–6 When the angelic hosts ("the sons of God") reconvene before the Lord, Satan also comes to renew his charges against Job. Satan is serving the purposes of God at this time.

2:1–3 These words are an exact echo of God's dialogue with Satan in 1:6–8, with the addition of the assertion that Job has remained faithful in the face of tragedy.

2:3 The phrase "movedst me against him" seems confusing when applied to God; we try to understand an infinite God with our finite minds and limited vocabulary. Ultimately, God is in control, and He is not pushed into these situations by Satan.

2:4–5 Satan is looking for that Achilles' heel, that weakness in Job, so that he can influence Job to turn from God. Perhaps when his health is gone, he will surrender to Satan.

2:6–8 Here is a picture of a man who had everything and is now reduced to nothing; even his health has failed him. We do not know for sure what disease Job has, but it is clear that it leaves him miserable and very ill.

2:9–10 These verses offer an indication as to why Satan does not kill Job's wife when he kills Job's children: She is helpful to Satan's cause in this situation. Still, Job does not bring any foolish accusations against

God. Job is not giving up; he is placing his life in the hands of a sovereign God—whatever comes his way.

2:11–13 Eliphaz, Bildad, and Zophar are true friends to Job, who come to comfort him during this difficult time. Job must have looked a mess, for at first his friends do not even recognize him. For seven days they simply mourn with him. As later passages will show, this is the most helpful thing they do for him.

3:1–10 When Job at last speaks, he curses the day of his birth. He is not cursing God, but it does sound like he is questioning why he was even born if he was going to have to live a life like this. Job is not a stoic, and God is not allowing these things to come upon his life to see if Job can sit there unmoved, emotionless. God has a purpose for all this suffering: to increase Job's faith. Although our common modern stereotype of Job is that of an incredibly patient man, he is more characterized by his perseverance than his patience. His prayers reveal many of the same thoughts and feelings that we all experience when we face suffering.

3:11–19 Job wishes he had been born dead, for it would be far better than the life he has. Job is here speaking out of frustration and not out of revelation. Job does not understand what he is talking about regarding death, for he has never experienced it.

3:20–26 Death itself seems more precious to Job than all the treasures of the world. He closes his monologue by questioning the meaning of life and contrasting its harshness to the presumed peace of the grave.

4:3–6 At first Eliphaz's words seem to affirm Job, as he reminds Job of how he has encouraged so many others in difficult times. But this affirmation turns to rebuke as he says, in effect, "Look, you have helped others through difficult times, but now you, the great counselor, can't even handle the difficult times you are going through. What's your problem, Job?"

4:6–7 Eliphaz says that the reason Job is going through these trials is that he is not innocent; only those who sin will go through times like this. This is a simplistic approach to Job's problem, but not a scriptural truth. Nevertheless, for the next thirty-six chapters, Job's friends are going to tell him this very thing—that his sins have caused his suffering.

4:8 Notice that Eliphaz comes across as being spiritually insightful. There is a measure of truth in that punishment will come for the wicked, but it is not always immediate. But wickedness is not the only reason for suffering.

4:9–11 Eliphaz's conclusion is that God will blast those who are evil just as He is doing to Job.

4:12–17 Eliphaz turns mystical as he builds up to the climax of his statement, claiming personal spiritual guidance, but his insight is less than profound. It doesn't take a mystic to recognize that God is more righteous than human beings.

4:18–21 Eliphaz seems to suggest that Job ought to expect destruction because of his own wrongdoing.

5:1 The saints to whom Eliphaz refers are angels.

5:2–5 Eliphaz's reference to those losing their homes and children is a none-too-subtle parallel of Job's misfortunes, which, Eliphaz contends, come to fools and simpletons—presumably like Job.

5:6 Eliphaz's point is that trouble doesn't spring out of nowhere, so clearly Job must have done something to bring it on himself.

5:8–16 Eliphaz turns holier-than-thou at this point, saying that if he were going through the things that Job is going through, he would repent before God.

5:17 God does chasten those He loves, but Eliphaz mixes truth with error, and that is destructive. The problem here is that Eliphaz assumes Job is guilty of some sin and this is God's reason for chastening him. But this is not the case.

5:18–27 Eliphaz's glib assurances—that if Job repents, all will again be well—only increase Job's pain. Here is an important lesson for us to learn from Eliphaz: When people are going through difficult times, the best thing to do is listen. Giving pious platitudes is of no help to suffering people.

6:4 Job has allowed the situations of life, and maybe even some of the words of his friends, to cloud his picture of God, for he now thinks that God is his enemy. Job has never experienced anything like this in his life, and now God is exposing him to his weakness so that his faith may grow out of these circumstances.

6:5–7 Animals make noise when their stomachs are empty. Job feels he has a right to complain because his life has become empty—even the so-called comfort from his friends is tasteless and sickening.

6:8–13 Job is so miserable that he asks God to end his life before his misery leads him to deny God's goodness. He has nothing to live for and no hope for his future.

6:14–18 Even Job's friends have failed him. They are like streams that flood in the winter, when no one needs them, and vanish in the dry season when they might do some good.

6:19–23 Just as desert caravans look in vain for an oasis, so Job looks in vain for comfort from his friends. Instead of supporting him at the only time he has needed it, they shrink back from his tragedy.

6:24–30 Job's friends are not speaking the truth. Rather, they are implying that Job is the dishonest one for not admitting that his troubles are his own fault.

7:6–11 As Job anticipates his life coming to a hopeless end, he addresses God directly. Not, however, in humble repentance, but rather in complaint. Job is not holding anything back.

7–9 Job compares death to the dissipating of a cloud, but the Bible does not teach that in death we enter a state of nothingness. Job's point is that, once dead, he is not coming back. There is no hope for a better earthly life next time.

7:12 Job questions God, asking Him why He is watching over his life so closely, like a watchman standing guard on board a ship, watching out for whales.

7:13–14 Job sees God as an adversary, not only allowing physical and emotional pain, but also sending terrifying nightmares so that Job cannot find comfort even in sleep.

7:15–16 When Job says he does not want to live forever, he is not making a theological statement about eternal life but simply stating that his life on earth is not worth living.

7:17 Job sees God's attention as a burden. In Psalm 8:4 David asks the same question, but in a positive light, seeing God's attention as an undeserved honor: "What is man, that thou art mindful of him? and the son of man, that thou visitest him?" Similar words; two different perspectives of God.

7:18–20 Job feels that with every step he takes, God is ready to strike out at him. He wonders why God has made him a target.

7:21 Adversity can lead to a warped concept of God; we see this happening with Job. He is unable to recognize God's forgiveness because of the cultural assumption Eliphaz has expressed in chapters 4–5: If God loves you, you will prosper. Job even goes so far as to tell God that He will be sorry when Job is gone, because He will no longer have anyone to pick on.

8:1–2 Bildad calls Job's pleas of innocence a bunch of hot air. This must have brought Job even greater pain.

8:5–7 Like Eliphaz in chapter 5, Bildad has a simple solution to Job's problems: If Job will confess his sins, then God will make him healthy, wealthy, and prosperous. Bildad's advice sounds like what many of the contemporary "health and wealth" teachers preach today, but he is only speaking a half-truth. God does bless the just *and* the unjust. And we must also fall back on the sovereignty of God; He is in control.

8:8–10 Bildad points to history and the experience of former generations to bolster his point. Job and his friends lived around the time of Abraham, which was only 250 to 300 years after the flood. When Bildad refers to what previous generations learned, he is probably thinking of how God destroyed all the wicked by a flood. Now Job, presumably because of his sin, is being wiped out as if by a flood.

8:20–22 Bildad calls for Job to plead his case before God. If Job is innocent, he has nothing to worry about. If Job is not innocent, then God will deal with him appropriately.

9:1–2 Job tells Bildad that his words are empty because even if Job could go before God, he couldn't win. All this righteousness that Eliphaz and Bildad are touting is out of reach for mere mortals, and even if one were innocent, who could beat God in an argument?

9:4–11 Not only is God wiser and more powerful than any human being, but He also is spirit and, as such, can be difficult for the human mind to comprehend.

9:12–13 At this point in the account, Job isn't sure that God is good, and if God is not good, then His having all that power is scary. Job is allowing his circumstances to cloud his picture of God.

9:14–20 Job believes he doesn't stand a chance with God; he can't even catch his breath and defend himself.

9:21–24 At this point in Job's perspective, it doesn't seem to matter if a person is good or evil, because God destroys both equally. In fact, it seems that Job sees God getting some kind of pleasure in destroying people, especially the innocent. Job clearly knows the greatness of God and His power but is struggling with the goodness of God. He is struggling because he sees the suffering of the innocent, including himself, which he can't understand.

9:25–31 Notice Job's faulty conclusion: If he is going to be punished regardless of his innocence or guilt, then why bother to repent?

9:32–33 While Job knows his desperate need for a mediator (daysman), he despairs of finding one. How rich we are who know that, as we are told in 1 Timothy 2:5, "there is one God, and one mediator between God and men, the man Christ Jesus."

9:34–35 Job sees God as a cruel taskmaster with His rod of discipline ready to strike anyone at His will, and Job is terrified of Him. Notice, as Job's picture of God gets more distorted, it is harder for him to truly love God.

10:1 Job is going to speak from his heart, and whatever comes out, let it be. He is not going to hold anything back.

10:2–7 Job knows that he is the work of God's hands, and yet it seems God despises him and loves the wicked.

10:8–9 Job now speaks of his own frailty, that God has created him out of the dust of the earth. Like a master potter, God has formed Job, and He has formed us, but these bodies of flesh will return to the dust of the earth.

10:12–17 Job sees himself as trapped. No matter what he does before God, it won't be good enough and he will be judged.

10:20–22 Job has had it; he can't take it anymore. So he cries out to God, asking God to leave him alone, to give him a break and let him try to enjoy the short time he has left.

11:1–12 Eliphaz was eloquent, but his words were only judgmental. Bildad was brutal as he accused Job of not being as innocent as he tried to make others believe. Now Job's third friend, Zophar, comes on the scene and blasts Job with stinging sarcasm. Zophar begins with rhetorical questions that let Job know he is not going to be able to justify himself.

11:3–5 Zophar is not going to let Job get away with his empty words. In Zophar's way of thinking, the things that have come upon Job's life show that Job is not pure. Since Zophar does not believe in Job's innocence, he is calling to God to show Job all the evil that is in him, that secret sin that has brought this catastrophe upon his life.

11:6–9 As if to attest to his own spiritual insight, Zophar tells Job that God has revealed that Job has received only half of what he deserves for his sin. Next Zophar takes Job to task for trying to understand God.

11:13–18 After all his rhetorical questions, Zophar offers his own simplistic answer: Job must get right with God, and the sun will once again shine on Job's life, a smile will return to his face, and he will be protected from his enemies just as a moat protects those living within the city walls.

11:19–20 According to Zophar, Job's friends will also return if he gets right with God. But if he doesn't, his life will come to an end.

12:1–2 Job's words here are a use of sarcasm. He tells Zophar that undoubtedly when Zophar dies, so, too, will die all the wisdom in the world.

12:3 Job lashes out at his friends' pride as he tells them that he understands just as much as they do, that he has not heard anything earth-shattering in their speeches.

12:4–5 It seems hard for Job's friends to be compassionate when things are going well in their own lives. They are making themselves out to be righteous, for they are blessed. And they are making Job unrighteous, for he is cursed. Those who come to comfort him are only mocking him.

12:6 Notice Job's argument against his friends' counsel. They have their theological answers to Job's problems, but Job calls for them to apply their theology to the real world and see if it still holds water. And he shows them that it doesn't, for the robbers are still prospering and the unrighteous seem to live in comfort.

12:7–12 Job says creation itself knows that God is free to do whatever He wishes with His creatures. Every breath is a gift of God.

12:13–25 Job is reaffirming that God is sovereign over nature, over nations, and over the lives of humans.

13:1–6 Job has had it with his friends' worthless counsel and does not want to hear their empty words any longer. He wants to hear only from God. This is why he calls for silence. While Job's friends think they are speaking for God, their counsel is wrong.

13:8–12 God will reprove Job's friends for their false counsel and their empty words, Job tells them, for their counsel is meaningless, of no help, and, most important, not of God.

13:15–19 This solid statement of trust in God comes seemingly out of nowhere from Job, who is still in his cave of despair. Even though Job has no idea why all this has happened to him, and though it seems quite unfair, he is now going to trust God with his life. Job is learning to trust God more and his faith is growing. He sees God as his salvation.

13:20–28 Before asking God to show him his error, Job asks God to remove all the adversity and let him rest awhile. Then Job concludes that God is punishing him for something done in his youth. This is a distorted viewpoint. God brings us through trials to stretch our faith, not for the purpose of revenge or intimidation.

14:1–2 The writer here uses several images one after another—birth, flowers, shadows—to make the point that human life is short when compared with eternity.

14:3–6 Since God alone knows the number of our days, Job holds God accountable for his own suffering. Here again, he sees God as his adversary and asks to be left alone.

14:7–12 Job concludes by bemoaning what he sees as the ultimate fate of every human being: death, which in his mind means the end of existence.

14:13–22 In the midst of his pain, Job expresses a beautiful longing for renewal and forgiveness. Despite this desire, however, Job concludes that there is no hope.

15:1 Each of Job's three friends has already had his say. Now Eliphaz begins round two with his second speech.

15:1–3 Eliphaz questions Job's wisdom. When he asks if a wise man would fill his belly with the wind, he is saying that Job's words are nothing more than a lot of hot air.

15:4–9 Eliphaz judges Job for refusing to admit that his sins have brought his troubles on him. As an attack on Job's credentials, Eliphaz asks if Job has some private access to God's counsel that is denied to his friends.

15:12–13 Eliphaz sees Job as a man who claims to be righteous but who is really entertaining sin. He sees Job's anger with God as another form of sin. The Bible gives many examples of the anger and frustration that God's people feel when things go wrong. Anger itself is not the problem; the problem comes when that anger prompts people to do and say things they should not.

15:14–16 Eliphaz is right to say that no one can attain righteousness on his or her own; even heavenly things are unclean compared to him.

15:17–26 Eliphaz falls back on what he has seen and the worldview he has been taught: that the wicked suffer their whole lives. He assumes that the converse is also true: If a man is suffering, he must be wicked. All of Job's prosperity has been taken away, just as happens to the wicked. Job has met the same fate as the wicked.

15:27 In Job's time, weight was a sign of wealth, because the rich were able to enjoy much more food than the common people. Job probably looked well fed before his troubles began, but by the time his friends arrived, he was probably skin and bones—so changed that at first they do not even recognize him.

15:31 In Eliphaz's eyes, Job is deceiving himself by claiming that he has done nothing to deserve his troubles. The things that are happening to Job are what Eliphaz has enumerated as the things that happen to wicked people. The implication is clear: Job is a wicked person.

15:32–33 Eliphaz's metaphors, of vines stripped of their grapes before they have matured and trees dropping their flowers before they have had time to develop into fruit, must have fallen hard on the ears of a man whose children died untimely deaths.

15:34–35 Because of his judgments against Job, all Eliphaz predicts for him now is barrenness; the only "children" Job will father are vanity and deceit.

16:1–2 Job's reply here addresses not just Eliphaz, who most recently spoke to Job, but also Bildad and Zophar.

16:3–4 Job blasts his friends for their insensitivity to his condition and calls them miserable comforters. He wants them to realize what they are doing by imagining they are in his shoes.

16:4 To shake one's head at someone is to say that their words are empty—the very thing Job's friends have been doing to him.

16:5 Job tells his friends that if they were in a similar situation, he would offer comfort instead of condemnation and encouragement instead of discouragement.

16:6–9 Job is not finding any comfort in his own words or in the words of his friends. He sees himself being eaten alive, wasting away to nothing, and God continuing to cause havoc in his life.

16:10–11 Job complains that God has given him wicked friends who are continually coming against him.

16:12–14 As a lion or tiger goes after its prey and grabs it by the neck to choke the life out of it, Job sees God doing this to him. In fact, Job sees himself as nothing more than a target on God's practice range; his suffering is tearing his guts out.

16:15–17 Job doesn't understand why this is happening to him; he feels that he doesn't deserve all of this suffering.

17:2–6 Job's many friends have forsaken him, and no one will speak up for him. Before this calamity, Job had been not only wealthy but also well respected. Others looked to him for help and direction. But now these same people look at him in disgust and begin to spit on him.

18:1–4 After hearing Job's complaint in chapters 16 and 17, Bildad steps up to have a second try at convincing Job of his friends' theology. Since Bildad sees Job as long-winded, he is upset that Job is speaking so harshly to his friends. This reveals a blind spot for Bildad because he and the others are equally harsh to Job. Bildad continues the theme of the others.

18:5–7 The extinguishing of lamps and fires signifies death. The verb *put out* suggests death at the hands of others. If that fate does not overtake a wicked man, perhaps his life will flicker out through weakness or illness, or even because his own schemes backfire, causing him to be cast down.

18:13 Job, with his blistered skin, must have identified with the wicked man whose skin is being eaten away by "the firstborn of death"—probably a poetic name for a deadly disease.

18:14–15 There is no safety for the wicked man, even in his own home. The brimstone is reminiscent of the destruction of Sodom and Gomorrah (see Genesis 19:24).

18:14 The "king of terrors" is the Canaanite god who was death personified. Mot devoured his victims. Isaiah turns this imagery around and prophesies that the Lord will swallow death forever (Isaiah 25:8), and the apostle Paul explains that this prophecy is fulfilled in Jesus Christ's resurrection from the dead (1 Corinthians 15:54).

18:16–19 The wicked man's roots—his ancestors and his descendants—do not thrive, and no one remembers him or his family once he is gone. He has no name, not only because his own name is forgotten, but also because his family name does not continue; none of his offspring or descendants survive.

18:20–21 Bildad may be thinking of how appalled he and Job's other friends were when they first saw Job in his misery. It is easy for Bildad to see how many of these horrors reserved for wicked men have befallen Job, and he concludes that Job either does not know God or at least is on the way to becoming estranged by God because of his complaints against Him.

19:4–8 Job sees himself as innocent before God no matter what his friends say, no matter how much they make themselves out to be righteous. Job's conclusion is that God is wrong. He can't understand why all this trouble has come upon him.

19:17 Even Job's own wife, who wasn't too supportive in the first place (see 2:9), is keeping her distance because of his offensive breath. Since we are told in chapter 1 that all of Job's children were killed, the mention of children in this verse may be a reference to his own brothers and sisters, who are ignoring him.

19:21–22 Although Job believed that God had brought this trouble on him, that is not the case. Satan is the one responsible for Job's misfortunes, even though God does allow them—for Satan cannot do anything without God's permission. When the enemy does something, it is not to build up, but to destroy.

19:23–24 Feeling that no one is really listening to him, Job longs for his words to be permanently recorded, possibly so that more unbiased readers might judge him less harshly than his friends do. And those words have indeed been recorded and passed down throughout the generations.

19:28–29 Job knows that no matter how much evil his friends speak against him, he is innocent. And as much as it hurts now, he knows that he will ultimately be vindicated. So he tells his friends to watch out because God will take vengeance; His wrath will come upon them for what they have done to him.

20:1–3 It is clear in Zophar's reply that he is very upset with Job's response. Job has insulted his character, just as Zophar has insulted Job.

20:4–5 Zophar returns to the refrain Job has heard from all his friends: comparing what happens to the wicked to what is happening in Job's life. The wicked may prosper, but only for a short time.

20:7–9 Eventually even the highest-ranking among the wicked will be valued no more than human waste; nobody will remember them.

20:12–17 The wicked savor evil the way a child might savor candy, but ultimately they will be left with a bad taste in their mouths.

20:17 Honey and butter represent a prosperous life. The land of Canaan was said to be a land flowing with milk and honey (Exodus 13:5).

20:18–19 Although the wicked may have every luxury, they won't enjoy it. All their hard work won't bring them satisfaction.

20:19 When Zophar talks of how the wicked treat the needy, he is implying that Job has oppressed the poor and repossessed homes by force. He has no proof of this. Maybe there were rumors to that effect, but more likely Zophar simply assumes Job's guilt to account for Job's current suffering.

20:20–21 The fate of one who indulges his greed is to experience more greed—so much that he can never be satisfied. Ultimately, there will be nothing more to acquire.

20:27–29 Zophar's summation of the fate of the wicked implicitly warns Job that if he continues to hide his sin, all these things will happen to him—and there is worse yet to come on Judgment Day.

21:5 Job must have looked awful. In fact, it seems that his friends have a hard time even looking at him. So Job calls them to take a good look at him, even though his appearance is shocking to those who see him.

21:6–12 Job contradicts Zophar's litany of what happens to the wicked by pointing to what really takes place in life. The wicked don't die young; they are profitable and powerful. They have many healthy children, their homes are safe, their livestock breed and are healthy, and they enjoy good times.

21:13 Just as Zophar goes to one extreme in saying that the wicked are always punished, Job goes to the other extreme and says that the wicked are always blessed. Neither is true; see Psalm 37:35–36. God is sovereign, and He has a purpose for everything.

21:14–16 Jesus, in Matthew 19:23–24, makes the same point that Job makes here when He says that it is easier for a camel to go through the eye of a needle than for a rich man to enter heaven. The point is not that rich people won't go to heaven but that wealth can blind our eyes to our need for God.

21:17–21 Job's friends have been blaming Job and his hidden sin for the death of his children. Job argues that God should punish the wicked and not their children.

21:22 Job seems to backtrack from his previous remark, acknowledging that it is presumptuous to try to teach God what to do.

21:23–26 God's ways are incomprehensible to Job. Why should one person live happily right up until his death, while another has nothing but misery in his life?

21:27–30 Job is fully aware that his friends are trying to prove that his hardships are evidence of his wickedness. He challenges them to ask anybody, from any part of the world; anyone will agree that the wicked prosper.

22:1–3 Eliphaz reminds Job that Job's actions do not benefit God at all. Job is not doing God a favor by being good.

22:4–5 The question of Job's goodness is a moot point, Eliphaz implies, because obviously Job is not being good—God wouldn't allow all these troubles to happen to a good man. This argument pervades the words of Job's friends.

22:6–9 Up until this point, Eliphaz and the other friends have been satisfied to list the consequences of sin and let Job draw the conclusion that, since he is suffering those consequences, he is obviously a sinner. But Job hard-headedly refuses to draw that conclusion, so now Eliphaz comes out and accuses Job directly. Eliphaz has no proof that Job did any of the things Eliphaz is about to accuse him of, but he is trying to figure out the ways of God by applying life's situations to them. So he has come to the conclusion that Job has become wealthy by strong-arming the poor—taking their clothes, refusing to give them food and water, and disregarding the plight of the widowed and fatherless.

22:12–14 Eliphaz accuses Job of trying to get away with some kind of evil when God isn't looking. There was a belief that when clouds covered the earth people could do what they wanted because God, up in heaven, couldn't see through them. Ironically, God *has* been looking at what Job does and has decreed Job blameless and upright (1:8; 2:3).

22:15–16 Eliphaz evokes the image of the flood, as Bildad had done earlier (8:11). Just as God swept away the wicked with the flood, so now He is deluging Job with judgment.

22:17–18 Eliphaz quotes Job's own plea for God to leave him alone (see also 7:20) and piously asserts that he, Eliphaz, has nothing to do with such wickedness.

22:19–20 The innocent rejoice in the suffering of the wicked, Eliphaz says. Since he has identified Job as wicked and himself as innocent, the implication is that Eliphaz is happy about Job's downfall.

23:1–7 Job believes that if he can talk with God, he will be vindicated and God will relieve him of his troubles.

23:8–10 Though Job cannot find God, he is just as convinced of his own innocence before God as his friends are convinced of his guilt. He is confident that he will not be found lacking. Job understands that trials are used to purify us, just as gold is refined in the refiner's fire so that all impurities are removed.

23:13–16 Job speaks of the sovereignty of God. Unfortunately, this knowledge does not comfort Job; it makes him afraid. He is afraid because he thinks that this all-powerful God is out to get him.

23:13 Job is right when he says that God does whatever He pleases. This does not negate our responsibility to pray, however. It is through prayer that God conforms our hearts to His. God does answer our prayers, but we don't fully understand how it all works. When God was going to destroy unbelieving Israel, Moses stepped in and interceded for them, and God spared them. Did God change His will? Or was Moses' heart so conformed to God's that his request was in line with God's will? We don't understand these things, but we do know that God invites, even commands, our prayers.

24:1–9 Having affirmed God's knowledge and God's power, Job questions in this chapter why God doesn't provide, in essence, a courtroom in which people might urge Him to use that knowledge and power to correct injustices. In short, why does a powerful God allow bad things to happen to good people? This section of verses includes some of the injustices that Job thinks God should correct.

24:10–12 Job has seen the wicked do all these things. He has seen how the poor must work hard without getting the rewards of their labor. Job hears the cries for help of the poor and oppressed—surely God must hear them, too. But, as Job sees it, God does nothing.

24:13–17 The wicked run from the truth, here described as light, because it exposes their evil deeds. They love the dark because they can get away with evil. Darkness is the natural environment of the wicked, just as daylight is the natural environment of the innocent.

25:3 Human kings may have large armies, Bildad points out, but God's forces—the angels and heavenly armies—are too numerous to count. A wealthy man may illuminate his home with candles, but that is only a pale reflection of God's light, the sun.

26:1–4 Job's words are sarcastic as he responds to Bildad. The *thou*, or *you*, is singular, not plural. Apparently Eliphaz and Zophar have already been silenced. What a comforting friend, wise and insightful, Bildad has been, Job says—meaning exactly the opposite. To speak so wisely must require inspiration—but from what spirit? Clearly Job is not buying his friends' implication that they (and not Job) speak for God.

26:5–8 Perhaps in contrast to belittling Bildad, Job now exalts God. Nothing escapes God's notice and God's control. God created and still upholds the skies; the earth stays where He put it, even though it seems to be suspended with nothing to hold it up. The water cycle is no less amazing: We take its transformation from liquid to vapor to liquid again as a matter of course, but if a rock did the same thing, we would be amazed!

26:9–13 The most commonplace of daily events are under God's control, Job says. When a cloud passes between earth and the moon, God is in control of it. When the sun rises over the eastern horizon and sets over the western horizon, God is in control. Storms that seem to shake the heavens and churn the waters are as nothing to God; He can blow them away with a single breath.

26:13 The "crooked serpent" is, like other sea monsters mentioned in the Bible, a poetic representation of storms and other wild forces of nature.

26:14 All this evidence of God's power can be seen in creation, and yet it is only the tiniest fragment of what God is doing. What we know of God's power is like a whisper compared to thunder—far too great for us to comprehend.

27:2–4 Although Job believes that God has denied him justice, he is committed to remaining truthful.

27:3 Job's mention of his own breath is a reference to his life. At creation, God breathed life into Adam (Genesis 2:7). Even while arguing that God has misjudged him, Job recognizes that life lasts only as long as God chooses to give it.

27:5–7 A good part of Job's truthfulness, in his mind, is standing by his statement that he has done nothing to deserve the troubles that have come on him. To give in

to these charges, Job says, *would* be wicked, because it would be a lie.

27:7 Job's friends have become his enemies through their false accusations, and finally Job wishes they would be punished for their lies about him.

27:16–17 When Job claims that the righteous will receive the wealth of the wicked, he is stating a principle of ideal justice. Ultimately, Job is convinced, God will punish evil and reward good. Although Job's experience at this point does not bear this happy thought out, Job knows enough of the character of God to cling to the conviction that justice will one day prevail.

28:1–11 Job now talks about those who go down into the earth to dig for precious stones and metals and bring them back up to the surface. It is dangerous work, but for those who are successful, the rewards outweigh the risks.

28:12–22 Wisdom is harder to find, and harder for people to value, than precious stones or metals, Job says. One can't mine wisdom from the ground like silver or gold, nor gather it from the ocean depths like pearls or coral. Nor can one buy wisdom with the riches that can be mined—with gold, silver, precious stones, coral, or topaz. As precious and valuable as these stones and metals may be, they are worthless when compared to wisdom. Wisdom originates from God. Thus, as we apply the Word of God to our lives, we are exercising wisdom. Unfortunately for Job, finding wisdom begins to seem like a hopeless endeavor.

29:1–10 Job reminisces about his past, about the good times and joy he had before all this trouble came upon his life. In those days, he walked in the light of God. His children, who are all dead now, used to run around his feet, and what joy their voices brought him. Luxuries like cream were as common as the dirt beneath his feet. Goodness at one time seemed to follow him wherever he went. Job had been a respected man who sat at the gate of the city as part of the city council. The young deferred to him and the aged stood in respect of him. Job's description here serves as a catalog of his losses.

29:11–17 Earlier Job's friends had accused him of oppressing the poor and taking advantage of the fatherless and widows. But Job contends that the opposite is true: He had a reputation as a good man because he helped the poor and fatherless, comforted the dying, and brought joy to the widow's heart. When people looked at Job, they saw righteousness and justice. He helped the disabled, befriended strangers, and stood against the wicked. He was a good man who practiced what he believed.

29:18–20 In those earlier times, Job had it all figured out. Since he was doing good, he expected that he would live to an old age and that his life would continue to be blessed. He would be like the righteous man described in Psalm 1, who is like a tree planted by streams of water. His reputation as the greatest man among all the peoples of the East (see 1:3) would be constant. But things are not working out as he has planned.

29:21–25 People used to gather and wait in line to hear the wisdom of Job. His words were refreshing to them; they stood drinking in his words. They were delighted when they won his approval. Job received a lot of respect from the multitudes of people who came to hear him. There is the idea here that when he spoke, you could have heard a pin drop. That is the way it was, but now things have changed dramatically.

30:2–10 These people who now mock Job live off the land and are not physically healthy. They basically take what they can find, even the garbage that people throw out. These people are hated by society and run out of town. No one wants them around, for they are troublemakers and very offensive.

30:11–14 Since God has taken away all of Job's wealth, people no longer feel the need to show respect to him. Young men once stepped aside on the path to let Job pass (29:8); now they block his way.

30:15 In the past, people were eager to win Job's approval and feared his disapproval (29:21–24); now it is Job who is afraid and humiliated.

30:20–23 It seems that God has closed His ears to Job's cry. Job is crying out for help, but things just seem to be getting worse and worse for him. He is certain now that he will be miserable for the rest of his life.

30:24–30 It seems unbelievable to Job that he, who has helped those in difficulty so often, should have no one to help him now. Yet this is the case; every hope for relief is disappointed, and his suffering goes on.

30:30–31 For Job, there are no more songs of joy; the only songs in his life are dirges, funeral songs associated with grief and dying.

31:1–4 Job contends that he has not looked with lust at any woman. Now this is not just by accident; Job made an intentional decision—a covenant or agreement with his eyes—not to look at a woman this way. This covenant, this conscious decision, affects all areas of Job's life, because he knows that God knows his every thought and action. The New Testament abounds with instructions to make a conscious decision for holiness; see 1 Peter 1:13–16. This is *practical righteousness*.

31:5–10 Job gives specific examples of his innocence, couching each in the same if/then structure: "If I have done this, then let me be judged for it." "If I have been involved in an adulterous relationship," says Job, "then let me be punished by my wife's unfaithfulness."

31:13–15 Job contends that he doesn't treat people differently because of their social status, the color of their skin, or their nationality. He acts this way because he acknowledges that God has created every human being in the same way, reflecting His own image.

31:16–23 Job says that he has never walked away from anyone in need but has come to the aid of such people and given them what they needed to live—be it food, clothing, even help against their enemies. Job has acted the way he has because of his fear of—his reverence and respect for—the Lord.

31:24–28 Job does not worship his wealth or place his confidence in it, nor does he turn to horoscopes or other astrological enticements, because he recognizes that both of these actions constitute idolatry and unfaithfulness to God.

31:27 The worship of the heavens—the sun, moon, and constellations—was very popular in the ancient world and, of course, was a pagan practice. That worship included kissing one's hand and throwing that kiss to the sun or moon.

31:29–32 Job claims that he has not gloated over his enemies' troubles or cursed them, and he has offered hospitality to household staff and strangers alike.

31:33–34 Job has lived his life in the open for all to see. He is not a hypocrite, trying to hide his sin.

31:35–37 Job underscores the seriousness of his claims by putting his name to them—possibly literally signing a document, or perhaps symbolically. And he wishes that his accuser, God, would put His charges in writing as well, so that Job could refute the charges one by one.

32:1 The three friends see the futility of arguing with Job more. Because Job will not agree that he has been wrong, that he has sinned and thus brought on this suffering, they see him as self-righteous.

32:2–3 Abraham's brother Nahor had two sons, Huz and Buz (Genesis 22:21). Elihu is a descendant of the family of Buz, making him a Buzite. Elihu is angered by Job's words, and he isn't too happy with Job's three friends, either, for they have condemned Job with no proof of sin. Elihu sees their reasoning as faulty.

32:4–10 Out of respect for men older than himself, Elihu had remained silent, but now that the three friends are giving up, Elihu can remain quiet no longer. He begins respectfully enough, acknowledging the older men's right to speak first. But he points out that age does not always equal wisdom; wisdom is given by the Spirit (or breath) of God, and the young can receive that wisdom as well. Elihu is eager to share his wisdom.

32:11–13 Elihu has listened patiently to the words of the three friends, but they have come up short and not convinced Job of his error. All they have done is put Job on the defensive.

32:14–17 Elihu hopes that Job will listen to him because he has not been part of the earlier arguments—and because he has something new to say. He doesn't see why he should be forced to remain silent just because the three friends have given up.

32:18–20 Elihu has so much to say that he is ready to burst.

33:1–7 Sometime earlier, Job had expressed a desire for a mediator between him and God (9:33). Elihu says that he is that man who can stand in the gap and bring Job and God together. He claims to be righteous, sincere, and Spirit-filled—in other words, someone God will listen to but also someone Job doesn't need to fear. Elihu is here describing the perfect mediator: truly righteous and truly human; see, for example, Hebrews 2:17; 7:26.

Looking back through history, we know that the perfect mediator described here is not Elihu but Jesus Christ.

33:8–11 Elihu accuses Job of falsely claiming to be sinless. Here he is misrepresenting Job, who has readily admitted that he is a sinner (7:21; 13:26). Further, Job regularly offers the appropriate sacrifices for sin (1:5). What Job has claimed is to be innocent of the kind of wickedness that deserves the punishment (as he perceives it to be) that he has received.

33:12–19 Elihu also accuses Job of claiming that God does not speak to humans. He lists many ways that God does in fact communicate: through dreams and visions, audibly or through the warnings of godly people, and even through pain, which can focus one's thoughts on God and on self-examination.

33:20–22 Job's friends had maintained that the things happening to Job were a direct result of sin in his life. Elihu's message is that God has brought this trouble upon Job because He is chastening him so that Job will confess his sin and get back on track. God does indeed sometimes use what C. S. Lewis called "the megaphone of pain" to get our attention and lead us back to Him. But Elihu is wrong in assuming that Job's suffering is God's rebuke and call to repentance; Job 1 and 2 have already made clear that the reason is quite different. In the same way, we would be wrong to assume that suffering is always God's rebuke for wrongdoing; see Luke 13:1–5 for Jesus' warning against that kind of judgment.

33:23–25 Elihu tries to encourage Job with the possibility that one of the angels will intercede with God on Job's behalf. Ironically, Job's troubles result from exactly the opposite: Satan's accusations against him.

33:26–30 The appropriate response, Elihu instructs Job, is to confess first to God and then to people that he has sinned and that God has given him another chance. In fact, Elihu says, Job's suffering is actually evidence of God's love, as it gives Job a chance to repent and be restored.

33:31–33 Elihu pauses to ask whether Job needs any clarification before he continues with his instruction. Presumably Job does not, because Elihu continues his lecture.

34:1–4 Elihu now turns to address those around him, inviting them to be partners in the process of assessing Job's situation.

34:5–9 Elihu summarizes Job's claims of injustice and then plays "good cop" to the three friends, saying Job has taken all their abuse, but Elihu is not going to do the same. Despite what Elihu claims, Job knows that the wicked will be punished and there is a profit in doing good. Once again, Elihu is misrepresenting what Job has to say.

34:10–15 Elihu begins to defend God, asserting that God does justice, not evil. No one supervises God; He holds us together and gives us the very breath we breathe.

34:16–20 At this point, Elihu turns back to speak directly to Job. He accuses Job of condemning God as unjust in His dealings with Job. Elihu contends that Job honors those in high positions, like kings, and yet he puts God down.

34:21–22 Evildoers can't get away with anything, at least in an ultimate sense; God knows what they are doing, Elihu reminds Job.

34:23 Although Job has been asking for a hearing before God, Elihu argues that hearings are unnecessary for a God who already knows everything.

34:24–28 It is certain that God will mete out justice, and that justice will be made public so that everyone can see what happens to people who reject God's laws and mistreat the poor.

34:29–30 Job has complained that God is silent when Job calls to Him. Elihu claims that it's God's right to remain silent; God maintains justice over the nations even when He is silent.

34:31–33 Elihu sets out a model of behavior for Job to follow, first with a hypothetical situation, and then more directly with a rhetorical question about Job's apparent refusal to repent.

34:34–37 Elihu seems to be thinking aloud as he summarizes Job's position: Everyone knows (so Elihu believes) that Job is a fool. Job deserves even more troubles than he has already received, Elihu contends, because Job not only is a sinner but also refuses to confess that sin and thus rebels against God's chastisement.

35:1–3 Elihu points out what he sees as an inconsistency in Job's complaint. Job claims that there is no benefit for not sinning, and yet he expects God to vindicate him for not sinning.

35:4–8 Elihu points out that God is far above human beings. God does not owe Job anything. Nor is God affected by how good or how bad Job is. While Job can't hurt God by his actions, he can very much hurt or help himself and others by what he does and what he says.

35:9–10 Many cry out for help during difficult times, but they look for their help in all the wrong places. They don't look to God, who will put a song in their hearts and give them hope and joy again.

35:11–16 Many people speak boldly about things they don't know. But God does not respond to them, because they are arrogant. Job is equally arrogant, Elihu says, and that is why God doesn't answer him.

36:1–4 Elihu has elevated himself to the position of spokesman for God—but God has not given him this position. Elihu claims he has obtained perfect knowledge through direct revelation from God, so Job had better listen.

36:7–8 Earlier Job had complained that God would not leave him alone (7:17–19). Elihu considers it a comfort to know that God's eyes are continually upon His people. The righteous God exalts, but the arrogant He afflicts.

36:9–12 Job is angry because God has brought a clear charge against him, but Elihu argues that God does warn people of their sins and brings trouble on them to get them to repent. If they do repent, they will prosper; if not, they will perish.

36:13–16 Elihu warns Job not to be like those who rebel against God's discipline but instead to recognize it as God's loving way of bringing Job out of sin and misery and into joy and comfort.

36:17–23 Elihu sees Job as being in danger of choosing evil rather than submitting to God's discipline. There is no one who teaches as God does. He is not wrong and He will never be wrong.

36:24–26 Humanity can know God because He has revealed Himself through scripture and through His creation. But we cannot understand God's thoughts and ways, nor can we fully grasp the truth that God is eternal. He has always existed.

36:24–29 Elihu points to the earth's atmosphere as an exhibit of God's wisdom, power, and provision. What follows is an accurate description of evaporation and distillation of water as rain, clouds, and, in the next chapter, cyclones.

36:30–37:13 Many feel that as Elihu is speaking to Job, in the distance a huge storm is forming. As Elihu is trying to make his point, he sees this storm and begins to draw illustrations on the power of God and His awesomeness.

37:14–20 Elihu again asks rhetorical questions as he challenges Job to reflect on God's power and control over creation.

37:21–24 Just as we find it difficult, almost impossible, to stare at the sun with our naked eyes, so, too, is it impossible to stand in the brightness of a holy and righteous God in our own righteousness. The only reasonable response to God's power and greatness is to revere Him.

38:1–40:2 For some thirty-five chapters, Job and his friends have spoken, but now it is time for God to speak. It is noteworthy here that God does not explain why He has done these things to Job. In fact, God asks Job a series of some seventy questions, and in the end, God's *answer* is far more important than an understanding of His *ways*. Simply speaking, God gives Himself as the answer.

38:1–3 Job has wanted to ask God questions, but God turns the tables and begins asking Job questions. Job has been looking and developing his ideas of God through life's situations instead of falling back on the truths of God. His picture of God has been clouded by life's circumstances, and God is going to clear things up.

38:4 God's initial question emphasizes His own preeminence. God asks Job whether he was around when the earth was created.

38:7 The angels, sons of God, were present at earth's creation and shouted for joy at what God had done. But Job was not around.

38:8–11 God set the boundaries for the waters without the help of Job.

38:12–15 Job was not around when God created the days and the light. God is trying to get Job to take his eyes off of the circumstances he finds himself in and to look back to his Creator, the source of true help and hope.

38:16 The ancients were not aware of the freshwater springs that are on the ocean floor, nor the channels and pathways located in the depth of the oceans, but God knew.

38:17–18 Job had wanted death to come upon him, for he saw death as a place of nonexistence (3:11–17). But he is wrong about that. God rebukes Job for speaking about something he knows nothing about.

38:22–23 Who understands how God controls the weather to influence the outcome of battles? God has used the elements of nature to bring about His will. In Judges 5 Barak defeats the army of Sisera when God causes a torrential rainfall, causing their chariots to be stuck in the mud so that they have to flee on foot. God causes hailstones to fall from the sky, destroying the Amorites, in Joshua 10. And in 1 Samuel 7 God uses thunder to confuse the Philistines, giving Israel the victory.

38:24 We know today that light can be divided into the light spectrum, but how did they know this back then? God knew because He created the light.

38:25–28 God reminds Job that He waters the wilderness, causing the vegetation to grow.

38:29–30 God did not just create life and sit back to watch what would happen; He is actively involved in sustaining His work.

38:31–38 Pleiades and Orion are winter constellations. The Great Bear, or Arcturus, is the fourth brightest star in the sky. Obviously Job has no control over them, nor can Job make it rain, but God can and He does.

38:39–41 God provides food for the various animals—even those Job will not go near.

39:1–4 God points to nature and how the animals give birth without the knowledge of Job, but God is aware.

39:5–8 God specifically mentions the wild donkey, but He is saying He cares for all the animals.

39:9–12 The word translated here as *unicorn* has also been translated as meaning a wild ox, a huge and fierce creature that could not be domesticated. And God is saying to Job, "If you can't stand before My creation, if you can't handle him, how can you stand before Me?"

39:13–18 The ostrich can stand seven to eight feet tall, weighing up to three hundred pounds. It is flightless, and it is without sense. But even though God did not give the ostrich wisdom, He gave it the ability to run.

40:1–2 God calls on Job to respond to all these questions He has put to Job.

40:3–5 Job had much to say before, when his eyes were focused on his situation. But now that God has his attention, he has very little to say. He rightly recognizes his error and is ready to listen to God.

40:6–7 Out of the storm, God again challenges Job to answer Him, using the same words He used earlier (38:3).

40:8 This time God addresses Job's primary complaint: that He has been unjust to Job (see 19:6).

40:9–13 Job has claimed to be just, so now God challenges Job to demonstrate his power to administer that justice.

40:14 If Job can demonstrate his power like God, then he can vindicate himself.

40:15–24 These verses make up the first of two poems that God speaks to Job, returning to the themes of chapter 39 and God's control over nature. The *behemoth* described here is an animal that God created, not a mythical being. It is an elephant, a rhinoceros, a water buffalo, or a hippopotamus. It is one of the most powerful of all God's creatures, but God is even more powerful. The area described as this creature's habitat is probably the region north of the sea of Galilee. The idea of any human capturing the behemoth is laughable, but God can certainly control it. Scholars aren't certain exactly what kind of creature the behemoth is. It is variously considered to be an elephant, a rhinoceros, a water buffalo, or a hippopotamus. It is a land animal that also lives in the water. It is also an herbivore; in other words, it eats grass. It is a massive creature that has a tail, or possibly a trunk, like a cedar tree. From the description that is given, it seems that the behemoth could be a dinosaur—possibly either a Brachiosaurus or an Apatosaurus.

41:1–21 The leviathan is powerful and untamable, with scary teeth—perhaps like a crocodile's. Apparently it is a reptile with a scaly back that is like a protective shield. To get within breathing range of the leviathan is to court disaster.

41:22–30 The leviathan is tough all over, practically invincible. Even its underbelly—usually the most vulnerable part of an animal—is as hard and as sharp as broken pottery.

41:33–34 Nothing on earth—and certainly not Job—is the equal of the leviathan. The last verse of this poem about the leviathan shifts from speaking of physical prowess to speaking of attitude and rank. It could be that the dragon that God is speaking of here is the same dragon found in the book of Revelation, Satan (Revelation 12:3–4, 7–9).

42:1–2 Notice the perspective that Job now has of God and his situation. Job recognizes the sovereignty of God and that He is in control of everything. God has shown Job that He not only created the heavens and the earth and all that dwells in them, but also sustains them. Everything is subject to His sovereign rule.

42:3 Job recognizes the foolishness of his words. Job spoke about issues he knew nothing about, and yet he sounded so sure of himself. God has redirected Job to fall back on the things he knows about God instead of coming up with foolish conclusions about life's situations. This is a typical response of many of us when

we are hurting. We take our eyes off God and what His Word has to say, and we come up with foolish words. If we will let God redirect us to fall back on the things we know about God through His Word, we, like Job, will find that His Word is full of wonder, hope, and comfort.

42:4–6 It is one thing to hear God but quite another thing to *encounter* Him. It is Job's encounter with God that causes him to see himself as a sinner, and he repents of his sin.

42:7 Job's friends have not represented God correctly, and here God holds them accountable for their actions. God is angry with Job's three friends because they have not spoken the truth about Him. They have reduced God to a cause-and-effect God, and they have assumed that they could both understand and predict all of God's actions. In essence, they have denied God's sovereignty by declaring that God must respond in a certain way to certain situations.

42:8–9 The three friends have spent much energy trying to convince Job of his sin and of his need to repent and offer sacrifices for that sin. How ironic it must seem when God tells them that *they* are the ones who need to offer sacrifices—and that God will accept those sacrifices for Job's sake and because of Job's righteousness.

42:10–11 When does God bless or restore Job? When he prays for his friends who abandoned him. Then they come rushing back, eager to comfort Job—and to eat his food (19:13–19). Why does God wait to bless Job until after Job prays for the friends who have attacked him? Job has had some bitterness toward his friends, as his replies to them have shown. But to pray for them he had to let go of that bitterness.

42:12–13 God blesses Job with even more wealth than he had before—twice as many sheep, camels, oxen, and donkeys as before. It seems that Job has the same number of children, but the reality is he has twice as many, for seven sons and three daughters were with the Lord.

42:14–15 Job treats his daughters with the same kindness as he treats his sons, even giving them an inheritance, which was unusual in those days.

42:16–17 Despite his friends' dire warnings that Job would die young (see 36:14) and leave no heirs (see 18:19), Job lives 140 more years and sees not only his grandchildren but also his great-grandchildren and great-great-grandchildren as well. That he dies "full of days" implies he enjoyed a long life.

THE BOOK OF

PSALMS

INTRODUCTION TO PSALMS ■ The book of Psalms has been called the "hymnbook" of the Old Testament. Depending on one's perception of a hymnal, the title can be misleading, or it can be quite accurate. Anyone who closely examines a traditional hymnal and reads the words of Martin Luther, Charles Wesley, Fanny Crosby, and others will find a wealth of biblical truth and weighty theological tenets.

AUTHOR ■ The psalms have a variety of authors. Almost half of the psalms (seventy-three) are attributed to David. Asaph (including his descendants, one of the clans of Levites assigned to oversee the music ministry of the temple) is credited with twelve psalms. Another music ministry clan, the sons of Korah, is identified with eleven psalms (although Psalm 43, which is unattributed, may have originally been an extension of Psalm 42 and is therefore added to the total). Two psalms are assigned to Solomon. One each is assigned to Moses, Heman, and Ethan. That leaves forty-nine psalms with no designated author.

OCCASION ■ The Hebrew title for the book means "praises." Overall, the content of the book is intended for prayer and praise, although there is much variety within those broad categories.

1:1–2 The first "book" within Psalms is the earliest of the five compilations. It is widely associated with David's life and reign. The placement of Psalm 1 does not appear to be coincidental. The work of editors seems clear from the fact that each book within the book of Psalms ends with a doxology. Similarly, Psalm 1 seems well chosen to emphasize a theme that will be ongoing. Throughout scripture God calls His people to set their standards higher than those of the world in general. People who commit themselves to God and are obedient to His clear instructions are promised rewards; those who reject Him can expect judgment. The word *blessed* describes the status of someone who has placed trust in the Lord and lives according to His commands. This desirable state is one of inner joy more than financial prosperity, although the two are sometimes intertwined. Blessedness results from committing to certain activities while avoiding others. Those desiring God's blessing must be careful of their worldly associations. While being a light to the world, they must not allow themselves to linger too long around ungodly influences, lest they be seduced. They are not to walk among the wicked, and they are to remain focused at all times on God's Word.

2:1 As with Psalm 1, the author and date of Psalm 2 are not known. The leaders of the early New Testament church attributed Psalm 2 to David (Acts 4:25), although their intent may simply have been to give him credit as the primary author of Psalms. The psalmist doesn't expect an answer to his opening question; he is simply pointing out that by resisting the one anointed by God, the nations are resisting the authority of God Himself—a futile effort. The psalmist's original readers would have been familiar with the political turbulence that frequently took place surrounding the rise of a new leader. Perhaps they recalled that in spite of David's credentials, the supporters of King Saul were still slow to accept him as their leader. Later, when Solomon's son Rehoboam

attempts to assert himself as a new king, the people strongly resist, and the kingdom is divided (1 Kings 12:1–24).

3:1–2 This is the first of the seventy-three psalms designated "of David." Psalms is divided into five books. Some people feel that each successive book is a compilation of songs assembled sometime after the previous collection. Book I may have been compiled during the time of David, so it isn't surprising to discover that all but four of the first forty-one psalms are attributed to him. In this case, the occasion of writing is included: when David fled from his son Absalom. The story of David fleeing from Absalom is told in 2 Samuel 15–18, but the sentiment expressed in the psalm is appropriate for anyone who has been betrayed or turned upon by a close friend or family member.

4:4–5 David had previously prayed for God to break the teeth of the ungodly. Here David's request is much warmer. He appeals to his opponents to not allow their anger to lead to sin, and he urges them to repent before God—to offer right sacrifices. Perhaps David's mind was indeed on Absalom as he wrote this, for it sounds like the plea of a parent worried that a grown child is in danger of harming himself.

4:7 David acknowledges that the joy God provides is greater than even the most festive times of regular life. He speaks from experience, but he hopes that others will discover the same truth.

5:1–3 This is a morning prayer of David, perhaps to accompany a regular morning sacrifice (Exodus 29:38–39). David has learned that it is always a good idea to present one's requests to God in the morning and then wait in expectation—especially on days that begin with sighing and cries for help.

5:4–6 David can take consolation because he understands the character of God. The Lord cannot tolerate evil, so He does not respond to people who willingly participate in arrogance, lies, and deceit. Some people begin their mornings proud of what they feel they have achieved or scheming to acquire more through less-than-honorable methods. David, however, expresses his feelings to God and waits for a response.

5:11–12 Those who seek God and take refuge in Him experience His protection, which allows them to be glad, sing, and rejoice. While on the run from King Saul, David had many times felt the surrounding protection of God. He knows for certain that the Lord's shield of favor is available to all who love and serve Him.

6:2–3 David's whole body is afflicted with pain. David is sick of being sick—worn out from groaning and weeping. With his bones in agony and soul in anguish, his whole being is in pain and he knows that only God can heal him. His question, "How long?" is asked frequently throughout the psalms.

6:4–5 David expresses his hope for healing because of God's unfailing love. He appeals to God, reasoning that he can continue to acknowledge God as long as he is living, but death will put an end to any praise he might offer.

7:1–2 The term *shiggaion* is used only twice in the Bible, here and in Habakkuk 3:1. It appears to be a musical term but has an undetermined meaning. In addition, the man named *Cush*, to whom David refers, is not known elsewhere in scripture. However, the additional note that he is from the tribe of Benjamin makes it likely that he might have been an associate of Saul. This makes sense in light of the psalm's description of being pursued by relentless enemies. David has great confidence in the Lord, but that doesn't make the attacks of his enemies any less unsettling.

7:10–13 David describes God as a warrior preparing for battle: sharpening His sword, stringing His bow, and lighting His arrows with fire.

7:14–16 Some people show blatant disregard for God and no desire for holy living. Such people "conceived mischief," but their time will come. Those who choose such a life cannot prevent trouble in their own lives.

7:17 Despite the very real threat David feels from his enemies, he concludes this psalm with praise to God—and an advance acknowledgment of God's willingness to act on behalf of His faithful people.

8:1–2 The introduction to Psalm 8 includes yet another ancient term: *gittith* (also found in the superscriptions of Psalms 81 and 84). The Hebrew word might be a reference to a winepress or to Gath, a Philistine city where David had spent some time (1 Samuel 21:10–15; 27:1–4). Its significance as a musical cue, however, is unknown. David begins with an acknowledgment that the earth is God's. Those who are observant see the majesty of God. The expanse and the order of the solar system reflect the design of a creator. Even the awe of small children as they encounter the wonders of the world gives praise to God.

8:3–5 When God's presence is not considered, people come up with distorted answers to the question, "What is man?" When one ponders the vast extent of the universe,

it is easy to feel small and insignificant, but God has bestowed much significance on humankind. In fact, the word translated as *angels* is *elohim*—one of the Hebrew names for God. Human beings have been crowned with glory and honor.

8:6–8 From the beginning, God has designated humankind to be the overseers of the earth (Genesis 1:28). People are privileged to rule over the other animals of the land, the sea, and the air. And this privilege is not to be taken lightly. It is still God's creation, and the people report to a higher master.

9:1–6 Like several of the preceding psalms of David, Psalm 9 deals with his struggles to endure the persecution of his enemies. David is eager to sing and rejoice because God has dealt with David's foes. They have been not only defeated but also rebuked, destroyed, and blotted out. Their ruin is endless, and soon there will not even be a memory of them.

9:7–10 David begins to extol the character of God. He affirms that the Lord is an eternal king, a righteous judge, and a stronghold and refuge for those needing help. People who seek God can count on Him to come through for them.

9:15–20 As for the nations, they will reap what they have sown. What they plotted against others will be their own downfall.

10:1 A case can be made that Psalms 9 and 10 were originally a single psalm. Some dispute this possibility because the two divisions have quite different themes and each section holds up on its own. However, in the span of Psalms 3–32, Psalm 10 is the only one lacking a superscription. And if the two are combined, they create an acrostic poem (a poem where each unit begins with a successive letter of the Hebrew alphabet), albeit roughly. Perhaps they were two songs meant to relate to each other, or maybe a single psalm was divided at a point in church history to facilitate its use in worship.

10:2–11 The psalmist (presumably David) goes into great detail about wicked people, describing both their attitudes and their actions. The people he writes about are arrogant, covetous, proud, self-centered, haughty, dishonest, and cruel. Their time is spent scheming, sneering, cursing, murdering innocent people, and otherwise preying on helpless victims. They scoff at God.

11:4–6 Even though earthly events may seem to be more chaotic and turbulent than usual, one's spiritual condition is as reliable as ever. God is still on His throne. Nothing has changed. He sees what is going on, He will judge what He sees, and it won't be pleasant for those who have defied Him.

11:7 This psalm ends with encouragement for the righteous—they may be shaken by the evil in the world, but they have nothing to fear from the Lord. Many believers comprehend that on a cognitive level, but David truly believed it and acted in faith that his righteous Lord would always be there for him. In David's case, God is not just a vague presence but a refuge in the truest sense of the word.

12:1-2 The superscription comments for this psalm, "upon Sheminith," are the same as for Psalm 6. David describes the all-too-common feeling of looking around and seeing that one's world has deteriorated into a sorry state. David is feeling somewhat alone in his commitment to God.

13:5-6 In spite of the somewhat bleak opening to the psalm, it concludes (like so many others) with the psalmist's expression of complete trust in God. The Lord may appear to be distant, but He isn't. David's enemies may have seemed triumphant, but they aren't. The fear of death may have been weighing on David's mind, but he is still alive and able to reach out in faith. David's steadfast God is still the source of unfailing love, salvation, and goodness. The circumstances of life might change, but the grace and mercy of God never will.

14:1 This psalm builds on several of the themes from previous psalms, particularly the contrast between the holiness of God and the foolishness of wicked people. Psalm 14 places more emphasis on the fools who ignore God. In contrast is Psalm 15, which focuses on the benefits of being among the righteous. David begins with a perceptive observation: Foolish people assume that God does not exist. That inner presumption, although entirely wrong, then results in corrupt and even vile outward actions. As those who *do* believe in God look on, they are disturbed and even horrified by such behavior.

14:4-5 The actions of the wicked people appear to be cold and calculated. They devour God's people as if they were eating bread—the modern equivalent might be "chewing someone up and spitting him out." And they never call on God. Such people are also portrayed as unsettled. While they won't personally acknowledge God, they can't help but see that He makes a significant difference in the lives of righteous people. Consequently, the evildoers are left with a sinking sense of dread.

15:1 With so many of the previous psalms expressing the writer's confusion, despair, and outrage over the fact that ungodly people seem to be running rampant while believers in God struggle to get by, Psalm 15 is a simple but powerful reminder of what is really important. The psalmist (presumably David) opens with a simple question: What does it take to find favor with God? What kind of people may approach Him and spend time with Him?

16:1-2 The superscription includes the first mention of a *michtam*, another presumed but undeterminable musical term. The word appears in later psalms (56–60), where David describes himself in personal peril. In this case, David may be experiencing a threat of some sort, although throughout most of the psalm he expresses overwhelming confidence and optimism. David affirms God as his refuge, an image he frequently uses (2:12; 7:1; 9:9). God is his solitary source of comfort and safety. David's expression of faithful confidence is so powerful that this psalm is later quoted by both Peter (Acts 2:25–28) and Paul (Acts 13:35). After the life,

death, and resurrection of Jesus, David's words about death take on a surprising new significance.

16:9-11 David doesn't have the same perspective of resurrection and eternal life as modern believers. Even so, he is assured and positive as he thinks about death.

17:1-3 Although David doesn't express his specific complaint for some time, he is again besieged by his enemies and is beseeching God's help. He desperately wants God's attention: He asks three different times for God to listen to him. David wants vindication in God's eyes. He affirms that his words come as a righteous request from honest lips. Only a person of real integrity would be able to challenge God to probe and test him, convinced that God will find no charge against him. In particular, David's resolve to control his mouth is reflective of Psalm 15.

17:9-14 The enemies surrounding David are serious threats: callous, arrogant, and compared to a lion crouching to spring at its prey. David is wise to turn to God for shelter, but he also prays that God will confront and deal with his wicked oppressors. Such people live only for what they can accumulate in this world. The righteous, however, know that God provides more than enough.

18:1-3 This is another psalm about David's praise to God in gratitude for His help in dealing with aggressive enemies. Psalm 18 is also found in its entirety (with only slight changes in wording) in 2 Samuel 22 as David's song of praise after being delivered from his enemies, including King Saul. Longer than any of the psalms that precede it, Psalm 18 opens with an introductory overture of praise containing a long string of terms to describe God: strength, rock, fortress, deliverer, buckler, horn of salvation, and high tower. These are all images of power, yet the God they describe is both accessible and personal.

18:4-6 David is in a desperate situation, writing of distress, destruction, and the likelihood of death. But rather than allow fear and panic to overwhelm him, David calls on God for help. God hears David's cries.

18:7-15 This vivid description includes imagery of God responding through the forces of nature, the intensity of an angry and powerful animal, and the accuracy of a soldier armed with arrows and bolts of lightning. The mention of cherub (angels) in biblical texts is frequently an indication of the presence of God.

18:16-19 David's foes had been too much to handle on his own, but his faith in God is not in vain.

18:20-24 Based on the fearful description of God, one might think David is afraid of Him. But David has a firm conviction that he has been living in obedience and faithfulness to God. The awesome power of God is directed against those who oppose Him, but it works in favor of those committed to living a righteous life.

18:25-29 David doesn't consider himself a special case to receive God's help and protection. He affirms that anyone who is faithful will witness God's faithfulness in return, and everyone who is blameless, pure, and humble stands to benefit from the righteous character of the Lord.

But those who display deceit or arrogance will view God in a vastly different manner. God's presence provides David assistance and abilities he cannot get anywhere else: light in darkness, strength, courage, and more.

18:30–50 David provides personal testimony to the difference God has made in his life. David acknowledges the perfection of God and the fact that the Lord is a unique entity who cannot be compared to anyone or anything else. It is God who empowered and sustained David to be victorious in battle. It is God who designated David to be king in spite of the initial resistance he received from Saul and others. And in response, David enthusiastically praises his Lord as saviour, avenger, and benefactor.

19:1–6 Humankind has always had a fascination with looking into the skies for weather forecasts, for getting one's bearings, for observation, for warning signs, and simply out of a sense of wonder. The message of the heavens is heard throughout the world. David begins by giving attention to the natural world that reflects God's glory and then moves on to the revealed Word of God—the source of many various potential blessings. David describes the simple repetition of day following night and the soothing sense of rhythm and regularity it provides, reflecting the concept that God is eternal and consistent and can be relied on. The creative description of the sun is that of a bridegroom arriving at his wedding and of a gleeful runner on track across the sky. David's viewpoint would have stood out from most others during his time. He credits God as being in control of the sun, while many pagan religions held that the sun *was* a god.

19:7–11 After looking into the heavens to witness the glory of God, David looks into the Word of God: its laws, statutes, precepts, commands, and ordinances. His experience is that an awareness of God's Word results both in practical help (wisdom, righteousness, and warning) and in positive, pleasant feelings (joy, enlightenment). By regularly examining the wonders of nature, someone can come to a broad and general belief that a creator must have designed the world. But to stop there can lead to much speculation and potentially erroneous theology. The living God responsible for creation is revealed throughout the pages of scripture. David knew to consult both sources for an accurate and more complete understanding of God.

19:12–14 David's knowledge of God inspires him to excel in his devotion to his Lord. He wants to rid his life of willful sins as well as hidden faults. David ends this psalm with a prayer that not only his words but also his inner thoughts would be pleasing to God, whom he acknowledges as his strength and redeemer.

20:1–5 This psalm is written for an assembled group to join the king in prayer preceding a battle. Significant spiritual preparation has already taken place. The king's prayers have been offered to God, along with sacrifices at the tabernacle (sanctuary). Battle plans have been made and David is mentally ready, but he wants to ensure that God is with him and that he has the support of the people. And indeed, the people are anticipating a joyous victory.

20:6 The singular voice may be that of David, the king. Or possibly it is a response assigned to a designated Levite participating in the worship ceremony. Even though the crowd is expecting victory, the credit goes to God even before the battle begins.

21:7 The crucial theme of Psalm 21 is found here. David's trust in God, in conjunction with God's love for David, creates a secure foundation for the psalmist. And his relationship with the Lord is the basis for all the other joys and blessings described throughout the psalm.

21:8–12 The second half of the psalm is a response by the assembled people in acknowledgment of and gratitude for God's deliverance. The king is recognized for his strength and success, but ultimately it is God's wrath and judgment that are responsible for the fall of Israel's enemies. By destroying the descendants of enemy leaders, a leader greatly minimizes the likelihood of that opposing nation becoming a danger anytime soon. Their continued plots and threats will be in vain.

21:13 This psalm ends with an echo of its beginning, this time with an affirmation of God's strength and praise for His power.

22:1–11 After two psalms that dwell on the strength of God and the victories experienced by David, Psalm 22 captures a quite different, more somber mood. According to the superscription, the psalm is intended to be set to an already established tune. Jesus quotes the opening line of this psalm while hanging on the cross. David's words in this psalm are surprisingly descriptive of Jesus' crucifixion. David expresses a cognitive understanding that God is present, that He always has been, and that He has always come through for His people throughout their history. However, David also writes of a personal experience of suffering during which his feelings do not mirror his cognitive truth. He feels abandoned by God and, like so many people throughout the ages, asks the question, "Why?" He cries out to God around the clock but detects no response. He is a target of scorn and ridicule, forced to listen to his enemies mock his faith, yet he tenaciously holds to what he knows to be true.

22:19–24 Jesus endured not only the physical agony of crucifixion but also the spiritual despair of taking on the sins of humankind. David, however, anticipates God's rescue from his own situation. Even before he detects God's deliverance, he is quick to praise God and affirm His faithfulness. Despite appearances, David knows God is fully aware of his situation and concerned about his safety. Consequently, David challenges his fellow Israelites to praise and revere God.

22:25–31 He wants to set a good example (fulfill his vows) for the people. David even expands his scope to include the ends of the earth and the nations. He hopes the entire world will respond when they hear how God has helped him. And if David does indeed foretell the crucifixion of his most famous descendant in this psalm, the news of God's deliverance and salvation will be heard by the entire world, as generation after generation continues to proclaim His righteousness. Of all the psalms, this one is quoted more than any other in the New Testament.

23:1–3 In what is undoubtedly the best known of the psalms, David uses the imagery of a shepherd to highlight God's blessings and protection of His people. It was rather common for kings of the time to be compared to shepherds. Although King David has firsthand experience in the role (1 Samuel 16:11–13; 17:34–35), in this psalm he is only one of the sheep in the fold of God. The prophets will later describe the distress of the people by using an absent-shepherd or bad-shepherd analogy (Isaiah 56:9–12; Jeremiah 25:34–38; Ezekiel 34:1–11; Zechariah 11:15–17). However, David's description of God is the epitome of a good shepherd—a title Jesus will later apply to Himself (John 10:11). As a shepherd, God provides for every need of His sheep. The green pastures and quiet waters are basic physical needs, but God also restores the soul, attending to the inner spiritual needs of humankind. Guidance is another essential role of ancient shepherds. In a land where many of the paths are rocky and treacherous, the safety of the sheep reflects on the reputation of the shepherd. God keeps David on paths of righteousness.

24:7–10 Portions of Psalms 96, 105, and 106 were used in conjunction with the return of the ark of the covenant to Jerusalem (1 Chronicles 15:1–16:36). It is possible that this psalm was also used on that occasion.

25:6–11 As he recalls his imperfections, David also calls upon God's mercy and love. He understands that God does not hold people forever responsible for their sins, but He both forgives them and forgets them. As a professed sinner, David needs God's instruction and guidance in order to discover God's way, which includes goodness, upright behavior, humility, love, and faithfulness. David doesn't attempt to hide or downplay his sin.

25:12–14 God's forgiveness will open the door to numerous blessings, including clear instruction throughout life.

25:15–21 David's afflictions and anguish have heightened his awareness of the need for God's direction. David uses one of his favorite symbols for God: his deliverer. The forces of life are pressing in on him, but he can still feel secure and protected.

26:1–3 This is David's prayer for vindication. In tone, it is not unlike Paul's defense of his ministry in 2 Corinthians 11, when the apostle attempts to distance himself from unrighteous peers and their false accusations. He doesn't want it to sound like he is boasting (2 Corinthians 11:10, 16–18, 21), but he needs to state some truths about himself strongly and clearly. So, too, David feels it necessary to defend himself. David's appeal is directed to God, so any misstatements or exaggerations will be quickly refuted. His claim to a blameless life doesn't suggest that he is sinless but rather that he has not intentionally taken advantage of others—one result of his unwavering faith in God. David invites God to examine his thoughts and feelings because he attempts to *continually* be aware of God's love and truth.

27:1 Fear is a universal emotion that frequently triggers a "fight or flight" response in people. When afraid, some people muster all the courage they can and stand their ground, whether or not it's a wise choice. At the first sign of trouble, others flee so they can live to fight another day. David begins this psalm with his own questions about fear and concludes it with another option for responding to fear that involves neither fighting nor fleeing. David has given the matter of fear more thought than most people, because he has already determined that God is his light, salvation, and strength. He will not stumble in the darkness, as many do. He has a deliverer and security, even during the times that are most alarming.

27:4–6 When faced with fear, David keeps his priorities straight—a lifetime relationship with God at the tabernacle. His eyes aren't directed toward the approaching enemy but rather toward the beauty of the Lord. Consequently, he has confidence that when trouble does come, God will protect and sustain him. Rather than panic, he can respond with songs and shouts of joy.

27:7–12 David prays that God will continue to be merciful and available, and he believes that God will be there during the worst of times, when even those closest to him might forsake him.

28:3–4 David makes a point not to associate with the wicked, and he purposefully attempts to distance himself from them in this prayer. He wants God to provide retribution for all the harm they have done. They seem particularly despicable because they will feign kindness toward others while they inwardly seethe with malice.

28:5–6 With little doubt that the actions of wicked people will bring about their judgment, David begins to praise God. At this point, David is convinced that God has indeed heard him.

29:1–2 David's focus begins and remains on the power of God. As the psalmist watches a powerful storm approach and roll through his location, he records his thoughts. The power of the approaching storm reminds David of the power of the Lord. He begins by challenging the mighty to attribute glory and strength to God. Most likely this is a reference to the angels who attend to the Lord. Possibly the comment is directed toward people who consider themselves "high and mighty" and who need to humble themselves before God.

29:3–7 The storm is referred to as "the voice of the Lord." First it thunders over the waters, which from David's perspective would have been the Mediterranean Sea. Then, in power and majesty, the storm blows into Lebanon, where it shatters mighty cedar trees. The earth appears to move beneath the fury of the storm. (*Sirion* is another name for mount Hermon. Lebanon is also a mountain.) Meanwhile, lightning flashes overhead.

30:1–3 The psalmist writes of being in the depths, of enemies eager to gloat over his vulnerable position, and perhaps even of a near-death experience. Yet God has responded with deliverance, healing, and life. The psalmist (presumed to be David) mentions some kind of physical ailment. One likely possibility, assuming that

David is the author, is that he is referring to his census of fighting men, evidently conducted out of a sense of pride (1 Chronicles 21). God had given David some options for his punishment. David's choice had resulted in the deaths of seventy thousand people, and had it not been for God's mercy, it would have included the divine destruction of Jerusalem. Immediately afterward, David provides great amounts of materials that would be needed to build Solomon's temple (1 Chronicles 22:2–5). Perhaps this is the incident David has in mind as he writes Psalm 30. Regardless of the origin of the psalm, it is a powerful reminder of the difference God can make in a person's life when things are going badly.

30:6–12 David's confession is true for many people. When life is going well and we are feeling secure, we lose the pressing need to turn to God. Then when we discover that we have lost touch with God, we become dismayed. Yet God's mercy is abundant. David's wailing in sackcloth quickly turns to dancing for joy. He senses that God prefers songs and praise to the silence that accompanies mourning. And in response to the fresh start that God has allowed him, David will be forever thankful.

31:6–8 When in affliction and anguish, many turn to idols, whether the false gods of Canaan or more contemporary idols of wealth, reputation, and pleasure. But David will not be distracted from his pursuit of God, and he is rewarded for his efforts.

31:9–18 When David gets specific about his situation, it is gut-wrenching to realize the depth of his suffering. He is distressed, in grief and anguish, weak, sick, hated by his enemies, avoided by his friends, broken off from any kind of human support system, and terrified. From time to time he can hear slander and conspiracies against him. And yet his trust in God is not shaken. David realizes that if God delivers him, then it discredits his enemies. Their lies and contempt will be silenced.

31:19–24 David concludes with confidence in God's deliverance. He uses his personal experience as grounds to exhort all God's saints to be faithful as well. They will do well to follow David's example of strength.

32:1–2 This is the first of thirteen psalms identified in the superscript as a *maschil.* (The others are 42, 44–45, 52–55, 74, 78, 88–89, and 142.) Like many of the other introductory terms, the meaning of the word has been lost. It is frequently assumed that a *maschil* is a poem intended for instruction or meditation. Additional speculation about this psalm is that it was originally a follow-up to Psalm 51, David's confession of his adultery with Bath-sheba. If true, Psalm 32 celebrates the relief that David feels after experiencing the forgiveness of God.

32:6–9 It is far better to voluntarily turn to God during such times than to react like a horse or mule, stubbornly resisting until being forced to respond because of a bit and bridle.

33:1–5 This is the first psalm since Psalm 10 that isn't specifically credited to David. It is a beautiful acknowledgment of the sovereignty of God, who deserves worship and praise from His people because they can always count on His faithfulness, righteousness, justice, and love.

33:6–9 God is the Creator, who spoke the stars and heavens into existence. The psalmist portrays God as placing the world's seas "as an heap." Just as God spoke to create the universe, His word continues to have power. As people begin to comprehend the unlimited power of God, they should respond with deep reverence.

33:10–11 People and nations have plans that don't always agree with those of the Lord. But God's plans will endure. When people are foolish and presumptuous enough to oppose God, He has no trouble countermanding their plans.

33:13–17 Rather than resisting God, it is far better to yield to Him and receive His blessing. God sees all. The Creator is aware of the actions and inner thoughts of those He created. Only God is capable of sure protection and safety, even though the people of the time looked to other things for security.

33:18–22 In a setting of frequent wars and famines, God is a constant hope for those who trust in Him. Because He sees all, He does not miss the faith and prayers of the righteous. For these He is a shield against calamity. They can learn to rejoice and receive His unfailing love, knowing they will receive His help whenever it is needed.

34:1–3 The introduction to Psalm 34 explains that it is written with a specific incident in mind. When David was running from King Saul and hiding out in Philistine territory, he began to feel threatened. As a diversion, he pretended to be insane, doodling on the city gate and drooling. The Philistines insisted that he leave, but he apparently posed no threat, so his life was not threatened (1 Samuel 21:10–15).

34:7 David affirms that the angel of the Lord will encircle and deliver those who trust God. It is interesting to note that in several stories of the Old Testament, the angel of the Lord turns out to be God Himself. But any of God's messengers are equipped to protect God's people.

34:8–10 Perhaps some people are on the verge of becoming more devoted to God. For them to go on about their lives without making that decision is like walking past an enormous feast without stopping to sample the food. David urges his readers to "taste and see that the LORD is good." The lions of the world have no guarantee of success, but those who faithfully seek the Lord will find all they need and more.

34:22 God's redemption and lack of condemnation of His people would have been emphasized for those hearing this psalm in the original Hebrew. The psalm is an acrostic. With one exception, the first letters of each stanza go through the Hebrew alphabet, a pattern that ends at verse 21. The additional final verse, then, would have drawn much attention to the psalmist's final statement—a promise well worth remembering.

35:4–8 David identifies his problem: People want him dead, or at the very least disgraced and ruined. He wants to see his enemies blown away like chaff in the wind, driven away by the angel of the Lord down a dark and slippery path. His is a prayer for a taste of one's own medicine. When evil people go to the trouble to trap someone, it is sweet irony if they are to accidentally be caught in their own traps. David has done nothing wrong to evoke their actions, yet those actions reveal their corrupt intent.

35:9–16 David's enemies had initiated conflict by ruthlessly repaying his good with evil, which disheartened him. When they got sick, however, David fasted and mourned for them in all sincerity, as if for a close relative. Still, when David faced his next difficult situation, they again gathered to mock him, slander him, and make his life as difficult as possible. So to be rescued from such people would delight David, and he would be quick to rejoice and thank God.

35:17–21 David has had enough. He asks God to stop merely observing and do something. These people have no reason to detest him. And it isn't just David whom they bother; they create havoc for other peaceful people in the land.

36:1–4 David is associated with a lot of psalms that feature a contrast between the behavior of the wicked (and the consequences of their actions) and the righteousness of those who seek the Lord (and the rewards for their faithfulness). In Psalm 36, however, David credits his insight on the matter to an oracle—a command or revelation from God. The prophets are usually associated with oracles, but in this case David has a clear epiphany on the subject that he has written so much about. The crux of the matter is that wicked people have no fear of the Lord. In this case, the root word for *fear* is less suggestive of fright than of anxiety or trepidation. Some people commit grievous injustices that apparently don't trigger any sense of dread or accountability to God. Instead, such people couch the severity of their sin with flattering and deceitful speech. They detect no reason to stop their evil actions, and the problem intensifies to the point where they can lie in bed and dream up new offenses to commit.

36:5–6 God has vast amounts of love and faithfulness. In David's imagery, God has mountains of righteousness and oceans of justice. It's no wonder that self-centered, coldhearted wicked people cannot connect with Him.

36:10–12 In David's continued clarity, he sees that the evildoers will meet defeat. In the meantime, he prays that he will not be confronted by the proud and the wicked. His wish is for God to continue to love and uphold the righteous people who know Him.

37:1–2 David makes a crucial observation about wicked people that will make a critical difference in how people view them. Whatever seems to be in their favor now won't be true for long, because they will soon wither like grass.

37:3–5 David points out that those who trust in the Lord have the opportunity and privilege of much more lasting results of their actions. And in the meantime, their relationship with God assures them of rewards

that have real value. They have a good place to live, in secure surroundings. They have the desires of their hearts because the source of their delight is God. "The land" is mentioned several times in Psalm 37 as a reward for the faithful. After God delivered Israel from Egypt and slavery, He guided them to the land that had been promised to Abraham. Under David's rule, the boundaries of that land continued to expand. The people's homes and surroundings were the result of God's direct blessing. And God's previous faithfulness in escorting them to the land was an assurance of His ongoing presence and involvement among them.

37:6 God's righteousness and justice are compared to sunshine. When we consider life in a Middle Eastern locale centuries before the introduction of air conditioning, the noonday sun was something that would get everyone's attention.

37:7–11 It seems that wicked people are getting away with lies, cheating, and deceit. When witnessing such injustice, God's people have one of two choices: They can worry and respond with great anger (a natural response), but that will only lead to more evil; or they can realize that God is aware of the problem and wait for Him to act. Only then will true justice be ensured.

37:12–22 David lists a series of contrasts between righteous and wicked people. In each specific instance, given enough time, the apparent success of evildoers comes to a crashing end. The effect of all that wickedness will never last. For the righteous, however, the blessings of God are both plentiful and eternal.

37:23–40 It is far better to focus one's energies on living a righteous life than to fret over the wicked. It's easy to get distracted by personal offenses, but it is much more beneficial to watch blameless and upright people and learn from their example. Then when one looks back over one's life, the love and faithfulness of God are more readily apparent.

38:1–4 This psalm fits in the "penitential" category (along with 6, 32, 51, 102, 130, and 143) and recounts David's inner turbulence while dealing with God's disfavor. (The exact nature of David's offense is unknown.) The hand of God is heavy on him, and God's dealings with David are described as piercing arrows.

38:5–12 David is overcome with both guilt and illness, including festering wounds and searing pain. He quickly confesses to foolishness. Still, the description of his physical and emotional misery is moving. The situation might not have been quite as bad if it had been between only David and the Lord. But David's suffering leads to his friends deserting him and his enemies taking the offensive against him, both of which add to his agony.

38:13–16 Yet David does not respond to criticism. He may not have literally placed his hands over his ears, but he describes himself as deaf and silent, unwilling to hear or reply to the malicious chatter of his enemies. Even in his defenseless position, he realizes his best option is to wait for God to answer, forgive, and reestablish his physical and spiritual health.

38:17–22 David had sinned, but he confessed and is now dealing with the aftereffects of what he has done. His enemies have also sinned, yet they continue in their iniquity. Their sin is more disturbing because they are persecuting David as he strives to do what is right. So David continues to beseech the Lord, seeking help in the one place he knows he can find it.

39:1–3 After David established himself as king over Israel and many of his battles were behind him, he spent considerable time organizing the military and spiritual leadership of Israel. He assigned three clans to oversee the music ministry, one of which was Jeduthun, also known as Ethan (1 Chronicles 25:1), who is mentioned in the superscription. David's self-imposed silence only causes inner turbulence. He continues to see wicked people around him, and he begins to burn with anger.

39:4–6 David comes to the realization that life is short. The days pass quickly, which should challenge people to put the events of life into a proper context. David realizes that the annoyance and anger he feels toward the wicked are fleeting, so he determines to focus on what he personally can accomplish while he has time.

39:7–13 Turning his attention back to God, David affirms his hope in the Lord while asking to avoid being ridiculed by foolish people. David confesses to sin, and realizing that God has every right to judge and discipline him, he determines to keep silent. Because each person's life is brief, David wants to restore his relationship with God as quickly as possible. From his perspective, death is quickly approaching, so his desire is to rediscover the joy of the Lord as quickly as possible.

40:1–3 God has answered David's prayer, and his personal tribulations seem to pale in comparison to his joy. We see that David's patience has been rewarded. He has regained his spiritual footing.

40:4–5 When people stop long enough to ponder what God has done for them, they discover it's impossible to think of everything. Therefore, to envy proud and irreligious people, or to pursue false gods, is all the more foolish.

40:12–15 It isn't that David's problems are over, but quite the contrary: He faces too many troubles to number. They continue to have a negative effect on him. Among his problems is the ongoing persecution from his enemies who want to take his life and in the meantime hound him verbally.

41:1–3 This psalm concludes the first section of the book of Psalms. In this section, David is credited with thirty-seven of the forty-one psalms, but in following sections David's influence is less pronounced. This final psalm of the section opens as the first one does, with a definition of what makes a person blessed (see 1:1). David is again writing from personal experience. From his sickbed, David expresses great confidence that God will heal him, deliver him from his enemies, and once again bless him.

41:4–9 David's enemies aren't all military foes. Some actually came to visit him while he was sick,

offered insincere words of comfort, and then left to slander him and wish that he were dead. While David is suffering, his enemies gather to fantasize about bad things happening to him. Their coldhearted attitudes must have been contagious; even those who had been David's trusted friends begin to forsake him. David's honest and uncensored description of being deserted and betrayed by so-called friends strikes a chord with many people. Indeed, as Jesus predicts His betrayal, He quotes David's words (see John 13:18).

41:10–13 Despite the betrayal he experiences, David continues to look to the future. He has confessed to God and reestablished his spiritual integrity. He fully expects God to raise him back up and enable him to confront those who hope to take advantage of him. This section of Psalms concludes with emphatic praise to the eternal Lord, the God of Israel. The first book within Psalms contains a varied story of a life—ecstatic joys, traumatic struggles, and all points in between. In this case it is David's life, although untold numbers of people throughout the centuries have related to his genuine expressions. Not everyone is a poet, but anyone can express honest feelings.

42:4–5 The psalmist has been prevented not only from attending worship services but also from taking part in his regular ministry there. Isolation and weeping have replaced fellowship, joy, and thanksgiving. Yet in the first of three identical choruses, he chides himself to overcome his negative mind-set (some scholars accuse him of self-pity) and instead place his hope in God.

42:6–7 Mountains and waters are the images used to portray the psalmist's feelings. He appears to be in a mountainous area, yet his desire is to be in the mountains around Jerusalem. That geographic region is also noted for waterfalls, so the psalmist uses the image to describe surging tides of trouble pouring over him.

43:1–2 In what is likely an extension of the previous psalm, the psalmist continues to attempt to make sense of his depressing situation. He has grown weary of the many accusations of his enemies (42:3, 10), and he seeks vindication from God. He is holding to his conviction that God is his stronghold, yet he finds it difficult to comprehend why he continues to be rejected, mournful, and persecuted.

43:5 The psalmist concludes with the refrain he has already used twice (see 42:5, 11). He continues to question his disturbed state of mind, but more importantly, he expresses his expectation that his hope in God will continue to result in praise as he waits for God to act.

44:1–3 It is always difficult to try to understand why bad things happen, especially to people who don't seem to deserve it. But for the early Israelites, the issue was even more poignant. Their covenant relationship with God is based on His promise that if they follow His instruction they will be blessed. For them to think they are being obedient and yet still experience signs of God's displeasure is indeed a dilemma. The psalmist addresses the situation in this psalm. He points out that the stories of God's provision and protection of His people have been passed from generation to generation as inspiration and encouragement.

44:9–12 For some reason, Israel's enemies have begun to be victorious. Israel has to retreat and is being plundered. The people feel that God has rejected them. It is a miserable feeling, like defenseless sheep being devoured by predators or worthless slaves being sold for almost nothing.

44:13–21 Surrounding nations have certainly taken notice of Israel's vulnerable state, which is both embarrassing and potentially dangerous. It would be easier to accept this vulnerable position if the people had been responsible for wrongdoing, but that is not the case. The psalmist affirms that Israel has not forgotten God or been unfaithful to Him. The people realize that God knows when they have strayed and that He cannot be fooled. So they will not attempt to do so.

44:22–26 The people are bewildered and hopeless. They cry out to God, pleading with Him to show Himself and see their suffering. They still have confidence in His unfailing love, even during their times of sorrow and confusion.

45:1 This psalm was written to celebrate the wedding of a king. The kings of Judah came from the line of David, which seems to be the case in this instance. The psalmist's praise for the king is profuse. He is moved by the event taking place, and he wants to put forth his best effort.

45:2–5 The psalmist extols both the character of the king (grace, truth, humility, righteousness) and the impressive and valiant actions of the king (victory, majesty).

45:9–15 The king stands beside his bride, dressed in gold. Ophir is thought to have been located in western Arabia. At this point the psalmist turns his attention to addressing the bride, advising her to shift her strongest loyalties from her family to her new husband. The king is stricken with her beauty, and she should honor him in return. The psalmist's description of the bridal court emphasizes not only its splendor but also the atmosphere of joy that prevails.

46:1–3 The introduction to this psalm contains an obscure term used only here and in 1 Chronicles 15:20: *alamoth*. Based on its usage, it is most likely a musical term. It may have to do with music in a higher register, such as high-pitched flutes, soprano voices, or young maidens with tambourines (see 68:25). This psalm, with its focus on the power and sovereignty of God, is similar to some of the previous psalms of David. But where David's are frequently intensely personal, this one is written with the nation of Israel in mind. Israel may have been facing some troublesome situations, but the psalmist envisions catastrophes to the extreme. Even if the mountains are to fall and the oceans are to rise, God will be there with His people, and they need not fear. Therefore, the Lord will surely see them through lesser problems.

46:5–7 The reference to "right early" could be to a distressing time. For those coming out of a long, dark, troubling night, it is a time of insecurity and fatigue. And for a city it is when attacks tend to take place. But God is there to help His people at dawn and throughout the day. The city offers the people a certain degree of protection, but God is their true fortress.

46:10–11 In the original language, the instruction to "be still, and know that I am God" is less a suggestion than an emphatic command. The intent is not "Quiet down and you'll discover God's presence," but rather "Quit what you're doing right now and acknowledge who God is." The last verse is a repetition of 46:7, likely a response by those in the worship ceremony. It is a closing reminder of God's ongoing presence and protection.

47:3–4 The subdued nations of Israel's history include some of the great powers of the world, not least among them the Egyptians and the Philistines. Israel's inheritance—the promised land—had been populated with many nations, some living in walled cities such as Jericho. Yet God overcame those peoples and fulfilled His promise to Israel.

48:1–3 This is the third consecutive psalm to emphasize the sovereignty of God.

48:4–7 The city was thought to have been impregnable before it had belonged to Israel. But David had the faith and skill to conquer and claim it, and he made it the capital city of a united Judah and Israel in 2 Samuel 5:6–10. Now, with God's temple there and the blessings of God on the city, it is even more impenetrable. Nations can band together and make an assault, but God's protection will send them fleeing in terror. The ships of Tarshish were a noted fleet that sailed the Mediterranean Sea, transporting goods from faraway places. Occasionally one of the ships would encounter a gale and experience an untimely end. The psalmist compares the destruction of Israel's enemies to the shattering and sinking of one of these mighty ships.

49:10–11 What the psalmist is saying would have been evident to everyone. Upon death, riches are worthless. Accumulated wealth remains for the living. Some people may be remembered longer than others if they prearrange for elaborate tombs or spend some of their money on something (such as land) that will bear their name. Still, the donor is left with a tomb for a house. He will never know when others see his fancy grave or hear his name connected with land or other possessions.

49:12–14 The psalmist points out that people have no advantage over animals when it comes to life cycles. Human beings see beasts of burden live and die, thinking little about it, but then seek fruitless ways to avoid the same end. A common image of the time was of death (personified) devouring the living (see Job 18:13; 24:19). In some cultures, the perception of death was that of a ravenous monster always on the prowl.

49:15–20 The point of this psalm is to challenge people to not allow themselves to become enamored by wealth and splendor. The privilege of the wealthy will not endure. Those who count on their riches have a common end. The upright, however, have a different outlook. Death is still a certainty, yet they can maintain the hope that God will not leave them in the grave.

50:1 This is the first psalm attributed to Asaph, one of the three men from whose families the temple musicians were assigned (1 Chronicles 25:1).

50:14–15 The people are encouraged to bring offerings of thanks to God (see Leviticus 7:11–15). Burnt offerings were sometimes offered routinely, perhaps with little thought. But a thanks offering was made in response to something God had done (healing, consolation, deliverance). The offering of thanks requires acknowledgment of God's involvement in one's life and sincere gratitude in response.

50:16–21 After correcting the worship habits of those who conscientiously want to honor God, the Lord addresses those who aren't so genuine in their motives. Some people worship along with the rest but have no regard for God's law. Their unrighteous acts are listed and include stealing, adultery, deceit, and slander. Because God has not yet taken action against them, this wicked bunch has the audacity to presume that silence gives consent. Not so, declares the Lord. This is the occasion for Him to refute their sinful actions personally and publicly.

51:1–7 This is the first of the psalms of David in the second book within Psalms (42–72) and is one of seven sometimes categorized as penitential. Its deeply personal and confessional tone is explained in the introduction. It was composed after David was confronted about his adultery with Bath-sheba (2 Samuel 12:1–25). David has avoided God for many months (considering that the baby he had conceived was already born). But when faced with the severity of his sin, his confession is unabashed. David makes no attempt to deny his sin or excuse his behavior. He readily admits that his actions were rebellious and sinful. Yet he is also confident that God is a source of mercy, unfailing love, compassion, and cleansing. David had gotten a married woman pregnant and then arranged to have her husband killed in battle, yet he realizes that his sin was against God. His propensity to sin reminds him of his sinful nature.

51:8–12 After God forgives him, David can again experience the joy and gladness that he has been missing. And after God has blotted out David's terrible offense, then David can renew his heart for God. David prays not only for a pure heart but also for a steadfast spirit and ongoing awareness of God's presence. After his grievous sin, he desires the joy of salvation and a renewal of his willingness to serve God.

51:13–17 David wants to be a good example for God in both teaching others and demonstrating praise. He has good insight into what God wants from him. Rather than animal sacrifices, God much prefers the sacrifice of a submissive spirit and humble heart.

51:18–19 David seems to comprehend that the king's behavior and spiritual integrity (or lack thereof) can affect God's perception of the nation as a whole. He closes his psalm with a prayer for the prosperity of Jerusalem and a time when the people's sacrifices will once again be righteous and pleasing to God. Some scholars have suggested that the last two verses may have been added to David's psalm at a later date, during Israel's exile. After a period away from home during which sacrifices were suspended, the desire to rebuild Jerusalem and reinstitute offerings would have been strong indeed.

52:1–7 Such people may appear to be securely entrenched in a community, and it may seem that no one is able to reason with them. But God is also affected by their actions, and righteous people can count on Him to act. He will have no trouble uprooting the wicked, who aren't as entrenched as they think. Those who watch will have the last laugh. The observers will have renewed reverence for God after witnessing the end of those who get ahead by putting others down.

52:8–9 In contrast to the wicked, who will be uprooted, David compares himself to an olive tree—securely rooted, productive, and anticipating long life. (Olive trees can live for centuries.) More importantly, he is flourishing in his relationship with God. His trust in God makes all the difference, and he promises to continue to praise the Lord and place his hope in Him.

54:1–2 The superscription mentions the Ziphims, inhabitants of the wilderness of Zith, south of Hebron. David had hidden from Saul in that desert, but the Ziphims operated as Saul's spies, monitoring David's movements and reporting back to the king (1 Samuel 23:15–25). However, such specifics aren't included in the psalm.

54:3–7 David voices his complaint: Ruthless, ungodly, aggressive men are trying to kill him. The Ziphims are little more than informants, but by the time of David's encounter with them, he had been on the run from Saul for a long time. During those years, he had undergone some periods of great faith and some other trying times, but God had sustained him through them all.

55:1–5 The introduction does not provide specifics about the event that inspired this psalm, but the psalm itself reveals a painful betrayal by someone who had been a close friend. The psalm may have been inspired by Absalom's revolt, during which several of David's trusted associates deserted him. One of note is Ahithophel (2 Samuel 15:12), perhaps the wisest advisor in the nation who, after Absalom fails to take his advice, realizes David will eventually regain the throne and commits suicide (2 Samuel 16:20–17:13, 23). However, no proof exists of this possibility, and scholars are left to speculate. David's appeal to God includes an account of both the treatment he is receiving from others and the inner turmoil it is creating within him. He describes a progression from anguish, to fear and trembling, to horror.

55:16–17 In the wake of such emotional trauma, David cries out to God evening, morning, and midday. David's regular prayer times are reminiscent of Daniel's faithfulness and commitment to pray three times a day (Daniel 6:10). We might say "morning, noon, and night," but David cites "evening, and morning, and at noon" because the Jewish day started at sundown.

55:18–21 Without God's support, David would feel vastly outnumbered, yet he remains unharmed. He knows his enemies have no fear of God, and he is no doubt distraught as he realizes that his former friend is now included among them.

55:22–23 David's response—and advice to others—is wise and appropriate. Those who cast their concerns on God will not be disappointed. God will simultaneously take care of the righteous while short-circuiting the work (if not the lives) of the wicked.

56:1–4 This is another of David's psalms where the superscription provides a clue to the source of his emotions. Gath was a Philistine city where David went to hide while trying to keep from being captured by King Saul. Though he eventually made a tentative alliance with the king of Gath (1 Samuel 27:1–7), an earlier visit hadn't been so amiable. When the people identified him as the one who had killed Goliath and many more of their soldiers, he quickly became persona non grata and even began to fear for his life. To extricate himself from the situation, he feigned madness. The Philistines forced him out of the city but did not harm him (1 Samuel 21:10–22:1).

56:7–9 David wants to ensure that God hears him correctly. After asking God not to let his persecutors escape, he wants God to keep track of his sorrows. He asks God to put his tears into a bottle. In other words, if God is well aware of David's situation, David trusts that the Lord will act to restrain the influence of his enemies.

57:4–10 He might be among beasts, but David expects to awaken at dawn with a steadfast heart and a song on his lips. He is eager to praise God and declare to other nations and peoples what God has done for him. God's love and faithfulness are unlimited, reaching to the heavens.

58:1–3 David asks rhetorical questions. Are the rulers of the nation speaking justly and acting uprightly? Everyone already knew the answer: no. The propensity for wickedness by such people could be traced back to the womb. So after a lifetime of practice, the injustice dispensed by such people is well orchestrated.

58:3–5 David compares the unjust leaders of the nation to serpents that are supposedly under the control of a snake charmer yet are no longer influenced by the music. The result is akin to having venomous cobras on the loose.

58:9 The original Hebrew of this verse defies clear interpretation. The underlying thought, however, appears to be that God's judgment on the people David has described will be sudden and swift—occurring in less time than it takes for a pot to feel heat when a flame is placed beneath it.

59:1–2 This psalm's superscription refers to the time when King Saul had ordered David's house watched so David could be killed while entering or leaving. But David's wife (Saul's daughter Michal) warns him, and he escapes through a window during the dark of night

(1 Samuel 19:11–18). However, the psalm itself doesn't appear to reflect such events. Some think, therefore, that a different psalmist updated the original psalm to apply to a later time in Israel's history. Whoever the writer is, he cites a common complaint found in the psalms: persecution by his enemies. He opens with an appeal for deliverance from such people, whom he classifies as evildoers and bloodthirsty men.

59:6–8 The psalmist describes his enemies as a pack of snarling dogs, prowling around for food. It would have been a fright-inducing scene for most people, but not to the psalmist's God, who would laugh and scoff at the pretension of such evildoers. And the knowledge that God feels no threat from the powers of the nations is assuring to the psalmist, who places his trust in God to minimize his fear.

59:9–12 The psalmist points out that as long as God goes before him as a fortress, he can remain impervious to the slander of others. He even has the presence of mind to realize that if God is to strike down the loudmouthed enemies all at once, the people of Israel might soon forget God's goodness and power. The psalmist wants them to suffer the consequences of their evil, to be sure, but far better to bide enough time to let them be "taken in their pride."

60:4–5 The intended meaning here is uncertain. Troops gathered around banners and then followed those banners out into battle. Perhaps the psalmist is asking God to gather His people and lead them to victory. It is also possible, however, that he is expressing frustration that God led them to defeat instead of victory. From this point on, the psalm is nothing but confident and hopeful. Since God's anger has led to Israel's defeat, nothing but His favor will restore them. God continues to love His people, and the psalmist (presumably David) calls on God to help and deliver them.

61:1–2 The theme of this psalm is yearning for God during a time of trouble, and it is written from the perspective of the king (presumed to be David). It appears to refer to specific events in David's life, but the specifics are not provided. If indeed the psalmist is David, this might have been when he was driven from his throne during Absalom's attempted overthrow of the kingdom.

61:3–5 The psalmist is able to trust God during this crisis because God has always been faithful in previous times of trouble. He desires a more permanent sense of closeness to God with the protection of both the sanctuary of God and the Lord's personal presence. He has made promises to God, and he is counting on God's promises (heritage) to His people.

62:1–4 The fact that this psalm is positioned between Psalm 61 and Psalm 63, coupled with the observation that opponents are attempting to cast down the psalmist, suggests that it is authored by a king (again presumed to be David). A king has many resources at his disposal, yet David's sole source of help and comfort is God. God is his security (rock), deliverance (salvation), and protection (defence). Humanity, on the other hand, is a continual source of chaos. People have repeatedly attempted to undermine David. He compares himself to a bowing wall that could easily be pushed down. The assaults of others are verbal as well. They bless him to his face but curse him and tell lies about him behind his back. They do not rest from their efforts to put him down.

62:9 The psalmist's description of human beings is in direct contrast to his image of God. The Lord is a rock and fortress; people are nothing. Even those who perceive themselves as wealthy and entitled will soon be deflated and forgotten.

63:1 According to the introduction of Psalm 63, David writes it in connection with being in the wilderness of Judah. It is a vague reference. David had attempted to hide from Saul in the wilderness (1 Samuel 23:14), although the fact that the psalm is also written from the perspective of a king suggests a later time in David's life. This might be another psalm written during the period when Absalom had forced David to leave Jerusalem (2 Samuel 15:23). The desert setting plays prominently in the psalm. David compares his longing for God to the thirst of a man wandering in a dry wilderness, desperate for water. For many people, the desire for God is a casual and occasional thing; for David, it is a matter of life and death.

63:6–8 David has fond memories of how God helped him in the past, and those memories fuel his faith for the future. He trusts God to sustain him now just as He has done throughout his lifetime.

64:8–10 Those who observe God's judgment of the wicked will have two responses. At first they will experience a scornful satisfaction because the evil people have gotten what they deserve. More importantly, though, they will then turn their attention to God, giving much thought to His justice and proclaiming the good things He has done. After realizing that evil does exist, but only for a short time, righteous people can then satisfy themselves with God's protection and learn to rejoice in their relationship with Him.

65:1–2 Psalms 65–68 have a similarity of thought and theme, as they focus on the gifts of God to His people. Praise and obedience are the appropriate responses to such a God. The vows to be fulfilled here are probably promises made to God by people during prayer when seeking His presence and help. The fact that God hears and responds to prayer draws people to Him.

65:5–8 The psalmist acknowledges God's power over creation. The Lord is Israel's hope, of course, but His works should have been apparent all around the world. God's control extends to the farthest seas and the mighty mountains of the world, as well as to the chaos among the nations. Go far enough in one direction, the psalmist realizes, and the sun is coming up. Face the other direction and go far enough, and the sun is setting. Throughout that entire span, the people should notice and revere the works of God, and they should respond in joy.

65:9–11 The area of Canaan was heavily dependent on rain to sustain life. Drought could be a death sentence. So the psalmist acknowledges God's part in abundantly providing the needed rains. The streams are filled with water, giving life to the land. Thankfulness for water naturally leads into thankfulness for crops and harvest. Some people think this psalm may have been used in conjunction with the barley harvest, during which the firstfruits were offered to God (Leviticus 23:9–14). It was an annual event that included both thanksgiving and celebration.

65:12–13 The all-too-rare greenness in the desert terrain is described as the hills rejoicing. Just as the psalmist had challenged people throughout the world to sing for joy in their knowledge of the Lord, he calls creation itself to join the song.

66:8–12 From the faithfulness of God in the distant past, the psalmist moves to the faithfulness of God in the recent past. His people had been through some difficult times, including prison, defeat, and other trials. But rather than being brought down by such experiences, the psalmist realizes that they have merely been refined, as when precious metal is treated with intense heat in order to remove any impurities. God is to be praised because He preserved His people through the trying times and eventually led them to abundant land.

67:1–2 Following the general theme of the previous two psalms, Psalm 67 requests God's favor, in this instance as a group prayer. The opening verses reflect the blessing taught to the priests in Numbers 6:24–26.

68:1–3 This psalm is a song of triumph. The first half of the psalm contains a number of references to Israel's exodus from Egypt and journey to the promised land. The song was probably used to commemorate Israel's victories throughout its history. Eventually the first-century church will adopt verse 18 as a reference to the resurrection and ascension of Jesus Christ (Ephesians 4:8). The psalmist points out that while those who love God are joyful as He rises to lead them, those who do not love God have no hope. No one can interfere with the progress of God. His opponents are blown away like a puff of smoke and melt like wax near a flame.

68:4–10 The joy of God's people is for good reason because God responds to their needs and hurts. He is Father and Judge, provider of fellowship for the lonely and the source of song among prisoners. Those who rebel against God find themselves in a sun-scorched land. The righteous, however, can be in a wasteland and still experience God's provision through pouring rain and abundant showers. The mention of the shaking earth and Sinai would have reminded the psalmist's listeners of their people's journey through the wilderness. "Confirm thine inheritance" is in reference to the promised land.

68:15–17 The land contained many impressive and majestic mountains (hills). The psalmist describes the jealousy the mountains felt toward mount Zion because that was where God had established His dwelling place, the temple. In His grand entrance into His city, God is accompanied by a procession of thousands upon thousands of angels, portrayed as riding chariots. The captives and gifts are associated with victory in battle—submission and tribute even from those who had rebelled and lost.

68:19–27 Enthroned in His city, God is praised by the psalmist. In His sovereignty, God regularly bears the burdens of His people, saves them from death, and allows them to rejoice in the defeat of their enemies. God's procession to the temple was a festive occasion involving the whole nation. The singers and musicians established a celebratory atmosphere, and they were followed by the tribes of the nation. Only four tribes are mentioned by name, but they are representative of large and small, north and south.

69:1–3 After the thrill and exultation of Psalm 68, Psalm 69 goes to the opposite extreme. David has sunk to a point where he can't get much lower. The psalm opens with a sequence of metaphors to describe his mood: waters in his soul, sinking in deep mire, swallowed up in deep waters. He can neither see God nor hear His voice; he receives no answer when he calls.

69:5–12 David admits he has sinned. He cares about how he carries himself as a believer in the Lord. He doesn't want to do anything that reflects badly on his Lord or impedes someone else's spiritual progress. He has wept, fasted, and dressed in sackcloth, yet he continues to suffer painful indignities: scorn, mocking, shame, insults, and even taunting songs from drunkards on the street.

69:13–21 As a young person, already anointed to be the next king and on the run constantly from King Saul, David had learned to wait for God's timing. Here his patience is displayed during his spiritual crisis. He will attempt to stay above water until the time of God's favor. He trusts God and counts on His mercy and love, yet his struggle is severe. He hopes for a quick resolution, and he continues to detail his circumstances in his prayer.

69:22–29 David's persecutors are absolutely merciless, and he begins to pray more for retribution against them than deliverance for himself. Essentially, he wants them to experience the same things he is feeling: weakness, isolation, and despair. Even worse, he wants God to judge them harshly by blotting them out of His book of the living. The book of the living (or book of life) is mentioned from time to time throughout scripture. It appears to be an image that represents a record of those whom God has declared righteous. New Testament references to this book suggest that those whose names are listed can anticipate eternal life with God (see Philippians 4:3; Revelation 3:5; 13:8).

70:1–3 This psalm appears to be a reworking of 40:13–17. David prays for God's hasty deliverance from a crowd of hostile enemies. They are mocking him while he is unable to retaliate, so David asks God to let them experience shame and confusion.

70:4 If David's deliverance is witnessed by others, they can then see for themselves that God is faithful and trustworthy. As a result, David's salvation might inspire the praise of many who believe in God.

70:5 David continues to be at the mercy of his enemies, but he has put his trust in a merciful God. He anticipates God's response soon—hopefully without further delay.

71:1–4 This psalm was written by someone who had the benefit, or perhaps the liability, of age. The psalmist looks back over his life and attests to his ongoing faith in God throughout the years. No introduction is provided. However, the next psalm is attributed to Solomon, which suggests to some scholars that this one may have been written from David's perspective as an older man. There is much to be said about an older person who continues to recognize his or her need for God. The psalmist expresses complete dependence on God. Surely the aggression of one's enemies seems even worse during old age, but God remains the psalmist's rock and refuge.

71:7–13 Some people assume the psalmist's problems are a sign that something is amiss in his spiritual life. Others simply want to attack while he is weak and it seems God has deserted him. But the psalmist doesn't overly concern himself with what others say or do. He may be older and weaker, but his God is as strong as ever.

71:14–24 Speaking with the wisdom of age, the psalmist continues to place his hope in God. He has not yet discovered the full extent of God's righteousness and salvation, but he has seen more than enough to proclaim God's goodness to others.

72:1–4 This is one of two psalms attributed to Solomon, the other being Psalm 127. As with many of the superscriptions throughout Psalms, there is much debate as to whether the designated writer is actually the author. Many argue that rather than being written *by* Solomon, Psalm 72 may have been written *for* Solomon. John Calvin even suggests that this psalm is David's dying declaration, recorded by Solomon for posterity. The content makes it an appropriate prayer or tribute for any king, and it is likely that it was used during various coronation ceremonies. The opening verses repeatedly emphasize a desire for justice and righteousness. Israel's king is in a position to help the poor and downtrodden as judge, provider, and protector.

72:5–7 The assurance of blessing and life beyond the sun and moon could apply to God; however, the poetic language may be intended to refer to the human king. In that case, the intent of the verses is that the righteous reign of a good king continues to influence many generations to come.

72:8–11 The boundaries of Israel were never larger than during the reign of Solomon. The psalmist anticipates the king's widespread influence that includes the Euphrates, Tarshish (modern Spain), Sheba (the Arabian Peninsula), and Seba (northern Egypt). The specific sites are not named to detail the outer boundaries of the kingdom but rather to suggest that it will have no limits. The king's enemies will be submissive, and many kings from around the world will bring him tribute.

72:18–20 These verses apply to the entire second book of Psalms, not just Psalm 72. A doxology concludes each of the five sections. The notation in verse 20 most likely referred at one time to a more limited collection of psalms that were all ascribed to David. The psalms of David do not end here, but they begin to be scarcer. Book III of Psalms begins with a long series of poems attributed to Asaph.

73:1–3 Book III of Psalms contains seventeen psalms, eleven of which are attributed to Asaph. However, several of the psalms contain references to events in Israel's history that would have been later than Asaph's lifetime, so there is good reason to believe that some of these psalms were penned by his descendants. This psalm demonstrates the difference one's acknowledgment of God can make in his or her spiritual outlook. The psalmist is surprisingly honest in describing his envy of prosperous people. The fact that they are also arrogant and wicked only intensifies his confusion.

73:4–12 The psalmist has paid close attention to prosperous people. Based on his observations, they are healthy, strong, and trouble-free. They have little in common with the average person, so they tend to be proud, insensitive, and self-centered. They have a sense of entitlement that surpasses earthly bounds and leads them to lay claim to heaven as well. Since it appears that the proud and selfish people aren't held accountable for their actions, others become enamored and even tempted to join their ranks. From the psalmist's perspective, such people seem to become ever wealthier and perpetually carefree. This distresses him.

73:15–20 At exactly the midpoint of his psalm, the psalmist has an epiphany. He goes to the temple and realizes he is only seeing half the story. He is glad that he hasn't spoken his thoughts out loud. When he is able to see things from God's viewpoint, he realizes where the wealthy, arrogant people are headed. They are not on solid ground; they are traveling a road to ruin and destruction. Those who terrify others will be faced with terrors of their own.

74:10–13 Sadly, the silence of God is offset by the jeering of Israel's enemies. The psalmist boldly suggests that God is sitting with His hands in His lap, and he urges the Lord to retaliate. The psalmist certainly does not doubt the power of God, who is Israel's only source of salvation.

74:14–17 The *leviathan* represents the forces of chaos, which are no match for the power of the Lord. Creation itself is under God's control, including seasons and heavenly bodies. God can create springs of water where none exist and stop mighty rivers in their tracks.

74:18–23 The psalmist has confidence that God will protect His people, even in their terrible situation. Adding to his confidence is the fact that God has established a covenant with Israel. For now, their enemies have the upper hand and demonstrate a continual uproar, but their clamor will not last forever. God will surely silence them as He protects and delivers Israel, His turtledove.

75:1 This psalm is an expression of confidence in God during a time when Israel is surrounded by arrogant and powerful nations. It opens with the psalmist's thanksgiving for God's presence. The connection between the nearness of God's name and people telling of His deeds can be understood in two ways. Perhaps it means that those who worship the name of God naturally begin to talk about the great things He has done. Or it may be the other way around: As people recall the wonderful deeds of God, they can't help but give thanks that He remains so near.

75:7–10 When God's judgment is pronounced, it is like a potent wine the guilty are forced to drink, replacing their self-confidence and arrogance with an intoxicating stupor. The psalmist wants no part of such judgment and commits himself to praise God for as long as he lives. It appears that he returns to God's voice in verse 10. Almost certainly it is God who intends to lift up the righteous while cutting off the horns of the wicked—their source of power and pride.

76:1–3 A victorious song celebrating the power of God, this psalm focuses on what God has done for Judah. The psalmist writes of God's deliverance from Israel's enemies after an aggressive action toward Jerusalem. (Both Salem and Zion are references to Jerusalem.) Some scholars attempt to pinpoint the exact battle the psalmist refers to, and their opinions vary. Others believe his intent is more general—that God has delivered His people from any number of warring nations.

77:1–4 The psalmist has turned to God in his misery and unease. He is spiritually and emotionally fragile—in distress, troubled, and overwhelmed. But prayer doesn't seem to help at first. In the past he has been able to rejoice at nighttime and sing of the deliverance of God; now, because of his personal troubles, he is simply unable to sleep.

77:10–20 The psalmist can't stop thinking about God's power that has been displayed time after time to deliver previous generations of His people. There is simply too much evidence of God's involvement in Israel's history for the psalmist to give up hope at this point. God is still holy, all-powerful, and a worker of miracles. No person, no force, no so-called god is greater. With renewed enthusiasm, the psalmist begins to recall one of God's greatest deliverances, the Exodus of the Hebrew people from Egypt. To begin with, God's involvement was evident in the fact that the Israelites had made it safely away from Egypt and into the well-protected confines of the promised land. But more than that, God's presence had been dramatically displayed through the miraculous parting of the Red Sea, thunder and lightning atop mount Sinai, earthquakes, and other means. Beyond a doubt, God had been with His people. Therefore, any doubts about God are unfounded. He is still a God of power and love who will deliver His people.

78:1–6 Several of the psalms recall God's deliverance of His people from Egypt as evidence of His strength, love, and care for Israel. However, few are as extensive as Psalm 78. The purpose of recalling God's previous faithfulness is to inspire and assure future generations.

The stories are to be passed along. In one sense, the teachings of God are parables and "dark sayings of old," yet not in any kind of mystical or secretive sense. They are clearly understandable. Jesus' parables are similar, as Matthew points out in Matthew 13:35 by quoting verse 2 of this psalm.

78:7–12 Hearing the facts about God's previous miracles is one thing; responding properly is another. Generations of Israelites had been stubborn and rebellious because they forgot the wonders of God. The goal for future generations is to not forget and to place faith in God and keep His commands.

78:13–16 In the psalmist's recap of the Exodus, He points out the great contrast between God's faithfulness and the people's lack of faith. God had made the waters of the Red Sea like a heap. When people complained of thirst in the wilderness, God had split rocks to create a source of flowing water. Such miracles that demonstrate God's unique power were performed purely for the benefit of His people.

78:30–33 Some of the people who disregarded God's provision and continued to crave other food were stricken with a plague and died (Numbers 11:33–34). God was attempting to lead them to a land flowing with milk and honey, yet the generation of those who began the journey died in futility and terror because they refused to acknowledge God's wondrous provision of food and water along the way.

78:34–41 The only thing that seemed to capture the Israelite's attention was God's anger. When a group of people died as a result of their sinful actions and attitudes, the survivors eagerly turned to God again. But their repentance was short-lived. They would continue to say the right words, but they were not sincere. Again and again they provoked God, but in His mercy He had not ultimately destroyed them.

78:42–64 The Israelites should have learned from God's dealings with the Egyptians. They had seen the series of plagues fall on Egypt—displays of God's anger, wrath, and hostility. And then He led His people like a shepherd leads sheep, through a path that took them right through a dried-up Red Sea to the promised land. Upon their arrival, He went before them to drive out the hostile nations and allow the Israelites to settle. In spite of everything God had done for them, the people were no better in the promised land than they had been in the wilderness. During the era of the judges, the Israelites were quick to forsake God and turn to idols. By the time of Samuel, God had allowed the ark of the covenant to be lost, and many Israelites were killed in battle.

79:1–4 This is one of the poems written during Israel's exile, recalling the tragic destruction of Jerusalem and the current helpless situation of the people. It is a perplexing state of affairs. Clearly the fall of Judah and the exile had been God's judgment on His people, and He had used the Babylonians to carry it out. But now, from the psalmist's standpoint, a bigger problem is the attitude of the heathen nations toward God. Jerusalem was God's

city, and the desecration of the temple was a particular insult. The Israelites had deserved punishment, and they had suffered for what they had done. But it seems that God's reputation is at stake. The mocking and scorn they continue to receive are also a derision of their God.

79:13 The Israelites had strayed and had been reprimanded for it, but the psalmist still believes that they are God's people, the sheep of His pasture. And as he looks to the future, he envisions not a continuation of suffering and exile but many successive generations all offering their praise to God.

80:1–2 Psalm 79 concludes with the concept of God as a shepherd and the people as sheep, and Psalm 80 begins with similar imagery. Further into the psalm, it becomes clear that the people *need* a shepherd—someone far more powerful than their enemies. In this case, the heavenly Shepherd is on a throne among angels, and His power is beyond question. So in his prayer for deliverance, the psalmist asks God to show His mighty power. The three tribes mentioned suggest that the psalm is referring to the northern kingdom. When the nation divided, Solomon's son Rehoboam was left with only the tribe of Judah. Geographically, portions of Benjamin were adjacent to Jerusalem—clearly as far south as Judah but still considered at that point a northern tribe. If indeed the psalmist writes of the northern tribes here, then the aggressors would have been the Assyrians.

80:8–11 The psalmist compares Israel to a vine that God had uprooted in Egypt and grafted into the promised land. At first its influence had been only positive, providing grapes and valuable shade to a large area. The sea is most likely the Mediterranean, and the river probably the Euphrates.

80:18–19 The writer once again appeals for God's deliverance and restoration.

81:5 *Joseph* is a term for the northern kingdom (as opposed to Judah)—not a personal reference to the Old Testament patriarch. The reference to the language they don't understand is to the tongues of the various nations that Israel encounters.

81:13–14 God had allowed the Israelites to go their own way, and they had suffered for it. Yet He is eager for the situation to improve. He promises immediate victory over their enemies if the people will listen and obey.

81:15–16 At this harvest celebration, the people would have certainly responded to the closing verses of being fed with the finest wheat rather than finding themselves cringing before God. The honey from the rock is, in this case, a product of bees that had made their nests among the rocks. In many instances, however, when the Bible speaks of honey it is a reference to a sweet concoction made from the fruit of the date palm.

82:1 With the opening of Psalm 82, the reader is immediately faced with a question: Who are the gods the psalmist writes about? To the nations surrounding Israel, such a reference would make them think of their own pantheon of gods, much like the Greek deities thought to operate from atop mount Olympus. Even the kings of many secular nations were often referred to as gods. The Israelites might have conceivably thought of angels among the great assembly of God.

83:1–8 David writes a number of psalms imploring God to intervene when he is being attacked by numerous personal enemies. This psalm is similar to those of David, but here the threat is to the nation of Judah as a whole; the enemies are not individuals but foreign nations. The psalmist appeals to God to take action, and as he provides more details, the situation is indeed critical. Israel's enemies have formed a coalition with the goal of completely obliterating the nation. The list of enemies includes several nations that have regularly initiated conflict (Edomites, Moabites, Ammonites, Philistines, and Assyrians), along with some less familiar names. If the psalmist writes of a specific historic event, it is not recorded elsewhere in scripture. It may be that he lists a number of nations that have oppressed and corrupted Israel, intending for them to be representative of *all* of Israel's enemies.

83:13–16 The power of God has not diminished, so the psalmist wants to see his nation's enemies blown away like chaff in the wind. God's pursuit could be like fire spreading through wood or a deadly storm rolling in, resulting in both terror and shame. But the goal is not simply the removal of enemies; the desired result is that people will witness the power of God and turn to Him.

83:17–18 The list of nations represents much power in the ancient world.

84:1–4 After someone has experienced a rich and rewarding relationship with God, it changes the person's perspective on life. Psalm 84 is an expression of longing by the psalmist to be closer to God and *remain* close. The opening verses appear to focus on the temple building with its courts, yet by the end of the psalm it becomes clear that it is the presence of God Himself that the writer desires. Worshippers tend to feel closer to God at the temple. A person's approach to God is heightened through priestly intercession, and praise and worship take on a more public, communal feel. The psalmist is even jealous of the birds that nest in and around the temple, living among the priests.

84:11–12 Being in the presence of God at His temple is akin to standing in the brightness of the sun, yet being shielded and protected at the same time. To those who can stand before Him blameless, God will grant blessing and deny nothing good. Trust in God, however, is essential in receiving what He has to offer.

85:7–13 God's mercy is unfailing, and His salvation is always available. He offers guidance that results in peace for those who listen and obey. But the pursuit of folly prevents people from benefiting from God's wisdom. The psalmist emphasizes the gifts of God by describing them in pairs: mercy and truth, righteousness and peace, truth and righteousness. Even more than pairs, they appear to be married together. Despite the current troubles of his nation, the psalmist maintains confidence that God

will still provide good things for His people. The Lord's righteousness will prevail.

86:1–7 Of all the psalms in Book III of the biblical book of Psalms (Psalms 73–89), this is the only one attributed to David. While many of the previous psalms are appeals to God on a national level, Psalm 86 is the prayer of an individual concerning his personal troubles. David expresses his general state of mind. He is poor and needy, but the specifics of his situation aren't revealed until later. First he wants to appeal to God for mercy and protection. David's trust is in God and he is quick to seek help, but his current situation has robbed him of joy. He is counting on God's love and forgiveness, fully expecting an answer.

86:11–14 David desires instruction from God. He wants to know truth and to cultivate an undivided heart. God has loved him and delivered him, and he wants to praise and glorify the Lord as a result. Only then does David get to the crux of the matter: He is being personally attacked by numerous unrighteous people who want his life. But his specific complaint doesn't matter; he has already entrusted himself to God, so the nature of the problem is inconsequential. God can handle it.

87:4–6 Psalm 87 stands out because of its inclusion of nations that are persistent enemies of Israel. The Babylonians and Philistines have been aggressive foes. *Rahab* is a name for the upper Nile region of Egypt (originating in mythological references). *Ethiopia* is the area that is now southern Egypt, northern Ethiopia, and Sudan. And *Tyre* is the representative city of Phoenicia. These nations have created havoc and suffering for Israel. In other psalms, they are the nations the psalmists might ask God to destroy. Here, however, they are being granted citizenship in God's city and given privileges associated with birthright. The psalmist makes it clear that the reason these peoples are invited into the rolls of the city of God is because they acknowledge the Lord.

87:7 The springs typify the blessings of God. Therefore, the musicians of the nations will acknowledge that God is the source of all good things.

88:6–8 David's suffering appears to be a consequence of God's anger. The psalmist is overcome with personal misery that is further complicated when his friends abandon him in his pain. It feels like being trapped in a deep and dark pit with no escape.

88:9–12 Day after day, the afflicted psalmist cries out to God. His is not just an emotional plea; he uses reason as well. He is eager, almost desperate, to experience the wonders of God and to respond with praise. If he is pushed any further, to the point of death, he will regret being no longer able to worship.

88:13–17 The psalmist will not give up on God. His cry echoes those in verses 1 and 9. He continues to pray each morning, even as he keeps wondering why God seems so distant. His problems began during his youth, and he is still seeking relief. Yet despite all his efforts, nothing has resolved the problem.

88:18 The writer's despair from the ongoing terrors he has suffered is too much for his friends. His companions have deserted him. Still, he will continue to cry out to God day and night, awaiting the Lord's intervention in his life.

89:1–4 This final entry in Book III of the biblical book of Psalms is another that scholars find difficult to date or to link to a historic event. It begins as a bold and confident expression of praise to God, but it takes a sudden shift at verse 38 and concludes as a lament. The psalmist begins with acknowledgment of God's great love and faithfulness, characteristics that are evident both in heaven and on earth and will be noticed by all generations of people. He then introduces the covenant God had established with David—a theme the psalmist will soon return to.

89:5–16 God is to be praised for many reasons. His work in creation is evident throughout the heavens, the earth, and the seas. The mountains (Tabor and Hermon) sing for joy in response. No other being can compare to the Lord. His works are apparent everywhere. He destroyed Egypt (Rahab)—just one example of His great power. His character and qualities influence and inspire humanity.

89:17–18 The psalmist uses a couple of metaphors for Israel's king. The human ruler serves as both a horn (a symbol of power) and a defender. Then the psalmist reviews the covenant that has been established between God and David.

89:19–37 David receives the support and blessings of God. He is victorious in all his battles. He calls God *Father*, and the Lord bestows on him the entitlements of a firstborn son. No one will be more successful as king. As a result, God promises to establish David's line forever. As it turns out, David's descendants aren't as faithful as they should be, and some blatantly disregard God's commands. They will receive God's punishment for their disobedience, but even so, God will not break His covenant with David. Israel can count on God's promises to endure forever.

89:38–45 The reality of life does not seem to fit the promises God has made, and the psalmist begins to bemoan his nation's situation. The current king ("thine anointed") has not proven faithful to God, and therefore God has become angry and rejected him. God's relationship with this king is antithetical to His relationship with David. This king experiences not only defeat in battle but also the scorn of his enemies. The nation has been plundered. Its former splendor has disappeared, and the king is impotent to do anything about it. From all appearances, it looks as if God has gone back on His covenant.

90:1–2 This psalm is attributed to Moses, which makes it several centuries older than the other psalms. It begins with an acknowledgment of the eternal God—the Creator of the world and everlasting dwelling place for humanity. He is the source of everything people need. "From everlasting to everlasting" is an expression to emphasize God's eternity.

90:7–9 The holiness of God quickly becomes evident to sinful humans, so the shortness of their lives is spent in struggle. When people sin and offend God, they may experience God's wrath. Some people spend the entire span of their lives feeling that God is angry with them, and they try to keep their secret sins hidden, to no avail.

90:10 The life span of seventy or eighty years is respectable. A study of Egyptian mummies has suggested that an Egyptian from the same approximate time period had an average life expectancy of forty to fifty years. However, if a person's years are filled with nothing but trouble and sorrow, then long life is nothing to cherish.

90:11–14 Sin will always be offensive to God, and people will continue to sin. But rather than attempting to hide sin and provoking God's anger, Moses entreats God both for instruction that will lead to accumulated wisdom and for divine compassion. If human life is but a day in the time frame of God, then let the morning begin with God's unfailing love that results in lasting joy and gladness.

91:1 The psalmist uses two of the most laudable names for God: *most High* and *Almighty*. In doing so, the psalmist begins a reasoned argument for why people can feel secure even during times of trouble. Rather than using first person to speak only of his own experiences, he uses third person to indicate that the comforting protection of God is available to anyone willing to seek God's guidance.

91:8–10 It is critical to take refuge in God; it's what makes the difference between security and susceptibility to danger. While in His protection, righteous people observe the demise of the wicked. No ultimate harm will befall someone if he or she takes refuge in the mighty God.

91:11–13 The Lord commissions angels to care for His people. However, this is the Old Testament's sole mention of angels in a guardian capacity. The psalmist uses well-known dangers (lions and dragons) to symbolize human attackers.

92:1–3 After the return from exile, the worship ceremonies of the Israelites included a weekly schedule of psalms sung to accompany the morning offerings. Psalm 92 is the song used each sabbath morning. Praising God is not merely an obligation but a privilege—and not a privilege to be taken for granted. The psalmist reminds the people that it is good to praise God and to make music for Him. The poetic expression of the writer can be confusing to modern ears. The point of verse 2 is not to detach the love of God from His faithfulness and to set aside different times to acknowledge each one. Rather, God's love and faithfulness are intertwined, and people should proclaim them all the time (morning and night).

92:10–11 Speaking from personal experience, the psalmist attests to the positive results of God's presence in his life. These verses sound as if they may have been written by a king. The word *horn* is a metaphor for power. *Oil* symbolizes joy and blessing. The writer's different senses (sight, hearing) detect the faithfulness of God all around him.

93:5 Human kings can issue orders on a whim and misuse power, but God doesn't. The Lord has established statutes to be followed, but they have proven to be beneficial to His people and will endure. The holiness that sets God above all other beings is both attractive and enduring. His rule will never end.

94:1–2 Few things in life are as disturbing as seeing people commit intentional offenses against others, knowing that their actions are wrong, and then laugh because they continue to get away with their cruel behavior. The writer has such an experience, and his psalm is a plea for God to take vengeance on unrepentant evildoers.

94:8–11 The psalmist realizes that God *is* aware of the situation. The One who created eyes and ears can surely see and hear what is going on in the lives of His creation. More than that, God knows every thought that passes through the human mind, no matter how futile those thoughts may be. Through the psalm, the writer issues a warning to wicked people, exhorting them to become wise and avoid the punishing discipline of God.

94:12–15 God's discipline can be a wonderful gift that turns people from potential trouble and allows them to share everything God has to offer. Continued wickedness becomes a pit that consumes those who never change their behavior, but righteous people need not fear judgment. God will not allow faithful people to suffer forever at the hands of evildoers.

94:16–19 As troubling as it is to witness the evil around him, the psalmist finds help from God, who provides consolation for his anxiety and helps him maintain spiritual footing. Without God's intervention, he feels that his enemies might have been too much of a problem, possibly forcing him to his grave.

94:20–23 Retribution against the wicked people has not yet taken place, but the psalmist is certain it will occur. God will have nothing to do with a corrupt throne—those who create misery rather than administer justice.

95:8 An outward show of worship is not enough. The people are to recall and take warning from the stories of their ancestors, who had defied God along the way from Egypt to the promised land. The account of what happened at Meribah ("quarreling") and Massah ("testing") is found in Exodus 17:1–7. Those people had seen sign after sign that God was with them and leading them, yet they continued to complain and resist. As a result, an entire generation of people missed out on the peace and security that God offered them.

95:8–11 The psalm ends on a stark note, yet it is an appropriate ending. If indeed the Lord is the great King above all gods, He is due both outward worship and praise that wells up from a grateful heart. Hard hearts and stubborn wills will have severe consequences.

96:1–3 God's rule over the earth has been a recurring theme in the previous three psalms, and it will continue in this psalm. The psalmist calls the people to sing a new song to the Lord. The occasion for a new song may well have been a new action of God to benefit His people, perhaps a recent act of salvation. Whatever the occasion, the psalmist exhorts the people to sing praise to God and

to make sure other nations hear of all His glorious works among His people.

96:7–13 The thrice-repeated phrase "Give unto the Lord" echoes the three commands to sing to the Lord in the psalm's opening verses. The fact that the Lord reigns is cause for deepest reverence and trembling as well as exultant rejoicing. God will indeed judge the earth, and those devoted to His righteousness and truth have nothing to fear. Nature itself—heavens, seas, fields, and trees—will celebrate the justice of God. The psalmist is dealing with his present time, yet he is looking forward to the coming of the Lord. The cause for celebration will only increase when the Lord arrives to enforce His justice, righteousness, and truth.

97:7 Anyone who gets a clear picture of God will be shamed to have ever worshipped anyone or anything else.

99:2–3 God's reputation among His own people (Zion) causes other nations to exalt Him.

100:1–2 Psalm 100 concludes a series of psalms (93–100) that were all written to inspire people to praise God as Lord over all the earth. God's rule is the inspiration to make a joyful noise. The psalmist challenges all the earth to participate in glad worship and songs of joy.

100:3 People have good reason to praise God. To begin with, He *is* God—the one and only sovereign Lord—a fact to be acknowledged. In addition, He is the Creator. Created humanity should identify with their Creator. Beyond that, God initiated a loving relationship with His people. They are not just created beings left to fend for themselves; they remain in God's care as the sheep of His pasture. These are all observations that should motivate people to be joyful.

100:4 Joy should be shared with others in communal worship. The gates and courts are references to the temple. Worshippers have to go through one of several gates in order to get to the inner courts. All along the way to worship, then, people are to express praise and thanksgiving to God. Praise and thanksgiving are often linked, and for good reason. Praise is grateful acknowledgment of who God is, and thanksgiving is appreciation for what He has done.

101:1–8 This psalm is attributed to David, the first one so designated since Psalm 86. It is a royal psalm in which the king commits to be faithful in both his personal life and his rule over his house. The Lord is a God of love and justice, and for that reason David opens his psalm with praise. But almost immediately, he responds to the justice of God. He wants to devote himself, both privately and publicly, to model a blameless life. And once his heart is blameless, he is determined not to get involved with things that might corrupt it. The word translated *wicked* has the same root in Hebrew as the name *Belial*—a name regularly connected with evil (2 Corinthians 6:15). In many cases, the phrase *sons of Belial* is translated simply as *wicked men*.

102:1–5 The introduction to Psalm 102 is like no other. It neither identifies the author nor provides a clue as to its usage or historical setting. Instead, it simply announces the travail of an individual pouring out his sorrows to God. Although normally classified as an individual lament, some people think the psalm could have been used in group assemblies because the reason for the author's troubles appears to be a national catastrophe that would have affected others as well.

102:12–16 Here we discover the source of the psalmist's dismay: The holy city has been destroyed. But he has not given up on God. He reminds himself that God is eternal—enthroned forever and always worthy of receiving honor. In addition, God has always been, and will always be, compassionate. Therefore, the psalmist has confidence that God will again show favor to Jerusalem (Zion). The city will be rebuilt and renewed to reflect God's glory. Many of the same enemies who are currently taunting the psalmist (and Israel) will eventually have a change of heart. Nations and kings will be humbled and show respect to God.

102:17–22 Considering himself to be among the destitute, the psalmist anticipates God's response to his prayer. He is so sure of it, in fact, that he wants it on the record that God will indeed hear His people and release them from their woeful situation. If God is to rebuild Zion, it is only a matter of time until people will again assemble there to worship and praise Him.

102:23–28 Even though the psalmist has confident hope in soon witnessing God's intervention in Israel's situation, for the time being he will continue to suffer. He asks the eternal God to allow him to live awhile longer. People come and go, and the heavens and the earth will pass away also. But God remains unchanged, and those who choose to live in His presence will continue to experience His faithfulness. The psalmist yearns for a more lasting relationship with God. It is interesting, then, that the author of Hebrews quotes verses 25–27 in connection with Jesus as the eternal Creator (Hebrews 1:10–12). Those who place their trust in Christ can experience what the psalmist so strongly desires—life forevermore in relationship with a loving Lord.

103:1–2 This psalm celebrates the work of God as He forgives and acts on behalf of His people. It is attributed to David, who opens the song with personal praise. ("O my soul" was used as someone today might say, "Note to self.")

103:3–5 The verbs used to describe acts of God are revealing: David has been forgiven, healed, redeemed, crowned, satisfied, and renewed. He has experienced the love, compassion, blessing, and infusion of strength that only God can provide.

103:11–12 God receives no satisfaction from punishing human sin. He desires for people to forsake their iniquities and turn to Him. When they do, He gladly removes sin as far as the east is from the west. Nothing is greater than the love of God.

103:19–22 Regardless of human response to the Lord, God's rule is total and unquestionable. He is praised and obeyed by the mighty angels of heaven. Creation itself speaks its praise. How much more, then, should people respond to the love and mercy of such a mighty God?

104:1–4 The greatness of God described in Psalm 103 is also affirmed in Psalm 104, although this psalm has no superscription to identify the author, and there is no reason to presume the same person wrote both. The previous psalm focuses more on God's relationship with humanity, while this one dwells on the evidence of His sovereignty in the realm of creation. It is difficult not to recall the creation story of Genesis 1 while reading through this psalm. Beginning with a description of God Himself, the psalmist writes of the Lord's clothing, which includes honor, majesty, and light. Then moving right away to the *works* of God, the writer envisions the creation of the heavens as if God were setting up a tent. It's as if heaven is an upstairs level of earth where God can dwell, built on beams that have been laid across the oceans as a foundation. God moves as if in a chariot borne on the winds. Wind and fire are often included in descriptions of God's presence.

104:14–18 Grass and plants provided food. God's people received not just basic nourishments of bread and oil but also wine. Whether in the mountain heights, the pine and cedar forests, or the rocky crags, God's creation is evident. He provides for all His creatures wherever they are.

104:21–32 God's provision sustains the entire animal kingdom. His presence comforts; His absence terrifies. He supplies life and determines life spans, when it is time to return to the dust. And as impressive as His creation is, God is far greater.

104:33–35 Those who fail to connect with God in light of all He has done have no place in His world, and the psalmist prays that they will simply vanish from the earth. He, on the other hand, commits to sing praise as long as he lives, rejoicing in all that God has done and attempting to please Him with worship.

105:1–4 The writer praises God through a review of Israel's history, spanning the call of Abraham to the arrival of the Israelites in the promised land. No author is designated, although the first fifteen verses duplicate the content of 1 Chronicles 16:8–22, a passage that is associated with both David and Asaph. The psalmist challenges people to get involved in their relationship with God: to give thanks, call on God's name, tell other nations what He has done, sing, offer praise, recall His actions, take joy in Him, and continually turn to Him for strength and assurance.

105:5–6 The Lord is a God of wonders, miracles, and judgments. To prove his point, the psalmist recalls a series of stories from Israel's past. Addressing the people as both descendants of Abraham and children of Jacob, he begins a concise but systematic review.

105:7–11 God hasn't simply interacted with Abraham for a bit; He has established an eternal covenant with the patriarch. God's promises to Abraham are passed on, in turn, to Isaac, Jacob (Israel), and Joseph. They all look ahead to the fulfillment of the promise of the land they are to inherit.

105:12–22 When Israel was only a family, prior to becoming a nation, they were few in number, but God still watched over them. In the Genesis account of the story of Joseph (Genesis 37), it appears that Joseph's brothers had been in control when they sold their little brother into slavery. In retrospect it became clear that God was sending Joseph ahead of the rest of the family to Egypt. What began as one person's imprisonment and anticipated life sentence turns out to be God's plan to honor His promise to Abraham to build a nation of his descendants.

105:23–36 These verses review Israel's time in Egypt, during which a family of around seventy grew into a sizable nation.

105:37–45 These verses describe the Exodus. The silver and gold that Israel possessed were the result of gifts the Egyptians gave the people to induce them to hurry and leave, although God was behind the generous giving of Egypt (Exodus 12:33–36). All during Israel's time in the wilderness, God provided food, water, and a clear sign of His presence through a cloud and fire.

This particular review highlights only the positive aspects of the journey; the psalmist mentions nothing of Israel's rebellion. His point is to show how God had followed through with what He promised Abraham. Israel inherited a wonderful land that other nations had worked hard to cultivate. Ideally, the Israelites should then have worshipped and obeyed God in the new land. It didn't turn out that way, but perhaps the people who used Psalm 105 in their worship would get the point and not make the same mistakes.

106:1–5 In contrast to Psalm 105, this psalm deals with many of the same events but looks at the actions and reactions of the people. Consequently, it is not nearly as positive. Both psalms open with a command to give thanks to God, and the first five verses of Psalm 106 recall the faithfulness of God and the need to respond to His mighty acts.

106:6–13 Here begins a confession of sin that continues throughout the psalm. God remained faithful to His people throughout their history, but they repeatedly disobey and rebel. The psalmist recalls the Red Sea experience, when the people panicked and wanted to turn back, but God miraculously led them through the sea and then drowned the Egyptian army behind them. In response the Israelites believed God and praised Him, but they quickly forgot what He had done for them.

106:14–33 The attitude of the Israelites went from bad to worse as they moved on into the wilderness. They tested God and questioned the leadership of Moses and Aaron. When Moses was absent for a few days, they had Aaron create a golden calf. When they finally got to the promised land, they lacked the faith to enter. They rebelled against God in order to follow the gods of other nations. Their grumbling was so persistent and unrelenting that they provoked foolish words from Moses that kept him from entering the promised land. In each of those instances, God responded with a disciplinary action, but to no lasting effect. The people

felt sorry for a little while, but in a short matter of time they reverted to their whining and griping.

106:34–47 The people finally mustered enough faith to enter the promised land, but soon thereafter they again began to rebel against God. They did not evict the inhabitants as God had instructed. Instead, they mingled with the Canaanites and soon began to worship their various gods, which sometimes included atrocious acts. In response, God allowed Israel to be overpowered again and again, but the people would not make a permanent commitment to Him. Each time they cried out, He lovingly forgave them and sent help. But their faith never lasted long. Apparently Israel has found itself in a similar situation in the present time, because the psalmist asks God to "gather us from among the heathen." After the people saw their temple and the city of Jerusalem destroyed, Israel's exile in Babylon was certainly pitiable.

106:48 This is an added doxology to conclude Book IV in the biblical book of Psalms. Each of the five books ends with such a note of praise.

107:1–3 This section begins the last of the five books contained within the biblical book of Psalms. It is likely the final book compiled chronologically, so along with some additional psalms of David there are other songs that contain references to events later in Israel's history. This first half of the final book contains the shortest psalm, the longest psalm, and the series of fifteen psalms known as the Songs of Ascents (or Songs of Degrees). Psalm 107 opens with a call to worship. The reference to people gathering suggests that the psalm was written during or after the exile. If so, the enemy would have been the Assyrians and Babylonians.

107:4–32 Again and again, the psalmist describes people who find themselves in desperate situations. Then they cry out to God and He delivers them. In response, the psalmist encourages the people to give thanks to the Lord, whose love is repeatedly described as unfailing. The situations described by the psalmist are varied: people wandering in desert wastelands and needing food and water, shackled prisoners who have rebelled against God and find themselves subjected to hard labor, some who have rebelled and suffered physical near-death experiences as a result, and sailors who face frightening and turbulent storms at sea, battling waves the size of mountains. In each case, God is gracious and merciful as He forgives and delivers those who ask. Clearly, these four cases are representative of God's ability and willingness to help anyone in any situation. In return, people should give much consideration to God's unfailing love and offer Him their thanks.

107:33–38 In addition to the regular and willing deliverance of God that should be received with thanksgiving, the closing section of this psalm provides reasons to offer praise to the Lord. In God's sovereignty, He has power to change human situations. Rivers dry up and become deserts, or deserts are suddenly infused with water and become springs that sustain vineyards and human civilization.

107:39–43 These adversities are more than theoretical for the Israelites who have experienced droughts—usually following times when they had forgotten the Lord. God had always forgiven them and restored life to their land. And yet the people eventually go too far in their rejection of God. He allows them to wander in the wilderness. Many die, and the rest suffer. But God's discipline is temporary. He once more delivers His people, increasing the families of the upright and silencing the wicked. The psalmist's concluding challenge is for people to exhibit wisdom and give much thought to the tremendous love of God.

108:1–13 If we think of the psalms as songs, then Psalm 108 is a medley of Psalms 57 and 60. Verses 1–5 of Psalm 108 echo Psalm 57:7–11. Verses 6–13 are a repetition of Psalm 60:5–12. The two previous psalms are credited to David, as is Psalm 108. Combined as they are here, the psalm is a song of victory to celebrate God's incomparable love and faithfulness as displayed in His deliverance of Israel from their enemies. The first portion of the psalm expresses praise to God. David rejoices in having a steadfast heart, attributed to God's power and glory. His praise is followed by a prayer for continued triumph over the nation's enemies. God is sovereign over both Israel (Shechem, Succoth, Gilead, Manasseh, Ephraim, and Judah) and the enemies of Israel (Moab, Edom, and Philistia). Realizing that human power is worthless, David gives all credit to God.

109:1–5 Attributed to David, Psalm 109 is sometimes placed in the category of *imprecatory* psalms (those that call for harm to come to the enemies of God and His people). Not all scholars agree, however, that such a category should exist. Several psalms contain sections of imprecations yet still are categorized as praise, lament, or so forth. David wastes no time laying out his case before God. His enemies have been busy speaking lies and deceit, spouting hatred toward him. David has attempted to initiate friendship, but to no avail. He has given his opponents no cause to attack him, yet they do. Throughout it all, he continues to be a man of prayer.

109:6–20 The plural references are replaced here with the singular *he*. Some scholars feel that these verses recount the psalmist's enemies' words toward him. More probably, David switches to singular because his many enemies have a ringleader who incites them, and it is that individual who warrants the most attention. Or perhaps criticism of David is so widespread that addressing one person effectively speaks to *all* his critics. David wishes the worst on the person who has caused him so much suffering and grief, and he uses strong words to express his feelings. But David also includes why he is so intent on seeing this person suffer. This person is an evil man who takes advantage of the weak and helpless. He never blesses people but is always quick to curse. Cursing others is his nature—not just an outer shell like clothing but steeped into his flesh and bones. So David prays that the man's heartless mentality be strapped around him forever, like a belt (girdle).

109:21–31 David pours out his own condition to God. He is poor, needy, and heartsick. He has fasted until he became physically weak, and he is still an object of ridicule to his many accusers. Yet he continues to count on God to deliver him and leave his enemies in shame and disgrace. God will help the needy, and David is determined to continue to praise and honor Him.

110:2–3 Sending the rod is a way of promising an ever-increasing kingdom. The figure being addressed will have many supporters—willing volunteers to go with him into battle. Their comparison to morning and dew implies freshness, youth, strength, and significant numbers.

110:4 More than a mighty warrior, this lord is also a priest in the order of Melchizedek. From the time of the Exodus onward, priests had to come from the tribe of Levi. But Melchizedek predates the Mosaic Law. He was the king/priest to whom Abraham paid tribute after a battle (Genesis 14:17–20). The Messiah will be both priest and king, holding a position higher than those who serve in the Aaronic priesthood. His priesthood will be forever.

111:1–3 Scholars have long linked Psalms 111 and 112. Both are in the format of an acrostic poem, and the content is quite similar. It is possible that the same person wrote both psalms, probably after the exile. The two psalms are written in praise to God and with the intent of imparting wisdom among the worshipping community. The opening verses set the tone for extolling God. The reasons for praising God are many: His great works, His glorious and honorable deeds, and His enduring righteousness.

112:1–3 Continuing the theme of the previous song, Psalm 112 picks up where Psalm 111 leaves off. Those who fear God discover the joy of following Him and therefore are eager to praise Him. A righteous upbringing is beneficial to children, helping them to thrive. And in the thinking of the time, the way in which an upright person would be remembered forever was through his line of descendants. Prosperity is also tied in with righteousness.

112:4–9 Everyone experiences dark times, but the darkness doesn't last for those who remain gracious and compassionate. Generosity and justice certainly benefit those who receive such gifts, but those who administer them are rewarded as well. God provides such people with stability and security. When bad news comes, they need not fear.

113:7–9 When the Lord sees poor and needy people among the dust and ashes, He lifts them up. Israel's history contains no shortage of stories of barren women—a condition of utter humiliation and subsequent sorrow in their culture—who eventually conceive and rejoice at the powerful intervention of God.

114:1–2 The story of the Exodus was told and retold in Jewish songs and ceremonies. Numerous psalms refer to God's miraculous deliverance and protection of His people during that time. But Psalm 114 is one of the most unique, stylized portrayals on record of Israel's journey from Egypt to the promised land. The psalmist is apparently reviewing Israel's past from a point beyond the reign of Solomon. His distinction between Judah and Israel suggests that he is writing during the period of the divided kingdom. But when the people first came out of Egypt, they were still the house of Jacob.

114:5–7 It is as if the psalmist is interviewing various elements of creation to see what they think about the miracles God had performed. If rivers, seas, and mountains respond to the work of God, the implication is that people should notice and acknowledge the mighty deeds of the Lord as well.

115:1–3 Idolatry was a recurring temptation for the Israelites. They were surrounded by other nations with their various gods. And many times when some disaster or difficulty befell Israel, those nations would question the presence of Israel's God. The psalmist makes it clear that God deserves glory because of His love and faithfulness. He is an unseen God who rules from heaven, yet He is in complete control. This would have been a foreign concept to the polytheistic nations around Israel.

115:16–18 God is not only the Creator of heaven but also its owner. In His grace, He created the earth and then provided it as a dwelling for humanity. The dead no longer have voices with which to express appreciation, so the psalmist challenges people to offer their praise while they are able.

116:1 There are many reasons to love God. The reason cited in this case is God's protection during a difficult time in the psalmist's life. The writer had cried out for the mercy of God, and the Lord responded.

116:12–19 The psalmist is eager to repay the Lord for His goodness. He has been delivered, so he will worship God publicly and intently. The cup of salvation may have been a drink offering (Numbers 28:7, 10, 14, 31) to accompany the psalmist's thank offering. Even though he has been spared from death this time, he knows that God is well aware of the deaths of His faithful followers. After his recovery, the psalmist intends to gladly continue to fulfill his vows to God, setting a good example for everyone.

117:1–2 The psalmist opens by exhorting everyone to praise the Lord—not only all peoples but also all nations. This psalm is another reminder that God's great love extends far beyond the Jewish states of Israel and Judah. The psalmist associates God's great love with His enduring faithfulness, which is a common pairing in the psalms. And he concludes with the phrase so frequently repeated in this section of Psalms: "Praise ye the Lord" (or "Hallelujah").

118:1–4 This psalm is one of the more celebratory songs in the entire collection of Psalms. These verses may have been written in a call-and-response format to get all the worshippers involved.

118:8–12 The psalmist's enemies have been numerous and they swarm like bees around him. But calling on the name of the Lord results in a quick response. Therefore, seeking refuge in God is far preferable to placing one's trust in people—even princes who have soldiers and wealth at their disposal.

118:13–17 God is never at a loss for strength. The symbol of His power, His right hand, is always there for support. It's never too late to call on Him for help. The psalmist feels as if he is about to fall, yet God delivers him. As a result, shouts of rejoicing are heard throughout the land.

118:18–21 The psalmist interprets his difficult times as God's chastening, yet he is thrilled to be alive and still able to testify to God's work in his life. God has delivered him, so he will go to the temple and give thanks.

118:24 This is a frequently quoted verse, usually used to encourage rejoicing on any given day. Originally, however, it referred to a specific day of deliverance and victory.

118:29 The psalm ends as it began, with a call to give thanks to God for His goodness and everlasting love.

119:1–16 This is the longest of the psalms (by far), and it is also a distinctive work of art. It stands out from other psalms in that it focuses primarily on the Word of God, rather than the works of God or the character of God. The psalmist constructs his observations as an acrostic poem, comprised of twenty-two stanzas of eight verses each. Other psalms are also written as acrostics (Psalms 111 and 112). But in this case, each of the first eight verses begins with the first Hebrew letter, the next eight verses start with the second Hebrew letter, and so on through the alphabet. Almost every one of the 176 verses of Psalm 119 contains a reference to the Word of God. The psalmist uses eight different Hebrew terms for variety. The terms are used approximately the same number of times throughout the psalm (ranging from nineteen times to twenty-five times apiece). English translations vary, however, and the assortment of interpreted words include *word, law, decree, command(ment), statute, precept, promise, saying, judgment, testimony, way, path,* and perhaps others. The first three verses serve as an introduction: Those who keep God's laws are blessed. The psalmist immediately expresses a desire to be in that category of people. He wants a pure life. With God's Word as his internal guide, he can then recount God's laws to others. God's statutes are a source of joy for him as well as the subject of his meditations.

119:17–32 The psalmist is well aware of the influence of evil people. He mentions them several times in this psalm. Rather than allowing their influence to affect him, he prays for God's enlightenment and protection. Even though he is weary with sorrow, he chooses to cling to God's promises and continue to obey God's Word.

119:33–48 The writer's understanding of God's Word results in delight. Ignorance or disobedience, on the other hand, leads to selfish gain, worthless pursuits, and disgrace. The laws of God also provide great confidence. The psalmist is prepared to stand before kings to declare the truth God has revealed to him.

119:49–64 Those who steadfastly follow God are subject to mocking and perhaps even suffering at the hands of others. Yet the psalmist's comfort remains in God's laws. He feels indignation toward his tormentors, yet at night he focuses his thoughts on God and regains perspective on his life.

119:65–80 The psalmist writes from experience. He had previously gone astray and knew what it was like to be out of favor with God. It had ultimately become a positive experience for him, because after he returned to the Lord, he realized what was really important. Afterward he wouldn't have traded his commitment to God's laws for silver and gold. He also acknowledges God as his Creator and wants to spend his life telling others about the Lord, offering them truth and hope.

119:81–88 The psalmist admits to experiencing periods when he didn't feel the comfort and presence of God. His spiritual condition began to get dry and brittle like "a bottle in the smoke." But during such times he remained patient and persevering, faithfully looking and longing for the promises of God to return.

119:89–104 In spite of persistent attempts by his enemies to destroy him, the psalmist has nothing but good things to say about God's faithfulness. God had established the world, and He continues to sustain it by His Word. God's laws not only give the writer hope but also make him wiser than his opponents. With such wisdom, he is able to stay away from paths of evil.

119:105–120 The world can be a dark and evil place, but God's Word provides a lamp to one's feet and a light to one's path. Thanks to God's precepts, the psalmist has so far evaded the traps that have been set for him. His determined commitment to the light of God's Word allows him to rebuke the evildoers who keep trying to trip him up.

119:121–136 Sometimes people who devote much time and effort to studying scripture develop a kind of spiritual arrogance, but that is not the case for the psalmist. He realizes he will always have more to learn about God, and he remains a humble servant of God. He detests the arrogance of the evildoers and will have nothing to do with that attitude, leaving it to God to deal with the problem. In fact, he is so captivated by the Word of God that he weeps when he sees others disobey it.

119:137–152 The psalmist isn't committing to some set of randomly assembled rules. The Lord is a righteous God, and the laws He provides reflect His righteousness. The writer has thoroughly tested God's promises and has seen them work, even in the worst of circumstances. Not only are they functional and effective—they are a delight. But the psalmist has no run-of-the-mill commitment. In seeking God's truth, he calls out with all his heart. He is up before dawn and awake through the night to meditate on God's promises. Wicked people are nearby, but as long as God is nearer with His commands, the psalmist knows he will persevere.

119:153–168 Appealing to God for deliverance, the psalmist continues to profess his great love for God's law. He realizes that the wicked people who pursue him have no hope for deliverance, which gives him a greater appreciation for God's compassion toward him. He is being persecuted by powerful people who have no cause to do so, yet what really gets to him is the power of God's Word. Each new insight is like discovering valuable treasure. The reference to "seven times a day" is a way of saying "all the time," because seven is a number that indicates completeness or perfection. His focus on God provides a sense of peace even in trying times.

119:169–176 The psalm's closing stanza looks to the future. The psalmist intends to keep crying out to God, asking for help, praising Him, and singing. He wants God to continue providing understanding, deliverance, teaching, help, and delight. In return for continued life, he will offer continued praise. And yet after all the writer has said about his devotion to God, he concludes with a confession that he has strayed. In the context of everything else he has written, this is probably not so much an admission of falling away as an expression of the desire to be closer to his heavenly Shepherd.

120:1–2 Psalms 120–134 are identified as Songs of Degrees, or Songs of Ascents, a title that is not totally clear. The Jewish Mishna associates the fifteen psalms with the fifteen steps that led to the temple, where the Levites who led the music would sing the songs. More common is the belief that this group of songs was sung by people making pilgrimages to Jerusalem. Three such journeys for community-wide religious festivals were expected each year (Deuteronomy 16:16–17).

120:6–7 The psalmist concludes with a longing for peace. The wording suggests that he could have been a king. Most people might speak of conflict, disputes, arguments, or such. But in this case the alternative to peace is war.

121:5–8 God's protection is like shade in the hot and sometimes hostile climate of the Middle East. It was also thought at the time that too much exposure to the moon could cause problems as well. (English words such as *moonstruck* and *lunatic* are examples of such a belief.) But God's protection works day and night. In addition, God will watch the pilgrim for the round-trip—coming *and* going.

122:6–7 *Jerusalem* means "city of peace," an appropriate title in the days of David and Solomon. But those people who sang this psalm in the period following the exile of Israel would soon realize how turbulent the recent history of Jerusalem had been. The call to pray for the peace of Jerusalem probably has more significance in later years.

123:1–2 It is not uncommon for those who are devoted to God to suffer ridicule or contempt from those who are not believers. Such is the case described in Psalm 123. The source of the ridicule is not known, but the description is of one entire group of people being harassed by another large group. In such cases, it is difficult to ignore the verbal jeers, yet the psalmist has been able to divert his attention and place his eyes on the Lord. With no thought of personal revenge or frontier justice, he leaves the matter in God's hands. He compares his status to that of a servant or maiden, looking to the master or mistress of the house for mercy.

124:6–7 Using examples from the animal kingdom, the psalmist offers praise to God. Verse 6 summons the image of a vicious animal baring its fangs, but the terrible teeth have done no damage. Verse 7 expresses the joy a bird must feel after being momentarily trapped in a hunter's snare but then escaping to its freedom. And in this case, the snare is broken to be a threat no more. The images used by the psalmist of exposure to raging waters and wild animals would have been appropriate descriptions of Israel's captivity.

125:1–2 Psalm 125 is yet another of the Songs of Degrees (or Ascents) that celebrates the security that only God can offer. The psalmist differentiates between those who trust in the Lord and those who don't. The former group is compared to mount Zion on which Jerusalem was built, protected all around by surrounding mountains. Similarly, God surrounds His people to prevent them from being shaken by their circumstances.

126:4 The release from captivity was just a start. The psalmist prays for a restoration of Israel's fortunes. He thinks of the wilderness of the Negev with its seasonal streams. In hot weather they either reduce to a trickle or dry up completely, but when the rainy season arrives they fill up again. The psalmist wants Israel to once again overflow with God's blessing.

127:3–5 People should acknowledge their children as blessings of God, not merely products of their own biological design. In ancient culture, sons were especially valued. As male children grew, they provided help on the farms, protection against danger, and representation of the family. The more sons parents produced, the more they felt that God had blessed them.

129:1–2 After a series of positive and celebratory psalms (124–128), Psalm 129 is quite a contrast. The psalmist reflects on how Israel has suffered in the past. Although the nation has a long history of outside oppression, it has never been ultimately defeated.

129:3–4 The imagery here is harsh, with the nation personified as someone who has long furrows from foreign plows dug down his back. This is perhaps a reference to the recent Babylonian takeover of Jerusalem. But even as bad as that experience had been, God had eventually freed His people from their bondage.

130:1–4 Psalm 130 is one of the seven psalms in the *penitential* classification (along with Psalms 6, 32, 38, 51, 102, and 143). The psalmist expresses remorse for the sins he has committed and anticipates that God will forgive him and redeem him. The writer is crying out from his emotional depths, asking God to hear and be merciful. He realizes that God is not a heavenly recorder of wrongs—no one would ever be able to please Him. God chose to forgive the sins of His people, which is an astounding fact. The response, then, should be reverential fear of God—not cowering in panic or horror but willfully submitting to Him in worship and obedience.

130:7–8 The writer expands the scope of his prayer. No longer limited to his own situation, the psalmist challenges *all* of Israel to place their hope in God, seeking complete forgiveness and redemption.

132:6 *Ephratah* is a more ancient name for Bethlehem that eventually came to refer to an area *around* Bethlehem. The additional mention of the fields of the wood points to the more specific location of Kirjath-jearim, the place where the ark of the covenant was housed for twenty years after it was returned by the Philistines (1 Samuel 6:21–7:2).

132:7–9 Part of David's preparation involved moving the ark of the covenant from Kirjath-jearim to Jerusalem. The location of the ark soon came to be known as God's dwelling place and His footstool. The temple was eventually built and priests were assigned to care for all aspects of community worship.

135:1–2 This next section of psalms finishes up Book V and therefore the biblical book of Psalms as well. Of the sixteen psalms that remain, half of them comprise a series attributed to David. The remaining ones are anonymous. Although not designated as one of the Songs of Degrees (or Ascents), Psalm 135 appears to have been used for special occasions in the temple worship ceremonies. It begins and ends with the familiar cry to praise the Lord, and the psalm contains many specific reasons to do so. The first challenge to praise God goes out to the temple servants—the priests and Levites.

135:3–4 God is deserving of praise from His people. To begin with, He is good. In addition, He has reached out to people. He chose Jacob (Israel) and all Jacob's descendants (the Israelites) to be His treasured possession.

135:5–7 The people of the surrounding nations cannot make the same claims about their gods. God is sovereign and able to do whatever He wishes, yet He chooses to create, sustain, and bless His people. God's power is seen in all of nature—earth, skies, and seas. Clouds, wind, rain, and lightning are all part of His wonderful design. Rain was a particularly appreciated blessing of God in the climate and geography of the Middle East.

136:1–3 It seems clear from the structure of Psalm 136 that it was used for public worship, with a designated Levite reciting the first portion of each statement as a temple choir, or perhaps the worshippers in attendance, responded with, "for his mercy endureth for ever." The format of the psalm makes it unique, but its content is similar to that of Psalm 135. Both psalms begin with the affirmation that God is good and then detail ways to indicate that He is also great. He is God of gods and Lord of lords. With these initial observations, the accompanying triple command to give thanks in the first three verses is an emphatic opening.

136:23–26 This section summarizes the ongoing work of God. He never forgot His people when they were suffering. He had always delivered them from their enemies. He provided food and necessities, and His provision went beyond Israel. God had been Creator of the world, and His gifts were available to every living thing. There are many reasons to give thanks to God. But at the top of the list, as the psalmist reminds his listeners twenty-six times during this song, God should be thanked because His mercy endures forever.

137:1–3 Psalm 137 begins as a mournful recollection of Israel's time spent in Babylon, and it ends with a brutal imprecation against those responsible for the destruction of Jerusalem. The request of Israel's captors adds insult to injury. The Israelites were in great distress over the fall of their city and temple. They experienced the end of life as they had known it. They were powerless in a foreign land, and then the people there started asking to hear some of their native music, which heightened their despair. So they hung up their harps and opted for silence.

137:4–6 The people were far away from home, but they weren't about to forget what it had meant to them. They had taken much for granted in the final years of the monarchy, and they had suffered the consequences. But memories of Jerusalem—the setting of their temple, worship, feasts, celebrations, and more—had become their greatest source of joy. They even called down curses on themselves if they dared to forget their home city.

138:1–3 Here begins a series of the final eight psalms of David that have been recorded. In this song, David offers his praise to God for a number of reasons, and his praise is unrestrained. David gives God credit for the strength in his soul. He had called out to God, and God had answered him, resulting in his praise for God's love and faithfulness.

138:4–6 David's prayer is that *all* kings will hear the words of God and respond with praise, acknowledging His glory. Much will depend on their individual attitudes. God is highly exalted, yet He is always willing to respond to the lowly—those who humble themselves and seek His help. Those who attempt to exalt themselves in pride, however, miss out on God's compassionate help and support.

139:1–4 Psalm 139 is an amazing expression of God's loving familiarity with David and David's unrelenting devotion in return. David's description of God's awareness of his life might be off-putting for many people. God is watching when the psalmist wakes up, goes to bed, sits down, and gets up. He knows every word David says and thinks.

139:5–12 How does David feel about the close scrutiny of God? It depends on how one interprets his comments. When he writes of being beset, both behind and before, and of having the hand of God upon him, does he feel restricted? Protected? Is he describing futile attempts to carve out a little personal time and space for himself? Or is he speculating about the unlimited ability of God to watch over him wherever he might find himself—heights or depths, day or night, one side of the sea or the other? Either way, his musings have shown him that the omnipresence of God is both too lofty and too wonderful for him to absorb. David's use of the term *wonderful* is not what modern English speakers might assume. David uses this word in the sense of *wondrous* or *miraculous*—beyond human comprehension.

140:1–7 Much of David's life was spent on the run from people who wanted to see him dead. Psalm 140 recounts one such time when he cried out to God for help. David's adversaries are both evil and violent. He compares them to serpents, with sharp tongues and poison. They are cunning and devious, setting snares and traps. David prays for both rescue and protection.

140:12–13 David concludes with an affirmation of God's justice and His care for the poor and needy. Righteous and upright people ultimately have nothing to fear.

141:1–2 One of the insidious consequences of wickedness is that people are prone to instinctively return evil for evil. In Psalm 141, however, David prays that God will prevent him from responding in such a way to people who provoke him. In the opening verses, he compares his prayer to the worship ceremony that took place in the tabernacle, including the smoke of incense rising to God as a prayer and the lifting of his hands as might be done during an evening sacrifice.

141:3–4 David is aware of the actions and intentions of wicked people. They have gotten away with their evil behavior and are enjoying fine foods and an elegant lifestyle as a result. It is tempting to want to join them in their opulence, yet he wants nothing to do with them. He asks God to guard both his lips and his heart.

141:8–10 David declares his trust in God. God, as always, is his refuge. He will keep his eyes on God and trust Him for deliverance from death. He knows the snares of the wicked are still out there. With God in control, however, David will be able to travel in safety while the evildoers become entangled in their own traps.

142:1–3 Psalm 142 has common themes with others in the set. This is the only one of the series, however, that provides a clue in its introduction as to David's situation. As David writes this psalm (as well as Psalm 57), he appears to be thinking about the time when King Saul unexpectedly went into the cave where he was hiding (1 Samuel 24). When strong and powerful enemies threatened David, he turned to God for help. Not only did God hear David's cry, but He also responded with mercy and protection. God was a consistent guide and supporter even when David grew weak and found himself in danger.

142:5–7 With no other source of support, David turns to God as his sole refuge. Even in his desperation, he is counting on God to deliver him. Without God, David's enemies are too strong for him. But after God's intervention, David fully expects to gather with other righteous people in the land of the living to praise the name of God and thank Him for His goodness.

143:1–2 This prayer of David is classified among the *penitential* psalms, the final one of this category in the book of Psalms (along with 6, 32, 38, 51, 102, and 130). Although similar in content to many of David's other psalms, this one contains the acknowledgment that he is among the unrighteous people worthy of judgment, and he asks to be spared.

143:7–8 David's condition leads to his request for God to answer *quickly*. Those who go down to the pit are people who die. The darkness in David's life is severe. He needs light, so he asks God for relief by the morning. His trust remains in God, and he is eager for God to act.

144:1–2 Another psalm attributed to David, Psalm 144 combines the psalmist's praise for God with a request for deliverance. David immediately lists reasons God should be praised. Ever the military man, David notices the strong and powerful aspects of God. The Lord is a fortress, high tower, shield, and deliverer. He can be counted on for training and skill in battle, delivering His people, and subduing enemy nations. Yet David doesn't miss the point that the Lord is also a loving God.

144:3–11 God is concerned with humanity, however weak and temporal it may be—the same themes as in David's Psalm 8, where they are a bit more fully developed. David then asks to witness the strength of his mighty God in the form of rescue from his enemies. David's foes are liars and deceivers, so he wants God to scatter them with lightning and power. In return, David will play and sing a new song to acknowledge God's victory.

145:8–16 God is gracious, compassionate, slow to anger, and rich in mercy. His goodness and compassion are evident from everything He has created. People who identify and appreciate the work of God will not only praise Him for His works but also tell other people. God's kingdom is enduring and everlasting. People in need will especially be glad for the gifts of God. He is loving, He honors His promises, He uplifts the fallen, He provides food, and He is the source that can satisfy all desires.

145:17–21 David concludes this psalm with his final expression of praise to God, inviting every living thing to join him. Those who call on God will discover that He is near. Those who love God will be protected. But those who reject Him to continue to live in wickedness will eventually be destroyed.

146:1–2 When people need help, they have a choice. They can depend on other people or they can turn to God. This psalm offers praise to God because He is always dependable. Psalms 146–150 focus on praising God. Each of these songs that close out the Psalter both begin and end with the phrase "Praise ye the Lord" (or "Hallelujah").

146:3–4 Putting one's trust in people eventually leads to disappointment. All people, even those with power and influence, are mortal. Their ability to help is limited in both time and degree. Situations will arise where their power is insufficient. And their influence ends with death.

146:5–10 God is the Creator of all things, and He remains faithful. The people who need help most can always count on Him: the oppressed, the hungry, the prisoners, the blind, those who are bowed down, the alien, the fatherless, and the widows. God's love and help extend to all who are righteous. Those who are wicked, however, will find themselves frustrated. God should be praised regularly because His reign will last forever.

147:1–3 This psalm of praise is in regard to God's faithfulness to Israel after their exile. Immediately after the opening call to praise, the psalmist begins to recount the events after the people's release from captivity. He recalls the gathering of the exiles and the building (actually, the rebuilding) of Jerusalem. The people were brokenhearted to see what had been done to the city and how much repair needed to be done, but God was there to heal their wounded spirits.

147:4–9 The psalmist reminds everyone that the same God who helped them is the One who had created, numbered, and named the stars. The rain He provides supplies life-supporting water for both domestic and wild animals. His understanding and His power are unlimited. And while His power will be used to subdue the wicked, it will always provide support for the humble.

148:1–6 Psalm 148 is a call for everyone and everything to praise God. The writer exhorts those in the heavens to praise Him: angels and heavenly hosts, sun, moon, stars, clouds, and waters above the skies. All have been created and established by God, and He deserves their praise.

148:7–13 The psalmist beckons the great creatures of the sea, the elements (lightning, hail, snow, clouds, and winds), mountains, trees, wild and domestic animals, human rulers (kings and princes), and *all* people—young and old, male and female. Of everything the psalmist lists, nothing is worthy of praise except the name of the Lord. People have limited knowledge of heaven and earth, but God's splendor is unbounded.

149:1 Psalm 149 is a call for the entire community of Israel to offer praise to God. As God continues to act on behalf of His people, the appropriate response is to sing a new song of praise to Him.

149:2–9 The people should praise God for their salvation. Their praise should take various enthusiastic forms: dancing, music, songs during the night, and an overall attitude of gladness and rejoicing. In addition, the people should praise God because He has empowered them to be victorious. They have not sat idly waiting for God to remove their problems; they have taken up swords to protect their nation. The victory will always be God's, but His people are involved and faithfully committed to Him, which entails occasional struggles and conflicts with other nations.

149:6 The two-edged sword was a relatively new invention at this time. Earlier mentions of a sword in scripture, such as the time period of Joshua and the judges, frequently refer to a curved instrument with the outside edge sharpened. By this time, though, the sword had evolved into a straight weapon with both sides of the blade sharpened and able to inflict blows. With God providing victory and safety for His people, they should always be prepared to praise Him.

150:1–2 Psalm 1 appears to be positioned intentionally to introduce the book of Psalms. Similarly, this concluding psalm may have been written to close the book with a final emphasis on the importance of praise. Each book within the biblical book of Psalms ends with a short doxology. In this case, the final psalm serves as the doxology for Book V. The Israelites perceive that God has a temple in heaven as well as the one they are familiar with in Jerusalem, and here the writer calls for God to be praised in both locations. God is to be praised for the feats He had performed for Israel in His power and for His greatness that surpasses all others.

150:3–6 The long series of instruments listed includes strings, wind instruments, and percussion. When united, the result will be an enthusiastic accompaniment to praise, along with dancing. God, the Creator of all things, should be praised by everything that has breath. The psalm (and the book of Psalms) concludes with one final "Praise ye the Lord."

THE
PROVERBS

INTRODUCTION TO PROVERBS ■ As the preface to the book states, Proverbs is about wisdom. On one level, wisdom is a skill of living, a practical knowledge. Wise people know how to say the right thing at the right time and to do the right thing at the right time. They live in a way that maximizes blessing for themselves and others in the world that God created. But at a deeper level, wisdom is more profound than an ability to navigate life well. Indeed, it begins with a proper attitude toward God characterized by "fear." This is not the type of fear that makes someone run away, but it is more than respect. It is the awe that a person should feel when in the presence of the sovereign Creator of the universe. Proverbs is a book about wisdom, and it intends to make its reader wise.

AUTHOR ■ The book of Proverbs is associated with Solomon, Israel's wisest king. His writings—or his teachings put into writing by a scribe—form most of the book. It was revealed in 1 Kings 4:32 that Solomon spoke three thousand proverbs, and it is good to have the book of Proverbs to see what he was teaching. A few additional short sections come from other contributors: anonymous writers (22:17–24:22), Agur (chapter 30), and Lemuel (chapter 31).

OCCASION ■ The purpose of the book of Proverbs is stated in 1:2–3: to provide wisdom that, when applied, will lead to a godly life.

1:1 The opening verse establishes the credibility of the proverbs in this book by identifying them with Solomon, the wisest man (except for Jesus Christ) who ever lived. When Solomon took the throne, God gave him "a wise and an understanding heart; so that there was none like thee before thee, neither after thee shall any arise like unto thee" (1 Kings 3:12).

1:7 Fear connotes not only terror but also extreme reverence, respect, and awe, as well as recognition of the fact that we are completely reliant on God. Fear of the Lord brings humility, a lack of pride, and a willingness to listen to Him rather than seek our own way.

1:8 Wisdom begins when a child listens to his father and mother. The word *hear* in this text carries the idea of listening with the intent to obey. The implication here is that the parents are themselves wise and godly people.

1:10–12 The greatest threat any young person faces is that of being deceived into falling in with a group of people who do not love what God loves.

1:15–16 The warning is clear: The goal is not to get as close to a sinful lifestyle as possible and see how much of your Christian virtues you can keep. The goal is to stay off the path altogether.

1:17–19 It is foolish to try to trap a bird by setting a trap while the bird is watching. It is just as foolish to try to profit illegally. If you follow this path, you will self-destruct.

1:23 Despite the attitudes of the simple ones, scorners, and fools, wisdom continues to speak to them with a strong message of mercy: If you seek wisdom, it will not run from you.

1:29–31 Those who have chosen folly do not do so out of ignorance; they have made a conscious decision to do things their own way rather than doing things God's way.

1:32–33 The foolish will experience the pain and misery that come from doing things their own way, while the wise will enjoy security and freedom from fear.

2:10–11 Knowledge will become pleasant to the seeker. He will develop such a taste for it that he will pursue it more and more. The wisdom and discretion he gains will protect him from the folly that comes when one does not operate as a wise person in this world.

2:12–15 A wise person will be protected from falling in with a bad crowd. Only wisdom will keep a person from falling into this path.

2:16–19 A wise person will be protected from sexually immoral people. This protection does not come from living an ascetic lifestyle. The true solution comes from fearing the Lord and living for God's glory and seeking after wisdom as a way of life.

2:20–22 The end result is that the wise person will walk in a manner that pleases God. Those who do walk in this manner will have the promised blessing that all Israelites seek. But those who do not walk in this way will have the pain and misery that come from folly.

3:1–2 Because a young person does not have as much experience, he should heed the wisdom of his parents. The fruit of this obedience is a life that escapes the pain associated with foolishness.

3:5 This verse is not setting the mind in opposition to the heart but rather teaching that humanistic reasoning will not lead to wisdom. Only when a person's heart is fixed on God can a person begin to think properly.

3:6 Walking according to God's will puts someone in the position to have God lead the way and open the doors to the life that He desires.

3:9–10 The focal point of this verse is not the offering as much as it is the heart and motive behind the offering made to God. We give to God because we acknowledge Him as our provider. This giving from a heart of trust does have an apparent blessing associated with it: God will continue to abundantly provide. This principle is meant to establish a basic assumption, not an automatic response.

3:11–12 These verses are also cited in Hebrews 12:5–6. The child of God should not despise God's discipline. God's discipline is the way that God corrects His children and makes them better.

3:19–20 The earth is a place where the very wisdom of God became the logic and the order by which the world was created. Those who abandon wisdom run against the very structure by which the world was made.

3:21–26 Even when problems come to the wise, they know how to handle them. This is what wisdom brings to people—not escape from the sin of the world but the ability to handle problems as they come.

3:31–35 Those living with kindness and love toward others have no need to envy those who pursue easy prosperity by violence and crime. Such people miss out on God's friendship, blessing, grace, and honor. To envy the wicked is to envy those who are on a path to destruction.

4:1–4 The home is the primary place of education, especially moral education. The affectionate and pleading tone of these verses shows that parents who love their children make the best teachers.

4:7 Wisdom is the greatest possession anyone can have, and the young man should obtain it.

4:16–17 This passage presents in vivid colors the depravity of the wicked. They live for crime. It is their food, drink, and sleep. They do not commit crimes in order to live but live to commit crimes. Their punishment will be appropriate. Their greatest satisfaction is in making others fall, but they, too, shall fall and not know how or why.

5:1–2 The father appeals to the young man to pay attention to his teaching. Morality is always an issue of the heart. If one's heart remains pure, then one can maintain a life of integrity. Current history is littered with those who have failed to live with integrity and have lost their voice in the world.

5:3 The immoral woman uses flattery to draw the young man in. Her lips are filled with words that appeal to the pride of the man and pull him into an inappropriate relationship with her.

5:4–6 The bitter outcome of a relationship with an immoral woman is torment, disappointment, emotional suffering, and even death. In other words, there is no upside to this relationship; all it does is harm people. To join this woman on her path to destruction is to join with death. (The writer of Proverbs is not exaggerating when he says that consorting with an immoral woman can lead to death. In ancient Israel, sexual sin was punishable by death; see Leviticus 20:10.)

5:7–8 The father warns his sons not to stray from his warning. A contemporary image is that of a man guiding his sons through a minefield. The goal is not to get as close to danger as possible but rather to stay far away.

5:9–11 The sons, in staying away from the immoral woman, will not have to worry about their reputations, losing their money in fast living, or sexually transmitted diseases. The use of the plural in this passage has led many to believe that this woman could be a prostitute or someone who is involved with a whole immoral system that will draw this young man in and destroy him.

5:22–23 Those who abandon God's plan for marriage will suffer the pain that is associated with this lifestyle. There is no moral neutral ground—to consider this immoral action is a step toward death. Such a person will die for lack of discipline. In short, the man will sow the seeds of his own destruction if he follows this path.

6:6–11 In contrast with the hardworking ways of the ant, laziness leads to certain poverty and ruin. The lazy person places rest and sleep as the nonnegotiable in life. Sleep is meant to give the body energy for work; it was never intended to be a way of life. Laziness will siphon off resources until the slothful have nothing left.

6:12–14 The people referred to in these verses can best be described as hucksters. A huckster is someone who pretends to be a friend, who tells people all the things they want to hear. But he does this to get something in return. A huckster takes advantage of people. This person will use every deceit in the book to get his way. This lifestyle is one that God will not bless.

6:15 Because people who take advantage of others sow destruction in others' lives, they will reap destruction.

6:16–19 This passage enumerates things that God hates in a clear, numerical manner for easy memorization. The first five things mentioned in this list are body parts, set in a sequence that moves from the head to the feet. These five items concern general moral characteristics: pride, dishonesty, and a violent or manipulative character. The last two are types of people who specifically belong to a court or governmental system.

6:20–24 The final section of Proverbs 6 contains another warning about sexual immorality. The exhortation begins with the now-familiar appeal for the son to heed his father's words. The father's teachings function as a guide, guardian, and companion. They are meant to accompany the son wherever he goes. The father's teaching is to shed light on the moral decisions of life and to help the young man recognize when a woman seeks to pull him into her web of sin through seductive words.

6:30–35 The writer makes a comparison between adultery and theft. Even a thief who steals out of hunger must repay his victim seven times over. How much more will adultery bring down a harsh verdict on an adulterer—for this is the worst of all actions. The marriage bed is to be held in high honor, and those who violate this will be punished to the worst degree. The young man must understand this, for it will serve him well as he enters the world where this kind of behavior goes on.

7:1–3 As this section opens, the father urges the son to keep his commands. This is said with the same force that is often used of God's commands. In other words, what is about to be said has to be heeded and treated with the utmost respect.

7:6–13 To make his point in the most powerful manner, the father tells of an occasion when he observed a young man being seduced by an adulteress. When the father looked out his window, he saw a young man walking toward the house of an immoral woman at twilight. It is not clear whether he was intentionally going there or just passing by. The woman's loud, seductive, and inappropriate behavior shows that she is the type of woman he should run away from.

7:15–18 Having dealt with the young man's moral qualms, the adulteress promises a night of passion.

7:21–23 In his acquiescence, the young man is both passive, like an ox going to slaughter, and dim-witted, like a deer or bird going into a trap. He is about to pay the full price for this sin—his life.

8:1–3 Wisdom calls for an audience at the places where people need her message: from the heights by the road, at crossroads, and at entrances to the city. Her message is not just for the elite but for all people to hear.

8:12 Even though wisdom is accessible to everyone, it is still the deepest and most profound reality in the world. This is first seen by the way it deals with the world. Observe that wisdom claims to possess prudence, knowledge, and discretion—which carry the idea of sensible, careful behavior that arises from clear and wise thinking. Wisdom teaches how to live a balanced and careful life as opposed to a reckless life that leads to suffering the pain of folly.

8:15–16 The reach of wisdom is not just for independent followers of God. Wisdom is also meant to be used by the leaders of the world. Wisdom is essential for those who have been given the responsibility to lead in government.

8:22–31 This passage describes wisdom's role in creation. It is an important role because it sets the stage for the relationship between wisdom and the world. This passage could be divided into three parts: the birth of wisdom (8:22–26), wisdom's part in creation (8:27–29), and the joy of wisdom (8:30–31).

8:22–26 Wisdom claims to be the first principle of the world ever created and the pattern by which the world was created. The point here is that wisdom is the oldest of all principles in the world. As such, she holds a superior position in the world and should be valued higher than creation itself.

8:30–31 In the development of the world, wisdom found great joy. The creation of the world was in harmony with the logic of wisdom. Wisdom is an artisan, and the principles of wisdom are woven into the fabric of the created order. Thus, to truly understand the world around us, we need the wisdom of God.

8:32–36 These verses are a fitting ending to this chapter. Because the whole world is embedded with wisdom, it is very important to listen to wisdom. Those who listen become wise, but those who neglect to listen will suffer.

9:11–12 The promise of life and the statement of individual responsibility are a fitting conclusion to the call of wisdom. The joy and blessing that she offers are for the taking. Yet if someone rejects this message, he will bear the consequences of his folly all by himself, without help.

9:13–14 This passage outlines the way of folly. Like the adulteress (7:11), folly is loud, careless, and seductive.

10:1 The behavior of children helps shape the happiness of the parents. If children are wise, parents find joy; if they are foolish, parents are grieved. This is a warning both to parents, to instill wisdom in their children, and to children, to recognize that their actions have a direct impact on their parents' hearts.

10:2 Two possible paths for a young adult are contrasted. If he gains wealth through immoral means, that wealth will be limited to this life only. If he gains success through the right means, he will have more than just earthly prosperity; he will have eternal life. Wealth by itself has no redeeming value. To pursue wealth through immoral means is to do nothing but find emptiness in life and death in the end. For this reason, it is important to pursue righteousness rather than wealth.

10:5 A person who works when he is supposed to work will bring honor to his parents and ultimately bring glory to God. A lazy person will bring shame to his family.

10:6–11 The contrast between a righteous person and a wicked person is common in Proverbs. Solomon wants his son to understand this difference, so here he sets out to explain it using six contrasts.

10:12–17 The proverbs in these verses outline how righteousness would look lived out in contrast to wickedness lived out.

10:12 If wickedness is the driving motivation in life, then strife will be the fruit; the one who is righteous will not attack an offense but will cover that offense with love.

10:13–14 The wise use their tongues carefully, but fools bring suffering on themselves by their words.

10:15–16 In general, life is easier for the rich than for the poor, but wealth that is wrongfully gained will bring a person to ruin and death.

10:17 A sinful person who is seeking righteousness will listen to correction, while the one who rebels against wisdom leads others down the road to destruction.

10:18–32 This section is set up in what is called *chiastic* fashion, with parallel ideas set in mirror image to each other. A topic is introduced—in this case the tongue, which is destructive in a wicked person and positive in a godly person (10:18–21). Then a second topic is talked about—in this case the stability of the righteous over the wicked (10:22–25). Then a third topic is introduced—in this case laziness (10:26). Then the second topic is revisited—the stability of the righteous (10:27–30). Finally the first topic is revisited—the tongue (10:31–32).

11:1–3 God hates fraud, pride, and dishonesty but welcomes integrity.

11:4 Riches gained by the unrighteous will not help them on the Day of Judgment.

11:5–13 The dishonesty and ambition of the unrighteous will be their downfall, while the godly will be rescued—to the delight of those watching, because they know that godly people make good fellow citizens, while bad neighbors go around gossiping.

11:16–18 Ruthless people may get rich, but they can't buy the respect that is due to someone gracious and kind.

11:22 Beauty is no more a guarantee of a good life than is wealth. Beauty without character is like fancy jewelry on a pig.

11:23 Those who are living according to God's will have a desire to do what is right, while those who are unrighteous know that their ultimate outcome will be eternal death.

11:24–28 Those who are generous with what they have will find their rewards increasing, while those who are selfish and keep everything for themselves will end up with nothing.

11:29–31 People's wickedness doesn't affect only the people themselves; it also affects family and friends. If that is apparent already in earthly relationships, think how significant it will be in eternity.

12:2 The good man will obtain the favor of the Lord because he seeks God's wisdom. God blesses the one who lives for Him and condemns the one who pursues evil. God does not show His favor to those who spurn Him.

12:3 The good man will not seek to find his way in the world by manipulation. Instead, he seeks to establish himself in the righteousness of God. By doing this, he gives his life a sure and steady root upon which to grow.

12:4 The wife who is truly righteous has such an impact on a man that it makes him better and more respected in the world. The wife who is not righteous not only has to contend with her own wickedness but also is a curse to her husband.

12:9–11 A lifestyle of moderate comforts is far more desirable than the pretense of wealth. A good man cares for those who provide for him, even if they are only animals. The wicked take advantage of everyone and everything. True success comes by working hard rather than by looking for the get-rich-quick scheme.

12:16–22 This passage uses a form of repetition to make a point about the value of truth and the recklessness of lying. The issue of reckless words emerges twice. The issues of honesty and lying emerge three times. Two times the issues of trouble for the wicked and peace for the righteous are addressed. The parallels are not exact parallels, but instead they are loosely connected themes expressing similar ideas from slightly different points of view.

12:23–28 The final six proverbs of chapter 12 describe the characteristics of a life of wisdom.

13:4 Work ethic is a common topic in Proverbs. The point to be drawn here is that, as a principle, lazy people will not get what they desire, because what they desire is gain without effort. Diligent people, on the other hand, want to reap the results of hard work, and generally they do.

13:7–11 This passage deals with wealth and its deceptive nature.

13:8 The rich may be able to pay a ransom, but the poor don't have to worry about being kidnapped in the first place.

13:9–11 These verses reiterate one of the central issues of Proverbs: A person who pursues wisdom will gain a reward far more lasting than that of the person who pursues money at all cost.

13:17 A messenger is an example of a person charged with a serious responsibility. Just as an envoy is charged with representing someone and speaking the words of the one he represents, so, too, the faithful child of God must represent the wisdom of God and take it seriously. There are consequences for not being faithful.

13:20–21 It is essential to choose one's friends wisely. Just as good friends have good influences, a friend who gets into trouble generally gets his friends into trouble with him.

14:1 If a woman is wise, her home grows and gets better and better, but a woman who is foolish will bring pain and destruction upon her home.

14:2 There are two paths in life: the path of those who fear the Lord and the path of the foolish, who despise the Lord.

14:5–7 The way that a person speaks reflects the condition of his or her heart. It is wise to avoid liars and scorners, because their language reveals the foolishness of a heart that does not fear the Lord.

14:8 Those who fear God understand what they are doing and why they are doing it. In contrast, foolish people seek to hide the true intentions of their hearts.

14:10 Everyone knows the real state of his or her own heart, so when the wicked deny their need for forgiveness, they lie to themselves and to God.

14:11 Even though wicked people may amass things on this earth, destruction will come. Even though righteous people might not gain as much, in the end they will know the security of being right with God.

14:20–22 No one wants to be poor, and the poor do not garner the respect in the world that the rich do. But those who show kindness toward others, regardless of their social and economic standing, are blessed by God.

14:23–24 While it is true that many people are poor despite their best efforts, this is no excuse for not working. The principle remains that the fruit of real work is reward, but people who hate work and only talk a good game get nothing.

14:28–35 The health and well-being of a nation depend upon both the ruler and the governed. A ruler must be fair and, above all, must respect the rights of his people. The people, on the other hand, must have virtue in their lives or they will bring society into chaos. No government can succeed without the people, and no people can thrive if corruption and evil abound.

14:34–35 Wisdom is not just for personal gain—there is a national aspect to it as well. A nation's political health depends to a great degree on the moral integrity of its people. For this reason, political leaders are better served by people of integrity.

15:1–4 The ability to avert quarreling and to live in harmony with others is a virtue of wisdom. A wise person knows how to speak gently, appealingly, and truthfully.

15:9 God hates the religious practices of the wicked. What pleases God the most is not religious ceremony but a heart that pursues righteousness all the time.

15:10–12 God will allow a fool to suffer the complete consequences for all of his actions. Those who do not repent under this discipline and continue to reject it will die. This death could refer to spiritual death alone, but Proverbs makes it clear that both physical and spiritual death are included in the consequences. How foolish it is to reject correction!

15:13–14 A person's focal point should always be the heart and nothing else. A person cannot control his experience with this world from the outside in; it has to be from the inside out. A wise person seeks to understand the world from God's point of view, which brings joy to the heart.

15:15–17 A happy heart has a continual feast. In fact, to have a heart feasting on the joy, fear, and love of the Lord is better than a literal feast.

16:5 Wicked people will certainly not go unpunished. People can live entire lifetimes being prideful and powerful, appearing to be in charge and getting their way. But in the end, they will be humbled in the judgment of God.

16:6 Avoiding the problem of pride is a simple matter of fearing the Lord. God is a God of mercy and truth who has made atonement for the sin of the proud (Isaiah 53:5).

16:9 People make their plans, but God ultimately directs their steps. While these insights are valuable for anyone, they are especially relevant for human leaders. Solomon's son would be next in line for royal leadership, so it was important for him to understand how a king was to act.

16:12–13 If a king uses his position for personal profit, he ignores the justice of God and commits an utter abomination. Kings should acknowledge and reward those who speak the truth.

16:14–15 People should show proper respect for their king. The king controls the power of the nation, and the sword may fall on anyone who incites his wrath. It is far wiser to appease the king than to antagonize him.

16:16–17 Life is a series of choices, which is why Solomon emphasizes the importance of wisdom. People see the value of tangible things like gold and silver, yet wisdom and understanding are far more valuable.

16:18–19 Choosing positive but intangible qualities over the riches of the world requires humility. Those who take pride in their riches are destined for destruction.

16:20–24 A person's words reflect his or her inner motives. Wise words are instructive, pleasant, and life-giving. A wise heart guides one's speech. Wise words are as exciting and pleasurable as candy to a child.

16:32 Controlling one's temper reflects great inner power—more than that of a victorious military leader.

17:1 Peace resulting from the blessing of God is far preferable to acquired wealth that creates problems and suffering. Solomon had untold riches at his disposal, yet he understood that the simple essentials of life with quietness were better than great wealth accompanied by strife.

17:5 Those who mock or celebrate the sufferings of others display a cruelty that will certainly be punished. The offense is not only against their fellow human beings but also against God.

17:7 People's words should reflect their true natures. It quickly becomes evident when a foolish person attempts to be arrogant or when the leader of the nation is telling lies.

17:10 The wise person's pursuit of truth will include a willing acceptance of well-intentioned rebukes for things he or she has done wrong. Fools, on the other hand, tend not to be swayed no matter what happens. One hundred lashes would not turn foolish people from their corrupt ways.

17:13 Those who repay good with evil will soon find themselves plagued with evil.

17:16 Fools can collect money for schooling, but without a genuine desire for wisdom, the money goes to waste.

17:17–18 No one wants fools around during difficult times. That's when people seek the help of true friends. A real friend is more than just someone who vouches for another; a genuine friend is there around the clock.

17:19 Those who never resist the tendency to sin are quick to quarrel, and they will eventually fall hard, like an oversize gate in a city wall.

17:27–28 A wise person uses few words. Even fools can appear wise if they keep their mouths shut. By paying attention over time to what (and how much) a person says, one can determine whether that person is wise or foolish. Words are the fruit that reflect the quality of the heart.

18:1–2 The selfish pursuits of foolish people result in the frequent expression of their personal opinions. In the absence of wisdom, they are drawn to vanity and narcissism.

18:15 While many people adopt the behavior of the wicked, others see its limitations and commit to seeking wisdom instead.

18:20–21 While words can be misused in any number of ways, when used properly they can edify others. Just as food satisfies one's hunger, well-chosen words can be an equally pleasurable source of contentment. Wise people take their words seriously.

18:22 The book of Proverbs has much to say about the importance of avoiding the wrong women and forming relationships with spiritually strong women. This verse emphasizes the favor God will bestow on the husband of a good wife.

18:24 The choice of one's friends is a matter of wisdom versus folly. Those with many friends have little time for intimacy with any of them, and such people may be led astray by some of their many acquaintances. True friendships, however, can be much closer than family relations.

19:1 Honesty and integrity are crucial ingredients of the best possible life. Impulsiveness should be avoided.

19:2 Hard work in itself is not enough because people should have an awareness of what they are doing and why.

19:3 A respect for wisdom should underlie one's pursuits. Too often people go through life doing whatever they want to do, and then when things don't work out, they are quick to blame God.

19:5–6 Honesty is important at all times—not just when it is convenient. Witnesses need to speak the truth, even if they might profit in some way from a lie or half-truth. Similarly, in trying to impress rulers or people in power, the tendency is to tell them what they want to hear when truthfulness would serve a better purpose.

19:9 The sense of satisfaction that comes with finding wisdom should be enough in itself, but getting wisdom also prevents one from eventually being judged and punished for lying.

19:13 Contentment within the home must be a cooperative effort. One person can create misery for all the others, such as a foolish child or quarrelsome spouse.

19:15 One person's laziness has an effect on others as well, whether those others are family members or a wider community. It is difficult to effectively relate to people who would rather sleep than work.

19:19 When people fail to control their emotions, anger issues are not easily resolved. It can become a full-time job for someone to repeatedly deliver an angry friend or family member.

19:27–29 Sometimes parents do all they can do and the children still don't respond. So Solomon follows with some specific warnings for those who ignore what they have been taught, beginning with his own son. An ongoing refusal to respond to the teachings of God and one's parents will surely result in evil, penalties, and punishments.

20:1–3 It is difficult enough to avoid conflicts in life under the best of conditions, so it is the essence of wisdom to minimize problems whenever and however possible. One way is to avoid intoxication that might otherwise lead to brawling. Another is to keep from provoking those in power. People who avoid conflict are seen in a positive light because any fool can pick a fight.

20:15 People don't tend to acknowledge the real value of wisdom. Solomon reminds his son that wisdom is a precious commodity even rarer than gold and rubies.

20:16 Clothing served as a sort of IOU for debts in the ancient world (see Deuteronomy 24:10–14). Solomon warned to be careful whose debt one assumed.

20:27 People owe everything to God. He is the source of light and life. He knows everything about every person, and no one can hide anything from Him. Consequently, those with wisdom realize the importance of living before God in openness and honesty.

20:29 People are blessed with different gifts at different phases of life. Many bemoan losing the strength of youth when, in fact, they should rejoice at the accumulation of wisdom that comes only with age.

20:30 Wisdom helps people understand and endure the painful experiences of life. In time they see how their sufferings work to keep evil at bay and make them stronger individuals.

21:4 God hates haughty eyes and a wicked heart. Pride and arrogance are at the root of any number of other sins.

21:8 Sometimes it appears that wicked people are prospering, and others are tempted to emulate them. But that path always has an abrupt and destructive end. Upright conduct will yield much greater rewards.

21:10 Wicked neighbors are no better than contentious spouses. Such neighbors quickly lose the respect of others and find themselves alone after pushing away everyone they encounter.

21:11 Seeing a wicked person punished is an encouragement to faithful people. Wise people need not get to the point of punishment. They will learn from positive instruction and/or an occasional rebuke that keeps them on the right track.

21:13 Everyone is in need from time to time. People who ignore the needs of others usually discover in their own time of despair that no one responds.

21:17–20 Many of the habits of the wicked and foolish are evident: living only for pleasure, overindulgence in alcohol and fine food, gluttony, and more.

21:21–23 The behaviors of the righteous and godly are intertwined with the rewards: disciplined accumulation of life's necessities, long life, prosperity, honor, success in the struggles of life, control of one's words, and so forth.

21:30 The key to righteousness and understanding is to acknowledge and seek the superiority of the wisdom of God. No other "wisdom" can approach God's wisdom.

22:1 Integrity is integral to being a child of God. Given the choice of a good name or great wealth, people should always choose the former. Sadly, many are quite willing to sacrifice their reputation for financial gain.

22:2 People make distinctions based on wealth, but God doesn't. He created all people, and He does not prorate His love according to personal bank accounts.

22:7–9 These verses are a series of general observations rather than insights. Most people can look around and confirm that the rich rule over the poor, that borrowing money makes the borrower beholden to the lender, that those who act wickedly are in for trouble, and that those who are generous to others will be blessed with satisfaction.

22:10–12 Those who suffer because of quarrels and insults need to eliminate the source. Conversely, gracious speech has a positive effect, even attracting a king's ear. God values truth, and those who attempt to distort truth will ultimately be frustrated.

22:15 The "rod" mentioned here refers to a shepherd's tool used to guide the sheep away from a dangerous direction. It was not used in a harsh manner. Any discipline conducted in anger is improper. It is nevertheless important to discipline one's children. Acting foolishly is not only potentially embarrassing but frequently harmful as well. Loving parents will dedicate themselves to helping their children get beyond the allure of folly to discover the true joy of godly wisdom.

22:17–21 These verses are an introduction to this segment of Proverbs. The writer attests that his words are true and reliable, yet he wants his readers to respond not to him but rather to the wisdom of God.

22:22–27 The unknown writer offers a series of warnings. The poor and needy already have trouble enough, so we must not add to it by exploiting or pressuring them. We are to avoid relationships with easily angered people, or risk becoming like them ourselves. And we are not to be too hasty to cosign loans for others, or we may soon find ourselves impoverished.

22:28 Land in Israel was very important for survival. The ancient landmarks established boundary lines, and moving them was a subtle method of stealing property that belonged to someone else.

22:29 People who are skilled at what they do, and who do their work without complaining, will succeed. Soon they will be recruited to serve before kings.

23:4–5 Although God can use money and although money can bring some temporal benefits, it should never be a primary pursuit of one's life. Wealth is a temporal entity.

23:17–18 Sometimes it is easy to envy someone who seems to get away with wrongdoing. We are reminded to continue to obey God. Walking in the fear of the Lord brings true and lasting hope, life, and peace.

23:22–25 The way the son lives affects the joy of the parents. (The concept of buying the truth means that the truth is so important that it is worth any sacrifice to acquire and keep.)

23:26–28 The son is warned about the illusive allure of a prostitute or wayward wife. Such women are outwardly attractive to young men, yet they will draw the man into a trap from which he cannot easily escape.

23:29–35 The final verses of Proverbs 23 are a warning to stay away from the seduction of wine. The painful symptoms of overindulgence are listed in detail. Alcoholism affects one's body, causing the person to become disoriented, lose control, and disregard wisdom.

24:3–4 Just as a house is constructed and then filled with goods that make it livable, a commitment to wisdom builds up people, and ongoing knowledge edifies them and allows them to function together.

24:5–6 Wisdom makes people powerful because knowledge provides strength that goes beyond the physical. A group of wise people can achieve victory in whatever they do.

24:13–14 Wisdom's effect on the soul is comparable to honey's sweetness in one's mouth. Those who feast on wisdom will never lose their hope for the future.

24:15–16 These verses serve a twofold purpose: to warn the wicked and to encourage the righteous. It is foolish for the wicked to try to overpower the righteous because godly people have the strength and wisdom to endure difficult times.

24:17–18 The wicked, lacking strength in God, will be worn down by trials. It is important to remain humble even when one's enemies suffer the consequences of their sin. Another person's judgment is no occasion to gloat or rejoice.

24:19–20 The righteous should not desire to be like evildoers, who have no future. Sin and wickedness lead to death, so it is foolish to envy people involved in such things.

24:21–22 This is a call to fear both God and the king—to respect those in leadership, both divine and human.

24:26 The one who tells the truth does something that is right and pleasurable.

25:1 The collection of proverbs contained in chapters 25–27 was either compiled or rediscovered by King Hezekiah. The collection begins with a series of proverbs about kings.

25:2–3 While the king needs to search things out to understand them, God does not. Similarly, a king's subjects cannot fully understand the king.

25:4–5 Just as the dross needs to be taken away from silver before it can be used to create something, so, too, wickedness needs to be removed from the kingdom in order for it to be justly established.

25:6–7 It is foolish to try to exalt ourselves to make ourselves known before the king. If the king does not feel the same way, we will be publicly humiliated and cast down to a lower position than where we started.

25:8–10 These verses warn against bringing people too hastily into court. If we respond out of emotion, we may be made a fool of in front of all. The best thing to do is to bring our problems to our neighbors directly. There is a pragmatic reason for this: In the course of a trial, our own sins and failings will be brought to light.

25:15 Tough leaders are won over not by a show of force but through patience. All a fight does is embolden the ruler.

25:16–17, 27–28 These proverbs deal with having too much of a good thing. Too much of a pleasure can be a bad thing.

25:18–19 The one who would sell out his neighbor for his own personal gain is a deadly person to be around, and placing faith in such a person will only bring pain and complications.

25:20 Blithely overlooking someone's grief produces a reaction in that person in the same way that vinegar and soda react.

25:21–22 In ancient Middle Eastern cultures, revenge was a way of life. These verses offer another way of dealing with the enemy: Serve him and meet his needs. The idea of pouring burning coals on the enemy's head is not to wreak vengeance but to shock him with this response.

25:23 A person with a loose tongue is a storm of problems.

25:24 This verse cautions about the spiritual dangers that an unrighteous spouse poses to a household—a common theme in Proverbs. It is important to select one's husband or wife carefully.

26:12 Pride is so destructive that there is more hope for a fool than the prideful man.

26:13–16 The lazy person is condemned just like the fool. The lazy person is worthless for a variety of reasons: He makes excuses, he loves sleep over work, he is too lazy even to feed himself, and he is extremely prideful. (The fact that seven wise people are mentioned in verse 16 is no doubt symbolic; seven is the number representing perfection. In other words, when a lazy person is presented with perfect wisdom, he will pick his lazy attitude every time.)

26:17–22 Some people are simply maddening. They meddle in problems that they have no reason to be involved in. They cover their lies by saying they were only joking ("in sport"). They start quarrels and keep them going with their gossip, savoring the rumors they spread, destructive though such talk may be.

27:1–2 A boastful attitude is a foolish attitude, whether one is boasting about himself or what he will do in the future.

27:3–4 Resentment and envy are two attitudes that foster dangerous conflict.

27:7–10 The context of a person's life—whether he is "full" or "hungry"—determines how he hears what he hears. When tough things have to be said, it is more dangerous to leave and ignore those tough words than to stay and endure them. Through friendship people are challenged, changed, refreshed, and supported. Friendships already established in the family are worth trusting in and ministering to.

27:11–14 Solomon wants to know the joy of his child's obedience and the honor that comes from having wise children in the community. Marks of that kind of wisdom include anticipating and avoiding trouble, not being an easy target for swindlers, and saying the right thing at the right time.

27:15–16 If Solomon's son marries a contentious woman, her behavior will be a great annoyance in the home.

27:17–18 Godly friendships, as earlier proverbs have said, exhort and motivate people to be godly. In a similar way, mutual respect between boss and worker benefits both.

27:19–22 These proverbs deal with issues of the heart. The heart of someone is who that person really is. The desires that are in the heart are never satisfied. Verse 21 can be understood to mean that what people say about a person reveals his character, or that how a person responds to praise and flattery reveals his character. In either case, if foolishness has taken over the heart of someone, then that foolishness will be impossible to remove.

27:23–27 This chapter ends on a practical appeal: to have a shepherd's heart for the resources that God has entrusted to us.

28:1 The boldness of the righteous is equated to the boldness of a lion—which is a courage that stands up against any foe. What one gets when walking in the righteousness of God is the ability to stand up for what is right regardless of the foe.

28:2 If a leader takes advantage of his people and operates in an unfair manner, then they will rise up and there will be a conflict between leaders in the nation. The ruler who realizes this truth and pursues a righteous approach to leadership will rule over a stable land for a long time.

28:3 Under a bad leader, poverty becomes so widespread that the poor even prey on one another.

28:4–5 Individuals, as well as leaders, contribute to how society functions. A person who breaks the law is in essence endorsing all lawbreakers, while obeying the law is a vote for justice.

28:9–14 Practical righteousness involves joining prayer with obedience, setting a good example, and having the right perspective on success. It means taking responsibility for one's actions and consciously choosing right over wrong.

28:15–16 For a ruler, practical righteousness includes governing with integrity and compassion.

28:17–18 The consequences of unrighteousness—whether it be disregard for human life or any other crookedness—are fatal.

28:19–22 As a general rule, and in the long run, the trustworthy, hardworking person does better than the person chasing a get-rich-quick scheme—especially at the expense of others.

28:23–25 Without honest accountability, it is far too easy for greed to lead to conflict within the family and beyond.

28:26–29:2 It is wiser to abandon a self-centered perspective and use what one has to help others. This is especially true among those who rise to leadership roles and have the power to influence, for better or worse, the lives of many people.

29:3–8 These verses address some of Solomon's key themes in Proverbs: the impact children's behavior has on their parents, the importance of just rulers for a stable society, and the dangers of flattery. He again emphasizes the consequences of actions, the importance of caring for the poor, and the trouble a loose tongue can cause.

29:9–11 Solomon warns about the futility of taking a fool to court, explains how differently good and bad people react to the upright, and extols the wisdom of keeping one's temper.

29:12–13 Rulers are warned against listening to bad counsel and reminded that rich and poor are equal in the Lord's eyes.

29:15–24 Solomon concludes his proverbs with a review of how children's behavior reflects on parents; the impact of those in authority; the importance of taking correction; the dangers of thoughtless speech, temper, and pride; and the foolishness of aligning oneself with lawbreakers.

29:25–27 This final section of Solomon's wisdom ends by affirming that ultimately God's judgment trumps any judgment human beings may offer.

30:1–31:31 Chapter 30 marks the beginning of the final section of the book of Proverbs: the sayings of the

Massaites. Massa was a clan from the line of Ishmael that lived in north Arabia. The two men whose wisdom is recorded here were contemporaries of either Solomon or Hezekiah and probably were influenced greatly by the theology of Israel. Some have speculated that Agur (chapter 30) was a leader of the Massaites and that Lemuel (chapter 31) was probably the king of that region.

30:1–3 Agur, whose words are recorded in chapter 30, begins by acknowledging the frailty of humanity. He is weary. He feels stupid. He doesn't understand life. He lacks wisdom. All this is for one simple reason: He does not know God.

30:4 To highlight how little he knows, Agur asks a series of rhetorical questions. The great news is that there is an answer to Agur's questions: God and Jesus Christ.

30:7–9 Agur makes two requests of God: (1) that God would remove falsehood and lying from his life and (2) that God would give him neither poverty nor riches. He wants enough food to eat so that he will not profane God for not having enough, but he does not want so much that he forgets about God and lives only for himself.

30:10–17 It is important to Agur that truth be held high. He describes ways that deceit and falsehood are expressed in the world: by slandering a worker to his employer, by dishonoring parents, by self-righteousness, by arrogance, and by cruelty.

30:15–16 The reason there is so much deceitfulness and falsehood in the world is that the human heart is wicked and never satisfied. It is like a leech ("horseleach") that continually sucks the blood of its victim and is never satisfied. To describe this concept even further, Agur lists four more things that are never satisfied.

30:18–19 Agur sets forth a series of wonders about the world around us: an eagle in flight, a serpent slithering on a rock, a ship on the high sea, and a couple in love. Agur responds to each of these with a sense of awe.

30:20 Agur wonders how anyone who sees what God has made can act as if God's laws have no validity, continuing on in their evil ways.

30:21–23 Agur lists a series of things that would throw his world into disarray: political, moral, marital, and domestic chaos. The point is that certain structures are essential for society to function. There is a need for order, and this truth drives us to our need for God.

30:29–33 Agur lists four examples of creatures that demonstrate a certain authority: the head of a pride of lions, the greyhound (most other translations interpret this as strutting rooster), the nimble male goat, and the commander in chief of an army. Agur's point is that fools who have tried to present an impressive image or do harm need to stand quietly before God. To persist in their foolishness will inevitably cause problems.

31:1 This final chapter of Proverbs contains lessons that King Lemuel's mother taught him.

31:10–31 At one level, the poem that concludes Proverbs appears to be about a godly wife. On another level, when this chapter is taken in the context of the book of Proverbs, it could also be seen as a personification of wisdom. It is not intended to be a checklist by which a woman is to evaluate her worth. Instead, this is no doubt the expression of how wisdom would act if wisdom were a wife. All of the virtues extolled in the book of Proverbs are mentioned in this chapter: work, wise use of money, wise use of time, caring for the poor, planning ahead, respect for one's spouse, wise counsel, and fearing God. Both men and women can learn from these final proverbs.

31:19–20 The virtuous woman is also selfless and generous. She understands that it is the desire of God to care for the poor, and therefore she does it with all of her heart. At the heart of wisdom is a love for the poor.

31:25 At the end of the day, when people look at the virtuous woman, it will not be how she is dressed that will matter; it will be her strength and dignity. She can face the future confident that she is walking in integrity and that no matter what happens, she will respond with faith in God and faithfulness to her family.

31:27–29 The children of the virtuous woman honor her for her hard work and loving care for them, and they call her blessed. Her husband praises her. He realizes that there are others who have done much, but he tells her that she has surpassed all other women in the world.

31:30 At the heart of the virtuous woman is godly character. Even though she might be physically charming and beautiful, those qualities do not last. The key to her godly wisdom is the fact that she fears the Lord. This is the key application of the entire book of Proverbs (see 1:7).

ECCLESIASTES
OR, THE PREACHER

INTRODUCTION TO ECCLESIASTES ■ The underlying pursuit of the book as a whole is the meaning of life. The author explores the purpose of life and, more importantly, asks what humanity's purpose is as a creation of a sovereign God. Verse by verse through the book of Ecclesiastes, the author answers that question. The purpose of life, meaningless though it may feel, is to fear God and obey His commands.

AUTHOR ■ The question of authorship of Ecclesiastes is a debated subject. Traditional scholarly opinion is that Solomon is the writer of the book, and early church testimony supports this view. It wasn't until the seventeen hundreds that Solomon's authorship came into question. For those who favor Solomonic authorship, this is an elder Solomon reflecting back on the pursuits and teachings of much of his life.

OCCASION ■ The main purpose of the book of Ecclesiastes is threefold. First, it paints a picture of a sovereign God who controls everything in the world. Second, it highlights the meaninglessness of life apart from fearing and obeying the sovereign God. And lastly, the book provides wisdom and counsel for future generations rooted in the things the author learned throughout his life's pursuit of meaning.

1:1 As is common with many books of the Bible, Ecclesiastes begins with a superscription introducing what will follow as the words of the Preacher, the son of David, as scribed by the unknown narrator. It is this opening line that draws the initial correlation between the speaker and King Solomon.

1:3 The rhetorical question here is intended to engage the reader and further emphasize the meaninglessness of life. If everything is meaningless, then the obvious answer to the question posed is that people do not profit from their hard work. The word translated *profit* occurs nine times in the book of Ecclesiastes, but it does not occur anywhere else in the Bible.

1:4 The vanity or meaninglessness mentioned in verse 2 is applied here to humanity's toil by appealing to the cyclical, unchanging world in which we live. Although time is progressing and generations come and go, nothing else is changing.

1:5–8 When viewing examples here of the cycles of nature, it's no doubt that the writer's tone is one of pessimism and weariness—his life exists within this repetitious cycle.

1:12–13 While the narrator establishes the tone and theme in the prologue, it is the Preacher's first-person reflections that form the bulk of the book. The Preacher briefly introduces himself and then moves into his initial reflection on his quest for wisdom. He points out that he isn't just trying to gain some additional insight into the world around him but that he has been tasked with trying to gain all the wisdom under heaven. He describes this as a burdensome task given him by God.

1:15 This proverb supports the idea that what is wrong with the world cannot be righted by humankind. The crooked imagery attests to the perversity of the human condition. Because of the fallen world and sin's presence, the human heart knows only evil unless affected by God. The prophet Isaiah uses this same imagery when he talks about the coming Messiah in Isaiah 40:4.

1:13–18 The reflection in verses 13–15 is repeated in verses 16–18. This passage is one of the key texts used to argue Solomon's authorship because of Solomon's pursuit of wisdom. Whether Solomon is the author or not, the comparison is important because it raises the question, If the wisest person in the world finds everything meaningless, what hope does anyone else have to reach a different conclusion?

2:1–8 The Preacher's pursuit moves from wisdom to a selfish pursuit of pleasure, but he doesn't leave the reader guessing as to his quest's findings—this pursuit also proves to be meaningless. Among the ways he pursues meaning in pleasure are drinking and engaging in folly; building mansions and expansive grounds; and employing servants and amassing animals, treasures, singers, and concubines.

2:9–11 The Preacher's pursuits were greater than those of anyone around him, yet he was able to maintain his wisdom throughout, since the pleasures were a part of his greater quest for the meaning of life. In his pursuit of worldly pleasures, he didn't hold back from anything he desired, but it was all in vain, because he reached the same conclusion that his pursuit of pleasure was meaningless, with no profit.

2:12–16 Not only do the wise and the fool face the same fate, but their deaths render them one and the same—forgotten. Such futile thoughts leave the writer hating all he has worked for in his life. Contrasting wisdom and folly is not unique to the writer of Ecclesiastes, as it is a common characteristic of proverbial writings. What stands out in the Preacher's comparison, however, is that he concludes that the lives of both the wise and the fool result in the same fate (death), thus nullifying the importance of wisdom.

2:17–23 The thought that work might provide some semblance of meaning is negated by the fact that in death a person's life's work will be passed on to someone else. However, the Preacher doesn't simply stop with the conclusion that work is rendered futile in death. Because one's work holds no long-lasting value, all the present pain, toil, and sleepless nights it creates are futile as well. In the Preacher's observation, these two factors—the present and future futility of work—support his conclusion that work also is meaningless.

2:26 It is up to God to determine who will have the ability to enjoy the small pleasures of life. But the Preacher finds even these pleasures of God to be meaningless in the grand scheme of things.

3:1–8 The overarching theme in this passage is the sovereignty of God, whose hand controls everything. Humanity's limitations and futility are made most evident in comparison to God's sovereignty. Part of what frustrates the Preacher about the futility of life is that everything is out of his control.

3:11 This verse seems to stand in opposition to the burdened feeling of verse 10. The first line of the verse reflects on the beauty of God's timing and the eternal perspective He brings. However, the second part of the verse, as well as the context of the verses surrounding it, attests to the frustration the Preacher feels at being unable to understand God's plans and His timing.

3:12–14 Because everything is orchestrated in God's timing, humanity is resigned to settle with enjoying those lesser pleasures of daily life mentioned in 2:24. The timeline God has set in motion cannot be altered.

3:15–22 The Preacher adds justice to the list of things that God will bring to pass in His timing, at which point He will bring justice to both the wicked and the righteous. This idea of future judgment directs the Preacher's thoughts toward death.

4:1–3 The Preacher laments the oppression he sees everywhere, the powerlessness of those being oppressed. But as with many of his other observations, he simply concludes that in lieu of such oppression it would be better to be dead. And beyond that, it would be better still to have never been born and never exposed to the wicked world. He feels crippled in the face of oppression and hopeless to bring about any change.

4:2 This is the first in a series of "better than" statements appearing in the succeeding verses (4:3, 6, 9, 13; 5:5; 6:3). In each instance, the writer emphasizes the negativity of something by comparing it favorably to something else.

4:7–8 If a life spent toiling away in vain isn't meaningless enough, the Preacher makes the point that the one who labors away *alone* is even worse off.

4:13 Having paused to voice his thoughts on the predetermined structure of time and those who live burdened lives, the Preacher returns once again to his subject of futility. While meaninglessness remains the foundation for his conclusions, this verse picks up where 2:23 ends.

4:15–16 The tone in these verses is reminiscent of 2:12–17, making the point that wisdom is no better than folly and power is no better than being powerless. Furthermore, because each shares the human condition

of imperfection, it is highly likely that the young ruler will become like the older one in time.

5:1–6 Amid his discourse on futilities, the Preacher includes a word of caution. God's holiness is not among the meaningless; therefore enter into the place of worship with caution. In this passage, wisdom most certainly trumps folly, and the Preacher gives three examples of worship wherein caution is key: sacrifice, prayer, and vows.

5:5 This "better than" statement relates to taking spiritual vows. Because vows are not a mandatory part of worship, he who never makes a vow is better off than he who cannot keep the vows he makes. Jesus makes a similar warning in Matthew 23:16–22.

5:8–9 The Preacher enters into a discourse on the meaninglessness of wealth. But he begins by warning that while God's divine authority is to be feared, human authority is by nature corrupt and therefore worthy of caution. The drive for profit controls one's desire for power, the perfect segue into the Preacher's observation on the futility of wealth.

5:13–17 These two scenarios illustrate the conclusion that wealth leads to evil. The first scenario is the evil of hoarding all of one's wealth. No pleasure can come from money that is hoarded. The same can be said of losing one's money. If a person depends on money for happiness, then when it is lost the person has nothing and can pass on nothing to his offspring. Whether one's riches are hoarded or stolen, in the end it makes no difference.

5:18 Earlier in his writing, the Preacher observes that because all of life is meaningless, one must seek pleasure in the simple things such as eating, drinking, and enjoying one's work (2:24–26; 3:12–13, 22). When wealth is involved, however, even those small pleasures aren't possible. The blind pursuit of wealth nullifies even the simplest of pleasures.

5:19–6:2 The only exception to the futility of wealth is when it is a gift from God. Just as some are able to find pleasure in their work because God allows it (2:24–26), so some are able to find pleasure in their God-given wealth. The Preacher considers these people to be a fortunate few.

6:3–6 In this case, the "better than" statement has to do with a stillborn baby who has never known anything of the unfairness of the world. That child is better off than the rich man who can't enjoy his wealth.

6:10–12 Humanity can only understand so much, so an increase in words is an increase in meaninglessness. The two rhetorical questions that close this section focus on two thoughts that plague the writer: the uncertainty of the future and the uncertainty of death. Only God knows the certainty of such things, and coming to this conclusion has been the long, arduous journey of the pursuits the Preacher has relayed in prior verses.

7:1 This section of wise counsel begins with several pieces of advice written in the form of proverbs. This pattern will continue throughout most of the verses that follow. The use of this literary style is just one of the elements of Ecclesiastes that convinces some of Solomon's authorship.

7:1–14 These verses function as a response to the rhetorical question of 6:12. The Preacher includes a series of proverbs to present some of the values he has found in an otherwise meaningless life. Two dominant themes are prevalent, and neither theme is new to Ecclesiastes: death (7:1–2, 4, 8) and the wisdom/folly relationship (7:4–7, 9–12).

7:15–22 This second section of proverbs focuses on the limitations of humanity. The Preacher warns against the extremities of life, especially when it comes to pursuing righteousness and wisdom or wickedness and folly. Righteousness and wisdom don't guarantee a longer life than those of the wicked or the foolish. And no one is perfect, so the endless pursuit of perfection will leave one empty-handed. It is the Preacher's advice that people should search for balance in life.

7:23–24 This is a two-verse interlude in which the Preacher reminds the reader of the pursuit of meaning he has been engaged in for much of his life. These two verses also serve to set up the counsel that will follow, in which the action of seeking and finding, or more often *not* finding, is of utmost importance.

8:1 The initial list of proverbial reflections in chapter 7 wraps up with rhetorical reminders to the reader that the Preacher's quest for wisdom has proven that indeed no person can attain it.

8:2–3 God alone controls everything that happens in the world, from the timing of everything to the administration of justice. However, that does not negate the power the king has been given. Just as a person is expected to obey God, the same expectation goes for obeying the king.

8:7–9 Because of the corruption of the world, there is no guarantee that obeying the king will keep someone out of trouble, again pointing out wisdom's limitations in the grand scheme of things. One's view of the authorship of Ecclesiastes determines how the Preacher's insight in this passage is to be interpreted. If the Preacher is not Solomon and not a king, then he is speaking from one subject of the court to another. However, if Solomon is the author, then his advice stems from his personal experience as king and how he expects a king to be treated.

8:10–13 This concept of justice for the wicked was previously mentioned in 3:16–22. It seems evident that the wicked are not receiving the punishment they seem due. And even worse than that, the Preacher concludes that the lack of justice is simply encouraging people to continue acting in evil ways. The only hope one has is that in the end God will enact His justice.

8:15–16 These verses repeat the now-familiar refrain that all one can do is take pleasure in the small things of eating, drinking, and working.

8:17 Humankind's inability to understand God and the way He chooses to work in the world is one of the main themes of the Preacher's discourse. For the other instances when he makes this point, see 3:11; 7:25–29; 9:12; and 11:5.

9:1–6 Reiterating 8:10–15, being righteous and wise doesn't mean one is in control of his or her fate. Supporting this point are five pairs of opposites, all of whom share the same fate—death. Inasmuch as the wicked and righteous share the inevitability of death, God's sovereign judgment is still pending, and it is in that judgment that the difference between the wicked and the righteous will be seen in the end.

9:7–12 Seek pleasure in the little things of life—like eating and drinking, being pampered, and enjoying one's wife—because they will all be impossible after death. While humanity won't find ultimate purpose in these activities, some pleasure will be gained from enjoying them. No one knows when hard times might come.

9:13–16 A short story closes this section of miscellaneous advice demonstrating that in the end everything is futile. The subject of the story is a poor man, but he is wise. He saves an entire city of people only to be forgotten along with the wisdom he shared. This story sums up the Preacher's underlying point that in the end everything, including wisdom, is meaningless.

9:17 To bring his discourse to a close, the Preacher dedicates the final chapters of his work to a series of proverbs covering a wide range of topics. Though these proverbs may seem random, they center on the same few themes: wisdom versus foolishness, dealing with the king, seeking pleasure in the small things, uncertainty of the future, and impending death. They also exhibit the Preacher's undeniable skepticism that foolishness has the ability to taint wisdom.

10:5–7 These verses demonstrate what happens when a ruler is full of foolishness. A foolish decision in leadership leads to a messed-up world.

10:8–11 These proverbs seem unrelated, but each proves an argument the Preacher has been making throughout his teaching: Life is unfair, even for the wise.

10:12–15 If these proverbs sound familiar, it may be because they have parallels in the book of Proverbs. See Proverbs 10:8, 21; 15:2; and 18:7 for these comparisons.

10:16–20 The Preacher will readdress the king in verse 20, but he pauses momentarily to offer two bits of seemingly random advice: Don't be lazy, and sometimes money does lead to happiness by paying for the things that bring enjoyment. The latter seems a contradiction to the earlier section on the meaninglessness of wealth.

11:3–6 These images from nature support the idea that the future is out of human control and in the control of God.

11:7–9 These verses include the most hopeful tone the Preacher has displayed in regard to youth, but he quickly brings the reality of youth's fleeting nature to view. The pattern of verses 7–8 (enjoy your youth, but death is coming) is repeated in verse 9, with the addition of judgment accompanying death.

11:10 The Preacher seems to have been praising youthfulness and encouraging his readers to enjoy it because of its carefree state. But then in the same breath he calls youth meaningless. These discontinuities in the text are not unusual and support the notion that Ecclesiastes covers more questions than answers as the writer wrestles with the meaning of life and God's sovereign work in the world.

12:1–7 The symbolism here illustrates old age and the destruction of the body it brings, all culminating in death. God is in view as the main subject of these verses, because He is the controller of time. The metaphors end with the symbolism of man returning to his state as dust of the ground—a reversal of man's beginning as described in Genesis 2:7 and 3:19. Verse 7 concludes the Preacher's words.

12:8 The switch to the third-person narrative voice in this verse marks the end of the Preacher's discourse and the beginning of the conclusion of the book. For those who hold to Solomon's authorship, these closing verses are from an older Solomon, wise and repentant, reflecting back on the pursuits that dominated his youth. Those who do not consider Solomon the author of this book argue that this shift in perspective simply closes the Preacher's discourse and returns to the voice of the narrator.

12:13–14 These verses summarize the overarching message of the book: Fear God and keep His commandments. Even in light of the futile elements of human life, we are to live in the reality of God's presence and judgment. We will give account to Him for what we do with our journey, though disillusionment may be inevitable. While we may call something "meaningless," we will not truly understand what matters and what doesn't until God reveals it in His judgment of life. He has the final word.

THE
SONG OF SOLOMON

INTRODUCTION TO SONG OF SOLOMON ■ Song of Songs (or Song of Solomon), for the most part, is a book of poems about romantic love.

AUTHOR ■ The title "Song of Songs" suggests that it is the greatest of all songs. There is disagreement among scholars as to whether Solomon wrote Song of Songs, but he is mentioned in the book and many credit him with part of its authorship, if not all.

OCCASION ■ The Song celebrates sexuality in its proper context. While some apply it as an allegory of spiritual truths (for example, the relationship of God and Israel or of Christ and the church), here it is treated as poetry that describes a love relationship between two people.

1:1 While the majority of Song of Songs is love poetry, the first verse serves as a superscription describing the contents of the book. This verse mentions Solomon, who is mentioned two other times. While there is disagreement as to Solomon's authorship, this may indicate that he wrote some of the poems included here.
1:2–4 The poetry begins when the woman takes the initiative to ask for a kiss. The woman also invites the man to get away with her to a private place; the words used in this case refer to an inner chamber. While this is the first entreaty of this kind, it is a theme that appears again.
1:11 The use of *we* doesn't indicate that the man will have a hand in creating the jewelry but rather that he will only enhance her beauty with these gifts of jewelry.
1:15 The beloved's eyes are compared to doves. While it is obvious that this is a flattering statement, we can't be sure what trait of an ancient dove relates to a woman's eyes, whether it is the color, the softness, or the fact that doves are known for faithfulness to their mates.
1:17 The trees mentioned—cedar and fir—were known for their fragrance.
2:2–3 Verse 2 opens with a simile that is then interpreted. Thorns are unattractive and invite anything but intimacy. So in this description, the man is clearly raising his beloved above her peers.
2:7 While this warning can be interpreted as specific instructions regarding one man, it is also interpreted as a strong warning to the woman's peers not to rush their own journey to love. It is repeated in 8:3–4.
2:10–13 Winter in Palestine runs from October to April, the only time rain falls. Since these rains end in April, the timing for the occasion of this poem is probably around May. The woman notes the end of winter and the beginning of springtime in many ways: The rains have ended, the flowers have blossomed, singing has begun, and the turtledove is cooing.
3:1–5 The scene changes throughout this section. What is described here may be more like a dream sequence than an experience unfolding in a chronological way. Verse 2 begins the woman's search for her love—something that happens again in chapter 5.

3:6–11 While in some of the previous poems it is left to interpretation where a poem ends or begins and how much connection exists between them, these verses are clearly a section unto themselves. The only other marriage poem in the Bible is recorded in Psalm 45.
3:11 *Daughters of Zion* is a phrase unique to this book, but it is clearly an alternate for the often used *daughters of Jerusalem*. It is not clear, however, whether the crown mentioned here pertains to a coronation crown or if it is a special wedding crown reserved for this occasion.
4:1 This chapter can be divided into several poems, but thematically they are tied closely together. In verses 1–7 the man declares the woman beautiful. In verses 8–9 he draws her to him, proclaiming his love. Then from verse 10 through the first verse of chapter 5, the poetry focuses on the image of a garden.
4:8 Several mountains are mentioned here. Hermon is perhaps the most well known. It lies in the northern region of Israel. Amana and Shenir are part of the Lebanon range that connects to Hebron in northern Israel. The groom is inviting his bride closer. He wants her close to him and safe from threats, here described as lions and leopards (or panthers).
4:10–11 The groom calls his love his *sister*. In the ancient Near East, *sister* was at times an affectionate term for one's wife.
4:15 While confirming the man's satisfaction with his wife, this verse introduces a new image associated with her body—a well or fountain.
4:16 Here is the woman's invitation for her groom to enjoy her virginity. She invites him in, using symbolic language with openly sexual overtones. These words refer to the satisfaction of one's sexual appetite.
5:1 This verse documents the man's satisfaction after the couple's experience. The last part of the verse is attributed to the daughters of Jerusalem. It is an invitation for the couple to enjoy their partnership with gusto, drinking their fill of love even to the point of intoxication.
5:2–6 The man calls his beloved by four terms of affection: *sister, love, dove, undefiled.* While getting back up from bed was more involved in the ancient world (dirt

floors that would dirty her bare feet, less sophisticated door locks that were difficult to latch and unlatch), the woman's hesitation to answer the door costs her the opportunity to be with her lover.

5:7 The mistreatment she experiences doesn't even seem to faze her. In contrast, she had previously been assisted in her search by the watchmen (3:3). In this case, it is likely that the watchmen represent the social difficulties the woman works her way through in order to get to the object of her desire.

5:8–16 Earlier in this chapter, the woman's focus is exclusively on herself and her own comfort, but in these verses she focuses exclusively on the man. He had earlier described her as he was addressing her; here she describes him, yet she is addressing the daughters of Jerusalem. In ancient Near Eastern literature, physical descriptions of one's lover, as found here, were almost exclusively male descriptions of females.

5:11 The comparison to gold implies great value, especially since gold had to be imported to Palestine.

5:15 The image of pillars of marble implies that his legs are strong.

5:16 It was customary to describe another's physical characteristics from top to bottom, but after working her way down, she goes back up to his lips once more. This, along with 1:2, suggests that she is particularly attracted to his mouth—both his kisses and his sweet words.

6:11–13 Some disagree as to who is speaking here. Most likely the woman is talking, and the man invites her to turn to him in verse 13.

6:12 This may be the most confusing verse in the book. The wording varies widely among the different Bible translations. There are two things that most commentators agree on, however. First is the difficulty of the text. And second is the fact that it reflects passion so powerful that someone gets carried away with it.

7:1–2 This passage is considered even more intimate than that of the honeymoon (4:1–15). The groom begins with her feet, perhaps because she is dancing. While his comparison of her navel to a goblet and her belly to a mound of wheat does not sound flattering from a modern perspective, these descriptions show how his wife satisfies him.

7:4–10 The man compares his wife's eyes to Heshbon, which is a beautiful area to the east of the Dead Sea. He also compares her to a palm tree. In verse 8 his desire to climb the tree and take hold of its fruit indicates his desire to be intimate with her and enjoy her breasts.

8:6 The seal indicates ownership and personal identification. One kind of seal was a cylinder. This seal was common in Mesopotamia and was rolled across clay to leave an impression. The seal more common in Palestine, called a signet, was simply pressed into clay to make an impression.

8:13–14 After the man calls out to the woman, her words are reminiscent of earlier images—the roe (gazelle) or young hart (stag; see 2:9, 17). And she finishes the book in a familiar way—by calling him away to solitude and intimacy.

THE BOOK OF THE PROPHET
ISAIAH

INTRODUCTION TO ISAIAH ■ The book of Isaiah is a potentially intimidating challenge for novice Bible readers, but it is a rich and rewarding pursuit for those willing to delve into it. Its sixty-six chapters comprise the fifth longest book of the Bible in terms of word count. But even more daunting than its sheer length is the prophetic nature of the writing. The author writes of events that cover centuries, and it can be difficult in places to tell if he speaks of the present, the near future, or the long-range future. Yet while the prophet's narrative can be a bit confusing in places, large portions are quite clear in presenting a merciful God who does not give up on His people even though they have been repeatedly rebellious and wayward.

AUTHOR ■ The name *Isaiah*, meaning "Salvation of Yahweh," is closely related to the name *Joshua* ("Yahweh is salvation"), which is the Old Testament equivalent of the name *Jesus*. However, not much is known about the prophet other than what he reveals in his book. Little more is known about his personal life. Justin Martyr recorded the tradition that Isaiah died a martyr's death at the hands of King Manasseh, sawed in two (possibly the source of the reference in Hebrews 11:37).

OCCASION ■ Isaiah's purpose in writing is described during a vision in which he receives his calling from God (6:6–10). He is instructed to speak to his people, even though most are spiritually rebellious and disobedient and will not listen to him. (Jesus later quotes this very passage to explain why He uses parables to teach the people [Matthew 13:13–15].) Isaiah faithfully brings God's word to the people, warning anyone who will listen of what is to come.

1:1 The kings listed are all from the southern kingdom of Judah. Isaiah's ministry lasted into the reign of King Hezekiah, who took the throne no later than 716 BC and ruled until 686 BC. Isaiah 6:1 reveals that Isaiah received his calling in the year that King Uzziah died, which was 740 or 739 BC. Therefore, Isaiah's ministry was no less than twenty-three years and may well have lasted fifty years or longer.

1:1 Most of the other Old Testament prophets spoke of bringing *the word* of the Lord to the people. Isaiah is unusual in stating that what he is presenting is a *vision*, although there are a few other exceptions (see Obadiah 1). Isaiah's father, Amoz (who is not the same person as the prophet Amos), is mentioned several times in this book.

1:2–10 Isaiah's presentation is essentially an arraignment, a legal accusation argued before the judges of heaven and earth. His unfavorable comparisons of his people span the gamut from a senseless ox to the iconic cities best known for wickedness: Sodom and Gomorrah.

1:11–15 Isaiah's questions reveal that although the people have a pretense of religious commitment, their prayers and offerings are devoid of meaning, and God is not pleased with them.

1:16–23 Jerusalem (the faithful city) has become corrupt, along with the values of its inhabitants. The rulers take bribes and do not defend the helpless. Still, if the people repent and submit to God in obedience, they can prosper. If not, they will not survive the coming judgment.

2:2–3 Isaiah writes of the last days. Some debate the time frame of the last days with much speculation, but all that can be safely presumed is that the reference is to a period of time after Jesus' incarnation that will culminate with His second coming. More important than *when* this will occur is *what* the people of God can expect. Isaiah describes an elevation of the mountain of the Lord's temple, which had been built on the spot where Abraham had attempted to offer Isaac. In the Bible, mountains often symbolize stability and are often associated with divinity. Isaiah's description indicates that one day the kingdom of the Messiah will be preeminent over all the kingdoms of the earth. The nations (Gentiles) will desire to know God's truth and will stream to the house of God, resulting in an unprecedented time of peace.

2:4 Although the Messiah is not named in this passage, later portions of Isaiah (chapters 7, 9, 11, 53) will be quite specific about His character and the role He will play in all this. In this instance, He fulfills the role of judge. This portion of Isaiah regarding the Messiah's future kingdom is repeated almost verbatim in Micah 4:1–3. We don't know if one writer borrowed from the other or if they both drew from the same source.

2:5 Isaiah challenges the house of Jacob (Judah and Jerusalem) to walk in the light of the Lord. The existing situation is bleak. Isaiah's account of God's people might have described any of the surrounding unbelieving nations. In fact, they have adopted various superstitions, idolatry, and occult practices from numerous places.

2:7–9 The people have wealth and resources, but rather than seeing such things as blessings, those assets further turn their hearts away from God.

2:11–22 The people's arrogance will be destroyed along with their dependence on wealth and idols, and it will be a turbulent transition. Isaiah warns that people will flee to caves and hide among the rocks. They will again acknowledge God, but their change of attitude will begin with a sense of great dread. The result, however, will be the disappearance of all idols and their exaltation of God alone.

3:1–3 God's people reject the government of their good, caring, beneficent God, so He removes all supply and support from Judah and Jerusalem through a series of foreign invasions. Included in their losses will be food, water, all leadership of any consequence, honor, skill, and respect. Within a hundred years of the death of Isaiah, this prophecy is fulfilled when Babylon breaches the walls of Jerusalem, destroys the city, and carries off most of the people.

3:4 In place of qualified leadership, Judah will get leaders who are mere children. The reference is usually less in regard to physical age than to the person's maturity level. *Boys* refers to those without wisdom and experience. However, this prophecy comes true literally when Manasseh succeeds his father, Hezekiah, as king at age twelve. During Manasseh's fifty-five-year rule, he acquires the designation of the most wicked ruler in the history of Judah.

3:5–7 Isaiah describes a terrible breakdown of social order: young against old, crude against honorable, neighbor against neighbor, and individual against individual. People will be desperate for leadership, but no one will be qualified.

3:8–14 In their confusion and disarray, the people will remain arrogant, plundering the poor and continuing to parade their sin. The problem will be widespread, but there will be exceptions. Isaiah assures righteous people that things will end well for them.

3:15–26 As the men of Judah fall in battle, the women will lose every pretense of arrogance and symbol of finery, reduced to desperation and groveling.

4:1 God's warning that He is about to remove stay and staff (3:1) from Judah is initially confirmed by the Assyrian invasion but is demonstrated even more emphatically by the subsequent Babylonian domination.

4:2–6 Isaiah's writing takes a sudden shift. He moves abruptly from talking about the nation of God as ruins to a section where every phrase seems to insist on the future fulfillment of the kingdom of God. Something has happened. There is a new day beyond the disgrace of the people of the old covenant, and Isaiah is serving as a herald of that coming day. The difference is the appearance of the branch of the Lord—Israel's Messiah. Those who come to the kingdom by His name are holy in Him. Their names have been duly recorded. God has washed away their filth. It is not the trappings of wealth that ensure survival (3:18–23) but the purifying fire of God in the judgment poured out on His Messiah.

4:2 Some people believe that in this case the *branch* of the Lord signifies believers—the remnant of humanity who repent and are therefore beautiful and glorious. However, in chapter 11 Isaiah will use a branch analogy where the indication is clearly in reference to God's Messiah, Jesus.

4:5–6 Eventually the day will come when God's divine presence will be evident to the senses. God will be the ever-present light, with no need for artificial lighting. Believers know this in their best moments, but someday they will recognize God's presence clearly and continually.

5:1–7 Vineyards were important commodities in ancient Judah. When someone went to the trouble of planting a vineyard, he expected to eventually reap fruit from his labor. So the song of the vineyard is a prophetic parable, and there is no doubt as to its meaning.

5:1–7 The vineyard of the Lord represents the house of Israel. God has taken great care of His vineyard. He has done all He can, but still the vineyard does not yield fruit as it should. God looks for the fruit of justice but finds bloodshed. He desires righteousness but hears instead an outcry from the oppressed, poor, and powerless. Therefore, God will remove His protection, and what had once been a beautiful vineyard will be trampled and destroyed. With no further blessing (rains) or cultivation, it will become a wasteland.

5:7 In this case, *Israel* refers to the southern kingdom (which is most often referred to as *Judah*). After the northern kingdom's fall to the Assyrians, *Israel* continued to refer to the people of God wherever they were.

5:8–10 This is a direct pronouncement of woe upon the people. They have ignored God in many ways, including failure to acknowledge that He owns their land and established laws to protect the poor throughout the generations. Families could legally lease their land to others for income, but it was supposed to eventually revert to the original family. The people of Judah, however, disregarded God's instructions and joined house to house and field to field.

5:13–17 Since so many refuse to exercise justice and righteousness, God Himself will enact those standards—beginning with His people! His righteous judgment will include exile, hunger and thirst, the death of many, and the humbling of the rest. And through His demonstration of justice, God will be exalted.

5:24–30 God is the One who pronounces judgment, but the means of affliction will be nations that are far away. Isaiah is clear on the matter: God is angry, and His anger is not easily diffused. The Lord is portrayed as whistling for distant nations to come, and when they do they roar as lions, growling as they seize their prey. The once-prosperous land of Judah will be a site of darkness and distress.

6:1–4 During a vision, Isaiah is shown the throne room of God. He sees the Lord on the throne, surrounded by mysterious fiery angelic creatures. This is the only biblical mention of seraphim, although some of the heavenly beings mentioned in Revelation have a similar description (Revelation 4:6–8). Some consider the seraphim to be the angels closest to God since that is how they are described here. Where angels appear in the Bible, they almost always insist that people focus on God.

6:5 As soon as Isaiah witnesses the glory of God, he senses that he is in mortal danger. Even Moses, when he had asked to see God, had been told that no one could see God's face and live (Exodus 33:20). Isaiah immediately acknowledges his sin and the sin of the community in which he lives.

6:6 The live coal is a symbol. When God established the day of atonement ceremony, one duty of the high priest was to take coals from the altar into the most holy place and burn incense there (Leviticus 16:11–14). Isaiah is witnessing the actual heavenly temple.

6:8–13 Isaiah must have experienced an immediate inner change. When he hears the invitation of God, he volunteers at once to go and serve. God does not provide many specifics, but the severity of Isaiah's mission is clear: He is being sent to people who will not listen or respond to him, yet he is to continue his work until their nation is destroyed. Israel and Judah have been like a mighty oak, but eventually they will fall and only a stump will remain. Still, the stump will be the holy seed—the remnant of believers from which the tree will grow again. All is not lost, but the near future will not be pleasant.

6:8 Though it may seem that Isaiah's calling comes after he had already started to prophesy, since it is placed in chapter 6, it is doubtful that Isaiah worked as a prophet for a time prior to receiving his heavenly calling. He probably simply waited until this point in his narrative to relate the events of his call. The despair of the first five chapters is somewhat offset by this unmistakable experience with the Lord God Almighty, still on the throne and enlisting people to do His work, even during times of national peril and failure.

7:1–2 Ahaz is not one of Judah's better kings. He brings much trouble on the nation by encouraging false worship. In this section, he is shown as weak and frightened, and for good reason. The northern kingdom of Israel has formed an alliance with the Syrians, and they are bearing down on Jerusalem.

7:2 Sometimes the nation of Israel was referred to as *Ephraim*, because that particular tribe of Israel was large and centrally located among the others. Consequently, the battle described in this section came to be known as the Syro-Ephraimite War. The alliance of Syria and Ephraim had been formed to defend against the expanding empire of Assyria—a useless action since Assyria will be God's instrument in executing His judgment.

7:9–16 God emphasizes the certainty of His message in two ways. First, He encourages Ahaz to strengthen his spiritual commitment. Then He gives Ahaz permission to ask for a sign to confirm that the word of Isaiah is the true promise of God. Ahaz expresses reluctance to make such a request, claiming that he does not want to test the Lord. Actually, it is his lack of commitment that is testing God's patience, so God chooses a sign: A virgin will conceive and bear a son named *Immanuel* ("God with us").

7:17–20 Although Judah will not fall to the Assyrians, they will suffer from the presence of such a powerful enemy. The Assyrians will arrive like swarms of flies and bees. The Assyrian king will humiliate Judah like a razor shaving off a warrior's hair and beard—an ultimate humiliation at this point in history.

7:21–25 The glut of milk and honey might sound promising at first, but it actually predicts a shortage of young animals to nurse and the pollination of flowers in fields that should have been growing crops. This less flattering scenario is confirmed by the prediction of briers and thorns.

8:1–2 Isaiah is to father a son and give the child a Hebrew name that designates the coming of an invading army. It is an intriguing name and the longest personal name in the Bible: *Maher-shalal-hash-baz*. The name is a battle cry, meaning "quick to the plunder, swift to the spoil." Some people try to make the case that this child of Isaiah's is the child predicted in 7:14, but the name is a far cry from *Immanuel*. And unless Isaiah has a second wife, the child-of-a-virgin requirement is out of the question because the prophet already had one child (7:3).

8:4–10 Before this new child of Isaiah's can develop any significant speech patterns, the Assyrians will have defeated both the armies that are threatening Judah: Aram and Israel (mentioned here as King Rezin of Aram and King Pekah son of Remaliah of Israel; 2 Kings 15:37). Judah will not be unscathed; Assyria is portrayed as a large devouring bird of prey. But God will be with Judah, and Assyria will not prevail.

8:12–14 Unbridled fear can lead to various problems. But such problems can be prevented if one's source of fear is properly placed. Those who fear God—who regard Him as holy and live to do His will—can be spared many other fears.

8:18–22 Even the powerful Assyrian Empire is no threat for those who place their trust in God. But those without God exhibit a pathetic existence. Without the genuine source of truth, they seek advice from mediums. When they get distressed and hungry, they curse their leaders and their God. And still they perceive only distress, darkness, and gloom.

9:2–7 The gloom Isaiah warned of in 8:22 is temporarily offset by this foretelling of a great light to come. This great light will accompany the birth of a child, and the reader immediately recalls Isaiah's recent promise of Immanuel (7:14). In retrospect, it becomes clear what Isaiah means in these prophecies. Yet for his original audience, Isaiah's words must have sounded almost too good to be true, and most likely confusing as well. The Wonderful Counsellor is to be a descendant of Adam, yet He is also mighty God and everlasting Father. And His other title, Prince of Peace, must have been puzzling in light of the war and destruction Isaiah had been predicting. Clearly Isaiah is bringing good news, yet it must have been a bit mystifying to his generation.

9:13 After a short passage about this person who will reign on David's throne, Isaiah goes right back to why God's anger against Israel has not relented. The people have simply refused to turn to the Lord.

9:14–18 The nation is beginning to deteriorate, but in their pride the people presume they will rebuild the nation even better than before. Wickedness is pervasive among young and old, rich and poor. So God is about to deal with both the head (elders and the well-to-do) and tail (false prophets) of Israel.

10:1–4 Within this woe is a promise. Those who have been preying on others will be brought to justice. Their options are limited: be taken captive or be included among those who will be killed.

10:5 Israel has a false sense of strength that is exposed when a mightier adversary (Assyria) threatens. But Israel's greatest adversary is God Himself. Isaiah makes it clear that in this case God's anger is not quickly turned away (9:12, 17, 21; 10:4). Assyria only *appears* to be the threat to Israel; that powerful nation is actually the hand of God.

10:6–19 Even though God chooses to use Sennacherib and the formidable military might of the Assyrians, Assyria will also be judged. They have no respect for the things of God, and they take it for granted that Jerusalem will be next on their list of easy conquests. God will allow them to trouble Judah, but only to a point. When God completes His work of judgment against His own people, Assyria will find itself powerless against Him.

10:16 The leanness mentioned here implies a wasting disease. The intensity and proximity of the Assyrian threat are better detailed in 2 Kings 19:35–37, where an angel of the Lord puts to death 185,000 Assyrian soldiers overnight, followed by the withdrawal of Sennacherib. Perhaps the deaths are connected to this disease.

10:20–25 The remnant of God's people who survive and endure will have the opportunity to witness the end of God's anger and again learn to rely on Him alone.

10:32–34 The Assyrians will do ample damage to Judah before being miraculously repelled by the power of God. They barrel through many of the cities but only get close enough to Jerusalem to shake their fists before being cut down like a lofty tree.

11:1 During Isaiah's vision of his calling from God, he had been told that the nation will be destroyed like a large tree cut down, leaving only a stump (6:11–13). Here he again writes of a stump, but the imagery is a little different. In this case, the stump is of Jesse. The kings of Judah had all descended from Jesse's son David, yet the time will come when it seems that the line has ended. But from that stump a branch will one day spring up. It is a marvelous fact that God's Son will be born from the line of the kings of Judah.

11:2–5 This prophetic section of Isaiah provides insight into the character of Christ as king. He will be filled with the Spirit of God. He will have no hint of the corruption that seems to permeate human positions of power. Instead, the qualities of righteousness and

faithfulness will be so clearly attributed to Him that they are called His girdle (or belt). One day His righteousness will result in the frightening vengeance of God against the wicked.

11:6–16 The influence of this Prince of Peace (9:6) is described in idyllic images. Fierce predators and their prey will become happy inhabitants of the kingdom. Children can safely play around cobra (cockatrice) nests. All who are ruled by the king will have perfect security. This blessing is not just restricted to Judah and Israel: The whole earth will be full of the knowledge of the Lord. Through the knowledge of this ruler from the root of Jesse, peace will be extended far beyond the borders of Israel.

12:1–6 God's people will be called out of captivity, and all their adversaries will be overwhelmed. In response, people will offer widespread and unbridled praise to God. Praise seems especially meaningful after God's people have been delivered from a particularly difficult experience. Praise had been abundant after the Lord delivered the Israelites from Egypt and when David united the kingdom after the civil war between Israel and Judah. Later generations will praise God during the days of Ezra and Nehemiah, when they return to their homeland after several decades in captivity.

13:1–11 Ruthless and arrogant, Babylon is considered the glory of kingdoms (13:19). But the might of Babylon at its pinnacle is no match for the power of the Lord God Almighty. Isaiah declares its certain destruction.

13:15–16 The haughtiness and ruthlessness so prevalent in Babylon will be replaced by terror and anguish. As revealed here, some of the actions taken against Babylon will be horrendous.

13:17 The superpowers of Isaiah's day were the Assyrians and the Persians. There was not always a clear succession of one empire falling and being replaced by the next. Rather, various nations coexisted for periods and had numerous coalitions and conflicts. For example, there was an alliance between the Medes and Babylonians in the late 600s BC, but about fifty years later the Medes were absorbed by the Persians, who then conquered Babylon. Various opinions exist, but it is likely that Isaiah's reference is to an early conquest of Babylon by the Assyrians in 689 BC rather than its more notable defeat by the Persians in 539 BC.

13:19–22 There is general agreement that the *Babylon* in verse 19 refers to the city rather than the empire, sometimes referred to also as Babylon or as Babylonia. The people's arrogance and sense of immortality will be shattered. After centuries of existence and influence, Babylon will come to an inglorious end. History confirms that Babylon does indeed become a ghost town by the seventh century AD, verifying Isaiah's prophecy.

14:1–2 Though Isaiah's prophecy includes the future destruction of Babylon, for Isaiah's original audience, the nation is a threat to Israel and Judah. What a surprise and comfort it must have been for them to hear the prediction that one day, thanks to God's great compassion, He will reestablish Israel and people will flock there from all nations.

14:12–17 This is sometimes said to be a biblical account of Lucifer's pride that caused him to be cast out of heaven, but there is no basis for this in the text. This poetic description of the king of Babylon (identified in 14:4) stands as a warning for anyone who allows ambition to override commitment to the service of others.

14:24–27 As Babylon is powerful, so is Assyria. Yet this nation, too, will be crushed. God has planned it, so it is certain to happen.

14:28–32 Isaiah's oracle warns the Philistines, here identified as Palestina, against rejoicing so quickly at the demise of their enemies. The fall of one enemy leader might be cause for celebration, but victory is tentative because others will arise to replace the fallen leader. The Philistines won't even have the honor of dying in battle. Instead, they will be afflicted with famine.

15:1 The Moabites were frequently at odds with the Israelites. During Israel's exodus from Egypt, Moabite king Balak had hired Balaam to curse the Israelites, but God didn't allow him to do so (Numbers 22). Moabite women had attempted to seduce the Israelites (Numbers 25:1–9). During the era of the judges, Moab had oppressed and financially burdened Israel until Ehud assassinated Moabite king Eglon (Judges 3:12–30). Saul and David had both defeated Moab, but Solomon had been persuaded by one of his wives to worship the Moabite god Chemosh (1 Kings 11:1, 7).

15:1–5 The origin of Moab can be traced back to the child conceived as a result of the incestuous relationship between Lot and his older daughter (Genesis 19:30–38). Moab is going to be destroyed, but not because of its ethnic heritage. The Lord despises the Moabites' false gods and high places of idolatry. He hates the way they have repeatedly turned against His people with violence. Yet Isaiah appears to demonstrate a heart of sympathy for Moab in distress. Entire cities (Ar and Kir) will fall in a single night. Even armed men trained for danger will be filled with fear in the face of a far more powerful enemy.

15:5 This is not the first time God's sympathy has been recorded for Moab. Israel had not been permitted to destroy Moab on the way to the promised land (Deuteronomy 2:9), nor was Moab among the nations that were to be dispossessed by Joshua and his generation during the conquest of Canaan. Ruth had been from Moab, returning to Israel with Naomi to eventually become the great-grandmother of David and be included in the genealogy of Christ (Ruth 4:13–22). It is clear that God's mercy extends beyond the borders of Israel.

16:1–6 Moab would have done well to unite with Judah (send lambs) because Judah will escape the conquest of the Assyrians (10:24–25). Instead, Moab will experience great suffering (15:6–9; 16:7–12).

17:3 Syria was one of the great ancient nations. It was common for an entire nation to be referred to by the name of its leading city, so Syria is called *Damascus*. (Similarly, Israel is sometimes referred to as *Ephraim* after its prominent tribe.) When a key city falls, the entire nation feels the humiliation of the defeat.

17:1–6 At one time Israel and Syria had been impressive nations. But here Isaiah compares them to a human body wasting away, a field that has already been harvested, and an olive tree picked clean except for a few remaining olives that can't be reached. Damascus is captured by Tiglath-pileser, a king of ancient Assyria, in 732 BC. Shortly afterward, the kingdom of Israel and its capital city of Samaria will also be subdued. All that will be left of Syria is just a small percentage of the fruitfulness that she once enjoyed, proving the accuracy of Isaiah's prophecies.

17:7–14 After trouble arrives, the people will forsake their idols and turn to God—something they could have done all along but refused to do. Their once-popular fertility cults will no longer be a pleasant diversion. In such a time of great trouble, God alone is a rock of refuge.

18:1–2 As Isaiah turns his attention to nations farther away from Israel, his description becomes more exotic: wings (strange insects, perhaps), vessels of bulrushes, scattered and peeled (clean-shaven, perhaps) people. The land of Ethiopia, south of Egypt, was essentially the remotest portion of known geography for those living in the Near East at this point in history.

18:1–3 Perhaps Ethiopia, sometimes referred to as Cush, had sent its envoys to Israel to broach the idea of forming an alliance against Assyria. No further evidence of any such proposal exists, although it was, after all, described as a terrible nation. The Ethiopians are not alone in their desire to resist Assyria, so Isaiah's message is directed to all people.

19:1–4 Egypt has a history with Israel. God had long ago removed His people from Egypt, but the influence of Egyptian idolatry had continued. Egypt remained a formidable power largely because of the Nile that provides constant water in a land where such a resource is rare. The Nile allows Egypt to produce grain for much of the world, and Egypt takes great pride in the Nile.

19:5–17 Isaiah warns that the Nile will one day dry up, causing many previously stubborn people to humble themselves before God in the midst of their great suffering. None of Egypt's leaders or presumed powerful idols can keep the mighty river flowing to deliver the nation from disaster.

19:22–24 The long-range prediction for Egypt is positive. God has a wonderful plan of grace that includes the Egyptians. It must have been quite shocking for Isaiah's original audience to hear that Assyria and Egypt, like Israel, will someday be embraced by God. They will all know and fear the Lord, and somehow they will all worship together.

20:1–6 As the Assyrians move into Philistine territory, capturing the city of Ashdod, God gives Isaiah an unusual assignment: The prophet is to remove his clothing and sandals and minister three years this way. These actions are symbolic of what will happen to Egypt and Ethiopia. Their people will be led away to Assyria, naked and humiliated. Anyone who had looked to Egypt for support against Assyria (as Judah had been tempted to do) will be disappointed and frustrated.

20:2 It is debated whether or not Isaiah was completely naked for this three-year period, though it seems that way. Still, some people presume a sense of propriety would be necessary and believe that the prophet was expected to remove his *outer* clothing. Either way, whether Isaiah was totally nude or only in his loincloth undergarment, it would have been both disconcerting for the prophet and attention-getting for those who saw him. For anyone who may have presumed him to be among the lunatics who run about scantily dressed, the fulfillment of his prophecy would be especially emphatic.

21:2–5 Isaiah describes his vision of the destruction of Babylon (identified in verse 9) as a source of anguish, making him bowed over, dismayed, and appalled. What a contrast with the way others, oblivious to the coming destruction, live around him.

21:9 Babylon is only mentioned by name, which helps explain the "desert of the sea" reference in verse 1. Babylon referred to their southern region as "the land of the sea," so Isaiah seems to indicate their impending defeat by the Assyrians. Babylon will eventually rise against Assyria and rule in glory for a short time, but then the Medes and Persians will rise to power.

21:10 Isaiah leaves no doubt that God is the source of his vision.

21:11–12 Although Edom is not mentioned by name, its identity is known because of *Seir*, the residence of Esau's descendants and another name for Edom. Isaiah agrees that another morning is coming but adds that another night will follow immediately afterward. In other words, their circumstances are not likely to improve.

22:1 In this list of God's pronouncements directed at Assyria, Babylon, Edom, and other nations, it is unsettling to see one against Jerusalem as well. Jerusalem sits on a hill, intended to be a place of great spiritual value. It is supposed to be a light to the surrounding nations. But the people have rejected God, their source of spiritual strength and insight. Consequently, Isaiah addresses the city as a valley.

22:3 Because Jerusalem has persistently committed evil, its people will face discipline from the Lord. The leaders will attempt to flee the city to save themselves rather than stand firm in faith, but they will be captured. Isaiah is not speaking symbolically; his words are literally fulfilled. When the Babylonians siege Jerusalem, King Zedekiah and his entire army try to sneak out of the city, but they are pursued and captured. The Babylonians make Zedekiah watch as they kill his sons, and then they blind him (2 Kings 25:1–7).

22:12–13 God instructs His people to weep, mourn, put on sackcloth, and humble themselves. And although He is the One who will bring the day of disaster, the people will not respond to Him. They attempt to prepare for conflict but refuse to acknowledge God or repent.

22:15–25 Shebna is a high-ranking official who was involved in dealing with the Assyrians when they threatened Jerusalem (2 Kings 18:17–19:37). But instead of a godly humility, Jerusalem's leaders appear to have a strange arrogance and even a hedonistic fatalism. Shebna attempts to establish the glory of his name in a potential day of disaster for the people of God. As a result, he is replaced by another man, Eliakim, who has more concern for the good of those who are looking for responsible leadership. Eliakim is an honorable and successful leader for a while, but even *his* time of influence will be limited.

23:1–5 Tyre was a location known for its ships and merchants at a time when many nations counted on trade with the Phoenicians. If Tyre was to fall, numerous other powers would suffer as well. Isaiah lists Tarshish (very likely located in Spain), Chittim (Cyprus), and Egypt among those who will feel the effect of Tyre's destruction. Even the seas are personified as mourning the loss.

23:5–6 Tyre will face a generation or more of trouble, and its fall will create more than economic concerns for its allies. The description is similar to that of the death of a loved one. Egypt will be in anguish. Tarshish will wail.

23:13 No matter how respected a person or nation may be in the opinion of humanity, a refusal to acknowledge God will result in failure and dishonor. No nation's security is assured. Even the Babylonians (here identified by their most powerful territory, Chaldea) have been bested by the Assyrians.

23:15–18 Babylon will again become a world power, and Tyre will also revive after seventy years. In the meantime, however, Tyre is portrayed as a forgotten prostitute in a pitiful journey through the cities of the world, singing songs of better days. And when Tyre *is* eventually reestablished, it will be to benefit the people of the Lord. Even this proud city will be used to accomplish God's purpose.

24:1–4 All the lands of the earth are aware of God and His majesty. Everyone has been given a conscience that is more or less informed concerning the ways of God (Romans 2:15). All should seek to further understand and experience God's presence because all are guilty before the Lord and without excuse for breaking the relationship with the Almighty Father. Eventually people in every territory will face the Lord's righteous wrath in judgment.

24:3–5 It is important to understand why God would do such a thing—completely lay waste and plunder the earth. It is because people have totally defiled the earth through disobedience and utter disregard for His laws. God established a covenant with His people, and they have broken it.

24:6–16 As a curse consumes the earth, the time for partying comes to an end. Wine loses its appeal, and the tambourines are put away. The singers, dancers, and merry-hearted people return to their homes as joy turns to gloom for those who do not know the Lord. There will be exceptions, although very few. However, those few who escape God's judgment on the wicked will respond with shouts of joy and praise.

24:16–23 People who remain disobedient will be so furious that the very pit of destruction will seem to swallow up all the inhabitants of the earth. Once-powerful authorities and rulers in high places will be called to account. At long last the wicked oppressors, both in heaven and on earth, will be shut away for eternity as the Lord Almighty reigns on mount Zion and in Jerusalem. It will be a day of great vindication for those who trust in the Lord's unfailing righteousness.

25:1 The Lord is capable of silencing a victory song in a moment and stopping the onslaught of the mightiest power. And when His people see such powerful demonstrations of God's protection, the result is spontaneous praise.

25:2–8 The destroyed city is probably representative of all the cities or nations that have defied God throughout the ages. Israel's victory is not just another instance of "the little guy" able to survive another day with a massive military force arrayed against him. This time those ruthless powers are facing utter defeat. God's victory will be world-changing and life-giving. The veil of misery and confusion will be lifted. Death will be defeated, and tears will all be wiped dry.

26:1–3 Isaiah records a song to the glory of the city of God, thus directing the reader's attention to the kingdom of heaven. This chapter provides a lens through which present-day believers can anticipate the ultimate victory of God on behalf of His people in the coming day of the Lord. Believers need to live in the light of that event every day of their lives. As they become more steadfast, God provides perfect peace.

26:19 Not only shall the remnant of Israel and Judah be saved, but also the inhabitants of the world will love the judgments of God and learn the way of righteousness. Even the righteous dead shall live, and their bodies shall rise because of the conquering Lord.

27:1 Many of the nations surrounding Israel had legends and mythologies that included their gods doing battle with sea monsters, of which leviathan was one of the best known. But Isaiah uses the image of the great sea monster to symbolize the powerful nations that show more regard for such mythologies than for the God of Israel. When it comes down to a matter of conflict, no other power can rival the power of the Lord.

27:1 From the opening chapters of the Bible, serpents have represented evil and opposition to God. Sin entered the world as Adam and Eve were deceived by the serpent and disobeyed God (Genesis 3). But no sooner did that take place than God announced that the seed of the woman would eventually crush the serpent's head. The slaying of leviathan is another portrayal of God's triumph over an evil serpent.

27:1–6 By slaying the serpent, God protects His kingdom, which is symbolized by a vineyard to which God devotes much personal attention (see 5:1–7). In that day of the Lord's deliverance, Israel's influence will be greatly expanded. Jacob will take root, growing to eventually fill the world with fruit.

27:8–13 The rough east wind may be a reference to the Babylonians. For a while, Jerusalem will be desolate and forsaken. But the day will come when the people of Israel will be again gathered one by one and return to worship God in Jerusalem.

28:1–4 As Isaiah begins a series of woes, the first is directed to *Ephraim*, another name to indicate Israel (the northern kingdom). The nation is portrayed as both a drunkard and a fading flower. It is a proud nation yet is past its prime and soon to be humbled by the Lord's hailstorm, destructive wind, and flooding downpour. Many of Isaiah's prophecies concerning Israel will be fulfilled with the invasion by Assyria in 722 BC, after which most of the population is carried away into captivity.

28:5–8 Israel will have a remnant of people who are protected by God. That holy remnant will turn to the Lord Almighty and find Him to be beautiful and glorious. In contrast, the drunken priest and prophet will find no help from the God they are supposed to represent. They will still claim to bring a prophetic vision, but since their own lives are covered with filth, who will believe them?

28:9–13 Perhaps the misguided priests and prophets feel they are being talked down to by Isaiah and respond by taunting. If so, Isaiah is not fazed. He acknowledges that they don't have to listen to him, but they will soon be forced to learn their lesson from foreign oppressors—the Assyrians. Instead of growing little by little in the way of righteousness, they will little by little fall away and eventually be utterly broken.

28:15–22 The covenant to cheat death is something the people of Judah (mistakenly) imagine will protect them from the grave, but the truth is that their covenant with death will be annulled. No other gods or religions can save them. Consequently, it is appropriate for them to stop mocking Israel (the northern kingdom) and realize their own peril.

28:16 *Corner stone* is a term that frequently applies to the Messiah, Jesus Christ (Zechariah 10:3–4; Acts 4:9–11; Ephesians 2:19–20; 1 Peter 2:4–8). It is unclear whether Isaiah intends this particular reference to be messianic. Perhaps he is simply affirming that God will ensure justice and righteousness in Judah.

28:23–29 Isaiah uses a number of analogies to assure his listeners that their coming troubles will only be temporary. Just as planting requires first breaking up the soil to be effective, and just as certain seeds must be beaten or ground to break the outer shell, God's people need to be broken in order for them to become useful and productive. Hard times will be necessary to effect positive change, but the difficulties will not be permanent.

29:2 After addressing Israel (28:1–13) and then Judah (28:14–29), Isaiah's narrative narrows to the city of Jerusalem, addressed here by the name *Ariel*. This name can mean either "lion of God" or "altar hearth." In the context of Isaiah's message, the latter definition is more appropriate. Just as Jerusalem had been the place where people brought their animal offerings to be burned in sacrifice, the city itself will soon be a site of bloodshed and burning.

29:3–4 God is going to bring judgment on faraway nations and on the northern kingdom of Israel, and then He is going to judge the very center of His presence on earth during the days of the kings—the city of Jerusalem. His people have become haughty, and He is going to humble them.

29:5–8 When the Assyrians approach, it may seem that disaster is imminent for Jerusalem, but God will provide divine protection. The invaders will become like a bad dream that vanishes with the dawn of a new morning.

29:9–16 This is a description of a spiritual daze. The prophets are a disgrace to their titles. Worship is not sincere but rather confused and hypocritical. What passes for wisdom is neither genuine nor lasting. It is a ludicrous situation: People who reject the leadership of God are like lumps of clay questioning the work of the potter.

29:17–24 Isaiah interjects a reminder that better days are ahead, when Zion will experience real joy. It will be a time of widespread divine healing. The deaf will hear and the blind will see. Even the land will have a vast increase in yield. Those previously subdued by the powerful will be vindicated, and the poor will celebrate their deliverance. All of the redeemed will glorify God. Even those who have gone astray in spirit will be brought back to an understanding of and receptivity to spiritual instruction. This exciting announcement of hope stands out for the faithful remnant of God's people.

30:1 Isaiah returns to his series of woes, now directed to rebellious children. God has a long history of delivering His people in times of trouble, but the Israelites are like children who never seem to learn to trust Him.

30:1–2 Rather than turn to God for deliverance, the people of Judah seek help from Egypt. Egypt has tangible assets—chariots, horses, and soldiers—while God is all-powerful but invisible. People still make the same mistake of trusting what can be seen.

30:3–7 The people's plan isn't God's plan, so it will surely fail. Isaiah sees clearly that Egypt will be no help to Judah against the Assyrians.

30:8–14 Judah is like a child who will not listen to wise advice. The people resent the seers and prophets who pass along the message of God to them, so God instructs Isaiah to write down their words as a witness against them.

30:15–17 The wise course of action is to repent and wait quietly and faithfully for God to act, but the people are unwilling to hear. Instead, they run toward the clamor of Egyptian power, forgetting the God who created them and who had, on a previous occasion, rescued them from the hand of Egyptian oppressors.

30:18–26 The sad fact of the people's actions is that all the time they are seeking help from foreign human powers, God yearns to show them grace and compassion. The very reason for their adversity and affliction is to help them recognize truth. He wants them to acknowledge their prophets (teachers) again. He

wants them to hear His voice and dispose of their idols. He wants to bless them with rain and food. He wants to bind up their injuries and heal their wounds.

30:33 Tophet was a location south of Jerusalem associated with fire and burning. It was where, on occasion, children were sacrificed to Molech, a god of the Ammonites. The Assyrians will be disposed of like a load of wood readily consumed by fire, except the source of heat in their case is the breath of the Lord.

31:1–3 Turning to Egypt is an offense to God. In Israel's history, Egypt was a place of bondage, a nation of idolatry, a symbol of commitment to the things of this world. God had done things through Moses that were far beyond the capabilities of just a man with a staff in his hand. Great waters had parted. Water had come from a rock. And a nation of God's people had been liberated from a great oppressor. Now those people are attempting to go back voluntarily rather than recall what God has done and trust Him to continue to deliver them.

31:4–9 God is not intimidated by any adversary. He will come down to fight on mount Zion and shield Jerusalem from harm. Just as the angel of death had passed over homes in Egypt with the sign of blood on the doorposts, God will see that danger passes over Jerusalem in the days to come. Assyria certainly appears to be the stronger power by far, yet it will fall as Jerusalem stands.

32:1–8 In his writing, Isaiah moves back and forth between his present time and the messianic age. Israel and Judah had recently known very few good kings, so Isaiah again looks to the future to describe a different kind of leader yet to come. Much good can come from an excellent king. A ruler who leads in righteousness provides stability and protection even during a time of shifting circumstances. And God's future king does more than that. He gives sight and hearing. He helps people discern what really matters. He showers them with gifts from heaven. When such a leader arrives, it will become clear how incompetent previous leaders have been.

32:9–15 Isaiah offers people a happiness that does not turn to panic when the grape harvest fails. No harvest of wine can produce the kinds of results among God's people that are available from the Spirit of God.

33:1 The sixth and final woe in this section (28:1; 29:1; 29:15; 30:1; 31:1) is directed toward the destroyers (probably referring to Assyria). The destroyer will eventually be destroyed, and the betrayer will be betrayed. According to the sovereign plan of the Lord, Assyria will have its day, but like all the powers that have come before, it will then fall.

33:2–6 The righteous remnant of people realize that the God of Israel controls all their affairs with His mighty hand. They can be happy as they wait for the Lord and His grace to be their salvation in times of trouble.

33:7–13 The nearness of destruction will terrify the sinners in Zion. Brave men will weep. Highways will be empty as people fear to travel. Once-plush areas of land will become like deserts. The people who have made plans apart from God will be subject to burning and consumption.

33:14–24 Those who continue to place their faith in God will behold His great beauty in a land that stretches to the horizon. The humble servant of the Lord will find refuge, but the proud cannot dwell there. The Lord Himself will be king, judge, and lawgiver. For the time being, however, Jerusalem is like a ship in disrepair, nowhere near ready to go to war. Its future might be glorious and secure, but it will first experience additional strain and conflict.

34:1–4 The destruction described in this section is massive and vivid. The coming of the Lord's mighty vengeance will go beyond the destruction of the peoples of the earth and will include the very heavens being rolled up like a scroll as stars seem to fall from the sky.

34:5–17 Why is Idumea (Edom) singled out in this passage as representative of all the nations that will face the sword of the Lord? One likely possibility is that Edom took great joy at the harsh discipline of God against His people. The descendants of Esau had long shown disdain for the people who descended from Esau's twin brother, Jacob.

34:14 God has a jealous love for His people (Exodus 20:5). He may discipline them and even use unbelieving nations to do so. But those nations dare not celebrate the shame of the people of God. The Lord will not stand for their pride, their boasting in their idols, their unbelief, and their immorality. They are likely to end up as Edom does in this passage: destroyed, desolate, deserted, and never to rise again.

35:1–10 With chapter 35 comes an abrupt change from the previous chapter. Isaiah brings marvelous news. A day is coming when people will be able to see what they have only been able to see by faith. Land that is currently parched and dry shall be fruitful, with refreshing streams of clear water for thirsty lips. People will be strengthened, encouraged, and healed. A highway—the way of holiness—will be made available for the redeemed and those the Lord has ransomed who travel to Jerusalem. Dangers will be removed, and the general atmosphere will be one of gladness and joy.

36:1 The reigning king in Judah is Hezekiah—one of the godlier kings of the southern kingdom. Hezekiah's nation has watched the Assyrians get nearer and nearer in their conquests—seemingly unstoppable. Now these powerful enemies are at the threshold. The northern kingdom of Israel has fallen, and much of Judah has already suffered from Assyrian domination. It looks as if Hezekiah and Jerusalem will be next. Another description of these events is found in 2 Kings 18–20. Isaiah's account was written first and may have been the source for the author of 2 Kings. It is also possible that both writers drew from yet another (unknown) source.

36:1–3 The king of Assyria at this time is Sennacherib. After he captures a number of Judah's well-defended cities, he sends a message to Hezekiah by way of his field commander. The Assyrian official goes to a public place where the leaders of Jerusalem and the populace as a whole can hear his message. Speaking in the language of the common people (36:11–12), he delivers a frightening warning that contains much truth interlaced with lies and half-truths, all designed to inspire fear among the Judahites and make them less likely to support Hezekiah in resisting the Assyrians.

36:4–7 The people of Judah had a tendency to place their trust in foreign alliances and considered going to Egypt for help against Assyria, but not even Egypt can stand up to Assyria. (God had told Isaiah as much.) The Assyrians greatly outnumber those in Jerusalem, and the people might feel more insecure than usual because Hezekiah has removed many of the idolatrous high places and altars where they tended to go instead of worshipping God at the temple.

36:12 If the Assyrians conducted a lengthy siege against Jerusalem, it wouldn't be just the leaders who suffered, but everyone within the city. The Assyrian field commander makes sure the people of Judah are aware that they might soon be forced to consume their own body wastes for lack of other options.

36:13–20 The Assyrian field commander adds some lies into his argument as he tries to dissuade the people from counting on the faith of King Hezekiah. He says that trusting in their Lord will not work for the people of Judah—a wicked falsehood. To even attempt to compare Judah's God to the idols of other nations is a horrible deception. An earnest and humble request for God's help will not be wasted breath. God hears the pleas of His people, as will be clear in the chapters that follow.

36:21–22 The field commander finishes his speech, and the people remain silent as Hezekiah had instructed them—probably not the response the Assyrians had hoped for. The underlying theme of the message has been, "Fear Assyria and its king and surrender now." Three palace officials with torn clothing (a sign of mourning) deliver the message to King Hezekiah.

37:1–4 Hezekiah shows great wisdom in responding to this crisis situation. He, too, tears his clothes and puts on sackcloth in a demonstration of repentance. He goes to the temple and sends for Isaiah, realizing that the words of the Assyrian messenger have been deeply offensive to God.

37:5–7 When Isaiah receives God's reply for King Hezekiah, the first instruction is to not be afraid. Assyria will be soundly defeated, not due to any military competence on the part of Judah, but because God will intervene in those international affairs. God informs Isaiah that Sennacherib will return to Assyria, where he will be killed.

37:8–13 The king of Assyria makes a hasty retreat. Before he leaves, however, he receives word that Egypt is sending troops to help Judah, and he sends another threatening message to Hezekiah. Sennacherib is quite confident that Judah's God poses no more threat to him than all the other gods he had confronted in other nations.

37:14–20 When Hezekiah reads the second letter from Sennacherib, he returns to the temple to lay his problem (literally) before God and to pray. In doing this, he recognizes the great power of Assyria but also acknowledges that the power of his God is much greater still, and rightly, he asks for God's deliverance.

37:36–38 In a single night, an angel of the Lord kills 185,000 Assyrian soldiers. With his army decimated, the next morning Sennacherib returns to Assyria the way he had come. Eventually he is assassinated by two of his own sons.

38:1–6 Isaiah's historical accounts concerning Hezekiah are not in chronological order. Hezekiah's near-death illness must have occurred prior to his encounter with Sennacherib described in chapters 36–37. One indication of this is the fact that God's decision to extend Hezekiah's life is accompanied by His promise to deliver Hezekiah and Jerusalem from the Assyrians, so they must have still been a threat to Judah at that time.

38:2–3 Hezekiah turns to God with a plea for deliverance from this trouble. He attests to his own faithfulness as he weeps bitterly. The fact that Hezekiah can stand before God and point to his devotion is a good indication that he is indeed attempting to live a righteous life. Many kings of Judah are remembered primarily for doing evil in the sight of the Lord, but Hezekiah is a positive exception (although he is far from perfect, as Isaiah will record in chapter 39).

38:7–8 In answer to Hezekiah's heartfelt prayer, God sends Isaiah back to the king to tell him he will have another fifteen years of life. The reversal of the prophet's message is so rapid (see 2 Kings 20:1–11) that perhaps Hezekiah is a bit reluctant to accept the good news at face value, so Isaiah gives him a sign from God. The sign is fascinating: A shadow that has just come down ten degrees on a sundial is reversed and goes back *up*.

38:10–20 Anyone who has been unexpectedly freed from an immediate death sentence is likely to be dumbfounded. Hezekiah expresses his emotions in a psalm-like work with the first stanza describing his initial feelings of despair and the second stanza focusing on praise and elation.

39:1 It seems likely that Isaiah positioned the accounts as he did because Hezekiah's encounter with the Babylonian leaders segues into the prophet's next chapters foretelling a Babylonian captivity to follow.

39:2 Hezekiah welcomes his visitors and hides nothing from them. He naively shows them everything about Jerusalem that might make it attractive to the invading force of a foreign power.

39:5–7 Speaking through Isaiah, God declares that the time will come when everything of worth in Jerusalem will be taken by Babylon. Even descendants of the king will be carried off, and nothing will be left. This was likely a surprising prophecy to Hezekiah. The predominance of Assyria made it the likely candidate to conquer smaller nations. But from this point onward, through the writing of Isaiah, the Babylonian captivity is in view.

40:1 While God will continue to correct His people, His word from this point forward is filled with much comfort. Yet this is not a comfort defined by the spiritual equivalent of a plush sofa but rather a deeper sensation that demands careful attention because it comes at a great cost.

40:1–2 God provides His prophet with not only a *message* to deliver to the people but also clear instructions as to the *emotions* to accompany the message. Isaiah is to speak tenderly to the people as he brings them an uplifting prophecy of comfort.

40:3–5 Despite the optimism of Isaiah's message, Jerusalem will continue to face great difficulties for decades to come after Isaiah. When will this good news arrive for the people of God? It will first be announced by a special prophet who will be a voice crying out for the people to prepare the way of the Lord. In the short term, this voice is probably that of Isaiah. But centuries later, this figure will be identified as John the Baptist for an entirely different generation of God's people (Matthew 3:1–3).

40:6–8 God is eternal and everlasting, as opposed to humanity, which is like grass in its fleeting existence. This is a world of the perishing. People come and go in the blinking of an eye. But God provides permanence through His Word, which stands forever.

40:18–20 When people begin to comprehend the reality of God, all idolatry seems foolish. God is the eternal Creator, Savior, and Deliverer. Idols, in contrast, must be man-made. Care must be taken that they don't too quickly rot or fall over. Any glory of the idol comes from gold overlay and silver adornment. Yet God's people have repeatedly forsaken His leading and turned to such idols.

40:21–27 The Lord made all things, visible and invisible. The most impressive rulers do not faze Him. He can bring the high and mighty to nothing, and He can raise up the poorest slave to sit among princes. He is familiar with each individual star throughout the universe, so it should be no surprise that He is just as knowledgeable of each human being He has created.

40:28–31 God is not only *aware* of the struggles of His people but also is actively *involved*. The affairs of life are demanding, but God is consistently present to provide strength to the weary and power to the weak. With the renewed energy He provides, God's people can soar on wings like eagles and run without wearing down.

40:28–31 God is the One who was at work behind all of the power struggles and international events in the Near East in the eighth century BC. The people of Judah may have seen only a powerful king with an unstoppable army bearing down on them from the East, but Isaiah is trying to make them aware that God was behind the situation. The Lord takes no pleasure in disaster, but He works all things according to the perfection of His holy will.

41:3 The observation that the threat from the East moved on unfamiliar ground ("by the way that he had not gone with his feet") suggests that Isaiah is no longer talking about Assyria. The new power in the East is most likely Cyrus, the Persian leader whom the prophet will soon identify by name (44:28–45:1). In addition, Isaiah has already said that the Medes will conquer Babylon (13:17–19). A later reference to Cyrus speaks of him coming from the north (41:25) because that is the site of his Babylonian conquests. Worldly powers will continue to shift, but God remains in control of them all.

41:5–10 As trouble approaches, people will respond in different ways to the power of God. Those who don't know Him will be fearful, forming alliances and turning to the worship of other gods. But God's people can respond differently. God tells them not to panic. He will not only be with them but also strengthen and help them.

41:8–16 God's plan for His nation Israel is no insignificant part of His overall design for the glory of His name and the redemption of the elect. It will be from Israel that one special servant will come as the only Redeemer of His people. God had called Israel into being for a purpose, and He had never abandoned that purpose for His chosen ones. He was always with them and would continue to help them.

41:17–24 Strong enemies will continue to try to destroy God's people and undermine His plan. But God is able to defeat all such enemies, seen and unseen, and even demonstrate His strength through the weakness of His people. Through Isaiah, God foretells all that will happen. Then He challenges the nations and their idols to do the same, proving that their gods are worth nothing.

41:25–29 God will allow the Babylonians to conquer His people and carry them from Judah into exile, but God's people will then see Babylon defeated by Cyrus and the Medes. And one day the Lord will send a herald of good news—a servant who will bring good news of redemptive love to God's people.

42:1–4 Isaiah describes a specially designated representative of God on whom God will bestow His Spirit. God's servant will faithfully promote justice until it is achieved throughout the earth. In the meantime, he will not add to the burdens of the weak, who are described as bruised reeds and flickering candles ("smoking flax").

42:1–17 Isaiah provides four servant songs: the first here, with three others to follow. Sometimes, as in this case, the servant he refers to will be the coming Messiah. On other occasions, he writes of Israel as the servant of God. His intended meaning is usually clear based on the descriptions he provides and the context of what he is saying.

42:5–9 Israel and Judah *should* have been a light for the Gentiles, but as it turned out, they were the ones who were actually blind and in desperate need of a savior. They had seen and heard God working among them, yet they paid no attention.

42:8–12 This is definitely good news that should result in praise among all the nations. Kedar was an Arabian area noted for its nomadic peoples and their flocks. The "inhabitants of the rock" are sometimes translated as

Sela, an Edomite capital south of the Dead Sea. Edom, like Judah, had previously received Isaiah's words of warning (34:5–17), yet here they are invited to sing a new song to the Lord.

43:1–5 In their condition, the only effective savior for Judah will be the Lord Himself, and in this section God promises them the best thing He can—that He will be with them as they go through the challenges they face. Yes, they will still have to deal with deep waters and flames, but the floods will not overwhelm them and the fires will not consume them. Even when Egypt and Ethiopia fall, God will save Israel. With words filled with love and commitment, God tells His people not to be afraid.

43:1 This great promise of God to summon His people will be fulfilled at several levels. First, Isaiah is prophesying an exile to Babylon, after which many of God's people will eventually be restored to the land under the leadership of Ezra, Nehemiah, and others. Second, after the coming of Jesus Christ and the outpouring of the Holy Spirit upon the church, people of faith will be gathered to the Lord in an amazing way. Finally, at the second return of Christ, the Lord will gather His people and take them home for good in His eternal kingdom.

43:6–13 God's people will be carried away to faraway nations, but God will gather them when their exile is over. It will be an act of redemption, salvation, and love. It will also be a demonstration of God's great power.

43:14–19 Even before the people go into Babylonian captivity, God assures them of their release. The Israelites have always seen their exodus from Egypt as a historical high point, but God tells them to stop focusing on the past so they can see the new thing He is doing that will be even better.

43:20–28 Some people are likely to ask the question, If God is going to gather His people eventually, why would He go to the trouble of having them experience the pain of being conquered and forcibly leaving their land? Isaiah has already pointed out several times that the people are stubborn and unrepentant. Here God compares them (unfavorably) to wild animals. God is receiving more acknowledgment from jackals and owls than from the people who supposedly worship Him. After their exile, they will be much more receptive to the love and commitment He continually shows them.

44:1–5 It is common knowledge that people need water to live, but those dwelling in the ancient Near East were more regularly reminded of that fact than modern people who have access to clean water regularly. Without water, there is no life. God uses this fact to teach that without His Spirit, there can be no spiritual life. Without the Spirit of God, people are first bone dry in a spiritual sense, and eventually dead in their sins.

44:4–5 The Lord is the provider of both needs: the water that sustains physical life and the Holy Spirit who bestows blessings to those who know God. Isaiah foretells the day when large numbers of people (springing up like grass and willows, sometimes understood as poplar trees) will turn to God. Not only that, but their reluctance will disappear and they will again *desire* to be known as believers in the Lord.

44:9–20 There is only one true God, but the world has never had a shortage of false gods. Isaiah has already noted the futility of idol worship in a number of places (see 40:18–20; 41:7, 21–24), but this section is one of the longer and more explicit descriptions. The images here point out the ridiculous nature of the idea that an object a person builds can then provide miracles for that person. People's minds were so spiritually cloudy that no one questioned the logic of praying to a block of wood.

44:28 Isaiah has already written that the Medes will bring the rule of the Babylonians to an end (13:17–22). More details are provided in 41:2–4, 25. But here Isaiah provides the name of the Persian leader: Cyrus. Isaiah ministered during the eighth century BC, long before the birth of Cyrus, which leads some people to question this particular account. Those who aren't convinced of the reliability of predictive prophecy believe that the specific mentions of Cyrus must have been added to the narrative at a later date—perhaps even after the release of the exiled people of Israel. Others believe the omniscience of God was at work in Isaiah's writing and that the prophet's ability to be so exact only proves that he spoke for the Lord.

45:1 An *anointed one* is someone chosen by God for a special task of deliverance and salvation for God's people. It is highly unusual to see the title applied to a non-Israelite emperor, yet God is able to use a wide variety of resources to accomplish His will. He will bring Cyrus to power by removing the obstacles that stand in his way (including the Babylonian Empire). God is more than capable of calling such a person for the benefit of His people Israel, even though the individual may not personally acknowledge God.

45:1–3 After defeating the Medes in 549 BC and Babylon in 539 BC, Cyrus is well established as the leader of the Persian Empire. History may give Cyrus the credit for his accomplishments, but Isaiah declares that it was God who went before Cyrus to level mountains, break down strong gates, and accumulate wealth.

45:9–13 Whatever benefited Cyrus in his rise to power would eventually benefit Israel. To question God's methods was as useless as a lump of clay challenging the skill of the potter. As Creator of heaven and earth, surely God was a more than competent architect of plans to deliver His people.

45:21–25 One of the end results of God's will is the deliverance of His people. But in addition, the population reaching to the ends of the earth can turn to Him to be saved. Every knee will bow and every tongue will attest to the strength and righteousness of Israel's God.

46:1–7 It's clear in the images included here that idol worship is a lot of work for the participants. People have to provide the gold and silver for the image, as well as pay a craftsman to create it. Then they have to transport the finished product with some difficulty, either carrying

it on their shoulders or transferring it to a beast of burden. When they get it to the desired location, they then have to be sure to anchor it. Finally, they pray to it—all to no avail. All the while it is God who has carried His people, not the other way around. Israel's God had carried His people from cradle to grave. He is always available to sustain and rescue them. There is no comparison between Yahweh and these idols.

46:1 *Bel* is not synonymous with *Baal* of the Canaanites, although the two were similar in influence in their respective cultures because they were the prominent deities. Bel is also known as Marduk. Nebo was the son of Bel and the god of wisdom.

46:8–13 The Babylonian leaders will fare no better than their gods. God's purpose will soon be revealed and accomplished. He will summon a bird of prey from the east (Cyrus). As a result, the Babylonian rebels will be defeated and salvation will come to the people of God.

47:1–7 God portrays the nation of Babylon as a young virgin girl sitting in the dust, having lost not only her throne but also everything that had made her attractive. Forced to work and to roam, she will be subject to nakedness and shame. Sitting in darkness and silence, Babylon will have time to contemplate how it has arrived at such a state. God makes that point clear: He allowed His people to be overpowered by Babylon, but the Babylonians had shown them no mercy. Soon Babylon will be on the other end of the power scale and will seek the mercy of stronger powers.

47:8–10 Babylon is a proud nation, thinking itself invincible. The people practice magic and sorcery, and they feel their secret knowledge gives them an advantage. They are wicked at heart, even though they think no one is aware of their evil actions.

47:11–13 Isaiah provides few details regarding the transition between Babylonian rule and the conquest of Babylon by Cyrus of Persia. The event is noted in Daniel 5, with a little more said about the feast of Babylonian leader Belshazzar with a hand writing on the wall one night and his replacement by Darius the Mede the next day. (Darius may be another name for Cyrus, or perhaps a different leader appointed by Cyrus.)

48:1–4 When it comes to arrogance and stubbornness, Babylon is no worse than God's people. God observes that the muscles in His people's necks are iron, and their foreheads are brass. They pride themselves in being associated with God and having a long, magnificent spiritual history. But in reality, they have strayed from God's truth and righteousness.

48:5–7 God reveals some things ahead of time so this generation of people cannot claim that their idols brought about those events. At other times He withholds sharing His plans so that His people cannot claim to know the hidden things of God. Both methods serve to direct His people's focus back to Himself.

48:8–22 Despite repeated rebellion among His people, God remains committed to them, ultimately for the glory of His own name. In the meantime, He continues to love them as He attempts to test and refine them through their struggles. Much of that refining process will be accomplished through the approaching Babylonian captivity, but Israel's testing will have limits. They can count on being released from their future captivity, although it is still tragic that such an action is necessary. If Israel had been obedient, they could have had peace, righteousness, fertility, prosperity, and more. Because of their lack of faithfulness, however, they will suffer much.

49:1 The servant songs of Isaiah are among the most exciting features of this impressive book of prophecy. The first of four songs for God's servant is found in chapter 42. The other three songs are found in this chapter, chapter 50, and chapter 52. (Scholars vary as to how many verses of each chapter the songs include, whether the first six, seven, or thirteen verses.) These songs and the surrounding material foretell a servant of God who will be a deliverer not just of Israel but of all the nations. In fact, the emphasis of Isaiah's writing shifts to the point that neither Babylon nor Cyrus is mentioned again. The people of God are still in a captivity of sorts, but it is less the harsh physical captivity of specific nations and more of a spiritual bondage that only a special agent of God can remedy.

49:1–4 The figure at the center of Isaiah's songs is the personification of the faithful Israel. As the songs progress through the book, it becomes clearer that this perfect image of Israel will actually come as a person with an appeal that extends far beyond the nation of Israel. The song included in the opening of this chapter is initially addressed to the distant nations—Gentile territory.

49:5–7 The work of the servant will result in salvation reaching the ends of the earth. Nevertheless, he will first be deeply despised—a theme that will be further developed in Isaiah's remaining songs (chapters 50 and 52).

49:8–13 The promises here include the land being restored and firmly established, prisoners of sin and death receiving their liberty, the hungry being fed and satisfied, and streams of living water becoming available for those who thirst. In retrospect, it is easy for modern believers to see that many of Isaiah's prophecies describe the life and ministry of Jesus Christ. For the original hearers, however, those promises must have seemed wonderful, yet also mysterious and possibly confusing.

49:20–26 Israel will undergo a period of bereavement, yet when times improve she will discover great numbers of descendants she was not aware of prior. She will even be a strong and positive influence on Gentile nations. Normally captives are not expected to ever be rescued, but God will certainly deliver His people from the hands of their captors.

49:25 This section may be an instance where both short-term and long-term fulfillments occur in regard to the same prophecy. When the people of Israel were released from Babylonian captivity and returned to their homeland, it might have seemed that Isaiah's prophecy was coming true. Yet at that time they were weak and disorganized, and they demonstrated no influence on

other nations. It would seem that Isaiah, then, was also referring to a future event.

50:1–3 A shift of address is made between Isaiah 49 and 50. In chapter 49, Israel is addressed as a mother. But as chapter 50 begins, God is addressing children— perhaps the faithful remnant among His people—and explaining that He has allowed their mother to be sent away for a while because of her sins. It is not unlike a husband declaring a divorce, which was accepted at this time in Israel's history (Deuteronomy 24:1–4). But in the case of God and His people, the divorce is only temporary (see Isaiah 54:5–7; Jeremiah 3:6–13). God could easily have protected His people, but they had repeatedly refused to call on Him.

50:4 The narrative now shifts to the perspective of God's servant once again in the third of the four servant songs of Isaiah. Israel is in a desperate state, yet the people are not helpless. The wonder of the Gospel is that God, in His justice, comes again as God in His mercy. Unlike the other people of Israel, the servant of God welcomes instruction and is never rebellious. His words bring life. His ear listens to the voice of the Lord morning by morning. He stands on the side of the covenant people and never turns back from his mission to love God.

50:7–9 What will be different about the servant to enable him to remain strong while others falter? He knows where to turn for strength. His help will come from God. As long as God is his vindication, he will never be overcome or put to shame.

51:1–3 God has a long, reliable record of proving that He can deliver His people even when things seem hopeless. Citing one such instance, He tells the people to recall the story of Abraham. Sarah and Abraham had wanted a child throughout their entire lifetimes, but Sarah had been unable to conceive. God waited until Sarah was well past childbearing age, so that when she got pregnant there could be no doubt that God was the One responsible for the miraculous event. Through Isaac, and then Jacob (Israel), comes a nation that inherited the promises God had initially made to the faithful Abraham. In time that nation turns away from the Lord. But God's point is that just as He had been able to create a great number of people from the aged Abraham and barren Sarah, so, too, can He restore them even when all they see are ruins and wastelands.

51:7–11 Without the love and power of God, humanity has no chance of life, even for a moment. But by the strength of the Lord, His redeemed will be forever kept alive. They will come to Zion with joyful singing. The return under Cyrus will be only temporary, but one day a heavenly Zion will be made available to them forever.

51:9 *Rahab* is a reference to Egypt. Egypt's association with the dragon is similar to the link between leviathan (27:1) and some of the Canaanite nations.

51:10 This verse includes references to Israel's exodus from Egypt: "dried the sea" and "made the depths of the sea a way for the ransomed to pass over."

51:12–16 God is the only guarantee for the people to gain for themselves what they cannot acquire by their own strength. He is the Creator who set the heavens in place, laid the foundations of the earth, and controls the raging sea. He can surely remake His people and secure for them blessings that will never be taken away.

51:17–20 The people of Judah are hearing both good news and bad news from God through the lips of Isaiah. They will certainly experience the wrath of God, symbolized by potent wine that causes them to stagger. Alcoholic intoxication can be a deadly thing, but even more devastating is to be drunk on one's pride and false delusions of safety. For a while the people of Judah will be inconsolable as they undergo famine, violence, and ruin. They have sinned, and they will suffer the consequences.

51:21–23 God's wrath will not last. After a time, He will deliver Israel as He passes the cup of wrath to her enemies. For God's people, it will be like waking from a fitful sleep to greet the day with a message of truly wonderful news. Their enemies will threaten them no more.

52:1–6 The people can dress in beautiful garments again, feeling anew the thrill of freedom and redemption. Shaking off the dust of the past, they will arise as a glorified city of God. They had previously been at the mercy of Egypt, and more recently Assyria had been a major threat. But God has demonstrated His sovereignty by delivering them from both worldly superpowers. Babylon will be next, but the Babylonian Empire will be no more a problem for God than any previous threat.

52:7–8 Not surprisingly, messengers bearing good news from far away were well received in ancient times. Watchmen were stationed to hear and report updates. But the best news that Judah could hear is a simple message: The God of Israel reigns.

52:7–8 Any good news is reason for celebrating. Judah's release from Babylon is one such example. But the emphasis on peace and salvation suggests that here, too, Isaiah is looking beyond his own times to the coming of the Messiah and His kingdom. At that time people can see the Lord return to Zion with their own eyes.

52:9–12 God's deliverance of Judah will get the attention of all nations. His people will burst into song in response to God's comfort, redemption, and salvation. He will call them out of unclean places, personally escorting them both before and behind.

52:13 Any lasting positive change among God's people must come about through the work of God's servant. This section is the last (and longest) of the four servant songs in Isaiah. It is also probably the best known because various portions of it are frequently cited throughout the New Testament.

52:13–15 God's servant will not look like a specially designated leader of humanity. In fact, his appearance will be appalling and disfigured. Perhaps this is a reference to Jesus' disfigurement on the cross. Or the point might be simply that the Messiah will not be a physically striking figure. Still, the servant's ministry will be effective. World leaders will acknowledge the truth of his message, and ultimately he will be raised up and highly exalted.

53:1–6 The actions of the servant are for the benefit of humanity. He is standing in the place of weak and sinful people. He carries the grief they should feel. He receives the wounds they should receive as a result of their transgressions. He takes the weight of the Lord's crushing justice in response to human iniquity. He endures the punishment so people can have peace. People have wandered away from God, but the servant pays the penalty for their iniquity.

53:4 It is evident in Isaiah's writing, and becomes even clearer in the New Testament, that humanity's penalty is not owed to any person or spiritual force other than God the Father. From the beginning, God made it clear that justice demanded consequences for sin. But through a plan between the heavenly Father and His Son (the servant in Isaiah), the death penalty fully deserved by sinful humanity was paid by Jesus Christ. Because of the great mercy of God, believers have the gift of freedom and eternal life.

53:5–12 Isaiah's final song about God's servant speaks with precision about the final days and moments of the life of Jesus Christ. Among other things, Jesus was pierced (John 19:33–34); wounded (Matthew 26:67–68; 27:26–31); silent (Matthew 27:12–14); with the rich in His death (Matthew 27:57–60); and numbered among transgressors (Luke 23:32–43).

53:9–10 He has done nothing wrong, yet he will face oppression, the corrupt judgment of his human peers, physical death, and, finally, the grave. If this all seems unjust for the servant, it must be emphasized that he is acting to ensure God's justice. Isaiah makes it clear: It is the Lord's will for him to suffer.

54:6–8 God seems to have abandoned His people for a short time, but after hiding His face for a moment, He extends His great compassion and kindness as He renews His relationship with them.

54:9–10 God has been angry with His sinful and unrepentant people, but He recalls His previous promise to Noah (Genesis 9:12–17) and determines not to take action that will destroy them.

54:13–17 God promises that His people will be safe from all enemies. Tyranny and terror will be far removed. This promise has never been perfectly fulfilled because God's people throughout the ages have had to contend against ungodly people and forces. Yet no weapon directed against the church can ultimately prosper. One day the perfect peace of God will be realized.

55:1–6 God extends an open invitation for all to come to Him. This invitation begins, in a very literal sense, with a call extended to the people of Judah after their captivity in Babylon. On a broader level, however, it is an appeal for them to return to God.

55:2–3 Idolatry is like a spiritual diet of junk food when God is offering fresh bread. No matter how hard people may work, they are not likely to be satisfied if their efforts have no lasting purpose. God's spiritual food and drink is His Word. It costs nothing, but it does require a listening ear.

55:3 God reminds His people of the covenant He had made with David. God had promised David that one of his descendants would be on the throne of an everlasting kingdom (2 Samuel 7:8–9, 16). It appears for a while that the dynasty of David has come to an end when Judah falls to Babylon and the people are carried away as captives, but in the New Testament Paul will quote this verse from Isaiah as proof that Jesus is the One from the line of David who will fulfill God's former promise (Acts 13:34).

55:4–6 In light of this leader who will eventually arrive, the invitation to come is extended to everyone. God's people will become a beacon that will attract other nations.

55:10–11 People don't have to understand the mind of God. In fact, it is impossible to do so. God's thoughts and ways are far beyond human capacity to comprehend. Yet God's Word and works never fail. Isaiah compares them to rain. Water falls from the sky as rain and snow and evaporates back into the atmosphere. Yet as it follows that simple cycle, it waters the earth, causes seed to sprout in the soil, and provides food for everyone on earth. Similarly, God's Word falls on people and returns, and as it does, it accomplishes all that God intends it to do.

55:12–13 These are indeed assuring words for people coming out of exile. After decades of captivity and dejection, they can expect joy and peace, with even nature seeming to burst into song around them. It will be a historic event that will stand as an everlasting sign of God's power and love for His people.

56:3–8 The people of Israel and Judah have developed a sense of special status in their relationship with the Lord. God's intentions to rescue His elect will broaden to include foreigners and eunuchs, two groups that have never before had full privileges in Israel. Among other restrictions, foreigners and eunuchs had not automatically been allowed to worship with the Israelites (Deuteronomy 23:1–3), but that is about to change.

56:9–12 God's plan reflects His love and mercy toward all people. Unfortunately, Israel's leaders have not yet developed the same attitude toward others. Like the prophet Jonah, they do not want to witness the fullness of God's mercy if it means that people who have long been their enemies will also be able to find peace with God and receive His greatest blessings. The leaders have drifted away from a real understanding of the plan of God and have turned instead to furthering their own private interests. They make no effort to help the weak and confused but rather plan great things for themselves while focusing on sleeping and drinking. The result will be an invasion of beasts that, here again, symbolize foreign nations.

57:1–5 God is not willing to ignore the widespread sin and idolatry among those who claim to be His people. In a culture that should have known purity and faithfulness to the Lord, the people are linked to sorceresses, adulterers, and prostitutes. Their pursuit of idolatrous practices has exposed them to numerous habits that God had prohibited in their law. While they mock other people, they participate in magic, rebellion, lying, lust, and even child sacrifice.

57:6–10 There is an irony in the fact that the people are faithful to their false gods while ignoring the living Lord. The imagery is graphic. The people of Israel are depicted as shamefully leaving a marriage bed to partake of affairs with various other lovers, among them the Ammonite god Molech, to whom parents sometimes offer their own children. Even though such a lifestyle becomes quite wearisome after a while, the people will not give it up.

57:11–13 God's promises are sound. Those who turn to Him for strength and deliverance will inherit the land and find refuge. Those who don't, however, will be left on their own. Since the people insist on worshipping false gods, the Lord will direct them back to those useless forms of wood and stone when trouble comes. They will discover too late that the power of idols disappears with a mere wisp of wind.

57:14–15 God's plan for humanity is always substantially better than what people tend to choose for themselves. Those who choose to pursue idolatry have to remain in good standing with those gods by providing regular gifts and offerings. God is in need of nothing, yet rather than remaining in His holy place, He willingly reaches out to provide help, strength, and fellowship for those who are contrite and lowly in spirit.

57:16–21 Rather than enforcing lingering and lasting punishment, God instead offers healing, guidance, and comfort. Those who respond to Him discover peace and restoration. But those who remain unrelenting in their wickedness are unable to find peace and will continue to suffer.

58:1–3 The people are apparently oblivious to the extent of their spiritual lethargy. They claim to seek God's will, proclaiming eagerness to hear what He has to say. They even go to the point of blaming God for not noticing their religious acts.

58:3–5 The people want to claim some religious credit for their fasts, yet the purpose of fasting is to focus on the things of God rather than the usual comforts of life. The Israelites ended up quarreling with one another and fighting on their fast days, revealing themselves to be self-centered and violent. Yet here they still expect God to respond to their requests.

58:6–10 Had the people truly been listening to God's voice, they would have known what they should be doing: fighting injustice (rather than each other), freeing the oppressed, feeding the hungry, sheltering the homeless, clothing those in need, and taking care of their own family members. If they had done these things, they would have noticed an immediate difference:

light in their darkness, healing, righteousness, and clear responses from God to their cries for help.

58:11–14 With a genuine concern for worship and the welfare of others, God's people will discover the ongoing strength and guidance of the Lord. Even in a desert setting, they will be like lush gardens. The ruins of their city will be rebuilt. Rather than having a reputation for quarreling and exploitation, they will be known as rebuilding and restoring their city. Keeping the sabbath will not be a joyless obligation but a time of true delight. Instead of dry and tasteless religion, the people will be blessed with joy and feasting. All their holiest desires will be satisfied, and a new day will come for following generations.

59:2 Sin is sometimes defined as "separation from God," which is an accurate description here.

59:3–8 When the Lord speaks about the sin of His beloved people, He does not ignore the depth and ugliness of it. Here He speaks of bloodstained hands, lying lips, and discomfiting involvement with spiders and snakes. Attempting to hide behind one's sinful lifestyle without being exposed is no more successful than attempting to make clothing from cobwebs. Those who wallow in their sin find neither contentment nor peace.

59:9–11 The people begin to admit the truth. They describe seeking light but not finding it. As a result, they are attempting to feel their way in the dark, stumbling like blind people as they do. Justice and deliverance seem unattainable. They are both angry and mournful, yet for all they are able to accomplish on their own, they may as well be dead.

59:12–15 The people acknowledge that their sin is against God. Their offenses are numerous and include rebellion, treachery, rejection of the Lord, instilling oppression, and lying. The standards by which their society was founded—justice, righteousness, and truth—are now nowhere to be found.

59:15–16 This is a distressing situation, but not a hopeless one. The people may not realize it, but the Lord knows that they lack the power to solve their problems. No one else is capable of intervening and dealing with the lack of righteousness; God will solve the problem Himself.

59:17–19 Righteousness and salvation are so integral to the Lord that they are described as His breastplate and helmet. For those who repent of their sin, God will be a certain redeemer. But those who continue to resist Him will discover that the Lord's garments also include vengeance and zeal. They will face His wrath and retribution.

60:1–3 Israel is instructed to prepare for a great influx of people from other nations to stream into Zion. The hostility between Israelite and Gentile will come to an end, and the grace of God can be embraced by those who had once been strangers to Zion. This must have been a difficult concept for the Israelite people of Isaiah's time to comprehend. Gentiles had not been considered in right relation with God without first becoming circumcised Israelites. But the image portrayed by the prophet here is by no means threatening. God's fulfillment of His promises will somehow bring something much better than His people had previously known.

60:6 In Isaiah's time, seeing camel caravans in the area was the equivalent of someone today seeing a UPS truck in the neighborhood. It was a sign that something good was being delivered from a great distance.

61:1 Some of the prophecies in these chapters seem to apply to a still-future time, but others are fulfilled with the first advent of Jesus. This opening verse of Isaiah 61 would have been good news at any time, of course. Most likely the *me* was first thought to be Isaiah, or it might have been believed to be the servant of the Lord whom Isaiah had foretold. But centuries later all doubt is removed. This is the passage that Jesus reads in a Nazareth synagogue very early in His ministry. After reading the passage, He sits down and tells those in attendance that the prophecy has been fulfilled in their hearing (Luke 4:16–21).

61:1 Isaiah's readers were probably a bit in the dark, being unable to fully understand his promises involving the coming of the Messiah. Similarly, when Jesus arrived on earth, He promised to return. Consequently, today's believers remain a bit in the dark as to their expectations involving His second coming. In retrospect it appears that Isaiah addresses both events: the initial incarnation of Jesus and His subsequent return to earth. In places it is debatable as to which occasion the prophet is referring to.

61:1–7 This is a grand announcement. Ancient ruins will have new life. Strangers and foreigners will find their place in the drama of bountiful blessing. Faithful people will serve as priests of the true and living God, supported by the wealth of many nations. Shame and dishonor will be replaced by sounds of everlasting joy that cannot be contained.

61:2 This period of rejoicing will not come about due to God's mere excusing of human wrongdoing. Human sin cannot be overlooked. God's day of vengeance, as Isaiah had previously noted, will still be very real. God's justice will not be preempted. The penalty for disobedience requires a just and holy atoning sacrifice. Jesus will be not only the prophet who announces the coming good news but also the sacrifice that satisfies divine justice and reconciles people to God.

61:8–11 God is clear that He not only loves justice but also hates iniquity. Yet after sin is atoned for, God will reward faithfulness and bless the people and their descendants. Those who respond to His forgiveness will experience great delight at a level best compared to the delight of a bride or groom preparing for a formal wedding ceremony. The Lord will continue to cause praise and righteousness to spring up like shoots in a fertile garden.

62:1–5 Jerusalem and Zion had once displayed God's glory but in time had fallen away and earned names such as *Forsaken* and *Desolate*. God is not content to have

His cherished land bear that reputation, so He will act to restore and rename Zion. The new names associated with the area will be *Hephzi-bah* ("My delight is in her") and *Beulah* ("Married"). The surrounding nations will no longer see Jerusalem as a wasteland but as a crown of splendor and a royal diadem. The land is portrayed as a bride, thrilled to approach her wedding, with God as the bridegroom.

62:6–7 God exhorts the people not to rest until Jerusalem is again recognized as the pride of the earth. But more than that, God urges them to give *Him* no rest until that day. They are supposed to keep praying until He establishes Jerusalem in full. Like watchmen, they are supposed to be ever vigilant in their watchfulness and expectation. The prophets serve as a type of spiritual watchmen (see, for instance, Ezekiel 3:16–21; 33:1–9).

62:8–9 Israel's history has involved many cycles of oppression by enemies with interspersed periods of freedom. Foreigners had eaten their grain, drunk their wine, and killed their loved ones. But here is the promise that the day will come when the enemies of Jerusalem will never again take control of the city.

62:10–12 The people are to anticipate the arrival of their Savior. Their preparation will involve both work (clearing a pathway and building the highway) and celebration (raising a standard, or banner). The nations (Gentiles) will be involved, too—not just the Jewish people. *All* believers will be deemed holy people and redeemed ones. Together they will give Zion new names.

63:1–6 A figure is described coming from Edom, one of Israel's regular enemies to the south. (Bozrah was one of Edom's key cities.) The figure identifies himself as the Lord. He is a solo warrior, stained with the blood of His vanquished enemies. His blood-spattered clothing is reminiscent of those who trod on grapes in a winepress. The Lord goes into battle alone because no one else can accomplish the victory. When no one else is capable, God is mighty to save. And the result of the battle is significant: It prompts the arrival of the year of God's redemption.

63:7–14 Although the imagery here is violent, the response is one of prayer and praise. It is the power of God that effects salvation and deliverance, as Isaiah (speaking for the nation) recalls in 63:7–64:12. God had repeatedly proven His faithfulness to Israel in the past. Their distress is His distress, so He had lifted them up and carried them for many centuries. Though they had rebelled against Him, He remains committed to them. His people had always needed Him, although sometimes they realized it more than others, as in the days of Moses when mighty waters parted before them and each day's food fell from heaven. On later occasions, they would remember such times and realize how far away they had drifted from God, causing them to cry out for Him.

63:15–19 The prophet asks God to look down from heaven and renew His zeal, power, tenderness, and compassion among His people. He also confesses that the problem is that the people's hearts have become hardened. Those who had once lived in peace and joy will see their enemies trample down the temple. The appeal is to God's reputation: If the people who were called by His name are permanently overthrown by other powers, it will seem that God is helpless.

64:1–5 God had always been in control, but many times His government of all things was subtler than His people would have preferred. By His continual providence, He works through countless ways to achieve His holy will, rarely drawing enough attention to Himself to be noticed. Isaiah prays for a clearer manifestation of God's presence.

64:5–12 Isaiah makes no attempt to downplay the sin of the people, yet he boldly asks for God's forgiveness. Only God is the Father. Only God is the Potter who can make things right amid the broken lives of His clay vessels. Only God can change the land that has become a desert back into the flourishing garden it had been before. Only God can rebuild a city that has been left in ruins.

65:1–2 When God responds to Isaiah's prayer, He explains that He has not been as silent as the people think. He has revealed Himself, but the people weren't seeking Him. He had said, "Here I am," but the people had made no attempt to listen. He had extended His hands many times, but the people remained obstinate.

65:3–5 God knows why the people had not heard Him. They had been too busily involved with pagan practices while disregarding their own laws. And while doing so, they had developed a smugly superior attitude. They were certainly religious, but they had completely lost touch with the one true God.

65:4 Sitting among the graves was often connected with practices of ancestor worship. People who tried to contact the dead would frequently spend time where the person was buried in the belief that the message would be clearer.

65:8–12 Not everyone had defied God. A remnant of people continued to seek Him, so He will show mercy to them. Israel is compared to a cluster of grapes that is going bad. But before tossing out the entire bunch, the good ones will be picked and kept. The people had not valued God's prior promises to Abraham (63:16), but those assurances are still in effect. The line of Abraham's descendants through Jacob (Israel) will continue. Those who seek the Lord will continue to be blessed. The locations mentioned—Sharon and Achor—were both fertile and geographically pleasing areas. But the unrepentant people who had forsaken God will not share in the blessing. Because they followed pagan gods, they will be destined for destruction.

65:13–20 One group of people will eat, drink, rejoice, and sing. Another group will go hungry and thirsty, experience shame, and wail in anguish. But after that separation is made, God's people begin to experience entirely new things. They get a new name, with their previous sins forgiven and forgotten. God will even create new heavens and a new earth. Jerusalem will be renewed, with no more weeping or early death.

65:21–25 Homes will be established with fruitful vineyards. The blessings of God will be so effective that work and child rearing are completely fulfilling pursuits. Even before a prayer leaves the people's lips, God will answer it. The dangers of nature are suspended as wolves and lambs, lions and oxen mingle together. The protection of the Lord will ensure complete security and satisfaction.

66:1–3 Throughout his entire writing, Isaiah has been faithfully relating what God has told and shown him, and he makes that point clear again as he closes. A prophet is nothing at all unless he is an authoritative spokesperson for God. The Lord—the speaker in this section—has heaven for a throne and earth as a footstool. He has no need for people to build Him a house (temple). He does not go hungry, whether or not animals are burned on altars.

66:2–3 Worship ceremonies should have inspired the people to keep their hearts and minds focused on the Lord, but the Israelites had gradually lost their love for God. Yet they had continued to pray and sacrifice as mere rituals, and their actions became blatantly offensive to the Lord. What God desires from His people is not a thoughtless sacrifice but rather a contrite spirit and a sense of humility.

66:3 In graphic terms, God points out that the people have lost any sense of distinguishing the holy from the unholy. Dogs and pigs are unclean animals, and the very thought of using them in a sacrifice should have been horrific. The people's sacrifices have become little more than animal abuse, and God deems their so-called devotion to Him the equivalent of idol worship.

66:3–4 Throughout Isaiah, God has made clear distinctions between the righteous and the wicked, and the prophet's writing concludes with yet another instance. Those who choose their own ways and delight in abominations will experience great dread as the judgment of God comes upon them. He has spoken, but they neither listen nor respond.

66:5–6 Judgment is for those who reject God. But others will hear His Word and respond in fearful reverence. The obedient have been hated, mocked, and scorned by the wicked. Yet God has seen and heard it all, and He will mete out terrible punishment for the evil that has been done.

66:11–12 The faithful are in for a surprise. God will renew His land and His people, and it will be both sudden and delightful. It will be like the joy of having a child, but without the discomfort of labor pains. Zion will give birth to her children, and a new nation will be born in a day. The people will have Jerusalem as a mother.

66:13–14 God Himself will provide the comfort that a mother offers her child. The righteous will be rewarded with new life and joyful hearts. The previous injustices of life are brought to an end with God's just and fair judgments.

66:15–16 The Lord will be coming with fire and sword in His judgment. His fury and judgment will be widespread. Isaiah never attempts to downplay the severity of this horrible news. Yet the reality of God's furious judgment is offset by another reality.

66:18–21 When Jerusalem is reestablished, God's grace and mercy will extend to all nations. The righteous will be sent out to faraway lands, where people will hear of God's love and travel to Jerusalem to worship Him, bringing back with them others from Israel who have been relocated. Some of those from other nations will even become priests and temple workers.

66:22–24 In His original call for Abraham to leave Ur and go to an as-yet-unrevealed land, God had promised that all peoples on earth would be blessed through the great nation that Abraham would become (Genesis 12:1–3). This final image in Isaiah describes the fulfillment of that promise. God will establish new heavens, a new earth, and an enduring kingdom. With the unrighteous removed in the judgment of God, the righteous remnant of all humankind will bow down to worship the Lord in joy and peace.

THE BOOK OF THE PROPHET

JEREMIAH

INTRODUCTION TO JEREMIAH ■ The Old Testament book of Jeremiah is considered one of the canon's major prophets and is named after the book's author, the prophet Jeremiah. By word count, Jeremiah is actually the longest book of the Bible, with even more words than Psalms, making it the lengthiest prophetic work in the canon. It follows the work of another major prophet, the book of Isaiah, and precedes the short poetic work Lamentations.

AUTHOR ■ The book of Jeremiah is highly autobiographical, and more can be learned about the prophet from his work than from any other historical source. Jeremiah was a Judean from the town of Anathoth, located about three miles outside of Judah's capital city, Jerusalem. We don't know when he was born, but he probably died in Egypt after the exile of 586 BC.

OCCASION ■ Jeremiah's prophecy takes place during the reigns of Judah's last five kings: Josiah, Jehoahaz, Jehoiakim, Jehoiachin, and Zedekiah. This is the time leading up to the Babylonian invasion of 586 BC, when Jerusalem falls. The historical events surrounding Jeremiah's prophecies are recorded in 2 Kings 21–25 and 2 Chronicles 33–36.

1:1–3 As is customary for the prophetic books of the Bible, the book of Jeremiah begins with a brief biographical introduction to the prophet. Jeremiah, for whom the book is named, was called to be a prophet of the Lord as a teenager in 627 BC, and ministered in that capacity for forty years. He grew up in Anathoth, a city about three miles northeast of Jerusalem. Anathoth was one of the Levitical cities, but there is no evidence that Jeremiah functioned as a priest. His name means "Yahweh loosens" (referring to the womb) or "Yahweh exalts."

1:5 This verse specifies God's personal involvement in Jeremiah's life. The verb *formed* means "to create or craft," like a potter (see chapter 18). God carefully designed and crafted Jeremiah in the belly of his mother. *Sanctified* means "made holy, set apart." Before Jeremiah came out of the womb, he was chosen to be on God's side, but he still has to be obedient. *Ordained* here means "gave." Jeremiah was designed and set apart by God so that God could give his life away.

1:9 Touch is important to God; He is not a distant being. God touches Jeremiah in order to put His words on his lips.

1:11–12 To confirm his calling, God reveals two visions to Jeremiah. The first sign is an almond branch. The almond is the first tree to greet the spring. Everything seems dormant, but God is watching, waiting to open. When Jeremiah sees the blossom, he will anticipate the fulfillment of God's Word.

1:13–16 The second vision, a boiling, seething pot, is a sign that judgment will come from the north, from Babylon. A flash flood will engulf the land and burn everything it touches, and the armies of Babylon will use the old invasion route of the Assyrians to invade Judah. Although this vision is tied to Israel's political future, God's judgment is deeply theological. Judah commits the gravest of sins by burning sacrifices to other gods and bowing down to them.

2:2–3 Jeremiah uses metaphors to remind Israel of their former relationship with God, a literary trend that will continue throughout his prophetic work. The first is espousal, or marriage. From God's perspective, the honeymoon phase was during the wilderness wandering, a time when Israel depended heavily on God. Another of Jeremiah's metaphors is harvest. Israel is the firstfruit of God's labor. Other fruit will come as other nations become God's people, but Israel was the first.

2:4–13 God brings a series of charges against Israel as if in a courtroom. The defendants are the house of Jacob and all the families of the house of Israel. The witnesses are the heavens.

2:5 Among the charges against Israel, God names two crimes: forgetting the Lord and vanity, or pursuing useless causes, specifically idolatry. He asks why Israel would abandon Him.

2:8 The leaders and priests are just as guilty as the rest of Israel in transgressing against God, which causes a breakdown in public life and a collapse in public institutions.

2:8, 11 Israel follows after things from which it cannot profit: the idols of the Canaanites.

2:10–12 God expresses the absurdity of idolatry. He notes that never before has a nation traded gods, and asks even the heavens to be astonished and afraid.

2:13 Israel's choosing idols over God is like working tirelessly for dirty water instead of letting fresh water flow to her.

2:14–28 As he has done previously, Jeremiah uses metaphors to describe Israel's behavior. Slavery is the first.

2:14 God had freed Israel from slavery, but the people became slaves again because they were continually drawn into compromising and dangerous alliances with Egypt and Assyria.

2:16 The cities mentioned here were in Egypt.

2:20, 23, 32–33 The metaphor of a harlot, an unfaithful wife, is familiar in the Old Testament. Israel was God's adored bride, but she was unfaithful. She was a Baal worshipper, a cult preoccupied with fertility whose worship practices included prostitution.

2:22–23 Israel's salvation could not be accomplished by her own means, and God claims she is in denial of her sin.

2:23–25 The dromedary, also translated as she-camel, was known to be unreliable and easily disturbed, and even violent when in heat. She sniffs out the scent of the male and chases him instead of vice versa. Likewise, Israel is so intent on pursuing her lusts that the idols do not have to seek her—she finds them. God portrays Israel as having given up on trying to resist such behavior.

2:26 The metaphor of the thief who is exposed applies not just to the common people of Israel but also to its leaders, the kings, princes, priests, and prophets who also worship Baal.

2:27–28 Stocks, or trees, represent female Canaanite deities; stones represent male Canaanite deities. Israel should be ashamed, humiliated, and embarrassed at her own behavior.

2:30–31 Despite God's efforts to discipline Israel, she continues to misbehave and to ignore Him.

2:32–33 God describes Israel as a bride who forgot her wedding attire—the jewelry and sash that marked her as being married. Israel has become so accomplished at her harlotry that she teaches the wicked women her ways.

2:34 The people's sins include taking the lives of innocent people who have done no wrong.

2:35–37 Because Israel will not accept guilt, even though God has tried repeatedly to restore her, God responds the only way His justice allows: by promising judgment. Israel will be put to shame by Egypt and Assyria.

3:1–2 God asks a rhetorical question about the law of marriage and divorce to continue the imagery of unfaithful Judah. The law prohibits the return of the first husband to his wife because, socially, the woman is considered defiled and rendered unacceptable. According to the law, then, God does not have to accept Judah if she chooses to turn back from her unfaithful ways. In other words, there is no provision in the law for God and Judah to be reconciled.

3:4–5 Judah's harlotry is more brazen than the Israelites'; its people speak admiringly of God and continue to turn to Him even in the midst of their idolatry.

3:6–25 Jeremiah recounts the history of faithless Israel, the northern kingdom, in contrast to Judah, the southern kingdom.

3:6–8 God judges Israel, and Assyria takes the northern kingdom into exile; God sends Israel away with a writ of divorce.

3:8–11 Judah not only follows Israel's faithless example but also feigns allegiance to Yahweh. In this way, Judah's treachery is worse than Israel's.

3:12–14 God assures hope to unfaithful Israel through an extraordinary invitation that goes against the earthly law. The people's opportunity to return to God is based not on their becoming acceptable but on God's accepting them. The one condition, however, is that Israel has to acknowledge its guilt and sin.

3:15–19 Among the things God promises the people if they will return to Him are that leaders and rulers will not be unjust but will feed the people knowledge and understanding; the people will be cleansed from all idolatry; God's throne will no longer be an ark but a city; He will bring a remnant of Israel and Judah home to Zion; the sons of Abraham will be joined by all the nations; and they will inherit the most beautiful of all the nations.

3:21–25 The weeping heard here is characteristic of Baal worship. Perhaps the cries are heard from the high places because Josiah destroyed their idols as part of his reform. Perhaps the people are weeping because they are saddened by the consequences of their sin. The people have loved wrongly and badly, and have done so from their youth.

4:1–4 This part of God's invitation through His prophet Jeremiah highlights three additional actions of repentance: Remove all idols and cast off all other loyalties; swear obedience to the true, living God; and have hearts that are receptive to God's Word. The images of breaking up fallow ground and circumcising hearts are akin to the idea of confession and exposing one's sins before God. Fallow ground is unplowed, hard land. The crusty earth has to be plowed so that the seed will germinate. Breaking up the ground is equivalent to not planting among thorns, since one function of plowing is the removal of noxious weeds that inhibit a fruitful harvest. Jeremiah warns that if such repentance does not occur, God will judge.

4:5–6 Jeremiah warns that an invader from the north (Babylon) is coming to destroy Judah and bringing God's judgment.

4:7–9 Jeremiah's prophecy includes metaphor sprinkled with an exhortation for the people to repent and reminders of the reasons for their situation.

4:10 Jeremiah is anguished at this message he must bring.

4:11–13 Jeremiah employs the metaphor of a dry, scorching wind—not the gentle breeze that aids the winnower at harvesttime, but a blast that will strike down everything in its path—to describe the judgment that awaits Israel and the reason it is certain. Threatening clouds also foretell impending darkness and devastation.

4:14–18 This section closes with another exhortation to repent and a reminder that this invasion is God's justice.

4:19–21 Jeremiah's prayer of lament gives evidence as to why he has been nicknamed "the weeping prophet." Jeremiah is intensely troubled. He is anxious and convulsing over what will happen to Jerusalem. Jeremiah's agony reflects God's agony. God lives with great heartache and turmoil. He doesn't like the idea of judgment, but He is committed to making a holy people. He is anxious for His people to obey Him, and He can't overlook their sin.

4:22–26 God resumes speaking, claiming that His people no longer know Him. The next verses remind listeners of the condition of the universe before God formed creation out of chaos. The connection between these verses and Genesis 1 is unavoidable. God looks and sees the conditions of the universe prior to creation: The earth is formless and void; there is no light in the heavens; there is neither man nor bird. All that exists is barrenness and wilderness—the murky conditions of the beginning.

4:27–28 The destruction of Jerusalem is likened to the creation coming undone and returning to a state of chaos. That which was proclaimed good by God is now evil. All of creation will pay the price for Judah's sin. God's comments also remind listeners of His actions in Noah's time, when He took disciplinary action but chose not to completely destroy creation.

4:30–31 Some people try like harlots to allure the invaders, but neither sweet-talking nor cries of agony will ward off the attackers or change God's mind.

5:1–2 As with Abraham at Sodom (see Genesis 18), Jeremiah unsuccessfully tries to find one righteous person to persuade God to spare Judah.

5:3–6 The prophet comments on the truth of God's only remaining option: judgment in the face of Judah's refusal to repent.

5:10 The metaphor here is of resources that have been used in an ungodly way and must be dealt with. Regardless of how God's justice will be enacted, however, God reminds us (see 4:27–28) that He will not destroy the nation completely.

5:12 One of the lies spread by people from both the northern and southern kingdoms is that God won't judge them, even though He has proved otherwise in the lives of their ancestors.

5:13 Some of God's own prophets have taken on the same complacent spirit as the people and no longer fear God. But Jeremiah, a prophet who continues to speak God's truth, is quick to remind them that no one can escape God's judgment.

5:14 God has chosen Jeremiah to speak His harsh truth to the people, and God will make that truth effective.

5:15–17 God's judgment will come in the form of an invasion from a foreign nation (see Deuteronomy 28:49) that will overpower Judah, bring unfamiliar language and customs, and take everything Judah has for its own.

5:18–19 It will be the nation of Babylon that fulfills the prophecy of Judah's punishment. As before, however, God says through His prophet that He will not completely destroy the people but only discipline them for their sins.

5:20–22 God reminds His people, who have stopped listening to Him, of His nature and power: He is the Creator.

5:22–25 Unlike the sea, God's people have stopped responding to His law, yet they still continue to enjoy the fruits of creation until God chooses to withhold them.

5:26 The nation's sin is so bad that it entraps others.

5:27–29 Judah's sin leads to corruption that causes the innocent and powerless to suffer, and God responds with punishment. Kings, princes, prophets, and priests—all of them are out for their own gain, proclaiming peace where none exists.

5:30–31 Judah's leaders are blamed for turning away from God, allowing sin to affect the entire community and nation, and doing nothing to repent and restore justice.

6:1–3 Jeremiah belongs to the tribe of Benjamin, so he sends this particular warning of God's approaching justice to his own tribe. As he previously warned (5:15), this justice is coming from the north.

6:4–7 Justice against Jerusalem appears to be coming in the form of a well-planned, premeditated attack on a nation that has continually defied God.

6:8–9 God likens His power and ability to completely destroy the people to those of a good harvester who picks all the grapes off a vine.

6:10–21 This section both condemns Judah for not heeding Jeremiah's warnings and expands on the reasons provided earlier for God's judgment.

6:10–11 The people are accused of not hearing the word of their Creator, and the Lord has had enough.

6:12–13 Jeremiah prophesies specific details of what can be expected from the Babylonian invasion, and again God blames each of the citizens of Judah for the nation's collective sin.

6:14–15 God's accusations toward the religious leaders are telling: They perform rituals and chant words, but their spirits are not pure.

6:16–20 The people of Judah had the chance to listen to the priests and prophets who spoke truth and to return to the true God, but they refused and chose to continue sacrificing to God while living in a way that did not bring Him glory.

6:24–26 Peace and normal life for the nation are quickly coming to an end.

6:27–30 Jeremiah's final metaphor of this chapter likens his search for people who do not deserve God's judgment to a metalworker searching for good, strong metal among weaker metal. The process includes hot fires stoked with bellows; the metalworker burns and burns without finding any good metal.

7:1–2 This event could have been at the beginning of Jehoiakim's reign, when, despite Josiah's restoration of the temple and true worship, cultic practice was again the norm. The temple gate was the most sacred and public place in Jerusalem. Jeremiah's message would have been very upsetting to the establishment, but the nation's leaders were clearly at fault for leading the people down a path of such disobedience.

7:3–4 The first two commands of this chapter are designed to get the attention of the people of Judah. They are repeated twice, the second repetition filling out the first. To amend one's ways means to make good, do well, do right, do what is pleasing.

7:5–7 Truly amending one's ways involves practical elements of everyday life: practicing justice, loving one's neighbor, caring for orphans and widows, and not walking after false gods.

7:8 The people of Judah are failing to do what is right, and they are worshipping the wrong god to their own ruin. They are being selfish, exploiting people for their own gain. They are dealing in lies and deceptions, which is the opposite of being faithful and true.

7:9–11 The deception that the people are trusting in is the notion that they can do anything they want and then find safety in God's temple.

7:12–14 God uses Jeremiah to remind the people that the presence of the Lord's temple didn't save the people of Shiloh, so they shouldn't expect it to save them, either.

7:15 Just as God exiled the Israelites in the northern kingdom, the people of Judah can expect the same fate if they don't repent and turn back to Him.

7:18 "Queen of heaven" is a reference to the worship of any number of Babylonian goddesses (see 44:17; see also 2 Kings 21; 23:4–14; Amos 5:26). This worship of these goddesses often appealed more to women, and one of the customs involved making cakes in the goddess's image. The fact that people are making cakes in the privacy of their homes as a form of worship to a false god and then showing up at the temple in public to worship Yahweh is the ultimate form of hypocrisy.

7:21–22 God knows the offerings are futile if the people's hearts aren't engaged in worshipping Him.

7:23–24 What God cares about is obedience, as He told their ancestors when He led them out of slavery in Egypt. A key word in the text is the Hebrew word *shema*. It appears eight times in chapter 7 and is translated as both "listen" and "obey."

7:25–28 God desires a simple obedience from a heart devoted to Him. But no matter how often God sends this message to His people, they reject Him and His messenger.

7:30–31 Among Judah's sins is the practice of child sacrifice. The valley of Tophet, or Hinnom, was just outside the city of Jerusalem to the south. This was a garden of the Canaanites and later a center of Baal worship.

7:32 Jeremiah says that the valley of Tophet will become the valley of slaughter and will be a dumping ground for all the bodies of people who die in the coming invasion.

7:32–34 The valley of the son of Hinnom will become Jerusalem's garbage dump, and the ruined land will be devoid of all joy.

8:3 The final word leaves no comfort—death will be better than life for those who survive the Babylonian invasion.

8:4–6 True wisdom involves being aware of the health of one's spiritual life and, if necessary, correcting course immediately. Judah hasn't been doing that.

8:7 The metaphor of the birds (*turtle* is translated elsewhere as *dove*) knowing their migratory patterns implies that people—who have much more intimate relationships with God—should know their role with God but do not.

8:8–9 Not even the ability to literally write down the law of the Lord is immune from corruption. The scribes take out their red markers and trim God's Word to what is acceptable to them. Their pen has changed truth into lies. Others reject God's Word completely. The people are caught in their own trap.

8:10 The giving away of the wives and fields is a reference to the coming exile, when the invaders will take what matters most to the leaders of the nation.

8:11–12 The spiritual leaders are guilty of lying to the people about the gravity of their sins, a lie that should have brought about feelings of guilt and shame. However, the priests and prophets feel no guilt about their misleadings, and it is because of this lack of a repentant heart that God will punish them.

8:14 Being inside a city means protection inside the city walls, but once resources run out or spoil, the people will suffer from starvation and likely die.

8:15–16 Peace is no longer an option, and the invaders from the north are coming as Jeremiah prophesied.

8:17 God compares the coming destruction to poisonous snakes that can't be charmed—there is no way to resist the fatal strike.

8:18–20 Jeremiah grieves over Jerusalem's fate. He laments that his people question God's presence and recalls God's warning about worshipping other gods. Because of their failure to repent, the people now face inevitable judgment.

8:21–22 Jeremiah believes the people's salvation is within reach, that all they have to do is repent, but they are acting like salvation isn't possible. The metaphor he uses is "balm in Gilead," a reference to medicine from a neighboring town that the people were unable to get.

9:1 This section closes with a picture of how much pain Jeremiah is in for his people: The weeping prophet wants his eyes to become never-ending streams of tears for their suffering.

9:2 Disgusted at the spiritually adulterous people around him, Jeremiah wishes for reprieve from his situation and his people.

9:3–6 God describes His people as so treacherous that no one can rely on anyone, making trust and true community impossible.

9:7–9 The only recourse God has is to refine the people (see 6:27–30) because of their deceitfulness and their actions toward one another.

9:10–11 The punishment will be so thorough that even nature will mourn, and only dragons—translated elsewhere as *jackals*, animals that thrive in the wasteland—will be left.

9:12–16 The people of Judah are in a situation of facing severe judgment because they did not choose wisely. The people should have chosen to keep God's law and listen to His voice instead of worshipping the idols of other nations. Because they chose poorly, they are subjected to bad food and water and will be destroyed as a community.

9:17–21 God tells the people to prepare not only the current generation for mourning but also the following generation, because the losses will be so great and continuous.

9:22 The massiveness of the destruction is seen in the prophecy that corpses will not even be buried, an indicator of how completely incapacitated and humiliated Judah will be—the people won't even be able to bury their own dead.

9:23–24 The theme of wisdom, a common theme in the book of Jeremiah, appears again. True wisdom means not trusting in human and earthly resources. Evidence of following the true God will be seen not in earthly treasures but in lovingkindness, justice, and righteousness.

9:25–26 These verses emphasize God's thoughts about religious actions versus true righteousness; even people who think they are of the true religion (the circumcised) are no better than those who are not, and all will be punished equally.

10:1–16 The opening verses of chapter 10 are a satirical contrast of God and idols. Such writing is not uncommon to the Old Testament, and the prophet Isaiah often employs similar rhetoric in his writing (see Isaiah 44:9–20). Later in the book of Jeremiah, the prophet reiterates verses 12–16 (see 51:15–19).

10:1–16 True wisdom recognizes the difference between the impotence of idols and the majesty of God. The first part of this section emphasizes how idols are made by people (10:3–5, 8–9, 11, 14–15), but the true God is like no other (10:6–7, 10, 12–13, 16). The words *vain, vanities* (10:3, 8), and *vanity* (10:15), a form of which is also used in 2:5, mean "emptiness," "vapor," "nothingness."

10:17 Chapter 10 closes with a lament about the coming destruction of Jerusalem. The prophecy describes the people as having bundles of wares or belongings, and it warns them to be prepared to leave because the exile is at hand.

10:19–21 Jeremiah expresses his great distress, using the language of nomadic shepherds to indicate that he speaks of the pain of loss of civilization and community for all the people of Judah.

10:22–25 The judgment is coming from the north as prophesied, and it is a necessary action from God to restore righteousness to His people. The chapter closes with Jeremiah's prayer that God will pour out His wrath on all of the people of Judah. Jeremiah no longer seeks God's mercy and forgiveness for the people, because the prophet knows that the people have regressed so far into their sin that they deserve the punishment of God's justice.

11:1–8 Jeremiah communicates to the people that they have broken the covenant between them and God that was made with Moses on mount Sinai. This covenant was to be foundational to the people and dependent on their hearing and obeying the words of the true God.

11:9–11 Instead of keeping the covenant, the people have chosen to follow other gods, and their punishment is now inescapable.

11:12 God predicts that the people will not find refuge from this destruction in Him and will thus turn to idols for help, which will not come.

11:14–15 God insists that the people are so far gone in their sin that having Jeremiah pray for them or performing rituals in the temple will not restore the people's hearts.

11:16–18 Throughout the book of Jeremiah thus far, we have experienced Jeremiah's emotional and spiritual anguish over the condition of his people, but this is the first time the listener understands the physical danger Jeremiah is in because of his prophecies. Jeremiah knows of this danger because God reveals it to him.

11:19 The tree refers to Jeremiah, and the fruit is the prophetic message he delivers. The people want Jeremiah dead so that they don't have to listen to his warnings any longer.

11:22 God responds to Jeremiah's plea for protection from his enemies by declaring that He will punish them. The punishment God declares is death by the sword to the young men and death by famine to the harassers' children. By killing their descendants, God makes sure no one will remember Jeremiah's enemies, just as the enemies want to make sure no one remembers the prophet.

12:1–2 Jeremiah hears God's reassurance, but he has more to say to God and more questions for Him. Through prayer, the prophet enters God's metaphorical courtroom, carrying a complaint against God. Desiring to plead his case and discuss matters of justice, he appeals to God's righteous and just character. Jeremiah's statements capture age-old feelings and questions: Why do good things happen to bad people? He finds it disturbing that these people are wicked and yet successful. And because God withholds any sense of justice, they are allowed to grow and even produce fruit. Jeremiah argues that their success is no accident.

12:6–13 God says to consider His grief. God laments over His people, His inheritance. Judah roared at God like a lion. She became like a speckled bird of prey whose plumage attracted the jealousy of other nations. The shepherds of Judah—the invading army—ruined God's vineyard. God's gift of a land flowing with milk and honey became desolate, and no one cared. So God has no choice. He forsakes and abandons Judah in the same way that she has forsaken Him. God gives His people over to their enemy (see 46:6–7). In the midst of Jeremiah's confusion and anger, God is saying, "Have you ever thought about how I feel?" The words *my* and *me* are repeated a dozen times. Jeremiah's tragedy is God's tragedy in miniature. Jeremiah's rejection by his family parallels the nation's rejection of God.

13:3–5 Jeremiah is commanded to go to the Euphrates and hide the girdle in the crevice of a rock. This would have meant a very long journey for Jeremiah, and the people of Judah may have been aware of his actions. In any case, Jeremiah obeys the word of God.

13:6–7 Jeremiah is commanded to retrieve the girdle. Once again he obeys, only to find that the girdle is ruined. It is totally worthless and no longer fit to accomplish its intended purpose.

13:8–9 The girdle is a spiritual symbol of Judah's relationship to God. God gives a word that matches each action in reverse order. First, God says He will destroy the pride of Judah and Jerusalem in the same way the belt was destroyed.

13:10 God points out the reason for Judah's destruction: She refuses to listen to His Word. The people instead "walk after other gods," ignoring and neglecting their relationship with God in the same way that Jeremiah had neglected the girdle, and the people of Judah have hidden themselves from God in the same way that Jeremiah hid the girdle.

13:12–14 These verses tell a parable of wine bottles. There are several references to wine in the book of Jeremiah. The wine bottle, or wineskin, referred to here is a large earthenware container, and it symbolizes the people of Judah. These bottles are to be filled with wine, but God adds a twist: The inhabitants of Judah will be filled not with wine but with drunkenness, which is symbolic of their addiction to idolatry. In the coming time of crisis, the inhabitants of Judah will be so inebriated by their sin that they will destroy one another like wine bottles that collide and break, and God will not intervene to stop them.

13:19 The people might seek refuge, but Jeremiah warns that all the cities of the Negev, the area to the south of Jerusalem, are barricaded so that fleeing fugitives will not be able to find a place to hide.

13:20 Dethroned kingship is a metaphor for judgment. God opposes the proud: Those who exalt themselves will be brought down. No one is exempt from the Lord's hand of judgment and discipline, which is coming from the north as prophesied.

13:21–27 The final picture is a lament over the disgrace to come upon Jerusalem.

13:21 The judgment will come by the hands of the Babylonians, the very people whom Judah courted as companions, and it will be painful, like the pains of labor.

13:22–23 In the midst of their sin, the people have forgotten God and resorted to falsehood. And worst of all, they have no hope of change. Judah can no more change its evil ways than the Ethiopian the color of his skin or the leopard its spots.

13:24, 26–27 Babylon will scatter the people like stubble (or straw) in the wind, a reference to exile, because of their behavior.

14:1–6 A drought will come over Judah that is so powerful that all classes of people, all animals, and even the earth will be affected and cry out in anguish.

14:7–9 Jeremiah connects this drought (verse 4) to God's judgment and intercedes with God on behalf of the people, appealing to his own sense of justice despite the nation's sinful ways, asking God not to forsake them.

14:10–12 God rejects Jeremiah's plea, citing the people's consequences for their own wandering feet. Although they may be feeling pain and remorse now, based on their history it is likely they will wander away again.

14:13–16 Jeremiah points out that other prophets are testifying to the people about peace and the prospect of being spared, but God calls them false and insists that both the false prophets and the people listening to them will face His justice.

14:17 Jeremiah again weeps over the physical and spiritual state of the nation. His tears represent the hopelessness of the people of Judah if they don't repent of their sins.

14:18 Death is all around Jeremiah, both in cities and in the country as a result of the famine and the diseases that accompany it.

14:19 Seeing the death and destruction around him, Jeremiah questions God's rejection of the nation.

14:22 In the midst of pleading with God, Jeremiah admits that God alone controls creation and has the power to make it rain; the false idols the people worship can do nothing to remedy the situation.

15:1 God's wrath continues to burn against the nation of Judah. Even though Jeremiah's generation attempts to repent, God's justice requires that the flagrant sins of past generations be vindicated. Perhaps Moses, who interceded for the nation at the giving of the law—can appeal to God for mercy. Or Samuel, who interceded for Israel as they cried for a king. But God knows that the repentant words from Jeremiah are no match for the hearts of the people, and He says neither Moses nor Samuel can make Him change His mind.

15:2 The people will face four different judgments: death, the sword, famine, and captivity.

15:7 The fan—translated elsewhere as a winnowing fork—was used to separate and scatter the chaff from the wheat. In this case, it has a dual purpose of separating the ungodly and inflicting death.

15:10 Jeremiah is perplexed by Israel's condemnation of him. In spite of the fact that he is not a lender or a borrower, he is deemed to be a contentious leader; he pities his own mother for giving birth to one who has become such a curse upon the name of Israel.

15:12 God's reference to iron and steel from the north is symbolic of the prophetic sweep of force by Nebuchadnezzar's armies as they converged upon Jerusalem to steal away Israel's dreams of glory.

15:13–14 As with any domination of one nation over another, the buildings are leveled and the temple is destroyed. The people are humiliated and carried off to Babylon to serve their new king and his many pagan gods.

15:15 Jeremiah's petition consists of four imperatives: remember, visit, take vengeance, and do not take away. He is not asking for revenge but for justice and lawfulness. Expressing his anxiety about death, he fears being taken away. He tells God not to be too patient, too slow to anger. He wants God to unleash His judgment against Judah right away.

15:16 Jeremiah reminds God that he has filled his stomach with God's words. He is probably referring to the discovery of the law in the temple during Josiah's reign. When God's Word was found, Jeremiah devoured it. He is satisfied with God's Word in the same way we are satisfied by a delicious meal. But now, being called by God's name is like swallowing a bitter pill.

15:17 Jeremiah reminds God that he has not gone the way of the crowd. Literally, he doesn't sit in the secret counsel of the mockers or revelers. He sits alone because God's hand is upon him. He is filled with anger at the sin of Judah and perhaps his own afflictions.

15:20–21 The second part of God's response to Jeremiah is more reassuring. These words reiterate what God tells Jeremiah in chapter 1, when Jeremiah was a young boy. God reaffirms that He is with him. Three powerful verbs—*save, deliver,* and *redeem*—describe God's presence. God is reliable and will stand by His messenger.

16:1–9 The opening verses of this chapter include another object lesson in which Jeremiah's life situation mimics the state of the nation. God uses Jeremiah's call to celibacy and bachelorhood as a picture of the relationship that is ending between God and the people, and the sorrow and loneliness that the people will soon experience.

16:8–9 The days of children playing and villages celebrating are long gone. In God's judgment, He is going to take from Israel its voice of gladness. By obeying God's instruction to avoid participating in mourning or in celebratory events, Jeremiah's life is a model for the people of how God feels toward them.

16:10–12 God prepares Jeremiah for the questions he will field in response to the gravity of his message. His answer is to be that Israel's forefathers forsook Him and turned to idols. But the idolatry didn't stop with their ancestors; the people are also guilty of their own sins.

16:13 God prophesies to the people that they will be cast out of their sacred promised land, a land they have now inhabited for almost a thousand years.

16:16–18 Despite the people's sins, God will once again show them mercy. But that is in the distant future. First, they must pay the price for their wickedness, and the price has doubled: They now must pay the penalty for their forefathers and for their own iniquities.

16:19–21 The coming judgment is, as before, offset by the promise of hope, restoration, and future blessing. Jeremiah prophesies a season when people from all nations will return to God, realize the absurdity of their idolatrous practices, and recognize God's power and might.

17:5–6 Those who trust in human flesh and human strength are cursed. These words are addressed primarily to the people of the covenant. At the time, the nation was surrounded by superpowers—Egypt, Assyria, and the rising Babylon. Judah kept trying to make alliances with these nations, especially Egypt, to achieve national security. But God warns that the person who trusts in the strength and power of humankind and whose heart turns away from God will be cursed. Such an individual will lead a dry, lonely, isolated, withered life. This is revealed in the three metaphors in verse 6: a heath (shrub) in the desert, parched places in the wilderness, and a land of salt without inhabitants.

17:8 The tree stands in contrast to the desert shrub of verse 6. One is destined for life, the other for death. One has a root system that brings nourishment; the other does not. One has adequate water; the other does not. One sees the good; the other does not. One has no fear or anxiety; the other is always desperate. Those who place their trust in humankind to find security will find their source of comfort lacking. The only way to avoid these things is to trust completely in the Lord.

17:9–10 Misplaced trust is symptomatic of a deeper problem, the source of which God reveals in the next verses. The human heart is naturally bent toward sin, and it is the root of not only misplaced trust but also every other way in which people sin against God. While people may not be able to discern why their hearts produce the type of deceit they do, God can discern and will judge according to the state of one's heart.

17:11 The proverb of the partridge is a reminder to all who hear it that coming upon wealth by unjust means does not earn the favor or blessing of God.

17:14 Jeremiah reflects on the condition of his own heart and makes his petition to God. He realizes that he needs God's help to cure his heart and deliver him from his sins.

17:17–18 Although Jeremiah's trust in God wavers at times, in these verses he displays complete trust that God will not turn away from him. He also prays that God will act justly on his persecutors but keep him from harm.

17:19–27 Jeremiah delivers a sermon about the importance of keeping the sabbath. Notice the repeated mention of the word *gate* in this passage. The public gate is the entryway into the city. It is from the gates to the city that Jeremiah preaches.

18:5–6 The meaning behind the scene at the potter's house is obvious to Jeremiah: God is the potter, and the house of Israel is the clay, but the clay has become spoiled through idolatry and sin. The people of Judah have forsaken God to pursue worthless and empty idols. As a result, the pot is not turning out the way God had intended. It has spiritual flaws and character defects. So He will crush the clay and begin again, remolding and reshaping His people.

18:7–10 God speaks a word of judgment on Judah beginning here. He informs the people that their response is very important in determining His actions. While He may plan to destroy a nation, if that nation repents, He will relent or possibly change His mind. Likewise, if God plans to do good to a nation but that nation does evil, then God will send judgment instead of blessing.

18:11 God informs Judah that He is planning calamity, but His exhortation is to repent—it is not too late to change God's course of action.

18:12 Sadly, the people of Judah have no intention of changing their evil ways. They want to follow their own plans and are unwilling to turn from the stubbornness of their evil hearts.

18:13–15 God speaks through Jeremiah, as He has been doing, asking the people rhetorical questions and making statements reminiscent of those in chapter 2. God asks how His people could have forgotten their true identity, but He also laments that they have done so by worshipping idols and other gods.

18:16–17 God will leave the people of Judah to endure His absence during their judgment.

18:18 The people attempt to discredit Jeremiah's message from God and plot to kill him.

18:19–23 Although the threat that the people make against him is only verbal, Jeremiah has had enough. The lament that ends this chapter is different from the previous ones (see 11:18–23; 15:10–21; 17:14–18). Jeremiah had interceded for the people before, but this time he asks God to do justice, honor His loyalty, and punish the people.

19:1 The metaphor of the potter and the clay, introduced in the previous chapter, resumes with God having Jeremiah buy a piece of pottery.

19:2–9 These verses reinforce the reality of the people's idolatrous sins against God and the judgment that God will enact as punishment.

19:11–15 Judah has become so hardened there is nothing left for God to do but to break the pot. A spoiled vessel can be reshaped on the potter's wheel (see 18:1–6), but once it becomes hardened it is beyond reconstruction and is fit only for breaking. Jeremiah's act is a sign proclaiming that just as he broke the pot, so God will destroy Jerusalem and its inhabitants.

20:1–2 When one of the religious leaders, Pashur, hears what Jeremiah has said, he has Jeremiah physically abused.

20:3–6 Upon his release, Jeremiah renames Pashur *Magor-missabib*, which means "terror on every side," an indicator of how Judah will soon be surrounded by Babylonian invaders. Jeremiah's message from God is clear: Because the religious leaders no longer recognize the words of the true God, judgment will come harshly and completely.

20:7–18 This passage includes one of Jeremiah's numerous laments to God. The cost to Jeremiah for his boldness is great, and his confidence gives way to despair.

20:7–10 Jeremiah sets out his complaint. On one level, he complains about his unjust treatment. He is the

object of public ridicule, a laughingstock. He is mocked, and his obedience has resulted in reproach and derision all day long.

20:9 Jeremiah trusts God, but in these verses he admits feeling like God has taken advantage of him. The prophet feels he is in a no-win situation. If he speaks God's word of judgment, he is the object of mockery, ridicule, and hostility. If he doesn't speak, then God's Word is like a burning fire in his body that he is unable to contain.

20:11 The key word in verses 7–12 (used three times) is *prevail*, which means "to overcome." In verse 7 God prevails over Jeremiah. In verse 10 Jeremiah's enemies are looking to prevail. But here it is determined that Jeremiah's enemies will *not* be able to prevail.

20:13 Jeremiah's lamenting is broken for a moment by a doxology. The prophet gives way to praise and breaks into song. How can Jeremiah sing in the midst of his afflictions? Jeremiah states that he sings because God delivers the soul of the *poor*. This word is used to describe the destitute, the day laborers of the ancient world who were completely dependent on others for their survival. What is delivered is the needy soul, not the needy body. In the midst of afflictions, people must depend on God.

20:18 The reason Jeremiah laments so deeply lies in this question: Why was I ever born if all I experience is trouble and sorrow? What a contrast to God's statement to Jeremiah in his youth, when He promised He knew Jeremiah in his mother's womb (see 1:5). At one time, Jeremiah had hope, purpose, and direction, but his life has become a series of afflictions. Sorrow is the only thing he knows.

21:3–7 Instead of receiving a word of assurance from Jeremiah, Zedekiah receives a word of judgment: The God who did wonderful things for Israel in the Exodus will now stand against the nation. Furthermore, Nebuchadnezzar will kill Zedekiah and the rest of the war's survivors.

21:8–9 It will be up to the people whether they stay in the city and die or are exiled to Babylon to live.

21:10 God makes His plan for Jerusalem and its inhabitants clear—it will be overtaken by the enemy and burned.

21:11–14 After the word of judgment, there is an exhortation for the king. The king is supposed to uphold justice and righteousness and the rights of the poor, the needy, and the afflicted. He is to uphold the integrity of the court system so that innocent blood will not be shed.

22:1–30 This chapter relates the stories of four kings—Josiah, Shallum (also called Jehoahaz), Jehoiakim, and Coniah (also called Jehoiachin and Jeconiah)—who not only forsake the Lord but also are guilty of not doing the things they were supposed to do according to the law and the Word of God. These leaders of Judah exalted themselves and exploited their people for their own personal gain.

22:1–3 God sends Jeremiah directly to the palace to deliver clear directions to the nation's leaders: Dispense justice and righteousness and care for the socially weak and powerless.

22:4–5 The king's conduct is decisive for the wealth or woe of the entire social system. If he acts according to God's command, then his royal power will be guaranteed. If he fails to do so, the house of David will be terminated.

22:6–7 God contrasts two images to explain the results of either following His instructions or choosing to disobey them. The kingdom will be plush and fertile if the leaders obey, or it will be like a desert if they do not.

22:8–9 What happens to Judah depends on what the leaders choose to do. But the royal house forsakes God's covenant, and a description of the judgment to come follows in the text.

22:10–12 The first king to succeed Josiah is his son Shallum (also called Jehoahaz), but his reign lasts only three short months before he is exiled to Egypt.

22:13–19 The second king to follow Josiah is Jehoiakim, another of his sons. Jehoiakim fights against Babylon and enters into a dangerous political exploitation that evokes the anger of that nation.

22:14 Jehoiakim uses people and exploits the poor to surround himself with comfort and luxury.

22:15–16 Jeremiah contrasts Jehoiakim with his father, Josiah, who was just and righteous.

22:18–19 After his death, Jehoiakim will be treated like a donkey because of his sin. There will be no funeral or lament.

22:20–23 These verses remind listeners of how God has continually tried to reach out to leaders, but they refuse to listen. They prosper and live in comfort (the mention of *cedars* refers to houses made of the finest timber possible), but their judgment is forthcoming.

22:24–30 The third king to follow Josiah is Coniah (also called Jehoiachin and Jeconiah), the son of Jehoiakim and grandson of Josiah. Coniah begins his rule in 598 BC but is exiled to Babylon in 597, reaping the curse of his father's corrupt politics.

22:24–26 God claims that if Coniah was a ring on His hand, He would pull it off, ending the relationship between the two of them and, consequently, the house of David. Ultimately this separation happens when Coniah is exiled.

22:26–30 With Coniah's exile, the royal line comes to an end and the land is forfeited. Although Coniah has several sons, he might as well have been childless: None of his descendants will succeed him as king.

23:1–2 The leaders of Judah are supposed to care for their people as shepherds care for their flocks. However, the kings and other leaders of Jeremiah's day were not good shepherds. Rather, they destroyed and scattered the sheep of God's pasture (see 10:21).

23:5–6 These verses are a word of hope in the midst of great sorrow: Jeremiah prophesies that God will bring a leader who will exemplify godly leadership and rule in stark contrast to the four kings previously mentioned in chapter 22.

23:5 In the midst of failure, the Lord makes a promise to Judah: One is coming who will sit on the throne of David and rule with wisdom, justice, and righteousness. The phrase "a righteous Branch" is one that in the Old Testament signals the idea of a Messiah who will fulfill the salvation God intended for His people.

23:6 The name of the coming king will be *The Lord Our Righteousness*, and under his rule, both the northern and southern kingdoms will prosper in peace and safety.

23:9–10 The focus shifts here from the kings to the prophets of Judah, the nation's spiritual leaders. These men occupy a very important position in Israel. They speak in the name of the Lord. As seen in 18:18, Judah's prophets are proclaiming one thing about the spiritual state of the nation, but it conflicts with the words of the Lord that Jeremiah delivered. Jeremiah will be vindicated in time, but in these verses he has a painful message for the brothers who share his vocation: Their bad leadership has fostered immorality in the nation.

23:11 Both prophet and priest are profane—polluted, twisted, and defiled—and the holy temple has become the site of sexually oriented fertility rites.

23:12 Following other patterns throughout Jeremiah, at the end of this statement of sin, God assures He will judge the false prophets.

23:13–14 The comparison with Samaria is designed to shame the southern prophets. Judah is worse than Samaria because the idolatry of Jerusalem is more shameful than the Baal worship of Samaria. In fact, the evil so repulses God that in His eyes Judah is no different than Sodom and Gomorrah.

23:23–24 Contrary to what the false prophets teach, God is capable of being both active in the midst of the people to save and protect them, and holy and just in His dealing with sin.

23:26–27 One characteristic of false prophets God points out is that they simply repeat what they hear each other say.

23:28 False prophets contrast to the Word of the Lord like chaff to wheat. The idle dreams and self-induced visions of the false prophets are like chaff—they lack substance. But the Word of God is like wheat—it has a nourishing quality.

23:29 The Word of God is powerful, like a refining fire that burns within us. It is also like a sledgehammer that shatters selfish dreams and stubborn hearts.

23:30–32 God wants His people to know His rejection of those who speak falsely in His name.

23:34 God addresses the false prophets' telling of oracles. He reiterates that anyone proclaiming a message in God's name that isn't from God will face His punishment.

23:35–37 With so many people claiming to be delivering oracles from God, no one is able to discern His true message, so God tells Jeremiah to stop using the common phrase "the burden of the Lord"—elsewhere translated "the oracle of the Lord"—in order to discern the true prophets from the false.

23:38–40 God's word to Jeremiah concerning the false prophets closes with the assurance that all false prophets will be cast from God's presence in exile and shame.

24:1 The opening verses of chapter 24 reveal that some captivity has taken place. Sources show that this captivity refers to Nebuchadnezzar taking captives in 597 BC.

24:2–10 Jeremiah sees a new image that serves as a message from God to His people: a basket with good and bad figs. The good figs represent the people who have been promised restoration, and the bad figs are the ones who have not. The frightening message the fig image symbolizes is that for some people, even exile and imprisonment will not return them to God.

25:1–3 The fourth year of Jehoiakim is 605 BC. By this time, Jeremiah has been a prophet for twenty years, so many people have had the opportunity to hear him.

25:4–7 Jeremiah has been consistent in the prophecies he has delivered against the people's bad behaviors and their worship of false gods, but they still have refused to listen.

25:8–9 Because of the people's disobedience, God will send Babylonian forces, led by King Nebuchadnezzar, to invade Jerusalem from the north. This event is the fulfillment of the invasion Jeremiah has been prophesying about repeatedly throughout the book of Jeremiah.

25:10 The destruction to the city will be so bad that significant life events, such as marriages and harvests, will cease.

25:12 After seventy years of punishment, God will also punish the captors and other nations for the same sins for which Judah is guilty.

25:13–14 Conquering another nation and exploiting its citizens for labor is not just treatment, so even though God uses the invading nations for His purpose, their actions will not go unpunished.

25:15–26 God invokes another image to symbolize His judgment of nations other than Judah—a cup filled with God's fury. God instructs Jeremiah to take the cup of God's fury to a list of nations for them to consume. Unlike the clay pots Jeremiah broke in front of Judah's leaders (see 19:10), this vision most likely symbolizes the message God wants to send the sinful nations.

25:16, 27 The message of drinking to excess is interesting, almost as if there is a connection between the leaders being unable to control themselves and the punishment that they have brought upon themselves.

25:28–29 God makes it clear that the choice to drink of His fury is no longer theirs; because of their past actions, God will force them to drink so that they will face the fullness of His fury.

25:33 The destruction, as previous warnings have stated, will be so great that it will be impossible to bury the dead, much less mourn for them.

25:34–36 God's forthcoming judgment appears to be particularly centered on leaders, those who are shepherding their followers. (In 3:15 God endows Judah

with a special gift when He says, "And I will give you pastors according to mine heart, which shall feed you with knowledge and understanding." The word *pastors* is translated elsewhere as *shepherds*. These shepherds, however, are not the same. They are the leaders of the offending nations. Beginning with the Egyptian Empire and then the Assyrian Empire and then the Babylonian Empire, these nations surrounded Judah and sought her destruction. God invites humiliation upon these proud, arrogant leaders. Their penalty is watching the Lord destroy the shepherd's pasture—the land, agriculture, and prosperity they sought.)

25:37–38 The final two verses of chapter 25 remind people of how dependent they are on God: It is His decision when people experience peace or horror. (Chapter 25 marks the end of Jeremiah's prophetic warnings of God's judgment against the people of Judah, which began in chapter 2. By this point, the Babylonian invasion has taken place, and God's judgment is being poured out on the nation.)

26:1–2 God, as He has done previously, has Jeremiah take His message to the public and the religious leaders by returning to preach in the temple courtyard.

26:4–5 God repeats all the ways He has tried to communicate with His people: through His own voice, through His law, and through prophets He sent again and again.

26:6 The message is clear: God wants peace and a relationship with His people, and He will wait until the last resort to punish them back into obedience. If they refuse to listen, then they will endure a fate like a city before them: Shiloh.

26:7 This verse is powerful in its specificity: Everybody hears Jeremiah speaking in the house of the Lord.

26:12–13 Jeremiah responds to the people's threats by saying that their salvation from the prophecy he has delivered depends on their choice to repent and behave differently, a repeated theme throughout Jeremiah's sermons.

26:14–15 Regardless of whether the people choose to repent, Jeremiah insists that the message he speaks is God's, not his own, and that if they kill him, the entire city will suffer the consequences.

26:16 With a newfound perspective, the people—leaders included—change their minds and acknowledge that Jeremiah does speak on behalf of God.

26:17–23 The elders remind the people of similar prophecies in the past when God demanded they repent or face judgment. Sometimes the people listened and repented, and sometimes they killed the prophet.

26:24 In the case of Jeremiah, the wisdom of the elders prevails. They choose to look at how God has acted in the past, and they decide that repentance is God's wish and message to His people. Jeremiah's life is spared.

27:1–2 Jeremiah, as he has many times before, receives word from the Lord, this time instructing him to speak out against the nations that are planning to fight back against Nebuchadnezzar's invading forces.

Jeremiah's message to the people is this: Get ready to put yourselves into submission. God has Jeremiah use yet another visual aid to symbolize His message: this time a yoke. The prophet is commanded to wear a yoke around his neck, similar to the wooden yokes worn by oxen. Jeremiah becomes a walking illustration of the bondage the nations will endure by coming under the yoke of Nebuchadnezzar.

27:3 The audience for Jeremiah's message is a group of kings from surrounding nations who are trying to come up with a way to respond to Nebuchadnezzar.

27:3–8 Despite the kings' desire to resist the invasion, God makes it clear that He has orchestrated Nebuchadnezzar's attack and is delivering His people over to Babylon.

27:9–10 God offers a series of warnings against false prophets. Anyone who proclaims the nations will avoid Nebuchadnezzar's rule is lying, and any leader who believes those falsehoods will be completely destroyed.

27:12 Jeremiah reiterates God's message to Judah's king, Zedekiah, because it is imperative that he hears the true message over that of the false prophets.

27:13–16 These verses repeat the distinction between the messages both sets of prophets are preaching. Jeremiah has the same warning against false prophets for the priests to hear.

27:16–18 Some prophets have been saying that vessels from the temple seized by the invaders will quickly be restored to the people. These items are valuable—not to mention sacred—and will be scattered in the chaos of invasion and enslavement.

27:19–20 Contrary to what the false prophets are saying, God declares that even the remaining temple relics will not join the people where they are in exile. Perhaps this separation of the people from their objects associated with God, their holy relics, is part of their discipline and chastisement.

27:21–22 The true prophets, God says, will not be worried about what is left behind and where those relics end up; eventually all will be restored to Jerusalem.

28:1–4 Hananiah claims to hear God saying the captivity will last only two years instead of seventy, and he speaks specifically about the same two things in Jeremiah's previous prophecy: yokes and vessels.

28:1, 5 Hananiah's prophecy directly contradicts Jeremiah's, and Hananiah is sharing it publicly with all the religious leaders.

28:6–9 Jeremiah supports Hananiah graciously, saying he wishes Hananiah's words were true, but they aren't. Jeremiah restates the prophecy he received from God.

28:10–11 Hananiah reacts fiercely, taking the yoke off Jeremiah's neck and breaking it. He is not backing down from his false prophecy. Notice that Jeremiah does not resist, protest, or make a scene.

28:12–13 Jeremiah receives a rebuke from God to pass on to Hananiah. He may have broken the yokes of wood, but his angry outburst has severe consequences: yokes of iron.

29:5–7 God wants His people to make families and become members of their communities, seeking God's will for the city of Babylon and its welfare.

29:10–11 God's message for the people is clear and powerful: The exile will be seventy years, but He has plans to be with them. Although their exile and captivity are a result of their own sinful ways, they still belong to God, and He sends them this word of hope through His prophet.

29:12–13 The Israelites will survive their situation, and their relationship with God will be restored, allowing them to once again communicate with Him and hear His voice.

29:14 Repeatedly in Jeremiah's earlier sermons, God voices His frustrations that the people of Judah no longer hear their Creator and that they turn to false gods and prophets for guidance and worship. God now tells the people that eventually they will again hear and respond to Him, and He will restore to them everything they lost. In the midst of God's judgment and punishment, the mercy and redemption He planned for His people are slowly coming into view.

29:15 In Babylon, the people are susceptible to false prophets promising them quicker relief from the seventy-year punishment God promised.

29:16–19 God reminds the people, as He has so many times previously, not to listen to the false prophets. Further, He explains that the people who remain in Judah, who were not taken captive, will still face punishment. The punishment declared for them is familiar: sword, famine, and plague (see 14:12).

29:20–23 God names two particular false prophets who are misleading the exiles in Babylon: Zedekiah and Ahab. Jeremiah prophesies that both will die, and the memories of their fate will live on in the lives of the exiles as a reminder of their blasphemy and sin.

29:24–29 Jeremiah writes a letter to the false prophet Shemaiah. Shemaiah had written letters to the people still in Jerusalem and to Zephaniah the priest. As part of his letter to Zephaniah, he reminded the priest that part of his role included taking prisoner every madman who acted like a prophet. At the root of Shemaiah's question to the priest is why the prophet Jeremiah has not yet been taken prisoner, since he is continuing to deliver God's messages to the exiles—messages that contradict those of Shemaiah and other false prophets. Zephaniah reads this letter to Jeremiah.

29:30–31 After he hears Shemaiah's letter, Jeremiah writes to the exiles again, this time delivering God's message of condemnation against Shemaiah for his attack on God's prophet.

30:1–3 The phrase *the days come* is found throughout Jeremiah 29–33 (see also 31:27, 31, 38; 33:14–15). God announces that days are coming and with them the promise of restoration. The people will be returned from captivity, and their land and fortunes will be returned to them. Everything will be reversed: sin, exile, barrenness, and even the exiles' desire to turn away from God. God wants His people to know these days are coming and instructs Jeremiah not only to tell the people but also to write the message down.

30:4–7 Immediately after God's proclamation of a coming day when fortunes will be restored, there is a word of judgment. The coming day of the Lord is a day of both salvation and judgment. It is going to be a day of glory for some but one of dire judgment for others. This is what Jeremiah means by "the time of Jacob's trouble": There will be intense pain, pictured here by a strong man buckled over like a woman in childbirth. But God's people will be saved; exile in Babylon is not the final chapter of their story. For God's people, judgment precedes salvation.

30:16 God says He will judge Judah's enemies. Instead of benefiting from their attack on God's people, they can expect a similar fate. All who devour, enslave, plunder, and prey upon others will be devoured, enslaved, plundered, and given as prey.

30:17 God's people will be miraculously healed and restored. (Sickness and healing are metaphors for what happens to God's people in exile. The restoration comes and a miracle occurs—a terminal condition is reversed. Why does God do this? He restores and heals because His name is at stake. Judgment and discipline are necessary in the sanctifying process. Sickness is not the end; there will be complete healing. God's goal is salvation, even though it is completely unmerited and undeserved.)

30:21 Instead of being oppressed or invaded, the people will be led by one of their own, someone humble enough to be called by God—exactly the opposite of the false prophets whom God called out in previous chapters.

30:22 This verse references God's original covenant with Abraham (as does the promise of offspring in verse 20). The fulfillment of God's covenant is possible because of the cleansing, refining work God has done for His people. The future tense of the verse is a reminder that God can bring about the same restoration again.

30:23 This verse serves as a reminder of the consequences of disobedience, sin, and wickedness.

31:1 All of the families of Israel will be reunited as one family under God.

31:3–4 God's love for His people is the same as the marriage kind of love He mentions in 2:2. God again describes Israel in marriage terms and promises that she will be returned to a state of celebration and happiness (see 18:13).

31:5–6 Before too long the people will again farm and harvest their own land, and regular worship of the true God by all in the community will be restored for the first time since the division of the northern and southern kingdoms.

31:10 The restoration will be so whole and permanent that Israel will be able to share the truth of it with other nations as evidence of God's choice to restore His people.

31:15 Ramah was a town north of Jerusalem, where many of the Israelites saw home for the last time before being deported. The crying of the mother for her children signifies both weeping over lost exiles and the northern kingdom's weeping over the loss of some of its tribes. All those who heard Jeremiah's prophecies—whether they actually lived them out or not—could imagine the torment one would feel in these circumstances.

31:16–17 God has a word for those who weep in despair: Their toil and pain are not in vain. The ones who are lost will return. Reality seems dire, and truly it is, but God's Word promises restoration and hope.

31:20 God asks a rhetorical question: Does Ephraim still belong to Me? This is reminiscent of God's earlier question about Judah: Is she still My wife even though she acts like a harlot? The answer is an emphatic *yes.* God still knows, owns, and yearns for His children, and He will act with mercy toward them.

31:33 An essential characteristic of the new covenant is a new heart, and thus a new obedience. The people did not obey the old covenant, and thus their hearts were not changed. With the new covenant, God writes His character on the hearts of His people, using the pen, or influence, of the Holy Spirit. Then, once hearts are transformed, actions follow—God Himself lives through His people.

31:34 The new covenant creates a new community, a restored humanity, and a new way of relating. This is a unique relationship between God and His chosen people, the Israelites. Under the old covenant, the life of God was mediated through the offices of priests and prophets. This verse will see its fulfillment in Christ's death, when the veil is removed from the entrance to the most holy place (see Matthew 27:50–51), giving all who believe a direct relationship with God through Jesus, the Mediator.

31:34 An important element of the new covenant is a new sense of acceptance and freedom. Under the old covenant, the sacrificial system provided the means for confession and forgiveness for sins. In the new covenant, however, true forgiveness is achieved through God's promise not to remember the sins of His people. This forgiveness is later achieved through the atoning death of Jesus, the Son of God.

31:38–40 Chapter 31 closes with a final pronouncement. The city of Jerusalem will be rebuilt, and it will be larger than before. The ground upon which such suffering and destruction had occurred at the will of God will remain sacred to Him and to His people.

32:6–8 God informs Jeremiah that his cousin Hanameel is going to offer to sell him a field in Anathoth, Jeremiah's hometown, just outside of Jerusalem. God's prediction is fulfilled, and Hanameel approaches Jeremiah because, as a family member, the prophet has the right to buy the field and keep it in the family.

32:9–14 The text records the entire transaction with great specificity: The purchase price is seventeen shekels of silver (roughly seven ounces), and witnesses are called in to verify the signing of the deed and the exchange of money. Then the deed is given to Baruch for safe storage.

32:15 Buying a field in Anathoth in the middle of an invasion seems foolish, and yet Jeremiah's response is one of obedience and confidence in the Lord. He is confident that houses, fields, and vineyards—the most common elements of economic life—will again be bought and sold in the land of Judah. He makes a long-term investment based upon a future hope. Furthermore, his purchase shows the people that God's prophet believes there will be life after the exile in Babylon.

32:16–17 After purchasing the land, Jeremiah prays. The prayer begins with praise and a doxology to God's character and name. God created the heavens and the earth with His outstretched arm. Nothing is too difficult for this great and mighty God.

32:18–19 In his prayer, the prophet recognizes God's fidelity and justice, to which Jeremiah has been witness.

32:20–23 Jeremiah speaks of God's great power in the Exodus and the conquest of the land. But God's people do not obey Him, so the outstretched arm that saves Judah will judge her.

32:24–25 The prophet concludes his prayer by conveying what is happening to Judah at that time: The land is being invaded, and in the midst of it God has Jeremiah purchase land in front of witnesses. Jeremiah hints at an unasked question underlying his prayer: I know that You are a great and powerful God, but are You sure You have this right? Buy a field in Anathoth?

32:26–27 God answers Jeremiah by asking a rhetorical question: "Is there any thing too hard for me?" The word *hard*, or *difficult*, is often translated *wonderful*. In the Old Testament it is always used to refer to the great and miraculous deeds of God (see Genesis 18:13–14; Joshua 3:5). God reminds Jeremiah that He is the God of wonderful things in the past and the God of wonderful things in the future.

32:28–35 God goes on to outline the terrible judgment that will come upon Judah and Jerusalem as a result of their aforementioned idolatry and Baal worship. Judah's guilt is certain, and her discipline must be severe.

32:36–37 Despite the impending judgment, God promises, as He has in the past, that He will not completely destroy His people and that He eventually will bring restoration and healing. The Babylonian invasion is not a random act of violence. It is the will of God, again described by the trilogy of sword, famine, and pestilence or plague.

32:37–38 God reassures Jeremiah with a phrase that would have been quite familiar: "They shall be my people, and I will be their God" (see 31:33).

32:39–41 The restoration of the people will include the renewal of their hearts and will be so powerful that it will last for several generations. God also guarantees a continued relationship between Him and His people.

32:42 The coming renewal is as much a part of God's plan for the Israelites as is the current punishment He is inflicting on them.

32:43–44 God's response is His way of reassuring Jeremiah that buying land is exactly the right thing to do, both as God's prophet sending a message of faith to his people and as a member of a nation that will endure and eventually be restored to full civic life.

33:2–3 God speaks to Jeremiah, reminding the prophet of His true character as Creator and Sustainer of all and inviting Jeremiah to an ongoing relationship with Him.

33:4–5 God lets Jeremiah know He is aware of the destruction happening to the people of Judah. Reflecting on the pain of invasion and war, God reiterates that He allowed the Babylonian invasion to happen as a way of cleansing Judah of its wickedness.

33:6–13 These verses comprise another message of hope for the future: God will restore both His people and their holy city, Jerusalem. God's specificity about restoration matches His specificity about destruction.

33:14–15 God reiterates that He will restore both Israel and Judah. During that restoration, He will choose a particular familial line, the branch of David, from which the Messiah will emerge to bring justice and righteousness to the earth.

33:16–18 Judah and Jerusalem will know a new level of salvation and safety. Under this new reign, Israel will always have a leader, and access to God will be assured.

33:20–21 God emphasizes His point in the same way He does in 31:36–37, by the unrealistic *if/then* statement. Since God is the Creator and Sustainer of all creation, and will be for all eternity, the promises He makes with His people are also eternal.

33:23–26 God addresses a claim that foreign nations are making about Israel and Judah: that God has abandoned them. God explains that His attachment to His people is as certain and predictable as day and night and the turning of the seasons. (Repeatedly throughout the book of Jeremiah, God asserts Himself as Creator and Sustainer of the earth and all that is in it. By doing so, God not only reminds His people of His faithfulness to them and His inability to abandon them despite their sins, but also contrasts His character with the false gods His people have experimented with.)

34:1–7 At the time King Nebuchadnezzar invades Jerusalem, God has a message to communicate through His prophet Jeremiah. The message, intended for Zedekiah, the king of Judah at that time, is that the invasion he is experiencing is the work of God. Jeremiah prophesies that Zedekiah will be captured, come face-to-face with Nebuchadnezzar, die a peaceful death, and be buried with dignity. Given how God had warned the people of countless corpses they wouldn't be able to bury, much less with formal rites and rituals of mourning, this message must have come as a comfort to Zedekiah.

34:8–22 This passage tells a story that highlights a significant broken promise.

34:11 Owners of servants (slaveholders) obey the king's command, but their initial action of loyalty is soon followed by a reversal, when the leadership reneges and takes back the slaves.

34:12–16 God responds to the leadership's reversal by reminding Jeremiah's listeners of their agreement regarding servants. God had released the people of Israel from bondage. He was faithful to His covenant and did not turn back. Zedekiah, too, released servants, but he was not faithful to his covenant. This theme of fickleness and inconsistency is found throughout the book of Jeremiah. A promise is given and a promise is broken.

34:17 God does not take kindly to the people's breach of covenant, and Zedekiah and his officials will suffer a harsh judgment. God, as He has on multiple occasions, refers to the triad of destruction He has promised—sword, pestilence, and famine—throughout Jeremiah's oracles. The implication is that God holds back the floodwaters of judgment, but there comes a point when He opens the gates.

34:18–22 The consequences of God's judgment will be brutal, and to express how brutal, He refers to the ritual of confirming a covenant (or agreement) by cutting a calf in two and walking between the pieces. The ritual signifies that anyone who breaks the covenant should become like the calf that is split in two. All those involved in breaking the agreement about the freeing of the servants—the officials of Judah, the officials of Jerusalem, the court officers, the priests, and all the people—are guilty. Their punishment will be as severe as indicated in the message of the halved calf.

35:3–5 Jeremiah brings the entire family into the temple of the Lord, a very holy and public place.

35:6–11 The Rechabites refuse to drink. Even though Jeremiah gives them permission to do so, and even though they have already compromised a bit by moving into the city for fear of the Babylonians, the Rechabites remain faithful to the covenant vow of Jonadab. (The Rechabites are mentioned in more detail in 2 Kings 10, where we read that Jehonadab, also known as Jonadab, the son of Rechab, joins himself to Jehu when Jehu ruthlessly slaughters the worshippers of Baal. Jonadab, who is zealous for the Lord much like Jehu, institutes strict disciplines for his family. They are nomads living in tents, not houses, and they do not raise crops. They do not plant vineyards, and they do not drink any wine. The Rechabites are metalworkers, but we don't have enough additional information to know exactly why they took the vows of Jonadab.)

35:12–16 The key words in these four verses are *hearken* (or listen) and *obey*. Both of these words come from the same Hebrew word, *shema*. This term means more than merely hearing; it means to hear and then put into practice what one has heard. God reveals the lesson by contrasting the Rechabites and Zedekiah. The Rechabites listened; Zedekiah does not. The Rechabites made a promise and remained faithful; Zedekiah made a promise and broke it. The specific details of the Rechabite way of life shouldn't be the focus of the story. What is important is the fact that the Rechabites lived in obedience and integrity. God repeatedly spoke to Judah and sent His prophets to them with the message

of repentance, but Judah did not listen. The Rechabites, on the other hand, listened and continued to obey even after 240 years.

35:17–19 Not only is there a contrast in fidelity in the stories of the Rechabites and Zedekiah, but there also is a contrast in results. Here we observe two different destinies. For Judah, the result of failing to listen will be judgment and disaster. The people will lose their land and cities and be carried off into exile. But the Rechabites will never lack a man to stand before God. The Davidic line was cut off with Zedekiah, but the line of the Rechabites will continue. Two different stories of covenant loyalty end in two different destinies.

36:1–2 God tells Jeremiah to record everything He says to him concerning Israel, Judah, and all the nations on a scroll. Scholars think these writings, as a result of God's commandment, comprise all of Jeremiah's preachings from 627 to 605 BC (chapters 1–25 of the book of Jeremiah).

36:8–10 Jeremiah and Baruch obey God's command: The text records three readings of the scroll that are dictated by Jeremiah, including one near the new gate, the same gate mentioned in chapter 26. Verse 9 states that the people are fasting, which probably indicates that the Babylonian invaders have already made progress in overtaking the city. The particular chamber mentioned in verse 10 is associated with a powerful political family. Even though a large crowd is present, it is obvious that God is targeting the leadership of the nation.

36:11–13 When Michaiah, son of Gemariah, hears the Word of the Lord being recited in the temple, he takes it seriously. He goes back to the king's house and tells all the officials, one of whom is his father. The officials listen to Michaiah.

36:12–32 Jeremiah faces much trouble in his lifetime, but there are times when God sends people to rescue him. The officials mentioned in this passage may well have been the very ones who rescued Jeremiah in chapter 26. Gemariah and Michaiah are instrumental in protecting Jeremiah and Baruch when King Jehoiakim burns the scroll and seeks to kill Jeremiah. Then after the fall of Jerusalem in 587 BC, Nebuchadnezzar himself gives word to the captain of the bodyguard to protect Jeremiah from harm. When the choice is given to Jeremiah to go to Babylon or stay in the land, he attaches himself to Gedaliah, the son of Ahikam.

36:23–24 Jehoiakim's response contrasts with the response of the earlier officials in this chapter. They hear the words of God and fear Him, but the king hears the same words but does not fear. His response also contrasts with the response of his father, Josiah, seventeen years earlier. Josiah had been presented by Shaphan (Josiah's secretary) with the scroll of Deuteronomy, rediscovered in the temple. Hearing the Word of God, Josiah tore his clothes (see 2 Kings 22:11). A generation later, the scenario is repeated between the sons. Josiah's son, Jehoiakim, is presented with a scroll by Shaphan's son, Gemariah. His response is completely different. Jehoiakim does not tear his garments. Instead, he tears the pages of the scroll, and the text specifically notes his servants do not tear their garments.

36:30–32 God has a new message for Jeremiah to deliver to Jehoiakim: Destroying the scroll did not destroy the message of God. Because Jehoiakim did not listen, he is going to die, and his family will suffer the effects of the Babylonian invasion. The final verse of the chapter describes Baruch and Jeremiah re-creating and elaborating on the original scroll.

37:1 Chapter 37 returns to the reign of Zedekiah, the king who breaks the promise of the servants' freedom. Zedekiah has been made king by the invading king of Babylon, Nebuchadnezzar.

37:2–3 Although Zedekiah and his people have continued to sin and to ignore the way of the Lord, even after being reminded of God's words through Jeremiah, he still asks Jeremiah to intercede for them.

37:4–5 At this point in the story, Jeremiah is still a free man, and reinforcements are coming for Judah to help fight the Babylonians.

37:6–10 God responds to Zedekiah's request for intercession: The reinforcements are not going to help, and Jerusalem is still going to fall to the Babylonians. Reinforcements cannot thwart the will of God.

37:11–12 The supporting army from Egypt helps for a time, and during that brief period, Jeremiah goes out to take possession of the land he had purchased from his cousin.

37:13–15 As Jeremiah is leaving, a member of the army thinks Jeremiah is deserting Jerusalem and going to join the Chaldeans (Babylonians). Despite Jeremiah's protests, he is arrested and thrown in a jail in the house of a man named Jonathan, where he is mistreated. Jeremiah's harsh treatment might have been because he was suspected of being a deserter, but there is also the possibility that it is because of his role as God's prophet and the message of judgment he had been preaching for years.

37:16 This dungeon is possibly a cistern, an underground chamber created to collect water.

37:18–19 After answering the king's question, Jeremiah continues, asking Zedekiah to justify his imprisonment. Why is he imprisoned, Jeremiah asks, while the so-called prophets who prophesy peace and contradict Jeremiah are free, even though the current circumstances in Judah prove the false prophets lied?

37:20–21 Jeremiah asks the king not to return him to the jail at Jonathan's house, where he is treated badly. Zedekiah agrees, and although he keeps Jeremiah captive, the prophet is imprisoned in better conditions as long as the siege in Jerusalem allows.

38:1–3 The chapter opens with a list of men who hear Jeremiah prophesying about the coming justice of God by sword, famine, and pestilence. According to his prophecy, joining the Chaldeans (the largest tribe of Babylonians at this time) is a way to keep one's life. Since Jerusalem is going to fall to Babylon, if the people

go ahead and surrender, they may be allowed to continue to live in their homes rather than be exiled when they are defeated.

38:7–13 It is likely that many people knew of Jeremiah's situation. But the text is specific about the one person who acts to ease his suffering: Ebed-melech the Ethiopian, a palace official. *Ebed-melech* means "servant of a king." This man is a foreigner from Ethiopia and a government official with no legal rights in Judah. None of Jeremiah's own people care enough about him or his message to fight for him, but Ebed-melech goes against popular opinion and asks the king to pardon Jeremiah's life. When he is granted permission, he pulls Jeremiah out of the pit.

38:14–16 Jeremiah finds himself in a familiar position: face-to-face with King Zedekiah. Jeremiah uses the opportunity to bargain for his life, pointing out to Zedekiah that in the past, even when Jeremiah told the truth about God's prophecy, Zedekiah didn't take actions to repent or change his behavior. Zedekiah promises, in the name of the true creator God, to neither order Jeremiah's death nor leave him to the whims of the mob like he did previously.

38:17–18 Apparently satisfied that his life is not in danger, Jeremiah reveals God's latest word. Jeremiah informs Zedekiah that if he turns himself over to the officers of the invading army, he and his family will live and the city's destruction will not be as vast as it has the potential to be. However, if Zedekiah continues to resist, the Chaldeans (Babylonians) will destroy the city completely and even kill Zedekiah.

38:19 Zedekiah confesses his distrust of the alliances that formed in war and indicates that he doesn't trust his fellow countrymen to deliver him to Nebuchadnezzar safely.

38:20–23 Jeremiah assures the king that he must follow God's direction or face specific consequences: The remaining harem in Judah—Zedekiah's wife and daughters—will be brought to the officers of the invading Babylonian army (including the largest tribe of Chaldeans), where they will be raped, forced into marriage, and possibly killed. Furthermore, Zedekiah will be killed, and the city will be completely destroyed by fire.

38:24–26 Zedekiah instructs Jeremiah to keep this message to himself, because this information can be used against the king. The king does not want his court to know that he truly trusts Jeremiah's prophecy, so he asks Jeremiah to lie about the purpose of their meeting.

38:27–28 Jeremiah seems to support the king's secrecy and ultimately survives this event. However, as the next chapters reveal, Zedekiah does not heed God's Word, and the city of Jerusalem does fall to the Babylonian forces.

39:1–3 The Babylonians storm the city of Jerusalem for thirty months before finally breaking through the city walls in July of 586 BC, marking the fall of the city. With the fall of Jerusalem, both nations of divided Israel have been conquered: Israel, the northern kingdom, was conquered by the Assyrians in 722 BC; and Judah, the southern kingdom, is conquered with this event in 586 BC.

39:6–7 Conquering kings believed it served no good purpose to keep the conquered king and his family alive. Sooner or later, any vestige of leadership or family was likely to attempt to retaliate. For this reason, Nebuchadnezzar disposes of Judah's leaders and Zedekiah's sons, burns the palaces to the ground, and gouges out the eyes of Zedekiah before presenting him as a trophy before the Babylonians.

39:9–10 The strongest of the people who are still in the city after its destruction are captured as exiles and begin their thousand-mile journey on foot to the great city of Babylon in the modern-day country of Iraq. The poorest and weakest citizens of Judah are left behind in the destroyed city, where they are given what remains of the vineyards and fields.

40:1–3 Nebuchadnezzar's bodyguard, Nebuzar-adan, knows that Jeremiah is a prophet from the Lord who has spoken an advanced warning of calamity for Jerusalem. He takes Jeremiah to a place north of Jerusalem, where exiles are taken and assessed for their worth, and speaks with him there. Nebuzar-adan acknowledges the work of God in the invasion and conquering that have just occurred.

40:4–6 Nebuzar-adan offers Jeremiah a choice: come to Babylon or stay behind with Gedaliah, the new leader of the land formerly known as Judah. Jeremiah chooses to return to Mizpah, near Jerusalem, to be with Gedaliah, whose name means "watchtower" or "lookout."

40:7–8 The forces in the field are groups of Jewish troops who have not yet been captured. When they learn that Gedaliah has been appointed governor of the land by Nebuchadnezzar, they go to him in the city of Mizpah.

40:9–10 Gedaliah tells the Jews not to fear the Chaldeans (the largest Babylonian tribe). Further, he instructs them to stay and harvest crops. It seems that the people can resume their lives under Nebuchadnezzar's reign.

40:11–12 When other people from Judah, who are neither displaced by the war nor exiled, hear of Gedaliah's community, they join the group, remembering that Gedaliah is the son and grandson of godly men who had served Josiah. These people also begin harvesting crops.

41:1–3 Three months after Jerusalem's capture and Gedaliah's appointment as leader of the Jewish community, Ishmael brings ten men to Mizpah and kills Gedaliah and all the people who are with him. Ishmael kills Gedaliah during a hospitality meal, while eating bread together. The inclusion of this fact in the text reveals what a cowardly and unjust act Ishmael committed. But it only gets worse.

41:4–9 On the day after the murders of Gedaliah and the Jews who had been with him, eighty men from Shechem (in Samaria) come to visit Gedaliah and to worship. Ishmael greets them, acting as if he is mourning Gedaliah's death. He lures the men into the city, where he kills them and dumps their bodies into a pit or cistern. Ten are spared because they bribe Ishmael, further

evidence that Ishmael is nothing but a self-motivated killer. The pit is described as being a particular one made by King Asa (see 1 Kings 15:22; 2 Chronicles 16:6).

41:10–15 Ishmael, continuing his atrocities, captures all the Jews who are under Gedaliah's protection, with the intention of carrying them across the river Jordan into the area known as Jordan. Ishmael plans to take them to the Ammonites, a reference to the ancient residents of the modern city of Amman, Jordan. To the rescue, however, is Johanan, the leader of what is left of a small Jewish army allowed to protect the city from further assault and one of the men who had tried to warn Gedaliah of Ishmael's threat. He puts together a group and rescues the kidnapped. The people are glad when they see Johanan coming, further indicating his status as a good community member. After he rescues the Jews from Ishmael, Johanan goes after him, and Ishmael flees to the Ammonites.

42:1–3 The remnant of people from Jerusalem have been through one traumatic experience after another, and all the people want is security. Faced with the absence of the only leader they have had since the invasion and destruction of their land and the exile of their fellow citizens and family members, they turn to Jeremiah. They want him to intercede with God on their behalf because so few of them remain and they need God's guidance. They know they can no longer trust Jerusalem to protect them—the city's walls have been torn down in the war.

42:4 Jeremiah, who for many years has acted as an obedient prophet to the people of Jerusalem, also shows the leadership of a priest by ministering to them. He assures them that he will pray for them, and he will not hold back a word of God's answer.

42:5–6 The people's response to Jeremiah's assurance that he will pray for them and share God's answer with them seems to indicate that at least this remnant has learned to be responsive to the word of the Lord received through Jeremiah. The people promise to obey the message no matter what it is.

42:10–12 God's message is consistent with what He has said all along: The worst is over, and God will nurture them as they restore and rebuild their city. Nebuchadnezzar is no longer a threat, and because of God's will for His people, He will work through Nebuchadnezzar to support the people in their restoration efforts.

42:13–14 The people's restoration is dependent on their staying where they are in the midst of the destroyed remains of Judah and Jerusalem. God knows the people are considering leaving the land and moving to Egypt for an easier life.

42:15–19 Although God has said the people have a choice to remain or flee, He implies that their minds are already made up, and predicts the same three kinds of destruction present throughout the book of Jeremiah. They can expect to face swords, famine, and pestilence (or plague) if they flee. God's message is clear: Don't go to Egypt.

42:20–22 Jeremiah seems to know that despite the promises the people make in verses 5–6 to obey God's message no matter what, they might as well have already left. Disobedience to Jeremiah's messages has become a pattern. (The people cannot let go of their old thoughts about God. Just as they thought rituals would save them no matter what the condition of their hearts—see 7:21–29—they think that because Jerusalem has been destroyed, God is no longer with them. They need to understand that Jerusalem is merely a symbol of God's protection. They look at their reality—the large majority of Jews in exile and their new leader, Gedaliah, murdered—and logic tells them it is time to give up on the promised land. In their immediate struggle, they fail to understand that God wants them to stay in Jerusalem to remain the faithful remnant, that He has not deserted them, and that He will not remove His hand of protection.)

43:1–3 Jeremiah speaks words of truth and warning to the remnant of people from Jerusalem, and yet they do the exact opposite of God's command. Azariah and Johanan are the first to voice resistance to the word of the Lord, calling Jeremiah a liar.

43:4–7 Despite Jeremiah's words of hope, the people flee to Egypt. Those who flee include all the leaders (even Johanan, who had acted so honorably in previous situations), everyone who had been rescued after Gedaliah's murder, and Jeremiah and Baruch. (Prophets were stoned if their prophecies did not come to pass. The very idea that Jeremiah has survived all these years is a testimony that his prophecies are true. This fact should have been proof enough for the people to listen to him. But instead, the Jewish remnant retreats back to the land God had miraculously led them out of a thousand years earlier. The people journey back to the Red Sea to the place called Tahpanhes, the modern-day Suez Canal. Pharaoh had a palace at this juncture of the Mediterranean and the Red Seas.)

44:2–6 In this message are the same elements that have been present throughout the book of Jeremiah. God summarizes where they have been: He punished His people in many ways because of their persistent sin, and He sent prophets again and again. But the result is the same: The people turn away from God and His Word and follow their own ideas about safety and prosperity in other places with other gods. Because of this behavior, Judah and Jerusalem are in ruins.

44:7–9 God expresses His anger with His people by asking a series of rhetorical questions about their actions up to this point.

44:10 The people have not gotten God's message, have not realized their sin, and have not learned to commit themselves to Him.

44:11–14 In the same pattern seen throughout the book of Jeremiah, God follows the statement of reality with the consequences. This time, even though only a remnant of Judah remains, God abandons them to the consequences

of their decisions. They will die in Egypt by sword, famine, and pestilence (or plague). None who went to Egypt will return to Judah, except for a few refugees.

44:15–19 The people respond to Jeremiah by telling him they are going to ignore him. At this point, one would expect deep and mournful repentance. But instead, they tell Jeremiah they will no longer listen to him. Their defiance has become an open act of rebellion, and they justify it by saying that when they used to worship the other gods, they did not suffer. They admit to preparing flat bread images of Ishtar (the "queen of heaven"), the Egyptian goddess of love and fertility. Their baked goods became a creative new act of burnt offering, and they topped off their bread by hosting wine parties dedicated to their favorite deities.

44:20–23 Jeremiah responds to the people's latest argument by saying God was watching the entire time. He endured their behavior as long as He chose to, and when He decided to teach the people their sins were unacceptable to Him, He allowed them to be punished.

44:27–28 In a reversal of the hopeful promise of 29:11, God assures the people He is watching over them for harm and not for good. The few who will emerge from Egypt will have no doubt about God's power.

44:29–30 In his final words of prophecy, Jeremiah speaks of a sign. Egypt's Pharaoh-hophra (Pharaoh Hophra) will also fall under the growing dominion of King Nebuchadnezzar, which comes to fruition in 569 BC.

45:1–3 Jeremiah's message to Baruch was written in the fourth year of Jehoiakim's reign (see Jeremiah 36), almost twenty years before Baruch went to Egypt with Jeremiah. The letter addresses some of the complaints Baruch is having about his role in Jeremiah's ministry.

45:4 This verse echoes the phrasing of 1:10, with language of building, breaking down, planting, and plucking up. The fact that these themes sustained themselves through all these years is evidence of the consistent message of God and the loyal obedience of Jeremiah. It is not surprising that, given Jeremiah's enemies and his own honest times of frustration with God, Baruch would also have such struggles.

45:5 The name *Baruch* means "blessing," and this is what Baruch is to Jeremiah. He came from a distinguished family. He might have had a moment where he sought great things for himself and questioned his role in Jeremiah's ministry, but he counted the cost and gave it all up in order to bless Jeremiah. Baruch's work ensured that Jeremiah's prophecies and story would survive for generations.

46:1–2 During Jehoiakim's reign, Jeremiah receives a word from God concerning Egypt. The first two verses reference the battle of Carchemish, fought in 605 BC by Egypt and Assyria against the growing power of Babylon and King Nebuchadnezzar.

46:6–9 The rivers are referenced for their benefits but also for their uncontrolled power, and the leaders are encouraged in their futile battle.

46:10 Ultimately God is in control, and because of His justice, He allows Egypt to be defeated at Babylon's hands.

46:13–15 God goes on to explain that Nebuchadnezzar is the king who will lead the Babylonians in Egypt's destruction. Egypt can prepare itself, but the invasion is going to come, and Egypt will suffer as the Lord decreed.

46:19 The people who survive the invasion will be taken prisoner and marched away from their homelands, which will be destroyed.

46:20–21 Egypt is described as a beautiful heifer, symbolizing the nation's size, strength, and importance as a world power that had dominated the nations even before 1800 BC, until the rise of Assyria in 722 BC. God's description of Egypt is of one that prospered for a while but was unprepared for the invasion and unable to defend itself.

46:22–24 The Babylonian army will march 550 miles, like a swarm of grasshoppers or locusts, attacking everything in sight, until it achieves the coveted title of world dominator. Destruction will be real, and Egypt will be subjugated to Babylon.

46:25–26 The gods of the Egyptians will be punished, as will the pharaoh, and then everyone will be turned over to Babylon. The destruction will not be complete or permanent, however; Egypt will rise again.

46:27–28 The chapter closes with God's simple yet sustaining assurance that the sons of Jacob will not be consumed during the ravage of war. God will continue to discipline, correct, and punish them, but He will not remove them from their coveted position as God's chosen people.

47:2 God's message to the Philistines is similar in that the invader is also Babylon. The image of a flood indicates that the invasion will be severe and widespread. The prophet Jeremiah describes the onslaught of Babylonian siege as a mighty torrent of water, sweeping through the land and consuming everything in its path.

47:3 Philistia will be so overpowered that parents won't be able to save their children.

47:5 Those who survive will become captives of the Babylonians and will be shaved bald as part of their enslavement. Likewise, cutting is an act of mourning for some pagans.

47:6–7 It is unclear who is asking God to sheathe His sword—it could be the Philistines themselves wondering if such harsh justice is necessary, to which God responds *yes*. Or it could be Jeremiah, wondering how God could allow such devastation to take place. When will God step in to restore order and peace?

48:1 As in each of the prophecies for the nations, Moab's coming destruction is described as if it has already happened. The oracle to Moab is lengthy because of Israel and Judah's long history with the country. The judgment begins with the word *woe*, indicating a time of mourning has come.

48:7 Much as he accused Judah and Egypt, God specifies that Moab trusts too much in its own achievements;

consequently, its false god Chemosh, priests, and princes will suffer.

48:8–9 No city in the entire country will survive the invasion, and all the citizens of Moab will either die or be captured.

48:10 God is so intent on fulfilling the nation's judgment that He takes a break from detailing its sins to motivate His instrument, the Babylonians, to act swiftly.

48:14–17 The idea that Moab's warriors will be able to defend against God's justice is laughable. When God decrees His judgment for Moab, it is time for the people to begin their mourning for the nation and expect to see examples of its destruction.

48:18 Cities on hills are often the safest and manage to avoid destruction, but God calls those in Dibon, who survived the initial destruction, to come down from the hill and experience it for themselves. God links the destruction of the country to that of the individual citizens.

48:21–24 These verses list all the communities in Moab that are destroyed.

48:25 The imagery of a mature stag that loses its horns (or a person whose arm is broken) is used to describe the crippled state of Moab.

48:26 As in Jeremiah 25, God describes Moab as drinking uncontrollably from a cup. The people's gluttony leads to their illness and destruction.

48:27–28 When Israel was weak, Moab took advantage of that weakness. Now God instructs the Moabites to flee their cities and take up refuge in hiding places like animals.

48:29–30 In addition to being idol worshippers and opportunists, the Moabites are also arrogant and prideful. But God observes that this pride is misplaced and futile.

48:31–32 As a result of Moab's misplaced pride, the mourning for the nation will be thorough, as seen by the specific groups God is mourning for, and the mourning will be even more intense than other instances known in history.

48:33 The winepresses that once kept Moab in economic prosperity will quit working, and no income will be produced.

48:34–35 The destruction will be far-reaching. Jeremiah prophesies that Moab will be destroyed as a people because of its idolatry.

48:36–39 God mourns as if at a funeral for a nation that once prospered but now is destroyed. The survivors wear the markings and the behaviors of slaves horrified at their state.

48:40 The eagle is an often-seen image of destruction in biblical texts.

48:41–42 The invasion brings great pain, and the country of Moab will be destroyed because of its arrogance.

48:43–45 Anyone who lives in Moab will experience punishment, and escape is impossible. The destruction moves from city to city throughout the country, and the destruction and harm are intense.

48:46 The god that the Moabites had worshipped fails them, and the Moabite children are taken captive by the invading nation, a method of destroying an entire culture. History shows that the people of Moab will assimilate into other cultures and cease to have a genetic identity.

49:4 The people once boasted in the beauty of their lands, but Jeremiah prophesies that those lands will be destroyed. God points out the futility of that misplaced boasting, pride, and arrogance.

49:7–8 As with Moab and Egypt, Edom's residents are urged to flee, perhaps even into nooks and crannies (depths or caves) like animals. Jeremiah mentions Teman and Dedan in 25:23, specific areas within Edom. The reference to Esau here is because Edomites are descendants of Esau.

49:9–11 *Gleaning*, a common practice, meant leaving part of the harvest behind so the poor could come behind and get some harvest for themselves. God says that even thieves take only until they have enough. But what God will do to Edom is strip it completely bare, leaving nothing behind, not even what people try to hide. As with Moab and Ammon, however, God promises to save a few, namely, the most vulnerable: orphans and widows.

49:12 God references His own righteous character to assert His next pronouncement, and He seems to be continuing an earlier theme of contrasting those who are responsible with those who are innocent. The cup of fury (see 25:15–38; 48:26–28) will be drunk by those who deserve God's wrath. But God says the orphans and widows will be safe. God then rhetorically asks the listener: Are you innocent? Will you be acquitted? And the answer is an emphatic *no*.

49:19 God lets listeners know that His wrath is coming like a lion approaching a well-tended pasture. In biblical times, this pasture would house vulnerable sheep. Upon God's approach, all will run and leave the sheep untended. As in any agrarian society, anyone or anything attacking livestock would be dealt with. But no one can dispute or stand up against God's just wrath.

49:20–21 God urges all to listen to what is coming: Edom will be conquered, and people will be taken captive. The fall of the mighty city will not go unnoticed.

49:23 The third nation prophesied against in chapter 49 is Damascus. The cities mentioned here, Hamath and Arpad, are both in the Damascus region. Shame and anxiety have come to these people because they have heard of the Lord's coming judgment.

49:28 The fourth group of prophecies in this chapter is against two nomadic communities in Arabia, Kedar and Hazor. Both tribes will come under Nebuchadnezzar's control.

49:31–33 Nomadic tribes move from place to place simply by moving their poles and tents, so God points out that they are an easy target, with no gates or bars for protection. These people depend upon their flocks for travel, food, and trade. God warns that these flocks will be destroyed or taken by the invaders, and the people left will be dispersed. The area where these nomads used to

congregate will be so devastated that only scavenging animals like dragons (or jackals) will be there.

49:34 The final set of prophecies in this chapter, against Elam, is one that Jeremiah shared when Zedekiah was still king of Judah. Elam is mentioned in Genesis as one of the sons of Shem, who was Noah's son (Genesis 10:1, 22). The Elamites were known as a warring people, constantly at odds with the Hebrews.

49:35 God's wrath is specific to the skill Elam is known for: archery. God describes His judgment as breaking Elam's bow and its finest archers.

49:36–37 The metaphor of four winds indicates how complete the destruction will be and how far flung the Elamites will be. God indicates no hope for anyone trying to survive.

49:38–39 Rather than others being worshipped in Elam, God will be restored as the rightful leader and king, and eventually God will restore Elam itself.

50:1 Babylon, clearly identified as the target of God's words, is often referred to by the name of its largest tribe at this time, the Chaldeans.

50:2 God pronounces to all the nations, probably through Jeremiah, that Babylon will cease to be the invader and will itself be conquered. Babylon's god, Merodach (or Marduk), has been destroyed.

50:3–4 Just as Judah was invaded from the north, so Babylon will be invaded by the Persians. Just like the nations prophesied about in the book of Jeremiah, Babylon will become a wasteland and no one will remain.

50:8–10 Amid the chaos of war, as God plans His wrath against Babylon, He allows the exiles to leave Babylon. The Chaldeans are linked with Babylon; they will not escape punishment.

50:11 It becomes evident why God intends to punish the people whom He had used to be His punishers. God has established throughout the book of Jeremiah that nations prosper when He allows them to prosper. When a nation forgets God as the source of blessing, peace, safety, and prosperity, and its people begin to look to themselves, their allies, and false gods as sources of those things, God must intervene. God is angry that Babylon enjoyed the role He gave it in refining His people.

50:14–16 Because of God's wrath, Babylon is now an easy target for anyone who wants to conquer it. The city's civic life no longer exists, and its defenses are literally gone.

50:17–20 Turning His attention back to His people, whom He refers to as sheep, God reminds the listener that His flock has been conquered before. God will punish this last invader, just as He did the first one. As this happens, Israel and Judah can rest easy; the cleansing God wants for them has occurred, and God is pardoning those who have survived.

50:21 God uses two sarcastic names for areas of Babylon: *Merathaim*, which means "double rebellion," and *Pekod*, which means "visitation." It is no surprise, then, that God uses such names in ordering their destruction.

50:22–24 War breaks out against Babylon just as God intended.

50:25–27 God speaks as if He personally is outfitting the invading Persian army and inviting it to do whatever it wants to Babylon and Chaldea.

50:28 The consequences of war have come to Babylon: Its own citizens are now fugitives and refugees. This is the justice of God.

50:29–32 These verses reiterate what God is allowing to happen to Babylon. Now is the time to conquer this nation that has been so destructive to so many. Invading armies will succeed, and Babylon's people will suffer. This harsh justice is specifically because of the arrogance with which Babylon conducts its affairs.

50:33–34 God reminds the listener of His work on behalf of His people. God needs to perform a work on His people, and He does so through Babylon's armies. But those soldiers themselves are also subject to the will and the work of God.

50:35–38 God asserts, as He has previously, the destruction that will come against the Chaldeans and the Babylonians, but this time He is specific about who will suffer: inhabitants, princes or officials, wise men, prophets, warriors, horses, chariots, and foreigners. Drought will also come. This punishment is coming because of Babylon's love of idols.

50:39–40 As a result of the destruction, only scavenging animals will remain where Babylon used to be.

50:44 The image that God uses to describe His wrath in 49:19—a lion—reappears here.

50:45–46 God has spoken: The people of Babylon will be destroyed, and those who survive will become captives. The entire world will see the humiliation and suffering of the nation that has been so mighty for so long.

51:3–5 God talks to the Babylonians and then instructs the invading Persians. As He has stated before, the Chaldeans (Babylon) will be destroyed, and any injustices that occurred to God's people while they were being refined by God are now avenged.

51:6 God instructs some people to flee Babylon because the wrath of God is coming. But why are some instructed to flee as if they are innocent? God is speaking to His people from Judah and Israel who have been captured and kept as slaves in Babylon. The destruction of Babylon is certain, and He doesn't want them to endure such wrath twice.

51:9 Any attempt by the people of Babylon to recover from God's actions toward them will be futile (see 10:19; 15:18; 30:12–13), because it is God's will that they be destroyed beyond healing.

51:10 The remnant of Israel and Judah see the destruction of Babylon as vindication for injustices they endured from the Babylonians during their own punishment from God.

51:11–12 Even more forces are awakened against Babylon to perform the Lord's work, and this particular people, the Medes, fulfill an earlier prophecy that they will participate in Babylon's fall.

51:13–14 Babylon's placement near rivers has allowed it to amass great fortune, but the end has come by the hand of the Lord.

51:15–16 God reminds the listener of His work as Creator and Sustainer of all creation. This section is highly reminiscent of not only Genesis but also earlier passages in Jeremiah, where God contrasts His nature as true God against the false, created gods Judah has turned to.

51:17–19 God is the Creator, and people are the created; when human beings try to create as God creates, they reveal their foolishness. The idols and gods they create from their own limited minds are worthless, and those who do such things will be punished. God is the one true God.

51:20–24 God uses anyone He wishes to do His work. In this case, He must punish those Babylonians and Chaldeans who let themselves act of their own wills and not of the will of God.

51:25–26 The ones who have been so mighty are now at the mercy of God and will not survive their punishment.

51:27–29 In this version of the war party against Babylon, three new groups are recruited: Ararat, Minni, and Ashchenaz. Their task on behalf of the Lord is as clear as the others have been: Destroy Babylon in the name of the Lord.

51:34–36 The voice shifts to that of a survivor of Judah, detailing what has happened at the hands of Nebuchadnezzar. God willed and allowed Judah to be invaded by Babylon, but Babylon acted as much out of its own arrogance and greed as it did out of respect for God's will. For the injustices that occurred in the midst of God's punishment, the survivors want retribution.

51:37–44 The Judah survivors' desire is fulfilled; the mighty, fearsome Babylon will be utterly destroyed. Many of the same phrases of destruction that have been applied to other nations in the book of Jeremiah now apply to Babylon.

51:45–46 As He did earlier in this chapter, God instructs the Jews and Israelites who are living in Babylon as exiles that He is about to punish Babylon. He has prophesied this so word will get to His people in the coming years.

51:47–48 The fact that God is speaking to His people personally and trying to comfort them with details of Babylon's destruction indicates that, as seen earlier in Jeremiah, the prophet and priest functions still exist even after war and exile. God wants His people to know that the coming wrath is targeted toward Babylon.

51:49–50 The reason for God's punishment of Babylon is that its people were excessive in their treatment of Judah. Now vengeance must be had for the Jews who were killed. Those Jews who survived must now flee and remember the Lord and Jerusalem.

51:52–53 Babylon's punishment is coming because of its arrogance and its worship of false idols. Her former power cannot save her.

51:57–58 Babylon's leaders become drunk with arrogance and power, so much so that they will not survive. The city itself will not survive either; its walls will be destroyed, and its remains will be burned down.

51:59–61 This chapter closes with a specific message from Jeremiah to a man named Seraiah (Baruch's brother). Jeremiah is communicating to the Babylonians while traveling with the exiled Jews. Jeremiah writes all these messages in a single book (or scroll) and instructs Seraiah to read every bit of it as soon as they get to Babylon.

52:1–3 The reader is taken back to a time when the king who ended up accompanying Judah into Babylonian exile, and who was brutally killed as a prisoner of war, is just coming to the throne at age twenty-one. Despite Jeremiah's prophecies about God's anger and coming wrath, Zedekiah, like his predecessor, Jehoiakim, continues to lead the nation in sin. God then punishes Judah as He promised. Apparently, for a time, Zedekiah rebels unsuccessfully against Nebuchadnezzar.

52:4–7 These verses explain in detail how Jerusalem falls to the Babylonians. In the ninth year of Zedekiah's eleven years as king, Nebuchadnezzar arranges his army around Jerusalem, cutting off traffic in and out of the city. After six months, the people are out of food, and the Babylonian troops break through the city wall.

52:8–11 Babylonian troops are supported by the Chaldeans, who capture Zedekiah and bring him to Nebuchadnezzar for sentencing. In a brutal fashion not uncommon in war, Zedekiah is forced to watch as all his sons are killed. He is then blinded and imprisoned in Babylon, remaining there until he dies.

52:13–14 About a month after the Babylonian invasion, Nebuchadnezzar sends his chief into Jerusalem to burn not only the temple but also all the large houses he can find, including Zedekiah's. This is the culmination of progressive actions Nebuchadnezzar has been taking to conquer Judah. This is the end. The Chaldeans destroy the city walls.

52:15–16 As seen earlier in Jeremiah's prophecies, huge numbers of people who haven't already been captured are taken prisoner. But, as also mentioned before, the poorest and the weakest are left behind.

52:17–23 These verses list in detail items that are taken from the temple. These are the items the exiles are longing for in 27:16–22.

52:24–27 Additional information is provided about some of the people who are captured: They are of religious and civic importance—leaders of the people who have just been conquered. Like Zedekiah, they are taken to Nebuchadnezzar and killed.

52:27–30 With the death of the leaders whom Nebuchadnezzar captured, the exile can begin. At least three waves of exile are listed here.

52:28–30 Forty-six hundred of Jerusalem's finest are bound into slavery to serve out their lives in subservience to King Nebuchadnezzar. Little do they know that God will use them as an object lesson to the world, to prove His uncompromising mandate for sovereignty in their lives, and to prove the severe and widespread consequences of bowing in worship to false gods. In every generation, we disappoint God with new ways of disobeying Him. Yet in new ways every generation, He proves His faithfulness to us and proves that His loving-kindness is everlasting.

52:31–34 The final verses of the book of Jeremiah show that despite the destruction of Jerusalem and its temple, and the death and exile of so many of its citizens, a king of Judah remains alive. This king (though in name only) is Jehoiachin, and Nebuchadnezzar's son Evil-merodach takes him out of prison. Probably as a gesture of good will, Evil-merodach improves Jehoiachin's living situation by giving him new clothes, allowing him to share meals, and providing him an allowance. Even among prisoners there is hierarchy, and the improvement in Jehoiachin's situation is an indication of hopefulness that closes this powerful book.

THE LAMENTATIONS
OF JEREMIAH

INTRODUCTION TO LAMENTATIONS ■ Wedged between two of the major prophet works—the books of Jeremiah and Ezekiel—is the short, five-chapter poem titled Lamentations. The book's name reveals what it is—a poem of lament. It records in grave detail and sorrow the aftermath of one of the lowest points in the history of the Israelites. But it also provides one of the greatest testimonies of God's justice and mercy.

AUTHOR ■ There is a tradition that the prophet Jeremiah wrote this book, and thus it has its place in the Bible following the book of Jeremiah. However, no author is named in this specific book itself, and there is no place in the rest of the Bible where this writing is attributed to Jeremiah.

OCCASION ■ Lamentations was most likely written soon after 586 BC, shortly after the fall of Jerusalem at the hands of the Babylonians. The author is reflecting on what he sees around him, making it most likely that the city's fall was recent at the time the book was written. In this work, he alludes to the future redemption God promised His people, but that redemption has not happened yet, and the wounds of their sins and consequences are still fresh.

1:1–8 The introductory chapter to the book of Lamentations focuses on the depth of the author's grief over Jerusalem's destruction. These verses catalog some of Jerusalem's losses. Among them are abundance, allies, a home, worship, prestige, courage, and prosperity. But despite all the tragedy the author notes, he quickly acknowledges that the destruction isn't undeserved.

1:8–11 Judah's sin has devastating consequences, not just for the state of the nation, but in the lives of its inhabitants. The author's grief is rooted largely in how much he cares for Judah's people and the sorrow he feels regarding their downfall.

1:8–10 The people are shamed after their idolatry is exposed. The people's sin also leaves them defiled, and the unclean aren't allowed to enter the presence of God. Their worship is tainted. One of the worst consequences of the Babylonian invasion for the city of Jerusalem as a whole is the desecration of the temple. The holiest place on earth has been invaded by a group of pagans who never even would have been allowed inside it.

1:11 A devastating consequence of the nation's sin, probably one of the most strongly felt by the people of Judah, is the famine caused by how long the city was held captive before being overtaken. The cause of Judah's grief and destruction isn't a mystery—it is a direct effect of the sin in which they had been living for many years.

1:12–13 While the suffering of the nation is undoubtedly deserved, and long overdue because of their sin toward God, God doesn't exact suffering on them for punishment's sake alone. At this time idolatry was rampant, and God had to remind the people who their true God was. The severity of their punishment is to get their attention and turn them back to Him.

1:14–15 God gave His people the freedom to make their own choices, but they became slaves to the consequences of their sins. No matter how much one suffers inwardly as a result of sin, nothing is as humbling a wake-up call as being crushed in the presence of one's enemy. And that is exactly what Judah experiences when its capital city is destroyed.

1:18–19 The people of Judah come face-to-face with the consequences of their sins, and this stark reality leads them to some confessions: God is righteous and acts rightly, and we were wrong to rebel against His Word.

2:1–9 The results of God's righteous and just anger are described in a series of powerfully descriptive verbs that capture the severity of God's anger against Jerusalem. The gates and walls of the city literally crumble, mimicking what happened to the people as well.

2:1–10 These verses mention more than forty times how God was personally involved in Jerusalem's downfall and what happened to the people within its walls. This repeated mentioning of God's control reiterates that although King Nebuchadnezzar may have commanded the attack on the city, it was ultimately God's judgment that orchestrated the events.

2:11–13 The author describes his own reaction to the events at hand—one of both torment and a sorrowful understanding of the justice of God. He understands that God's discipline is appropriate for the sin of the people of Jerusalem, but that doesn't make it any easier for him to stomach the city's destruction. He is admittedly without words of comfort in the face of the people's suffering.

2:14–17 There were many false prophets who were telling the people that they had nothing to fear (see Jeremiah 27–28). In the wake of the city's destruction, however, it becomes evident that these prophecies were false. Although Jerusalem's enemies gloat in the face of its downfall, the enemy's involvement in Jerusalem's destruction is secondary to God's.

2:18–21 The people are encouraged to wail and mourn at the consequences of their sin, the worst of which is the suffering of the innocent, especially their children (see 1:5, 16; 2:11–12). Because of the faithlessness of the people of Jerusalem, this holy city has been destroyed. The people who survived the attack were taken off into Babylonian captivity. Their situation is one of complete hopelessness. But God is a faithful God. It is in this truth that hope for the nation of Judah rests.

3:1–24 This chapter opens with an identification of a man who is afflicted. Most scholars see this man as a personification of the city of Jerusalem, much like the widow mentioned at the opening of the book. Others think, however, that the author is simply referring to himself and his own desperation.

3:21–24 From a picture of hopelessness and suffering, this section marks a powerful transition from the desperation in Judah to the hope of God. This hope is rooted in the fact that God didn't destroy everyone; therefore He hasn't completely abandoned His people. Just as God was faithful to bring the judgment and destruction He had promised, He will also be faithful in the mercy and renewal He promised.

3:25–39 The goodness of God is still evident. The people's suffering doesn't change this aspect of God's character. By the same token, God is in control, even during times of grief.

3:40–66 Included in this section is a catalog of sufferings, which can seem out of place after the previous section of verses that focus on hope in God's goodness, faithfulness, and control. Suffering is still the reality for this nation, but the author trusts that the characteristics of God's mercy will return and bring relief to those who seek God's forgiveness.

3:52–58 For those who consider Jeremiah the author of this book, these verses seem to be an obvious description of an event from Jeremiah's life recorded in Jeremiah 38:6–13 when he was attacked, thrown into a dungeon (or cistern), and left to die. Just as God rescued him from that situation, he prays that God will rescue the nation from its suffering.

3:59–66 As if the sufferings of the nation aren't enough, the author once again finds himself being attacked and persecuted by his enemies. He knows, however, that the Lord is capable of delivering him, and he prays that God will rescue him and punish his attackers.

4:1–2 This chapter opens with a description of the costs of the people's rebellion against God in imagery they would understand. Although their lives had once been as valuable as gold, they are now as dispensable as everyday pottery.

4:3–5 The people's rebellion has physical costs. The children are starving, and people who were once considered royalty are sleeping in dunghills on the streets.

4:6 This is a comparison of the situation in Jerusalem to that in Sodom, but in this case the author says Jerusalem is worse off in that her suffering lingers in contrast to Sodom's sudden destruction (see Genesis 18–19).

4:7–12 These verses paint a picture of what the suffering in Jerusalem is like following the Babylonian siege. Bejeweled princes are sickly and roam the streets unrecognizable and covered in filth. People are constantly dying of starvation due to famine, and the author again notes the horrific scene of women cooking their children for food to survive. All of this is a result of what is referred to as God's fierce anger.

4:14–16 This section gives specifics about the causes for God's judgment. Those who were supposed to be the example of holiness and the mediators between the people and God were leading the people astray with lies and corrupt practices. The priests who survive the Babylonian attack are left to wander the streets and are shown no honor.

4:17 Jeremiah 37:5–7 reports that the people of Jerusalem will look to Egypt to ally with them against Babylon. Here, this prophecy comes to pass. After the attack, some of the people who survived and weren't taken into captivity sought refuge in Egypt, where they would be free to continue their idolatrous practices (Jeremiah 44:7–30).

5:1–13 These verses describe the people's condition at the time of this prayer. Their property (inheritance) is gone, they are exiled to a foreign land, and they are impoverished and at the mercy of their enemies. Everyone has suffered in some way. There are six different people groups, all of whom have experienced extreme suffering. The entire nation feels God's punishment on an individual level.

5:14–18 The prayer shifts to the topic of emotional suffering. There is no joy among the people, and their hearts are faint because of what they have endured. More important than physical healing, the people's spirits need to be restored to the joy of the Lord they once knew.

5:19 This verse is the crux of the prayer that makes up the surrounding section and reveals the foundation of the author's hope. God is the only One with power to right the people's punishment and bring physical and emotional healing to the nation.

5:21–22 The author prays for restoration and for God, in His mercy, to turn the people's hearts back to Him if mercy is in His plan. He also recognizes, however, that God, in His sovereignty, may not choose to lift the punishment and show mercy, but it is his prayer that that is not the case.

THE BOOK OF THE PROPHET

EZEKIEL

INTRODUCTION TO EZEKIEL ■ Ezekiel was a prophet caught up in the turmoil of his time. He was among ten thousand exiles carried off to Babylon in the second of three deportations from Judah (2 Kings 24:14). He and his wife settled in a Jewish community established near Nippur, on the Kebar Canal. God's people needed a prophet in Babylon because, with some wonderful exceptions, they carried all the spiritual baggage from the years of idolatry and apostasy that began their ruin.

AUTHOR ■ Ezekiel was a priest, and his priestly orientation comes through in his prophecies. More than any other prophet, he depicts the consummation of the kingdom of God in terms of a new temple and revitalized worship. His prophetic call came at age thirty, which would have made him a young eyewitness to the spiritual reforms during the reign of King Josiah. Although he is unable to serve as priest in a traditional capacity due to his relocation (and the subsequent destruction of Jerusalem's temple), his spiritual preparations are still put to use as God calls him to be a prophet during a crucial time of Israel's history.

OCCASION ■ God's people were caught in the maw of conflict between world powers Egypt and Babylon. International tensions overshadowed the circumstances of many smaller states and turned the lives of countless individuals and families upside down. Ezekiel's world was turbulent, which makes his message surprisingly relevant for today.

1:1 Ezekiel was among a group of expatriate Jews living in Babylon along the river of Chebar at Tel-abib. It was his thirtieth year, the age at which a priest should be beginning his official service to God (see Numbers 4:3). He is far away from the temple in Jerusalem, but God has not forgotten him.

1:2–3 This passage marks a shift from first person to third person, likely the insertion of an editor to provide objective dating for Ezekiel's call and/or to make the opening more consistent with other prophetic books. The date would have been July 31, 593 BC. It may seem strange that this account is dated according to the reign of Jehoiachin, a king who ruled only three months and accomplished nothing. Yet Jehoiachin is perceived as the last of the kings in the Davidic line. Those who follow are Babylonian appointees. Archaeological evidence suggests that the Jews in Jerusalem as well as Babylon acknowledged Jehoiachin as the true king, even after his exile.

1:4–9 In there land of Israel's enemies, while God's people are in captivity, Ezekiel receives a magnificent vision. A sudden storm blows in, accompanied by wind, lightning, and fire. In the center of the fire are four creatures, each with four faces. They will be identified later as *cherubim*, a specific rank of angels.

1:10–14 Each of the four faces of the creatures is significant: The lion is chief of the wild animals, the ox chief of domestic animals, the eagle the primary bird, and human beings chief of all animals. The four faces orient the beings in all directions, so they therefore have no need to turn while navigating. They move, literally, like lightning: They are both brilliant and quick. The description of these cherubim may have appeared less bizarre to Ezekiel's original audience than to modern ears. The iconography of the ancient Near East included figures that had more than one head, multiple sets of wings, human bodies with animal heads, and so forth.

However, no symbols have been discovered that match Ezekiel's depiction.

1:15–21 The prophet's portrayal of the wheels by which these creatures move from place to place is fascinating and puzzling. The beings are able to move in any direction, including leaving the ground. In Hebrew and Greek, the same word can be used for wind and spirit, so the *whirlwind* (see 1:4) is associated with the movement of God's Spirit. No prophet writes of the Spirit as much as Ezekiel. This energizing power of God directs him from place to place, at least in his visions. And the movement of the four creatures is in response to the Spirit.

1:22–28 Ezekiel now describes a gemlike firmament—an expanse or platform above the creatures upon which the throne of God will rest. The throne of sapphire is reminiscent of Moses' description of seeing God on mount Sinai (Exodus 24:9–11). Even describing the sound the creatures make is a challenge for Ezekiel. He likens it to three different things: the roaring of waters, the voice of the Almighty, and the tramp of a great army on the march. Yet these amazing sights and sounds are only a prelude to what is to come. Ezekiel's attention is arrested first by a voice from above, and then by a figure like that of a man, sitting on a dazzling throne. The shining brilliance of the figure prevents Ezekiel from seeing anything other than a general shape, yet the prophet leaves no doubt that he is witnessing the terrible majesty of Yahweh. In response, he falls facedown before the Lord God.

2:1–5 Throughout the entire book of Ezekiel, God never addresses the prophet by name. Instead, he uses the term *son of man*, which highlights Ezekiel's humanity in contrast to the Lord's divine glory. God is sending Ezekiel to speak to his own people, the Israelites. But at this point in their history, they are rebellious, obstinate, and stubborn. They are subjects revolting against their

King and children rebelling against their Father. But they are about to discover a real prophet among them. The problem with false prophecy is that it is invariably rosy and frequently proven false by real-life events. Ezekiel, on the other hand, will provide stark promises of divine wrath, and the people will see his prophecies come to pass.

2:3 References to *Israel* can be confusing. The name originated with Jacob (Genesis 32:27–28). By the end of Genesis, phrases such as "tribes of Israel" (Genesis 49:16) or "children of Israel" (Genesis 50:25) indicated the people of God. Centuries later, after Solomon's death, the tribes divided. The ten northern tribes continued to be known as *Israel,* while the southern tribes comprised *Judah.* Technically, the Jews exiled to Babylon were from Judah, but they were the only ones to return to their homeland after captivity. From that point, biblical writers again use *Israel* to refer to them, as Ezekiel does. And while the term *Jew* is by definition someone from the kingdom of Judah, it soon broadens to include any of the citizens of the remnant of Israel after the exile.

2:8–10 God warns Ezekiel of the danger of getting caught up in the rebellious attitude of his people. He offers him something to eat, and Ezekiel no doubt expects some kind of food. Instead, he is handed a scroll with a message of lament, mourning, and woe.

3:1–3 Jeremiah had written of eating the words of God (Jeremiah 15:16), but Ezekiel goes beyond metaphor to a more concrete (and most likely unpleasant) experience, as he is instructed to fill his stomach. The message certainly isn't appealing, yet the taste of the scroll is sweet. The sweetness must have come from the prophet's encounter with the Word of the Lord itself. Opening one's life to God's Word and God's will is humanity's highest privilege and the greatest conceivable satisfaction.

3:4–7 Had Ezekiel been sent to some other people, they might be expected to respond, as the Assyrians listened to Jonah. But the people of Israel had a long habit of rejecting God, so Ezekiel should expect the same response and not take it personally.

3:8–11 God promises to help toughen up His prophet. (The name *Ezekiel* means "God strengthens.") We speak in terms of "facing" difficult situations; it is Ezekiel's face that is hardened to help the prophet cope with his listeners. And it is at this point revealed that Ezekiel's assignment is to preach to the community of exiled Hebrews.

3:16–21 Ezekiel is not to be evaluated based on the *results* of his prophecies but rather on his faithfulness in speaking for God. Ezekiel's role as a prophet is like that of a watchman for a city. It is his job to sound an alarm after being made aware of an approaching threat. All Ezekiel has to do is pass along God's message to the people. They might respond and be spared a tragedy, or they might ignore the message and suffer the consequences. God's truth is a fragrance of life to those who are being saved and an odor of death to the defiant. The results are not under Ezekiel's control, but the prophet *will* be held responsible for speaking the truth clearly.

4:1–2 Ezekiel received his call to be a prophet in 593 BC. The Babylonians would destroy the city of Jerusalem in 586 BC. Many of Ezekiel's first assignments were to predict the fall of Israel's beloved city. If the previous section (Ezekiel 2–3) seems repetitive in its depiction of the Jews as hard of heart and obstinate in their refusal to humble themselves before the Lord, this section will prove equally repetitive in describing God's determination to punish Jerusalem for the Jews' betrayal of His covenant. God first tells Ezekiel to construct a model of the city of Jerusalem. The prophet would have drawn a map of the city on soft clay and then allowed it to harden under the Middle-Eastern sun. Jerusalem was on a hill, so any attempt to overtake the city would require ramps to transport battering rams and other weapons to the walls. Conquering a walled city was no easy task, so enemy armies would usually lay siege to the city first in order to weaken its resistance. Ezekiel's model of the city includes the ramps, weapons, and surrounding armies.

4:4–8 After spending 390 days turned toward the northern kingdom, Ezekiel reverses sides to deal with the sin of Judah—a forty-day commitment this time.

4:9–11 Ezekiel's next sign involves baking bread using an unusual combination of ingredients: grain and vegetables. The intent is to simulate a siege diet, much like those remaining in Jerusalem would be forced to eat. The shortage of available grain required making bread out of whatever could be found. The daily allotment is only eight ounces. Water is rationed as well, with Ezekiel only allowed about two-thirds of a quart each day.

4:12–17 Ezekiel doesn't balk at any of God's instructions until he is told to cook his meals using human excrement for fuel. This distasteful practice would be part of life under siege. But Ezekiel had always striven to uphold his principles as a priest, so God is sympathetic to his request and grants the prophet a concession. Ezekiel's symbolic actions in Babylon are to reflect the horrific conditions of life in Jerusalem. It is important not to overlook the qualifying phrase in verse 17. The people are certainly suffering, but their situation is because of their sin.

5:1–4 Ezekiel's symbolic demonstration continues with a severe haircut. He is instructed to remove his hair and beard. Normally priests were forbidden to shave their heads (Leviticus 21:5), so the action would have drawn attention. But the haircut is just the beginning. More significant is what Ezekiel is told to do with the hair; he is to weigh it and divide it into thirds. After his observation of the siege periods, he is to burn one-third of the hair inside the city (his clay representation). Another third is to be stricken with a sword and placed around the city. The final third is to be tossed into the wind. But Ezekiel is to hold back a few strands. No one in Jerusalem is going to weather the siege well. The people will either die from plague or famine inside the city, be killed outside the city, or be scattered by God to faraway places. Any survivors who may have remained complacent are represented by the few strands of hair first held back by Ezekiel but eventually added to the fire.

5:5–17 God's frustration with Israel is evident, and for good reason. The Israelites are supposed to be a light to the Gentiles, an example of higher standards. Yet they have degenerated to the point where they don't even meet the standards of the nations around them. Even after thousands of people have been carried away in two large deportations, the remaining Israelites continue to offer sacrifices to Canaanite gods. As one awful consequence, they are going to be driven to cannibalism as Jerusalem is besieged and their food supplies dwindle to nothing. Although the Babylonians are the instrument of their fall, God makes it clear that He is the One responsible for what is happening. However, the terrible circumstances will not last forever. God will see His people through, even in their desperate situation.

6:1–3 Ezekiel's oracle to the mountains of Israel begins with God's pronouncement of judgment on the high places around Jerusalem. While the people in Jerusalem will eventually hear what Ezekiel is preaching in Babylon, the Hebrews already exiled in Babylon realize they are implicated in Jerusalem's sins and have already suffered punishment for them. Other than the object of worship, idol worship in the high places is not dissimilar to worship at the temple. People burn sacrificial animals on an altar of earth, stone, or wood that is usually overlaid with bronze. This offering for the benefit of the particular god at that site is accompanied by incense burned in incense altars, creating a pleasing aroma for the god. But Yahweh is about to thoroughly devastate such idolatrous worship. The exposure of corpses as punishment is among the curses spelled out for those who betray God's covenant (Deuteronomy 28:26). Yet God will spare some of the people to bring them to a right mind and restore them to a life of faith. There is a terrible irony in that those who are restored first have to be cast out of the land the Lord has given them and stripped of all the privileges that have been theirs as His people. But that's what it will take for some people to know that He is Lord.

7:1–6 "The four corners of the land" is an all-encompassing reference. Disaster will befall the entire nation of Israel, but God's judgment is no more than God's justice. Israel has committed detestable acts and will receive only what is deserved.

7:7–9 When Ezekiel spoke of "the day," his listeners would have known what he was talking about. Other prophets (Amos, Isaiah, Joel, Zephaniah, and others) had already spoken and written of the day of the Lord. Ezekiel's prophetic ministry falls squarely in line with these other prophets who warned of God's terrible judgment if His people did not repent and return to Him. Although Ezekiel speaks of "the day" in present tense here, it will still be about six years before his prophecy is fulfilled. Yet the likelihood of the event taking place in the future is just as certain as if it had already happened. Similarly, in the New Testament we read of certain promises of God yet to come but spoken about as if they had already occurred.

7:10–14 Ezekiel now begins to describe the appalling effects of the day of the Lord. However, the reader needs to be aware of the examples of hyperbole—the use of exaggeration for effect (the way we might say, "He lost a ton of weight"). For instance, Ezekiel says that no one will be left after God's judgment, yet he will soon speak of the survivors. Ezekiel does not explain what he means about the rod that has blossomed. Perhaps it is a reference to Nebuchadnezzar or other oppressive rulers who will soon dominate Israel. What is clear, however, is that the economic consequences of God's judgment will be catastrophic. All the normality of daily life—buying and selling, for example—will be forgotten as Judah is driven from their land.

7:15–18 Sword, pestilence, and famine have been recurring themes in Ezekiel so far (see 5:12; 6:12) as the three forms of death associated with siege warfare. And the few who escape death won't be able to rejoice. They carry with them their own guilt and God's anger toward them on account of their rebellion. They will be overwhelmed, powerless, and psychologically devastated.

7:23–25 The city of Jerusalem has been spared for some time, and even under Babylonian control life is not particularly unpleasant at first. But Jerusalem will eventually be destroyed and associated with bloodshed. Those who don't die will be subject to chains—captivity and exile.

7:26–27 This will be a time of mischief upon mischief. Jerusalem's prophets will have no visions. The priests will offer no teachings. The ancients (elders) will provide no wise counsel. Not even the king will be spared indignity and despair. The people will have nowhere to turn as they realize that they are bereft of help. Jerusalem had been Israel's pride and joy. Its destruction will be their most agonizing memory.

8:1 This vision takes place some fourteen months after Ezekiel's initial vision in 1:1. The date would have been September 18, 592 BC, still several years prior to the fall of Jerusalem at the hands of Babylon. The fact that the elders are gathered at Ezekiel's home indicates that they recognize his prophetic authority.

8:2 As in his first vision (see 1:26–27), Ezekiel sees a general shape of a man, fiery and bright—another manifestation of Yahweh Himself. The details of this vision continue through 11:24, so one must wonder what the elders observed as Ezekiel witnessed what God was showing him.

8:3–4 The Lord assumes a form Ezekiel is familiar with (a hand) to lift him up. While remaining bodily in Tel-abib with the elders, Ezekiel is taken to Jerusalem in visions. Ezekiel first sees the north gate of Jerusalem's temple. Three gates lead from the outer court to the inner court, the north gate being the one used by the king and likely the most prominent. An idol stands in full view. The pathetic sight of an idol in the temple is soon contrasted with the glory of God Himself in the fullness that Ezekiel had previously witnessed (see 1:26–28).

8:14–18 Tammuz is a Babylonian fertility god who is particularly appealing to women. The women are mourning because tradition held that Tammuz had been banished to the underworld. Moving on from the inner room to the entrance of the temple, Ezekiel sees about twenty-five men worshipping the sun. Sun worship is nothing new in Judah (2 Kings 23:5, 11), but it has never been more brazen than in this temple setting. The temple faced the east, so logistically, to bow to the sun in the east, one had to turn his back to the temple. Yahweh is being displaced in His own sanctuary. Corrupted worship of God and crimes against other humans go hand in hand, so it is not surprising that Ezekiel notes the violence that fills the land. The phrase "the branch to their nose" is not used elsewhere in scripture, and its meaning is uncertain. It may be a reference to some pagan ritual or perhaps a disrespectful gesture.

9:1–5 The men who are summoned are most likely angels sent to execute God's sentence. Six have weapons, the seventh a writing kit. The six executioners will accomplish their work through the Babylonian army. The seventh is assigned to mark the people of the city who lament the detestable acts taking place throughout Jerusalem. The mark is the *taw*, the last letter of the Hebrew alphabet. Jeremiah would have been one of the inhabitants of Jerusalem at this time, so he and a minority of other citizens would not have been complicit in Jerusalem's apostasy. God's judgment will therefore make appropriate distinctions between those who participate in idolatry and sin and those who are grieved by such things.

9:6 Those with the mark are to be spared, but no one else. The widespread destruction, including women and children, is a feature of the holy war—a divine war against a wicked people. There is no mention of adult men because they will have been killed in combat.

9:7–11 Ezekiel fears that this judgment of God might do away with Israel altogether. Galilee and Transjordan had been lost in 733 BC. Samaria and what was left of the northern kingdom fell and its people were carried off in 721 BC. Little territory was left around Jerusalem. But the section concludes with the reminder that every true believer has been marked—a remnant will be spared. Israel has defied God in the most brazen and disgusting ways by forsaking Him for the ridiculous mythologies of other cultures. Their spiritual apostasy has led to a culture of violence and injustice. As severe as their judgment will be, it will be nothing they don't deserve.

10:1–22 The angel who had been given the task of marking the righteous is next assigned to bring the fire of Yahweh's judgment upon Jerusalem. The cherubim seemed to accompany the Lord's chariot, which was parked to the south of the temple—perhaps because of the idol that stood in the north gate. God is planning to depart from the temple. The cloud, representing the glory of the Lord, first moves from its established position in the most holy place to the threshold of the temple. Soon it moves from the threshold to the place where the cherubim are assembled outside. It is significant that the temple is called

the Lord's house at precisely the moment He is leaving it. It is at this point that Ezekiel identifies the creatures he had seen in his initial vision (chapter 1) as cherubim. The Bible maintains a close connection between cherubim and the presence of God. Large images of cherubim stood above the ark of the covenant, the physical sign of God's enthroned presence in the temple (Exodus 25:18-22), and the temple was filled with carvings of cherubim (1 Kings 6:29, 35). In the Old Testament, Yahweh is routinely portrayed as borne by cherubim. Ancient Israelites expected that wherever cherubim were found, God would also be present (Psalm 18:10; 80:1).

11:1–4 More evidence of the wickedness within the temple is seen as Ezekiel is shown another group of men. (The Jaazaniah here is not the same as in 8:11.) They are arrogant and self-confident, presuming that, as meat in the pot, they are secure and protected in Jerusalem—unlike the exiles in Babylon. The repeated command to prophesy indicates urgency.

11:5–12 As always, the Lord's gaze penetrates human motives. The group of men is placing confidence in Jerusalem, but the city will provide no safe haven. They will be driven out to suffer either death or captivity. In fact, the city's leadership will become the target of mass executions after the Babylonians overrun the city (2 Kings 25:18–21). The people *will* know that Yahweh is the Lord eventually.

11:13 The death of Pelatiah, one of the men Ezekiel had witnessed in the temple, is intriguing. It seems that he actually dies, not in the vision that Ezekiel is having, but *while* Ezekiel is prophesying. If so, his death would have symbolized what would soon come to pass for the rest of his peers. Ezekiel acknowledges the significance of Pelatiah's death and expresses fear that God will completely destroy the remnant of Israel.

11:14–19 The people with Ezekiel in Babylon are a remnant, and God will eventually return them to Israel. Those who remained in Jerusalem had somehow come to believe that *they* were the favored few, even with their inferior leadership established by the Babylonians after two previous deportations of Israel's principal citizens. God contradicts their assertion. A new exodus will take place, this time comprised of the exiles returning to Israel.

11:20–21 As God had promised previous generations of Israelites (Exodus 6:7), He again affirms that they will be His people and He will be their God. Ezekiel will have more to say about the renewed covenant later on. For now, however, judgment remains his primary theme.

11:22–25 The glory of God continues its progress out of the temple, ascending to a place above the mount of Olives east of Jerusalem. The vision concludes and Ezekiel is again set down in Babylon, where he reports to the exiles what he has seen and heard. Humanly speaking, it was easy for the people in Jerusalem to believe that Yahweh had favored them and rejected those in exile. But Ezekiel's vision demonstrates that the situation, in fact, is precisely the reverse. God is departing His temple and leaving behind those who give Him no thought. Instead, He will restore those in exile who have a humble and submissive mind toward Him.

12:1–2 Ezekiel has just related a detailed vision to the exiles, but God knows the people remain resistant and rebellious, so He has Ezekiel act out what those in Jerusalem will soon undergo.

12:3–11 As the exiles watch, the prophet packs his belongings, digs through the wall of his house to retrieve them, puts them on his shoulder, and carries them off. When people ask what he is doing, Ezekiel is to explain that it is a sign of what will soon take place in Jerusalem: Babylonians will break through the walls of the city, and most of the remaining survivors will be exiled. Evidently the exiles in Babylon still believe fervently in the security of Jerusalem, as do those who remained there. They do not accept that their exile has been divine punishment for their sins. The complete destruction of Jerusalem will not directly affect the circumstances of the exiles already in Babylon, but it will dash their hopes of a speedy return home.

12:12–16 Babylon will be the instrument of the fall of Jerusalem, but Yahweh is the Judge. The reason the prince (King Zedekiah) will not see is because he will be blinded by the Babylonians (2 Kings 25:7). Eventually the remnant of people who survive will acknowledge their sin and God's hand in the matter.

12:17–28 Continuing his symbolism of the situation at home, Ezekiel is to publicly eat and drink while trembling. His actions symbolize the anxiety and despair of the people not just in Jerusalem but in its surrounding towns as well. Yet people are slow to acknowledge harsh truths. The prevailing attitude among the exiles is that Ezekiel's prophecies are not coming true and that he must certainly be talking about a distant time in the future. God's response is that every vision (of His true prophets) will indeed be fulfilled and there will be no further delay.

13:4–5 The false prophets are portrayed as foxes in the desert, an image of destruction. They prophesy what people want to hear—peace and safety—so no one feels motivated to repent or to expect the coming judgment of the Lord. Ezekiel is trying to repair and rebuild Israel; other prophets are merely capitalizing on its spiritual ruin.

13:6–7 Divination was a widespread practice posing as a science, by which the practitioner presumed to learn what the gods intended in the future by studying animal livers, the stars, or some other symbol. The practice was forbidden in Israel because the Israelites were supposed to maintain godly character and faithfulness to God's covenant, leaving their future in His hands.

13:8–9 The consequences of prophesying falsely are severe indeed. The false prophets will face loss of membership in the assembly, have their names struck from the census register, and lose their right to the land, since they will not participate in the return of the exiles to Judah and Jerusalem. Theirs will be permanent excommunication.

13:17–23 Israel had female prophetesses as well as male prophets, so it stands to reason that there would be a number of female false prophets. It is surprising, therefore, that Ezekiel provides one of the very few judgments against women found in the Old Testament prophets. The language Ezekiel uses is clear enough to verify that Israel's magic and divination practices are wrong and offensive to God, but obscure enough to prevent stating exactly what those methods are. It seems likely that some of the exiles had adopted Babylonian magical ideas.

14:4–5 God knows that the elders of Israel in Babylon are still involved in idolatry, although it is perhaps more covert than before (in their hearts). They found Babylon to be far wealthier, more prosperous, and more powerful than their own nation, and they have been tempted to imitate Babylonian ways. But attempting to combine recognition of Yahweh's lordship with recourse to other gods is a bad idea. The gods of the Babylonians could tolerate other loyalties, but not the one, living, and true God of Israel. The Ten Commandments lead off with, "Thou shalt have no other gods before me" (Exodus 20:3). The reason, of course, is because other gods are false, foolishness, and unreal. The Babylonians had so many gods that it's difficult to know which particular ones might have been most appealing in Israel at this time. Excavations in Canaan have uncovered large numbers of small statuettes of Babylonian and Egyptian deities. So the elders of Israel have come to Ezekiel, not planning to submit their lives to the Lord in true faith, but to consult the prophet as if he were merely a fortune-teller. They want an answer to a question, and then they fully intend to return to the lives they have been living. They aren't looking for their covenant God to speak to them His truth. Considering their spiritual state, one might not expect God to reveal *anything* to them. In this instance, however, He promises to answer their inquiry directly, although it will not be the kind of answer they are hoping for.

14:6 This is the first of very few calls to repentance in Ezekiel that may seem to contradict the earlier statement that the prophet will not be preaching for repentance (3:26). Indeed, the die has been cast for Israel: This generation will be judged, and there is no hope left for it. Still, repentance remains God's desire for His people.

14:12–19 God assures Ezekiel of the inexorable and merciless judgment that awaits those who rebel against Him. Although the Lord speaks generally, it is Israel who is being addressed here. (His judgments for other nations will come later.) The particular judgments listed are the typical curses of the covenant for those who prove unfaithful to God: famine, wild beasts, sword, and pestilence (Leviticus 26; Deuteronomy 32).

14:14–20 Noah, Daniel, and Job were all conspicuously godly men who lived outside of Israel. The Israelites seem to presume that because there were heroically good people among them, they will be exempt from judgment. God had agreed to spare Sodom if only ten righteous people could be found (Genesis 18:26–32), but He did not intend to establish some kind of divine law or principle that would be observed in every case.

14:21 The sad fact that God addresses *Jerusalem's* great sin makes the judgment even worse. The people had known His truth, so their judgment will be heavier. The one consoling consequence will be that the exiles in Babylon will see the new exiles come from Jerusalem. When they realize how faithless and wicked they were, they will also acknowledge that God is entirely just in destroying the city. The impiety of the newcomers will be evident to the entire Israelite community in Babylon.

15:2–5 The vine is woody, but the wood is virtually useless. It is too soft even to use for making pegs.

15:6–7 The nation has been burned at both ends and charred in the middle by the first two Babylonian incursions into the Holy Land. It was customary at the time for invading armies to burn the cities they captured, so this allegory merges into a literal account of Jerusalem's future. Nothing is left but to cast the remaining wood into the fire to be consumed.

16:5–8 Yahweh is depicted as a passerby who spies the abandoned girl in an open field, helpless and near death, and chooses to make her live. The girl grows up to become a beautiful young woman. She is mature but still naked, creating a completely different situation. Yahweh preserves the young woman's purity and marries her.

16:8 The custom of spreading a corner of a garment over one's intended is mentioned in Ruth 3:9. The Lord's relationship with Israel had long before been described as a marriage, and Ezekiel's hearers would have known he was speaking about Yahweh's covenant to be Israel's God. The allegory and the theology merge at the end of this verse.

16:9–14 Yahweh dresses His bride and bedecks her in fine jewelry. The blood washing from her suggests virginal bleeding, the effect of the first lovemaking. At this point Israel is an innocent maiden. As her husband, the Lord lavishes luxuries upon her. The previously abandoned baby girl is now a queen—and fed and clothed as one. Her beauty, status, and fame are all Yahweh's doing. She owes everything to Him. Some of the language of this section, such as *broidered work* and *fine linen*, is also found in previous descriptions of the tabernacle, its curtains, and the priestly robes. The fine leather of her sandals is mentioned elsewhere in the Bible only in regard to the tabernacle and temple. Even the special food can be compared to the Israelites' sacred offerings.

16:15–19 Despite His great generosity and love for His bride, Yahweh begins to speak as a betrayed husband. His wife has begun to use her beauty for purposes other than for the pleasure of her husband. The verb meaning "to act as a prostitute," or some derivative, occurs twenty-two times in this chapter and may be regarded as the key word of the passage.

16:20–22 As if prostitution weren't bad enough in itself, the bride of Yahweh also participates in child sacrifice, the ultimate cultic crime. Involvement in such a barbaric act requires both a pagan mind-set and the most extreme repudiation of Yahweh's covenant. The practice seems to have first been introduced to Israel in the seventh century BC, in the northern kingdom (2 Kings 17:17), spreading to Judah during the reign of Ahaz (2 Kings 16:3) and becoming rampant during the reign of Manasseh (2 Chronicles 33:6). Josiah took steps to eliminate Israel's participation (2 Kings 23:10), but after his death the practice returned (Jeremiah 32:35). Israel, who had been rescued as an unloved and abandoned baby, is killing her children.

16:23–31 The details of Israel's promiscuous actions continue. Here prostitution is a metaphor for military and political alliances with other nations, each of which represents a failure to trust the Lord. The order in which other nations are mentioned—Egypt, Philistia, Assyria, and Babylon (Chaldea)—reflects Israel's history. Each of these relationships proved harmful, yet Israel moved from one such affair to another. In the original language, Ezekiel's description is more explicit than what is interpreted in most Bible translations. Israel's effort to attract other lovers is brazen. Even the pagan nations around her are shocked by such behavior.

16:32–34 In spite of her repeated conscientious efforts, Israel doesn't make a good prostitute. The point of prostitution is to make money, yet Israel paid others to be involved. The money is a reference to the bribes and tribute Israel gave to foreign powers over the years. Israel would not have *wanted* to make those imposed payments, but Ezekiel sees it all as the result of her philandering.

16:35–43 After the husband's case is made and Israel's betrayal has been exposed, the sentence is pronounced. In an ironic twist, the wayward wife who uncovered her nakedness without shame to entice her various lovers will be stripped and shamed before them. Her fortune has come full circle. She who began naked and abandoned by her parents will find herself naked and abandoned by the Lord.

16:38–42 Adultery is a capital offense in the Mosaic Law. In this case, the sentence would be carried out by Israel's paramours. Yet once the punishment has been inflicted, God's holy wrath will be satisfied. Ezekiel often reminds his readers that God's judgment is not a fit of divine temper, but rather the exercise of His holy justice.

16:43 Ezekiel can't seem to emphasize enough throughout his writing that what is happening to Israel is a result of her own actions. He makes the point again that Israel has ignored and forgotten the grace of God, His covenant, and His kindness to her.

16:44–58 God compares Jerusalem to other notable cities in history. Samaria had been the capital of the northern kingdom of Israel until the Assyrians conquered it during the previous century. What compounded Judah's sin was that the people had witnessed the fall of Samaria—punishment for the betrayal of Yahweh's covenant—and still did not repent.

16:46–55 Perhaps surprising is the comparison between Jerusalem and the city of Sodom with its sins of arrogance, self-centeredness, and lack of concern for the poor and weak. The noted city of sin had nothing on Jerusalem in those regards. It is hard to know what is meant by the restoration of Sodom, although it is meant as a backhanded rebuke of Jerusalem. The point is that since Jerusalem's wickedness is greater than Sodom's or Samaria's, those cities should be restored if Jerusalem is.

16:59–63 As is so common in the prophetic books, the Lord looks beyond Judgment Day to the new work of grace He will perform among His people. The restoration of Jerusalem will be a humbling experience. Sodom and Samaria are portrayed as being united with Jerusalem—a picture of universal salvation also common to prophetic books. The original covenant God made was with Israel, not with other nations, but the nations will not be left out in the end.

17:1–2 Ezekiel's third allegory approaches the style of a fable where animals and inanimate objects talk and act with human characteristics. This allegory is much more like a riddle. In fact, the word *riddle* used here is the same word used to describe Samson's riddle to the men in his wedding party (Judges 14:12). The literary style would have had an impact on Ezekiel's listeners because they would not have been able to figure it out until he provided them with the meaning.

17:3–4 The allegory begins with a precise description of an eagle that breaks off the top of a cedar tree and carries it away. Babylon had long gone to Lebanon for wood, so the tree in Ezekiel's allegory represents Israel. The top of the tree (the leadership of the nation) had been carried away (deported to Babylon in 598 BC).

17:5–9 The seed of the land is Zedekiah, the member of the royal family whom the Babylonians placed on the throne as their puppet king in Jerusalem. For a time Zedekiah was loyal to Babylon, indicated by the branches turned toward the eagle. But then a second eagle appeared, also powerful, yet not described quite as impressively as the first one. If the vine then sent its roots out toward the second eagle rather than the first, would it survive? Ezekiel's question is confusing, so he provides the answer first and then the explanation.

17:9–10 The vine will *not* thrive; it will wither. The second eagle represents Egypt. After a while, the galling yoke of subjection to Babylon begins to provoke thoughts of rebellion from Zedekiah. Egypt, a long-standing enemy of Babylon, is nearby. In this context, the east wind would have been the siroccos that heat Palestine from the desert.

17:20–21 Zedekiah's loyalty to the wrong eagle results in the Babylonian army bearing down on Jerusalem in 586 BC. After being forced to watch the execution of his sons, Zedekiah is blinded and taken captive to Babylon. His army, seeking to escape, is caught and destroyed. The rest of the population, with the exception of a few poor people left to tend the fields, is sent into exile. The details are found in 2 Kings 25.

17:22–24 This allegory has a surprise ending, as the Lord promises the eventual restoration of the remnant of Israel. He will choose and plant another shoot from the top of a cedar tree (provide another king). The positive influence of this new king will be felt around the world. The Lord will eventually cause Babylon to fall and restore life to the nation of Israel.

18:1–2 Ezekiel 18 is one of the better-known sections of this mostly unfamiliar book. In this section, the prophet clarifies God's attitude toward sin and who is responsible. Afterward, Ezekiel returns to his message of judgment on Judah and Jerusalem. Ezekiel illustrates that someone cannot begin to really understand human existence until he or she acknowledges that each life belongs to God. The emphasis throughout the chapter will be on the *individual* life. The proverb here suggests a world of fatalism, which is by no means true. Every single person will one day stand before a personal God, and He will judge each one accordingly. Jeremiah had cited the same proverb (Jeremiah 31:29), but both he and Ezekiel foretell an end to its popularity. The belief that God will hold future generations accountable for the sin of an ancestor is not accurate.

18:3–4 As I live means that the Lord charged the nation by an oath taken symbolically upon His own life. God judges each person according to his or her holiness. It is evident that the use of *die* in this context is a reference to spiritual death—death that continues in the world to come.

18:5–13 God provides Ezekiel with some illustrations to help his listeners clarify their thinking. The first describes a righteous man who has an unrighteous son. The father not only avoids actions that are clearly sinful; he also chooses to act honorably in everything he does. The son, however, is violent and disregards both civil and spiritual laws. The unrighteous son will answer for his own sins; his father's righteousness will be of no help to him. The biblical language used in verse 9 and other places is often questioned. God isn't saying, through Ezekiel, that a person deserves life rather than death because he or she follows God's laws. Works of faith do not accumulate points for anyone. Rather, such actions are the proper response of anyone whom God has already delivered from the fear of death. It is due only to God's deliverance, not a person's actions, that he or she will live.

18:14–18 This illustration is a reverse of the one that precedes it: The father is the sinful party, but the son refuses to follow in his father's offensive footsteps. The father will be judged for his wrongdoings, but the son will certainly not be punished for the father's sins. He will be treated by God as the righteous man he is.

18:19–23 The Lord expects objections to what Ezekiel is proclaiming and prepares the prophet with a good response: "The soul that sinneth, it shall die." If a wicked person turns away from sin and starts obeying God, the Lord will show forgiveness.

18:25–31 The people are accusing God of being unfair. Ezekiel ends this particular oracle with a plea for his audience to accept responsibility for their own destiny. What may be true for the generation as a whole need not be true of any specific individual. His call for them to receive a new heart and spirit refers to the seat of thoughts, attitudes, and desires. God will have to make the change, but the individual must initiate the desire. Faith, repentance, and obedience are at the same time divine gifts and human duties.

19:1 Several laments can be found throughout the Old Testament—dirges composed and sung at the death of an individual or over the destruction of a nation. (The book of Lamentations is a series of five laments.) One of the general features of a Hebrew lament is the "once. . . now" pattern that contrasts the glories of the past with the misery, indignity, and shame of the present. Such is the pattern of Ezekiel 19. In addition to using the term *Israel* rather than the more accurate *Judah* in this passage, Ezekiel also uses *princes* to indicate Judah's kings. The plural indicates that Ezekiel has in view not just Zedekiah but probably the whole series of unrighteous rulers who have led Judah to its final catastrophe.

19:2–3 The lion imagery, referring to Judah, had been used since the days of the patriarchs (Genesis 49:8–9). The lion was a symbol of rule, and Judah was the tribe that would rule over the other tribes of Israel, so Ezekiel's reference is to the kings of Judah.

19:10–14 Ezekiel's shift of imagery from lion to vine is yet another tie-in to Genesis. In Jacob's prophecy concerning his son Judah (more than fifteen hundred years previously), the boy's future is portrayed in terms of both the power of a lion and the fruitfulness of the vine (Genesis 49:8–11). After God's subsequent covenant with David, Judah had seen twenty-two kings from David to Zedekiah. But during that time, the kings of the house of Judah and David had become arrogant. They ruled Judah without regard to their obligations to God or the people of Israel. Consequently, the line of royalty came to an end (temporarily) because there was no strong branch left on the vine fit for a ruler's scepter. It is important to note that this lament is for the people of Israel, not just the kings. It is *about* the kings, but it will be sung *by and for* the people.

20:5–8 God reveals information through Ezekiel that had not been provided earlier in the scriptural account. In making a covenant with Israel, God had made it absolutely clear that there could be no compromise with idolatry. Any such practice is a denial of the one true and living God, and a repudiation of the revelation God had provided about Himself. However, Israel in Egypt was hardly a devoted and faithful people waiting patiently for the promises of God to be fulfilled. Rather, they were idolaters who had adopted the religious practices of the Egyptians.

20:9–12 Yahweh does not punish Israel as she deserves. Her idolatry notwithstanding, He is gracious and brings her out of Egypt. The sabbath is a sign in that it is a regular weekly reminder of God's covenant. It became a perpetual reminder of Yahweh's goodness in delivering His people from the seven-day workweek by which slaves were exploited in the ancient world. It is frequently proposed that the commandment to keep the sabbath originated at Sinai, along with most of the other laws. By this way of thinking, God's people would have been under no obligation to keep one day holy prior to their wilderness experience. Yet Ezekiel clarifies that God gave *all His laws* to Israel in the wilderness—that is, they were all formally codified at that time. Israel had already abided by certain civil laws (prohibitions to kill, lie, steal, etc.) and religious regulations (the offering of sacrifices, prohibitions to worship idols, etc). It is reasonable to believe, therefore, that observing the sabbath was also among their already established practices, even though it is not mentioned specifically until Exodus 16:21–30.

20:18–26 God gives Israel's children (the next generation) another chance to follow Him more faithfully. That generation enters the promised land, but they prove to be hardly more faithful than their parents had been. Reading through the passage, it is impossible to miss the repetition Ezekiel uses as a literary device to emphasize God's patience in light of Israel's persistent denial of God's covenant, their disobedience to His commandments, and their ongoing profanation of His sabbath.

20:27–29 Ezekiel begins to make a transition from the history of Israel to its current state. One might think that the one place where Israel would have been faithful to God was the promised land itself—a beautiful place God gave the people in spite of the fact that they did not deserve such a gift. Yet they quickly adopted Canaanite idolatry as they had practiced Egyptian idolatry previously. Ezekiel's point is that the people of his time are descended from blasphemers and idolatry is in their national DNA. Now they are in Babylon, surrounded by yet another pantheon of idols. English speakers miss the relevance of the question in verse 29. *Bamah*, the word meaning "high place," is sounded several times in Ezekiel's phrasing. The implication is that the current generation of Israelites is still seeking out high places to worship other gods, even in Babylon, as their ancestors had repeatedly done.

20:30–31 Even more offensive than anything their forefathers had done, this group of Israelites has become involved in idolatry to the point of child sacrifice—a monstrous outrage against the holiness of God. Yet they have the audacity to come to Ezekiel hoping to get some specific answer from the Lord! Rather than serving God, they expect God to serve them.

20:32–44 The people are out calling on idols, and God is going to judge them. The Babylonian exile is, in a way, a repetition of Israel's history of slavery in the wilderness. But in Babylon, the people will be purified and then restored to the promised land in a second exodus—a return from exile and a new beginning. Their restoration will have nothing to do with their achievement or performance. As always, it will be entirely due to God's grace, mercy, and faithfulness to His Word.

20:45–49 As God continues to speak to the people through Ezekiel's oracles, it isn't certain that even Ezekiel is aware of the meanings at first. Clearly his listeners aren't making sense of the imagery because they accuse him of just telling stories. But God will soon supply the proper interpretations: Fire represents war; the south is Judah; the green tree symbolizes righteous people; the dry tree stands for the wicked people.

21:1–7 The Babylonian armies will be the sword God uses. The route they take from Babylon will result in Judah/Jerusalem being to the south. Consequently, there will be much reason to groan. Ezekiel's symbolic sighing will pique the people's curiosity and make a point, but the time is coming when they and all of Israel will sigh (groan) for real. And a fact of war and other circumstances is that sometimes righteous people suffer in the punishment visited upon a wicked nation.

21:8–18 The proper interpretation of verse 10 is unclear. Perhaps the Jews first imagined that the image of Yahweh brandishing His sword would have been good news. In this case, however, He is not preparing to defend and avenge Israel. Just the opposite: God is preparing to destroy Jerusalem. The sword will soon be handed to Nebuchadnezzar. In response, Ezekiel's sighing escalates into howling and striking his thigh, for good reason.

21:19–24 Nebuchadnezzar will arrive at a crossroad and seek direction through divination, beseeching his gods, and other signs. Then he will choose the route that takes him to Jerusalem for conquest. But since God is telling Ezekiel exactly what will happen, it is clear that the choice is not Nebuchadnezzar's at all, but God's. Usually divination methods were used in cases where one of two choices needed to be made: go to war or not, attack this way or that, and so forth. Examining the liver of animals (hepatoscopy) was one standard technique of divination that was very popular with the Babylonians. Also, arrows would be marked with various symbols and drawn from a bag, not unlike drawing straws. And it was around this time that astrology—the effort to discover the future in the stars—was being developed in Babylon. The ancients were fascinated with attempting to know the future. But God's people were forbidden from such practices. The future was to be left to God; people were to concern themselves with faith and obedience in the present.

21:25–27 The Jews might have thought themselves safe from Babylonian attack because they had sworn loyalty to Nebuchadnezzar. But after the oath of loyalty was broken by Zedekiah (2 Chronicles 36:13), they should have had no expectation of security. Zedekiah was the profane and wicked prince. The threefold repetition of *overturn* is the ultimate Hebrew superlative. The outcome will definitely not be pleasant.

21:22–32 Ezekiel's prophecies of judgment against *other* countries (besides Israel/Judah) will begin in earnest in chapter 25. But Ammon is the only one mentioned in chapters 1–24. Perhaps it is the single

exception for the contrast that could be made. Ammon had joined Israel in rebellion against Babylon, and their people must have heaved a sigh of relief when the Babylonian army attacked Jerusalem rather than their town of Rabbah. The diviners in Ammon were forecasting good news for their nation. But the truth of the matter is that the sword will soon strike them as well. And while Israel will eventually recover from its tragedy to receive a future that includes the blessings of God, Ammon is to disappear, never to rise again.

22:6 A reference to blood, or bloodshed, occurs seven times in the first sixteen verses. The terms are not limited to literal physical violence committed against another person, but also include, by extension, *any* harm done to another. Ezekiel begins his case with the sins of the leaders of the nation, but the problem isn't limited to them.

22:7–12 The list of specific accusations is only a sampling that represents a cross section of violations of God's law. Taken together as Israel's way of life, they reveal that the people have forgotten Yahweh. So the sins are not presented simply as specific violations of God's covenant but rather as evidence that the people have lost all interest in honoring the God who had brought them into covenant with Himself. Still, this is among the longest lists of sins found anywhere in the Bible. The offenses cover a broad spectrum: religious idolatry, taking bribes, demanding sex from menstruating women, incest, and more. They are listed with no sense of one sin being more or less harmful than another, not as an arrangement on a continuum of evil. They are all sins, so all are offensive to God. And sin *will* be punished.

22:13–16 The image of Yahweh striking His hands together is a gesture to indicate both His anger and His order to put an end to all such behavior. Israel may have forgotten God, but He has not forgotten her.

22:17–22 All proper punishment has three purposes. First is *retribution*, paying back what is deserved and balancing the scales of justice. Human beings have a sense of retributive justice because they are created in the image of a just and holy God, who will by no means clear the guilty. The second aspect of punishment is *correction*, by which a person learns not to commit the same sin again. A driver who has just received a ticket is much more likely to slow down the next time he or she is on the same stretch of highway. And the third purpose of punishment is *purification*. God doesn't simply want His people to correct their errant behavior; He wants to create in them a new heart, a new mind, and a new attitude. Yet punishment is not pleasant. Here, as in other places, it is compared to a refiner's fire that will burn away the dross and leave what is valuable.

23:1–8 It is not uncommon to find instances of Israel or Judah compared to a prostitute, in that the people reject a loving God to pursue false gods and the idols of other nations. But nowhere is the imagery as stark as in this portion of Ezekiel. He uses some of the coarsest and crudest language in the Bible. In Jewish tradition, this chapter of Ezekiel was among the last to be taught to young men because of its potential to offend. But, of course, that is exactly the point. Ezekiel describes two sisters: Aholah and Aholibah, who represent Samaria and Jerusalem (the capital cities of Israel and Judah). Both women engaged in prostitution from a young age, beginning while they were in Egypt. More recently, however, Aholah (Samaria) had become enamored with the Assyrians. At that time the Assyrian Empire was among the greatest powers in the world. Israel (the northern kingdom) wants to emulate Assyria and copies both its cultural and religious practices.

23:9–10 This instance of prostitution is, in fact, adultery. Assyria turns out to be a cruel lover. The Assyrians destroy Israel in 721 BC, depopulating the land and scattering the population across the great empire. Ezekiel's audience had come from the southern kingdom of Judah. They had probably heard of Israel's demise; after all, the northern kingdom had virtually disappeared from the face of the earth. It was not hard for the people of Judah to assume that Israel had done something to offend God and that He had dealt with them. But Judah wrongly assumes that God is not so angry with them.

23:11–21 Ezekiel declares that God is in fact even angrier with Judah than He had been with the north. Their spiritual lust and prostitution had continued more intensely than ever, even after they witnessed the Lord's furious response to the behavior of the northern sister. Judah has no excuse for continuing infidelity, but the people's attitude is portrayed as the lust and fascination of a young woman for a dashing, handsome lover.

23:22–35 Yahweh has finally turned away from His wife in disgust, proclaiming that Judah will face the same end as her northern sister. The lovers to whom she had given herself will be the instruments of her destruction. She will undergo the same foreign invasion and conquest that Israel had suffered a century and a half previously. The bond between Judah and the surrounding nations had never been a satisfying one, yet the severing of that bond would be horrific. Ezekiel's depiction of foreign armies stripping off the clothes and fine jewelry of their victims is more literal than symbolic. In certain chronicles written by conquering nations during this time, the brutality of the treatment of prisoners was a source of pride.

23:36–48 The numerous accusations against Aholah and Aholibah appear all the more heinous in the context of promiscuous seduction. The picture is of women who can't get enough, losing all standards as their loyalties shift from one foreign country to another. Judah's adultery was shameless, and in the Law of Moses the punishment for adultery was death. Unrepentant actions are about to have consequences.

24:1–2 As Ezekiel completes the section of his writing having to do with the judgment of Judah, he provides yet another date. The siege on Jerusalem will begin on January 5, 587 BC, but the city won't fall until August 14,

586 BC, so the people there are in for more than a year and a half of turmoil.

24:3–12 Ezekiel had previously cited a proverb indicating that the inhabitants of Jerusalem viewed the city as a cooking pot and themselves as the meat, worthwhile and protected (see 11:3). God's message in this passage is that, yes, the city might be a cooking pot, but it is a place where the people will be confined and consumed. In this case, the pot is encrusted due to heat applied for so long and at such a high temperature that only a scummy residue remains. To gather the pieces seems to suggest the depopulation of the city. And no lot is cast because the casting of lots presumes the Lord's active involvement in the people's lives. Yahweh is no longer accommodating the people's presumption that they have special status before Him. Based on Ezekiel's earlier personal involvement with his prophecies, it is likely that he acts out this one as well: filling a cooking pot with water, placing choice pieces of meat in it, setting fire beneath it, and so on. The pot would have been heated until the meat burned away and only bones were left. The visible blood is a witness to Jerusalem's crimes. And like a modern self-cleaning oven, great heat is used to char the remnants on the sides and bottom of the pot until they can be brushed away.

24:13–14 After Ezekiel's parable ends, God abandons the metaphor and makes His point clearly. The Lord's previous attempts to cleanse His people had failed, but after undergoing this traumatic experience they will be clean again. God's wrath is not an unreasonable response to their persistently lewd conduct.

24:15–17 Ezekiel had acted out a number of his prophecies, including lying on his side for a portion of each day for weeks at a time (see 4:1–8) and shaving his head (see 5:1–4). But nothing he had done so far compared to the personal toll the next object lesson required of him. God tells him his wife will die. Although not certain, the circumstances appear to be that his wife had died suddenly and unexpectedly. What *is* clear is that her death was Yahweh's doing, despite the fact that Ezekiel loved her very much. Five traditional (though not biblically mandated) acts of mourning are mentioned: sighing, removing one's turban (normal wear for a priest), going barefoot, covering one's mouth, and eating special (less flavorful) food. Ezekiel is denied several of these outward traditions. He is permitted his grief, but not the public demonstration of it.

24:20–24 Jerusalem was the delight of Israel's eyes and God's as well. The popular theology of the time was that as long as the temple stood, the nation was safe. But when it fell, the people would be too affected to even mourn properly. While Ezekiel has every right to mourn his wife's death, the exiles have little justification to mourn the downfall of Jerusalem. The destruction of their prized city is fair punishment for their horrific crimes against God.

24:25–27 With the fall of Jerusalem, God's judgment is executed. Ezekiel's duty in preparing his people for the event is fulfilled. Therefore, his period of imposed silence comes to an end. Now the prophet, after a six-year ministry of preaching the doom of Jerusalem, is free to speak again and resume a normal life. He will next turn his attention to God's judgment concerning other nations.

25:1-3 Ezekiel has shown so far that Judah certainly deserves God's judgment, but the surrounding nations are just as guilty of wrongdoings and atrocities.

25:8-11 Moab had also been delighted to see Jerusalem fall. Their response was a bit more understandable than that of the Ammonites because they had been dominated politically and militarily by Israel throughout much of their history. Still, they had been aware that God had intervened on Israel's behalf in times past. Their sin was to deny Israel's election, to suppose that Yahweh was unable or unwilling to act on behalf of His people. It isn't surprising, though, that they failed to acknowledge that Israel was unlike any of the other nations. Israel had come to have the same view of herself, motivated by a great desire to be just like those other nations (see 20:32). Moab, too, will fall to the desert tribes, beginning with its key cities.

26:1-6 Tyre (Tyrus) was only one hundred miles from Jerusalem, originally situated on an island in the Mediterranean Sea about six hundred yards off the coast, connected by what was then a narrow man-made causeway. (It has since expanded due to winds and tides to create a peninsula.) The date of Ezekiel's pronouncement against Tyre (February 3, 585 BC) came several months after the fall of Jerusalem, which would have been approximately the time that Ezekiel and the exiles were hearing the news. At the same time, Nebuchadnezzar was initiating a siege of Tyre. The many nations that will oppose Tyre include the various ethnic groups within the Babylonian army because imperial armies were comprised of soldiers from various conquered peoples.

26:7-18 Tyre's (Tyrus's) mainland settlements, unprotected by the sea, will naturally be the first to suffer attack. Still, the protective walls require a siege—in this case, a siege of thirteen years. The final destruction of Tyre will not occur until the time of Alexander the Great. The word *isles* refers to other maritime peoples who will identify with a seafaring and trading city like Tyre. It is dreadful to consider that if the powerful Tyre can fall, the same can happen to them. The Babylonian appetite for new lands is voracious. Also, Tyrian control of the seas had provided stability. Now there is uncertainty.

26:19-21 As had been true with the fall of Jerusalem, the Babylonian army is the implement of destruction, but Nebuchadnezzar is only fulfilling the will and action of the Lord. Yahweh uses first-person language, and He speaks of more than mere physical death. The Israelites, as every other ancient Near Eastern people, had a doctrine of the world to come. They would have identified a number of phrases as references to judgment and the next life: "into the pit" and "the deep." The city of Tyre (Tyrus) itself will never entirely cease to be. It exists today. But it never recovers significance or becomes the great nation-state it once was.

27:1-24 At this point, Ezekiel begins a lament for Tyre (Tyrus). In a description of the glories of the past, Tyre is likened to a magnificent ship. The description is poetic in its mention of many of the very best products that Tyre shipped throughout the Mediterranean: Lebanon cedars, ivory, and so forth. An actual ship would not, for example, have had linen sails. Tyre's glory is accented by the geographic breadth of its servants and trade associations. This list is a historic review rather than a current list of allies. Israel, for example, had been destroyed about a century and a half previously.

27:25-36 The glory of Tyre (Tyrus) will soon come to an end. If Tyre is a ship, she is going to wreck at sea and sink, and her demise will be hard to watch. It is interesting to note that the reason for Tyre's fall is not described much in terms of her various sins, although it is clear that the city is guilty of slave trading and pagan practices. However, Ezekiel's accusations have more to do with a location that is simply wealthy, fat, and sassy. Tyre's prosperity rests on the sea trade that she has come to dominate. She is accustomed to the luxuries of life. And worse than that, she is proud of herself—a theme that Ezekiel will continue to develop.

28:1-5 Ezekiel's prophecy gets a little more personal. He turns his attention to the king of Tyre (Tyrus), although in an absolute monarchy of the ancient world, the fate of the king and the kingdom were so intertwined as to be virtually indistinguishable. The people tended to admire and support a king who was responsible for the nation's prosperity and greatness, and they would consider an oracle against such a leader to be directed at themselves as well. In Ezekiel's day, the king of Tyre was Ethbaal II ("Baal is with him"), a clever man who amassed power and wealth as a result. Many people use such worldly wisdom to great advantage, but he isn't as wise as he *thinks* he is. Normally the Mesopotamian-Syrian states believed a king was *appointed* by the gods but not actually a god himself. Perhaps Ethbaal II is attempting to elevate his status among the people, or it could be that Ezekiel uses such language to indicate that the king has a far too high opinion of himself, that he is "playing God," so to speak.

28:6-7 The glory of Tyre (Tyrus) and the presumed wisdom of its leader will both disappear with the coming of "the terrible of the nations"—Babylon. The king, in his arrogance, has now reckoned with Yahweh.

28:8-10 The Phoenicians, like the Israelites, also practiced circumcision, though for different reasons and at a different time of life. For one of their leaders to die at the hands of uncircumcised foreigners was the ultimate indignity. No historical record has been found detailing the fall of Tyre (Tyrus), but it is not unreasonable to assume that after a thirteen-year siege, the king of Tyre would have been executed, if not tortured first, for creating so much trouble for Babylon.

28:20-23 Zidon was the second city to Tyre in Phoenicia. In fact, this is the only place in the Old Testament where the city is mentioned without its tie-in to Tyre, so it seems logical that it would be a partner in this oracle of doom. Zidon would not be spared the same destruction that was in store for Tyre.

28:24–26 This short section is almost exactly halfway through the portion of Ezekiel's prophecies concerning the grim futures of Israel's enemies (25–32). It is also the pivot around which the entire section turns. God is dealing with Israel, but these other nations are also being judged so Israel will be freed from their influence, both spiritually and politically. This section paves the way for the third section of Ezekiel (33–48): Israel's return from exile and the renewal of the life of God's people in the promised land. The Israelites in Babylon understood the difficult, and usually expected, fate of captives. But the Lord will not be prevented from delivering His people and blessing them again in the land, even if it means the destruction of entire nations.

29:6–7 Through the centuries, Israel had occasionally sought help from Egypt against her enemies, always in defiance of the warnings of Yahweh. Beseeching Egypt had not helped against the Assyrians, and it will do no good against the Babylonians either. Ezekiel's image is that of a person leaning on a staff, but the staff is a weak reed that quickly gives way under weight.

29:8–16 God will humble Egypt. The nation won't cease to exist as some of Israel's other enemies, although it will become a small, insignificant kingdom.

29:17–21 In the next of Ezekiel's dated prophecies concerning Egypt, Babylon is shown as doing the Lord's work, though hardly by her own intention. Still, the reward for her pains is the wealth of Egypt. Not much of the historical record exists for this portion of Egyptian history, but it appears that the pharaoh had to contribute large amounts of money to Babylon to help fund its siege of Tyre (Tyrus). Meanwhile, Israel begins to regain strength.

30:1–26 Just as Ezekiel had given a lament for Tyre (Tyrus; see chapter 27), so also he relates one for Egypt, a nation that had never before suffered a catastrophic invasion. The Assyrians, at the height of their power, had managed to render Egypt a client state for a time, but Egypt had weathered that storm. However, the day of the Lord is approaching. Babylon will invade in 568 BC, crushing the might of Egypt while devastating all her allies. Even after the fall of Babylon, Egypt will remain a Persian colony until 404 BC, and after that will fall to Alexander the Great in 332 BC.

31:1–18 In a lengthy metaphor, Ezekiel likens Egypt to a great cedar tree of Lebanon. But then, Assyria had also been a great tree, a wonder to behold and without equal. It had then been cut down, never to recover. Egypt, too, will fall and fare only slightly better in the aftermath.

32:1–32 Ezekiel concludes this section with a lament for Egypt's pharaoh, describing Egypt's fall in the most sweeping terms. Egypt has been a dominant power, but God will soon dominate Pharaoh. The final scene is one of a number of fallen powers, Egypt among them, buried together in the pit in various stages of ignominy and shame.

33:1–9 This section begins the third and final segment of Ezekiel's writings. Most of what he has said so far has been somber. The first section (1–24) dealt with God's judgment on Judah. The second section (25–32) covered the judgment of Judah's enemies. With those matters behind, however, his look to the future is hopeful and positive. In the final chapters of his book, he foresees Israel's restoration and prosperity as the people again receive the blessings of God. Ezekiel has already explained that God designated him a watchman (see 3:16–21), but he reiterates the concept. The logic is clear and unassailable: If a watchman warns of impending catastrophe but the people ignore his warning, they have no one to blame but themselves for the disaster that overtakes them. The watchman is to blame only if he detects the danger but fails to sound the warning.

33:10–11 Ezekiel has been a conscientious watchman. He sounded the warning. In response, the people see that their suffering is a result of their sins, and they are depressed and discouraged about their situation. Their pessimism is understandable. After all, they had been exiled from their homeland, and Ezekiel had for years been forecasting Jerusalem's catastrophic devastation. But was theirs a state of repentance or simply sorrow?

33:23–29 Some of the Israelites remained in the area of Jerusalem, even though the city was in ruins. These are the poorest of the Israelites whom the Babylonians had three times left behind (2 Kings 25:12), yet they have the mind-set that they have managed to outlast the others. They even compare themselves to Abraham: If God had given the patriarch—one man—the land, then certainly a group of them had the right to it. But comparing themselves to the righteous Abraham isn't appropriate. Ezekiel quickly lists a number of their ongoing sins and what the consequences of those sins will be. Jeremiah's account confirms Ezekiel's prophecy: The lives of the people left behind go from bad to worse. An abortive rebellion leads to the flight of many to Egypt and an increase in poverty. When the exiles eventually return from Babylon, the people who had remained in Judah are found eking out a hardscrabble existence.

33:30–33 The exiled Israelites in Babylon don't fare much better. They come to recognize Ezekiel as an authentic prophet of God. He enjoys a newfound popularity as people come to him to hear what God has to say. But God sees through their spiritual facade. Then, as now, the recognition of truth is not always coupled with the willingness to obey. Ezekiel faithfully proclaimed God's truth, but the people saw him as no more than an entertainer and responded in the same way they might to a singer or musician. Eventually, however, they see God's Word come to pass and acknowledge that when Ezekiel spoke they were hearing the words of the Almighty Himself.

34:1–6 Ezekiel had previously placed responsibility for Israel's pathetic spiritual condition on its leaders (see 22:6–12). Here God has him prophesy against the nation's *shepherds*. When modern believers hear the word, they tend to think of pastors or ministers, but Ezekiel's hearers would have immediately thought of their kings, not prophets or priests. The likening of kings to shepherds was commonplace in the ancient Near East. The kings of Israel and Judah are compared to shepherds who are glad to benefit from the food and wool available to them yet refuse to take care of the flock that provides those assets. Of the forty-two kings who ruled from Saul to Zedekiah (about 1030 BC to 586 BC), very few were consistently faithful to their responsibility as overseers of God's people. Another handful were moderately faithful, but most were completely insensitive to the needs of the people as they used the position only to aggrandize themselves. Israel's exile is the direct result of the malfeasance of her kings.

34:7–16 Yahweh is about to take matters into His own hands. He will hold the incompetent shepherds accountable for their unfaithfulness. His primary interest, however, is not to punish the rulers but rather to rescue His sheep from them. Utterly unlike the selfish reigns of Israel's kings, Yahweh will attend to the needs of His people and provide for them.

34:17–24 Those who are wealthy and powerful—"the fat and the strong" (verse 16)—will continue to take advantage of the poor and weak people. In fact, the matter will not be ultimately resolved until God provides a new shepherd, one akin to His servant David. This will be a single person who perfectly embodies the kingly ideal. It may have seemed that the collapse of Judah, the capture of her kings, and the exile of her people to Babylon had signaled the end of God's covenant with the house of David. However, Ezekiel's pronouncement of God's promise reveals that the covenant with David has by no means been revoked. The promise is still in force. David's descendant will again sit on his throne.

34:25–31 With the appointment of this new king, the Lord will establish a covenant of peace with Israel. Ezekiel lists a number of images of blessing and prosperity that the covenant will bestow upon the people of God (Leviticus 26; Deuteronomy 28). Everything God had promised Israel will eventually be realized.

35:1–15 Israel and Edom were two mountainous nations that shared a long history of animosity and conflict (with Israel tracing its roots to Jacob and Edom going back to Esau). This section of Ezekiel contrasts their respective destinies. After the fall of Jerusalem, Judah is left with an economy in shambles and a lack of effective government or military. Edom, encouraged by the Babylonians, takes advantage of Judah's vulnerability and invades at that time, taking whatever the Babylonians haven't already removed and annexing portions of the land. It might seem that this particular passage should have accompanied the previous section of judgments against foreign nations (chapters 25–34). However, the promise of Edom's destruction, coming immediately after the destruction of Jerusalem, serves as the background for a prophecy of Israel's restoration. Mount Seir is symbolic of the entire nation of Edom. The two

nations Edom has in its sights are Israel and Judah. The Edomites are celebrating the desolation of Jerusalem; even worse, they slaughter the Jews they catch fleeing from the Babylonians. But soon Edom's punishment will fit their crime as they experience similar desolation. Those who use their strength to take advantage of others are rarely popular. When Edom eventually faces the same crisis for which they had ridiculed Israel, the rest of the world takes a perverse delight in their misery. The entire book of Obadiah (short though it is) is devoted to a similar prophecy against Edom.

36:1–7 Just as mount Seir represents Edom (chapter 35), the mountains of Israel stand for the entire nation. Ezekiel does not provide a date for this prophecy, but it is clear that it is given after the destruction of Jerusalem while Judah is at the mercy of her enemies. God's message to Israel is just the opposite of the accompanying prophecy to Edom (and other nations). In fact, it was probably hard for many people to believe such a promise, considering Israel's current circumstances: nation and temple in ruins, people in exile, kings dead or imprisoned.

36:8–18 God is renewing the blessings previously spelled out in His covenant with Israel, including increased fertility of the land and the people. The people have done nothing to deserve it. They had defiled Israel, and when God removed them from that defiled land, their continued inappropriate conduct caused other nations to profane God's name. The assumption of Israel's enemies is that Israel's God must not be very powerful if He can't save His people from such indignities.

36:19–23 The Lord loves His people and will deliver them even though Israel has done nothing to deserve His mercy. Ezekiel makes it clear that Yahweh is not rewarding the people for their goodness, because they haven't been good or faithful for a long time. Rather, God is acting to show the holiness of His own name, His faithfulness to His own Word.

36:24–38 God's faithfulness to His Word is seen in the promises here, which are another form of the same promises previously given in Deuteronomy 30:6–8. And as the Spirit of God works among the people, many will respond with deep contrition.

37:3–6 The Lord's question to Ezekiel is intended to start the prophet thinking about life after death. Next Ezekiel is instructed to address the long-dried-up bones, to prophesy to them. More specifically, he is told to tell the bones that God is planning to make them live again. The word translated as *prophesy* (literally, "to speak for God") occurs seven times throughout the passage.

37:7–10 The obvious question is, what possible good is it to make such an effort? So much time has passed and the bones are so dry that they are not even connected to one another. They are loose bones, not intact skeletons. Yet Ezekiel does as he is told. In response to Ezekiel's prophesying, the bones not only come together to form complete skeletons but also grow tendons, flesh, and skin. However, they still have no breath until God instructs Ezekiel to prophesy once more, after which the former pile of bones rises to form a vast army.

37:11–14 This vision, as it turns out, is Yahweh's response to the hopelessness and despair of His people. Ezekiel's vision demonstrates that for God's people, hope is never gone.

37:15–17 After the vision of the valley of dry bones, God provides Ezekiel with yet another depiction of Israel's restoration. God instructs him to take two sticks (representing Israel and Judah) and join them together. It is not clear exactly how he does this, but the result is the appearance of a single stick, demonstrating that the nations will again be one. *Israel* had previously been the name of the northern ten tribes. Sometimes *Ephraim* was used as a synonym because it was the principal tribe (from which all the northern kings had come) and it covered the geographical area of Samaria, the capital of the northern kingdom. But Israel had been conquered and absorbed into surrounding nations more than a century ago. Judah was all that was left of the original nation of Israel. In the view of all the prophets, including Ezekiel, Judah had inherited the title of *Israel* and remained a divinely chosen people in covenant with Yahweh.

37:18–23 Like the meaning of the valley of dry bones, this, too, would have been hard for Ezekiel's audience to understand and almost too good to believe. God is promising not only a political/social restoration but also spiritual renewal. The phrase "so shall they be my people, and I will be their God" reflects God's covenants with Abraham and Moses, and some say it is a succinct way to describe New Testament salvation.

37:24–26 God's people will be united under a single king. He is called David because he will be a leader from the house of David. Modern believers may recall David's adultery and fall and the miserable second half of his reign. But David was a man after God's own heart. It was under his reign alone in the history of Israel that the nation was free of idolatry and polytheism—a remarkable achievement in a world where the great number of gods made religion without idols seem a contradiction in terms.

38:1–3 Magog, Meshech, and Tubal were three grandsons of Noah (Genesis 10:2), and the peoples who descended from them are still known to Ezekiel's contemporaries. Magog (which probably means "land of God") is thought to have been a land in western Asia Minor, though that is not certain. Meshech and Tubal are two relatively small nations of Cappadocia (present-day Turkey). Ezekiel has already mentioned the latter two locations in passing (27:13; 32:26). Meshech had a warlike reputation due to frequent conflicts with the Assyrians (Psalm 120:5–7). The name *Gog* seems to have been derived from the name of a powerful king of Lydia (western Asia Minor) in the first half of the seventh century BC. So Ezekiel refers to two separate nations with the king from a third—a great force gathering to invade the south sometime in the future.

38:4–16 Gog's great army will be enlarged by mercenary troops from a variety of other nations that span the farthest reaches of the known world, all united to invade the promised land where Israel lives in safety. Ironically, Gog and his legions will be following Yahweh's orders. Sheba and Dedan are caravan trading nations, one to the east and one to the west, hoping to profit at Israel's expense by buying plundered goods to resell to their trading partners.

38:17–23 This assault on Israel will be the fulfillment of other predictions made by Old Testament prophets. The description of the Lord putting an end to Gog's aggression is universal and cosmic. The entire earth is involved; all creatures tremble. The account of warfare in Revelation reflects many of the same events: earthquake (Revelation 11:13), fire and hail raining down from heaven (Revelation 8:7; 20:9), and birds eating the flesh of the enemies of God (Ezekiel 39:4; Revelation 19:17–21). There is evidence that the beast of Revelation is to be understood as Gog.

39:1–16 This chapter is a repeat of Ezekiel 38, but with more emphasis on Gog's destruction than the attack on Israel. It will be total annihilation, with no survivors to bury the dead and even the homelands of the invading armies laid to waste. Ezekiel's reference to "the day" ties in with other biblical prophecies about the day of the Lord. On that day, God will reverse which side does the plundering and looting. The burial of enemy soldiers will take seven months, but the ritual purification of the land (including removing all bones) will take much longer.

39:17–29 With such an image of the victory God will give His people, it should have been abundantly clear that it isn't for any want of power on Yahweh's part that Israel falls prey to the Babylonians. He is judging His people, but the long-range result will be a restored house of Israel—a transformed and spiritually renewed people living in communion with God and in willing obedience to Him.

40:1–4 Ezekiel has been given some very specific visions to proclaim to the people of God exiled in Babylon, not least among them the fall of Jerusalem and the confident expectation of being freed to return to their homeland. Others of his visions were much more symbolic than specific, such as the valley where a pile of dry bones sprang to life. His vision of a future temple has been interpreted both ways. Some people consider the closing chapters of Ezekiel a description of an actual temple to be built in Jerusalem at some point in the future. (Its description and measurements do not match those of any previous temple.) But a number of reasons arise from the biblical text to discourage such a viewpoint. The high mountain position suggests the dwelling of God, and we may assume that Ezekiel intends for us to understand that he is looking southward toward Jerusalem (although the city is not specifically mentioned). However, there is no high mountain north of Jerusalem, or anywhere in Israel for that matter. In addition, the design of the temple is highly stylized or idealized: Its dimensions are dominated by multiples of five, with twenty-five a common number and everything exactly proportioned. It is not unlike the description of the heavenly Jerusalem found in Revelation 21—a description so fabulous it is impossible to visualize. The date would have been April 28, 573 BC, but of equal significance is the *way* Ezekiel's vision is dated. The fact that it is twenty-five years after Ezekiel's exile may be a subtle reference to the year of jubile (jubilee). Every fifty years all enslaved Israelites were to be freed (Leviticus 25:8–13). The twenty-fifth year would mark the turning point when people no longer looked back to the catastrophe of the exile but looked forward to their restoration instead. The vision invites comparison to Israel's deliverance from bondage in Egypt (Exodus 12:2).

40:5–47 Ezekiel's descriptions are not illustrated. His audience has only his words. Modern readers may find the temple section of his writing repetitive or overly detailed, but that was the only way the prophet could attempt to describe the splendor he witnessed. He needed to provide many details to help his listeners/readers form appropriate pictures in their minds. As his celestial host proceeds to measure the temple, Ezekiel records not only the measurements but also a number of observations. Starting at the east gate, they move into the outer court and its north and south gates before continuing to the inner court with its gates and special rooms.

40:48–42:20 Ezekiel, as a priest, is able to enter the holy place, but he remains there as the angel goes alone into the most holy place. Additional side rooms surround the temple in three layers. The cherubim carved into this temple have only two faces rather than the four that Ezekiel had previously seen firsthand (see 1:10). Finally, Ezekiel is shown the priests' rooms. This surely must have been an inspiring vision for the people of Israel. As they will eventually discover, the temple they had known is completely gone. When it is reconstructed after the exile, even the foundation has to be rebuilt. Impressive buildings are still a measure of the greatness of a city. The reputation of Paris would be diminished without its Eiffel Tower, Notre-Dame, and Arc de Triomphe. Rome is enhanced by the Colosseum, St. Peter's Basilica, the Trevi Fountain, the Spanish Steps, and the Pantheon. Jerusalem without the temple was just not the city it should be, and Ezekiel envisioned a marvelous temple indeed.

43:1–5 Ezekiel discovers that another attribute of this new temple is its permanence. Israel is still in shock over the loss of its first temple—the one Solomon had built. It will soon be reconstructed by Zerubbabel, but it will also fall. Later a third temple will be built, this time supervised by Herod during the time of Jesus. It will have the shortest existence of all and be destroyed by the Romans only a few years after its completion. The temple Ezekiel describes, however, will be the dwelling place of God forever. This is a powerful vision. Ezekiel had previously described the glowing, fiery radiance that indicated the presence of God, and he had heard angels'

wings that sounded like the movement of a great army. It is significant that the glory of the Lord enters this new temple through the east gate, for it was from the east gate that His glory had departed in Ezekiel's former vision (see 10:18–19). A great reversal is taking place as the complete manifestation of God's divine majesty returns to take its place among His people. The filling of the temple with the glory of the Lord is a phenomenon previously seen in the days of Solomon (1 Kings 8:10–11) and in one of Isaiah's visions (Isaiah 6:1–4).

43:6–8 The presence of Yahweh is further confirmed by His voice. The reference to the house (temple) as the place for the soles of His feet recalls the ark of the covenant in earlier passages as the Lord's footstool (1 Chronicles 28:2). While the ark is the embodiment of the Lord's presence in the old temple and viewed as Yahweh's throne, it is not prominent in this new visionary temple. The temple itself is God's throne and dwelling place. The shift of emphasis away from the ark to God's more widespread presence is also reflected in Jeremiah's writing (Jeremiah 3:16–17). Some translations use the word *tabernacle*, which derives from a verb sometimes translated "I will live." The word has a biblical history that recalls the place of the tabernacle and the temple as an embodiment of God's presence among His people. It is just as applicable for the present and future as well. When John writes that the Word became flesh and *dwelt* among us (John 1:14), he is conveying the same idea that, in Jesus Christ, God was present among humanity. The nature of the defilement mentioned is unclear. Various sources have speculated that the problem might have involved the tombs of kings being placed too near the temple (although no evidence of such a practice exists), some kind of cult that worshipped the dead, or memorials being built nearby that detracted from a single-minded focus on Yahweh. Whatever the specific problem was, it was yet another way Israel had betrayed God's covenant.

43:9–12 In this visionary description of the future consummation of salvation, the people of God are still summoned to live in holiness. Even when all is complete, obedience and loyalty to the Lord are expected. The end of history is connected to the responsible actions of the Lord's people. Ezekiel is challenged to keep the description of the new temple before the people, who are still mourning the fall of Jerusalem's temple. It is the next best thing possible to snapping a photo of what he had seen and showing the snapshot to encourage and strengthen those who see it. Ezekiel's regular descriptions also remind the people that they had strayed away from God in the first place, creating the problems they eventually faced. However, they are now able to enjoy God's presence again, thanks to His forgiving grace.

43:13–27 Unlike the gods of the surrounding territories, Yahweh has no interest in a temple where He can enjoy basking in the glory of His surroundings. Israel's temple has an ongoing function to be the place where people worship the Lord and where He fosters holiness among them. Yahweh desires fellowship with His people, which necessitates their purity and righteousness. Ezekiel next makes a transition from describing the incredible temple to providing regulations that will govern worship. The altar needs to be properly dedicated.

44:1–31 There is no mention of a high priest in this section, although the prince who abides in the temple with God is mentioned frequently in the material that follows, beginning in 44:3. The priests will not only attend to the temple but also serve as preachers, teachers, and rulers of the people.

45:1–12 The division of land is summarized, and it will be covered in greater detail in 48:1–22. Great emphasis is placed on justice in the land. The king will rule justly and for the sake of the people, not himself, and private land will be protected from royal confiscation.

45:13–46:24 This section specifies the offerings to be made and the feasts to be celebrated in the new temple. They are similar to, but not identical with, the regulations in the Law of Moses. In addition are guidelines for other public services and daily offerings. Ezekiel's vision is, in a sense, a map of holiness. Every detail serves to emphasize an ideal worship depicted in forms that are understandable and meaningful to his contemporaries. The Lord draws near and invites His people to come near to Him, but He does not cease to be the God of terrible holiness. His people must revere Him accordingly.

47:1–2 As Ezekiel finishes describing his vision of a future temple, he also concludes his lengthy book. In this section, he depicts the river flowing out of the temple and explains how the land is to be divided among the tribes. Numerous references to a river of life are found throughout the Bible. The theme begins in Genesis, as four rivers flow through the garden of Eden, and continues to the final chapter of scripture that describes a river, clear as crystal, flowing from the throne of God. The latter example, written by John, appears to derive in a substantial way from Ezekiel's description in this passage. All ancient Near Eastern temples faced east, and Israel's was no exception. The worship was conducted according to completely different principles, of course, but the sanctuary would have looked familiar to that culture. As Ezekiel returns from the kitchens in the outer court of the temple to the sanctuary itself in the inner court, he sees a small stream of water gushing out from beneath the slab of stone at the base of the main doorway. The east gate had been closed, so the flow of water is diverted to the south side of the gate structure. Ezekiel exits through the north gate.

47:3–12 As Ezekiel watches, his angelic escort does periodic depth checks. After walking about one thousand cubits (a standard Hebrew cubit was 17.5 inches), the water is ankle deep. Another one thousand cubits, and it has become knee deep. Another stretch, and it is waist deep. At the fourth measurement (by that time, well over a mile away from the temple), the water has become an impassable stream—both too deep and too wide to cross. No mention is made of tributaries, so the stream appears to become larger through a miraculous effect. The physical topography of Israel would have required that a literal river cross valleys and ascend and descend mountain ranges before it could drop several thousand feet to the basin of the Dead Sea. What Ezekiel sees is a miraculous river in a vision. During Ezekiel's time, as is true today, little life could be found in the Dead Sea. It has no exits, and the water that gathers there is filled with various toxic materials, including salts. But Ezekiel witnesses flowing water that will freshen the sea and soon have it teeming with life.

47:13–20 The division of the territory as viewed by Ezekiel is considerably different from the boundaries that God had given Joshua centuries before. The boundaries described are essentially those that Israel possessed during the time of David and Solomon, except that the land east of the Jordan is not included in Ezekiel's vision. This time the division is to be equitable, where originally some tribes had considerably more land than others.

47:21–23 Under the Law of Moses, aliens could become circumcised and gain membership in the community, yet they were banned from owning land, which relegated them to something of an outsider status. But with the ability of outsiders to join the community *and* possess land, the distinctions between them and the native Israelites are entirely eliminated.

48:1–29 Ezekiel's description of the allotment of the land is so idealized that it ignores the topography of Canaan. Each tribe's designated segment runs east and west, from one side of the promised land to the other. Near the center of those bands is one strip reserved for the city, the sanctuary, the priests, and the prince. Seven tribes will be situated north of that strip, and five tribes south. A number of intriguing details come to light in Ezekiel's depiction. For one, the sons of Jacob's two wives (Rachel and Leah) are positioned nearest the central reserve and the sanctuary. The children by handmaids Bilhah and Zilpah are further removed.

48:30–35 The names of the tribes connected with the twelve gates of the city do not match the names in the land allotment (48:1–29). The land division is as before, with Joseph being replaced by his two sons (Manasseh and Ephraim) and with Levi omitted (because the Levites were distributed for ministry among the other tribes). But the *gates* include a gate for Joseph and one for Levi, reverting to the twelve original sons of Jacob (Israel). Finally, we find a great ending to a great book. The continuing story of the kingdom of God is a story of the presence of the Lord. Because of Israel's unbelief and disobedience, she had forfeited the presence of God. But the new epoch would herald the arrival of Immanuel—God with us.

THE BOOK OF
DANIEL

INTRODUCTION TO DANIEL ■ The book of Daniel contains some of the best-known stories in the Bible, but it also provides some of the most challenging and intriguing passages to attempt to comprehend. Some of the prophets had sent warning of a judgment of God's people to come; others are present at the end of the captivity to help encourage and empower the beleaguered exiles. But Daniel goes into exile along with his countrymen and provides an insider's view of Judah's experiences in the faraway land of Babylon.

AUTHOR ■ Daniel came from a royal family. He is compared with Noah and Job in terms of faithfulness to God and righteousness (see Ezekiel 14:14). Daniel also demonstrates great wisdom, always giving God complete credit.

OCCASION ■ Daniel describes events that occurred during one of the worst situations the people of God ever experienced. The nation of Israel had fallen to the Assyrians more than one hundred years earlier, but Judah survived. Yet the people of Judah continue to refuse to heed God's warning and soon face humiliating defeat themselves. The Babylonians breach the walls of Jerusalem, ransack the temple, and carry off most of the population in a series of deportations. Daniel is among the first group taken. His writing offers much assurance in that even though circumstances are bad, God is still with His people.

1:1–2 Daniel has a bleak opening. Within the first two verses, the beloved city of Jerusalem falls into the hands of one of the most terrifying empires on earth. The temple's holy items are carted away and placed among the idols of Babylon. To make things worse, it is the Lord who has given Jerusalem over to its enemies. The captivity that results is a God-designed plan to chastise His people for their ongoing rebellion. The year is 605 BC. Judah's king at the time is Jehoiakim.

1:4 Being handsome and without blemish, Daniel and his three peers clearly have genetics working for them. But they also are noted for their quickness to learn and their aptitude for accumulating wisdom. They are expected to assimilate quickly into Babylonian culture by absorbing the language and literature of their new home. They are also given Babylonians names.

1:6–7 Daniel is one of four young men mentioned by name who are taken from Judah. At the time, these young men are probably about fifteen or sixteen years old. Nothing is said of their parents, but the Babylonians wouldn't have hesitated in breaking up families to carry off exiles.

1:6–7 A change in names had spiritual as well as cultural significance. The Hebrew names all acknowledged characteristics of the awesome God of Judah. *Daniel* meant "God is my Judge." *Hananiah* meant "Yahweh is gracious." *Mishael* meant "Who is like God?" *Azariah* meant "Yahweh is my helper." The newly assigned names, in contrast, acknowledged various Babylonian deities: Bel, Aku, and Nego/Nebo.

1:8 This verse is key in understanding who Daniel truly is. In his situation, many young people would quickly succumb to exotic opportunities and temptations, especially in a setting where it appears that righteous behavior does not matter. Yet Daniel never loses his resolve to live a holy life for the Lord.

1:18–20 At the end of the three-year training period (1:5), Nebuchadnezzar interviews each of the young men who have gone through his program. Daniel and his three friends are clearly exceptional. *Ten times better* is not a quantitative term. Just as people today think in terms of "a perfect 10" at an Olympic event, or judge an extremely attractive person as "a 10," the number had similar meaning in ancient times. *Ten* was a number that represented fullness or completeness.

2:1–13 This account occurs during the second year of the reign of Nebuchadnezzar, yet Daniel and his friends are put into the king's service after three years of training (1:5, 18). This seems to be a discrepancy. However, in the Babylonian system, a king's years of service are counted the same way people today number birthdays. Even though Nebuchadnezzar might have been well into his third year chronologically, his reign was two years old. Also, at this point in his narrative (from 2:4 to 7:28), Daniel shifts from Hebrew to Syriack (or Aramaic). Syriack was a widespread language, understood by many diverse peoples. (Nebuchadnezzar's advisors, for example, were probably from different nations, and according to 2:4, they spoke in Syriack.) Daniel reverts to Hebrew for chapters 8–12.

2:11 The response of Nebuchadnezzar's magicians reveals their worldview. They perceive a distinct separation between gods and people. From their perspective, gods stay in their world, and it is the responsibility of humans to reach out to them. The magicians' statement sets the stage for the rest of the book of Daniel, which explains the Gospel message in terms that can be understood by the Gentile world of the Babylonian culture. Daniel will go on to describe how God enters the world of humanity to rescue people. Every story told from this point forward demonstrates how God interacts with this world. The second half of Daniel's book describes more specifically how and when God will come to the world in the person of the Messiah.

2:12–13 The king's order to have all the wise men of Babylon put to death includes Daniel, Shadrach, Meshach, and Abed-nego. This apparent crisis is divinely orchestrated to create a supposedly impossible situation through which God's plan for the world will be revealed.

2:14–23 Daniel asks for a bit more time so that he might do what the king has asked. Even though Nebuchadnezzar had just accused his court magicians and sorcerers of attempting to stall for time (2:8), it seems that he respects Daniel's request.

2:17–18 Daniel and his three Hebrew friends realize this is a divine challenge that they face, so they turn to God for clarity. They appeal to Him for mercy and wisdom, and He provides the solution.

2:22–23 God enables Daniel to be wise and discerning, and Daniel uses his wisdom to seek God's help. In return, God makes known to Daniel something that Daniel couldn't possibly discern on his own. Daniel's knowledge of Nebuchadnezzar's dream will allow many people to live who otherwise would have been put to death. Thus Daniel also praises God for revealing Nebuchadnezzar's dream to him.

2:24–28 When Daniel is called back in to speak to Nebuchadnezzar, he gives God full credit before the king. Daniel makes it patently clear that no human—not wise men, enchanters, magicians, or diviners—could have given Nebuchadnezzar the answer he sought. Yet his God is in heaven and can reveal mysteries. Daniel elevates the focus from humanity to God. Through Daniel, God is letting Nebuchadnezzar know that God is at work in the world, revealing His glory. This is the Lord's world, the future is in the Lord's control, and even the ability to see and understand what the Lord is saying requires divinely inspired insight.

2:29–31 This dream both humbles and frightens Nebuchadnezzar. This is no mere nightmare that results from indigestion or an active imagination. It is a divine revelation. God is allowing Nebuchadnezzar to come face-to-face with a future not under his control but the Lord's. As Daniel goes on to interpret the dream, Nebuchadnezzar will receive the first of several lessons concerning the sovereignty of God.

2:31–35 The statue is made of different kinds of metal. Nebuchadnezzar sees a stone that is cut out, but not by human hands. The stone smashes into the statue and breaks it into pieces, which are quickly swept away by the wind like chaff (husks) at threshing time. The stone, however, grows into a huge mountain that fills the whole earth.

2:32, 36–38 The head of gold on the statue in Nebuchadnezzar's dream symbolizes Babylon. Nebuchadnezzar is the leader of the most glorious of all the kingdoms in the world. Yet it will not be a lasting kingdom.

2:32, 39 The statue's belly and thighs of brass represent Greece. Just as brass is stronger than silver,

Alexander the Great will dominate the leaders of the Medes and Persians (who had conquered Babylon). Yet the Greek Empire will be less glorious than the Persian Empire had been.

2:33, 40–43 Stronger still will be the Roman Empire, represented by the statue's legs of iron. At a point in the future, the Romans will arise and conquer all the surrounding kingdoms. Yet again there will be a diminishing of the glory of the kingdom. In addition, this fourth kingdom will be divided. Portions will be as strong as iron, but other parts will be like clay—and iron and clay certainly don't mix well. The imagery is most appropriate. As it turns out, the mighty Roman Empire will lack unity as it is plagued by civil wars, social unrest, and moral relativism.

2:39 The nations that conquer Babylon (the Medes and Persians) will be inferior to Babylon. They will be stronger but not as glorious. Daniel is letting Nebuchadnezzar know that his days are numbered. The kingdom he has established will fall to another.

3:1 Nebuchadnezzar has been told that he is the king of kings—the head of gold (2:37–38). It is commonly thought that the king's pride leads him to then make a statue of himself in complete gold. Perhaps he is so prideful that he misses the point of the dream (the destruction of the kingdom) and hears only that he is the king of kings. The statue, then, communicates that his kingdom is beautiful and will last forever.

3:3–6 A close reading reveals that the unveiling of Nebuchadnezzar's statue is shrouded in religious overtones. He is not just introducing the image as a token of remembrance; he is presenting a new religion.

3:8–18 The accusations made by these Babylonians include the claim that the Jews are not serving Nebuchadnezzar's gods. Nowhere in Nebuchadnezzar's decree did he stipulate that everyone had to serve his gods, but these men add it to their list of charges. It is likely that the accusers are jealous of the prior success of Shadrach, Meshach, and Abed-nego, because the charges are certainly exaggerated. In reality, the three Hebrews have not disregarded the king or defied his position. They are three of Nebuchadnezzar's greatest assets and more than willing to serve on his staff. But in that culture, no king could afford to easily dismiss accusations of treason against those close to him.

3:12 It seems that most people have no problem with Nebuchadnezzar's new ruling. When the music plays, they bow as they have been ordered. This naturally exposes anyone who doesn't bow, as is the case with Shadrach, Meshach, and Abed-nego.

3:12–13 Where is Daniel? His three friends are left to themselves to deal with a high-pressure situation. We aren't given that information, but it would be safe to assume that considerable time has passed between Daniel 2 and Daniel 3. Ninety-foot-tall gold statues are not quickly constructed. Daniel's responsibilities would have grown in the interim.

3:19–20 Most likely the order for the furnace to be heated to seven times its usual temperature implies that it is to be heated to its maximum heat. In this situation, having the men bound serves no good purpose other than the psychological strategy of removing control from them and preventing them from even minimally shielding themselves from the heat. Nebuchadnezzar is parading his strength for all to see. He wants the totality of his power to be made known so that the three young men and everyone observing will know that he is the most powerful man on earth.

3:22–23 The punishment for Shadrach, Meshach, and Abed-nego is intended to be severe, as is proven when a number of their captors die just from tossing the three into the flames. The judgment intended for the Hebrews falls instead on some of Nebuchadnezzar's most valiant warriors. As for the three who have so deeply angered the king, they are about to astonish him.

3:24–25 Not only does God preserve Shadrach, Meshach, and Abed-nego; He joins them in the furnace. Some people think the fourth figure may be the preincarnate Christ. Nebuchadnezzar can only speculate as to the fourth figure, calling him the Son of God.

4:1–2 The positive opening of this chapter temporarily shields the fact that Nebuchadnezzar has been through a horrendous experience. However, the experience has taught him about his own sin and the nature of God, so he records the lesson for all the governors in his kingdom so they will not make the same mistake he has.

4:3 Nebuchadnezzar acknowledges the signs he has observed (2:5–6, 19), God's intervention in this world, God's eternal kingdom, and God's rule over the earth. For the first time in this record, the Babylonian leader acknowledges a greater kingdom. Such acknowledgment reflects a significant change in Nebuchadnezzar, demonstrating the extent of his humility.

4:4–7 Nebuchadnezzar begins his story by explaining that everything in his life and kingdom was going well—then he had another dream. The previous dream of Nebuchadnezzar's—the image made of different metal (2:31–35)—had no small effect on the king. But this one is apparently even more influential. His staff of wise men are no more helpful in this case than they had been before (2:10–11). Why Nebuchadnezzar always waits to ask Daniel is unknown, although his tendency to do so repeatedly proves that the Lord enlightens Daniel in ways that none of the other magicians, enchanters, astrologers, and diviners can come close to matching.

4:8–9, 18–19 Since this chapter is written from Nebuchadnezzar's perspective, Daniel's Babylonian name (Belteshazzar) is used. However, in most other cases, Daniel's Hebrew name is used, and that is the name by which he is best known.

4:10–18 It is likely that Nebuchadnezzar has a sense of what his dream means, which is probably why it troubles him so much. He may even have enjoyed the first part of the dream as he saw himself as the great tree that touched the sky and provided shelter and sustenance

for so many. If so, he is surely unsettled as the dream unfolds and strange events begin to occur.

4:20–22 The tree in the dream is a symbol for Nebuchadnezzar, yet as dominant as Nebuchadnezzar has become, he is still merely a human. Heavenly forces are at work over which he has no control. At a single command by a holy messenger, the great tree is cut down. God's action will be the result of the king's refusal to recognize that it is the Lord who rules. Nebuchadnezzar has acknowledged that Daniel's God is a strong God, and he notes that Daniel and his friends have benefited from serving their God. But Nebuchadnezzar has always stopped short of *submitting* to Daniel's God.

4:26 When Daniel tells Nebuchadnezzar that the king needs to acknowledge that "the heavens do rule," he is using a figure of speech that substitutes a place for a person. Similarly, someone today might say that an action made by the president is made by Washington or the White House.

4:27 Daniel's approach is tactful and humble. He doesn't leap right to accusations and judgment; he starts with the opportunity for repentance. He lays out the option for the king to start right away to cease his wickedness and serve God by showing mercy to the weak. In that case, maybe the king's prosperity will continue.

4:33 Nebuchadnezzar's sentence begins immediately. A fragmentary cuneiform tablet in the British Museum refers to Nebuchadnezzar, apparently during this part of his life. It states that "life appeared of no value to" Nebuchadnezzar, that "he does not show love to son and daughter," and that "family and clan does not exist" for him any longer.

4:36–37 God does indeed allow Nebuchadnezzar to prosper again. This time he doesn't make any attempt to take credit for his fame. Instead, he exalts and glorifies the King of heaven. Had he done so earlier, in response to Daniel's advice, he might have avoided a lot of misery.

5:1–4 At least six years have passed between chapters 4 and 5. It appears that Daniel's high-profile position in the king's court has come to an end. After the death of Nebuchadnezzar, his successor is his son Evil-merodach. This son rules for two years until he is assassinated and replaced by Neriglissar. After Neriglissar, Evil-merodach's brother-in-law, an Assyrian named Nabonidus, takes control of the kingdom. As new king, Nabonidus establishes a home in the oasis that is now the location of Saudi Arabia. He appoints his son Belshazzar to reign as vice-regent and handle the business of Babylon.

5:2–4 As Daniel will eventually make clear, Belshazzar cannot plead ignorance. He knew about Nebuchadnezzar's decrees and the holiness attached to the Jewish goblets (5:22–23). He just doesn't care. In a mockery of God, he uses the temple's sacred vessels for his party, passing out wine to impress his nobles as well as their female companions. Even worse, as they drink they praise their gods.

5:5–6 Belshazzar's defiance of God has been public; so, too, is God's condemnation of Belshazzar. In front of all his guests, the king turns pale, goes limp, and is gripped by fear to the point of terror. Then, after the experience of seeing the hand come and go, Belshazzar is left with a message he can't comprehend.

5:7–9 Belshazzar promises to promote anyone who interprets the handwriting to third place in the entire kingdom. Belshazzar is responsible to Nabonidus, so the top two places are already filled.

5:11 In addressing Belshazzar, the queen refers to "thy father, the king." The usage of *father* cannot be assumed to mean a biological relationship or even a relationship in terms of one generation to the next. The word was sometimes used in referring to a person's lineage. The Jews often spoke of Abraham as their father. Similarly, Nebuchadnezzar could be considered a father by any number of people, not merely his biological children.

5:13–17 Belshazzar goes through the proper protocol of flattering Daniel, briefly summarizing the situation for him and offering him great rewards for his much-needed help. Daniel is more confrontational with Belshazzar than he had been with Nebuchadnezzar, and for good reason. Belshazzar had ignored the lesson of the past and in a matter of a few years openly defied God.

5:22 Daniel isn't telling Belshazzar anything about Nebuchadnezzar the king doesn't already know. A mighty ruler who leaves the throne for a while to live in the fields, eat grass, and grow animal-like hair and nails is not quickly forgotten. Belshazzar knows the story, but he hasn't heeded the lesson of Nebuchadnezzar. Because Belshazzar refuses to honor God, his defiant party is the last one he will ever have.

5:25–31 The words the hand had written on the wall—*Mene, Mene, Tekel, Upharsin*—essentially mean "Number," "Weigh," and "Divide." The message that no one else could determine is quite clear to Daniel: The days of Belshazzar are numbered, his life has been weighed (evaluated) by God, and because he is found deficient, his kingdom will be divided as the Medes and Persians take over. Simply put, the end is at hand for the king.

6:1–4 Throughout the book of Daniel so far, kings have come and gone while Daniel's service to God, as well as to his human rulers, has remained consistent. It seems clear that the godly wisdom demonstrated by Daniel in his youth has carried into his senior years as well. He serves as one of three key leaders to whom another 120 officials report. This leadership structure is used by the new king, Darius, so that he can protect his interests. In other words, Darius is wisely attempting to avoid losing his kingdom to a rebel group or having the wealth of his kingdom pilfered by an unscrupulous, unsupervised overseer.

6:2–3 Daniel's integrity becomes evident when you compare verses 2 and 3. At first King Darius is cautious about placing too much power in the hands of any one person. But when he sees how Daniel lives and works, he trusts him to have even more power without fear that he will misuse it.

6:6–9 Scripture doesn't say that Darius is flattered at the proposal, but he also doesn't appear to need much coaxing. Although it is a despicable attempt to get rid of Daniel, the plan is an intelligent one. Darius had structured his leadership team to protect the kingdom from disloyal people, and at face value it appears that this proposal will support the king in his desire. Once the king puts the decree into writing, it becomes an unalterable law. Not even Darius himself can revoke it.

6:10 Daniel is well aware of the king's signing of the decree. He understands the consequences of breaking it. But Daniel truly believes what he has been communicating to Nebuchadnezzar and Belshazzar: God is sovereign and in control.

6:14–16 It appears that Darius searches for legal loopholes but can find no way to avoid sentencing Daniel to the punishment as set forth in the decree. The king has little recourse but to order Daniel thrown into the lions' den, yet in that moment it becomes clear how much Daniel's faithfulness to his God has influenced Darius. It is admirable that Daniel displays faith that God will deliver him, whether in life or in death. But as a result of his consistent faith, even *Darius* suggests that Daniel's God might deliver him.

6:19–20 The lions' den is an enclosure with no visual access. Daniel is apparently lowered into it, a stone is laid over the top, and the king seals it with his signet ring. In the morning, Darius is surprisingly optimistic. He doesn't just call out to Daniel; he asks a question that demands a response.

6:22 Daniel has defied a Persian law and submitted to what was intended to be the Persian death penalty. So God's deliverance of Daniel is more than simply a reward for his steady faith. It is also God's divine declaration of Daniel's innocence based on the law of the Lord and an emphatic demonstration that God's law is to be feared over any human law.

6:24 The scheme against Daniel is revealed for what it is: a malicious attempt to murder an innocent man. Historians have learned that Persian law dictated the destruction of entire families of people who were harmful to the kingdom. It may be that in a culture of violence and vengeance, it was believed that the children of an offender might attempt vengeance when they grew up.

6:26–27 Just as the Lord made Himself known to Nebuchadnezzar and Belshazzar in phenomenal ways, so, too, He persuades Darius of His unequaled power.

7:3–4 Daniel will later be told that the beasts represent kingdoms (7:17), so his description is more to differentiate their qualities and characteristics than to detail their specific physical appearances.

7:4 The description of the lion implies that the figure began as a wicked being, fell from earthly glory, and was restored to normal. Nebuchadnezzar immediately comes to mind after his account provided in chapter 5, although some people believe this will be a king yet to come.

7:5 The bear is powerful and vicious, but with a tendency to be slow and lazy. It is raised up on one of its sides, perhaps indicating a walking position. And it has been feeding on another animal, having been given permission to conquer.

7:6 The four-headed, four-winged leopard is swift and fierce and has the ability to cover a lot of territory quickly. The biblical concept of multiple heads frequently symbolizes different kingdoms or regions, so the creature is perhaps a single kingdom with four regions.

7:10 The books that Daniel sees opened may be the same books mentioned in Revelation 20:11–15. God's judgment is based on the deeds recorded in these books. God notices the injustices done in this world, and they will not go unpunished.

7:17 The four beasts in Daniel's dream appear to correspond with the four sections of the great statue of Nebuchadnezzar's first dream (2:31–35). The descriptions of the four creatures lend credence to their representation of Babylon, Medo-Persia, Greece, and Rome. Much debate takes place as to the significance of the ten horns and the final, boastful horn. Many people connect this section of Daniel with John's writing in Revelation and believe that Daniel's dream describes the end-times Antichrist (called the "beast" in Revelation) and the false prophet who serves as a type of prime minister for him.

7:23–27 The angel reveals that the fourth creature is a cruel beast that will control ten kingdoms and conquer the world. His reign of terror will last for "a time and times and the dividing of time." In Aramaic (or Syriack), the use of the word *time* refers to the passing of one year (4:16). A common interpretation of the phrase, then, is to consider *a time* as one year, *times* as two years, and *the dividing of time* as half a year, yielding a total of three and a half years.

7:26–28 After the violent reign of this figure, God's heavenly court will assemble to strip him of power and destroy him once and for all. The people of God will then be given control of all the kingdoms of the world. God will be acknowledged as the true King, ensuring everlasting peace and contentment. It is a satisfying ending, to be sure, yet the dream completely overwhelms Daniel.

8:1–3 This vision occurs during the third year of Belshazzar's reign, which is about two years after the dream Daniel described in chapter 7. The location in the vision is Shushan (or Susa), a city in the heart of the Medo-Persian Empire that will later become a common vacation spot for King Darius. So during the final years of the Babylonian Empire, Daniel is shown a vision of the destruction of the Persian Empire that will follow.

8:7–8 The he goat strikes the ram and quickly overpowers it. When Persia comes up against Alexander the Great, it falls hard and fast. Alexander will go on to conquer most of the populated world before he is thirty. His combination of strength, speed of conquest, and youth will stand out in history. Daniel's vision continues as he sees the goat grow in fame, but it suddenly has its large horn broken off. In place of the severed horn

grow four other horns. History confirms that Alexander became quite proud and exalted himself. Yet by the age of thirty-three, he had died (the cause of which is widely disputed). After his death, the Greek nation is split into four states, each with a different leader.

8:12 History sheds light on this prophetic vision. One of the leaders who rises to power after Alexander the Great is a man named Antiochus Epiphanes. He has an intense dislike of the Jews, persecuting them, killing their high priest, and entering their temple to have pigs sacrificed to him because he believes he is the Messiah. In the ultimate insult, he corrupts and twists the entire religious system of the Jews so that it serves him. The religious corruption initiated by Antiochus Epiphanes will actually turn out to be a worse experience for the Jews than their exile. In Babylon, they mourned because they knew their temple and city were being neglected. But later, when they see their religion perverted and a false messiah desecrating their temple, it is heart-wrenching.

8:19 Gabriel's reference to *the end* should be interpreted from Daniel's perspective, not a modern one. The Jewish people are undergoing a time of God's discipline. They are currently exiled in Babylon, and Daniel is discovering that this won't be the worst of it. It is a couple of centuries before the horrors of Antiochus Epiphanes fall on them, but soon thereafter the consequences for the sins of Israel will come to an end.

8:19 Daniel is about to be shown (in chapter 9), that shortly after the events described in this vision will come a Messiah.

8:23–25 Antiochus Epiphanes is a picture of the end-times Antichrist (the beast in Revelation). The description here is applicable to both figures. Both feel superior and spread deceit. Both are especially destructive because they establish their power while people feel secure. Only later do they reveal their true natures. And eventually both will be destroyed, but not by human power. (Antiochus isn't killed; he eventually dies of tuberculosis.)

8:26 Daniel is asked to seal the vision—not to discuss it with anyone. The reason, he will discover, is that he is about to receive another vision that will take precedence. Daniel can see some of the behind-the-scenes operations of God's kingdom, but the Lord doesn't want people motivated to come to Him out of fear. The next vision will reveal the coming of an anointed one, a Messiah, who acts out of compassion and offers salvation.

9:1 The date here reveals that fourteen years have passed between Daniel's previous recorded vision (chapter 8) and this prayer. At the end of chapter 8, Daniel is left exhausted, sick, and confused about what he has witnessed. He has been shown that God is going to bring the kingdoms of humanity to an end and that He is going to discipline the Jewish people. Seemingly, those fourteen years have been a time of searching for Daniel. He has not questioned that both discipline and judgment are deserved, yet God has promised that they will not last forever. So Daniel is seeking to discover when God will restore His glory.

9:5–6 God's people have sinned in many ways. They have been wicked and rebellious, ignoring God's commandments. When God sent prophets to confront them about their sin, the people had rejected them. They had persistently lived for themselves, not for God.

9:15–16 Daniel asks God to turn away His anger from Jerusalem. This is not a personal request. Rather, Daniel is asking God to reestablish His glory in the world. Ever since God allowed the Babylonians to conquer Jerusalem and take away the people, there has been no specific physical location where God is acknowledged and worshipped. Daniel's request is not just to get "home" but rather to see the glory of Jerusalem restored and an end to God's name being mocked by pagan nations.

9:20–23 Daniel is still in prayer in the evening when the angel Gabriel appears to him in swift flight. Daniel recognizes the angel from his previous vision (8:15–26).

9:24–27 This passage has been described as one of the most difficult passages in the Bible. Gabriel begins to depict a unit of time comprised of seventy weeks, during which God will bring about redemption for His people. Numerous theories abound as to what this message really means. Some consider each week to be a seven-year period. If so, much of what Gabriel says begins to fit a historic time line starting when a decree is passed to rebuild Jerusalem (which is described in Ezra 7:12–26) and carrying through to Jesus' ministry.

9:26–27 If the ruler here is the same as the boastful horn mentioned in 7:20–22, the final week will begin with the contract made by this malicious leader. He will break his covenant midway through, and great suffering will ensue for God's people. But after a period of time, God will remove him from leadership and make all things right.

10:1 Cyrus was the great king over the entire Persian Empire, which at this time included Israel. Darius, who ruled at the same time, may have served under Cyrus as emperor. During Cyrus's first year, he passes a decree allowing the Jews to return to Judah and rebuild Jerusalem (Ezra 1:1–4). This final vision of Daniel's occurs two years later.

10:4 A biblical reference to the "great river" usually means the Euphrates, but Daniel clarifies that he is beside the Hiddekel (or Tigris). There he sees a heavenly figure whose description is similar to that of Jesus in Revelation 1:12–16. Some people have suggested that it is indeed a preincarnate appearance of Jesus, but the difficulty this figure faces in spiritual warfare would not have been true of the Lord (10:13).

10:5–6 The figure is bedecked in linen (a sign of purity) and a gold belt (worn by royal leaders). His body is like beryl, a shiny and transparent gold-colored stone. His face is like lightning, his eyes like lamps of fire. His arms and feet have a gleam like polished brass. His voice is unusually powerful.

10:11 The angel addresses Daniel as a man who is "greatly beloved." God honors Daniel because his heart

is not callous. The Lord values the pain that Daniel feels as a result of the people's sin.

10:12–13 There has been a long delay between Daniel's petition and the angel's response due to a three-week battle with the prince of the Persian kingdom. Clearly this is a hostile and aggressive spiritual being, perhaps working to affect the kingdom of Persia for evil.

10:21 The Babylonians thought their gods had a Tablet of Destiny that foretold their history. Gabriel's reference to the scripture of truth may have suggested Daniel's awareness of such a Tablet, and it could have been the angel's way of assuring Daniel that God is sovereign and has the future in His hand. In any event, Gabriel is about to reveal some truth about the future to Daniel (11:2). The purification of the nation will include punishment and persecution. God's plan includes the temporary emergence and dominance of various nations along with individual world leaders who exert a certain amount of control.

11:2 Four kings will arise in Persia, the fourth creating conflict against Greece. The three Persian leaders who follow Darius are Cambyses (530–522 BC), Smerdis (522 BC), and Darius I (522–486 BC). However, the Persian Empire had a total of thirteen leaders, and opinions vary as to whether the three referred to here are the consecutive kings after Darius or the three most prominent leaders who succeed him. Also debated is the identity of the fourth Persian king, although much evidence points to Xerxes I (486–465 BC). He is a strong king whose empire and wealth grow to large proportions. Eventually he seeks to attack Greece and incorporate the nation into his empire, but he fails miserably. His antagonism may have been the primary catalyst for the fall of Persia to Greece more than a century later.

11:18–19 Many interpret the accounts in this passage as describing the historical period in which the king of the north, Antiochus, is stalled in his efforts against Egypt. He begins to tangle with the Roman army that is beginning to make some serious advancements in the area. The Romans first defeat Antiochus and then require him to pay heavy fines for his attacks, which places an economic strain on his country. When Antiochus returns home, he is killed by an angry mob who resent paying so much to Rome.

11:20–21 Seleucus IV, son of Antiochus III, is the one who sends out a tax collector in an attempt to pay Rome the taxes its leaders have demanded. That tax collector, however, kills Seleucus in an attempted coup. He is unsuccessful, yet his actions leave the throne open to other contenders. The person who comes out on top is Antiochus IV Epiphanes. The rightful heir to the throne, a man named Demetrius, is being held hostage in Rome until his nation's taxes are paid. So Antiochus seizes the leadership role; he is not *given* the honor.

11:36 Up until this point in Daniel's vision, the events described appear to have been fulfilled by very specific events in history between Daniel's time and the modern day. In fact, the amazing accuracy has led some scholars to believe that Daniel must have lived in the second century BC and backdated his prophecy. The literary technique was not unusual at the time, but a close study of numerous additional aspects of Daniel's writing has convinced other scholars of its much earlier date, its reliability, and the reliability of his predictive prophecy. As Daniel repeatedly tells King Nebuchadnezzar, God is a revealer of mysteries (2:22, 28, 29). The precision of Daniel's visions only confirms this fact.

11:36 Here, Daniel's prophecy makes an almost imperceptible shift. He continues to write about the king of the north and the king of the south, but the events no longer correlate, as many believe, to what has been recorded about Antiochus Epiphanes. In addition, his language adopts a grander scale than previously, and he begins to speak of end times. It is difficult to state with certainty exactly what Daniel knew at the time and intended to communicate, but several scholars believe he must be writing of the last-days Antichrist.

11:37–39 Translations vary here. Some say that the figure described has no desire for women, which would indicate that he is so consumed with himself that no other relationships matter. Other translations say that he has no desire for the god loved by women. In this case, the reference might be to a Babylonian fertility god named Tammuz. (The only overt biblical mention of this god is in Ezekiel 8:14.) His following was much like the one that would follow for the Greek god Adonis. No matter the translation, the only god that appeals to this individual is power. His religion is based on his ability to conquer. As he accumulates more and more power, it confirms his misassumption that he is the one and only god.

11:45 The end-time ruler's headquarters is right in the heart of Israel. As troubling as this might have been to Daniel, as soon as this fact is revealed, it is also confirmed that this ruler's success will be limited. His time of conquest will quickly be concluded. When God finally takes action against him, his end is inevitable.

12:4 In ancient times, an official document was concealed or put in a safe place after being sealed. Gabriel instructs Daniel to close and seal what he has seen and heard. When later generations are ready to increase their knowledge, this book will be available to them.

12:5–8 Daniel is on the bank of the river (see 10:4). He overhears two angels, one on either bank of the Hiddekel (Tigris). One asks how long it will take to fulfill these astonishing things and is told it will be a period of three and a half years.

12:11–12 God's people will be persecuted for 1,290 days (three and a half years), beginning with the cessation of Jewish temple rites and the desecration of the temple. This is a long time for people to remain faithful to God. And even beyond the 1,290 days is another forty-five-day period during which people are to patiently persevere. No explanation is provided for the different lengths of time mentioned (1,290 days vs. 1,335 days). Conceivably, a forty-five-day period might pass between the time God puts an end to the suffering of His people and His ultimate destruction of the person responsible for it.

12:13 The best Daniel can do in response to all he has seen is to continue on until the end. He has faithfully served his God throughout his long life. In return, he is promised rest and eventual resurrection, after which he will receive everything God has in store for him.

THE BOOK OF

HOSEA

INTRODUCTION TO HOSEA ■ In our present age, fixed truths, moral absolutes, divine imperatives, sure hope, and life-transforming power often seem to be overshadowed by uncertainty, insecurity, and subjectivism. Yet in the story of Hosea, we are confronted with the truth about God's persistent and unlikely love for an unfaithful people, the Israelites, even as we marvel at the tragic and remarkable beauty of one prophet's unconditional love for his faithless wife that exemplifies the love story between God and humanity.

AUTHOR ■ Hosea's prophecy may have existed first simply in spoken form; then later it may have been gathered together in written form by disciples or scribes. Still, this work is traditionally attributed to Hosea, the son of Beeri (1:1). We don't know much about the prophet's life except for the little that we learn from chapters 1 and 3.

OCCASION ■ When Hosea is called to serve as God's prophet, Israel is in a state of rebellion. Based on the kings reigning during his prophecy (1:1), we know that the nation of Israel has been split by civil war (1 Kings 12) and that Hosea is sent to the northern kingdom of Israel, which is characterized by corrupt kings, crime, and compromised morality (Hosea 4:1–2).

1:1 The book of Hosea provides its readers with some important facts that ground the story in its historical context. God calls Hosea during the reigns of Uzziah, Jotham, Ahaz, and Hezekiah, kings of Judah, and during the reign of Jeroboam II, king of Israel. Israel has been split from civil war (see 2 Kings 13:12–13), and the people are pursuing nearly everything except God. Even its kings are often quite corrupt. Hosea is a contemporary of Amos, Isaiah, Jonah, and Micah—other Old Testament prophets charged with declaring God's love and faithfulness in the face of Israel's wayward rebellion.

1:2–3 What the Lord requires of Hosea is shocking indeed: to forsake the natural hopes he may have for a happy marriage and instead consign himself to endure the emotional anguish and dishonor of a wife who will be persistently unfaithful.

1:2 The Lord's instruction to Hosea has been widely taken to mean that the Lord commands Hosea to marry a woman of ill repute, perhaps a prostitute. Some scholars maintain that the whole account of Hosea and Gomer is only a parable and not a description of what actually happened. It is a story to make a point. Another view suggests that perhaps Gomer is not a prostitute but that instead the term *adulterous wife* is used metaphorically, as *prostitution* is used metaphorically to refer to Israel's spiritual adultery. The most natural reading is to take the story literally.

1:4–9 The names that the Lord requires Hosea and Gomer to give to their children express the Lord's intention in the most decisive and unmistakable way. The name *Jezreel* means "God sows" and declares God's intention to punish Israel for its unfaithfulness to Him. *Lo-ruhamah* means "not loved," as the Lord is prepared to not love Israel anymore because the people have broken His covenant. *Lo-ammi* means

"not my people." This harsh denial of Israel's place as God's nation is ultimately what the Lord is warning this generation of Israelites about: Their fate is based on their unfaithfulness.

1:10–2:1 God's promise to restore His people in relationship with Himself is fulfilled, at least in large part, in the gathering of the Gentiles into the church after Pentecost (Romans 9:22–26). It is this promise of restoration that is prophetically enacted in Hosea's relationship with Gomer.

2:2–13 The Old Testament prophets devoted an immense amount of their preaching to what the modern church has neglected almost altogether: the judgment and the wrath of God. The centerpiece of the prophetical preaching is God's divine wrath against sin and the impending doom of those who betray His covenant and do not believe His Word. Hosea describes the punishment that God intends to put upon Israel in stark uncompromising terms: God will make Israel like a desert, blocking her path with thornbushes; strip her naked; slay her with thirst; and ruin her vines and fig trees.

2:16–17 What comes out of one's mouth is a representation of what is in the heart (see Proverbs 13:3; 16:23). Thus by calling God *Baali*, the people are in essence showing that they have given their hearts to false worship. Yet God will cleanse them, and they will address God in terms of a deep love relationship rather then abandoning Him in false worship. Israel will call God *Ishi*, or *my husband*—a term of endearment and relationship. Thus the restoration will be great.

2:18 Despite Israel's unfaithfulness, God is going to pursue her again, and this time the marriage covenant will be stronger—one that will bring an eternal relationship. This new covenant will be one in which love will rule. It is the beginning of an unprecedented relationship of love between God and His people. It is a new covenant.

2:21–23 God promises to reverse the famine of 2:9 by making what has become a wilderness a land that meets the needs of His people. God is going to respond to the people's call for help by providing for them.

3:1 God requires Hosea to reclaim his wife, Gomer, though she is an adulteress. This command is extraordinary considering how seriously God takes faithfulness, but He gives Hosea a model in His own love for the unfaithful Israelites. The general view of this passage is that Hosea must purchase his wife, who is on sale as a slave, perhaps for debt. God describes how the Israelites were unfaithful to Him. The Lord's love cannot be extinguished even by the people's outright apostasy.

4:1–3 In this passage, Hosea is laying out a prophet lawsuit—a charge from the Lord that comes with evidence and judgment. The charges are fairly straightforward and damning. "There is no truth, nor mercy, nor knowledge of God in the land" (see Proverbs 24:2). There is instead plenty of transgression—cursing, lying, murder, stealing, adultery—that is already bringing about negative consequences for the people and even the land (Isaiah 33:9; Jeremiah 4:28). The land mourning is likely a reference to a drought, and the death of the animals is mentioned in other Old Testament prophecies (see Jeremiah 4:25; 9:10).

4:5–6 Hosea explicitly says that the priests have perverted the law of God. In fact, under their false teaching, Israel is perishing for lack of knowledge. No doubt that teaching included a great deal of paganism (drawn from the surrounding culture), a radical undermining of the authority of God's law, and a relaxed take on the standards of holiness God requires.

4:9–14 The fact that the priests have greater responsibility and consequent accountability does not absolve the rest of the Israelites. God will punish both the priests and the people for their wickedness. Like Gomer, the Israelites will give themselves over to prostitution. This part of the prophecy describes how God will punish the Israelites for their persistent unfaithfulness—through depriving them of prosperity and joy and by launching a full-scale attack on the Baal cult.

5:1–5 Hosea calls again to get the people to listen—there is judgment against them, and God wants their full attention. These opening verses renew the fact that God is making a direct charge against Israel's leaders, the priests, and even the royal family. Tabor and Mizpah are places associated with worship of Baal.

5:3–4 God sees everything and declares that Israel is defiled, or unclean. This image points back to Hosea's unclean wife, whom God calls Hosea to love in spite of her unfaithfulness. Israel's sin is so tremendous that it prevents the people from returning to God even if they want to, a concept that resurfaces in the New Testament (see Mark 3:29; 1 John 5:16).

5:6–7 God has withdrawn from receiving the people's sacrifices. This is one of the curses that God long ago promised to visit upon those unfaithful to His covenant

(see Deuteronomy 31:18). The month (or New Moon festivals) that will devour the people and their fields likely refers to pagan rituals that are mentioned elsewhere (see Isaiah 1:14).

5:8–10 Ephraim is reduced to waste, and Judah acquires a territory of Benjamin by military force. This action violates the sacred tribal land allotments that God's covenant had fixed and is what Hosea is probably talking about when he says Judah's leaders "remove the bound" (or move boundary markers). These actions of violation provoke God's wrath (see Proverbs 22:28).

6:1–3 In the midst of the despair of God's withdrawing His life-giving presence from His people, there is a glimmer of hope and forgiveness. God will return to bless His people. Hosea has been hammering away at Israel with his message of doom and the grim promise that the people are about to fall under God's unrelenting judgment. And now, in the next breath, Hosea proclaims the compassion and mercy of God and His willingness to forgive His people in spite of the wrongs they have committed against Him.

6:1–3 God is a God of great mercy, and He will forgive and restore human beings to fellowship with Himself— even when they are guilty of every manner of sin against Him—if they will repent. Even when they have defied His grace, spurned His commandments, and abused His gifts, His grace reaches the heights and the depths. Just as Christ would be raised on the third day, so the image of Israel's revival and restoration to live in God's presence is described.

6:11–7:2 Israel, on account of its disobedience and disloyalty to the Lord, is teetering on the brink of extinction. God's desire to "return the captivity," translated elsewhere as *restore the fortunes*, is a reference to the same healing and restoration described in 6:1. Israel's real hope lies in the sovereign God who knows how to deliver His people, as He has so often in the past. But instead of trusting in this, the people are putting faith in the sort of diplomatic maneuvering that never brings true success.

7:9–10 Israel has for so long beckoned to the world of sight and ignored the unseen realities of the life of faith and of God's covenant that the people now have become totally blind and deaf to those realities. Their faith is so feeble that they are completely cut off from understanding what faith in God alone gives. No amount of evidence can make Israel realize what total folly the people have chosen for themselves.

7:11 The Israelites persist in making terrible decisions that only further their destruction. Hosea pictures Ephraim in its clumsy waywardness like a dove flapping every which way. The context for what Hosea is referencing is the foreign policy decisions that Israel made to play off Egypt and Assyria (see 2 Kings 15:19–20; 17:3–6).

7:14 The howling or wailing is a reference to the worship of Baal (see 1 Kings 18:28), and God calls the people out on the duplicity of their cry for help, implying that they are actually calling for Baal.

7:16 Israel's arrogance and failure to call on the one true God make the nation a laughingstock even among its enemies in Egypt.

8:1 The theme of this chapter is to prepare the Israelites for the punishment that they are about to receive. The trumpet signals the approaching danger. The eagle is more accurately translated as a *griffon vulture,* which signifies that death is already settling over Israel and the birds of scavenging are taking their places.

8:5–7 The calf-idol of Samaria refers to the two calves at Bethel and Dan (see 1 Kings 12:28–30), and these man-made impostors will be destroyed just as they have brought about the destruction of Israel.

8:14 Again and again Hosea says this: Israel calls upon the Lord to save her, but she will have God only on her own terms. She has no intention of living according to the commandments of God. She wants His forgiveness and His help, but she does not want to be ruled by Him and by His law. The name *Maker* for God refers to His election of Israel from among the nations, not their physical creation (see Psalm 100:3; Malachi 2:10).

9:2 The harvest the people seek from this harlotry will not produce prosperity for the nation. In fact, their produce will not sustain them at all. God will keep the product of their harlotry from feeding the nation.

9:7–8 The false prophets have continually deceived the people, promising them that days of destruction will never come. They have escaped this day of judgment for only so long, but now it is upon them. In God's purpose, the days of judgment are inevitable. Hosea gives to the false prophets the title they claim for themselves: "the prophet" and "the spiritual man." Yet these prophets are not God's men, and they do not have the Spirit of God in them. They are mad and crazy prophets who speak destructive lies to the people. They lead the people astray.

9:10 Baal-peor was the location of a shrine to Baal in the plains of Moab, some twelve miles northeast of the Dead Sea (see Numbers 25:1–9). After Balaam failed to bring a curse down on Israel, the Israelites brought one down on themselves by yielding to the temptation to have sexual relations with Moabite women. A plague began in Israel, and the plague did not come to a stop until the priest Phinehas took a spear and ran it through the bodies of an Israelite man and a Moabite woman. By calling the attention of Israel to this incident, the people will see that their apostasy to Baal began before they entered the promised land.

9:14 Israel had attributed its fertility to Baal, and now barrenness is the only appropriate judgment. Since the people turned to Baal for life, the only logical consequence is for God to give them over to death. Thus God will remove the fertility of the land.

9:16–17 Israel is so cursed that life will not be given to its people. God will show them how cursed they are as a nation. They will be wanderers among the nations—exiled and forced to live as aliens and strangers in the world. They will lose their blessing, their home, and their

fertility. In short, they will live cursed because they have rejected God and turned to Baal.

10:1 Israel and its reach are compared to a vine, a metaphor Jesus Himself used when describing the life of God's children.

10:8 The people will be so distraught and desperate in the face of destruction that, in the absence of both of their false saviors, they will cry out to the mountains to cover them up and for the earth itself to consume them.

10:10–13 Long before, when God made His covenant with Israel during the days of Moses, He had promised the people that if they fully obeyed Him, they would be set high above all the nations and all manner of blessing would be poured out upon them. But at the same time, the Lord promised Israel that if she betrayed His covenant and proved disloyal to Him, then He would curse her and deprive her of all of those blessings.

10:12–13 God is in control and will give Israel what she deserves—divine judgment. It is not what God wants to do, but it is what Israel has sown with her wicked ways. The prophet says that if Israel will trust and obey the Lord, the nation will prosper; but because she has disobeyed Him and His covenant, she is suffering and faces destruction.

11:2–4 God cared for the needs of the nation—describing Israel as His child and His animal.

11:5 Hosea warns that the Exodus will be undone and Israel will return to its former condition of slavery. Yet this time the captivity will not be in Egypt but in Assyria.

11:7 The Israelites are deepening their rebellion against God. The reality is that the more they deepen their rebellion, the more they depend upon false religious practices to get them through. Therefore, there will not be the type of deliverance that God had provided in the past. They will feel the sting of this rebellion.

12:2–5 Hosea employs legal language to describe God's case against Israel—laying out God's charge against Israel. Hosea brings up examples from Israel's past, as well as Judah's, in which Jacob rebelled and wrestled to get his way.

12:6 Hosea returns, as he has previously, to his crucial themes of love, justice, and patience, commanding Israel to return to the Lord in repentance as Jacob did.

12:8 The Lord unmasks Israel's pride through Hosea and warns His children never to imitate Israel in her fundamental and tragic blasphemy. God shows through Israel what pride can do and, by recording it in scripture, warns His children to stand against it. Israel's spiritual pride is plain dishonesty. It is the big lie of Israel's life. Pride is false security. Ephraim has boasted and taken credit for its economic prosperity, luxurious lifestyle, and success, when in fact it is God's favor the people have enjoyed.

12:9 The feast referred to in this text is the feast of tabernacles (see Leviticus 23:33–44). This verse looks ahead to the time when Israel's people will be scattered from their homeland.

12:11 The obvious answer to God's rhetorical question is that there is nothing besides sin in Gilead. *Gilead* represents all the country east of the Jordan, and *Gilgal* represents the land west of the Jordan. They both have sinned and sacrificed to Baal. And in both, God has shown forth His mercies.

12:12–13 God shifts the focus of His complaints from the Exodus and pre-Exodus to the message of the prophets. Hosea will pick up this shift in the opening of his next complaint. Once again, God declares that He will undo the Exodus and return Israel to the status of no longer being a nation. God speaks of a return to wilderness rather than a return to slavery. God asserts His sovereignty over the people.

13:1–3 God continues to describe His people's unfaithfulness in terms of their idolatry. He recognizes that despite the consequences of their sin, they persist in it by making even more idols. He compares them to the morning cloud (or mist), suggesting that rather than being preserved by God and made a great nation as He had promised to Abraham, they will surely pass away.

13:9–16 The Lord solemnly makes the point and swears that Israel's boasting will be overturned, her cities in ruins, and her security gone. This is the tragedy of pride.

13:10–13 The God who gives can take away, and the God who gives and is not properly acknowledged promises to take away as part of His judgment upon dishonesty and ingratitude. This, then, is the Lord's warning through Hosea, His prophet: Pride is a hopeless illusion that will certainly be shattered.

13:14–16 Scholars disagree over the precise meaning of the ransom described by God. Some suggest that it points ahead to Christ paying the ransom for His people (see 1 Corinthians 15:55). However, in Hosea's context, that is in the future. Ultimately in this Old Testament instance, the Lord decides against paying the ransom, declaring that He will have no compassion. The images here are truly ghastly—the people will bear their guilt, and even little ones and pregnant women will be subject to the violence.

14:1–3 Hosea is still desperate to have Israel hear God's plea to return to Him. He reiterates the theme of the book—that the people's sins have been their downfall—and encourages them to turn to God in repentance. Hosea's last chapter is a reprise of a main theme of his preaching from the very beginning of the book: It is a call to repentance, an invitation to Israel to repent of her sins.

14:2 As Hosea has already declared, God demands sincerity of heart. Repentance is not merely the recognition of one's own sin. It will not be enough for Israel to recognize that she has disobeyed the Lord and betrayed His covenant. Even Pharaoh confessed that he had sinned in not letting Israel go from Egypt after the plague of hail. But he did not really repent. Repentance, as God requires it, is not merely sorrow and remorse for sin. Judas was so overcome by sorrow when the enormity of his betrayal of the Lord Jesus came home to him that he committed suicide, but he had no repentance.

14:3 Israel must believe that nothing besides God can save her. Repentance is a change of will and behavior—just as Israel denounces her sin, she also draws near to God, in whom the fatherless find compassion. Repentance begins with a change of mind and heart about sin. Sin becomes not a thing to be loved but a thing to be abominated. In Psalm 51 David expresses the mind of every man or woman whom the Spirit of God has brought to a true repentance. Repentance wants nothing so much as to be right with God and to walk with God. Repentance is a turning away from sin to God for pardon and forgiveness.

14:9 This final verse of Hosea is an editorial note, reminding the reader to take careful heed of the message of the book and repeating that message succinctly.

THE BOOK OF
JOEL

INTRODUCTION TO JOEL ■ The book of Joel is an intriguing book, beginning with the fact that we know little about the author, his historical time frame, or even whether he was writing to the northern kingdom of Israel or the southern kingdom of Judah. We are left, then, with the words themselves—the brute force of the message of the divine author. We may be unaware of the specifics of Joel's personal information or the audience to whom he writes, yet he delivers the message of God with boldness and clarity.

AUTHOR ■ *Joel* (meaning "Jehovah is God") is a popular name in the Old Testament, with a dozen other men bearing the same name. However, little is known about the prophet Joel.

OCCASION ■ Joel writes in response to a devastating attack by locusts. But the destructive insects are described as an invading army, symbolizing the potentially greater destruction awaiting those who do not heed the words of the prophet and repent. Then, beyond the immediate situation in the land, Joel writes of the day of the Lord, when judgment will come to the enemies of God's people and Israel will eventually be restored.

1:1–2:11 The terrible arrival of a swarm of locusts is the catalyst for Joel's writing. In his opening section, he responds to the great destruction, calling on the people to mourn. Such a sobering event should also remind them that an even worse time of suffering is in store for those who refuse to humble themselves before God.

1:2 Joel addresses the elders of the nation because they should have borne a special responsibility to clothe themselves with humility before God and seek His mercy on behalf of the people. Yet they are the ones who have allowed the spiritual state of the nation to decline, so they probably feel the effects of the crisis just as much as anyone.

1:4, 10–12 Wave after wave of locusts have overrun the nation's crops, and that is in addition to a drought. With the failure of all the other crops (corn, wheat, barley, fig, pomegranate, palm, apple, and so forth), the situation is indeed dire.

1:5 For a nation characterized as drunkards, the loss of the grape harvest is particularly disheartening.

1:6–7 It is rather common in scripture, as well as in other ancient literature, to read of invading armies described as swarms of locusts. In Joel's case, it appears he has reversed the imagery. He describes a literal invasion of locusts in terms of a human army attacking. In terms of the effects on an agrarian society, locusts could be every bit as merciless and cruel as enemy soldiers.

1:13 Joel exhorts the priests to demonstrate appropriate behavior, considering the situation they are in. They are to dress for mourning—in dark, rough sackcloth rather than their usual clothing. Instead of offering their usual prayers, they are to howl or wail.

1:14 Joel will soon, in 2:12–13, clarify that it isn't the actions being taken that will appease the wrath of God but rather the proper attitudes of the people.

1:15 The Hebrew words for *almighty* and *destruction* sound quite similar, so Joel's statement here has added

impact. Specific historic events are associated with the day of the Lord, including Israel's fall to Assyria and Babylon's subsequent conquest of Judah.

1:16–20 This is a time for the people of God to come before Him with the truth. It is a time to speak to Him about their trials and to acknowledge Him as the only One who can ever provide food, shelter, safety, and joy. Such an acknowledgment should occur *before* disaster strikes, but even in the depths of their despair, God's people can call on Him for help. No such help can be found from any other source.

2:3 The analogy to locusts is a fitting one. The land will lie beautiful and plush, so much so that it is compared to the garden of Eden, but by the time the army has passed through, all that will be left is a desert wasteland. A comparison to fire is appropriate to describe utter loss.

2:4–11 The appearance of this army will stun those who see it. The noise and destruction will dishearten all observers. Nothing can be done to stop its progress. It is described as marching straight ahead, plunging through defenses, scaling walls, and even entering private homes. The impact of the aggression will shake the earth. In response, entire nations will be in anguish and become pale with fear.

2:12 When the day of the Lord arrives, there is nothing people can do to stop God's judgment. However, it is never too late for *God* to act. Speaking through His prophet, God provides a note of hope for those remaining in a situation that appears completely hopeless. He invites the wayward people to return to Him "also now" (or "even now," in another translation). However, such a return will accomplish nothing if it is based on hypocrisy or empty ceremony. God knows the hearts of people and sees through insincerity.

2:12–17 After a rather distressing section pertaining to a current plague of locusts and an even worse similar scourge to come, Joel at last offers some hope to the readers and listeners. Yes, the coming day of the Lord will be dreadful, but there are things the people can do to avoid its potentially terrifying consequences.

2:28–29 God speaks through His prophet of a great day to come, when His Spirit will be poured out—not just upon Israel but also on all faithful believers. The power of God will be felt by young and old, men and women. God's plan will be known through dreams, visions, and prophecies. When that day arrives, the effect will be so dramatic that onlookers will presume the recipients of God's Spirit are drunk (see Acts 2:13).

2:28–32 The date of the future events described by Joel is left a mystery. God's promise of the future will come "afterward." As it turns out, some of Joel's prophecy from this section will be remembered and applied in connection with the arrival of the Holy Spirit on Jesus' followers shortly after the Lord's death and resurrection (see Acts 2:14–21).

2:28–32 When Joel 2 is quoted by Peter (Acts 2:17–21) and Paul (Romans 10:13), it becomes clear that the ultimate fulfillment of the prophecy will be a *heavenly* Jerusalem and mount Zion. And from the New Testament perspective, another important detail is drawn out of the shadows and brought into clear light: The Lord Jesus Christ is the Son of God, who died on the cross for sinners and rose again. He is the Lord of the resurrection. It is His name people must own in order to receive the fullness of salvation that comes by the grace of their merciful God.

3:2–5 The charges that God brings against the nations are quite severe. For one thing, they have ransacked the wealth of Israel. They are also guilty of scattering God's people to the various lands of the time. And while it is true that they were acting under the auspices of God's control, they treated their captives horribly. The remaining specific charges that are included in the narrative are some of the worst imaginable offenses, with human trafficking and child prostitution among them.

3:9–11 Joel tells the nations to rouse their warriors. If they are going to be foolish enough to oppose the Lord of Israel, they may as well prepare for it. Their tools for everyday living should be converted into weapons of war.

3:14–16 God's judgment of the nations is connected with the day of the Lord, and afterward the Valley of Jehoshaphat ("God's judgment") will become the "valley of decision." As prophesied in 2:10, this event is said to be accompanied by great signs in the skies—a darkening of the sun, moon, and stars—and a shaking of the earth.

3:17 Joel's closing description portrays such a positive outlook for Jerusalem that it must be a reference to a yet-future time. Certainly, Jerusalem has not yet experienced a period where it could be said that foreigners will never again invade her. But someday the city will truly be holy—set apart for the glory of God. Joel's description anticipates Revelation 21–22 and the description of the new Jerusalem.

3:19 Those who remain hostile toward God and His people (symbolized by Israel's persistent enemies, Egypt and Edom) will lack water and life. Those who have shed innocent blood will be left a desolate desert wasteland.

3:20–21 Judah will be forgiven of her past sins, and God's presence will be with His people forever. When the day of the Lord arrives, one age will end and another, eternal one will begin. The Lord's coming will overwhelm the current created order, and by the plan and power of God, there will be a new heaven and a new earth fit for a renewed population of resurrected bodies. For the new Israel, the age of discipline will finally yield to the age of perfect delight.

THE BOOK OF

AMOS

INTRODUCTION TO AMOS ■ The prophet Amos was a contemporary of Old Testament prophets Hosea and Isaiah. He stood for justice in an era of Israel's history in which the nation was politically strong but spiritually weak.

AUTHOR ■ The first verse of this book attributes the writing to a man named Amos. Though his prophecy is directed to Israel, the northern kingdom, Amos himself is from Tekoa, a town in Judah, five miles south of Bethlehem. His work as a shepherd and gardener implies he belongs to the working class until the Lord commissions him to be one of His prophets.

OCCASION ■ Amos's ministry falls in the first half of the eighth century BC, during the last half of the reign of Jeroboam II (793–753 BC). Israel is enjoying a measure of domestic affluence and international power that she has not known since the reign of Solomon. Israel and Judah have expanded to the point that they encompass nearly all the land that David and Solomon controlled two centuries before. It is a time of military conquest and economic prosperity. It is also a time of moral darkness.

1:1–2 Even though Israel is in a time of prosperity, God's prophet knows Jeroboam's kingdom is not far from total extinction after his death. The roar from Zion is probably of a lion about to pounce, ready to lunge at its victim, Israel. Israel has voluntarily cut herself off from the temple in Jerusalem and its worship, but that is where the Lord's presence is represented. Part of what the Lord holds against Samaria, the capital of Israel, is the sanctuaries the people have built rather than attending the temple in Jerusalem.

1:3 Notice that God condemns the nations not for their false worship or religious practices but for their violations of the obligations they owe to other human beings—in Syria's case, her barbarity and inhumanity in war.

1:9, 11 Tyrus is accused of slave trading, but the sin for which she is to be destroyed is her violation of the covenant she made with another nation, apparently Israel. This is a sin she shares with Edom, which is also condemned for violations of brotherhood.

1:11 Edom has already been implicated in slave trading, but the fourth sin for which God is angry is like Tyrus's: a violation of family bonds. Edom is indeed Israel's brother, descended from Esau as Israel is from Jacob, and Isaac is the grandfather of both. But Edom has long harbored animosity toward Israel.

1:12 The cities of Edom—Teman to the south and Bozrah to the north—are mentioned to make the point that the entire country will suffer God's wrath, from top to bottom.

1:13–2:3 The last two nations, Ammon and Moab, are condemned for atrocities committed against the most vulnerable, fragile, and helpless of human beings: pregnant women and their unborn children in the first case and dead bodies in the second. And the Ammonites did this for temporal advantage, to enlarge their borders. They stepped on the weak to advantage themselves.

2:4–16 The two oracles of judgment in chapter 2— against Judah and Israel—show the progress of apostasy,

or the abandonment of one's faith. Things are not as bad in Judah during Amos's ministry as they are in Israel, but eventually Judah will be guilty of all the sins that Amos accuses Israel of in verses 6–12. At best, relations between the divided kingdoms—Israel to the north and Judah to the south—took the form of a peaceful coexistence. But more often, the two kingdoms interacted with outright hostility and sometimes war. Amos's Israelite audience would have enjoyed his message thus far. They would have been glad to hear of the Lord's judgments to befall their surrounding enemies and glad to learn that Judah was going to suffer.

2:6–16 The remaining verses of chapter 2 describe Israel as guilty of the same crimes against humanity that the pagan nations around her have been accused of. Israel has blatantly disobeyed the commandments of God's Word, involving herself in incestuous and promiscuous sexual relations, especially, no doubt, in regard to fertility rites at the temples and shrines. Amos represents Israel as deliberately throwing off the claims of the Lord.

2:13–16 God's wrath is inescapable, regardless of anyone's earthly wealth, power, or talent. As before, with the other nations, God's judgment will come in the form of an attack by a stronger nation. This will prove to be Assyria, just a few decades later. The Assyrian theory of conquest is the complete devastation of a nation, the depopulation of its territory, and the terrorization of its remnants.

3:1 The opening words of chapter 3 are repeated in 4:1; 5:1; and 8:4. Amos speaks to Israel as one nation, though the nation has long ago been divided and its people have been addressed separately already in this prophecy. The verses following will make it clear, however, that Israel, the northern kingdom, is chiefly in Amos's view.

3:3–6 The questions in this passage make a point. The coming of God's judgment is certain. Just as nature moves when it has purpose and need, so will God's justice move on His people. The blowing of a trumpet, a ram's horn, would have been familiar to the people of Amos's day. While the preceding questions rhetorically point to a *no* answer, the questions in verse 6 point to a *yes* answer. Perhaps the last question makes the main point: These people are not expecting disaster and do not see themselves in Amos's question.

3:8 Just as one pays attention when a lion roars, so the Lord's prophet cannot ignore or fail to deliver His Word.

3:11 Israel's strongholds and fortresses—the things she has trusted for protection—will prove little obstacle to the Assyrians. Neither will Israel's wealth be her protection.

3:14–15 The image of Bethel, a name that means "house of God," is combined with a variety of other houses. When the house of God falls, no house remains. Israel's great houses are monuments to her corruption and her ill-gotten wealth.

4:4 Amos taunts the Israelites by saying that all they are accomplishing with their worship is the multiplying of their sins and the deepening of their judgment. He exaggerates their practices as if they are doing almost nothing but making pilgrimages to Bethel and Gilgal. The implicit question becomes, what good is all of this doing?

4:6–11 This section is marked by the first-person pronoun *I* and the refrain that the people have not returned to God even with all He has done to draw them back. There is a deliberate contrast between what Yahweh has done and what Israel is doing. Israel has been busy rebelling against the Lord; the Lord has been busy seeking to bring her to repentance. All of the catastrophes listed in this section—hunger, drought, plague, pestilence, war, etc.—have been signs of God's wrath, and Israel has ignored them all.

4:12–13 The God whose justice and judgment Israel must now face is the sovereign Lord who controls nature. Israel cannot withstand the Lord when He comes in judgment.

5:4–5 Instead of empty rituals, God wants His people to seek Him. Bethel, Gilgal, and Beer-sheba are important sites in Israel's history. Apparently all three cities held shrines to which Israelites made faithful pilgrimages—even Beer-sheba, which lay at the southernmost end of Judah. But the people had been commanded to go to Jerusalem to worship. Amos is once again pointing out the futility of Israel's religious practices. Her people worship, but instead of following God's guidelines, they make their own rules. They offer worship that offends the Lord rather than pleases Him.

5:6 The "house of Joseph" is a reference to the northern kingdom of Israel. Regions were often identified by their principal tribe. In this case, that tribe is Ephraim, made up of the descendants of one of Joseph's sons.

5:7–11 This passage has a unique structure. Verse 7 characterizes Israelite life as unjust and unrighteous, something that Amos has already established. Verses 8–9 function as a kind of doxology, describing God in terms of His power and majesty. He alone can save Israel from the disaster that looms. Then the characterization that began in verse 7 continues in verses 10–11. By the middle of verse 11, the announcement of judgment begins.

5:12–13 In essence, the religion of the Israelites does not touch their lifestyles; they are heedless of the claims of justice and God's law.

5:14–15 The people must do certain things if they indeed want to be the people of God they claim to be. The Israelites mistakenly believe God to be on their side, even while they are disconnected from their true spiritual state.

5:18–20 These verses include the earliest recorded use of the expression *day of the Lord*. It will occur many more times in the prophets of the Old Testament and again in the New Testament. But clearly it is already a familiar phrase by this time as a religious figure of speech. Because of their disconnection from God's view of their spiritual state, the Israelites think that the Day of the Lord will bring happiness and triumph to them when, in fact, it will bring disaster.

5:25–26 The prophet makes the point, as he has previously done, that Israel's sacrifices are disconnected from her faith relationship with God. The people of Israel seem to think that as long as they offer Yahweh sacrifices, all will be well, no matter their obedience in other areas of life. Amos is reminding them that their own history is the disproof of that idea.

5:27 The place beyond Damascus is Assyria, which eventually defeats the northern kingdom of Israel.

6:1 As he has done before, Amos presents Israel as serenely confident of God's approval without good reason to be so confident. Zion, a synonym for the capital city of Judah, seems to be a reference to the whole southern kingdom. Samaria, capital city of the northern kingdom, is used in the same way to represent the whole kingdom of Israel.

6:2 These cities may have fallen during Amos's lifetime or before. Either way, he lifts these cities up as a reality check to Israel, to show that trusting in her own supremacy may be a futile effort.

6:3 Amos accuses his nation of causing "the seat of violence to come near," or bringing a "reign of terror," by its disobedience.

6:9–10 Israel's military self-confidence will be turned into a cruel joke. The picture is that of ten men who have survived the terrors of the siege so far and are found taking refuge together in a single home—probably a large home. This is a picture of the wealthy of Samaria, but even these will die, probably of disease, a feature of siege warfare.

7:2 Repeatedly throughout this section, Amos refers to the nation of Israel as *Jacob*. This is a common custom in the writings of the Old Testament. Nations are sometimes identified by the name of their ancestors. Jacob is the forebear of the twelve tribes of Israel.

7:9–10 Amos's message is the last straw for the priest Amaziah. Amaziah not only wants to punish Amos, but also wants to discredit him and get rid of him. The quickest path to this goal is creating trouble for Amos with the current government. For Amaziah to say that the land cannot bear Amos's words is simply to say that these words should not be tolerated.

7:11 Amaziah exaggerates, as do most people who wish to cast someone else in a bad light. Amos never predicted that Jeroboam would die by the sword (in fact, he died of natural causes), but Amos had said enough about the nation's sins and God's impending judgment by military conquest that it was only a small step to saying that Amos predicted Jeroboam's death.

7:12–15 The treatment that Amos receives reveals animosity and superiority on the part of Amaziah. The insinuation is that Amos is preaching in Israel because the money is better in the wealthy north. Amaziah is judging Amos by his own standards. He thinks of his own work as simply a job, and he imagines it to be the same for Amos. Amos clarifies the issue. He is not a prophet for hire; he is called by God. This sets him apart from Amaziah, a bureaucrat doing the king's bidding.

7:16–17 While Amaziah wants Amos to stop prophesying against Israel, he receives prophecy not only a against Israel but also against his own family. The last line of the curse is the explanation of the previous four: Israel will be conquered and its people sent into exile. The other punishments can all be explained as typical effects of military conquest and exile. In any case, events will prove which of the two men has been speaking the truth and is a servant of the true living God.

8:3 Amos has already referred to music in Israel's temple worship (5:23), but when the Lord's judgment falls, the only music to be heard at Israel's sanctuaries will be howling. Dead bodies will be scattered everywhere.

8:10 Amos compares the people's mourning to that found at the funeral of an only son, which would have been understood by Amos's listeners to be an ultimate and bitter loss.

8:12 The Israelites will stagger from one sea to another. This reference implies the Dead Sea to the Mediterranean, which is a way of saying that this judgment will affect all of Israel.

8:14 Samaria's shame is a contrast to the mention of Jacob's pride in verse 7. It refers to the false gods that have been added to Yahweh's worship at Israel's shrines.

To swear by a god is to commit themselves to the reality of that god and its power to help them. Israel's lack of true repentance shows that in that same day, they will still be found calling on other gods and looking to their idols as well as to Yahweh.

9:1–4 These verses contain the fifth and last of the visions that God gives Amos—this one of the destruction of the temple. (The first four visions are recorded in chapters 7–8.) The pillars of the temple support the roof, and the cut stone thresholds are at the bottom of the great doors. The picture here is of the complete collapse of the temple from top to bottom. One of Israel's sanctuaries is in view, probably the principal one at Bethel. The picture of the building collapsing on the worshippers indicates that Israelite worship is conducted in some significant measure inside the sanctuary, in the Canaanite fashion, not outside in the court in the orthodox fashion prescribed in the Law of Moses.

9:5 The Nile's rising and falling is used as an image of destruction in 8:8. Here the Nile serves as another image of the totality of the Lord's judgment—like a flood that covers the land before it recedes, it leaves nothing but destruction behind.

9:7 Here the Lord begins to speak in the first person, asking two rhetorical questions that place Israel, spiritually speaking, on equal ground with all others. Israel is no more exempt from God's judgment than the people of Ethiopia. Israel, by her lack of faith and her betrayal of God's covenant, has become just like these other people instead of the people of God she was called to be. Since the Philistines and the Syrians were hated enemies of Israel, the comparison would have been particularly galling to Amos's audience.

9:13–14 This is a description of a time of unprecedented bounty. The picture is of fields so fertile and harvests so large that the reapers will still be gathering the grain as the soil is being turned over for the next planting. And the image of wine flowing downward from the hills where the grapes are grown is, again, a picture of unimaginable plenty.

9:13–15 Amos closes with a promise that when the people of God are restored and resettled in the promised land to enjoy the blessings and benefits of God's favor, they will never be judged again. The judgment of the nation is upon them. This has been Amos's primary theme from the beginning of the book, but when the Day of Judgment is past and Israel is restored, it will be for good.

THE BOOK OF

OBADIAH

INTRODUCTION TO OBADIAH ▪ The book of Obadiah is the shortest of the Old Testament, yet its brief message has numerous applications far beyond its relevance to Edom. Obadiah provides a warning to anyone who mistakenly believes that sin will go unnoticed (and unpunished), but he also offers confidence that for those who continue to seek God, the Lord is able to both forgive and deliver.

AUTHOR ▪ Personal facts are scarce concerning the prophet Obadiah. He provides no family references or pertinent locations that enlighten the reader as to his biography. Even his name (meaning "worshipper of the Lord") was a common one in his day. At least a dozen Old Testament men are named Obadiah.

OCCASION ▪ Obadiah has a single purpose in writing: to bring God's message of judgment to the people of Edom. The nation's deeply rooted sense of pride will result in its certain downfall.

---

1 The concise writing of Obadiah is a pointed accusation against the nation of Edom. Israel and Edom had a long and interwoven history. Sometimes they had joined as allies against a common enemy. More often, however, the original rivalry between Jacob (Israel's forefather) and Esau (Edom's forefather) created ongoing conflicts between the two nations. In fact, Edom had taken perverse pleasure in seeing God's people suffer and had even acted aggressively against them during a vulnerable time. What Edom didn't realize, however, was that Judah's fall was a result of God's judgment on His people. Obadiah now reveals that God will certainly judge Edom as well and that judgment will be severe.

3–4 Edom was located along a span of wilderness that stretched from the southern tip of the Dead Sea to the northern portion of the Red Sea. It was mountainous territory where the inhabitants lived among rocky cliffs, confident of their security and the impenetrability of their cities. It is as if they feel untouchable, high among the stars.

4 Edom's pride could be seen in a variety of ways. Israel had requested permission to travel through Edom during their exodus from Egypt, but the Edomites had marched out with a large and powerful army to deny them passage (Numbers 20:14–21). Later, when Israel was an established nation of its own, the Edomites waited until other people attacked Israel and then invaded and took prisoners (2 Chronicles 28:16–21). And when Jerusalem eventually fell to the Babylonians, the Edomites cheered and celebrated (Psalm 137:7–8).

5–9 During a typical theft, the robbers will leave behind some of the person's belongings, but Edom's loss will be total. Even worse, those whom Edom considers close friends and allies will prove deceitful. The very people whom they trust enough to sit around the table and share a meal with will destroy them with alarming treachery. The wisdom and power of the most accomplished descendants of Esau will not be adequate to anticipate this trouble nor deliver their countrymen from a horrifying slaughter.

10–14 When nonbelievers observe God's people undergoing a period of corrective discipline, they may perceive that God has no abiding love for those who worship Him, but it is never wise to gloat over those whom the Lord has called His special possession. He will stand up for them in the day when He comes to judge and will bring upon the heads of their enemies the very vengeance those people had sought for them. Edom will learn this lesson too late, as the people find themselves covered with shame and destroyed.

15 Jesus will later teach that we should treat others the way we want to be treated (Matthew 7:12). The prophet Obadiah records a twist of this truth, pronouncing that as Edom has treated God's people, so shall Edom be treated.

16–18 After contributing to the (temporary) defeat of Jerusalem, the Edomites had apparently celebrated with strong drink. But the cup of God's fury (see Isaiah 51:17) is in store for them to drink. Edom represents all the nations who have opposed God—they all will one day completely disappear from existence, while Jerusalem is restored. The house of Esau will have no survivors.

19–21 Mount Zion (Jerusalem) will be delivered, once again holy and home to the house of Jacob (Israel). Surrounding land that had been ceded to other nations will be reclaimed and restored. People will be called out of exile to resettle in their homelands. Deliverers will be assigned to help govern, but the kingdom will be the Lord's.

THE BOOK OF

JONAH

INTRODUCTION TO JONAH ■ Jonah is the only prophet who is recorded as having run away from God. In this way, Jonah is not known for his piety but for his prodigality. Jonah, in his rebellion, disobedience, and hardness of heart, is a man who typifies the rebellion of Israel as described by other prophets. Ironically, the name *Jonah* means "dove," a bird often associated with peace.

AUTHOR ■ Very little is said of the prophet Jonah outside of the book of Jonah itself. It does seem safe to conclude that the Jonah in 2 Kings 14:25 is the same person who is the subject of the book of Jonah, especially since both are identified as the son of Amittai. The book of Jonah does not name its author. While it is about Jonah, there is no specific claim as to whether Jonah actually wrote it.

OCCASION ■ Jonah is a prophet in the northern kingdom of Israel during the first half of the eighth century BC. His predecessors are Elijah and Elisha. The ministries of Hosea and Amos immediately follow that of Jonah.

1:1–2 The description of Nineveh as "great" probably refers to its size and its influence, but its sins were great as well. The city of Nineveh is located on the Tigris River, more than five hundred miles to the northeast of Israel.

1:3 Rather than going east toward Nineveh, Jonah goes west toward Tarshish, which seems to have been located on the western coast of Spain. Jonah flees from God's presence, a truth repeated twice. Jonah is not trying to flee the literal presence of God, but he is attempting to avoid his own role as a prophet.

1:5 Each sailor is praying to his own gods for deliverance. These pagan sailors likely worshipped gods they thought influenced the seas on which they traveled.

1:6 The ship's captain is irritated to find Jonah sleeping while the rest of the crew members work to stay alive during the storm. He doesn't ask Jonah to help cast the cargo overboard, but he does command Jonah to pray to his God. The text does not reveal whether Jonah obeys the captain's orders.

1:7 The captain and the sailors understand the storm to be a religious matter. When praying doesn't stop the storm, they try another religious technique: casting lots (a way to make the kind of random decisions you would drawing straws or throwing dice) to find the person whose sin has caused the problem. The lots land on Jonah and identify him as the culprit.

1:9–10 In his answer to their questions, Jonah separates himself religiously from the sailors but apparently reveals insight into his mission. From his responses, the sailors immediately know that Jonah has indeed caused the storm and that his sin has endangered the entire ship's crew.

1:11 The response of the sailors—who are appalled at Jonah's disobedience—shows that even the pagans are shocked at how this man has chosen to defy God. They, too, are experiencing the consequences of Jonah's actions, so they ask Jonah what to do to appease the wrath of his God.

1:12–14 Jonah tells the sailors to throw him overboard and the sea will calm. Given the intensity of the storm, this request would have made his death seem a certainty. Some believe this shows repentance on Jonah's part, but others feel that Jonah wants to die to avoid God's command to confront Nineveh. Many scholars agree that by the time the sailors throw Jonah into the sea, they are praying to Jonah's God.

1:15–16 As Jonah sinks beneath the waves, the winds cease and the sea calms down. This confirms for the sailors that Jonah's God is the only true God. Thus we see the sailors worshipping by sacrificing and declaring their faith in God. In trying to avoid preaching to the Ninevites, Jonah has unwillingly preached to the sailors, and they come to faith in his God.

1:17 The fish that God provides has become the focus of this story, yet it is simply a provision of the Lord. The miracle is not in the fish itself or in the details of how the fish swallowed Jonah; the miracle is God's grace toward Jonah, saving him from almost certain death in order that Jonah may receive all that God's call on his life has to offer.

1:17 Jesus refers back to Jonah's plight (using the name *Jonas*) in the belly of the fish in Matthew 12:39–41, comparing Jonah's three days and nights to the three days and nights the Son of man spends in the earth. This is called the sign of the prophet Jonah.

2:10 There is little emphasis on the actual fish itself in this passage, perhaps because the fish is obedient to his commission. Jonah's prayer is answered, and he is not only expelled from the fish but also returned to dry land.

3:3 The mention of a three-day journey refers to how long it would take to walk around Nineveh.

3:4–6 Jonah's message is simple, to the point, and frightening: In forty days, Nineveh will fall. Just like the sailors in chapter 1, the people of Nineveh take Jonah's words of imminent divine judgment seriously—they believe. The faith of the Ninevites is not simply a fear of judgment. They call a fast and put on sackcloth—a sign of helplessness and despair.

3:10 God takes note of Nineveh's repentance because it involves more than mere words or token gestures. The Ninevites have changed more than outward appearances; they have changed their evil ways.

4:1–3 In spite of the repentance of Nineveh, Jonah is angry with God. Jonah is not hesitant to explain, and he protests to the Lord in prayer. Instead of learning this lesson about God's loving and merciful character, he complains that he would rather die than live.

4:5–8 Jonah could have chosen to walk away from his suffering and join the Ninevites in their worship of God, but he allows his anger to keep him in discomfort and isolation. He once again begs God to let him die.

4:9 For the second time in this chapter, God offers the opportunity for Jonah to examine his anger; and again Jonah chooses anger over any other emotion. He is so adamant about his anger that he insists upon keeping it and wishes to die.

THE BOOK OF

MICAH

INTRODUCTION TO MICAH ■ Sometimes called the prophet of the poor, Micah is a contemporary of Isaiah and speaks a similar message, though, as recorded in the Bible, shorter. King Hezekiah initiates sweeping spiritual and moral reforms in Judah in response to the preaching of Micah and Isaiah, but unfortunately these reforms are short-lived.

AUTHOR ■ The first verse of this book ascribes the authorship to Micah, a prophet about whom we know very little outside of what is revealed through this prophecy. The prophet is mentioned in only one other place in the Bible, in Jeremiah 26:17–19. In this account, Micah is described as a prophet during the reign of King Hezekiah. When Micah prophesied a bad end for Jerusalem, the king repented, saving Jerusalem from the destruction Micah had prophesied.

OCCASION ■ The first verse of this prophecy identifies the monarchies under which Micah prophesies—Jotham, Ahaz, and Hezekiah. This places Micah in the eighth century BC. The prophecy references the destruction of Samaria and the invasion of Sennacherib in 701 BC, which would agree with that chronology.

1:1 Micah begins with the announcement of judgment because of sins against God and unfaithfulness to God's covenant. This is a major theme of the prophets, leading up to the destruction of the northern kingdom in 722 BC and the devastation and exile of the southern kingdom some 150 years later. This lesson also reveals the nature of God's divine justice, the ferocity of divine wrath, and the final and conclusive judgment of all people at the end of the world.

1:1 The kings listed reign from 742 BC to 686 BC. It is widely thought that Micah mentions only the southern kings—though he mentions the northern kingdom (Samaria) as well as the southern (Jerusalem)—because he did not regard the northern kings as legitimate and did not want to dignify them by mentioning them by name.

1:2 The call goes out to the entire earth, even though the message concerns Samaria primarily and Jerusalem to a lesser degree. They are all being summoned to a trial to face the Judge of all the earth.

1:5–7 The specific sins will be enumerated in chapters 2 and 3 and again in chapter 6, but here the case is put generally as rebellion. The capital cities are mentioned both to represent the entire nation and because they are where the living embodiment of the corruption that has destroyed the nation originated. The punishment on Samaria and Jerusalem foreshadows punishment for all people who worship idols.

1:8 The description of the prophet stripped of clothes is not a picture of penitence but of exile. Exiles, barefoot and naked, were forced to tramp miserably away from home in long lines under the supervision of enemy soldiers. The same idea is expressed with the howling of the dragons (or jackals). This implies the wilderness, which is what Judah will be reduced to.

1:10 The mention of Gath is significant because the city does not exist at this time, having been destroyed by Sargon. The idea, as any Israelite of this era would immediately

realize, is that the house of David is now falling, just as the house of Saul had done before. Dust is a symbol of abject humiliation and defeat (see Genesis 3:14).

1:15 This allusion is literary, not literal. As David had to flee from Saul to the cave of Adullam (see 1 Samuel 22:1), so the sons of David—the kings and the nobles (the glory of Israel)—will be driven out.

2:1 The reference to the light of morning alludes to the time of day when the courts meet. The indication is that the people in power are controlling the courts, which should be a place of justice for all, not just the powerful.

2:7 The first half of this verse shows what the false prophets are teaching, and the second half reveals Micah's response to that teaching. The message of the false prophets amounts to an assurance that because God is love, Israel has nothing to fear. But Micah explains that while God is gracious, He is also a God of judgment to those who do not believe in or obey Him.

2:11 Micah mocks the message preached by the false teachers as simply another version of what people want to hear. He is properly cynical of the base motives of the false teachers.

2:12–13 Historically there have been two different interpretations of these verses. Some see them as a further prophecy of woe and judgment. Most, though, take the verses to be a message of hope and consolation, a promise of at least a temporary deliverance—a direct prophecy of the deliverance of Jerusalem from Sennacherib's invading army in 701 BC. The sheep pen, or fold, is Jerusalem. The Shepherd of Israel is gathering His flock to protect it from marauders.

2:13 Micah's contemporary listeners would have noticed a similarity between this description of the Lord breaking open the way and David's reference to the Lord breaking out against His enemies (the Philistines) in 2 Samuel 5:20, 24. In other areas of scripture, God is the One who breaks open a way to save His people.

3:1–4 Chapter 3 contains three oracles of judgment of equal length and identical in form, with the same theme in every case—corrupt leadership. Micah is the person speaking. He uses imagery to show that the leaders are, in effect, consuming people for their own gain.

3:4 There is a startling new development in this oracle—the fact that the Lord will punish these false teachers in keeping with their crimes. The oppressed cry out to these leaders, and they do not answer or help them. So when the leaders cry out to God for help, He will not answer them. This indicates a point of no return.

3:6 Divination, or fortune-telling, is forbidden to the people of God (Deuteronomy 18:10). It is considered a betrayal of the sufficiency of God's revelation and a serious mistaking of the way to live a life pleasing to God.

3:7 In Micah's day, the false prophets held equal social status with God's prophets, if not a higher status because of the popularity of their message. Yet one hundred years later, these same false prophets will be walking through the ruins of Jerusalem like unclean lepers.

3:9–12 This is a third oracle against the corrupt leadership of the people. This last oracle speaks to the leadership in general, adding the priests, by name, to the leaders and false prophets.

3:12 This is the only verse in the Old Testament that is cited word for word somewhere else in the Old Testament (Jeremiah 26:18), some one hundred years later. The Lord relents because of Hezekiah's faithfulness.

4:1 The prediction that opens chapter 4 is similar to other instances in the Old Testament Prophets such as Isaiah 2:2–4 and Hosea 3:5. The opening mention of the last days is used in the New Testament also to refer to the future when God will bring all prophecies to fruition (1 Timothy 4:1; 2 Timothy 3:1; 1 Peter 1:5; Jude 18). There is debate about whether these days refer to a time before Christ comes again or the time after Christ actually has returned.

4:1–5 Almost every ancient Near Eastern religion and deity had a mountain dedicated to it, and most often a temple stood on that mountain (or hill, as the case may be). In this era, the mountain symbolizes God's bringing of order over chaos, access to heaven, and His presence on earth. The Lord's mountain rising above the others means that Yahweh will reign supreme as the nations come to recognize and honor Him as the true God.

4:9–11 The suffering of the people in the coming captivity is foreshadowed here. Some Bible translations interpret *king* and *counsellor* as a reference to human figures and thus interpret the question in verse 9 as sarcasm. But if verse 9 parallels verse 11, it suggests that these words are a reference to God. In this understanding, the question is rhetorical. Has God perished? Of course not.

4:11–13 There is a twist here. While these nations think they are destroying Israel on their own, in reality God is using them to punish and purify His people. While their actions are being used by Him at this time, eventually He will punish these nations for both their actions and their intentions.

5:3 Israel's distress will continue until the Messiah comes. The *remnant*, or the rest, is the same idea as in Isaiah 11:11–12 and Zechariah 10:10, the gathering of those who have been dispersed because of exile or defeat.

5:5–6 The Assyrian invasion in 701 BC is likely the context of this oracle, for several reasons: First, Nimrod (Babylon) is an inferior power, so this must describe a time when Babylon is subject to Assyria. Also, Assyria is used as the representative of the forces of hostility to the kingdom of God, which supports the idea that Assyria is in an era of power. Finally, the term *principle men* is one the Assyrian king Sargon used for his leaders.

5:7 The previous oracle links the earlier prophecies with the coming of the Messiah. In the oracle beginning here, the Messiah will expand His kingdom through the nations of the world by means of the remnant.

5:9–14 The destruction in Micah's own day comes by means of the Assyrian invasion, and it will continue with the exile to Babylon (which has already been foretold). The specific details of the destruction highlight God's anger at Israel's worship of false gods.

5:14 The word translated *destroy* is the same word used in Leviticus concerning the punishment of sin in the camp in order to maintain a holy people (Leviticus 17:10; 20:3).

6:8 The idea expressed here represents one of Micah's chief emphases. The failure of Israel's faith is demonstrated in the people's indifference to justice and mercy toward others, especially toward those who are poorer or weaker than themselves.

6:9 In the broader legal analogy found in this passage, this verse is the sentencing phase. The rod mentioned is a picture of the Assyrians, who will attack and who will function as God's chastisement of His people.

6:10–14 The wealthy who are called out here are the royal family, the land barons, and the military elite. We have already heard of their unjust treatment of the middle class in 2:2, 8–9, and 3:11.

6:13–16 These judgments are the very curses that God had long before promised—in Deuteronomy and Leviticus—to visit upon His people if they proved unfaithful to His covenant with them.

7:1–2 The image here would be familiar to Micah's agricultural society—a vinedresser and orchard manager who, after long and patient labor, finds his vineyard stripped by vandals. God feels the same way when He comes to delight in His people and finds, instead, so much sin.

7:2 The last part of this verse can sound like a manhunt, but it is actually a reference to the way fellow citizens are mistreating each other.

7:3–4 Micah calls the best of the leaders and judges a brier, and a group of them like a hedge of briers—an agricultural touchstone that the original audience would understand. Briers keep people or animals from harvesting ripe fruit—they leave painful cuts and scratches on those who try. In this case, the briers are obstructing justice.

7:4–6 These verses repeat the idea that one should not trust in his own protection, because God is the only source of protection, safety, and peace. Even the most intimate human relationships snap under strain, and each one looks out for oneself, as is happening to these people.

7:8–13 This section opens almost like a psalm, with Jerusalem telling her enemy not to gloat. She is being punished justly for her sins; but precisely because the Lord always does what is right, the remnant within Israel who acknowledge their sin and repent will once again enjoy the Lord's favor.

7:11 The idea of walls here is not to imply defensive fortifications. These walls are more like the walls that surround a vineyard. Their mention speaks to Jerusalem's prosperity, not her self-defense.

7:12 This is the fulfillment of God's ancient promise to Abram (Genesis 15:18) in a broader and still more glorious form—the promise extends not just to the area but to the people in that area.

7:14 Bashan and Gilead are both known for their rich pastures, and thus they build upon the image of a shepherd. They are places fit for a king's sheep to graze. Israel doesn't possess these places anymore; they have been lost to her because of her infidelity to God. But Micah is asking that Israel be restored. It is not a presumptuous request, because God has already promised that Israel's former dominion will be restored to her (4:8). Micah's prayer is that God's Word, His promise, will come true.

7:15 The stories of the Exodus are faith affirming for the people of Israel. They remember God's mighty acts as He freed His people and miraculously led them toward the land He had promised them.

7:16–17 The images of nations with deaf ears and hands on mouths represent a sense of awe and even a sense of being put in one's place. In fact, all the images in these verses are of people who recognize the greatness of Israel's God.

7:17–20 Micah sings the praises of the true God but at the same time is educating his listeners and readers about the character of God.

THE BOOK OF

NAHUM

INTRODUCTION TO NAHUM ■ Nahum is a book that calls into reckoning Judah's enemy, Nineveh. A careful reading of this book reveals that the author has a high view of God and His Word; he preaches against idolatry, immorality, injustice, and all manner of sin.

AUTHOR ■ We don't know many facts about Nahum, but there is no reason to doubt he is the primary author of the material that bears his name. From his writing style we can assume he was born into a family with enough means to provide him literary training.

OCCASION ■ Nahum witnessed the reduction of his nation to vassalage during the early campaigns of Assyria. These events, a prelude and a means to the judgment of both Judah and Nineveh, are part of the process that accomplishes the restoration of God's people.

1:1 Throughout this book, Nahum's prophecies deal with Nineveh's doom, its eventual defeat, and its destruction.

1:2–10 Nahum begins his prophecy with a two-part hymn that sets forth the theme and depicts key elements of God's nature. God is a God of justice, who will punish the wicked and avenge His own. He is a sovereign and mighty God who, although He is long-suffering, will defeat His guilty foes and, though He is beneficent, will destroy those who plot against Him. The rehearsal of these general truths concerning the character and work of God provides a foundation for their application to the world situation of Nahum's day.

1:8–10 God, in His judicial wrath, will come against His enemies like a victorious commander pursuing his foes to the farthest recesses of the earth. Like men entangled in thorns or overcome with their own drunkenness, they will be easily overthrown. God's fiery wrath will consume them like fire. They will not devise their devious plot a second time. The ruins of Nineveh show abundant evidence of the intensity of the conflagration that consumed the fallen city. Whatever application these verses have to God's enemies in general, it is obvious that Nahum's prophetic pronouncements have a particular relevance for Nineveh.

1:11 The description of the counsellor as *wicked* carries the idea of *worthless*. It speaks of a character of life so totally reprobate that the term came ultimately to apply to Satan himself (2 Corinthians 6:14–15).

1:14 Nahum's use of the word *name* is particularly appropriate, as it here connotes *existence*. Nineveh (Assyria) will be destroyed and left without descendants.

1:14–15 With the pronouncement of the irreversible decision of divine judgment, there is a good word for Judah. Nahum's prophecy is a near-historical realization of Isaiah's. Isaiah foresees the day when an oppressed Israel will be freed at last from oppressors and invaders, and its people will not only hear the message of the Lord's salvation but also experience the everlasting serenity that comes with His presence in royal power in their midst (Isaiah 52:1–10).

2:1 Each of the imperatives in this verse produces a staccato effect and lends urgency and dramatic appeal

to the scene. Nahum's admonitions are probably to be understood as irony, perhaps with a touch of sarcasm. Because Nineveh's doom has already been announced in chapter 1, all such efforts are obviously destined for failure as God restores His own.

2:3–10 Nahum's description of the attack against Nineveh begins with a consideration of its attackers. In these verses, there is a clear pattern describing the siege: the enemy's assembling of his forces, the initial advance, the all-out attack, and its aftermath. The scene progresses from one of preparation and advance to one of conflict.

2:8–10 Conquered Nineveh is said to be like a pool of water. The simile is effective and appropriate. The city lay in a favorable location with an adequate water supply. But now the blessing has turned into a curse at the hands of the enemy. The panicked masses flee from the waters and the crumbling city.

2:11 In an extended metaphor (or allegory), Nineveh is compared to a lions' den, now no longer the lair of an invincible predator or a den of refuge for its cubs but reduced to ashes. Nineveh will be judged for its selfishness, rapacity, and cruelty.

3:1–7 Nahum writes his second description of Nineveh's certain doom in the elements of a woe oracle. The initial *woe* is a word drawn from a lamentation for the dead. It constitutes a formal denunciation of the doomed city.

3:2–3 Whether reporting what he has seen in a vision or merely envisioning the future scene, Nahum's portrayal of the coming battle is one of picturesque brevity using vivid images.

3:6 The word translated *filth* denotes something that is detested. A strong word, it is usually reserved for contexts dealing with aberrations connected with pagan worship. The word carries with it the idea of loathing. The thought is that despoiled Nineveh will be treated as an abominable thing.

3:8 As described here, No, better known as Thebes, was surrounded by a strong defensive wall and a water system that included lakes, moats, canals, and the Nile.

In the past, Thebes had been able to boast of the help of not only all Egypt but also its seventh-century allies: Ethiopia (Sudanese Cush), Put (perhaps the fabled land of Punt in coastal Somaliland), and Lubim (Libya). None of these, however, supplied strength and protection for Thebes at this time.

3:14–19 These verses form the second portion of an extended taunt song that functions as satire. Nahum's sarcasm is evident throughout. He prophesies that Nineveh's enemy will sweep through the city like a horde of devouring locusts. Nineveh's merchants and officials flee, and her sleeping leaders are compared to shepherds who have nodded off to sleep and allowed the sheep (the Ninevites) to be scattered (in flight or in exile). The choice of this motif as the final one for the book may suggest, as many commentators have observed, that the "sleep" (or "slumber") of the shepherds/officials is death.

3:14–19 Nahum predicts the burning of the city (1:10; 2:13), a fact confirmed by archaeological excavation. Nahum's emphasis on the destruction of Nineveh's temples is also confirmed by excavations. Minute details concerning the events of the final days before Nineveh's fall—such as the drunkenness (1:10; 3:11), cowardice, degeneracy (3:4), and desertion (2:8; 3:17) of the city by its leadership—are also abundantly recorded in the ancient traditions. Nahum's prophecies concerning the final slaughter of Nineveh's citizens (3:3) and the looting of the city (2:9–10), its utter destruction (2:10; 3:7), and the virtual disappearance of its people are facts confirmed in the ancient records.

3:14–19 Nahum's words have been dramatically precise in their fulfillment. They find corroboration in the findings of archaeologists who note the hasty strengthening of the walls at strategic defensive positions. The fall of the city due to water (1:8; 2:8) has been attested both by archaeologists and ancient historians. Unusually heavy rains were known to have given difficulty to Nineveh, which was served by three rivers: the Tigris, the Khosr, and the Tebiltu. A high-water season and a sudden storm, accompanied by the swelling of any or all three rivers, would account for the fulfillment of Nahum's prophecy.

THE BOOK OF

HABAKKUK

INTRODUCTION TO HABAKKUK ■ Like Nahum, Habakkuk begins by referring to his message as an oracle, or a message, placed upon his heart by God. Like Nahum, Habakkuk assures his readers that what he is about to relate is not from his own ingenuity but is from God. Unlike Nahum, however, Habakkuk does not state that his message is specifically directed at any one individual or group of people, though he will devote a great deal of space to a denunciation of the Chaldeans, which is a representation of the Babylonians.

AUTHOR ■ We don't know anything more about Habakkuk than what can be gleaned from this book. We do know, however, that his authorship of this message was accepted from very early on.

OCCASION ■ While Habakkuk may differ from the other prophets in terms of whom he addresses in his message, he is similar in that he is troubled by the disobedience of his people. In Habakkuk's case, however, rather than pleading with God for more time or with the people for more attention, he questions why God's judgment hasn't already fallen on his nation.

1:1–4 The nature of Habakkuk's complaint to God, begun in the invocation and elaborated in the statement of the problem, describes his society as a place characterized by general spiritual and ethical havoc.

1:5–6 God tells Habakkuk to look at the nations. God is already at work in and behind the scenes of earth's history to set in motion events that will change the whole situation. And when Habakkuk learns what is to happen, he will be utterly amazed. Why? Because God will raise up the Chaldeans to discipline Habakkuk's people.

1:7–11 The Lord reassures the prophet of His sovereign control. Since God's prophet will be surprised at the announcement about the Chaldeans, God goes on to supply a brief résumé of their character and potentially devastating power.

1:9 Contrary to Habakkuk's complaint, God assures His prophet that He sees all that comes to pass and hears the prayers and complaints of His people. Habakkuk's own word is sent back to him. Has Judah done violence? It shall in turn suffer violence at the hands of a violent nation whose well-trained and battle-seasoned army will move forward with such precision that the whole striking force will march as one to achieve its objectives, at the same time taking many captives.

1:10–11 Although the language here is exaggerated to make a point, in light of the ancient records it is not inappropriately exaggerated. Many texts could be cited concerning the Chaldeans' successful campaigning. The picture of Chaldean armed might is of one who holds all his foes in contempt and mocks them. Such a nation knows no god but strength.

1:12 Habakkuk simply cannot reconcile God's use of the Chaldeans, a people more corrupt than those they are to judge, to punish His people. He begins his second perplexity with an invocation in which he expresses his consternation. Faced with the prospect of destructive judgment, perhaps even the death of the nation itself,

Habakkuk cries out to Israel's God, the Holy One of her salvation, who alone is her refuge in such times.

1:13–17 Habakkuk has reservations. He cannot comprehend why a holy God plans to use a nation more wicked than the nation He desires to punish. From the prophet's perspective, he has to wonder, once this plan is put into operation, will not a helpless humankind always be at the mercy of these God-commissioned agents of chastisement? Habakkuk's fears are not unfounded, for the Chaldean war machine was effective enough to gain for them political dominance across the northern part of the Fertile Crescent and through the Levant to the borders of Egypt.

2:1 Habakkuk ends his complaint with a statement of his renewed confidence in God and his intention to assume the role of a watchman. As a city watchman mans his post atop the walls to look for the approach of danger or a messenger, or to keep watch over current events, Habakkuk will assume the role of a prophetic watchman, taking his post to watch for the Lord's reply.

2:5–8 God's answer takes the form of a logical argument: If it is true that the arrogant have ungodly desires and never come to enjoy the blessings of God, how much more certain is it that the qualities accompanying such an attitude will ultimately betray them? The underlying implication is clear: The Chaldeans' selfishness and success will be their undoing.

2:9–10 This second woe underscores the Chaldeans' capacity for cunning schemes against humankind. Building on the imagery in the first woe (2:6), the Chaldean is portrayed as one who achieves wealth through violence and evil means.

2:11 The stone walls and beams refer to the Chaldeans' building projects. In the end, the Chaldeans will have no lasting empire.

2:12–14 The image of construction found in the second woe is continued in the third. The chief materials used in constructing the city are seen for what they are: bloodshed and injustice. Such conduct is an affront to a holy and righteous God. It marks the Chaldeans as those who, unlike the righteous who reflect God's standards, are arrogant and presumptuous.

2:15–16 The fourth woe begins with an invective formed with a strong allegory. The Chaldean is a man who gives his neighbor a drink in seeming hospitality, but the cup contains wrath and is designed to get its partaker drunk. The giver of the drink is forced to take his own drink and suffer the disgrace of exposure.

2:18 In drawing the woe oracles to a close, Habakkuk deliberately changes the order he has previously employed by beginning with the reason for the threatened judgment. The religious orientation of the Chaldean is now examined and shown to be without foundation. His idolatrous polytheism is seen to be worthless. Since idols are only humankind's creation, to put one's trust in them is to trust one's own creation rather than the Creator.

3:1–2 Having heard and understood God's principles of judgment and their application, Habakkuk returns to the matter of Judah's judgment. This begins his prayer psalm, a composition to be set to music for use in worship.

3:3–15 Habakkuk has prayed for God's mercy in the midst of judgment. He does so on the basis of his consideration of God's past redemptive acts for His people, some of which he now rehearses for all to contemplate.

3:3–7 In a graphic simile, the brilliance of God's glory is detailed. The association of the glory of the Lord with Sinai is unmistakable; the point here, however, may be that the same glory that was seen at mount Sinai and traveled with the people on their journeys (Exodus 40:34–38) now moves in surpassing brilliance ahead of them.

3:8–11 Addressing God personally, Habakkuk asks whether His actions against the waters are out of anger. All three words for wrath here characterize God's judicial activity against anything that opposes His will. Yahweh is portrayed metaphorically as Israel's mighty warrior who appears in His battle chariot, armed with bow, club, arrows, and spear. This is no cosmic battle between deities; Yahweh comes as Israel's champion against human opponents.

3:8–15 The second poem is a victory ode that sings of the mighty strength of Israel's Redeemer. His power

is displayed at the waters of testing (3:8–9), unleashed in the natural world (3:9–11), and viewed by the enemy (3:12–15). Whereas the first two sections deal in a general way with the entire Exodus event, the final section fixes its attention on the initial stage of the Exodus.

3:8–15 These verses constitute a victory song. He who had acted in both judgment and deliverance for Israel in the past can be counted on to do so once again, for both Israel and His prophet. Thus Habakkuk's final prayer of praise to Israel's Redeemer stands not only as a unified composition but also as the climax to the whole prophecy.

3:8 The waters here probably refer to God's activities in the entire Exodus event. The theme of water is prominent not only in the triumph at the Red Sea but also in the passing through the Jordan (Joshua 3–4).

3:9–11 The scene here changes from preparation to engagement in battle. The predominant image in this description of nature's response is the agitation of cosmic waters. The description fits well with the details of the crossing of the Jordan.

3:14–15 Habakkuk's psalm ends here on a note of redemption. Israel's God, who brought them through the waters of testing with a mighty power that left all nature in convulsion, and who led His people in triumph, is the One who has been with them since the deliverance out of Egypt.

3:16–18 Habakkuk ends his prophecy with affirmations of personal commitment and praise. Having been dramatically reminded of the past exploits of God against the wicked and His saving intervention on behalf of His people, the prophet is overwhelmed. Now that he understands who God is and the principles and methods of His activities, it is enough for Habakkuk.

3:18 The words translated *rejoice* and *joy* here represent strong emotions; Habakkuk used them previously to express his anxiety over the unbridled avarice of the Chaldeans (1:14–15). Here he underscores his repentant heart and triumphant faith. Together these words express his resolve not merely to rest in the Lord's will through everything that will come to pass but to rejoice fully in his saving God.

3:19 Borrowing phraseology from the repertoire of ancient Hebrew poetry, Habakkuk closes the account of his spiritual odyssey on a high note of praise. The order is significant. Whatever strength he has he owes to the One who is his strength; but basic to everything is the fact that Yahweh is his Lord and his Master, the center of his life.

THE BOOK OF
ZEPHANIAH

INTRODUCTION TO ZEPHANIAH ■ Zephaniah denounced the materialism and greed that exploited the poor. He was aware of world conditions and announced God's judgment on the nations for their sins. Above all, God's prophet had a deep concern for God's reputation and for the well-being of all who humbly trusted in Him.

AUTHOR ■ Although some concern has been raised with regard to many passages in the book that bears his name, Zephaniah has generally been accepted as the author of most of this book. Zephaniah traces his lineage four generations to a certain Hezekiah. Jewish and Christian commentators alike have commonly identified this Hezekiah with the king by that name, though this is not conclusive.

OCCASION ■ The occasion for Zephaniah's prophecy lies in the deplorable spiritual and moral condition of Judah in the early days of Josiah's reign. Taking the throne as an eight-year-old, Josiah finds himself the head of an immoral society. As Zephaniah writes, he is cognizant of the conditions that will surely spell the end of Judah itself (2 Kings 23:26–27).

1:1–3 God's prophet warns of a universal judgment that will one day descend upon the earth and all that is on it. The pronouncement is solemn; its phraseology is at first reminiscent of the flood (Genesis 6:17; 7:21–23). The disaster envisioned here, however, is more cataclysmic, for every living thing that dwells on the land, air, and sea dies. Man's sin is weighty, involving not only himself but his total environment.

1:4–6 Zephaniah alludes to the creation. His catalog of death is arranged in inverse order to God's creative work: humankind, beasts, the creatures of the air, and those of the sea (see Genesis 1:20–27). The coming destruction will begin with humans, who have denied their Creator and involved in their sin all that is under their domain. Because of their idolatry and apostasy, Judah and Jerusalem will find God's hand of chastisement stretched out against them.

1:7–13 In light of the pronouncements of judgment, Zephaniah issues exhortations to Judah. Since the coming of judgment is certain, it is time for them to examine their spiritual condition.

1:8 Israel's leadership has adopted a foreign lifestyle, including its dress or strange apparel. There could be a veiled threat here. Do they prefer foreign attire? They will soon see the specter of foreign uniforms throughout the land. The threat is literally carried out (for examples, see 2 Kings 23:31–35; 24:10–16; 25:1–21).

1:14–18 Zephaniah's exhortations based on the surety of the coming judgment are amplified with further information concerning the day of the Lord. In language bordering on the later apocalyptic genre, he tells of frightful conditions in the natural world and terrible destruction throughout the earth. For this section describing the day of the Lord, Zephaniah has drawn upon the works of Isaiah, Jeremiah, Ezekiel, and Joel, but he is particularly indebted to Joel (see Joel 2:1–11).

2:1 To *gather together* means to come together in genuine repentance and submission to the will of God.

Zephaniah's plea is urgent, for God's decree is settled and will soon be put into effect.

2:4 Philistine presence in Canaan had been reported since the days of the early patriarchs. The region was made up of city-states—Gaza, Ashkelon, Ashdod, Ekron, and Gath—four of which are mentioned here.

2:5–7 Zephaniah calls these Philistine settlers *Cherethites*, a name associated with the Philistines (perhaps an early tribe or a branch). According to Zephaniah, the prosperous seacoast district will become pastureland dotted with caves for Israelite shepherds and folds for their flocks. It will belong to the remnant of Judah.

2:8 Zephaniah's pronouncements of judgment turn to Judah's eastern neighbors across the Jordan, the nations of Moab and Ammon. Like the Philistines, these nations are numbered among Israel's traditional foes. According to Genesis 19:30–38, both Moab and Ammon are descendants of Lot, Abraham's nephew. They were conceived incestuously with Lot's daughters through a scheme set by the young women. Later in Israel's history, the Ammonites join the Moabites in hiring Balaam to curse the Israelites. Both nations harass the Israelites in the days of the judges, and Saul and David fight against them.

2:9 Zephaniah condemns both the Moabites and Ammonites for their pride and their blasphemous insults against God and His people. He predicts that both nations, which have often worked together, will be treated like Sodom and Gomorrah—the whole area will be turned into a perpetual wasteland, overrun with weeds and pocked by salt pits.

2:13–15 Zephaniah's fourth message against the foreign powers swings around to the north—Assyria's capital city, Nineveh, will be rendered desolate, fit only for animals. The reason for the demise of Assyria in general and of Nineveh in particular is haughtiness. Centuries later, the city's ruins are unrecognizable.

3:2 This verse describes a lifestyle and social structure at variance with God's character and laws. Zephaniah charges God's people with refusing to obey God's commandments and with unwillingness to learn from chastisement. They have neither concern nor time for God and His standards.

3:3–4 Even the priests of Jerusalem are defiled. Those who were charged with the purity of God's house and the sanctity of His law have violated both. With bold metaphors Zephaniah exposes Jerusalem's leaders for what they are.

3:5–7 Zephaniah reminds his hearers of Judah's ultimate leader. In contrast to Jerusalem's corrupt leadership, the Lord is righteous. Unlike the wicked who know no shame, He does no iniquity. With the light of each new day, He brings evidence of His unfailing justice.

3:9–20 Zephaniah turns from judgment to its outcome—God's blessing of the people of the world. In a vivid and varied metaphor, the prophet portrays a courtroom scene in which God first rises as witness on His own behalf and before the assemblage, and then presides as judge to deliver His righteous sentence. The double emphasis on judgment and hope is prominent in Zephaniah. Rather than being irreconcilable themes, judgment and hope are two aspects of one divine perspective.

3:18–20 Zephaniah closes his prophecy on the highest of notes. Not only is that which he has just recorded the word of the Lord, but the whole prophecy is as well. God Himself has spoken.

THE BOOK OF

HAGGAI

INTRODUCTION TO HAGGAI ■ Haggai's message, so effective in shaking the Jews of 520 BC from their lethargy, has an abiding relevance for all who fail to seek first the kingdom of God and His righteousness. The book of Haggai consists of four addresses.

AUTHOR ■ We know very little about Haggai outside of the four months of ministry described in this writing. He is mentioned in the book of Ezra.

OCCASION ■ Haggai's purpose is clear. The exiles who returned to Jerusalem after their captivity in Babylonia have failed to complete the temple. Haggai calls these citizens to repentance and to action.

1:1 Zerubbabel son of Shealtiel is the second in a line of Jewish governors. According to Jeremiah 40:7, Gedaliah was the first governor. The last mentioned in the Bible is Nehemiah (Nehemiah 8:9). The term *governor* suggests an overseer. Joshua the son of Josedech (or Jehozadak) is here designated the high priest.

1:2–6 The prophet highlights the indifference of the people, chiding the returned exiles and their fellow countrymen for putting their own interests ahead of the Lord and the temple. The result has been calamitous, for the more they seek self-satisfaction, the less they achieve it.

1:7 This verse repeats verse 5. The people need to reflect on their ways. Their indifference leads to instruction so that the impasse might be resolved and the temple construction begun. Haggai once more urges Zerubbabel, Joshua, and presumably the people to remember with seriousness their past failures and the remedy about to be announced.

1:8–9 The cause of the disastrous conditions facing the people, hinted at in verse 4, is articulated here: God's house is in ruins. The command to rebuild is in strong antithesis to those who, in verse 2, insist that the time for rebuilding Yahweh's house has not yet come.

1:9–11 As though to reinforce His point that the promised glory has been frustrated by Judah's indolence and self-centeredness, Yahweh reiterates that the people have sought much for themselves but with meager results. As long as the temple remains unfinished, the people can continue to expect poverty and lack of fulfillment.

1:13 This is an assurance of God's presence among the people. This assurance finds expression in His supernatural movement among them. Governor, priest, and people alike respond to the kindling of their dormant spirits by setting to work.

1:14 The people here are referred to as a remnant. The notion of a remaining few who will survive both apostasy and judgment to become the nucleus of a restored nation is pervasive in the Old Testament.

1:15 The date here reveals a twenty-three-day interval between the time the message to rebuild is first proclaimed (1:1) and the time of its execution (1:14). We can't know with certainty the reason for the delay, but it may have been as simple as tending to harvest.

2:1–3 Twenty-six days have passed since construction began, and already the differences are becoming painfully evident. No one will be more aware of the contrast between Solomon's temple and the structure under construction than those old enough to have experienced the Solomonic temple so ruthlessly destroyed by the Babylonians sixty-six years earlier. To these people, Haggai addresses his question. He concludes that they view the new building as inconsequential compared with the old.

2:9 Once the people have brought their precious belongings to the temple, Yahweh will fill it with His glory. The house's glory will be greater than before.

2:13–14 These verses present a converse case. Granted, unclean things don't become clean by virtue of their association with the clean. However, will things that are clean become contaminated by the unclean? The answer is an unqualified *yes*. The example is the corruption caused by contact with a corpse. The dead body mentioned here isn't linked with something in the immediate context of this passage. The point is that God's people can pollute, and have polluted, themselves because of their ungodly associations.

2:16–17 The community's moral and spiritual defilement calls for divine discipline. From the very beginning of their postexilic life, before the foundations of the temple were laid some sixteen years earlier, the people had suffered Yahweh's wrath because of their self-service. This chastening marks their whole life until Haggai, called by God, urges them to forsake their shortsighted materialism and resume the work of building a house for Yahweh.

2:18–19 Haggai refers back not to the initial groundbreaking for the temple in 536 BC (2:15) but to the renewal of construction exactly three months earlier. This reference provides a backward glance focused on the refounding of the temple and subsequent events. In spite of this backward glance, however, these verses relate to the present and future. The date of the laying of the foundation is the date of the oracle, the twenty-fourth day of the ninth month. The seed has already been sown, and the fruit trees promise rich production in the season to come, but the growing season is a future event. In the midst of December, there is little on which to subsist. But there is a promise of better days ahead. Even though the vestiges of the people's previous disobedience remain to make their existence most uncomfortable, all this will change. God will begin a new age of prosperity.

2:20–23 This fourth and final message of Haggai is received and delivered on the very same day as the third, but to Zerubbabel alone. The apocalyptic language focuses on the destruction of all things hostile to the rule of Yahweh, a destruction that cannot be separated from the last clause of 2:19. In verse 19, the promise to bless from that very day finds its expression in the end-times hope outlined here. In terms reminiscent of his second oracle, the prophet speaks of a shaking of heaven and earth and the overthrow and shattering of human kingdoms (2:6–7). The difference in the two addresses is the result of the shaking. In 2:7 it results in tribute to Yahweh in His temple. Here it is a defeat of the nations so severe in its results that no one and no thing remains but Yahweh and His own sovereign ruler.

2:23 Focused on the future, the prophet introduces the climax of his message by relating it to "that day." Since the context indisputably is apocalyptic in nature, the Zerubbabel to whom the oracle is directed cannot be the governor whom Haggai has so frequently addressed. Rather, one must see Zerubbabel as a prototype of one to come who will be Yahweh's servant and chosen vessel.

THE BOOK OF
ZECHARIAH

INTRODUCTION TO ZECHARIAH ■ The books of Haggai, Zechariah, and Malachi were composed in the postexilic period of Israel's history to offer hope to a people whose national and personal lives had been shattered by the Babylonian destruction of Jerusalem and captivity of the people. Zechariah goes beyond Haggai's burden for the immediate, earthly situation of the postexilic community and sees, through a vision and dream, the unfolding of divine purpose for all of God's people and for all the ages to come.

AUTHOR ■ At least thirty people mentioned in the Bible bear the name Zechariah, which means "The Lord remembers." The prophet and author of this book, however, is further identified as being the son of Berechiah and grandson of Iddo (1:1). He was born during Judah's captivity in Babylon and returned to Jerusalem with a group led by Zerubbabel. Iddo was a priest during that time (Nehemiah 12:1–7), and Zechariah eventually succeeds his grandfather in that role.

OCCASION ■ After about seventy years of exile in a foreign land, God's people are released to return to their homeland, only to discover that the walls and temple of Jerusalem have been demolished. Projects are planned for reconstruction, but the people need much encouragement and faith during this period. As both prophet and priest, Zechariah brings assurance of God's faithfulness and hope for the future of His people.

1:1 Zechariah, here identified as the son of Berechiah and grandson of Iddo, is also mentioned in Ezra (5:1; 6:14) and Nehemiah (12:16). However, both of those citations imply that the prophet is the son of Iddo, and neither mentions Berechiah. It is likely that Zechariah's father died and young Zechariah was raised by his grandfather. This would also explain why Zechariah succeeds Iddo as priest (see Nehemiah 12:10–16).

1:2–4 Zechariah begins his book with a solemn exhortation to learn from history. God had been extremely displeased with the generations past because they had stubbornly refused to heed the appeal of their prophets to turn to the Lord. The "evil ways" reference is not to incidental sins but to a whole pattern of rebellion and disloyalty.

1:7 The date here equates to February 15, 519 BC, on the modern calendar—approximately three months after the initial call of Zechariah (see 1:1) and two months after Haggai's last revelation (Haggai 2:10, 20). Significant events around this time that may have bearing on elements of Zechariah's first vision are (1) the return of Darius to Persia from Egypt (through Palestine) and (2) the approaching of New Year's Day, a time when Zerubbabel will be crowned as Judah's king, restoring a Davidic successor to the throne (see Haggai 2:20–23).

1:8 The myrtle is a fragrant, decorative shrub that sometimes reaches the size of a tree. It is used in connection with the feast of tabernacles and in postbiblical times in betrothal celebrations. Its perpetual greenness and aromatic qualities provide a suitable setting for the inauguration of the Lord's domain, which is everlasting and pleasant in every way.

1:8–11 The mission of the rider of the red horse (and presumably all four horsemen) is to walk across the whole earth. To walk to and fro through the earth is to assert sovereignty over it (see Genesis 13:17; Job 1:7; Ezekiel 28:14). Here the Lord, through the symbolism of four cavalry charges, announces that He is Lord of all.

1:12, 16 Jeremiah had already referred to a seventy-year period, dating its end with the demise of the Babylonian (Chaldean) kingdom (see Jeremiah 25:11–12). It is clearly understood, however, that the seventy years have a flexible starting and concluding date because their termination is also connected to the completion of the second temple, which verse 16 refers to here. The completion of Jerusalem's second temple takes place in 516 BC, exactly seventy years after the destruction of Solomon's temple in 586 BC.

1:18–21 Zechariah's vision contains two elements (four horns and four carpenters or craftsmen), so the interpretation is divided into two parts. In response to the query about the horns, the angelic interpreter first asserts that they are scatterers of Judah, Israel, and Jerusalem. Under further interrogation, he adds that the horns are associated with the nations. The nations had used their horns (military might) to effect the dispersion of God's people.

1:21 The task of the carpenters is to bring down the nations, to nullify the effect of their great power. The ultimate result will presumably reverse the scattering so that the dispersed can return again to their land.

2:6–7 In the language of the prophets, *Zion* is a key term used to refer to the end-times kingdom. The phrase *the four winds* suggests that exiles will be returning from all directions, not only from the north.

2:10–13 The reason for the joy here is that the Lord is coming and will live in Zion's midst. Haggai and Zechariah share this theology of divine presence, a note that was especially meaningful in the days of the regathered community struggling to build a temple worthy of God's dwelling place. But Zechariah is particularly concerned with orienting this theological truth to the age to come, when all nations (not just Israel and Judah) will join themselves to the Lord and be His people. In addition, God will take the land of Judah as His special allotment in all the created universe.

3:1–3 How and why Satan became God's adversary remains a mystery, but it is plain throughout scripture that he is subservient to the sovereignty of God. The idea that Satan is a previously upright being employed by God who then departed from that role to become the adversary of God finds no support in the Bible. In fact, the New Testament teaching is the opposite: "The devil sinneth from the beginning" (1 John 3:8).

3:8–9 The stone placed before Joshua may be taken to be the foundation of the second temple. It isn't uncommon for a stone to be used as a messianic symbol throughout the Bible (see Isaiah 28:16). But the stone in Zechariah's oracle is unique; it has seven eyes. In biblical numerology, the number seven signifies fullness or completeness, so the seven eyes suggest omniscience or undimmed vision. In the following vision, Zechariah will identify the seven eyes as the eyes of the Lord, which take in everything that is happening on the earth (see 4:10).

4:2–3 The prophet sees in this vision a golden candlestick (menorah) flanked by two olive trees, the whole of which symbolizes the Spirit of the Lord. The candlestick, or menorah, was traditionally located on the south side of the holy place in the temple. Its purpose was to illuminate the interior of the holy place (see Exodus 25:37), and it also represented the illumination of the presence of the Lord Himself.

4:2–3 The major source of lamp oil in ancient Palestine was the olive, so it is not surprising that two olive trees appear in Zechariah's vision to provide that fuel. It is important to note that the trees are not to the left and the right of the candlestick, but they flank the reservoir. The oil could not go straight to the cups but had to be mediated through the upper container that received it directly from the trees.

4:11–14 Zechariah has faithfully described what he has seen, yet he cannot understand its significance. At this point, the messenger declares that the olive trees are the two anointed ones who stand by the Lord of the earth. It is important to connect these two anointed ones with the trees that symbolize them. They are not just anointed, but they are anointed with the oil of these trees.

5:3–4 The connection of the scroll (flying roll) with the dwelling place of the Lord leads to the conclusion that the scroll contains the covenant document that binds God and the nation together. The interpretation of the vision is filled with covenant terminology and motifs that make it certain that the scroll either is the Jewish Torah or contains covenant texts of the Torah. The unidentified speaker immediately equates the scroll with the *curse*—a technical term referring to the sanctions of covenant documents.

5:8 The woman is identified as *wickedness*. The woman's danger is most apparent, for no sooner has the interpreting messenger pronounced her name than he slams the heavy cover down upon the ephah to be certain that she cannot escape. The ephah has become not only a means of conveyance but also a cage.

6:1–3 In this vision, Zechariah sees four chariots emerging from between two mountains. In the Old Testament, a chariot was not just a mode of transportation; its primary use was as a war machine.

6:1–6 The four chariots in the vision reflect the worldwide extent of their travels. They are sent forth to reclaim all the earth for the Lord, a result that follows the splitting of the mountain in the day of the Lord (see 14:10). Zechariah witnesses the arrival of the four chariots between the two mountains, having come there from heaven. (The chariots are to go throughout the earth, though it doesn't appear that they are dispatched north, south, east, and west. Due to the geography of Palestine, one must go north even to go to the northwest or northeast. Assyria, Babylon, and even Persia were all considered "north" of Palestine, even though they don't appear quite that way on a map.)

6:12–13 The Word of the Lord through Zechariah is directed specifically to Joshua, thus distinguishing him from another man called the branch. There is no doubt as to the identity of the branch. Converging lines of identification within Zechariah (4:7–10) and elsewhere (Isaiah 11:1; 53:2; Jeremiah 33:15; Haggai 2:23) make it certain that Zerubbabel is in view. As a direct offspring of the line of David, he is well qualified to sit on the royal throne of Judah.

7:2–3 A group of travelers arrives to inquire about a religious matter. For a number of years, the travelers' community has fasted and wept in the fifth month (in observance of the destruction of Solomon's temple, a disaster that occurred almost exactly seventy years earlier). The next anniversary is just a few months away, and the travelers are asking if it is appropriate to create holy days to observe occasions that have arisen in the post-Mosaic period.

7:3 It is evident that progress is well under way on the temple by the date of this oracle. The priesthood is active there with some degree of formality and legitimacy, although it is also clear that the temple is not completely finished (see 8:9).

7:4–6 God's response is a sharp rebuke. The people's fasting and mourning has for seventy long years been an empty exercise designed to enhance not the Lord but rather those who participated. Their religion has become one of outward show with no inner content. God points out that just as they eat and drink for their own satisfaction, so, too, do they fast. Their religious activity is centered on themselves, not their holy and loving God.

7:8–10 The Lord reviews the basis for true worship, including fasting, by appealing to earlier canonical principles that provide its moral and spiritual framework. Such appeals to justice, mercy, compassion, and proper treatment of one another were abundant throughout the texts available to the people of that time, especially in the writings of Moses.

7:11 Past generations had responded to the word of witness from the prophets by "giving a shoulder of stubbornness" and "making their ears heavy"—the literal translations of the phrases in this verse.

7:12–14 The result of the past generations' stubborn refusal to listen was predictable: The Lord sent great wrath against them. The land had become desolate as a result, so much so that it appeared to be virtually uninhabited (see Ezekiel 36:32–36). What had once been a place flowing with milk and honey had become a desert devoid of life and pleasure. Unless Zechariah's audience understands the abhorrence with which the Lord views superficial and self-serving religious observance, the people can expect the same calamitous results as those experienced by their forefathers.

8:7 References to the east and west indicate the rising and setting of the sun, suggesting that future immigrants to Jerusalem will come from places throughout the world, not just the nearby surrounding areas.

8:9–13 It is important for the people to shoulder the responsibilities requisite to the fulfillment of God's promise. Their deliverance and return will depend wholly on God's grace, but present and future prosperity in the land will be directly related to their obedience and hard work. So this section is bracketed with the Lord's repeated challenge to "let your hands be strong."

8:10–12 Zechariah alludes to the days of social and economic distress in Judah (unemployment, no payment of wages, social unrest, etc.) before the people rearranged their priorities and began to put the Lord and His temple at the center of their community life.

8:14–17 The painful experience the Lord previously brought on Judah had been a disciplinary action to produce consciousness of sin and a desire for repentance, and it had accomplished its intent. The Lord was then able to do good again to Judah, and the people could live where truth and justice were restored and valued.

8:19 At the beginning, only one city sent its representatives (7:2); but at the end, all the languages of the nations will be represented (8:23). And fasting in sorrow (7:3) will be turned into feasting for joy.

8:20–22 The idea of the nations converging at Jerusalem to worship the Lord at His temple is a major eschatological theme. Zechariah has already affirmed this explicitly in the oracle following an earlier vision (2:11). He will have more to say about the matter in chapter 14. No prophet excels Zechariah in his presentation of the universal pilgrimage of nations and their confession of the Lord's kingship.

8:23 The number *ten* is not to be taken literally but rather is symbolic in the Bible of totality or compre-hensiveness. So urgent will be the desire of many people that they will hold on to the people of God ("take hold of the skirt" or clutch at the sleeve) with no intention of letting go.

9:3–4 Zechariah notes that Tyrus (or Tyre) has amassed and hoarded great revenues of silver and gold but will soon see its power and possessions taken away.

9:5–6 The list of Israel's enemies includes a series of Philistine city-states: Ashkelon, Gaza, Ekron, and Ashdod. The once-proud Philistia will be shamed and embarrassed.

9:7–8 Zechariah declares that Philistia will be thoroughly chastened and purified, becoming a remnant for God, like a clan in Judah. By Zechariah's time, the Jebusites have been totally assimilated into Judah. One day Ekron (perhaps representing all of Philistia) will have the same privilege. The Philistines (and by extension the preceding nations as well) will feel the awesome wrath of the Lord, but those who are left—a small remnant—will then be included within the covenant of God.

9:9–13 This passage of scripture is one of the most messianically significant passages in the Bible, in both the Jewish and Christian traditions. Judaism sees in it a basis for a royal messianic expectation, while Christianity sees a prophecy of the triumphal entry of Jesus Christ into Jerusalem on the Sunday before His crucifixion (see Matthew 21:5; John 12:15). Both agree that a descendant of David is depicted here, one who, though humble, rides as a victor into his capital city of Jerusalem. On first reading, it appears that the Christian interpretation does not square exactly with Zechariah's prophecy. Although Jesus is described as entering Jerusalem in precisely the manner envisioned by Zechariah in 9:9, He dies within days of the event, never having made any active claim to the throne of David. The New Testament account shows that the servant who will someday be exalted as King must first suffer and die on behalf of those who will make up His kingdom in the ages to come.

10:2 Zechariah is still looking to the future, because in his own day, Judah had suffered a devastating crisis of leadership in both her spiritual and political life. Throughout their history, Israel and Judah had turned to illicit religious channels such as idols and diviners, all of whom delivered nothing but falsehood and emptiness.

10:4 God foresees Judah as the source of four elements: the corner(stone), the nail or peg, the battle bow, and the oppressor or ruler. These should be interpreted in the context of the warfare that prevails here rather than in terms of construction.

10:8 Zechariah shares a well-established tradition when he looks at the eschatological (end-times) deliverance of Israel in terms of exodus (see Isaiah 43:1–7; Haggai 2:4–5). In this case, the process of regathering will begin when the Lord signals for His people to return. Once they gather, they will multiply as they did in the days of Moses, and the pitiful postexilic remnant will once more become the mighty and innumerable host of God (see 2:4; 8:4–5).

11:1–3 The objects that Zechariah mentions under the guise of trees and animals are the same as the ones he calls shepherds. This poem that opens the chapter, then, turns out to be a lament for the destruction of the evil shepherds, who, as previously noted, represent kings (see 11:8, 17). So the cedar tree of Lebanon, the oak of Bashan, and the fir (pine) tree are symbols of powerful rulers.

11:8 Zechariah eradicates the three shepherds—a clue that he is reliving the Lord's own experience in Israel's history and that his removal of the leaders is symbolic. *One month* is best viewed as meaning a short time rather than a specific point in history when three key leaders all fell within a literal period of thirty days.

11:12–13 When the time comes for Zechariah to be compensated for his services, he is offered thirty pieces of silver—the pittance paid for a slave who had been gored to death (see Exodus 21:32). This is actually the Lord being appraised, and only His service is considered, not His intrinsic value. Therefore, the silver is like refuse because of the insulting attitude it represents.

11:17 The Lord is not oblivious to the shepherd who abuses and exploits his people. The woe-judgment that comes upon him will be a sword that wounds his arm and his right eye. Without the arm to carry the sheep and the eye with which to search and find, the shepherd truly is worthless—not only in a moral sense but in a practical, functional sense as well. Why the shepherd is not killed is unclear, but he is so severely incapacitated that he can no longer function.

12:2 The mighty Lord will use His chosen people Judah as an instrument by which He does battle with the nations and brings them under His dominion. This is what is meant in describing Jerusalem as a "cup of trembling" (an "intoxicating drink" in one translation). The nations will drink of Jerusalem—partake of her in hostility and conquest—but will end up inebriated.

12:5–6 Judah's rulers will realize that the people of Jerusalem have been their greatest strength. The Lord of hosts used them as a discomfit to their enemies and has guaranteed that the nation will survive. The rulers will themselves become a "hearth of fire among the wood" and a "torch of fire in a sheaf," incinerating all the surrounding woods that threaten Israel.

12:9–10 Once the Lord has accomplished His work of judgment on the nations and secured Judah and Jerusalem from them, He will begin a work of grace among the redeemed. The spirit of grace will be poured out on God's people, though they little deserve it. In fact, the Lord must extend His grace to enable His people to seek it in the first place.

12:11 The great mourning of Hadadrimmon is believed to be the expression of sorrow that took place after the violent and premature death of King Josiah, when he foolishly interposed his tiny army between the Egyptians and the Assyrians (see 2 Kings 23:29–30). The tragic event was commemorated from that time on (2 Chronicles 35:25).

12:11–14 Usually community or corporate repentance is standard, but in this case it appears that each member and entity of the community feels individually culpable and must individually give account before God.

12:12 Nathan was the third son of David. Though the kings of Judah after Solomon until the exile were all descendants of Solomon (see 1 Chronicles 3:10–16), a change occurred after the return from exile, and royal descent began to be traced through Nathan.

13:1–2 Judah's lamentation of repentance will result in its forgiveness, followed by purification and cleansing described with the metaphor of a fountain that gushes forth. The cleansing is widespread and removes sin and iniquity, idols in the land, false prophets, and the underlying spirit of impurity that has been so pervasive.

13:7–9 After addressing problems in the priesthood and among the so-called prophets, Zechariah turns his attention to the monarchy. As he has previously done, he refers to Israel's kings as *shepherds*. After a bold assertion by the Lord that the shepherd-king is an associate comes a poignant command to strike the leader so that the flock will be scattered. This action will cause not only the leaders of the community to suffer the blow of the Lord's righteous indignation but also the flock (described as "little" or insignificant).

14:4–5 When all seems lost, the Lord leads His people forth and parts the mount of Olives by the very act of treading on it, not unlike the way Moses parted the Red Sea to deliver the Israelites. The splitting of the mountain creates a new valley through which the people will flee. This is no mere earthquake, however, but a shaking of the whole universe as the Lord comes in judgment.

14:8 One result of the Lord's coming will be life-giving waters that flow from Jerusalem. The meaning of the Hebrew indicates that these are not waters that give life but waters that are moving and fast-flowing, as well as sparkling.

14:9 The Jewish Shema (see Deuteronomy 6:4–5) is the very heart of Israel's covenant faith—a confession of the Lord's self-consistency as well as His uniqueness and exclusivity. Zechariah makes unmistakable reference to the Shema here. The original statement of monotheism, however, breaks out of an exclusively Jewish viewpoint and speaks of the oneness of God on a universal scale. There is no reference to *our* God because the Lord will be the one and only God of *all* the nations.

14:10–11 Jerusalem will continue to be the center from which the grace of God will radiate to all the earth. To express the continued centrality of Israel, Zechariah visualizes the leveling of the remainder of the Holy Land and the elevation of Jerusalem so that the city stands high above in a position of eminence and security.

14:12–15 All those who have persecuted and tormented God's people will be inflicted with a horrible plague or pestilence of some kind that attacks both humans and animals. In addition to the plague's grotesque physical consequences, it will trigger a panic among the people, causing them to lash out and destroy one another. It appears that the plague and its related events best fit chronologically with the conflict described in 14:3–8, before the elevation of Jerusalem (14:9–11).

14:9, 16–19 After the great fire that marks the beginning of the Lord's reign, the survivors among the nations acknowledge Him as King and come regularly to offer Him homage. This is not to suggest, however, that they have undergone conversion in the religious sense. The word used for *worship* in verse 16 can mean only to bow down or do obeisance.

14:17 The particular occasion of pilgrimage is the feast of tabernacles, one of the three annual events in Israel's calendar when the Lord's able-bodied people are to appear before Him at the central sanctuary. Immediately after the celebration, the Levites will lead the assembly in a great ceremony of covenant renewal (see Nehemiah 9:1–38) that culminates in a solemn commitment by the people to reaffirm their covenant allegiance to the Lord (Nehemiah 9:38; 10:29).

14:18–19 In the Bible, Egypt is frequently a symbol of the world at large (see Isaiah 27:13; Revelation 11:8).

Therefore, it is not distinguished here from the nations just mentioned but appears as a synonym for them.

14:20–21 Zechariah describes a number of transformations to take place "in that day." What was unclean—horses, lowly pots—will be elevated. These examples point to the fact that "there shall be no more the Canaanite in the house of the LORD of hosts." In this case, the Canaanite symbolizes what is most reprehensible to God. The Canaanites are a cursed people (see Genesis 9:25) and are to be annihilated by the conquest of Israel if they won't turn to Yahweh (Joshua 3:10). To think of their participation in the worship of God at all is scandalous, and to envision their doing so within the holy precincts of the temple is incomprehensible. Yet in the day of the Lord, all are welcome because they all will be the people of God.

MALACHI

INTRODUCTION TO MALACHI ■ The book of Malachi is a summons to repentance and revival. In six disputations, the prophet summons the people to forsake their spiritual doldrums and halfhearted commitment to the Lord and return to an active faith and the practice of devotion to God.

AUTHOR ■ Some have wondered if Malachi's name, which means "my messenger," could be a title rather than a name. But there is no reason to believe that Malachi is written by anyone other than Malachi himself.

OCCASION ■ The concerns raised by Ezra and Nehemiah in their work of reformation are some of the same that Malachi mentions: spiritually mixed marriages, the neglect of tithing, disregard for keeping the sabbath, the corruption of the priesthood, and social injustice. Some scholars suggest that it is likely Malachi preached before the reforms of Ezra and Nehemiah, preparing the way for them.

1:1 This writing is identified as an oracle, one given through *Malachi*, a name that is Hebrew for "my messenger." The oracle is addressed to the nation of Israel. In this writing, the people who make up that nation are also referred to as *Judah* (2:11; 3:4) and *Jacob* (1:2; 2:12; 3:6).

1:3 The term *hate* probably refers to a rejection. God selected Israel and rejected Edom as His chosen people.

1:4–5 Edom, though a little country, was often used as an emblem for all the enemies of Israel. At no point in Israel's history is Edom an ally, as are (at one time or another) most of the other nearby nations. Prophets such as Ezekiel and Obadiah speak against Edom (see Ezekiel 25:12–14; Obadiah 1–7). The region is gradually overrun and by the middle/late fifth century has become a non-nation, but in Malachi's time, the Edomites have not yet been thoroughly destroyed.

1:6 God is credited with this message. The phrase "saith the Lord of hosts" is used often in this disputation. Malachi is attacking the priests, after all. They would be almost certain to react badly to Malachi's criticism, so it is important for him to emphasize that his message is from the Lord.

1:8 The priests are violating the law that requires the best and the first of all the people's property be given to God. The firstborn, the firstfruits, and the most excellent of one's property belong to God. This is a test of faith because the best animals are, of course, the best breeding stock, and in order to give that stock away to God, one has to believe it is better to honor the Lord than to seek material prosperity.

1:11 There will be a time when the whole world will worship the Lord. Malachi is interested in the future fulfillment of the plan of salvation.

1:12–14 The priests are guilty of profaning the name of the Lord and of doing their jobs in a spirit of boredom, and the people seem to prefer it that way.

1:14 The moniker *great king* is a common title in some ancient texts and refers to the king over all the other lesser kings—the emperor. The Lord is the great King

who will enforce the penalties of His covenant upon those who betray its requirements.

2:1–2 Curses are threatened upon the priests for their unbelief and disobedience. A primary role of the priests—pronouncing blessing—will become futile. The priests will pronounce blessing, as with the Aaronic benediction (see Numbers 6:23–27), but the people will get curses instead.

2:4 The text of this covenant is found in Numbers 25:11–13, and its language is spread throughout Malachi 2:1–8, as is the blessing of Levi found in Deuteronomy 33:8–11. No Israelite would have missed the connection.

2:6–7 Malachi says that a faithful minister turns many from sin and communicates the knowledge and the instruction of the Lord. He does this, Malachi says, because he himself walks with the Lord.

2:8–9 The hearts of the priests in this day are contrary to the way Malachi says they should be. The priests teach without power, even tailor their messages to certain people's advantage and to others' disadvantage. The people have stumbled, and the law is up for sale. Israel is sinking into spiritual doldrums and, from there, might eventually sink into spiritual death.

2:10 Malachi reminds the people of their special relationship to God, their Father. Israel must live in obedience to God and in union with one another as brothers and sisters, at least in God's family. In this, the Israelites are breaking faith.

2:13 The tears probably refer to loud displays of emotion during sacrifices. Many religions of the day believed that these protestations of earnestness would influence God to act. What is scorned here is emotion intended to manipulate God.

2:14–16 The same word is used to describe two kinds of marital sins—improper intermarriage and improper divorce. Marriage is regarded as a covenant. It takes on features like those of God's covenant with His people; it requires fidelity on the part of the covenant partners.

2:17 The statement that those who do evil are good in the eyes of God is one of irony. It is not likely that anyone is actually saying or even thinking this. The point is that it doesn't seem that God is doing anything about this evil. Does it matter to Him?

3:1 God promises to respond in the form of a messenger.

3:2–5 The ministry of the messenger described in this passage is clearly the ministry of a divine figure. He does the things that only the Lord has the power and the authority to do.

3:6–7 It is God's immutability that explains why Israel, though generation after generation has violated God's covenant, has not been destroyed. The Lord is a merciful God, faithful to His covenant and to the promises He made to be Israel's God.

3:8 The tithe is the requirement to give a tenth of one's income to the Lord. The offerings are gifts above the tithe. Giving of these things is a symbol of recognition that all one has belongs to God.

3:9–11 Either the people are holding back part of what they owe by law or not everyone is giving a tithe. Since the tithes are the allotment of the priests and Levites, the people's disobedience causes them hardship.

3:14 The mourning the people mention is probably the same kind of ritual mourning mentioned in 2:13. Malachi condemns the people for a show of mourning and penitence before the Lord that is nothing but an attempt to manipulate Him.

3:15 The idea of tempting, challenging, or testing God refers to those who openly do what God forbids. Their actions test to see if God will respond. The people referred to here—in some translations called *evildoers* or *wicked*—are simply those who are doing other kinds of evil than the insolent and complaining Israelites are doing.

3:16 This verse contains the only narrative in the book of Malachi. The people described here (obviously a distinct minority among Israel as a whole) are pious, faithful, and devout. They stir one another up to love and good deeds, and the Lord takes special notice of their spiritual conversation.

3:16 The *book of remembrance*, or *scroll*, is probably a document that contains the names of all those who ascribe to some written commitment to the Lord. Another possibility is that it is a scroll akin to "the books," in which are written the record of the lives of men and women, or even to "the book of life," in which are found the names of those whom God has saved.

4:1 The metaphor of burning, or fire, is often used to describe the effects of the Lord's judgment. Malachi has already referred to a refiner's fire in 3:2. The fire renders the wicked into stubble. *Stubble*, used here as a term of agriculture, is what is left when everything valuable has been taken away—the leftovers after the field has been cut down with a scythe.

4:3 This image connotes a reversal of fortune. The wicked, who generally ride in triumph over the righteous in this world, will be trampled under the feet of the righteous in the day of the Lord. This, too, is a frequently employed image of divine judgment. The prosperity of the wicked is overtaken in a moment.

4:5 This verse promises the coming of Elijah, the quintessential prophet. Does this mean he will return in person? In Matthew 11:7–10 and 17:10–13, we read Jesus' interpretation of this text. In both cases, Jesus mentions John the Baptist as the "Elias" (or "Elijah") of whom Malachi speaks.

4:6 The sense here is not merely that when the Messiah and the day of the Lord come, they will usher in a new harmony in family relationships. The mention of parents and children is a way of saying that when the day of the Lord comes, He will turn everyone back to faithfulness to the covenant. This is a promise of great revival.

THE GOSPEL ACCORDING TO

MATTHEW

INTRODUCTION TO MATTHEW ■ Matthew's author used a number of literary devices that indicate a Jewish audience. His writing captures a strong sense of messianic expectation and fulfillment. Matthew made much of fulfilled prophecy in his narrative. Quoting heavily from the Old Testament, Matthew claimed that fifteen Old Testament prophecies were fulfilled in Jesus' ministry. He showed great interest in Jesus' teaching on the Law of Moses. Jesus' statement that He came to fulfill the law rather than abolish it is found exclusively in Matthew (5:17–20).

AUTHOR ■ Our earliest records claim that the apostle Matthew wrote this Gospel. Early church tradition was almost unanimous in this regard. While there remains some continuing discussion about Matthew's authorship, the Gospel itself was accepted without question by the early church and incorporated into the New Testament canon.

OCCASION ■ It is obvious that Matthew's Gospel was addressed to a Jewish-Christian audience or community. Matthew presented Jesus to this audience as God's messianic King.

1:1–17 Matthew begins his theological argument for the messiahship of Jesus in proper Jewish style, with an appropriate genealogy—although it is a theologically shaped one. It is obvious from a comparison of other Old Testament genealogies (1 Chronicles 1–9) that Matthew leaves out some levels of Jesus' family tree and repeats some names. To emphasize the theological impact of this genealogy, he begins with its most significant elements—"Jesus Christ, the son of David, the son of Abraham." Matthew numbers the generations from Abraham to Jesus as three groups of fourteen. This has generated much speculation. Though we cannot be certain of Matthew's meaning, he seems to take it for granted that his first-century Jewish readers will understand. The genealogy of Matthew differs from that of Luke. Matthew traces a heritage from Abraham through David to Jesus through the royal or legal lineage. His goal is to show that Jesus is the legitimate King of Israel. Luke also follows the line of David and Abraham but traces his genealogy from Jesus through Mary all the way back to Adam. Luke's genealogy, like Matthew's, is meant to fulfill a theological purpose, demonstrating that Jesus is the Savior for all people everywhere.

1:18 Joseph is "espoused" to Mary. This indicates something similar to modern engagement, only with a stronger legal implication. It was, in fact, the beginning of the marriage "ceremony." The pledge was as legally binding as the marriage contract. It could only be broken according to the Jewish laws of marriage and divorce. In this case, since it appears that Mary is no longer considered clean because she is pregnant with Jesus, it is within the law for Joseph to divorce her.

1:21 The virgin birth of Jesus is fundamental to the Christian faith and to Matthew's theology. Throughout this section, Matthew emphasizes the role of the Holy Spirit. He wants his readers to know that this conception is unusual, that it transcends the purely historical and earthly, that Jesus' conception and birth involve the direct involvement and action of the divine. The central point in this birth narrative is not simply that Jesus is born of a virgin, true as that may be, but that His conception and birth are the result of direct divine intervention (the Holy Spirit) and are an integral part of God's saving activity in history.

1:22–23 Matthew argues that Jesus' birth is a fulfillment of prophecy, namely, Isaiah 7:14. For Jewish ears, this is a powerful argument demonstrating that Jesus is a fulfillment of God's prophetic activity, that He has a legitimate place in God's promises to Abraham, and that He, in fact, stands in the direct line of God's redemption.

2:1 Matthew sets this account of the wise men in a historical context—during the reign of Herod the king (Herod the Great, AD 47–4 BC). Because we know the date of Herod's death, a key event in this story, we have a firm time marker—one that is somewhat surprising. If Jesus was born while Herod was still ruling, then Jesus was born before 4 BC. Herod the Great was not popular with the Jews because he was only half Jewish and was known to be a violent (and some would say irrational) ruler.

2:12 Being warned in a dream not to return to Herod, the wise men leave for their own home country. Herod and the chief priests do not receive Jesus and pay Him homage, but Gentiles from afar worship Him. Matthew continues to work this theme into his Gospel.

2:14–15 Matthew cites Hosea 11:1 as his second fulfillment prophecy. While this Hosea text pertains to the nation of Israel, Matthew uses it in regard to the Messiah. In doing this, he emphasizes that what is happening to Joseph, Mary, and Jesus is not an accident; it is part of God's ongoing work of salvation throughout history.

2:16–18 Herod's response to the possible presence of the Messiah is to have all male children in Bethlehem who are two years old and under killed. Matthew cites Jeremiah 31:15 as a prophetic reference to this. Again, Matthew takes an Old Testament text and paraphrases it. This text is the third of the fulfillment texts in Matthew.

2:19–23 An angel of the Lord tells Joseph to return to Israel. After Herod's death no one is appointed king, but Herod's son Archelaus becomes governor over Judea. Archelaus, like Herod, is not a pure Jew; he is half Idumean and half Samaritan. Because of Archelaus's reputation, Joseph goes to Galilee, the district in the north over which Archelaus is *not* governor. Joseph and his family settle in Nazareth.

3:2 John the Baptist's message is a short statement with significant theological content. It is exactly this message that Jesus came preaching (4:17). Each word is loaded with meaning.

3:3 Matthew's quote stresses that John's ministry takes place in the wilderness, away from the religious establishment. It is in the wilderness that John is preparing for the ministry of the Messiah, whose ministry also begins outside of Jerusalem's influence.

3:4 John's clothes set him apart from the religious leaders of the day. His dress is that of a desert monk (and his diet that of a desert survivalist), reminiscent of the great prophet Elias (also known as Elijah, 2 Kings 1:8). The religious leaders would have worn fine garments reflecting their high position.

3:7–10 When the Pharisees and Sadducees come out for baptism, John severely warns them to repent because judgment (an axe) is ready to take place over them. They will be judged by God for their rejection of the Messiah.

3:17 Immediately when Jesus is baptized, God gives His approval. Again we notice the activity of the Holy Spirit in the life and ministry of Jesus, reinforcing the aspect of divine intervention. On this occasion the Holy Spirit descends on Jesus like a dove, giving visual manifestation of His presence. Following that, a loud voice proclaims that Jesus is the Son of God and that God is pleased with Him. Jesus' baptism plays a significant role in affirming Jesus' Sonship.

4:1–10 There is a strong connection here between Israel's ancient story and Jesus' story. Jesus' forty days in the wilderness are analogous to Israel's forty years of wandering in the wilderness. The three Old Testament passages Jesus cites are all from Israel's wilderness wanderings. When put to the test, Jesus succeeds where Israel had failed. This seems to be the central analogy in the temptation account.

4:13 After visiting Nazareth, Jesus goes to Capernaum. From this point on, Capernaum becomes Jesus' home base. (All four Gospels inform us that Jesus moves to Capernaum at this point.) John adds that during the journey, Jesus spends a few days in Samaria, where He speaks to the woman at the well about living water (John 4:1–42).

4:18–22 All four of the New Testament Gospels describe the calling of the first disciples. Peter and Andrew were brothers, as were James and John. They worked as partners in the fishing business. When Jesus calls the two groups of brothers, they immediately leave their fishing boats and their families and follow Jesus. The emphasis on "straightway" (or immediately)

stresses the radical nature of the discipleship to which they are called by Jesus.

5:4 Only those who mourn truly understand the need for comfort. The background to this beatitude is Isaiah 61:2–3. This passage is in the context of God's promise of restoration for those who repent. Although this beatitude carries the concept of mourning in general, within the context of Jesus' ministry the mourning is specifically for personal sin and estrangement from God.

5:5 The Greek word translated *meek* means gentle, humble, considerate, and unassuming. Jesus did not simply have in mind those who were gentle and kind but rather those who were humble and downtrodden and oppressed.

5:10 Righteousness in the Jewish sense had to do with a person's relationship with God. The righteous were in a right relationship with God. Because of that relationship, disciples would be persecuted. Persecution was synonymous with discipleship in the first three centuries of the Christian faith.

5:17 The fact that Jesus intends to fulfill Jewish law is vitally important to His ministry. In fact, He repeats the saying twice in a parallel form. But what exactly does Jesus mean by *fulfill*? The word translated *fulfill* can mean to accomplish, to complete, to finish, to bring to an end, to validate, to confirm, to establish, to uphold, or to bring out the intended meaning.

5:21 The expression "ye have heard that it was said" is repeated multiple times in upcoming verses. The use of this phrase was a typical device by which the teaching rabbis demurred from pitting their views against scripture, or even readily commenting on scripture. It was their custom to refer back to the teachings and conclusions of previous rabbis with the expression, contrasting their views with the rabbinic tradition rather than scripture. Jesus sets His teaching against the rabbinic tradition by using this same traditional saying but then drawing His conclusions from scripture, correcting the rabbinic tradition. Jesus' teaching, therefore, carries a much stronger scriptural authority. It is no wonder that at the end of the Sermon on the Mount, the crowds are astonished because He teaches with authority (7:29).

5:23–26 These verses drive home the point that God wants more than mere sacrifice. He wants love, mercy, and righteousness. This teaching reinforces Jesus' message that love comes before the strict literal performance of the commandments. This does not diminish the need to respect and keep the commandments. It does demand the correct understanding of their meaning.

5:29–30 The plucking out of the offending right eye or cutting off of the right hand is a Hebrew idiom or hyperbole stressing the seriousness of the action or offense.

5:31–32 Unlike the previous two antitheses, this one is not based on one of the commandments but arises out of the command against adultery. Jesus will again comment on divorce in 19:3–12, where He is tested by the Pharisees on Deuteronomy 24. The debate on Deuteronomy 24 was obviously one that engaged the scribes and Pharisees considerably.

5:43–48 The command to love your neighbour is drawn directly from Leviticus 19:18, and later Jesus will teach that this is the second most important commandment. The second part of rabbinic teaching, to hate your enemy, is not commanded or taught directly, but it may be a summary drawn from such passages as Psalms 26:5; 139:21–22; Deuteronomy 7:2; 30:7. Following centuries of aggression against Israel's enemies in the occupation of Canaan and Palestine, it is natural that Jews would see hating one's enemy as a legitimate attitude. Jesus' response is a radical departure from current Jewish attitudes toward enemies.

6:1–8 The main thrust of this section is that a disciple's piety, almsgiving, and prayer are not to be like those of the hypocrites who did their righteous deeds to be seen and admired by others. The disciple's prayer is also to be different from that of the Gentiles.

6:5 Public prayer can be a challenge, especially to the one leading the prayer. There is the danger of it being said to impress others rather than being addressed to God. Here Jesus takes exception to the prayers of both the Jews and the Gentiles.

6:7 In regard to "the heathen" (or Gentiles), the "vain repetitions" (babbling, rambling) are apparently attempts to manipulate God into fulfilling some desire of the petitioner by repeating a supposed magic formula, not merely the repetition of words. We learn from Jesus' instruction and His own religious lifestyle that prayer is an important aspect of a disciple's righteousness.

6:9–13 These verses contain what is commonly referred to as the Lord's Prayer. Some take exception to this name and prefer to call this the Model Prayer. Certainly it is intended to be a model prayer—Jesus' words opening verse 9 indicate this clearly—but in contrast to model prayers taught by others (John the Baptist to his disciples), this is Jesus' model prayer, so it can legitimately be referred to as the Lord's Prayer. From what we know of Judaism in Jesus' day, His model prayer is shaped by the prayer tradition and pattern of the synagogue. The primary concern is a redemptive theme, not concern for mundane, earthly matters.

6:16–18 Again Jesus contrasts a disciple's righteous behavior with that of the Jewish leaders whose fasting had become a performance of righteousness. Fasting is an interesting subject. This is a Jewish practice that is more traditional than biblical in the sense that fasting was not commanded but practiced. We read of people in scripture fasting, but nowhere does it seem that it is commanded. Rabbinic tradition informs us that the stricter Jews fasted regularly on special days such as Mondays and Thursdays. From what we learn in the Gospels, Jesus is neither proposing that disciples fast nor condemning the practice of fasting. He simply speaks out against hypocritical fasting, which had as its goal to be noticed.

7:1–5 Apparently the tendency to judge one another was widespread in the first century and has been common in religious groups throughout history. Although Christianity should be an exception to this weakness (the basic ethical foundation to the Christian faith is that disciples, being children of God, should love one another since love is the fulfillment of the law, and God is love [see John 13:34–35; 1 John 3:11; 4:7–8]), human nature still leaves Christians open to the sin of unfairly judging others.

7:7–11 The next pitfall disciples face is the loss of faith. Jesus encourages His disciples to keep on asking, seeking, and knocking, for true faith never loses heart and quits. Disciples are to be like their heavenly Father. They are to love one another and be constant in their faith.

7:12 The Golden Rule, as this saying is commonly known, is not unique to Jesus or Christianity, for it is found in most religions in some form. In Judaism it is found in the negative form. One ancient Jewish rabbi, Rabbi Hillel, summarized it as follows: "What is hateful to yourself, do to no other." The Christian form as given by Jesus is, however, more positive and powerful than the negative form, which does not deny the good intention of the negative form. This proverbial saying is simply another way of expressing the fundamental kingdom ethic of loving one another. The Golden Rule, expressing the law of love, is what the law and prophets were all about.

7:13–20 This section addresses the problem of false teachers and commitment to the teachings of Jesus. We are again introduced to the Jewish idiom of two opposing ways—here, one way is narrow, the other way broad. The narrow way is the more difficult. Jesus knows that the road ahead for disciples will entail opposition and even serious persecution. Faced by such difficulties, disciples will be tempted to choose the easier way, perhaps that of retaining their Jewish religion based on law rather than following God in freedom.

7:21–23 Jesus is fully aware that many will follow Him—but on their own terms or when it is convenient. Obedience to the will of God will be the hallmark of true discipleship. In the context of the Sermon, with its heavy emphasis on righteousness as a right relationship with God and His will, it is not surprising that Jesus closes with this teaching. Failure to submit to and do the will of God will result in Jesus' denial of a disciple.

7:24–27 The parable of the two builders provides a powerful conclusion to this section on commitment to the will of God, as well as to Jesus' emphasis on the necessity of doing the will of God.

7:28–29 When Jesus finishes teaching, the crowds are astonished at the authority with which He spoke to them. A statement like this can be found at the conclusion of each of the great discourses in Matthew. In each of these formula endings to the teachings of Jesus, Matthew draws attention to the authoritative role of Jesus. This is one of Matthew's tools that emphasizes the unique character of Jesus.

8:1–3 Leprosy was a common ailment in the ancient world and one Israel had encountered throughout its history. It was a most dreaded illness. Biblical leprosy is not the same as modern leprosy (Hansen's disease). In the Bible, the word *leprosy* refers to a variety of skin ailments, some serious and some not—but all rendered their sufferers unclean. Thus the issue of leprosy has as much to do with ritual uncleanness as it does with great danger to health or imminent death.

8:5–13 The centurion was a soldier in command of one hundred soldiers. Groups of Roman soldiers were posted throughout the empire. The encounter between Jesus and this man introduces a major theme that Matthew develops throughout his Gospel: The Jewish religious leaders who should have believed in Jesus do not, and the Gentiles, who had no real reason to believe, do (remember Herod and the wise men of 2:1–12).

8:14–17 Upon entering Peter's house in Capernaum and learning that Peter's mother-in-law is ill with a fever, Jesus heals her. Many others hear of this and gather at Peter's house. Jesus heals all who are sick and demon possessed. The citation is obviously of Isaiah 53:4 but is apparently a free translation by Matthew. The brevity of this section, describing the powerful miracles of Jesus, highlights the incomparable authority of Jesus as the Messiah.

8:23–26 The sea of Galilee was surrounded by hills and was susceptible to sudden and violent storms. Matthew indicates that the sea was extremely rough and dangerous. The disciples' frantic reaction is a natural one. Jesus' response and His reference to little faith pick up on one of Matthew's themes: people of little faith who should have great faith. Jesus' response to the disciples' fear is found five times in Matthew (6:30; 8:26; 14:31; 16:8; 17:20) and is well translated "O ye of little faith."

8:27 The disciples marvel that Jesus can still the sea, and they ask the rhetorical question, "What manner of man is this, that even the winds and the sea obey him!" The answer is obvious—this man is not an ordinary man, because only God can command the waves and sea and they obey the command.

8:29 In contrast to the Jewish leaders in Matthew (scribes and Pharisees), here at least two demons recognize Jesus as the Son of God. The little expression "before the time" indicates the Jewish understanding of an end-time judgment. The demons recognize that in Jesus the end is already near.

8:31–34 In keeping with their request, Jesus casts the demons out and they enter a herd of pigs, causing them to rush over the cliff into the sea. The Gergesenes obviously do not understand and are fearful of Jesus, possibly believing Him to be a powerful magician. They ask Him to leave the area. The fact that they had a herd of pigs indicates that they are Gentiles, not Jews.

9:1–8 Returning to His own city (Capernaum), Jesus enters a house and a paralytic is brought to Him. Jesus does a startling thing for the man—He forgives his sins. The cross of Jesus overshadows this section; Jesus can forgive sins for He is the Son of God. It would be much easier to heal a man than to forgive his sins. The forgiveness of sins was the greater gift of the Messiah, connecting His ministry to His primary reason for coming, that is, to die on the cross for sins.

9:9–13 Publicans (tax collectors) were despised for their avarice, being self-serving and dishonest. Furthermore, they were the agents of the despised Roman power. They were considered by the Jews to be among the worst of sinners. In fact, Jews viewed publicans to be as lowly as the Gentiles. Jesus tells the Pharisees that His purpose in coming is not to call those who see themselves as righteous but to call sinners who see their need. This passage draws attention to the growing antagonism between the Pharisees and Jewish leaders and Jesus.

9:18–19 The story regarding the ruler (Mark and Luke reveal his name as Jairus, a ruler in the synagogue) is abruptly broken off for a while by the intrusion of the woman with the twelve-year hemorrhage.

9:20–22 It is obvious that this story is about the simple faith of the woman. She is convinced that if she can only touch the fringes of His garment, she will be healed. Jesus acknowledges her faith and encourages her to take heart, for her faith has made her well. Instantly she is healed.

9:23–26 Jairus's faith is the point of this section, indicating that some of the Jewish leadership believed. By the time Jesus gets to Jairus's house, the girl is dead. When Jesus says the girl is not dead, the crowd laughs because they know she is dead. Jesus knows, however, that her death is not permanent, for He is about to raise her up from death.

9:27–31 In striking contrast to the Jewish leaders, two blind men recognize Jesus and confess their faith by calling Him the son of David. (Matthew's reference to *two* blind men is significant in a Jewish context because two witnesses were required for any testimony.) Jesus asks whether these men really believe He can heal them, and they confess they do. They not only demonstrate great faith but acknowledge Him as Lord, something the Jewish leaders refused to do. Jesus immediately restores their sight. Again Matthew demonstrates the necessity of great faith in Jesus and the acknowledgment of His lordship.

9:37–38 With the observation that the harvest is plentiful, Jesus means that there are many people who will believe in the gospel of the kingdom. The scribes and Pharisees should have been laboring in the kingdom but were more interested in their religious position. Jesus' instruction is for the disciples to pray for the Lord of the harvest to send laborers into the ministry of the kingdom.

10:1–4 Matthew refers to Jesus' closest followers as the twelve "apostles." The term *apostle* means "one sent out," or "a person commissioned to go." Notice that Matthew groups the names into six groups of two. In similar fashion, in Luke 10:1, Luke records Jesus' sending of seventy disciples in groups of two.

10:5–15 Jesus' instruction to take no provisions on the journey and to stay with those who welcome them is within the tradition of traveling rabbis or teachers in both the Jewish and Gentile cultures. Traveling or itinerant teachers and philosophers were common in the Jewish world, and good Jewish communities were expected to welcome and care for such itinerant rabbis (Romans 15:19–24; 1 Thessalonians 2; 2 John; 3 John). Jesus speaks with gravity to those who do not accept the apostles and the message they preach, comparing them to Sodom and Gomorrha.

10:16–23 Because of their testimony, the disciples will be hated and faced with death. The apostles are not to be overly concerned as to how to react in such circumstances, for the Holy Spirit will give them the words they need. You can hear throughout this text not only Jesus' concern for His disciples but also Matthew's concern for his community as they testify to their faith in a hostile Jewish and Gentile context. Persecution is sure to arise and threaten.

10:24–33 Jesus warns His disciples that they should expect nothing less than what He, their teacher, will receive from the Jewish leaders. Since the Jewish leaders had attributed His power to Satan (9:27–34), they would also malign Jesus' disciples. Jesus warns the apostles not to fear those who could, and would, kill them, but rather to fear the One who has the power to destroy both body and soul in hell—God Himself.

10:34–39 Jesus explains that His coming will bring suffering for those who believe in Him. Parents and family will turn against the disciples because of Jesus. The radical nature of messianic discipleship is that disciples must choose Jesus before all family allegiance. Those who will not choose Jesus over all others are not worthy disciples. Jesus adds a brief statement about disciples taking up their crosses and following Him. He will again take up this thought in 16:24–28. Taking up one's cross is a picture of being willing to die for Jesus—it means far more than accepting one's responsibilities.

10:40–42 Jesus assures the apostles that whoever receives them and their message receives both the Son and the Father. Jesus follows this with a proverbial saying about the righteous receiving their just reward. Jesus' closing statement in this section sets the scene for a discussion Matthew will take up in chapter 18, namely, that of taking care of the "little ones." At first glance this might be construed as a reference to children, but Jesus will later describe these little ones as those who believe in Him (18:6).

11:2–6 Jesus' response to John's question draws attention to His messianic ministry. He has been doing what had been prophesied the Messiah would do (Isaiah 35:5–6; 61:1–3; Luke 4:16–19): healing the sick, blind, lame, and deaf, and taking care of the poor. Jesus'

messianic ministry should have been all the witness John and his disciples needed.

11:7–19 Jesus continues the discussion on John the Baptist by asking what kind of person the Jews had set out to see when they went to the Jordan River to witness John's baptisms. His somewhat colloquial language reflects that they had not gone out to see a weak person but a bold prophet. Jesus cites Malachi 3:1 in support of John's ministry of preparing the way for the Messiah. Following this He pays John a great compliment—there is no one greater than John.

11:20–24 Chorazin and Bethsaida were small towns just to the north of the sea of Galilee and the town of Capernaum. Jesus had performed powerful signs in those towns, but the people refused to believe in His ministry and messiahship. If the miracles performed in these two cities had been performed in the Gentile towns of Tyre and Sidon, the Gentiles would have believed. Because a great revelation had been made to these places, a great accountability would be required of them.

11:25–30 This passage must be seen in the context of Jewish rejection of Jesus and His message. The learned ones rejected Jesus' message; the poor, needy, and humble ones believed and followed Him.

12:1–8 Matthew records that it is on the sabbath that Jesus and His disciples are traveling through the corn fields. The disciples, being hungry, pluck corn to eat. To the Pharisees, this was a serious violation of the sabbath law—resting from all work on the seventh day—as recorded in Exodus 20:10; 34:21; and Deuteronomy 5:14. Rabbinic tradition listed at least thirty-nine classes of work the rabbis saw covered by this law. The overzealous literal application of the legal principle obviously overlooked a deeper principle to which Jesus holds the Pharisees. He corrects their understanding by referring to two examples in the Jewish writings (Torah) that were obvious exceptions to the legal application of the law. Furthermore, He finally explains the place of the law in God's purpose.

12:9–14 Matthew's use of the expression "their synagogue" sets the synagogue of the Jews in contrast to the community of believers, namely, the church. When a man with a withered hand appears, the Pharisees take advantage of this to raise another question and accuse Jesus regarding lawful activity on the sabbath. In this instance, Jesus knows that rabbinic practice permits the rescuing of an animal on the sabbath (Luke 14:5). Arguing that it is far more important to heal a person than an animal, Jesus heals the man's withered hand. The Pharisees, obviously dissatisfied with Jesus, take council on how to destroy Him.

12:15–21 Jesus withdraws. Rather than incite the Pharisees further, Jesus seeks out quieter climes away from areas where the Pharisees frequented, but He continues His healings. Matthew draws attention to one of the Servant Songs in Isaiah (Isaiah 42:1–4) to demonstrate that Jesus, as the Messiah, is involved in messianic works.

12:22–28 When a blind demoniac acknowledges Jesus as the "son of David" (a term that had come to refer to the Messiah and was Matthew's favorite title for Jesus), the Pharisees take exception, charging that it is by the power of Beelzebub, the prince of the devils, that Jesus casts out demons. Jesus' startling reply is this: Since He is indeed casting out demons by the power of the Spirit of God, then the kingdom of God has come. Not that it *will* come, but the kingdom has already come and is upon them.

12:31–32 The blasphemy against the Holy Spirit that is unforgivable is a denial of the working of the Holy Spirit in God's system of atonement. Jesus considered this blasphemy even worse than blasphemy against Himself. To reject the saving power and work of the Holy Spirit is ultimately to reject God's working His salvation in the individual.

12:33–37 Jesus closes this encounter with the Pharisees with a pronouncement of judgment on them for the careless words they had just uttered. In their haste to deny Jesus, they had in fact blasphemed the very working of God through His Holy Spirit. Their words, uttered in the heat of their hatred, were not thought about, and through their cavalier treatment of Jesus and the Holy Spirit, they had brought judgment on themselves.

12:39–42 Unlike the people of Nineveh, the scribes and Pharisees would not believe and repent. The sign of Jonas (Jonah) here is the analogy between Jonas (Jonah) in the belly of the large fish and Jesus' burial and resurrection.

12:43–45 Jesus concludes this encounter with a parable of an unclean spirit leaving a man and returning to find his house clean. The spirit returns with seven more spirits and moves into the house. Jesus compares the generation of the scribes and Pharisees with this spirit. Those who do not respond will find in the end that their situation is worse than it was in the beginning. Obviously, Jesus has in mind that by refusing His message, the scribes and Pharisees face certain judgment.

12:46–50 This is the first reference to Jesus' family in Matthew. The last reference to Mary was in chapter 2. The next reference to family will be in 13:55–56, where the Jews attempt to find Jesus' significance in His family of origin by asking if He's the carpenter's son, if His mother is Mary, and if His brothers are James, Joseph, Simon, and Judas. In this encounter with His family, Jesus is not rejecting them but demonstrating that kingdom relationships take precedence over physical relationships. The section serves as a transitional passage, as Matthew moves on to the third discourse and the teachings on the kingdom.

13:3–9, 18–23 The parable—the simple analogy of a farmer sowing seed in Palestine—is about how a person hears and understands the message of the kingdom. The point is that in order for the message of the kingdom to germinate and flourish, the mind has to be prepared for hearing about and understanding the kingdom. A stubborn and rebellious heart cannot receive the Word.

13:10–15 Parable teaching was a favored rabbinic teaching style. The Jews were familiar with parable teaching. Jesus explains that the crowds surrounding Him are expecting some teaching, though they are not ready for the deeper matters of the kingdom or willing to understand the true spiritual nature of the kingdom. Jesus is well aware that the crowds are willing to hear Him but are not willing to hear His message. His understanding of the mysteries of the kingdom is not in step with theirs.

13:16–17 In contrast to the stubborn Jewish leaders, the disciples believe. To them the secret things of the kingdom will make sense. For this reason, Jesus teaches in parables. The Jewish leaders who are looking for the wrong kind of kingdom will still find some message in Jesus' parables, but the disciples who believe will be in a position to receive and accept the deeper spiritual nature of the kingdom.

13:24–30 This parable, like the parable of the sower, receives additional attention and explanation by Jesus (13:36–43). The parable is also similar to the kingdom parable of the dragnet (13:47–52). The parable of wheat and tares explains that in the kingdom of God one can expect a mixed crop. This is first because of human fallibility and weakness. But also, Satan is busy working on human minds. He plants seeds, sometimes of false teaching, sometimes of doubt. Whatever the case, a mixed crop is the result. The parable emphasizes that the judgment of crops (a person's faith) is beyond the disciples and must be left to the reaper himself (Jesus). Even the well-meaning individual can judge a person too soon.

13:31–32 In this time, the mustard seed was considered the smallest of seeds. The size of the mustard seed would have been well known among those hearing Jesus tell this parable. The size and slow growth of the mustard seed are an excellent metaphor for the humble beginnings of the kingdom. The Jews expect a triumphant arrival of the kingdom and expulsion of the Gentile enemy, but that is not how the kingdom of God is going to work. The Messiah came not to a princely house but to the house of a lowly carpenter. The beginnings of the kingdom are in fact small—12 apostles and about 120 other believers (Acts 1:13–15). Despite its humble beginnings, the kingdom slowly matures and grows significantly. The mysterious growth of the kingdom is due to the working of God's grace and power in human lives, not the result of human intervention and work.

13:33 Baking bread was an everyday experience in ancient days, especially among the Jews. It is widely known that leaven spreads throughout the loaf, but the maturing of the leaven takes time. Hurry the process, and you end up with a lump of hard bread that is useless and inedible. Give the leaven time, and it produces a wonderful loaf of bread. So it is with the message of the kingdom. Interfere with the process of slow leavening and growth, and you end up with a catastrophe. Give the power of God time to work in people, and do not expect too much too soon.

13:44–46 These two parables are similar in meaning and application. The kingdom is of inestimable value, and those who find it are greatly enriched. However, the richness of the kingdom is not out on the surface to be seen by all. Perhaps the most significant message of these parables is that when one finds the richness of the kingdom, one must be prepared to give up everything to attain it. Matthew will develop this point later when he narrates Jesus' encounter with the rich young ruler (19:16–30).

13:47–50 Jesus sets this parable in the context of the end of the age by emphasizing that the angels will come to separate the evil from the righteous and throw the evil into the fire of judgment (typical Jewish and rabbinic images of the final judgment). It is a sobering thought that one's attitude toward Jesus and His kingdom involves final judgment.

13:52 This conclusion is in the form of a proverbial saying. The scribes, the learned scholars of the law, should have been trained for the purpose of revealing all the mysteries of the kingdom. However, the scribes of Jesus' day are blinded by their reaction to Jesus and the nature of His message and kingdom. Jesus has revealed the richness and mysteries of the kingdom—both the old thoughts of the kingdom and the new ideas and thoughts of the kingdom. His disciples, by learning from Him about the kingdom, can bring together the promise of the old covenant with the fulfillment of the new.

14:1–12 The description of John's death is a flashback, prompted by Herod's speculation that Jesus might be John the Baptist raised from the dead. This Herod is Herod Antipas, one of the sons of Herod the Great. He is identified by Matthew as the tetrarch and by Mark as the king.

14:13–21 The narrative of the miracle of the feeding of more than five thousand people has more than historical significance. It drives home the point that Jesus, as the Messiah, could take care of His people. The feeding of the five thousand has an obvious connection to God feeding the children of Israel with manna in the wilderness after they left Egypt. It also has insights into the messianic banquet at the end of time when God's redeemed will sit at God's banquet table and be sustained.

14:22–33 This miracle is not so much about the natural elements, other than Jesus' power over them, as it is about Peter and the disciples' faith. The narrative indicates that Peter initially steps out in faith, but his faith wavers, resulting in his sinking into the sea. But Jesus saves him. It is easy to find fault in Peter for his wavering faith, but where were the other disciples?

15:1–20 The Pharisees were experts in interpreting the tradition of the elders, but that was not the same as the actual Torah (Genesis, Exodus, Leviticus, Numbers, and Deuteronomy). Translating this into contemporary contexts, human interpretations are opinions and not the law or doctrine itself. These traditions in themselves

are good, but when they are put on the same level as God's law, then humankind's opinion has been set on the same level as God's Word. This is the mistake the religious leaders have made. Jesus' condemnation of the Pharisees is scathing. He likens them to the Jews in Esaias's (Isaiah's) day who honored God with their lips but whose hearts were far away from God (Isaiah 29:13). The Jews in Isaiah's day had taught their own opinions and thoughts on an equal level with the sacred scriptures. The Pharisees were blind guides leading blind men, resulting in everyone falling into a pit. It is not what goes into the mouth that defiles people, but instead what proceeds out of their hearts and mouths.

15:21–22 This section continues the story of the need for faith, and the lack of faith, on the part of the Jewish leaders. Jesus leaves Capernaum and travels west into the Gentile region of Tyre and Sidon, where He is met by a Canaanite woman whose daughter is possessed by a demon. In her plea to Jesus, she acknowledges that Jesus is the Lord and messianic King.

15:23–28 The point of this narrative is this: The Jews, who should have accepted Jesus and believed in Him, did not, but this Gentile woman, who had no reason to believe in Jesus, did. Jesus finds great faith where no one would have expected it, but no faith where it should have been. The lesson for the members of Matthew's community is that they, too, should not ignore the Gentiles among whom they live, for one can find faith also among the Gentiles.

15:29–38 The point of this narrative is that Jesus can take care of the needs of His people, no matter how little they have and how great the need. A secondary lesson is that the disciples' faith still needs much maturing.

16:1 The Pharisees are now joined by the Sadducees to continue the attack on Jesus. These two theological and political enemies join together in their opposition to Jesus, illustrating their frustration and desperation. The request for a sign (from heaven, which also meant from God) is intended to trap Jesus and provide evidence that they might use against Him.

16:4 Jesus' strident rebuke likens the Pharisees and Sadducees to an adulterous generation, which has all the evidence it needs yet still rebels against God. Therefore, they are guilty of committing spiritual adultery. This is the second time Jesus refers to the sign of Jonas (Jonah; see also 12:40). In both cases, Jesus is referencing His resurrection from the dead. Jonas (Jonah) was in the belly of the fish for three days and nights, and Jesus will be in the grave for the same period.

16:5–12 Jesus warns the disciples to beware of the leaven (yeast) of the Pharisees and Sadducees. The disciples associate this with physical bread, which they have forgotten to bring with them. Reminding them of His miracles with the five thousand and four thousand, Jesus warns them again. Finally, the disciples understand Jesus' warning regarding the Pharisees' and Sadducees' teaching and refusal to believe, and the need they have for faith.

16:13–20 The confession of Peter is a crucial turning point in the Gospel accounts. It is only here in Matthew, though, that the high status in the church is assigned to Peter at the end of the passage. Jesus' response recognizes that Peter's understanding is the result of the revelation of God. The hand of the Father can be seen in the process that has led to Peter's understanding.

16:22 Peter's rebuke demonstrates that he does not understand the full implication of Jesus' messianic ministry as the suffering servant described by Isaiah (Isaiah 53) and of God's purpose for Jesus.

16:23 Jesus' response is a strident rebuke. A paraphrase of Jesus' response might read, "Peter, you are a hindrance to God's purpose for me. You are functioning under the influence of Satan." Jesus' purpose, contrary to human tendencies, was not to take the easy solution to the problem.

16:25–27 Martyrdom was a very present reality to Christians in the first century. In fact, by the second century of Christianity, discipleship held the threat of martyrdom for many. Jesus adds a dramatic note to the discussion. Those who seek to save their lives by denying Him will be judged by this at the end of the age.

17:1–13 The fact that this section appears in all three synoptic Gospels immediately after Jesus' prediction of His death is striking. The passion prediction must have left a dark cloud over the disciples. They needed encouragement and hope. The transfiguration and God's approving statement regarding Jesus provide a ray of light and encouragement for the immediate circle of disciples (Peter, James, and John) and for Matthew's readers, too.

17:14–21 It is the lack of faith, or weak faith, of the disciples that is at the center of this story. Jesus is again working to build the faith of His disciples. His comment that faith can move mountains is a Hebrew proverb that meant faith can move immovable obstacles. The emphasis is not on the literal moving of mountains but on the insurmountable problems that the disciples and all Christians face in life.

17:22–23 Jesus again tells His disciples that He must be delivered into the hands of men and be killed, and then be raised by the power of God. Matthew reveals that the disciples are greatly distressed because they are still struggling with the fate of the Messiah.

17:24–27 Jesus as the Son of God does not need to pay this tax, for sons are free of taxation. But to show His regard for the temple and all it really stood for, Jesus pays the tax anyway. However, the disciples and Matthew's community need to know that Jesus is greater than the temple, and whereas before His death the temple had been a focal point of Jewish faith, now it is Jesus who is the center of faith.

18:1–5 Still struggling with the true nature of the kingdom, the disciples are concerned with who will be greatest in the kingdom. Jesus' answers demonstrate that the disciples are struggling with matters of position, power, and authority. His response that the disciples should be like little children indicates that greatness in the kingdom has nothing to do with power and position but everything to do with one's attitude toward self and others.

18:6–9 The discussion on humility is developed by Jesus to reflect on how disciples treat one another and influence other disciples. To cause a vulnerable disciple to stumble or lose his or her faith in Jesus is a serious matter, the judgment of which is compared to having a millstone tied around one's neck and being cast into the depths of the sea and drowned. It seems from other references (Revelation 18:21) that this figure of speech may have been an idiom in Judaism for severe condemnation.

18:10–14 To demonstrate further that all disciples are vulnerable, Jesus uses the illustration of the man who had one hundred sheep, of which one got lost. Jesus concludes that this analogy reflects the love and concern of the Father in heaven for any one lost sheep. Disciples are vulnerable to stumble and be lost. Disciples must be concerned for the vulnerable and lost and be sensitive to the needs of fellow disciples. Being prideful and seeking greatness are not fitting for the kingdom. Having concern for fellow disciples, those who are vulnerable and easily lost, is key to kingdom understanding.

18:15–20 The principles laid down by Jesus in this section are essential to resolving ruptured personal relationships and mediating conflict. The instruction on how to handle such matters is firmly set in the threefold procedure established in Deuteronomy 19:15–21: (1) The process begins first on the personal level; (2) then it proceeds to the second level of two witnesses; (3) finally, the matter is brought before the community of believers. In Deuteronomy 19:17, the final community level is considered the same as being in the presence of the Lord. Note Jesus' teaching that where this process is followed in His name, there He is present.

18:21–22 This section begins with Peter asking how often he should forgive another person. Peter recognizes that forgiveness is vital to the process of church discipline and restoration of broken relationships. His suggestion of forgiving seven times is generous. Rabbinic teaching suggested three times as the standard. Peter has chosen a favored Jewish number for completeness, but Jesus responds with a greater number—seventy times seven—indicating that there is no limit to the number of times one should be willing to forgive.

18:21–35 The principles of Christian forgiveness are as essential to successful church community life as are the ones for resolving conflicts involving sin, as depicted in the previous section. Whereas the previous section initially presupposed a lack of repentance and focused on the other party, this section focuses on the first person, or the self. It asks not what the other person should have done, but what we should be doing.

18:23–35 The powerful parable that Jesus teaches drives home the need for Christians to learn how to forgive. In the parable, the first servant owes the king an unpayable debt, ten thousand talents, estimated by some to be in the high millions or even billions of dollars in present-day currency. The other debt mentioned is only one hundred denarii, about one hundred days' wages. The application of this parable is timeless, applying to the first disciples, Matthew's community, and all Christians today.

19:3–6 This discussion is set in the context of the Pharisees attempting to test and trap Jesus. This discourse on divorce and remarriage is not the final testament on the issue but a serious answer to a trap by the Pharisees. Certainly, Jesus touches on several major issues in the debate on divorce and remarriage, but only within the context of the Pharisees' question. Jesus' response moves the argument back beyond Moses' permission for divorce to God's ideal for marriage. Marriage is to be for life, and what God has joined, no one is to break apart (Genesis 2:24).

19:7–9 The Pharisees' return argument is that Jesus has spoken in opposition to Moses. Jesus corrects them by showing that what Moses had given was not a command but permission. The Pharisees had attempted to place Jesus in opposition to Moses and the law. Jesus again, as in the Sermon on the Mount, demonstrates that the Pharisaic interpretation of the law does not take into consideration the real spirit of the purpose of the law. Moses' permission was purely because of human hardness of heart.

19:12 Jesus' response speaks of three groups of eunuchs—two literal, one metaphorical: (1) those born impotent and therefore eunuchs; (2) those made eunuchs by others as in the case of the Ethiopian eunuch of Acts 8, sometimes occurring in slavery; (3) those who choose to live celibate lives for the kingdom as in the case of the apostle Paul (1 Corinthians 7:8). Jesus' response to the disciples' concern again illustrates the radical nature of discipleship in the kingdom. Disciples are to live by God's ideals rather than permissiveness resulting from sinful weakness.

19:13–15 This little section in which the disciples seek to drive children away provides Jesus with another occasion to remind the disciples that the kingdom belongs to those who have learned to be humble like children. It is not uncommon for disciples to bring worldly standards of greatness into the kingdom. Followers of Jesus throughout the centuries have struggled with the principle of humble servant leadership, with many seeking positions in the church for the wrong reasons—personal importance rather than humble service.

19:21–22 Jesus' instruction to the young man gets to the heart of his problem—riches. When he learns that discipleship in the kingdom involves placing kingdom matters and discipleship above personal possessions, the young man goes away sad, for the cost of discipleship is too high. His reaction reminds us of Jesus' teaching in the Sermon on the Mount, that your heart will be where your treasure is (6:21).

19:23–24 Jesus continues the discussion begun by the young man. He does not say it is impossible for a rich person to enter heaven but only that it is difficult.

Illustrating how difficult it would be for a rich person to enter the kingdom, Jesus uses the analogy of a camel going through the eye of a needle. Attempts to soften this statement by interpreting *camel* and *eye of a needle* in a more reasonable way fail to grasp the irony of Jesus' statement. He is using exaggeration to make a point.

19:27–29 Peter, troubled by Jesus' seemingly harsh statement, asks what will happen to them, for they have given up all for the kingdom. Jesus responds that in the new world they will sit on thrones with Jesus and judge the world with Him. All who give up everything for Jesus and the kingdom's sake will inherit eternal life.

19:30 Jesus concludes this discussion with the proverbial statement that the first will be last. Given the context of the rich young man, one must assume that the first must be in reference to the rich who believe that because of their position in life they should be privileged. In the kingdom, this is not the case, for it is the humble who benefit from the kingdom, not the proud (5:1–12), and it is the humble servants who are greatest in the kingdom (18:1–4).

20:1–16 The householder (who represents God) hires a series of workers at different times of the day. He promises the first a day's wages. At the close of the day, he pays all the workers the same wage, but those who were hired first are upset that they worked longer for the same pay received by those who were hired later. The householder's closing remarks demonstrate a great principle of grace: Can't I do what I want with what belongs to me? Do you resent my generosity toward others? Jesus closes the parable by returning to the proverb He spoke of in 19:30, but in this case He reverses the order—the last will be first.

20:17–19 As Jesus draws near to Jerusalem, He again instructs the twelve regarding His death, burial, and resurrection. This time, though, He elaborates briefly on several other things: His suffering, His condemnation by the Jewish leadership, His trial before the Gentiles, and the mocking and scourging He will receive.

20:20–28 We see again in this section the difficulty the disciples have understanding the true nature of discipleship and the kingdom. On this occasion, the mother of James and John asks Jesus for positions of honor for her sons in the kingdom. We should not think too poorly of this mother or of the other disciples for being indignant over her request. The temptation to see leadership positions as power rather than opportunities to serve still exists today in the church.

20:29–34 As Jesus and the disciples are passing through Jericho, they see two blind men. The two blind men call out to Jesus, referring to Him as the son of David and begging Him to heal them, which He does. The narrative draws attention to the fact that even the blind recognize Jesus as the Messiah, yet the seeing—Pharisees, scribes, and Sadducees—do not recognize the Messiah. This narrative fits in well with the preceding discussion of the greatest being last and the least being first.

21:1–11 Jesus' entry into Jerusalem is a turning point in the Gospel narrative. It ends His Galilean ministry and journey to Jerusalem and begins the tragic passion narrative. It is an event marked by the capriciousness of the people and manifests a mixture of truth and irony. The truth is that Jesus really is the Messiah. The irony is that His very identity as the Messiah is the reason He is rejected by the Jews, particularly the Jewish leadership. When He enters Jerusalem, He is welcomed as the son of David but is almost immediately rejected as the Messiah and mocked by the people. When Jesus shows that He is a different kind of Messiah than they expected, He is rejected.

21:4–7 Jesus arranges His ride into Jerusalem to fulfill Zechariah 9:9, an Old Testament passage that was interpreted with reference to the Messiah by the rabbis. Matthew's use of Zechariah 9:9 is one of the ten fulfillment passages unique to his Gospel. He combines Zechariah 9:9 with Isaiah 62:11.

21:8–9 The crowd welcomes Jesus jubilantly, spreading their garments on the road for Him to ride into Jerusalem in kingly style and crying, "Hosanna to the son of David," followed by a blessing from Psalm 118:26. The term *Hosanna* in Aramaic means "O save" or "God save," but it had come to be a simple term of praise. The people praise Jesus as their King, their Messiah. Yet they also recognize Him merely as the prophet from Nazareth.

21:12–17 Matthew records the cleansing on the same day that Jesus is acknowledged as King, indicating that the cleansing is a messianic duty. Jesus quotes Isaiah 56:7 as His authority for overturning the tables of the moneychangers and the seats of the pigeon sellers. Consideration of the verses surrounding Isaiah 56:1–7 adds to the significance of Jesus' actions. Particularly notable is the fact that Isaiah 56 refers to the Gentile inclusion in God's kingdom. There in the temple, Jesus continues His ministry of healing the blind and the lame. However, when the chief priests see the wonderful miracles of Jesus and hear the children acclaiming Jesus as the son of David, they are indignant and rebuke Jesus. Jesus responds by referring to Psalm 8:2, with His declaration that perfect praise can come from the mouths of babes or children.

21:18–22 The barren fig tree is a lesson on faith. However, it is also a lesson on the absence of faith. The presence of leaves indicates that the early fruit of the fig should have been present, but Jesus finds none. The harshness of His condemnation is symbolic of His condemnation of the Jewish leaders for their lack of faith. Faith should have been the trademark of the Jewish religious leaders but had not been a typical response from them.

21:24–27 Jesus' question backs the Jewish leaders into a corner, for if they claim John's baptism was from heaven, they will blacken their own eyes because they didn't believe John. If they answer that his baptism was from men, the crowds that followed John could turn on them. Stymied, they simply respond that they do not know. In similar fashion, Jesus answers that He will not tell them by what authority He acts. This exchange illustrates well the growing tension and opposition from the Jewish leadership and Jesus' firm response.

21:28–32 The next parable involves two sons— one initially refuses to work but then works; another initially agrees to work but never goes. The first son represents the tax collectors, prostitutes, and general sinners who turn away from God but then repent. The second represents the Jewish leaders who claim to be righteous but do not repent. Those who should inherit the kingdom will not, but those who do not deserve the kingdom receive its benefits. Jesus gets very personal by speaking directly to the Jewish religious leaders. He confronts them about their character assassination of Him and John the Baptist as well as their refusal to repent.

21:33–46 The parable of the wicked tenants is again a reference to the religious leaders who should take care of the master's vineyard but do not. When the master sends servants, the tenants kill the servants and then go on to kill the heir of the master who comes in the master's name. When asked by Jesus what should happen to the wicked tenants, the chief priests and Pharisees rightly respond that the wicked tenants deserve death. What they do not see is that Jesus is referencing them in the parable. Jesus' next comment is a scathing rebuke—the Jews will lose the kingdom of God, and the Gentiles will receive it. Finally, the chief priests and Pharisees see that Jesus is speaking about them. If not for fear of the crowds, they would arrest Him.

22:1–14 This chapter continues Jesus' condemnation of the Jewish leaders with the parable of the marriage feast. It also includes further discussion with the Pharisees and Sadducees, which leads into Jesus' scathing condemnation of the scribes and Pharisees in chapter 23. Demonstrating Matthew's end-times perspective, this parable is addressed as a parable of the kingdom of heaven and draws heavily on the Jewish concept of a final banquet to which those who are righteous and worthy are invited. The book of Revelation likewise draws on this concept (Revelation 19).

22:6 Some say that the king sending out his army to punish the offenders might be a reference to the judgment and destruction of the scribes, Pharisees, and Jerusalem that are described in greater detail in chapters 23–25. This might not be the case since the figure of kings sending soldiers out to punish offenders was a common one in ancient parables and narratives.

22:11 Of the many who do respond to the invitation, one man is present who is not wearing a wedding garment. Questions exist among scholars as to whether the king had provided the wedding garments for his guests and whether this was a common practice. These details are not mentioned in the parable. It is, after all, simply a parable rather than a historical account. Not all the details are necessary to the story, nor are they pertinent to the lesson of the parable. What is pertinent to the lesson is that the man is not properly attired for a wedding and is thrown out.

22:14 The final verse of this parable gets to the heart of things—many are called (invited), but few are chosen. Many are called, but only those characterized by faith and righteousness are the chosen.

22:15–22 The question of the Pharisees places Jesus between the horns of a dilemma. Whichever way He answers the question, He will be in trouble with some group of leadership. If He answers that it is permissible to pay taxes to Rome, He will meet with opposition from the crowds as well as the Pharisees—the Roman tax was despised by the Jewish nation. If He answers that tax should not be paid to the Romans, He will meet with opposition from the Herodians and the Romans themselves.

22:23–33 Jesus' answer to the Sadducees is both direct and stern—the Sadducees' problem is that they know neither the scriptures (a serious challenge and insult) nor the power of God (which addresses the core of the Sadducees' problem with the resurrection). Jesus' challenge to the Sadducees regarding their lack of knowledge comes directly from scripture the Sadducees have to accept—Exodus 3:6, 15. Since these verses are in the present tense, the implication is that at the time God was speaking these words to Moses, Abraham, Isaac, and Jacob, they were alive, even though centuries had passed since their deaths were recorded in Genesis. This could be possible only if the resurrection was real and true. Jesus' point, then, is that to deny the resurrection is to misunderstand scripture. This is quite a challenge to a group that defines itself by its attention to scripture. Rather than undermine Jesus' standing as a teacher, the Sadducees reinforce it, for the crowds are astonished by Jesus' teaching.

22:34–40 One wonders what must have motivated this particular question. Perhaps it was Jesus' previous teaching that seemed to be contrary to the scribes' interpretation of the Torah (5:17–48). Jesus' answer, though, gets to the heart of the law by way of an orthodox path. He quotes part of the Shema (Deuteronomy 6:4–9), a passage that was quoted twice every day by all serious Jews. Jesus then follows this with a quotation from Leviticus 19:18. A close examination of the Ten Commandments reveals that loving God and one's neighbour is what the Ten Commandments and the Torah are all about. Jesus' final comment that the law and the prophets depend on these two commandments leaves the lawyer silent. Neither the lawyer nor the Pharisees have a response.

22:41–46 Jesus' question is not simply one designed as a clever trap for the Pharisees but is one with serious implications for His own identity and calling as the Messiah. The question does, however, pose a serious interpretive problem for the Pharisees. How could David call the Messiah his Lord (Psalm 110:1) when the Messiah was to be a human descendant of his? The core of Jesus' question addresses the issue of a human being (a son of David) being the divine messianic Lord (which

is what Psalm 110:1 implies). This question and how it is answered lies at the very core of Matthew's Gospel and theology. Disciples must believe that Jesus (a human being) is at the same time a divine being (this is what the virgin birth narrative demonstrates) and the divine Messiah.

23:1–36 Jesus begins His significant judgment by acknowledging the scribes and Pharisees as teachers of the Torah, but He warns the disciples not to imitate their actions. The problem is that the scribes and Pharisees make their interpretation of keeping the Torah a matter so strict that no one can bear the burden of their interpretation. Furthermore, the Pharisees make a show of their position and righteousness in contrast to drawing people's attention to their God and His laws. The point Jesus is stressing in this passage is that the disciples have only one true interpreter and teacher of the Torah—Jesus—not the scribes and Pharisees. Likewise, the disciples have only one spiritual Father, and that is God Himself. The scribes and Pharisees are not to be seen as the spiritual fathers of the disciples. Jesus' closing condemnation adds even more gravity to the woes. His inclusion of the whole generation brings the Jewish populace into the condemnation, for they side with the scribes and Pharisees in the events leading up to Jesus' crucifixion.

24:1–2 The disciples are so shocked by Jesus' condemnation of Jerusalem that as they near the temple— the bastion of Judaism—they draw Jesus' attention to it. Jesus responds in a manner intended to help the disciples see that the temple, however important it was to Judaism, is not to play a part in the messianic kingdom and ministry. The temple is to be destroyed.

24:4–14 Jesus warns that many will falsely predict His coming, but before such an event, the gospel has to be preached throughout the world. Jesus encourages His disciples not to be misled by wars, earthquakes, and other such events, which false prophets will use to lure followers away. He encourages His disciples to endure such catastrophes and persecutions; those who endure will be saved in the end (He is speaking of final, eternal salvation—not the present salvation we enjoy in the Christian life). The point Jesus is making to the disciples in this section is that they should not be led astray by false predictions or claims that Jesus has come or is about to come. They are not to confuse the destruction of Jerusalem and the temple with the end of the world or the coming of the Son of man.

24:15 Jesus begins His discussion of the destruction of Jerusalem by making reference to language and events with which all Jews were familiar, the language of Daniel 9:27 and 12:11—the "abomination of desolation." Most scholars identify this event with the destruction of Jerusalem by the Romans in AD 70. The historical accounts of the Roman siege and destruction of Jerusalem fit well with the language used by Jesus in this section.

24:23–27 Jesus repeats His previous warning—that He will come just as the lightning strikes, suddenly and without warning. At this point, Jesus has twice warned His disciples not to interpret world events as signs of His eschatological coming.

24:36 Typically, the pronouns *this* and *these* refer to what is closest at hand in time or in space. Note that in this verse, Jesus speaks of *that* day or hour. The pronoun *that* indicates something further away in time or space. In 24:32–35 the signs are for what is closer or nearer. The context of the discussion and the interpretation of the warning signs point to the judgment and destruction of Jerusalem rather than the second coming of Christ. Knowing that Jesus has taught the imminence of the fall of the temple, the disciples naturally assume the imminence of Jesus' second coming. In their minds, the two are inseparable. They can't conceive of the fall of Jerusalem apart from the end of the age, as the question of 24:3 indicates. Nevertheless, although Jesus teaches the imminent fall of Jerusalem, He does not teach the imminence of His second coming. He leaves the latter to the undetermined future.

24:42 This verse gets to the heart of Jesus' teaching about the unexpected coming of the Son of man. The disciples are to be ready, watchful, and alert, for they do not know on what day their Lord will come. As the thief does not announce in advance his coming, so the Son of man will not announce His coming in advance. Therefore the disciples must always be ready.

24:45–51 The faithful and wise servant is the one who, when His master comes home, is busy doing what he is supposed to be doing. Jesus highlights the point by warning that the unfaithful and foolish servants are hypocrites who will be punished. This is a clear warning that eternal punishment awaits those who are not ready and waiting expectantly.

25:1–13 The Greek word often translated as *virgin* can also be translated as *maiden* or *young woman*. In the context of Jesus' parable, the emphasis indicates that these are young, unmarried women—similar to today's bridesmaids. Of the ten maidens, five are prepared and five are not. The unprepared are excluded from the marriage feast. The connection of the marriage feast with the end-times banquet anticipated by Judaism and Christianity is obvious. Disciples who are not prepared will be excluded from that banquet. Why wouldn't the wise maidens lend oil to the foolish maidens? Why not help those in need? The necessities this parable illustrates—personal faith, repentance, baptism, personal holiness, personal service, and personal preparedness—can't be borrowed.

25:14–30 In this parable, the talent is an amount of money. A master leaving on a journey entrusts an amount of money to each of his three servants. The first two servants trade and double the investment. The third one, for fear of his master, buries his talent of silver and returns it to his master. The master casts this third servant into outer darkness (again, indications of the final judgment are evident in this parable). The other two servants are rewarded for their diligence. The point of the parable is that disciples must use the giftedness

that they have, whatever it may be. Disciples do not all have the same giftedness, but all disciples must use what they have in service of the Master. Being involved is part of being prepared.

25:31–46 In this parable, the warnings of Jesus regarding watching, being alert, and being ready reach a disturbing high point. The reference to the final judgment is obvious and clear. The sheep, those on the right hand, are blessed and inherit the kingdom prepared for them from the beginning of the world. The goats, on the other hand, are cursed and cast into eternal fire. But what are the criteria for this judgment? What has the one group done that the other group has not? The goats are so busy with their religion and hypocritical worship of God that they do not take time for the poor and helpless. The sheep recognize that true worship of God involves taking care of the poor and helpless (Micah 6:6–8; James 1:27).

26:1–2 Matthew's mention of the passover is not intended to simply provide a time reference. Instead, it sets the purpose of the passion narrative in a specific theological framework. Central to the original passover event was the lamb whose blood, smeared on the doorposts, saved the Israelites from death (Exodus 12–14). Here in the Gospel, Jesus is the Lamb prepared for the deliverance and redemption of humanity.

26:6–13 This event occurs in the home of Simon the leper, only mentioned in the New Testament on this one occasion. The fact that Simon has been cured is implied by the fact that they are meeting in his home, something that would not have been permissible otherwise under Jewish law. Simon lived in Bethany, a small town two miles from Jerusalem on the eastern slope of the mount Olivet. A woman anoints Jesus with ointment that is obviously very expensive. The theological point of this narrative is that Jesus interprets the woman's action in light of His approaching death and burial—not simply as an act of devotion. That is not to say that the woman made that connection—she has acted only out of love. Nevertheless, in the context of His imminent passion, Jesus breathes new meaning into her love.

26:14–16 Judas makes plans to betray his Lord. The sum of the betrayal agreement is thirty pieces of silver, a sum considered by scholars to be the equivalent of the price of a slave. The insubstantial sum has led some to suggest that Judas's motivation for the betrayal is not greed but possibly disappointment in Jesus' messiahship. Some have suggested that Judas might have been motivated by the same frustrations seen in the zealots who were looking for a militant political messiah who would lead them in victory over their Roman overlords.

26:17–18 Jesus sends His disciples to find a man in whose home Jesus intends to eat the passover. Apparently, Jesus has made some arrangement with the man, but we are not informed regarding all the details.

26:26–29 Jesus intends this institution, often referred to as the Lord's Supper, to be a way for the disciples (and later the church) to commemorate His death. As the passover was intended to be a perpetual commemoration of God's deliverance of Israel from Egypt, so the Lord's Supper is intended to be a perpetual commemoration of Jesus' death. The eating of the Supper is intended to be a proclamation of His death as well as an interpretation of that death. The bread and wine are intended to symbolize His body and blood given for the deliverance of humankind from bondage to sin. Just as the annual passover rite memorialized and personalized the passover in Egypt and deliverance from Egypt, the Lord's Supper likewise not only memorializes the death of Jesus but personalizes it as well.

26:30–35 This sad narrative stresses the tragic frailty of human effort. We don't know exactly what prompts Jesus to warn the disciples of the frailty of their faith, but His warning indicates His knowledge of their coming weakness and denial. Jesus' statement about scattering sheep suggests He may have intended the events that followed to be seen as a fulfillment of the prophecy in Zechariah 13. Nevertheless, Jesus' warning of the falling away of the disciples obviously disturbs them. First Peter and then all the disciples deny that they will fall away and disown Jesus. Jesus, however, forewarns Peter of his disowning Him.

26:36–46 This poignant narrative stands as a monument to Jesus' agony and fear of suffering and dying as a human and also as a monument of His willingness to submit to the will of His Father in heaven. Adding to the tragedy of this occasion is that this is the last account of Jesus spending time with His disciples before dying on the cross. At the moment that He needs them most, they fail Him miserably.

26:47–56 Judas arrives with a great crowd armed with swords and clubs as though Jesus were a robber or insurrectionist. Judas, by agreement with the mob members, kisses Jesus to identify Him as the One they are seeking. The Eastern kiss was a sign of greeting.

26:59–61 The hypocrisy for which Jesus has condemned the scribes and Pharisees comes to the forefront in the false testimony the Sanhedrin seeks against Jesus. After several attempts to gather enough testimony against Jesus to condemn Him to death, which is their purpose, they finally get two false witnesses to come forward with statements that Jesus had claimed to be able to destroy the temple and rebuild it in three days. Obviously they were taking several strands of Jesus' teachings and weaving them into ridiculous charges.

26:62–64 When Jesus refuses to answer the charges of the high priest, the high priest places Him under oath and asks Him whether He is the Christ, the Son of God. Jesus' answer is actually a direct answer in the affirmative, a Hebrew idiom that indicates a qualified yes. Jesus' additional comments are drawn from Daniel 7:13 and Psalm 110:1. They are so loaded with apocalyptic symbolism that the high priest immediately understands what Jesus is claiming—to be the One seated "on the right hand of power," and the One who will come in judgment

on them. The word *power* implies God but adheres to the Jewish tradition of not saying God's name out loud.

26:66–27:2 After requesting the death penalty, those present in the Sanhedrin begin to mistreat Jesus. Their evil scheming has come to fruition. However, the Jews under Roman rule did not have the authority to carry out their condemnation of death. Only the Romans could carry out that sentence. That is why, after Matthew's description of Peter's denial of Jesus, Jesus is led bound to Pilate, the Roman governor.

27:6 What is ironically tragic is that the chief priests recognize earnings from betraying someone as blood money. They know they cannot put the money into the treasury since these kinds of earnings are condemned in the Torah (Deuteronomy 23:18). Yet they have knowingly provided the money for this very reason, to betray Jesus. Their duplicity apparently does not trouble them. It is no wonder Jesus condemns them as "whited sepulchres" full of decaying bodies (Matthew 23:27).

27:11 Pilate asks Jesus if He is the king of the Jews. Notice he does not ask Jesus if He is king over Israel, which could seem a more politically threatening title. Pilate's political sensitivity to Roman concerns, and his ability to see that this was a Jewish matter, frames the question. Jesus' answer to Pilate, "Thou sayest," implies a simple yes.

27:12–14 When Pilate questions Jesus further, He remains silent, reminiscent of the prophet Isaiah's description of the Messiah as a silent lamb led to slaughter (Isaiah 53:7).

27:15 At the feast, it is the governor's practice to release a Jew from prison. Although we have no external evidence for such practice other than the Gospels, this seems in accord with what the governor would have done in order to show some sort of clemency to the Jews. The person to be released would be someone meeting the crowd's request.

27:19–25 Romans paid much attention to warnings from divination and dreams, like the one Pilate's wife had. As Pilate attempts to remove himself from the process by symbolically washing his hands, he is indicating publicly that he does not find Jesus worthy of death. The crowd's statement, that the blood of Jesus will be on their hands and those of their children, was a well-accepted expression from the Old Testament that spoke to full responsibility in an act (Lamentations 5:7).

27:26 The scourging with the Roman lash, which contained sharp objects for tearing the flesh, was commonly administered to those about to be crucified, possibly to so weaken them that they would not linger on the cross indefinitely. After having Jesus scourged, Pilate hands Him over to his soldiers to be crucified. Had Jesus been a Roman citizen, His death by crucifixion would have been prohibited.

27:27–38 After mocking Jesus in the worst manner, the Roman soldiers take Jesus out to Golgotha, the place of the skull, to crucify Him between two robbers. These men were possibly insurrectionists or bandits.

27:32 Simon, the man from Cyrene (North Africa) who carries Jesus' cross, was in all probability a Jewish pilgrim to the passover feast. Tradition has it that Simon later became a Christian.

27:34 The drink offered to those dying on the cross was sometimes mixed with gall—which could be a bitter, poisonous or noxious substance—which might explain why Jesus refuses to drink it when He tastes it. Most likely though, it was spoiled or bitter wine. Later, when offered vinegar on a sponge (27:48), He drinks it. Vinegar was a form of sour or cheap wine, which was known to relieve thirst better than water.

27:45 From the sixth to the ninth hour (from noon to 3:00 p.m.), there is darkness over all the land, possibly meaning the region of Judea. The darkness is similar in significance to a divine judgment over the land.

27:46 Twice in Matthew's account, Jesus cries out with a loud voice, here and in verse 50. The first time He adds the words in Aramaic, but Matthew translates them for us into Greek: "My God, my God, why hast thou forsaken me?" Scholars have been divided over exactly what Jesus meant by this expression in which He quotes Psalm 22:1, a lament psalm. (Lament psalms were characterized by a similar structure: first a complaint, then trust, then deliverance, and finally praise.) Matthew offers no explanation for Jesus' cry.

27:54 Perhaps the most important event in this section of the Gospel narrative is the comment of the Roman centurion and his companions—"Truly this was the Son of God." These people saw what the Jewish leaders did not see. Luke adds that the centurion praises God and claims Jesus' innocence (Luke 23:47).

27:62–66 The guard is to make the tomb secure. This is the sabbath, and by now Jesus has been in the tomb all of Friday night. It is certain that the guard would have inspected the tomb. The tomb's being made secure must have implied some sort of official seal. The resurrection of Jesus was not then something unknown, unexpected, or unpredicted. The Jewish authorities knew about it, they did not believe it, and they expected the disciples to make some effort to steal the body. Any attempt to steal the body was, therefore, rendered highly improbable.

28:1–2 It is because of the resurrection of Jesus on Sunday that Sunday became the holy and special day of worship for Christians (Acts 20:7; 1 Corinthians 16:2). The day became known as the Lord's day (Revelation 1:10). The two women go to the tomb, most likely to mourn the death of Jesus. As in the previous chapter, there is a great earthquake, signifying some divine intervention, and an angel appears and rolls back the stone, unsealing the mouth of the tomb. It certainly would have been too heavy for two women to roll it back.

28:8 The women leave quickly with mixed emotions—fear and great joy. Fear because remarkable and strange things have happened. Jesus has risen! An angel appeared! There was a great earthquake! Any one of these events would cause fear in most people. But they are also filled with great joy—Jesus is not dead, and He is going to meet the disciples in Galilee.

28:11–15 It isn't surprising that the duplicitous chief priests and the Sanhedrin would have to do something to keep the guards at the tomb quiet. As they have done before, they are willing to pay a bribe to achieve their purposes. They tell the guards to say that the disciples had come during the night and stolen the body. The chief priests will take care of any concerns of the governor that the soldiers did not adequately guard the tomb. As a result, the story of the disciples stealing the body of Jesus spreads quickly. However, it is surprising that no disciple ever confesses to stealing the body of Jesus or knowing of those who did steal the body, even under dire circumstances—persecution and martyrdom.

28:18–20 This final passage is a key to the whole Gospel narrative. It concerns making disciples of all nations. Matthew's Jewish community would need to know Jesus had commissioned His apostles for this purpose—including Matthew's readers. The eleven disciples meet Jesus on a mountain in Galilee, just as Jesus had instructed them through the two women. In commissioning His disciples and sending them out as apostles to make disciples of all nations, Jesus promises to always be with them. The apostles will not be alone as they preach; Jesus will be with them in power and spirit.

THE GOSPEL ACCORDING TO

MARK

INTRODUCTION TO MARK ■ The book of Mark is the shortest of the four Gospels and is considered by many to be the oldest. It may well have served as a source for the Gospels of Matthew and Luke. It was the opinion of the early church that Mark, the author, recorded the Gospel that Peter preached.

AUTHOR ■ The writer of Mark never identifies himself, yet no serious suggestion of an author other than Mark has been put forward. John Mark was a young disciple who had traveled with Paul and Barnabas on their first missionary journey (Acts 13–14) but deserted them. His actions later caused such a rift between the two missionaries that they went their separate ways (Acts 15:36–41). Yet Mark's subsequent spiritual growth and faithfulness eventually earned Paul's trust once more (2 Timothy 4:11).

OCCASION ■ Mark probably wrote from Rome to an audience primarily comprised of Gentile Christians to provide them with a defense of the Gospel and encourage them in their faith. The content of the Gospel contains several indications of Mark's Roman and Gentile audience. He uses ten Latin words, some of which are found nowhere else in scripture; he makes a point to explain Jewish traditions; no genealogy is found for Jesus, as in Matthew and Luke; and he doesn't go into geographic or historic detail because his audience would not have been familiar with such Palestinian matters.

1:2–3 The prophets had foretold not only a Messiah to come but also a messenger—an Elias (or Elijah)—to prepare the way. Mark quotes from Isaiah 40:3 and Malachi 3:1. He inserts these reminders to introduce John the Baptist.

1:6 Mark's physical description of John the Baptist—his unique diet and style of dress—creates an additional connection between the new prophet and the Old Testament Elias (Elijah; see 2 Kings 1:8).

1:7 Even though John must have been a powerful presence, his message of repentance is based on the anticipation of "one mightier than I." John's comment about his own unworthiness to unloose Jesus' sandals—the work of a slave—is a vivid image of the homage he pays to Jesus and the work He will do.

1:9–13 Even though John had proclaimed Jesus to be much greater than himself, Jesus came to be baptized by John. At this time, God makes a statement about Jesus that He has never made about anyone after the fall of Adam. Because of the prevalence of sin, no human being can please God. Yet Jesus came to do for us what we are unable to do for ourselves.

1:13 Mark mentions wild beasts present in the wilderness. God had placed Adam in a beautiful and peaceful garden over which he had dominion, yet Adam lost that privilege due to his sin. Jesus is sent into a dangerous setting yet overcomes physical dangers and spiritual temptations to reestablish the kingdom of God on earth—a kingdom marked by peace and righteousness (Isaiah 11:6–9; 35:9). It seems clear that Jesus' spiritual temptations are severe, because angels are there to minister to Him and encourage Him.

1:14 Jesus begins His public ministry as John the Baptist is completing his. John has been put in prison and will not emerge alive (6:17–29).

1:15 Jesus continues John's message that the kingdom of God is near and that people should repent and believe the good news (see also Matthew 3:1–2). The good news is twofold: (1) Because of Jesus, the kingdom of God has come to earth; and (2) through Jesus, salvation is given to all who believe. The only way to enter God's kingdom is by believing the good news that Jesus came to take the punishment of humankind. Through belief in Him, the very righteousness of God will be bestowed as a person is reconciled to Him.

1:21–28 Jesus' authority as a teacher is authenticated by the power He displays. The first miracle Mark records is the casting out of an evil spirit from a possessed man at a synagogue in Capernaum. The crowd is already amazed at Jesus' teaching, but becomes even more astounded when He rids the troubled man of the evil spirit. Note that the demon knows exactly who Jesus is—in regard to both His humanity ("Jesus of Nazareth") and His divinity ("the Holy One of God"). And even though Jesus sternly commands the spirit to keep quiet, news about Jesus quickly spreads.

1:29–34 When Jesus and His followers leave the synagogue, they presumably go to the home of Simon and Andrew for their sabbath meal. There they find Simon Peter's mother-in-law in bed with a fever—a very serious condition in the first century. Jesus' healing allows her to rise immediately and begin to wait on her guests—an honor for a woman during this time. The sabbath ended at sundown, at which time "all the city was gathered" at the house.

1:35–39 Even after the long healing session at Simon Peter's house (see 1:34), Jesus arises very early the next morning and finds a solitary place to pray. His solitude doesn't last long, however, because the crowds are soon looking for Him again. But Jesus opts to move on to other places. He has come to spread the Word of God—not just to heal the sick.

2:1–12 Jesus returns to Capernaum. Again huge crowds assemble to hear Him speak. This time He is in a house, and it is filled beyond capacity. Most Palestinian homes had one to four rooms, and the crowd at this one fills the house and sprawls outside.

2:3–4 While Jesus is speaking, five men arrive: four carrying a fifth who is paralyzed. When they realize they can get nowhere close to Jesus, they improvise a plan to go through the roof. Many first-century homes had an outside staircase leading to a flat roof made of branches and sod. It would not be difficult to make an opening in the roof and lower their friend.

2:5–7 Considering the unusual entrance of the man (2:4), Jesus' first words to him are surprising. For one thing, Jesus surely knows the man has come for physical healing, not spiritual forgiveness. For another, His words trigger a negative response from the scribes among the crowd. Jesus perceives the faith of the five men, and Mark frequently associates the presence of faith with the performance of miracles by Jesus. Even though Jesus uses the passive voice in making His statement, His intent is not missed by skeptical listeners. The Jews believed that only God was capable of forgiving sin. Similar claims by anyone else were blasphemy (irreverent, profane, impious speech about God that held a sentence of death for those found guilty [Leviticus 24:16]).

2:10 This is the first place in Mark where Jesus calls himself "the Son of man," although Jesus will use this term as His favorite self-designation. The vagueness of the phrase carries overtones of both humanity and deity (Daniel 7:13–14). By using it, Jesus forces people to make up their own minds about Him. If He had spoken publicly of being the Messiah (Christ), it would have quickly created problems in the politically and religiously charged culture of the time.

2:21–22 The fasting of the Pharisees was not necessary because it represented an old way of doing things. With the onset of the kingdom of God on earth, certain things were going to change. The traditions of scribal Judaism were like the old garment and the old wine bottle. The "old" was not inherently wrong, but its time had passed. The old ways would not smoothly merge with Jesus' new teachings; they had to be replaced with something better.

2:23–26 The Old Testament clearly forbade work on the sabbath (Exodus 20:8–11), but the scribes had so meticulously defined "work" that they had a list of thirty-nine different prohibitions. Third on their list was "reaping," which is their accusation against Jesus and His disciples. Since Jesus' followers were only feeding themselves, Jesus has a ready response. He refers His accusers to the story of David (1 Samuel 21:1–6), who used consecrated bread out of the tabernacle to feed his men.

2:27–28 Jesus emphasizes that the sabbath was created to refresh people—not to enslave them with legalistic restrictions.

3:1–6 For the Pharisees, sabbath observance was one of the most important elements in Judaism and a noticeable distinction between Jews and Gentiles. When Jesus begins to challenge their long-held standards, they become enraged. And when the conflict isn't quickly resolved, they even begin to plot to kill Him.

3:6 The irony here is that while Jesus is doing good on the sabbath, His opponents are plotting murder.

3:11–12 Again Jesus encounters evil spirits (1:23–24, 34). This time they are acknowledging Him as the "Son of God," but He forces them to remain quiet about His identity.

3:13–19 Mark has already written about Jesus' call of Andrew, Simon, James, John (1:14–20), and later Levi (2:13–14). Here he provides the list of the twelve disciples chosen from the rest. They would be designated *apostles*, meaning "sent ones," in contrast to crowds of other disciples who followed Jesus as well. They would be the first to understand His plan of redemption and to spread the good news of that plan around the world.

3:22–27 Jesus says it is foolish to think that someone possessed by the prince of the devils would go around casting demons out of other people. He uses three consecutive short parables to make His point. The first two are self-explanatory. The third one, however, can be confusing. The "strong man" is a reference to Satan, who possesses a number of people. The one capable of entering his house and carrying off his possessions is Jesus, who came to earth and began setting people free by exorcising demons. He will soon break the hold of sin and death for good with His sacrificial death.

3:28–30 To understand these verses, we have to understand the context. Jesus has recently cast out a number of demons using the miraculous power of God. But the scribes accuse Jesus of acting under the power of evil. Jesus explains that those who attribute the power of the Holy Spirit to Satan have no way of being forgiven. This sin is apparently quite rare because it requires being faced with the power of Jesus and then declaring it the work of the devil.

3:31–35 As Jesus faces skeptics and doubters both within and outside His family, we see quite a difference in scale. Jesus' family members thought He was crazy, yet they weren't as off-base as the scribes. Jesus' response shows a shift in thinking. Jesus is now speaking of God's family, not His own human family unit. This passage surely encouraged Mark's Gentile readers, as it does modern Christians. It is difficult to think of a more meaningful symbol than inclusion in the family of God.

4:3–9 Jesus begins and ends the parable by telling His audience to listen thoughtfully, indicating that the meaning of parables is not always self-evident. The parable of the sower is short, clear, and true to what is known about Palestinian agriculture. Unlike the modern method of planting, seeds were first sown and then plowed underground. The sower held a quantity of seed in an apron with one hand and used his other hand to broadcast it. Naturally, some seeds would fall on the hardened path through the field, some where the soil was too shallow, and some among thorns. (The stones and thistles that infest Palestinian fields to this day are legendary.)

4:10–12 The parables are the means through which God provides two opposing works: revelation and concealment. In the revelation of the kingdom of God, His people are trained and instructed in the requirements of the kingdom. In the concealment of the kingdom, those who oppose God are prevented, as a form of punishment, from ever understanding the true nature and requirements of the kingdom. Unless one understands this dual purpose of the parables, there will be no proper interpretation, and therefore the clear and intended meanings of the parables will be lost.

4:13–20 Jesus' explanation of the parable provides surprising insight. The symbolism of the sower is not explained, but the context indicates he is Jesus. The seed is the Word of God. Soils are different kinds of hearers. Birds represent Satan. Thorns are the worries of life. Jesus seems to say that there are those who can hear His message, respond for days, months, or even years, and still not have the gospel take root in their lives. But those who hear and respond will bear spiritual fruit, with varying yields.

4:26–29 The point of this parable is that as the disciples work to cast the seed of the Gospel, the ultimate results are the work of God. The sowers are not in charge of the hearts of the people, nor can they change others. All they can do is cast the seed and trust God for the outcome. Followers of Jesus must understand that they do not cause the harvest but must spread the seed.

4:30–32 Although an herb, the mustard plant begins as a tiny seed and can grow to heights of ten to twelve feet with a stalk three to four inches in diameter. It is clear that the mustard plant symbolizes the extreme contrast between the tiny beginning and ultimate result of the kingdom of God. Mark is writing his Gospel at a time near the beginning of the growth cycle when the kingdom might not have appeared very significant in contrast to other earthly kingdoms such as the Roman Empire. Yet this parable points to a much greater impact to come.

4:35–41 Most of the recorded miracles of Jesus were healings and exorcisms. This miracle, however, is important because it establishes Jesus' authority over nature just as His healings show His power over humanity. Jesus is the Lord of nature as much as He is the Lord of individuals. The disciples know Jesus is a great man with great power, yet they never imagined *this* kind of power could exist. They are astounded, but their faith remains weak.

5:7 The demon within the man recognizes Jesus and is afraid. In contrast to the disciples' recent fear that was based on their ignorance, the demon's fear is a result of knowing with whom he is dealing.

5:9 The spirit gives his name as *Legion*, which was a term used to describe a Roman force of four thousand to six thousand men. It is unclear whether the word in

this sense refers to a proper name, an arrogant boast, or an attempt to avoid providing an actual name. The usual interpretation is that many demons actually possessed this man.

5:13 The demon(s) realize Jesus is in complete control of what is going to happen. Rather than being cast out of the area, they beg to move into a nearby herd of swine. When Jesus grants them permission, the entire group of two thousand pigs runs directly into the lake and drowns.

5:18–19 The man, now freed of his demonic tormentors, is most grateful. He begs to go with Jesus, an indication that he realizes Jesus is not only a miracle worker but someone to be followed. Jesus denies his request but gives him a different mission—one that is assigned to every disciple.

5:21–24 Jesus and the apostles have come back across the sea of Galilee after His healing of the demon-possessed man in Gentile territory. He is quite possibly back in Capernaum, and certainly among another Jewish crowd that knows His reputation and is eager to be around Him. One who comes with a specific request is a synagogue ruler named Jairus, but his request is not for himself. He knows of Jesus' reputation for laying hands on people to heal them, and his twelve-year-old daughter (5:42) is near death.

5:25–34 One person in the crowd actually shouldn't be there: a woman with a twelve-year bleeding issue. Mark isn't specific as to her problem, but it may have been uterine bleeding, which would have made her ceremonially unclean. She would have been an outcast for twelve years, with people having no contact with her, and yet here she is among the crowd. Her desperation is understandable. She had been to numerous doctors and had only gotten worse.

5:30 The miracle is extraordinary because it takes place without conscious effort on Jesus' part.

5:40–43 Consider that Jesus could have made a public display of bringing the girl back to life, silencing and shaming His critics. But it is a private moment, an amazing miracle to be witnessed only by those with considerable faith. At Jesus' command, the dead girl immediately stands up and walks.

6:1–6 Because He is a well-known speaker and healer, Jesus is invited to speak at His hometown synagogue. A large crowd is there. The people are amazed at His teaching, but not in a positive way. Instead, they question His credentials. They knew Him better than anyone and were aware that He had never studied with a rabbi. They consider Him nothing more than an ordinary craftsman—no different than His brothers and sisters, and no better than anyone else in Nazareth.

6:7–13 At this time, Jesus sends out the disciples to share the message He has been preaching. They travel in pairs, which was a common Jewish practice. Jesus gives them authority to speak for Him and power over evil spirits. Jesus' instructions suggest the urgency of their mission and the necessity of trusting God for provisions.

6:14–16 When Herod hears of the power of Jesus and His followers, he grows worried that John the Baptist has risen from the dead, so Mark provides us with the account of John's death.

6:17–18 It seems that Herod has fallen in love with his sister-in-law, Herodias, and has divorced his wife and convinced Herodias to divorce her husband in order to get married. John has criticized the marriage, and Herodias wants to have him killed.

6:21–29 Herodias sees an opportunity for revenge at Herod's birthday banquet. She has her daughter (named Salome, according to the historian Josephus) perform a dance for the assembled group of leading men of Galilee. Because he enjoyed the show so much, Herod promises the young dancer anything. At her mother's urging, she asks for the head of John the Baptist on a platter. With all eyes on him, Herod has little choice but to comply, even though he is distressed. John's disciples come to claim his body and bury him.

6:31–34 After their return from ministering to the surrounding villages, the apostles are weary. They had hoped to retreat to a quiet place and rest, but the crowds won't allow it. Even when they leave on a boat, the people note the direction they are headed and get there ahead of them. But arriving to find large crowds doesn't upset Jesus. Instead, He sees their spiritual need, has compassion, and begins to teach them.

6:34 The word translated *compassion* is used in the New Testament only by or about Jesus. It is an emotion that compels action, not merely a feeling of pity. Jesus saw not only physical need but also spiritual lostness. So first He feeds the crowds with His teaching and then addresses their physical hunger.

6:35–37 The disciples see a problem arising and try to head it off. But rather than sending the people home, Jesus tells the disciples to feed them. Having just returned from their mission, they should have had a sense of what God was capable of doing. But rather than using faith, they figure out how much it would cost to feed everyone and determine it can't be done!

6:38–44 Jesus has the disciples collect whatever food they can find, which turns out to be meager indeed. The loaves are smaller and flatter than modern bread. The fish are dried and salted. And the head count is five thousand men (plus women and children).

6:45–48 The disciples were tired before this event, so afterward they must have been exhausted. Jesus has them get in a boat and head toward Bethsaida. He was going to spend a little more time with the people and then have a private time of prayer. From His prayer spot on the mountainside, Jesus can probably see His followers struggling to row against the wind.

6:51 The notation that the disciples were "sore amazed" makes the point that they should have learned by now that nothing is beyond the power of Jesus, because the power of Jesus is the power of God.

7:1–2 This time the Pharisees' complaint is that Jesus' followers eat meals before washing their hands. The issue is not one of hygiene but of ritual purity and is an excellent case in point to describe how oral law had become much more stringent than what Moses had recorded.

7:5–9 In response to the scribes and Pharisees' query, Jesus quotes Isaiah 29:13 to clarify that external observance of religious ceremony is no substitute for inward piety. Their insistence on external righteousness is not in accordance with the scriptures, and they are missing the whole point. It is they who are unclean and not Jesus' disciples. But Jesus doesn't stop with the Isaiah passage. He labels His critics as hypocrites and accuses them of substituting human tradition for God-given law.

7:10–13 Jesus gives a specific example to show how ludicrous the traditions of the Pharisees and scribes have become. It seems that it had become common practice to make an offering of one's financial wealth and devote it to God by invoking a vow ("Corban"). It sounds quite spiritual and selfless. But what such an action actually meant was that the person would retain his wealth throughout his life, and it would go to the temple/priests when he died. If his parents needed assistance in their old age, the person could refuse to provide funds because they were set aside for God. This twisted tradition was just a way to sidestep the clear command to honor one's mother and father.

7:15 Jesus makes it clear that food is not the real issue of defilement. Impurity, He says, is not the result of failing to follow a ritual but rather is the condition of an unredeemed and unregenerate heart.

7:21–22 Jesus explains that the source of uncleanness is already inside a person. His point is that uncleanness is moral rather than ritual.

7:25 A woman finds out Jesus is in the area and rushes to ask Him to heal her daughter who is possessed by an evil spirit. Prostration was a sign of both grief and reverence. By falling at His feet, the woman is showing the utmost respect for Jesus.

7:29–30 Although this account says nothing about the woman's faith, it is certainly implied in Jesus' statement. Jesus responds to her and grants her request. When she gets home, she finds her daughter well, with the demon gone.

7:32–35 A group brings a deaf and mute man to Jesus, but He takes the man aside, away from the crowd. Jesus is going to heal the man but doesn't want the crowds to misinterpret the miracle. The miracle will be a sign authenticating Him as being the Messiah, not an indication that the earthly kingdom of God had arrived in its fullness and everyone could expect to walk around in perfect bodies. This miracle illustrates a running theme in Mark: Only those who have ears to hear can speak with faith.

8:1–3 Jesus and His disciples are still in the region of the Decapolis, a group of cities populated mainly by Gentiles. Crowd after crowd forms to see and hear Him. In this case, a group has been with Him for three days.

Mark doesn't even mention whether Jesus is teaching or healing. Instead, he moves right to the compassion Jesus feels for the people, who are surely hungry after such a long time.

8:4 The disciples are woefully shortsighted. As soon as Jesus expresses the desire to feed the crowd, they immediately respond with the impossibility of finding enough bread "in the wilderness."

8:8 The word used to indicate a basket here is not the same as the one used previously (6:43). This time the reference is to a large basket made of wicker or rope, used for carrying provisions. So the seven basketfuls of leftovers in this account may well have contained more than the twelve basketfuls in the previous miracle.

8:11–12 The "sign" the Pharisees request here is not another healing, exorcism, or feeding. They want to see some kind of apocalyptic manifestation (the sun disappearing, angels appearing, or some similar sign) that will prove beyond all doubt that Jesus has God's approval. Jesus' response is likely a sigh of anger because He knows they aren't sincere in their request—they only want to trip Him up and lessen His influence on the crowds. Jesus did not perform miracles to convince the hard-hearted; He used them to cure those in need and to show compassion to those hurt by sin.

8:14–15 As Jesus and the disciples go back across the sea, He warns them to beware of the "leaven" (or "yeast") of the Pharisees and Herod. Most references to yeast or leaven in the New Testament are symbolic references to evil. (Matthew 13:33 is one exception.) Just as a little yeast changes the complete nature of dough, so too a slight influence of pharisaical teachings could corrupt the truth of the Gospel.

8:22–26 Because of where it is in the narrative, this miracle should be considered an object lesson—a physical demonstration of the spiritual condition of Jesus' disciples. Some people of Bethsaida ask Jesus to heal a blind man. Jesus applies saliva to the man's eyes, lays His hands on him, and asks what he sees. The man's vision has improved because he can see the shapes of men, but they look like walking trees. Jesus again places His hands on the man, and this time the man can see clearly. Similarly, although the disciples' spiritual vision is not yet 20/20, they will eventually come to see clearly who Jesus is.

8:31 Up to this point, Jesus had been revealing the Messiah's power and authority. Here He begins to reveal His suffering role, clarifying for His followers what is involved in God's plan for the Messiah. It will involve not only suffering at the hands of others but ultimately His death as well. Jesus' teachings about His death are specific.

8:34–37 To deny oneself is not a call to asceticism, self-rejection, or self-hatred. Rather, it is to replace the desires of self with the will of God, to set aside all personal rights and live for the glory of God and the mission of extending His kingdom. Jesus challenges His listeners to think of long-term effects of their daily choices. Everyone either lives for self or lives for God. While living for self will have certain benefits, none come close to eternal life with a loving God.

8:38 Living for Jesus includes speaking up for Him, even when persecuted by a sinful and adulterous generation.

9:2 "Transfigured" refers to a radical change in form or appearance. In this account, it is a physical change, as Jesus' appearance is temporarily transformed from that of a human being to a divine being in all His glory. In other places where the word is used, it refers to a dramatic moral transformation from sinner to saint (Romans 12:2; 2 Corinthians 3:18).

9:4–13 Moses and Elias (Elijah) represent the law and the prophets. Jesus was the fulfillment of the ancient scriptures. Christianity would not be a new religion, nor a correction of Judaism. Rather, it is the fulfillment of what had been proclaimed through the Old Testament writings.

9:14–29 The disciples had previously been able to exorcise demons (6:13) and apparently assumed they could do so whenever they wished. But in this case, they lack faith. Spiritual power is not a resource that, once possessed, will always be available.

9:28–29 The disciples are frustrated and confused about not being able to cast out the demon on their own. While Jesus has spoken about faith on numerous occasions, here He adds the importance of prayer as well. The two go hand in hand. Prayer is the avenue to faith. The power the disciples lack can come only from God, and therefore is available only through faith and prayer.

9:30–31 Jesus is again seeking privacy for Himself and His disciples, but this time it is not due to danger from Herod (6:14) or the teachers of the law (9:14). Rather, He wants to continue to instruct His disciples about His upcoming betrayal, death, and resurrection. The word *delivered* means "given over" or "handed over." The same word is used to refer to Judas's betrayal of Jesus as well as the fate of the Old Testament prophets, John the Baptist, and eventually Jesus' disciples.

9:32–34 Mark again emphasizes the dullness of the disciples. By this time, they are even embarrassed to ask Jesus to explain what He means. Jesus knows their minds are on less noble things. When He asks what they are discussing, they won't respond. But Mark informs us that they are arguing about which of them is the greatest.

9:38–41 The disciples were accustomed to thinking of spiritual leadership in terms of exclusivity. The scribes and Pharisees, for example, were exclusive groups. So when the disciples come upon someone else driving out evil spirits in the name of Jesus, they instruct him to stop. And they tell Jesus, thinking He will be pleased. But Jesus makes it clear that anyone who does anything sincerely "in my name" is to be accepted as an ally. Jesus is beginning to promote a mind-set of acceptance rather than rejection.

10:1–9 Jesus is in the territory of Herod, so perhaps His questioners hope to get Him to say something that will incur Herod's displeasure, as John the Baptist had done. But Jesus counters their question with one of His own, which sends them back to their scriptures. He then explains that Moses wasn't by any means promoting divorce, yet he had allowed for it in extreme cases. It was God's intention for marriage to last a lifetime, yet He knew the hardness of the people's hearts and had created a contingency plan.

10:10–12 Jesus' comments are quite contrary to the traditions of Judaism at that time. According to Jewish law, a wife could commit adultery by having relations with another man; a man (single or married) could commit adultery against another man by having relations with that man's wife. But a husband could not be charged with adultery against his own wife by being unfaithful to her. By insisting that a husband can commit adultery against his own wife, Jesus greatly elevates the status of wives and women in general.

10:14–15 Jesus grows "displeased" with His disciples for their treatment of the young children. Anyone who comes to Jesus, regardless of age, should do so with the simple faith and trust of a child. He or she is not to be hindered but encouraged and supported. In ancient society, children were considered irrelevant, totally without social status. Here the traits of children that Jesus is probably referring to are their lowliness and dependence on others. In essence, He is telling His disciples they must be humble and absolutely dependent on God to enter the kingdom. These values help us find and enter the kingdom of God.

10:17–23 The story of Jesus and the rich man must be understood in light of the Jewish attitude toward riches. The dominant Jewish view was that wealth was an indication of divine favor and a reward for righteousness. Although provision was made for the protection and assistance of the poor, rarely was poverty associated with piety.

10:28–30 After Peter takes a stab at saying the disciples had tried to do as Jesus said, Jesus turns from warning to promise. Jesus is not encouraging people to walk away from their families, but He is telling His followers to keep their priorities straight. Following Jesus can be costly, because along with blessing comes persecution. Yet, ultimately, the eternal rewards will far outweigh any sacrifices made in order to obtain them.

10:37–40 The disciples are still anticipating an earthly reign, and they want positions of authority when the time comes. In Jewish thought, the right hand of the king was the place of greatest prominence; his left hand was the second most coveted seat. But James and John are missing the point. Jesus doesn't rebuke them directly but indicates that they do not realize the implications of their request.

10:41–45 By aspiring to positions of greatness, the disciples are thinking like Gentile rulers. And as a result, dissension runs through their ranks. Jesus emphatically

states that His disciples must be like servants—even slaves.

10:46–51 When Jesus and His disciples reach Jericho, they encounter a blind man name Bartimaeus among a large crowd. Bartimaeus addresses Jesus as "son of David." The crowd tries to shush the blind man, but he is determined to get Jesus' attention. Jesus finally calls him forward. Mark provides the interesting detail of the man casting off his garment (possibly used as a pallet), showing that Bartimaeus is casting aside everything to stand before Jesus. He has real and passionate faith. And when Jesus asks what he wants, he is quick with his response.

10:52 Again Mark emphasizes the importance of faith. The man calls out to Jesus, and Jesus saves him. His eyes are opened. He is healed physically and saved spiritually. And he immediately begins to follow Jesus.

11:1–6 Jesus is not improvising as He goes along. Jesus' choice of a donkey's colt is very important because it demonstrates an unusual level of humility. Those who rode donkeys were usually people of humble means. If a king rode a donkey into a city, it was to proclaim peace rather than to declare war. Therefore Jesus enters Jerusalem making a statement of humility and peace. He is not coming to claim the military or political leadership of Israel. Without such a display of humility by Jesus, we would never be able to understand the level of humility that God loves and expects from us.

11:7–10 The crowds recognize the significance of Jesus' entrance into Jerusalem and respond with signs of respect. The spreading of garments pays homage to royalty (2 Kings 9:13), as does the waving of branches. The verbal shouts are additional signs of honor. Although Jesus demonstrates complete humility in what He is doing, He is also fulfilling the mission He has come to do and is glorifying God in the process. So God ensures that, at least for this short ride into Jerusalem, Jesus receives worship and honor.

11:17 While the pilgrims in Jerusalem would have benefited from the services of the moneychangers and animal sellers, the temple was not a proper location to conduct business. Even if the merchants weren't price gouging, they were "thieves" in the sense that they were robbing the Gentiles of unhindered worship opportunities.

11:27–28 Upon Jesus' return to the temple, He is confronted by a delegation of chief priests, scribes, and elders from the Sanhedrin—the Jewish religious ruling body. They want to know by whose authority He had driven out the temple moneychangers and animal sellers.

11:29–30 Rather than defend His actions, Jesus answers their question with a question of His own, posed to show that their motives are not about seeking the truth as much as about staying in power and maintaining popularity. He isn't attempting to evade their question but rather to establish the source of His authority in the spiritual realm.

11:30–33 At issue is the authority of John the Baptist. The clear implication of Jesus' question is that John's ministry was divinely authorized. And if so, since John had endorsed the ministry of Jesus, then the religious leaders should recognize Jesus' authority. Of course, the religious authorities would never concede that John was a prophet from God. But John had been popular with the crowds, so the religious leaders don't dare voice their opinion.

12:1–9 This parable of the wicked husbandmen is very similar to a prophecy of Isaiah (Isaiah 5:1–7). In both cases, the vineyard clearly represents Israel, and the owner represents God. In the Isaiah account, the problem was that the vineyard failed to produce the fruits of righteousness. In Jesus' variation, the problem is with the husbandmen (the religious authorities) who refuse to serve the owner due to their wickedness (greed, dishonesty, violence, and murder).

12:12 The religious leaders who continue to oppose Jesus realize this parable is about them. If Jesus was right, it meant that God would soon reject them. But rather than change their opinion, they are all the more determined to have Jesus arrested. This is an irony in Mark's Gospel; while previous parables concealed the truth from the religious leaders, this one reveals it to them and so provokes Jesus' crucifixion.

12:13–17 A short time later a group of Pharisees and Herodians goes to Jesus in an attempt to "catch him in his words." Although what they say about Jesus is true, Mark reveals their shady motives by showing that it is insincere flattery. Jesus sees right through their hypocrisy and calls them on it. Ironically, Jesus doesn't have a coin, but His opponents do. The insertion of this fact might be another indication that they implicitly recognized the authority of the emperor, thereby exposing themselves as hypocrites.

12:25 Jesus teaches that resurrection life will be different from earthly life. "As the angels" may indicate either a sexless state or an emphasis on serving and worshipping God. Relationships in heaven will be of such a degree that they will satisfy better than the best relationships on earth. Sin, grief, and loss will be left behind as believers experience the surpassing joy of new and more powerful relationships.

12:26–27 Addressing the Sadducees' disbelief in resurrection, Jesus quotes from Exodus 3:6. When God spoke in present tense of being the God of Abraham, Isaac, and Jacob, He indicated that those patriarchs were still alive—an implication of resurrection. And to make things perfectly clear, Jesus emphasizes that the Lord is not God of the dead but of the living.

12:28–31 Jesus quotes from Deuteronomy 6:4–5 (the first part of the Jewish *Shema*) and Leviticus 19:18. In doing so, He teaches that in loving God and one's neighbour, a person fulfills the entire law of God. Jesus brings together the commands to love God and to love fellow human beings.

12:34 By deeming the man "not far from the kingdom of God," Jesus is encouraging him to go the rest of the way with wholehearted devotion.

12:38–39 Jesus refutes the showiness that has come to symbolize proper worship. The reference to "long clothing" (like flowing robes) probably refers to the *tallith*, a shawl worn during formal prayers and ceremonies. Some scribes might have worn one to attract attention.

12:41–44 The amount of each of the widow's two mites would have been one sixty-fourth of a denarius—a denarius being equal to a day's wage. Jesus observes her selfless gift and points out that the amount of a gift is weighed by how much remains for one's personal use afterward. The widow's giving of everything she has to live on demonstrates her absolute trust in God—a far more significant gift than anyone else had given.

13:1–4 Jesus acknowledges the greatness of the buildings but predicts a day when "there shall not be left one stone upon another." Naturally the disciples want more details, so Jesus gives His followers signs to look for—but not specifics (13:7–14).

13:5–6 In Jesus' expansive answer to the disciples' questions, He identifies signs that will indicate the coming destruction of Jerusalem and/or the end of the world. It's interesting to note that Jesus' first warning sign is deceit—many people will come claiming to be the Christ and recruit a lot of followers.

13:8 Earthquakes and famines will only be the beginning of the problem. The reference to "sorrows" (often translated "birth pains") should have been familiar to any Jewish people with a knowledge of their scriptures. It was a common metaphor to symbolize anticipation of a significant event (see Isaiah 13:8; 26:17–18; Jeremiah 4:31; 50:43; Hosea 13:13; Micah 4:9–10).

13:9, 11–13 The followers of Jesus will be opposed and handed over to the courts, where they will be sentenced to punishment or death. The Gospel will be rejected as the religious establishment seeks to silence the message of Jesus.

13:10 None of these signs can silence the Gospel. Even in the midst of horrendous times and catastrophic events, God's Word will continue to be preached, and His kingdom will advance.

13:14–23 "The abomination of desolation" is a phrase found in Daniel's prophecies (Daniel 9:27; 11:31; 12:11). The word *abomination* indicates something repulsive to God and His people. *Desolation* suggests that as a result of its profanation, the true people of God abandon the temple. Daniel's prediction came true when Antiochus IV Epiphanes of Seleucid Syria erected a statue of Zeus Olympus in the Jerusalem temple in 167 BC. Jesus' use of the phrase most likely refers to the coming profanation of the temple by the Romans just prior to its destruction in AD 70. During this siege, Titus would enter the most holy place and remove various items, taking them to Rome to adorn his victory procession. However, a second meaning can also be taken to refer to a future sacrilege by another profane and oppressive person, possibly the "man of sin" Paul writes about in 2 Thessalonians 2:1–12.

13:28–29 Jesus compares the coming of the Son of man with the approach of summer. Jesus uses a fig tree in His example because so many other trees in Palestine are evergreens. But the fig tree loses its leaves in winter, and the reappearance of leaves is a sign of summer. Similarly, the signs Jesus has been describing are certain to lead to His return.

13:30 "This generation" refers to the contemporaries of Jesus. Some of them—particularly some of His disciples—will not die until the events of 13:5–23 have taken place, including the destruction of the temple. To a limited extent, here Jesus answers the question asked in 13:4.

13:32–33 No one except God knows the exact time of the coming of Christ. But by referring to the event as "that day," Mark taps into the richness of the Old Testament writings about the day of the Lord—a day of judgment for both Israel and the surrounding nations (Amos 5:18–20; Zephaniah 1:7, 14–16). The day marks the end of the present evil age and the beginning of the coming age of righteousness.

14:3 While Jesus is reclining at the table (the traditional posture during more formal meals and dinner parties in that time and culture), a woman approaches Him. That is unusual in itself, because Jewish women didn't normally attend banquets for men except as servants. But in addition, she breaks an alabaster box of very expensive spikenard (aromatic oil probably imported from India) and pours the entire contents on Jesus' head. Mark doesn't explain the woman's motives. (John indicates this woman is Jesus' friend Mary [John 12:3].)

14:10–11 In stark contrast to the woman's devotion to Jesus (14:3–9), Mark inserts Judas's decision to betray Jesus at this point. Mark has only mentioned Judas once previously, and that was in a list of the disciples (3:19). Nothing is said of Judas's motive. Judas's cooperation sets in motion the religious leaders' plan to have Jesus put to death.

14:17–20 Jesus has already made it clear that He will be betrayed and put to death. The observation that Jesus' betrayer is a close friend is intended to show the extent of Judas's crime. In ancient Semitic society, eating together was one of the most meaningful indications of friendship. Few actions were more despicable than betraying a friend at, or immediately after, a shared meal.

14:19–21 The very celebration of passover is a reminder that death is necessary to provide salvation. Yet the one who betrays Jesus will face a horrible consequence. At the time, all the disciples are afraid Jesus might be talking about them.

14:22–24 At some point during this passover, Jesus institutes a new meal for His followers. It begins with giving thanks, followed by the proclamation that the bread is Jesus' body and the cup (wine) His blood. Up until this point, passover recalled the lamb that was slain to preserve life just prior to Israel's exodus from Egypt. In the future, however, the celebration would become a remembrance of the body of Jesus offered up as our substitute and His blood shed to provide the forgiveness of our sins.

14:31 The vehemence of Peter's affirmation of loyalty makes his failure all the greater. The fact that scripture portrays its main characters with such honest and unflattering examples is one indication of its trustworthiness.

14:37–41 The disciples, as usual, are lost as to what is really happening. When Jesus checks on them, they are sleeping off a good meal. Even after Jesus specifically asks them to pray with Him, they fall asleep a second and a third time.

14:47–49 We know from John's account of this story that the disciple with the sword is Peter (John 18:10). He makes an initial futile effort to defend his Master, but he is a fisherman, not a soldier. Jesus repairs the damage Peter has done to the servant's ear (Luke 22:51) and then addresses the crowd. His comments point out the wickedness and deception of His adversaries.

14:51–52 The unusual notation about the young man who ran away naked has led to much speculation that he was John Mark, the author of the Gospel. The upper room where Jesus had celebrated passover might have been owned by Mark's mother, and Mark could have followed the group after dinner. The word translated *naked* could mean completely naked or wearing only a loincloth.

14:53–59 The religious leaders have made an arrest but have no evidence to formally charge Jesus. The trial should have been public, but they are trying to get it done under the cover of night. Before imposing a death penalty, Jewish law required the agreement of two (if not three) witnesses, but no two people will agree. The religious leaders' scheme is backfiring, so Jesus has no need to speak. His silence during this period fulfills prophecies such as Psalm 38:13–14 and Isaiah 53:7.

14:60–62 Jesus is leaving no doubt—neither for His accusers nor for His followers. Not only is He the Messiah, but He is also going back to His Father and will return to earth one day in all His power.

14:63–64 Rending (tearing) one's clothes was usually a dramatic symbol of grief or alarm; in this case it is an official act expressing indignation. By claiming to sit at God's right hand, predicting a return from heaven, and using the divine name "I am" (14:62), Jesus is clearly claiming to be God. The priest accused Jesus of blasphemy and "condemned him to be guilty of death."

14:65 The irony in this verse becomes apparent in retrospect. The hostile crowd beats Jesus and challenges Him to "prophesy" because they think He can't. Yet their very actions are fulfilling His own previous prophecy (10:33–34) as well as Old Testament prophecies such as Isaiah 50:6; 53:3–5; and Micah 5:1.

14:66–72 Peter tries to remain anonymous. To his credit, he has at least tried to stay close to Jesus. While there, however, Peter denies Christ. As soon as his third denial leaves his mouth, a rooster crows a second time and Peter recalls Jesus' prediction. In response, Peter weeps. His great failure is recorded in all four Gospels. There is no attempted cover-up of the fact that the man who insightfully confessed Jesus' messiahship at Caesarea Philippi (8:29) later denies Him three times.

15:2 Pilate's first question to Jesus gets right to the heart of the charge. The phrase "King of the Jews" doesn't appear in Mark until this point, yet it is used five times in chapter 15. By doing so, Mark calls attention to the fact that Jesus died as the King of the Jews.

15:7–11 Mark records another irony with his account of Barabbas. After showing how the religious leaders have gone to such lengths to position Jesus as a threat to Rome, Pilate then places Him up against an already convicted insurrectionist. It seems that Pilate is attempting to see that Jesus is set free. Pilate's attempt to release Jesus is probably based less on motives of humanity and justice than on his contempt for the men who are railroading Jesus. It surely wasn't hard for a politically astute ruler to see that the Jewish leadership was envious of Jesus and that the entire procedure was a sham.

15:17–18 Purple cloth was very expensive, so the color purple is associated with royalty. The crown of thorns is a mocking parody of the emperor's laurel wreath. The soldiers' shout, "Hail, King of the Jews," is an imitation of their salute, "Hail, Caesar the Emperor."

15:21 We know that Jesus started toward Golgotha bearing His own cross (John 19:17). But the fact that Simon is recruited to help Him carry it indicates that Jesus must be very weak at this point.

15:22 *Golgotha* is a Greek form of the Aramaic word for "skull." None of the Gospel writers provide a location or description of the place. Both Jews and Romans customarily executed people in public places, but outside the city.

15:24 Crucifixion was one of the most horrifying forms of execution ever devised. After being stripped and flogged, the victim was lashed and/or nailed to a wooden pole. Death usually came slowly as a result of exposure and exhaustion. Inasmuch as no vital organ was damaged, it often took two or three days for the subject to die, although death could be hastened by breaking the legs, making breathing much more difficult. The usual practice was for the condemned person to carry the crossbar to the place of execution, where he was affixed to it before being hoisted upon the vertical pole that was permanently fixed.

15:27 The word translated *thieves* probably means "insurrectionists" or "rebels." Perhaps these men were among the group Barabbas was involved with (15:7).

15:33 Mark records two apocalyptic signs that accompany the death of Jesus. The first is eerie darkness for three hours (noon until 3:00 p.m.). The second is described in verse 38.

15:38 The second of Mark's recorded apocalyptic signs occurs at the moment of Jesus' death. The tearing of the temple veil (or curtain) represents the climax of the replacement of the temple motif throughout Mark (11:12–25; 13:2; 14:58). The death of Jesus removes the barrier to the most holy place, opening the door to God.

15:39 Jesus' death has an immediate effect on one of the people closest to Him—a Roman centurion. Although crowds have mocked and taunted Jesus while He has hung on the cross, the centurion sees the way Jesus dies and is convinced of His deity. The fact that a Gentile is the first to recognize that Jesus' status as Son of God is confirmed through His suffering is quite significant. In fact, it foreshadows the expansion of the Gospel mission beyond the Jews into the Gentile nations.

15:40–41 Mark introduces a group of female disciples, three who are named, who are observing Jesus' death from afar. Members of their group will also be at His burial and later at the empty tomb. Although Jesus has been forsaken by His male disciples, these women display great strength and courage.

15:42–47 The Romans did not always permit burials of executed criminals, often leaving the bodies on the cross to rot or be devoured by animals and birds. But the Jews believed a quick and decent burial of the dead—including enemies and criminals—was an act of piety.

16:1–2 Due to the onset of the sabbath, the women who have followed Jesus' ministry have not been able to attend to His body after His death as they wished. But they are ready to go at sunrise on Sunday morning. They are prepared to anoint His body with oils and spices that were probably bought immediately after sunset the previous night when stores opened briefly after the close of the sabbath.

16:3–6 Having been concerned about how they would roll away the stone from the tomb, the women discover they had worried for nothing. The stone is already rolled away—not to make their access easier but to reveal that Jesus is no longer there. The young man wearing a white garment is an angel who confirms that Jesus has indeed risen from the dead. This unexpected event fills the women with alarm. They are not only startled but afraid as well.

16:7–8 The angel tries to comfort the women by assuring them they will see Jesus again and by giving them directions. The oldest and most reliable versions of Mark's Gospel do not include any post-resurrection accounts of Jesus, but Mark makes it very clear in this passage that Jesus has risen. His body has not been stolen or misplaced. He has been resurrected and is alive again. The events of the early morning are a shock to the women.

16:9–20 Because the other Gospels provide such full accounts of appearances of Jesus after His resurrection, it is curious and somewhat frustrating that Mark's writing stopped at 16:8. Perhaps he had written more, but his ending was lost. The scribes who added verses 9–20 pulled from other scriptures as well as historical witnesses to the post-resurrection lives of the apostles. Therefore, the events recorded here are true but not a part of Mark's original record.

THE GOSPEL ACCORDING TO

LUKE

INTRODUCTION TO LUKE ■ As author of this Gospel and its sequel, the book of Acts, Luke is responsible for over a fourth of the content of the Greek New Testament. He brings a distinctive perspective to the writing as well. While many of Jesus' followers had the reputation of being "unlearned and ignorant men" (Acts 4:13), Luke's writing in his opening paragraph displays the sophisticated style of Greek historians. He then moves into smooth, everyday vernacular. His eye for detail is evident in numerous places.

AUTHOR ■ Luke doesn't identify himself in either of the books he wrote, but there has been little dispute that he was the author of both. He was a physician (Colossians 4:14), and notes specifics in several of Jesus' healings that other writers do not. Aside from the Colossians reference, Luke is mentioned only two other times in the New Testament (2 Timothy 4:11; Philemon 24).

OCCASION ■ Evidence points to Luke being a Gentile believer who wrote for a Gentile audience. The primary recipient of both his books was "most excellent Theophilus" (Luke 1:3; Acts 1:1), a title that suggests someone of wealth and authority—perhaps a ranking official. Luke tended to give details about Jewish locations that wouldn't have been necessary for Jewish readers. These and other clues suggest that Luke's intent was explaining the story of Jesus to Gentiles.

1:1–2 Luke immediately acknowledges that numerous people have been writing about Jesus, but he wants to ensure his readers that they will have a trustworthy account based on eyewitness testimony.

1:3 Luke personally sets out to investigate carefully before writing. "Most excellent" was a title of respect. While nothing is known of Luke's recipient, Theophilus, he may have been a Roman official who became a Christian. He very well might have been a Gentile, and perhaps even Luke's financial backer. Regardless, since Luke is writing to an individual concerned with the truth of the gospel of Jesus, his Gospel is appropriate for all interested readers.

1:5–11 Many priests were available to serve in the temple, so various duties were assigned by "lot." The duties were allocated according to the divisions of priests (see 1 Chronicles 24). When it came time for the order of Abia's (Abijah's) division to perform the temple duties, Zacharias was chosen for the very high privilege of burning the incense, which he did either in the morning or in the evening. This was such a high privilege that it might be done by a priest only once in a lifetime. It was a very coveted task. Some of the priests would never have the honor of going into the holy place alone and providing fresh incense that burned continually on the special altar before the most holy place. But while Zacharias is there, the angel Gabriel appears to him.

1:12–17 After getting past the initial shock and fear, Zacharias hears that his wife, Elisabeth, will soon have a child—a very special child, whose purpose will be to prepare the people for the coming of the Lord. He will be filled with the Holy Spirit inside his mother's womb (1:41, 44). While it's understandable from a human perspective that Zacharias has difficulty believing this amazing thing is happening to him, there are a number of examples of supernatural births in the Old Testament with which he is certainly familiar. Abraham and Sarah had a son in their old age, as did Hannah and the parents of Samson.

1:20 Zacharias is understandably confused and skeptical because of his and Elisabeth's advanced age. Because of his doubts, and to signify that something special has indeed occurred, Zacharias's ability to speak is temporarily suspended. It will be restored when the promised child is born.

1:21–25 The people outside the temple are growing restless. Zacharias is supposed to lead a blessing when he comes out, and it shouldn't have taken very long to light the incense. In addition, the people waiting would be well familiar with the story about the sons of Aaron, who were put to death because they had performed this very function with an improper attitude (Leviticus 10:1–2). Even after Zacharias emerges from the temple, it takes them all awhile to determine what has happened. But it doesn't take long for Gabriel's prophecy to come true.

1:32–33 Gabriel's announcement to Mary is significant for many reasons, including the declaration that Jesus will be the Messiah who will fulfill God's promise to King David. This promise is recorded in 2 Samuel 7, particularly in verses 10–16. Nathan's prophecy from God was that King David's family (of which Jesus would be a descendant) would rule forever.

1:34 Mary is quite a contrast to Zacharias in age, gender, and marital status. Yet Gabriel gives her a similar impossible prediction. After her initial surprise at being addressed as "highly favoured" (1:28), she is also confused at how she can be pregnant having never had sex. This is an additional contrast: Zacharias had been somewhat doubtful, but Mary is only seeking clarification in order to comply with God's message.

1:36–37 Both Mary and Elisabeth are learning that nothing is impossible with God. Gabriel identifies them as relatives, but their relationship is never explained. We aren't told how much each woman knew of the other's story prior to Mary's visit.

1:41–45 No sooner did Mary greet Elisabeth than Elisabeth's child "leaped in her womb." Filled with the Holy Spirit, Elisabeth immediately recognizes the importance of the child Mary will bear, as well as the significance of the son she is carrying.

1:46–55 Mary's song, called the Magnificat, reflects a great depth of spiritual understanding. Her praise is buoyed with numerous Old Testament references and allusions. It begins with her personal expression of humility and expands to reflect God's grace to His chosen people, Israel.

1:56 Elisabeth is six months pregnant when Mary arrives (see 1:36), and Mary stays three months. We can speculate that she was present for the birth of John, after which she returned home to complete her own pregnancy.

1:59–63 In first-century Middle Eastern culture, being named after a father or other family member indicated intent to follow in his steps. But John will not become a priest like Zacharias. He will have his own distinct ministry.

1:65 The first to hear of these astonishing events (and to respond in awe) are not the religious elite in Jerusalem but simple people living in the hill country. The announcement foreshadows the later ministries of Jesus and John, who come not to the healthy and the righteous, but to the sick and to sinners (see Matthew 9:12–13).

1:67–79 As Elisabeth and Mary had done previously, Zacharias uses his renewed power of speech to praise God. His Spirit-inspired proclamation is more prophetic than Mary's, laying out John's purpose in life as well as his relationship to Jesus. Like Mary, Zacharias focuses on God's plan for the nation of Israel.

1:80 Luke's concluding statement for this account, though short, summarizes about thirty years of John's life. John's spiritual strength will be developed in solitude for eventual use in his public ministry.

2:1–20 The details of Jesus' birth are surprisingly scarce in the Bible. Mark and John ignore them altogether. Matthew provides a few stories surrounding the birth. Luke is the only Gospel writer to cover the birth itself.

2:1–4 The taxing (or census) was a painful reminder that the Jewish people were under the rule of a pagan power. Yet it serves to send Mary and Joseph to Bethlehem, the place where the prophet Micah had long ago predicted the Jewish Messiah would be born (see Micah 5:2). The journey from Nazareth to Bethlehem is more than sixty miles and would have taken at least three days.

2:5 Luke points out that Mary was Joseph's "espoused wife" at this point. Matthew calls them husband and wife (Matthew 1:19, 24), titles that were used as soon as an

engagement was formally announced. To ensure the purity of the bride, the engagement was followed by a one-year period of abstinence—after which a ceremony would be held, the relationship would be consummated, and the couple would begin living together.

2:8 The ancient Egyptians looked down on shepherds (Genesis 46:33–34), yet Israelite leaders such as David and Moses were shepherds. God Himself is described as a shepherd (see Psalm 23).

2:12 The promised sign was not meant to convince the shepherds of the truth of the angelic announcement. Surely the splendor of the heavenly host was convincing enough. This sign is for the purpose of identification. The shepherds would recognize God's Messiah by His swaddling clothes and unusual crib—circumstances unique to His birth. In addition, these circumstances powerfully identify Jesus with the shepherds. The Lord seemingly has no roof over His head and no house to dwell in. Neither do the shepherds, who sleep under the stars as they care for their flocks (2:8). Jesus is poor and of no reputation, as are they. And Jesus is said to be both the sacrificial Lamb of God (see Isaiah 53:4–7; John 1:29) and our Shepherd (see Ezekiel 34:23; John 10:14).

2:21–40 At least three ceremonies were required after the birth of a child: (1) The circumcision was to take place the eighth day after a son's birth (see Leviticus 12:3), after the mother's seven days of ceremonial uncleanness. The child was usually given a name at this time. (2) A second ceremony involved the presentation and consecration of a firstborn son (see Exodus 13:1–2, 12). (3) Finally, there was the purification of the mother, celebrated forty days after a son's birth or eighty days after having a daughter (see Leviticus 12:1–8). The scene captured in this passage is the second ceremony.

2:34–35 Simeon is the first to acknowledge the suffering that will come to Jesus and those connected to Him.

2:36–37 Anna is of the tribe of Aser (Asher), one of the ten lost tribes of Israel, which were scattered in the Assyrian captivity. She is also a prophetess and was married for seven years before her husband died. She lived the rest of her long life as a widow.

2:41–52 This is the only biblically recorded incident from the life of Jesus between His birth and adult ministry.

2:49–50 Although Jesus' parents don't understand what He means, Jesus is already preparing for His adult mission. At age thirteen, Jewish males joined the adult community. It seems that at this crucial time in his life, Jesus does not want to miss the opportunity to sit in the temple and learn things His parents cannot teach Him.

2:52 The story of Jesus and His parents in Jerusalem (2:41–51) is bracketed by two similar notations about the growth of Jesus (see 2:40). Just as all humans do, Jesus went through a growth process—not just physically, but spiritually, intellectually, and relationally as well.

3:2–4 Some people consider John the Baptist to be the last of the Old Testament prophets. Luke associates

John's ministry with Esaias (Isaiah) and his prophecy of the voice in the wilderness preparing the way for the Lord (see Isaiah 40:3–5).

3:5–6 Luke extends the Old Testament quotation to include Isaiah 40:5, which states that all humanity will see God's salvation. This passage is especially significant from Luke's Gentile perspective because it foretold the coming of not just Israel's deliverer but someone who will enable *all* humankind to see "the salvation of God," which is a key theme for Luke.

3:7 The Gospels do not record a single miracle performed by John. He does not heal, so far as we know. Those people who witnessed his ministry testified that John, unlike Jesus, never performed signs (see John 10:41). This must mean that it is only John's preaching that attracts the multitude. He must have been a powerful preacher. (No doubt the messianic nature of his message caused a great deal of excitement.)

3:8 Like the prophets of old, John's message of repentance includes a call to both personal response and responsibility. He also tells his Jewish audience that they cannot count on their national heritage (having "Abraham to our father") to ensure God's favor.

3:10–14 Other Gospel writers provide more complete physical descriptions of John (see Matthew 3:4; Mark 1:6), but Luke alone shares some of the interaction between John and various groups in his audience. Surrounded by soldiers, tax collectors, and others, John speaks frankly. His answers to their questions demand justice, fair treatment, and generosity to those in need.

3:16 Although John has publicly declared his unworthiness to loosen the latchet of Jesus' shoes—a task designated for the lowest of slaves—Jesus still acknowledges John's ministry and comes to him to be baptized.

3:22 When God's voice from heaven calls Jesus His Son, the words suggest more than just a father/son relationship. When God established kings for Israel in the Old Testament, He invited them into a relationship of sonship (see 2 Samuel 7:14; Psalm 2:6–12). So here at Jesus' baptism, God designates Jesus as the King of Israel, confirming what Gabriel had told Mary prior to Jesus' birth (1:31–33). The final comment, "in thee I am well pleased," calls to mind Isaiah 42:1–4, the prophetic foretelling of the coming servant in whom God delights.

3:23–38 These verses contain Luke's genealogy of Jesus. Matthew provides one as well (Matthew 1:1–16), but the two versions have considerable differences. On the one hand, Matthew begins with Abraham and tracks the line of descent to Jesus—clearly something that would interest his Jewish readers. Luke, on the other hand, begins with Jesus and works back through history to Adam, suggesting a more Gentile-friendly message that Jesus' significance was for the entire human race, not just the Jewish nation. In addition, the difference in placement should be noted. Matthew begins his Gospel with Jesus' genealogy—His "credentials." Luke waits until he has introduced the public ministry

of Jesus, placing the genealogy between Jesus' baptism and temptation. Another key difference is that Matthew traces the royal line through David's son Solomon, while Luke traces it through Nathan, another of David's sons.

4:1–2 Jesus' baptism may have been a high point in His life, with the descent of the Holy Spirit and the voice of His heavenly Father expressing His love and approval. Yet the Spirit immediately leads Jesus into the wilderness to be tempted. It seems safe to presume that these temptations are a barrage by the devil who strikes when He is the weakest.

4:3–4 After forty days with nothing to eat, Jesus would be more than just hungry. A physical body deprived of food that long, apart from divine intervention, would be weakened to the point of near death. Yet Satan's taunt to turn a stone into bread is not effective. Jesus had a need for food as well as the power to meet that need, but He isn't there to eat, as indicated by His response. Jesus chooses to remain focused on God rather than fulfill His own desire at the moment.

4:5–8 For the second temptation, an offer of power and authority, the devil parades all the kingdoms of the world before Jesus in an instant. Both Jesus and Paul recognized Satan as the ruler of this world in the sense that he dominates fallen human beings through the power of sin and death (see John 12:31–32; 16:11; 2 Corinthians 4:3–4; Ephesians 6:12). However, while the devil may influence kings and kingdoms, he is not in control. Jesus is the One who is in sovereign control of history. Jesus' second response is a reminder to keep God foremost in one's thoughts.

4:9–12 Satan's third temptation features an acknowledgment of Jesus as the Son of God. For anyone else, a leap off the pinnacle of the temple would be certain suicide. Jesus has already twice used scripture to refute temptation (see 4:4, 8; Deuteronomy 6:13; 8:3), so this time the devil uses scripture, perhaps hoping to enhance his proposition (see Psalm 91:11–12). But Psalm 91 was not a promise of protection for Israel's Messiah. Rather, it was a promise of protection from God's wrath for all who take refuge in Him. The devil's motive may have been to disqualify Jesus as Messiah, weaken His faith and trust in God, bring about a premature introduction of Jesus as Messiah, or maybe even kill Him. Regardless of his intent, Jesus curtly rejects his proposal with a third quotation from scripture (see Deuteronomy 6:16).

4:23–24 Jesus points out that if His ministry were correctly understood, He would be rejected like all the other prophets of Israel's history. Prophets were often spurned, persecuted, or even killed (see 1 Kings 19:10; Jeremiah 35:15; 44:4–5; Acts 7:52).

4:29–30 When the crowd rushes Jesus from the synagogue and attempts to force Him off a nearby cliff, He does not escape by fleeing or by taking a back way out. Instead, Jesus walks "through the midst" of His opponents. Just as the waters of the Red sea parted to allow God's people to pass through them, so the angry crowd parts to allow Jesus to pass through their midst, unharmed and untouched. This is the one and only miracle they will witness.

4:31–32 As was the case in Nazareth, the people of Capernaum are amazed at Jesus' teaching. (There was a similar reaction immediately after Jesus delivered the Sermon on the Mount [see Matthew 7:28–29].) What is it that distinguished Jesus' teaching from that of the scribes and Pharisees and made His teaching authoritative, when their teaching was not? The difference seems to be a matter of substance rather than style. Jesus taught with personal authority. Hearing Him speak was like hearing from someone who authored a book, rather than someone who had simply read the book.

4:33–34 Despite screaming at Jesus in a loud and disruptive manner, the evil spirit recognizes Jesus' identity and purpose.

4:40 Sunset marked the end of the sabbath—and the expiration of the injunction against work on the sabbath.

4:42–43 Early the next morning, Jesus goes to a solitary place, yet the people keep coming. They desperately want Jesus to stay in Capernaum, but He is committed to a broader teaching ministry that will cover all of Galilee. The people want to see miracles, but He has come to proclaim the kingdom of God. The healings and exorcisms are not an end in themselves but are meant to demonstrate the powerful arrival of God's kingdom—a message that everyone needs to hear.

5:5 Simon's (Peter's) response suggests a hint of irritation, perhaps for three reasons. First, he and his partners are exhausted from working all night. Second, they had already washed their nets. If they do as Jesus asks, they will have to wash them all over again. Third, night was the best time to fish. If they failed to catch anything then, why should they hope to succeed in broad daylight, the worst possible time to fish?

5:14–15 By instructing the healed leper to show himself to the priests, Jesus meant for him to be a living testimony. Jesus also orders the man not to tell anyone else, but how does a healed leper explain his instantaneous recovery without giving credit to the man who helped him? So news about Jesus spreads even more.

5:16 Jesus continues to seek out solitary places where He can pray. His retreat for prayer is an expression of dependence upon His Father. It puts Jesus' successes in perspective, for He does everything in obedience to the Father's will and in the power of His Spirit (see 4:14). These times help Jesus keep His priorities in line with those of the Father.

5:17 Jesus begins to attract the attention of religious leaders who critique what He says. Luke includes a curious detail about the Pharisees in this account—they are sitting, even though the house is packed with people. In those days, sitting was a position of authority. A teacher did not stand to teach; he sat (see 4:20–21). The Pharisees' posture may indicate their skepticism of Jesus' authority.

5:23–24 There is no visible indication of sins being forgiven. One can claim the ability to pardon sin without having to prove it. But to command a paralyzed man to walk—the proof is visible. Jesus has set up this circumstance to show that He has the power both to forgive sins and to make the paralytic walk.

5:27–28 Publicans (or tax collectors) were a painful reminder of Israel's subjugation to Rome. Earlier, Luke hinted at one of the publican's most notorious injustices: collecting more than was required (see 3:12–13). Many publicans abused their position, charging excessive taxes and pocketing the profits. Luke himself later informs his readers of one case where a sinful publican repents and makes restitution for his misconduct (see 19:1–10). Since nothing in the immediate context suggests that Levi needed to make restitution for previous dishonesty, perhaps he was an upright and honest tax collector. Maybe that is why Jesus chooses him.

5:29–30 To celebrate, Levi hosts a banquet for Jesus, and according to Luke, the guest list includes both "publicans and. . .others." Matthew and Mark both identify the guests as "publicans and sinners" (Matthew 9:10; Mark 2:15). Horrified to see Jesus associating with those they consider beneath themselves, the Pharisees ask the disciples (not Jesus) why He engages in such conduct.

5:31–32 Jesus' answer reflects the difference between the heart of God and the heart of Pharisaism. The Pharisees thought that holiness required them to remain separate from sinners, to refuse to have contact with them. Jesus was holiness incarnate; yet His holiness was not diminished by contact with sinners. In order for God to call sinners to repentance, He found it necessary to have contact with them, which is the whole point of His incarnation—taking on human flesh, living among people, touching and being touched by them.

5:33 Apparently Jesus' response isn't what the Pharisees want to hear, so they press the point of Jesus' and John's differing practices. It is quite clear from their question that what John chose not to drink—namely wine—Jesus did.

5:36–38 Jesus tells two short parables to explain that sometimes new things must replace old things; trying to incorporate the two just doesn't work. The Pharisees are entrenched in old ways—trying to follow the law to the letter in order to obtain righteousness. This doesn't work, and it never will. Jesus and the "sinners" are happy; they're enjoying life and developing relationships. The guests are in the presence of the bridegroom, and it is a time to celebrate.

6:1–11 Luke's purpose in describing the escalating tension between Jesus and the Pharisees is to prepare his readers for the eventual rejection, arrest, conviction, and execution of Jesus. The Pharisees have already clashed with Jesus because He claims God's own authority (5:17–26) and because He associates with sinners (5:27–39). Now they reject Him because He does not keep the sabbath as they interpret it. These three issues will dominate the relationship between the Pharisees and Jesus, culminating in His crucifixion.

6:12–16 By this time, Jesus has attracted a number of followers. Seventy would soon be sent out to various towns (see 10:1) After spending a night in prayer, Jesus designates twelve of His disciples to become apostles. Luke has already recorded the call of Peter, Andrew, James, John, and Matthew (Levi). See 5:3–29. Now he completes the roster. It is noteworthy that every biblical list of apostles names Peter first and Judas last. Yet this does not suggest that Jesus recruited Peter to be "the rock" and Judas a traitor. It is likely that during their extended learning process Peter gradually rises to prominence, while Judas falls away to become a thief and betrayer.

6:18–20 A large number have come to benefit from Jesus' great healing power, yet Jesus uses this as an opportunity to teach. Luke indicates that Jesus' words were addressed primarily to His disciples.

6:20–26 Jesus does not attribute any intrinsic value to being poor, nor is there any automatic evil in being rich. Jesus says, "Blessed be ye poor," *not* "Blessed are all who are poor." Luke's account suggests that the poor in this case are the disciples who have chosen poverty in order to follow Jesus. It is not simply being poor that is blessed, but being poor for Christ's sake. Likewise, there is no intrinsic merit in being rejected and persecuted (6:22), but only in being thus treated on Christ's account (see 1 Peter 2:20). The joy of serving Jesus will more than compensate for the things disciples give up in order to serve.

6:27–49 Jesus' teaching is 180 degrees from what people are accustomed to hearing. Not only does He teach love for one's enemies; He refuses to justify retaliation or revenge for offenses. This is the context for the familiar Golden Rule (6:31). Jesus' challenge is to rise above the status quo of relationships and initiate a higher level of love and care.

6:38 In the Middle East, measures of grain were sometimes carried in the folds of loose clothing.

6:39–42 Status seeking and hypocrisy only cause difficulties in life: The blind have difficulty leading other blind people, students have difficulty rising above their teacher until they've learned to be like their teacher, and a fool finds it impossible to remove a speck of sawdust from someone's eye without first addressing the plank in his own eye.

6:43–45 Just as trees are recognized by their fruit, people are identified by their actions. People with good hearts can't help but produce good deeds, just as evil in one's heart will produce evil in one's life. And whatever is in the heart—good or bad—will certainly be reflected in one's speech.

6:46–47 It's easy to give lip service to Jesus; it's much harder to love enemies, freely give to someone who is trying to take from you, keep from judging others, and maintain a mind-set of humility. But genuine believers obey even the difficult commands of Jesus.

6:48–49 Jesus closes with a parable (also recorded in Matthew 7:24–27) in which one home builder digs a deep foundation on rock. The other doesn't even bother with a foundation. So when a torrent falls on the two homes, the first one stands firm while the second is completely destroyed.

7:2–5 The Jewish people didn't care for the Romans as a whole, but this particular centurion is an exception. Not only has he shown respect for the Jewish nation and helped with the construction of a synagogue, but he also values his servant—who might very well be Jewish.

7:6–8 Jesus accommodates the centurion's request (7:3). Yet while Jesus is en route, the centurion sends messengers to intercept Jesus. The centurion understands authority; he realizes Jesus doesn't need to enter his home in order to heal his servant.

7:11–16 Jesus' raising the widow's son calls to mind two similar incidents—one from Elijah's ministry (1 Kings 17:17–24) and one from Elisha's (2 Kings 4:18–37). In the case of Elijah, the parallels are especially striking. Both Jesus' and Elijah's stories involve a mother and son living in Nain. Each boy was the only son of a widow. Both were raised from the dead by a prophet of God. Afterward, both Elijah and Jesus presented the boys to their mothers. Both miracles proved that a true prophet of God was present. There is, however, one key difference: The more labored and time-consuming resurrections performed by Elijah and Elisha were overshadowed by Jesus' instantaneous demonstration of supernatural power.

7:14 The bier on which the son's body rests would not have had a top, assuming it was made according to Jewish tradition. Jesus' act of touching the bier is an unusual move since it would have rendered anyone else ceremonially unclean. With no fanfare, Jesus simply instructs the boy to arise.

7:22 Jesus doesn't openly declare Himself the Messiah—at least not as John may have hoped. Instead, He simply tells John's disciples to go back and report what they saw: blind and lame people healed, lepers cured, the dead raised, and the good news of the Gospel preached to the poor. These were all signs from Isaiah (Isaiah 29:18; 35:5–6) meant to signal the coming of God's salvation. In effect, Jesus is simply telling John to do what every first-century Jewish seeker needed to do—compare the prophecies of the Old Testament with the deeds and declarations of Jesus Christ.

7:28 Jesus does not seem at all upset by John's questioning; in fact, He gives John a glowing tribute after his disciples have gone. However, Jesus adds that the least person in the kingdom of God will be even greater than John. In other words, John *anticipated* the kingdom of God, but those who come after John understand more clearly the redemption Jesus brings through His sacrificial death and resurrection.

7:36–50 All four Gospels include an account of a woman washing Jesus' feet (see Matthew 26:6–13; Mark 14:3–9; John 12:1–8). Despite a few similarities, the story in Luke seems to be a different event from the one described in the other Gospels. We are not told precisely when or where this incident occurs.

7:36 This dinner invitation came at a time when the religious leaders were increasing their opposition against Jesus, so it is not clear what the Pharisee's intents were.

7:38 Since Jesus and the others eat while reclining at the table, His feet are away from the table rather than under it. So the woman washes His feet with her tears, dries them with her hair, and then anoints them with the perfume. The host (and perhaps many others) knows of the woman's reputation and assumes Jesus isn't much of a prophet if He doesn't know as well.

7:41–43 Jesus tells this particular story to make the point that those who are forgiven most love most.

8:2–3 Luke names three of Jesus' female sponsors who represent different backgrounds and social statuses: Mary Magdalene; Joanna the wife of Cuhza, Herod's steward (who may have been one of Herod's primary sources of information about Jesus and His ministry; see 9:7); and Susanna, who is not mentioned again in the scriptures. The women seem to share one thing in common: Jesus has miraculously delivered them from conditions for which there is no human solution. Some, like Mary Magdalene, were delivered from "evil spirits." Others were healed of "infirmities." They wanted to be of help to Jesus because they had experienced His help in their lives. Luke is clear that these women are not mere "hangers-on." They are active contributors to the proclamation of the Gospel. They also serve as confirmation that Jesus encourages women to serve in ministry. Luke's account of these women who followed Jesus is a fitting tribute to them and to their ministry. They are commended for their faithfulness and commitment to the Lord and for their partnership in the Gospel.

8:11–15 Imagine the disciples' confusion after first hearing this parable without the explanation. Thankfully, Jesus offers a clear interpretation in these verses. As He sows the Word of God, those who hear will respond in numerous ways. Some do not respond at all (the soil "by the way side"). Others respond enthusiastically at first but soon fall away (the rocky soil). Still others try to add His teachings to an already full life rather than changing priorities (the thorn-infested soil). Some, however, hear the Word, retain it, and become productive for God's kingdom (the "good ground").

8:19–21 Spiritual wisdom is not something to take for granted. It is acquired by careful listening, and it can be lost through apathy and inattention. Indeed, Jesus begins to define relationships in terms of those who hear God's Word and put it into practice—which matters even more to Jesus than blood relationships (see also John 7:5).

8:25 Every biblical account of Jesus' calming the storm is surprisingly short and succinct (see Matthew 8:23–27 and Mark 4:35–41). What comes through clearly, however, is Jesus' expectation that by now the twelve should have faith in Him. Even a raging storm that could terrorize experienced fishermen is no problem for Jesus. After He speaks, not only does the storm dissipate, but the sea immediately becomes absolutely calm. In response, the disciples are amazed and fearful. The disciples' amazed reaction suggests that what Jesus has just done is even more startling to them than the storm itself. They are beginning to catch on that maybe they've been scared of all the wrong things.

8:26–29 No sooner have Jesus and the disciples landed than they have another frightening encounter. In a relatively remote stretch on the other side of the sea of Galilee, they find a demon-possessed man living among tombs. He no longer wears clothes. People have tried to secure him for his own protection, but chains cannot hold him.

8:28 Although the demoniac falls at Jesus' feet, it is not an act of worship, as it will be once the demons are cast from him. The demons recognize Jesus' identity, and they acknowledge His superiority over them. They understand that He can do with them as He pleases. Their petitions, however, are addressed out of fear, as those of inferior beings to One who is infinitely superior—not in devotion or worship.

8:30–31 The name *Legion* suggests a multitude of demons.

8:32 It seems that the demons need to be embodied in something, if not someone.

8:39 Jesus refuses the man's request to join Him. Who better to not only describe but also demonstrate the healing power of God?

8:40 Although Jesus has sailed across the sea of Galilee, enduring a storm and facing off with a demon-possessed man, a crowd is still waiting for Him when He returns to the other shore.

8:44 The woman shouldn't even be there because her bleeding disorder makes her unclean. It is very likely a menstrual problem, so even if she can get Jesus' attention in the crowd, it would be horribly embarrassing to request healing.

8:46–48 Jesus will not allow the woman's faith to go unnoticed. As far as He is concerned, she is a positive example for everyone. In addition, she might come to feel guilty about "stealing a healing." Or perhaps others who hear her story might interpret the healing as magic rather than faith. So Jesus waits until the woman comes forward (trembling) and explains what she has done. He acknowledges her faith and sends her home in peace.

8:50 Jesus is clearly not fazed by the news that Jairus's daughter has died.

8:55–56 After raising the girl, Jesus tells her parents to feed her and not tell anyone what has happened. Perhaps the command for silence is directed to the faithless scoffers who wait outside (see Matthew 9:23–25). Not only do they miss seeing this outstanding miracle, but they are also denied the opportunity to hear about it firsthand. Lack of faith has many drawbacks.

9:1–5 One day Jesus gathers the apostles, puts them in pairs, and sends them out to "preach the kingdom of God." He gives them "power and authority over all devils. . .and diseases" and forbids them to take any provisions. They are to go village to village, in each place finding a willing host to allow them to stay and do their work. If none is found, they are to "shake off the very dust" from their feet—a gesture that demonstrates complete separation and disdain.

9:9 While there are people in remote villages who have not heard much about Jesus or His message, Herod certainly has. He is curious about Jesus. Herod is a Jew and probably knows something about the Messiah. He might have heard talk of the kingdom of God and feels threatened. He could be haunted by guilt and fear that John the Baptist (whom he had killed) has risen from the dead. Or maybe he just wants to see a miracle (see 23:8).

9:10–11 When the disciples return from their ministry, Jesus tries to provide them a place and time for a little retreat. But the crowds find them and gather, so Jesus continues to teach and heal.

9:12–14 As the day wears on and the crowds don't go home, the disciples urge Jesus to send them away. But He tells the disciples to feed the crowd. Despite having just returned from living day-to-day by God's provision, the disciples balk at this challenge. They see five thousand men (plus women and children) and only five loaves and two fish. They see no way to feed the crowd without going out to buy food for everyone.

9:17 It is not likely a coincidence that there are twelve baskets of leftovers—one for each spiritually shortsighted apostle.

9:20–22 Despite Peter's confession, the apostles are far from a complete understanding of their Master. Jesus instructs them not to breathe a word to anyone. He wants to provide them with a fuller understanding of the Messiah's role: He is to be a suffering servant rather than a military victor or political figure.

9:23–27 Jesus not only warns the disciples about His destiny with death; He begins to prepare them for their own future suffering. But He also promises that some of the disciples will personally witness God's kingdom.

9:30–31 Both Moses and Elias (Elijah) had departed the earth with some mystery. Moses was buried by God (Deuteronomy 34:6), and Elijah was carried to heaven in a whirlwind (2 Kings 2:11). These men speak to Jesus about His "decease," meaning His exit from earth and return to heaven. The word translated *decease* hearkens back to Moses' exodus from Egypt when he led God's people to freedom, an apt parallel for the work of Christ.

9:33 As the two heavenly visitors begin to leave, Peter proposes building shelters for them, possibly in an attempt to extend their stay. Or perhaps he thinks if Jesus' kingdom is established *now*, they will be able to avoid all the suffering, rejection, and death that Jesus has been telling them about (see 9:21–27). Whatever Peter's intent, Luke tells us he doesn't know what he is saying.

9:38–40 While Jesus, Peter, John, and James are away, the other nine apostles are asked by a desperate father to cast an evil spirit out of his son. Although Jesus has given His disciples authority to drive out demons (see 9:1), they are unable to help this young man.

9:41 Luke doesn't specify whom Jesus is addressing when He expresses frustration concerning a lack of faith. Very likely He is referring to the entire "generation," which would include the father, the people in the crowds, and even His disciples.

9:46–50 The apostles may not understand Jesus' teaching about His kingdom, but that does not stop them from arguing about who will have the highest position in it. In response, Jesus calls forward a small child as an example of the least on earth who will become the greatest in the estimation of God. This act must have reminded them of a stranger they had seen driving out demons in the name of Jesus. They had tried to stop him. (Quite an irony: They had been unable to cast out a demon [9:40] and equally unable to stop someone who could!) Jesus tells them not to interfere with those who are working toward the same goals as they are.

9:51 This is a reference to Jesus' ascension. Luke's Gospel describes the ministry of Jesus before His ascension; the sequel, Acts, reports what happens after Jesus' ascension (see Acts 1:2).

10:1 Three Gospels mention Jesus' earlier sending out of the apostles (see Luke 9:1–6), but only Luke tells of the sending out of seventy disciples. (Some manuscripts say that seventy-two went out rather than seventy.) And he provides considerably more detail about the appointing of the seventy than the mission of the twelve. While there are similarities between the two groups that were sent out, there are significant differences in the instructions given.

10:4 It can seem strange that Jesus would command the disciples to refrain from the normal social amenity of a friendly greeting on the road. His instruction actually suggests the urgency of the task: Instead of stopping for chitchat, He wants His followers to get to the business of spreading the good news. Just as Jesus is resolved to go to Jerusalem, so the disciples must be resolved to proclaim His message.

10:7–8 Jesus tells the larger group to eat whatever is set before them. Seemingly, Jesus is intentionally expanding His ministry—not only reaching into larger cities than before but also beginning to include Gentile territory. (Otherwise, there would have been no need to address the food issue.)

10:18–19 Jesus tells the overjoyed disciples that their ability to cast out demons is evidence of an even greater reality than they have imagined. They see their success only in terms of their having authority over the demons; Jesus is also watching their success and seeing Satan in the beginnings of his demise. Satan is falling down fast. The coming of Christ—and more specifically His sacrifice—spells Satan's defeat. The mission of the seventy is just a preview of what is to come.

10:20 Jesus doesn't want to diminish His followers' joy, but He does gently try to redirect it. If the destruction of Satan is good news and cause for rejoicing, their salvation is even better news and cause for deepest joy. Jesus tells His followers that they should rejoice in the fact of their salvation, rather than the fact of Satan's downfall and defeat. On another occasion, He goes so far as to speak of those who have the power to cast out demons yet who are nonetheless workers of "iniquity" (see Matthew 7:22–23).

10:21–24 Jesus is full of joy. Although He has "stedfastly set his face to go to Jerusalem" in order to die (see 9:51), He is filled with the Holy Spirit and praises God for revealing to the seventy what prophets and kings have long wished to see. He also thanks God for revealing spiritual insights that will remain hidden from the wise and educated.

10:25–27 Jesus is approached by a lawyer (religious legal expert) who asks Him about the scriptural prerequisites for inheriting eternal life. Jesus turns the question back on the man, whose answer comes from Deuteronomy 6:5 and Leviticus 19:18.

10:29–30 The parable of the good Samaritan is Jesus' response to the question, "And who is my neighbour?"

10:31–32 The Jewish priest and Levite, both of whom hold respected religious positions, choose to ignore a severely injured man on the road. The fact that they are going down the road suggests they are coming *from* Jerusalem and aren't rushing to some important obligation at the temple. Yet still they go out of their way to cross the road and avoid close contact.

10:37 In response to Jesus' penetrating question, the lawyer can't even bring himself to say, "The Samaritan." Nevertheless, this is the second time he answers Jesus correctly—and the second time that Jesus instructs him to *do* what he has said. The lawyer thought he was doing a good job of justifying himself by his works, but Jesus quickly shows him it isn't as easy as he thought. Love for God is demonstrated by love for others—*all* others.

10:38–39 This is the same Mary and Martha who are sisters to Lazarus, whom Jesus raises from the dead (see John 11:1–44).

10:41–42 It must have been difficult for Martha to hear that Mary had made the better choice. Jesus shows no anger toward Martha. Nor does He impose a stereotypical "woman's role" on either of the women. He merely tries to clarify what should have been the highest priority at that moment.

11:5–13 Having provided a model for prayer, Jesus moves to the motivation for prayer. To do this, He tells two parables: The first parable deals with one's request of a friend; the second deal with the request made of one's father. The first parable demonstrates the need for persistence in prayer. If people can be swayed to change their minds in response to their friends, even at inconvenient times, then how much more is a loving God willing to respond to His followers? The result of persistence is receiving as much as one needs. Yet it is important to ask, seek, and knock rather than assume God will drop all we need into our laps with no thought. In the second parable, Jesus teaches that God is like a father who wants only the best for his children. Human fathers give their children good things when asked, rather than potentially harmful substitutes. So a loving, heavenly Father who knows our needs will certainly provide much more for His children. But rather than give us everything we ask for (much of which is not necessarily needed or helpful), God provides the Holy Spirit to those who ask. With the wisdom, strength, and comfort provided by God's Spirit, there is little else we actually need.

11:17–20 Jesus' first argument points out the illogic of His critics. Why would anyone working in league with Satan go around removing evil spirits? It's as if Jesus asks, "Who willingly and knowingly shoots himself in the foot?" Jesus continues by reminding His skeptics about other Jewish people who drive out demons, as well as the Jewish belief that only the power of God can remove evil spirits. Then He brings the point home: If His critics are wrong and He is operating in the power of God, then they must admit that the kingdom of God has come and that Jesus is the Messiah. This is the very thing they most dread, and Jesus has just reminded them of the only reasonable conclusion: Jesus is the King, whom they refuse to receive.

11:21–22 Jesus' second argument is just as forceful as the first: Anyone who would attack Satan must be more powerful. No one can take away the possessions of a powerful man without first overpowering the person. The powerful man must first be overpowered, then disarmed, and finally bound, so that his goods can be plundered. Satan is indeed strong—so much so that he takes possession of certain people. But Jesus is stronger, capable of overpowering him and freeing those who have been bound.

11:24–26 For those in the crowd who may have been trying to remain neutral on the issue of casting out evil spirits, Jesus warns what can happen to those who try to cleanse themselves using their own power. The power of God is necessary to effectively and lastingly deal with the problem of sin and evil.

11:38–41 The concern here is one of ceremonial defilement. The washing overlooked by Jesus is one that was required by Pharisaical tradition, rather than by the law itself (see Mark 7:1–4). In all likelihood, Jesus intentionally passed on the opportunity to wash in order to challenge the Pharisees on their habits. He insists that they are focused on looks and external matters at the expense of the inward purity God desires. The problem with the Pharisees is not in what they believed, and not even in what they hoped to do, but in what they actually became and did. Their goals were noble and their presuppositions were essentially correct, but they were sidetracked. Instead of being the first to recognize Jesus as the Messiah, they were the first to reject Him. Rather than turning the nation to Him, they sought to turn the nation against Him.

11:42–44 Jesus excoriates the Pharisees for emphasizing minute points of law while missing the basic fundamentals. Jesus' second "woe" attacks the Pharisees' preoccupation with position, prestige, and praise. According to the third "woe," the Pharisees had become a source of defilement rather than purification.

12:1 Despite being surrounded by a trampling crowd of thousands, Jesus seems to ignore the masses and speaks directly to the disciples.

12:2–7 Jesus seems to suggest that despite knowing the truth, His disciples may be reluctant to speak out. Perhaps that's why He speaks of hidden things being made known and the fear of those who can physically threaten. But He also makes clear each person's worth and God's awareness of each person and situation. And He tempers His comments on the fear of God by addressing His listeners as "friends."

12:8–12 Jesus challenges His followers to stand firm for Him when the time comes, promising that He will be their heavenly advocate. The unforgivable sin of blasphemy against the Holy Spirit is better defined in Matthew 12:31–32 and Mark 3:23–30 as attributing the work of the Holy Spirit to Satan. If someone does not acknowledge the role of the Holy Spirit in faith and salvation, no other course of forgiveness exists. Indeed, it is the Holy Spirit who will instruct believers on what to say during times of trial and persecution.

12:14 Jesus is a rabbi, a teacher. He has not come to oversee probate court, and He lets the man know.

12:15–21 It is unclear to whom this parable is directed, whether the disciples, the crowd, or perhaps the questioner and his brother who are disputing their inheritance. Yet Jesus clearly identifies the root of the problem: greed. The parable teaches that a person's view of the future determines his or her present conduct. The rich man's failure is his refusal to recognize where his wealth has come from. Jesus clarifies that it is the ground that produces a good crop. God has provided the wealth but the man is seeking to cash it in and store it.

12:20 The rich man is a fool because he perceives his possessions as his security. He has great wealth, but doesn't use it for anyone except himself.

12:22 Concern for the future should not escalate into worry, according to Jesus. Just as rich people can become preoccupied with accumulating wealth, so can those of lesser means.

12:23–31 Jesus' statement that "life is more than meat" echoes His rebuke of the devil during His temptation (see 4:4). When we worry about clothing or food, we fail to focus on what is most important in life. Such worry is even more foolish when we consider God's marvelous provision for His creatures in nature. Believers should put God's kingdom first.

12:33–34 Jesus doesn't seem to regard His disciples as poor. His instructions here should be read as a general rule, not a broad-sweeping command. What is in one's heart is inextricably connected to his or her idea of treasure. In the long run, heavenly things endure as earthly ones deteriorate.

12:35 Keeping the lamps burning was important in a culture without electricity or streetlights.

12:36–40 Jesus tells two parallel stories, both of which emphasize the importance of readiness for His coming—yet with vastly different results. Both stories involve an unscheduled visitor. The difference, however, is the relationship between those in the house and the one who will be arriving. The faithful servants—those who are alert and ready—are rewarded for their watchfulness.

12:37 The image of a master attending to his servants was extremely countercultural in the first century.

12:39 In this second story, Jesus speaks of a homeowner who has no interest in visitors. In this case, the return of the Son of man is described in terms of an unexpected thief who breaks into the house.

12:41–48 Jesus doesn't respond directly to Peter's request for clarification, but He gives additional clues to what He means.

12:46–47 If directed to individuals, Jesus' words sound uncomfortably severe. Another interpretation, however, is that the nation of Israel is the "servant, which knew his lord's will." Because they are not ready to receive Jesus, they are "cut. . .in sunder" (that is, dispersed) and assigned a place with the unbelieving Gentiles. The church (including both believing Jews and Gentiles) will eventually be put in charge of the Master's possessions (see 12:44). Whether eagerly anticipating or dreading it, one's attitude toward the Lord's second coming is the result of his or her response to His first coming.

12:50 The passing of judgment is painful to God. In addition to not wanting anyone to perish (see 2 Peter 3:9), Jesus dreads His own "baptism" (death). His love for humankind will motivate Him to go through with it, yet not all the consequences will be positive.

12:49–59 Jesus continues with some alarming statements. He speaks of coming fire, the division of families, and the possibility of prison for those who don't reconcile with the magistrate. Jesus' ministry will not bring peace to everyone. He is going to judge sin, and unrepentant sinners will be punished before God's kingdom can ultimately be established.

13:1 Jesus still seems to be among the crowd first mentioned at the beginning of Luke 12. Some of those present bring up news of a recent tragedy: Pilate had ordered people to be killed while they were offering sacrifices in the temple.

13:2 Jesus confronts the unstated assumption that those killed were somehow guiltier of sin than others. A related common belief was that a person's prosperity was proportional to his or her piety.

13:3–5 Jesus brings up another tragedy well known to his audience: the collapse of a tower inside the wall of Jerusalem. The two events are quite similar. In both cases, people died suddenly and unexpectedly at places where they probably felt most secure. One group was offering sacrifices to God; the other was adjacent to a structure that had been erected for their defense. In both cases, Jesus emphatically refutes the assumption that the victims had done anything to expedite their deaths. Rather, He teaches His listeners to view the two events as symbolic of the kind of death that *everyone* who doesn't repent will face.

13:6–9 Jesus follows His comments with a parable about a fig tree. The lack of fruit certainly applies to Israel, as confirmed by other statements and parables by Jesus. Yet in spite of the nation's stubborn rebellion and sin, the parable emphasizes God's patience and an extended period of grace.

13:10 The setting abruptly changes from that of a crowded street to a synagogue where Jesus is teaching. (This is Luke's final mention of Jesus teaching in such a location.)

13:14 Previously, Pharisees who had opposed Jesus' healings on the sabbath had challenged Him personally. This time, the synagogue leader uses a different tactic—he starts telling the people to come for healings only on the six days suited for work.

13:22 Luke provides another reminder of Jesus' ultimate purpose: He is continuing toward Jerusalem, where He faces death.

13:24–27 Jesus doesn't respond to the question directly but rather begins to speak in terms of a door and limited time to enter. The door is narrow, but at least it is currently open. Salvation involves more than mere association with Jesus, such as sharing a meal or listening to His words. Some who assume entitlement to God's kingdom are considered "workers of iniquity" by Jesus. In the kingdom of God, many who consider themselves first will be last, and those who are last will become first.

13:31–33 Jesus will not be deterred from His mission—not even by rumors of Herod's desire to kill Him. While Herod is hoping to meet Jesus, he also fears Him, thinking He might be the resurrected John the Baptist, whom Herod himself had executed (see 9:7–9). Jesus isn't swayed. He gives the Pharisees a return message, though it is doubtful they will have the courage to deliver it.

13:34–35 Luke concludes this section with Jesus' statement of fondness for Jerusalem and its people. The fondness keeps Him moving toward the city, even knowing what He is meant to do there.

14:1–2 If it seems suspicious that Jesus is invited to eat with a prominent Pharisee, such suspicions are confirmed when we read He is being carefully watched. Also quite dubious is the diseased man coming to Him on the sabbath.

14:3 Jesus is aware of the trap and asks His fellow diners whether they believe it is lawful to heal on the sabbath. Since the sabbath forbade work, the rabbis typically debated whether it was lawful to do good, such as healing, on the sabbath. Different rabbis had different opinions. Generally it was considered that only life-threatening diseases or injuries could be treated on the sabbath.

14:5 Jesus knows the Pharisees wouldn't hesitate to make an exception to their sabbath traditions if one of their sons, or even one of their animals, needed help.

14:8–11 Certain seats, usually those nearest the host, were considered places of honor. (This was true not only for the Pharisees but throughout the Greco-Roman world.) It had become something of an art to secure one of the better seats at any occasion.

14:12–14 Jesus challenges the dinner guests to provide meals for those who cannot afford to throw parties—the poor, crippled, lame, and blind. When planning a banquet, the temptation is to invite those who are most likely to benefit us in return. Thus, one thinks first of inviting family members or rich friends, who will reciprocate in kind. We are tempted to give in order to get. Jesus teaches that this practice should be not only revised but reversed.

14:16–20 The parable Jesus tells confirms that, indeed, the leaders of Israel *should* be at the banquet. The invitations have been sent out well in advance of the event, and it appears that the recipients have responded that they will be coming. But when the big day arrives and a messenger is sent to escort them to the banquet hall, they all give reasons why they cannot attend. They are expecting the master of the banquet (who certainly must represent God) to excuse them.

14:21–24 In the end, the Pharisee's dinner guest is correct. It *will* be a blessing to eat at the feast in the kingdom of God (see 14:15). But the guest list will be very different from what any of those present can imagine.

14:25–27 It is customary for people to follow Jesus wherever He goes, but in this instance Jesus begins to talk about what it means to *really* follow Him as a disciple. His expectations seem high—perhaps exceptionally high at first. For someone who has taught love of enemies (see Matthew 5:42–44), Jesus' instructions to "hate" one's own family must sound peculiar indeed. But a true disciple will not put *anything* before a relationship with his Master—not even parents, a spouse, or children. In addition, discipleship includes a cross of one's own.

14:34–35 Jesus makes it clear that He expects commitment and dedication from His disciples. He is up front about this expectation. Better to have a few followers who finish what they start than a great number who lose their "savour" before getting the job done.

15:1–2 As Jesus continues to move toward Jerusalem, teaching as He goes, He begins to attract a crowd of publicans (tax collectors) and sinners. Jesus treats them with respect, and His willingness to associate with them draws criticism from the Pharisees.

15:3–7 Beginning with this passage, Jesus tells a series of three stories in response to the Pharisees' criticism. The first asks His listeners to put themselves in the place of a man who has one hundred sheep, but loses one. It is a story even the Pharisees can relate to. Most people have experienced the joy of finding something valuable they had considered lost. Jesus is using this universal feeling to explain that there is rejoicing in heaven when even one sinner repents.

15:11–12 This passage has come to be known as the parable of the prodigal son. The younger son who asks for his share of the estate might have received a third of the father's wealth. (The older son would have been entitled to a double portion.) The assets should not have gone to either son until the death of the father, yet the father grants the son's request.

15:13–15 It doesn't take long before the younger boy has squandered his wealth with "riotous living." Not only does he become the hired hand of a pagan landowner; his work involves feeding pigs—one of the most degrading jobs a Jewish person could think of.

16:1 Luke has a lot to say about wealth and possessions. In his Gospel, he addresses attitudes toward tax collectors, blessings on the poor, the sending out of disciples without provisions, invitation lists to banquets, and more. Here the topic receives yet more emphasis. In this parable, a rich man's steward has "wasted his goods"—not unlike padding an expense account or perhaps embezzling money.

16:3–7 The steward is panicked at first. He is too proud to beg and is not cut out to do manual work. So instead he comes up with a plan to make allies who will help him after he is out of work. He offers deep discounts to his master's clients, pulling each one of them into a conspiracy against his master.

16:8–9 In a surprise twist, the master *commends* the steward for acting shrewdly. How can a man who has just been defrauded by his employee commend such behavior? First, the unrighteous steward and his master both valued the same thing—shrewdness. That (and not the dishonesty) is what the master commends. Second, both steward and master are counted among "the children of this world," as opposed to "the children of light." Jesus' point is simply that His disciples are to use worldly wealth wisely to achieve eternal ends. If believers are to follow the steward's example at all, it should be to make friends by the use of material possessions. The unjust steward saw that his days were numbered, and he knew that he would not be able to take his master's money with him. He then began to use his master's money to make friends who would outlast his master's money. While we should have an eternal motivation deeper than mere survival, we can nevertheless use money in such a way that will last forever—by building relationships with people who will gratefully receive us in heaven.

16:10–13 The rest of Jesus' commentary seems to be a direct contrast with the actions of the steward. Anyone who can't be trusted with little certainly can't be trusted with much. If we're not trustworthy with worldly wealth and other people's property, how can we expect to be responsible with things that really matter? Jesus makes it clear that following God is an either/or decision. If He doesn't have our complete hearts, we aren't really serving Him.

16:16 The term "the law and the prophets" is a reference to the entire Old Testament. The Pharisees highly regarded the Law—the five books of Moses. But it was the prophets who spoke of the coming Messiah. They also had much to say about the "heart issues" of life. God's revelation in the Old Testament was not about seeking mere outward conformity—but inward conformity to the will of God. In valuing the law over the prophets, the Pharisees overlooked a significant portion of scripture.

16:18 The reference to divorce seems abrupt, but it is just one example of how the usually conservative and legalistic Pharisees have adopted a liberal interpretation to justify their own actions, expanding the parameters of acceptable reasons for divorce until their customs no longer reflect what God taught. Enabled by the Pharisees, men of the first century had the freedom to change wives at will.

16:22–23 The majority of the parable takes place after both men have died, when the contrast in life is reversed. Lazarus is carried to "Abraham's bosom," a term Jewish rabbis used for the home of the righteous. From hell (Hades), the rich man can see Lazarus in the distance and can even communicate with Abraham, but a great chasm prevents any other interaction.

17:1–2 Many times, sin is not a solitary problem. Temptations often arise when we get around other people. Jesus holds those accountable who lead others into sinful actions. His words as recorded by Luke are ominous, but a similar statement following the parable of the tares as recorded in Matthew 13:40–42 is even worse.

17:3–4 Forgiveness is first granted, and then it is experienced by those who repent. The point in this passage is that forgiveness is to be verbalized at the time the sinner repents.

17:5 Note the subtle shift from "disciples" (see 17:1) to "apostles."

17:7–10 If Jesus had the Pharisees in mind even while addressing His disciples in this chapter, the religious leaders would have bristled at the comparison to servants who had to clean themselves after working in the fields before they could prepare and serve supper.

17:14–17 Of the ten lepers, two things set the one who returns apart from the others. First, he praises God "with a loud voice." Second, he is a Samaritan. The inference is that the others are Jewish. Their actions are not overtly rude or malicious. After all, Jesus tells them to show themselves to the priests, who need to make an official ruling on the healing. Yet Jesus' questions to the one grateful leper indicate that taking the time to stop and express gratitude would have been appropriate.

17:19 Jesus' comment suggests salvation in addition to physical healing.

17:20–21 The Pharisees want Jesus to tell them about the timing of the coming of God's kingdom. Jesus answers that not only will they be unable to observe it, but they have already missed it because it is "within." Perhaps Jesus meant it was a spiritual, inner matter. Others think the word *within* is better translated *among*, in which case

Jesus meant that the kingdom of God was already in their midst because *He* was present. Why were the Pharisees unable to observe God's kingdom? Probably because their expectations of what it would be like were so distorted that they would never recognize the real thing. Jesus simply did not fit their preconceived expectations, and on the whole, they seemed to have no thought of changing those expectations. This was in spite of the fact that Jesus did produce many signs attesting His identity as Messiah (see John 9:16; 11:47; 12:37).

17:22 Jesus speaks to the Pharisees about His first coming (see 17:20–21), but to the disciples He talks about His second coming.

17:34 Jesus offers some examples to illustrate the suddenness of His coming. The first mentions "two men in one bed." The Greek is not gender specific but simply refers to two *people*. Far from offering any commentary on human sexuality, Luke is merely describing the day-to-day events that will be affected by Jesus' return. (A typical Jewish house did not have bedrooms as we know them today. Often the whole family slept together on the floor.)

18:8 It is only if we give up that we stand to miss out. When Jesus returns, He will be looking for faithful and ready people.

18:11–13 The Pharisee's words are a stark contrast to the publican (tax collector) who can't even hold his head up before God. The Pharisee not only does not want God's grace but disdains it. The reason, in his mind, is that he does not need it, for his righteousness (law-keeping as he defines it) is sufficient—indeed, more than enough.

18:14 Able to speak for God, Jesus declares the second man justified rather than the first. This parable helps explain why those who weep and mourn are blessed (see Luke 6:21).

18:18 The story of the rich young ruler drives home the point that we can do nothing to earn our place in the kingdom of God.

18:19 Jesus' point is not to affirm whether He is good or not but to challenge the man's concept of what is good. True goodness is perfection, so only God is good. We are all therefore dependent on God for salvation.

18:21–22 To his credit, the young man seems to realize that following the law (as he is convinced he has done) is not enough for salvation. But Jesus doesn't directly answer the young man's original question (18:18). Instead, He tells him what he needs to do to become a disciple. In that event, his earthly treasure will be gone—distributed to the poor—but he will have treasure in heaven.

18:26 The disciples are still thinking like the Pharisees, assuming that wealth and privilege are signs of God's favor. To them, this young ruler—who is rich, religious, and appears to be genuinely seeking God's kingdom—is more than qualified.

18:27 Some may interpret Jesus' answer to mean that salvation for the rich is impossible without God's help.

But the truth is, God's power is necessary for *anyone* to be saved no matter their possessions or wealth.

18:32–33 Luke reveals a new detail about Jesus' impending sacrifice: He will be rejected and crucified by the Gentiles. Writing for a Gentile audience, Luke highlights their own participation in the rejection and crucifixion of the Messiah.

18:35 According to Mark 10:46, the blind man is named Bartimaeus.

18:38 "Son of David" is a title for the Messiah, suggesting that Bartimaeus isn't spiritually blind.

18:39–42 The blind man (Bartimaeus) keeps yelling for Jesus until he annoys everyone around him. But it works. Jesus calls him forward, restores his sight, and declares that his faith has healed him.

19:1 Jericho was about seventeen miles from Jerusalem.

19:4 Climbing a tree does not seem compatible with a man of Zacchaeus's wealth and position—which indicates how desperate he is to get a glimpse of Jesus.

19:7 Throughout His ministry, Jesus never stopped receiving criticism for his association with publicans (tax collectors). We might even wonder if the people who complained included the apostles.

19:8 Jesus doesn't demand that Zacchaeus sell all his possessions to benefit the poor as He had the rich ruler. Zacchaeus's response is voluntary and generous.

19:11–27 Jesus' parable of the ten minas is usually considered another version of the parable of the talents found in Matthew 25:14–30, although there are considerable differences. In Luke's account, Jesus reveals the attitudes of the people toward the nobleman who left and came back as king. Also, in this version the servants are given the same amount of money (19:13) and told to put it to use. (A "pound" was equivalent to about one hundred days' wages.)

19:16–19 The first servant, who earned a tenfold return on his pound, is rewarded with responsibility over ten cities and verbal praise from his master. The second servant, with a profit of five times the original amount, receives charge of five cities (though no praise is noted).

19:20–24 The bulk of the parable dwells on the third servant. He expresses fear of the master to justify his inaction and is judged by his own words. His fear should have at least motivated him to invest the money in a bank account to get interest. Consequently, he loses his portion of money to the one who had proven to be faithful with the ten pounds.

19:27 Perhaps the citizens who bad-mouthed their leader (19:14) symbolize the unrepentant Israelites who rejected Jesus (in which case the servants may symbolize the disciples).

19:28 Jesus' arrival in Jerusalem comes at a time of heightened emotions. People close to Him have heard numerous comments about kingdoms and the Messiah and such. Perhaps they are hoping for something eventful to occur. After all, everyone knew from Old Testament writings that Jerusalem would be where the Messiah would be enthroned as king. In addition, it was passover when pilgrims gathered in Jerusalem and fueled the fires of messianic expectation.

19:35 The remaining distance to Jerusalem is negligible, and nothing is said of Jesus riding an animal at any other point in the Gospels. So why now? Jesus is not only declaring Himself to be the King who has been foretold, but also fulfilling prophecy to the letter (see Zechariah 9:9).

19:36–37 The crowds surrounding Jesus are likely comprised of His followers—not the city as a whole. And even among that crowd, no one fully understands what is going on.

19:38 The triumphal entry serves to publicly identify Jesus as the King of Israel. Many were wondering if He was the Messiah. His act of riding into Jerusalem on a donkey is His way of affirming His role as King of Israel and Son of God, thus His right to be worshipped by all people.

20:1 After arriving in Jerusalem, Jesus spends considerable time in the temple teaching the people and preaching the Gospel. The religious leaders, who had tolerated His ministry through gritted teeth as long as He had been a wandering rabbi, are now more concerned because He is in their center of operation. This is *their* territory, *their* turf.

20:2 The leaders' question is two-pronged, not simply one question put differently the second time. The first question has to do with Jesus' personal authority. Jesus is acting as though He owns the place—and so He does. The second question has to do with Jesus' official accreditation. These leaders seem to assume they are the accrediting agency. Jesus has not received their permission to come to town or take over the temple. If the nation's highest spiritual leadership has not authorized Jesus, then who has?

20:7 To profess such uncertainty must have been very frustrating for such self-proclaimed authorities.

20:9 Jesus continues by telling the parable of the vineyard. The vineyard represents Israel, and the owner, God.

20:10–12 The servants represent the prophets—men like John the Baptist, who had the authority to speak for God. As a divinely appointed spokesman for God, John proclaimed Jesus to be the Messiah. But Israel's leaders had rejected the prophets.

20:14 Jesus is the son in the parable. He owns the vineyard and has been sent by His Father to possess what is His.

20:16–18 The people hearing the parable are horrified. But Jesus cites another prophecy to verify His meaning (see Psalm 118:22; Isaiah 8:14–15). The stone that is overlooked and rejected by the builders of the nation will eventually become the "head of the corner" (or cornerstone). The stone will also be an object of judgment—one that opponents to the Gospel will continue to stumble over.

20:19 The religious leaders know Jesus is talking about them (see Matthew 21:46), but He is so popular

with the people that they can't do as they wish—that is, arrest Him on the spot. Instead, they resort to stealth and subversion. They watch Him closely and send spies to act nice and try to catch Him saying something they can use against Him.

20:23–25 Jesus' response surely takes everyone by surprise. No one expects Him to advocate paying tribute (taxes) to support the Romans. He acknowledges a distinction between government and God but doesn't assume they have to be in opposition to one another. Indeed, Jesus will soon give Caesar His very life, so taxes are a small matter.

20:33 The Sadducees didn't believe in the resurrection, so their query is almost certainly contrived, meant to be a stumper. Their argument is based on the assumption that life in the kingdom of God will be just like it is on earth. Consequently, the Sadducees assume that the present institution of marriage must continue on in the kingdom. Thus a woman who was married to seven brothers would be in a terrible predicament in heaven, for she would have to choose one of them to live with.

20:34–35 Jesus, however, distinguishes between this age and that age. He specifically mentions the "resurrection from the dead," when people neither experience death nor participate in marriage.

20:39–40 Jesus' answer is so powerful that even adversaries have to commend Him. The Pharisees and Sadducees are opponents; so naturally, the former enjoy the way that Jesus silences the latter. The praise of the Pharisees will be short-lived, however.

20:41–43 "Son of David" was a messianic title that all of Jesus' listeners would have been aware of. By citing this passage from Psalm 110, Jesus makes it clear that not only do the religious leaders have a grievance with Jesus, but more so, they are inconsistent with the Old Testament scriptures—even those written by their hero, King David.

20:44 While there is no explicit claim to deity in this particular passage, Jesus makes the rather intriguing point that the Messiah must be more than David's son and therefore more than Jewish expectations about the Messiah.

21:1–4 Jesus has just been warning His disciples about the abuses of the teachers of the law and their misplaced priorities. Among His specific charges are that they "devour widows' houses" (see 20:47), indicating a certain level of deceit in their dealings with helpless people. No sooner does He speak those words than He notices a widow making an offering. Her two small coins, each worth about one-eighth of a cent, surely seem pathetic in contrast to the showy gifts of the wealthy.

21:8 Jesus warns His followers to watch out for false messiahs. When times get bad, people always arise with answers. But the bad times He is describing will be the judgment of God, and no human solution will remedy the situation.

21:9–19 Jesus encourages His followers to be frightened neither by major world events nor by personal persecution. Yet His promise that "not an hair of your head" will perish must be viewed in light of the statement in verse 16 that some of the disciples will be put to death. Followers of Jesus will not perish *eternally,* though they may pay a high price for discipleship.

21:20–24 Jesus warns His followers not to flee to Jerusalem for safety when it is under siege. Normally people would flock to fortified cities during wartime, but Jerusalem will not stand. Its fall is to occur within the lifetime of the disciples who are with Jesus.

21:25–28 From the predictions of what will happen in and around Jerusalem, Jesus moves on to heavenly signs. Here He appears to be speaking specifically to His second coming, so the same signs produce quite different responses. Those who don't know Christ will faint with terror, while believers should stand with their heads lifted in anticipation of their final redemption.

21:29–31 Jesus intentionally chooses not to give His followers a list of specific times and dates. His parable of the fig tree explains why. Farmers and gardeners don't operate by calendar dates but in response to the conditions they observe. Jesus expects His disciples to be alert to the season of His return. He doesn't want them ignorant of what to expect, but neither does He want them to suspend their watchfulness until some specified date in the future.

21:33 Jesus speaks with an authority far greater than even the prophets had. He speaks as God. His words are divine revelation.

21:36 The antidote for all three dangers is to always watch and pray. An ongoing relationship with Jesus is the only way to face all that will take place.

22:3 Judas had been among the twelve when they were paired up to teach and heal (see 9:1–6). His faults prior to Jesus' betrayal didn't seem much worse than those of the other disciples. So perhaps the best explanation for what makes him decide to betray his Master is Luke's short comment: "Then entered Satan into Judas."

22:4–6 In the next section (22:7–13), Luke gives the account of Judas's agreement with the chief priests and officers just before the Lord's instructions concerning the preparation for the last supper. The order of events is significant, for had Judas known in advance the place where the passover was to be eaten, he could have arranged for Jesus' arrest there.

22:7–13 Jesus' instructions for finding a place to celebrate the passover are just as cryptic as those for acquiring a donkey to ride into Jerusalem (see 19:28–35). But Peter and John faithfully obey, and the upper room is secured.

22:17–20 Luke writes of Jesus taking first the cup, then the bread, and then the cup again. Current Lord's Supper sacraments normally begin with the bread and follow with the wine. But if Jesus were following a traditional passover celebration, there would have been four cups of wine during the dinner.

22:24–30 Luke records Jesus responds to His disciples' issue regarding who is the greatest among them with His own criteria of greatness. He exhorts His disciples to demonstrate servanthood and promises that their efforts will be rewarded—not only with their inclusion in His kingdom but also with authority. When Jesus tells His disciples that the greatest must be the servant of all, He is simply reminding them that they must be like Him. He is not asking them to do anything that He is not doing Himself.

22:31 At some point during the evening, Jesus singles out Peter and warns him of a specific temptation the disciples will face (the word *you* is plural in this verse). The word picture regarding wheat is this: In the process of getting from the fields into the storehouses, wheat is cut down, trampled, and tossed about. Jesus' followers can expect a similar experience before becoming productive members of the kingdom.

22:33–34 Peter thinks he is ready to withstand any kind of suffering—even death. But Jesus states, in no uncertain terms, that by morning light Peter will already have denied Him three times.

22:35–37 These verses raise numerous questions. Jesus had previously told the disciples not to take provisions with them when they went out (see 9:1–6). Is Jesus changing His mind? The key to proper interpretation is verse 37, which is a reference to Isaiah 53—a passage that details various aspects of an unpopular, suffering Saviour, as opposed to a victorious Messiah. In fact, Isaiah 53 was not even considered a messianic passage until after Jesus had died. The Greek word translated as *transgressors* here refers to rebels, those defiant of God. The fact that Jesus is later crucified between two criminals fulfills the prophecy of Isaiah 53:12, but it does so in a kind of symbolic way, leaving room for a more sweeping fulfillment. Jesus is numbered with the transgressors, but it could also be said that since Jesus is dealt with as a criminal, His disciples are regarded in the same way.

22:39 The mount of Olives was apparently a regular stop for Jesus—and it was a fairly secluded location. Perhaps Judas knew he could lead Jesus' opponents to Gethsemane without the likelihood of encountering Jesus' adoring crowds.

22:42 Jesus speaks of what is to come as a "cup." In other places in scripture, a cup is used as a visual image of the wrath of God (Habakkuk 2:16; Revelation 14:10). Jesus' agony is due to the cross that looms before Him. He is not in agony because He will be forsaken by men, but because He will be forsaken and smitten by God. Jesus is suffering because of His anticipation of bearing the sins of the world and the wrath of God that He would deserved.

22:44 Luke's record of Jesus sweating drops of blood is also unique to this Gospel. This may indicate a physical condition in which a person's stress response causes capillaries to break and blood to mix with perspiration. Alternatively, it may be a reference to the notion that Jesus is sweating so profusely that it is as if He is bleeding.

22:63–65 The guards are fulfilling Jesus' own words—that a prophet is persecuted, not praised, for his work.

Thus Jesus is here identified with the prophets who have gone before Him to Jerusalem, to be rejected and to die.

22:67 The law of that day had its own version of the fifth amendment, which prevented the accusers from forcing a man to testify against himself. However, the religious leaders want to force Jesus to acknowledge His claim to be the Messiah—and even more, to say that He is the Son of God. If so, then they could find Him guilty of blasphemy, a crime punishable by death.

22:68–71 Jesus affirms He is the Messiah. You can imagine the Sanhedrin's response when Jesus refers to Himself as the Son of man. This expression, found in Daniel's prophecy, implied not only humanity, but deity. Jesus' statement gives the Sanhedrin the grounds they need to accuse Jesus.

23:2 The religious leaders press three charges against Jesus, all of which are political (that is, against the state)—and none of which are religious: (1) stirring up unrest and rebellion; (2) opposing taxation by Rome; and (3) claiming to be a king.

23:3 Pilate appears to have been a savvy politician. He passes right over the first two charges. If Jesus were a revolutionary or a tax-dodger, the Romans would have found out about Him long ago. After all, Jesus taught publicly, day after day, making His views a matter of public record (see 22:52–53).

23:5–6 By mentioning Galilee, the chief priests have disclosed that Jerusalem is simply the most recent place where Jesus has caused unrest. Pilate delights in declaring that this case is not in his jurisdiction. The case must go to Herod the Tetrarch, for he is the one who rules over Galilee.

23:13–16 It seems that Pilate takes Jesus aside after He is brought back from Herod, in an attempt to satisfy himself concerning Jesus' guilt or innocence. After doing so, Pilate reiterates his belief in Jesus' innocence.

23:18–22 With Jesus again in Pilate's jurisdiction, Pilate tries three more times to convince the crowd to release Jesus. Yet they insist on releasing Barabbas, a convicted murderer, rather than Jesus, a man of peace.

23:23–25 Even after Pilate attempts to satisfy the crowd by having Jesus beaten, they still insist on His crucifixion.

23:26 Normally, convicted criminals carried their own crosses (the horizontal piece, that is) to the execution site, but Simon of Cyrene is commandeered by the Roman soldiers to carry the cross for Jesus. Presumably, the beatings and other demands of the evening have been too physically strenuous for Jesus. Simon was from a faraway place—Cyrene, a city in Africa (see Acts 2:10; 6:9)—and he was on his way into the city at the time. He was as removed from the rejection of Jesus as was possible.

23:27–30 Jesus' words to the women of Jerusalem—to weep for themselves and their children rather than for Him—places the sorrow on them as He tells them what

to expect: namely, the future destruction of Jerusalem, which will take a terrible toll on them and on their children.

23:33 *Calvary* means "the Skull." Crucifixions were gory and gruesome, yet Luke spares us many of those details. He says simply that Jesus is crucified along with criminals.

23:44–46 The sixth hour is noon, by Jewish time-keeping. So the darkness must have been eerie. Nevertheless, it provided an appropriate setting for the Saviour of the world to commit His spirit into the hands of His heavenly Father. Meanwhile, the curtain in the temple that veiled the most holy place and ark of the covenant is torn in half. Following the death of Jesus, people will henceforth be able to approach God boldly, without requirement of animal sacrifice or priestly intervention. Jesus forever fulfills both essential roles: sacrifice *and* priest (see Hebrews 4:14–16).

23:50–53 It is a member of the Sanhedrin who makes the official request to tend to Jesus' body. Joseph of Arimathaea (with the help of Nicodemus [John 19:38–40]) goes to Pilate, takes Jesus' body, prepares it with seventy-five pounds of spices and wrappings, and places it in his brand-new tomb (see also John 19:38–42). This was done in the final hours before sunset when the sabbath would begin and such a task would not be allowed.

24:1 The women who had wanted to anoint Jesus' body on Friday have been unable to do so, but they have marked the location of the tomb where He was laid (see 23:55). Perhaps they even noticed that someone had already anointed His body (since seventy-five pounds of spices had been used [see John 19:39]), but they want to see to it themselves.

24:4 The angels' clothing is fiercely radiant, probably allowing the women to see clearly that Jesus' body is not there.

24:9–12 The women return to tell the apostles, but the eleven don't believe them. Still, Peter decides to check out their story (along with John [see John 20:1–9]) and runs to the tomb. He sees the open tomb and wrappings for the body but registers no understanding or belief that something miraculous has happened.

24:13–35 By virtue of the length of this account, it seems that Luke places a great deal of importance on this incident.

24:13 We do not know the exact location of the small village of Emmaus, only its distance from Jerusalem. If the two men did not live in Emmaus, they may have been staying there, in the suburbs as it were, for the passover celebration. The huge influx of people may have necessitated finding accommodations outside the city.

24:16 The failure to recognize Jesus might only mean that Jesus appears to the men in His resurrected body. This could mean, for example, that the nail scars and other telltales of His identity were not apparent.

24:17–24 According to the two men, it was the third day since Jesus had died. This could be a reference to Jesus' words that He would rise again on the third day.

What was more, some of the women had gone out to the tomb and found it empty. They further claimed to have seen angels, but alas they did not see Jesus. The very things which seemed to point to the resurrection of Jesus had no impact on these two men at all.

24:25–26 Jesus gently scolds the two men for not comprehending what the prophets had written in light of all that had happened. They had a partial understanding, as did many of the Israelites of their day, but perhaps they chose to overlook the prophecies about the suffering of the Messiah while dwelling on the portions declaring His victory and glory.

24:32–34 The men get up at once, driven by a burning in their hearts, and return to Jerusalem to tell the eleven. By that time, Jesus has also appeared to Peter (24:34; see also 1 Corinthians 15:5), so they begin swapping their joyful stories.

24:36–37 While the disciples are discussing their experiences, Jesus appears again. Jesus' first words to this group are of peace. This is not their response, however. They are terrified, Luke tells us. Why are they not overjoyed? Why are they frightened and upset? The use of *terrified* suggests that the disciples are caught off guard, as though they never expected to see Jesus. They think He is a ghost. It is easier for the disciples to believe in a ghostly Jesus than in a Jesus who is literally and physically present. The issue really comes down to belief or unbelief. The disciples thought they really believed. They say that they believe (see 24:34). But their response seems to communicate something else.

24:36–43 The thrust of this passage is Jesus' provision of physical evidence for His resurrection. The first evidence is the Lord, standing before them. He is not, as they supposed, a ghost. He encourages them to touch Him and to see that He has flesh and bones. He also encourages them to look at His hands and His feet. The inference is clear that both His hands and His feet bare the nail prints which He had from the cross. In this sense, at least, His body is like the body He had before His death. Finally, Jesus eats some of the fish which they are eating, the final proof that His body is, indeed, a real one.

24:44–45 As Jesus reasons with the startled group, He opens their minds to allow them to understand what the biblical prophecies had meant. Paul will later reaffirm that it is only through God's revelation that *anyone* can properly interpret and understand the truths of scripture (see 1 Corinthians 2:6–16; 2 Corinthians 3:14–18).

THE GOSPEL ACCORDING TO

JOHN

INTRODUCTION TO JOHN ■ While the Gospels of Matthew, Mark, and Luke are identified together as the synoptic Gospels because of their similarities, the Gospel of John stands apart in style and in content. John's style is simple in vocabulary, yet it is profound and even sometimes poetic. As for content, he records events that the synoptic Gospels don't. Jesus' teaching also has a different focus. In the synoptic Gospels, Jesus' teaching focuses on the kingdom of God, but in John His teaching centers more on His own identity and how His presence manifests God the Father.

AUTHOR ■ The author of this Gospel does not identify himself by name, though he is referred to as the disciple "whom Jesus loved." Through the years, a variety of possible authors have been proposed, yet the apostle John, of the original twelve disciples, still seems the most likely candidate.

OCCASION ■ John states his purpose for writing in the Gospel's closing (see 20:30-31). The central theme of this Gospel is Jesus' revelation of God the Father and the connection that revelation enables between humanity and God. This Gospel is a call to faith as well as an encouragement to those continuing in their faith.

1:1 To begin, John draws the reader's attention to three truths about Jesus. (1) His *eternality.* John's opening words echo those of Genesis, where Moses writes, "In the beginning God" (Genesis 1:1). (2) His *distinctiveness.* When John says that "the Word was with God," the Greek word carries the idea of two persons who are intimately related or facing each other. John is saying that Christ was distinct from the Father and yet in union with Him. This was a stumbling block to the Jews of Jesus' day. They believed in one God. Then Christ came, declaring that He is God, yet distinct from God the Father. This is the foundation of the doctrine of the Trinity, the belief that there is one God who exists as three distinct "persons"—Father, Son, and Spirit. (3) His *deity.* John is not saying that Jesus is simply divine, as if He were an extension of God. John is saying that Jesus is God in bodily form, and He is God completely (see also 14:9).

1:4–5 Life and light are recurring themes in John's Gospel. John refers to Christ as the source of life more than fifty times. In addition, Jesus is the source of light. Some Bible translations, including the King James Version, say the darkness couldn't "comprehend" the light, while others say it couldn't "overpower" the light. The Greek word can mean either. It is possible that the author is making a play on words and that both meanings are intended.

1:14 This is perhaps John's most direct reference to the concept of incarnation—God becoming human. Jesus was not a man who became divine—He was divinity who took on humanity. This belief is central to Christianity. The word translated *dwelt* means "to pitch a tent" or "to take up residence"—an image referring back to the Old Testament when God was believed to reside first in the tabernacle and later the temple. Jesus lived among us for thirty-three years as the presence of God on earth. The "glory" of God is simply the sum of all of His attributes. Through His nature and work, Jesus revealed the grace and truth of God.

1:31–34 It is not that John did not know Jesus at all, but rather, he had not previously come to a full realization of Jesus' messiahship. How, then, did John come to know that Jesus was really the Messiah? He had been given a sign by God, and that sign was revealed at Jesus' baptism—the Spirit came down like a dove and rested on Jesus.

1:35–51 This passage names five witnesses who testify to the nature and work of Jesus Christ: John the Baptist (1:35–36), Andrew (1:37–40), Simon Peter (1:41–42), and Philip and Nathanael (1:43–51).

1:36–37 The designation "Lamb of God" is all the two disciples need to hear in order to understand who Jesus is. They recognize this as a reference to the One who takes away the sins of the world.

1:38 For the sake of the non-Jewish reader, the Gospel writer defines the word *Rabbi*—master or teacher. The word originally came from a root word meaning "a great man," but it came to be used of a respected teacher. By calling Jesus "Rabbi," they are showing their respect to Him. In asking where He is staying, they imply a desire to, in essence, set up an appointment to learn from Him.

1:41 Andrew's response is immediate. Notice that John translates *Messias* as "Christ" for his Greek readers. Both *Messiah* (Hebrew) and *Christ* (Greek) mean "anointed one" or "God's chosen instrument." By the first century, the term *Messiah* had come to refer specifically to the Saviour from King David's line who would deliver God's people.

1:42 Apparently Jesus already knows Simon, since He identifies the new disciple by name. Jesus gives him the nickname *Cephas,* an Aramaic word that John translates into Greek for his readers as "Peter" (*petros*). Both *Cephas* and *Peter* mean "rock" or "stone." Jesus is laying claim to Simon, hinting at his role in God's kingdom. Simon will be a key player for Jesus over the next three years.

2:3 Running out of wine was a critical situation, risking the host family's reputation. The fact that Mary alerts Jesus to the problem might suggest that she was related to the host family—in which case she was "in the know" about the lack of wine. The fact that she takes the problem to Jesus leads many to scholars to think that Joseph was dead by this time. As the firstborn son, Jesus would have become the head of the family upon His father's death—and thus responsible for His mother.

2:4 Jesus' response to Mary may seem harsh, but it is not. Calling her "woman" was roughly equivalent to calling someone a "dear lady." It was a respectful but distant term—a word that one would normally use to refer to a person who is not related but nevertheless deserves respect.

2:6 Stone waterpots were used for purification rites. The law required several types of cleansing, including the cleansing of hands and feet before a meal. That is probably what these pots were used for.

2:7 Filling the pots is no small task. When full, they will hold 180 to 240 gallons of liquid. Obeying Jesus' instructions meant several trips to the well and back.

2:11 For John, the significance of this miracle—indeed, his purpose in writing this entire Gospel—was to show Jesus as the self-revelation of God in all His glory.

2:15 Jesus makes a "scourge" because a whip is the best tool to move sheep quickly.

2:19–21 There are a couple of Greek words for *temple*. One usually refers to the temple grounds or larger courtyard area (*hieron*), while the other refers to the temple building itself (*naos*). Jesus uses the latter here. The distinction is important. Jesus is indicating that He is now the place God is dwelling on earth. The religious leaders, however, miss the point of Jesus' comment.

3:1 We are told two things about Nicodemus: (1) He is a Pharisee, a member of a Jewish movement devoted to keeping the Law of Moses, and (2) he is a ruler of the Jews, a part of the seventy-member Jewish ruling council called the Sanhedrin.

3:3 The famous construction "verily, verily" translates into the Greek word *amen*, which means "this is the binding truth."

3:3–4 Nicodemus fails to understand what Jesus means by "born again," as indicated by his literal interpretation of the words.

3:10 Jesus' point is that the truth has been in the scriptures all along.

3:14 A bronze snake on a pole was the means God used to grant life to the children of Israel when they were bitten during a plague of snakes (see Numbers 21:4–9). If they looked to the serpent that Moses held high, they survived. In the same way, Jesus must be lifted up—on the cross. There He will die and take on humanity's punishment for its sins. Nicodemus is being challenged to turn to Jesus for new birth, just as the ancient Israelites were commanded to turn to the bronze snake for new life.

3:15 The word *believe* means to place trust and faith in something. In this context, it means that one's entire relationship with God is resting on this one person, Jesus Christ.

3:16 One of the most famous verses in the Bible, this passage describes the true nature of God in relation to the world, the fact that God is love, and God's love extending past Israel to all the people of the world. The word *begotten* is probably better translated as "one of a kind" or "unique." Jesus is the One who is from God and therefore shares the nature of God. His glory is not just a part of God; He shares in the full nature of God.

3:18 Those who do not believe stood condemned prior to Christ. Now they just add to their judgment by rejecting Christ. The "name" of God's Son is significant; in first-century Judaism, someone's name represented his or her character or nature. Not to believe in the name of Jesus is to deny His character or nature.

3:31–35 John's Gospel offers five reasons why Jesus must gain greater emphasis: (1) Jesus came from heaven and therefore is above everyone on the earth, (2) Jesus speaks from a firsthand knowledge of God's kingdom, (3) Jesus says and does all that God would say and do on earth because Jesus *is* God, (4) Jesus speaks the words of God, and (5) Jesus is the sovereign ruler of the world and all that is in it.

3:36 Jesus is God the Father revealed; therefore, the central religious question is, who is the object of your faith? If Jesus is rejected as the focus of a person's faith, then that person has to face the consequences of sin—the eternal wrath of God. This wrath does not imply a sudden burst of anger but simply the reaction of God's righteousness to humanity's unrighteousness.

4:4 Samaria was sandwiched in between Judea to the south and Galilee to the north. The Jews and the Samaritans had an extreme prejudice toward each other, dating back as far as 450 BC. They only had dealings as a last resort and, if time and resources allowed, would probably go out of their way to minimize contact with each other. Jesus' purpose in going through Samaria has to do with His broader mission.

4:7 Going to the well was typically a task women did as a group. The fact that this woman goes alone says something about her reputation in the community. Jesus' request for a drink from her is a break in tradition for several reasons: In that day and time, men generally did not talk with women in public; rabbis did not talk to women; and Jews did not talk with Samaritans.

4:10 Jesus turns the tables with His response. At the beginning of this conversation, Jesus is thirsty, and the woman has the source to quench His thirst. Now Jesus turns their talk to the fact that she is thirsty, and He has the source to quench her thirst. The Greek phrase translated "living water" refers to a well fed by an underground spring—one that always produces fresh water.

4:11–12 Like Nicodemus (3:4), the woman misses a spiritual truth and responds instead to what she sees as a physical impossibility.

4:15 The woman's response seems to be motivated by a desire for convenience. Would this "living water" (4:10) keep her from having to walk out to the well each day?

4:20 The woman's question about where people should worship seems to be on a different track from the conversation up to this point. The Samaritans worshipped on mount Gerizim, and the Jews worshipped in Jerusalem.

4:21–24 Jesus responds to the woman's question with three truths: (1) Worship as she understands it will be rendered obsolete; (2) salvation springs forth out of Judaism, the source of the Old Testament scriptures and all the messianic promises they contain; and (3) true worship is based not on location but on the condition of the worshipper's heart.

4:26 The first person to whom Jesus declares His messiahship is a Samaritan, a woman, and a social outcast.

4:27 John makes the point that the disciples walked into the conversation as Jesus was declaring Himself to be the Messiah.

4:28 If the Greek word translated *men* means "male human beings" in this case (it can also mean "people"), it may indicate that the woman went to the men of the city because women in this culture did not hold any position of authority.

4:31–33 The misunderstanding between Jesus and the disciples regarding food is one that occurs throughout the Gospel of John—the things of the earth versus the things of heaven.

4:37–38 Jesus shares a key to understanding the work of God: In His kingdom, there will be some who sow and others who reap, and the work of God depends on both. Then Jesus gives the disciples their commission, explaining that they will be reaping a crop for which they have not worked. This is the first of many times that Jesus explains to the disciples their purpose. In fulfilling their calling, they are building on the works of others—Moses, John the Baptist, and, obviously, Jesus.

4:45 At first it seems that the Galileans believe in Jesus, but their belief is based on the miracles that Jesus does rather than who He is.

4:48 Jesus' rebuke is in response to the fact that people are looking for Him to do His tricks—His signs and wonders. They will not believe in Him based upon His Word. (Note the contrast with verse 42—the Samaritans believed based upon His Word.)

4:49–50 The nobleman reveals the limitations he believes Jesus faces. He asks Jesus to "come down" before his child dies because he believes that after death there is nothing Jesus can do. Yet when Jesus declares the child healed (without being present with the child), the man believes.

5:2 The pool near the gate had five entrances and was probably spring fed, which means that it would bubble up every time the fresh water came in. This bubbling is what the people would wait for, hoping to be healed.

5:8–9 With three simple commands, Jesus heals the man: "Rise, take up thy bed, and walk." Notice that the man says nothing of record. He does not argue with Jesus; he just jumps up, rolls up his bed, and walks. Why? Because Jesus spoke with the ultimate authority of God. At the end of verse 9, John offers what becomes a sticking point for the rest of Jesus' ministry—Jesus heals this man on the sabbath.

5:10–13 It's obvious from the religious leaders' response that they have more concern for their rules than for a miracle from God. They could not fathom that anything good might come outside their laws. In their view, their system was the system that the Messiah would come through, and anything outside of that system was surely evil.

5:14–15 Jesus' later words to the healed man make it appear as if this man's condition had been a result of some sin. We are given no further explanation, but it is interesting to the note the man's response once Jesus confronts him.

5:16 After the healed man identifies Jesus as the One who made him well (see 5:15), the conflict is set between Jesus and the religious establishment. The core of this conflict is a question of authority and who has it—Jesus or the Pharisees, the interpreters of the Jewish religious system.

5:17 Jesus' initial response reveals two important truths. First, God does not stop working on the sabbath, so neither will Jesus. Even after the creation of the world (see Genesis 2:1–3), God did not cease working altogether; He merely rested from the work of creation. Second, Jesus claims an exclusive relationship with God, whom He calls "My Father." Both elements of Jesus' response declare that He is God. Jesus does not bow to the Pharisees' authority; instead, He establishes His own authority and calls for them to submit to Him.

5:19–23 Jesus provides yet more reason to believe that He is God: (1) He implements God's will, (2) He exhibits God's power, (3) He judges with the same authority as God, and (4) He receives equal honor. All these things together leave no doubt that Jesus claimed to be one with God.

5:33–39 Jesus offers four sources of testimony to confirm His deity: John the Baptist, His own work, God the Father, and the scriptures.

5:36 Jesus' own work testifies to His deity. No one could do the miracles that Jesus did. Only God can do these miracles. Remember that the context for this discourse is Jesus' healing a man who was infirm for thirty-eight years (5:5–9).

5:37–38 God the Father testifies to the deity of Jesus Christ. God gave His witness at Jesus' baptism (see Matthew 3:16–17). The way to bear the witness of God is to believe in the Son; and if one fails to believe in the Son, one does not receive the witness of the Father.

6:1 This account probably comes from the later portion of Jesus' ministry in Galilee. Therefore, between verses 5:47

and 6:1, approximately six months to one year passed. For more of the Galilean ministry, see Matthew 4:12–15:20.

6:3 If we compare this verse to Mark 6, we discover that the disciples had just returned from their first ministry assignment. Now Jesus wants to debrief them on that experience.

6:9 Barley loaves were not like contemporary loaves of bread. They would have been more like muffins, which is why the boy had five for himself. The fish were probably pickled fish that were spread on top of the loaves. This was a common meal in that day—one that suggests this boy is probably impoverished, since barley loaves were the meal of the poor.

6:10 Greek has two different words that are sometimes translated "men." The first sentence of this verse uses *anthropos,* which typically means "humankind" in general. The last sentence uses *aner,* which usually means "male" human beings. John's wording indicates that the total number of people was far greater than five thousand.

6:11 In the Jewish catechism, the children are taught that if you do not thank God for your food, it is equal to stealing from God, for food is a gift from God. A typical Jewish thanks for a meal would have been something like this: "Blessed are you, O Lord our God, King of the universe, who brings forth bread from the earth."

6:14 The people's response is a reference to Deuteronomy 18:15–18, the promise to bless the children of Israel with a Prophet like Moses who will speak the words of God.

6:17–18 The sea of Galilee is six hundred feet below sea level, in a cuplike depression among the hills. When the sun sets, cooler air from the west sometimes rushes down over the hillside, churning the lake quite suddenly. Since the disciples are rowing toward Capernaum, they are heading into the wind.

6:26 The people saw the miracle but failed to recognize its significance: Here was the Messiah, putting Himself on display for all to fall before Him in repentance and worship. These people are coming to Jesus to have their needs met, not to be redeemed.

6:27 In that day, many people could not read, so when the king wanted people to understand that a decree was his, it would be "sealed." Jesus says that the Father has placed His seal, His mark of approval, upon Him as the sole dispenser of eternal life.

6:28–29 The people focus their attention on works, having no idea that salvation is a gift of God given by His grace and mercy, while Jesus responds with their need for faith.

6:34–35 In calling Himself the bread of life, Jesus is saying that people must partake of His nature and His life in order to have the hunger of the soul satisfied.

6:36 Jesus shifts gears a little and begins confronting the real problem—the people do not truly believe in Him. There is more to belief than simply seeing Jesus as a prophet, an earthly king, or a great man. He wants us to see Him as God in the flesh.

6:37–39 The role of the Father is to turn on the light of understanding in humanity. The role of the Son is to protect and preserve those who have come to Him.

6:41–42 Jesus' Jewish opponents have a problem with one aspect of His teaching: His claim of deity. The Jews grumble because Jesus' claim puts Him on par with God—the ultimate blasphemy. These men think that they know Jesus—the son of a Galilean carpenter. They know His mom and His dad, and they know where He came from. They refuse to accept that He is from God, and therefore they refuse to go through Him in order to get to God.

6:45 Jesus is referring to an Old Testament teaching found in Isaiah and Jeremiah (and implied in many other passages). See in particular Isaiah 54:13–14.

6:47–48 These verses provide the foundational point that Jesus wants to get across: Those who believe in Him will have eternal life. By referring back to manna, He says, in essence, that if you reduce God to nothing more than a source of physical provision, you have nothing.

6:50 Jesus provides the fundamental contrast with manna. Manna prolongs the death process, but the bread out of heaven gives life.

6:53 Notice that Jesus says that the Jews must not only "eat the flesh" but also "drink his blood," or there is no life. The latter would have been even more troublesome for Jesus' listeners than the former. To the Jews, drinking blood was a major offense.

6:54–58 Jesus promises three benefits for those who look to Him for salvation: (1) eternal life, (2) unity with Jesus, and (3) abundant life.

6:60 *Disciples* is a reference to all the people who are following Jesus at this point. By saying that Jesus' teaching is "hard," they are implying that it is difficult to accept.

6:61 When Jesus asks if His words "offend," He is using a word that describes an old-fashioned trap for an animal—a box held up by a stick with bait attached. Over time, this word developed the connotation of anything that trips someone up.

6:63 The central issue of true discipleship surfaces yet again: The words of Christ are the dividing line between life and death.

6:64 In this text, John includes an indirect reference to Judas. John wants us to see that not even Judas is beyond the knowledge of Jesus. Jesus is fully aware of the people's unbelief and fully aware of Judas's true nature.

7:1 The opening verse of chapter 7 explains why Jesus trained His disciples in Galilee rather than in Jerusalem. If Jesus were to perform a public ministry in Judea, it would create such a stir that His death would likely be carried out before the appointed time.

7:2 The feast of tabernacles had a twofold purpose: It celebrated the harvest that God provided each year and looked back to the provision God gave Israel while its people were living in tents in the desert. It looked to the present as well as to the past. During the celebration, all Jewish males were to come to Jerusalem, set up tents, and celebrate. The tents symbolized the tents in which the Israelites lived during their wandering (described in the book of Numbers).

7:3–5 Jesus has four brothers. The request they make here does not come from faith. (Notice the "if" in verse 4.)

7:6–9 Jesus gives two reasons for refusing His brothers' request. First, the timing isn't right. Revealing Himself in Jerusalem would precipitate His trial and death, and it's not yet time for that. Second, those He would teach in Judea would resent Him for revealing the sin in their lives. While His brothers would be free to go, such a visit would have greater ramifications for Him.

7:15 John doesn't focus on the content of Jesus' sermon but rather on the people's response to His teaching. The point of this passage is that Jesus teaches not before the religious leaders but before all the people. The religious leaders are astonished at the way Jesus handles the text of scripture, yet they point out that His teaching is not grounded in the systems of the day. In that day, all truly learned men had a teacher who authenticated them.

7:24 Jesus' healing of the man in chapter 5 was a symbol of the work of God in the life of every believer. But because these leaders are caught up in their own legalistic standards, they are not able to evaluate or understand Jesus at all. Their judgment is based on appearances and not on the heart behind the laws of God.

7:25–27 The fact that the Jewish leaders allow Jesus to speak publicly causes the people to wonder if the leaders believe that Jesus really is the Messiah. But they rule out this possibility based on a misinterpretation of Malachi 3:1 and portions of Isaiah 53. It was widely believed that the Messiah would appear out of nowhere. Since they know Jesus is from Nazareth, they decide He could not possibly be the Messiah.

7:28–29 Jesus, shouting His response, opens with what is perhaps deliberate sarcasm, as if to say, "So you think you know Me, do you?" Jesus' point is that He comes not from Nazareth but from God. He is not a self-proclaimed prophet but a sent one. The implication, then, is that these people do not know the God whom Jesus really comes from.

7:37–38 On the last day of the feast, Jesus gives Israel the call to faith that the entire Old Testament was longing for. The last day was the high point of the feast of tabernacles, a celebration of God's provision for the Israelites during their forty years of desert wandering. On the last day, a golden chalice was filled with water from the pool of Siloam and carried in a procession by the high priest back to the temple. As the procession approached the Water Gate, the door in the temple wall that gave access to the water hole, three blasts from the shofar—a special trumpet—were sounded. The water, offered to God at the time of the morning sacrifice, was an image of the Lord's provision of water in the desert and the promised pouring out of the Spirit in the last days—that is, the messianic age. It is on this day that Jesus proclaims Himself the source of water for thirsty people.

7:41–42 Others referred to Jesus as "the Christ" or Messiah. Yet others ruled Him out as Messiah on the basis that He came from Galilee rather than Bethlehem as was prophesied in Micah 5:2. They seem to have no idea that Jesus was, in fact, born in Bethlehem. Had they dug more deeply, they might have discovered that Jesus indeed qualified to be the Messiah.

7:44–46 The guards fail to seize Jesus because they are so awed by His words.

7:50–51 This is the same Nicodemus who had come to Jesus secretly in John 3. Unlike many of his peers, Nicodemus is open to the possibility that Jesus is from God. He offers a procedural defense of Jesus, saying that his fellow Pharisees are wrong to condemn Jesus without hearing His side of the story. By law they should at least give Jesus the chance to validate His claims.

7:53–8:11 Some Bible translations do not include this passage. While it was not a part of the earlier manuscripts of John, it is unlikely that it is totally fiction. It is probably an added snapshot of Jesus' ministry, inserted later from oral tradition.

8:6–8 The Bible does not reveal what Jesus writes on the ground. When He does speak, His answer is based on Deuteronomy 13:9 and 17:7, which instructed those who had witnessed a crime to be the first to inflict the punishment. Since the religious leaders are the ones who caught this woman, they are the ones who should actually make the first move. Jesus' response also suggests that you cannot accuse someone of something that you yourself are guilty of. The question is not whether or not the Law of Moses should stand in this case but whether or not these men are qualified to judge this woman. Their hearts are not bent on the glory of God but rather on causing Jesus' downfall. Their hypocrisy disqualifies them.

8:9 Notice the order in which the scribes and Pharisees leave: The older ones are the first to go. The retreat continues until only Jesus and the woman are left. Finally, she moves from being the object of an evil plot to the object of God's mercy.

8:10–11 In showing mercy, Jesus addresses both her position ("Neither do I condemn thee") and her practice ("Go, and sin no more"). Her position is forgiven, but she must now practice righteousness.

8:17–18 Since Jewish law requires two witnesses to confirm any testimony, Jesus is saying He has two witnesses: Jesus and the Father, because they are one. This should satisfy the demand of the law.

8:19–20 Jesus' statements would have been outrageous to those who did not believe in Him. The conflict for these religious leaders is building, yet God's timing is still in effect.

8:21 The tenor of Jesus' ministry changes as He begins to pronounce the judgment that the people of Israel will face for rejecting their Messiah. They cannot go where He is going because of their lack of faith in Him.

8:27–28 Because the leaders miss the point that Jesus was sent from God, Jesus predicts that His death on the cross will reveal who He really is.

8:31–32 To "continue" conveys the idea that a person will not fall away. True discipleship means that Jesus' teaching becomes part of the believer's life, a permanent influence. Jesus is not saying you must prove by staying the course that you have good enough faith. He is saying that as you continue in His teaching, then it becomes obvious that you are one of His true disciples.

8:33 In response to Jesus' definition of true faith, His listeners counter by touting their heritage as descendants of Abraham. They believed that because they were Jewish, they were inwardly free, even though as a nation they were outwardly in bondage. They failed to realize that God did not call the Jewish nation to a salvation meant exclusively for them; rather they were called to be the people through whom His salvation would come to the world.

8:34 Sin, according to Jesus, affects every aspect of our being—down to the very depth of who we are.

8:36 The only one who can set a slave free is the rightful holder of the family inheritance—only the father or the firstborn son. That means Jesus can set humanity free from the enslavement of sin.

8:48 In response to Jesus' bold claims, the Jewish leaders pose a question that reflects how they truly feel about Jesus. While there are other places in the Gospels where Jesus is accused of working under the power of Satan, this is the only place where He is accused of being a Samaritan.

8:49–50 Interestingly, Jesus does not respond to the accusation that He is a Samaritan (8:48). Jesus loved the Samaritans (see chapter 4). He does, however, flatly deny that He is demon-possessed. Jesus' only concern is with honoring God; He doesn't respond to attacks that have nothing to do with that role.

8:58–59 For these argumentative religious leaders, Jesus' claim is unmistakable. Jesus calls Himself "*I am*". That is the personal name of God used in the Old Testament when God spoke to Moses (Exodus 3:14). Jesus is saying, "I am God." Leviticus 24:16 states that anyone who claims to be God, and thus blasphemes God, should be stoned. This is why the men pick up stones with the intent to execute Jesus.

9:1–2 Some believed that any physical infirmity was a result of a sin committed by that person or someone related to that person. This idea may have been based on a misunderstanding of passages like Exodus 34:7.

9:4 Jesus' statement is a call to make the most of the time that God has given. There is an appointed amount of work that God has planned for Jesus, and Jesus must complete that work while He is here on earth (see also 17:4).

9:5 Jesus is the light of the world, the revelation of God on earth. He is showing the glory of God to everyone.

9:13–17 This is the first of three interrogations performed by the Pharisees in response to Jesus' healing of the man. Their questions center around the process Jesus used to perform the miracle. John reveals that this healing took place on a sabbath. In the Pharisees' view, Jesus had broken the prohibition against work on the sabbath in three ways: (1) He had healed a man, (2) He had made a clay pack, and (3) He had anointed the man. The Pharisees were concerned more about the rules than about God's glory.

9:18–23 The Jewish leaders interview the parents of the healed blind man, hoping to discredit the miracle by proving the man had not been born blind. Terrified, the parents only confirm their son was indeed born blind and then defer any other questions to him. They feared being excommunicated—that is, cut off from the synagogue. If they were cut off, they would not be able to work, they would be kicked out of their home, forced to live as outsiders, and not be welcomed into heaven when they died (or so the Jews of the day believed).

9:24–25 The leaders summon the healed man for a second round of questioning. Since they cannot deny that he was blind from birth, the only thing left is to attack the character of Jesus. If Jesus is a sinner, then it does not matter what miracle He performs—it is all evil. The one thing this man will not relinquish, though, is that he was blind and now he sees.

9:27 The man's question may be sarcastic. It was probably obvious that the religious leaders had no interest in becoming Jesus' disciples.

9:28–29 The idea of Moses and God conversing together conveys God's approval and blessing, which the religious leaders claim for themselves.

9:31–33 The healed man's reasoning is simple yet compelling: (1) We know that God does not hear sinners. (2) God hears those who do His will. (3) To heal someone blind from birth must be a miracle of God. (4) Since it is a miracle of God, the person who performed this miracle must have been obeying God because God heard Him. (5) Therefore, if Jesus were not from God, God wouldn't have empowered Him to work this miracle.

9:35 The word *believe* means "to trust." Keep in mind that when the man asks who the "Son of God" is, he has never actually seen Jesus. His eyes had been covered with clay, and then he was taken to the water, where he received his eyesight (see 9:6–7).

10:1–5 First-century sheepfolds were large enclosures, open to the sky, but walled around with reeds, stone, or brick to protect against robbers, wolves, and other beasts. At the doors of the large sheepfolds—some large enough to hold thousands of sheep—a porter, or doorkeeper, remained on guard. This doorkeeper would only admit those who had the right to enter. All those who climbed into the sheepfold some way other than by the door were robbers or attackers.

10:7–9 Jesus calls Himself the "door of the sheep." Anyone who wants to be a part of the kingdom of God must go through Him. When He refers to all who came before Him as "thieves and robbers," He is not teaching that Moses and the prophets were among that group. He is referring to more recent history—the teachers and leaders who are in power at the time.

10:11–15 Jesus continues to contrast Himself with the religious leaders of the day. He is the Shepherd; they are the hired help. There is a bond between the sheep and the shepherd. The true Shepherd cares for the sheep in such a way that He gives His all.

10:16 Those sheep who are "not of this fold" are the Gentiles. The Shepherd (Jesus) will bring them to the sheepfold, and they will become one with the Jewish believers. There will be a single flock, with a single Shepherd.

10:24 *Christ* is a title rather than a name. It's the Greek equivalent of the Hebrew *Messiah*. Both words mean "anointed one." The Jews want a champion leader like Judas Maccabeus (who famously recaptured the temple in 167 BC) to conquer Rome.

10:28–30 Jesus refers to His hand and to God's hand interchangeably—one more allusion to the truth that Jesus is fully God.

10:31–32 Previously when the leaders threatened to stone Jesus (8:13–59), He disappeared. This time He stays put and challenges their reaction to His words.

10:34–38 Jesus refers His accusers to Psalm 82:6, where God spoke to the unjust rulers, calling them "gods" and "children of the most High." They were His sons, His representatives on earth. The title *gods*, in this context, implies authorities or rulers. Jesus makes an argument from the lesser to the greater. If the men in Psalm 82 could be called sons of God without having performed any great works of God, could Jesus not rightly be called the Son of God, having manifested God's works?

11:1–2 Not much has been said about Lazarus until this miracle. In fact, more people know Mary and Martha, so John mentions them as a point of reference. Mary's anointing of Jesus' feet (see 12:1–8) must have been a well-known story by the time this Gospel was written, because John references it here even though the story hasn't appeared in this narrative yet.

11:3 The term of endearment in this passage signifies a close relationship. Jesus had healed others He had never met; surely He would come and heal this man who means so much to Him.

11:5–6 Notice the tension in these verses. Jesus has a deep affection for Lazarus and his sisters, yet He waits two days to respond to them. Why does He wait? In hindsight, it is clear that Jesus waits so that Lazarus will be dead when He arrives and so Jesus can raise him from the dead.

11:9–10 Jesus responds to the disciples' fear with the image of the safety that daylight offers. In Jesus' day, a person working at night would not be able to see well and would stumble around, accomplishing nothing. If that same person worked in the daylight, he could see. As long as the disciples are in the presence of the light, nothing will get in the way of their mission.

11:11–15 When Jesus describes Lazarus as asleep, the disciples miss His point. Lazarus is actually dead, not asleep, and they are charged with a divine mission to heal, not a mandate to escape danger.

11:17 In the Jewish tradition, four days was sufficient time to confirm that a person was dead. As was the custom of the day, relatives and neighbours had come to care for Lazarus's family during this time of grief. In addition, at most funerals, the family would hire a funeral band to play

sad music, as well as professional mourners. This would have meant a large gathering of people.

11:21–24 While perhaps not obvious at first, Martha's comments reflect a lack of faith. While she is sure that Jesus *could have* done something about Lazarus, now that he is dead, she is just as sure that Jesus can do nothing about the situation.

11:33 Amid Martha and Mary's grief, and the looming question of whether He had waited too long to intervene, Jesus is either deeply moved or deeply agitated. It may be that Jesus is weeping with them, or the word *troubled* could indicate that Jesus is upset at the lack of faith He encounters.

11:39–40 As Jesus stands before the grave, calling for the stone to be moved, Martha struggles to look beyond her circumstance and see the "glory of God" as Jesus promised. In this context, the *glory of God* does not refer to a grand light show. It is simply an authentic display of who God is. As throughout the Gospel of John, Jesus is that display of God's glory.

11:41–43 Jesus' prayer of thanks reaffirms the claim He has made throughout this section of John's Gospel—that He has been sent from heaven and is the physical manifestation of the Father.

11:44 The graveclothes on Lazarus were typical for that culture. Embalming was not a part of Jewish burial customs. The body was typically washed, dressed, and wrapped in linen, but it was not put into a coffin. Instead, it was carried into the tomb and left in a prepared place, perhaps a carved shelf or shallow grave. Spices and perfumes were placed in the graveclothes and in the tomb to mitigate the odor of decay. A separate piece of cloth covered the head.

11:48 The leaders do not deny the miracles of Jesus. Instead, they are preoccupied by the large numbers of people believing in Him. If Jesus' popularity goes unchecked, the status quo will be threatened. The more Jews who see Him as a king, the more likely Roman intervention becomes.

11:49–50 Caiaphas served as high priest for eighteen years (AD 18–36) by the appointment of Rome. Caiaphas seems to feel that having Jesus killed will help maintain the peace with Rome. Under Roman law, the Jews were allowed some measure of self-governance, but they were not given the authority to execute anyone.

11:53–54 With the commitment the leadership has made to end Jesus' life, the stakes have changed, and Jesus withdraws. It was the previous passover mentioned in John's Gospel at which Jesus healed the man who had been lame for thirty-eight years. He then declared Himself God, with full rights to break the man-made sabbath laws (see chapter 5). The conflict that surrounded that passover has only grown since then.

12:3 John's account is unique in its focus on Jesus' feet, which may have some connection to the foot-washing scene in chapter 13. Mary pours about twelve ounces of spikenard (perfume) on Jesus' feet. It was not uncommon for a special guest in that day to be anointed with a perfume when he arrived. The region was hot and dusty, and the people did not have showers in which to clean up—a douse of perfume helped the smell. However, Mary broke several customs of the day. First, she approached Jesus at the table. In that day, men and women dined at different tables. Second, she let her hair down in public. Women did not let their hair down in front of men; doing so was a kind of intimacy only to be shared between husband and wife. Third, she wiped His feet with her hair—certainly a social taboo in that day. In doing this, Mary placed all that she had at the feet of Jesus, humbling herself in front of Him and responding to Him with love and devotion. Her act also foreshadowed Jesus' death (see Matthew 26:12; Mark 14:8).

12:4–8 In defending Mary's actions, Jesus indicates that Judas needs to get his priorities straight. Nothing is to be more important than the glory of God. Nothing is to take center stage more than the worship of God.

12:10–11 Lazarus's presence is a living testimony to Jesus. A movement is continuing to form around Jesus that threatens the current religious leaders.

12:14–15 Jesus' entrance into Jerusalem fulfills the Old Testament prophecy of Zechariah 9:9.

12:20–22 The "Greeks" are probably Gentiles who worshipped the God of Israel but had not fully converted to Judaism. They have come to Jerusalem to celebrate the passover. Their presence in the story serves to signify that Jesus is the Saviour of the whole world.

12:23–28 Jesus' response to the Gentiles' inquiry is that the time has come for Him to be glorified. For the Jewish listeners around Him, Jesus' words might be mistaken for a rallying cry against Rome—which, of course, is not what Jesus has in mind.

12:28 After Jesus' declaration of allegiance, the Father speaks to Him in an audible voice. There are only two other times in the Gospel accounts where God speaks audibly—at Jesus' baptism (see Matthew 3:17; Mark 1:11; Luke 3:22; compare John 1:29–34) and at His transfiguration (Matthew 17:1–8; Mark 9:2–8; and Luke 9:28–36).

12:30 When Jesus says that God is speaking for the people's sake, He means that the Father did not speak from heaven because Jesus needed confirmation, but because the crowd needed confirmation that Jesus' death will bring glory to God.

12:32 "All men" does not mean that Jesus will draw to Him everyone ever created. It means that He will draw all those who put their faith in Him throughout history.

12:35–36 Jesus points to the urgent necessity of acting on the light that the people have. They must give up their preconceived notions and act on Jesus' revelations. In essence, one must first become a child of the light in order to walk in the light.

12:37–41 John shows his readers that Jesus' rejection by Israel is part of what God had said would happen, and therefore it is not a reason to deny that Jesus is the Messiah. Instead, it is a sign confirming that Jesus is the Messiah. John quotes from Isaiah 53:1 and 6:10. Both

passages talk about the blindness of Israel in relation to the Messiah.

12:42–43 There is a segment of people—even religious leaders—who believe, but they are afraid of the stigma of admitting it.

12:44–50 These verses summarize Jesus' teaching and public ministry. They are not a literal response to the leaders mentioned in 12:42. Rather, they probably come from a series of messages that Jesus had preached to the leaders—now condensed for the readers of this Gospel. The idea that Jesus cries out these words (verse 44) means that whenever they are spoken, they are shouted out. This signifies their importance.

13:1 The word *hour* refers to the whole period of the crucifixion, not just the hanging on the cross. John's point is that Jesus knows He is ending His full-time public ministry. For Jesus to love His own "unto the end" is another way of saying that His love will carry His followers through to the end. Ultimately, the cross is the place where Jesus' perfect, unconditional love is manifested.

13:2 John refers to Judas's betrayal but leaves out any details concerning it. Jesus is in the room with a man who is in a conspiracy with Satan to seek His execution.

13:3–7 When Jesus lays aside His outer garment and takes the towel to wash the disciples' feet, He is putting on the clothes and taking on the role of the lowest of servants. That is why Peter is so unsettled. His view of leadership could not contemplate a leader doing such a thing. He thought that leadership meant being served, not serving. Once Peter understands the cross, the foot washing will make more sense.

13:9–10 Jesus responds to Peter's request for a bath with a principle of forgiveness. If a person has taken a bath before he goes to a gathering at someone's house, when he arrives he does not need to take an entire bath again. All he needs is to have the dust of his feet washed off. The rest of his body is already clean. The point is that you do not need to go beyond what Jesus offers for salvation. His work is enough for a lifetime. That is why it is a perfect love.

13:20 If Jesus and God are one, then those whom Jesus sends out are included in that connection.

13:22 The disciples have labored together, yet they don't immediately suspect Judas. They are at a loss. This serves as a reminder that their lives and relationships were as complicated and mysterious as our own can sometimes be.

13:26 Jesus offers the sop (bread) dipped in sauce to Judas, signifying to the disciples the identity of the betrayer. Ironically, offering bread to a guest was a sign of friendship.

13:27–29 John mentions Judas being possessed by Satan, highlighting the fact that the conflict is not between Jesus and the Pharisees, or the Romans, or even Judas. It is between Jesus and Satan. So when Jesus speaks to Judas, He gives Satan the approval to start the chain of events that will bring about His crucifixion, though the disciples still don't understand the significance of those instructions and come to their own conclusions.

13:34 Jesus calls this a "new commandment," though God had already commanded the Jews to love each other (Leviticus 19:18). Jesus' command is new because His followers are to love each other even as Jesus loves them.

13:37–38 All four Gospels record the claim Peter makes to lay down his life for Jesus (see Matthew 26:35; Mark 14:31; Luke 22:33). His words echo those of Jesus when He describes the work of the shepherd laying down his life for the sheep (see 10:1–17). As bold as Peter's claim is on behalf of Jesus, Jesus predicts here Peter's denial—which happens that very night.

14:4–6 Jesus makes another *I am* statement, identifying Himself as "the way, the truth, and the life." In Jewish wisdom literature, following "the way" meant living by God's standards. Jesus is the only true path that leads to eternal life with God.

14:7 The disciples do not recognize Jesus for who He truly is. When Jesus tells them that they will know who He is eventually, He is referring to all that is to come—His resurrection, His ascension, the coming of the Spirit. Only after these things will they fully know Him, and in knowing Him they will know the Father.

14:10–12 Jesus makes three key observations: First, His unity with the Father begs the question, do the disciples believe He is one with God? Second, Jesus issues a call to faith, reminding them that only God could do the works that Jesus has done. Third, He explains that those who believe in Him will do His same works and even greater ones. The word *greater* indicates the idea of "greater in depth." What could be greater than raising the dead? Preaching the Gospel of eternal life.

14:13–14 The gap between the Father and the disciples is closed by Jesus. They now have access to the Father. They have the resources of heaven at their disposal.

14:16–17 The word translated *Comforter* means "one who comes alongside to intercede or to support." This is not the idea of a therapist's role but more like a lawyer who pleads a case for you. The helper is the "Spirit of truth"—that is, He reveals the truth to those who believe.

14:18–19 Because of His imminent resurrection and departure, Jesus is giving His disciples the Spirit, access to God, the ability to work the miracles of heaven, and a promise of abundant life on earth and eternal life in heaven. They are not orphans; they have a new home in heaven.

14:26 Things will get a little more difficult after Jesus' departure, but He will send the Holy Spirit to empower His disciples. They are required to obey, preserve, guard, and protect all that Jesus has taught. That is something that is impossible in the flesh. Yet with the Spirit's help, it can be done.

14:27 The discouragement of the disciples initiated this conversation, so Jesus reminds them of the peace that only He can give.

14:28 Jesus refers to His departure for the sixth time in this chapter. Each time, He has shown the disciples some theological error in their belief.

15:1–3 Jesus' words "I am the true vine" are another *I am* statement in this Gospel. The disciples are already connected to the vine, not on the basis of their works or adherence to the law, but based upon the word Jesus spoke to them. The idea that they are "clean" has to do with being purified from sins in order to be used by God. Unlike Old Testament Israel, which failed to produce the fruit of obedience, the disciples' hearts are cleansed from their sin so they can produce fruit.

15:11 Jesus tells the disciples all this so that they might experience the joy that He possesses. If they abide in Jesus, then they will have that perfect joy.

15:13 At one level, this verse defines the standard of love Jesus' disciples are to show to one another; at another level, it refers to Jesus' death on behalf of His friends. It is this level of sacrifice that Jesus wants the disciples to associate with love.

15:14 It might appear that Jesus is saying that you are a friend of Jesus if you are obedient; He tells the disciples that they are His friends "if ye do whatsoever I command you." However, it is not that their obedience makes them friends but rather that their friendship is characterized by obedience. The point is that Jesus lays down His life for them, and they, as a result of this love, become completely devoted to Him.

15:16 Jesus, out of His love, chose these men. Their relationship with God is a result of *His* choice, not theirs. The idea around the word *ordained* is that they have been set apart for a particular purpose: to bear fruit. Inherent to their salvation is their mission. This is true for every believer.

15:18–21 In order to help the disciples deal with the fear of future persecution, Jesus instructs them about suffering, identifying two reactions that "the world" (meaning, in this context, anyone not devoted to Jesus) will have to the disciples: hatred and persecution.

15:20 Everywhere Jesus went, He encountered a mixed reaction—those who hated what He said and those who believed. The disciples will receive similarly mixed reactions.

15:26–27 When Jesus goes to heaven, His testimony on earth will not go to heaven with Him but will stay and be proclaimed by the Holy Spirit. Not only will the Spirit bear witness, but the disciples will bear witness as well. In the face of these witnesses, Jesus' opponents will continue to reject the message just as they did when He walked the earth.

16:5–6 A major problem with the disciples is their self-focused minds. Sorrow has filled their hearts because it seems they are going to lose everything when Jesus goes away. This is the second time that Jesus has confronted the disciples' self-centeredness (see 14:28). They can't see past the persecution that is to come in order to appreciate the bigger picture of what Jesus is accomplishing through His departure.

16:8–11 The ministry of the Spirit to the world centers on the reproof of sin. The word *reprove* means "to expose, refute, or convince." The Spirit will also proclaim the end of Satan's reign, testifying that Satan and his system have already been condemned by God.

16:12–15 Jesus is beginning to draw His instruction to a close. It is time for them to endure the next few days. After that, the Spirit will work on their behalf.

16:20 The disciples' grief will not be *replaced* with joy but "turned into joy." The very event that plunges them into grief—Jesus' crucifixion—ultimately will lift them into joy.

16:21 Before a baby is born, there is sorrow and astounding pain. But once the baby is born, the focus suddenly shifts from pain to joy. The event becomes a day of celebration, to be commemorated every year of a person's life. It's not the event that changes but the *focus* of the event. And the birth becomes a greater matter than the sorrow or pain that precedes it. The sorrow is only temporary, but the joy is eternal.

16:24 "Full" joy is experienced by those who have an active prayer life with the Father. Their joy is strengthened because they are experiencing an ongoing relationship with the Father.

16:31–33 Observe Jesus' response to the disciples' hasty answer. In less than twenty-four hours, they will experience their first set of trials, and those trials will continue for the rest of their existence on earth. But Jesus wants them to fully understand that His peace will allow them to remain stable in the turbulent world around them. And the reason that His peace will do this is because His peace has overcome the world.

17:1 Today we often bow our heads in reverence when we pray. In the first-century Jewish culture, a common prayer posture was standing with eyes lifted to heaven. This signified two things: (1) that the person praying acknowledged God's place in heaven on the throne, and (2) that the person praying was coming to God with a clean and pure heart.

17:4–5 Jesus declares His perfect obedience to the Father. He finished the work that God called Him to do. Because of that, He prays that He will return to the union that He shared with the Father before He came to earth.

17:6 Jesus prays for the specific followers who were commissioned to bring the message of the Messiah to the world. These followers are described as those who kept the Word of God, which Jesus had made known to them.

17:9 Jesus is saying that the disciples are a part of His family, His true believers.

17:11–12 Jesus prays for protection for His disciples, that the Father will protect them in the same way that Jesus did while He was on earth. But even more than this, He will uphold them so they will remain an ever-visible representation of Christ on earth.

17:12 The "son of perdition" is Judas Iscariot. Judas's betrayal was predicted in the Old Testament (see Psalms 41:9; 109:4–13). The word *perdition*, sometimes translated "doomed to destruction," refers to someone who is utterly lost with no hope of ever being saved. A subtle point here is that the will of the Father

was accomplished in both Judas and the other eleven disciples.

17:17 This is the other side of the protection Jesus requests. Not only are the disciples to be protected from Satan, but they are also to be sanctified—that is, to be set apart for a specific purpose. It is the idea of being a holy vessel in the hands of the Master.

17:20–26 Jesus prays a threefold prayer for future generations of believers. First, He asks for unity, that His followers would know the oneness that exists between the Father and the Son. Because of Jesus' work with the disciples (revealing the Father), they have His life within them and are to be unified just as the Father and the Son are one. Second, Jesus prays for His followers to experience His full glory in heaven. Third, He prays that His followers will have His love within them. One of the functions of the Father's revelation was to place the unending love of God within those who believe.

18:4–5 Instead of putting up a fight, Jesus goes to these men before they can come to Him. Notice that the Gospel writer makes it clear that Judas is standing with the guards, not with the disciples. John also records yet another *I am* statement from Jesus, confirming His identity as God.

18:6 Close to seven hundred people fall to the ground in response to Jesus' statement—that is, because of the power of His name. This detail further highlights the fact that Jesus is offering Himself. It is God's will that He be arrested, not human will.

18:10–11 In Luke's Gospel we are told that Jesus heals Malchus (see Luke 22:50–51), but John focuses on Peter's mistake—Peter failed to see Jesus as being in control. Jesus rebukes Peter and tells him to put his sword away.

18:12 The Romans and the Jewish officers of the high priest—two groups that were more commonly in opposition to each other—worked together to arrest Jesus.

18:13 Annas, the father-in-law of Caiaphas, was a powerful man. For several years, he served as high priest, and then he continued his influence through his son-in-law's tenure as high priest. Annas's control of Caiaphas was no secret to the people.

18:15 John's Gospel moves from an introduction of the principal Jewish leaders to the story of Peter's failure—a story that shows how even with the best of intentions, it is impossible to be faithful to God in one's own power. Peter is following behind, accompanied by an unnamed disciple (who may not be one of the eleven). Other followers of Jesus are also referred to as disciples, for instance, Nicodemus (7:50) and Joseph of Arimathaea (19:38).

18:22 It was forbidden to strike a prisoner—a further illegality of Jesus' trial. The wording used here indicates that the officer hit Jesus hard, as one would strike an insubordinate criminal who was mouthing off to the authorities. There is a possibility that the officer used a stick rather than his hands.

18:28–40 It is at this point that Pilate is brought into the story. The Jews did not have the authority to enforce the death penalty. Therefore, they needed to have the Romans find Jesus guilty, and then the Romans could put Him on a cross.

18:29–30 Pilate's inquiry exposes the motives of the Jewish leaders. They tell Pilate, in essence, to "take our word for it." They are not interested in a trial, only an execution.

18:34–37 The exchange between Pilate and Jesus confirms that Pilate has no idea why Jesus is being accused. The interview does provide Jesus an opportunity to explain that He is indeed a king, but the kingdom of which He is a part of doesn't exist within earthly boundaries. Jesus is not subject to the affairs of this world. Even His wording—that He "came. . .into the world"—implies that He existed outside of it.

18:38–40 Pilate is suggesting that the truth cannot be found, that there is no absolute answer. Yet Jesus spoke the truth. Pilate finds no fault in Jesus, but the custom that makes releasing Barabbas a possibility negates Pilate's view of Jesus' innocence.

19:1 The Roman scourge was a stick wrapped in leather with long leather strips hanging off the end. Attached to the leather strips were bits of brass, lead, and bones filed to sharp points. The victim was strapped to the ground with his back up, tied to a post, or actually hung in the air. Scourging involved forty lashes on the back. This process could expose the arteries and even the internal organs. It shredded the skin. It was such a horrendous torture that no Roman citizen could ever legally be scourged—only the enemies of Rome. Many did not survive.

19:6–8 When Pilate reiterates that he has no official grounds on which to execute Jesus, the people explain their view on blasphemy. Pilate, scared and confused, makes his second attempt to free Jesus.

19:10–11 After Pilate reminds Jesus of his own power, Jesus responds, but only to put Pilate in his place. Any authority Pilate has is a delegated authority. Therefore, Jesus is not concerned about the outcome.

19:13–14 Pilate now resorts to political pressure by going to the Pavement, a place where official judgments were made. Any judgment made from the Pavement was permanent and binding. Pilate puts Jesus on display one more time with His robe, thorns, wounds, and blood. John's Gospel points out that it's almost the sixth hour. The passover celebration is at hand. A judgment needs to be made. Pilate wants to put the pressure of the decision on the Jewish leaders. If Jesus is going to be crucified, it will be because they made the decision.

19:15–16 In a purely hypocritical expression of loyalty to Caesar, the Jewish leaders call once more for Jesus' death.

19:17–18 John shows the crucifixion simply and clearly. His focus is the glory of Jesus, not the horror of the cross.

19:18 Jesus is hung between two thieves—an important detail because Isaiah 53:12 prophesied that the Messiah would be "numbered with the transgressors."

19:19–20 Pilate's sign, made for the top of the cross, becomes a center of controversy. Pilate believes Jesus to be innocent, yet for political reasons, he gives in to the crucifixion. It was a Roman custom to write the criminal's offense on the top of the cross, explaining the crime that warranted execution. Pilate's sign simply identifies Jesus as the King of the Jews and is written in Hebrew, Latin, and Greek so that all onlookers are able to read it.

19:21–22 It is unusual that such a sign carries no disgrace for the condemned. In this case, the disgrace is reserved for the Jewish leaders. They look guilty because they just crucified their King. In light of this, these Jews want the sign changed to put the offense back on Jesus—that He only *claimed* to be King. Pilate refuses, which may be a way of retaliating for the difficult position they put him in.

19:23–24 Jesus' "garments" would have included His shoes, belt, headdress, and outer cloak. The coat (inner garment) is one piece; therefore, the soldiers gamble to see who will get it, thus fulfilling Psalm 22:18.

19:26–27 Even on the cross, Jesus fulfills His duty as Mary's son in seeing to it that she is cared for. Jesus places her into the care of John. From this point on, John treats Mary as his own mother and cares for her.

19:32–37 Exodus 12:46 declares that the passover lamb is not to have any broken bones. Since the passover is a picture of the cross, Jesus was not to have any broken bones either.

19:38–42 Victims of crucifixion were often buried in a common grave. In Jesus' case, though, Joseph of Arimathaea and Nicodemus, two Jewish leaders who had become disciples of Jesus, ask Pilate for the body and take care of the funeral arrangements. Even in this, the scriptures are fulfilled. Isaiah 53:9 says that the Messiah would be a rich man in death. Though Jesus died the death of a wretched man, in a twist of circumstances, He was allowed to be buried in a rich man's tomb.

20:5 If Jesus' body had been moved by someone, then the "linen clothes"—that is, Jesus' burial clothes—would not be lying there. They would still be around the body. If someone stole the body, he or she would not likely unwrap it. The burial clothes are the first evidence of Jesus' bodily resurrection.

20:7 The second evidence of Jesus' resurrection that John offers is the carefully folded "napkin"—that is, Jesus' face cloth. While the body of the deceased was wrapped in strips of cloth, somewhat mummy-like, the face cloth was laid over the head. This piece of cloth is folded up and placed away from the wrappings. This is unlikely to be the work of grave robbers, who would not have taken the time to fold the cloth even if they chose to unwrap the dead body.

20:11–13 John's third piece of evidence for the resurrection is Jesus' own claim. John's account of

Mary's encounter with the two angels does not focus on Mary's reaction but on the angels' question. The angelic presence confirms this as a divine moment. They ask Mary a question, but not because the angels need the answer—Mary needs to know it. Mary thinks Jesus' body has been stolen. She thinks that Jesus is gone and has no idea what has taken place. The implication of the angels' question is that there is nothing to weep about. This is a day of rejoicing, not of tears.

20:19 To wish someone peace was to wish them all of the fullness and happiness that God intended. When Jesus uses this greeting, it carries a deeper significance because He wants the disciples to have the fullness of life and peace that is found in Him.

20:22 Jesus had promised that the Holy Spirit would come after the Ascension, but the event described here is not the same as the coming of the Holy Spirit described in Acts 2. Here Jesus is connecting the Holy Spirit with the mission of the disciples in anticipation of what will happen after His ascension.

20:24–27 Thomas was not with the other disciples in the room when Jesus gave the commission, though the other disciples obviously explained it to him. He responds with his famous skepticism, wanting physical confirmation. Jesus does appear again, announces peace, and then offers the physical evidence that Thomas has been looking for.

20:28–29 Jesus knows Thomas's doubts even though He wasn't in the room when Thomas voiced them. This is another way in which John's Gospel emphasizes Jesus' sovereignty over everything. He knows Thomas's doubts, and He meets Thomas at his point of need.

20:30–31 John states his purpose for writing his Gospel. He wants the reader to believe that Jesus is God manifested, that on the cross He bore all people's sin, and that when He rose from the dead, He gave humanity life.

21:1–14 After Jesus' resurrection, He is in His glorified body and only appears to those who know Him.

21:1–3 Seven disciples are fishing. They are not returning to their old trade, but they are continuing to fish in this transition time. They are no longer with Jesus daily, and yet the Holy Spirit has not come and empowered them to preach. They are waiting for their mission to start.

21:7–8 After the disciples' miraculous catch, John realizes that the man on the shore is Jesus. Who else controls the fish in the ocean? Note Peter's zeal in response. The rest of the disciples are left to carry the load of fish in by themselves as Peter is swimming to the shore.

21:12–14 By the time Jesus invites the disciples to eat breakfast, they all recognize Him. When this Gospel was written, years later, these kinds of statements offered proof for those who questioned whether the resurrection was a reality. John tells us that this is the third manifestation of Jesus to the disciples, and it is an experience filled with service and compassion.

21:15 Jesus' question addresses the heart of Peter's problem: He does not understand the nature of love. He loves Jesus with passion, enthusiasm, and emotion, but his love is lacking simple obedience. Peter's answer declares Jesus as the center of his affection. Jesus wants that love and affection channeled through the tending of His lambs. If Peter loves Jesus, then he will love and value the things that Jesus loves and values.

21:16 Jesus asks the question again, and this time His directive to Peter contains a different word—one having to do with nourishing, caring for, and treating the sheep as if they are an extension of his own body. It is more than just pet-sitting; it is engaged nurture.

21:17 Jesus asks the question a third time, which grieves Peter. He takes it personally that Jesus has not trusted his responses, but Jesus is restoring Peter. For each time Peter looked out for himself at the expense of obedience by denying Jesus (see 18:15–27), he will be restored. This last time, Jesus charges Peter to make sure he takes Jesus' lambs as his primary responsibility.

21:19 Jesus now addresses Peter's death. We know that Peter was indeed crucified. Church tradition claims that he asked to be crucified upside down because he did not want to die in the same way as Jesus. In light of this information, Jesus calls Peter to follow Him. The Greek word used here indicates that Peter is to follow Jesus constantly and consistently, not sporadically.

21:20–24 At one time, it was believed that Jesus' response to Peter's inquiry meant that John was going to live forever. Here, as Gospel writer, John clears up the rumor and says that Jesus was not giving a prophecy about the manner of John's death.

THE
ACTS OF THE APOSTLES

INTRODUCTION TO ACTS ■ One of the earliest titles for this book of the Bible was simply "Acts," with other early titles being "Acts of Apostles," "Acts of the Holy Apostles," and the popular "The Acts of the Apostles," which isn't really accurate. The acts of Peter and Paul are highlighted in this book, yet many of the other apostles are hardly mentioned.

AUTHOR ■ As was the case with his Gospel, Luke doesn't identify himself as the writer of Acts, though his authorship is seldom questioned. The information he provided in the book of Luke was a result of his research to verify the testimony of eyewitnesses (Luke 1:1–4). His involvement in Acts is even more personal. Much of this book, like Luke's Gospel, is written in the third person. But certain sections (16:10–17; 20:5–15; 21:1–18; 27:1–28:16) switch to first person. It is evident that Luke accompanied Paul on various legs of his missionary journeys. Luke was a doctor (Colossians 4:14) who had an eye for detail. He seems particularly interested in seafaring, and he provides vivid descriptions as he narrates. Many of his first-person accounts are of incidents occurring when Paul is traveling by ship.

OCCASION ■ Like his Gospel, Luke's book of Acts is addressed to Theophilus (1:1). The purpose of the Gospel narrative was so that readers would have an accurate account of what happened (Luke 1:4). With his follow-up book of Acts, Luke is sending his primary recipient (and perhaps his financial sponsor) a well-researched account of the spread of Christianity throughout both Jewish and Gentile communities. Since Luke was personally involved in the growth of the church, he was able to provide both an insightful historical overview and a corresponding apologetic emphasis.

1:1 Luke addresses this book to Theophilus as he did his Gospel. The use of the title "most excellent" (see Luke 1:3) suggests that Theophilus had a position of high social status. Perhaps he was a Roman court official with whom Paul was scheduled to meet. In his opening statement, Luke emphasizes that Jesus' earthly ministry was only a beginning. What Jesus had begun would continue to expand in geographic and spiritual significance.

1:2–5 Luke describes four stages of development that Christ instituted for disciples: First, He chose them; none of the apostles were self-appointed. Second, He commissioned them (see also Matthew 28:16–20), giving them specific instructions. Third, He showed Himself to them. It was no ghost or apparition that appeared to the disciples during the forty-day period following Jesus' resurrection. Fourth, He promised them the Holy Spirit, who would provide the power and authority they needed to carry out His instructions.

1:6–7 In his Gospel, Luke noted numerous times when the apostles either misunderstood Jesus or seemingly ignored what He was saying as they held their own discussions about position and power. It's not surprising that Jesus once again has to steer their attention to the need for simple obedience and witness rather than establishing rank in God's kingdom.

1:9 Some argue that the statement about Jesus being "taken up" reflects a prescientific view of cosmology, with heaven being somewhere above us and hell somewhere below. Yet such an argument seems to press the point too far. Christ's ascension is not about the order of the universe or the physical location of heaven. Rather, it shows a distinct break as Jesus leaves His

human companions and returns to His Father. He had been appearing and disappearing for forty days. What better way to show He would not be coming back than to let everyone observe His final departure into the clouds?

1:12–15 The number of believers who gather after Jesus' ascension is a meager 120. With the exception of Judas Iscariot, all the apostles are present. And by this time, Jesus' brothers, who previously hadn't believed in Him (see John 7:5), are also among the believers.

1:20 Peter quotes portions of Psalms 69:25 and 109:8. These psalms typologically predicted the betrayal of Jesus and what should be done in response. With Jesus no longer available to consult, and prior to the arrival of the Holy Spirit, the apostles were using scripture to guide their decision-making and discernment of God's will for their lives.

1:24–26 To ensure that the decision is God's and not theirs, the disciples pray and cast lots to decide. Casting lots may seem like tossing a coin to us, but it had long been a highly respected method of determining God's will (see Leviticus 16:7–10; 1 Samuel 14:40–42; Nehemiah 10:34; Proverbs 16:33). Yet it is interesting to note that scripture says nothing more of Matthias, the one chosen. In addition, this is the final mention of casting lots in the Bible. After the arrival of the Holy Spirit, such measures were no longer necessary. Some suggest that the apostles acted hastily and that Paul was intended to be the twelfth apostle. However, Paul would not have met either of the criteria they were using, and he was aware that his calling was quite unlike that of the others in Jesus' inner circle (see 1 Corinthians 15:7–8).

2:2–4 Two covenant promises are fulfilled on the day of Pentecost: God had promised to send His Spirit to the people of Israel (see Ezekiel 36:27) and to put His law in their minds and write it on their hearts (Jeremiah 31:33). In addition, God turns a harvest festival into a memorable event regarding the "harvest" that Jesus mentioned in Luke 10:2. Notably, the sound (a violent wind), fire, and speech that had been present atop mount Sinai occur once again on the day of Pentecost. Of the three, the speech was perhaps the most impressive sign of all. A group of uncultured and unschooled Galileans is suddenly able to present the Gospel in the various native languages of all the visitors gathered in Jerusalem for the feast.

2:5–11 Luke identifies fifteen people groups, listing them (approximately) in geographic order from east to west. The fact that they all hear the Gospel clearly explained in their own language represents the voice of God and the universality of the message.

2:14–15 Peter makes it clear that the phenomenon the crowds have witnessed is not the result of too much wine—especially not at 9:00 a.m.!

2:16–21 Peter quotes Joel 2:28–32 to explain what is happening. Joel is a rather gloomy book, written during a period when an invasion of locusts had destroyed every green plant, creating a national disaster for Israel's agrarian economy. Rather than soothing the people with promises of comfort, Joel told them that their situation would get worse. The locusts were a symbol of even more intense judgment to come. Yet in the midst of such gloom, Joel promised that God will pour out His Spirit and provide salvation for everyone who calls on His name.

2:23 Peter is addressing his fellow Jews and all those who live in Jerusalem (see 2:14). He holds his own people accountable for Jesus' death. However, it is important to note that the word *wicked* can also mean "lawless," and those without the law were the Gentiles.

2:24 The act of putting Jesus to death is soon overshadowed by God's action of raising Him from the dead.

2:25–33 Peter appeals to the Old Testament a second time, this time quoting Psalm 16:8–11, a psalm of David. Although it was written a thousand years before Christ and primarily understood as a reference to the Old Testament king of Israel, one portion could not possibly have referred to David. In Peter's speech, he points out that David's tomb is there in their midst, so David's body had certainly seen decay. Jesus is therefore the Holy One referred to in Psalm 16:10, who had overcome death and the grave as prophesied by David long ago.

2:34–35 Peter's quotation comes from another of David's psalms (Psalm 110:1). This verse is referenced in the New Testament at least twenty-five times. The first "Lord" is the Hebrew word *Yahweh*, referring to the great God of Israel. The second "Lord" is the word *adonai*, meaning an individual greater than the speaker. So David is saying that God invites another person, someone greater than David, to sit at His right hand. Peter again clarifies that this significant individual is none other than the Messiah.

2:41–47 In a modern setting, such growth might create numerous problems. Yet in its first days, it seemed that the early church was doing everything right. It was, and continues to be, a model for worship (both collectively in the temple and in smaller groups in homes), discipleship, caring for others, evangelizing, and serving. The "fear" (or godly awe) that fills the people is reflected in their attitudes, relationships, giving, and every other aspect of their lives.

3:2 This particular gate (Beautiful) is usually considered to be the Nicanor Gate—the main eastern gate to the temple precincts from the court of the Gentiles. According to legend, the gate was being transported by ship from Alexandria to Jerusalem when a terrible storm began. The gate was about to be jettisoned, and a man named Nicanor requested to be thrown overboard along with it. Miraculously, both survived the storm, and the gate was forever associated with the man. Josephus described the gate as being seventy-five feet tall with double doors made of Corinthian brass. The beggar must have appeared a pathetic creature indeed at the foot of this gleaming, magnificent gate.

3:6–7 Perhaps Peter recalled the day that Jesus raised Jairus's daughter from the dead (see Luke 8:54), because he doesn't merely tell the man to get up; he extends the command and then extended his hand to help.

3:8–10 The healed beggar's reaction is noteworthy. He praises God verbally while simultaneously walking and jumping. His physical enthusiasm is certainly praise as well. And as onlookers see the commotion and recognize the man who is leaping around, they are amazed.

3:11 Even in his unbridled enthusiasm, the healed beggar holds on to Peter and John. Solomon's porch, next to the outer court of the temple, was a roofed area supported by rows of tall stone columns. It is here that Peter, for a second time, finds himself surrounded by curious onlookers wanting an explanation for the awe-inspiring events they have witnessed (see 2:14–36).

3:13–15 Peter describes three specific ways that Jesus had suffered at the hands of the people: First, they—including those in the crowd—had demanded that Jesus be killed even after Pilate tried to exonerate Him. Second, they had demanded release of a murderer rather than God's own Son. Third, they had killed the very One who made life possible for them, but God had raised Him from the dead.

3:16 It was only through the power of Christ that Peter and John were able to heal the crippled man (see 3:6–7). So it must have been difficult for the people to hear that Christ's own suffering had been at *their* hands.

3:22–26 The people had missed the message of the prophets concerning Jesus; even Moses (whom they revered) had told them to look for a prophet like him (see Deuteronomy 18:15–19). Also, the other prophets from Samuel onward had reaffirmed Moses' message of a coming servant of God. Moses and the prophets had done as God had instructed; now it is up to the people to do the same by turning from their wicked ways.

4:1 Peter's teaching attracts the unwelcome attention of the Sadducees, who did not believe that people were resurrected after death (see Luke 20:27). The "captain of the temple" who accompanies the Sadducees held a priestly rank, second only to the high priest, and was responsible for the maintenance of law and order.

4:3–6 The purpose of Peter and John's overnight incarceration is to convene the Sanhedrin, a seventy-member council comprised of the high priest, members of his family, experts in the law (including scribes and Pharisees), and other respected members of the community (elders). They sat in a semicircle as they served as both the supreme court and senate of the nation of Israel.

4:8–12 Peter's response to the Sanhedrin is an emphatic demonstration of the courage Jesus had previously promised His followers (see Luke 21:12–15). There are three parts to his defense. First, he characterizes the healing of the crippled man as an act of kindness, brought about by the name of Jesus. Second, he draws attention to the fact that the same Sanhedrin trying his case had been responsible for the death of Jesus, but that God had vindicated Jesus by raising Him from the dead. Peter considers their actions a fulfillment of prophecy (Psalm 118:22). Jesus was the rejected stone that became the crowning piece of God's work. Third, Peter changes the subject from healing to salvation. The physical restoration of the crippled man is a picture of the salvation available to all people through Jesus.

4:13 The Sanhedrin is astonished at the courage of Peter and John. Jesus had been an insightful and formidable opponent of the religious authorities who had repeatedly debated and criticized Him. These two are clearly ordinary men—but then again, the religious leaders had underestimated Jesus as well (see John 7:15).

4:14 Because the healed man stands before the Sanhedrin, they cannot deny the miracle, but neither will they acknowledge it. Even such a convincing display could not penetrate the Sadducees' preoccupation with protecting their vested interests.

4:21 With all the people praising God for the miraculous healing of the crippled man, the council can see no way to punish Peter and John. So it threatens them more and then lets them go.

4:23–24 The believers "had all things common" (see 2:44), so all the other church members had a stake in what would happen to Peter and John. That the apostles are released with nothing more than a slap on the wrist is a cause for great rejoicing.

4:31 God acknowledges the believers' prayers, responding by shaking their meeting place and filling them all with the Holy Spirit. As a result, their boldness is intensified.

4:32–33 Since the arrival of the Holy Spirit on the day of Pentecost, every mention of the gathering of believers has emphasized their unity. Here they are "of one heart and of one soul." The proof of their love for one another is seen in their selfless giving. Despite their large numbers, none among the believers were in need of

anything because they didn't even claim possessions as their own. The willingness of those with wealth to share with others more than covered the needs of the group.

4:34–36 Generosity even reaches the point where some people sell their houses and property to donate to the needs of the church. One such person was named Joseph, yet he would become known throughout the rest of the New Testament as Barnabas, a nickname meaning "son of consolation."

5:1–3 From all appearances, Barnabas and Ananias did the same thing. Both sold a piece of property. Both brought the proceeds of the sale to the apostles. The only difference might appear to be that Barnabas brought all he received, while Ananias holds out a little for himself. Yet Ananias is guilty of dishonesty and deceit. He and his wife agree to misrepresent the selling price when reporting to the church.

5:4 According to Peter, the couple's sin isn't that they hold some of the money for themselves; that is their right. Instead, what they think is a subtle attempt to make themselves appear better is actually a lie to God.

5:11 The church members become fearful after hearing what happened (see also verse 5). The situation is a classic example of what Paul will later teach: "Be not deceived; God is not mocked" (Galatians 6:7). This story is a graphic reminder that there are no "little" sins.

5:12–14 The story of Ananias and Sapphira (5:1–10) had a positive impact on the community. Although Luke seems to say that no one else dared join the believers, this statement probably refers to those who would have been tempted to join out of curiosity or with less than total commitment. Sincere believers continued to be added to their number.

5:16 People begin to flock in crowds to Jerusalem as news spreads of the many wonderful things taking place.

5:17–18 The Sadducees aren't happy that the apostles have ignored their warnings to quit talking about Jesus (see 4:18, 21), so this time they have a larger group arrested and jailed. Luke records their real motive: "indignation" or jealousy. Clearly, God was at work among the believers in Jesus, and all the Sadducees could do was observe (and complain) as outsiders.

5:19–21 The apostles are supposed to be in prison overnight, but their sentence is commuted by an angel who releases them. Rather than take the opportunity to hide or escape, the apostles follow the angel's orders to go tell people about the Gospel.

5:22–25 The truly miraculous aspect of the apostles' prison break is that no one knows they are gone. The cells are still locked and the guards still at their posts. It isn't until the Sanhedrin assembles and sends for the apostles that they are discovered missing. Someone finally has to tell the council that the apostles are teaching in the temple courts—one of the most public places in Jerusalem.

5:26 To avoid a potential stoning by the people, the temple officials decide to use tact instead of force to summon the apostles.

5:29–32 Peter and the other apostles give the religious leaders a mini-sermon about the significance of Jesus and the Holy Spirit, and how the Jewish leaders had contributed to Jesus' death.

5:40–42 Rather than being despondent from the pain and shame of their punishment, the apostles rejoice that they have been deemed worthy of suffering in the same way that Jesus did. They have the honor of being dishonored.

6:1 With the number of disciples steadily increasing in the church, problems were to be expected. But discrimination should not have been among them.

6:2–3 The fact that the apostles seek out people known to be full of the Spirit and wisdom indicates that serving tables is just as much a spiritual calling as teaching and preaching. The apostles' plan is wise for other reasons as well. They do not merely appoint a committee; they empower a ministry team with the authority to get the job done. In addition, they choose seven people to oversee the new program rather than a single person. There is great wisdom in the plurality of leadership in the church, with ministry exercised in community.

6:5 The names listed here are Greek. The church selected people who would be most understanding of the problem of discrimination, striving to be inclusive rather than exclusive.

6:9 The "synagogue of the Libertines" may have been composed of descendants of Jewish prisoners of war enslaved by the Roman general Pompey when he conquered Palestine in 63 BC. Later released, they formed a synagogue community of "freedmen." It is unclear whether Luke has in mind one synagogue or two or more synagogues.

6:9–11 The topic of the argument with Stephen is not mentioned, but the members of the synagogue were no match for his wisdom. Yet rather than concede that he knows more than they do, they used the same tactic the Pharisees had used with Jesus: enlisting false witnesses to twist his words.

6:13–14 Stephen's supposed offense is a double charge of blasphemy: speaking against the temple and the Law of Moses. The Law was God's Word, and the temple was God's house. To speak against either was to speak against God Himself.

6:15 Many believe that Stephen's face glowed with divine glory much like Moses' did after he had spent time in the presence of God (see Exodus 34:29–35).

7:1–53 In response to the high priest's inquiry, Stephen launches into a lengthy sermon. In the panorama of God's dealings with His people, Stephen focuses on four main epochs of Israel's history, each one with a major character. In each case, Stephen's point is that God's presence cannot be limited to any particular place. On the contrary, the God of the Old Testament was a living God, a God on the move who was always calling His people to fresh adventures and always accompanying them wherever they went. As such, nothing Stephen has taught is out of line with the Old Testament.

7:2–8 Stephen focuses on Abraham. It was thanks to Abraham's obedience that the Hebrews first got to the promised land. Abraham left a comfortable home in Mesopotamia only because God told him to. He was later rewarded with land, a child of his own, and descendants too numerous to be counted. It was through Abraham that God's covenant of circumcision was established. God also shared with Abraham what would happen during the next phase of history—slavery in Egypt.

7:9–19 Stephen reminds his audience of Joseph's story. It was thanks to Joseph's obedience that the Israelites didn't starve during a seven-year famine. After four hundred years in Egypt, however, Joseph's descendants had grown into an immense force that threatened the Egyptian leaders who no longer remembered Joseph. Therefore, the members of the family of Israel (the Israelites) were enslaved.

7:20–43 Stephen recounts the story of Moses. God had told Abraham that his descendants would become slaves in Egypt but that He would punish the nation that enslaved them (see 7:6–7). It was thanks to Moses' reluctant obedience that the Israelites at last departed from Egypt and (after numerous trials and lapses of faith) finally made it to the promised land. Had Moses' parents obeyed Pharaoh's instructions, Moses would have been put to death as an infant. But through a series of God-directed events, he grew up as Pharaoh's grandson instead. He spent forty years in the palace, forty years in a lonely existence in the wilderness, and forty years leading his people. His final forty years were especially challenging because the people continually complained and even built a golden calf as soon as Moses was gone for a while.

7:44–50 Stephen considers David and Solomon. During their wilderness years and early days in the promised land, the Israelites had a portable tabernacle that allowed the priests to operate and the people to worship and offer sacrifices. David wanted to build a permanent structure for God, but his request was denied. Instead, God allowed Solomon to construct the temple. But Solomon realized at the time, and Stephen reiterates in his speech, that God cannot be limited to any physical space—not even a temple dedicated in His name (see 1 Kings 8:27).

7:54–56 While the council members react furiously, Stephen sees a vision of Jesus, which he describes aloud. His use of the title "Son of man" recalls how Jesus often referred to Himself, subtly combining the human and divine nature of His messianic role. (This is also the final use of the term in the New Testament.) The fact that Stephen sees Jesus standing at God's right hand may indicate that Jesus is waiting to receive Stephen into His presence.

7:57–59 The Sanhedrin was supposed to be a supreme-court-like body with strict rules and procedures. But here its members act no better than a lynch mob. They don't have the authority to carry out a death sentence, yet they drag Stephen outside the city and stone him.

8:3 Saul quickly moves from tending coats to leading full-scale persecution of believers. He is cruel and heartless, going from house to house and dragging off both men and women to be imprisoned—all in his desire to destroy the church. Paul's story is dropped abruptly at this point, but it will be picked up again in Acts 9.

8:4 It must have been difficult, if not traumatic, for believers in Jerusalem to disperse. Yet everywhere they went, they preached about Jesus and began to see positive things happening.

8:5–9 Philip's display of God's power is overshadowing the work of a sorcerer named Simon who had made a living in Samaria for a while.

8:10–12 Simon's boast to be the "great power" may have been a claim of divinity, or perhaps it was enough for him to claim an association with some unseen power. In either case, his ability to amaze the Samaritans with his magic comes to an end when they see Philip performing genuine miracles in the name of Jesus.

8:14–17 One great miracle has not yet been observed in Samaria. For some reason, the belief and baptism of the Samaritans were not accompanied by the receiving of the Holy Spirit, as all previous conversions had been. Why the delay? The centuries of hostility between the Jews and the Samaritans may help explain. The schism had formed long ago because of racial and theological differences. For the Samaritans to believe in the same Saviour and be baptized in the same Name as the Jews was an unprecedented event. The delay in the coming of the Holy Spirit allows Peter and John to witness their conversion so they can return to the church in Jerusalem and confirm God's work among their former enemies.

8:18–24 Judging from Simon's attempt to bribe Peter, it is doubtful that he had ever made a sincere decision to repent and follow Jesus. Even after Peter's harsh rebuke, Simon won't pray to God directly but looks for someone else to pray for him. The word *simony* arose from this story, meaning the buying or selling of ecclesiastical pardons, offices, and such. According to one early church tradition, Simon started the heresy of Gnosticism and led believers astray with his false teachings.

8:26–27 After such rousing success in Samaria, the angel's instructions to Philip seem to make little sense. Gaza is the most southerly of five Philistine cities near the Mediterranean coast. The road between Jerusalem and Gaza stretched through the desert for up to sixty miles. Why leave the crowds of eager-to-hear Samaritans to go into isolation in the wilderness? Yet Philip seems to respond without hesitation.

8:27 The eunuch was an important official, in charge of the queen mother's treasury. The Ethiopia mentioned here is not the contemporary country east of Sudan but rather an area that extended from southern Egypt into central Sudan. The queen's treasurer had traveled a great distance to worship in Jerusalem, but the fact that he was a eunuch may have prevented his inclusion in the ceremonies because Hebrew law forbade it (see

Deuteronomy 23:1). Perhaps he had gone all that way only to be turned away from the temple.

8:39 As soon as the two come up out of the water, Philip disappears under the power of the Spirit of the Lord. The Ethiopian never sees him again, but he leaves rejoicing. It appears that when the Ethiopian gets back home, he starts a family—not a physical one, but a spiritual one. The Christian church in Ethiopia sprang up and continued to grow, perhaps as a result of the Ethiopian's newfound understanding of the Gospel, although there is no direct proof.

8:40 Azotus is the Old Testament city of Ashdod. It was miles away from where Philip had been before. He then makes his way north to Caesarea, where he appears to settle (see 21:8).

9:1 Saul had previously been involved with the stoning of Stephen (see 7:58). Whether he actually participated in the killings of other believers is unknown, but this verse implies that he might have.

9:4 Jesus doesn't accuse Saul of persecuting the church; it is Jesus Himself who is being persecuted. Saul will later come to understand the close interrelationship between Jesus and His followers and will incorporate the concept into his Epistles.

9:10–14 Jesus is calling Saul to an exciting new ministry, but first He calls a believer named Ananias for a short-term assignment. Ananias had full knowledge of Saul's original mission—to persecute believers—so it is no small matter for him to approach Saul and treat him as a believing brother.

9:16 Over the course of his life, Saul was beaten eight times for his faith. Once he was pelted with rocks and left for dead. On various occasions he spent time in prison. Tradition says that eventually Saul was beheaded in Rome by order of Caesar.

9:20 During Saul's time in Damascus, he immediately begins to preach in the synagogues that Jesus is the Son of God. The antagonist of the believers had become a protagonist. The persecutor had become a proclaimer. Right from the start, Saul is a powerful witness and defender of the faith.

9:26 Back in Jerusalem, Saul is a man with no place to go. He, of course, wants to unite with the believers there, but they don't know what happened to him in Damascus.

9:26–27 Saul needs someone to reach out to him, as Ananias had done in Damascus. That person turns out to be Barnabas, the "son of consolation" (see 4:36–37). We aren't told that Barnabas received a vision or special divine instruction to provide the courage to meet with Saul. Perhaps he did it because he thought giving someone a chance for repentance and forgiveness was simply the right thing to do.

9:32–35 In Lydda, Peter comes across a man named Aeneas who has been paralyzed for eight years and is currently bedridden. We aren't told of any preliminary conversation between the two. It appears that Peter simply declares Aeneas healed in the name of Jesus and tells him to get up and walk, which Aeneas immediately does. In many of Jesus' miracles, healing had been in response to a person's declaration of faith. Yet there are other instances, such as this one, where the person makes no expression of faith prior to being healed. It appears that in some cases healing initiates faith.

9:36 Joppa was Judea's main seaport, only about twelve miles away from Lydda. The names *Tabitha* (Aramaic) and *Dorcas* (Greek) both mean "gazelle." Tabitha was a skilled seamstress who had a wonderful reputation for doing good.

9:39–40 The Bible records three instances when Jesus raised someone from the dead, but none of His followers had ever attempted a miracle of this magnitude. It is possible that the believers in Joppa have sent for Peter only for his consolation and prayer support during this difficult time, although it seems that they are expressing faith that he will perform a great miracle. Peter had been present when Jesus raised Jairus's daughter (Luke 8:51–56), and he follows much the same procedure here—sending out the mourners, kneeling down, and telling the woman to get up.

10:1–8 Previous sections of Acts have hinted at a ministry to the Gentiles. The great response of the Samaritans to Philip's preaching (see 8:4–8, 14–17) was a start, even though the Samaritans were ethnically and theologically related to the Jews. The conversion of the Ethiopian eunuch (see 8:38–39) was another positive sign of things to come. Now another noteworthy Gentile comes into the picture—a centurion named Cornelius.

10:11–12 Many (or perhaps all) of the animals, reptiles, and birds that Peter sees are not "clean" as defined in the Law of Moses (and many were specifically prohibited in Leviticus 11).

10:14–16 Peter's reaction is emphatic. His hardline stance is reminiscent of two previous occasions: once when Jesus had tried to tell the apostles of His impending death (Matthew 16:21–22) and again when Jesus tried to wash Peter's feet (John 13:6–8). It seems that Peter is still in the habit of trying to tell the Lord how things should be done in His kingdom. Even after a second and third command, Peter holds fast. Then the sheet disappears back into heaven.

10:17–18 Peter hardly has time to make sense of the vision before Cornelius's messenger arrives and calls out for him.

10:20 It is interesting to note that the word translated *doubting nothing* can also mean "to make no distinction." Peter is likely beginning to see the connection between his vision challenging the distinction between clean and unclean foods and the timely arrival of Gentile (unclean) visitors.

10:23 The invitation is certainly a step in the right direction. For one thing, Peter has been waiting for lunch and probably shares it with his three visitors. In addition, it is too late to begin the thirty-mile trip from Joppa back to Caesarea, so the three men need overnight accommodations. Most Jews wouldn't consider allowing Gentiles under their roofs, much less overnight. God is beginning to break down some of the divisive barriers.

10:27–28 Peter walks right into Cornelius's home, breaking down old taboos and setting an example for both the Gentiles there and the Jewish believers he has brought with him. By this time, it is clear that he has come to understand his vision as a sign that the Gentiles are no longer to be considered unclean.

10:30–33 Cornelius succinctly explains the reason he had sent for Peter. It is apparent that both Peter and Cornelius are not acting on their own instincts but following what God has instructed them to do.

10:34–43 Peter speaks to the crowd about Jesus' life and ministry, His death, and His resurrection. He emphasizes the divine plan behind the events that had played out during Jesus' time on earth.

10:39 Peter offers not only the facts about Jesus but also his personal verification as an eyewitness—both before and after Jesus' crucifixion.

10:42–43 Peter concludes with an image of Jesus as the One appointed as God's judge of humanity, yet makes it clear that forgiveness and salvation are available to anyone who believes in Him.

10:44–46 Peter is still speaking when the truth of his words is confirmed by the arrival of the Holy Spirit. The Jewish believers are amazed to see Gentiles speaking in tongues and praising God—which demonstrates Peter's wisdom in bringing them to be witnesses.

10:47–48 Philip had baptized the Ethiopian eunuch—who may have been a Jewish proselyte—in the solitude of the desert (see Acts 8:38). This, however, marks the first time Gentiles are baptized into the church along with Jewish believers. Apparently there is no objection, because Peter sees to their baptisms right away.

11:2–3 Upon his return to Jerusalem, Peter immediately receives criticism from the Jewish believers for visiting and eating with Gentiles. This accusation is somewhat reminiscent from the ones Jesus had regularly received from the religious leaders for eating with publicans (tax collectors) and sinners.

11:4–17 In explanation, Peter starts from the beginning and reviews his vision, Cornelius's visit from the angel, the coming of the Holy Spirit to the Gentile believers, and the unanimous decision to baptize them. He repeatedly emphasizes the work of God's Spirit as instrumental in bringing about the events.

11:18 Peter's critics relent and praise God. As hard as it was to understand at the time, God was offering salvation even to the Gentiles. And if God was removing the distinctions between Jews and Gentiles, what right did Peter—or anyone else—have to harbor old prejudices? The dispute is settled, but only temporarily. It will take a long while and many additional debates to work through all the obstacles to granting Gentiles the same rights and privileges of church membership that the Jews enjoyed.

11:19–30 At this point, Luke returns to the persecution that followed the stoning of Stephen. From here, Luke traces a different story line, starting with noteworthy events taking place in Antioch of Syria.

11:19 Antioch was the third largest city in the Roman world, after Rome and Alexandria. It lay three hundred miles north of Jerusalem, about fifteen miles inland from the Mediterranean Sea. Its population (estimated to be 500,000 to 800,000) included around 100,000 Jews along with a number of Gentile proselytes to Judaism. Antioch was also a popular hedonistic destination, accused by the Roman satirist Juvenal of having a corrupting influence on Rome itself. Yet it was here where some of the victims of the persecution in Jerusalem had settled and taught the Gospel.

11:25 Tarsus, where Saul is staying (see 9:30), was about ninety miles away, yet Barnabas goes there to invite him to Antioch as well. Tradition indicates that Luke was from Antioch, so it is possible that he was among the new converts who learned of the truth of Jesus from the lips of Barnabas and Saul during this time.

12:2–4 King Herod Agrippa I was the grandson of Herod the Great and a nephew of the Herod (Antipas) who had killed John the Baptist. He ruled Judea from a headquarters in Jerusalem from AD 41 to 44, the year he died.

12:3 The feast of unleavened bread, or passover, was one of three annual religious festivals that Jewish males were expected to attend. During passover, Jerusalem's population swelled with men loyal to their history and traditions. When Herod sees that the death of James pleases the people, he arrests and imprisons Peter. By now, most people knew that Peter was the leading apostle in the church and that he had been associating with Gentiles. He is the perfect target in Herod's ongoing quest for popularity.

12:6 Usually a prisoner's left hand was chained to a guard; however, Peter is chained to guards at *both* hands. Despite the very real threat to his life, Peter sleeps soundly—most likely an indication of his lack of fear or worry. Perhaps he had confidence in Jesus' previous prediction that he would grow to be an old man (see John 21:18).

12:7–9 Peter's rescue is so unlikely that at first he doesn't know if it is actually happening or if he is having another vision.

12:13–18 Peter's inability to get inside at first is comic in its true-to-life depiction. Even though committed church members are earnestly praying for Peter's release, they find it hard to believe when it actually happens. The servant girl is too excited to open the door, and the other believers are too skeptical to go see for themselves. Meanwhile, Peter keeps knocking until someone finally lets him in.

12:15 The assumption that the figure at the door is Peter's angel reflects the belief (based partially on Jesus' words in Matthew 18:10) that guardian angels oversee God's people and can take on the appearance of the person being protected. Another possibility is that the word *angel* is a reference to a person being dispatched by Peter with a message (the Greek word used here can mean either "angel" or "messenger"). A third possibility

is that the believers think Herod has already killed Peter, and the apostle's spirit is showing itself to them.

12:18–19 Herod discovers Peter is gone. He holds the guards responsible, probably assuming the only way Peter could have escaped was through their cooperation with him or through negligence. Either way, their sentence is death.

12:20–23 Luke's version of this account is quite concise, compared to that of the Jewish historian Josephus. It seems that Herod stood in the outdoor theater on a festival day, attired in a silver robe that gleamed in the sunshine. The people, eager to flatter him, went so far as to call him a god, and Herod said nothing to correct them. He was then immediately struck with stomach pains and had to be carried out of the theater. According to Josephus, he died five days later.

13:1–4 The commissioning of Barnabas and Saul marks a turning point in Acts. Until now, the church's contact with Gentiles has been almost incidental. But here, under the leading of the Holy Spirit, the prophets and teachers at Antioch send two dedicated church members into predominantly Gentile territory.

13:6–7 Paphos was the provincial capital on the western coast of the island. It is there where the Roman proconsul, a man named Sergius Paulus, hears about Barnabas and Saul and sends for them.

13:8–11 Luke refers to the proconsul's attendant as Elymas, a nickname that means "sorcery." Introduced in verse 6 as Bar-jesus, Elymas falsely claims to be a Jewish prophet. When he tries to sway the proconsul against Barnabas and Saul, he is struck temporarily blind. It was an appropriate attention-getter for someone who tried to blind others to the truth of God's Word. (Also, as Saul knew from experience, temporary blindness could lead to clear spiritual vision [see 9:1–19].)

13:12 This was another first for Christianity—the presentation of the Gospel to someone in authority in Roman aristocracy. The conversion of the proconsul also legitimized a direct ministry to the Gentiles.

13:13 After spending time in an area familiar to Barnabas, the travelers sail north to Pamphylia, Paul's home province—a 100-mile journey that would have taken Paul (as he is known from now on) and Barnabas from sea level to an elevation of 3,600 feet. John Mark's reason for leaving is not stated. He was young and may have been homesick or fearful of illness or other dangers of travel. Or because of his strong ties to the Jerusalem church, he might not have been entirely comfortable with the attention being given to Gentiles. If so, he would hardly be the only Jewish believer to express discontent in the weeks and months to come. But whatever the reason for Mark's leaving, it will later cause a rift between Paul and Barnabas (see 15:36–41).

13:14 Antioch in Pisidia is not to be confused with the Antioch that had sent Paul and Barnabas on this journey, or with another Antioch in nearby Phrygia. The popularity of the name was due to a ruler in 281 BC who had both a father and a son named Antiochus, and founded sixteen cities named in honor of them.

13:16–41 This passage records the longest of Paul's sermons (though no doubt in condensed form) to nonbelievers in Acts. The content is very similar to previous messages presented by Peter (2:14–39) and Stephen (7:2–53), providing a broad overview of Israel's history and concluding that Jesus was the fulfillment of all that had been promised.

13:20 Paul's reference to 450 years likely includes the 400 years spent by the Israelites in Egypt, 40 years in the wilderness, and about another decade spent conquering and settling the promised land.

13:33–37 Paul acknowledges the reverence the people hold for King David and says that God had raised up Jesus in much the same way He had raised up David as king—only God had raised Jesus to emphasize His victory over death and the grave.

13:38–39 Paul's closing statements regarding forgiveness, belief, and justification are explained more fully in his letters to the Romans and Galatians. His epistle to the Galatians was written to the people in this area—many of whom likely responded to this message in the synagogue.

13:42–44 The initial response to Paul's sermon is quite positive. He and Barnabas are invited to speak again the following week. In the meantime, numerous listeners seek them out to learn more.

13:46–52 Paul and Barnabas boldly rebuke the Jewish lack of faith and shift focus to the Gentiles. The Gentile believers are honored to be included in God's plan, but the Jewish resistance only increases as those who are jealous solicit support from prominent community members. As a result, Paul and Barnabas are persecuted and forced to leave the area. This event is a key turning point in Acts. The Jews, for the most part, reject the Gospel, so Paul turns to the Gentiles, who respond positively. This pattern will be repeated again and again until its climax in chapter 28.

14:1–7 A noted Roman road called the Via Sebaste ran from the port city of Ephesus westward to the Euphrates River. At Antioch in Pisidia (see 13:14), it branched into two roads. One went north through mountainous terrain to the Roman colony of Comana, about 122 miles away; and the other moved southeast across rolling country, past snowcapped mountains, and through the Greek city of Iconium, about eighty miles from Antioch in Psidia, and then ended another twenty-four miles later at the Roman colony of Lystra. Paul and Barnabas are literally at a fork in the road, and they choose the southeastern route that will take them to people in three very different types of cities in the southern area of the Roman province of Galatia.

14:1 Iconium sat on a high plateau surrounded by fertile plains and green forests, with mountains to the north and east.

14:3–7 God is with His representatives and enables them to perform great miracles as they stay in the city and speak boldly for Him. They continue to win over many people, but others side with the Jewish antagonists.

When Paul and Barnabas discover a plot to stone them, they finally move on, preaching wherever they go.

14:11–12 Without the benefit of Old Testament scripture or knowledge of the true God, the people of Lystra believe that Greek gods are walking among them.

14:14–17 Paul and Barnabas do everything in their power to dissuade the people from sacrificing to them. They tear their clothes to indicate extreme grief and distress. They assure the crowd that they are both just fellow human beings. They explain that all the good things that have occurred are the result of a living God.

14:19–20 A group of Jews who had opposed Paul in Antioch and Iconium show up, and before long, Paul's stoning that had been planned in Iconium is carried out in Lystra. It is no judicial execution of judgment; it is a lynching. Some people speculate that Paul actually died and came back to life, though no evidence exists to prove this theory. But equally miraculous is the fact that he is able to get up and return to the city after such an experience. He and Barnabas's next destination, Derbe, is about sixty miles away.

14:22 Paul is speaking from experience when he tells the disciples that they must enter the kingdom of God "through much tribulation." It certainly must have taken great courage for Paul and Barnabas to go back through the same cities that had sent hostile delegations to oppose them. Surely the believers recognize Paul and Barnabas's dedication.

14:23 Paul and Barnabas address the needs of the new churches by appointing elders. Paul will later declare that elders shouldn't be new converts (see 1 Timothy 3:6), so he may have chosen believers who had previously served in the Jewish synagogues and would have had a good working knowledge of scripture.

14:27–28 By the time Paul and Barnabas arrive in Antioch (in Syria), they have been gone the better part of two years. Here, they report that God's salvation has come to the Gentiles by faith—not by adapting to Jewish customs or performing any other kind of works. Paul and Barnabas stay a long time in Antioch and are probably glad for the opportunity to rest. Paul writes his letter to the Galatians from Antioch at about this time.

15:1–4 By the time the council in Jerusalem convenes, Gentiles have been joining the church for about ten years and are welcomed simply by baptism. The movement began with Cornelius, the God-fearing centurion whom Peter had baptized (see 10:23–48). What began as a trickle of Gentile conversions is fast becoming a torrent.

15:7–9 Peter alludes to his encounter with Cornelius, an experience that revealed to him that God makes no distinction between Jews and Gentiles.

15:11 Peter argues that since God's grace was the source of salvation for the Gentiles, it is all that is necessary for the Jews as well.

15:12 Paul and Barnabas relate the signs and wonders they had witnessed God perform among the Gentiles in the various places they had been. The emphasis is not on their efforts but on God's work.

15:13–18 Last to speak is James, one of the brothers of Jesus who came to faith after the resurrection. He came to be known as James the Just because of his piety, and he was the leader of the "mother church" in Jerusalem. The Jewish roots were still strong in the Jerusalem church, and if anyone was to back the proposal of the Pharisees, it would have been James. But James quotes Amos 9:11–12 to confirm the experience that the other speakers had described. The inclusion of the Gentiles is not a divine afterthought; the prophets had foretold it.

15:22–29 In their direct but tactful letter to Gentile converts, the council members make a number of points. First, they distance themselves from the Judaizers who had been teaching the necessity of circumcision for salvation. Second, they name Judas and Silas as delegates who will personally verify the content of the letter and minister to the Gentile Christians. Third, the council members share their unanimous decision not to require anything other than abstention from a few cultural practices that were particularly repulsive to Jewish Christians.

15:27 Judging from their names, Judas (Barsabbas) was probably a Hebrew-speaking Jew, and Silas (*Sylvanus* in Latin) was Greek-speaking and a Roman citizen (see 16:36–37).

15:30–33 Upon the messengers' arrival in Antioch, the believers there gather to hear the letter read. They are pleased with its positive message, and afterward Judas and Silas stay to strengthen and encourage them.

15:36–39 In spite of everything they have been through together, a problem arises between Paul and Barnabas, and they are unable to agree on a resolution. For reasons not stated by Luke, John Mark had left them shortly after beginning the first trip (see 13:13). Apparently Barnabas thought that Mark had since learned his lesson. Paul, however, felt Mark had deserted them. Luke makes no judgment about who is right or wrong. But the result is a doubling of outreach. Barnabas takes Mark (his young cousin) with him and goes to Cyprus—an area of familiarity where they will probably face little opposition.

15:40–41 Paul pairs up with Silas, one of the two representatives of the Jerusalem church who had returned with him to Antioch (15:22). After a short stay, Silas returns to Jerusalem. But the fact that he is again in Antioch may indicate his interest in the church there. Paul and Silas head north to Syria and Cilicia.

16:3–4 Paul and Silas are delivering news of the decision of the Jerusalem Council—that believing Gentiles don't need to be circumcised before joining the church. Yet Paul has Timotheus circumcised before taking him along. It is likely that he had not already been circumcised in deference to his father's Gentile culture. But in working with Jewish believers, it would appear callous and even sacrilegious for the son of a Jewish mother to be uncircumcised. So for the good of the ministry—not as a matter of legalism—Timotheus is circumcised.

16:6–8 Paul, Silas, and Timotheus soon find themselves in new territory as they set out across Galatia

(modern Turkey), heading west toward the Aegean Sea. They are told by the Holy Spirit not to enter Asia. When they consider going north through Bithynia, they are also prohibited. So they find themselves in Troas, a seaport on the Aegean Sea.

16:10 Here the writing shifts from third person to first person, indicating that Luke joins the group. Yet he doesn't join the party as a mere observer; he feels called by God to preach the Gospel with the others as well.

16:13 Luke does not mention a synagogue in Philippi, so the Jewish community must have been very small. But on the sabbath, when Paul and his companions seek a place to pray, they find a group of women by the river and start a conversation with them.

16:14 Lydia sold purple cloth—something only the wealthy could afford to buy. She worshipped God to the extent that she understood Him, but her understanding is greatly increased as Paul speaks and God opens her heart.

16:15 Lydia's invitation to Paul and his group indicates that she was a woman of means to have such space available. Lydia is the first known convert on the European continent, and her home may have become the first house church in Philippi.

16:19–21 Rather than being glad that the girl is no longer troubled by the spirit, her owners only see that their source of easy income is gone. Instead of admitting it is a money issue, they accuse Paul and Silas of promoting Jewish customs that aren't acceptable for Romans.

16:22–24 In response to the false allegations, the surrounding crowd joins the attack as Paul and Silas are stripped, beaten, and securely imprisoned.

16:27 When the jailer awakes to discover what has happened, he intends to kill himself because he knows the Roman authorities will do as much or worse. (Herod had previously ordered Peter's guards killed [see 12:19].)

16:28 The reason for the prisoners' reluctance to flee is not recorded. Perhaps the prisoners recognized the work of God in connection with the hymns and the miraculous nature of the earthquake.

16:29–30 The jailer is no longer the authority figure. He falls trembling before Paul and Silas, frees them, and then asks what he needs to do to be saved.

16:39–40 Paul and Silas's request is accommodated, although the magistrates do ask them to leave the city. So they make one more stop at Lydia's house to encourage the believers, and then move on.

17:1–2 After being asked to leave Philippi, Paul and Silas pass through two other prominent cities before deciding to stop in Thessalonica, about one hundred miles away.

17:2 The mention of a synagogue in Thessalonica may indicate the absence of one in the other towns, explaining why Paul and his companions pass through those locations before stopping. Despite their recent imprisonment, they don't alter their usual routine. When they arrive in Thessalonica, they go to the synagogue and speak to the people assembled there. The response must have been encouraging, because they have the opportunity to speak on three consecutive sabbaths. And based on other indications (see Philippians 4:14–16; 1 Thessalonians 2:8–9), they spent more than a few weeks there.

17:4 The appeal of the Gospel is widespread, reaching Jews, Gentiles, and a considerable number of prominent women.

17:5–6 As had been the problem previously, the Jewish leaders grow jealous and take action. When they can't find Paul and his companions at Jason's house where (apparently) they had been staying, they take Jason and some other believers as well. Little is said about Jason, although Paul had a relative of that name (Romans 16:21). Perhaps Jason knows more than he is telling about Paul and Silas, but if so, he does not let the crowd know.

17:10 By nightfall the believers in Thessalonica have reconnected with Paul and Silas and see them on their way to Berea, about fifty miles southwest of Thessalonica.

17:14–15 Rather than allow the situation to become a public spectacle as it had previously, the believers immediately escort Paul to Athens—about three hundred miles away and possibly a sea voyage. Since Paul is apparently the agitators' main target, Silas and Timotheus are able to remain in Berea for a while.

17:18 Stoics believed that the true essence of life was the ability to understand the rational order veiled by natural phenomena. Freedom and joy were the result of detaching from the outer world and mastering one's reactions to his or her environment. Stoicism didn't allow for sympathy, pardon, or genuine expression of feeling. Famous Stoics include Zeno, Seneca, Cicero, and Marcus Aurelius.

17:22–26 Paul finds a novel approach to present the Gospel. He had seen an altar inscribed with the words "To the Unknown God." The Athenians worshipped many gods, apparently afraid of overlooking one and suffering his wrath. Paul explains that he knows the God they don't—the God who made the world and everything in it, the Lord of heaven and earth. Paul's God does not live in temples or need anything from humans. He is the Creator who takes a personal interest in the lives of those He created.

17:28 To emphasize his point that God is more personal than all the idols strewn around Athens, Paul quotes two Greek poets familiar to his listeners. "For in him we live, and move, and have our being" were the words of Epimenides, a poet from Crete. (Paul quotes him again in Titus 1:12.) Then Paul quotes Aratus, a poet from Cilicia (Paul's homeland): "For we are also his offspring."

17:31–34 When Paul mentions the resurrection, he encounters resistance from some of his listeners. But he also has the attention of others who want to hear more and eventually become believers. However, no evidence exists that a church was formed in Athens as a result of Paul's visit.

18:6 Shaking "his raiment" was akin to shaking the dust off one's feet, as Jesus had instructed His disciples to do when they encountered resistance. Paul's time would be better spent moving on to someone who wanted to hear rather than continuing a fruitless debate with those whose minds are already made up (see Luke 9:5; 10:10–11).

18:7–8 Paul doesn't have to go far to find new opportunities to speak. Next door to the synagogue is the home of a believer where he can teach. In addition, the synagogue leader and his entire household become believers, which influences a number of other Corinthians as well.

18:12–13 Luke records one incident of resistance in Corinth. A group of Jewish people try to get Paul in trouble with the Roman authorities. They haul him to court and accuse him of trying to institute a new and unauthorized religion.

18:14–16 Paul does not even have to speak in his own defense. Instead, the deputy (proconsul) Gallio (the brother of the famed philosopher Seneca) rebukes the Jewish group and drives them out of court.

18:22 The church that Paul "saluted" is likely the mother church in Jerusalem. With this, Paul concludes his second missionary journey.

18:22–23 Luke devotes little attention to Paul's return visit to Jerusalem and Antioch. After spending an unspecified amount of time there, Paul sets out on what is to be his third missionary trip. Luke's abrupt summary of Paul's second journey (see 18–22) and the start of his third one seems to be intentional. The focus remains squarely on Ephesus, where Paul had a positive response at the end of his second trip. That's where he left Aquila and Priscilla while he returned to Jerusalem, and that's where he is heading—and will spend almost all of his time—on this third journey.

18:24 Apollos was a Jewish believer who knew the scriptures well and had heard about Jesus.

19:1–2 Upon his return to Ephesus, Paul finds other disciples who, like Apollos, have not experienced a full Christian conversion. They are believers, to be sure, but have never even heard of the Holy Spirit.

19:3–7 Paul begins with what they are familiar with— the baptism of John the Baptist. He explains that John had pointed the way to One coming after him, Jesus. Then Paul baptizes them in the name of Jesus. As he does, the Holy Spirit comes upon them and they start speaking in tongues and prophesying.

19:8–10 Paul spends three months speaking in the synagogue, but some of its members stubbornly refuse to believe and start publicly disparaging the Gospel. So Paul leaves with those who believe him and relocates his ministry to a local lecture hall for the next two years— his longest stay anywhere in his ministry. Word spreads about his teachings until everyone in Asia has heard the Gospel.

19:11–12 The power of God is becoming evident in contrast to other sources of power. Ephesus had earned a reputation as the magic capital of the world. So God does amazing things through Paul's ministry in order to validate his teachings. Handkerchiefs and other articles that Paul touched could be carried to sick or possessed people, and they would be healed.

19:13–16 A group of Jewish exorcists (the "seven sons of one Sceva") had been going around evoking the name of Jesus to try to cast out evil spirits. Perhaps they wanted to emulate Paul's ability, because they use his name as well, but their efforts backfire when one particular spirit challenges them. The possessed man single-handedly overpowers the whole group and leaves the exorcists bleeding and naked.

19:21–22 At this point, Paul feels led to make his way to Rome. He will spend a little more time in Ephesus and then take a roundabout route to Jerusalem in order to visit young churches and take up a collection for the believers in Jerusalem who are struggling financially. He sends two associates ahead of him to Macedonia. Erastus was another of Paul's fellow ministers (see 2 Timothy 4:20).

19:23–24 Paul was accustomed to resistance from religious skeptics, but in Ephesus he encounters opposition from merchants. His preaching is causing a significant drop in demand for idols of the goddess Diana (also known as Artemis).

19:25–28 Under the guise of loyalty to Diana, Demetrius (one of the local silversmiths whose business was suffering) calls a meeting and unites his fellow craftsmen.

19:29–34 Despite being worked into a frenzy, most of the people don't even know what is going on. Some are seizing anyone they can find who is associated with Paul. And when someone tries to quiet the people and establish order, they refuse to let him talk because he is a Jew. At this time, many people had yet to differentiate between Judaism and Christianity; both faiths were detrimental to the idol merchants.

19:35–41 Finally, the city clerk (whose position was comparable to a contemporary mayor) subdues the crowd and points out that the Christians have done nothing malicious or worthy of mistreatment. He knows Demetrius and the other craftsmen have been behind the pandemonium and explains how they can legally take appropriate steps to seek the justice they desire. He also warns that Rome could impose penalties or restrictions on the city if its citizens are prone to riot.

20:1 The "uproar" refers to the riot incited by Demetrius the silversmith and his fellow craftsmen (see 19:23–41). But that's not what prompts Paul's departure; he had already resolved to leave. Timotheus and Erastus are in Macedonia (see 19:21–22), so Paul sets out in that direction.

20:4 Paul rarely traveled alone. Luke lists several of his companions on this leg of his journey. They represented the different regions of Macedonia that were taking part in the collection to be delivered to believers in Jerusalem, who were suffering from a famine in the Middle East. The churches didn't just send money; they sent people to help as well.

20:5–6 The story picks up again with a first-person account, indicating that Luke has rejoined the group.

20:8–9 A young man named Eutychus is seated on a high window ledge, perhaps trying to get some fresh air due to the many lamps burning and the warmth of the crowded room. Fast asleep, Eutychus falls from the third floor. As a physician, Luke would have been able to confirm his death.

20:10 Paul throws himself on the body, wrapping his arms around the young man in a scene reminiscent of the Old Testament prophets Elijah (1 Kings 17:21) and Elisha (2 Kings 4:34–35). Just as Peter's faith in the power of God had brought Tabitha back to life (see Acts 9:40), Paul's faith restores life to Eutychus.

20:11–12 Paul returns to preaching and continues until dawn. Afterward, the friends of Eutychus take him home and feel immense comfort.

20:15–18 After several days of sailing, Paul and his companions arrive at Miletus. Ephesus is nearby, but Paul has determined not to return. He had spent almost three years with the Ephesians, and a visit would take more time than he has at his disposal. (He wanted to get to Jerusalem by Pentecost.) His recent run-in with the silversmith guild may have generated some legal complications as well. So rather than going again to Ephesus, he has the elders of the church meet him in Miletus.

20:20–21 Groups of antagonists are out to smear Paul's good name (see 17:5–9), so he begins by defending the sincerity of his motives and reminding the elders of his personal ministry in Ephesus. Paul's reference to teaching "from house to house" may indicate a number of house churches spread throughout the great city.

20:22–23 Paul continues by sharing his current plans. He doesn't know for certain what will happen, but he is anticipating "bonds and afflictions"—that is, imprisonment and other hardships.

20:24 Paul views his ministry the same way a runner sees a race. In spite of any obstacles he might face, his goal is to finish—to complete the task he has been given.

20:25 Paul doesn't anticipate visiting Ephesus again, although it seems that he does. Elsewhere, he refers to events that appear to have taken place after the ones recorded here (see 1 Timothy 1:3–4).

20:28–31 Paul reminds the elders that they are shepherds entrusted by the Holy Spirit with the flock of God. Wisely, he advises them to watch over themselves as well as their congregations. Soon the flock will come under attack from "wolves"—those who would distort the truth and attempt to lead others astray. Even some leaders will fall away from the faith (see 2 Timothy 4:9–10), so Paul warns them to always be on their guard.

20:36–37 After his farewell speech, Paul prays for the group, and there isn't a dry eye among them. Most upsetting is the elders' concern that they might never see Paul again.

21:7 The ship's next stop is at Ptolemais, where Paul and his group are able to connect with another assembly of believers. Groups like this one had probably sprung up about twenty-five years before, when persecution in Jerusalem had forced believers out into other communities.

21:10–13 Paul had been warned by other prophets against returning to Jerusalem. Agabus carries the same message, but he has a more emphatic means of communicating it. His symbolic binding of Paul, combined with his dire warning, understandably worries the group of believers. Paul, however, is more upset with their heartbreaking response than with the anticipation of potential trouble in Jerusalem. One thing that made Paul such a devoted and persistent messenger for God was his willingness to suffer and even die, if necessary.

21:14–15 Paul's next stop—Jerusalem—is only sixty-five miles ahead. Perhaps Paul is so determined to get there because he is carrying the money that had been collected from the other churches (primarily in Gentile territory). In doing so, he would be emphasizing the unity of the worldwide church, which was very important to him.

21:17 Paul refers to his delivery of the financial gift from the other churches in various epistles (see Romans 15:25–27; 1 Corinthians 16:1–4; 2 Corinthians 8–9). Luke makes no mention of it here, but later he acknowledges it as he records Paul's account of this moment (see 24:17).

21:19–20 Paul's report of the work of God among the Gentiles encourages the Jerusalem church leaders. They have good news as well: Thousands of zealous Jewish converts have been added to their number.

21:23–24 An ideal opportunity arises for Paul to prove his devotion to Jewish tradition: Four men of the church are preparing to conclude a vow they had made to God. Paul had recently done the same thing in Corinth (see 18:18). So the elders recommend that Paul join the four men in their rites of purification. In addition, he will pay for their offerings that were prescribed by Mosaic Law. Each man will bring two lambs, one ram, a meat or grain offering, a drink offering, and a basket of unleavened cakes and wafers (see Numbers 6:13–15). After each man's offering is presented to God, the man will shave his head and his hair will be placed in the fire of the fellowship offering (Numbers 6:16–18).

21:26 Paul has no problem accommodating the requests, and joins the men in their purification the next day. The ceremony was entirely voluntary and did nothing to compromise his Christian convictions. Yet his willingness to comply was proof that he wasn't promoting the cessation of Jewish rights and traditions.

21:30–32 The scene is so dangerous that the Roman "chief captain" (Claudius Lysias, according to 23:26) hurries out with sufficient forces to stop those who are beating Paul.

21:33–36 Claudius Lysias first arrests Paul and places him in a kind of protective custody, bound with two chains, most likely between two guards. He then tries to determine from the crowd who Paul is and the nature of his offense, but his efforts are futile due to inconsistent answers and ongoing pandemonium. The mob is still trying to get to Paul, and the soldiers have to actually carry him into the barracks and away from the chanting crowd.

21:37–38 Paul asks the captain for a favor, speaking in Greek, which surprises the Roman leader. Until that moment, Claudius Lysias thought he might have captured a terrorist—an Egyptian who spoke no Greek—who was on the loose. So Paul's words take Lysias aback.

21:40–22:2 Claudius Lysias grants Paul's request to address the crowd. Surprisingly, the crowd grows quiet—then even quieter when Paul addresses them in the most familiar language of the local people.

22:3 The crowd's complaint was that Paul wasn't "Jewish" enough, so he presents his life story with an emphasis on his Jewish upbringing. He was born a Jew in Tarsus but had spent much time in Jerusalem. He had been tutored by Gamaliel, the most eminent rabbi of the time, who had died just five years earlier. (Gamaliel's wisdom is demonstrated in 5:33–40.)

22:4–5 Initially, Paul had been as zealous as anyone in wanting to quash the spread of "the way" (Christianity). He did everything within his power to imprison and kill believers. The hostile crowd surely is with him up to this point of his address.

22:6–11 Next Paul shares his experience on the road to Damascus (see 9:1–19). He tells them about the light from heaven, the voice of Jesus that only he could hear, and the instructions to go into Damascus to wait for further instructions.

22:12–15 Paul's description of Ananias is exemplary: "a devout man according to the law." It was Ananias who had confirmed that Paul would be a witness to all men—which, by implication, included the Gentiles.

22:16 Paul's baptism wasn't the water baptism that had washed his sins away, although repentance and baptism are almost always closely linked in the New Testament. Paul had already submitted to Jesus and received the Holy Spirit (see 9:6, 17–19); his baptism was an outward verification of the inner change that had occurred.

22:21–22 So far the hostile crowd is still listening to Paul, but the explicit reference to Gentiles is bound to incite their anger. The crowd refuses to listen to any suggestion that Jews and Gentiles are equal and can come to God on identical terms.

22:24 Again the chief captain orders Paul indoors. His plan is to submit Paul to a brutal flogging and interrogation. The scourge consisted of strips of leather fastened to a wooden handle. Embedded in the leather were pieces of metal or bone. Sometimes a scourging crippled a person for life. Occasionally the victim died as a result.

22:29–30 The plans to have Paul whipped are immediately canceled. The chief captain is alarmed because he had almost committed a grievous injustice. He still wants to find out why Paul has been such a target for the Jews, but now it will be done by means of a trial rather than the use of force.

23:5–6 Paul quickly explains that he didn't realize that the order had come from the high priest. Some believe Paul had trouble seeing, in which case his poor vision might have prevented him from recognizing Ananias as the high priest. Besides, Paul had been out of Jerusalem for a while, and the position of high priest changed quite often. Other interpreters suggest that his reply was sarcastic and that Paul refused to recognize the authority of anyone who would use the office of high priest to promote unwarranted hostility. But his rapid shift from calling Ananias a "whited wall" to addressing the Sanhedren as "brethren" suggests sincerity. Whatever his motive, he apologizes and submits to the legal protocol (see Exodus 22:28).

23:7–10 The conflict between the Pharisees and Sadducees intensifies so that the Roman commander retrieves Paul by force.

23:11 After being a target of hostility for two different mobs on two consecutive days, Paul might have felt very disheartened. But the next night he receives affirmation from Jesus through a supernatural revelation encouraging him to keep going. He will indeed be traveling on to Rome, as he had hoped. Paul didn't experience visions often, so he must have appreciated this unusual blessing.

23:16–22 Luke reveals that Paul has a sister and nephew in Jerusalem, and the young man finds out about the ambush planned against Paul.

23:23 Remembering that Paul is a Roman citizen, the commander acts immediately. He dispatches two centurions and a detachment of two hundred soldiers, along with seventy horsemen and two hundred spearmen. If they encounter the forty assassins, a Roman contingent of 470 soldiers will have little trouble defeating them. Yet the soldiers aren't looking for a fight. They leave at 9:00 p.m., escorting Paul during the night toward Caesarea (a two-day journey) where he will be much safer.

23:24–25 Paul is being delivered to Antonius Felix, the ruling governor of Judea. The Roman commander sends a letter to be delivered along with Paul, which would have been expected.

23:26–28 Since Claudius Lysias is addressing his superior, he subtly changes over some of the details in his account. For example, Lysias didn't rescue Paul because he was a Roman citizen; he had been preparing to torture Paul during interrogation when he happened to find out about Paul's citizenship (see 22:24–29).

23:29 Lysias expresses his opinion that Paul is not guilty of any serious crime. There may have been some disagreement about Jewish law, but Paul certainly didn't deserve death or imprisonment.

23:31–32 The trip must have been strenuous—even for hardened Roman soldiers. They traverse thirty-five miles the first night, much of it across difficult terrain—including a long stretch that would have been ideal for an ambush. After arriving safely in Antipatris, the remaining distance to Caesarea (twenty-seven miles) is far less threatening. So the foot soldiers return to Jerusalem while the cavalry continue ahead with Paul.

23:33 The journey takes place without incident. The letter and the prisoner are delivered to Felix, who agrees to hear the case.

23:35 Paul is held in the palace of Herod until his accusers arrive to prosecute the case. This will prove to be one of Paul's more pleasant stays on his way to Rome. He will be in other prisons in the days to come.

24:2–10 Tertullus opens with what is known as a *captatio benevolentiae*, a flowery and flattering statement meant to capture the goodwill of the judge. He notes Felix's penchant for peace and his reforms, and promises to be brief so as not to weary the busy governor. Paul also begins with a *captatio benevolentiae*, but his is considerably more modest and moderate than Tertullus's (see 24:24). Then he jumps into his defense, refuting the accusations one by one.

24:11–12 Paul emphasizes that he is not a troublemaker and has at no time tried to instigate an insurrection. He had gone to Jerusalem as a pilgrim, not an agitator. He had cut his visits with other churches short in order to be in Jerusalem for the feast of Pentecost.

24:14–16 Paul stresses the similarities between what his prosecutors believe and his own beliefs. He points out that they worship the same God, have the same forefathers, believe the same scriptures, and maintain the same hope that God will resurrect the righteous and the wicked. The sect that his opponents accuse him of leading is actually a faith quite similar to their own.

24:17–18 Paul insists that he has done nothing to defile the temple. Not only was he unconnected to any kind of crowd or disturbance, but he was also ceremonially clean. It wasn't until the Jewish troublemakers from Asia showed up that a riot erupted.

24:19–20 Paul adds that the instigators from Asia should have been present to make their accusations against him.

24:23 Felix doesn't seem to consider Paul any kind of threat and allows him a minimum-security environment. Paul is still supervised by a centurion, yet he has a degree of freedom and opportunities for friends to visit.

24:26 Despite a lack of evidence against Paul, Felix isn't yet willing to release him, probably because there isn't anything in it for him. If Paul had been the average prisoner, he would have offered a bribe and been out in no time. But Paul is not about to pay for his own release.

24:27 Felix was forced to step down because of his mistreatment of his Jewish subjects.

25:3–5 Despite being more accommodating than Felix, Festus is no pushover. The Jews know they have no real case against Paul, so they beg to have him returned to Jerusalem, secretly planning to kill him along the way. Festus denies their request but offers a retrial in Caesarea instead. They have little choice but to comply.

25:9 Festus doesn't want to start his term by provoking the Jews if it can be helped. But like Felix, he has no evidence on which to convict Paul. His decision to consult the accused may seem unusual, but it was an accommodation of Paul's legal rights as a Roman citizen.

25:11–12 Paul's appeal to Caesar must have been a great relief for Festus. Not only would it get Paul out of Festus's jurisdiction in Caesarea, but it also meant Festus did not have to make a decision that would antagonize the Jews.

25:13 Marcus Julius Agrippa II was a descendant of Herod the Great. Rome had appointed him king over Caesarea Philippi, the territory adjoining Judea to the northeast. Agrippa was accompanied by his sister and consort, Bernice. They had tried to squelch rumors of an incestuous relationship by having Bernice marry Polemo II, the king of Cilicia, but she soon returned to Agrippa.

25:14–22 The governor's account appears honest and straightforward, yet the religious significance of the events has escaped him. He indicates that he believes Jesus to be dead, and he has no idea how to respond to Paul's claim that Jesus is alive.

25:24–25 Festus opens the proceedings by explaining why Paul is being brought before the crowd. This is not an official trial, yet Festus has to write the facts of Paul's case to be sent along with him to Rome. Festus is seeking advice from the group—especially from Agrippa. Festus also expresses his opinion that Paul has done nothing worthy of death.

26:1 Festus yields the floor to Agrippa, who gives Paul permission to speak. It is a dramatic moment. For four generations, the family of Herod had obstructed God's work through Jesus, John the Baptist, James the apostle, and now Paul. Yet here the Word of God is boldly proclaimed before the current Herodian leader. It is also a moment when the words of Jesus to His disciples—and later to Paul—are fulfilled (see Matthew 10:18; Acts 9:15).

26:2–3 God had revealed to Paul that he would be heard in Rome, so he has no need to press the case for his own innocence. Instead, he uses the opportunity to promote the Gospel to some of the leaders of the Roman Empire. What follows is the longest of Paul's five defenses recorded in Acts. Paul even asks for Agrippa's patience before he begins, knowing that he will not be brief. Paul's introductory remarks are complimentary, but not flattering. Agrippa was indeed "expert" in Jewish customs. Among other things, it was his job to oversee the treasury of the temple and to appoint the high priest.

26:6–7 Paul feels that his faith in Jesus is perfectly compatible with his Jewish upbringing; in fact, Jesus is the fulfillment of what the Jews had been anticipating for centuries.

26:9–11 Paul confesses his initial fervor to eradicate Christianity. At the time, he didn't believe that Jesus had risen or was the Messiah, and he was near-fanatical in opposing those who did. His reference to giving his "voice against them"—sometimes translated as "casting my vote"—is thought to be a figure of speech.

26:12–19 Paul's zealous persecution of Christians is what makes his conversion story so powerful.

26:25 Paul calmly denies the accusation of insanity, pointing out that everything he has said is a matter of common knowledge. The ministry, death, and

resurrection of Jesus had been public and were open to verification. In addition, anyone who compared the Old Testament prophecies with the historical facts concerning Jesus must acknowledge the truth of Christianity.

26:27 Paul knows Agrippa is aware of Jewish history and recent events concerning Jesus, so he requests the king's input. Paul's question seems simple enough, but Agrippa surely knows that if he admits to believing in the prophets, he will be asked if he agrees that Jesus has fulfilled their predictions.

26:28–29 It is not unreasonable to interpret Agrippa's response as an attempt to add some lightheartedness to the proceedings. Perhaps Paul's answer had a similar tone. He was clearly serious about his prayers for Agrippa as well as everyone else present and his desire for all of them to be like him. But his final words, "except these bonds," may have been delivered with a smile.

26:30–31 By standing, Agrippa indicates that the assembly is concluded.

26:32 Agrippa's closing comment confirms the previous results of Paul's trials. Paul had not been found guilty of any crime by the Jewish Sanhedrin (23:9), the Roman commander in Jerusalem (23:29), or two successive Roman governors in Caesarea (24:22–27; 25:25). Now, the king over the territory, a high-ranking Roman authority with long-standing connections to the Jewish people, can find no fault with Paul. Yet Paul still has another trial to withstand—this one before Caesar himself.

27:1 The book of Acts reverts back to first person at this point when Paul prepares to sail toward Rome. (Perhaps Luke has been near this whole time.) Little is known about "Augustus' band" (also known as the Imperial Regiment), but Julius, the centurion assigned to oversee Paul, would have been responsible for one-sixth of the regiment.

27:3 Paul is allowed to get off the ship and visit fellow believers at Sidon, their first stop. Perhaps Paul's Roman citizenship gave him certain privileges that other prisoners didn't receive.

27:7–12 "The fast"—that is, the day of atonement—was already past. In AD 59, the year Paul set out for Rome, the day would have been October 5. The Romans preferred not to sail after mid-September, and attempts made after the first of November were considered suicidal. Everyone agrees that it would be foolish to set out for Italy, but the fair havens isn't a good harbor. Many want to sail to Phenice, a location forty miles farther west. Paul warns the others that to continue will mean disaster, but the centurion has the final say.

27:13–15 The centurion's decision appears to be a good one at first. A gentle wind blows from the south, helping them along. But soon a raging wind comes out of the northeast, blowing the ship away from shore. A granary ship like theirs could be 140 feet long by 36 feet wide and 33 feet tall, but it wasn't designed for handling storms. The bow and stern were the same width, and it had no rudder, being steered instead by two large paddles coming from each side of the stern. A single mast with a large square sail made it impossible to make progress against a strong wind, which placed significant strain on the ship.

27:22–26 Paul explains that an angel had appeared to him, told him not to be afraid, and assured him that God would spare the lives of everyone on board. They will run aground and the ship will be destroyed, but all the people will survive.

27:27–30 It is no wonder morale is low. Imagine being at sea with 275 other people (see 27:37) and being tossed by ferocious weather for two weeks with no control over where you are going. It is enough to drive seasoned sailors to despair. When they realize they are coming upon land—still with no control—some pray for daylight while others try to sneak away in the lifeboat. Paul sees what is going on and alerts the centurion, and the soldiers scuttle the lifeboat.

27:39–41 The crew's plan was to run the ship onto the shore, but they hit an unseen sandbar. As a result, the bow is stuck fast in the sand while the stern is smashed into pieces by the pounding waves.

27:42–44 The centurion instructs those who can swim to make their way to shore first. The others find pieces of the battered ship and use them to float to shore. And just as Paul had promised, everyone arrives safely on the land.

28:1 *Melita* (Malta) meant "refuge," and it lives up to its name for Paul and his fellow shipwreck victims. They find themselves about five hundred miles west of Crete, where they had last put out to sea, and they are less than sixty miles away from Sicily, which is just off the southwest corner of the Italian mainland.

28:2 The term *barbarous people* does not necessarily carry negative connotations. In Paul's time, the term was used to indicate anyone who didn't speak Greek. It is evident from Luke's description of the Maltese people that they are far from barbaric. They extend kindness toward the stranded sailors, building a fire on shore to get them warm and dry.

28:3–6 The islanders, no doubt familiar with the species of snake that bit Paul, suppose the apostle had been a murderer intended to perish in the sea. They watch a long time for the effects of the poison, and when Paul shows no ill effects at all, they assume he must be divine.

28:10 Paul and the others have to wait out the winter on Melita. But three months later, when they are again ready to sail, the grateful people provide them with all the supplies they need.

28:11 Sailing in the Mediterranean resumes around mid-February, which is consistent with the three-month span spent on Melita. Another ship is in a nearby port—probably another grain ship since it, too, is Egyptian. Its figurehead is of Castor and Pollux, the twin sons of Zeus portrayed in the constellation Gemini. They are thought to protect sailors, and the sighting of Gemini in the night sky is considered a good omen. But by now the men traveling with Paul know something of the God who can really protect those at sea.

28:12–14 The first stop is a three-day layover in Syracuse, a major city on the eastern coast of Sicily. From there they continue north to Rhegium (now Reggio di Calabria), on the "toe" of the Italian mainland, just east of Sicily. A favorable wind the next day carries them 180 miles farther north to Puteoli (now Pozzuoli), a large port protected by the Bay of Naples. There a group of believers invites Paul to spend a week with them before going on to Rome, still seventy-five miles away. Evidently the centurion responsible for Paul has developed enough respect for him to allow him certain privileges.

28:15 News of Paul's approach precedes him. Believers from Rome come flocking to meet him and get as far as The three taverns (a way station thirty-three miles outside of Rome) and the Appii forum (forty-three miles from Rome). They would have traveled the famed Appian Way, one of the great Roman roads named after Appias Claudius. The Greek word used to describe these meetings is formal—the same word that would be used to describe an official city delegation going out to greet a general or king. Paul is being treated as one of the great heroes of the faith. He is encouraged, not at the attention he receives, but at the very sight of believers representing Jesus Christ in the heart of the Roman Empire.

28:16 As an indicator of the large degree of freedom Paul enjoys while awaiting trial, he is allowed to live by himself—although he is always under guard.

28:21–22 The local Jews say they haven't heard any bad reports about Paul. Perhaps they were being tactful; communication between Rome and Jerusalem was usually good, and it had been almost two and a half years since the riot that had led to Paul's arrest. Yet the Jewish leaders are curious about Christianity and eager to hear Paul's explanation.

28:23–24 A meeting is arranged, and a great number of people turn out to hear Paul, who spends the entire day teaching and encouraging them to believe in Jesus. True to the pattern in previous cities, some do believe and others refuse to.

28:26–27 As those Jews who rejected the Gospel are leaving, Paul quotes Isaiah 6:9–10. It was a prophecy that Jesus had once cited in reference to His ministry (see Mark 4:12).

28:28–29 Paul's last encounter with the Jews follows the same pattern found throughout Acts. Some respond favorably; most reject his message, leading Paul to take the good news to the Gentiles.

28:30–31 It may seem puzzling that Luke concludes his account without revealing Paul's fate, but it wasn't Luke's intent to write a biography of Paul. His purpose was to record the spread of the Gospel from Jerusalem to Samaria to the ends of the earth, and from its Jewish roots to the Gentile world (see Acts 1:8).

THE EPISTLE OF PAUL THE APOSTLE TO THE

ROMANS

INTRODUCTION TO ROMANS ■ It is easy to forget that the epistle to the Romans is a letter and not a theological treatise. It is so often used in doctrinal studies and pursuits that we may miss the heartfelt passion that the author, Paul, had for his readers, many of whom he had never met. It isn't the first of Paul's letters chronologically, though it is placed first among his epistles in the New Testament.

AUTHOR ■ Paul is the writer of this epistle. Skeptics have challenged the authenticity of some of Paul's other epistles, but Romans has never seriously been questioned.

OCCASION ■ Paul considered himself an apostle to the Gentiles (11:13), yet he had never been to Rome, the center of the secular Roman Empire. He was planning a visit on his way to Spain (15:23–24, 28) and was writing in anticipation of his arrival. Yet his epistle is far more than a casual letter. He lays out a fresh and clear explanation of God's plan of salvation for both Jews and Gentiles—one that has continued to inspire and motivate Bible readers for centuries.

1:1 Paul consistently begins his letters by identifying himself, as he does in this epistle. He had been called by Jesus to be an "apostle"—someone sent out bearing the authority of another. After Paul's conversion, it didn't take long for him to consider himself a "servant" (literally, a slave) of Jesus. He placed himself completely at Jesus' disposal, listening for and responding to his Master's commands.

1:2 The Gospel Paul describes had not just appeared out of nowhere; it had been promised long ago in the Old Testament scriptures. The prophets foretold the ministry and death of Jesus, yet many had missed the significance of their message.

1:3–4 Among the prophecies concerning the Messiah was the prediction that He would be not only a descendant of David, but also the Son of God. Jesus was declared to be the Son of God through the power of His resurrection from the dead.

1:5 Paul attributes two characteristics—"grace and apostleship"—to himself, though he uses the editorial "we." Apostleship is not something available to all believers, but rather a unique calling.

1:6–7 Believers form a family of brothers and sisters who are provided for by a heavenly Father. The call to be "saints" means to be set apart from the world. It is something not only desirable but also achievable for all Christians.

1:8 After Paul's salutation, he first expresses thankfulness for the Christians in Rome and their reputation for faithfulness. His reference to "the whole world" means *his* world—the Roman Empire. Note that while their faith inspires his gratitude, Paul doesn't thank them; he thanks God.

1:14–17 Paul makes three strong statements about his desire to preach in Rome. He is obligated, eager, and unashamed.

1:16 The word translated *believeth* means more than simply "intellectual assent." It refers to having confidence and placing one's trust in something.

1:19–20 The suppression of truth is, in this case, the occasion for God's wrath. His involvement with humankind should be evident by His creation, if nothing else. While all humans have a bent toward sin, those who suppress the truth are perhaps the worst of the bunch. Despite knowing the truth, these individuals grow comfortable with immorality, trying to justify or deny their sinful actions (as they have since Adam and Eve).

1:21–25 God is the source of truth and righteousness, so all alternatives (foolishness and idols) are but shallow substitutes. God's wrath targets the sin, not the person. Yet when people stubbornly refuse to repent, God will eventually allow their sinful desires to run rampant.

1:26–32 The list of "vile affections" is quite detailed and includes homosexuality, envy, murder, deceit, gossip, arrogance, and much more. Such actions are not committed in ignorance but in willful defiance.

2:1–16 In the previous section (1:18–32), Paul wrote about people's refusal to recognize God as revealed through His creation. Here Paul reflects on how people also reject God by ignoring His special revelation through scripture.

2:1 Paul uses a literary device, the diatribe, in which the writer addresses an imaginary pupil or rival ("O man") and makes his point by issuing bold statements and asking questions. In this case, Paul's point is that anyone who passes judgment on others is actually condemning himself or herself as well. It isn't so much the judging itself that is wrong (believers are instructed to discern harmful behaviors in passages like Matthew 18:15–17 and James 5:19–20); but, like Jesus, Paul warns against the danger of hypocrisy in evaluating other people.

2:3–5 Paul may have the Jewish people in mind here because they tended to look down on Gentiles while overlooking their own shortcomings. In any case, those passing judgment were doing so with stubbornness and an "impenitent heart." It is far too common to find those who cherish God's kindness, tolerance, and patience for themselves, yet are reluctant to extend them to others.

2:7–10 Even though people tend to be judgmental when they shouldn't be, God is frequently *not* judgmental when He *could* be. His mercy allows people to repent.

Rewards are in store for those who turn from evil and seek righteousness instead, but God's wrath awaits those who continue to reject truth.

2:17–20 Paul cites five positive distinctions that contributed to the Jewish people's pride. First, they were proud to be called Jews. The term was derived from their ancestor Judah. Not long after the word *Jew* first appeared in the scriptures, it became the national name Hebrews were proud to bear. Second, Paul acknowledges the Jewish reliance on their scriptures; they possess God's Word—the oracles of faith, revealed and recorded. Third, the Jews had a special relationship with God. He had made a covenant with them, delivered them from bondage in Egypt, and given them the promised land. Fourth, they were strong moralists with a clearly stated set of values, distinguishing right from wrong in the midst of a culture that encouraged hedonism and self-indulgence. Fifth, the Jews were very capable of teaching others. Not only did they discern right from wrong; they instructed others in the ways of God.

2:17–29 So far, Paul has demonstrated that no one is moral enough to earn salvation. Next, he anticipates the rebuttal: What about religious people? Won't God accept them? His answer in this section addresses the religious pride of the Jewish people of his time. They felt sure God regarded them with special favor because of their descent from Abraham and because they bore the mark of the Old Testament covenant: circumcision. Paul counters with a radical thought: Being Jewish is not a matter of race but of conduct.

2:25–27 The Jews had an unwarranted confidence in circumcision as a sign that they were special to God. Paul reminds his readers that circumcision was an outer sign meant to reflect an inner commitment to God. Circumcision meant nothing to those who neglected God's law. In fact, any uncircumcised person who kept God's Word was preferable to someone who was circumcised but ignored what God commanded.

3:1–2 Paul himself was a knowledgeable and well-trained Pharisee. And while it isn't a person's knowledge or Jewish status that leads to salvation (see Philippians 3:3–8), Paul still sees a crucial advantage to his Jewish heritage: namely, the "oracles of God."

3:9–20 Scripture had already addressed the subject of whether Jews or Gentiles had a better understanding of God's love and righteousness. Paul quotes a series of Old Testament scriptures (mostly from Psalms, with additions from Ecclesiastes and Isaiah) to show the widespread influence of sin.

3:22–24 From God's perspective, there is no difference between Jew and Gentile. Both are sinful. Nor is there a difference in how they can have a proper relationship with God: He justifies them freely, out of grace, because the death of Jesus paid for their sin. People are unable to do anything to contribute to their own justification, so God does it by His grace. We don't deserve it, but He loves us and initiates action.

3:25–26 Jesus' sacrifice (His blood) was the necessary atonement to pay for the sins of humankind—past, present, and future. The atoning sacrifice is referred to as *propitiation*. The great importance of such a sacrifice is that it appeases God's wrath so that we don't receive the condemnation that we deserve. God doesn't just overlook our sins; they are fully atoned for from this point forward. Additionally, He had left sins unpunished in the past, knowing that justice would be fulfilled when Jesus paid the price for them.

3:27 Paul has already clarified that justification has nothing to do with people's works; instead it is an act of God based on the sacrificial death of Jesus Christ. Observing the law is a positive action, yet it has nothing to do with justification.

3:27–31 Paul emphasizes that people are justified only by faith. In this section, he returns to a question-and-answer format.

4:1 Paul's question is intriguing: How, exactly, was Abraham justified? The Jews had grown so accustomed to thinking that adherence to the law was the way to God's favor that they could hardly conceive another way. But Abraham lived centuries before God provided the law. If Abraham could find God's favor without the law, so could other people.

4:3–5 Paul quotes scripture to remind his readers that Abraham's faith in God was "counted unto him for righteousness" (see Genesis 15:6). To have something "counted unto" someone means the recipient does nothing to earn what is received—just the opposite of working to get a paycheck.

4:9–11 In addressing the necessity of circumcision, Paul returns to the story of Abraham. His first-century readers knew the story well; Paul didn't need to spell out for them that God had declared Abraham righteous when he was eighty-six years old (see Genesis 16:16). Yet God did not instruct Abraham to receive the mark of circumcision until the patriarch was ninety-nine (Genesis 17:1, 11; 21:5). Abraham's circumcision had no direct connection to his righteousness before God.

4:12–13 There was no problem with circumcision being a sign of Jewishness, and through it the Jews could continue to honor Abraham as their ancestor. But circumcision was not proof of a person's righteous standing before God, and Abraham was also to be the father of those who came to God by faith and were not circumcised.

4:18–19 Just because justification is by faith alone does not mean it comes easily. Abraham waited a long twenty-five years between the time of God's initial promise to him and its fulfillment in the birth of Isaac. During that time, he was hoping "against hope." His body was as good as dead, yet God was at work, and Abraham became the father of the Jews physically and the father of many nations spiritually.

4:20–21 Abraham had faith, yet he maintained his faith through patient trust in God. So it is for all who come to God. After making a statement of faith, it is easy to waver when God doesn't respond exactly as we might hope. Ongoing faith is necessary.

5:1–11 Paul has shown that circumcision and adherence to the law are not necessary for salvation. As he begins to detail a number of benefits resulting from our justification, he first mentions peace—the awareness that we are no longer God's enemies and the confidence that comes from realizing we no longer need to struggle to gain His favor.

5:12–14 The "one man" is Adam. In his actions, Adam represented all human beings. Through his defiance of God, sin entered the world and death came to all people. No one born today has the capacity to live a life of perfect righteousness and obedience.

5:15–17 The judgment that Adam received for his sin is what each of us deserves for ours. Yet Adam is only the first of the two men Paul writes about. The second is Jesus. If people think facing condemnation as a result of Adam's sin is unfair, they must realize that receiving the gift made available through Jesus' sacrifice is even more undeserved. Yet God reaches out in love to offer His grace and righteousness.

5:18 Adam's trespass condemned humanity to spiritual and physical death; Jesus' sacrifice conquered death and the grave, providing eternal life for everyone. It is important not to take Paul's statement out of context, however. When he says that Jesus' act of righteousness brings life for "all," he is referring to the *opportunity* for salvation, not suggesting that everyone will be saved.

5:20–21 For those who seek restoration, forgiveness, and justification, there is no doubt they can find it. Paul makes it clear that the weight of our combined sin is no match for God's grace. For a period, sin had reigned and death was the result. But from now on, grace and righteousness reign, providing eternal life.

6:1–2 Paul asks the question he imagines some of his readers would raise at this point—then answers it with an emphatic *no*. Genuine followers of Jesus Christ cannot continue to live in sin without sensing their own guilt before God and repenting.

6:3 This is the first of three times in Romans 6:1–10 that Paul uses the word *know* to remind his readers that they have been joined with Christ (see also verses 6 and 9). Baptism involves a personal identification with Jesus and signifies inclusion into the covenant community of faith.

6:11–12 If dead to sin, a person can no longer allow it to control his or her life. Yet it requires a conscious decision to act in harmony with (and on the basis of) one's new relationship with Christ. When tempted to revert to one's old life, a believer must consider that person—and those behaviors—dead. That doesn't mean pretending the old nature has gone away when he or she knows perfectly well it hasn't. Rather, it means acknowledging that the former identity died with Christ—and willingly putting an end to its influence.

6:13 Rather than being offered to sin, one's body should be offered to God. Grace should rule a believer's life. Instead of giving in to sin and letting it rule, Paul suggests that Christians pursue a positive alternative. The entirety of one's life should be offered to God—limbs, organs, eyes, ears, hands, feet, thoughts, and

dreams. It is inconceivable that Christians should go back to their old ways of living by willfully persisting in sin and presuming on God's grace.

6:20–22 One of the best ways to keep a proper mindset is to look back from time to time and remember the quality of life when sin was still master. Everyone recalls things they aren't proud of, which should inspire greater motivation to pursue obedience and godly living.

7:1–3 Paul uses the metaphor of marriage to answer his own question. According to Jewish law, a woman could not divorce her husband. The only way she could be free to marry another man was if the first husband died. Otherwise, she would be considered an adulteress.

7:9–13 Paul's use of the phrase "without the law" was probably his way of saying, "before I realized what the law meant." Like the Pharisees who lived unaware of what the law really meant, Paul was "alive without the law" for a while. But after coming to see what the law really said, he was confronted with his sin.

7:14–25 The struggle that Paul describes in this section is common to all believers. The more mature the believer, the more aware of sin he or she becomes. The more progress a person makes toward sanctification, the more he or she will abhor sinfulness and see it for what it is.

7:24 The word translated *wretched* could also be interpreted "miserable" or "unhappy." There are times when all believers grow weary of their daily struggles and just want to give up. Surely, with all of Paul's exceptional trials, he must have felt the same way at times. Good and evil are battling it out within him, creating an inner conflict. Paul also confesses to feeling condemned. He realizes he deserves to have God's judgment of death pronounced on his sins. If he were in a court of law, he would plead guilty to the charges. It is a startlingly honest expression of emotion, yet few Christians can say they haven't had similar feelings.

7:25 Thankfully, despair isn't the end of Paul's story. He concludes the passage with an optimistic message of hope: Christ will rescue him from the dire state in which he finds himself. The key to understanding this turnaround is to comprehend the already-and-not-yet nature of the kingdom of God. Jesus inaugurated His kingdom at His first coming but will not consummate it until His second. Believers who live in between will experience the power of His coming in some measure, but not in full. Therefore, it is possible to be assured of victory in Christ yet still feel defeated from time to time.

8:2–4 The Mosaic Law was powerless to provide righteous standing before God. It remains a guide for how believers should live, yet Paul introduces a new law—the "law of the Spirit of life." The Old Testament law could define and prohibit sin, but it could never eliminate it. Our human nature could never empower us to live up to the law's standards.

8:15–16 As long as people cling to selfish desires and exclude God, they are unable to experience the relationship that He intends for them. But those who respond to the Spirit are led into an intimate relationship—one of Father and child. Jesus had addressed God as *Abba* ("Father") in

His prayers (Mark 14:36). Prior to that, no Jewish person would have addressed God with such a familiar term. Yet here Paul extends the privilege to all believers.

8:19–22 Creation itself is suffering. Just as Adam, Eve, and the serpent were recipients of the curse after the Fall (see Genesis 3:14–19), so was the earth. Rather than remaining the perfect paradise that God intended, creation is now in bondage.

8:23–25 Believers groan as well, waiting for the time when God will redeem them fully. God's plan is in action. The agreement has been made, and the initial stages have already begun; but the full significance won't be realized until resurrection. So the anticipation and assurance of this reality are believers' hope in the meantime.

8:26–27 The presence of the Holy Spirit in the life of the believer is the first of all the signs that God has begun His work. In addition, the Spirit acts on behalf of the believer, interceding to bring God and the believer closer together.

8:28 The world can be an evil place at times, yet God works in all things for good. This is not to suggest that God creates sin or evil; He works in spite of them. When tragedy befalls a believer, the church should not infer that God was responsible for the pain and confusion. Yet He can see His children through such times and teach them valuable lessons about His love and faithfulness.

8:29 The meaning of *predestinate* is debated. *Predestination* is sometimes called "election" and may refer to what God predetermined to do for those who call on His name (see Ephesians 1:4–6). If this is the case, then Paul is not suggesting that prior to creation God created a list of people destined for salvation. However, God's foreknowledge is more than simply knowing ahead of time what will happen. It has an added element of regarding with favor.

8:30 *Justification* (being declared righteous) is a matter of how God sees believers now. Throughout the Christian life, God's people should become progressively more Christlike. Similarly, they are also considered glorified. Ultimately, this means their human bodies will be transformed into a state like Jesus' glorious body (see Philippians 3:20–21).

9:1–33 The doctrine of predestination is one that many people avoid, but it is closely tied to the doctrine of God's sovereignty. Indeed, believers rejoice in God's sovereignty over sin, struggles, and eventual death. Yet many hesitate to accept His sovereignty with respect to salvation. In this section, Paul proclaims two paradoxical truths: (1) God is sovereign, and (2) people are responsible for their choices. Somehow both teachings are true, and God rewards believers' struggle to make sense of them.

9:7–9 Paul turns to history to show how God's sovereignty has been demonstrated throughout the centuries. He points out that Abraham's oldest child was actually Ishmael, yet God had proclaimed that His promise to Abraham would be fulfilled through Isaac.

9:10–13 As another demonstration of His sovereign choice, God opted to work through Jacob, the younger twin, rather than Esau. God's decree to do so came even before the birth of the twins (see Genesis 25:23);

it wasn't based on anything that Esau did wrong or that Jacob did right.

9:17–18 As a third example from Israel's history, Paul introduces Pharaoh. The hardening of Pharaoh's heart—which eventually led to Israel's exodus from Egypt—was part of God's sovereign plan.

9:19–21 It may seem unfair, if God is sovereign, for Him to hold us accountable for our choices. Paul isn't condemning honest questions here; he is referring to those who simply want to quarrel with God. That is not our right, any more than a piece of clay has a right to take issue with the potter.

9:22–29 God's sovereign choice had been prophesied a number of times. It had been foretold that God would call those who were not His people. Even when the nation of Israel rejected Him, He would deliver a remnant who would be saved. It was only God's mercy that kept Israel from being destroyed as completely as Sodom and Gomorrha.

9:30–33 The obtaining of salvation by the Jews and Gentiles had been much like the race between the tortoise and the hare. Many Jews zealously pursued a legalistic path to God's favor; yet they never achieved what they hoped for. The Gentiles, on the other hand, hadn't been looking for righteousness but had found it through faith in Jesus. The Israelites needed to quit depending on their own efforts and put their faith in God instead.

10:3–4 Hard work had made Paul's countrymen self-righteous, and when presented with the righteousness that is attainable only through Jesus, they were too proud to consider it. As the Messiah to whom the law and the prophets had pointed, however, Jesus put an end to the law.

10:5–8 Moses had taught that justification came by faith, emphasizing obedience out of love rather than legalistic commitment (see Deuteronomy 30:6–10). He had also stressed the nearness of God's law (see Deuteronomy 30:11–14). People don't have to go out of their way to receive insight from God; He has placed it in their mouths and hearts. So it is foolish pride to think that we can do anything to help bring the Messiah down from heaven or to raise Him from the dead. These actions were completely the work of God.

10:11 Paul again quotes Isaiah 28:16 to show that salvation is by faith (see also 9:33).

10:14 Salvation is a matter of hearing the truth of the Gospel and responding, so Paul credits those who were involved with spreading the message.

10:18 But what if Israel hadn't heard God's message? Paul answers this question by quoting from Psalm 19. The psalmist describes how God reveals Himself through both what He has created (19:1–6) and what He has revealed in His written Word (19:7–11). The Israelites had heard God's message; they just hadn't responded.

10:19–20 Perhaps Israel didn't understand what God was trying to tell them. Paul quotes two Old Testament passages (Deuteronomy 32:21 and Isaiah 65:1) to show that the Gentiles (a "foolish nation") had figured it out. The Jews believed themselves to be far superior to the Gentiles and must have felt a bit insulted at Paul's insinuation.

11:2–4 Paul reminds his readers of the story of Elias (Elijah), who had served God during a time when many of the Israelites had abandoned the Lord and turned to idols. Even then, God had a remnant of faithful people, seven thousand strong (see 1 Kings 19:9–18).

11:5–6 Paul is convinced that another remnant of faithful Jewish believers exists during his time. The existence of such a remnant is evidence of the grace of God.

11:7–10 Paul cites the examples of Moses (Deuteronomy 29:4) and David (Psalm 69:22–23), who had written about their people being unable to see what God was doing in their midst. Yet even during such bleak times, the nation had endured because of a remnant of those faithful to God.

11:11–12 Paul insists that the rejection of the Jews was partial, passing, and with purpose. A remnant continued to believe, the rejection wouldn't last forever, and some good would actually come from it. Israel's transgression allowed the Gospel to be delivered to the Gentiles. As a result, a sense of jealousy developed among the people of Israel. When the Jewish people saw God's acceptance of the Gentiles, many would repent and come to God as well. Indeed, Paul's use of the word *fulness* indicates a positive future for Israel.

11:22–24 The Jewish nation should not see the inclusion of the Gentiles as a threat. Just the opposite. If God could make a wild branch become productive, it will be no trouble for Him to restore some of the natural branches. All the Jews needed to do was show the same degree of repentance and faith as the Gentiles, and they would quickly be reattached to their source of growth and productivity. Ultimately, the restoration of a Jewish person was an easier process than the call of a Gentile to faith, because the knowledgeable Jew understood the need for forgiveness.

11:25–27 Paul begins wrapping up this section by reminding his readers that God's sovereignty is undeniable. Even while Israel was rejecting Him, God was opening the doors of salvation to the Gentiles. And the long-range results of this would be the salvation of Israel.

11:30–32 Paul further demonstrates that God's mercy is unfathomable. His love and mercy overflowed to the Gentiles, allowing them access to His kingdom. And He used the inclusion of the Gentiles to get the attention of the Jews. God continues to show His mercy, even after His people reject Him and harden their hearts to His love.

11:33–36 Finally, Paul shows that God's mind is unsearchable. At this point, it seems Paul stops preaching and starts worshipping. He notes that people, as finite creatures, are incapable of fully comprehending the infinite God. Much of what we believe must simply be taken on faith. Yet that which we cannot grasp with our minds, we can entrust to God with all of our hearts.

12:2 What God offers is not mere improvement but the radical transformation of sinners into saints, allowing them to exchange their filthy rags of sin for the royal robes of righteousness in Christ. Holy living involves the body, mind, and spirit.

12:6 When people think of prophecy, many immediately think of foretelling the future. While that is one aspect of the gift, a wider sense includes the revelation of the Holy Spirit to a believer concerning the will of God. For example, when an important decision needs to be made, the gift of prophecy might allow someone to know for certain what God wants His church to do.

12:6–8 Paul identifies seven of the gifts of the Holy Spirit in this passage.

12:7 The gift of service, or "ministry," is the ability to support others inside and outside the family of God. The believer with this gift is motivated to demonstrate Christ's love by meeting practical needs and giving assistance. (The Greek word for *service* [*diakonia*] is the root for our word *deacon*.) Teaching is the ability to clearly explain what God has revealed.

12:9–21 The overriding theme in the rest of this section is the importance of love and how genuine love affects the believer's behavior.

13:1–5 Paul's instructions for his readers to submit to the governing authorities ("higher powers") take on greater significance in light of the fact that there were few Christians in authority at the time. Those in charge were largely unfriendly or even hostile to the church. Yet Paul viewed the governing authorities not only as having been established by God but also as being the ministers of God. The Greek word Paul uses here is the same one used to describe the work of a pastor or elder. Paul also reminds his readers that the purpose of the state is to restrain evil and promote a just social order. Government originated as an ordinance of God. While it cannot redeem the world, it can nevertheless set boundaries for human behavior. The state is not a remedy for sin, but it is a means to restrain sin.

13:8 No one ever comes to the point in his or her Christian life where it can be said, "I have loved enough." Paul ties together love for one another with fulfillment of the law. According to scripture, love cannot operate on its own without an objective moral standard.

13:9–10 A person who truly loves will not commit adultery, for example, because real love shows respect and restraint. If someone allows physical passion to sweep him or her into an affair, then that person loves too little rather than too much. Why does love sum up all the other commandments? Paul says it's because love does not harm its neighbour. The final five of the Ten Commandments address sins that hurt other people: murder, adultery, stealing, giving false testimony, and coveting (see Exodus 20:13–17). The essence of love is to serve one's neighbour. So the demonstration of love does away with the need to spell out all the individual "Thou shalt nots" of the law.

13:12–14 With each passing day, Jesus' return draws nearer. As believers anticipate that return, Paul reminds them to be aware of their behavior. He provides the image of taking off nightclothes and putting on the armour of light, suitable daytime equipment for soldiers of Christ. As the time grows shorter, the need for love takes on greater urgency.

14:1–12 Scripture is clear as to whether many things are right or wrong. But in this section, Paul addresses those "gray" issues.

14:4–8 Believers suffer when they compete with one another. No one is self-sufficient, so all of us need to acknowledge the right of other believers to worship in different ways. Rather than being critical of one another, people should attend to their own spiritual conditions and devote themselves to God.

14:10–12 Paul reminds his readers that there will indeed be a day of judgment when everyone will stand before God and give an account. In the meantime, judgment of one another is a useless exercise.

14:13–23 A problem between "strong" and "weak" Christians is the exercise of one's religious freedom with callous disregard for how others might be affected. In the first century, when one group was sensitive to dietary restrictions and whether or not meat had been sacrificed to idols, and another group had no concern about such things, sharing a meal together could be awkward. Christian freedom is not license. If one's exercise of freedom impairs the growth of others, it's better to voluntarily do without such exercise. Paul recognized that believers develop at their individual paces. People are not required to reach total agreement in all matters of church function, and they should learn to respect differences of opinion.

15:1–2 In some of Paul's other writings, he warns against becoming intent on pleasing other people (for example, see Galatians 1:10; 1 Thessalonians 2:4). Those who are too concerned with pleasing others are in danger of falling away from God. That's not what Paul means when he writes of sacrificing one's rights and pleasing "his neighbour." The other instances refer to pleasing people instead of God. In this case, the desire to find favor with other believers is so that God will be pleased as they continue to grow spiritually.

15:7–12 Jesus has already accepted both the stronger and weaker believers, so now they need to learn to accept one another. He has already set the example to follow; and because of His willingness to set aside His own rights and privileges, He brought salvation not only to the Jews but to the Gentiles as well.

15:15–16 Paul describes his work as a priestly ministry. A priest was responsible for offering sacrifices on behalf of the people, and Paul had been able to offer to God a great number of Gentile converts. Although the Gentiles were excluded from sharing in the temple sacrifices at Jerusalem, they were "living sacrifices" (see 12:1).

15:23–28 Having clarified his ministry for his readers, Paul outlines his future travel plans, specifying three destinations: Jerusalem, Rome, and Spain. Assuming he would travel by sea, going to these locations would require a journey of three thousand miles—an ambitious undertaking given the difficulties of first-century transportation.

15:26–27 Paul and others had collected a special offering from a number of Gentile churches in Greece. Now he wants to deliver the gift to the Jewish believers in Jerusalem who are suffering from a severe famine. In particular, the gift of the Macedonian churches was significant for a number of reasons. First, it fulfilled the request of the apostles to remember the poor (see Galatians 2:10). Second, it demonstrated the solidarity of God's people across various geographic regions and economic levels. Third, it broke down racial and social barriers. Paul recognizes the gift from the Gentile churches to the Jewish believers as a powerful demonstration of the oneness of the body of Christ.

15:28 As for Paul's hopes to see Spain, we don't know if he ever made it. The entire Iberian Peninsula was under the control of Rome and had many flourishing Roman colonies. But if Paul took that trip between his first imprisonment in Rome and the later one that led to his death in AD 64, it was not recorded anywhere.

15:30–33 Paul concludes this section with a heartfelt request for prayer for safety in his travels, deliverance from his enemies, and above all, the opportunity to visit with the church in Rome. He does not pray in order to bend God's will to his but rather to align his plans with God's will.

16:1–13 A significant point about Paul's list is that it is comprised of people of different rank and ethnicity. There are Jews and Gentiles, men and women, slaves and free people. Aristobulus was a grandson of Herod the Great and a friend of Emperor Claudius. Narcissus was a rich and powerful freed slave who served as the secretary to Claudius. Amplias, on the other hand, was one of several common slave names on Paul's list. Rufus may have been the son of Simon of Cyrene, the bystander who had been unexpectedly forced into Roman service to carry the cross of Jesus to Calvary (see Mark 15:21). Yet there is great unity within the diversity. Four times in this chapter Paul describes the believers at Rome as being "in Christ." Twice he uses "sister" or "brethren" as a metaphor for the familial unity of the body of Christ. Paul's list of names also includes nine women. Tryphena and Tryphosa may have been twin sisters (based on the similarities in their names). Their names mean "dainty" and "delicate" respectively, yet Paul praises them for working hard for the Lord—a phrase that indicates working to the point of exhaustion. Clearly, Paul was not the male chauvinist some have made him out to be. He appreciated the gifts and ministries of women, and he commended them for their service to him and to Christ.

16:1–16 When it comes to lists of names in the Bible—whether tribes, genealogies, the great gallery of faith in Hebrews 11, or others—many people have a natural tendency to skip over them. Yet in most cases, there are valuable lessons to be discovered by those who slow down and take a look. In this passage, twenty-six people are mentioned by name, and there are twenty-one titles attached to the various names (sister, servant, helper, etc.). Some names are familiar; many are not. Yet a quick look at the people and Paul's comments may provide some surprising insight.

16:25–27 Paul's doxology is a final reminder that the mystery of God had been revealed through Jesus Christ. What had been written in the law and proclaimed by the prophets could at last be fully understood. And for that, God is due praise and glory forever.

CORINTHIANS

INTRODUCTION TO 1 CORINTHIANS ▪ During his second missionary journey, Paul remained in Corinth for about eighteen months (about AD 51–52), teaching and establishing the church there. He then returned to his home base at Antioch and subsequently set off on his third missionary journey. He traveled to Ephesus, the key city in the Roman province of Asia, where he remained for three years, establishing churches there and in the surrounding regions. Paul considered himself the spiritual father of the Corinthian church (4:14–15). It was his love for the believers that motivated him to confront them so directly concerning spiritual and moral issues. Personally, he had experienced weakness, fear, and trembling in his previous association with the church (2:3), but Paul knew it was the power of God that would sustain both him as the messenger and the Corinthian believers as a body.

AUTHOR ▪ The epistle of 1 Corinthians both begins and ends with an identification of Paul as the author (1:1; 16:21). The early church was quick to affirm his authorship, and few modern scholars dispute it.

OCCASION ▪ A delegation from Corinth (Stephanas, Fortunatus, and Achaicus [16:17]) came to Paul with a financial gift from the church. They probably also brought a list of questions from the church, since Paul answers these questions in his letter (7:1). The report of these three men, along with a report from members of the household of a woman named Chloe (1:11), and perhaps a report from his fellow missionary Apollos (1:12; 16:12), prompted Paul to write the letter.

1:1 As was customary for first-century letters, Paul begins by identifying himself and his recipients and then provides a brief greeting. He refers to his apostleship as well as his calling, both credentials that attest to his being sent out by God. Later in the letter, he will reveal that his authority is questioned, so from the beginning he establishes his credibility.

1:3 The usual Greco-Roman greeting was "rejoice" or "be well" (*chairein*). Paul gives a distinctly Christian greeting by using a similar-sounding Greek word: *grace* (*charis*). *Peace* (*shalom* in Hebrew; *eirene* in Greek), on the other hand, was the typical Jewish salutation. So Paul combines Greek and Jewish greetings, and he acknowledges their theological overtones by citing the origin of both: the one, true, living God revealed in Jesus Christ.

1:4–9 Paul expresses thankfulness for the believers in Corinth, even though he will soon confront them with a number of shortcomings. Paul trusts God's character and faithfulness to see the Corinthians through their human frailties and flaws.

1:12 Foremost among the reasons for division among the Corinthians was a tendency to align themselves with different Christian leaders, as if it were a contest. Paul names four leaders here, and it's not surprising that they would have appealed to different personalities. Some believers aligned themselves with Paul—probably those of Greek ancestry, who wanted to be loyal to the one who founded their church. Others aligned themselves with Apollos (see Acts 18:24–28). Educated in Alexandria and known for his oratorical abilities and knowledge of the Old Testament, he would have appealed to the intellectuals. Cephas (that is, Peter) probably appealed to those of Jewish background. Perhaps they were attracted to the forcefulness of his personality or the fact that he had spent three years with Jesus. Finally, one group professed devotion only to Christ—perhaps with

an air of superiority. Yet they were using the name of Jesus to separate themselves from others in the church.

1:22–24 At the time, wisdom was perceived as less a matter of genuine intellect than an ability to articulate a clever-sounding worldview addressing the grand themes of life. Two philosophers could expound on their opinions and reach quite different conclusions, yet both be considered wise. God's wisdom had little to do with such showiness. The simple message of the gospel was God's wisdom, yet some people continued to look for wondrous signs and others for hidden truths.

1:25–31 God's "foolishness" is wiser than all of humanity's wisdom. God intentionally chooses "foolish" and "weak" things to accomplish His will, undermining the arguments of the "wise" and "strong." Thus, credit for a believer's wisdom and strength belongs to God.

2:1–5 Paul credits God for everything in his ministry. Though well educated and knowledgeable, he does not package his message in pretentious speech or high-sounding eloquence. The content of his message is powerful enough without trying to bolster it in manipulative ways. But by humbly refusing to make a dazzling presentation of the Gospel, Paul allows his readers to see the supernatural nature of what he is preaching. Paul doesn't want the attention to be on him, but on God.

2:6 As Paul continues to differentiate between various kinds of wisdom, he explains that the believer's wisdom is mature—not at all like what was being presented as wisdom in the world. The difference is due to the work of the Holy Spirit. In Paul's day, many tried to approach God through reasoning and argument. The result was *apatheia*—an impersonal deity with no ability to feel. They saw God as detached and remote, and the preaching of Christ (with its emphasis on suffering and reconciling the world to Himself through death on a cross) seemed incomprehensible and foolish.

2:7–10 God's wisdom had been hidden, but what was once secret has now been revealed and made accessible. Without the Spirit's enlightenment, however, a person is incapable of realizing the truth about God.

2:15–16 Paul concludes this section with a question from Isaiah: "Who hath known the mind of the Lord?" And the answer, from a New Testament perspective, is that with the Holy Spirit's help, *all* believers can know the mind of Christ. Elsewhere, Paul shares his definition of the mind of Christ (Philippians 2:5–11), and it is not mystical or mysterious. The mind of Christ is characterized by an attitude of humility and sacrifice.

3:1–2 The church in Corinth was immature. Although its members had been Christians for several years, they were still babes in the faith. They should have possessed a mature hunger for real Christian teaching, but they still wanted "milk" (probably a reference to justification and all the other benefits of a Christian relationship) instead of "meat" (the solid truths of Christianity: choosing righteousness, making sacrifices, submitting to others, and so forth).

3:5–9 Paul had sown the seed of God's Word in Corinth, and a church had sprung up. Apollos had come along later to "water" the young church. But Paul makes it clear that only God is responsible for any growth. The Corinthians needed to see that Paul and Apollos had played different—but equally important—roles in the ministry of the church. To argue about which leader was more important made about as much sense as cheering for one farmer over another.

3:10 Paul uses the illustration of a building to further clarify his point. Jesus is the foundation of anything a believer hopes to construct. Paul had laid that foundation in the sense that he had first preached the Gospel in Corinth. Apollos (see 3:5) contributed to the subsequent growth by building on the foundation—strengthening the Corinthian Christians.

3:11–15 Not every builder has the same results. Those who work with valuable materials—the truths of God—have a lasting ministry. Those who settle for less will not see the same results. The references to wood, hay, and straw probably represent work based on the limited human wisdom Paul described in chapter 2.

4:1 Having told the Corinthians how *not* to treat apostles, Paul brings the discussion full circle and encourages the believers to view their spiritual leaders as stewards (servants)—stewards entrusted with "the mysteries of God."

4:2–5 Ultimately, both the leaders and the other church members would have to give an account to the Lord. It meant little to Paul how the Corinthians regarded his ministry, because all that really mattered was God's divine assessment.

4:14–21 There was an antidote to pride, but it wasn't popular in first-century culture. Paul doesn't use the words *lowliness of mind* (humility) here as he does in other places (see Philippians 2:3), but that is the heart of the matter. According to Greek philosophy, humility was a trait associated with slaves—a sign of weakness not to be associated with men of character. Paul (in imitation of

Jesus) had a completely different philosophy—one that prized humility.

5:1–2 The Greek attitude toward promiscuity was rather lax. To most Gentiles, it was a small matter whether someone frequented brothels or had an extramarital affair. The Greek word for *fornication*, when used by the church, referred to numerous sexual sins they found inappropriate, such as adultery and homosexuality. One of the few specific requests the early church leaders made of Gentile converts was to abstain from sexual immorality (Acts 15:20, 29). Yet one of the church members in Corinth was living with his father's wife—most likely his stepmother. It is possible that the man's father had already died and that he and the woman were approximately the same age. But the relationship was still considered incestuous. Even pagan society looked down on such a bond, and it was prohibited by Roman law. Yet members of the Corinthian church took pride in the tolerance they showed by allowing the relationship.

5:5 Paul doesn't address the immoral man (see 5:1) but rather scolds the church as a whole for allowing the problem. And since it hadn't taken action, he dictates what should be done: excommunicating the man for his own good and the good of the church. It was a severe punishment. Yet Paul later makes a reference to a similar event (2 Corinthians 2:5–11), perhaps even referring to the same situation—in which case the man does repent and returns to good standing in the church.

5:9–13 In a previous letter (one that has never been found), Paul had apparently dealt with a similar problem, but the church members had misinterpreted his instructions. So here he reiterates his point and makes himself very clear. It is not right to judge those *outside* the church. The church has a ministry to those people. If outsiders choose to ignore the truth of the Gospel, then God will be their judge. Paul's point is to disassociate with immoral people *within* the church.

6:2–3 Christians have access to the wisdom of God through the Holy Spirit. They will one day rule with Christ and even judge angels (Jude 6). Yet the Corinthians couldn't even settle their own minor disputes.

6:5 Instead of feeling proud of their legal victories in secular courts, the Corinthian Christians should be ashamed of airing their problems in the public arena. Paul writes that such behavior is an ineffective witness for Christ.

6:7–8 Even if the Corinthian believers can't settle a matter to their satisfaction within the church, for the good of the Gospel they should be willing to be wronged. No offense is severe enough to sacrifice one's Christian witness to nonbelievers.

6:9–20 Corinth had a reputation for sexual promiscuity. Prostitution was rampant, much of it connected with the large temple of Aphrodite, the Greek goddess of love. Many Corinthian men no doubt visited prostitutes before they became believers, and it appears that some continued to do so even afterward. (In which case, it is no wonder they had little to say about a man living with his stepmother [5:1–5].)

6:12–13 Paul responds to two specific arguments from the Corinthians. First was the social argument that everyone else was doing it. They didn't want to be left out of the citywide parties occasionally held at Aphrodite's temple. Second was the philosophical argument that sex didn't really matter, since food and sex were physical things, not spiritual things (a philosophy known as dualism). The physical body would eventually pass away, leaving only the spirit, so what people did with their bodies was of no lasting concern. Paul refutes both arguments.

6:15–20 The Spirit of God dwells in the bodies of believers, so even their physical lives should honor God. This principle holds true for more than just sex. Freedom in the Christian life is never an excuse to live however one wants.

6:18 Sexual purity is one of God's most precious gifts. Sex goes beyond mere biology or physiology and encompasses the totality of one's humanity. So Paul is not being prudish in his instructions. Rather, he is attempting to lift this wonderful gift of God above the cultural standards that tend to debase and demean it. Many people settle for a cheap imitation of what God intends for sex. In pursuit of selfish gratification, they sacrifice true freedom and miss the ultimate fulfillment of sexual fidelity within the covenant of marriage.

6:20 Everyone else may be doing the wrong things (the social argument—see 6:12), but believers are not their own. They have been bought with a price and therefore should glorify God with their bodies.

7:1–16 Having just told his readers to flee from sexual sins, Paul turns to the option of marriage. In previous correspondence, he had received questions about the subject—no surprise, since Greek cultural values distorted scriptural teachings on marriage at both ends of the scale. On the one hand, dualism taught that body and spirit were completely separate entities within a person. If nothing done to the body had a lasting spiritual effect, why not freely engage in hedonism? Another philosophy was asceticism, where one sought to purify his spirit by depriving his body of any pleasure—sexual or otherwise. Having already addressed hedonism (chapters 5–6), Paul turns his attention to the ascetics.

7:12–16 With the rapid growth of the church, it is not surprising that guidelines were needed for when one spouse becomes a believer and the other doesn't. Paul says if the unbelieving spouse leaves, the believer is no longer bound to the marriage. Yet if the unbeliever is willing to continue in the marriage, the Christian is not to leave his or her spouse. The godly influence of one spouse on the other may result in the other's salvation.

7:17–24 Becoming a Christian changes a person's spiritual life and outlook, yet it doesn't mean a person will change in every way. Gentiles remain Gentile. Servants may remain servants (but are under no obligation to do so if they can obtain their freedom). Similarly, happily single people need not rush out looking for a mate, and married believers need not pursue singleness. Instead, everyone should attempt to do whatever God directs.

7:25–29 Paul preferred the single life, yet he insists it is not the only way for people to be faithful to God. However, ministry was foremost on Paul's mind. His reminder that there is little time may be a reference to Jesus' return. In any case, Corinth was prosperous at the time, and believers there had not yet faced the persecution that would eventually come.

7:34 A single person is freer to serve God. Marriage is a commitment to another person, and such a commitment requires time and attention. People can serve God whether they are married or single, but God is not honored by the neglect of a spouse.

8:4–6 Paul says that idols have no objective spiritual existence, so in reality the meat had been dedicated to nothing. The God of the Bible is the provider of all things. Although other people recognized various gods and goddesses, none of those so-called deities had anything to do with the creation, sustenance, or redemption of the world. Therefore, a Christian was free to eat meat that had been sacrificed to an idol because the idol had no spiritual power or authority.

8:7–8 Although there was no theological basis for refusing to eat sacrificed meat, the fact remained that some of the Christians in Corinth could not in good conscience do so in the privacy of their own homes, much less in the pagan temples of the city. Many had no doubt been involved with idol worship and ceremonial sacrifices before converting to Christianity, and they wanted nothing to do with that past. They would have felt compelled to abstain from anything associated with such ceremonies.

8:9 In consideration of those who continued to struggle with the sacrificed meat, Paul asks other believers to willingly abstain from the practice as well. Even though they had freedom in Christ, the highest calling for the believer is love.

9:1–2 If anyone was skeptical about Paul's right to be an apostle, it shouldn't have been the Corinthians. Paul's credentials were not only that he had seen the living Jesus on the road to Damascus, but also that he had begun the church in Corinth.

9:3–6 Paul was a proven apostle, and apostles had rights. Although the church should have been supporting him, he never demanded it even though other churches were taking care of the expenses of their leaders—and the leaders' wives as well.

9:7–14 It was common sense that someone who did so much work should be recompensed in some way. Soldiers were paid for their service to the nation. Gardeners ate the fruit they planted. Shepherds drank their animals' milk. People were sure to feed the oxen that turned the mill wheels. A priest got a share of what was offered at the temple. So how much more should a church take care of its spiritual leader?

9:12 Paul's argument is strong that he should be entitled to certain rights and privileges in return for the work and service he is doing for others. Yet he refuses to demand anything because of his high regard for the Gospel of Christ.

9:18 Paul doesn't require financial support, because he is more than satisfied with the reward he has received—the privilege of preaching the Gospel without charge. If he were performing his ministry for money, he wouldn't find it nearly as fulfilling.

9:19–22 Paul's willingness to minister without remuneration gives him great freedom. He doesn't have to submit expense reports or give answer to a patron. He uses his Christian freedom to live for Christ as fully as possible. When around fellow Jews, he adheres to Jewish customs and dietary restrictions, even though he feels no spiritual obligation to do so. When among Gentiles, he adapts to their practices and menus. When around immature believers, he practices no spiritual freedom that might cause them to stumble in their progress. In devotion to Jesus, Paul attempts to be "all things to all men."

9:24–27 Paul's readers were familiar with the Olympics in Greece, as well as the nearby Isthmian Games that took place every two or three years, so they would have understood Paul's athletic metaphors. A runner intent on winning will deny himself certain things while in training. Similarly, a boxer toughens himself to endure the blows he will receive. If such efforts result in victory, the outcome is worth all the training and sacrifice. Likewise, Paul is more than willing to deny himself certain things if the result is the ongoing progress of other believers in their spiritual journeys. He is in the race to win.

10:1–5 When believers fail to exercise self-control, they expose themselves to danger, as evidenced by the Israelites' wandering in the wilderness. Paul lists four privileges that could have led to subsequent blessings for the Israelites, but didn't: (1) They were guided by God's presence (Exodus 13:21–22); (2) they escaped the Egyptians by crossing the parted sea (Exodus 14:21–29); (3) they feasted on manna and quail in the desert (Exodus 16); and (4) they were supernaturally given water (Exodus 17:1–7).

10:7–10 Despite all the blessings they received, the Israelites proved faithless in four ways: (1) They repeatedly complained about their conditions in the desert (Exodus 17:2–3); (2) they committed idolatry by worshipping the golden calf (Exodus 32:1–6); (3) their grumbling turned into rebellion, resulting in a widespread plague (Numbers 16:41–50); and (4) they engaged in sexual immorality (and pagan worship) with women of Moab (Numbers 25:1–9).

10:12–13 Everyone faces occasional temptations. No one is exempt. Believers confront many of the same temptations that others have endured throughout history, yet we can experience God's faithfulness during such times. Paul assures his readers that God will not give them more than they can handle, provided they rely on His strength and yield to the power of His Spirit.

10:18–20 Jewish believers would have understood that after the Old Testament sacrifices, those who ate the sacrificial meat in the temple communed with the Lord and appropriated the temporary forgiveness that was associated with those animal sacrifices. Similarly, pagan sacrifices were not only offered to idols, but part of the meat was given back to the worshipper so he or she could hold a feast, with the belief that the god himself

would be a guest. So while a believer need not be overly concerned about the meat itself, he or she should not participate in the pagan festivals. The idols may have been only wood and stone, but they had real spiritual forces behind them that believers were to avoid.

10:23–24 Paul summarizes his argument of the last three chapters: Love for others should dictate a believer's choices and behaviors.

10:25–26 Regarding meat sacrificed to idols, what a believer did in his or her own home was of no concern. To a Christian, it was just a piece of meat. If believers were invited out to dinner where the meat was served, they could eat it in good conscience. But if a fellow believer was at the dinner and was troubled by what was served, the more mature believers should refuse to eat, lest the weaker one compromise his or her own conscience.

11:2–16 During Paul's day, it was customary for a woman to wear a veil (similar to a scarf) covering the head and hanging down over her neck. No respectable woman would think of appearing in public without it. In addition, the prevailing first-century attitude toward women was that they were inferior and subordinate to men. Jewish women, for example, could attend synagogue, but they were segregated from the men. Greek women were not allowed to attend school. So as women joined the church, they experienced similar discrimination. While the question of whether a woman should have her head covered or have a particular hairstyle does not dominate conversations in many churches today, it was a very sensitive matter for the early church. Would the church impose discrimination and second-class status onto its female members? Would women have all the same rights as men—including dress and hairstyles? Or would some middle ground need to be reached?

11:11–16 According to Paul, men and women cannot operate independently of one another. For a male writing in the first century, Paul's teachings were radically progressive. He was one of the first advocates of a role for women in church leadership, but he also wanted to ensure that both women and men submit to God and act appropriately.

11:17 Paul usually acknowledges what a church is doing right before correcting its members or challenging them to do better. But when it comes to the Corinthians' behavior during the Lord's Supper, Paul can find nothing good to say.

11:18–22 The early church met weekly for a kind of potluck supper called the Agape Feast, which ended with Communion. But at Corinth, the wealthy people (who didn't have to work until sunset as did the poorer manual laborers) would go early and eat their fill, leaving little, if anything, for those who needed the food most. Some would drink their fill to the point of drunkenness. The very meal that was supposed to bring people closer to one another and to God had become an embarrassment—and yet another source of division.

11:23–34 Paul reminds the Corinthians of the proper procedure and purpose of the Lord's Supper. He also instructs the believers to examine themselves before participating. They should not see the meal without seeing the body and blood of Jesus. And he tells them to consider the others involved. A believer's spiritual rebirth makes him or her a member of a spiritual family. There is no time that a Christian should be more aware of this fact than during the solemn reminder of the Lord's Supper.

12:1 The Greek word translated *gifts* is *charismata*, the source of our word *charismatic*. The word could also be interpreted as "gifts of grace." Paul says that the church is to be a charismatic, Spirit-gifted community.

12:2–3 Many of the Corinthians came from pagan backgrounds. But the idols they once worshipped were mute and offered no help or direction. The Holy Spirit of God, in contrast, would provide them with knowledge and spiritual substance.

12:8–11 This list of spiritual gifts (see also verses 28–30) is not exhaustive. Paul provides other lists (see Romans 12:6–8; Ephesians 4:11–13).

12:12–13 Paul emphasizes the importance of unity in the body of Christ. The church, though comprised of many members, is intended to be a single unit, an organic whole regardless of racial or religious backgrounds (Jews or Greeks) or social standing (slave or free).

12:14 Unity is not the same as uniformity. Various groups within Christianity, and even within denominations, will have different opinions that should be respected as long as all agree on the great orthodox spiritual truths that all Christians share.

12:15–20 No physical body can function as all-seeing, all-hearing, or all-smelling. So why should the church expect to function with a focus on only one spiritual gift? People are not all the same, their gifts will differ according to God's will, and believers should learn to accept one another. They are called to celebrate their diversity within the unity of the church, which provides a place of belonging for a wide range of followers of Jesus Christ.

12:21–28 The various members of the body of Christ are not just to tolerate one another. As with the parts of the human body, mutual interdependence is critical to proper operation. The effectiveness, health, and vitality of the church are dependent on how well its various members function together as a whole. No individual has the right to say to another, "I don't need you." And whether or not church members realize it, each person is indispensable for collective effectiveness in the world. Indeed, unity and interdependence create a richness and texture for the collective witness of the church.

12:29–30 Not everyone can preach. Not everyone can sing. Not everyone can teach. But everyone is gifted to do *something*. Apparently, the problem in Corinth was a rivalry among spiritual gifts and a jealousy that caused some people to covet the gifts of others. There was no unity, no positive diversity, and certainly no interdependence.

13:1–3 Charity (or love) is absolutely necessary if the church is to function as God intends. People can use their Spirit-given gifts—they can speak in angelic tongues, understand deep mysteries, give all their possessions to the poor, and sacrifice their very bodies—but actions performed without love count for nothing.

13:4–7 The word *love* is tossed around in literature, music, and advertising. Surely it was much the same in ancient Corinth, especially with its rampant promiscuity. Yet Paul provides a description of charity (or love) that has nothing to do with hearts and flowers. True Christian charity is action in response to the conviction of one's heart and mind.

13:8–13 Most likely, arguments about spiritual gifts centered on those that were most apparent: speaking in tongues, prophecy, healing, and so forth. It would have been quite clear who had those gifts in contrast to the gifts of faith, helping others, or administration. So Paul clarifies that just because a gift is from God and is used for the good of the church doesn't mean it is permanent. The time will come when these gifts are no longer needed. Prophecies will cease. Tongues will be stilled. Knowledge will pass away. Only three will always remain: faith, hope, and charity. And charity is the greatest of the three.

13:12 Paul compares a believer's image of God to what he or she might see in a mirror of the time. The reflection is helpful, but far from satisfying. It only makes the person wish for a clearer view.

14:1 Paul begins by making himself clear that people should be eager to receive the gifts of the Holy Spirit. And he reiterates what he had just written about the importance of charity (or love) in connection with spiritual gifts.

14:2–5 Apparently believers at Corinth were enamored with the gift of speaking in tongues. Paul assures them that this gift has its place, yet it needs to be used with love and discretion. He contrasts the gift of tongues with that of prophecy. The role of the New Testament prophet was to discern God's message to the church through the Holy Spirit. Early believers had no Bibles for reference; even Old Testament scrolls were costly and difficult to secure. So the role of the prophet was vital. Furthermore, the person speaking in tongues didn't know what he or she was saying, nor did the church. Only the person speaking in tongues felt edified, whereas prophecy edified all who heard.

14:6 Paul asks the Corinthians to suppose he had come to them speaking only in tongues they could not understand. Clearly, they would have needed knowledge and instruction—the same is true for the newer believers currently in their midst.

14:8 As a third example of the difference between prophecy and tongues, Paul refers to a military trumpet giving signals to the soldiers. If it is unclear whether the signal is to advance or retreat, how can the army function?

14:13–25 Paul never tells the Corinthians *not* to speak in tongues. But he is firm in clarifying the right way to use the gift. He insists that gifts that benefit the church should always have preference over those that only edify the individual. Those who take undue pride in the gift of tongues think they are the mature segment of the church, but Paul says they are thinking like children.

14:26–28 Paul writes that all spiritual gifts should be used in an orderly, helpful, productive manner. The public expression of speaking in tongues should be limited to two or three people, with interpretations for each one. Otherwise, the person(s) should worship silently and privately.

14:34–35 Paul's words for women have caused much debate, but he doesn't seem to be saying that *all* women should be silent at *all* church functions. He had previously validated their participation in prayer and prophesying (see 11:5, 13). Most likely his comments were intended to reduce potential confusion in the worship services. It might be that some of the women were asking questions or initiating debates over what was said. One theory is that Paul is referring to women married to believers, in which case he is asking them to let their husbands speak for both of them. Others think Paul is simply asking the women to keep quiet just as (by limiting the number to three) he was asking some of those who would otherwise speak in tongues or prophesy to keep quiet (see 14:28).

14:39–40 Paul reiterates the right and the privilege of putting all of the gifts of the Spirit into practice—as long as they are carried out properly. He isn't just expressing his opinion, but using *his* gift to let the Corinthians know how God feels.

15:1 Paul assures the Corinthians that they had indeed received the Gospel. Salvation is a gift from God. No one ever discovers it on one's own or accomplishes it by clever insight, imaginative thinking, or hard work. In addition, the Gospel is the foundation on which they stand.

15:3–8 The Corinthian believers had based the weight of their lives, hopes, and dreams of heaven on what Paul had originally preached to them. According to Paul, the most important message is that Jesus died for the sins of humankind, was buried, rose from the dead, and made numerous undeniable appearances.

15:9 After His resurrection, Jesus had appeared to Peter, the eleven remaining apostles (still referred to as the twelve), James, a group of more than five hundred, and others. Peter had denied Jesus. James had doubted Him. And Paul was the worst of them all.

15:12 The debate over the resurrection of the dead had been going on for a long time. It was a major point of contention between the Pharisees (who believed in the resurrection) and the Sadducees (who did not).

15:13–19 Paul insists on two options: Either Jesus was resurrected, or He wasn't. If Christ had *not* been resurrected, then nobody else would be either. And that would also mean that Christianity was a lie and all preaching was in vain. Sin would still reign. Attempting to live a victorious life on earth with no anticipation of eternal life was simply pitiable.

15:22–28 Paul declares the truth: Jesus has indeed been raised from the dead. Adam's sin has separated all humankind from God, but Jesus' sacrifice has redeemed all people and restored an intimate relationship. Jesus has been resurrected, and all believers will follow Him into eternal life after their deaths. The resurrection of Jesus is God's ultimate victory over sin and death.

15:31–34 No one could question Paul's commitment to his belief in Jesus' resurrection. He proved it by facing danger every day. The "beasts at Ephesus" probably means the angry mob that tried to find him (see Acts 19:28–31). His point is that it would be foolhardy to keep putting his life on the line for a faith that ended at his death. But the reality of resurrection makes a difference in how believers should live.

15:39–44 There are all kinds of "bodies"—human, animal, heavenly, and so on. The resurrection body will differ from the earthly body in that it will be glorious, imperishable, and spiritual.

15:45–49 Human beings bear the likeness of Adam in a natural body that eventually returns to the dust of the earth. But after death, believers can look forward to receiving an eternal body that bears the likeness of Christ.

15:50–57 Paul tells his readers why they shouldn't fear death. For believers, it is only a passageway to immortality and eternal life with God. Jesus has removed the sting of sin and the power of death. Victory over death is assured. Whether believers are dead or alive when Jesus returns, their bodies will be changed.

15:58 Rather than speculate about matters that God has already taken care of, Christians should stand firm and get to work. The assurances of God should not lull them into self-satisfaction but motivate them to greater love and service.

16:1 Before closing his letter to the Corinthians, Paul wants to answer one final question. Someone had asked about the collection he was taking for the church in Jerusalem. There is no additional information to be found about what he had told the Galatian churches.

16:2 The first day of the week was not yet called the Lord's day, even though Christians had already begun assembling on that day in memory of the resurrection of Jesus. And it was never called the sabbath, which was Saturday, the day Jews met for worship. Paul simply tells the Corinthians to bring their financial gifts on "the first day of the week."

16:3 The church in Jerusalem had been suffering from persecution. The churches in Greece and Galatia owed their existence to those whom God had called from Jerusalem to go out and minister. It was natural for them to help their sister church financially.

16:4 When Paul wrote, he did not yet know if he would personally take the collection back to Jerusalem. As it turns out, he does (see Acts 21:17; 24:17).

16:5–9 Paul closes by sharing some of his plans with the Corinthian believers—including his desire to spend a considerable amount of time with them. His phrasing shows that although he was making plans, his ultimate itinerary depended on God. He demonstrates that a believer can use God-given wisdom to keep moving ahead rather than waiting for detailed knowledge of God's will before even getting started.

16:10–19 Paul acknowledges his fellow ministers, as he usually does in his letters. He is thankful for Timotheus (Timothy), Apollos, Stephanas, Fortunatus, Achaicus, and Aquila and Priscilla. Divided loyalties between church leaders was one of the problems at Corinth (see 1:11–12), but Paul always gave credit to *everyone* whom he saw at work for God—whether they were ministering alongside him or elsewhere.

THE SECOND EPISTLE OF PAUL THE APOSTLE TO THE

CORINTHIANS

INTRODUCTION TO 2 CORINTHIANS ■ This epistle from Paul to the Corinthian church is a follow-up letter to 1 Corinthians. The topics he discusses are similar, particularly the concern over the false teachers who continued to plague them. Though Paul addresses both general principles and issues specific to the Corinthian community, there is much here for the church today.

AUTHOR ■ Paul not only identifies himself as the author of 2 Corinthians (1:1; 10:1) but also provides more autobiographical information than in any of his other letters.

OCCASION ■ After establishing a church at Corinth (Acts 18:1–11), Paul continued to correspond with the believers there. Some of the correspondence between them has never been discovered (1 Corinthians 5:9; 7:1; 2 Corinthians 2:4; 7:8). In 1 Corinthians, Paul had addressed specific issues that had been raised in previous communications. He firmly advised the church how to handle its problems.

1:1 The fact that Paul opens this letter by identifying himself as Christ's apostle "by the will of God" is significant. In later sections, he will address the fact that some in Corinth were challenging his call to be an apostle. Paul may have been away from the Corinthians and uncertain about their response to his previous letter(s), but at least he had Timothy with him. Timothy was a regular comfort to Paul in his travels. Even though he was quite young when Paul recruited him, Paul considered the young minister a brother.

1:3 Paul could experience great comfort because of his understanding of God. All three titles he uses for God are assurances for Paul and believers as well. Paul will have much to say about suffering in this letter, but he begins with the outcome of his sufferings: comfort.

1:4–7 Paul makes it clear that believers will sometimes share in the sufferings of Jesus, but they will also share in the comfort that only God can provide.

1:10–11 Paul notes that his own weaknesses and limitations only cause God's power to be more apparent. This is a point he will emphasize throughout this letter.

1:12–14 Paul's boasting had a present dimension. He could declare a clear conscience regarding his conduct among believers and nonbelievers. But it also had a future dimension that looked ahead to the Day of Judgment when Christ would return to establish His kingdom. When that time came, Paul could take pride in his association with the Corinthian church, and the believers could be proud of him. Conversely, Paul's opponents might be proud and boastful now, but they would be silenced in the day of the Lord.

1:18–20 Paul makes it clear that God's promises are sure. God keeps His word. Likewise, those who serve Him must also keep their word. It would be wrong if Paul had made a foolish promise he had no intention of keeping; but it was quite different to make plans that were subject to the will of God and leading of the Holy Spirit.

2:5–6 Paul refers to a specific individual—perhaps the man who was excommunicated for having an improper relationship with his father's wife (see 1 Corinthians 5:1–5). But it is just as likely it was someone whom Paul had confronted on his most recent visit to Corinth. Whatever the case, it appears that one individual had reacted in an unseemly manner toward Paul. The church members had apparently rushed to Paul's defense to censure the man by excluding him from their fellowship. It also seems that the man had repented, yet the church had not reinstated him (perhaps thinking Paul would want it that way).

2:7–11 Paul was not one to hold grudges. As long as the church failed to reinstate the offender, the believers would not have unity and would be vulnerable to Satan's attacks. In entreating the church to extend forgiveness, Paul shows concern for both the individual and the church as a whole. Excluding someone from fellowship is a drastic action—necessary at times, but not to become a regular solution for all problems in the church.

2:12–13 Even Paul was subject to the pressure of seemingly endless responsibility and accountability. He was always quick to share news of his associates and how much they meant to him. In this case, he has failed to connect with Titus in Troas, which leaves him without any peace of mind. Even though he felt that God had opened a door to that city, Paul doesn't linger long.

2:17 Paul refuses to cater to the whims of his listeners. Unlike others, he didn't minister for the money. He could therefore speak simply and sincerely.

3:4–6 Those who held to the old covenant focused only on the letter of the law. The new covenant initiated by Jesus, however, provides access to the Spirit of God and to life. And it is the Holy Spirit who provides Paul's competence.

3:12–18 Paul uses the veil that Moses had worn over his face (see Exodus 34:29–35) to symbolize the spiritual "vail" over the hearts of many of the Jewish people. In their devotion to the old covenant, they were unable to see the glory that was available to them. The Spirit of God is the One who lifts the veil and enables believers to behold the glory of God in the face of Christ.

And it is the hope of glory that emboldens believers to proclaim the Gospel. With the veil removed, all believers should reflect the glory of the Lord.

4:5–6 Paul never tries to make himself the object of attention but faithfully keeps his focus on Jesus Christ as Lord.

4:7 Paul describes the wonder of the Gospel—that human believers carry the glory of God within them—as having "treasure in earthen vessels." Clay jars are weak, fragile, and subject to being broken. But like the pitchers used by Gideon's army (see Judges 7:15–25), they may be broken for a purpose. When the jar is broken, the light within shines brightly and does not go unnoticed. Indeed, it may have a powerful effect. Numerous people throughout Christian history have been "broken," only to reveal the great power of the Spirit of God.

4:8–9 The believer is not as fragile as he or she may appear. Paul knew from personal experience that it was possible to be (1) hard-pressed without being crushed; (2) "perplexed, but not in despair"; (3) persecuted, but not abandoned; and (4) struck down, but not destroyed. A believer's afflictions do not result in complete failure or destruction.

4:16–18 Paul finds comfort in knowing that while his physical body is deteriorating, his inner spirit is being renewed daily. In fact, his body is being destroyed at a more rapid pace than most due to the abuses he receives as an apostle determined to spread the Gospel. Still, he can see the unseen glory ahead of him.

5:1 Like a tabernacle or tent, the earthly body is temporary and far from perfect. At death, believers leave behind their physical bodies and are provided vastly superior heavenly bodies. The frailty of the human frame is replaced by the permanence of an eternal dwelling place.

5:9–10 The physical body will perish, but the deeds a believer has done in it (whether good or bad) are the basis for future judgment. The resurrection of Jesus should remind people of their own future resurrection, as well as Jesus' promise to return to earth to subdue His enemies. He will then judge everyone according to their deeds, so believers should desire to please God as they live in their earthly bodies.

5:12–13 If Paul's readers thought he was out of his mind ("beside ourselves"), he wants them to know it is because he is determined to please God. If they believed him and considered him sane, he let them know it is for their sake that he speaks as he does. Paul and other true apostles are motivated by the love of Christ.

5:16–17 Just as believers come to see Jesus through a different lens—as Saviour and Lord rather than simply a notable rabbi who had lived and died—so Paul encourages them to see one another differently. According to Paul, believers are new creatures and should be acknowledged as such. Christians dare not view others merely by outward appearances.

5:18–20 Apart from Christ, all people are dead in their sin, enemies of God, and alienated from Him. They do not seek God, but He seeks them through His Son. As sinners acknowledge their sin and trust in Jesus for forgiveness and eternal life, they are reconciled to God. Those who know and trust God are given the privilege and responsibility of proclaiming the Gospel.

6:1–2 Paul knew the Corinthian church had been divided into competitive cliques. Some were looking to their leaders or their spiritual gifts as a basis for boasting. They needed to experience true salvation and then grow up in unity and maturity. Otherwise, they received the gift of God's grace in vain.

6:11–13 In both of his letters to the Corinthians, Paul hints at divisions within the body of believers. Here he gets right to the point. The Corinthians had a serious problem regarding their relationships. They had distanced themselves from Paul and other genuine apostles, while at the same time drawing close to those who sounded good but twisted the truth of the Gospel. Paul urges those in the church to open their hearts to him.

6:14–18 As Paul continues, his language becomes stronger. His instruction to not be yoked with unbelievers is not just a warning but also an intimation that such illicit intimacy with unbelievers already exists. Christians cannot be yoked together with unbelievers in God's work. Christians are to pursue righteousness; unbelievers are accustomed to lawlessness. Christians have been exposed to the light of God's truth; non-Christians remain in darkness. The distance between the two is so significant that they find no basis for a partnership in spiritual ministry.

7:2–4 Paul is surprisingly upbeat in this passage. What enabled him to write with such confidence after so many wrongs had been committed against God and against him? Instead of writing off the Corinthian church and moving to his next ministry opportunity, Paul states his desire to restore the relationship he once had with the Corinthians. More than that, Paul feels great pride because of his association with the believers in Corinth.

7:13–16 Another source of joy for Paul is seeing how excited Titus was after he had delivered Paul's difficult message. Paul had boasted about what kind of believers the Corinthians were. The fact that they responded so well had been a tremendous relief for Titus, and seeing Titus's enthusiasm is pure delight for Paul.

8:1 Starting here and continuing through chapters 8–9, Paul turns to the second major reason for writing this letter: He is gathering a collection for the poor and persecuted believers in Jerusalem and wants to encourage the Corinthians to give generously. By way of incentive, he points to the generosity of the churches in Macedonia. Paul had already told them about this collection in his previous letter (see 1 Corinthians 16:1–4). Perhaps the Corinthians had begun to lose heart at the prospect of contributing, due to the problems in their own church. But since Paul has just heard of their renewed excitement, he broaches the topic again.

8:3–7 The Macedonians *first* gave themselves to the Lord and then to the apostles. They realized the great significance of their salvation and gave back to God what they had. They gave generously, voluntarily, gratefully, and joyfully. They set a high standard for other churches to imitate. The Corinthian church had many strong points, and Paul challenges its members to add generosity to the list. Yet he makes it clear that he is not commanding them but rather encouraging them to give as proof of their love.

8:8–9 The ultimate example of selfless giving is the Lord Jesus Christ, demonstrated by His atoning work on the cross of Calvary. He was infinitely rich in the presence of His Father yet gave it all up during His incarnation (Philippians 2:5–8). Because of His sacrificial life and death, He made all who trust in Him exceedingly rich.

8:10–12 Paul is convinced that generous giving works to the donor's advantage. The Corinthians had been the first to begin to give, and if they were not yet ready with their contribution, it was time to finish the matter. Paul refuses to use guilt to prompt the Corinthians to give more than they are able, but he doesn't hesitate to urge them to finish what they had started.

8:13–15 Paul concludes his exhortation to give by setting forth two governing principles. The first is the principle of equality. The world operates according to a structure by which the rich get richer and the poor get poorer. But the biblical model is one in which political and economic power is used not to oppress the helpless but for the good of those who are powerless. Paul never suggests that people give up their rights to own private property or live on exactly the same standard as everyone else. But when one believer has plenty and sees another believer in need, he or she should seek to narrow the disparity rather than widen it. The second principle that Paul promotes is reciprocity. He suggests that although one group of believers may *now* have an abundance and the ability to help another group in need, there may come a day when the tables are turned and they find themselves in need. Generosity shown toward a brother in need may result in generosity from that same brother at a later time.

9:6–15 Paul concludes this section of his letter with a number of principles concerning generosity and giving. First, he quotes a proverb about sowing and reaping. Giving generously is the way to have an abundant return, and the key is an attitude of delight. Second, Paul states that when someone shows grace to others by giving, God replenishes the grace so that he or she has more to give. Third, when people sow generously, they reap more than monetary gain. Cheerful giving transcends financial matters and results in a harvest of righteousness. Finally, Paul suggests that no matter how generous one's giving, it pales when compared with the generosity of God, who gave His only Son. Even when writing about money, Paul's mind remains on the cross of Christ. The gift of salvation should never cease to produce awe and gratitude.

10:1–2 This passage begins with an accusation leveled against Paul in his absence: Some said he was only bold

and authoritative when writing letters and would be far less impressive in person (see also verse 10). Paul's response demonstrates considerable meekness.

10:3–6 Paul rebuts the use of worldly tactics in the church. The world relies on certain things for authority: education, status, personal connections, oratorical skill, and so forth. The church, however, uses different "weapons." The only authoritative source of doctrine is the Word of God, so Paul battles against all arguments and pretensions that oppose God's truth. Paul understands that scripture is the basis for Christian living. The final test of any proposed "truth" is whether or not it results in obeying Christ's commands. If the Corinthian believers learned to be more diligent and obedient, then Paul would be better able to confront the acts of disobedience being committed by the false apostles.

10:9–11 Paul's critics said his letters were just a forceful attempt to cover for his lack of personal charisma. But the false apostles were judging by their own standards rather than conforming to biblical ones. They sought to elevate themselves by misrepresenting their own accomplishments and minimizing the value of others. While honest, Paul is never self-promoting.

10:12–18 Paul's attention is always given to building up the church—not to his own reputation, image, or power.

11:5–6 The Corinthians had been naively tolerant of the false teachings of the self-proclaimed apostles. Since Paul now has their attention, he quickly sets himself apart from those he calls the "chiefest apostles." Was he inferior to the others, as some had charged? Not at all. While the false apostles were proud of their speaking ability, Paul doesn't purport to be a trained speaker. What set him apart from (and above) the others is the content of his message.

11:7–12 The false apostles had no problem finding people to support them financially, while Paul demands no payment from the Corinthians—a fact that led Paul's critics to charge that his ministry was worthless. But if this is true, Paul retorts, then he is robbing the Macedonian churches, because they willingly supported him. Paul's decision to serve without expecting payment verifies that the gift of the Gospel is free—and proves that the so-called "chiefest apostles" (see 11:5) were operating out of greed and self-interest.

11:13–15 Paul follows with some of his harshest words for the false apostles. Not only were they deceitful, but they were servants of Satan who masqueraded as enlightened leaders.

11:21–22 Paul's comparison here has to do with the Jewish credentials of the leaders in Corinth. They may have been Hebrews, Israelites, and descendants of Abraham, but Paul is also those things—plus more (see Philippians 3:4–6).

11:23–33 Paul's comparison is the crucial difference: the personal price paid to serve others. Here Paul far outperforms the false apostles with his lengthy, detailed list of sufferings. Several of the incidents included here are also mentioned in Acts. Others we know nothing about. For instance, Acts only tells of one shipwreck of Paul—not three—and it occurred *after* the writing of this letter. Clearly, scripture reveals only a small percentage of all that Paul experienced at the hands of others. As the Corinthian Christians read this list of Paul's sufferings, surely they realized that these were genuine credentials.

12:2–4 Although Paul begins to write in third person, he eventually makes it clear that he is referring to himself. He can't be sure whether he has undergone a bodily experience as well as a spiritual one, yet he is certain of what has taken place.

12:7 Paul's weakness is evident in what he refers to as a "thorn in the flesh." It was probably some sort of Satan-inspired, God-allowed physical malady. After being privileged to witness heavenly events, even Paul would be tempted to become arrogant, and this impediment was a continual reminder that it was God's grace that kept Paul active—not Paul's own strength or wisdom. Paul never reveals the problem with which he was forced to contend. It seems likely that it was more than a mere irritation, but rather a nagging, persistent, painful problem—perhaps something that affected his appearance and caused embarrassment. It's also likely that it affected his spirit, attitude, and outlook.

12:10 Rather than removing Paul's thorn, God gave Paul sufficient grace to sustain him throughout his lifelong affliction.

12:11–13 Like an attorney just before the jury deliberates, Paul provides his readers a closing argument before ending his letter. He shouldn't have had to defend himself so thoroughly, and he feels foolish for doing so. But his action was necessary because the Corinthians hadn't come to his defense as quickly as they should have.

12:14–18 Paul reminds the Corinthians yet again that he intends to visit them soon and assures them that he is not coming with an expectation of personal gain. In fact, he wants to ensure that neither he nor his associates place any financial demands on the believers in Corinth.

12:20–21 As their spiritual father, Paul plans to provide for them rather than vice versa. Yet he also suspects he might find a number of problems when he arrives. Up to this point, Paul has been defending his actions to the Corinthians, but now he explains that they will be held accountable for their actions.

13:1–4 According to the Mosaic Law, any legal accusation had to have more than one witness (see Deuteronomy 19:15). Paul was accusing the Corinthians of improper behavior, so it was significant that this would be his third visit. Each time, he came with an accompanying witness. He was prepared, if necessary, to be a strict disciplinarian when he arrived this time.

13:5–9 Although Paul tells the Corinthians to "examine" themselves, he doesn't provide a checklist of any kind for them to consider. They were to simply confirm their relationship with Jesus and their commitment to God's truth. Paul never suggests anything is necessary for one's salvation other than Christ.

13:10 Paul's frankness with the Corinthians has a specific purpose: He wants to give them the opportunity to repent and straighten out their spiritual lives before his arrival. If they do, he will have no reason to be harsh with them. If they don't, he will use his God-given authority to discipline them.

13:11–14 Paul ends this deeply personal letter with a positive appeal and a reminder of God's grace, love, and fellowship. His final benediction is an assurance of the work of God the Father, God the Son, and God the Holy Ghost.

GALATIANS

INTRODUCTION TO GALATIANS ■ The book of Galatians is a centerpiece of New Testament theology that had a great influence during the Protestant Reformation. (Martin Luther's *Commentary on Galatians* ranks with the most influential books to come out of the Reformation.) Galatians is the only one of Paul's letters addressed to a group of churches rather than to a single location. The epistle has been called a spiritual Magna Carta due to its masterful explanation and defense of justification by faith alone.

AUTHOR ■ The style of writing and the method of thinking are so true to those of Paul that few scholars throughout the centuries have questioned his authorship. The early church held a strong and unwavering belief that Paul was the writer.

OCCASION ■ The epistle to the Galatians was written to emphasize the complete sufficiency of justification by faith alone in one's relationship with God. The Galatian churches (where many new believers were Gentiles) were being strongly influenced to add traditional Jewish beliefs and practices to their newfound faith. While it was quite natural for Jewish believers to continue to worship as they always had in the past, to require the same for Gentiles was, to Paul, tantamount to promoting a different gospel (1:6).

1:1 Since Paul will be addressing weighty problems in the church, he begins by identifying himself as an apostle. He opens other letters with a similar reminder that he is one who has been sent (for other examples, see Romans 1:1; 1 Corinthians 1:1; Ephesians 1:1), but here he places special stress on his authority and the fact that he is speaking for God.

1:8–9 No human credentials were strong enough to discredit the truth of the Gospel—and for that matter, no divine credentials either. Anyone who attempts to teach things contrary to the Gospel of Jesus Christ is to be eternally accursed—*anathema*, in Greek. Paul felt so strongly about this offense that he states the curse twice.

1:10 Paul is writing with the authority of God, by revelation of Jesus Christ, yet he also draws from personal experience. His question suggests that he had been accused of tailoring his message to please his audience.

1:17 Paul's comment about the other apostles may sound a bit arrogant at first, but it is not intended to be. He will soon express respect for the other apostles' ministries as equal to his own (2:7–10). Yet since his apostolic calling and commission had been questioned, he makes it clear that he did not derive his authority from the other apostles, but from God. It was *not* true, as his critics were seemingly suggesting, that Paul had first been taught by the apostles but had then broken ranks with them on the issue of circumcision and had begun to follow his own path.

1:18 Paul's return to Jerusalem as a Christian is described in Acts 9:26–30. The believers in Jerusalem were understandably suspicious of their former enemy, but Barnabas helped them overcome their fears and introduced Paul to them. Paul took fifteen days to get to know Peter. The word that is translated *abode with him* can also mean "interviewed," which is almost certainly just as accurate in this context. It is easy to envision

Peter providing Paul with firsthand information about Jesus and to imagine Paul's active mind interrupting, questioning, seeking clarification, and so forth.

2:1 The book of Acts mentions two different visits that Paul and Barnabas made to Jerusalem (Acts 11:29–30; 15:2). Scholars are divided as to which of the trips is referred to here, yet evidence is strong for the earlier visit.

2:6–10 Paul acknowledges the roles of the Jerusalem apostles, yet he refuses to revere them as some were wont to do. He knew that any wisdom or power that *he* had came from God and knew it would be true of the other church leaders as well. He realized they all had their callings to attend to. His was among the Gentiles—the uncircumcised. Peter's was among the Jews. Many other apostles are not mentioned, although Thomas, for example, is believed to have gone to India to minister.

2:11–14 The fact that the apostles were human beings with their own frailties and weaknesses becomes apparent. Paul and Barnabas had been ministering primarily to Gentile believers in Antioch, a prominent city in Syria. Peter had visited and demonstrated hypocrisy. Paul confronts Peter publicly and challenges his attitudes and actions.

2:17–18 Paul is probably suggesting that if believers forsake all thought of justification by their own works of the law and turn instead to Christ's righteousness, they are likely to be considered sinners by others who have legalistic mind-sets.

2:19 What Paul means by being "dead to the law" is that he has died to sin. He has died to the law as a means of justification, of peace with God, and of acceptance by God. He has died to the self-righteousness that comes from knowing the letter of the law and not the Spirit of God. And he has determined to live his life for the Lord, not to fulfill the requirements of the Jewish laws and traditions.

2:21–22 Paul observes that since it required the death of Jesus Christ to purchase his peace with God, then clearly salvation has nothing to do with his own effort or acts of righteousness. It was the grace—the free gift—of God that achieved his justification. The law had nothing to do with providing righteousness.

3:3–5 Paul intentionally leaves no middle ground between justification by faith and justification by works (2:15–16). The inclusion of any works at all as a prerequisite for salvation becomes justification by works. Here Paul provides clearer insight into the Judaizers' error: Whatever they might have said about faith and the cross, they really believed that their own effort alone made possible the fulfillment, consummation, and completion of salvation.

3:6–9 Paul conveys that scripture says it was Abraham's *faith* that justified him and produced a life of obedience. It wasn't his obedience that gave him proper standing before God and made him righteous. And in that respect, Abraham stands as the quintessential believer—an example for both Old Testament and New Testament people of God.

3:13–14 All who were under the curse—even Gentiles—can now avoid the just punishment for sin and instead receive peace with God and a righteous status before Him. The Holy Spirit is God's pledge of everlasting life and the source of power by which believers can live new lives for God. This justification before God is the "blessing of Abraham" that Paul has been describing.

3:15–18 Paul uses an argument based on the nature of covenants. When two people sit down and write out a legal agreement, one of them does not have the right to change the terms of the contract at some future date. Even more binding are the covenants of God. After He made a covenant with Abraham, He wasn't going to renege. And God's promise wasn't just to Abraham but included his descendants as well. Abraham's faith had been credited to him as righteousness (3:6), and that arrangement was not going to be annulled or modified—not even by the Law of Moses that came afterward.

3:21–24 The fact that the law came later and had a less direct manner of revelation than God's promise to Abraham is one of Paul's arguments for why it did not supersede or set aside the promise of justification by faith. But Paul then adds that the function of the law was actually to serve the interests of God's promise to bring people to faith in God and in Christ, the Son of God.

3:28 Judaism in many ways was a religion of exclusion. Women, Gentiles, and slaves did not have the same rights or access to God as Jewish men. The temple in Jerusalem was a series of concentric courtyards. Gentiles could not go farther than the outer "court of Gentiles," and women could go no farther than the next "court of women." Jewish men were allowed the next step into the "court of Israel," but only priests could enter

the temple building itself. Paul's point here is that the Gospel breaks down all such boundaries, allowing equal access to God's presence and equal access to salvation for all people, regardless of their race, gender, or social status.

4:5–7 Paul acknowledges the contribution of the Trinity in the process of salvation. Not only did God send His Son, but He also sends the Spirit of His Son. Believers don't just receive peace with God—though that alone is a priceless gift—but they also become God's sons and daughters.

4:16–20 The Galatians had been influenced by the zealous efforts of the Judaizers, which dismayed Paul. He challenges them to be just as faithful to the Gospel when he is absent from them as when he is present. Paul's imagery in verse 19 is powerful. He would have at least had the attention of all the mothers in the church by comparing his ministry to childbirth. Giving birth is a joyful experience, because once the trauma is over and the pain has subsided, the parent has a child to be proud of. But in Paul's metaphor, he is being forced to start over and "birth" the same child. It's no wonder he is feeling perplexed.

5:2 Paul was circumcised, and when working among Jewish believers, he even had his coworker Timothy circumcised (Acts 16:1–3). But in Galatia, where his opponents are insisting that circumcision is a requirement for the salvation of Gentile believers, Paul insists even more strongly that it isn't. In fact, he says, getting circumcised would be like a personal offense to Jesus. Adding *any* human requirement to the work of salvation accomplished by Jesus is wrong.

5:4 Those who don't stand firm in the freedom and liberty that Christ provides (5:1) are in danger of falling away from grace. That doesn't mean God writes off such people but that they voluntarily give up their freedom by seeking justification by the law—exactly the reason it is such an offense to their Saviour.

5:13 In contrast to Paul's feelings toward the Judaizers, he tenderly implores the Galatians to remain free but not to misuse their "liberty" (freedom). It would be quite natural for some people, after hearing someone repeatedly emphasize that following the law is not what God expects, to go to the other extreme and ignore all spiritual rules (antinomianism). But Paul immediately clarifies himself and challenges the Galatians to celebrate their liberty by serving and loving one another.

5:14 In this context, Paul's reference to "all the law" means more than just a list of dos and don'ts. Rather, it is the entirety of the spirit, intention, and direction of all the commandments of God. As strongly as Paul had just stressed that the law is *not* the means of justification, it is interesting to note how much he continues to value it as the guideline for how we are to live.

5:19–21 Paul's list of sins addresses four distinct problem areas: The first three terms refer to sexual immorality, the next two to false gods, the next eight to various sins of personal conflict, and the final two to drunkenness. It also appears that this is not intended to be a complete list but rather a representation of common problem areas. This list is quite similar to those Paul provides in other epistles (see 1 Corinthians 5:9–11; 6:9–10; 2 Corinthians 12:20–21; 1 Timothy 1:9–10). The striking similarities have caused Bible scholars to wonder if these lists were circulating among Jewish and Christian ethical teachers and if Paul incorporated them into his letters.

5:22 In the starkest of contrasts, Paul shifts from the acts of human, sinful nature to a list of the fruit of the Spirit in a believer's life. Love is first on the list, which makes sense because Paul has already said that love is how genuine faith expresses itself (5:6). Some Bible expositors have written that love is actually the only item on the list, with the other named characteristics being how love is expressed in a believer's life. Experience would suggest that where there is true love for God and fellow human beings, joy and peace cannot be far behind.

6:2 When Paul says to "bear ye one another's burdens," the word he uses almost certainly means "support."

Paul intends for spiritually mature people to assist (not overlook) weaker, growing believers.

6:3–5 Although Paul had been making a strong argument in favor of justification by faith alone, he still acknowledges the importance of personal responsibility. Not only should each person carry his or her own load, but believers can take pride in themselves. Indeed, there is a future aspect to what Paul writes here; perhaps he is thinking in terms of believers being judged according to their works. When Judgment Day comes, the evaluation will be based not on how well one person did in comparison to another but how well each person did in light of God's calling and provision.

6:14 While the Judaizers took great pride in external religious symbolism, Paul's only "glory" is in the reality of Jesus' crucifixion and its results. Paul once had a list of honors and accomplishments (Philippians 3:4–6). Although religious in nature, they had drawn his heart away from God, so now he considers them crucified. They had lost their charm and allure to Paul, just as he had lost the respect of many who once admired him. For those who rejected Jesus, Paul was an object of either complete disinterest or active contempt.

EPHESIANS

INTRODUCTION TO EPHESIANS ■ The book of Ephesians is a powerful and uplifting contribution to the canon of scripture. Lacking any specific rebuttals of false doctrines, and addressed primarily to Gentile believers, it has long been beloved by seekers and new believers. Its doctrinal foundation has made it a favorite of Bible scholars as well.

AUTHOR ■ Paul is the named author of this book. The logic, the structure of the book, the emphasis on the grace of God, and the full acceptance of Gentile believers are distinct indications that Ephesians was indeed written by the apostle Paul.

OCCASION ■ Although some of Paul's epistles address specific problems within a particular church, Ephesians doesn't. Rather, it challenges the reader to set a higher standard for living—the imitation of God (5:1). Paul was writing to a prominently Gentile church and makes clear that its members have been fully reconciled to God and are entitled to every spiritual blessing that He offers (1:3; 3:16–19).

1:4–5 The salvation of humankind was no afterthought. God knew that human beings would be guilty and inveterate sinners, so He provided a way for sin to be removed, the record cleansed, and perfect righteousness reestablished. Still, that was not all. God loved human beings so much that He chose to include them in His family—not only as servants or friends but as His sons and daughters.

1:7–10 God is by no means a stingy Father. Believers are lavished with wisdom and understanding. They are made privy to the mystery of His will. While they may not know all the specifics, they can have absolute confidence that all things are proceeding according to God's plan and will ultimately conclude with a universal demonstration of the glory and divine dominion of Jesus.

1:11–12 The same plan that enables any person's forgiveness and adoption embraces the farthest reaches of the cosmos and everything that happens in it. The salvation of each and every believer is subsumed into God's larger, greater plan for the world and for humankind. The God who planned, accomplished, and applied Christ's salvation to each believer is the same God who now controls the march of history as, day by day and event by event, history moves toward the consummation of all things.

1:13–14 The believers in Ephesus were recipients of everything God had promised and were well aware of their inheritance. Yet they could not yet see or experience those things fully. Paul instructs them to wait and look to the future in confident hope. To prevent them from becoming discouraged in the meantime, the Holy Spirit is present among them to assure them that God will someday deliver everything He has promised.

1:15–16 Here, as in a number of other places in the New Testament, the point is made that true faith in Christ is evidenced by showing love for fellow Christians.

1:20–23 Believers have access to the same power of God that Jesus had. At one point, Jesus appeared to be at the mercy of Pontius Pilate; now He is King of kings and Lord of lords. Here Paul hints at spiritual forces of darkness as he writes of power, might, and dominion. He will later be more specific (3:10; 6:12–13). Yet whether human or spiritual, current or future, no ruler can ever compare to the power and authority of Jesus Christ.

2:1–3 The original sin that permeates human existence is no small problem. It is human nature to sin—to rebel against God rather than trust Him or please Him. Sin comes from deep within and leaves no part of the person untainted, including his or her desires and thoughts. Sin is not just a matter of misdeed but also of an unrighteous state of mind and unrighteous attitudes and motives. People are born in this sinful condition—even if they desire to escape, they are unable to do so in their own power.

2:8 Salvation is only by God's grace, which Paul emphasizes with repetition. Believers owe God the entirety of their salvation— both its provision by God and Christ and its appropriation by the individual.

2:10 Paul has written of predestination and God's sovereignty (1:4–6); here he confirms that God prepared in advance for His workmanship—those He created and who responded in faith to His Son—to do good works. Yet Paul points out that good works are a *result* of salvation, not the *reason* for it.

2:14–22 The unity created by Jesus established a oneness among believers that transcended Israel and Judaism. Gentiles are no longer outcasts, but neither are they Jewish proselytes. Rather, they are fellow citizens with the Jews and equal members of God's household. All believers are part of the same structure, where Jesus is the cornerstone that both supports and unites all the other components. And that structure, or building, as it turns out, is a temple where God resides.

3:2–5 Paul frequently emphasizes that he receives his insight into the Gospel by direct revelation from Jesus. He is not being boastful but rather defensive. He knew he had critics who disputed his authority as an apostle. They falsely claimed that he had been taught by the other apostles yet had strayed from their teaching by opening the Gospel to the Gentiles. So Paul inserts regular reminders that he writes and speaks with the authority of Christ.

3:6–9 Although the ultimate mystery is salvation in Christ, one surprising aspect of the mystery is that salvation is lavished on the Gentiles as well as the Jews, resulting in a single unified spiritual body.

3:10 The church does not exist for itself but for the glory of God. It serves that purpose by demonstrating the wisdom, grace, goodness, justice, and holiness of God as sinners are transformed by the Gospel of Christ and become unified in love. Such a magnificent transformation is bound to be noticed—not only by people who see the changes that the love of Christ can make in a believer's life, but also by rulers and authorities in the heavenly realms.

3:12 Perhaps one of the church's most overlooked privileges is the right to approach God freely and confidently. For centuries God's people had to offer blood sacrifices and go through priests for access to God. And closeness to God evoked great fear. Modern believers tend to take for granted the perpetual nearness of God they have through prayer and the Holy Spirit.

3:14–17 Paul continues to acknowledge all three persons of the Trinity. He prays to the Father, asking for power from the Holy Spirit and the presence of Christ in the hearts of the Ephesians. Father, Son, and Spirit are intertwined, each relating to the believer in a harmony of grace and love.

3:20–21 Paul wraps up this first half of his letter with a short doxology. As he reflects on the things he has written about—all that God has poured out on His people—Paul cannot help but stop and give God the glory for it. No matter how much believers can comprehend and imagine what God has done for them, He has actually done even more.

4:1–2 The biblical concept of humility, or meekness, has nothing to do with weakness. It can take great inner strength and the help of God's Spirit to set aside one's rights in favor of a weaker party or the common good. Yet this is the model set by Jesus (2 Corinthians 10:1; Philippians 2:5–8) and one that believers should determine to imitate.

4:3 Even godly believers will struggle from time to time, which is why Paul challenges them to make an effort. Even though the Holy Spirit makes unity possible among people, it requires determination on their part as well.

4:7–10 Christian unity is not a matter of imposing a dreadful sameness upon all believers or reducing individuals to the status of a single cog on a large wheel. As each person applies his or her individual gifts, the resulting variety produces complex and magnificent harmony.

4:11–16 It is through the grace of the triumphant Christ that each person receives spiritual gifts (4:7–10), and Paul mentions a few of them. Yet it should be noted that the gifts Paul names are those directly having to do with the life of the church as a body. They are the gifts that Christians benefit from when they meet *together*.

4:17–19 One thing Paul insists that the Ephesian Christians do is reject their old ways of life, even though many of their peers are still involved in such things. Paul suggests that the darkness of unbelievers is not necessarily due to a lack of knowledge about God or the inability to understand. Rather, it is a hardness of heart and unwillingness to repent that prevents their salvation.

4:20–24 Paul explains that even after placing one's faith in Jesus, a struggle continues between the old self and the new. Although believers die to sin, change their priorities, and begin to live for Jesus, the complete transformation doesn't take place at once. Paul refers to the old self as dead and destroyed (Romans 6:2), because Christ effectively removed people from the sentence of sin and death. Yet the influence of sin continues, and believers must *choose* to ignore the evil desires that remain within them (Romans 6:11–14). Those choices must be made every single day, no matter how long a person lives as a Christian.

4:25–32 To ensure everyone understands what he is saying, Paul gets more specific about exactly what should be discarded as believers begin to live as new creations. First on his list is falsehood. Truth is of utmost importance in Christian doctrine and practice. Lies distort the Gospel and poison personal relationships. Yet the deeper such habits have been embedded, the more difficult they are to eradicate.

5:1 Paul continues what he started in chapter 4 as he spells out practical ways to live a more righteous life. He has already said to put on the new self that was created to be like God (4:24). Here he states the same concept in a different way by saying to imitate God, to be followers of Him.

5:2–12 Paul's intent in verse 3 is most likely that certain things shouldn't even be *mentioned* in Christian company. Rather than being regularly exposed to and beginning to tolerate common sins, Paul recommends that believers keep themselves removed as much as possible, remaining tender and sensitive.

5:21–24 Paul begins by telling believers to submit to one another out of their reverence for Christ. He sets out a particular order of submission in relationships: Wives are to submit to their husbands, children to their parents (6:1), and servants to their masters (6:5). The concept of submission is used in regard to Jesus submitting to His parents, demons submitting to the power of the disciples, citizens submitting to governing authorities, Christians submitting to God, and so forth.

5:25–31 It should be noted that as soon as Paul instructs wives to submit to their husbands, he explains what is expected of the husband in the relationship. Husbands are expected to show the same love for their wives that Christ has for the church. They are to love their wives as their own bodies. If marriage were merely a matter of hierarchy, no one would want to leave the comfort of his or her own home to become one flesh with a spouse.

5:32–33 No one can fully comprehend the mysterious metaphor of Christ as a husband and the church as His bride. Yet we need not have a full understanding to know what Paul means here. Again Paul sets an immensely high standard for Christians—in this case, Christian husbands—to live up to.

6:1–2 Honoring parents involves more than mere obedience. It is possible to obey grudgingly, moodily, or only because one has to. Such responses do not honor parents. The one commandment with a promise is the fifth of the Ten Commandments (Exodus 20:12; Deuteronomy 5:16). This is only one of many places in the New Testament where a law is cited from the Old Testament as something believers must obey. Some people promote the idea that the commandments of God have been supplanted by a vague and general law of love. Such an idea never occurred to Paul.

6:5–8 Paul makes a strong argument, pointing out that believers all have the same Master to whom they will someday give an account. By faithfully serving their earthly masters, servants also please their Lord in heaven.

6:9 Both servants and masters are instructed to keep their focus on Jesus. Servants are not to obey simply because doing so might ingratiate themselves with their masters. And masters are not to mistreat their servants, because in one sense, they are actually fellow servants. Paul's exhortations are very general; he doesn't provide a long list of dos and don'ts. As in many other places in scripture, it is assumed that if the conscience is awakened and love is ruling in the heart, people will know what to do and how to behave.

6:11–12 Paul acknowledges adversarial spiritual forces that are under the control of a dark and scheming spiritual leader. Paul has already referred to the devil a couple of times in this epistle (2:2; 4:27), and here he gets more specific.

6:13–18 As the sword is a weapon, so is prayer. In fact, prayer is given the most prominent place and the most space in Paul's description of a fully armed Christian soldier. The importance of prayer is seen in verse 18, with the repeated emphasis on *all*: *all* prayer and supplication with *all* perseverance for *all* the saints.

6:18 To pray "in the Spirit" means to pray with the guidance and assistance of the Holy Spirit. While continuing to stand firm, a believer is also to pray and to keep alert.

6:19 The "mystery" Paul refers to means, as before, the Gospel itself (1:9; 3:3–4, 9; 5:32). It is something that would not be known unless God had revealed it. Now it is able to be embraced by Jews and Gentiles alike.

6:20 The reference to an ambassador bound in bonds would have been interpreted as an oxymoron. An ambassador was entitled to diplomatic immunity. The arrest of an ambassador would have been a grave insult to the king who had sent him and also would have reflected poorly on the leader of the country who had imprisoned him.

6:21–22 Much of Paul's closing is verbatim to what he writes in his closing statement to the Colossian church (Colossians 4:7–8). The two letters were probably written at about the same time and were possibly both carried by Tychicus to different groups of Christians living in the Roman province of Asia.

6:23–24 Paul opened his letter with the words *grace* and *peace* (1:2); here he closes with the same sentiment. If this closing sounds a little less personal than those of some of his other letters, perhaps it is because Paul intended for this one to circulate among several different churches in the same area—to people whom he hadn't even met. Still, his wish for all who read it is an undying love for the Lord Jesus Christ. It is more than a sign-off. Indeed, it would be difficult to think of a more relevant blessing—and challenge—for all who profess faith in God.

PHILIPPIANS

INTRODUCTION TO PHILIPPIANS ■ Paul's letter to the church in Philippi is remembered for its joyful tone of gratitude against the stark background of the fact that Paul was in prison while writing. Paul writes about the peace, joy, and contentment he finds in Christ, regardless of his situation or circumstances.

AUTHOR ■ According to Philippians 1:1, the apostle Paul is the writer of this letter. The theology and personal comments fit with what we know of Paul from other writings in the New Testament. Early church fathers and historians also affirmed Paul's authorship.

OCCASION ■ When Epaphroditus visited Paul, he brought news of troubles in the Philippian church: The Judaizing threat had appeared (Jewish Christians claiming Gentiles must first become Jews in order to be saved), financial troubles and other problems were creating doubts about the Philippians' newfound faith, and discord had surfaced in the church. Knowing they were in need of help, they asked Paul to send them Timothy, but he could not come immediately. However, Paul sent back with Epaphroditus this letter full of thanksgiving and encouragement, instruction and correction, and doctrine and exhortation.

1:1 Paul's use of the word *saints* refers to all the Christians in the Philippian community of faith rather than to a super-spiritual subset, as the term sometimes implies today. Paul also mentions the church officers here, a distinction from his other letters. These people were perhaps instrumental in raising the generous offering that was sent to Paul. They will also likely be the ones who ensure that the Philippians follow Paul's instructions in the letter. The fact that this church had these types of leaders, particularly deacons, indicates that it was well established.

1:3–4 Paul's mention of joy is significant. His was not an easy situation, yet he found joy in the midst of it. Joy is a key theme in this letter (1:19, 25–26).

1:7–8 The Philippians had shared God's grace with Paul by supporting him as an evangelist and defender of the faith. In both verses 5 and 7, Paul uses a Greek word meaning "to share" or "to partner with." Sharing in God's grace means they share a common experience of Christ's love. Through their experiences, they formed an unbreakable bond. His affection for them is visible evidence of this bond.

1:13–14 The praetorians, or palace guards, were an elite force serving as the emperor's bodyguards. As Paul meets one after another of these soldiers, the knowledge of the Gospel begins to spread among them. A number of them become Christians, and as a result, they begin to spread the Gospel themselves.

1:18–19 Paul rejoices because the Gospel is advancing and for an additional reason—the hope of his own deliverance. When Paul writes about his salvation, some take him to mean his release from prison. However, the language he uses is most likely a reference to eternal salvation. In other words, trials and difficulties are part of the means the Lord employs to carry us safely to the end of our pilgrimage. Most scholars believe Paul is quoting from Job 13:16.

1:28–30 The Philippians were facing opposition. There does not seem to have been a large community of Jews in Philippi—there was no synagogue—so local opposition would likely have come from Gentiles. Here Paul makes a statement mirroring a theme that runs throughout his writings—those who wish to live godly lives will suffer persecution.

2:4–5 The true obstacle to unity of heart and mind is not based on differences of opinion but is due to selfishness and vanity. Shifting attention away from oneself to others—which, of course, is what Jesus Christ did—is the key to Christian unity. The fact that Paul has to tell the Philippians this, and later appeal to some members of the church to get along with one another, is proof that Christian unity does not come without effort and attention. Loving unity is as difficult to fulfill as any other part of sanctification.

2:7 The Greek words translated as Jesus making himself "of no reputation" have led some to believe that Jesus stopped being divine. However, that is not a principle taught elsewhere in the New Testament, and it cannot be the meaning here. Jesus' deity is affirmed both before and after His incarnation—His taking on of human flesh (John 1:1–2, 14, 18). It is Jesus' humility and obedience in the face of His true identity that brings such meaning to His actions.

2:9 The focus switches to God's role. Jesus humbled Himself, but God exalted Him. Jesus' teachings include references to this principle—that when we humble ourselves, God will lift us up (Mark 9:35).

2:10 Paul's mention of every knee bowing to God may be a reference to Isaiah 45:23. Paul cites the same text in Romans 14:11, in reference to the Day of Judgment. Both the doomed and the saved will make this confession.

2:12 The phrase "work out your own salvation" is another way of saying "obey." To work out one's salvation is to apply oneself to living in a manner worthy of the

Gospel of Christ. It is a theme of this whole section. The idea of obedience also connects this statement to the previous verses, which emphasize Christ's obedience, even to the point of death.

2:15 How can Christians be described as blameless while remaining sinful and still in need of daily confession? Throughout the Bible, terms like *blameless* are applied to people who, while not sinless and perfect, are faithful. A Christian falls short of perfection, to be sure, but he or she is not content with anything but perfect purity and a faultless life.

2:22 Paul compares Timothy to a son, but that does not mean that he is Paul's biological son. It was common in those days for the relationship between a rabbi and a disciple to be described as that of a father and a son.

2:25–28 Paul seems to expect a favorable outcome to his legal troubles but decides it necessary to send Epaphroditus (who earlier served as the Philippians' emissary to Rome, to inquire after Paul's welfare and to bring him their gift of financial support). Though the journey between Philippi and Rome took roughly forty days, news had reached the Philippians of Epaphroditus's illness. In sending Epaphroditus home, Paul not only ensures the delivery of this letter but also tends to the natural desire of Epaphroditus to be with his family and friends.

3:3 This verse sums up much of Paul's teaching that believers in Jesus, whether Jew or Gentile, are the true inheritors of the covenant God made with Abraham and Israel. When one becomes a Christian, he or she does not abandon the God of Israel—on the contrary, Abraham's God becomes one's own.

3:4–6 The Judaizers who were troubling the church in Philippi probably expected their Jewish credentials to add authority to their messages. But Paul points out that he has all those credentials and more. He was born from a pure family line of Israelites, he was a strict Pharisee, and he was zealous for the Jewish and Pharisaic viewpoint to the point of being a persecutor of the church in his earlier days.

3:7–11 There is much to gain when one gains Christ. Paul writes that a person gains justification (righteousness before God), sanctification (the transformation of life), and glorification (resurrection from the dead).

3:10 True righteousness can be obtained only by abandoning one's own effort and turning in faith to Jesus. Because of humanity's sinfulness, true righteousness can only be a gift; it will never be an achievement. One receives not only righteousness by faith in Christ but the transformation of life. He or she becomes more Christlike—more and more each day, rejecting sinful desires. To be sure, there will be suffering, as with Christ, and for the same reason—because it is by this means that life is renewed and God's will is made perfect.

3:17–19 It is a common theme in the Bible, and certainly in Paul's letters, that believers should imitate those who live godly lives and beware of those who do not. Paul wants his readers to be as conscious of their own failings as he is of his, and as dependent upon God's grace to keep going on as he knows he must be.

4:2–3 The fact that Paul mentions Euodias and Syntyche by name is an indication of how serious Paul perceives the situation to be in Philippi. The disunity in the church, to which these women obviously were contributing, was a problem that needed to be dealt with directly. Paul does not leave the women to overcome their dispute by themselves. He enlists others in the church to help them. Paul obviously believes the unity of the church is more important than whatever had separated these women from each other.

4:8 It is safe to assume that this list is not definitive but is representative of the kinds of things a believer should focus his or her mind on. The connotation of the verb used to conclude ("think") is that our minds should *continually* be thinking about these kinds of things.

4:14–16 To make sure that the Philippians understand the measure of his appreciation for their generosity, Paul tells them that he has not forgotten the unique place they have had in his heart from the beginning, some ten years before, when they generously supported his ministry when no one else did. The significance of the mention of Thessalonica is that it is the next major town on the Roman road from Philippi to Athens. So Paul had scarcely left Philippi before their gifts reached him.

4:17–19 Paul's greatest interest is not in what he can receive from the Philippians' generosity but in what they will receive from giving. The term he uses to describe the return on their investment in him can mean the profit gained in business, and here it means something like the interest that would accrue on someone's investment account. While the Philippian church was not a wealthy church, the gifts the believers sent Paul were a great blessing to him and fully met his needs. More important, they were pleasing to God, and they reflected the Philippians' faith in the truth that God would take care of them.

4:20 This verse functions as a kind of doxology before Paul sends his final greetings.

4:21–22 Assuming Paul was in Rome, his reference to "every saint in Christ Jesus" refers to all the believers there in the Roman Christian church (Romans 16:1–15).

4:23 Paul gave his life to proclaim the good news of Jesus; he traveled the world with that message. He was Christ's ambassador, preaching to everyone who would listen that God was, in Christ, reconciling the world to Himself. He began this letter with this grace, and he ends with it as well (compare with 1:2).

THE EPISTLE OF PAUL THE APOSTLE TO THE

COLOSSIANS

INTRODUCTION TO COLOSSIANS ■ The New Testament letter to the Colossians presents the person and work of Jesus Christ as the Saviour, the Creator, and the Sustainer of the universe and the total solution for humanity's needs, both for time and eternity.

AUTHOR ■ We can confidently assert that Paul was the author as the letter identifies (1:1; 4:18).

OCCASION ■ Paul's purpose in writing Colossians was threefold: (1) to express his personal interest in the Colossians (1:3–4; 2:1–3); (2) to warn them against reverting to their old pagan vices (3:5 and following); and (3) to counteract a particular theological heresy that was being promoted within the church at Colossae (2:4–23). The Colossian heresy wore the mask of Christianity, but it was false.

1:1–8 Paul introduces himself as an apostle by God's will. By doing this, he establishes his authority and the Colossians' responsibility to listen. This description further stresses that Paul's position as an apostle is not something he had sought or earned. It was a calling (see also 1 Corinthians 1:1; Galatians 1:1; 2 Timothy 1:1). Paul and Timotheus (Timothy) had evidently never been to Colossae and did not know the church personally (2:1–2); they had heard of the faith that existed among the Colossians and of their love for all the saints.

1:9–10 Paul prays for two things for the Colossians: (1) that his readers would have a full knowledge of God's will and (2) that, as a result, they might live in a manner worthy of the Lord. Both are necessary. Verse 9 without verse 10 is incomplete and falls short of the will of God, but verse 10 without verse 9 is impossible.

1:9–14 Paul moves from thanksgiving to petition. Paul's prayers are not only brief and explicit but spiritually strategic in nature. To counter the false knowledge of the heretics, Paul prays for a full and more penetrating knowledge of God's will.

1:15 Jesus is the manifestation of God. To know what God is like, one must look at Jesus (John 1:14–18; 12:45; 14:7–11; Hebrews 1:3). He is the firstborn of every creature. This is not saying that Jesus was the first to be created by God; *firstborn* refers instead to Jesus' preeminent position over all creation.

1:16 Jesus is the Creator and Sustainer of the universe. Paul is describing the all-encompassing scope of Christ's authority—thrones, dominions, principalities, and powers—which includes the invisible world of angels and demons. (With the Colossian heresy in mind, Paul stresses the hierarchy of angelic powers.)

1:17 Jesus is before all things. Note that Paul says Jesus *is* before all things rather than *was*. This is Paul's way of saying what Jesus said Himself in John 8:58. It also hearkens back to God's claim to Moses to be the "I AM" (Exodus 3:13–14).

1:18 Paul affirms Christ's superiority and supremacy over a new creation, the church. The Colossians must recognize that the Creator of the cosmos is also the supreme head of the church as their Saviour. He is the source, power, and originating cause of the life of the church.

1:19–22 God is pleased that His "fulness" dwells in Christ. *Fulness* means "the sum total." *Dwell* means "to reside, to settle down." Most expositors understand this as a powerful affirmation of Christ's deity (which it is), but the context of this verse is about the work of reconciliation. It might be better to understand *fulness* in reference to God's plan of reconciliation. Paul is declaring that the fullness (fulness) of God's saving provision resides totally in the work of Christ through His blood on the cross. Nothing else can be added to the work of the Son.

2:1–3 Paul's message is for everyone. The treasures of wisdom and knowledge are hidden in Christ, but not in the sense that they are concealed. Instead, they are stored up in one place only, and that is in Christ alone.

2:9 Paul says that the full nature of God dwells within Jesus. This means Jesus is completely full of the divine nature; there is not one aspect of His nature that is lacking any divinity. When Christ came to earth, God came to earth.

2:10 As a result of Christ's character, believers are complete in Him because they become partakers of Him. Salvation is not just a philosophy; it is not just an event. It is the partaking of the very nature of Christ. We do not become God, but His righteousness lives within us.

2:11–15 Paul uses three descriptions of what happened at the Colossians' salvation: (1) *Circumcision*. Paul tells his readers that they have been spiritually circumcised already in Christ, and there is no need to be circumcised physically. (2) *Burial*. This is the identification with the death of Christ. It signifies the completion of the death process. The death of Christ was the moment that our punishment was lifted, and sin was dealt a deathblow. (3) *Resurrection*. The resurrection of Jesus signifies the new life of a believer. Because God raised Jesus from the dead, every believer has been given new life. Salvation is complete.

2:16–17 The Colossians were facing legalism. Believers are not to follow certain rules in order to maintain their faith; they choose their practices and lifestyles *because* of their faith. Therefore, they are able to live out the intent of the law rather than just the rules of it. This law represents the "shadow of things to come," that is, Jesus.

3:5–10 The Colossians must, as a result of being alive in Christ, be in the daily process of putting sin to death in their own lives. While through the work of Jesus believers stand righteous before God, they are still responsible to grow into that position of righteousness. They must put aside personal and public sins.

3:11 Paul makes a transition from one's union with Christ to union with one another. Race, religion, and class are no longer barriers to the body; now everyone is one in Christ.

3:13 We are to pattern our grace on the forgiveness we have received from God—God forgave us before we ever could have asked for it. He gave grace, not on the basis of our merit or even our request, but on the basis of His love while we were still in rebellion toward Him. Christ is the standard for forgiveness.

3:14 Of all the things the believer is to put on, the governing agent is charity (love). The charity that Paul is talking about is God's selfless love that seeks to do the best for people who deserve only death. It is this kind of love that unites Christians.

3:15 When Paul refers to the peace of Christ, he is not talking about an internal feeling of serenity as much as a result of doing the right thing. When humanity rebelled, God sought to make peace by sacrificing His own Son. That same trait must rule us.

3:18 The wife is to submit to her husband. It is a voluntary action by the wife, not a forced action by the husband. It is not a position of inferiority but rather a different role on the same team. The essence of this verse means that a wife finds her identity not apart from her husband but in conjunction with her husband.

3:19. The word *love* here is the self-sacrificing love that causes one to place the needs of others above his or her own. A husband is to give love and self-sacrificially meet his wife's needs. It is not the role of the husband to dominate his wife and treat her like a slave. He should treat her as more important than himself.

3:22–4:1 Paul's instruction moves from family relationships to the relationship between servant and master. This is a relationship of obedience and authority. Typically, this command is linked to employees and employers, but there are other relationships in life that apply. One would be the teacher-student relationship. Another might be the civil law and the citizen. There is a principle in this text that could govern anywhere a person is subject to authority.

4:2 The Colossians must understand that they are fully dependent on Christ for everything. This dependence is seen through a life of continual prayer. Paul's instruction is to "continue in" (or be dedicated to) prayer—continually faithful, not lacking in endurance. Paul charges the believers to pray with alertness. This is a picture of vigilance and undistracted focus.

4:17 Paul's words to Archippus are an encouragement to faithfully do what he has been called to do without shrinking back.

THESSALONIANS

INTRODUCTION TO 1 THESSALONIANS ■ First Thessalonians is a short letter written to a predominantly Gentile church of new converts. It provides all the basic requirements for holy living (a regular "walk" with God) as well as great insight into the importance and specifics of the anticipated return of Jesus. As such, it is a worthwhile study for believers of all ages.

AUTHOR ■ Early church authorities agreed that Paul is the author of this epistle, and little serious opposition has been raised since. With the possible exception of Galatians (for which the date is debated), this is most likely Paul's first letter among those that are included in scripture.

OCCASION ■ The church at Thessalonica was facing persecution, yet it was continuing to grow and had developed a dynamic testimony of faith. Paul's letter was an effort to comfort and motivate the believers there with the truth of the Lord's sure return.

1:1 The greeting first identifies the writer, Paul. It also identifies his companions, Silvanus (Silas) and Timothy. *Silas* was probably an Aramaic name, and *Silvanus* a Roman one. Silvanus had accompanied Paul on his second missionary journey (Acts 15:40). Timotheus (Timothy) was a younger man, the son of a Jewish Christian mother and a Gentile father (Acts 16:1; 2 Timothy 1:5). Paul may have led Timotheus to Christ, and he was a mentor to the younger man (1 Timothy 1:2).

1:7–9 Macedonia and Achaia were Roman provinces that comprised what is now Greece. Because of the faithful witness of the Thessalonians, the Gospel was heard through the entire land like the peal of a trumpet. The change in the lives of the Thessalonians was clearly evident. Many had been idolaters, and some probably continued to battle the pull of their past. Yet they had welcomed God's message by faith and were putting their trust in Jesus.

1:9–10 The Gospel had revealed the foolishness of the Thessalonians' faith in empty idols and pointed them to the truth of the living God. They did not put off their old life *in order* to be saved; it was their understanding of and belief in the message of the Gospel that led to salvation.

2:1–6 A believer's personal life speaks powerfully to the nature of his or her ministry in regard to the motives, methods, and means used to accomplish the work of God. Paul had spent time with the Thessalonians. They knew not only what he said but also who he was. Consequently, Paul refers to their knowledge of his life numerous times in this letter (see 1:5; 2:11; 4:2).

2:6 As an apostle of God, Paul spoke with authority. Others might have misused the position, yet Paul was always a good steward of the weighty authority he had. He never attempted to wield it to make himself look better, to manipulate his message, or to intimidate his listeners. Some of his critics had used those tactics, but Paul knew *he* hadn't. Even more important, the Thessalonians could attest to his conscientious use of authority (2:3).

2:7–12 In this section, Paul compares his ministry to both a loving mother (with an emphasis on gentleness and willingness) and a concerned father (focused on instruction backed up by godly example). The mother he describes as a nursing mother, and the care she shows is the same word used of birds covering their eggs with their feathers. There is not only devotion involved in Paul's meaning but a loving tenderness as well.

2:8 The word Paul uses for this degree of love and affection is very strong and rarely used, though it is found in the parental inscriptions on some ancient graves of small children. Paul was serious about his feelings for the Thessalonians, and those feelings led to his willingness to work hard and share his very life with the recently converted Christians.

2:15–16 Paul's statement here can sound like religious bigotry until one remembers that Paul was among the very group he is describing. Though he doesn't go into detail here as he does in other places, his conversion had been so sudden and life-changing that the Christian persecutors he had once partnered with were the same ones who immediately tried to hinder his newfound zeal for Christ.

3:6 All of the concern and anxiety Paul felt toward the condition of the church in Thessalonica was alleviated by the return of Timotheus (Timothy) with an encouraging report. The word Paul uses here for Timothy's good news is the same that he usually uses in reference to the Gospel. It reflects here what a rejuvenating effect Timothy's report had on Paul.

3:9 Paul had been instrumental in getting the Thessalonian church started, yet he takes no credit for it. In fact, he thanks God for the believers' influence on *him*—not the other way around! Paul was a thankful servant, one who always lived with the perspective of God's hand on his life. His heart was filled with gratitude for the work of God in the lives of others.

3:11 Paul prays that God would remove obstacles that might prevent his return to Thessalonica. He is referring to the spiritual opposition he had experienced (2:18), so his prayer is for both God the Father and the Lord Jesus to clear the way. There are circumstances where no amount of human desire or effort will accomplish the desired results, and Paul is quick to turn to God's fatherly care to achieve what is best for him.

4:1–2 Paul is exhorting the Thessalonians to rise to a level of holiness in their daily living. Even though they were doing well, Paul encourages them to improve their consistency even more. By using the word *walk* (or *live*), Paul puts an emphasis on *actions*, but then he immediately adds that it is to please God, which demonstrates the importance of *motives*.

4:5 It isn't just active sexual immorality that is to be avoided, but all passionate lust as well. Even then, mere avoidance is not enough. Christians are instructed to maintain control over their bodies in a way that is both holy and honorable. Clearly, one way to avoid sexual impurity is through marriage and a proper understanding of sex as God designed it. Scripture sets marriage apart from the motives, ideas, and values of a world that does not know God.

4:6–7 Paul's reference to one's brother is unusual. Essentially every other time he uses the word, he intends it as a synonym for *believer*. In this context, however, he seems to refer to a fellow human being—either male or female. His message is that inappropriate sexual behavior has victims. Adultery on the part of one spouse betrays the other. Premarital sex robs both parties of the gift of virginity at marriage. And verification of its destructive nature is the fact that God will exact punishment on all such sins.

4:17 Believers who are alive will be "caught up" in the air (the words actually mean "seized" or "snatched")

together with the resurrected dead. Clouds make an appropriate meeting place for God's people during this event because clouds are frequently associated with the presence and glory of God.

5:6–8 Believers should remain spiritually awake. Paul compares essential Christian qualities to a soldier's armour, as he does in his letters to Rome (Romans 13:12) and Ephesus (Ephesians 6:10–18). The call to sobriety and watchfulness is also part of a soldier's discipline. And in this context, Paul groups faith, hope, and love, as he is prone to do.

5:9–11 In a final dramatic contrast, Paul compares salvation to God's wrath. The fact that God has appointed believers to receive salvation is the basis for there not being a need to fear the day of the Lord and the reason they should be alert and sober. On the day of the Lord, unbelievers will experience the wrath of God as never before, and believers will experience their salvation in a way not yet realized.

5:16–18 Maintaining a joyful spirit, having a prayerful mind, and exhibiting a thankful attitude are not random goals; they are God's will for believers. Such things depend on one's focus and faith in God—His person, plan, principles, promises, and purposes set forth in scripture.

5:19–22 Paul concludes his list with instructions that relate to worship. The Holy Spirit is frequently likened to fire in scripture (see Matthew 3:11; Acts 2:3–4). The warning about quenching the fire of the Spirit is clearly a prohibition against hindering the work, ministry, and gifts of the Holy Spirit. And Christians should not disparage any authoritative revelation—neither those that were delivered through the gift of prophecy in the first-century church nor those that have been preserved by the Holy Spirit in scripture.

THESSALONIANS

INTRODUCTION TO 2 THESSALONIANS ■ The second letter to the Thessalonian church is a timely follow-up to 1 Thessalonians and, as such, deals with the same concerns for the believers in Thessalonica. (See the introduction to 1 Thessalonians.) Yet some in the church were not responding to the first epistle, so 2 Thessalonians has a more urgent tone.

AUTHOR ■ Most scholars support the authorship of Paul as stated in 1:1.

OCCASION ■ The persecution of the Thessalonian church seems to have intensified since the previous letter (1:4–5). So Paul writes this follow-up epistle from Corinth after Silas and Timotheus (Timothy) inform him of the recent developments in Thessalonica.

1:6 Because God is absolutely righteous (just), He will do what is right. He will recompense tribulation to those who have persecuted believers, as well as reward those who remain faithful to Him. He may not take action during a believer's lifetime, but each devoted follower can be assured that God will certainly not ignore or tolerate sin and rebellion.

1:8 Paul continues to explain the vengeance (judgment) of God. The Greek word used to describe judgment of those who cause trouble suggests a full and complete punishment—a vindication of God. The essence of heaven is being in the presence of God. So although it is difficult for sinful humans to understand, the ultimate punishment is eternal removal from the presence of God.

1:9–10 These verses are perhaps Paul's clearest indication of an ongoing eternal punishment for the wicked. The reference to "everlasting destruction" suggests that Paul does not mean annihilation, but perpetual punishment. Just as believers can look forward to eternal life with God in heaven, those who reject God face eternal death.

1:11–12 Paul's marvelous description of the return of Christ is intended to provide comfort for the suffering believers in Thessalonica. Yet Paul wants the truth of the second coming not only to comfort their hearts and minds but also to impact their hands and feet. Believers are to take hope in the future yet continue to minister in the here and now. So Paul's prayer is a call to action.

2:1–5 Word was spreading through the congregation that the return of Jesus had already taken place. Naturally, there was a significant degree of concern and alarm. Paul identifies the false reports and offers a slight rebuke in his reminders of teachings they should have known. The rumors that were spreading should not have shaken the faith of the Christians in Thessalonica.

2:6–8 Paul's first two proofs that the day of the Lord has not yet arrived are the absence of both the widespread rebellion against God and the "man of sin" (2:3). And here he adds an additional proof: the continuing restraining power of God. The reason the

man of sin has not yet made his appearance is because God continues to prevent it. The time is not yet right. When God's restraint is withdrawn, the wicked one will soon be revealed.

2:15 The Thessalonians had begun to waver in their faith, so Paul reminds them to stand firm. God-breathed teachings had been handed down to His people and incorporated into apostolic traditions. In turn, Paul has handed those teachings on to the Thessalonian believers. They are true and dependable—a means for standing firm against all kinds of trials.

2:16–17 As a result of God's great love, believers receive two wonderful gifts: everlasting consolation and good hope. In the midst of the Thessalonians' struggles, these gifts would keep them looking forward to permanent consolation and everything else God has promised His people. They could hardly have asked for anything that would be more appreciated.

3:1 As he had done at the end of his previous letter (1 Thessalonians 5:25), Paul again asks the believers for prayer for himself and his associates. Paul's team had spread the Gospel to Thessalonica and then moved on to carry it to new places. Who better than the Thessalonians, who were currently experiencing the work of God among them, to pray for Paul's ongoing ministry elsewhere? Paul writes with apostolic authority to help the Thessalonians deal with their problems, yet he readily confesses his own inadequacy and the need for God's enablement.

3:2–4 Paul makes a sharp contrast between human lack of faith and God's faithfulness. He assures the Thessalonians that they can count on God for spiritual strength and protection at any time, and he is confident they will continue to faithfully follow the truths they have been taught. The Christian life is more than just a good feeling; it is confidence in God. Paul's confidence is not in the physical stamina of the Thessalonians to endure but in God's ability to sustain them in growth and obedience.

3:6 Paul has nothing to do with promoting the sit-around-and-wait-for-Jesus philosophy, and he orders his readers to have nothing to do with those who refuse to work and who twist the teaching of scripture. The word used for Paul's instruction is the same as would be used for a military officer barking out commands. He is quite firm on the topic.

3:7–10 Paul isn't asking the Thessalonians to do anything he doesn't do himself. Even while performing his ministry among them, he had provided for himself and had not expected handouts. It's not that he doesn't think he has the right to expect help (1 Corinthians 9:3–4, 6), but it is more important to him to set an example for the believers. Paul models appropriate Christian behavior for the Thessalonians and challenges them to imitate it. And it is more than a request; he insists on it as a moral necessity. As for those who are unwilling to work, Paul recommends letting them go hungry.

3:16–17 The Thessalonians' disputes could be settled by the ultimate Peacekeeper. Yet it requires a real commitment to Christ to experience peace at all times and in every way.

3:18 Until this point in his letter, Paul has been dictating to a secretary. But as was his custom—as readers discover here—he takes the pen and writes a short section in his own handwriting.

THE FIRST EPISTLE OF PAUL THE APOSTLE TO
TIMOTHY

INTRODUCTION TO 1 TIMOTHY ■ First Timothy is a letter from a faith mentor to one of his dearest disciples. It is a look into the first-century relationships that made up the early church and the issues with which the believers grappled.

AUTHOR ■ ■ The author of this letter introduces himself as the apostle Paul. Of all the letters of Paul, the pastoral epistles (1 Timothy, 2 Timothy, and Titus) are by far the most disputed in terms of authorship. Differences of language, style, and theology have caused many scholars to doubt that Paul was the original author. Some believe that a disciple of Paul wrote these after his death. Others think he may have had one of his missionary companions write out these letters (see Romans 16:22), and this scribe left his own stylistic mark. In any case, the differences are not as great as is sometimes supposed, and there are many features of the letter consistent with Paul's language and style. Evangelical scholars continue to assert that these letters came from the apostle's hand.

OCCASION ■ Paul wrote this letter from Macedonia sometime after being released from his first Roman imprisonment—around AD 63–64. Paul had left his protégé, Timothy, to minister at the church in Ephesus (1:3). At this particular time, the church was plagued by false teachers and dissension. Paul was going to be delayed in returning to Ephesus to be with Timothy and guide him in person, so he wrote this letter to offer guidance on how to choose and strengthen the leaders of the church and train them to preserve godliness and reject false teaching.

1:1 Paul identifies himself by noting the authority with which he writes. He is an apostle, an envoy, one sent with a specific mission. While all Christians are called to serve God, the first-century use of the term *apostle* referred to a very specific group—those who had accompanied Jesus. While Paul had not been one of the twelve disciples, his conversion experience brought him face-to-face with Jesus (Acts 9:1–9). In Acts 13:2 the Holy Spirit calls Saul (Paul) and his companion, Barnabas, to the missionary work recorded in the book of Acts. This further legitimizes Paul's claim to be an apostle.

1:2 Paul identifies his recipient as one so dear he is like a son in the faith. Paul reserves this designation for Timothy and for Titus (Titus 1:4). Timothy had grown up in Lystra, a Galatian city Paul visited on both his first and second missionary journeys. It was on this second journey that Paul requested Timothy to serve with him (Acts 16:1–3).

1:3 The very fact that Paul refers to "other" doctrine (false doctrine) reveals that at this point in the first century there was a core of Christian doctrine already widely accepted and agreed upon.

1:6–7 The teachers of the law Paul discusses may have been Gentiles or Jews. Whichever they were, though, they failed the test of love outlined in the previous verses. What they were teaching was not tightly connected to the scriptures. Their discussions were meaningless. While they wanted to be seen as authorities, they did not have a handle on the content and meaning of the law.

1:8–11 Paul discusses the law. Throughout his New Testament writings, Paul maintains the position that the law does not make people right with God or provide forgiveness of sins. The law only serves to point out the sin of humanity so that people can realize their need for

God and thus be forgiven and made clean. That is the lawful use Paul refers to in verse 8. The list following verse 8, then, makes up those who refuse to see what the law reveals—their need for God's redemption through Jesus.

1:17 This verse serves as a kind of spontaneous doxology not uncommon in Paul's writing. There is no known external source for this doxology, so it is reasonable that Paul himself wrote it. It highlights God's nature as eternal (no beginning or ending), immortal and invisible (existing as a spirit), and the one true God.

1:20 The two men singled out by Paul—Hymenaeus and Alexander—had evidently been members of the church. Hymenaeus had claimed the resurrection had already take place (2 Timothy 2:17–18). Alexander was possibly the coppersmith mentioned in 2 Timothy 4:14. When Paul says he handed these men over to Satan, it means they were removed from the church. This practice, while a part of church discipline, was not simply about punishment. The hope was that the men would see their error and return.

2:8 While contemporary prayer is often accompanied by bowed heads and closed eyes, the first-century posture for Jews and early Christians was often with hands reaching up and face looking upward toward heaven. Thus, lifting one's hands in prayer indicated a calling out to God.

2:11–12 The instruction regarding women being silent in church is likely a specific remedy to the situation Timothy was facing in Ephesus. While it was customary for only men to lead prayer in Jewish worship, it is somewhat unusual that Paul specifies only the men to pray. Elsewhere (1 Corinthians 11:5 for instance) Paul gives guidelines for women both praying and prophesying, so the directive across the board is not for women to always keep silent.

3:2 Paul lists several qualifications for the bishop (or overseer, elder). The qualification of "blameless" is an opening summary of the character of the bishop. It speaks to a reputation that contains no flaw that could be grounds for accusations.

3:3 A bishop should be "not given to wine, no striker" (that is, not a drunk or violent). There are obvious reasons that a bishop is not to be an immoderate drinker—it would stand in the way of many of the characteristics already listed.

3:4–5 This is not saying that in order to be a church leader the bishop must have children, but his management style at home (which will inform his style in the church) should be compassionate, effective leadership. Note that the children of the bishop aren't merely to obey, but to obey with "gravity" (or out of respect). This distinction reflects on the manner in which the bishop manages his children.

3:6 Paul's admonition that the bishop not be a "novice" Christian is quite understandable. Because of the new faith and the quick leadership, a novice Christian may get a distorted view of himself.

3:12 The "husband of one wife" requirement doesn't mean that a deacon *must* be married. Instead, it speaks to his faithful character within his relationships.

4:12 While Paul refers to Timothy's youth, that may have communicated a different concept to the early church than to today's readers. Some suppose that Timothy could have been as old as forty when he was leading this congregation.

4:15–16 Timothy was to give attention to, not neglect, his giftedness in his ministry. Paul promises that God will use Timothy's perseverance in sound doctrine to save him and Timothy's proclamation of that doctrine to save those who hear the message.

5:3–4 Considering the historical context of the first century—the low status of women, the importance of the husband in the family inheritance, the obstacles for widows to make money—a widow was often unable to support herself. If a widow has no family to support her, Paul suggests that the church should fill in the gap. On the other hand, if the widow has children or extended family, then the family should carry the primary responsibility.

5:5–6 To clarify which widows are truly in need of the church's support, Paul offers these parameters: the widow who is left entirely alone yet continues to live out her faith. His reference to the widow who seeks "pleasure" may refer to widows who resort to prostitution to support themselves.

5:7–8 In the general culture of this day, even outside of the Christian community, there was an acceptance that children were to shoulder the burden of caring for their parents. Paul's exhortation here protects the church community from the shame of being less responsible for its own than the pagan worshipers around them.

Those who deny assistance to their aging parents and grandparents are disgraceful not only to their families but also to their faith.

5:11–12 It seems harsh that younger widows should be excluded from ongoing church assistance, but this refusal on Paul's part isn't based on a lack of mercy. It may be that the vows required of an older widow who is cared for by the church included a vow not to remarry, thus Paul's reference to their "first," or former, faith. By requiring younger widows to remain in circulation, these guidelines offer them another life with marriage and family.

5:15 The reference to those who had already turned toward Satan may not mean a complete departure from the church so much as individuals who had entered into the behaviors that Paul describes in the previous verses: sensual desires, idleness, gossip, and so on.

5:17 In contemporary churches, the term *elder* has become specifically defined to include certain leadership roles and functions. Keep in mind that at the time Paul wrote to Timothy, these roles were not so fully defined. All of the older men were to be revered. Even more reverence was offered for those who rose in leadership. When Paul instructs Timothy regarding honor for the elders, this likely means both respect and financial remuneration.

6:1–2 Servants—noncitizens who served Roman citizens—were common in the Roman Empire of the first century. Slavery in the Roman Empire, though certainly a degrading institution, was very different than the slavery in the American South that most readers are familiar with. It was not based on race. Many servants were drawn from the ranks of prisoners of war. Others sold themselves into slavery for financial reasons. Working as a servant in a wealthy household was considered better than living in poverty and destitution. Servants could achieve very high social status, even serving as managers of large estates.

6:9–10 It seems apparent that Paul is not talking in theory about people falling away from the faith because of greed. There may have been those in the congregation at Ephesus with whom he or Timothy had firsthand experience. Paul's warning about the love of money should not be interpreted as the idea that Christians should disregard financial issues. It is more of a warning against greed than against money management. Certainly there are plenty of New Testament scriptures that encourage good money management.

6:20–21 Paul closes both of his letters to Timothy with similar instructions about guarding his ministry. When Paul writes of what has been entrusted to Timothy's care, the idea is almost like a deposit made into a bank. It is deposited there in order to be kept safe and to sometimes even earn interest. In the same way, Timothy's ministry in Ephesus was given to his care. He is to keep it safe and allow it to return on the investment.

THE SECOND EPISTLE OF PAUL THE APOSTLE TO

TIMOTHY

INTRODUCTION TO 2 TIMOTHY ■ Paul wrote this letter to Timothy—someone who came to faith through Paul's ministry, then worked as a colleague, and finally took on a leadership role at the church in Ephesus. The instructions in this letter serve to give Timothy guidance in leading the church, which includes battling with false teachers.

AUTHOR ■ The author of this letter introduces himself as the apostle Paul. Of all the letters of Paul, the pastoral epistles (1 Timothy, 2 Timothy, and Titus) are by far the most disputed in terms of authorship. Differences of language, style, and theology have caused many scholars to doubt that Paul was the original author. Some believe that a disciple of Paul wrote these after his death. Others think he may have had one of his missionary companions write out these letters (see Romans 16:22), and this scribe left his own stylistic mark. In any case, the differences are not as great as is sometimes supposed, and there are many features of the letter consistent with Paul's language and style. Evangelical scholars continue to assert that these letters came from the apostle's hand.

OCCASION ■ When Paul wrote this letter, he was in prison in Rome and had been deserted by most of his colleagues. He was also aware that his life was reaching its end and may have had some sense of passing on the torch of leadership. Timothy was in Ephesus, troubled by corrupted doctrine that was affecting his congregation. Paul reached out to Timothy through this letter to offer guidance and to connect and communicate as old friends will do.

1:1 The author identifies himself as the apostle Paul. *Apostle* means "one who is sent." This is a title of authority. While all Christians are called to serve God, the first-century use of this term referred to a very specific group—those who had accompanied Jesus. While Paul had not been one of the twelve disciples, his conversion experience brought him face-to-face with Jesus (Acts 9:1–9).

1:4 Paul's mention of Timothy's tears is probably a reference to the last time they were together—possibly when Paul was taken to prison in Rome. While this may seem an out-of-place reference considering the Western culture in which men are often pressured against expressing strong sentimental emotion, the first-century Judean culture held a different bias.

1:9–10 Some believe these verses are an early Christian hymn or confession. The truths included here fit so well within Paul's text, though, that some have concluded that even if it is a part of a hymn text, Paul may have written the hymn himself.

1:11–12 In the face of his own persecution, Paul embraced his role as a spokesperson for the message of grace, the gospel, and he denies being ashamed of it. The basis of Paul's boldness, however, is not personality or even character—it is God Himself. Paul's relationship with God, in whom he believes, is the key to his ability to stand in the middle of difficult circumstances without being destroyed by them.

1:12 Paul's mention of that which he has committed or entrusted to God is actually a financial concept, like a deposit at a bank. It paints the picture of someone giving his or her valuables to a friend to hold in safekeeping.

1:13 This verse opens with Paul's reference to what Timothy has heard from him. That would encompass all of the teaching shared between this mentor and

his protégé—not simply what has been written in this particular letter thus far.

2:1 Paul's encouragement for Timothy to be strong is not simply an exhortation for Timothy to gather his own self-will and bravado. The fact that Timothy is to be strong in "the grace that is in Christ Jesus" tempers self-will with the enabling of the indwelling Spirit. Timothy's strength will find its source in grace.

2:2 Paul had entrusted the message to Timothy and now commands Timothy to entrust it to others who will faithfully protect and proclaim it. The witnesses Paul mentions are probably all those who had heard Paul's teaching along with Timothy.

2:3–4 Suffering is as common to the Christian as it is to the soldier. In order to please a commanding officer, both the soldier and the Christian will abandon the conveniences of civilian life for the sake of a higher calling. They will endure.

2:14 Not only is Timothy to remember Paul's teaching (2:7), but he is also to remind others of it. Fighting or debating over terminology is useless. The phrase "before the Lord" increases the seriousness of the warning.

2:19 The building metaphor seems to be one of Paul's favorites. In this case, the foundation refers to the church, which has received God's seal, or mark of ownership. The first inscription that Paul quotes is from Numbers 16:5. The context for this statement is a rebellion led by a man named Korah. It occurred during the time that the Israelites were on their journey to the promised land (Numbers 16:1–5). The second inscription is not a direct quote from the Old Testament, yet it carries the same theme: that God knows the difference between those who are truly His and those who claim another truth.

2:22–25 Paul instructs Timothy to flee from youthful lusts, including the desire to win arguments by quarreling. Since Paul and Timothy knew each other well, Paul could fashion his advice specifically for his young friend. The passions mentioned here are not merely sexual but include all the extremes of youth. As Paul often does, he contrasts what Timothy should *flee from* with what he should *follow*: righteousness, faith, love, and peace.

3:1 The "last days" referred to the time immediately preceding Jesus' return. But in a broader sense, the last days actually encompass the whole era between Jesus' ascension back into heaven and His second coming.

3:2–4 The vice list here includes eighteen indictments. Perhaps the first one listed, "lovers of their own selves," governs the rest of the list. Paul includes being disobedient to parents in company with more offensive sins—a sober reminder of the wickedness of every sin, even those we may consider less offensive. There isn't an obvious structure to this list, though a theme could be those who substitute personal pleasure for God.

3:8–9 Jannes and Jambres are not names you will find in the Old Testament. They were the traditional names given to the Egyptian magicians who contested Moses before Pharaoh (Exodus 7:11, 22) and became symbols of those who oppose the truth. Just as those magicians were exposed in their trickery, those who stand against the truth in Ephesus will be exposed.

3:16–17 Paul provides two indispensable characteristics of scripture: (1) It is inspired by God—God breathed it out. (2) It is profitable to prepare godly people for every good work. This preparation for every good work happens in four ways: doctrine (teaching), reproof (rebuking), correction, and instruction (training). The first two are related more to doctrine. The second two are related more to practice. If all scripture originated with God, who cannot lie (Hebrews 6:18), then it is true.

4:3–4 "Itching ears" is a phrase that describes those who no longer want the simple truth or sound doctrine. Instead, they want novelty and entertainment. While Paul

has already described the false teachers who harassed Timothy's church, here he is turning the tables and highlighting the audience that is attracted to those false teachers. In understanding that audience, though, it makes sense that the teachers who are willing to satisfy that itch for novelty build their popularity by substituting fantastic myths for the truth.

4:10–11 Demas, according to Colossians 4:14, was a close associate of Paul's. The wording here gives the impression that Demas actually deserted Paul on a personal level. When Paul writes that Demas loved the world, he uses the same verb as in verse 8 (*agapao*)—meaning a deep longing or affection. Perhaps it was while mentioning those who had left him that Paul was reminded of Mark, who had rejoined Paul's ministry.

4:12 Tychicus may have hand delivered this letter to Timothy in Ephesus. In fact, it might have been Paul's intention for Tychicus to relieve Timothy so that Timothy could visit him.

4:17 Paul's reference to the Gentiles hearing his message may simply be a metaphor, since Rome was the center of the Gentile world. In the same way, his rescue from the lion's mouth may also simply be a word picture of escaping great danger (Psalm 22:21; Daniel 6:20) rather than a symbol of Nero or Satan or an allusion to the amphitheater in which Christians were killed by hungry lions as some have supposed.

4:19 Prisca (Priscilla) and Aquila were Paul's friends and ministry colleagues. The couple is always mentioned together in the Bible (Acts 18:2, 18, 26; Romans 16:3–4; 1 Corinthians 16:19), and most often Prisca's name is mentioned first. Paul first met them in Corinth and stayed with them for a year and a half, learning from their wisdom. They also influenced other first-century church leaders, like Apollos (Acts 18:24–28).

4:22 Finally, as Paul opens the letter with grace (1:2), he also closes this letter with the wish that Timothy would be accompanied by the grace of God and His Spirit.

TITUS

INTRODUCTION TO TITUS ■ The books of Titus and 1 and 2 Timothy comprise Paul's pastoral epistles—not an entirely accurate name for the three letters. Titus and Timotheus (Timothy) were not pastors, at least not by the modern definition. Still, both Timothy and Titus were Paul's associates who did a lot of legwork for him, and his letters to them about the expectations of church leaders are valuable guidelines for spiritual leadership.

AUTHOR ■ The author of this letter introduces himself as the apostle Paul. Of all the letters of Paul, the pastoral epistles (1 Timothy, 2 Timothy, and Titus) are by far the most disputed in terms of authorship. Differences of language, style, and theology have caused many scholars to doubt that Paul was the original author. Some believe that a disciple of Paul wrote these after his death. Others think he may have had one of his missionary companions write out these letters (see Romans 16:22), and this scribe left his own stylistic mark. In any case, the differences are not as great as is sometimes supposed, and there are many features of the letter consistent with Paul's language and style. Evangelical scholars continue to assert that these letters came from the apostle's hand.

OCCASION ■ Titus is not mentioned in Acts, as many of Paul's other associates are, but his name appears in various epistles. Paul's ministry had initiated Titus's conversion to Christianity, and the Gentile convert soon had taken on the responsibility of traveling and ministering with Paul and at other times on his own. This was one of the latter cases as Paul had left Titus in Crete while the apostle was elsewhere (perhaps Corinth). Paul desired to stay in touch with his protégé and offers him some practical advice for overseeing a church.

1:1 The openings of Paul's letters are all very similar. Paul usually begins by identifying himself as a servant of Christ. But in Titus, he calls himself a servant of God. This single exception is not too surprising when looking at the writings of Paul as a whole. He frequently gives credit to more than one person of the Trinity in a single passage, viewing the three as one God at work among humankind. A servant of Christ is certainly a servant of God.

1:5 Crete is an island of more than three thousand square miles in the Mediterranean Sea. Paul's ministry there is not recorded in Acts. Paul's visit was apparently shorter than he wished, so he left Titus there with significant work to do: answer questions, smooth out problems, appoint elders, and so forth.

1:6–9 Paul's list to Titus contains many of the same prerequisites for bishops (elders) as does his list to Timothy. The behavior of a bishop (elder) is an important aspect of his or her life, including how the person interacts with a spouse, family, fellow church members, and outsiders. Both public and private lives are under constant scrutiny.

1:10–11 The need for competent and spiritually mature bishops (elders) was essential because of the threats presented to the believers at Crete. They faced the same problems as other churches, yet those who opposed the truth seemed to be in full force in Crete.

1:12 Paul quotes the poet Epimenides, who had lived in Crete in the sixth century BC. Even though the people of Crete were well aware of their culture's ethical and spiritual shortcomings, Paul knew the power of the Holy Spirit to transform lives. He maintains just as high a spiritual standard in Crete as anywhere else. Yet in order

for the believers to persevere and overcome, they had to resist the influence of the false teachers and hold fast to the truth of the Gospel.

1:13–2:1 Paul challenges Titus and the bishops (elders) to silence the false teachers by refusing them opportunities to speak in the church—and rebuking them emphatically. They are also to preempt the false teachers by proclaiming the genuine Gospel that *will* have lasting value for their hearers.

2:9–10 Servants (slaves) were noncitizens who served Roman citizens, and they were common in the Roman Empire during the first century. (Perhaps as many as half of the people in the Roman Empire were servants.) Many lived as members of the household in which they served. They were usually paid and occasionally had the opportunity to earn their freedom. Paul tells them to behave in a godly way toward their masters so that the Gospel would be attractive.

2:13 Paul moves from a perspective on the present to the future. Believers can choose to go against the moral tide of society, not only because of the first appearance of Christ, but also because they eagerly anticipate His second appearance. Jesus' first coming was a historical reality; His second coming is a blessed hope that should affect all aspects of present-day life.

3:1–2 Paul lists a number of specific qualities expected of Christians: (1) to be subject to rulers and authorities; (2) to be obedient; (3) to be ready to do every good work; (4) to slander no one; (5) to be peaceable; (6) to be gentle; and (7) to show complete courtesy to all people.

3:3 Paul lists characteristics that had been evident prior to the believers' awareness of Jesus: (1) foolishness,

(2) disobedience, (3) being deceived by pleasures, (4) enslavement, (5) malice, (6) envy, and (7) both being hated and hating others.

3:8–11 Paul isn't just expressing his opinions. He instructs Titus to affirm these teachings—to insist on them. They are not only excellent and profitable for anyone who heeds them—they are also faithful. Even after salvation, those who want to experience the abundant life that God offers must be careful to maintain good works. God makes all things possible, but believers must be disciplined and willing.

3:12–15 Paul had worked with Tychicus and spoke highly of him on numerous occasions (Acts 20:4; Ephesians 6:21; Colossians 4:7). Nothing more is said of Artemas in the Bible. Apparently Paul was sending one of these men to Crete to minister for a while, allowing Titus to take a break and meet him in Nicopolis.

3:13 Before leaving, Paul requests Titus's help for Apollos and Zenas, who were traveling through the area. Scripture identifies Apollos as a spiritually discerning and devoted church leader (Acts 18:24–28; 1 Corinthians 1:12; 3:5), but this is the Bible's only mention of Zenas. His title of "lawyer" might have meant one of two things: If a Jewish reference, it would mean Zenas was trained in the law and had been a rabbi. If a Gentile reference, it would suggest that he was a person of high standing in Rome who had converted to Christianity.

3:14 Although the people of Crete had a propensity for laziness (1:12), Paul challenges the believers to provide for their daily necessities. This devotion to doing good could then be spread to people like Apollos and Zenas, who were doing God's work full-time and could benefit from the help of fellow Christians.

THE EPISTLE OF PAUL TO

PHILEMON

INTRODUCTION TO PHILEMON ■ Of the thirteen epistles traditionally attributed to Paul in scripture, his letter to Philemon is the most personal. Most were written to entire churches. The three pastoral epistles (1 and 2 Timothy and Titus) were to individuals but had churchwide applications. Philemon, too, contains public greetings and was intended to be read publicly. Philemon's situation was very specific, yet Paul's advice, as usual, contains wisdom appropriate for all believers.

AUTHOR ■ Paul identifies himself as the author (verses 1, 9, 19), and there is nothing in the letter theologically or grammatically to suggest otherwise.

OCCASION ■ Paul had come upon a runaway servant (slave) named Onesimus and had convinced him to return to his owner, Philemon. This letter is Paul's appeal to Philemon to forgive the servant and accept him back into the household.

---

1 In most of Paul's salutations, he identifies himself as an apostle of Christ. In this instance, however, such an opening would have been too strong. He is asking a favor rather than attempting to impose his position to coerce Philemon's decision, so he identifies himself as "a prisoner of Jesus Christ." He appears to be a prisoner of the Emperor Nero, but he was in chains because of his faithfulness in speaking for Jesus.

2–3 Paul will soon be asking a specific favor of a specific person, yet he begins with a greeting that includes the entire church. The specific appeal is to Philemon, but the importance of forgiveness and acceptance of others is applicable to all believers.

7 Philemon had a track record of encouraging believers. He had refreshed the "bowels" (hearts) of many people already; and Paul will soon ask him to refresh *his* heart by granting his request (verse 20).

8–10 Paul chooses not to demand the desired response from Philemon, although he feels he has the right to do so. He prefers to appeal to Philemon in love. It isn't until this point in the letter that he even mentions Onesimus by name. The servant had apparently become a Christian after conversing with Paul, based on Paul's reference to him as his son.

11 Paul uses a play on words. The name *Onesimus* means "profitable" or "useful." So Paul is essentially saying, somewhat tongue in cheek, that Philemon's "profitable" servant had temporarily become unprofitable but was now ready to live up to his name.

12–14 Paul genuinely likes Onesimus. He would like to recruit him as an assistant, much the way he had with Timotheus (Timothy) and Titus. But it is a matter of law, as well as moral obligation, for Paul to return Onesimus to Philemon. Onesimus had already broken

faith with Philemon and had possibly stolen from him as well. Had Paul kept Onesimus rather than sending him back, it would have amounted to yet another theft from Philemon. The servant needed to seek forgiveness from his master and offer restitution.

15–16 Paul wants Philemon to see Onesimus with new eyes. It had been wrong for Onesimus to run away, but the experience had led to his conversion, which created an interesting new development. Onesimus had left Colossae as the property of Philemon, but he is returning as a beloved brother. On a spiritual level, Onesimus and Philemon are now equals. On a human level, they will need to come to an agreement about how they can continue to interact.

17–19 Paul does all he can on Onesimus's behalf. He promises to personally pay any unsettled debts to Philemon, and he asks Philemon to receive Onesimus as if he were Paul himself. The fact that Paul wrote this letter personally would have made his promise legally binding.

20–22 Paul expresses confidence that Philemon will grant his request and even go beyond that. Aside from taking back his fugitive servant, what more could Philemon do other than set him free? And finally, Paul writes that he will soon be making a visit. The expectation of seeing the apostle in person soon might be additional motivation for Philemon to settle the matter.

23–25 The people with Paul are essentially the same people he mentions at the close of Colossians (Colossians 4:10–14). And his short benediction ends this letter in very much the same way he concludes all his other letters—with a prayer for the grace of the Lord Jesus Christ.

HEBREWS

INTRODUCTION TO HEBREWS ▪ The book of Hebrews is rightly identified as a letter (or "epistle") because it was written to a specific group of people to address problems and concerns of that community. Like a letter, it contains some personal comments and greetings (13:22–25). But in contrast to most other New Testament letters, Hebrews is fundamentally a sermon—a word of exhortation (13:22). It can be read aloud in less than an hour and, like most sermons today, is structured around the citation, exposition, and application of scripture.

AUTHOR ▪ No one can say with certainty who wrote Hebrews. Some attribute it to Paul, yet in every other Pauline letter, the apostle opens by identifying himself. In addition, the author's statement about hearing the Gospel from others (2:3) does not jibe with Paul's other statements that emphasize his receiving the Gospel directly from Christ (Galatians 1:11–12, for example). Furthermore, the language, style, and theological perspective are very different from Paul's found elsewhere. Other educated guesses for authorship include Barnabas, Luke, and Apollos. Perhaps the best perspective comes from the insight of the early Christian theologian Origen: Concerning the author of Hebrews, he commented, "God alone knows."

OCCASION ▪ The original recipients of this letter, as the title indicates, were Jewish Christians. They had suffered persecution for their new faith and had stood firm at first. But as time passed, they had begun to waver and were tempted to return to the comfort of their old, familiar ways. Some had apparently already made the decision to leave the Christian faith and return to Judaism, which placed added pressure on the ones who were still in the church.

1:1 The first sentence of the Hebrews sermon is an opening salvo. The author immediately begins to set Jesus Christ high above everyone and everything that people might otherwise trust for salvation and security.

1:2–3 The full deity of Jesus Christ is made evident in that He is the Creator of all things, His nature is the same as that of God the Father, and He does what only God can do. After completing His great work of redemption, He is again in heaven at the place of highest honor and authority—God's right hand (alluding to Psalm 110:1–2). The observation that Christ "sat down" indicates that His work of offering the sacrifice is finished.

1:4–6 The point the writer is making is that the angels, who were exalted by certain people, worshipped Jesus. Christ is not equal to angels; He is their object of worship. This point is made stronger by the writer's reminder that Jesus is the "firstbegotten" (firstborn) of God—a title less about birth order than about position, authority, and preeminence.

1:7 Not only do angels worship Christ, but they are also His servants—God controls them as He does the winds and the flames. Angels could announce Jesus' birth in Bethlehem and attend to Him in the garden of Gethsemane, but they couldn't take His place in living and dying for the salvation of humankind.

1:13–14 Angels serve not only God and Christ but also human beings—those who will inherit salvation. Some angels minister in the very presence of God, but only Jesus Christ sits at God's right hand. In addition, here is found the first of many indications in Hebrews that "salvation" is more than the believer's initial commitment. The author will repeatedly speak of salvation as something believers are yet to inherit.

2:5 After stating a clear warning, the author returns to the theme he had begun in chapter 1: the superiority of Jesus Christ to the angels. He wants his readers to consider the world to come, and he makes it clear that this is what he has been talking about all along. If indeed the Hebrew believers were being influenced by members of the Essene communities, they would be presented with teachings that included the exaltation of angels in the end times.

2:5–8 The image portrayed by Psalm 8, which is quoted in these verses, is far different from that of some people who see human beings as merely specks in the universe, lost amid the vast cosmos. The psalmist and the writer of Hebrews acknowledge that humans are not only created in the image of God but also given authority to oversee creation.

2:9–10 At first it may appear odd to consider that God *made* Jesus perfect, since Jesus *is* God. The answer is that Jesus was made "perfect," or complete, in His *humanity*. As a human being, He was conceived and born without sin. He lived without sin. And by His obedient suffering, He became the perfect sacrifice for sin and so achieved complete or "perfect" humanity—the position of glory that Adam and Eve failed to achieve because of their rebellion against God.

2:17–3:1 Jesus' experience perfectly qualifies Him to act as High Priest—an intercessor between sinful humankind and a perfect God. No one can rightly claim that God doesn't understand how he or she feels, because Jesus lived through everything any human being can face—and worse. The writer of Hebrews will have more to say on this topic later in the letter. Jesus helps in a very real way by seeing His people through whatever they are facing. He relates to human suffering because of His incarnation. He had to take on human form in order to die, and by doing so, He also experienced the emotions, pains, and temptations common to all human beings.

3:2–6 As the writer contrasts Moses with Jesus, his imagery makes his point. Moses was a faithful servant in God's house, but Christ was the builder. Moses was never anything more than a worker in the house over which Jesus ruled as the Son of God. Jesus is clearly superior to Moses.

3:7–11 The Jewish Christians receiving this letter would have been more familiar with Psalm 95 than most modern readers. The section quoted by the writer of Hebrews is the latter half of the psalm. What came before (Psalm 95:1–6) was a rousing call to worship God with joy, thanksgiving, and gratitude.

4:1 Another word the author uses frequently is *promise*, and the first of its appearances in Hebrews is found in this verse. He uses the word to encompass the world to come, eternal life, and the final consummation of salvation. This promise was made to God's people in the ancient epoch and is still being made to believers. The author of Hebrews clarifies that the promise will be fulfilled in the next world for those, and only those, who have followed the Lord Jesus with persevering faith all the way to the end of their lives. People in the church whose faith flags and who turn away from following the Lord forfeit that promise.

4:9–11 The author uses a word that might literally be rendered "sabbathment" but is translated "rest." The word is found nowhere else in the Bible and has been detected in no earlier uses than this one. The writer may have invented the word to define what he was talking about. No doubt the term evoked in his mind a connection to the weekly sabbath. Just as God rested from His work on the seventh day of creation, so He now invites believers to enter into His rest, signifying both His presence and salvation. Just as the seventh day of creation represented the completion of God's work and a time of rest, so the sabbath-rest for believers symbolizes the consummation of their salvation and entrance into God's rest.

4:13 God sees every action. He knows every thought and attitude. No matter how hard people try to hide their sins, the truth will eventually come to light and they will be expected to give an account. How much better it is to respond to God and await His rest.

4:14–16 Jesus didn't just step symbolically into God's presence in the temple; He went through the heavens to literally be in the presence of God. And His qualifications as High Priest are unsurpassed. Not only had He been the spotless, perfect sacrifice whose blood was shed, but He had also shared the human experience with those whom He was defending. He knew the exact temptations they faced and the weaknesses they felt. He felt the full force of human difficulties and understands them better than people do, from God's perspective.

5:1 Jewish religious purists might have ruled out Jesus as a likely high priest simply because of the fact that He was from the tribe of Judah, when the priests were required to be descendants of Levi. So in this section, the author takes care to establish that Jesus is in every way fitted to be the believers' great High Priest.

5:4–10 The writer of Hebrews drops in a couple of references to Melchisedec, the king/priest who had associated with Abraham centuries before. This is another example of how the author tends to briefly introduce a topic before delving into it later. His full discussion about Melchisedec comes in chapter 7. At this point, however, where Jesus is being compared to Aaron as a high priest, it should be noted that Melchisedec served as priest long *before* the law was given—before Aaron was even born.

6:4–6 Numerous Bible passages affirm that a genuine believer is in no danger of ever losing his or her salvation, including the final verses of this section (6:16–20). The Hebrew Christians appear to have been genuine believers: They had been enlightened, had reveled in the Word of God, had shared in the Holy Spirit. The author clearly desires for his hearers to repent.

6:13–18 All believers throughout the centuries have been heirs to God's promise to Abraham. And they have the same guarantee that the promise will be honored. God cannot lie, and He has no need to take an oath to ensure His trustworthiness. Yet He did so (Genesis 22:15–18), perhaps as a concession to the human tendency toward disbelief. And since there is nothing greater in the universe, God swore by Himself. There is no stronger assurance available.

6:19 The symbol of our assurance is an anchor—strong and secure. So when scripture speaks of the hope believers have in God, the concept is a far cry from the fingers-crossed, against-all-odds "hope" of which many people speak. Biblical hope in God refers to the certainty that God's promises will all be fully fulfilled. It is a source of ongoing encouragement.

6:19–20 The writer will have much more to say about the work of the priests and how Jesus' ministry compares. But at this point, he makes one very important observation: He says that Jesus entered the most holy place behind the veil in the temple. The privilege of doing so was given only to the high priest.

7:1–3 Melchisedec is proof that there were other priests of God besides the Levitical priests (who wouldn't exist for a number of centuries). Levitical priests would proudly trace their ancestry back to Aaron to justify their authority, yet Melchisedec did not depend on a genealogical right to be a priest. His is the example that foreshadows the ministry of Jesus.

7:4–7 The author points out that people acknowledged the authority of their priests by bringing a tithe. At the same time, they took great pride in being descendants of Abraham. Yet, as the author notes, Abraham offered a tithe to Melchisedec. Symbolically, then, the Levitical priests (through Abraham) deferred to the priesthood of

Melchisedec. Jesus was not a high priest in the tradition of Levi/Aaron but rather in the order of Melchisedec, which was clearly greater.

7:21 The author reminds his readers that for Christ, the priesthood is forever. The Law of Moses had made no provision for any such priesthood. This reference by the psalmist (Psalm 110:4) is obviously not the Levitical priesthood of the law.

7:22–25 As the author identifies Jesus as the king/priest who had come, his argument begins to make sense. Although from the tribe of Judah rather than Levi, Jesus still qualifies as a priest in the same way Melchisedec did. He is the One who lives forever and continues to intercede before God on behalf of human beings.

7:26–28 Jesus is superior to the Levitical priests in that He does not need to offer sacrifices on His own behalf. Jesus Christ is a high priest who is holy, harmless, and undefiled. And He only needed to offer a single sacrifice to God. The sacrifice of Himself was once for all. Its effectiveness covered past, present, and future. The Levitical priesthood was not the last word in salvation; Jesus is.

8:1–6 Despite all the emphasis many of his readers were placing on the Mosaic Laws, the author clearly shows their limited vision. Jesus, he explains, is not just one more in a long line of priests. Jesus, in fact, is the original and true Priest. His heavenly priesthood was the blueprint the earthly priests were expected to model. The Levitical system was a copy of the true priesthood; the work of the Old Testament priests was but a shadow of the real thing.

8:7 The first-century Jews wanted to believe that the covenant between God and Moses was a lasting one, and they were continuing to try to live according to those rules and regulations. But if that were so, queries the author of Hebrews, why did God later promise a new and better covenant?

9:1–5 The author reviews the basic setup of the tabernacle. The furnishings in the holy place and most holy place ("Holiest of all") were described in great detail in Exodus 35–40. However, most people never got to see those items, because only the priests were allowed within those enclosed portions of the tabernacle (and later the temple).

9:6–8 The author recalls the events of the day of atonement (Leviticus 16)—the most solemn day of the Hebrew year. The letter to the Hebrews was almost certainly written prior to the destruction of the temple in AD 70, so the observance of the day of atonement would still have been an annual ritual. It would have been just as significant for the Jewish Christians as for any Jews—perhaps more so.

9:11–14 Jesus' death was no random tragedy or act of circumstance. It was an intentional and spiritual sacrifice. Although He died on a cross outside the walls of Jerusalem, His sacrifice is represented as having been offered directly to God in heaven. And the author

is intentional about acknowledging the triune God in the work of securing the salvation of humankind.

9:15 The term *mediator* is used as a synonym for *guarantor*. The author continues to allude to the promised eternal inheritance that no one has yet received, but believer's ongoing faith in Christ ensures that they will one day be given everything God has promised.

9:16–17 The Greek word for *testament* could mean "covenant" or "last will and testament," and the prior reference to "eternal inheritance" (9:15) also brings to mind the concept of a will. A person draws up a will however he or she wishes, and it doesn't take effect until after the death of the person. Similarly, God initiated all the biblical covenants—with Abraham, Moses, and David, and the new covenant being described by the writer of Hebrews. People have nothing to offer God, so He is the originator. People *are* expected to respond, however.

9:18–22 Death is important. In the Levitical system, it was the death of the sacrificial animal—the shedding of blood—that effected God's forgiveness. When the covenant with Moses was confirmed, blood was required to be sprinkled in various places (Exodus 24:1–8).

9:23–24 This is the contrast the writer has been making all along. Christ's sacrifice was not a copy of the real one, and it was not offered in a temple that was a copy of the real one. Quite the opposite: The earthly priestly system was a copy of the genuine one. Christ's sacrifice was the blood of the perfect, divine substitute, and it was offered in the heavenly sanctuary.

9:25–26 The earthly priests had to enter the tabernacle again and again, year after year, to reenact the ceremony and offer more blood. Not so with Christ. The author describes Jesus' sacrifice as a onetime event that does not need to be repeated.

10:8 The author is quite purposeful here as he specifies sacrifices, offerings, burnt offerings, and sin offerings rather than grouping all sacrifices together. He indicates the entire sacrificial ritual of the Mosaic Law, aware that his readers were striving to use such methods to deal definitively with their sin before God. He has no quarrel with worshippers who offer sacrifices while acknowledging their trust in the Lord as the true Redeemer. He takes issue, however, with those who hope that the act of sacrifice will itself cleanse them from guilt.

10:10 As the author begins to wrap up this portion of his argument, he repeats a number of key points in summary. He again uses a favorite phrase to describe Jesus' sacrifice: "once for all."

10:11–12 The author reminds his readers that the work of the Levitical priests was never really done, yet Jesus completed His work and sat down at the right hand of God the Father.

10:13–18 The author's point is clear: Those who insisted on animal sacrifice as a means of salvation would never find God's favor. But those who place their faith in Jesus will experience the true salvation that God promises and Christ guarantees—a permanent and full forgiveness of sins. The author repeats his scriptural basis (Jeremiah 31:31–34).

10:19–22 No amount of animal sacrifice would ever entitle a worshipper to enter the most holy place ("the holiest"), yet the blood of Jesus was sufficient to allow people to be in God's very presence. It is a renewed and cleansed person who is invited to stand before God. The invitation includes the criteria of sincerity, assurance of faith, and cleansing from a guilty conscience.

10:23 In response to God's promise of forgiveness (10:17), the author again presents his persistent theme: the necessity of holding unswervingly to one's faith, ever looking ahead to what has been promised.

10:24–25 The author notes that Christianity was not intended to be a solitary religion; it is a fellowship of saints. Believers are *collectively* looking to the future. As they do, they are to spur one another on to deeper love and positive actions and to continue to encourage one another and meet together.

10:37–38 Shrinking back from one's faith has always been a problem, as the author points out by quoting from Habakkuk 2:3–4. He takes the liberty of transposing the two lines to place more emphasis on the warning. The quote also reinforces his point that the just (or righteous) have always lived by faith—both in the Old Testament system and after the completed work of Christ.

11:1 The author defines *faith*: being sure of what we hope for and believing the evidence of what we do not see. This definition echoes Paul's observation that hope that is seen is no hope at all (Romans 8:24–25).

11:4 The author provides insight into the Cain and Abel story (Genesis 4:1–16). Many people assume that God received Abel's offering because it involved a blood sacrifice and rejected Cain's because it did not. Yet both Hebrews and Genesis suggest that Cain's real sin was tokenism. Abel offered the very best of what he had, while Cain offered only a sampling when he should have given the firstfruits of his crop to God. It was a faulty attitude that led to the rejected offering.

11:5–7 The author provides a second definition of *faith* (the first definition is found in verse 1): a belief that God exists and rewards those who diligently seek Him. Enoch was spared death because his faith pleased God, and Noah (and his family) was spared because he believed God and acted on something he had not yet seen.

11:8–10 Several examples of Abraham's faith are mentioned. To begin with, he left his homeland solely because God promised to lead him somewhere else. He didn't even know where he was going! But when he arrived, and God promised him the land as an inheritance, he lived there as if it were his even though he never possessed it during his lifetime. (All he actually owned was a small burial plot.) He lived much of his life as a stranger in someone else's country.

11:23–25 Moses is another top figure in Israel's history. And as is the case in numerous instances, the faith of the parents is shown to be influential in the subsequent birth and life of an important spiritual figure.

Of course, Moses didn't get off to such a good start. After he was raised by Pharaoh's daughter, his murder of an Egyptian overseer declared his loyalty to the Israelites (Exodus 2:11–15). The short-lived pleasures of the Egyptian court were not to be compared with the eternal inheritance to be enjoyed by those who trust the Lord and do His will.

11:30–31 Faith was just as important after arriving in the promised land as it had been in getting there. Just two examples are provided: the falling of the walls of Jericho and the faith of Rahab, the woman who helped the Israelites and the only survivor (with her family) of the fall of Jericho. The first-century Jewish believers were most likely jolted a bit to be reminded of the faith of a Gentile prostitute—and God's vindication of her—as an example that they would do well to follow.

11:39–40 The final two verses of Hebrews 11 are often misunderstood. The author's clear statement is that the faithful people of Old Testament times did not receive what had been promised to them. All believers continue to look to the future for a better country, a better resurrection. One of the last things the author will write is that all believers continue to look for the city that is to come (13:14). All who place their faith in God are to be made perfect *together*—old and new.

12:1 After providing such an abundant and commendable group of examples in Hebrews 11, the author tells his audience to imagine being surrounded by those heroes as they live out their faith in the first-century world. The historical figures could be perceived as a cheering section that would give the modern believers a home-field advantage of sorts.

12:10–11 No one enjoys being disciplined by an authority figure. When God takes action to get a person's attention, it is not usually pleasant. But neither is it lasting. As soon as the person responds, the disciplinary action is quickly replaced by righteousness and peace.

12:14 Peace within the Christian community is not something that occurs automatically or that should be taken for granted. Believers are to make every effort to ensure they have a holy lifestyle on an individual basis and a peaceful coexistence with others in the church. Otherwise, people lose sight of God and the things that matter.

12:15 Each Christian must seriously pursue holiness and help other believers do the same. It is important to deal with sin as it arises, or it will quickly become a bitter root that spreads quickly to affect many.

13:1–2 Most likely the author's comments are in regard to believers, since he begins with the mandate to continue loving one another as brothers. So the strangers whom the Hebrew Christians were to entertain were probably fellow believers from other places. Whether fellow Christians or not, it is clear that believers should not confine Christian love only to those they know well.

13:3 The command to visit prisoners might be primarily in regard to believers who had been imprisoned on account of their faith. Underlying all these commands is the golden rule to treat others as one would like to be treated (Matthew 7:12). Brotherly love is more than verbal expressions of regret for others' situations; it requires putting oneself in the situation of another and responding the way one would desire to be treated.

13:8 Any correct understanding of the theology of Hebrews—and scripture as a whole—must acknowledge that Christ did not begin to be His people's Saviour or object of their faith when He came into the world as the son of Mary. What He accomplished by His incarnation, suffering, obedience, death, and resurrection was the basis for the relationship He had held with His people since the days of Adam and Eve. Otherwise, it could not be said that Christ is the same yesterday, today, and forever.

13:10–14 For believers coming from a Jewish background, the situation in the first-century church must have been quite difficult. They were being asked to downplay the importance of the temple and all its ceremonies. Christians had none of the visible accoutrements that signified a religion to most people of their time—including temples, altars, and priests. Their pagan neighbours thought they were atheists, and their Jewish peers would have scorned their faith without all the outward signs of religious ceremony. So the author of Hebrews reminds his readers that they do indeed have an altar, a priest, and a temple. . .in heaven.

13:15–16 Animal sacrifices are no longer necessary. Rather, believers are to offer God a sacrifice of praise—a confession of His sufficiency and a commitment to do good works. The good deeds have nothing to do with acquiring salvation but are in response to the forgiveness and righteousness God provides.

13:17 In retrospect, considering how determinedly the author has tried to explain the dangers of reverting to old ways and rejecting Christ, and considering his persuasive argument to convince his readers to remain true to their faith, it seems safe to assume that the near schism within the church had already created some tension between those members and the leaders. So the author issues a clear call for obedience to those watching over the spiritual integrity of the church. Their work was demanding enough without a lot of opposition from within.

13:20–25 The author has given his audience a lot to think about. His final benediction is a beautiful summary and reminder that Jesus Christ's shed blood and resurrection are the foundation of God's work in saving people and enabling them to live holy lives. The distinction he makes here is what separates Christianity from all other faiths and philosophies: the conviction that Jesus Christ is *the* way, *the* truth, and *the* life.

THE GENERAL EPISTLE OF

JAMES

INTRODUCTION TO JAMES ■ James's instructions echo those found in the Old Testament, but they also repeat Jesus' own teachings. James is teaching new believers what it means to live out their faith in Christ as Lord. (The Greek word *pistis*, translated as *faith*, appears fifteen times in the letter.)

AUTHOR ■ James was the natural son of Joseph and Mary and the younger half brother of Jesus, since they shared a mother but not a father. James is always mentioned first in the lists of Jesus' siblings (Matthew 13:55; Mark 6:3), indicating that he was most likely the eldest of Jesus' half siblings. He is also mentioned in Acts 15:13; 21:18; 1 Corinthians 15:7; Galatians 1:19; 2:9, 12; James; and Jude.

OCCASION ■ James was a Jewish Christian writing to a Jewish Christian audience. The letter is replete with Old Testament teachings and allusions, but it is clear that James wrote from a distinctly Christian perspective and from the experience of one who had spent time with Jesus. The audience was a group of Christians who were experiencing persecution for their faith. James wrote to them to encourage them in the face of trials and to help them know how to stand firm in the faith.

1:1 The writer of the letter simply introduces himself as James. As the most prominent leader in the first-century church in Jerusalem, he would not have needed to explain who he was. Yet instead of clinging to his position, or even to his blood relationship with Jesus, James calls himself a servant. His authority doesn't come through his position as leader or apostle (Galatians 1:19) but as "a servant of God and of the Lord Jesus Christ."

1:2 James addresses his "brethren" (Greek: *adelphoi*) many times in his letter, setting the tone of both pastor and fellow believer. He moves quickly from a joyful greeting to a difficult command—be joyful in the midst of trials.

1:3–4 How can joy and trials coexist? The one experiencing the trial knows that the end result is a stronger character and faith. James says patience is developed through trials. God gives believers the ability to endure with patience, and the testing develops patience and a stronger faith. It's a lifestyle that leads to a mature and whole spiritual journey. The word *perfect* does not mean "without fault," but "whole," "complete," or "mature."

1:5 Wisdom is a key tool to knowing how to deal with difficult situations. In acknowledging the need for wisdom, James points believers toward God's grace. God's nature is to give generously and without reservation. James's call to live by faith goes out to everyone.

1:13–15 James is clear: (1) Temptation does not come from God. This passage speaks to the holy character of God. God is not tempted by evil, and He is never the source of temptation. (2) Temptation is not sin. Responding inappropriately to temptation is sin, and unconfessed sin brings death. But simply being tempted is a different matter.

1:19–25 James condemns dormant, unapplied knowledge. He calls for people to listen to a message of truth

and then live a life consistent with that message, and he offers guidelines for what that might look like. The pressure that trials create may make believers quick to react in anger; James says to act differently. These verses are key for the letter because they point to a faith that results in changed behavior.

1:26–27 James says one's religion is worthless if it is without fruit. As just one example, he says that if faith doesn't change the way a person speaks, then that believer deceives himself. James mentions three areas in which genuine faith will be demonstrated, though it is by no means an exhaustive list: the tongue, one's care for the unfortunate, and purity.

2:8 James writes about the "royal law," the same law he speaks of in 1:25. James refers to the Mosaic Law but adds the definer *royal* to reiterate the significance of the law of Christ, the King—the One who fulfilled the Old Testament law.

2:13 James calls for mercy, not judgment. Mercy and forgiveness are supernatural activities. They are extreme demonstrations of loving our neighbour as ourselves.

2:14–17 James does not advocate a works-based salvation. Workless faith and faithless works are equally dead. James's main concern is consistency of faith, evidenced by its fruit. True faith is active belief and active trust, which result in a changed life. The example here shows that action is necessary; otherwise words are empty. What use are words without obedience?

2:18 James argues for theological unity: faith *and* works. He essentially says faith without works is impossible. The way people see someone's faith is by how he or she lives it out.

2:19–20 James emphasizes the uselessness of faith without its accompanying deeds by saying that even the devils believe in the triune God—but they do not obey.

2:21–24 James points to the example of Abraham, who obeyed out of trust and belief in God. In the beginning of

Abraham's narrative, he showed that he trusted God. His faith was made perfect (as opposed to a hollow faith) as a result of his obedience.

2:25 Even the prostitute Rahab acted in obedience that resulted from trust and belief (Joshua 2:4–21; 6:22–25). Christians can find narratives throughout the Old Testament of people demonstrating that genuine faith is always accompanied by obedient actions.

3:1–6 James opens chapter 3 with an instruction that not many should become teachers. His address is to those who seek positions of leadership in the church, likely those who would presume to teach primarily for prestige. His warning is against pride, reminding those who think they should have authority to stay humble. James follows this specific address with general thoughts on living with wisdom and humility. He uses the tongue as an example of being able to control oneself and live wisely.

3:8 The tongue is "unruly," meaning it is unstable and its ability to do evil can never be fully restrained. It is important for believers to be aware of its power in order to avoid careless words. The tongue is also a deadly poison (a reference to Psalm 140:3). Words can harm those who speak them, poisoning them through bitterness, and they can harm those they are spoken to or about by wounding like a snake's bite.

3:14–16 James highlights the problem of inconsistency in the life of a believer. One who is truly wise cannot harbor bitterness, envy, strife, or selfish ambition. Twice he mentions envy and strife, two sides of the same coin. Envy comes when someone selfishly wants what another has, and this leads to strife, a point James further makes in chapter 4.

4:2 When people are given over to selfish ambition or pleasures, division and fighting occur. James suggests that people fight because they don't get what they want. Here James also references Jesus' words in Matthew 5:21–22 when he says that the believers murder and envy.

4:4 James exchanges his comforting greeting "my brethren" (see 1:2; 2:1, 14; 3:1) with "ye adulterers and adulteresses." By using these powerful words, followed by the imagery of enmity with God and friendship with the world, James is accusing his readers of spiritual unfaithfulness. Echoing Jesus' statement in Matthew 6:24, James makes this strong point: Christians have to make a choice; they cannot love both God and the world's values.

4:11 James continues an emphasis on relationships among believers. He highlights again the importance

of controlling the tongue by refusing to harm another's reputation, something that would break a relationship.

4:13–17 James offers a powerful warning to those who think they are in control of their lives: Presumptuous living is dishonoring to God. The problem James points to is the tendency *not* to include God in the planning. No one should presume even to have the opportunity to travel, conduct business, and pursue success without recognizing that life itself is a gift from God. Self-sufficient boasting is evil because it disregards a need for God.

5:1–6 James's words of warning emphasize an eternal perspective. He condemns self-indulgence in the present, reminding the rich that their luxury comes at a greater price than they are willing to realize.

5:7–8, 10 The word translated here as *patient* occurs multiple times. James uses the prophets as an example of exhibiting patience while suffering as a result of following God's will.

5:11 James returns to the notion of perseverance. Job's patience is the same word used in 1:3–4, a strong endurance in the face of trials.

5:13–15 In closing, James circles back to his opening call for prayer. He points to praying in all circumstances: whether facing trouble or in happy times. He also directs those who are sick to call church leaders to pray. Notice that it is not the faith of the sick person that James mentions but the faith of those who pray. Presumably, the sick person exercises faith by calling the elders.

5:15–16 James dispels a widespread belief that illness is caused by a person's sin. He writes "if," indicating that sin could be a factor contributing to one's sickness, but it is not necessarily the cause. He also tells his readers to confess sins to one another, reminding believers of their call to bear one another's burdens (Galatians 6:2).

5:17–18 James calls the prayer of a righteous person effective and uses Elias (Elijah) as his example. In 1 Kings 17:1 the prophet Elias (Elijah) spoke with Ahab, the wicked king of Israel. Elias (Elijah) prophesied that there would be no rain for three years as a sign of God against Ahab's wickedness. Three years later, in 1 Kings 18:1, God sent him back to Ahab promising rain again. Elias (Elijah) was not supernatural; he was human. What set him apart was that he prayed earnestly.

5:19–20 James offers a picture of Christian community in which members are accountable to one another. James's letter closes with a continued concern for living out a faith that works and also with concern for the welfare of others.

PETER

INTRODUCTION TO 1 PETER ■ First Peter is a great book to shatter any false expectations about who God is and what it means to serve God. It gives us realistic expectations about what this world has to offer and what perspective can help us through the tough times.

AUTHOR ■ This letter was written by Peter, one of Jesus' twelve disciples, who became a leader of the first-century Christian church. Like other New Testament writers who penned their letters with the help of scribes (see Romans 16:22; Galatians 6:11), Peter may have dictated the letter to Silas, who improved the style and quality of the Greek.

OCCASION ■ Peter writes to believers living in Asia Minor to encourage them to faithfully endure persecution in light of the glorious salvation Christ had accomplished for them and to see their suffering as a normal part of their service to God.

1:4 Peter highlights the point of inheritance. The believer's hope is not simply in going to heaven but in the inheritance awaiting them there. It is imperishable; it cannot be destroyed. It is also undefiled, or sin-free. It is unimpaired by time and will not lose its value. Finally, it is unconditionally reserved—guarded. The point of a reservation is that it's guaranteed.

1:5 Believers not only have a protected inheritance, but they are also a protected people. If God is going to protect their inheritance in heaven, then He is going to protect them on earth as well.

1:6 Peter's point is that in this world there will be trials, but these trials are momentary in the grand view of eternity. The faith displayed during trials will be the faith that will one day deliver us from this world.

1:7 Suffering is a tool in the hands of God to bring about revelation and glory. Jesus is our example. Through Him, God revealed His character and put His glory on display.

1:8–9 Believers love Christ and believe in Christ even though they have never seen Him. As a result, they will gain salvation from the world that they are living in.

1:13 Peter uses the metaphor of someone girding his loins to illustrate working in the field or preparing for battle. In the first century, if a man wanted to work in the field, he would gather up his robe and pull it between his legs, then tie it around his waist. This would get the excess cloth out of the way so he could work. Similarly, a warrior would gather up his clothes and tuck them into his waist to fight more effectively.

1:16 Peter quotes Leviticus 11:44, a verse from the passage outlining the dietary laws that set the Jews apart from the cultures around them. Today we are not bound by these laws. Instead, we are bound by our commitment to imitate the character of Jesus.

1:18–19 We are told that after seeing us exactly as we are, God redeems us, or purchases us out of slavery. Redemption came in the form of Jesus' blood. Peter draws on the image of the Old Testament sacrificial system—offering animal sacrifices to maintain peace with God. The animals offered were to be without any blemish (Leviticus 3:1)—in His perfection, Jesus fit the bill.

1:20–21 Because of our redemption, we have faith and hope in God. We can partake of this faith and hope because of the resurrection of Jesus. The resurrection was the sign that God was satisfied and redemption was complete.

2:1–2 Peter says we must put aside our natural responses to the world around us. The sins listed here are the enemies of love. When we see what God has done for us, it should humble us and cause us to reach out to others with the same love. We should crave this new way of life.

2:6–8 The truth that Peter has just proclaimed about Christ is not new. Both Isaiah 28:16 and Psalm 118:22 teach that there will be those who reject this stone and those who accept this stone. Rejection can lead to injury. To stumble means to get hurt.

2:9–10 We have an identity, a mission, a useful purpose, and a new lifestyle because of Christ. We are to tell the world how God transitioned us from death to life and that this is a transition of love, mercy, kindness, and compassion. We are "peculiar" people not in the sense of being odd, but as being special to God.

2:11 Notice how Peter describes the believers: as strangers and pilgrims. The word *stranger* means a person who is not a part of the life of society in which he or she is presently living. In a spiritual sense, this is true of Christians. The term *pilgrim* carries the idea of temporarily dwelling in a land with no intention of putting down roots. Certainly, this is how Christians look at their sojourn on earth.

2:14 In this life, the believer is to submit to human authorities in attitude and in action. Our distinctness from our culture does not mean we are above the structure of the world. The government is sent by God to punish evil and praise good behavior, to keep lawlessness from ruling.

2:18 According to most historians, almost half the population of the Roman Empire was some type of slave or servant. This was a key to the economic stability of the Roman Empire. The servants mentioned here are likely domestic helpers. This is why many preachers apply this passage to employees.

2:22–23 Peter offers a snapshot of the service of Jesus in the face of suffering by quoting Isaiah 53:9, part of the description of the suffering Messiah. Jesus never sinned, yet He was accused and punished severely. In the midst of that, Jesus did not respond in kind. He was verbally and physically abused, yet He did not threaten abuse in return.

2:25 We were a straying people who wandered away from God. Jesus suffered for us so that we might be able to be pulled toward God and live for Him and live out His sacrificial love for this world.

3:3–4 Peter is not condemning a woman for dressing nicely, but he makes the point that women should not make their looks the sum total of their worth. He contrasts those who focus on external beauty with those who focus on the inner attitude. This part of the woman's life must be adorned with a meek (or gentle) and quiet spirit.

3:7 Peter addresses husbands. They are to live with their wives by trying to understand their needs. The husband is to be a student of his wife so that he can care for her and love her according to who she is specifically. Peter's mention of the wife as the "weaker" vessel is not an insult toward women or a statement of the moral or spiritual superiority of men (as some throughout church history have claimed). *Weaker* refers instead to the fact that women are generally physically weaker than men, and so a husband's role is to ensure that his wife is protected, cared for, and treated with dignity and honor.

3:16 We must have a conscience that is pure. To maintain that clear conscience, we must live with integrity in this world so any accusations against us won't stick.

3:18–22 Jesus' suffering brought about salvation. Just as Noah's family passed through the water and was delivered, when we pass through the waters of baptism and all that they symbolize, we are delivered. Peter rids his readers of any magical ideas about baptism by making it plain that the efficacy of baptism does not lie in the outward symbolism but in the inner response of faith toward God.

4:1 When a person has "ceased from sin," this does not mean that person has become perfect. Peter is saying that the moment we share in God's understanding of suffering and we step up and begin to suffer for what is right, we are no longer pursuing the flesh but instead are living for the will of God.

4:2–6 There are two reasons we should embrace suffering: (1) The time is over for us to live for the lusts of the flesh. Every sin mentioned in verse 3 is a

sin of personal pleasure. When people seek to live for righteousness in this world, they stop living simply for their own pleasure. They live, instead, aware that they will give an account to Jesus for their lives. (2) There is a reward that will follow—eternal life. Redemption cannot be stopped even if the world treats us like the scum of the earth.

4:9 *Hospitality* means to show love to strangers—a high value in ancient Near Eastern society (as it is today in the Middle East). In Peter's day, there were many traveling preachers who moved from town to town and may have arrived unannounced at believers' homes. Since many Christians were very poor, having another mouth to feed would have been an enormous personal sacrifice. Hospitality is not just an act; it is a selfless act.

4:14–16 Here we find a message of hope—suffering in this world is not a sign of sin but a sign of blessing. The reproaches (or insults) Peter mentions being reproached for the name of Christ. The blessing has at its root the idea of being refreshed. The idea behind the "spirit of God" resting on you is that God is applying His glory to your life so that when you suffer, His glory is being seen. In other words, your suffering is a usable moment in the hands of God, for God is allowing His glory to rest upon you. We can be agents of God's glory—in other words, the expression of His character and nature.

4:17–18 These verses make a simple point—if the trials the church is undergoing are severe, how much more severe will be the judgment awaiting the wicked. The word *judgment* used with reference to the church means the ongoing process of dealing with sin rather than the final pronouncement of judgment.

5:1–4 Rather than using the position to *tell* people what to do, the elder should *show* them an example of what to do. Elders must show the flock how they are to live. When Jesus comes, there will be a reward for all those who served the way Peter describes here. This reward is an unfading crown of glory; their work will not go unrecognized by God.

5:6–7 Peter makes his case that humility is needed toward leaders and each other; it stands to reason that we must be humble in our relationship with God. The "mighty hand of God" is an image that is used frequently in the Bible. Here it refers to what Peter stated in 4:17—namely, that God is at work in the lives of His children, using the trials of the world to deal with their sin. To humble yourself under the mighty hand of God is to acknowledge the trial that you are in and to surrender to the process rather than running away. We are to be ready to have God give us the honor in His time rather than fighting for it on our own schedule.

5:10–11 Peter offers one more piece of helpful advice—look to the future. This suffering is for a short time compared to eternity. This is such great news that Peter ends in words of praise.

PETER

INTRODUCTION TO 2 PETER ■ Late in the first century, the church was in an increasingly vulnerable position. In addition to the continuing threat of persecution, false teachers began to arise and distort the true message. At the same time, the apostles, who had established the church and provided its early leadership, were beginning to die off or suffer martyrdom. This letter deals with the problems that come when false teachers sneak into the Christian fold with the goal of turning people away from the message of Christ and enticing them with their own false message grounded in worldly wisdom and human achievement.

AUTHOR ■ The writer of this book identifies himself as Peter, one of Jesus' twelve disciples. Many have questioned Peter's authorship because of language differences with 1 Peter, among other things. However, conservative scholars, while acknowledging the difficulties of the letter's authorship, still agree that Peter is a likely option.

OCCASION ■ Peter's goal in writing is to fortify the church against false teaching. He wants to give the standard of truth to the church so that once he and the rest of the apostles are gone, the church will be able to stand strong against heresy. In order for the standard of truth to be established, Peter must show the true knowledge of God, the nature of the false teachers, and how to stand firm in the midst of both.

1:1 Peter clarifies that he is writing to all believers rather than to one specific church. He states that the faith the church has received is the same faith the apostles received. Not only is it the same faith, but it also arises from the same source—the righteousness of Jesus Christ.

1:2 The "knowledge" Peter refers to is an intimate and experiential knowledge of God. It is best illustrated in the kind of familiarity that comes through a marriage relationship. The more people know and experience God, the more they experience His grace and peace.

1:5 The word translated *add* originally meant to pay the expenses of a chorus in staging a play, but it came to mean providing support or aid of any kind (generally rich or lavish support provided at one's own expense). In the context of this verse, it carries with it the idea of cooperating with God as He produces these important qualities in His children.

1:8 Peter refers to a believer's knowledge of Jesus. This is a knowledge that is forged in a relationship, not a simple acknowledgment or familiarity with a set of information.

1:9 Peter describes the fallout of someone who does not pursue the traits described in verses 5–7. That person is blind, shortsighted, and suffers from amnesia. He or she cannot see the reality of the present world, the inheritance that waits, or what Jesus has done for him or her in the past.

1:16–18 Peter refers to the event that is often called the transfiguration (Mark 9:2–8). Jesus brought Peter, James, and John to a mountain, and He physically changed before them, revealing His glory. Elias (Elijah) and Moses—both key figures in the story line of the Bible—appeared with Jesus. This was a defining moment for the apostles.

2:1–3 False teachers will face judgment before God, since they have denied the One who bought them. They

have refused the redemption offered them and influenced others to do the same. Peter's use of "the way of truth" may be an allusion to Psalm 119:30.

2:9 Through the examples in the previous verses, Peter is demonstrating that while false teachers experience limited success, no one will have to endure them forever. God will judge the false teachers, and He will deliver the righteous.

2:10 This verse reveals the two main problems with the false teachers. First, they engage in overt immorality. And second, they despise authority. Peter describes them as presumptuous and self-willed. The idea around the word *presumptuous* is that of recklessness. It carries the thought of people who are so arrogant and so bold that they will do whatever they want, no matter the cost.

2:12–13 Peter compares these teachers to unreasoning animals. Rather than living by the Spirit, they simply follow their own fallen instincts—and, like wild animals, they are caught and destroyed. The fact that they are carousing in broad daylight would have been an offense not only to the Christian community but to the first-century Roman culture at large.

2:14 Peter describes the nature of the false teachers as constantly immoral. When Peter says that these teachers have "eyes full of adultery," he doesn't mean they are looking to commit adultery as much as the fact that they believe that everything in the world belongs to them, and they want to have it all.

2:18 This verse describes the true method of the false teachers and the content of their teaching. Their words are empty. They are vain. They have no value. These teachers have nothing beneficial to say, yet they say it with great pride and arrogance.

2:20–21 Knowledge creates responsibility (see James 3:1, where teachers are said to receive a stricter judgment).

Those who have heard and understood the message, yet willfully reject it, will be judged more harshly than those who have never heard or understood. The false teachers had heard the Gospel, knew the Gospel, and could even speak the Gospel message, yet they never obeyed it.

3:3–4 Peter refers to the false teachers as "scoffers" because they deride, or attack, God's truth—starting with the return of Jesus. They snidely wonder, *Where is Jesus? I thought He said He would return.* Their implication is that God has not had an active part in the history of the world. Things have continued to simply go their way, and He has not kept His promise.

3:8 This is a reference to Psalm 90:4. This psalm was written by Moses and was a foundational psalm in early Christian teaching. Within Peter's context, it emphasizes the fact that God is not bound by time. The false teachers are incorrect in their assumption that because Jesus has not yet returned, He isn't going to at all.

3:9 The "longsuffering" (patience) of God shouldn't be interpreted as a lack of involvement but instead as the ultimate involvement, because God is using this time to draw humanity to Himself. When Peter says that God doesn't want anyone to perish, it does not imply that all will enter the kingdom of heaven—verse 7 reveals God's judgment. But Peter is saying that the Lord is longsuffering toward those who are not mockers and not opposed to the will of God—as he has described the false teachers.

3:12 We must be a part of what God is doing on the earth. Waiting for that day is not a lack of activity, but it is active waiting as believers participate in God's kingdom.

3:13–14 If God is preparing a new world in which righteousness is the controlling factor, those who want to live in that new world will desire righteousness in their current lives. Peter wants his readers to focus on the peace that comes from walking in full harmony with God. He also says to be diligent, spotless, and blameless. This is an image from the Old Testament. The passover lamb could not have any spot or blemish. In regard to his readers, Peter is saying that when Jesus returns, He must find believers living pure lives on earth.

3:15–16 Peter refers to Paul's writings, saying he and Paul are preaching the same message. Peter places Paul's writings in the same category as all of the scriptures—which in this case refers to the Old Testament.

3:17 Peter's final words are of warning and direction: It is the responsibility of the believer to be on guard. This means a believer must be personally vigilant over his or her own spiritual life.

3:18 In closing, Peter turns his attention to the spiritual growth of his readers—in the grace and knowledge of Jesus. He opens this letter praying that grace and peace will be multiplied to his readers (1:2). At the closing, then, he comes full circle, instructing them to continue to grow in grace and also in knowledge. His inclusion of knowledge here is a reminder that dealing with false teaching requires tending to one's own knowledge of the truth.

JOHN

INTRODUCTION TO 1 JOHN ■ The New Testament book we refer to as 1 John is a letter to a community of faith. Much of this letter is written to combat heresy regarding the identity of Jesus. The conflict over this heresy caused part of the congregation to split from the rest. John writes to ground the community in a true picture of not only Jesus' identity but the identity of the children of God in light of who Jesus is.

AUTHOR ■ Determining the author of 1 John is somewhat different from determining the author of 2 and 3 John. In the case of 1 John, no author is identified in the work itself. However, the author does identify himself as an eyewitness of Jesus' ministry. He also speaks with an apostolic kind of authority and writes in a similar style to that of the Gospel of John. There is good evidence, both historical and internal, that supports the traditional view of John the apostle as the author.

OCCASION ■ John appears to be writing to a community to which he is well known (and to which he may belong). Because this Christian community has undergone a serious split, and a substantial part of the community has withdrawn from fellowship over doctrinal issues, John writes to reassure them of their faith. The group that has split off is continuing to propagate its own beliefs, seeking to persuade more community members to join them. John writes to warn members of the community to resist the proselytizing efforts of these false teachers by bolstering their understanding of the truth.

1:4 John states his purpose for writing: that the joy of all these witnesses may be full. This joy will come from continuing fellowship with one another and with the Father and the Son, as opposed to breaking that fellowship by siding with false teachers.

1:5 This is a description of one of God's qualities—completely sinless. It is also the introduction of the imagery of light and darkness—important images in John's theology.

1:7 This verse introduces the counterclaim to verse 6—if we actually do walk in the truth, we will be assured of fellowship with God. In this context, *fellowship* is something shared between believers as a result of a righteous lifestyle.

1:9 The confession John writes about is an ongoing lifestyle of confession, not just a onetime confession at conversion (as this verse is often applied). John's readers have already experienced conversion.

2:1 This is the picture of someone coming alongside to represent us, like a mediator.

2:2 The word John uses to describe the work of Jesus—translated *propitiation*—involves the idea of a sacrifice for sins that turns away the divine wrath. Jesus does not turn away God's wrath by ignoring one's sin but by offering His own punishment in one's stead—His life.

2:3 John answers the question, "How do we know that we know God?" John's answer is that obedience to God's commands gives the assurance that one has come to know God.

2:4–5 According to John, this person's claim to know God is false; it's those who obey God's Word who truly know Him. In this case, God's *word* is a reference not only to the facts of the scriptures but to God's ethical demands. It is these demands a believer will attempt to

obey (but presumably the false teachers would not be concerned about obeying).

2:7 This verse refers to the teaching specified as the "new commandment" of John 13:34–35 (that believers should love one another).

2:8 The light/darkness contrast is a little broader here than in John's Gospel (John 1:5). In the Gospel, the light refers to Jesus Himself. In this context, though, the obedience of John's readers is a part of the light that is shining.

2:9, 11 The use of the verb *hateth* may seem strong, but for John, the failure to show love for others in the Christian community to which one belongs is a very serious matter. Such a person may be described as spiritually blind (John 9:39–41). Some see the description here as a reference to Proverbs 4:19, with its description of the wicked who stumble in the darkness.

2:12–14 John addresses his readers directly as "little children." He writes to assure them that their sins have been forgiven. This is a reference to the whole group (little children) followed by two subgroups (fathers and young men). Whether these two subgroups are distinguished by age or spiritual maturity is not clear, but John's words are applicable to all.

2:15 John presents only two alternatives: A person either loves the world or loves the Father. In this case, *the world* does not refer merely to creation or to the world's population for whom Christ died (John 3:16). Instead, this use of *the world* represents those who stand against John and the teachings of Christ.

2:16 John defines everything the world has to offer: (1) The "lust of the flesh." This probably does not refer simply to sensual desires (lustfulness or promiscuity). It refers to everything that is the desire of human beings—all that meets their wants and needs. (2) The "lust of the eyes." This is more than merely human desires; this is related to what we want for ourselves. We see it, and we want to have it. (3) The "pride of life" has to do with our possessions and accomplishments, those things we brag about, even if only in our minds.

2:27–28 John reminds his readers that the Holy Spirit resides in them. The "anointing" they have received is the indwelling presence of the Holy Spirit. This provides assurance that they do also indeed reside in Him—Jesus.

3:1 The concept that John uses here to describe God's relationship to believers, as a father to children, points on the one hand to God's personal, relational, and loving nature. On the other hand, it defines the status of Christians: They are members of God's household.

3:5 John reminds the readers of the basics they all know: that Jesus came to take away sins. He also affirms Jesus' sinlessness. This, in turn, leads into the issue of sin for those who reside in Jesus.

3:6 This verse, along with verse 9, can seem to mean that genuine Christians do not sin. Obviously, this is not the case, as John points out in 2:1. More likely John is saying that genuine Christians do not continue to sin with no remorse.

3:15 John writes that the person who hates a fellow believer is as guilty as if he or she had murdered that believer. This is strong language, but failure to show love to fellow believers is a serious matter to John. It is an indication that eternal life is not present within the individual. Once again, one's behavior is a measure of one's spiritual status.

3:19 By expressing love for one another, Christians assure themselves that they belong to the truth, because the outward action reflects the inward reality of one's relationship with God.

3:22–24 John closes the chapter by specifying God's commandment to believe in Jesus and love one another. The person who does these things, the genuine believer, is in a mutual and reciprocal relationship with God. The assurance of this mutual relationship between God and the believer is God's Spirit. The believer's assurance is based on three things: (1) believing in Jesus, (2) loving one another, and (3) the gift of God's indwelling Spirit.

4:13–14 The indwelling of the Spirit leads a person to testify to what God the Father has done through His Son, who was sent to be the Saviour of the world. This expression recalls the testimony of the Samaritan woman at the well in John 4, which led to the same confession about Jesus by the Samaritans (John 4:42).

4:17–18 Fear and mature love are mutually exclusive. A Christian who fears God's punishment (on the Day of Judgment) needs to grow in his or her understanding of love.

5:1 Once again (echoing 4:2–3) John stresses that confession of Jesus as the Christ is the standard that determines whether or not one is fathered by God. The second part of this verse reads like a proverb: If one loves the parent, one will love the child. While this is likely a general statement applying to any parent, in the present context it has application to loving God and loving God's children.

5:2 At face value, this verse says just the opposite of 4:20. Instead, these two verses are like looking at the same coin from two different sides. They both work together.

5:4 John uses the word *overcometh*. He has already used this same word to describe victory over Satan in 2:13–14 and over the false teachers (described as false prophets) in 4:4. Here John most likely has in mind victory over the false teachers.

5:8 John calls on three witnesses to support his claims about Jesus: the Spirit, the water, and the blood. In the previous verses, the Spirit was listed separately from the water and the blood, but here they stand together.

5:11 God's witness (mentioned in verse 9) is revealed. The witness is the eternal life that John and his readers possess, while the false teachers do not. It is important to remember that in John's debate with the false teachers, the controversy is not over the *reality* of eternal life (whether it exists at all) but over which side of the debate *possesses* it. John began with a testimony that the eternal life had been revealed (1:2), and it is consummated here with the acknowledgment of that eternal life as the final testimony in his case against the false teachers.

5:12 Possession of eternal life is connected to one's relationship to God's Son. The contrast between the readers of the letter, who are being reassured that they do indeed possess eternal life, and the false teachers, who in the opinion of John do not, is once again portrayed in stark terms: Someone either has the Son—He is present in the person's life—and thus has eternal life, or does not have the Son, in which case he or she does not have eternal life.

5:13 John begins his conclusion by telling his readers why he has written the letter. Once again John writes to reassure his readers that they possess eternal life.

5:21 John's closing can seem rather abrupt. It is possible that he is offering a general warning against idolatry. However, John has spent virtually the whole letter discussing, in one form or another, the false teachers who are continuing to trouble the community. It is likely that *idols* is a reference to the false image of Jesus that these teachers are putting forth.

THE SECOND EPISTLE GENERAL OF

JOHN

INTRODUCTION TO 2 JOHN ■ Second John is a personal letter written to warn a sister congregation some distance away. In its original Greek manuscript, it is shorter than any other New Testament book, except 3 John. The length of both 2 and 3 John is governed by the size of a single sheet of papyrus, which would have measured about 25 by 20 centimeters.

AUTHOR ■ As with the Gospel of John, the author does not explicitly identify himself as the apostle John. Instead, he uses the designation *the elder*. He obviously assumes the readers know him. However, the style of writing is unmistakably similar to that of 1 John. Also, as early as the second century, Christian historians and theologians recognized the author as the apostle John, one of the original twelve disciples.

OCCASION ■ The purpose of this letter is to warn its readers of the missionary efforts of false teachers and the dangers of welcoming them whenever they should arrive.

---

3 John's greeting, while it fits the standard format of a first-century letter, also contains a significant amount of reassurance for the readers. Rather than wishing or praying for his readers to have grace, mercy, and peace with them (for instance, "May grace be with you"), he promises that these three important elements of faith, specifically from the Father and the Son, will certainly be with his readers.

6 John explains what the love of God consists of: obedience to God's commandments. (This coordinates with 1 John 5:3.) Believers express their love for God by obeying His commandments and especially by loving one another.

7, 9 The deceivers (false teachers) are described as those who have gone beyond the apostolic eyewitness testimony about Jesus. Such a person does not have God, as opposed to the individual who remains in the apostolic teaching about Jesus.

8 John urges his readers not to lose what they have worked for, which refers to their pastoral and missionary efforts in their community and surrounding communities. If the false teachers are unopposed and

allowed to recruit in the community to which John is writing, all the effective work accomplished up to this point by the recipients of the letter would be in danger of being lost. Thus there would be no basis left on which to be rewarded.

11 John's command not to welcome, or greet ("biddeth"), these individuals is not intended to represent an insult. In this context, to greet someone means to greet him or her as a fellow Christian; and this is impossible, because as far as John is concerned, the false teachers are not genuine believers. Therefore, they should not be publicly greeted as such. Giving one of the false teachers' representatives a greeting in public could be construed as giving endorsement to that person's views about Jesus. This would be, in effect, to share in his evil deeds.

13 John sends final greetings. It is significant that it is "the children" of the elect sister, and not the sister herself, who send the greetings here. This probably refers to members of a sister church to which 2 John is written. Evidently John is staying in that community while writing this letter.

THE THIRD EPISTLE GENERAL OF

JOHN

INTRODUCTION TO 3 JOHN ■ Third John, like 2 John, is written in the standard correspondence format for the first century. It is slightly shorter than 2 John and is the shortest book of the New Testament. It is one of only a few New Testament letters to be addressed to a named individual.

AUTHOR ■ As with the Gospel of John, the author does not explicitly identify himself as the apostle John but instead uses the designation *the elder*. As early as the second century, though, Christian historians and theologians recognized the author as the apostle John, one of the original twelve disciples.

OCCASION ■ John wrote this letter to commend two church leaders, Gaius and Demetrius, and to send a warning about Diotrephes, a man who opposed John's leadership.

1–2 As in 2 John, John refers to himself as "the elder." The addressee's name, *Gaius*, was common in the Roman Empire, and it is unlikely that the person addressed here is the same as one of those with that name associated with Paul (Acts 19:29; 20:4; Romans 16:23; 1 Corinthians 1:14).

2 John affirms that Gaius is well-off spiritually. He prays that Gaius's physical health would match his spiritual health. Notice, it is the spiritual health that is to be the standard by which one's physical health is measured—not the other way around.

9 Diotrephes appears to be an influential person (perhaps the leader) in a local church known to Gaius, but to which Gaius himself does not belong. John's description of Diotrephes suggests an arrogant person who has refused to acknowledge John's prior written communication. This communication probably concerns the traveling missionaries mentioned in the next verse, and Diotrephes has refused to acknowledge John's authority to intervene in the matter. (For Diotrephes this may have been an issue of John's authority and local jurisdiction over such things.)

10 The church mentioned here, which John says he may visit, is not the same as the one mentioned in verse 6, to which John apparently belongs (or of which he is in charge). It seems probable that Gaius belongs to (or is in charge of) one local church while Diotrephes is in another. If John visits, he will expose Diotrephes's behavior. Since Diotrephes made unjustified charges against John, John will bring charges of his own against Diotrephes.

12 Demetrius is apparently someone Gaius has not met. He has a good reputation, and it is possible he is the leader of the traveling missionaries. John commends Demetrius to Gaius.

13–14 As in the closing of 2 John, John says that he has many things to write to Gaius but prefers to speak in person. It appears that John anticipates a personal visit in the near future. This may be the same visit mentioned in connection with Diotrephes in verse 10. Gaius's church and Diotrephes's church may have been in the same city or in neighboring towns, so that John anticipates visiting both on the same journey.

JUDE

INTRODUCTION TO JUDE ■ Truth and discernment are two key themes of this book. A believer's security in God's love opens and closes the letter, but the meat of the content pertains to the false teachers in the believers' midst and the need for believers to stand firm in the truth.

AUTHOR ■ The author of this letter is Jude, the brother of James. Most likely these brothers are the same brothers listed in Matthew 13:55 and Mark 6:3 as Jesus' half brothers (born to Joseph and Mary after Jesus' birth). It was common in the history of the church to shorten the name of Judas to Jude, in the interest of changing one's name from that of the great betrayer, Judas Iscariot. While these two brothers did not have faith in Jesus as Lord during His lifetime (John 7:5), they became leaders in the first-century Christian church, and each wrote a New Testament letter.

OCCASION ■ This epistle is a passionate plea for the readers to contend for their faith. In light of a growing heresy in the church that understood grace as a license for immorality, Jude wrote to an unidentified group of Christ followers to call them back to faith.

---

1 Jude describes himself as a servant (or slave; Greek: *doulos*) of Jesus Christ. A servant in this culture was a lifelong loyal servant of his master. He also identifies himself as the brother of James, the half brother of Jesus. This kind of introduction is an act of humility on Jude's part; he is not touting his familial connection with Jesus but rather stressing his faith in Jesus.

3–4 Jude's original purpose for writing had changed. Rather than being a relaxed letter to friends, this letter deals with a problem: the introduction of false doctrine into the community.

5–7 Jude offers three examples of God's judgment on those who failed in contending for their faith. In doing so, he sheds light on the nature of the false teachers.

9–10 Jude tells us that the angel Michael did not even speak in his own authority to the devil. This is a reference to a story not included in scripture but that was probably well known to Jude and his readers. The story centers on who had jurisdiction over Moses' body after he died, the angel Michael or the devil. The point Jude is likely making here is that Michael did not act on his own authority even against the devil but rather left that task to God Himself. (The words attributed to Michael here may have been drawn from Zechariah 3:2.) If Michael was this careful in how he spoke and acted, how much more so should mortal men watch their words in light of God's power? Yet these false teachers were cavalier in their attitudes, theologies, and philosophies.

12–13 Jude describes these troublesome teachers as self-focused feasters, waterless clouds (making empty promises), fruitless trees (twice dead because they came

to faith, then fell away), waves carrying impurities to the beach (see Isaiah 57:20), and shooting stars that fall into the darkness.

14–15 These verses announce judgment by quoting 1 Enoch, a Jewish book written between the Old and New Testaments and not included in the Christian Bible. The man Enoch, however, is mentioned in Genesis 5 as the descendant of Adam through Seth, Adam's son born after Cain and Abel. One of Enoch's claims to fame is as the father of Methuselah. The other is that rather than record his death, the scriptures say that Enoch walked with God and God simply took him from the earth (Genesis 5:18–24). While it may seem strange to read a New Testament quote from a book not included in the scriptures, it is important to remember that this book was valued by both Jude and his readers, and that the New Testament canon had not been formalized when Jude was writing this letter. Jude does not claim that it is scripture but simply describes a scene recorded in it.

17–19 Jude warns the community of danger by quoting the apostles. We can't know which of the apostles' writings Jude's readers were aware of, but we can certainly see from the New Testament scriptures available to us that the apostles often warned of false teachers (see Acts 20:29; 2 Corinthians 11:3; Colossians 2:4; 1 Timothy 4:1–3; 1 John 2:18–19).

24–25 In his final words of praise, Jude describes God as worthy of all honor for eternity past and future. Yet in His completeness, He saves us, protects us, and uses us to reach out to others and share the lifesaving news of the Gospel.

THE REVELATION

OF ST. JOHN THE DIVINE

INTRODUCTION TO REVELATION ■ The word *revelation* means "unveiling," or "disclosure." This is a book that reveals how the person, righteousness, and judgment of Jesus are going to be revealed in all of the fullness and power of God. Understanding a symbolic book like this requires putting together whole sections rather than reading select verses in isolation. The meaning of Revelation comes from unfolding the entire book chapter by chapter. The message is God's sovereignty over all.

AUTHOR ■ As with most New Testament books, through the centuries there has been discussion as to the author of this letter. While the writer identifies himself as John (1:1), some have wondered if it is safe to assume that this means the apostle John. Many of the arguments on this topic center around the language differences with the other New Testament books attributed to the apostle (the Gospel of John and 1 John). There has been no irrefutable evidence, though, to sway conservative scholars from accepting John's authorship.

OCCASION ■ Since so many of the images in Revelation are often interpreted in relation to governments and political leaders, discussions about when the book was written focus on which emperor was ruling at the time. Many suggest that Nero must have been ruling, but most suggest that John wrote during the time of Domitian, which would have placed the writing of this vision letter around AD 90–95. One of the biggest supports for this date is the fact that emperor worship—which is repeatedly alluded to in John's visions—was a much greater issue during Domitian's rule than during Nero's.

1:1–2 The first two verses of Revelation reveal three things: (1) This book is a revelation of Jesus Christ and His sovereign control of the universe, (2) John is the one who received this revelation, and (3) his letter is an eyewitness account.

1:5 John provides a threefold description of Jesus. First, He is the "faithful witness." Jesus was faithful in the past to carry out God's plan of redemption, and He will be faithful in the future, too. Second, Jesus is the "first begotten of the dead." Because Jesus was faithful, God raised Him from the dead. This is the ultimate in hope for the believer, because all those who place their faith in Jesus can be assured of rising from the dead as well. Third, Jesus is the "prince of the kings of the earth." Even though John's readers were dealing with cruel rulers who seemed to be in ultimate control, Jesus has supreme control over the earth.

1:7 John states that this same Jesus who loves us, releases us from sin, includes us in the kingdom, and makes us able to serve God will also come again. At the return of Jesus, the people will mourn the judgment that is coming as a result of their sin.

1:8 John gives several titles to God the Father, each conveying the depth and strength of God: First, He is the "Alpha and Omega," a name that refers to the eternal, unchanging nature of God. *Alpha* is the first letter of the Greek alphabet, and *omega* is the last. Second, He is the One "which is, which was, and which is to come." God, although living outside of time, still dwells in time and interacts with those living in the present, the past, and the future. Third, God is "the Almighty." He has His hand on everything and is in complete control.

1:10 Some say that the "Lord's day" is a figurative reference to the final Judgment Day. More likely it is simply a reference to Sunday, the new day of worship (as opposed to Saturday, the Jewish sabbath). John says he was "in the Spirit," which suggests a state of mind in which he was open to the Spirit's leading.

1:15 Jesus is looking at the world with the eyes of judgment. The feet—glowing with power—represent the reality that Jesus will execute judgment personally. The fact that His voice sounded like "many waters" indicates that He spoke with authority and power (see Ezekiel 43:2).

2:1–4 The church at Ephesus is committed to doctrinal purity; the believers have persisted as disciples of Jesus. Yet their love for truth is stronger than their passion for Jesus. The concept of not staying true to their "first love" may mean not only their love for Jesus but also their love for each other.

2:5 The Ephesian church receives two commands: (1) They must consider how far they have fallen, and (2) they must repent. If they don't, Jesus will pronounce judgment, and their effectiveness as a church will be lost.

2:6 All that is known of the Nicolaitans is found here. Some speculate that the Nicolaitan heresy was spawned from Nicolas, one of the seven chosen to serve the widows in the Jerusalem church (see Acts 6). Others believe this group was not associated with Nicolas but used his name to gain credibility.

2:7 The statement "He that hath an ear, let him hear" is used throughout these letters to the churches. It means that if individuals understand the real meaning of what they hear, then they must respond.

2:8–9 Jesus identifies the believers of Smyrna by the distresses they have experienced—suffering, poverty, and slander. Christianity was outlawed at this time, and believers were held in contempt for their refusal to worship the Roman emperor. This passage refers to those who call themselves Jews but are not, indicating that being a Jew has more to do with how a person lives than with one's heritage or bloodline. This is key to interpreting Revelation. One who understands John's use of the Jewish nation to mean the new nation of faith—the church—will interpret passages relating to the Jews as symbolic references to the church as a whole.

2:12 To the church at Pergamos, Jesus is described as the One with a "sharp sword," an image that symbolizes the Word of God. The sword also served as a symbol of Rome, so the use of this image serves as a reminder that Jesus' authority exceeds any earthly power.

2:14 The Pergamos church allowed false teachers to exist in their presence. John references the Old Testament story of a king named Balak, who tried to hire the prophet Balaam to curse the Israelites. When Balaam's attempt failed (see Numbers 22–24), he advised Balak to tempt the Israelites to worship idols—the ensuing consequences would have the same effect as a curse (Numbers 31:15–16). Both behaviors attributed to the church at Pergamos—eating food sacrificed to idols and engaging in sexual immorality—were connected to idol worship.

2:18 This description of Jesus' eyes and feet highlights His all-knowing nature and His commitment to hunt down and conquer evil (see also 1:14–15).

2:19–20 While the church at Thyatira is celebrated for its good works, it is also accused of tolerating Jezebel—probably an alias that John uses to relate this woman to the wicked Old Testament queen by the same name (see 1 Kings 16:30–31). This woman's teaching pulls people into immorality and idolatry.

2:24–26 There are those in Thyatira who have not succumbed to Jezebel's false teaching, and they are commended. The reference to "none other burden" probably indicates any further service beyond their calling to be disciples of Jesus. The reward for their perseverance will be authority in Jesus' name.

3:1 Unlike the judgments of the preceding churches, the judgment against the church at Sardis is stated immediately.

3:2 The city of Sardis was twice overtaken by enemies because of its failure to remain on watch.

3:4–5 Most likely the white garments represent justification through faith in Jesus. The few faithful individuals mentioned here have done nothing to forfeit that justification, thus staining their clothes. Also, they will be confessed before the Father, which means they will be acknowledged as belonging to Jesus and thus allowed to enter into heaven. Finally, they will not have their names erased. In some ancient cities, everyone had their names written in a book, and when they died their names were crossed out or erased. Jesus is saying that

those who overcome will not have their names erased, because they will never die. Eternal life is their destiny.

3:9 The Jews will bow before the believers in Philadelphia as a testimony to the reality that Jesus is the Messiah. The implication is that with the life and death of Jesus, the definition of God's chosen people has changed. It is not a matter of family heritage but of faith in Jesus.

3:14–16 The judgment against the church at Laodicea is given because they are "lukewarm." The water in Laodicea came from a hot spring, so it was indeed lukewarm. In this case, of course, it is the spiritual condition of the church that is being described. Rather than denying Christ, they made an empty profession.

3:17–18 The Laodicean believers claimed to need nothing, yet they were "poor, and blind, and naked." These three accusations were direct hits at the industries of Laodicea: banking, medicine, and clothing. Banks cannot alleviate the bankruptcy of the soul. Wool cannot cover the nakedness of sin. Eye salve cannot cure the blindness toward the Gospel. Thus, to trust in the things of the world is foolish. Only Christ can actually take care of spiritual poverty, blindness, and nakedness.

3:20 This well-known verse includes a word picture of Jesus asking to be let in. The phrase "sup with him" does not describe a meal shared with a stranger but rather a meal shared among friends who know each other well.

3:21 The reward offered here is unlike the wreaths or crowns already mentioned. Instead, this is an invitation to rule with Jesus.

4:5 The "seven" lamps of fire are not like the candlesticks mentioned in 1:12–13; these are outdoor torches, which John identifies as the seven Spirits of God (a reference to the Holy Spirit [see Zechariah 4:1–10]).

4:7 Each creature has a different face: lion, calf, man, and eagle. These symbols show that all of creation is represented before the throne; thus all of creation is worshipping God.

4:10 In addition to the angels, the elders also worship. They fall before God in reverence and lay their crowns before Him. All of their actions—throwing themselves down, offering crowns—communicate God's greatness. They are placing themselves below Him.

5:1 Sealing a scroll was not an unusual practice. Some scrolls may have had seven seals on the outside that had to be broken in order to unroll the parchment. In this case, though, it seems each seal opens a section of the scroll.

5:4 When no one can be found to break the seals, John weeps. The kind of weeping described here is a loud, wailing grief.

5:5 The phrase "Lion of the tribe of Juda" is found only here in the Bible. In Genesis 49:9 Jacob speaks a prophecy over each of his sons. When he speaks of Judah, he refers to him as a lion cub. Jesus, of course, finds His ancestry in the tribe of Judah. The "Root of David" means that Jesus was born into the family line of David. Both Matthew and Luke give genealogies of Jesus, tracing Him through David's bloodline (Matthew 1; Luke 3).

5:7 This is the high point of John's vision—the Son of God takes the scroll from the hand of God. This means that the plan of God is ready to be carried out and that Jesus is the One who will implement the plan.

5:8 The only appropriate response to this moment is praise. In this case, the beasts and elders employ music and fragrance. Harps are often associated with worship in Revelation. The vials symbolize the prayers of saints who have died by persecution.

5:9–10 *New* in this case is not a descriptor of timing but of quality. This song is meant for this particular situation, not simply reused from another. It celebrates the fact that Jesus is worthy to take the scroll. The song also acknowledges that the redeemed belong to God.

6:8 The fourth horse is described as "pale," signifying a sickly green color, the color of a corpse. This horseman is not holding a weapon of any kind, but his name is Death, and he is followed by "Hell"—that is, Hades, the place of departed spirits. As with the third horseman, permission is given to cover 25 percent of the earth in destruction.

6:9 The next seal marks a change. The first four reflect the coming of a particular kind of destruction. The fifth involves the prayers of a particular group of people— the persecuted. Notably, no one is summoned to "come and see" in this case (see 6:1, 3, 5, 7). These souls are under an altar—they are already dead. John gives two reasons why these souls have been killed: (1) because of the Word of God (that is, the message of Jesus) and (2) because of the testimony (the faith they lived out) they had been given by Jesus.

6:11 The souls are told to rest until the full number of martyrs is reached. This does not imply that God has a certain quota of martyrs who must to die before He will enact His justice, but it does indicate that more people will be sacrificing their lives for Him.

6:14–17 The events described in this passage will affect everyone on earth and cause widespread panic. John captures the hopelessness of the situation: It is clear that no person has control of his or her own fate; each is at the mercy of the powerful Sovereignty of heaven and earth.

7:1 The fact that the angels are standing at "the four corners of the earth" implies that they cover the whole earth. Prior to this point, John has not described any winds that need to be held back, so these angels may be holding back all that was released in the first four seals. In any case, they are stopping the natural order of the world. The sun is not shining, the stars are not shining, meteors are falling, and now the wind has stopped blowing.

7:2–3 This angel instructs the four angels holding the winds to hold back their damage until the servants (slaves) of God are identified by a seal on their foreheads. This seal will mark them so that they will not be hurt during the judgment of God.

7:4 Many interpreters hold that the 144,000 people represent Israel. Keep in mind, though, that John is sending this letter to dispersed Christians, not all of whom are Jewish. Also, John has made statements elsewhere

that can be interpreted to mean that God's chosen people are no longer identified by heritage or ancestry, but by faith (see 2:9; 3:9). As a result, some interpret this 144,000 as the faithful of the Christian church.

7:9 Many think this verse describes the rapture, when God will remove His church from the world. Others believe it refers to those who have been killed during the unleashing of evil. Either way, these are people who have come from the world and are now rescued from their misery and are in the presence of the Lord.

7:13–14 An elder asks and answers his own question about the identity of the throng in white robes. The now familiar phrase "great tribulation" could mean the ongoing tribulation these people previously faced on earth, as opposed to a specific future period often referred to as "the tribulation."

7:15–17 The elder describes the fate that awaits these worshippers. They will be provided for, and even shepherded, by the Lamb. Reminiscent of Psalm 23, Jesus will provide for them, and the sorrows and difficulties of this life will be left behind.

8:2 These are specific angels who stand before God, endowed with the responsibility of carrying out justice on the earth. The trumpets are instruments of that judgment.

8:4–5 The prayers ascend from the angel's hand, uniting heaven and earth. Fire from the altar is added, thus adding the power of God to the prayers.

8:13 After the first four trumpets and judgments, a flying angel (other translations refer to the creature as an eagle) proclaims three woes, perhaps in light of the three trumpets yet to sound. This is a curse and a proclamation of things to come. The appearance of this angel provides an interlude amid the trumpet judgments.

9:3–5 In addition to the smoke, locusts pour out, representing God's judgment, just as they did in the plagues in Egypt and in Joel's prophecy (Joel 2:25). In this case, though, the locusts are prohibited from plant life—their typical food source. These locusts are given power, presumably by God, to sting like scorpions. They can go after, but not kill, those without God's seal. The five-month period of torment may correspond to the typical life span of the locust, or it may simply be a way to communicate that the torment will last a few months. This is how the number five is used elsewhere in scripture (see Acts 20:6; 24:1).

9:7–9 The description of the locusts combines human and animal features, revealing them to be more akin to demons than insects. The significance of the comparison to horses is that the locusts are prepared for battle like horses—that is, they are determined to accomplish the task. The "crowns" may symbolize the authority to act and to get things done. The teeth reveal more about the creatures' fierceness than their physical description. And the breastplates reveal how well protected they are. The loud noise made by their wings indicates their great number.

9:11 At the time John was writing this letter, the emperor of Rome liked to think of himself as the incarnation of the god Apollo—who, interestingly, was known as the god over locusts. The locusts in this verse are from the underworld, and thus they represent the power of evil being used by God, a message that would be relevant to John's readers. Both names listed here, *Abaddon* and *Apollyon*, can be translated as *destruction*.

9:17–19 It is not certain whether John is describing three different colors of breastplates or breastplates that are each three colors. However, the description of the horses—heads like lions, tails like snakes—indicates the ferocity and danger of this army. These warriors are bent on total destruction.

9:18–19 The riders do not seem to play any active part in the destruction; it is the horses who breathe the fire, smoke, and brimstone (or sulfur) on the people.

9:20 John transitions from the cavalry to those who survive the plagues. Notice that his description of their idols underscores the appalling fact that even in light of the destruction all around them, they fail to repent.

10:2 The book is open, which means that what is in the book is about to be read and executed. The fact that the angel places one foot on the sea and the other foot on the land shows that he has authority over the entire earth.

10:4 John intended to write down what the voice said, but he is instructed not to. Apparently this seal is meant to hide what has been said.

10:5–7 This angel is identified as the same one in verse 2. He swears an oath by raising his right hand, a gesture common in both ancient and contemporary days. His oath is that when the seventh trumpet is blown— when all is done that needs to be done—there will be no delay before the fulfillment of God's plan.

11:3–6 The two witnesses have the ability to protect themselves from attack. They can prevent rain and perform miracles if necessary, like turning water to blood and causing plagues. These references bring to mind Moses and Elijah, who exhibited these types of miracles (see Exodus 7:19–20; 1 Kings 17:1).

11:7–8 The witnesses' ability to protect themselves is temporary. When their job is done, they are killed by what is referred to as "the beast" from the abyss. The beast is a prominent figure in the last half of Revelation. It is empowered by Satan and filled with evil. For those who interpret Revelation literally, the killing of the witnesses will happen in Jerusalem, where Jesus was crucified. Jerusalem is also referred to as Sodom and Egypt, one a city famous for immorality and the other a country known for holding God's people in bondage.

11:9 The fact that the corpses lay for three and a half days without being buried is an act of shame. Given the customs of the day, John's original readers would have understood the disgrace of no proper burial.

11:10 The general population rejoices that the witnesses are dead. Because of their message and their power, the forty-two months that they spent on the earth were horrible for the unrepentant. Therefore, their deaths seem almost like a holiday—people exchange gifts and celebrate. But this only happens for three and a half days.

11:11–12 First, God breathes life into the two witnesses; then He calls them to heaven. All those watching are seized by fear. In a sense, this is a review of the Gospel— new life and the conquering of death. While we can't be sure if everyone in the crowd watching hears God call out, or if just the two witnesses hear His voice, it is obvious to everyone that those who were dead have found new life.

11:13–14 Those who had celebrated the death of the two witnesses have now experienced an earthquake that collapses part of the city and kills seven thousand. The unrepentant now honor God's power and authority.

11:15–19 The seventh trumpet is not just one short event; it comprises the rest of God's judgment and then the final end of the age with the coming of the new heaven and earth. It also serves as a prompt for the next series of visions recorded by John.

12:1–2 In the first of the seven signs, a woman is described as a picture of Israel. She has been called by God and is "clothed with the sun," meaning she reflects the power of God. The moon is "under her feet," indicating that she is the nation God has marked as special. Her twelve crowns correspond to the twelve tribes of Israel. She is with child—a picture of the Messiah. Her labor pains represent the struggles that were a part of the life of Israel.

12:4 Some see this passage as a reference to Satan taking one-third of the angels with him when he fell from heaven. Others think it simply represents a show of power by the dragon. He has only one goal in mind: to destroy the child (who is an image of the Messiah).

12:5 This is not a picture of a tyrannical rule as much as it is shows the firm power of a king. The child is immediately caught up into heaven—that is, He ascends into heaven. This ascension indicates that the Son is waiting for the day when He will rule.

12:6 The 1,260 days, or three and a half years, show up again (see 11:1–3). In this case, the woman hides for this duration.

12:10–12 The announcement of salvation and of Satan's ultimate expulsion from heaven is spoken in first person plural ("the accuser of *our* brethren"). It is probably proclaimed by a group of angels, but any of the heavenly members in the vision could be the source.

12:13 When Satan realizes that he can't reach the child, he goes after the woman. In other words, Satan sets out to persecute Israel.

12:15–17 Two more attempts are made by Satan. First, he spits floodwaters to sweep the woman away from her wilderness safe house, but the earth swallows the floodwaters. Then, when he is unable to attack, he goes after her children—that is, he turns on the church.

13:4 The people will begin to worship Satan the beast. This is the ultimate in blasphemy. The question, "Who is like unto the beast?" may be a reference to Psalm 35:10, highlighting their blasphemous worship.

13:7 The beast focuses his attack on those who believe in the one true God. The situation John describes is such that, if it continues, there will be no believers left on the earth.

13:10 This verse contains instructions. If you are marked for arrest, do not resist. If you are to be killed, do not fight back. A day of reckoning is coming, and you are to wait for that day. The point is to leave the fighting to God.

13:11–17 The second beast, the false prophet, will be able to mimic the prophets of the past by calling down fire from heaven. Everyone who is not a true believer will be fooled by his power. He will encourage people to make an image of the beast so that all can worship him in their homes. In this way, he will have the entire world consumed with the first beast, the one with the restored head, the Antichrist. He will be a household word, even a way of life.

13:18 For centuries, people have searched for the meaning behind the number 666. Since numerical values were often applied to letters in the ancient world, many have looked for a name that, when converted to numbers, would equal 666. No solutions to that equation have been widely accepted. And in truth, this number may represent some symbolism that has thus far not been taken into account.

14:1 God prevents the plan of the beast from coming to fruition by sealing 144,000 people, thus keeping them from being killed by the beast. He will seal them with a sign on their foreheads.

14:4–5 John offers five characteristics of the worshippers: First, they are sexually pure—they are not married and have not allowed themselves to indulge in sexually immoral relationships. Second, they are devoted to Jesus. Third, they were purchased as firstfruits—that is, the first of the harvest offered to God as an act of worship. Fourth, they are righteous. When the text states that "no guile" is found in their mouths, it means that their words and actions are just as righteous as their hearts. Fifth, they are blameless—that is, they are beyond reproach.

14:8 The second proclamation in this passage is that Babylon has fallen. God is going to do away with the beast's empire. Notice the terminology: This nation makes people drink the wine of its immorality. Every thought and every desire of this nation are so wicked and evil that its heart is bent on destroying God.

14:9–12 The third proclamation is that punishment awaits those who take the mark of the beast and worship him. Keep in mind that the mark of the beast is not just a number—it is a religion and a life philosophy. Those who receive the mark of the beast will drink of the wine of God's wrath (a reference to God's power to punish and the totality of His anger) and experience eternal and continual torment with fire and brimstone (a reference to hell).

14:16 Because there is no mention of wrath, those who interpret the person on the cloud as Jesus hold that this reaping is the time when the followers of God are being brought to heaven. For those who hold that the one doing the reaping is an angel, this harvest is undefined.

14:17–20 This is most likely a picture of judgment, since it is a winepress of wrath. We aren't told who presses the grapes, but the huge amount of blood that pours from the winepress—enough to reach the height of horses' bridles stretching for nearly two hundred miles—reveals a devastating judgment. The precise distance is not the main concern here; it is the immeasurable extent of God's judgment falling on those who refuse to believe.

15:2 Unlike the sea of glass in 4:6, this one is mixed with fire. Some have speculated that this "sea" represents the evil in the world, with those who have overcome that evil standing beside it. Others have supposed that this "sea" is the same one mentioned in 4:6—a glass-like platform that surrounds God's throne (here with the added element of God's anger, as represented by fire).

15:7 The word translated *vials* is the same word used for the vials (bowls) that contained the prayers of the saints in 5:8. The seven vials will be described in the upcoming chapters, and they symbolize the final events of God's punishment of those who reject Him.

16:1 The loud voice from the temple indicates that the actions about to take place are being controlled by God. In the same way, the judgments about to fall will strike those who have directly scorned God.

16:2 The first vial is a physical attack against all of the people who worship the beast—one that will render them useless.

16:2–3 Not only do the people get sores, but the water is turned to blood, much as it had been during the famous plagues of Egypt (Exodus 7:17–21). Earlier in Revelation, during the second trumpet (8:8–9), the water was turned to blood, but this is different. In this case, *all* the oceans of the world are turned to blood; life can no longer be sustained. Also, this is "the blood of a dead man," meaning it has already coagulated. It is thick and stale and useless.

16:4–7 When the third vial is poured out by the angel, the rest of the water supply is affected—the rivers and the streams. The "angel of the waters" is not mentioned anywhere else in the Bible.

16:8–9 In some of the past judgments described in Revelation, the sun has been diminished (6:12; 8:12; 9:2). But in this judgment, the intensity of the sun increases so much that it is scorching people.

16:12 The sixth plague removes the water from the Euphrates. This might not seem like such a bad thing given the fact that the river is filled with blood. But it is important because the next judgment is the great war of Armageddon that will destroy the armies of the beast once and for all. Drying up the riverbed removes an important obstacle for attacking armies.

16:16 *Armageddon* probably stands for *Har Mageddon*, which means "the mountain of Megiddo." There is no known mountain with this name, so some have considered it to be merely an element of John's vision—a symbol of God's judgment. Others, however, identify it as the plain that lies beside the ancient city of Megiddo.

16:17 When the seventh angel pours his vial of wrath upon the earth, a loud voice comes from the throne in the temple, shouting, "It is done." This is similar to the announcement of Jesus at His death (see John 19:30). In this context, God is saying there will be no more judgment—the serpent and all evil are being punished on the earth.

17:3 The scarlet beast is presumably the same beast described in 13:1, with seven heads and ten horns and labeled with blasphemous names.

17:5 This is one of several times in Revelation that people are identified by a mark or seal on their foreheads (see 7:3; 9:4; 14:1). Rather than understanding the woman's name as being *Mystery*, her name *was* a mystery. More explanation is given later in this chapter (see verses 15–18). *Babylon*, the next thing written on her forehead, is not used to identify a place but to identify a godless culture. Not only is this woman evil herself; she gives birth to evil. Identified as the mother of all prostitutes, she represents the source of all of the immorality in the world. In addition, she is the source of all of the evil that seeks to desecrate God.

17:6 The woman is drunk with the blood of the saints, which implies she is responsible for their deaths. The language here is not that of something done long ago but rather something that is still continuing.

17:8 Several times in the angel's explanation, the beast is described, with some variations, as the one who "was, and is not, and yet is." This is a way of saying that he has been resurrected, but it is a false resurrection. It is probably meant to stand in contrast to the description of Jesus in 1:4. This beast lived, died, and is going to come back to life—a sign of false divinity. But in the end, this coming back serves the purpose of his final destruction.

17:10–11 Whether interpreted as a ruler, a nation, or a symbol of evil, this eighth king refers to the beast himself. Somehow, he belongs to the seven yet rules again. The angel's interest in this explanation, though, doesn't seem to be in identifying the beast in a definite way. The focus seems to be that this beast is on his way to destruction at the hand of God.

17:12–14 The ten horns represent ten kingdoms as a confederacy that will rule with the beast for a short period of time. They will be completely united with the beast in opposition to the Lamb, but they will be defeated.

17:18 The angel offers some clues to the prostitute's identity. She is a great city who rules over the kings on the earth. In John's day, this certainly would have been taken as a reference to Rome. Alternatively, it may be seen as an organized world religion or simply as a reference to organized humanity living outside of the law of God.

18:6–8 These verses seem to be addressing those who can impose justice. They are a request for punishment, not simply according to the degree that Babylon inflicted pain, but double that. The punishment is not according to Babylon's cruelties but according to her demand for luxury. As extravagantly as she has lived, so let her punishment be.

18:9–11 While no one runs to Babylon's rescue, there are some who mourn her passing—namely, those who profited from her.

18:12–13 Most of the merchandise listed here is easily recognizable today. The precious stones could include granite. The colors of the cloth—scarlet and purple—are associated with splendor, royalty, and also sin. Thyine (or citron) is a hardwood well known for its deep grain. The mention of slaves denotes what we would refer to today as human trafficking.

18:21 This image is reminiscent of the Old Testament prophet Jeremiah's actions in Jeremiah 51:63, which are also a picture of the destruction of Babylon. When the millstone is thrown down, it is done with violence. The judgment comes in an intense, destructive moment that changes the foundation of life forever.

18:22–23 These verses list what will never happen again in light of Babylon's destruction. Musicians won't play, craftsmen won't practice, and everyday life—like grinding grain into flour, marrying, and even lighting lamps in homes—will cease.

18:24 The deaths of prophets and saints and all those killed on earth have been attributed to Babylon. In light of such a designation, many believe that the destruction represents the destruction of not just one city or power but all the world's cities that have chosen to operate outside of God's laws.

19:3–6 When the multitude sings out a second time, a picture of smoke rising from the battle is a sign of the permanence of the destruction. Then, for the final time in Revelation, the twenty-four elders and four living creatures—those who have been described as the ones closest to God's throne—take part in the worship.

19:7 Throughout the scriptures, the picture of a bride has often represented God's faithful people. Isaiah spoke of Israel as God's bride (Isaiah 54:6). Here the bride is a picture of the church, and the Lamb is a picture of Jesus. Redeemed believers are welcomed into heaven, and they have the privilege of having union with Christ forever.

19:10 The angel's words make several things clear: (1) Angels are not to be worshipped, (2) angels are fellow servants with Christians in bearing witness to Jesus, and (3) the testimony about Jesus is the spirit of prophecy.

19:12 Jesus' blazing eyes relate to judgment; His many crowns indicate His position as King of kings and Lord of lords.

19:13 Jesus' blood-dipped robe is that attributed to God in Isaiah 63:1–6. First-century rabbis claimed God would wear this kind of robe on the day of His vengeance on Rome.

19:15 The sword extending from Jesus' mouth is His true weapon, not His armies. The iron rod depicts His absolute authority. Finally, the winepress of God's wrath is an image of judgment also used in 14:19–20.

19:17–21 These verses paint a picture of final disaster. An angel appears in midair and calls to the birds to come and feast on the flesh of everyone—that is, everyone who took the mark of the beast, including the beast himself and his false prophet. This is a judgment scene that exhibits the power of the Word of God. Christ's victory over those who oppose Him is total. The Antichrist and the false prophet are thrown into the fiery lake of burning sulfur—this is complete destruction.

20:4–6 The typical form of execution in first-century Rome was beheading with an axe or sword. In this case, though, the language probably implies more generally those who were martyred for their faith, whatever the method. John also remarks on the perseverance of these sufferers: They had not worshipped the beast nor received his mark. Because of this, they were mistreated by the authorities of the world and thus will be given authority by God. They are resurrected to rule with

Jesus—which John calls the "first resurrection." The rest of the dead will come to life after the thousand years is complete; however, he does not refer to that as the second resurrection. Instead, he only speaks of a "second death," from which these martyrs are saved.

20:10 The devil is thrown into the lake of fire and brimstone to accompany the beast and false prophet who are already there. Their torment will be continuous. God had promised Eve that the serpent would be dealt with eventually, and that promise is fulfilled here (see Genesis 3:15).

20:11 This throne is distinguished from the other thrones mentioned in Revelation in that it is large and white. It is such a powerful place of righteousness that nothing will be able to stand before it.

20:13 No one will be overlooked in this judgment. All those who have died, no matter their fate, will be called up.

20:14 The power that held physical bodies in bondage (death) and the place where all the wicked went until the Day of Judgment (hell, alternately translated "Hades") will both be destroyed in the "lake of fire." There is no reason for death and Hades to exist anymore, because sin is finally being removed from the earth.

21:2 The new Jerusalem is described as a bride coming down from heaven. The bride is completely prepared, at her best for her husband.

21:3–4 The great pronouncement is that God is now living among His people. Heaven and earth have joined together to make one place. All of the misery that the children of God had to endure on their way to heaven will be wiped away. God will restore every believer.

21:6 God will forever be the source of the water of life—free of charge. His eternal nature provides people with the new life necessary for participating in this new world.

21:7–8 Those who do not succumb to evil and remain true to God will engage in a complete relationship with God. There are those who will not, however, and their fate is the second death in the lake of fire (as described in the previous chapter). The list given here opens with "the fearful"—that is, cowards, the opposite of those who persevered and conquered.

21:9 This is a reference not only to the "bride" of the Lamb, but to the "wife" of the Lamb. This parallels the idea of God's work being complete. The wedding has taken place, and the relationship is solidified.

21:10–11 John again sees Jerusalem descending from heaven. The city is described as a clear jewel. The stone that is now known as jasper is not transparent, so the term *jasper* may have been applied to a different stone in John's day. Nevertheless, the description here of the city of God is that of a beautiful, costly jewel.

21:12–14 Walls, though unnecessary in a world without enemies and natural disasters, still denote a protected and safe place. The twelve gates, guarded by angels and labeled with the twelve tribes of Israel, can easily be seen as a fulfillment of God's promises to His chosen people throughout history. The gates are positioned to reflect the way the twelve tribes encamped around the tabernacle in Numbers 2. The mention of the twelve apostles indicates the inclusion of the Christian church, the redeemed of God.

21:15–16 The angel measures the city, and while it is described as square, it is actually an even cube, given that the height is also the same as the length and width—about fourteen hundred miles each.

21:18 The new Jerusalem's walls are made of jasper. In 4:3 God is described as jasper, so there may be an allusion here to God as the city's protector.

21:21 The gates into the city are not only made of pearl, but each is one giant pearl. And again, as in 21:18, the main street is pure gold, clear and perfect.

21:22–27 These verses reveal three things missing from the new Jerusalem: the temple, the sun and moon, and the presence of sin. There is no temple because the Lord dwells in this place; God is the temple.

22:5 The idea that the inhabitants will reign with God is not to indicate that there will be multitudes to reign over, for everyone there will be a child of God. But it is an indication that everyone there will be considered royalty, children of the King.

22:6 While the angel's claim that the words are reliable and trustworthy could simply apply to the immediately preceding verses, it is likely that it can be understood as a claim for this whole book of visions. This prophecy is of God.

22:7 The quote in this verse can be attributed to Jesus. In this case, *quickly* means not so much that these events will happen sooner rather than later but that they are the next events on God's schedule.

22:12–13 Jesus repeats His promise to "come quickly" and to reward each person according to the life he or she has lived. He also states the same claim that was attributed to God in 1:8. In this case, Jesus adds two additional descriptive phrases, but all three statements come to the same thing—He is the beginning and the end.

22:14–15 These words are probably spoken by John, but this is not completely certain.

22:16–17 Jesus describes Himself as both the root of David (that from which David's bloodline sprang) and a descendant of David (that which sprang from David's bloodline). He is the One who came before David and before the great political empire of Israel. He is also the One who is the human descendant of David. He is the center of everything. Jesus' claim to be the "bright and morning star" may be a reference to Numbers 24:17, a prophecy stated by Balaam, who claimed a star would come out of the family of Jacob, father of the twelve tribes of Israel.

22:18–19 The warning here covers both those who would add to John's prophecy and those who would diminish it. Neither will be tolerated.

22:20–21 John closes this prophecy with both a promise from Jesus that He is coming and a prayer from John that Jesus will come. Jesus is described as the One who testifies to these prophecies and confirms His intent to return. This must have resonated greatly with those first-century Christians enduring persecution, wondering about God's timetable, praying that their good deeds would not be forgotten by God, even if they were disdained by their own culture and government.

THE HOLY LAND
TODAY

5 10   20 30 Miles
5 10 20 30 40 Km

Mediterranean Sea

LEBANON

Sour (Tyre)

Kiriath Shemonah

Al Qunaytira

Dimashq
(Damascus)

GOLAN
HEIGHTS
*(occupied
by Israel)*

SYRIA

Akko

Haifa

Nazareth

Teverya

*Sea of
Galilee*

Dara

Afula

Irbid

Hadera

Jenin

Beth-shean

Jordan River

Netanya

Nablus

WEST
BANK

As Salt

Az Zarqa

Tel Aviv-Yafo

Karama

Amman (Rabbah)

Ramallah

Ariha (Jericho)

Ashdod

Jerusalem

Ashqelon

Bayt Lahm
(Bethlehem)

Madaba

Qiryat Gat

Dead Sea

AZA
TRIP

Ghazzah
(Gaza)

Al Khalil
(Hebron)

Beersheba

Arad

ISRAEL

Kerak
(Kir-hareseth)

JORDAN

Dimona

El-Gi

Maan

EGYPT

SAUDI
ARABIA

Elat

N

Copyright © 2007 by Barbour Publishing, Inc.

Black Sea

Caspi

Magog
Gomer
Ashkenaz

ASIA MINOR
Heth
Mesech
Togarmah
Mash?
Madai

Lud
MESOPOTAMIA
Asshur
Nimrod
Javan
Tubal

Dodanim?
Aram
Zemarites
Arvadites
Hamathites
Sinites
Arkites
Sidon
Hivites
Girgashites
Jebusites
Amorites
Arphaxad
Elo

Caphtorim
Kittim

Mediterranean Sea
Canaan

Put?
Naphtuhim
Uz?
ARABIA
Per
G

Lehabim?
Egypt

Pathrusim
Red Sea
Dedan

WESTERN MEDITERRANEAN NATIONS

Tiras?

Tarshish?
Elishah?

0   250   50
0   300 km

Cush

AFRICA

Raamah?

Havilah?

Sabtah?
Uzal?
Sheba?
Haza

Seba?

Ophir?

NATIONS OF THE ANCIENT WORLD

Descendant of Ham
Descendant of Shem
Descendant of Japheth

0   100   200   400 mi
0   200   400   600 km   Copyright 2007 © by Barbour Publish